The American Nation

THE American Nation

PRIMARY SOURCES

Edited by Bruce P. Frohnen

Liberty Fund

INDIANAPOLIS

This book is published by Liberty Fund, Inc., a foundation established to encourage study of the ideal of a society of free and responsible individuals.

𒂼𒄄

The cuneiform inscription that serves as our logo and as the design motif for our endpapers is the earliest-known written appearance of the word "freedom" (*amagi*), or "liberty." It is taken from a clay document written about 2300 B.C. in the Sumerian city-state of Lagash.

"Address to the First Annual Meeting of the Women's State Temperance Society," by Elizabeth Cady Stanton. Reprinted from *History of Woman Suffrage,* vol. 1, 493–97. New York: Arno & The New York Times, 1969. Used by permission of Ayer Company Publishers.

Cover art: From Réunion des Musées Nationaux / Art Resource, N.Y.

C 10 9 8 7 6 5 4 3 2 1
P 10 9 8 7 6 5 4 3 2 1

Library of Congress Cataloging-in-Publication Data
The American nation : primary sources / edited by Bruce P. Frohnen.
    p. cm.
   Includes bibliographical references and index.
   ISBN 978-0-86597-729-7 (hardcover : alk. paper)—
   ISBN 978-0-86597-730-3 (pbk. : alk. paper)
   1. United States—History—Civil War, 1861–1865—
   Sources.   2. Reconstruction (U.S. history, 1865–
   1877)—Sources.   3. United States—History—
   1865–1921—Sources.   4. United States—History
   —1919–1933—Sources.   5. United States—
   History—1933–1945—Sources.   I. Frohnen, Bruce.
   E173.A747 2009
   973.7—dc22   2008029605

Liberty Fund, Inc.
8335 Allison Pointe Trail, Suite 300
Indianapolis, Indiana 46250–1684

Contents

Alphabetical Table of Contents

Alphabetical List of Authors

EDGAR W. CHARLES,
JULIUS A. DARGAN,
ISAAC D. WILSON,
JOHN M. TIMMONS,
FRANCIS HUGH
    WARDLAW,
R. G. M. DUNOVANT,
JAMES PARSONS CARROLL,
WM. GREGG,
ANDREW J. HAMMOND,
JAMES TOMPKINS,
JAMES C. SMYLY,
JOHN HUGH MEANS,
WILLIAM STROTHER
    LYLES,
HENRY CAMPBELL DAVIS,
JNO. BUCHANAN,
JAMES C. FURMAN,
P. E. DUNCAN,
W. K. EASLEY,
JAMES HARRISON,
W. H. CAMPBELL,
T. J. WITHERS,
JAMES CHESNUT, JR.,
JOSEPH BREVARD
    KERSHAW,
THOS. W. BEATY,
WM. J. ELLIS,
R. L. CRAWFORD,
W. C. CAUTHEN,
D. P. ROBINSON,
H. C. YOUNG,
H. W. GARLINGTON,
JOHN D. WILLIAMS,
W. D. WATTS,
THOS. WIER,
H. I. CAUGHMAN,
JOHN C. GEIGER,
PAUL QUATTLEBAUM,

W. B. ROWELL,
CHESLEY D. EVANS,
WM. W. HARLLEE,
A. W. BETHEA,
E. W. GOODWIN,
WILLIAM D. JOHNSON,
ALEX. MCLEOD,
JOHN P. KINARD,
ROBERT MOORMAN,
JOSEPH CALDWELL,
SIMEON FAIR,
THOMAS WORTH GLOVER,
LAWRENCE M. KEITT,
DONALD ROWE BARTON,
WM. HUNTER,
ANDREW F. LEWIS,
ROBT. A. THOMPSON,
WILLIAM S. GRISHAM,
JOHN MAXWELL,
JNO. E. FRAMPTON,
W. FERGUSON HUTSON,
W. F. DE SAUSSURE,
WILLIAM HOPKINS,
JAMES H. ADAMS,
MAXCY GREGG,
JOHN H. KINSLER,
EPHRAIM M. CLARKE,
ALEX. H. BROWN,
E. S. P. BELLINGER,
MERRICK E. CARN,
E. R. HENDERSON,
PETER STOKES,
DANIEL FLUD,
DAVID C. APPLEBY,
R. W. BARNWELL,
JOS. DAN'L POPE,
C. P. BROWN,
JOHN M. SHINGLER,
DANIEL DU PRE,

A. MAZYCK,
WILLIAM CAIN,
P. G. SNOWDEN,
GEO. W. SEABROOK,
JOHN JENKINS,
R. J. DAVANT,
E. M. SEABROOK,
JOHN J. WANNAMAKER,
ELIAS B. SCOTT,
JOSEPH E. JENKINS,
LANGDON CHEVES,
GEORGE RHODES,
A. G. MAGRATH,
WM. PORCHER MILES,
JOHN TOWNSEND,
ROBERT N. GOURDIN,
H. W. CONNER,
THEODORE D. WAGNER,
R. BARNWELL RHETT,
C. G. MEMMINGER,
GABRIEL MANIGAULT,
JOHN JULIUS PRINGLE
    SMITH,
ISAAC W. HAYNE,
JNO. H. HONOUR,
RICH'D DE TREVILLE,
THOS. M. HANCKEL,
A. W. BURNETT,
THOS. Y. SIMONS,
L. W. SPRATT,
WILLIAMS MIDDLETON,
F. D. RICHARDSON,
B. H. RUTLEDGE,
EDWARD MCCRADY,
FRANCIS J. PORCHER,

T. L. GOURDIN,
JOHN S. PALMER,
JOHN L. NOWELL,
JOHN S. O'HEAR,
JOHN G. LANDRUM,
B. B. FOSTER,
BENJAMIN F. KILGORE,
JAS. H. CARLISLE,
SIMPSON BOBO,
WM. CURTIS,
H. D. GREEN,
MATTHEW P. MAYES,
THOMAS REESE
    ENGLISH, SR.
ALBERTUS CHAMBERS
    SPAIN,
J. M. GADBERRY,
J. S. SIMS,
WM. H. GIST,
JAMES JEFFERIES,
ANTHONY W. DOZIER,
JOHN G. PRESSLEY,
R. C. LOGAN,
FRANCIS S. PARKER,
BENJ. FANEUIL DUNKIN,
SAMUEL TAYLOR
    ATKINSON,
ALEX. M. FORSTER,
WM. BLACKBURN
    WILSON,
ROBERT T. ALLISON,
SAMUEL RAINEY,
A. BAXTER SPRINGS,
A. I. BARRON,
A. T. DARBY.

Attest: BENJ. F. ARTHUR,
        Clerk of the Convention.

South Carolina Ordinance of Secession, 1860

South Carolina Declaration of Secession, 1860

Mississippi Ordinance of Secession, 1861

Mississippi Declaration of Secession, 1861

Virginia Ordinance to Repeal the Ratification of the Constitution of the
United States of America, 1861

Missouri Act Declaring the Political Ties Heretofore Existing between the
State of Missouri and the United States of America Dissolved, 1861

Ordinance of the Kentucky Convention, 1861

*On November 10, 1860, just four days after the presidential election, the South Carolina
legislature called for a convention to consider the state's secession from the Union. Less
than two months later, South Carolina officially seceded. Ten more states would follow.
A legislative session called by Missouri's governor and a convention of citizens in Kentucky also passed ordinances of secession, though in these latter cases the Union governments continued to exist as well as secessionist elements seated in the Confederate legislature. Four states, South Carolina, Georgia, Mississippi, and Texas, also issued separate
declarations setting forth their reasons for secession. All assumed a right of states to secede
and a stance portraying the federal government as an aggressor for violating Southern
states' rights and acting against Southern interests.*

South Carolina Ordinance of Secession

December 20, 1860

AN ORDINANCE

To dissolve the Union between the State of
South Carolina and other States united with
her under the compact entitled "The Constitution of the United States of America."

*We, the People of the State of South Carolina, in Convention
assembled, do declare and ordain, and it is hereby declared
and ordained,*

That the Ordinance adopted by us in Convention, on the
twenty-third day of May, in the year of our Lord one thousand seven hundred and eighty-eight, whereby the Constitution of the United States of America was ratified, and also, all
Acts and parts of Acts of the General Assembly of this State,
ratifying amendments of the said Constitution, are hereby
repealed; and that the union now subsisting between South
Carolina and other States, under the name of "The United
States of America," is hereby dissolved.

D. F. JAMISON, *Del. from Barnwell, and Pres't Convention.*

Thos. Chiles Perrin,	W. Peronneau Finley,
Edw. Noble,	J. J. Brabham,
J. H. Wilson,	Benj. W. Lawton,
Thos. Thomson,	Jno. McKee,
David Lewis Wardlaw,	Thomas W. Moore,
Jno. Alfred Calhoun,	Richard Woods,
John Izard Middleton,	A. Q. Dunovant,
Benjamin E. Sessions,	John A. Inglis,
J. N. Whitner,	Henry McIver,
James L. Orr,	Stephen Jackson,
J. P. Reed,	W. Pinckney Shingler,
R. F. Simpson,	Peter P. Bonneau,
Benjamin Franklin	John P. Richardson,
Mauldin,	John L. Manning,
Lewis Malone Ayer, Jr.,	John J. Ingram,

And to avoid misconstruction, the last clause of the fifth section of said act, which authorizes the person holding a warrant for the arrest or detention of a fugitive slave, to summon to his aid the *posse comitatus,* and which declares it to be the duty of all good citizens to assist him in its execution, ought to be so amended as to expressly limit the authority and duty to cases in which there shall be resistance or danger of resistance or rescue.

4. That the laws for the suppression of the African slave trade, and especially those prohibiting the importation of slaves in the United States, ought to be made effectual, and ought to be thoroughly executed; and all further enactments necessary to those ends ought to be promptly made.

places under its exclusive jurisdiction, and situate within the limits of States that permit the holding of slaves.

ART. 3. Congress shall have no power to abolish slavery within the District of Columbia, so long as it exists in the adjoining States of Virginia and Maryland, or either, nor without the consent of the inhabitants, nor without just compensation first made to such owners of slaves as do not consent to such abolishment. Nor shall Congress at any time prohibit officers of the Federal Government, or members of Congress, whose duties require them to be in said District, from bringing with them their slaves, and holding them as such during the time their duties may require them to remain there, and afterwards taking them from the District.

ART. 4. Congress shall have no power to prohibit or hinder the transportation of slaves from one State to another, or to a Territory in which slaves are by law permitted to be held, whether that transportation be by land, navigable rivers, or by the sea.

ART. 5. That in addition to the provisions of the third paragraph of the second section of the fourth article of the Constitution of the United States, Congress shall have power to provide by law, and it shall be its duty so to provide, that the United States shall pay to the owner who shall apply for it, the full value of his fugitive slave in all cases when the marshal or other officer whose duty it was to arrest said fugitive was prevented from so doing by violence or intimidation, or when, after arrest, said fugitive was rescued by force, and the owner thereby prevented and obstructed in the pursuit of his remedy for the recovery of his fugitive slave under the said clause of the Constitution and the laws made in pursuance thereof. And in all such cases, when the United States shall pay for such fugitive, they shall have the right, in their own name, to sue the county in which said violence, intimidation, or rescue was committed, and to recover from it, with interest and damages, the amount paid by them for said fugitive slave. And the said county, after it has paid said amount to the United States, may, for its indemnity, sue and recover from the wrong doers or rescuers by whom the owner was prevented from the recovery of his fugitive slave, in like manner as the owner himself might have sued and recovered.

ART. 6. No future amendment of the Constitution shall affect the five preceding articles; nor the third paragraph of the second section of the first article of the Constitution; nor the third paragraph of the second section of the fourth article of said Constitution; and no amendment shall be made to the Constitution which shall authorize or give to Congress any power to abolish or interfere with slavery in any of the States by whose laws it is, or may be, allowed or permitted.

And whereas, also, besides those causes of dissension embraced in the foregoing amendments proposed to the Constitution of the United States, there are others which come within the jurisdiction of Congress, and may be remedied by its legislative power; and whereas it is the desire of Congress, as far as its power will extend, to remove all just cause for the popular discontent and agitation which now disturb the peace of the country, and threaten the stability of its institutions: Therefore,

1. *Resolved by the Senate and House of Representatives of the United States of America in Congress assembled,* That the laws now in force for the recovery of fugitive slaves are in strict pursuance of the plain and mandatory provisions of the Constitution, and have been sanctioned as valid and constitutional by the judgment of the Supreme Court of the United States; that the slaveholding States are entitled to the faithful observance and execution of those laws, and that they ought not to be repealed, or so modified or changed as to impair their efficiency; and that laws ought to be made for the punishment of those who attempt by rescue of the slave, or other illegal means, to hinder or defeat the due execution of said laws.

2. That all State laws which conflict with the fugitive slave acts of Congress, or any other constitutional acts of Congress, or which, in their operation, impede, hinder, or delay the free course and due execution of any of said acts, are null and void by the plain provisions of the Constitution of the United States; yet those State laws, void as they are, have given color to practices, and led to consequences, which have obstructed the due administration and execution of acts of Congress, and especially the acts for the delivery of fugitive slaves, and have thereby contributed much to the discord and commotion now prevailing. Congress, therefore, in the present perilous juncture, does not deem it improper, respectfully and earnestly to recommend the repeal of those laws to the several States which have enacted them, or such legislative corrections or explanations of them as may prevent their being used or perverted to such mischievous purposes.

3. That the act of the 18th of September, 1850, commonly called the fugitive slave law, ought to be so amended as to make the fee of the commissioner, mentioned in the eighth section of the act, equal in amount in the cases decided by him, whether his decision be in favor of or against the claimant.

The Crittenden Compromise, 1860

After the 1860 elections had been held, but before the new Congress was seated, the old, lame duck Congress met to attempt one last compromise to save the Union. The best-known effort was led by Kentucky senator John J. Crittenden. The Crittenden Compromise was actually a joint resolution seeking a series of amendments to the American Constitution. Crittenden's resolutions would have expanded on the Missouri Compromise of 1820 and enshrined its provisions in the Constitution, declaring that territory held or acquired by the United States would be free from slavery if north of latitude 36° 30' and open to chattel slavery if south of that line—a line the Crittenden Compromise would have extended to the Pacific Ocean. In addition, the Crittenden Compromise would have provided for congressional compensation to slave owners unable to recover fugitive slaves owing to abolitionist action, protected slaveholding in the District of Columbia, prevented Congress from prohibiting the interstate transportation of slaves, and provided that none of its provisions could thereafter be amended or repealed. The measures garnered majorities but failed to achieve the necessary two-thirds majority in either house of Congress.

The Crittenden Compromise

December 18, 1860

A joint resolution (S. No. 50) proposing certain amendments to the Constitution of the United States.

Whereas serious and alarming dissensions have arisen between the northern and southern States, concerning the rights and security of the rights of the slaveholding States, and especially their rights in the common territory of the United States; and whereas it is eminently desirable and proper that these dissensions, which now threaten the very existence of this Union, should be permanently quieted and settled by constitutional provisions, which shall do equal justice to all sections, and thereby restore to the people that peace and good-will which ought to prevail between all the citizens of the United States: Therefore,

Resolved by the Senate and House of Representatives of the United States of America in Congress assembled, (two thirds of both Houses concurring,) That the following articles be, and are hereby, proposed and submitted as amendments to the Constitution of the United States, which shall be valid to all intents and purposes, as part of said Constitution, when ratified by conventions of three fourths of the several States:

ARTICLE 1. In all the territory of the United States now held, or hereafter acquired, situate north of latitude 36° 30', slavery or involuntary servitude, except as a punishment for crime, is prohibited while such territory shall remain under territorial government. In all the territory south of said line of latitude, slavery of the African race is hereby recognized as existing, and shall not be interfered with by Congress, but shall be protected as property by all the departments of the territorial government during its continuance. And when any Territory, north or south of said line, within such boundaries as Congress may prescribe, shall contain the population requisite for a member of Congress according to the then Federal ratio of representation of the people of the United States, it shall, if its form of government be republican, be admitted into the Union, on an equal footing with the original States, with or without slavery, as the constitution of such new State may provide.

ART. 2. Congress shall have no power to abolish slavery in

ABRAHAM LINCOLN'S ELECTION to the American presidency in 1860 shattered a truce among America's sectional interests that had become increasingly fragile and tenuous. Lincoln won a majority of electoral votes, but none from a Southern state. Moreover, he failed to poll a majority of the popular vote, though he did win the most votes of any candidate in that four-way race. Numerous leaders in the South had made clear that they viewed Lincoln as an enemy because of his oft-stated conviction that slavery should be put on the road toward extinction, as well as his Republican Party's explicit opposition to reopening the African slave trade or expanding slavery into the territories. Some threatened that Lincoln's election to the presidency would cause slaveholding states to secede in short order. And so they did. By February 1861, seven states (South Carolina, Mississippi, Florida, Alabama, Georgia, Louisiana, and Texas) had seceded. Four more states (Virginia, Arkansas, Tennessee, and North Carolina) would secede after the Confederate attack on the Union-controlled Fort Sumter in Charleston harbor in April of 1861. The four remaining slaveholding states (Delaware, Kentucky, Maryland, and Missouri) along with West Virginia, which was carved out of Virginia at this time, remained in the Union but were the source of political and military instability. Indeed, in both Missouri and Kentucky secessionist elements formed their own governments loyal to the Confederacy.

There were a number of last-ditch efforts to stave off war. And leaders of the Confederacy insisted that no war was necessary—the North must simply recognize the right of any state to secede if it so desired, and peace would ensue. The issue of secession's legality had been debated for decades and was settled only on the battlefield.

Disagreements abound as to the ultimate cause and moral status of the Civil War. Was it about slavery or states' rights? Or perhaps both, and made more virulent on account of the ever-widening gulf between Northern and Southern ways of life? Before coming to any of these conclusions, one would do well to examine the constitutional arguments presented by both sides during secession and the Civil War itself.

This section includes official documents regarding secession, as well as political speeches and military orders related to the conflict and issues underlying it.

Alabama Secession Convention Flag, 1861. Alabama Department of Archives and History, Montgomery, Alabama.

Battle of Franklin, Tenn., November 30, 1864. Library of Congress, Prints and Photographs Division, LC-USZC4-1732.

PART ONE　The Civil War

Note on the Texts

As with the previous volume, *The American Republic: Primary Sources,* the editor has sought to make as few changes as possible in the texts included, so as to convey the flavor as well as the content of the writings. Further, because the materials in this volume are from time periods closer to our own, very few changes were required. Asterisks inserted without clear meaning or intent have been deleted, as have marginalia, extraneous quotation marks, and page numbers from previous editions that had been inserted in various texts. Some of the longer titles have been shortened in accordance with modern usage. Headings in which the original text used anachronistic fonts or, for example, all capital letters, have been modernized and standardized. Only those footnotes deemed necessary for understanding the text have been reproduced.

maintain chronological consistency than in the first. Consequently, in this work there is somewhat greater overlap of eras among the documents. Moreover, in a very few cases it was necessary to present documents from eras before that which is the focus of this volume. For example, it would be confusing to readers to avoid presentation of the original statement of the Monroe Doctrine in "America in the World," despite its dating from well before the Civil War, because that doctrine has been central to debates concerning America's proper attitude toward international affairs and conflicts. In addition, Elizabeth Cady Stanton's "Address to the Woman's State Temperance Society" is presented, despite its having been delivered before the Civil War. This is because Stanton and that speech had influence beyond the Civil War era, because

they presented arguably the most lucid and powerful statement of prohibition assumptions and ideology, and because Stanton herself embodied an important element in reform movements—the ties between abolitionism, prohibition, and the struggle for women's rights.

Thanks are owed to the members of this volume's editorial board, especially to Dr. Danton Kostandarithes, whose assistance went well beyond the call of duty. I also wish to thank the following for their assistance: Amy Ruark, Raymond McAuliffe, and Michael Thiefels. As always, my greatest thanks and my greatest debts belong to my wife, Gloria Antonia Frohnen, for reasons that include but go far beyond the many ways in which she made possible the completion of this work.

program put forward by the Progressives themselves during the height of their influence.[2] Direct documentary knowledge of Progressive legislative and constitutional enactments such as the direct election of senators would increase students' understanding of the entire history of American public life. Likewise, the relationship between various political ideologies and the debate between so-called isolationists and internationalists—a relationship which changed radically at least once during the era represented in this volume—would be shown to be more complex, and more worthy of serious thought and investigation, by examination of relevant pronouncements and enactments.

A few words are required regarding editorial interpretation. As with the first work, this volume eschews editorial commentary on the contents of the documents presented. It presents only brief, historically oriented headnotes, intended to provide readers with the most basic information needed to understand the documents themselves. Given the breadth of material covered, it was necessary to organize the volume around themes. But those themes were chosen with the intention of providing a framework for the documents that does not necessitate or even push the reader toward any particular ideological conclusions. Whether one sees consolidation as a good or a bad thing, it can be agreed among students of all stripes that the era covered in this volume was one in which the power of the federal government increased and gained greater clarity, in which industrialization and the construction of national markets took place, in which regional movements opposed to consolidation, as well as truly national reform movements, were formed, in which a conflict of visions produced genuine conflict regarding race, ethnicity, and culture in America, and in which the United States came to play a far greater role in international affairs. The goal is simply to show the variety of positions and policies that shaped American public life during the era between the Civil War and World War II.

ORGANIZATION OF THE WORK

This work is in seven parts. As in the previous volume, each part is composed of selections of public writings intended to illustrate the major philosophical, cultural, and policy positions at issue during crucial eras of American political and cultural development.

2. See especially James Allen Smith, *The Spirit of American Government* (New York: Macmillan, 1907).

The first part, "The Civil War," provides documentary evidence of the positions of both sides as to the causes of that war, as well as the intentions behind eventual emancipation of African Americans and the impact of the war itself on American public life. The second part, "Reconstruction," provides materials illustrating the nature and purpose of the programs initiated by the victorious states at the end of the Civil War, as well as reactions to that program in the Southern states that were these programs' target. The third part, "Consolidating Markets," includes materials showing the contested nature of the government's role in American economic expansion and the growth of national markets for goods and services. The fourth part, "Consolidating Culture?" includes materials illustrating the various cultural conflicts—regarding race, religion, ethnicity, ideology, and culture—that characterized the late-nineteenth and early-twentieth centuries. The fifth part, "Reform Movements," provides materials on the various reform movements that influenced public life and policy during this era, focusing on the constitutional changes they sought and achieved. The sixth part, "Consolidating Government," traces the development of the federal administrative and welfare state through various legal, constitutional, and intellectual crises and developments. The seventh part, "America in the World," provides materials tracing developments in America's public position regarding the role it can and should take in international affairs.

This volume ends with the opening of the Second World War. While it would, perhaps, be helpful to include documents from beyond this era, it was judged prudent to stop there. Reasons for this decision include the need to keep the volume to some kind of manageable length, the existence of many courses in contemporary American history that begin at or immediately following World War II, and the general recognition that America's participation in that war significantly altered its role in the world and the nature of debates regarding the nature of its people and the proper role of its government.

As with the previous volume, the placement of specific selections within this work is intended to answer two pedagogical needs: that of chronological consistency and that of issue focus, so that readers may see particular topics of importance in sufficient depth to give them serious examination. Given the increased complexity and prevalence of public debates, particularly concerning the role of government, during the era covered in this second volume, it proved more difficult to

Introduction

This volume continues the work begun with *The American Republic: Primary Sources*. Like that work, this one seeks to make available within the covers of one volume the most crucial documents necessary for understanding the variety of policies and viewpoints driving American public life during an important, substantive part of its history. Picking up with the onset of the Civil War, documents in this volume will take students and other readers through the onset of World War II and America's entrance into yet another major new phase in its existence.

For decades now, a host of debates have continued concerning the purpose, nature, and impact of the major popular, legal, and ideological movements shaping the United States during the period from approximately the onset of the Civil War through World War II. Was Reconstruction a noble, failed attempt to protect and empower African Americans in the South by reforming Southern institutions, a self-interested attempt to gain power and wealth for one political party and region through cynical appeals to abstract ideals, or a Utopian experiment in radical politics? Were national markets in goods and services the natural outgrowth of individual initiative and the American spirit of enterprise, or the creation of powerful interests? Is American culture intrinsically racist, ideologically intolerant of racial and cultural connections that might dilute a common emphasis on individual choice, or racially and culturally ambivalent? Were American reform movements homegrown or spawned by immigrants who brought with them European political habits and notions of class? Did the Great Depression necessitate establishment of the national welfare and administrative state, or was this a matter of ideological choice? Was America's entry onto the world stage an inevitable consequence of its growing power, or a conscious choice, spawned by commitment to, and dreams of, universal peace and justice?

Such questions abound in discussions of these critical periods, but too rarely are informed by close reading of the public documents and pronouncements through which American thought has been expressed and policy made. In particular, the recent turn to social history has uncovered a great deal of information regarding the daily lives of Americans during the Civil War and through World War II. Unfortunately, this information often has come at the expense of in-depth study of crucial, relevant documents. The massive evidence marshaled by Raoul Berger in his landmark volume *Government by Judiciary* concerning the intentions of the framers of the Fourteenth Amendment, for example, has been all but ignored in the legal literature.[1] Indeed, the history of the Fourteenth Amendment, which promised all Americans due process of law, equal protection of the laws, and the privileges and immunities of American citizenship, has become part of the ideological debate it was intended to illuminate.

The debate continues over whether public figures and policy makers after the Civil War sought to treat race as a set of intractable differences government should treat as guides to public policy, conventional differences public institutions should eliminate, or cultural differences government and society should respect. Almost unnoticed has been the specifically constitutional debate over which branch of government—Congress, the president, or the courts—should have primary responsibility for defining and enforcing the rights set forth in the Fourteenth Amendment. Thus re-presentation of key speeches and statutes relevant to that amendment's passage remains imperative.

If students are to understand how and why the Supreme Court has gained increased power in the American system, they must be able to consult, directly, the relevant documents. The same may be said for the late-nineteenth-century growth of national markets, aided by Supreme Court decisions as it was opposed by an organized set of political actors (the Populists in particular) whose political program too often is reduced by commentators to issues of class struggle. Again, there has not been sufficient attention paid to actual party platforms and reforms.

In addition, while the work of the so-called Progressive historians has changed opinions greatly among academics concerning the nature and intent of the American founding, most students gain little exposure to the actual political

---

1. Berger, Raoul, *Government by Judiciary: The Transformation of the Fourteenth Amendment* (Indianapolis: Liberty Fund, 1997).

Illustrations

South Carolina Declaration of Causes of Secession

December 20, 1860

DECLARATION OF THE IMMEDIATE CAUSES WHICH INDUCE AND JUSTIFY THE SECESSION OF SOUTH CAROLINA FROM THE FEDERAL UNION.

The People of the State of South Carolina, in Convention assembled, on the 26th day of April, A.D. 1852, declared that the frequent violations of the Constitution of the United States, by the Federal Government, and its encroachments upon the reserved rights of the States, fully justified this State in then withdrawing from the Federal Union; but in deference to the opinions and wishes of the other slaveholding States, she forbore at that time to exercise this right. Since that time, these encroachments have continued to increase, and further forbearance ceases to be a virtue.

And now the State of South Carolina having resumed her separate and equal place among nations, deems it due to herself, to the remaining United States of America, and to the nations of the world, that she should declare the immediate causes which have led to this act.

In the year 1765, that portion of the British Empire embracing Great Britain, undertook to make laws for the government of that portion composed of the thirteen American Colonies. A struggle for the right of self-government ensued, which resulted, on the 4th July, 1776, in a Declaration, by the Colonies, "that they are, and of right ought to be, FREE AND INDEPENDENT STATES; and that, as free and independent States, they have full power to levy war, conclude peace, contract alliances, establish commerce, and to do all other acts and things which independent States may of right do."

They further solemnly declared that whenever any "form of government becomes destructive of the ends for which it was established, it is the right of the people to alter or abolish it, and to institute a new government." Deeming the Government of Great Britain to have become destructive of these ends, they declared that the Colonies "are absolved from all allegiance to the British Crown, and that all political connection between them and the State of Great Britain is, and ought to be, totally dissolved."

In pursuance of this Declaration of Independence, each of the thirteen States proceeded to exercise its separate sovereignty; adopted for itself a Constitution, and appointed officers for the administration of government in all its departments—Legislative, Executive and Judicial. For purposes of defence, they united their arms and their counsels; and, in 1778, they entered into a League known as the Articles of Confederation, whereby they agreed to entrust the administration of their external relations to a common agent, known as the Congress of the United States, expressly declaring, in the first article, "that each State retains its sovereignty, freedom and independence, and every power, jurisdiction and right which is not, by this Confederation, expressly delegated to the United States in Congress assembled."

Under this Confederation the War of the Revolution was carried on, and on the 3d September, 1783, the contest ended, and a definitive Treaty was signed by Great Britain, in which she acknowledged the Independence of the Colonies in the following terms:

"*Article* 1.—His Britannic Majesty acknowledges the said United States, viz: New Hampshire, Massachusetts Bay, Rhode Island and Providence Plantations, Connecticut, New York, New Jersey, Pennsylvania, Delaware, Maryland, Virginia, North Carolina, South Carolina and Georgia, to be FREE, SOVEREIGN AND INDEPENDENT STATES; that he treats with them as such; and for himself, his heirs and successors, relinquishes all claims to the government, propriety and territorial rights of the same and every part thereof."

Thus were established the two great principles asserted by the Colonies, namely: the right of a State to govern itself; and the right of a people to abolish a Government when it becomes destructive of the ends for which it was instituted. And concurrent with the establishment of these principles, was the fact, that each Colony became and was recognized by the mother Country as a FREE, SOVEREIGN AND INDEPENDENT STATE.

In 1787, Deputies were appointed by the States to revise the Articles of Confederation, and on 17th September, 1787, these Deputies recommended, for the adoption of the States, the Articles of Union, known as the Constitution of the United States.

The parties to whom this Constitution was submitted, were the several sovereign States; they were to agree or disagree, and when nine of them agreed, the compact was to take effect among those concurring; and the General Government, as the common agent, was then to be invested with their authority.

If only nine of the thirteen States had concurred, the other four would have remained as they then were—separate, sovereign States, independent of any of the provisions of the Constitution. In fact, two of the States did not accede to the Constitution until long after it had gone into operation among the other eleven; and during that interval, they each exercised the functions of an independent nation.

By this Constitution, certain duties were imposed upon the several States, and the exercise of certain of their powers was restrained, which necessarily implied their continued existence as sovereign States. But, to remove all doubt, an amendment was added, which declared that the powers not delegated to the United States by the Constitution, nor prohibited by it to the States, are reserved to the States, respectively, or to the people. On 23d May, 1788, South Carolina, by a Convention of her people, passed an Ordinance assenting to this Constitution, and afterwards altered her own Constitution, to conform herself to the obligations she had undertaken.

Thus was established, by compact between the States, a Government, with defined objects and powers, limited to the express words of the grant. This limitation left the whole remaining mass of power subject to the clause reserving it to the States or to the people, and rendered unnecessary any specification of reserved rights.

We hold that the Government thus established is subject to the two great principles asserted in the Declaration of Independence; and we hold further, that the mode of its formation subjects it to a third fundamental principle, namely: the law of compact. We maintain that in every compact between two or more parties, the obligation is mutual; that the failure of one of the contracting parties to perform a material part of the agreement, entirely releases the obligation of the other; and that where no arbiter is provided, each party is remitted to his own judgment to determine the fact of failure, with all its consequences.

In the present case, that fact is established with certainty. We assert, that fourteen of the States have deliberately refused for years past to fulfil their constitutional obligations, and we refer to their own Statutes for the proof.

The Constitution of the United States, in its 4th Article, provides as follows:

"No person held to service or labor in one State, under the laws thereof, escaping into another, shall, in consequence of any law or regulation therein, be discharged from such service or labor, but shall be delivered up, on claim of the party to whom such service or labor may be due."

This stipulation was so material to the compact, that without it that compact would not have been made. The greater number of the contracting parties held slaves, and they had previously evinced their estimate of the value of such a stipulation by making it a condition in the Ordinance for the government of the territory ceded by Virginia, which now composes the States north of the Ohio river.

The same article of the Constitution stipulates also for rendition by the several States of fugitives from justice from the other States.

The General Government, as the common agent, passed laws to carry into effect these stipulations of the States. For many years these laws were executed. But an increasing hostility on the part of the non-slaveholding States to the Institution of Slavery has led to a disregard of their obligations, and the laws of the General Government have ceased to effect the objects of the Constitution. The States of Maine, New Hampshire, Vermont, Massachusetts, Connecticut, Rhode Island, New York, Pennsylvania, Illinois, Indiana, Michigan, Wisconsin and Iowa, have enacted laws which either nullify the Acts of Congress or render useless any attempt to execute them. In many of these States the fugitive is discharged from the service or labor claimed, and in none of them has the State Government complied with the stipulation made in the Constitution. The State of New Jersey, at an early day, passed a law in conformity with her constitutional obligation; but the current of anti-slavery feeling has led her more recently to enact laws which render inoperative the remedies provided by her own law and by the laws of Congress. In the State of New York even the right of transit for a slave has been denied by her tribunals; and the States of Ohio and Iowa have refused to surrender to justice fugitives charged with murder, and with inciting servile insurrection in the State of Virginia. Thus the constitutional compact has been deliberately broken and disregarded by the non-slaveholding States, and the consequence follows that South Carolina is released from her obligation.

The ends for which this Constitution was framed are declared by itself to be "to form a more perfect union, establish justice, insure domestic tranquility, provide for the common defence, promote the general welfare, and secure the blessings of liberty to ourselves and our posterity."

These ends it endeavored to accomplish by a Federal Government, in which each State was recognized as an equal, and had separate control over its own institutions. The right of property in slaves was recognized by giving to free persons distinct political rights, by giving them the right to repre-sent, and burthening them with direct taxes for three-fifths of their slaves; by authorizing the importation of slaves for twenty years; and by stipulating for the rendition of fugitives from labor.

We affirm that these ends for which this Government was instituted have been defeated, and the Government it-self has been made destructive of them by the action of the non-slaveholding States. Those States have assumed the right of deciding upon the propriety of our domestic institutions; and have denied the rights of property established in fifteen of the States and recognized by the Constitution; they have denounced as sinful the institution of Slavery; they have permitted the open establishment among them of societies, whose avowed object is to disturb the peace and to eloign the property of the citizens of other States. They have encour-aged and assisted thousands of our slaves to leave their homes; and those who remain, have been incited by emissaries, books and pictures to servile insurrection.

For twenty-five years this agitation has been steadily in-creasing, until it has now secured to its aid the power of the Common Government. Observing the *forms* of the Consti-tution, a sectional party has found within that article estab-lishing the Executive Department, the means of subverting the Constitution itself. A geographical line has been drawn across the Union, and all the States north of that line have united in the election of a man to the high office of President of the United States whose opinions and purposes are hostile to slavery. He is to be entrusted with the administration of the Common Government, because he has declared that that "Government cannot endure permanently half slave, half free," and that the public mind must rest in the belief that Slavery is in the course of ultimate extinction.

This sectional combination for the subversion of the Con-stitution, has been aided in some of the States by elevating to citizenship, persons, who, by the Supreme Law of the land, are incapable of becoming citizens; and their votes have been used to inaugurate a new policy, hostile to the South, and de-structive of its peace and safety.

On the 4th March next, this party will take possession of the Government. It has announced, that the South shall be excluded from the common Territory; that the Judicial Tri-bunals shall be made sectional, and that a war must be waged against slavery until it shall cease throughout the United States.

The Guaranties of the Constitution will then no longer exist; the equal rights of the States will be lost. The slavehold-ing States will no longer have the power of self-government, or self-protection, and the Federal Government will have become their enemy.

Sectional interest and animosity will deepen the irritation, and all hope of remedy is rendered vain, by the fact that pub-lic opinion at the North has invested a great political error with the sanctions of a more erroneous religious belief.

We, therefore, the people of South Carolina, by our del-egates, in Convention assembled, appealing to the Supreme Judge of the world for the rectitude of our intentions, have solemnly declared that the Union heretofore existing be-tween this State and the other States of North America, is dissolved, and that the State of South Carolina has resumed her position among the nations of the world, as a separate and independent State; with full power to levy war, con-clude peace, contract alliances, establish commerce, and to do all other acts and things which independent States may of right do.

Mississippi Ordinance of Secession

January 9, 1861

AN ORDINANCE
TO DISSOLVE THE UNION BETWEEN THE STATE OF MISSISSIPPI AND OTHER STATES UNITED WITH HER UNDER THE COMPACT ENTITLED "THE CONSTITUTION OF THE UNITED STATES OF AMERICA."

The people of the State of Mississippi, in Convention assembled, do ordain and declare, and it is hereby ordained and declared as follows, to-wit:

SECTION 1ST. That all the laws and ordinances by which the said State of Mississippi became a member of the Federal Union of the United States of America be, and the same are hereby repealed, and that all obligations on the part of the said State or the people thereof to observe the same, be withdrawn, and that the said State doth hereby resume all the rights, functions and powers which, by any of said laws or ordinances, were conveyed to the government of the said United States, and is absolved from all the obligations, restraints and duties incurred to the said Federal Union, and shall from henceforth be a free, sovereign and independent State.

SECTION 2ND. That so much of the first section of the seventh article of the Constitution of this State as requires members of the Legislature, and all officers, executive and judicial, to take an oath or affirmation to support the Constitution of the United States, be, and the same is hereby abrogated and annulled.

SECTION 3RD. That all rights acquired and vested under the Constitution of the United States, or under any act of Congress passed, or treaty made, in pursuance thereof, or under any law of this State, and not incompatible with this Ordinance, shall remain in force and have the same effect as if this Ordinance had not been passed.

SECTION 4TH. That the people of the State of Mississippi hereby consent to form a Federal Union with such of the States as may have seceded or may secede from the Union of the United States of America, upon the basis of the present Constitution of the said United States, except such parts thereof as embrace other portions than such seceding States.

Thus ordained and declared in Convention the 9th day of January, in the Year of Our Lord One Thousand Eight Hundred and Sixty-one.

W. S. BARRY, *President.*

F. A. POPE, *Secretary.*

IN TESTIMONY of the passage of which, and the determination of the members of this Convention to uphold and maintain the State in the position she has assumed by said Ordinance, it is signed by the President and Members of this Convention this the fifteenth day of January, A.D. 1861.

Adams County—A. K. Farrar, J. Winchester.
Attala—E. H. Sanders.
Amite—D. W. Hurst.
Bolivar—M. H. McGehee.
Carroll—J. Z. George, W. Booth.
Claiborne—H. T. Ellett.
Coahoma—J. L. Alcorn.
Copiah—P. S. Catching, B. King.
Clarke—S. H. Terral.
Choctaw—W. F. Brantley, W. H. Witty, J. H. Edwards.
Chickasaw—J. A. Orr, C. B. Baldwin.
Covington—A. C. Powell.
Calhoun—W. A. Sumner, M. D. L. Stephens.
DeSoto—J. R. Chalmers, S. D. Johnston, T. Lewers.
Franklin—D. H. Parker.
Green—T. J. Roberts.
Hinds—W. P. Harris, W. P. Anderson, W. B. Smart.
Holmes—J. M. Dyer, W. L. Keirn.
Harrison—D. C. Glenn.
Hancock—J. B. Deason.
Issaquena—A. C. Gibson.
Itawamba—R. O. Beene, A. B. Bullard, W. H. H. Tison, M. C. Cummings.
Jasper—O. C. Dease.
Jackson—A. E. Lewis.
Jefferson—J. S. Johnston.
Jones—J. H. Powell.
Kemper—O. Y. Neely, T. H. Woods.
Lawrence—W. Gwin.
Lowndes—George R. Clayton.
Leake—W. B. Colbert.
Lauderdale—J. B. Ramsey, F. C. Semmes.
Lafayette—L. Q. C. Lamar, T. D. Isom.

Marshall—A. M. Clayton, J. W. Clapp, S. Benton, H. W. Walter, W. M. Lea.
Madison—A. P. Hill.
Monroe—S. J. Gholson, F. M. Rogers.
Marion—H. Mayson.
Noxubee—Israel Welsh.
Neshoba—D. M. Backstrom.
Newton—M. M. Keith.
Oktibbeha—T. C. Bookter.
Perry—P. J. Myers.
Pike—J. M. Nelson.
Panola—J. B. Fiser, E. F. McGehee.
Pontotoc—C. D. Fontaine, J. B. Herring, H. R. Miller, R. W. Flournoy.
Rankin—Wm. Denson.
Sunflower—E. P. Jones.

Simpson—W. J. Douglas.
Smith—W. Thompson.
Scott—C. W. Taylor.
Tallahatchie—A. Patterson.
Tishomingo—A. E. Reynolds, W. W. Bonds, T. P. Young, J. A. Blair.
Tunica—A. Miller.
Tippah—O. Davis, J. H. Berry, J. S. Davis, D. B. Wright.
Washington—J. S. Yerger.
Wilkinson—A. C. Holt.
Wayne—W. J. Eckford.
Warren—W. Brooke, T. A. Marshall.
Winston—J. Kennedy, W. S. Bolling.
Yallobusha—F. M. Aldridge, W. R. Barksdale.
Yazoo—H. Vaughan, G. B. Wilkinson.

Mississippi Declaration of Causes of Secession

January 9, 1861

A DECLARATION
*OF THE IMMEDIATE CAUSES WHICH INDUCE
AND JUSTIFY THE SECESSION OF THE STATE
OF MISSISSIPPI FROM THE FEDERAL UNION.*

In the momentous step which our State has taken of dissolving its connection with the government of which we so long formed a part, it is but just that we should declare the prominent reasons which have induced our course.

Our position is thoroughly identified with the institution of slavery—the greatest material interest of the world. Its labor supplies the product which constitutes by far the largest and most important portions of the commerce of the earth. These products are peculiar to the climate verging on the tropical regions, and by an imperious law of nature none but the black race can bear exposure to the tropical sun. These products have become necessities of the world, and a blow at slavery is a blow at commerce and civilization. That blow has been long aimed at the institution, and was at the point of reaching its consummation. There was no choice left us but submission to the mandates of abolition, or a dissolution of the Union, whose principles had been subverted to work out our ruin.

That we do not overstate the dangers to our institution, a reference to a few facts will sufficiently prove.

The hostility to this institution commenced before the adoption of the Constitution, and was manifested in the well-known Ordinance of 1787, in regard to the Northwestern Territory.

The feeling increased, until, in 1819–20, it deprived the South of more than half the vast territory acquired from France.

The same hostility dismembered Texas and seized upon all the territory acquired from Mexico.

It has grown until it denies the right of property in slaves, and refuses protection to that right on the high seas, in the Territories, and wherever the government of the United States had jurisdiction.

It refuses the admission of new slave States into the Union, and seeks to extinguish it by confining it within its present limits, denying the power of expansion.

It tramples the original equality of the South under foot.

It has nullified the Fugitive Slave Law in almost every free State in the Union, and has utterly broken the compact which our fathers pledged their faith to maintain.

It advocates negro equality, socially and politically, and promotes insurrection and incendiarism in our midst.

It has enlisted its press, its pulpit and its schools against us, until the whole popular mind of the North is excited and inflamed with prejudice.

It has made combinations and formed associations to carry out its schemes of emancipation in the States and wherever else slavery exists.

It seeks not to elevate or to support the slave, but to destroy his present condition without providing a better.

It has invaded a State, and invested with the honors of martyrdom the wretch whose purpose was to apply flames to our dwellings and the weapons of destruction to our lives.

It has broken every compact into which it has entered for our security.

It has given indubitable evidence of its design to ruin our agriculture, to prostrate our industrial pursuits and to destroy our social system.

It knows no relenting or hesitation in its purposes; it stops not in its march of aggression, and leaves us no room to hope for cessation or for pause.

It has recently obtained control of the Government, by the prosecution of its unhallowed schemes, and destroyed the last expectation of living together in friendship and brotherhood.

Utter subjugation awaits us in the Union, if we should consent longer to remain in it. It is not a matter of choice, but of necessity. We must either submit to degradation, and to the loss of property worth four billions of money, or we must secede from the Union framed by our fathers, to secure this as well as every other species of property. For far less cause than this, our fathers separated from the Crown of England.

Our decision is made. We follow their footsteps. We embrace the alternative of separation; and for the reasons here stated, we resolve to maintain our rights with the full consciousness of the justice of our course, and the undoubting belief of our ability to maintain it.

Virginia Ordinance to Repeal the Ratification of the Constitution of the United States of America

April 17, 1861

An ORDINANCE to repeal the ratification of the Constitution of the United States of America, by the State of Virginia, and to resume all the rights and powers granted under said Constitution.

The people of Virginia, in their ratification of the Constitution of the United States of America, adopted by them in Convention, on the twenty-fifth day of June, in the year of our Lord, one thousand seven hundred and eighty-eight, having declared that the powers granted under the said Constitution, were derived from the people of the United States, and might be resumed whensoever the same should be perverted to their injury and oppression, and the Federal Government having perverted said powers, not only to the injury of the people of Virginia, but to the oppression of the Southern slaveholding States,

Now, therefore, we, the people of Virginia, do declare and ordain, That the ordinance adopted by the people of this State in Convention, on the twenty-fifth day of June, in the year of our Lord one thousand seven hundred and eighty-eight, whereby the Constitution of the United States of America was ratified; and all acts of the General Assembly of this State ratifying or adopting amendments to said Constitution, are hereby repealed and abrogated; that the union between the State of Virginia and the other States under the Constitution aforesaid is hereby dissolved, and that the State of Virginia is in the full possession and exercise of all the rights of sovereignty, which belong and appertain to a free and independent State.

And they do further declare, That said Constitution of the United States of America, is no longer binding on any of the citizens of this State.

This ordinance shall take effect and be an act of this day, when ratified by a majority of the votes of the people of this State, cast at a poll to be taken thereon, on the fourth Thursday in May next, in pursuance of a schedule hereafter to be enacted.

Done in Convention in the City of Richmond, on the seventeenth day of April, in the year of our Lord one thousand

eight hundred and sixty-one, and in the eighty-fifth year of the Commonwealth of Virginia.

Missouri Act Declaring the Political Ties Heretofore Existing between the State of Missouri and the United States of America Dissolved

October 31, 1861

An act declaring the political ties heretofore existing between the State of Missouri and the United States of America dissolved.

Whereas the Government of the United States, in the possession and under the control of a sectional party, has wantonly violated the compact originally made between said Government and the State of Missouri, by invading with hostile armies the soil of the State, attacking and making prisoners the militia while legally assembled under the State laws, forcibly occupying the State capitol, and attempting through the instrumentality of domestic traitors to usurp the State government, seizing and destroying private property, and murdering with fiendish malignity peaceable citizens, men, women, and children, together with other acts of atrocity, indicating a deep-settled hostility toward the people of Missouri and their institutions; and

Whereas the present Administration of the Government of the United States has utterly ignored the Constitution, subverted the Government as constructed and intended by its makers, and established a despotic and arbitrary power instead thereof: Now, therefore,

Be it enacted by the general assembly of the State of Missouri, That all political ties of every character now existing between the Government of the United States of America and the people and government of the State of Missouri are hereby dissolved, and the State of Missouri, resuming the sovereignty granted by compact to the said United States upon the admission of said State into the Federal Union, does again take its place as a free and independent republic amongst the nations of the earth.

This act to take effect and be in force from and after its passage.

Approved, October 31, 1861.

I hereby certify the above and foregoing to be a full, true, and perfect copy of the original roll. In testimony whereof I have hereto set my hand and the great seal of the State of Missouri, this 2d day of November, 1861.

[SEAL.]   B. F. MASSEY, *Secretary of State.*

An act ratifying the Constitution of the Provisional Government of the Confederate States of America.

Whereas the Congress of the Confederate States of America have, by an act entitled "An act to aid the State of Missouri in repelling invasion by the United States, and to authorize the admission of said State as a member of the Confederate States of America, and for other purposes," enacted that "the State of Missouri shall be admitted a member of the Confederate States of America, upon an equal footing with the other States, under the Constitution for the Provisional Government of the same, upon condition that the said Constitution for the Provisional Government of the Confederate States shall be adopted and ratified by the properly and legally constituted authorities of said State": Now, therefore,

Be it enacted by the general assembly of the State of Missouri, as follows:

SECTION 1. The general assembly of the State of Missouri, for and in behalf of the people thereof, do hereby accept the provisions of an act of the Congress of the Confederate States of America, as set forth in the preamble to this act, the State of Missouri hereby adopting and ratifying the Constitution for the Provisional Government of the Confederate States of America as a member of said Confederacy upon an equal footing with the other States under said Constitution.

Ordinance of the Kentucky Convention

November 20, 1861

Whereas the Federal Constitution, which created the Government of the United States, was declared by the framers thereof to be the supreme law of the land and was intended to limit the powers of said Government to certain general specified purposes, and did expressly reserve to the States and people all other powers whatever; and the President and Congress have treated this supreme law of the Union with contempt, and usurped to themselves the power to interfere with the rights and liberties of the States and the people against the expressed provisions of the Constitution, and have thus substituted for the highest forms of rational liberty and constitutional government, a central despotism, founded upon the ignorant prejudices of the masses of Northern society, and, instead of giving protection with the Constitution to the people of fifteen States of this Union, have turned loose upon them the unrestrained raging passions of mobs and fanatics, and because we seek to hold our liberties, our property, our homes, and our families, under the protection of the reserved powers of the States, have blockaded our ports, invaded our soil, and waged war upon our people for the purpose of subjugating us to their will; and

Whereas our honor and our duty to posterity demand that we shall not relinquish our own liberty, and shall not abandon the right of our descendants and the world to the inestimable blessings of constitutional government: Therefore,

Be it ordained, That we do hereby forever sever our connections with the Government of the United States, and, in the name of the people, we do hereby declare Kentucky to be a free and independent State, clothed with all power to fix her own destiny and to secure her own rights and liberties; and

Whereas the majority of the legislature of Kentucky have violated their most solemn pledges, made before the election, and deceived and betrayed the people; have abandoned the position of neutrality assumed by themselves and the people, and invited into the State the organized armies of Lincoln; have abdicated the government in favor of the military despotism which they have placed around themselves, but can not control, and have abandoned the duty of shielding the citizens with their protection; have thrown upon our people and the State the horrors and ravages of war, instead of attempting to preserve the peace, and have voted men and money for the war waged by the North for the destruction of our constitutional rights; have violated the express words of the Constitution by borrowing five millions of money for the support of the war, without a vote of the people; have permitted the arrest and imprisonment of our citizens and transferred the constitutional prerogatives of the executive to a military commission of partisans; have seen the right of habeas corpus suspended without an effort for its preservation, and permitted our people to be driven in exile from their homes; have subjected our property to confiscation, and our persons to confinement in the penitentiary as felons, because we may choose to take part in a contest for civil liberty and constitutional government against a sectional majority waging war against the people and institutions of fifteen independent States of the old Federal Union, and have done all these things deliberately against the warnings and vetoes of the governor and the solemn remonstrances of the minority in the senate and house of representatives: Therefore,

Be it further ordained, That the unconstitutional edicts of a factious majority of a legislature thus false to their pledges, their honor, and their interests, are not law, and that such government is unworthy of the support of a brave and free people; and that we do therefore declare that the people are thereby absolved from all allegiance to said government, and that they have a right to establish any government which to them may seem best adapted to the preservation of their rights and liberties.

SECTION 1. The supreme executive and legislative power of the provisional government of this Commonwealth, hereby established, shall be vested in a governor and ten councilmen, one from each of the present Congressional districts, a majority of whom shall constitute a quorum to transact business. The governor and councilmen to be elected by the members of this convention in such manner as this convention may prescribe.

SEC. 2. The governor and council are hereby invested with full power to pass all laws necessary to effect the objects contemplated by the formation of this government. They shall have full control of the army and navy of this Commonwealth, and the militia thereof.

SEC. 3. No law shall be passed, or act done, or appointment made, either civil or military, by the provisional government, except with the concurrence of a majority of the council and approval of the governor, except as herein specially provided.

SEC. 4. In case of a vacancy in the gubernatorial office, occasioned by death, resignation, or any other cause, the council shall have power to elect a governor, as his successor, who shall not, however, be a member of their own body.

SEC. 5. The council hereby established shall consist of one person selected from each Congressional district in the State, to be chosen by this convention, who shall have power to fill all vacancies from any cause from the district in which such vacancy shall occur.

SEC. 6. The council shall have power to pass any acts which they may deem essential to the preservation of our liberty and the protection of our rights, and such acts, when approved by the governor, shall become law, and as such shall be sustained by the courts and other departments of the government.

SEC. 7. The governor shall nominate, and, by and with the advice and consent of the council, shall appoint all judicial and executive and other officers necessary for the enforcement of law and the protection of society under the extraordinary circumstances now existing, who shall continue in office during the pleasure of the governor and council, or until the establishment of a permanent government.

SEC. 8. The governor shall have power, by and with the consent and advice of the council, to conclude a treaty with the Confederate States of America, by which the State of Kentucky may be admitted as one of said Confederate States upon an equal footing in all respects with the other States of said Confederacy.

SEC. 9. That three commissioners shall be appointed by this convention to the Government of the Confederate States of America, with power to negotiate and treat with said Confederate States for the earliest practicable admission of Kentucky into the Government of said Confederate States of America, who shall report the result of their mission to the governor and council of this provisional government, for such future action as may be deemed advisable, and, should less than the full number attend, such as may attend may conduct such negotiation.

SEC. 10. So soon as an election can be held, free from the influence of the armies of the United States, the provisional government shall provide for the assembling of a convention to adopt such measures as may be necessary and expedient for the restoration of a permanent government. Said convention shall consist of one hundred delegates, one from each representative district in the State, except the counties of Mason and Kenton, each of which shall be entitled to two delegates.

SEC. 11. An auditor and treasurer shall be appointed by the provisional government, whose duties shall be prescribed by law, and who shall give bond with sufficient security for the faithful discharge of the duties of their respective offices, to be approved by the governor and council.

SEC. 12. The following oath shall be taken by the governor, members of the council, judges, and all other officers, civil and military, who may be commissioned and appointed by this provisional government: "I, ——, do solemnly swear (or affirm), in the presence of Almighty God, and upon my honor, that I will observe and obey all laws passed by the provisional government of Kentucky. So help me God."

SEC. 13. The governor shall receive, as his salary, $2,000 per annum, and the councilmen, $5 per diem, while in session, and the salary of the other officers shall be fixed by law.

SEC. 14. The constitution and laws of Kentucky, not inconsistent with the acts of this convention, and the establishment of this government, and the laws which may be enacted by the governor and council, shall be the laws of this State.

SEC. 15. That whenever the governor and council shall have concluded a treaty with the Confederate States of America, for the admission of this State into the Confederate Government, the governor and council shall elect two Senators, and provide by law for the election of members of the House of Representatives in Congress.

SEC. 16. The provisional government hereby established shall be located at Bowling Green, Ky., but the governor and council shall have power to meet at any other place that they may consider appropriate.

Done at Russellville, in the State of Kentucky, this 20th day of November, in the year of our Lord 1861.

(Signed)   H. C. BURNETT,
President of the convention, and member from Trigg County.
R. McKEE,
Secretary, and member from Louisville.
T. L. BURNETT,
Assistant secretary, and member from Spencer County.
T. S. BRYAN,
Assistant secretary, and member from Christian County.
W. M. COFFEE, of Ballard County.
A. D. KINGMAN.
W. J. LUNSFORD.
J. J. CUNNINGHAM, of Grayson County.
JOHN J. GREEN.
J. P. BURNSIDE.
GEORGE W. MAXSON.
ROBERT S. FORD, of Hardin County.
WILLIAM JOHNSTON, of Hardin County.
WILLIAM W. THOMPSON, of Hart County.
W. S. SHOWDY, of Hart County.
J. J. GROVES, of Hart County.
J. W. CROCKETT, of Henderson County.
B. W. JENKINS, of Henry County.
L. M. LOWE, of Hopkins County.
GREEN MALCOLM, of Jefferson County.
B. K. HORNSBY, of Jefferson County.
WILLIAM K. DANIEL, of Jessamine County.
D. P. BUCKNER, of Kenton County.
C. BENNETT, of Livingston County.
C. N. PENDLETON, of Logan County.
JAMES M. BEALL, of Logan County.

JOHN W. MALONE, of Logan County.
E. D. RICKETTS, of Louisville, First district.
J. A. PENTON, of Louisville, Second district.
GEORGE P. TALBOT, of Louisville, Third district.
J. G. P. HOOE, of Louisville, Fourth district.
H. W. BRUCE, of Louisville, Fourth district.
R. L. COBB, of Lyon County.
WILLIS B. MACHEN, of Lyon County.
GEORGE R. MERRITT, of Lyon County.
J. C. GILBERT, of Marshall County.
WILLIAM E. RAY, of Marion County.
L. M. RAY, of Marion County.
MICHAEL McARTY, of Marion County.
JOHN BURNAM, of Warren County.
J. H. D. McKEE, of Anderson County.
JAMES A. McBRAYER, of Anderson County.
W. TOWSLEY, of Ballard County.
J. P. BATES, of Barren County.
R. W. THOMAS, of Barren County.
N. A. SMITH, of Barren County.
W. K. EDMUNDS, of Barren County.
C. W. PARRISH, of Barren County.
J. W. EVARTS, of Barren County.
WILLIAM F. BELL, of Barren County.
S. S. SCOTT, of Barren County.
W. R. CUNNINGHAM, of Bourbon County.
SAMUEL H. McBRIDE, of Boyle County.
DORSEY B. BOWERS.
WILLIAM N. GAITHER.
JAMES W. MOORE.
HARDY S. LYPERT.
L. K. CHILTON.
JOHN J. THOMAS.
ROBERT McKEE.
STEPHEN EDWARDS.
P. C. BARNETT.
D. MATHEWSON, of Calloway County.
P. S. HAMLIN, of Calloway County.
T. M. JONES, of Calloway County.
ALEXANDER WESSON, of Calloway County.
FRANCIS W. DODDS, of Calloway County.
WILLIAM T. MATHES, of Calloway County.
C. A. DUNCAN, of Calloway County.
A. J. HOLLAND, of Calloway County.
H. L. GILTNER, of Calloway County.
THOMAS T. BARRETT.

ROBERT J. BRECKINRIDGE.

J. S. GIBBON.

R. B. ALEXANDER.

E. R. WOODWARD, of Metcalfe County.

E. M. BRUCE, of Nicholas County.

J. J. CONOVER, of Owen County.

OWEN DORSEY, of Oldham County.

GEORGE W. JOHNSON, of Scott County.

A. KEENE RICHARDS, of Scott County.

WILLIAM B. CLARK, of Simpson County.

B. W. WILLIAMS, of Simpson County.

T. L. BURNETT, of Spencer County.

J. A. RUSSELL, of Todd County.

W. B. HARRISON, of Todd County.

G. LINE, of Todd County.

H. H. POSTON, of Trigg County.

W. H. MURTRIE, of Trigg County.

ROBERT WOLDRIDGE, of Trigg County.

ANDREW CUNNINGHAM, Jr., of Trigg County.

J. Y. NEWKIRK, of Trimble County.

WILLIAM D. RAY.

WILLIAM J. PAYNE, of Union County.

S. D. BLACKBURN, of Warren County.

SANDFORD LYNE, of Woodford County.

JOHN W. ARNETT.

ROBERT A. BRECKENRIDGE, of Washington County.

WARREN LYTTLETON JENKINS, of Webster County.

THOMAS S. BRYAN, of Christian County.

J. F. BELL, of Calloway County.

A. R. BOONE, of Graves County.

H. M. ROSE, of Graves County.

J. A. PERTLE, of Graves County.

J. D. SCAFF, of Graves County.

JOHN RIDGWAY, of Graves County.

BLANTON DUNCAN, of Louisville.

PHILIP B. THOMPSON, of Mercer County.

Z. McDANIEL, of Monroe County.

W. N. WAND, of Muhlenburgh County.

A. F. WILLIAMS, of McCroskin County.

JOHN M. JOHNSON, of McCroskin County.

WILLIAM G. BULLITT, of McCroskin County.

H. H. HUSTON, of McCroskin County.

JOHN Q. A. KING, of McCroskin County.

WILLIAM E. MINER, of Nelson County.

JOHN C. BRODHEAD, of Nelson County.

JOHN J. DENNIS, of Calhoun, McLean County.

J. L. GREGORY, of Calhoun, McLean County.

Constitution of the Confederate States of America, 1861

On February 4, 1861, a convention of delegates from the seceding states convened in Montgomery, Alabama. They drafted a provisional constitution in four days and ratified a permanent document a month later. That document repeats much of the U.S. Constitution, but with important differences. In addition to provisions protecting chattel slavery against any legislative encroachments, either in the Confederate states or territories, the Confederate Constitution also limited the president to one six-year term, provided the president with a limited line-item veto, and forbade the use of tariffs to promote industry. Several provisions strengthened the capacity of state legislatures to check officials of the central government. Of particular note is the Confederate Constitution's preamble, which, while following the basic pattern of the original Constitution, refers to "each State acting in its sovereign and independent character" and invokes "the favor and guidance of Almighty God."

Constitution of the Confederate States of America

March 11, 1861

We, the people of the Confederate States, each State acting in its sovereign and independent character, in order to form a permanent federal government, establish justice, insure domestic tranquility, and secure the blessings of liberty to ourselves and our posterity—invoking the favor and guidance of Almighty God—do ordain and establish this Constitution for the Confederate States of America.

ARTICLE I

Section 1

All legislative powers herein delegated shall be vested in a Congress of the Confederate States, which shall consist of a Senate and a House of Representatives.

Section 2

1. The House of Representatives shall be composed of members chosen every second year by the people of the several States; and the electors in each State shall be citizens of the Confederate States, and have the qualifications requisite for electors of the most numerous branch of the State Legislature; but no person of foreign birth, not a citizen of the Confederate States, shall be allowed to vote for any officer, civil or political, State or Federal.

2. No person shall be a Representative who shall not have attained the age of twenty-five years, and be a citizen of the Confederate States, and who shall not, when elected, be an inhabitant of that State in which he shall be chosen.

3. Representatives and direct taxes shall be apportioned among the several States, which may be included within this Confederacy, according to their respective numbers, which shall be determined, by adding to the whole number of free persons, including those bound to service for a term of years, and excluding Indians not taxed, three-fifths of all slaves. The actual enumeration shall be made within three years after the first meeting of the Congress of the Confederate States, and within every subsequent term of ten years, in such manner as they shall by law direct. The number of Representatives shall not exceed one for every fifty thousand, but each State shall have at least one Representative; and until such enumeration shall be made, the State of South Carolina shall be entitled to choose six; the State of Georgia ten; the State of Alabama nine; the State of Florida two; the State of Mississippi seven; the State of Louisiana six; and the State of Texas six.

4. When vacancies happen in the representation from any State, the Executive authority thereof shall issue writs of election to fill such vacancies.

5. The House of Representatives shall choose their Speaker and other officers; and shall have the sole power of impeachment; except that any judicial or other Federal officer, resident and acting solely within the limits of any State,

may be impeached by a vote of two-thirds of both branches of the Legislature thereof.

Section 3

1. The Senate of the Confederate States shall be composed of two Senators from each State, chosen for six years by the Legislature thereof, at the regular session next immediately preceding the commencement of the term of service; and each Senator shall have one vote.

2. Immediately after they shall be assembled, in consequence of the first election, they shall be divided as equally as may be into three classes. The seats of the Senators of the first class shall be vacated at the expiration of the second year; of the second class at the expiration of the fourth year; and of the third class at the expiration of the sixth year; so that one-third may be chosen every second year; and if vacancies happen by resignation, or otherwise, during the recess of the Legislature of any State, the Executive thereof may make temporary appointments until the next meeting of the Legislature which shall then fill such vacancies.

3. No person shall be a Senator who shall not have attained the age of thirty years, and be a citizen of the Confederate States; and who shall not, when elected, be an inhabitant of the State for which he shall be chosen.

4. The Vice President of the Confederate States shall be President of the Senate, but shall have no vote unless they be equally divided.

5. The Senate shall choose their other officers; and also a President *pro tempore* in the absence of the Vice President, or when he shall exercise the office of President of the Confederate States.

6. The Senate shall have the sole power to try all impeachments. When sitting for that purpose, they shall be on oath or affirmation. When the President of the Confederate States is tried, the Chief Justice shall preside; and no person shall be convicted without the concurrence of two-thirds of the members present.

7. Judgment in cases of impeachment shall not extend further than to removal from office, and disqualification to hold and enjoy any office of honor, trust or profit, under the Confederate States; but the party convicted shall, nevertheless, be liable and subject to indictment, trial, judgment and punishment according to law.

Section 4

1. The times, places and manner of holding elections for Senators and Representatives, shall be prescribed in each State by the Legislature thereof, subject to the provisions of this Constitution; but the Congress may, at any time, by law, make or alter such regulations, except as to the times and places of choosing Senators.

2. The Congress shall assemble at least once in every year; and such meeting shall be on the first Monday in December, unless they shall, by law, appoint a different day.

Section 5

1. Each House shall be the judge of the elections, returns, and qualifications of its own members, and a majority of each shall constitute a quorum to do business; but a smaller number may adjourn from day to day, and may be authorized to compel the attendance of absent members, in such manner and under such penalties as each House may provide.

2. Each House may determine the rules of its proceedings, punish its members for disorderly behavior, and with the concurrence of two-thirds of the whole number expel a member.

3. Each House shall keep a journal of its proceedings, and from time to time publish the same, excepting such parts as may in their judgment require secrecy; and the yeas and nays of the members of either House, on any question, shall, at the desire of one-fifth of those present, be entered on the journal.

4. Neither House, during the session of Congress, shall, without the consent of the other, adjourn for more than three days, nor to any other place than that in which the two Houses shall be sitting.

Section 6

1. The Senators and Representatives shall receive a compensation for their services, to be ascertained by law, and paid out of the treasury of the Confederate States. They shall, in all cases, except treason, felony, and breach of the peace, be privileged from arrest during their attendance at the session of their respective Houses, and in going to and returning from the same; and for any speech or debate in either House, they shall not be questioned in any other place.

2. No Senator or Representative shall, during the time for which he was elected, be appointed to any civil office under the authority of the Confederate States, which shall have been created, or the emoluments whereof shall have been increased during such time; and no person holding any office under the Confederate States shall be a member of either House during his continuance in office. But Congress may, by law, grant to the principal officer in each of the Executive Departments a

seat upon the floor of either House, with the privilege of discussing any measures appertaining to his department.

Section 7

1. All bills for raising revenue shall originate in the House of Representatives; but the Senate may propose or concur with amendments, as on other bills.

2. Every bill which shall have passed both Houses, shall, before it becomes a law, be presented to the President of the Confederate States; if he approve, he shall sign it; but if not, he shall return it, with his objections, to that House in which it shall have originated, who shall enter the objections at large on their journal, and proceed to reconsider it. If, after such reconsideration, two-thirds of that House shall agree to pass the bill, it shall be sent, together with the objections, to the other House, by which it shall likewise be reconsidered, and if approved by two-thirds of that House, it shall become a law. But in all such cases, the votes of both Houses shall be determined by yeas and nays, and the names of the persons voting for and against the bill shall be entered on the journal of each House respectively. If any bill shall not be returned by the President within ten days (Sundays excepted) after it shall have been presented to him, the same shall be a law, in like manner as if he had signed it, unless the Congress, by their adjournment, prevent its return; in which case it shall not be a law. The President may approve any appropriation and disapprove any other appropriation in the same bill. In such case he shall, in signing the bill, designate the appropriations disapproved; and shall return a copy of such appropriations, with his objections, to the House in which the bill shall have originated; and the same proceeding shall then be had as in case of other bills disapproved by the President.

3. Every order, resolution or vote, to which the concurrence of both Houses may be necessary, (except on a question of adjournment,) shall be presented to the President of the Confederate States; and before the same shall take effect, shall be approved by him; or being disapproved by him, shall be re-passed by two-thirds of both Houses, according to the rules and limitations prescribed in case of a bill.

Section 8

The Congress shall have power—

1. To lay and collect taxes, duties, imposts, and excises, for revenue necessary to pay the debts, provide for the common defence, and carry on the government of the Confederate States; but no bounties shall be granted from the treasury; nor shall any duties or taxes on importations from foreign nations be laid to promote or foster any branch of industry; and all duties, imposts, and excises shall be uniform throughout the Confederate States:

2. To borrow money on the credit of the Confederate States:

3. To regulate commerce with foreign nations, and among the several States, and with the Indian tribes; but neither this, nor any other clause contained in the constitution, shall ever be construed to delegate the power to Congress to appropriate money for any internal improvement intended to facilitate commerce; except for the purpose of furnishing lights, beacons, and buoys, and other aids to navigation upon the coasts, and the improvement of harbors and the removing of obstructions in river navigation, in all which cases, such duties shall be laid on the navigation facilitated thereby, as may be necessary to pay the costs and expenses thereof:

4. To establish uniform laws of naturalization, and uniform laws on the subject of bankruptcies, throughout the Confederate States; but no law of Congress shall discharge any debt contracted before the passage of the same:

5. To coin money, regulate the value thereof and of foreign coin, and fix the standard of weights and measures:

6. To provide for the punishment of counterfeiting the securities and current coin of the Confederate States:

7. To establish post-offices and post-routes; but the expenses of the Post-office Department, after the first day of March in the year of our Lord eighteen hundred and sixty-three, shall be paid out of its own revenues:

8. To promote the progress of science and useful arts, by securing for limited times to authors and inventors the exclusive right to their respective writings and discoveries:

9. To constitute tribunals inferior to the Supreme Court:

10. To define and punish piracies and felonies committed on the high seas, and offences against the law of nations:

11. To declare war, grant letters of marque and reprisal, and make rules concerning captures on land and water:

12. To raise and support armies; but no appropriation of money to that use shall be for a longer term than two years:

13. To provide and maintain a navy:

14. To make rules for the government and regulation of the land and naval forces:

15. To provide for calling forth the militia to execute the laws of the Confederate States, suppress insurrections, and repel invasions:

16. To provide for organizing, arming, and disciplining

the militia, and for governing such part of them as may be employed in the service of the Confederate States; reserving to the States, respectively, the appointment of the officers, and the authority of training the militia according to the discipline prescribed by Congress:

17. To exercise exclusive legislation, in all cases whatsoever, over such district (not exceeding ten miles square) as may, by cession of one or more States and the acceptance of Congress, become the seat of the government of the Confederate States: and to exercise like authority over all places purchased by the consent of the legislature of the State in which the same shall be, for the erection of forts, magazines, arsenals, dockyards, and other needful buildings: and

18. To make all laws which shall be necessary and proper for carrying into execution the foregoing powers, and all other powers vested by this Constitution in the government of the Confederate States, or in any department or officer thereof.

Section 9

1. The importation of negroes of the African race, from any foreign country other than the slaveholding States or Territories of the United States of America, is hereby forbidden; and Congress is required to pass such laws as shall effectually prevent the same.

2. Congress shall also have power to prohibit the introduction of slaves from any State not a member of, or Territory not belonging to, this Confederacy.

3. The privilege of the writ of *habeas corpus* shall not be suspended, unless when in cases of rebellion or invasion the public safety may require it.

4. No bill of attainder, *ex post facto* law, or law denying or impa[i]ring the right of property in negro slaves shall be passed.

5. No capitation or other direct tax shall be laid, unless in proportion to the census or enumeration hereinbefore directed to be taken.

6. No tax or duty shall be laid on articles exported from any State, except by a vote of two-thirds of both Houses.

7. No preference shall be given by any regulation of commerce or revenue to the ports of one State over those of another.

8. No money shall be drawn from the treasury, but in consequence of appropriations made by law; and a regular statement and account of the receipts and expenditures of all public money shall be published from time to time.

9. Congress shall appropriate no money from the treasury except by a vote of two-thirds of both Houses, taken by yeas and nays, unless it be asked and estimated for by some one of the heads of departments, and submitted to Congress by the President; or for the purpose of paying its own expenses and contingencies; or for the payment of claims against the Confederate States, the justice of which shall have been judicially declared by a tribunal for the investigation of claims against the government, which it is hereby made the duty of Congress to establish.

10. All bills appropriating money shall specify in federal currency the exact amount of each appropriation and the purposes for which it is made; and Congress shall grant no extra compensation to any public contractor, officer, agent or servant, after such contract shall have been made or such service rendered.

11. No title of nobility shall be granted by the Confederate States; and no person holding any office of profit or trust under them, shall, without the consent of the Congress, accept of any present, emolument, office or title of any kind whatever, from any king, prince, or foreign state.

12. Congress shall make no law respecting an establishment of religion, or prohibiting the free exercise thereof; or abridging the freedom of speech, or of the press; or the right of the people peaceably to assemble and petition the government for a redress of grievances.

13. A well-regulated militia being necessary to the security of a free state, the right of the people to keep and bear arms shall not be infringed.

14. No soldier shall, in time of peace, be quartered in any house, without the consent of the owner; nor in time of war, but in a manner to be prescribed by law.

15. The right of the people to be secure in their persons, houses, papers, and effects, against unreasonable searches and seizures, shall not be violated; and no warrants shall issue but upon probable cause, supported by oath or affirmation, and particularly describing the place to be searched, and the persons or things to be seized.

16. No person shall be held to answer for a capital or otherwise infamous crime, unless on a presentment or indictment of a grand jury, except in cases arising in the land or naval forces, or in the militia, when in actual service in time of war or public danger; nor shall any person be subject for the same offence to be twice put in jeopardy of life or limb; nor be compelled, in any criminal case, to be a witness against himself; nor be deprived of life, liberty, or property without due

process of law; nor shall private property be taken for public use, without just compensation.

17. In all criminal prosecutions, the accused shall enjoy the right to a speedy and public trial, by an impartial jury of the State and district wherein the crime shall have been committed, which district shall have been previously ascertained by law, and to be informed of the nature and cause of the accusation; to be confronted with the witnesses against him; to have compulsory process for obtaining witnesses in his favor; and to have the assistance of counsel for his defence.

18. In suits at common law, where the value in controversy shall exceed twenty dollars, the right of trial by jury shall be preserved; and no fact so tried by a jury shall be otherwise reexamined in any court of the Confederacy, than according to the rules of common law.

19. Excessive bail shall not be required, nor excessive fines imposed, nor cruel and unusual punishments inflicted.

20. Every law, or resolution having the force of law, shall relate to but one subject, and that shall be expressed in the title.

Section 10

1. No State shall enter into any treaty, alliance, or confederation; grant letters of marque and reprisal; coin money; make any thing but gold and silver coin a tender in payment of debts; pass any bill of attainder, or *ex post facto* law, or law impairing the obligation of contracts; or grant any title of nobility.

2. No State shall, without the consent of the Congress, lay any imposts or duties on imports or exports, except what may be absolutely necessary for executing its inspection laws; and the nett produce of all duties and imposts, laid by any State on imports or exports, shall be for the use of the Treasury of the Confederate States; and all such laws shall be subject to the revision and control of Congress.

3. No State shall, without the consent of Congress, lay any duty on tonnage, except on sea-going vessels, for the improvement of its rivers and harbors navigated by the said vessels; but such duties shall not conflict with any treaties of the Confederate States with foreign nations; and any surplus revenue, thus derived, shall, after making such improvement, be paid into the common treasury. Nor shall any State keep troops or ships-of-war in time of peace, enter into any agreement or compact with another State, or with a foreign power, or engage in war, unless actually invaded, or in such imminent danger as will not admit of delay. But when any river divides or flows through two or more States, they may enter into compacts with each other to improve the navigation thereof.

ARTICLE II

Section 1

1. The executive power shall be vested in a President of the Confederate States of America. He and the Vice President shall hold their offices for the term of six years but the President shall not be re-eligible. The President and Vice President shall be elected as follows:

2. Each State shall appoint, in such manner as the legislature thereof may direct, a number of electors equal to the whole number of Senators and Representatives to which the State may be entitled in the Congress; but no Senator or Representative or person holding an office of trust or profit under the Confederate States, shall be appointed an elector.

3. The electors shall meet in their respective States and vote by ballot for President and Vice President, one of whom, at least, shall not be an inhabitant of the same State with themselves; they shall name in their ballots the person voted for as President, and in distinct ballots the person voted for as Vice President, and they shall make distinct lists of all persons voted for as President, and of all persons voted for as Vice President, and of the number of votes for each, which lists they shall sign and certify, and transmit, sealed, to the seat of the government of the Confederate States, directed to the President of the Senate; the President of the Senate shall, in the presence of the Senate and House of Representatives, open all the certificates, and the votes shall then be counted; the person having the greatest number of votes for President shall be the President, if such number be a majority of the whole number of electors appointed; and if no person have such majority, then, from the persons having the highest numbers, not exceeding three, on the list of those voted for as President, the House of Representatives shall choose immediately, by ballot, the President. But in choosing the President, the votes shall be taken by States—the representation from each State having one vote; a quorum for this purpose shall consist of a member or members from two-thirds of the States, and a majority of all the States shall be necessary to a choice. And if the House of Representatives shall not choose a President, whenever the right of choice shall devolve upon them, before the fourth day of March next following, then the Vice-President shall act as President, as in case of the death, or other constitutional disability of the President.

4. The person having the greatest number of votes as Vice

President, shall be the Vice President, if such number be a majority of the whole number of electors appointed; and if no person have a majority, then, from the two highest numbers on the list, the Senate shall choose the Vice President; a quorum for the purpose shall consist of two-thirds of the whole number of Senators, and a majority of the whole number shall be necessary to a choice.

5. But no person constitutionally ineligible to the office of President shall be eligible to that of Vice President of the Confederate States.

6. The Congress may determine the time of choosing the electors, and the day on which they shall give their votes; which day shall be the same throughout the Confederate States.

7. No person except a natural born citizen of the Confederate States, or a citizen thereof at the time of the adoption of this Constitution, or a citizen thereof born in the United States prior to the 20th of December, 1860, shall be eligible to the office of President; neither shall any person be eligible to that office who shall not have attained the age of thirty-five years, and been fourteen years a resident within the limits of the Confederate States, as they may exist at the time of his election.

8. In case of the removal of the President from office, or of his death, resignation, or inability to discharge the powers and duties of the said office, the same shall devolve on the Vice President; and the Congress may, by law, provide for the case of removal, death, resignation, or inability, both of the President and Vice President, declaring what officer shall then act as President; and such officer shall act accordingly, until the disability be removed or a President shall be elected.

9. The President shall, at stated times, receive for his services a compensation, which shall neither be increased nor diminished during the period for which he shall have been elected; and he shall not receive within that period any other emolument from the Confederate States, or any of them.

10. Before he enters on the execution of his office, he shall take the following oath or affirmation:

"I do solemnly swear (or affirm) that I will faithfully execute the office of President of the Confederate States, and will, to the best of my ability, preserve, protect, and defend the Constitution thereof."

Section 2

1. The President shall be commander-in-chief of the army and navy of the Confederate States, and of the militia of the several States, when called into the actual service of the Confederate States; he may require the opinion, in writing, of the principal officer in each of the executive departments, upon any subject relating to the duties of their respective offices; and he shall have power to grant reprieves and pardons for offences against the Confederate States, except in cases of impeachment.

2. He shall have power, by and with the advice and consent of the Senate, to make treaties; provided two-thirds of the Senators present concur; and he shall nominate, and by and with the advice and consent of the Senate, shall appoint ambassadors, other public ministers and consuls, judges of the Supreme Court, and all other officers of the Confederate States whose appointments are not herein otherwise provided for, and which shall be established by law; but the Congress may, by law, vest the appointment of such inferior officers, as they think proper, in the President alone, in the courts of law, or in the heads of departments.

3. The principal officer in each of the executive departments, and all persons connected with the diplomatic service, may be removed from office at the pleasure of the President. All other civil officers of the executive departments may be removed at any time by the President, or other appointing power, when their services are unnecessary, or for dishonesty, incapacity, inefficiency, misconduct, or neglect of duty; and when so removed, the removal shall be reported to the Senate, together with the reasons therefor.

4. The President shall have power to fill all vacancies that may happen during the recess of the Senate, by granting commissions which shall expire at the end of their next session; but no person rejected by the Senate shall be re-appointed to the same office during their ensuing recess.

Section 3

1. The President shall, from time to time, give to the Congress information of the state of the Confederacy, and recommend to their consideration such measures as he shall judge necessary and expedient; he may, on extraordinary occasions, convene both Houses, or either of them; and in case of disagreement between them, with respect to the time of adjournment, he may adjourn them to such time as he shall think proper; he shall receive ambassadors and other public ministers; he shall take care that the laws be faithfully executed, and shall commission all the officers of the Confederate States.

Section 4

1. The President, Vice President, and all civil officers of the Confederate States, shall be removed from office on impeach-

ment, for and conviction of, treason, bribery, or other high crimes and misdemeanors.

ARTICLE III

Section 1

1. The judicial power of the Confederate States shall be vested in one Supreme Court, and in such inferior courts as the Congress may, from time to time, ordain and establish. The judges, both of the Supreme and inferior courts, shall hold their offices during good behavior, and shall, at stated times, receive for their services a compensation which shall not be diminished during their continuance in office.

Section 2

1. The judicial power shall extend to all cases arising under this Constitution, the laws of the Confederate States, and treaties made, or which shall be made, under their authority; to all cases affecting ambassadors, other public ministers and consuls; to all cases of admiralty and maritime jurisdiction; to controversies to which the Confederate States shall be a party; to controversies between two or more States; between a State and citizens of another State, where the State is plaintiff; between citizens claiming lands under grants of different States; and between a State or the citizens thereof, and foreign states, citizens or subjects; but no State shall be sued by a citizen or subject of any foreign state.

2. In all cases affecting ambassadors, other public ministers and consuls, and those in which a State shall be a party, the Supreme Court shall have original jurisdiction. In all the other cases before mentioned, the Supreme Court shall have appellate jurisdiction both as to law and fact, with such exceptions and under such regulations as the Congress shall make.

3. The trial of all crimes, except in cases of impeachment, shall be by jury, and such trial shall be held in the State where the said crimes shall have been committed; but when not committed within any State, the trial shall be at such place or places as the Congress may by law have directed.

Section 3

1. Treason against the Confederate States shall consist only in levying war against them, or in adhering to their enemies, giving them aid and comfort. No person shall be convicted of treason unless on the testimony of two witnesses to the same overt act, or on confession in open court.

2. The Congress shall have power to declare the punishment of treason; but no attainder of treason shall work cor-

ruption of blood, or forfeiture, except during the life of the person attainted.

ARTICLE IV

Section 1

1. Full faith and credit shall be given in each State to the public acts, records, and judicial proceedings of every other State. And the Congress may, by general laws, prescribe the manner in which such acts, records, and proceedings shall be proved, and the effect thereof.

Section 2

1. The citizens of each State shall be entitled to all the privileges and immunities of citizens in the several States; and shall have the right of transit and sojourn in any State of this Confederacy, with their slaves and other property; and the right of property in said slaves shall not be thereby impaired.

2. A person charged in any State with treason, felony, or other crime against the laws of such State, who shall flee from justice, and be found in another State, shall, on demand of the executive authority of the State from which he fled, be delivered up, to be removed to the State having jurisdiction of the crime.

3. No slave or other person held to service or labor in any State or Territory of the Confederate States, under the laws thereof, escaping or lawfully carried into another, shall, in consequence of any law or regulation therein, be discharged from such service or labor: but shall be delivered up on claim of the party to whom such slave belongs, or to whom such service or labor may be due.

Section 3

1. Other States may be admitted into this Confederacy by a vote of two-thirds of the whole House of Representatives and two-thirds of the Senate, the Senate voting by States; but no new State shall be formed or erected within the jurisdiction of any other State; nor any State be formed by the junction of two or more States, or parts of States, without the consent of the legislatures of the States concerned, as well as of the Congress.

2. The Congress shall have power to dispose of and make all needful rules and regulations concerning the property of the Confederate States, including the lands thereof.

3. The Confederate States may acquire new territory; and Congress shall have power to legislate and provide governments for the inhabitants of all territory belonging to the

Confederate States, lying without the limits of the several States; and may permit them, at such times, and in such manner as it may by law provide, to form States to be admitted into the Confederacy. In all such territory, the institution of negro slavery, as it now exists in the Confederate States, shall be recognized and protected by Congress and by the territorial government: and the inhabitants of the several Confederate States and Territories shall have the right to take to such territory any slaves lawfully held by them in any of the States or Territories of the Confederate States.

4. The Confederate States shall guarantee to every State that now is, or hereafter may become, a member of this Confederacy, a republican form of government; and shall protect each of them against invasion; and on application of the legislature, (or of the executive, when the legislature is not in session,) against domestic violence.

ARTICLE V

Section 1

1. Upon the demand of any three States, legally assembled in their several conventions, the Congress shall summon a convention of all the States, to take into consideration such amendments to the Constitution as the said States shall concur in suggesting at the time when the said demand is made; and should any of the proposed amendments to the Constitution be agreed on by the said convention—voting by States—and the same be ratified by the legislatures of two-thirds of the several States, or by conventions in two-thirds thereof—as the one or the other mode of ratification may be proposed by the general convention—they shall thenceforward form a part of this Constitution. But no State shall, without its consent, be deprived of its equal representation in the Senate.

ARTICLE VI

1. The Government established by this Constitution is the successor of the Provisional Government of the Confederate States of America, and all the laws passed by the latter shall continue in force until the same shall be repealed or modified; and all the officers appointed by the same shall remain in office until their successors are appointed and qualified, or the offices abolished.

2. All debts contracted and engagements entered into before the adoption of this Constitution shall be as valid against the Confederate States under this Constitution, as under the Provisional Government.

3. This Constitution, and the laws of the Confederate States made in pursuance thereof, and all treaties made, or which shall be made, under the authority of the Confederate States, shall be the supreme law of the land; and the judges in every State shall be bound thereby, anything in the Constitution or laws of any State to the contrary notwithstanding.

4. The Senators and Representatives before mentioned, and the members of the several State legislatures, and all executive and judicial officers, both of the Confederate States and of the several States, shall be bound by oath or affirmation to support this Constitution; but no religious test shall ever be required as a qualification to any office or public trust under the Confederate States.

5. The enumeration, in the Constitution, of certain rights, shall not be construed to deny or disparage others retained by the people of the several States.

6. The powers not delegated to the Confederate States by the Constitution, nor prohibited by it to the States, are reserved to the States, respectively, or to the people thereof.

ARTICLE VII

1. The ratification of the conventions of five States shall be sufficient for the establishment of this Constitution between the States so ratifying the same.

2. When five States shall have ratified this Constitution, in the manner before specified, the Congress under the Provisional Constitution shall prescribe the time for holding the election of President and Vice President; and for the meeting of the Electoral College; and for counting the votes, and inaugurating the President. They shall, also, prescribe the time for holding the first election of members of Congress under this Constitution, and the time for assembling the same. Until the assembling of such Congress, the Congress under the Provisional Constitution shall continue to exercise the legislative powers granted them; not extending beyond the time limited by the Constitution of the Provisional Government.

Adopted unanimously by the Congress of the Confederate States of South Carolina, Georgia, Florida, Alabama, Mississippi, Louisiana and Texas, sitting in Convention at the capitol, in the city of Montgomery, Alabama, on the Eleventh day of March, in the year Eighteen Hundred and Sixty-One.

HOWELL COBB,
President of the Congress.

South Carolina.—R. Barnwell Rhett, C. G. Memminger, Wm. Porcher Miles, James Chesnut, Jr., R. W. Barnwell, William W. Boyce, Lawrence M. Keitt, T. J. Withers.

Georgia.—Francis S. Bartow, Martin J. Crawford, Benjamin H. Hill, Thos. R. R. Cobb.

Florida.—Jackson Morton, J. Patton Anderson, Jas. B. Owens.

Alabama.—Richard W. Walker, Robt. H. Smith, Colin J. McRae, William P. Chilton, Stephen F. Hale, David P. Lewis, Tho. Fearn, Jno. Gill Shorter, J. L. M. Curry.

Mississippi.—Alex. M. Clayton, James T. Harrison, William S. Barry, W. S. Wilson, Walker Brooke, W. P. Harris, J. A. P. Campbell.

Louisiana.—Alex. De Clouet, C. M. Conrad, Duncan F. Kenner, Henry Marshall.

Texas.—John Hemphill, Thomas N. Waul, John H. Reagan, Williamson S. Oldham, Louis T. Wigfall, John Gregg, William Beck Ochiltree.

Extract from the Journal of the Congress

Congress, *March 11, 1862 [1861].*

On the question of the adoption of the Constitution of the Confederate States of America, the vote was taken by yeas and nays; and the Constitution was unanimously adopted, as follows:

Those who voted in the affirmative being Messrs. Walker, Smith, Curry, Hale, McRae, Shorter, and Fearn, of Alabama, (Messrs. Chilton and Lewis being absent); Messrs. Morton, Anderson, and Owens, of Florida; Messrs. Toombs, Howell Cobb, Bartow, Nisbet, Hill, Wright, Thomas R. R. Cobb, and Stephens, of Georgia, (Messrs. Crawford and Kenan being absent); Messrs. Perkins, De Clouet, Conrad, Kenner, Sparrow, and Marshall, of Louisiana; Messrs. Harris, Brooke, Wilson, Clayton, Barry, and Harrison, of Mississippi, (Mr. Campbell being absent); Messrs. Rhett, Barnwell, Keitt, Chesnut, Memminger, Miles, Withers, and Boyce, of South Carolina; Messrs. Reagan, Hemphill, Waul, Gregg, Oldham, and Ochiltree, of Texas, (Mr. Wigfall being absent).

A true copy:

J. J. HOOPER,
Secretary of the Congress.

Congress, *March 11, 1861.*

I do hereby certify that the foregoing are, respectively, true and correct copies of "The Constitution of the Confederate States of America," unanimously adopted this day, and of the yeas and nays on the question of the adoption thereof.

HOWELL COBB,
President of the Congress.

Farewell Speech to Congress, *Jefferson Davis,* 1861

Inaugural Address, *Jefferson Davis,* 1861

Jefferson Davis served in the House of Representatives, as a regimental commander in the Mexican-American War (1846), as a U.S. senator, and as secretary of war before return-ing to the Senate in 1857. A powerful defender of Southern institutions and interests, Davis was not considered in the forefront of the call for secession, remaining in the Senate until his own state of Mississippi seceded. He did, however, heed his state's decision to secede, and his farewell address to Congress is a defense of that decision. Davis actually delivered two inaugural addresses, the first (reproduced here) as the appointed president of the provisional government of the Confederate States of America, the second, a year later, as the Confederacy's first (and only) formally elected president. Davis's inaugural as provisional president was held in Montgomery, Alabama. After Virginia seceded from the Union, the Confederate capital was moved to Richmond, and Davis's inaugural as duly elected president of the Confederacy was held in that city's Capitol Square, at the foot of an equestrian statue of the first president of the United States, George Washington.

Farewell Speech to the United States Congress

January 21, 1861

Jefferson Davis

Mr. DAVIS. I rise, Mr. President, for the purpose of an-nouncing to the Senate that I have satisfactory evidence that the State of Mississippi, by a solemn ordinance of her people in convention assembled, has declared her separation from the United States. Under these circumstances, of course my functions are terminated here. It has seemed to me proper, however, that I should appear in the Senate to announce that fact to my associates, and I will say but very little more. The occasion does not invite me to go into argument; and my physical condition would not permit me to do so if it were otherwise; and yet it seems to become me to say something on the part of the State I here represent, on an occasion so solemn as this.

It is known to Senators who have served with me here, that I have for many years advocated, as an essential attribute of State sovereignty, the right of a State to secede from the Union. Therefore, if I had not believed there was justifiable cause; if I had thought that Mississippi was acting without sufficient provocation, or without an existing necessity, I should still, under my theory of the Government, because of

my allegiance to the State of which I am a citizen, have been bound by her action. I, however, may be permitted to say that I do think she has justifiable cause, and I approve of her act. I conferred with her people before that act was taken, coun-seled them then that if the state of things which they appre-hended should exist when the convention met, they should take the action which they have now adopted.

I hope none who hear me will confound this expression of mine with the advocacy of the right of a State to remain in the Union, and to disregard its constitutional obligations by the nullification of the law. Such is not my theory. Nullification and secession, so often confounded, are indeed antagonistic principles. Nullification is a remedy which it is sought to ap-ply within the Union, and against the agent of the States. It is only to be justified when the agent has violated his consti-tutional obligation, and a State, assuming to judge for itself, denies the right of the agent thus to act, and appeals to the other States of the Union for a decision; but when the States themselves, and when the people of the States, have so acted as to convince us that they will not regard our constitutional rights, then, and then for the first time, arises the doctrine of secession in its practical application.

A great man who now reposes with his fathers, and who has been often arraigned for a want of fealty to the Union, advocated the doctrine of nullification, because it preserved the Union. It was because of his deep-seated attachment to the Union, his determination to find some remedy for existing ills short of a severance of the ties which bound South Carolina to the other States, that Mr. Calhoun advocated the doctrine of nullification, which he proclaimed to be peaceful, to be within the limits of State power, not to disturb the Union, but only to be a means of bringing the agent before the tribunal of the States for their judgment.

Secession belongs to a different class of remedies. It is to be justified upon the basis that the States are sovereign. There was a time when none denied it. I hope the time may come again, when a better comprehension of the theory of our Government, and the inalienable rights of the people of the States, will prevent any one from denying that each State is a sovereign, and thus may reclaim the grants which it has made to any agent whomsoever.

I therefore say I concur in the action of the people of Mississippi, believing it to be necessary and proper, and should have been bound by their action if my belief had been otherwise; and this brings me to the important point which I wish on this last occasion to present to the Senate. It is by this confounding of nullification and secession that the name of a great man, whose ashes now mingle with his mother earth, has been invoked to justify coercion against a seceded State. The phrase "to execute the laws," was an expression which General Jackson applied to the case of a State refusing to obey the laws while yet a member of the Union. That is not the case which is now presented. The laws are to be executed over the United States, and upon the people of the United States. They have no relation to any foreign country. It is a perversion of terms, at least it is a great misapprehension of the case, which cites that expression for application to a State which has withdrawn from the Union. You may make war on a foreign State. If it be the purpose of gentlemen, they may make war against a State which has withdrawn from the Union; but there are no laws of the United States to be executed within the limits of a seceded State. A State finding herself in the condition in which Mississippi has judged she is, in which her safety requires that she should provide for the maintenance of her rights out of the Union, surrenders all the benefits, (and they are known to be many,) deprives her-

self of the advantages, (they are known to be great,) severs all the ties of affection, (and they are close and enduring,) which have bound her to the Union; and thus divesting herself of every benefit, taking upon herself every burden, she claims to be exempt from any power to execute the laws of the United States within her limits.

I well remember an occasion when Massachusetts was arraigned before the bar of the Senate, and when then the doctrine of coercion was rife and to be applied against her because of the rescue of a fugitive slave in Boston. My opinion then was the same that it is now. Not in a spirit of egotism, but to show that I am not influenced in my opinion because the case is my own, I refer to that time and that occasion as containing the opinion which I then entertained, and on which my present conduct is based. I then said, if Massachusetts, following her through a stated line of conduct, chooses to take the last step which separates her from the Union, it is her right to go, and I will neither vote one dollar nor one man to coerce her back; but will say to her, God speed, in memory of the kind associations which once existed between her and the other States.

It has been a conviction of pressing necessity, it has been a belief that we are to be deprived in the Union of the rights which our fathers bequeathed to us, which has brought Mississippi into her present decision. She has heard proclaimed the theory that all men are created free and equal, and this made the basis of an attack upon her social institutions; and the sacred Declaration of Independence has been invoked to maintain the position of the equality of the races. That Declaration of Independence is to be construed by the circumstances and purposes for which it was made. The communities were declaring their independence; the people of those communities were asserting that no man was born—to use the language of Mr. Jefferson—booted and spurred to ride over the rest of mankind; that men were created equal—meaning the men of the political community; that there was no divine right to rule; that no man inherited the right to govern; that there were no classes by which power and place descended to families, but that all stations were equally within the grasp of each member of the body-politic. These were the great principles they announced; these were the purposes for which they made their declaration; these were the ends to which their enunciation was directed. They have no reference to the slave; else, how happened it that among the items of arraignment made against George III was that he endeavored to do just what the North has been endeavoring of late to do—to stir up insurrection among our slaves? Had the Declaration announced that the negroes were free and equal, how was the Prince to be arraigned for stirring up insurrection among them? And how was this to be enumerated among the high crimes which caused the colonies to sever their connection with the mother country? When our Constitution was formed, the same idea was rendered more palpable, for there we find provision made for that very class of persons as property; they were not put upon the footing of equality with white men—not even upon that of paupers and convicts; but, so far as representation was concerned, were discriminated against as a lower caste, only to be represented in the numerical proportion of three fifths.

Then, Senators, we recur to the compact which binds us together; we recur to the principles upon which our Government was founded; and when you deny them, and when you deny to us the right to withdraw from a Government which thus perverted threatens to be destructive of our rights, we but tread in the path of our fathers when we proclaim our independence, and take the hazard. This is done not in hostility to others, not to injure any section of the country, not even for our own pecuniary benefit; but from the high and solemn motive of defending and protecting the rights we inherited, and which it is our sacred duty to transmit unshorn to our children.

I find in myself, perhaps, a type of the general feeling of my constituents towards yours. I am sure I feel no hostility to you, Senators from the North. I am sure there is not one of you, whatever sharp discussion there may have been between us, to whom I cannot now say, in the presence of my God, I wish you well; and such, I am sure, is the feeling of the people whom I represent towards those whom you represent. I therefore feel that I but express their desire when I say I hope, and they hope, for peaceful relations with you, though we must part. They may be mutually beneficial to us in the future, as they have been in the past, if you so will it. The reverse may bring disaster on every portion of the country; and if you will have it thus, we will invoke the God of our fathers, who delivered them from the power of the lion, to protect us from the ravages of the bear; and thus, putting our trust in God, and in our own firm hearts and strong arms, we will vindicate the right as best we may.

In the course of my service here, associated at different times with a great variety of Senators, I see now around me some with whom I have served long; there have been points of collision; but whatever of offense there has been to me, I leave here; I carry with me no hostile remembrance. Whatever offense I have given which has not been redressed, or for which satisfaction has not been demanded, I have, Senators, in this hour of our parting, to offer you my apology for any pain which, in heat of discussion, I have inflicted. I go hence unencumbered of the remembrance of any injury received, and having discharged the duty of making the only reparation in my power for any injury offered.

Mr. President, and Senators, having made the announcement which the occasion seemed to me to require, it only remains for me to bid you a final adieu.

Inaugural Address

February 18, 1861

Jefferson Davis

Gentlemen of the Congress of the Confederate States of America, Friends, and Fellow-Citizens:

Called to the difficult and responsible station of Chief Executive of the Provisional Government which you have instituted, I approach the discharge of the duties assigned to me with an humble distrust of my abilities, but with a sustaining confidence in the wisdom of those who are to guide and to aid me in the administration of public affairs, and an abiding faith in the virtue and patriotism of the people.

Looking forward to the speedy establishment of a permanent government to take the place of this, and which by its greater moral and physical power will be better able to combat with the many difficulties which arise from the conflicting interests of separate nations, I enter upon the duties of the office to which I have been chosen with the hope that the beginning of our career as a Confederacy may not be obstructed by hostile opposition to our enjoyment of the separate existence and independence which we have asserted, and, with the blessing of Providence, intend to maintain. Our present condition, achieved in a manner unprecedented in the history of nations, illustrates the American idea that governments rest upon the consent of the governed, and that it is the right of the people to alter or abolish governments whenever they become destructive of the ends for which they were established.

The declared purpose of the compact of Union from

which we have withdrawn was "to establish justice, insure domestic tranquillity, provide for the common defense, promote the general welfare, and secure the blessings of liberty to ourselves and our posterity"; and when, in the judgment of the sovereign States now composing this Confederacy, it had been perverted from the purposes for which it was ordained, and had ceased to answer the ends for which it was established, a peaceful appeal to the ballot-box declared that so far as they were concerned the Government created by that compact should cease to exist. In this they merely asserted a right which the Declaration of Independence of 1776 had defined to be inalienable; of the time and occasion for its exercise they, as sovereigns, were the final judges, each for itself. The impartial and enlightened verdict of mankind will vindicate the rectitude of our conduct, and He who knows the hearts of men will judge of the sincerity with which we labored to preserve the Government of our fathers in its spirit. The right solemnly proclaimed at the birth of the States, and which has been affirmed and reaffirmed in the bills of rights of States subsequently admitted into the Union of 1789, undeniably recognize in the people the power to resume the authority delegated for the purposes of government. Thus the sovereign States here represented proceeded to form this Confederacy, and it is by abuse of language that their act has been denominated a revolution. They formed a new alliance, but within each State its government has remained, the rights of person and property have not been disturbed. The agent through whom they communicated with foreign nations is changed, but this does not necessarily interrupt their international relations.

Sustained by the consciousness that the transition from the former Union to the present Confederacy has not proceeded from a disregard on our part of just obligations, or any failure to perform every constitutional duty, moved by no interest or passion to invade the rights of others, anxious to cultivate peace and commerce with all nations, if we may not hope to avoid war, we may at least expect that posterity will acquit us of having needlessly engaged in it. Doubly justified by the absence of wrong on our part, and by wanton aggression on the part of others, there can be no cause to doubt that the courage and patriotism of the people of the Confederate States will be found equal to any measures of defense which honor and security may require.

An agricultural people, whose chief interest is the export of a commodity required in every manufacturing country, our true policy is peace, and the freest trade which our necessities will permit. It is alike our interest, and that of all those to whom we would sell and from whom we would buy, that there should be the fewest practicable restrictions upon the interchange of commodities. There can be but little rivalry between ours and any manufacturing or navigating community, such as the Northeastern States of the American Union. It must follow, therefore, that a mutual interest would invite good will and kind offices. If, however, passion or the lust of dominion should cloud the judgment or inflame the ambition of those States, we must prepare to meet the emergency and to maintain, by the final arbitrament of the sword, the position which we have assumed among the nations of the earth. We have entered upon the career of independence, and it must be inflexibly pursued. Through many years of controversy with our late associates, the Northern States, we have vainly endeavored to secure tranquillity, and to obtain respect for the rights to which we were entitled. As a necessity, not a choice, we have resorted to the remedy of separation; and henceforth our energies must be directed to the conduct of our own affairs, and the perpetuity of the Confederacy which we have formed. If a just perception of mutual interest shall permit us peaceably to pursue our separate political career, my most earnest desire will have been fulfilled. But, if this be denied to us, and the integrity of our territory and jurisdiction be assailed, it will but remain for us, with firm resolve, to appeal to arms and invoke the blessings of Providence on a just cause.

As a consequence of our new condition and with a view to meet anticipated wants, it will be necessary to provide for the speedy and efficient organization of branches of the executive department, having special charge of foreign intercourse, finance, military affairs, and the postal service.

For purposes of defense, the Confederate States may, under ordinary circumstances, rely mainly upon their militia, but it is deemed advisable, in the present condition of affairs, that there should be a well-instructed and disciplined army, more numerous than would usually be required on a peace establishment. I also suggest that for the protection of our harbors and commerce on the high seas a navy adapted to those objects will be required. These necessities have doubtless engaged the attention of Congress.

With a Constitution differing only from that of our fathers in so far as it is explanatory of their well-known intent, freed from the sectional conflicts which have interfered with the pursuit of the general welfare, it is not unreasonable to expect that States from which we have recently parted may seek to unite their fortunes with ours under the Government which we have instituted. For this your Constitution makes adequate provision; but beyond this, if I mistake not the judgment and will of the people, a reunion with the States from which we have separated is neither practicable nor desirable. To increase the power, develop the resources, and promote the happiness of a confederacy, it is requisite that there should be so much of homogeneity that the welfare of every portion shall be the aim of the whole. Where this does not exist, antagonisms are engendered which must and should result in separation.

Actuated solely by the desire to preserve our own rights and promote our own welfare, the separation of the Confederate States has been marked by no aggression upon others and followed by no domestic convulsion. Our industrial pursuits have received no check. The cultivation of our fields has progressed as heretofore, and even should we be involved in war there would be no considerable diminution in the production of the staples which have constituted our exports and in which the commercial world has an interest scarcely less than our own. This common interest of the producer and consumer can only be interrupted by an exterior force which should obstruct its transmission to foreign markets—a course of conduct which would be as unjust toward us as it would be detrimental to manufacturing and commercial interests abroad. Should reason guide the action of the Government from which we have separated, a policy so detrimental to the civilized world, the Northern States included, could not be dictated by even the strongest desire to inflict injury upon us; but otherwise a terrible responsibility will rest upon it, and the suffering of millions will bear testimony to the folly and wickedness of our aggressors. In the meantime there will remain to us, besides the ordinary means before suggested, the well-known resources for retaliation upon the commerce of an enemy.

Experience in public stations, of subordinate grade to this which your kindness has conferred, has taught me that care and toil and disappointment are the price of official elevation. You will see many errors to forgive, many deficiencies to tolerate, but you shall not find in me either a want of zeal or fidelity to the cause that is to me highest in hope and of most enduring affection. Your generosity has bestowed upon me an undeserved distinction, one which I neither sought nor desired. Upon the continuance of that sentiment and upon your wisdom and patriotism I rely to direct and support me in the performance of the duty required at my hands.

We have changed the constituent parts, but not the system of our Government. The Constitution formed by our fathers is that of these Confederate States, in their exposition of it, and in the judicial construction it has received, we have a light which reveals its true meaning.

Thus instructed as to the just interpretation of the instrument, and ever remembering that all offices are but trusts held for the people, and that delegated powers are to be strictly construed, I will hope, by due diligence in the performance of my duties, though I may disappoint your expectations, yet to retain, when retiring, something of the good will and confidence which welcome my entrance into office.

It is joyous, in the midst of perilous times, to look around upon a people united in heart, where one purpose of high resolve animates and actuates the whole—where the sacrifices to be made are not weighed in the balance against honor and right and liberty and equality. Obstacles may retard, they can not long prevent the progress of a movement sanctified by its justice, and sustained by a virtuous people. Reverently let us invoke the God of our fathers to guide and protect us in our efforts to perpetuate the principles which, by His blessing, they were able to vindicate, establish and transmit to their posterity, and with a continuance of His favor, ever gratefully acknowledged, we may hopefully look forward to success, to peace, and to prosperity.

By the time Lincoln delivered his first inaugural address, seven states had seceded from the Union and formed themselves into the Confederate States of America, complete with its own Constitution and provisional president. Lincoln, meanwhile, had been brought to the capital in secrecy and under military guard. Dangers of the time did not, however, stop Lincoln from riding to the capitol building in an open carriage, accompanied by the outgoing president, James Buchanan. Criticized by some for not making more overt attempts at reconciliation with the seceding states up to this time, Lincoln nonetheless struck a conciliatory tone in this speech, which contains some of his best-known allegorical phrases.

First Inaugural Address

March 4, 1861

Abraham Lincoln

Fellow-Citizens of the United States:

In compliance with a custom as old as the Government itself, I appear before you to address you briefly and to take in your presence the oath prescribed by the Constitution of the United States to be taken by the President "before he enters on the execution of this office."

I do not consider it necessary at present for me to discuss those matters of administration about which there is no special anxiety or excitement.

Apprehension seems to exist among the people of the Southern States that by the accession of a Republican Administration their property and their peace and personal security are to be endangered. There has never been any reasonable cause for such apprehension. Indeed, the most ample evidence to the contrary has all the while existed and been open to their inspection. It is found in nearly all the published speeches of him who now addresses you. I do but quote from one of those speeches when I declare that—

I have no purpose, directly or indirectly, to interfere with the institution of slavery in the States where it exists. I believe I have no lawful right to do so, and I have no inclination to do so.

Those who nominated and elected me did so with full knowledge that I had made this and many similar declarations and had never recanted them; and more than this, they placed in the platform for my acceptance, and as a law

to themselves and to me, the clear and emphatic resolution which I now read:

Resolved, That the maintenance inviolate of the rights of the States, and especially the right of each State to order and control its own domestic institutions according to its own judgment exclusively, is essential to that balance of power on which the perfection and endurance of our political fabric depend; and we denounce the lawless invasion by armed force of the soil of any State or Territory, no matter what pretext, as among the gravest of crimes.

I now reiterate these sentiments, and in doing so I only press upon the public attention the most conclusive evidence of which the case is susceptible that the property, peace, and security of no section are to be in any wise endangered by the now incoming Administration. I add, too, that all the protection which, consistently with the Constitution and the laws, can be given will be cheerfully given to all the States when lawfully demanded, for whatever cause—as cheerfully to one section as to another.

There is much controversy about the delivering up of fugitives from service or labor. The clause I now read is as plainly written in the Constitution as any other of its provisions:

No person held to service or labor in one State, under the laws thereof, escaping into another, shall in consequence of any law or regulation therein be discharged from such service or labor, but shall be delivered up on claim of the party to whom such service or labor may be due.

It is scarcely questioned that this provision was intended by those who made it for the reclaiming of what we call fugitive slaves; and the intention of the lawgiver is the law. All members of Congress swear their support to the whole Constitution—to this provision as much as to any other. To the proposition, then, that slaves whose cases come within the terms of this clause "shall be delivered up" their oaths are unanimous. Now, if they would make the effort in good temper, could they not with nearly equal unanimity frame and pass a law by means of which to keep good that unanimous oath?

There is some difference of opinion whether this clause should be enforced by national or by State authority, but surely that difference is not a very material one. If the slave is to be surrendered, it can be of but little consequence to him or to others by which authority it is done. And should anyone in any case be content that his oath shall go unkept on a merely unsubstantial controversy as to *how* it shall be kept?

Again: In any law upon this subject ought not all the safeguards of liberty known in civilized and humane jurisprudence to be introduced, so that a free man be not in any case surrendered as a slave? And might it not be well at the same time to provide by law for the enforcement of that clause in the Constitution which guarantees that "the citizens of each State shall be entitled to all privileges and immunities of citizens in the several States"?

I take the official oath to-day with no mental reservations and with no purpose to construe the Constitution or laws by any hypercritical rules; and while I do not choose now to specify particular acts of Congress as proper to be enforced, I do suggest that it will be much safer for all, both in official and private stations, to conform to and abide by all those acts which stand unrepealed than to violate any of them trusting to find impunity in having them held to be unconstitutional.

It is seventy-two years since the first inauguration of a President under our National Constitution. During that period fifteen different and greatly distinguished citizens have in succession administered the executive branch of the Government. They have conducted it through many perils, and generally with great success. Yet, with all this scope of precedent, I now enter upon the same task for the brief constitutional term of four years under great and peculiar difficulty.

A disruption of the Federal Union, heretofore only menaced, is now formidably attempted.

I hold that in contemplation of universal law and of the Constitution the Union of these S[t]ates is perpetual. Perpetuity is implied, if not expressed, in the fundamental law of all national governments. It is safe to assert that no government proper ever had a provision in its organic law for its own termination. Continue to execute all the express provisions of our National Constitution, and the Union will endure forever, it being impossible to destroy it except by some action not provided for in the instrument itself.

Again: If the United States be not a government proper, but an association of States in the nature of contract merely, can it, as a contract, be peaceably unmade by less than all the parties who made it? One party to a contract may violate it—break it, so to speak—but does it not require all to lawfully rescind it?

Descending from these general principles, we find the proposition that in legal contemplation the Union is perpetual confirmed by the history of the Union itself. The Union is much older than the Constitution. It was formed, in fact, by the Articles of Association in 1774. It was matured and continued by the Declaration of Independence in 1776. It was further matured, and the faith of all the then thirteen States expressly plighted and engaged that it should be perpetual, by the Articles of Confederation in 1778. And finally, in 1787, one of the declared objects for ordaining and establishing the Constitution was *to form a more perfect Union.*

But if destruction of the Union by one or by a part only of the States be lawfully possible, the Union is *less* perfect than before the Constitution, having lost the vital element of perpetuity.

It follows from these views that no State upon its own mere motion can lawfully get out of the Union; that *resolves* and *ordinances* to that effect are legally void, and that acts of violence within any State or States against the authority of the United States are insurrectionary or revolutionary, according to circumstances.

I therefore consider that in view of the Constitution and the laws the Union is unbroken, and to the extent of my ability, I shall take care, as the Constitution itself expressly enjoins upon me, that the laws of the Union be faithfully executed in all the States. Doing this I deem to be only a simple duty on my part, and I shall perform it so far as practicable unless my rightful masters, the American people, shall withhold the requisite means or in some authoritative manner direct the contrary. I trust this will not be regarded as a menace, but only as the declared purpose of the Union that it *will* constitutionally defend and maintain itself.

In doing this there needs to be no bloodshed or violence, and there shall be none unless it be forced upon the national authority. The power confided to me will be used to hold, occupy, and possess the property and places belonging to the Government and to collect the duties and imposts; but beyond what may be necessary for these objects, there will be no invasion, no using of force against or among the people anywhere. Where hostility to the United States in any interior locality shall be so great and universal as to prevent competent resident citizens from holding the Federal offices, there will be no attempt to force obnoxious strangers among the people for that object. While the strict legal right may exist in the Government to enforce the exercise of these offices, the attempt to do so would be so irritating and so nearly impracticable withal that I deem it better to forego for the time the uses of such offices.

The mails, unless repelled, will continue to be furnished in all parts of the Union. So far as possible the people everywhere shall have that sense of perfect security which is most favorable to calm thought and reflection. The course here indicated will be followed unless current events and experience shall show a modification or change to be proper, and in every case and exigency my best discretion will be exercised, according to circumstances actually existing and with a view and a hope of a peaceful solution of the national troubles and the restoration of fraternal sympathies and affections.

That there are persons in one section or another who seek to destroy the Union at all events and are glad of any pretext to do it I will neither affirm nor deny; but if there be such, I need address no word to them. To those, however, who really love the Union may I not speak?

Before entering upon so grave a matter as the destruction of our national fabric, with all its benefits, its memories, and its hopes, would it not be wise to ascertain precisely why we do it? Will you hazard so desperate a step while there is any possibility that any portion of the ills you fly from have no real existence? Will you, while the certain ills you fly to are greater than all the real ones you fly from, will you risk the commission of so fearful a mistake?

All profess to be content in the Union if all constitutional rights can be maintained. Is it true, then, that any right plainly written in the Constitution has been denied? I think not. Happily, the human mind is so constituted that no party can reach to the audacity of doing this. Think, if you can, of a single instance in which a plainly written provision of the Constitution has ever been denied. If by the mere force of numbers a majority should deprive a minority of any clearly written constitutional right, it might in a moral point of view justify revolution; certainly would if such right were a vital one. But such is not our case. All the vital rights of minorities and of individuals are so plainly assured to them by affirmations and negations, guaranties and prohibitions, in the Constitution that controversies never arise concerning them. But no organic law can ever be framed with a provision specifically applicable to every question which may occur in practical administration. No foresight can anticipate nor any document of reasonable length contain express provisions for all possible questions. Shall fugitives from labor be surrendered by national or by State authority? The Constitution does not expressly say. *May* Congress prohibit slavery in the Territories? The Constitution does not expressly say. *Must* Congress protect slavery in the Territories? The Constitution does not expressly say.

From questions of this class spring all our constitutional controversies, and we divide upon them into majorities and minorities. If the minority will not acquiesce, the majority must, or the Government must cease. There is no other alternative, for continuing the Government is acquiescence on one side or the other. If a minority in such case will secede rather than acquiesce, they make a precedent which in turn will divide and ruin them, for a minority of their own will secede from them whenever a majority refuses to be controlled by such minority. For instance, why may not any portion of a new confederacy a year or two hence arbitrarily secede again, precisely as portions of the present Union now claim to secede from it? All who cherish disunion sentiments are now being educated to the exact temper of doing this.

Is there such perfect identity of interests among the States to compose a new union as to produce harmony only and prevent renewed secession?

Plainly the central idea of secession is the essence of anarchy. A majority held in restraint by constitutional checks and limitations, and always changing easily with deliberate changes of popular opinions and sentiments, is the only true sovereign of a free people. Whoever rejects it does of necessity fly to anarchy or to despotism. Unanimity is impossible. The rule of a minority, as a permanent arrangement, is wholly inadmissible; so that, rejecting the majority principle, anarchy or despotism in some form is all that is left.

I do not forget the position assumed by some that constitutional questions are to be decided by the Supreme Court, nor do I deny that such decisions must be binding in any case upon the parties to a suit as to the object of that suit, while they are also entitled to very high respect and consideration in all parallel cases by all other departments of the Government. And while it is obviously possible that such decision may be erroneous in any given case, still the evil effect following it, being limited to that particular case, with the chance that it may be overruled and never become a precedent for other cases, can better be borne than could the evils of a different practice. At the same time, the candid citizen must confess that if the policy of the Government upon vital questions affecting the whole people is to be irrevocably fixed by decisions of the Supreme Court, the instant they are made in ordinary litigation between parties in personal actions the people will have ceased to be their own rulers, having to that extent practically resigned their Government into the hands of that eminent tribunal. Nor is there in this view any assault upon the court or the judges. It is a duty from which they may not shrink to decide cases properly brought before them, and it is no fault of theirs if others seek to turn their decisions to political purposes.

One section of our country believes slavery is *right* and ought to be extended, while the other believes it is *wrong* and ought not to be extended. This is the only substantial dispute. The fugitive-slave clause of the Constitution and the law for the suppression of the foreign slave trade are each as well enforced, perhaps, as any law can ever be in a community where the moral sense of the people imperfectly supports the law itself. The great body of the people abide by the dry legal obligation in both cases, and a few break over in each. This, I think, can not be perfectly cured, and it would be worse in both cases *after* the separation of the sections than before. The foreign slave trade, now imperfectly suppressed, would be ultimately revived without restriction in one section, while fugitive slaves, now only partially surrendered, would not be surrendered at all by the other.

Physically speaking, we can not separate. We can not remove our respective sections from each other nor build an impassable wall between them. A husband and wife may be divorced and go out of the presence and beyond the reach of each other, but the different parts of our country can not do this. They can not but remain face to face, and intercourse, either amicable or hostile, must continue between them. Is it possible, then, to make that intercourse more advantageous or more satisfactory *after* separation than *before?* Can aliens make treaties easier than friends can make laws? Can treaties be more faithfully enforced between aliens than laws can among friends? Suppose you go to war, you can not fight always; and when, after much loss on both sides and no gain on either, you cease fighting, the identical old questions, as to terms of intercourse, are again upon you.

This country, with its institutions, belongs to the people who inhabit it. Whenever they shall grow weary of the existing Government, they can exercise their *constitutional* right of amending it or their *revolutionary* right to dismember or overthrow it. I can not be ignorant of the fact that many worthy and patriotic citizens are desirous of having the National Constitution amended. While I make no recommendation of amendments, I fully recognize the rightful authority of the people over the whole subject, to be exercised in either of the modes prescribed in the instrument itself; and I should, under existing circumstances, favor rather than oppose a fair opportunity being afforded the people to act upon it. I will venture to add that to me the convention mode seems preferable, in that it allows amendments to originate with the people themselves, instead of only permitting them to take or reject propositions originated by others, not especially chosen for the purpose, and which might not be precisely such as they would wish to either accept or refuse. I understand a proposed amendment to the Constitution—which amendment, however, I have not seen—has passed Congress, to the effect that the Federal Government shall never interfere with the domestic institutions of the States, including that of persons held to service. To avoid misconstruction of what I have said, I depart from my purpose now to speak of particular amendments so far as to say that, holding such a provision to now be implied constitutional law, I have no objection to its being made express and irrevocable.

The Chief Magistrate derives all his authority from the people, and they have referred none upon him to fix terms for the separation of the States. The people themselves can do this if also they choose, but the Executive as such has nothing to do with it. His duty is to administer the present Government as it came to his hands and to transmit it unimpaired by him to his successor.

Why should there not be a patient confidence in the ultimate justice of the people? Is there any better or equal hope in the world? In our present differences, is either party without faith of being in the right? If the Almighty Ruler of Nations, with His eternal truth and justice, be on your side of the

North, or on yours of the South, that truth and that justice will surely prevail by the judgment of this great tribunal of the American people.

By the frame of the Government under which we live this same people have wisely given their public servants but little power for mischief, and have with equal wisdom provided for the return of that little to their own hands at very short intervals. While the people retain their virtue and vigilance no Administration by any extreme of wickedness or folly can very seriously injure the Government in the short space of four years.

My countrymen, one and all, think calmly and *well* upon this whole subject. Nothing valuable can be lost by taking time. If there be an object to *hurry* any of you in hot haste to a step which you would never take *deliberately,* that object will be frustrated by taking time; but no good object can be frustrated by it. Such of you as are now dissatisfied still have the old Constitution unimpaired, and, on the sensitive point, the laws of your own framing under it; while the new Administration will have no immediate power, if it would, to change

either. If it were admitted that you who are dissatisfied hold the right side in the dispute, there still is no single good reason for precipitate action. Intelligence, patriotism, Christianity, and a firm reliance on Him who has never yet forsaken this favored land are still competent to adjust in the best way all our present difficulty.

In *your* hands, my dissatisfied fellow-countrymen, and not in *mine,* is the momentous issue of civil war. The Government will not assail *you.* You can have no conflict without being yourselves the aggressors. *You* have no oath registered in heaven to destroy the Government, while *I* shall have the most solemn one to "preserve, protect, and defend it."

I am loath to close. We are not enemies, but friends. We must not be enemies. Though passion may have strained it must not break our bonds of affection. The mystic chords of memory, stretching from every battlefield and patriot grave to every living heart and hearthstone all over this broad land, will yet swell the chorus of the Union, when again touched, as surely they will be, by the better angels of our nature.

Proclamation Calling the Militia and Convening Congress,
   Abraham Lincoln, 1861

Proclamation of Blockade against Southern Ports,
   Abraham Lincoln, 1861

Message to Congress in Special Session, *Abraham Lincoln, 1861*

When secessionist forces fired on Fort Sumter on April 12, 1861, Congress was not in session. At this time the federal army numbered at most 16,000 men, making it necessary for the federal government, if it wished to prosecute a war, to call upon the states, with their large, if ill-trained and ill-equipped, militias (today's National Guard) for troops. Within three days President Lincoln commenced calling up the militia. He also called Congress—specifically authorized under Article I, Section 8 of the Constitution to raise and support armies—into special session, but not until July 4. In the meantime Lincoln declared a blockade of Southern ports. Normally, blockades were issued only against foreign nations, so Lincoln's action in effect recognized the South's separate status from the Union. Such a move was necessary, however, if the North was to stop the South from receiving supplies from countries, such as Great Britain, that had refused to abide by any lesser move declaring Southern ports closed to foreign commerce.

Lincoln's actions were not everywhere greeted with praise. Some in the North argued he had asked for too few troops, yet four Southern states that until then had remained in the Union seceded immediately upon learning that their militia would be required to join in fighting secessionists. Questions concerning Lincoln's use of war powers were raised consistently during the war and after. His Message to Congress outlined his view of the war's opening, including the circumstances surrounding the surrender of Fort Sumter and his view that the individual states had only those powers reserved to them in the Constitution.

Proclamation Calling the Militia and Convening Congress

April 15, 1861

Abraham Lincoln

BY THE PRESIDENT OF THE UNITED STATES
OF AMERICA:
A PROCLAMATION.

WHEREAS the laws of the United States have been, for some time past, and now are opposed, and the execution thereof obstructed, in the States of South Carolina, Georgia, Alabama, Florida, Mississippi, Louisiana, and Texas, by combinations too powerful to be suppressed by the ordinary course of judicial proceedings, or by the powers vested in the marshals by law:

Now, therefore, I, ABRAHAM LINCOLN, President of the United States, in virtue of the power in me vested by the Constitution and the laws, have thought fit to call forth, and hereby do call forth, the militia of the several States of the Union, to the aggregate number of seventy-five thousand, in order to suppress said combinations, and to cause the laws to be duly executed.

The details for this object will be immediately communicated to the State authorities through the War Department.

I appeal to all loyal citizens to favor, facilitate, and aid this effort to maintain the honor, the integrity, and the existence of our National Union, and the perpetuity of popular government; and to redress wrongs already long enough endured.

I deem it proper to say that the first service assigned to the forces hereby called forth will probably be to repossess the forts, places, and property which have been seized from the Union; and in every event, the utmost care will be observed, consistently with the objects aforesaid, to avoid any devastation, any destruction of, or interference with, property, or any disturbance of peaceful citizens in any part of the country.

And I hereby command the persons composing the combinations aforesaid to disperse, and retire peaceably to their respective abodes within twenty days from this date.

Deeming that the present condition of public affairs presents an extraordinary occasion, I do hereby, in virtue of the power in me vested by the Constitution, convene both Houses of Congress. Senators and Representatives are therefore summoned to assemble at their respective chambers, at twelve o'clock, noon, on Thursday, the fourth day of July next, then and there to consider and determine such measures as, in their wisdom, the public safety and interest may seem to demand.

In witness whereof, I have hereunto set my hand, and caused the seal of the United States to be affixed.

Done at the City of Washington, this fifteenth day of April, in the year of our Lord one thousand eight hundred and sixty-one, and of the Independence of the United States the eighty-fifth.

[L. S.]   ABRAHAM LINCOLN.

By the President:

WILLIAM H. SEWARD, *Secretary of State.*

Proclamation of Blockade against Southern Ports

April 19, 1861

Abraham Lincoln

BY THE PRESIDENT OF THE UNITED STATES
OF AMERICA:
A PROCLAMATION.

WHEREAS an insurrection against the Government of the United States has broken out in the States of South Caro-

lina, Georgia, Alabama, Florida, Mississippi, Louisiana, and Texas, and the laws of the United States for the collection of the revenue cannot be effectually executed therein conformably to that provision of the Constitution which requires duties to be uniform throughout the United States:

And whereas a combination of persons, engaged in such insurrection, have threatened to grant pretended letters of marque to authorize the bearers thereof to commit assaults on the lives, vessels, and property of good citizens of the country lawfully engaged in commerce on the high seas, and in waters of the United States:

And whereas an Executive Proclamation has been already issued, requiring the persons engaged in these disorderly proceedings to desist therefrom, calling out a militia force for the purpose of repressing the same, and convening Congress in extraordinary session to deliberate and determine thereon:

Now, therefore, I, ABRAHAM LINCOLN, President of the United States, with a view to the same purposes before mentioned, and to the protection of the public peace, and the lives and property of quiet and orderly citizens pursuing their lawful occupations, until Congress shall have assembled and deliberated on the said unlawful proceedings, or until the same shall have ceased, have further deemed it advisable to set on foot a blockade of the ports within the States aforesaid, in pursuance of the laws of the United States and of the law of nations in such case provided. For this purpose a competent force will be posted so as to prevent entrance and exit of vessels from the ports aforesaid. If, therefore, with a view to violate such blockade, a vessel shall approach, or shall attempt to leave either of the said ports, she will be duly warned by the commander of one of the blockading vessels, who will indorse on her register the fact and date of such warning, and if the same vessel shall again attempt to enter or leave the blockaded port, she will be captured and sent to the nearest convenient port, for such proceedings against her and her cargo as prize, as may be deemed advisable.

And I hereby proclaim and declare that if any person, under the pretended authority of the said States, or under any other pretence, shall molest a vessel of the United States, or the persons or cargo on board of her, such person will be held amenable to the laws of the United States for the prevention and punishment of piracy.

In witness whereof, I have hereunto set my hand, and caused the seal of the United States to be affixed.

Done at the city of Washington, this nineteenth day of April, in the year of our Lord one thousand eight hundred and sixty-one, and of the Independence of the United States the eighty-fifth.

[L. S.]   ABRAHAM LINCOLN.

By the President:

WILLIAM H. SEWARD, *Secretary of State.*

Message to Congress in Special Session

July 4, 1861

Abraham Lincoln

Fellow-citizens of the Senate and House of Representatives:

Having been convened on an extraordinary occasion, as authorized by the Constitution, your attention is not called to any ordinary subject of legislation.

At the beginning of the present Presidential term, four months ago, the functions of the Federal Government were found to be generally suspended within the several States of South Carolina, Georgia, Alabama, Mississippi, Louisiana, and Florida, excepting only those of the Post Office Department.

Within these States, all the Forts, Arsenals, Dock-yards, Custom-houses, and the like, including the movable and stationary property in, and about them, had been seized, and were held in open hostility to this Government, excepting only Forts Pickens, Taylor, and Jefferson, on, and near the Florida coast, and Fort Sumter, in Charleston harbor, South Carolina. The Forts thus seized had been put in improved condition; new ones had been built; and armed forces had been organized, and were organizing, all avowedly with the same hostile purpose.

The Forts remaining in the possession of the Federal government, in, and near, these States, were either besieged or menaced by warlike preparations; and especially Fort Sumter was nearly surrounded by well-protected hostile batteries, with guns equal in quality to the best of its own, and outnumbering the latter as perhaps ten to one. A disproportionate share, of the Federal muskets and rifles, had somehow found their way into these States, and had been seized, to be used against the government. Accumulations of the public revenue, lying within them, had been seized for the same object. The Navy was scattered in distant seas; leaving but a very small part of it within the immediate reach of the govern-

ment. Officers of the Federal Army and Navy, had resigned in great numbers; and, of those resigning, a large proportion had taken up arms against the government. Simultaneously, and in connection, with all this, the purpose to sever the Federal Union, was openly avowed. In accordance with this purpose, an ordinance had been adopted in each of these States, declaring the States, respectively, to be separated from the National Union. A formula for instituting a combined government of these states had been promulgated; and this illegal organization, in the character of confederate States was already invoking recognition, aid, and intervention, from Foreign Powers.

Finding this condition of things, and believing it to be an imperative duty upon the incoming Executive, to prevent, if possible, the consummation of such attempt to destroy the Federal Union, a choice of means to that end became indispensable. This choice was made; and was declared in the Inaugural address. The policy chosen looked to the exhaustion of all peaceful measures, before a resort to any stronger ones. It sought only to hold the public places and property, not already wrested from the Government, and to collect the revenue; relying for the rest, on time, discussion, and the ballot-box. It promised a continuance of the mails, at government expense, to the very people who were resisting the government; and it gave repeated pledges against any disturbance to any of the people, or any of their rights. Of all that which a president might constitutionally, and justifiably, do in such a case, everything was foreborne, without which, it was believed possible to keep the government on foot.

On the 5th of March, (the present incumbent's first full day in office) a letter of Major Anderson, commanding at Fort Sumter, written on the 28th of February, and received at the War Department on the 4th of March, was, by that Department, placed in his hands. This letter expressed the professional opinion of the writer, that re-inforcements could not be thrown into that Fort within the time for his relief, rendered necessary by the limited supply of provisions, and with a view of holding possession of the same, with a force of less than twenty thousand good, and well-disciplined men. This opinion was concurred in by all the officers of his command; and their *memoranda* on the subject, were made enclosures of Major Anderson's letter. The whole was immediately laid before Lieutenant General Scott, who at once concurred with Major Anderson in opinion. On reflection, however, he took full time, consulting with others upon the country, the distinct issue: "Immediate dissolution, or blood."

And this issue embraces more than the fate of these United

States. It presents to the whole family of man, the question, whether a constitutional republic, or a democracy—a government of the people, by the same people—can, or cannot, maintain its territorial integrity, against its own domestic foes. It presents the question, whether discontented individuals, too few in numbers to control administration, according to organic law, in any case, can always, upon the pretences made in this case, or on any other pretences, or arbitrarily, without any pretence, break up their Government, and thus practically put an end to free government upon the earth. It forces us to ask: "Is there, in all republics, this inherent, and fatal weakness?" "Must a government, of necessity, be too *strong* for the liberties of its own people, or too *weak* to maintain its own existence?"

So viewing the issue, no choice was left but to call out the war power of the Government; and so to resist force, employed for its destruction, by force, for its preservation.

The call was made; and the response of the country was most gratifying; surpassing, in unanimity and spirit, the most sanguine expectation. Yet none of the States commonly called Slave-states, except Delaware, gave a Regiment through regular State organization. A few regiments have been organized within some others of those states, by individual enterprise, and received into the government service. Of course the seceded States, so called, (and to which Texas had been joined about the time of the inauguration,) gave no troops to the cause of the Union. The border States, so called, were not uniform in their actions; some of them being almost *for* the Union, while in others—as Virginia, North Carolina, Tennessee, and Arkansas—the Union sentiment was nearly repressed, and silenced. The course taken in Virginia was the most remarkable—perhaps the most important. A convention, elected by the people of that State, to consider this very question of disrupting the Federal Union, was in session at the capital of Virginia when Fort Sumter fell. To this body the people had chosen a large majority of *professed* Union men. Almost immediately after the fall of Sumter, many members of that majority went over to the original disunion minority, and, with them, adopted an ordinance for withdrawing the State from the Union. Whether this change was wrought by their great approval of the assault upon Sumter, or their great resentment at the government's resistance to that assault, is not definitely known. Although they submitted the ordinance, for ratification, to a vote of the people, to be taken on a day then somewhat more than a month distant, the convention, and the Legislature, (which was also in session at the

same time and place) with leading men of the State, not members of either, immediately commenced acting, as if the State were already out of the Union. They pushed military preparations vigorously forward all over the state. They seized the United States Armory at Harper's Ferry, and the Navy-yard at Gosport, near Norfolk. They received—perhaps invited—into their state, large bodies of troops, with their warlike appointments, from the so-called seceded States. They formally entered into a treaty of temporary alliance, and co-operation with the so-called "Confederate States," and sent members to their Congress at Montgomery. And, finally, they permitted the insurrectionary government to be transferred to their capital at Richmond.

The people of Virginia have thus allowed this giant insurrection to make its nest within her borders; and this government has no choice left but to deal with it, *where* it finds it. And it has the less regret, as the loyal citizens have, in due form, claimed its protection. Those loyal citizens, this government is bound to recognize, and protect, as being Virginia.

In the border States, so called—in fact, the middle states—there are those who favor a policy which they call "armed neutrality"—that is, an arming of those states to prevent the Union forces passing one way, or the disunion, the other, over their soil. This would be disunion completed. Figuratively speaking, it would be the building of an impassable wall along the line of separation. And yet, not quite an impassable one; for, under the guise of neutrality, it would tie the hands of the Union men, and freely pass supplies from among them, to the insurrectionists, which it could not do as an open enemy. At a stroke, it would take all the trouble off the hands of secession, except only what proceeds from the external blockade. It would do for the disunionists that which, of all things, they most desire—feed them well, and give them disunion without a struggle of their own. It recognizes no fidelity to the Constitution, no obligation to maintain the Union; and while very many who have favored it are, doubtless, loyal citizens, it is, nevertheless, treason in effect.

Recurring to the action of the government, it may be stated that, at first, a call was made for seventy-five thousand militia; and rapidly following this, a proclamation was issued for closing the ports of the insurrectionary districts by proceedings in the nature of Blockade. So far all was believed to be strictly legal. At this point the insurrectionists announced their purpose to enter upon the practice of privateering.

Other calls were made for volunteers, to serve three years, unless sooner discharged; and also for large additions to the regular Army and Navy. These measures, whether strictly legal or not, were ventured upon, under what appeared to be a popular demand, and a public necessity; trusting, then as now, that Congress would readily ratify them. It is believed that nothing has been done beyond the constitutional competency of Congress.

Soon after the first call for militia, it was considered a duty to authorize the Commanding General, in proper cases, according to his discretion, to suspend the privilege of the writ of habeas corpus; or, in other words, to arrest, and detain, without resort to the ordinary processes and forms of law, such individuals as he might deem dangerous to the public safety. This authority has purposely been exercised but very sparingly. Nevertheless, the legality and propriety of what has been done under it, are questioned; and the attention of the country has been called to the proposition that one who is sworn to "take care that the laws be faithfully executed," should not himself violate them. Of course some consideration was given to the questions of power, and propriety, before this matter was acted upon. The whole of the laws which were required to be faithfully executed, were being resisted, and failing of execution, in nearly one-third of the States. Must they be allowed to finally fail of execution, even had it been perfectly clear, that by the use of the means necessary to their execution, some single law, made in such extreme tenderness of the citizen's liberty, that practically, it relieves more of the guilty, than of the innocent, should, to a very limited extent, be violated? To state the question more directly, are all the laws, *but one,* to go unexecuted, and the government itself go to pieces, lest that one be violated? Even in such a case, would not the official oath be broken, if the government should be overthrown, when it was believed that disregarding the single law, would tend to preserve it? But it was not believed that this question was presented. It was not believed that any law was violated. The provision of the Constitution that "The privilege of the writ of habeas corpus, shall not be suspended unless when, in cases of rebellion or invasion, the public safety may require it," is equivalent to a provision—is a provision—that such privilege may be suspended when, in cases of rebellion, or invasion, the public safety *does* require it. It was decided that we have a case of rebellion, and that the public safety does require the qualified suspension of the privilege of the writ which was authorized to be made. Now it is insisted that Congress, and not the Executive, is vested with this power. But the Constitution itself, is silent as to which, or who, is to exercise the power; and as the provision

was plainly made for a dangerous emergency, it cannot be believed the framers of the instrument intended, that in every case, the danger should run its course, until Congress could be called together; the very assembling of which might be prevented, as was intended in this case, by the rebellion.

No more extended argument is now offered; as an opinion, at some length, will probably be presented by the Attorney General. Whether there shall be any legislation upon the subject, and if any, what, is submitted entirely to the better judgment of Congress.

The forbearance of this government had been so extraordinary, and so long continued, as to lead some foreign nations to shape their action as if they supposed the early destruction of our national Union was probable. While this, on discovery, gave the Executive some concern, he is now happy to say that the sovereignty, and rights of the United States, are now everywhere practically respected by foreign powers; and a general sympathy with the country is manifested throughout the world.

The reports of the Secretaries of the Treasury, War, and the Navy, will give the information in detail deemed necessary, and convenient for your deliberation, and action; while the Executive, and all the Departments, will stand ready to supply omissions, or to communicate new facts, considered important for you to know.

It is now recommended that you give the legal means for making this contest a short, and a decisive one; that you place at the control of the government, for the work, at least four hundred thousand men, and four hundred millions of dollars. That number of men is about one tenth of those of proper ages within the regions where, apparently, *all* are willing to engage; and the sum is less than a twentythird part of the money value owned by the men who seem ready to devote the whole. A debt of six hundred millions of dollars *now,* is a less sum per head, than was the debt of our revolution, when we came out of that struggle; and the money value in the country now, bears even a greater proportion to what it was *then,* than does the population. Surely each man has as strong a motive *now,* to *preserve* our liberties, as each had *then,* to *establish* them.

A right result, at this time, will be worth more to the world, than ten times the men, and ten times the money. The evidence reaching us from the country, leaves no doubt, that the material for the work is abundant; and that it needs only the hand of legislation to give it legal sanction, and the hand of the Executive to give it practical shape and efficiency. One of the greatest perplexities of the government, is to avoid receiving troops faster than it can provide for them. In a word, the people will save their government, if the government itself, will do its part, only indifferently well.

It might seem, at first thought, to be of little difference whether the present movement at the South be called "secession" or "rebellion." The movers, however, well understand the difference. At the beginning, they knew they could never raise their treason to any respectable magnitude, by any name which implies *violation* of law. They knew their people possessed as much of moral sense, as much of devotion to law and order, and as much pride in, and reverence for, the history, and government, of their common country, as any other civilized, and patriotic people. They knew they could make no advancement directly in the teeth of these strong and noble sentiments. Accordingly they commenced by an insidious debauching of the public mind. They invented an ingenious sophism, which, if conceded, was followed by perfectly logical steps, through all the incidents, to the complete destruction of the Union. The sophism itself is, that any state of the Union may, *consistently* with the national Constitution, and therefore *lawfully,* and *peacefully,* withdraw from the Union, without the consent of the Union, or of any other state. The little disguise that the supposed right is to be exercised only for just cause, themselves to be the sole judge of its justice, is too thin to merit any notice.

With rebellion thus sugar-coated, they have been drugging the public mind of their section for more than thirty years; and, until at length, they have brought many good men to a willingness to take up arms against the government the day *after* some assemblage of men have enacted the farcical pretence of taking their State out of the Union, who could have been brought to no such thing the day *before.*

This sophism derives much—perhaps the whole—of its currency, from the assumption, that there is some omnipotent, and sacred supremacy, pertaining to a *State*—to each State of our Federal Union. Our States have neither more, nor less power, than that reserved to them, in the Union, by the Constitution—no one of them ever having been a State *out* of the Union. The original ones passed into the Union even *before* they cast off their British colonial dependence; and the new ones each came into the Union directly from a condition of dependence, excepting Texas. And even Texas, in its temporary independence, was never designated a State. The new ones only took the designation of States, on coming into the Union, while that name was first adopted for the old ones, in, and by, the Declaration of Independence. Therein the "United Colonies" were declared to be "Free and Independent States"; but, even then, the object plainly was not to declare their independence of *one another,* or of the *Union;* but directly the contrary, as their mutual pledge, and their mutual action, before, at the time, and afterwards, abundantly show. The express plighting of faith, by each and all of the original thirteen, in the Articles of Confederation, two years later, that the Union shall be perpetual, is most conclusive. Having never been States, either in substance, or in name, *outside* of the Union, whence this magical omnipotence of "State rights," asserting a claim of power to lawfully destroy the Union itself? Much is said about the "sovereignty" of the States; but the word, even, is not in the national Constitution; nor, as is believed, in any of the State constitutions. What is a "sovereignty," in the political sense of the term? Would it be far wrong to define it "A political community, without a political superior"? Tested by this, no one of our States, except Texas, ever was a sovereignty. And even Texas gave up the character on coming into the Union; by which act, she acknowledged the Constitution of the United States, and the laws and treaties of the United States made in pursuance of the Constitution, to be, for her, the supreme law of the land. The States have their *status* IN the Union, and they have no other *legal status.* If they break from this, they can only do so against law, and by revolution. The Union, and not themselves separately, procured their independence, and their liberty. By conquest, or purchase, the Union gave each of them, whatever of independence, and liberty, it has. The Union is older than any of the States; and, in fact, it created them as States. Originally, some dependent colonies made the Union; and, in turn, the Union threw off their old dependence, for them, and made them States, such as they are. Not one of them ever had a State constitution, independent of the Union. Of course, it is not forgotten that all the new States framed their constitutions, before they entered the Union; nevertheless, dependent upon, and preparatory to, coming into the Union.

Unquestionably the States have the powers, and rights, reserved to them in, and by the National Constitution; but among these, surely, are not included all conceivable powers, however mischievous, or destructive; but, at most, such only, as were known in the world, at the time, as governmental powers; and certainly, a power to destroy the government itself, had never been known as a governmental—as a merely administrative power. This relative matter of National power, and State rights, as a principle, is no other than the principle of *generality,* and *locality.* Whatever concerns the whole, should be confided to the whole—to the general government; while, whatever concerns *only* the State, should be left exclusively, to the State. This is all there is of original principle about it. Whether the National Constitution, in defining boundaries between the two, has applied the principle with exact accuracy, is not to be questioned. We are all bound by that defining, without question.

What is now combatted, is the position that secession is *consistent* with the Constitution—is *lawful,* and *peaceful.* It is not contended that there is any express law for it; and nothing should ever be implied as law, which leads to unjust, or absurd consequences. The nation purchased, with money, the countries out of which several of these States were formed. Is it just that they shall go off without leave, and without refunding? The nation paid very large sums, (in the aggregate, I believe, nearly a hundred millions) to relieve Florida of the aboriginal tribes. Is it just that she shall now be off without consent, or without making any return? The nation is now in debt for money applied to the benefit of these so-called seceding States, in common with the rest. Is it just, either that creditors shall go unpaid, or the remaining States pay the whole? A part of the present national debt was contracted to pay the old debts of Texas. Is it just that she shall leave, and pay no part of this herself?

Again, if one State may secede, so may another; and when all shall have seceded, none is left to pay the debts. Is this quite just to creditors? Did we notify them of this sage view of ours, when we borrowed their money? If we now recognize this doctrine, by allowing the seceders to go in peace, it is difficult to see what we can do, if others choose to go, or to extort terms upon which they will promise to remain.

The seceders insist that our Constitution admits of secession. They have assumed to make a National Constitution of their own, in which, of necessity, they have either *discarded,* or *retained,* the right of secession, as they insist, it exists in ours. If they have discarded it, they thereby admit that, on principle, it ought not to be in ours. If they have retained it, by their own construction of ours they show that to be consistent they must secede from one another, whenever they shall find it the easiest way of settling their debts, or effecting any other selfish, or unjust object. The principle itself is one of disintegration, and upon which no government can possibly endure.

If all the States, save one, should assert the power to *drive* that one out of the Union, it is presumed the whole class of seceder politicians would at once deny the power, and denounce the act as the greatest outrage upon State rights. But suppose that precisely the same act, instead of being called "driving the one out," should be called "the seceding of the others from that one," it would be exactly what the seceders claim to do; unless, indeed, they make the point, that the one, because it is a minority, may rightfully do, what the others, because they are a majority, may not rightfully do. These politicians are subtle, and profound, on the rights of minorities. They are not partial to that power which made the Constitution, and speaks from the preamble, calling itself "We, the People."

It may well be questioned whether there is, to-day, a majority of the legally qualified voters of any State, except perhaps South Carolina, in favor of disunion. There is much reason to believe that the Union men are the majority in many, if not in every other one, of the so-called seceded States. The contrary has not been demonstrated in any one of them. It is ventured to affirm this, even of Virginia and Tennessee; for the result of an election, held in military camps, where the bayonets are all on one side of the question voted upon, can scarcely be considered as demonstrating popular sentiment. At such an election, all that large class who are, at once, *for* the Union, and *against* coercion, would be coerced to vote against the Union.

It may be affirmed, without extravagance, that the free institutions we enjoy, have developed the powers, and improved the condition, of our whole people, beyond any example in the world. Of this we now have a striking, and an impressive illustration. So large an army as the government has now on foot, was never before known, without a soldier in it, but who had taken his place there, of his own free choice. But more than this: there are many single Regiments whose members, one and another, possess full practical knowledge of all the arts, sciences, professions, and whatever else, whether useful or elegant, is known in the world; and there is scarcely one, from which there could not be selected, a President, a Cabinet, a Congress, and perhaps a Court, abundantly competent to administer the government itself. Nor do I say this is not true, also, in the army of our late friends, now adversaries, in this contest; but if it is, so much better the reason why the government, which has conferred such benefits on both them and us, should not be broken up. Whoever, in any section, proposes to abandon such a government, would do well to consider, in deference to what principle it is, that he does it—what better he is likely to get in its stead—whether the substitute will give, or be intended to give, so much of good to the people. There are some foreshadowings on this subject. Our adversaries have adopted some Declarations of Independence; in which, unlike the good old one, penned by Jefferson, they omit the words "all men are created equal." Why? They have adopted a temporary national constitution, in the preamble of which, unlike our good old one, signed by Washington, they omit "We, the People," and substitute "We, the deputies of the sovereign and independent States." Why? Why this deliberate pressing out of view, the rights of men, and the authority of the people?

This is essentially a People's contest. On the side of the Union, it is a struggle for maintaining in the world, that form, and substance of government, whose leading object is, to elevate the condition of men—to lift artificial weights from all shoulders—to clear the paths of laudable pursuit for all—to afford all, an unfettered start, and a fair chance, in the race of life. Yielding to partial, and temporary departures, from necessity, this is the leading object of the government for whose existence we contend.

I am most happy to believe that the plain people understand, and appreciate this. It is worthy of note, that while in this, the government's hour of trial, large numbers of those in the Army and Navy, who have been favored with the offices, have resigned, and proved false to the hand which had pampered them, not one common soldier, or common sailor is known to have deserted his flag.

Great honor is due to those officers who remain true, despite the example of their treacherous associates; but the greatest honor, and most important fact of all, is the unanimous firmness of the common soldiers, and common sailors. To the last man, so far as known, they have successfully resisted the traitorous efforts of those, whose commands, but an hour before, they obeyed as absolute law. This is the patriotic instinct of the plain people. They understand, without an argument, that destroying the government, which was made by Washington, means no good to them.

Our popular government has often been called an experiment. Two points in it, our people have already settled—the successful *establishing*, and the successful *administering* of it. One still remains—its successful *maintenance* against a formidable internal attempt to overthrow it. It is now for them to demonstrate to the world, that those who can fairly carry an election, can also suppress a rebellion—that ballots are the rightful, and peaceful, successors of bullets; and that when ballots have fairly, and constitutionally, decided, there can

be no successful appeal, back to bullets; that there can be no successful appeal, except to ballots themselves, at succeeding elections. Such will be a great lesson of peace; teaching men that what they cannot take by an election, neither can they take it by a war—teaching all, the folly of being the beginners of a war.

Lest there be some uneasiness in the minds of candid men, as to what is to be the course of the government, towards the Southern States, *after* the rebellion shall have been suppressed, the Executive deems it proper to say, it will be his purpose then, as ever, to be guided by the Constitution, and the laws; and that he probably will have no different understanding of the powers, and duties of the Federal government, relatively to the rights of the States, and the people, under the Constitution, than that expressed in the inaugural address.

He desires to preserve the government, that it may be administered for all, as it was administered by the men who made it. Loyal citizens everywhere, have the right to claim this of their government; and the government has no right to withhold, or neglect it. It is not perceived that, in giving it, there is any coercion, any conquest, or any subjugation, in any just sense of those terms.

The Constitution provides, and all the States have accepted the provision, that "The United States shall guarantee to every State in this Union a republican form of government." But, if a State may lawfully go out of the Union, having done so, it may also discard the republican form of government; so that to prevent its going out, is an indispensable *means,* to the *end,* of maintaining the guaranty mentioned; and when an end is lawful and obligatory, the indispensable means to it, are also lawful, and obligatory.

It was with the deepest regret that the Executive found the duty of employing the war-power, in defence of the government, forced upon him. He could but perform this duty, or surrender the existence of the government. No compromise, by public servants, could, in this case, be a cure; not that compromises are not often proper, but that no popular government can long survive a marked precedent, that those who carry an election, can only save the government from immediate destruction, by giving up the main point, upon which the people gave the election. The people themselves, and not their servants, can safely reverse their own deliberate decisions. As a private citizen, the Executive could not have consented that these institutions shall perish; much less could he, in betrayal of so vast, and so sacred a trust, as these free people had confided to him. He felt that he had no moral right to shrink; nor even to count the chances of his own life, in what might follow. In full view of his great responsibility, he has, so far, done what he has deemed his duty. You will now, according to your own judgment, perform yours. He sincerely hopes that your views, and your action, may so accord with his, as to assure all faithful citizens, who have been disturbed in their rights, of a certain, and speedy restoration to them, under the Constitution, and the laws.

And having thus chosen our course, without guile, and with pure purpose, let us renew our trust in God, and go forward without fear, and with manly hearts.

July 4, 1861.

In response to rioting in Baltimore, along the most important railroad supply line into Washington, D.C., Lincoln authorized General Winfield Scott to suspend the writ of habeas corpus, allowing him to imprison suspected subversives without charge. Lincoln later would expand this suspension to other areas. Supreme Court chief justice Roger Taney (sitting as an appellate court judge) declared Lincoln's suspension of the writ of habeas corpus unconstitutional in ex parte Merryman—*a decision that was ignored. Congress did not immediately embrace Lincoln's suspension of habeas corpus, taking no action in regard to it until, in 1863, it gave its authorization and set guidelines for future suspensions.*

Proclamation Suspending Writ of Habeas Corpus

September 15, 1863

Abraham Lincoln

BY THE PRESIDENT OF THE UNITED STATES
OF AMERICA.
A PROCLAMATION.

Whereas the Constitution of the United States has ordained that the privilege of the writ of *habeas corpus* shall not be suspended unless when, in cases of rebellion or invasion, the public safety may require it; and

Whereas a rebellion was existing on the 3d day of March, 1863, which rebellion is still existing; and

Whereas by a statute which was approved on that day it was enacted by the Senate and House of Representatives of the United States in Congress assembled that during the present insurrection the President of the United States, whenever in his judgment the public safety may require, is authorized to suspend the privilege of the writ of *habeas corpus* in any case throughout the United States or any part thereof; and

Whereas, in the judgment of the President, the public safety does require that the privilege of the said writ shall now be suspended throughout the United States in the cases where, by the authority of the President of the United States, military, naval, and civil officers of the United States, or any of them, hold persons under their command or in their custody, either as prisoners of war, spies, or aiders or abettors of the enemy, or officers, soldiers, or seamen enrolled or drafted or mustered or enlisted in or belonging to the land or naval forces of the United States, or as deserters therefrom, or otherwise amenable to military law or the rules and articles of war or the rules or regulations prescribed for the military or naval services by authority of the President of the United States, or for resisting a draft, or for any other offense against the military or naval service:

Now, therefore, I, Abraham Lincoln, President of the United States, do hereby proclaim and make known to all whom it may concern that the privilege of the writ of *habeas corpus* is suspended throughout the United States in the several cases before mentioned, and that this suspension will continue throughout the duration of the said rebellion or until this proclamation shall, by a subsequent one to be issued by the President of the United States, be modified or revoked. And I do hereby require all magistrates, attorneys, and other civil officers within the United States and all officers and others in the military and naval services of the United States to take distinct notice of this suspension and to give it full effect, and all citizens of the United States to conduct and govern themselves accordingly and in conformity with the Constitution of the United States and the laws of Congress in such case made and provided.

In testimony whereof I have hereunto set my hand and caused the seal of the United States to be affixed this 15th day of September A.D. 1863, and of the Independence of the United States of America the eighty-eighth.

[SEAL.]   ABRAHAM LINCOLN.

By the President:

WILLIAM H. SEWARD, *Secretary of State.*

Message to Congress on Gradual Abolishment of Slavery,
   Abraham Lincoln, 1862

Proclamation Revoking General Hunter's Emancipation Order,
   Abraham Lincoln, 1862

Emancipation Proclamation—1862, *Abraham Lincoln*

Emancipation Proclamation—1863, *Abraham Lincoln*

Lincoln's opposition to the institution of slavery was well known; he had first proposed a plan for gradual emancipation in 1849. But he did not portray the war as one intended to free the slaves. Indeed, fearing lest border, slaveholding states might secede, he repeatedly denied that such was his goal. But Congress itself, in the Confiscation Act of 1861, had authorized emancipation of slaves used in the Confederate war effort. When General John C. Frémont, Union commander in the Western Division, declared all slaves in Missouri "forever free," Lincoln asked Frémont to limit his action to conform with the Confiscation Act. Frémont refusing, Lincoln, on August 30, 1861, revoked the proclamation and relieved him of command. Increasingly, however, Lincoln embraced limited forms of emancipation as a means of preserving the Union, thus delivering speeches such as that of March 6, 1862, reproduced here.

On May 9 of the following year, General David Hunter, commanding federal forces holding a series of Union-controlled enclaves along the South Atlantic coast, issued a proclamation declaring every slave in South Carolina, Georgia, and Florida to be free and eligible for military service. Like Frémont, Hunter claimed that his action was one of military necessity. But Lincoln reserved decisions of this magnitude for himself. Moreover, Lincoln had already made at least two appeals to border states to accept compensated emancipation, a policy he deemed less likely to win favor if Hunter's actions were allowed to stand. But his third appeal, made at a meeting between Lincoln and border state leaders on July 12, 1862, also met with rejection. It was in this context that Lincoln decided to issue his Preliminary Emancipation Proclamation. Lincoln waited for a Union victory on the battlefield, which he felt he had after the Battle of Antietam, and then informed Confederate states, through his Preliminary Proclamation, that he would free all slaves in those states still in rebellion, as of January 1, 1863. The Emancipation Proclamation made good on this word, at least officially. The Proclamation declared free only those slaves essentially out of reach of Union forces, leaving all others in bondage. The Proclamation did, however, spawn a flood of slave escapes and was part of a wider movement toward emancipation that culminated in the Thirteenth Amendment.

Message to Congress on Gradual Abolishment of Slavery

March 6, 1862

Abraham Lincoln

GRADUAL ABOLISHMENT OF SLAVERY.

MESSAGE

FROM THE

PRESIDENT OF THE UNITED STATES,

IN RELATION TO

Co-operating with any State for the gradual abolishment of slavery.

March 6, 1862—Committed to the Committee of the Whole House on the state of the Union, and ordered to be printed.

Fellow-citizens of the Senate and House of Representatives:

I recommend the adoption of a joint resolution by your honorable bodies, which shall be substantially as follows:

"*Resolved,* That the United States ought to co-operate with any State which may adopt gradual abolishment of slavery, giving to such State pecuniary aid, to be used by such State in its discretion, to compensate for the inconveniences, public and private, produced by such change of system."

If the proposition contained in the resolution does not meet the approval of Congress and the country, there is the end; but if it does command such approval, I deem it of importance that the States and people immediately interested should be at once distinctly notified of the fact, so that they may begin to consider whether to accept or reject it. The federal government would find its highest interest in such a measure, as one of the most efficient means of self-preservation. The leaders of the existing insurrection entertain the hope that this government will ultimately be forced to acknowledge the independence of some part of the disaffected region, and that all the slave States north of such part will then say, "the Union for which we have struggled being already gone, we now choose to go with the southern section." To deprive them of this hope substantially ends the rebellion; and the initiation of emancipation completely deprives them of it as to all the States initiating it. The point is not that *all* the States tolerating slavery would very soon, if at all, initiate emancipation, but that while the offer is equally made to all, the more northern shall, by such initiation, make it certain to the more southern that in no event will the former ever join the latter in their proposed confederacy. I say "initiation," because in my judgment gradual, and not sudden, emancipation is better for all. In the mere financial or pecuniary view, any member of Congress, with the census tables and treasury reports before him, can readily see for himself how very soon the current expenditures of this war would purchase, at fair valuation, all the slaves in any named State. Such a proposition on the part of the general government sets up no claim of a right by federal authority to interfere with slavery within State limits, referring as it does the absolute control of the subject in each case to the State and its people immediately interested. It is proposed as a matter of perfectly free choice with them.

In the annual message last December I thought fit to say "the Union must be preserved; and hence all indispensable means must be employed." I said this not hastily, but deliberately. War has been made, and continues to be, an indispensable means to this end. A practical re-acknowledgment of the national authority would render the war unnecessary, and it would at once cease. If, however, resistance continues, the war must also continue; and it is impossible to foresee all the incidents which may attend and all the ruin which may follow it. Such as may seem indispensable, or may obviously promise great efficiency towards ending the struggle, must and will come.

The proposition now made, though an offer only, I hope it may be esteemed no offence to ask whether the pecuniary consideration tendered would not be of more value to the States and private persons concerned than are the institution and property in it, in the present aspect of affairs?

While it is true that the adoption of the proposed resolution would be merely initiatory, and not within itself a practical measure, it is recommended in the hope that it would soon lead to important practical results. In full view of my great responsibility to my God and to my country, I earnestly beg the attention of Congress and the people to the subject.

ABRAHAM LINCOLN.

Washington, *March 6,* 1862.

Proclamation Revoking General Hunter's Emancipation Order

May 19, 1862

Abraham Lincoln

BY THE PRESIDENT OF THE UNITED STATES
OF AMERICA:
A PROCLAMATION.

Whereas there appears in the public prints what purports to be a proclamation of Major General Hunter, in the words and figures following, to wit:

Headquarters Department of the South,
Hilton Head, S.C., May 9, 1862.

General Orders No. 11.—The three States of Georgia, Florida, and South Carolina, comprising the military department of the South, having deliberately declared themselves no longer under the protection of the United States of America, and having taken up arms against the said United States, it becomes a military necessity to declare them under martial law. This was accordingly done on the 25th day of April, 1862. Slavery and martial law in a free country are altogether incompatible; the persons in these three States—Georgia, Florida, and South Carolina—heretofore held as slaves, are therefore declared forever free.

(Official)   David Hunter,
                              Major General Commanding.

Ed. W. Smith, Acting Assistant Adjutant Gen'l.

And whereas the same is producing some excitement and misunderstanding, therefore,

I, ABRAHAM LINCOLN, President of the United States, proclaim and declare, that the Government of the United States had no knowledge, information, or belief, of an intention on the part of General Hunter to issue such a proclamation; nor has it yet any authentic information that the document is genuine. And further, that neither General Hunter, nor any other commander, or person, has been authorized by the Government of the United States to make proclamations declaring the slaves of any State free; and that the supposed proclamation, now in question, whether genuine or false, is altogether void, so far as respects such declaration.

I further make known that whether it be competent for me, as Commander-in-Chief of the Army and Navy, to declare the slaves of any State or States free, and whether, at any time, in any case, it shall have become a necessity indispensable to the maintenance of the Government, to exercise such supposed power, are questions which, under my responsibility, I reserve to myself, and which I cannot feel justified in leaving to the decision of commanders in the field. These are totally different questions from those of police regulations in armies and camps.

On the sixth day of March last, by a special message, I recommended to Congress the adoption of a joint resolution to be substantially as follows:

Resolved, That the United States ought to coöperate with any State which may adopt a gradual abolishment of slavery, giving to such State pecuniary aid, to be used by such State in its discretion, to compensate for the inconveniences, public and private, produced by such change of system.

The resolution, in the language above quoted, was adopted by large majorities in both branches of Congress, and now stands an authentic, definite, and solemn proposal of the nation to the States and people most immediately interested in the subject matter. To the people of those States I now earnestly appeal—I do not argue—I beseech you to make the arguments for yourselves—You cannot, if you would, be blind to the signs of the times—I beg of you a calm and enlarged consideration of them, ranging, if it may be, far above personal and partisan politics. This proposal makes common cause for a common object, casting no reproaches upon any. It acts not the Pharisee. The change it contemplates would come gently as the dews of heaven, not rending or wrecking anything. Will you not embrace it? So much good has not been done, by one effort, in all past time, as, in the providence of God, it is now your high privilege to do. May the vast future not have to lament that you have neglected it.

In witness whereof, I have hereunto set my hand and caused the seal of the United States to be affixed.

Done at the City of Washington, this nineteenth day of May, in the year of our Lord one thousand eight hundred and sixty-two, and of the Independence of the United States the eighty-sixth.

[SEAL.]   ABRAHAM LINCOLN.

By the President:

WILLIAM H. SEWARD, *Secretary of State.*

Emancipation Proclamation

September 22, 1862

Abraham Lincoln

BY THE PRESIDENT OF THE UNITED STATES
OF AMERICA:
A PROCLAMATION.

I, ABRAHAM LINCOLN, President of the United States of America, and commander-in-chief of the army and navy thereof, do hereby proclaim and declare that hereafter, as heretofore, the war will be prosecuted for the object of practically restoring the constitutional relation between the United States and each of the states and the people thereof, in which states that relation is or may be suspended or disturbed.

That it is my purpose, upon the next meeting of Congress, to again recommend the adoption of a practical measure tendering pecuniary aid to the free acceptance or rejection of all slave states, so called, the people whereof may not then be in rebellion against the United States, and which states may then have voluntarily adopted, or thereafter may voluntarily adopt, immediate or gradual abolishment of slavery within their respective limits; and that the effort to colonize persons of African descent with their consent upon this continent or elsewhere, with the previously obtained consent of the governments existing there, will be continued.

That on the first day of January, in the year of our Lord one thousand eight hundred and sixty-three, all persons held as slaves within any state or designated part of a state, the people whereof shall then be in rebellion against the United States, shall be then, thenceforward, and forever free; and the Execu-

tive Government of the United States, including the military and naval authority thereof, will recognize and maintain the freedom of such persons, and will do no act or acts to repress such persons, or any of them, in any efforts they may make for their actual freedom.

That the Executive will, on the first day of January aforesaid, by proclamation, designate the states and parts of states, if any, in which the people thereof, respectively, shall then be in rebellion against the United States; and the fact that any State, or the people thereof, shall on that day be, in good faith, represented in the Congress of the United States by members chosen thereto at elections wherein a majority of the qualified voters of such state shall have participated, shall, in the absence of strong countervailing testimony, be deemed conclusive evidence that such state, and the people thereof, are not then in rebellion against the United States.

That attention is hereby called to an act of Congress entitled "An act to make an additional article of war," approved March 13, 1862, and which act is in the words and figure following:

"Be it enacted by the Senate and House of Representatives of the United States of America in Congress assembled, That hereafter the following shall be promulgated as an additional article of war, for the government of the army of the United States, and shall be obeyed and observed as such:

"ARTICLE—. All officers or persons in the military or naval service of the United States are prohibited from employing any of the forces under their respective commands for the purpose of returning fugitives from service or labor who may have escaped from any persons to whom such service or labor is claimed to be due, and any officer who shall be found guilty by a court-martial of violating this article shall be dismissed from the service.

"SEC. 2. *And be it further enacted,* That this act shall take effect from and after its passage."

Also to the ninth and tenth sections of an act entitled "An act to suppress insurrection, to punish treason and rebellion, to seize and confiscate property of rebels, and for other purposes," approved July 17, 1862, and which sections are in the words and figures following:

"SEC. 9. *And be it further enacted,* That all slaves of persons who shall hereafter be engaged in rebellion against the Government of the United States, or who shall in any way give aid or comfort thereto, escaping from such persons and taking refuge within the lines of the army; and all slaves captured from such persons or deserted by them, and coming under the control of the Government of the United States; and all slaves of such persons found *on* [or] being within any place occupied by rebel forces and afterwards occupied by the forces of the United States, shall be deemed captives of war, and shall be forever free of their servitude, and not again held as slaves.

"SEC. 10. *And be it further enacted,* That no slave escaping into any state, territory, or the District of Columbia, from any other state, shall be delivered up, or in any way impeded or hindered of his liberty, except for crime, or some offence against the laws, unless the person claiming said fugitive shall first make oath that the person to whom the labor or service of such fugitive is alleged to be due is his lawful owner, and has not borne arms against the United States in the present rebellion, nor in any way given aid and comfort thereto; and no person engaged in the military or naval service of the United States shall, under any pretence whatever, assume to decide on the validity of the claim of any person to the service or labor of any other person, or surrender up any such person to the claimant, on pain of being dismissed from the service."

And I do hereby enjoin upon and order all persons engaged in the military and naval service of the United States to observe, obey, and enforce, within their respective spheres of service, the act and sections above recited.

And the Executive will in due time recommend that all citizens of the United States who shall have remained loyal thereto throughout the rebellion shall (upon the restoration of the constitutional relation between the United States and their respective states and people, if that relation shall have been suspended or disturbed) be compensated for all losses by acts of the United States, including the loss of slaves.

In witness whereof, I have hereunto set my hand, and caused the seal of the United States to be affixed.

Done at the city of Washington this twenty-second day of September, in the year of our Lord one thousand eight hundred and sixty-two, and of the Independence of the United States the eighty-seventh.

[L. S.]   ABRAHAM LINCOLN.

By the President:

WILLIAM H. SEWARD, *Secretary of State.*

Emancipation Proclamation

January 1, 1863

Abraham Lincoln

BY THE PRESIDENT OF THE UNITED STATES
OF AMERICA:
A PROCLAMATION.

WHEREAS, on the twenty-second day of September, in the year of our Lord one thousand eight hundred and sixty-two, a proclamation was issued by the President of the United States, containing, among other things, the following, to wit:

"That on the first day of January, in the year of our Lord one thousand eight hundred and sixty-three, all persons held as slaves within any state or designated part of a state, the people whereof shall then be in rebellion against the United States, shall be then, thenceforward, and forever, free; and the Executive Government of the United States, including the military and naval authority thereof, will recognize and maintain the freedom of such persons, and will do no act or acts to repress such persons, or any of them, in any efforts they may make for their actual freedom.

"That the Executive will, on the first day of January aforesaid, by proclamation, designate the states and parts of states, if any, in which the people thereof, respectively, shall then be in rebellion against the United States; and the fact that any state, or the people thereof, shall on that day be in good faith represented in the Congress of the United States, by members chosen thereto at elections wherein a majority of the qualified voters of such states shall have participated, shall, in the absence of strong countervailing testimony, be deemed conclusive evidence that such state, and the people thereof, are not then in rebellion against the United States."

Now, therefore, I, ABRAHAM LINCOLN, President of the United States, by virtue of the power in me vested as commander-in-chief of the army and navy of the United States, in time of actual armed rebellion against the authority and Government of the United States, and as a fit and necessary war measure for suppressing said rebellion, do, on this first day of January, in the year of our Lord one thousand eight hundred and sixty-three, and in accordance with my purpose so to do, publicly proclaimed for the full period of one hundred days from the day first above mentioned, order and designate as the states and parts of states wherein the people thereof, respectively, are this day in rebellion against the United States, the following, to wit:

Arkansas, Texas, Louisiana, (except the parishes of St. Bernard, Plaquemines, Jefferson, St. John, St. Charles, St. James, Ascension, Assumption, Terre Bonne, Lafourche, St. Mary, St. Martin, and Orleans, including the city of New Orleans,) Mississippi, Alabama, Florida, Georgia, South Carolina, North Carolina, and Virginia, (except the forty-eight counties designated as West Virginia, and also the counties of Berkeley, Accomac, Northampton, Elizabeth City, York, Princess Ann, and Norfolk, including the cities of Norfolk and Portsmouth,) and which excepted parts are for the present left precisely as if this proclamation were not issued.

And by virtue of the power and for the purpose aforesaid, I do order and declare that all persons held as slaves within said designated states and parts of states are, and henceforward shall be, free; and that the Executive Government of the United States, including the military and naval authorities thereof, will recognize and maintain the freedom of said persons.

And I hereby enjoin upon the people so declared to be free to abstain from all violence, unless in necessary self-defence; and I recommend to them that, in all cases when allowed, they labor faithfully for reasonable wages.

And I further declare and make known that such persons, of suitable condition, will be received into the armed service of the United States to garrison forts, positions, stations, and other places, and to man vessels of all sorts in said service.

And upon this act, sincerely believed to be an act of justice, warranted by the Constitution upon military necessity, I invoke the considerate judgment of mankind and the gracious favor of Almighty God.

In witness whereof, I have hereunto set my hand and caused the seal of the United States to be affixed.

Done at the city of Washington this first day of January, in the year of our Lord one thousand eight hundred and sixty-three, and of the Independence of the United States of America the eighty-seventh.

[L.S.]   ABRAHAM LINCOLN.

By the President:

WILLIAM H. SEWARD, *Secretary of State.*

Gettysburg Address, *Abraham Lincoln, 1863*

One of the most famous speeches in American history, The Gettysburg Address was not even the main attraction of the event at which it was delivered. Lincoln was asked to make a few remarks at the official dedication of the cemetery for Union war dead from the battle of Gettysburg. The featured speaker was the then-famous orator, Edward Everett. But it is Lincoln's speech, now carved on the Lincoln Memorial, which has become the subject of historical study and legend.

The Gettysburg Address

November 19, 1863

Abraham Lincoln

Address delivered at the dedication of the
    Cemetery at Gettysburg.

Four score and seven years ago our fathers brought forth on this continent, a new nation, conceived in Liberty, and dedicated to the proposition that all men are created equal.

Now we are engaged in a great civil war, testing whether that nation, or any nation so conceived and so dedicated, can long endure. We are met on a great battle-field of that war. We have come to dedicate a portion of that field, as a final resting place for those who here gave their lives that that nation might live. It is altogether fitting and proper that we should do this.

But, in a larger sense, we can not dedicate—we can not consecrate—we can not hallow—this ground. The brave men, living and dead, who struggled here, have consecrated it, far above our poor power to add or detract. The world will little note, nor long remember what we say here, but it can never forget what they did here. It is for us the living, rather, to be dedicated here to the unfinished work which they who fought here have thus far so nobly advanced. It is rather for us to be here dedicated to the great task remaining before us—that from these honored dead we take increased devotion to that cause for which they gave the last full measure of devotion—that we here highly resolve that these dead shall not have died in vain—that this nation, under God, shall have a new birth of freedom—and that government of the people, by the people, for the people, shall not perish from the earth.

November 19, 1863.   ABRAHAM LINCOLN.

Message to the Congress of Confederate States, *Jefferson Davis*, 1864

Act to Increase the Military Force of the Confederate States, 1865

Founded on the doctrine of states' rights, the Confederacy found itself engaging in increasingly centralizing conduct over the course of its unsuccessful war of secession. The armies of the Confederate states were outnumbered throughout the war, and the relative numbers became increasingly lopsided in the Union's favor, with increasing numbers of Confederate soldiers deserting and conscription methods (never popular) becoming increasingly onerous, particularly given the much smaller white population of the Southern states. Confederate president Jefferson Davis repeatedly issued messages and speeches intended to rally the people, restating the principles of the Confederate cause and predicting eventual victory. But conditions continued to worsen, eventually leading to calls for arming African Americans. Some of these proposals included emancipation. All were resisted until very late in the war when General Robert E. Lee, among others, threw his support behind calling on slaves to provide various services to the war effort—including labor, transport, and perhaps even fighting. On February 10, 1865, Congressman Ethelbert Barksdale of Mississippi introduced the act reproduced here. The bill was passed on March 13, succeeding by just one vote in the Confederate Senate. The March 23 executive order implementing the act required that the Confederate government gain the approval of slaves' masters for their military service.

Message to the Congress of Confederate States

May 2, 1864

Jefferson Davis

To the Senate and House of Representatives of the Confederate States of America:

You are assembled under circumstances of deep interest to your country, and it is fortunate that coming, as you do, newly elected by the people and familiar with the condition of the various localities, you will be the better able to devise measures adapted to meet the wants of the public service without imposing unnecessary burthens on the citizen. The brief period which has elapsed since the last adjournment of Congress has not afforded sufficient opportunity to test the efficacy of the most important laws then enacted, nor have the events occurring in the interval been such as materially to change the state of the country.

The unjust war commenced against us in violation of the rights of the States, and in usurpation of power not delegated to the Government of the United States, is still character-ized by the barbarism with which it has heretofore been conducted by the enemy. Aged men, helpless women and children, appeal in vain to the humanity which should be inspired by their condition for immunity from arrest, incarceration, or banishment from their homes. Plunder and devastation of the property of noncombatants[,] destruction of private dwellings and even of edifices devoted to the worship of God, expeditions organized for the sole purpose of sacking cities, consigning them to the flames, killing the unarmed inhabitants, and inflicting horrible outrages on women and children, are some of the constantly recurring atrocities of the invader. It can not reasonably be pretended that such acts conduce to any end which their authors dare avow before the civilized world, and sooner or later Christendom must mete out to them the condemnation which such brutality deserves. The suffering thus ruthlessly inflicted upon the people of the invaded districts has served but to illustrate their patriotism. Entire unanimity and zeal for their country's cause have been preeminently conspicuous among those whose sacrifices have been greatest. So the Army, which has borne the trials and dangers of the war, which has been subjected to privations and disappointments (tests of manly fortitude far more severe than the brief fatigues and perils of actual combat), has been the center of cheerfulness and hope. From the camp comes the voice of the soldier patriots invoking each who is at home, in the sphere he best may fill, to devote his whole energies to the support of a cause in the success of which their confidence has never faltered. They, the veterans of many a hard-fought field, tender to their country, without limit of time, a service of priceless value to us, one which posterity will hold in grateful remembrance.

In considering the state of the country, the reflection is naturally suggested that this is the Third Congress of the Confederate States of America. The Provisional Government was formed, its Congress held four sessions, lived its appointed term, and passed away. The Permanent Government was then organized, its different departments established, a Congress elected, which also held four sessions, served its full constitutional term, and expired. You, the Second Congress under the Permanent Government, are now assembled at the time and place appointed by law for commencing your session. All these events have passed into history, notwithstanding the threat of our prompt subjugation, made three years ago, by a people that presume to assert a title to govern States whose separate and independent sovereignty was recognized by treaty with France and Great Britain in the last century and remained unquestioned for nearly three generations. Yet these very Governments, in disregard of duty and treaty obligations which bind them to recognize as independent Virginia and other Confederate States, persist in countenancing by moral influence, if not in aiding by unfair and partial action, the claim set up by the Executive of a foreign Government to exercise despotic sway over the States thus recognized and treat the invasion of them by their former limited and special agent as though it were the attempt of a sovereign to suppress a rebellion against lawful authority. Ungenerous advantage has been taken of our present condition, and our rights have been violated, our vessels of war detained in ports to which they have been invited by proclamations of neutrality, and in one instance our flag also insulted where the sacred right of asylum was supposed to be secure; while one of these Governments has contented itself with simply deprecating, by deferential representations, the conduct of our enemy in the constantly recurring instances of his contemptuous disregard of neutral rights and flagrant violations of public law. It may be that foreign governments, like our enemies, have mistaken our desire for peace, unreservedly expressed, for evidence of exhaustion, and have thence inferred the probability of success in the effort to subjugate or exterminate the millions of human beings who in these States prefer any fate to submission to their savage assailants. I see no prospect of an early change in the course heretofore pursued by these Governments; but when this delusion shall have been dispelled, and when our independence, by the valor and fortitude of our people, shall have been won against all the hostile influences combined against us, and can no longer be ignored by open foes or professed neutrals, this war will have left with its proud memories a record of many wrongs which it may not misbecome us to forgive, some for which we may not properly forbear from demanding redress. In the meantime it is enough for us to know that every avenue of negotiation is closed against us; that our enemy is making renewed and strenuous efforts for our destruction, and that the sole resource for us as a people secure in the justice of our cause, and holding our liberties to be more precious than all other earthly possessions, is to combine and apply every available element of power for their defense and preservation.

On the subject of the exchange of prisoners I greatly regret to be unable to give you satisfactory information. The Government of the United States, while persisting in failure to execute the terms of the cartel, make occasional deliveries of prisoners and then suspend action without apparent cause. I confess my inability to comprehend their policy or purpose. The prisoners held by us, in spite of humane care, are perishing from the inevitable effects of imprisonment and the homesickness produced by the hopelessness of release from confinement. The spectacle of their suffering augments our longing desire to relieve from similar trials our own brave men who have spent so many weary months in a cruel and useless imprisonment, endured with heroic constancy. The delivery, after a suspension of some weeks, has just been resumed by the enemy; but as they give no assurance of intent to carry out the cartel, an interruption of the exchange may recur at any moment.

The reports of the Departments, herewith submitted, are referred to for full information in relation to the matters appertaining to each. There are two of them on which I deem it necessary to make special remark. The report of the Secretary of the Treasury states facts justifying the conclusion that the law passed at the last session for the purpose of withdrawing from circulation the large excess of Treasury notes heretofore issued has had the desired effect, and that by the 1st of July the amount in circulation will have been reduced to a sum not exceeding $230,000,000. It is believed to be of primary importance that no further issue of notes should take place, and that the use of the credit of the Government should be restricted to the two other modes provided by Congress, viz, the sale of bonds and the issue of certificates bearing interest for the price of supplies purchased within our limits. The law as it now stands authorizes the issue by the Treasury of new notes to the extent of two-thirds of the amount received under its provisions. The estimate of the amount funded under the law is shown to be $300,000,000, and if two-thirds of this sum be reissued, we shall have an addition of $200,000,000 to our circulation, believed to be already ample for the business of the country. The addition of this large sum to the volume of the currency would be attended by disastrous effects and would produce the speedy recurrence of the evils from which the funding law has rescued the country. If our arms are crowned with the success which we have so much reason to hope, we may well expect that this war can not be prolonged beyond the current year, and nothing would so much retard the beneficent influence of peace on all the interests of our country as the existence of a great mass of currency not redeemable in coin. With our vast resources the circulation, if restricted to its present volume, would be easily manageable, and by gradual absorption in payment of public dues would give place to the precious metals, the only basis of a currency adapted to commerce with foreign countries. In our present circumstances I know of no mode of providing for the public wants which would entail sacrifices so great as a fresh issue of Treasury notes, and I trust that you will concur in the propriety of absolutely forbidding any increase of those now in circulation.

Officers have been appointed and dispatched to the Trans-Mississippi States, and the necessary measures taken for the execution of the laws enacted to obviate delays in administering the Treasury and other Executive Departments in those States, but sufficient time has not elapsed to ascertain the results.

In relation to the most important of all subjects at the present time—the efficiency of our armies in the field—it is gratifying to assure you that the discipline and instruction of the troops have kept pace with the improvement in material and equipment. We have reason to congratulate ourselves on the results of the legislation on this subject, and on the increased administrative energy in the different bureaus of the War Department, and may not unreasonably indulge anticipations of commensurate success in the ensuing campaign.

The organization of reserves is in progress, and it is hoped they will be valuable in affording local protection without requiring details and detachments from active force.

Among the recommendations contained in the report of the Secretary of War, your attention is specially invited to those in which legislation is suggested on the following subjects, viz:

The tenure of office of the general officers in the Provisional Army, and a proper discrimination in the compensation of the different grades.

The provision required in aid of invalid officers who have resigned in consequence of wounds or sickness contracted while in service.

The amendment of the law which deprives officers in the field of the privilege of purchasing rations, and thus adds to their embarrassment, instead of conferring the benefit intended.

The organization of the general staff of the Army, in relation to which a special message will shortly be addressed to you, containing the reasons which compelled me to withhold my approval of a bill passed by your predecessors at too late a period of the session to allow time for returning it for their reconsideration.

The necessity for an increase in the allowance now made for the transportation of officers traveling under orders.

The mode of providing officers for the execution of the conscript laws.

The means of securing greater dispatch and more regular administration of justice in examining and disposing of the records of cases reported from the courts-martial and military courts in the Army.

The recent events of the war are highly creditable to our troops, exhibiting energy and vigilance combined with the habitual gallantry which they have taught us to expect on all occasions. We have been cheered by important and valuable successes in Florida, northern Mississippi, western Tennessee, and Kentucky, western Louisiana and eastern North Carolina, reflecting the highest honor on the skill and conduct of our commanders and on the incomparable soldiers whom it is their privilege to lead. A naval attack on Mobile was so successfully repulsed at the outer works that the attempt was abandoned, and the nine months' siege of Charleston has been practically suspended, leaving that noble city and its fortresses imperishable monuments to the skill and fortitude of its defenders. The armies in northern Georgia and northern Virginia still oppose with unshaken front a formidable barrier to the progress of the invader, and our generals, armies, and people are animated by cheerful confidence.

Let us, then, while resolute in devoting all our energies to securing the realization of the bright auspices which encourage us, not forget that our humble and most grateful thanks are due to Him, without whose guidance and protecting care all human efforts are of no avail, and to whose interposition are due the manifold successes with which we have been cheered.

JEFFERSON DAVIS.

Act to Increase the Military Force of the Confederate States

February 10, 1865

A BILL

To be entitled An Act to increase the military force of the Confederate States.

The Congress of the Confederate States of America do enact, That in order to provide additional forces to repel invasion, maintain the rightful possession of the Confederate States, secure their independence and preserve their institutions, the President be and he is hereby authorized to ask for and accept from the owners of slaves the services of such number of able-bodied negro men as he may deem expedient for and during the war, to perform military service in whatever capacity the General-in-Chief may direct.

SEC. 2. That the President be authorized to organize the said slaves into companies, battalions, regiments and brigades, under such rules and regulations as the Secretary of War may prescribe and to be commanded by such officers as the President may appoint.

SEC. 3. That while employed in the service the said slaves shall receive the same rations, clothing and compensation as are allowed in the Act approved February 17th, 1864, and the Acts amendatory thereto, "to increase the efficiency of the army by the employment of free negroes and slaves in certain capacities," and the compensation so allowed shall be made to the owner or to the slave as the owner thereof may elect.

SEC. 4. That nothing in this Act shall be construed to authorize a change in the relation which the said slaves shall bear towards their owners as property, except by consent of the States in which they may reside, and in pursuance of the laws thereof.

Last Order, *Robert E. Lee, 1865*

Increasingly outnumbered and suffering increasingly frequent and important defeats, Confederate general Robert E. Lee finally accepted defeat and surrendered to Union general Ulysses S. Grant on April 9, 1865. The surrender took place at Appomattox Court House, near where Lee's dwindling army of thirty thousand men, less than half of them battle-worthy, had been cornered after weeks of retreats, rear-guard actions, and disappointed searching for supplies. Grant had promised that Confederate officers would be allowed to keep their sidearms, and all who owned their horses would be allowed to keep them. All of the soldiers would be allowed to go home unmolested after promising not to take up arms against the government of the United States. Returning to his camp from Appomattox, Lee was cheered by his troops. He expressed like sentiments for his soldiers in his final order, which effectively, though not officially, ended the war. Several Southern armies in addition to Lee's "Army of Northern Virginia" would surrender in short order, and Confederate president Jefferson Davis would be captured on May 10, 1865, by Union troops in Georgia as he attempted to escape to Texas to meet up with Confederate troops there.

Last Order

April 10, 1865

Robert E. Lee

NEAR APPOMATTOX COURT-HOUSE, VA.,

April 12, 1865.

MR. PRESIDENT: It is with pain that I announce to Your Excellency the surrender of the Army of Northern Virginia. The operations which preceded this result will be reported in full. I will therefore only now state that, upon arriving at Amelia Court-House on the morning of the 4th with the advance of the army, on the retreat from the lines in front of Richmond and Petersburg, and not finding the supplies ordered to be placed there, nearly twenty-four hours were lost in endeavoring to collect in the country subsistence for men and horses. This delay was fatal, and could not be retrieved. The troops, wearied by continual fighting and marching for several days and nights, obtained neither rest nor refreshment; and on moving, on the 5th, on the Richmond and Danville Railroad, I found at Jetersville the enemy's cavalry, and learned the approach of his infantry and the general advance of his army toward Burkeville. This deprived us of the use of the railroad, and rendered it impracticable to procure from Danville the supplies ordered to meet us at points of our march. Nothing could be obtained from the adjacent country. Our route to the Roanoke was therefore changed, and the march directed upon Farmville, where supplies were ordered from Lynchburg. The change of route threw the troops over the roads pursued by the artillery and wagon trains west of the railroad, which impeded our advance and embarrassed our movements. On the morning of the 6th General Longstreet's corps reached Rice's Station, on the Lynchburg railroad. It was followed by the commands of Generals R. H. Anderson, Ewell, and Gordon, with orders to close upon it as fast as the progress of the trains would permit or as they could be directed on roads farther west. General Anderson, commanding Pickett's and B. R. Johnson's divisions, became disconnected with Mahone's division, forming the rear of Longstreet. The enemy's cavalry penetrated the line of march through the interval thus left and attacked the wagon train moving toward Farmville. This caused serious delay in the march of the center and rear of the column, and enabled the enemy to mass upon their flank. After successive attacks Anderson's and Ewell's corps were captured or driven from their position. The latter general, with both of his division commanders, Kershaw and Custis Lee, and his brigadiers, were taken prisoners. Gordon, who all the morning, aided by General W. H. F. Lee's cavalry, had checked the advance of the enemy on the road from Amelia Springs and protected the trains, became exposed to his combined assaults, which he bravely resisted and twice repulsed; but the cavalry having been withdrawn to another part of the line of march, and the enemy massing heavily on his front and both flanks, renewed the attack about 6 p.m., and drove him from the field in much confusion.

The army continued its march during the night, and every effort was made to reorganize the divisions which had been shattered by the day's operations; but the men being depressed by fatigue and hunger, many threw away their arms, while others followed the wagon trains and embarrassed their progress. On the morning of the 7th rations were issued to the troops as they passed Farmville, but the safety of the trains requiring their removal upon the approach of the enemy all could not be supplied. The army, reduced to two corps, under Longstreet and Gordon, moved steadily on the road to Appomattox Court-House; thence its march was ordered by Campbell Court-House, through Pittsylvania, toward Danville. The roads were wretched and the progress slow. By great efforts the head of the column reached Appomattox Court-House on the evening of the 8th, and the troops were halted for rest. The march was ordered to be resumed at 1 a.m. on the 9th. Fitz Lee, with the cavalry, supported by Gordon, was ordered to drive the enemy from his front, wheel to the left, and cover the passage of the trains; while Longstreet, who from Rice's Station had formed the rear guard, should close up and hold the position. Two battalions of artillery and the ammunition wagons were directed to accompany the army, the rest of the artillery and wagons to move toward Lynchburg. In the early part of the night the enemy attacked Walker's artillery train near Appomattox Station, on the Lynchburg railroad, and were repelled. Shortly afterward their cavalry dashed toward the Court-House, till halted by our line. During the night there were indications of a large force massing on our left and front. Fitz Lee was directed to ascertain its strength, and to suspend his advance till daylight if necessary. About 5 a.m. on the 9th, with Gordon on his left, he moved forward and opened the way. A heavy force of the enemy was discovered opposite Gordon's right, which, moving in the direction of Appomattox Court-House, drove back the left of the cavalry and threatened to cut off Gordon from Longstreet, his cavalry at the same time threatening to envelop his left flank. Gordon withdrew across the Appomattox River, and the cavalry advanced on the Lynchburg road and became separated from the army.

Learning the condition of affairs on the lines, where I had gone under the expectation of meeting General Grant to learn definitely the terms he proposed in a communication received from him on the 8th, in the event of the surrender of the army, I requested a suspension of hostilities until these terms could be arranged. In the interview which occurred with General Grant in compliance with my request, terms having been agreed on, I surrendered that portion of the Army of Northern Virginia which was on the field, with its arms, artillery, and wagon trains, the officers and men to be paroled, retaining their sidearms and private effects. I deemed this course the best under all the circumstances by which we were surrounded. On the morning of the 9th, according to the reports of the ordnance officers, there were 7,892 organized infantry with arms, with an average of seventy-five rounds of ammunition per man. The artillery, though reduced to sixty-three pieces, with ninety-three rounds of ammunition, was sufficient. These comprised all the supplies of ordnance that could be relied on in the State of Virginia. I have no accurate report of the cavalry, but believe it did not exceed 2,100 effective men. The enemy were more than five times our numbers. If we could have forced our way one day longer it would have been at a great sacrifice of life, and at its end I did not see how a surrender could have been avoided. We had no subsistence for man or horse, and it could not be gathered in the country. The supplies ordered to Pamplin's Station from Lynchburg could not reach us, and the men, deprived of food and sleep for many days, were worn out and exhausted.

With great respect, your obedient servant,

R. E. LEE,
General.

His Excellency JEFFERSON DAVIS.

GENERAL ORDERS, } *ADDENDA.*
No. 9.

HDQRS. ARMY OF
NORTHERN VIRGINIA,
April 10, 1865.

After four years of arduous service, marked by unsurpassed courage and fortitude, the Army of Northern Virginia has been compelled to yield to overwhelming numbers and resources. I need not tell the brave survivors of so many hard-fought battles, who have remained steadfast to the last, that I have consented to the result from no distrust of them. But, feeling that valor and devotion could accomplish nothing that could compensate for the loss that must have attended the continuance of the contest, I determined to avoid the useless sacrifice of those whose past services have endeared them to their countrymen.

By the terms of the agreement officers and men can return to their homes and remain until exchanged. You will take with you the satisfaction that proceeds from the consciousness of duty faithfully performed; and I earnestly pray that a merciful God will extend to you his blessing and protection.

With an increasing admiration of your constancy and devotion to your country, and a grateful remembrance of your kind and generous considerations for myself, I bid you all an affectionate farewell.

R. E. LEE,
General.

Johnson's Veto of the Freedmen's Bureau, from *Harper's Weekly,* April 14, 1866; drawn by Thomas Nast.

(below) The Freedmen's Bureau, from *Harper's Weekly,* July 25, 1868; drawn by A. R. Waud. Library of Congress, Prints and Photographs Division, LC-USZ62-105555.

WELL BEFORE FIGHTING ended on the Civil War's battlefields, conflict stirred in the North regarding how the South should be reintegrated into the Union. The issue first surfaced only five days after Virginia seceded from the Union, when its thirty-five western counties sought separation from Virginia and reintegration with the Union, which they achieved as West Virginia in 1863. But the process of "reconstruction," which at times aimed to alter fundamentally the governments and societies of the former Confederacy, continued for more than a decade and remains an issue to this day. According to popular legend (now disputed) Reconstruction's formal end came when the Democratic and Republican parties struck a deal allowing the Republican presidential candidate, Rutherford B. Hayes, to take office after the disputed election of 1876 in exchange for the withdrawal of federal troops from the Southern states, public works projects in the South, and other concessions. Thereafter a series of Supreme Court cases and legal and constitutional challenges in the South sought to undo Reconstruction. From its inception until its end, Reconstruction was the subject of intense debate and sometimes violent conflict. The program first set forth by Abraham Lincoln, then championed by his successor, Andrew Johnson, drew criticism from Radical Republicans convinced that it did too little for African Americans, too little for Northern interests, and too little to fundamentally reform governments in the South. The program also drew extensive opposition, particularly from white Southerners who labeled it dictatorial and intrusive in character. And white Southern opposition took a variety of forms, from mob violence to contradictory legal and constitutional documents.

Proclamation of Amnesty and Reconstruction, *Abraham Lincoln*, 1863

Veto Message with Wade-Davis Proclamation and Bill,
    Abraham Lincoln, 1864

Wade-Davis Manifesto, 1864

Lincoln's Proclamation of Amnesty and Reconstruction, greeted warmly in the North at the time, set forth the first official plan of Reconstruction, seeking to expedite formation of loyalist governments. In it Lincoln offered all but the highest officers in the Confederacy amnesty in exchange for an oath of allegiance to the United States. Lincoln also set forth his "10 percent plan," according to which any state in which at least 10 percent of those qualified in 1860 to vote agreed to abide by congressional laws and presidential proclamations regarding the end of slavery would be deemed the true government of that state. This would allow for the retraction of military government and, with congressional consent, the seating of the state's congressional delegation. Radical Republican congressmen Henry Winter Davis, of Maryland, and Benjamin F. Wade, of Ohio, opposed what they saw as the plan's leniency. Their Wade-Davis bill would have required that half the white male citizens of any seceded state take an oath of loyalty to the Union before civil government could be reestablished in that state. The bill also required that freed slaves be given the right to vote—a right denied most African Americans in Northern states. Lincoln refused to sign the bill, letting it die at the end of the congressional session, on the grounds that he should not be tied to a single, inflexible plan of restoration for each seceded state. The Wade-Davis Manifesto was a response to this pocket veto. Published in the New York Tribune, *it defended the more stringent requirements of the bill and accused Lincoln of dictatorial conduct in his control over reconstruction policies.*

Proclamation of Amnesty and Reconstruction

December 8, 1863

Abraham Lincoln

BY THE PRESIDENT OF THE UNITED STATES
OF AMERICA:
A PROCLAMATION.

Whereas, in and by the Constitution of the United States, it is provided that the President "shall have power to grant reprieves and pardons for offences against the United States, except in cases of impeachment"; and

Whereas, a rebellion now exists whereby the loyal state governments of several states have for a long time been subverted, and many persons have committed, and are now guilty of, treason against the United States; and

Whereas, with reference to said rebellion and treason, laws have been enacted by congress, declaring forfeitures and confiscation of property and liberation of slaves, all upon terms and conditions therein stated, and also declaring that the President was thereby authorized at any time thereafter, by proclamation, to extend to persons who may have participated in the existing rebellion, in any state or part thereof, pardon and amnesty, with such exceptions and at such times and on such conditions as he may deem expedient for the public welfare; and

Whereas, the congressional declaration for limited and conditional pardon accords with well-established judicial exposition of the pardoning power; and

Whereas, with reference to said rebellion, the President of the United States has issued several proclamations, with provisions in regard to the liberation of slaves; and

Whereas, it is now desired by some persons heretofore engaged in said rebellion to resume their allegiance to the United States, and to reinaugurate loyal state governments within and for their respective states: Therefore—

I, ABRAHAM LINCOLN, President of the United States, do proclaim, declare, and make known to all persons who have, directly or by implication, participated in the existing rebellion, except as hereinafter excepted, that a full pardon is hereby granted to them and each of them, with restoration of all rights of property, except as to slaves, and in property cases where rights of third parties shall have intervened, and upon the condition that every such person shall take and subscribe an oath, and thenceforward keep and maintain said oath inviolate; and which oath shall be registered for permanent preservation, and shall be of the tenor and effect following, to wit:—

"I, ———, do solemnly swear, in presence of Almighty God, that I will henceforth faithfully support, protect, and defend the Constitution of the United States and the Union of the States thereunder; and that I will, in like manner, abide by and faithfully support all acts of congress passed during the existing rebellion with reference to slaves, so long and so far as not repealed, modified, or held void by congress, or by decision of the supreme court; and that I will, in like manner, abide by and faithfully support all proclamations of the President made during the existing rebellion having reference to slaves, so long and so far as not modified or declared void by decision of the supreme court. So help me God."

The persons excepted from the benefits of the foregoing provisions are all who are, or shall have been, civil or diplomatic officers or agents of the so-called Confederate government; all who have left judicial stations under the United States to aid the rebellion; all who are, or shall have been, military or naval officers of said so-called Confederate government above the rank of colonel in the army or of lieutenant in the navy; all who left seats in the United States congress to aid the rebellion; all who resigned commissions in the army or navy of the United States and afterwards aided the rebellion; and all who have engaged in any way in treating colored persons, or white persons in charge of such, otherwise than lawfully as prisoners of war, and which persons may have been found in the United States service as soldiers, seamen, or in any other capacity.

And I do further proclaim, declare, and make known that whenever, in any of the States of Arkansas, Texas, Louisiana, Mississippi, Tennessee, Alabama, Georgia, Florida, South Carolina, and North Carolina, a number of persons, not less than one tenth in number of the votes cast in such state at the presidential election of the year of our Lord one thousand eight hundred and sixty, each having taken the oath aforesaid, and not having since violated it, and being a qualified voter by the election law of the state existing immediately before the so-called act of secession, and excluding all others, shall reëstablish a state government which shall be republican, and in nowise contravening said oath, such shall be recognized as the true government of the state, and the state shall receive thereunder the benefits of the constitutional provision which declares that "the United States shall guaranty to every state in this Union a republican form of government, and shall protect each of them against invasion; and on application of the legislature, or the executive, (when the legislature cannot be convened,) against domestic violence."

And I do further proclaim, declare, and make known that any provision which may be adopted by such state government in relation to the freed people of such state, which shall recognize and declare their permanent freedom, provide for their education, and which may yet be consistent as a temporary arrangement with their present condition as a laboring, landless, and homeless class, will not be objected to by the National Executive.

And it is suggested as not improper that, in constructing a loyal state government in any state, the name of the state, the boundary, the subdivisions, the constitution, and the general code of laws, as before the rebellion, be maintained, subject only to the modifications made necessary by the conditions hereinbefore stated, and such others, if any, not contravening said conditions, and which may be deemed expedient by those framing the new state government.

To avoid misunderstanding, it may be proper to say that this proclamation, so far as it relates to state governments, has no reference to states wherein loyal state governments have all the while been maintained. And, for the same reason, it may be proper to further say, that whether members sent to congress from any state shall be admitted to seats constitutionally rests exclusively with the respective houses, and not to any extent with the Executive. And still further, that this proclamation is intended to present the people of the states wherein the national authority has been suspended, and loyal state governments have been subverted, a mode in and by which the national authority and loyal state governments may be reëstablished within said states, or in any of them; and, while the mode presented is the best the Executive can suggest, with his present impressions, it must not be understood that no other possible mode would be acceptable.

Given under my hand at the city of Washington the eighth day of December, A.D. one thousand eight hundred and sixty-three, and of the Independence of the United States of America the eighty-eighth.

ABRAHAM LINCOLN.

By the President:

WILLIAM H. SEWARD, *Secretary of State.*

Veto Message with Wade-Davis Proclamation and Bill

July 8, 1864

Abraham Lincoln

BY THE PRESIDENT OF THE UNITED STATES: A PROCLAMATION.

WHEREAS, at the late session, congress passed a bill to "guarantee to certain states, whose governments have been usurped or overthrown, a republican form of government," a copy of which is hereunto annexed;

And whereas the said bill was presented to the President of the United States for his approval less than one hour before the *sine die* adjournment of said session, and was not signed by him;

And whereas the said bill contains, among other things, a plan for restoring the states in rebellion to their proper practical relation in the Union, which plan expresses the sense of congress upon that subject, and which plan it is now thought fit to lay before the people for their consideration:

Now, therefore, I, ABRAHAM LINCOLN, President of the United States, do proclaim, declare, and make known, that, while I am (as I was in December last, when by proclamation I propounded a plan for restoration) unprepared by a formal approval of this bill, to be inflexibly committed to any single plan of restoration; and, while I am also unprepared to declare that the free state constitutions and governments already adopted and installed in Arkansas and Louisiana shall be set aside and held for nought, thereby repelling and discouraging the loyal citizens who have set up the same as to further effort, or to declare a constitutional competency in congress to abolish slavery in states, but am at the same time sincerely hoping and expecting that a constitutional amendment abolishing slavery throughout the nation may be adopted, nevertheless I am fully satisfied with the system for restoration contained in the bill as one very proper plan for the loyal people of any state choosing to adopt it, and that I am, and at all times shall be, prepared to give the executive aid and assistance to any such people, so soon as the military resistance to the United States shall have been suppressed in any such state, and the people thereof shall have sufficiently returned to their obedience to the constitution and the laws of the United States, in which cases military governors will be appointed, with directions to proceed according to the bill.

In testimony whereof, I have hereunto set my hand, and caused the seal of the United States to be affixed.

Done at the city of Washington this eighth day of July, in the year of our Lord one thousand eight hundred and sixty-four, and of the Independence of the United States the eighty-ninth.

[L.S.]   ABRAHAM LINCOLN.

By the president:

WILLIAM H. SEWARD, *Secretary of State.*

A Bill to guarantee to certain States whose Governments have been usurped or overthrown a Republican Form of Government.

Be it enacted by the Senate and House of Representatives of the United States of America in Congress assembled, That in the states declared in rebellion against the United States, the President shall, by and with the advice and consent of the Senate, appoint for each a provisional governor, whose pay and emoluments shall not exceed that of a brigadier-general of volunteers, who shall be charged with the civil administration of such state until a state government therein shall be recognized as hereinafter provided.

SEC. 2. *And be it further enacted,* That so soon as the military resistance to the United States shall have been suppressed in any such state, and the people thereof shall have sufficiently returned to their obedience to the constitution and the laws of the United States, the provisional governor shall direct the marshal of the United States, as speedily as may be, to name a sufficient number of deputies, and to enroll all white male citizens of the United States, resident in the state in their respective counties, and to request each one to take the oath to support the constitution of the United States, and in his enrolment to designate those who take and those who refuse to take that oath, which rolls shall be forthwith returned to the provisional governor; and if the persons taking that oath shall amount to a majority of the persons enrolled in the state, he shall, by proclamation, invite the loyal people of the state to elect delegates to a convention charged to declare the will of the people of the state relative to the reëstablishment of a state government subject to, and in conformity with, the constitution of the United States.

SEC. 3. *And be it further enacted,* That the convention shall consist of as many members as both houses of the last constitutional state legislature, apportioned by the provisional governor among the counties, parishes, or districts of the state, in proportion to the white population, returned as electors, by the marshal, in compliance with the provisions of this act. The provisional governor shall, by proclamation, declare the number of delegates to be elected by each county, parish, or election district; name a day of election not less than thirty days thereafter; designate the places of voting in each county, parish, or district, conforming as nearly as may be convenient to the places used in the state elections next preceding the rebellion; appoint one or more commissioners to hold the election at each place of voting, and provide an adequate force to keep the peace during the election.

SEC. 4. *And be it further enacted,* That the delegates shall be elected by the loyal white male citizens of the United States of the age of twenty-one years, and resident at the time in the county, parish, or district in which they shall offer to vote, and enrolled as aforesaid, or absent in the military service of the United States, and who shall take and subscribe the oath of allegiance to the United States in the form contained in the act of congress of July two, eighteen hundred and sixty-two; and all such citizens of the United States who are in the military service of the United States shall vote at the head-quarters of their respective commands, under such regulations as may be prescribed by the provisional governor for the taking and return of their votes; but no person who has held or exercised any office, civil or military, state or con-

federate, under the rebel usurpation, or who has voluntarily borne arms against the United States, shall vote, or be eligible to be elected as delegate, at such election.

SEC. 5. *And be it further enacted,* That the said commissioners, or either of them, shall hold the election in conformity with this act, and, so far as may be consistent therewith, shall proceed in the manner used in the state prior to the rebellion. The oath of allegiance shall be taken and subscribed on the poll-book by every voter in the form above prescribed, but every person known by, or proved to, the commissioners to have held or exercised any office, civil or military, state or confederate, under the rebel usurpation, or to have voluntarily borne arms against the United States, shall be excluded, though he offer to take the oath; and in case any person who shall have borne arms against the United States shall offer to vote he shall be deemed to have borne arms voluntarily unless he shall prove the contrary by the testimony of a qualified voter. The poll-book, showing the name and oath of each voter, shall be returned to the provisional governor by the commissioners of election or the one acting, and the provisional governor shall canvass such returns, and declare the person having the highest number of votes elected.

SEC. 6. *And be it further enacted,* That the provisional governor shall, by proclamation, convene the delegates elected as aforesaid, at the capital of the state, on a day not more than three months after the election, giving at least thirty days' notice of such day. In case the said capital shall in his judgment be unfit, he shall in his proclamation appoint another place. He shall preside over the deliberations of the convention, and administer to each delegate, before taking his seat in the convention, the oath of allegiance to the United States in the form above prescribed.

SEC. 7. *And be it further enacted,* That the convention shall declare, on behalf of the people of the state, their submission to the constitution and laws of the United States, and shall adopt the following provisions, hereby prescribed by the United States in the execution of the constitutional duty to guarantee a republican form of government to every state, and incorporate them in the constitution of the state, that is to say:

First. No person who has held or exercised any office, civil or military, except offices merely ministerial, and military offices below the grade of colonel, state or confederate, under the usurping power, shall vote for or be a member of the legislature, or governor.

Second. Involuntary servitude is forever prohibited, and the freedom of all persons is guaranteed in said state.

Third. No debt, state or confederate, created by or under the sanction of the usurping power, shall be recognized or paid by the state.

Sec. 8. *And be it further enacted,* That when the convention shall have adopted those provisions, it shall proceed to reëstablish a republican form of government, and ordain a constitution containing those provisions, which, when adopted, the convention shall by ordinance provide for submitting to the people of the state, entitled to vote under this law, at an election to be held in the manner prescribed by the act for the election of delegates; but at a time and place named by the convention, at which election the said electors, and none others, shall vote directly for or against such constitution and form of state government, and the returns of said election shall be made to the provisional governor, who shall canvass the same in the presence of the electors, and if a majority of the votes cast shall be for the constitution and form of government, he shall certify the same, with a copy thereof, to the President of the United States, who, after obtaining the assent of congress, shall, by proclamation, recognize the government so established, and none other, as the constitutional government of the state, and from the date of such recognition, and not before, Senators and Representatives, and electors for President and Vice-President may be elected in such state, according to the laws of the state and of the United States.

Sec. 9. *And be it further enacted,* That if the convention shall refuse to reëstablish the state government on the conditions aforesaid, the provisional governor shall declare it dissolved; but it shall be the duty of the President, whenever he shall have reason to believe that a sufficient number of the people of the state entitled to vote under this act, in number not less than a majority of those enrolled, as aforesaid, are willing to reëstablish a state government on the conditions aforesaid, to direct the provisional governor to order another election of delegates to a convention for the purpose and in the manner prescribed in this act, and to proceed in all respects as hereinbefore provided, either to dissolve the convention, or to certify the state government reëstablished by it to the President.

Sec. 10. *And be it further enacted,* That, until the United States shall have recognized a republican form of state government, the provisional governor in each of said states shall see that this act, and the laws of the United States, and the laws of the state in force when the state government was overthrown by the rebellion, are faithfully executed within the

state; but no law or usage whereby any person was heretofore held in involuntary servitude shall be recognized or enforced by any court or officer in such state, and the laws for the trial and punishment of white persons shall extend to all persons, and jurors shall have the qualifications of voters under this law for delegates to the convention. The President shall appoint such officers provided for by the laws of the state when its government was overthrown as he may find necessary to the civil administration of the state, all which officers shall be entitled to receive the fees and emoluments provided by the state laws for such officers.

Sec. 11. *And be it further enacted,* That until the recognition of a state government as aforesaid, the provisional governor shall, under such regulations as he may prescribe, cause to be assessed, levied, and collected, for the year eighteen hundred and sixty-four, and every year thereafter, the taxes provided by the laws of such state to be levied during the fiscal year preceding the overthrow of the state government thereof, in the manner prescribed by the laws of the state, as nearly as may be; and the officers appointed, as aforesaid, are vested with all powers of levying and collecting such taxes, by distress or sale, as were vested in any officers or tribunal of the state government aforesaid for those purposes. The proceeds of such taxes shall be accounted for to the provisional governor, and be by him applied to the expenses of the administration of the laws in such state, subject to the direction of the President, and the surplus shall be deposited in the treasury of the United States to the credit of such state, to be paid to the state upon an appropriation therefor, to be made when a republican form of government shall be recognized therein by the United States.

Sec. 12. *And be it further enacted,* That all persons held to involuntary servitude or labor in the states aforesaid are hereby emancipated and discharged therefrom, and they and their posterity shall be forever free. And if any such persons or their posterity shall be restrained of liberty, under pretence of any claim to such service or labor, the courts of the United States shall, on habeas corpus, discharge them.

Sec. 13. *And be it further enacted,* That if any person declared free by this act, or any law of the United States, or any proclamation of the President, be restrained of liberty, with intent to be held in or reduced to involuntary servitude or labor, the person convicted before a court of competent jurisdiction of such act shall be punished by fine of not less than fifteen hundred dollars, and be imprisoned not less than five nor more than twenty years.

SEC. 14. *And be it further enacted,* That every person who shall hereafter hold or exercise any office, civil or military, except offices merely ministerial, and military offices below the grade of colonel, in the rebel service, state or confederate, is hereby declared not to be a citizen of the United States.

Wade-Davis Manifesto

August 5, 1864

To the supporters of the government.

We have read without surprise, but not without indignation, the Proclamation of the President of the 8th of July, 1864.

The supporters of the Administration are responsible to the country for its conduct: and it is their right and duty to check the encroachments of the Executive on the authority of Congress, and to require it to confine itself to its proper sphere.

It is impossible to pass in silence this Proclamation without neglecting that duty; and, having taken as much responsibility as any others in supporting the Administration, we are not disposed to fail in the other duty of asserting the rights of Congress.

The President did not sign the bill "to guarantee to certain States whose Governments have been usurped, a Republican form of Government"—passed by the supporters of his Administration in both Houses of Congress after mature deliberation.

The bill did not therefore become *a law*: and it is therefore *nothing.*

The Proclamation is neither an approval nor a veto of the bill; it is therefore a document unknown to the laws and Constitution of the United States.

So far as it contains an apology for not signing the bill, it is a political manifesto against the friends of the Government.

So far as it proposes to execute the bill which is not a law, it is a grave Executive usurpation.

It is fitting that the facts necessary to enable the friends of the Administration to appreciate the apology and the usurpation be spread before them.

The Proclamation says:

"And whereas the said bill was presented to the President of the United States for his approval less than one hour before the *sine die* adjournment of said session, and was not signed by him—"

If that be accurate, still this bill was presented with other bills which were signed.

Within that hour, the time for the sine die adjournment was three times postponed by the votes of both Houses; and the least intimation of a desire for more time by the President to consider this bill would have secured a further postponement.

Yet the Committee sent to ascertain if the President had any further communication for the House of Representatives reported that he had none; and the friends of the bill, who had anxiously waited on him to ascertain its fate, had already been informed that the President had resolved not to sign it.

The time of presentation, therefore, had nothing to do with his failure to approve it.

The bill had been discussed and considered for more than a month in the House of Representatives, which it passed on the 4th of May; it was reported to the Senate on the 27th of May without material amendment, and passed the Senate absolutely as it came from the House on the 3d of July.

Ignorance of its contents is out of the question.

Indeed, at his request, a draft of a bill substantially the same in all material points, and identical in the points objected to by the Proclamation, had been laid before him for his consideration in the Winter of 1862–1863.

There is, therefore, no reason to suppose the provisions of the bill took the President by surprise.

On the contrary, we have reason to believe them to have been so well known that this method of preventing the bill from becoming a law without the constitutional responsibility of a veto, had been resolved on long before the bill passed the Senate.

We are informed by a gentleman entitled to entire confidence, that before the 22d of June in New-Orleans it was stated by a member of Gen. Banks's staff, in the presence of other gentlemen in official position, that Senator Doolittle had written a letter to the department that the House Reconstruction bill would be staved off in the Senate to a period too late in the session to require the President to veto it in order to defeat it, and that Mr. Lincoln would retain the bill, if necessary, and thereby defeat it.

The experience of Senator Wade, in his various efforts to get the bill considered in the Senate, was quite in accordance with that plan; and the fate of the bill was accurately predicted by letters received from New-Orleans before it had passed the Senate.

Had the Proclamation stopped there, it would have been only one other defeat of the will of the people by an Executive perversion of the Constitution.

But it goes further. The President says:

"And whereas the said bill contains, among other things, a plan for restoring the States in rebellion to their proper practical relation in the Union, which plan expresses the sense of Congress upon that subject, and which plan it is now thought fit to lay before the people for their consideration—"

By what authority of the Constitution? In what forms? The result to be declared by whom? With what effect when ascertained?

Is it to be a law by the approval of the people without the approval of Congress at the will of the President?

Will the President, on his opinion of the popular approval, execute it as law?

Or is this merely a device to avoid the serious responsibility of defeating a law on which so many loyal hearts reposed for security?

But the reasons now assigned for not approving the bill are full of ominous significance.

The President proceeds:

"Now, therefore, I, ABRAHAM LINCOLN, President of the United States, do proclaim, declare, and make known, that, while I am (as I was in December last, when by proclamation I propounded a plan for restoration) unprepared, by a formal approval of this bill, to be inflexibly committed to any single plan of restoration—"

That is to say, the President is resolved that the people shall not *by law* take *any* securities from the Rebel States against a renewal of the Rebellion, before restoring their power to govern us.

His wisdom and prudence are to be our sufficient guarantees!

He further says:

"And, while I am also unprepared to declare that the Free-State Constitutions and Governments already adopted and installed in Arkansas and Louisiana shall be set aside and held for naught, thereby repelling and discouraging the loyal citizens who have set up the same as to further effort—"

That is to say, the President persists in recognizing those shadows of Governments in Arkansas and Louisiana, which Congress formally declared should not be recognized—whose Representatives and Senators were repelled by formal votes of both Houses of Congress—which it was declared formally should have no electoral vote for President and Vice-President.

They are the mere creatures of his will. They cannot live a day without his support. They are mere oligarchies, imposed on the people by military orders under the forms of election, at which generals, provost-marshals, soldiers and camp-followers were the chief actors, assisted by a handful of resident citizens, and urged on to premature action by private letters from the President.

In neither Louisiana nor Arkansas, before Banks's defeat, did the United States control half the territory or half the population. In Louisiana, Gen. Banks's proclamation candidly declared: "*The fundamental law of the State is martial law.*"

On that foundation of freedom, he erected what the President calls "the free Constitution and Government of Louisiana."

But of this State, whose fundamental law was martial law, only sixteen parishes out of forty-eight parishes were held by the United States; and in five of the sixteen we held only our camps.

The eleven parishes we substantially held had 233,185 inhabitants; the residue of the State not held by us, 575,617.

At the farce called an election, the officers of Gen. Banks returned that 11,346 ballots were cast; but whether any or by whom the people of the United States have no legal assurance; but it is probable that 4,000 were cast by soldiers or employees of the United States military or municipal, but none according to any law, State or National, and 7,000 ballots represent the State of Louisiana.

Such is the free Constitution and Government of Louisiana; and like it is that of Arkansas. Nothing but the failure of a military expedition deprived us of a like one in the swamps of Florida; and before the Presidential election, like ones may be organized in every Rebel State where the United States have a camp.

The President, by preventing this bill from becoming a law, holds the electoral votes of the Rebel States at the dictation of his personal ambition.

If those votes turn the balance in his favor, is it to be supposed that his competitor, defeated by such means, will acquiesce?

If the Rebel majority assert their supremacy in those States, and send votes which elect an enemy of the Government, will we not repel his claims?

And is not that civil war for the Presidency, inaugurated by the votes of Rebel States?

Seriously impressed with these dangers, Congress, *"the proper constitutional authority,"* formally declared that there are no State Governments in the Rebel States, and provided for their erection at a proper time; and both the Senate and the House of Representatives rejected the Senators and Representatives chosen under the authority of what the President calls the Free Constitution and Government of Arkansas.

The President's Proclamation *"holds for naught"* this judgment, and discards the authority of the Supreme Court, and strides headlong toward the anarchy his Proclamation of the 8th of December inaugurated.

If electors for President be allowed to be chosen in either of those States, a sinister light will be cast on the motives which induced the President to "hold for naught" the will of Congress rather than his Government in Louisiana and Arkansas.

That judgment of Congress which the President defies was the exercise of an authority exclusively vested in Congress by the Constitution to determine what is the established Government in a State, and in its own nature and by the highest judicial authority binding on all other departments of the Government.

The Supreme Court has formally declared that under the 4th section of the IVth article of the Constitution, requiring the United States to guarantee to every State a republican form of government, *"it rests with Congress to decide what Government is the established one in a State";* and *"when Senators and Representatives of a State are admitted into* the councils of the Union, the *authority* of the *Government under which they are appointed,* as well as its republican character, *is recognized by the proper constitutional authority, and its decision is binding on every other department of the Government,* and could not be questioned in a judicial tribunal. It is true that the contest in this case did not last long enough to bring the matter to this issue; and, as no Senators or Representatives were elected under the authority of the Government of which Mr. Dorr was the head, Congress was not called upon to decide the controversy. Yet the right to decide is placed *there."*

Even the President's proclamation of the 8th of December, formally declares that "Whether members sent to Congress from any State shall be admitted to seats, constitutionally rests exclusively with the respective Houses, and not to any extent with the Executive."

And that is not the less true because wholly inconsistent with the President's assumption in that proclamation of a right to institute and recognize State Governments in the Rebel States, nor because the President is unable to perceive that his recognition is a nullity if it be not conclusive on Congress.

Under the Constitution, the right to Senators and Representatives is inseparable from a State Government.

If there be a State Government, the right is absolute.

If there be no State Government, there can be no Senators or Representatives chosen.

The two Houses of Congress are expressly declared to be the sole judges of their own members.

When, therefore, Senators and Representatives are admitted, the State Government, under whose authority they were chosen, is conclusively established; when they are rejected, its existence is as conclusively rejected and denied; and to this [judgment] the President is bound to submit.

The President proceeds to express his unwillingness "to declare a constitutional competency in Congress to abolish Slavery in States" as another reason for not signing the bill.

But the bill nowhere proposes to abolish Slavery in States.

The bill did provide that all *slaves* in the Rebel States should be *manumitted.*

But as the President had already signed three bills manumitting several classes of slaves in States, it is not conceived possible that he entertained any scruples touching *that* provision of the bill respecting which he is silent.

He had already himself assumed a right by proclamation to free much the larger number of slaves in the Rebel States, under the authority given him by Congress to use military power to suppress the Rebellion; and it is quite inconceivable that the President should think Congress could vest in him a discretion it could not exercise itself.

It is the more unintelligible from the fact that, except in respect to a small part of Virginia and Louisiana, the bill covered only what the Proclamation covered—added a Congressional title and judicial remedies by law to the disputed title under the Proclamation, and perfected the work the President professed to be so anxious to accomplish.

Slavery as an institution can be abolished only by a change of the Constitution of the United States or of the law of the State; and this is the principle of the bill.

It required the [new] Constitution of the State to provide

for that prohibition; and the President, in the face of his own proclamation, does not venture to object to insisting on *that* condition. Nor will the country tolerate its abandonment—yet he defeated the only provision imposing it!!

But when he describes himself, in spite of this great blow at emancipation, as "sincerely hoping and expecting that a constitutional amendment abolishing Slavery throughout the nation may be adopted," we curiously inquire on what his expectation rests, after the vote of the House of Representatives at the recent session, and in the face of the political complexion of more than enough of the States to prevent the possibility of its adoption within any reasonable time; and why he did not indulge his sincere hopes with so large an installment of the blessing as his approval of the bill would have secured.

After this assignment of his reasons for preventing the bill from becoming a law, the President proceeds to declare his purpose *to execute it as a law by his plenary dictatorial power.*

He says:

"Nevertheless, I am fully satisfied with the system for restoration contained in the bill as one very proper plan for the loyal people of any State choosing to adopt it; and that I am, and at all times shall be, prepared to give the Executive aid and assistance to any such people so soon as the military resistance to the United States shall have been suppressed in any such State, and the people thereof shall have sufficiently returned to their obedience to the Constitution and the laws of the United States; in which cases Military Governors will be appointed, with directions to proceed according to the bill."

A more studied outrage on the legislative authority of the people has never been perpetrated.

Congress passed a bill; the President refused to approve it, and then by proclamation puts as much of it in force as he sees fit, and proposes to execute those parts by officers unknown to the laws of the United States and not subject to the confirmation of the Senate!

The bill directed the appointment of Provisional Governors by and with the advice and consent of the Senate.

The President, after defeating the law, proposes to appoint without law, and without the advice and consent of the Senate, *Military* Governors for the Rebel States!

He has already exercised this dictatorial usurpation in Louisiana, and he defeated the bill to prevent its limitation.

Henceforth we must regard the following precedent as the Presidential law of the Rebel States:

"Executive Mansion,
"Washington, March 15, 1864. }
"*His Excellency* Michael Hahn, *Governor of Louisiana.*
"Until further orders, you are hereby invested with the powers exercised hitherto by the Military Governor of Louisiana. Yours.   "Abraham Lincoln."

This Michael Hahn is no officer of the United States; the President, without law, without the advice and consent of the Senate, by a private note not even countersigned by the Secretary of State, makes him dictator of Louisiana!

The bill provided for the civil administration of the laws of the State—till it should be in a fit temper to govern itself—repealing all laws recognizing Slavery, and making all men equal before the law.

These beneficent provisions the President has annulled. People will die, and marry and transfer property, and buy and sell: and to these acts of civil life courts and officers of the law are necessary. Congress legislated for these necessary things, and the President deprives them of the protection of the law!

The President's purpose to instruct his Military Governors "to proceed according to the bill"—a makeshift to calm the disappointment its defeat has occasioned—is not merely a grave usurpation but a transparent delusion.

He cannot "proceed according to the bill" after preventing it from becoming a law.

Whatever is done will be at his will and pleasure, by persons responsible to no law, and more interested to secure the interests and execute the will of the President than of the people; and the will of Congress is to be *"held for naught,"* "unless the loyal people of the Rebel States choose to adopt it."

If they should graciously prefer the stringent bill to the easy proclamation, still the registration will be made under no legal sanction; it will give no assurance that a majority of the people of the States have taken the oath; if administered, it will be without legal authority, and void; no indictment will lie for false swearing at the election, or for admitting bad or rejecting good votes; it will be the farce of Louisiana and Arkansas acted over again, under the forms of this bill, but not by authority of *law.*

But when we come to the guarantees of future peace which Congress meant to enact, the forms, as well as the substance of the bill, must yield to the President's will that *none* should be *imposed*.

It was the solemn resolve of Congress to protect the loyal men of the nation against three great dangers, (1) the return to power of the guilty leaders of the Rebellion, (2) the continuance of Slavery, and (3) the burden of the Rebel debt.

Congress *required* assent to those provisions by the Convention of the State; and if refused, it was to be dissolved.

The president "holds for naught" that resolve of Congress, because he is unwilling "to be inflexibly committed to any one plan of restoration," and the people of the United States are not to be allowed to protect themselves unless their enemies agree to it.

The order to proceed according to the bill is therefore merely at the will of the Rebel States; and they have the option to reject it, accept the proclamation of the 8th of December, and demand the President's recognition!

Mark the contrast! The bill requires a majority, the proclamation is satisfied with one-tenth; the bill requires one oath, the proclamation another; the bill ascertains voters by registering, the proclamation by guess; the bill exacts adherence to existing territorial limits, the proclamation admits of others; the bill governs the Rebel States *by law,* equalizing all before it, the proclamation commits them to the lawless discretion of military Governors and Provost-Marshals; the bill forbids electors for President, the proclamation and defeat of the bill threaten us with civil war for the admission or exclusion of such votes; the bill exacted exclusion of dangerous enemies from power and the relief of the nation from the Rebel debt, and the prohibition of Slavery forever, so that the suppression of the Rebellion will double our resources to bear or pay the national debt, free the masses from the old domination of the Rebel leaders, and eradicate the cause of the war; the proclamation secures neither of these guaranties.

It is silent respecting the Rebel debt and the political exclusion of Rebel leaders; leaving *Slavery* exactly where it was by law at the outbreak of the Rebellion, and adds no guaranty even of the freedom of the slaves he undertook to manumit.

It is summed up in an illegal oath, without a sanction, and therefore void.

The oath is to support all proclamations of the President during the Rebellion having reference to slaves.

Any Government is to be accepted at the hands of one-tenth of the people not contravening *that oath.*

Now that oath neither secures the abolition of Slavery, nor adds any security to the freedom of the slaves the President declared free.

It does not secure the abolition of Slavery, for the proclamation of freedom merely professed to free certain slaves while it recognized the institution.

Every Constitution of the Rebel States at the outbreak of the Rebellion may be adopted without the change of a letter; for none of them contravene that Proclamation; none of them establish Slavery.

It adds no security to the freedom of the slaves.

For their title is the Proclamation of Freedom.

If it be unconstitutional, an oath to support it is void. Whether constitutional or not, the oath is without authority of law, and therefore void.

If it be valid and observed, it exacts no enactment by the State, either in law or Constitution, to add a State guaranty to the proclamation title; and the right of a slave to freedom is an open question before the State courts on the relative authority of the State law and the Proclamation.

If the oath binds the one-tenth who take it, it is not exacted of the other nine-tenths who succeed to the control of the State Government; so that it is annulled instantly by the act of recognition.

What the State courts would say of the Proclamation, who can doubt?

But the master would not go into court—he would seize his slave.

What the Supreme Court would say, who can tell?

When and how is the question to get there?

No habeas corpus lies for him in a United States Court; and the President defeated with this bill its extension of that writ to this case.

Such are the fruits of this rash and fatal act of the President—a blow at the friends of his Administration, at the rights of humanity, and at the principles of republican government.

The President has greatly presumed on the forbearance which the supporters of his Administration have so long practiced, in view of the arduous conflict in which we are engaged, and the reckless ferocity of our political opponents.

But he must understand that our support is of a cause and not of a man; that the authority of Congress is paramount and must be respected; that the whole body of the Union men of Congress will not submit to be impeached by him of rash and unconstitutional legislation; and if he wishes our support, he must confine himself to his executive duties—to obey and execute, not make the laws—to suppress by arms armed Rebellion, and leave political reorganization to Congress.

If the supporters of the Government fail to insist on this, they become responsible for the usurpations which they fail to rebuke, and are justly liable to the indignation of the people whose rights and security, committed to their keeping, they sacrifice.

Let them consider the remedy for these usurpations, and, having found it, fearlessly execute it.

B. F. WADE, Chairman Senate Committee.

H. WINTER DAVIS, Chairman Committee.

House of Representatives on the Rebellious States.

Special Field Order no. 15, *William Tecumseh Sherman*, 1865

As General William Sherman marched his Union army through Georgia, he collected in his wake an ever-growing number of former slaves who chose to follow his army rather than remain on the plantations on which they had been held in bondage. As he prepared to turn his army northward, Sherman sought to unburden himself of these refugees. On January 12, 1865, Sherman, along with Edwin M. Stanton, the secretary of war, met with twenty leaders (mostly clergymen) of the African American community in Savannah. Four days later, with the approval of President Lincoln, Special Field Order no. 15 was issued, confiscating roughly 400,000 acres of land along the coasts of South Carolina, Georgia, and Florida and distributing it to refugees, who would farm it.

Special Field Order no. 15

January 16, 1865

William Tecumseh Sherman

Headquarters Military Division of the
  Mississippi, in the Field, Savannah, Georgia,
  January 16, 1865.

1. The islands from Charleston south, the abandoned rice-fields along the rivers for thirty miles back from the sea, and the country bordering the St. John's River, Florida, are reserved and set apart for the settlement of the negroes now made free by the acts of war and the proclamation of the President of the United States.

2. At Beaufort, Hilton Head, Savannah, Fernandina, St. Augustine, and Jacksonville, the blacks may remain in their chosen or accustomed vocations; but on the islands, and in the settlements hereafter to be established, no white person whatever, unless military officers and soldiers detailed for duty, will be permitted to reside; and the sole and exclusive management of affairs will be left to the freed people themselves, subject only to the United States military authority, and the acts of Congress. By the laws of war, and orders of the President of the United States, the negro is free, and must be dealt with as such. He cannot be subjected to conscription, or forced military service, save by the written orders of the highest military authority of the department, under such regulations as the President or Congress may prescribe. Domestic servants, blacksmiths, carpenters, and other mechanics, will be free to select their own work and residence, but the young

and able-bodied negroes must be encouraged to enlist as soldiers in the service of the United States, to contribute their share toward maintaining their own freedom, and securing their rights as citizens of the United States.

Negroes so enlisted will be organized into companies, battalions, and regiments, under the orders of the United States military authorities, and will be paid, fed, and clothed, according to law. The bounties paid on enlistment may, with the consent of the recruit, go to assist his family and settlement in procuring agricultural implements, seed, tools, boots, clothing, and other articles necessary for their livelihood.

3. Whenever three respectable negroes, heads of families, shall desire to settle on land, and shall have selected for that purpose an island or a locality clearly defined within the limits above designated, the Inspector of Settlements and Plantations will himself, or by such subordinate officer as he may appoint, give them a license to settle such island or district, and afford them such assistance as he can to enable them to establish a peaceable agricultural settlement. The three parties named will subdivide the land, under the supervision of the inspector, among themselves, and such others as may choose to settle near them, so that each family shall have a plot of not

more than forty acres of tillable ground, and, when it borders on some water-channel, with not more than eight hundred feet waterfront, in the possession of which land the military authorities will afford them protection until such time as they can protect themselves, or until Congress shall regulate their title. The quartermaster may, on the requisition of the Inspector of Settlements and Plantations, place at the disposal of the inspector one or more of the captured steamers to ply between the settlements and one or more of the commercial points heretofore named, in order to afford the settlers the opportunity to supply their necessary wants, and to sell the products of their land and labor.

4. Whenever a negro has enlisted in the military service of the United States, he may locate his family in any one of the settlements at pleasure, and acquire a homestead, and all other rights and privileges of a settler, as though present in person. In like manner, negroes may settle their families and engage on board the gunboats, or in fishing, or in the navigation of the inland waters, without losing any claim to land or other advantages derived from this system. But no one, unless an actual settler as above defined, or unless absent on Government service, will be entitled to claim any right to land or property in any settlement by virtue of these orders.

5. In order to carry out this system of settlement, a general officer will be detailed as Inspector of Settlements and Plantations, whose duty it shall be to visit the settlements, to regulate their police and general arrangement, and who will furnish personally to each head of a family, subject to the approval of the President of the United States, a possessory title in writing, giving as near as possible the description of boundaries; and who shall adjust all claims or conflicts that may arise under the same, subject to the like approval, treating such titles altogether as possessory. The same general officer will also be charged with the enlistment and organization of the negro recruits, and protecting their interests while absent from their settlements; and will be governed by the rules and regulations prescribed by the War Department for such purposes.

6. Brigadier-General R. Saxton is hereby appointed Inspector of Settlements and Plantations, and will at once enter on the performance of his duties. No change is intended or desired in the settlement now on Beaufort Island, nor will any rights to property heretofore acquired be affected thereby.

By order of Major-General W. T. Sherman,

L. M. DAYTON, *Assistant Adjutant-General.*

Second Inaugural Address, *Abraham Lincoln*, 1865

Last Public Address, *Abraham Lincoln*, 1865

Tens of thousands of people stood in a mud-filled Pennsylvania Avenue on a stormy day to see Lincoln inaugurated as president for the second time and to hear a speech Lincoln himself considered among his best. By this time, the war was almost over (Lee would surrender on April 9), but the carnage of civil war, with over six hundred thousand soldiers dead, had been enormous, and the travails of Reconstruction were just beginning. Two days after Lee's surrender, Lincoln would deliver his last public address, to a crowd of well-wishers gathered outside the White House. Addressing his policies for Reconstruction, Lincoln made his public statement in support of African American suffrage. Three days later Lincoln was shot dead by John Wilkes Booth, who had been in the audience at both the second inaugural and this last speech.

Second Inaugural Address

March 4, 1865

Abraham Lincoln

Fellow-Countrymen:

At this second appearing to take the oath of the Presidential office there is less occasion for an extended address than there was at the first. Then a statement somewhat in detail of a course to be pursued seemed fitting and proper. Now, at the expiration of four years, during which public declarations have been constantly called forth on every point and phase of the great contest which still absorbs the attention and engrosses the energies of the nation, little that is new could be presented. The progress of our arms, upon which all else chiefly depends, is as well known to the public as to myself, and it is, I trust, reasonably satisfactory and encouraging to all. With high hope for the future, no prediction in regard to it is ventured.

On the occasion corresponding to this four years ago all thoughts were anxiously directed to an impending civil war. All dreaded it, all sought to avert it. While the inaugural address was being delivered from this place, devoted altogether to *saving* the Union without war, insurgent agents were in the city seeking to *destroy* it without war—seeking to dissolve the Union and divide effects by negotiation. Both parties deprecated war, but one of them would *make* war rather than let the nation survive, and the other would *accept* war rather than let it perish, and the war came.

One-eighth of the whole population were colored slaves, not distributed generally over the Union, but localized in the southern part of it. These slaves constituted a peculiar and powerful interest. All knew that this interest was somehow the cause of the war. To strengthen, perpetuate, and extend this interest was the object for which the insurgents would rend the Union even by war, while the Government claimed no right to do more than to restrict the territorial enlargement of it. Neither party expected for the war the magnitude or the duration which it has already attained. Neither anticipated that the *cause* of the conflict might cease with or even before the conflict itself should cease. Each looked for an easier triumph, and a result less fundamental and astounding. Both read the same Bible and pray to the same God, and each invokes His aid against the other. It may seem strange that any men should dare to ask a just God's assistance in wringing their bread from the sweat of other men's faces, but let us judge not, that we be not judged. The prayers of both could not be answered. That of neither has been answered fully. The Almighty has His own purposes. "Woe unto the world because of offenses; for it must needs be that offenses come, but woe to that man by whom the offense cometh." If we shall suppose that American slavery is one of those offenses which, in the providence of God, must needs come, but which, having continued through His appointed time, He now wills to remove, and that He gives to both North and South this terrible war as the woe due to those by whom the offense came, shall we discern therein any departure from those divine attributes which the believers in a living God always ascribe to Him? Fondly do we hope, fervently do we pray, that this mighty scourge of war may speedily pass away. Yet, if God wills that it continue until all the wealth piled by the bondsman's two hundred and fifty years of unrequited toil shall be sunk, and until every drop of blood drawn with the lash shall be paid by another drawn with the sword, as was said three thousand years ago, so still it must be said "the judgments of the Lord are true and righteous altogether."

With malice toward none, with charity for all, with firmness in the right as God gives us to see the right, let us strive on to finish the work we are in, to bind up the nation's wounds, to care for him who shall have borne the battle and for his widow and his orphan, to do all which may achieve and cherish a just and lasting peace among ourselves and with all nations.

Last Public Address

April 11, 1865

Abraham Lincoln

April 11, 1865

We meet this evening, not in sorrow, but in gladness of heart. The evacuation of Petersburg and Richmond, and the surrender of the principal insurgent army, give hope of a righteous and speedy peace whose joyous expression can not be restrained. In the midst of this, however, He, from Whom all blessings flow, must not be forgotten. A call for a national thanksgiving is being prepared, and will be duly promulgated. Nor must those whose harder part gives us the cause of rejoicing, be overlooked. Their honors must not be parcelled out with others. I myself, was near the front, and had the high pleasure of transmitting much of the good news to you; but no part of the honor, for plan or execution, is mine. To Gen. Grant, his skilful officers, and brave men, all belongs. The gallant Navy stood ready, but was not in reach to take active part.

By these recent successes the re-inauguration of the national authority—reconstruction—which has had a large share of thought from the first, is pressed much more closely upon our attention. It is fraught with great difficulty. Unlike the case of a war between independent nations, there is no authorized organ for us to treat with. No one man has authority to give up the rebellion for any other man. We simply must begin with, and mould from, disorganized and discordant elements. Nor is it a small additional embarrassment that we, the loyal people, differ among ourselves as to the mode, manner, and means of reconstruction.

As a general rule, I abstain from reading the reports of attacks upon myself, wishing not to be provoked by that to which I can not properly offer an answer. In spite of this precaution, however, it comes to my knowledge that I am much censured for some supposed agency in setting up, and seeking to sustain, the new State Government of Louisiana. In this I have done just so much as, and no more than, the public knows. In the Annual Message of Dec. 1863 and accompanying Proclamation, I presented *a* plan of re-construction (as the phrase goes) which, I promised, if adopted by any State, should be acceptable to, and sustained by, the Executive government of the nation. I distinctly stated that this was not the only plan which might possibly be acceptable; and I also distinctly protested that the Executive claimed no right to say when, or whether members should be admitted to seats in Congress from such States. This plan was, in advance, submitted to the then Cabinet, and distinctly approved by every member of it. One of them suggested that I should then, and in that connection, apply the Emancipation Proclamation to the theretofore excepted parts of Virginia and Louisiana; that I should drop the suggestion about apprenticeship for freed-people, and that I should omit the protest against my own power, in regard to the admission of members to Congress; but even he approved every part and parcel of the plan which has since been employed or touched by the action of Louisiana. The new constitution of Louisiana, declaring emancipation for the whole State, practically applies the Proclamation to the part previously excepted. It does not adopt apprenticeship for freed-people; and it is silent, as it could not well be otherwise, about the admission of members to Congress. So that, as it applies to Louisiana, every member of the Cabinet fully approved the plan. The Message went to Congress, and I received many commendations of the plan, written and verbal; and not a single objection to it, from any professed emancipationist, came to my knowledge, until after the news reached Washington that the people of Louisiana had begun to move in accordance with it. From about July 1862, I had corresponded with different persons, supposed to be interested, seeking a reconstruction of a State government for Louisiana. When the Message of 1863, with the plan before mentioned, reached New-Orleans, Gen. Banks wrote me that he was confident the people, with his military co-operation, would reconstruct, substantially on that plan. I wrote him, and some of them to try it; they tried it, and the result is known. Such only has been my agency in getting up the Louisiana government. As to sustaining it, my promise is out, as before stated. But, as bad promises are better broken than kept, I shall treat this as a bad promise, and break it, whenever I shall be convinced that keeping it is adverse to the public interest. But I have not yet been so convinced.

I have been shown a letter on this subject, supposed to be an able one, in which the writer expresses regret that my mind has not seemed to be definitely fixed on the question whether the seceded States, so called, are in the Union or out of it. It would perhaps, add astonishment to his regret, were he to learn that since I have found professed Union men endeavoring to make that question, I have *purposely* forborne any public expression upon it. As appears to me that question has not been, nor yet is, a practically material one, and that any discussion of it, while it thus remains practically immaterial, could have no effect other than the mischievous one of dividing our friends. As yet, whatever it may hereafter become, that question is bad, as the basis of a controversy, and good for nothing at all—a merely pernicious abstraction.

We all agree that the seceded States, so called, are out of their proper practical relation with the Union; and that the sole object of the government, civil and military, in regard to those States is to again get them into that proper practical relation. I believe it is not only possible, but in fact, easier, to do this, without deciding, or even considering, whether these States have even been out of the Union, than with it. Finding themselves safely at home, it would be utterly immaterial whether they had ever been abroad. Let us all join in doing the acts necessary to restoring the proper practical relations between these states and the Union; and each forever after, innocently indulge his own opinion whether, in doing the acts, he brought the States from without, into the Union, or only gave them proper assistance, they never having been out of it.

The amount of constituency, so to to [sic] speak, on which the new Louisiana government rests, would be more satisfactory to all, if it contained fifty, thirty, or even twenty thousand, instead of only about twelve thousand, as it does. It is also unsatisfactory to some that the elective franchise is not given to the colored man. I would myself prefer that it were now conferred on the very intelligent, and on those who serve our cause as soldiers. Still the question is not whether the Louisiana government, as it stands, is quite all that is desirable. The question is "Will it be wiser to take it as it is, and help to improve it; or to reject, and disperse it?" "Can Louisiana be brought into proper practical relation with the Union *sooner* by *sustaining,* or by *discarding* her new State Government?"

Some twelve thousand voters in the heretofore slave-state of Louisiana have sworn allegiance to the Union, assumed to be the rightful political power of the State, held elections, organized a State government, adopted a free-state constitution, giving the benefit of public schools equally to black and white, and empowering the Legislature to confer the elective franchise upon the colored man. Their Legislature has already voted to ratify the constitutional amendment recently passed by Congress, abolishing slavery throughout the nation. These twelve thousand persons are thus fully committed to the Union, and to perpetual freedom in the state—committed to the very things, and nearly all the things the nation wants—and they ask the nation's recognition, and its assistance to make good their committal. Now, if we reject, and spurn them, we do our utmost to disorganize and disperse them. We in effect say to the white men "You are worthless, or worse—we will neither help you, nor be helped by you." To the blacks we say "This cup of liberty which these, your old masters, hold to your lips, we will dash from you, and leave you to the chances of gathering the spilled and scattered contents in some vague and undefined when, where, and how." If this course, discouraging and paralyzing both white and black, has any tendency to bring Louisiana into proper practical relations with the Union, I have, so far, been unable to perceive it. If, on the contrary, we recognize, and sustain the new government of Louisiana the converse of all this is made true. We encourage the hearts, and nerve the arms of the twelve thousand to adhere to their work, and argue for it, and proselyte for it, and fight for it, and feed it, and grow it, and ripen it to a complete success. The colored man too, in seeing all united for him, is inspired with vigilance, and energy, and daring, to the same end. Grant that he desires the elective franchise, will he not attain it sooner by saving the already advanced steps toward it, than by running backward over them? Concede that the new government of Louisiana is only to what it should be as the egg is to the fowl, we shall sooner have the fowl by hatching the egg than by smashing it? Again, if we reject Louisiana, we also reject one vote in favor of the proposed amendment to the national constitution. To meet this proposition, it has been argued that no more than three fourths of those States which have not attempted secession are necessary to validly ratify the amendment. I do not commit myself against this, further than to say that such a ratification would be questionable, and sure to be persistently questioned; while a ratification by three fourths of all the States would be unquestioned and unquestionable.

I repeat the question. "Can Louisiana be brought into proper practical relation with the Union *sooner* by *sustaining* or by *discarding* her new State Government?["]

What has been said of Louisiana will apply generally to other States. And yet so great peculiarities pertain to each state; and such important and sudden changes occur in the same state; and, withal, so new and unprecedented is the whole case, that no exclusive, and inflexible plan can safely be prescribed as to details and colatterals. Such exclusive, and inflexible plan, would surely become a new entanglement. Important principles may, and must, be inflexible.

In the present "*situation*" as the phrase goes, it may be my duty to make some new announcement to the people of the South. I am considering, and shall not fail to act, when satisfied that action will be proper.

Constitution of Indiana, Article XIII, 1851

Black Code of Mississippi, 1865

While slavery had become a specifically Southern institution well before the Civil War, African Americans were subjected to numerous legal and constitutional disabilities throughout the North. States in what is today the Midwest were particularly insistent on discouraging African Americans from living within their borders. Such laws, the first of which was enacted in Ohio in 1804, banned African Americans from owning property, entering into contracts, and even residing in the state. The Indiana Constitution was part of a trend of increasing severity in such laws before the Civil War. Limits on African American rights in the North continued to be a sore spot for white Southerners opposed to post–Civil War legislation aimed at enfranchising and empowering their former slaves. Black Codes such as that in Mississippi bound African Americans to (generally agricultural or domestic) labor contracts, forbade free movement and voting, and sought to restrict social and educational as well as political conduct among African Americans.

Constitution of Indiana, Article XIII

November 1, 1851

ARTICLE XIII
NEGROES AND MULATTOES

SECTION 1. No negro or mulatto shall come into, or settle in, the State, after the adoption of this Constitution.

SEC. 2. All contracts made with any negro or mulatto coming into the State, contrary to the provisions of the foregoing section, shall be void; and any person who shall employ such negro or mulatto, or otherwise encourage him to remain in the State, shall be fined in any sum not less than ten dollars, nor more than five hundred dollars.

SEC. 3. All fines which may be collected for a violation of the provisions of this article, or of any law which may hereafter be passed for the purpose of carrying the same into execution, shall be set apart and appropriated for the colonization of such negroes and mulattoes, and their descendants, as may be in the State at the adoption of this Constitution, and may be willing to emigrate.

SEC. 4. The General Assembly shall pass laws to carry out the provisions of this article.

Black Code of Mississippi

December 2, 1865

MISSISSIPPI
AN ACT to regulate the relation of master and apprentice, as relates to freedmen, free negroes, and mulattoes.

SECTION 1. It shall be the duty of all sheriffs, justices of the peace, and other civil officers of the several counties in this State, to report to the probate courts of their respective counties semi-annually, at the January and July terms of said courts, all freedmen, free negroes, and mulattoes, under the age of eighteen, in their respective counties, beats, or districts, who are orphans, or whose parent or parents have not the means or refuse to provide for and support said minors; and thereupon it shall be the duty of said probate court to order the clerk of said court to apprentice said minors to some competent and suitable person on such terms as the court may direct, having a particular care to the interest of said minor: *Provided,* That the former owner of said minors shall have the preference when, in the opinion of the court, he or she shall be a suitable person for that purpose.

SEC. 2. *Be it further enacted,* That the said court shall be fully satisfied that the person or persons to whom said minor shall be apprenticed shall be a suitable person to have the charge and care of said minor, and fully to protect the interest of said minor: *Provided,* That the said court shall require the said master or mistress to execute bond and security, payable to the State of Mississippi, conditioned that he or she shall furnish said minor with sufficient food and clothing; to treat said minor humanely; furnish medical attention in case of sickness; teach, or cause to be taught, him or her to read and write, if under fifteen years old, and will conform to any law that may be hereafter passed for the regulation of the duties and relation of master and apprentice: *Provided,* That said apprentice shall be bound by indenture, in case of males, until they are twenty-one years old, and in case of females until they are eighteen years old.

SEC. 3. *Be it further enacted,* That in the management and control of said apprentices, said master or mistress shall have the power to inflict such moderate corporal chastisement as a father or guardian is allowed to inflict on his or her child or ward at common law: *Provided,* That in no case shall cruel or inhuman punishment be inflicted.

SEC. 4. *Be it further enacted,* That if any apprentice shall leave the employment of his or her master or mistress, without his or her consent, said master or mistress may pursue and recapture said apprentice, and bring him or her before any justice of the peace of the county, whose duty it shall be to remand said apprentice to the service of his or her master or mistress; and in the event of a refusal on the part of said apprentice so to return, then said justice shall commit said apprentice to the jail of said county, on failure to give bond, to the next term of the county court; and it shall be the duty of said court at the first term thereafter to investigate said case, and if the court shall be of opinion that said apprentice left the employment of his or her master or mistress without good cause, to order him or her to be punished, as provided for the punishment of hired freedmen, as may be from time to time provided for by law for desertion, until he or she shall agree to return to his or her master or mistress: *Provided,* That the court may grant continuances as in other cases: *And provided further,* That if the court shall believe that said apprentice had good cause to quit his said master or mistress, the court shall discharge said apprentice from said indenture, and also enter a judgment against the master or mistress for not more than one hundred dollars, for the use and benefit of said apprentice, to be collected on execution as in other cases.

SEC. 5. *Be it further enacted,* That if any person entice away any apprentice from his or her master or mistress, or shall knowingly employ an apprentice, or furnish him or her food or clothing without the written consent of his or her master or mistress, or shall sell or give said apprentice ardent spirits without such consent, said person so offending shall be deemed guilty of a high misdemeanor, and shall, on conviction thereof before the county court, be punished as provided for the punishment of persons enticing from their employer hired freedmen, free negroes or mulattoes.

SEC. 6. *Be it further enacted,* That it shall be the duty of all civil officers of their respective counties to report any minors within their respective counties to said probate court who are subject to be apprenticed under the provisions of this act, from time to time as the facts may come to their knowledge, and it shall be the duty of said court from time to time as said minors shall be reported to them, or otherwise come to their knowledge, to apprentice said minors, as hereinbefore provided.

SEC. 7. *Be it further enacted,* That in case the master or mistress of any apprentice shall desire, he or she shall have the privilege to summon his or her apprentice to the probate court, and thereupon, with the approval of the court, he or she shall be released from all liability as master of said apprentice, and his said bond shall be cancelled, and it shall be the duty of the court forthwith to re-apprentice said minor; and in the event any master of an apprentice shall die before the close of the term of service of said apprentice, it shall be the duty of the court to give the preference in re-apprenticing said minor to the widow or other member of said master's family: *Provided,* That said widow or other member of said family shall be a suitable person for that purpose.

SEC. 8. *Be it further enacted,* That in case any master or mistress of any apprentice, bound to him or her under this act, shall be about to remove, or shall have removed, to any other State of the United States, by the laws of which such apprentice may be an inhabitant thereof, the probate court of the proper county may authorize the removal of such apprentice to such State upon said master or mistress entering into bond, with security, in a penalty to be fixed by the judge, conditioned that said master or mistress will, upon such removal, comply with the laws of such State in such cases: *Provided,* That said master shall be cited to attend the court at which such order is proposed to be made, and shall have a right to resist the same by next friend or otherwise.

SEC. 9. *Be it further enacted,* That it shall be lawful for any freedman, free negro, or mulatto, having a minor child or children, to apprentice the said minor child or children, as provided for by this act.

SEC. 10. *Be it further enacted,* That in all cases where the age of the freedman, free negro, or mulatto cannot be ascertained by record testimony, the judge of the the county court shall fix the age.

Sec. 11. *Be it further enacted,* That this act take effect and be in force from and after its passage.

Approved November 22, 1865.

AN ACT to amend the vagrant laws of the State.

Section 1. *Be it enacted by the legislature of the State of Mississippi,* That all rogues and vagabonds, idle and dissipated persons, beggars, jugglers, or persons practicing unlawful games or plays, runaways, common drunkards, common night-walkers, pilferers, lewd, wanton, or lascivious persons, in speech or behavior, common railers and brawlers, persons who neglect their calling or employment, misspend what they earn, or do not provide for the support of themselves or their families, or dependants, and all other idle and disorderly persons, including all who neglect all lawful business, habitually misspend their time by frequenting houses of ill-fame, gaming-houses, or tippling shops, shall be deemed and considered vagrants, under the provisions of this act, and on conviction thereof shall be fined not exceeding one hundred dollars, with all accruing costs, and be imprisoned, at the discretion of the court, not exceeding ten days.

Sec. 2. *Be it further enacted,* That all freedmen, free negroes and mulattoes in this State, over the age of eighteen years, found on the second Monday in January, 1866, or thereafter, without lawful employment or business, or found unlawfully assembling themselves together, either in the day or night time, and all white persons so assembling themselves with freedmen, free negroes or mulattoes, or usually associating with freedmen, free negroes or mulattoes, on terms of equality, or living in adultery or fornication with a freed woman, free negro or mulatto, shall be deemed vagrants, and on conviction thereof shall be fined in a sum not exceeding, in the case of a freedman, free negro, or mulatto, fifty dollars, and a white man two hundred dollars, and imprisoned, at the discretion of the court, the free negro not exceeding ten days, and the white man not exceeding six months.

Sec. 3. *Be it further enacted,* That all justices of the peace, mayors, and aldermen of incorporated towns and cities of the several counties in this State shall have jurisdiction to try all questions of vagrancy in their respective towns, counties, and cities, and it is hereby made their duty, whenever they shall ascertain that any person or persons in their respective towns, counties, and cities are violating any of the provisions of this act, to have said party or parties arrested, and brought before them, and immediately investigate said charge, and, on conviction, punish said party or parties, as provided for herein. And it is hereby made the duty of all sheriffs, constables, town constables, and all such like officers, and city marshals, to report to some officer having jurisdiction all violations of any of the provisions of this act, and it shall be the duty of the county courts to inquire if any officers have neglected any of the duties required by this act, and in case any officer shall fail or neglect any duty herein it shall be the duty of the county court to fine said officer, upon conviction, not exceeding one hundred dollars, to be paid into the county treasury for county purposes.

Sec. 4. *Be it further enacted,* That keepers of gaming-houses, houses of prostitution, prostitutes, public or private, and all persons who derive their chief support in employments that militate against good morals, or against law, shall be deemed and held to be vagrants.

Sec. 5. *Be it further enacted,* That all fines and forfeitures collected under the provisions of this act shall be paid into the county treasury for general county purposes, and in case any freedman, free negro or mulatto shall fail for five days after the imposition of any fine or forfeiture upon him or her for violation of any of the provisions of this act to pay the same, that it shall be, and is hereby, made the duty of the sheriff of the proper county to hire out said freedman, free negro or mulatto, to any person who will, for the shortest period of service, pay said fine or forfeiture and all costs: *Provided,* A preference shall be given to the employer, if there be one, in which case the employer shall be entitled to deduct and retain the amount so paid from the wages of such freedman, free negro or mulatto, then due or to become due; and in case said freedman, free negro, or mulatto cannot be hired out, he or she may be dealt with as a pauper.

Sec. 6. *Be it further enacted,* That the same duties and liabilities existing among white persons of this State shall attach to freedmen, free negroes and mulattoes, to support their indigent families and all colored paupers; and that in order to secure a support for such indigent freedmen, free negroes, and mulattoes, it shall be lawful, and it is hereby made the duty of the boards of county police of each county in this State, to levy a poll or capitation tax on each and every freedmen, free negro, or mulatto, between the ages of eighteen and sixty years, not to exceed the sum of one dollar annually to each person so taxed, which tax, when collected, shall be paid into the county treasurer's hands, and constitute a fund to be called the Freedmen's Pauper Fund, which shall be applied by the commissioners of the poor for the maintenance of the poor of the freedmen, free negroes, or mulattoes of this State, under such regulations as may be established by the boards of county police in the respective counties of this State.

SEC. 7. *Be it further enacted,* That if any freedman, free negro, or mulatto shall fail or refuse to pay any tax levied according to the provisions of the sixth section of this act, it shall be *prima facie* evidence of vagrancy, and it shall be the duty of the sheriff to arrest such freedman, free negro, or mulatto, or such person refusing or neglecting to pay such tax, and proceed at once to hire for the shortest time such delinquent tax-payer to any one who will pay the said tax, with accruing costs, giving preference to the employer, if there be one.

SEC. 8. *Be it further enacted,* That any person feeling himself or herself aggrieved by the judgment of any justice of the peace, mayor, or alderman in cases arising under this act, may within five days appeal to the next term of the county court of the proper county, upon giving bond and security in a sum not less than twenty-five nor more than one hundred and fifty dollars, conditioned to appear and prosecute said appeal, and abide by the judgment of the county court; and said appeal shall be tried de novo in the county court, and the decision of said court shall be final.

SEC. 9. *Be it further enacted,* That this act be in force and take effect from its passage.

Approved November 24, 1865.

AN ACT to confer civil rights on freedmen, and for other purposes.

SECTION 1. *Be it enacted by the legislature of the State of Mississippi,* That all freedmen, free negroes, and mulattoes may sue and be sued, implead and be impleaded, in all the courts of law and equity of this State, and may acquire personal property, and choses in action, by descent or purchase, and may dispose of the same in the same manner and to the same extent that white persons may: *Provided,* That the provision of this section shall not be so construed as to allow any freedman, free negro, or mulatto to rent or lease any lands or tenements except in incorporated towns or cities, in which places the corporate authorities shall control the same.

SEC. 2. *Be it further enacted,* That all freedmen, free negroes, and mulattoes may intermarry with each other, in the same manner and under the same regulations that are provided by law for white persons: *Provided,* That the clerk of probate shall keep separate records of the same.

SEC. 3. *Be it further enacted,* That all freedmen, free negroes, and mulattoes who do now and have heretofore lived and cohabited together as husband and wife shall be taken and held in law as legally married, and the issue shall be taken and held as legitimate for all purposes; that it shall not be lawful for any freedman, free negro, or mulatto to intermarry with any white person; nor for any white person to intermarry with any freedman, free negro, or mulatto; and any person who shall so intermarry shall be deemed guilty of felony, and on conviction thereof shall be confined in the State penitentiary for life; and those shall be deemed freedmen, free negroes, and mulattoes who are of pure negro blood, and those descended from a negro to the third generation, inclusive, though one ancestor in each generation may have been a white person.

SEC. 4. *Be it further enacted,* That in addition to cases in which freedmen, free negroes, and mulattoes are now by law competent witnesses, freedmen, free negroes, or mulattoes shall be competent in civil cases, when a party or parties to the suit, either plaintiff or plaintiffs, defendant or defendants; also in cases where freedmen, free negroes, and mulattoes is or are either plaintiff or plaintiffs, defendant or defendants, and a white person or white persons is or are the opposing party or parties, plaintiff or plaintiffs, defendant or defendants. They shall also be competent witnesses in all criminal prosecutions where the crime charged is alleged to have been committed by a white person upon or against the person or property of a freedman, free negro, or mulatto: *Provided,* That in all cases said witnesses shall be examined in open court, on the stand; except, however, they may be examined before the grand jury, and shall in all cases be subject to the rules and tests of the common law as to competency and credibility.

SEC. 5. *Be it further enacted,* That every freedman, free negro, and mulatto shall, on the second Monday of January, one thousand eight hundred and sixty-six, and annually thereafter, have a lawful home or employment, and shall have written evidence thereof as follows, to wit: If living in any incorporated city, town, or village, a license from the mayor thereof; and if living outside of any incorporated city, town, or village, from the member of the board of police of his beat, authorizing him or her to do irregular and job work; or a written contract, as provided in section sixth of this act; which licenses may be revoked for cause at any time by the authority granting the same.

SEC. 6. *Be it further enacted,* That all contracts for labor made with freedmen, free negroes, and mulattoes for a longer period than one month shall be in writing, and in duplicate, attested and read to said freedman, free negro, or mulatto by a beat, city or county officer, or two disinterested white persons of the county in which the labor is to be performed, of which each party shall have one; and said contracts shall be taken and held as entire contracts, and if the laborer shall quit the service of the employer before expiration of his term of service, without good cause, he shall forfeit his wages for that year up to the time of quitting.

SEC. 7. *Be it further enacted,* That every civil officer shall, and every person may, arrest and carry back to his or her legal employer any freedman, free negro, or mulatto who shall have quit the service of his or her employer before the expiration of his or her term of service without good cause; and said officer and person shall be entitled to receive for arresting and carrying back every deserting employé aforesaid the sum of five dollars, and ten cents per mile from the place of arrest to the place of delivery; and the same shall be paid by the employer, and held as a set-off for so much against the wages of said deserting employé: *Provided,* That said arrested party, after being so returned, may appeal to a justice of the peace or member of the board of police of the county, who, on notice to the alleged employer, shall try summarily whether said appellant is legally employed by the alleged employer, and has good cause to quit said employer. Either party shall have the right of appeal to the county court, pending which the alleged deserter shall be remanded to the alleged employer or otherwise disposed of, as shall be right and just; and the decision of the county court shall be final.

SEC. 8. *Be it further enacted,* That, upon affidavit made by the employer of any freedman, free negro, or mulatto, or other credible person, before any justice of the peace or member of the board of police, that any freedman, free negro, or mulatto legally employed by said employer has illegally deserted said employment, such justice of the peace or member of the board of police shall issue his warrant or warrants, returnable before himself or other such officer, to any sheriff, constable, or special deputy, commanding him to arrest said deserter, and return him or her to said employer, and the like proceedings shall be had as provided in the preceding section; and it shall be lawful for any officer to whom such warrant shall be directed to execute said warrant in any county of this State; and that said warrant may be transmitted without indorsement to any like officer of another county, to be executed and returned as aforesaid; and the said employer shall pay the costs of said warrants and arrest and return, which shall be set off for so much against the wages of said deserter.

SEC. 9. *Be it further enacted,* That if any person shall persuade or attempt to persuade, entice, or cause any freedman, free negro, or mulatto to desert from the legal employment of any person before the expiration of his or her term of service, or shall knowingly employ any such deserting freedman, free negro, or mulatto, or shall knowingly give or sell to any such deserting freedman, free negro, or mulatto any food, raiment, or other thing, he or she shall be guilty of a misdemeanor, and, upon conviction, shall be fined not less than twenty-five dollars and not more than two hundred dollars and the costs; and if said fine and costs shall not be immediately paid, the court shall sentence said convict to not exceeding two months' imprisonment in the county jail, and he or she shall moreover be liable to the party injured in damages: *Provided,* If any person shall, or shall attempt to, persuade, entice, or cause any freedman, free negro, or mulatto to desert from any legal employment of any person, with the view to employ said freedman, free negro, or mulatto without the limits of this State, such person, on conviction, shall be fined not less than fifty dollars and not more than five hundred dollars and costs; and if said fine and costs shall not be immediately paid, the court shall sentence said convict to not exceeding six months' imprisonment in the county jail.

SEC. 10. *Be it further enacted,* That it shall be lawful for any freedman, free negro or mulatto, to charge any white person, freedman, free negro or mulatto, by affidavit, with any criminal offence against his or her person or property, and upon such affidavit the proper process shall be issued and executed as if said affidavit was made by a white person, and it shall be lawful for any freedman, free negro or mulatto, in any action, suit or controversy pending, or about to be instituted in any court of law or equity of this State, to make all needful and lawful affidavits as shall be necessary for the institution, prosecution or defence of such suit or controversy.

SEC. 11. *Be it further enacted,* That the penal laws of this State, in all cases not otherwise specially provided for, shall apply and extend to all freedmen, free negroes and mulattoes.

SEC. 12. *Be it further enacted,* That this act take effect and be in force from and after its passage.

Approved November 25, 1865.

AN ACT to punish certain offences therein named, and for other purposes.

SECTION 1. *Be it enacted by the legislature of the State of Mississippi,* That no freedman, free negro or mulatto, not in the military service of the United States government, and not licensed so to do by the board of police of his or her county, shall keep or carry fire-arms of any kind, or any ammunition, dirk or bowie-knife, and on conviction thereof in the county court shall be punished by fine, not exceeding ten dollars, and pay the costs of such proceedings, and all such arms or ammunition shall be forfeited to the informer; and it shall be the duty of every civil and military officer to arrest any freedman, free negro, or mulatto found with any such arms or ammunition, and cause him or her to be committed for trial in default of bail.

SEC. 2. *Be it further enacted,* That any freedman, free negro, or mulatto committing riots, routs, affrays, trespasses, malicious mischief, cruel treatment to animals, seditious speeches, insulting gestures, language, or acts, or assaults on any person, disturbance of the peace, exercising the function of a minister of the gospel without a license from some regularly organized church, vending spirituous or intoxicating liquors, or committing any other misdemeanor, the punishment of which is not specifically provided for by law, shall, upon conviction thereof in the county court, be fined, not less than ten dollars, and not more than one hundred dollars, and may be imprisoned at the discretion of the court, not exceeding thirty days.

SEC. 3. *Be it further enacted,* That if any white person shall sell, lend, or give to any freedman, free negro, or mulatto any fire-arms, dirk or bowie-knife, or ammunition, or any spirituous or intoxicating liquors, such person or persons so offending, upon conviction thereof in the county court of his or her county, shall be fined not exceeding fifty dollars, and may be imprisoned, at the discretion of the court, not exceeding thirty days: *Provided,* That any master, mistress, or employer of any freedman, free negro, or mulatto, may give to any freedman, free negro, or mulatto, apprenticed to or employed by such master, mistress, or employer, spirituous or intoxicating liquors, but not in sufficient quantities to produce intoxication.

SEC. 4. *Be it further enacted,* That all the penal and criminal laws now in force in this State, defining offences and prescribing the mode of punishment for crimes and misdemeanors committed by slaves, free negroes, or mulattoes, be,

and the same are hereby, re-enacted and declared to be in full force and effect, against freedmen, free negroes, and mulattoes, except so far as the mode and manner of trial and punishment have been changed or altered by law.

SEC. 5. *Be it further enacted,* That if any freedman, free negro, or mulatto, convicted of any of the misdemeanors provided against in this act, shall fail or refuse for the space of five days, after conviction, to pay the fine and costs imposed, such person shall be hired out by the sheriff or other officer, at public outcry, to any white person who will pay said fine and all costs, and take said convict for the shortest time.

SEC. 6. *Be it further enacted,* That this act shall be in force and take effect from and after its passage.

Approved November 29, 1865.

AN ACT supplementary to "An act to confer civil rights upon freedmen," and for other purposes.

SECTION 1. *Be it enacted by the legislature of the State of Mississippi,* That in every case where any white person has been arrested and brought to trial by virtue of the provisions of the tenth section of the above-recited act, in any court in this State, upon sufficient proof being made to the court or jury, upon the trial before said court, that any freedman, free negro, or mulatto has falsely and maliciously caused the arrest and trial of said person or persons, the court shall render up a judgment against said freedman, free negro, or mulatto for all costs of the case, and impose a fine not to exceed fifty dollars, and imprisonment in the county jail not to exceed twenty days; and for a failure of said freedman, free negro, or mulatto to pay or cause to be paid all fines, costs, and jail fees, the sheriff of the county is hereby authorized and required, after giving ten days' public notice, to proceed to hire out at public outcry at the court-house of the county said freedman, free negro, or mulatto for the shortest time, to raise the amount necessary to discharge said freedman, free negro, or mulatto from all costs, fines, and jail fees aforesaid.

SEC. 2. *Be it further enacted,* That this act shall take effect and be in force from and after its passage.

Approved December 2, 1865.

U.S. Constitution, Thirteenth Amendment, 1865

Freedmen's Bureau Bill, 1865

Second Freedmen's Bureau Bill, 1865

Veto of the Second Freedmen's Bureau Bill, *Andrew Johnson,* 1866

Civil Rights Act of 1866

Recommended by Congress for state ratification on January 31, 1865, the Thirteenth Amendment freed slaves held in Delaware and Kentucky, enshrined the Emancipation Proclamation's freeing of other slaves in the Constitution, banned other forms of involuntary servitude (other than for convicted felons), and empowered Congress to enforce its provisions. But this did not address the predicament of freed slaves and Union loyalist whites in the South, where they were subjected to extreme economic and political deprivations. To this end Congress established the Bureau for the Relief of Freedmen and Refugees, or "Freedmen's Bureau," as an agency within the War Department. The bureau distributed food, clothing, and medicine. It also undertook projects intended to educate freedmen, settle them on confiscated land (which it administered), facilitate marriages, and maintain records regarding freedmen's conditions. Several Southern states responded by passing Black Codes. Congress thereupon sought to extend the bureau's tenure and increase its ability to protect African American rights. Congress also passed the Civil Rights Act, which declared all African Americans to be citizens and guaranteed them a number of corresponding rights. To the surprise of observers at the time, President Andrew Johnson vetoed both bills, objecting to what he argued was an unconstitutional continuation of war measures in time of peace and continued treatment of states that had been returned to the Union as conquered territories. Congress fell two votes short of the two-thirds majority needed to pass the Second Freedmen's Bureau Bill over the president's veto but did override his veto of the Civil Rights Act.

U.S. Constitution, Thirteenth Amendment

December 18, 1865

SECTION 1

Neither slavery nor involuntary servitude, except as a punishment for crime whereof the party shall have been duly convicted, shall exist within the United States, or any place subject to their jurisdiction.

SECTION 2

Congress shall have power to enforce this article by appropriate legislation.

Freedmen's Bureau Bill

March 3, 1865

An Act to establish a Bureau for the Relief of Freedmen and Refugees.

Be it enacted by the Senate and House of Representatives of the United States of America in Congress assembled, That there is hereby established in the War Department, to continue during the present war of rebellion, and for one year thereafter, a bureau of refugees, freedmen, and abandoned lands, to which shall be committed, as hereinafter provided, the supervision and management of all abandoned lands, and the control of all subjects relating to refugees and freedmen from rebel states, or from any district or county within the territory embraced in the operations of the army, under such rules and regulations as may be prescribed by the head of the bureau and approved by the President. The said bureau shall be under the management and control of a commissioner to be appointed by the President, by and with the advice and consent of the Senate, whose compensation shall be three thousand dollars per annum, and such number of clerks as may be assigned to him by the Secretary of War, not exceeding one chief clerk, two of the fourth class, two of the third class, and five of the first class. And the commissioner and all persons appointed under this act, shall, before entering upon their duties, take the oath of office prescribed in an act entitled "An act to prescribe an oath of office, and for other purposes," approved July second, eighteen hundred and sixty-two, and the commissioner and the chief clerk shall, before entering upon their duties, give bonds to the treasurer of the United States, the former in the sum of fifty thousand dollars, and the latter in the sum of ten thousand dollars, conditioned for the faithful discharge of their duties respectively, with securities to be approved as sufficient by the Attorney-General, which bonds shall be filed in the office of the first comptroller of the treasury, to be by him put in suit for the benefit of any injured party upon any breach of the conditions thereof.

Sec. 2. *And be it further enacted,* That the Secretary of War may direct such issues of provisions, clothing, and fuel, as he may deem needful for the immediate and temporary shelter and supply of destitute and suffering refugees and freedmen and their wives and children, under such rules and regulations as he may direct.

Sec. 3. *And be it further enacted,* That the President may, by and with the advice and consent of the Senate, appoint an assistant commissioner for each of the states declared to be in insurrection, not exceeding ten in number, who shall, under the direction of the commissioner, aid in the execution of the provisions of this act; and he shall give a bond to the Treasurer of the United States, in the sum of twenty thousand dollars, in the form and manner prescribed in the first section of this act. Each of said commissioners shall receive an annual salary of two thousand five hundred dollars in full compensation for all his services. And any military officer may be detailed and assigned to duty under this act without increase of pay or allowances. The commissioner shall, before the commencement of each regular session of congress, make full report of his proceedings with exhibits of the state of his accounts to the President, who shall communicate the same to congress, and shall also make special reports whenever required to do so by the President or either house of congress; and the assistant commissioners shall make quarterly reports of their proceedings to the commissioner, and also such other special reports as from time to time may be required.

Sec. 4. *And be it further enacted,* That the commissioner, under the direction of the President, shall have authority to set apart, for the use of loyal refugees and freedmen, such tracts of land within the insurrectionary states as shall have been abandoned, or to which the United States shall have acquired title by confiscation or sale, or otherwise, and to every male citizen, whether refugee or freedman, as aforesaid, there shall be assigned not more than forty acres of such land, and the person to whom it was so assigned shall be protected in the use and enjoyment of the land for the term of three years at an annual rent not exceeding six per centum upon the value of such land, as it was appraised by the state authorities in the year eighteen hundred and sixty, for the purpose of taxation, and in case no such appraisal can be found, then the rental shall be based upon the estimated value of the land in said year, to be ascertained in such manner as the commissioner may by regulation prescribe. At the end of said term, or at any time during said term, the occupants of any parcels so assigned may purchase the land and receive such title thereto as the United States can convey, upon paying therefor the value of the land, as ascertained and fixed for the purpose of determining the annual rent aforesaid.

Sec. 5. *And be it further enacted,* That all acts and parts of acts inconsistent with the provisions of this act, are hereby repealed.

Approved, March 3, 1865.

Second Freedmen's Bureau Bill

December 4, 1865

AN ACT to amend an act entitled "An act to establish a Bureau for the relief of Freedmen and Refugees," and for other purposes.

Be it enacted by the Senate and House of Representatives of the United States of America in Congress assembled, That the act to establish a Bureau for the relief of Freedmen and Refugees, approved March three, eighteen hundred and sixty-five, shall continue in force until otherwise provided by law, and shall extend to refugees and freedmen in all parts of the United States, and the President may divide the section of country containing such refugees and freedmen into districts, each containing one or more States, not to exceed twelve in number, and, by and with the advice and consent of the Senate, appoint an Assistant Commissioner for each of said districts, who shall give like bond, receive the compensation, and perform the duties prescribed by this and the act to which this is an amendment; or said bureau may, in the discretion of the President, be placed under a Commissioner and Assistant Commissioners, to be detailed from the army, in which event each officer so assigned to duty shall serve without increase of pay or allowances.

SEC. 2. *And be it further enacted,* That the Commissioner, with the approval of the President, and when the same shall be necessary for the operations of the bureau, may divide each district into a number of sub-districts, not to exceed the number of counties or parishes in such district, and shall assign to each sub-district at least one agent, either a citizen, officer of the army, or enlisted man, who, if an officer, shall serve without additional compensation or allowance, and if a citizen or enlisted man, shall receive a salary of not less than five hundred dollars nor more than twelve hundred dollars annually, according to the services rendered, in full compensation for such services; and such agent shall, before entering on the duties of his office, take the oath prescribed in the first section of the act to which this is an amendment. And the Commissioner may, when the same shall be necessary, assign to each Assistant Commissioner not exceeding three clerks, and to each of said agents one clerk, at an annual salary not exceeding one thousand dollars each, provided suitable clerks cannot be detailed from the army. And the President of the United States, through the War Department, and the Commissioner, shall extend military jurisdiction and protection over all employés, agents, and officers of this bureau in the exercise of the duties imposed or authorized by this act or the act to which this is additional.

SEC. 3. *And be it further enacted,* That the Secretary of War may direct such issues of provisions, clothing, fuel, and other supplies, including medical stores and transportation, and afford such aid, medical or otherwise, as he may deem needful for the immediate and temporary shelter and supply of destitute and suffering refugees and freedmen, their wives and children, under such rules and regulations as he may direct: *Provided,* That no person shall be deemed "destitute," "suffering," or "dependent upon the government for support," within the meaning of this act, who, being able to find employment, could by proper industry and exertion avoid such destitution, suffering, or dependence.

SEC. 4. *And be it further enacted,* That the President is hereby authorized to reserve from sale or from settlement, under the homestead or pre-emption laws, and to set apart for the use of freedmen and loyal refugees, male or female, unoccupied public lands in Florida, Mississippi, Alabama, Louisiana, and Arkansas, not exceeding in all three millions of acres of good land; and the Commissioner, under the direction of the President, shall cause the same from time to time to be allotted and assigned, in parcels not exceeding forty acres each, to the loyal refugees and freedmen, who shall be protected in the use and enjoyment thereof for such term of time and at such annual rent as may be agreed on between the Commissioner and such refugees or freedmen. The rental shall be based upon a valuation of the land, to be ascertained in such manner as the Commissioner may, under the direction of the President, by regulation prescribe. At the end of such term, or sooner, if the Commissioner shall assent thereto, the occupants of any parcels so assigned, their heirs and assigns, may purchase the land and receive a title thereto from the United States in fee, upon paying therefor the value of the land ascertained as aforesaid.

SEC. 5. *And be it further enacted,* That the occupants of land under Major General Sherman's special field order, dated at Savannah, January sixteen, eighteen hundred and sixty-five, are hereby confirmed in their possession for the period of three years from the date of said order, and no person shall be disturbed in or ousted from said possession during said three years, unless a settlement shall be made with said occupant, by the former owner, his heirs, or assigns, satisfactory to the Commissioner of the Freedmen's Bureau: *Provided,* That whenever the former owners of lands occupied under General Sherman's field order shall make application for restoration of said lands, the Commissioner is hereby authorized, upon the agreement and with the written consent of said occupants, to procure other lands for them by rent or purchase, not exceeding forty acres for each occupant, upon the terms and conditions named in section four of this act, or to set apart for them, out of the public lands assigned for that purpose in section four of this act, forty acres each, upon the same terms and conditions.

SEC. 6. *And be it further enacted,* That the Commissioner shall, under the direction of the President, procure in the name of the United States, by grant or purchase, such lands within the districts aforesaid as may be required for refugees and freedmen dependent on the government for support; and he shall provide or cause to be erected suitable buildings for asylums and schools. But no such purchase shall be made, nor contract for the same entered into, nor other expense incurred, until after appropriations shall have been provided by Congress for such purposes. And no payments shall be made for lands purchased under this section, except for asylums and schools, from any moneys not specifically appropriated therefor. And the Commissioner shall cause such lands from time to time to be valued, allotted, assigned, and sold in manner and form provided in the fourth section of this act, at a price not less than the cost thereof to the United States.

Sec. 7. *And be it further enacted,* That whenever in any State or district in which the ordinary course of judicial proceedings has been interrupted by the rebellion, and wherein, in consequence of any State or local law, ordinance, police or other regulation, custom, or prejudice, any of the civil rights or immunities belonging to white persons, including the right to make and enforce contracts, to sue, be parties, and give evidence, to inherit, purchase, lease, sell, hold and convey real and personal property, and to have full and equal benefit of all laws and proceedings for the security of person and estate, including the constitutional right of bearing arms, are refused or denied to negroes, mulattoes, freedmen, refugees, or any other persons, on account of race, color, or any previous condition of slavery or involuntary servitude, or wherein they or any of them are subjected to any other or different punishment, pains, or penalties, for the commission of any act or offence, than are prescribed for white persons committing like acts or offences, it shall be the duty of the President of the United States, through the Commissioner, to extend military protection and jurisdiction over all cases affecting such persons so discriminated against.

Sec. 8. *And be it further enacted,* That any person who, under color of any State or local law, ordinance, police, or other regulation or custom, shall, in any State or district in which the ordinary course of judicial proceedings has been interrupted by the rebellion, subject, or cause to be subjected, any negro, mulatto, freedman, refugee, or other person, on account of race or color, or any previous condition of slavery or involuntary servitude, or for any other cause, to the deprivation of any civil right secured to white persons, or to any other or different punishment than white persons are subject to for the commission of like acts or offences, shall be deemed guilty of a misdemeanor, and be punished by fine not exceeding one thousand dollars, or imprisonment not exceeding one year, or both; and it shall be the duty of the officers and agents of this bureau to take jurisdiction of, and hear and determine all offences committed against the provisions of this section, and also of all cases affecting negroes, mulattoes, freedmen, refugees, or other persons who are discriminated against in any of the particulars mentioned in the preceding section of this act, under such rules and regulations as the President of the United States, through the War Department, shall prescribe. The jurisdiction conferred by this and the preceding section on the officers and agents of this bureau shall cease and determine whenever the discrimination on account of which it is conferred ceases, and in no event to be exercised in any State in which the ordinary course of judicial proceedings has not been interrupted by the rebellion, nor in any such State after said State shall have been fully restored in all its constitutional relations to the United States, and the courts of the State and of the United States within the same are not disturbed or stopped in the peaceable course of justice.

Sec. 9. *And be it further enacted,* That all acts, or parts of acts, inconsistent with the provisions of this act are hereby repealed.

> SCHUYLER COLFAX,
> *Speaker of the House of Representatives.*
> LA FAYETTE S. FOSTER,
> *President of the Senate, pro tempore.*

I certify that this act did originate in the Senate.
> J. W. FORNEY, *Secretary.*

Veto of the Second Freedmen's Bureau Bill

February 19, 1866

Andrew Johnson

MESSAGE
OF THE
PRESIDENT OF THE UNITED STATES,
RETURNING
Bill (S. 60) to amend an act entitled "An act to establish a Bureau for the relief of Freedmen and Refugees," and for other purposes, with his objections thereto.

FEBRUARY 19, 1866—Read and ordered to be printed.

To the Senate of the United States:
I have examined with care the bill which originated in the Senate, and has been passed by the two houses of Congress, to

amend an act entitled "An act to establish a Bureau for the relief of Freedmen and Refugees," and for other purposes. Having, with much regret, come to the conclusion that it would not be consistent with the public welfare to give my approval to the measure, I return the bill to the Senate with my objections to its becoming a law.

I might call to mind, in advance of these objections, that there is no immediate necessity for the proposed measure. The act to establish a Bureau for the relief of Freedmen and Refugees, which was approved in the month of March last, has not yet expired. It was thought stringent and extensive enough for the purpose in view in time of war. Before it ceases to have effect, further experience may assist to guide us to a wise conclusion as to the policy to be adopted in time of peace.

I share with Congress the strongest desire to secure to the freedmen the full enjoyment of their freedom and property, and their entire independence and equality in making contracts for their labor; but the bill before me contains provisions which, in my opinion, are not warranted by the Constitution, and are not well suited to accomplish the end in view.

The bill proposes to establish, by authority of Congress, military jurisdiction over all parts of the United States containing refugees and freedmen. It would, by its very nature, apply with most force to those parts of the United States in which the freedmen most abound; and it expressly extends the existing temporary jurisdiction of the Freedmen's Bureau, with greatly enlarged powers, over those States "in which the ordinary course of judicial proceedings has been interrupted by the rebellion." The source from which this military jurisdiction is to emanate is none other than the President of the United States, acting through the War Department and the Commissioner of the Freedmen's Bureau. The agents to carry out this military jurisdiction are to be selected either from the army or from civil life; the country is to be divided into districts and subdistricts, and the number of salaried agents to be employed may be equal to the number of counties or parishes in all the United States where freedmen and refugees are to be found.

The subjects over which this military jurisdiction is to extend in every part of the United States include protection to "all employés, agents, and officers of this bureau in the exercise of the duties imposed" upon them by the bill. In eleven States it is further to extend over all cases affecting freedmen and refugees discriminated against "by local law, custom, or prejudice." In those eleven States, the bill subjects any white person who may be charged with depriving a freedman of "any civil rights or immunities belonging to white persons"

to imprisonment or fine, or both, without, however, defining the "civil rights and immunities" which are thus to be secured to the freedmen by military law. This military jurisdiction also extends to all questions that may arise respecting contracts. The agent who is thus to exercise the office of a military judge may be a stranger, entirely ignorant of the laws of the place, and exposed to the errors of judgment to which all men are liable. The exercise of power, over which there is no legal supervision, by so vast a number of agents as is contemplated by the bill, must, by the very nature of man, be attended by acts of caprice, injustice, and passion.

The trials, having their origin under this bill, are to take place without the intervention of a jury, and without any fixed rules of law or evidence. The rules on which offences are to be "heard and determined" by the numerous agents are such rules and regulations as the President, through the War Department, shall prescribe. No previous presentment is required, nor any indictment charging the commission of a crime against the laws; but the trial must proceed on charges and specifications. The punishment will be—not what the law declares, but such as a court-martial may think proper; and from these arbitrary tribunals there lies no appeal, no writ of error to any of the courts in which the Constitution of the United States vests exclusively the judicial power of the country.

While the territory and the classes of actions and offences that are made subject to this measure are so extensive, the bill itself, should it become a law, will have no limitation in point of time, but will form a part of the permanent legislation of the country. I cannot reconcile a system of military jurisdiction of this kind with the words of the Constitution, which declare that "no person shall be held to answer for a capital or otherwise infamous crime unless upon a presentment or indictment of a grand jury, except in cases arising in the land and naval forces, or in the militia when in actual service in time of war or public danger"; and that "in all criminal prosecutions the accused shall enjoy the right to a speedy and public trial, by an impartial jury of the State or district wherein the crime shall have been committed." The safeguards which the experience and wisdom of ages taught our fathers to establish as securities for the protection of the innocent, the punishment of the guilty, and the equal administration of justice, are to be set aside, and, for the sake of a more vigorous interposition in behalf of justice, we are to take the risks of the many acts of injustice that would necessarily follow from an almost countless number of agents, established in every parish or county, in nearly a third of the States of the Union, over whose decisions there is to be no supervision or control by the federal courts. The power that would be thus placed in the hands of the President is such as in time of peace certainly ought never to be intrusted to any one man.

If it be asked whether the creation of such a tribunal within a State is warranted as a measure of war, the question immediately presents itself whether we are still engaged in war. Let us not unnecessarily disturb the commerce, and credit, and industry of the country, by declaring to the American people and to the world that the United States are still in a condition of civil war. At present there is no part of our country in which the authority of the United States is disputed. Offences that may be committed by individuals should not work a forfeiture of the rights of whole communities. The country has returned or is returning to a state of peace and industry, and the rebellion is, in fact, at an end. The measure, therefore, seems to be as inconsistent with the actual condition of the country as it is at variance with the Constitution of the United States.

If, passing from general considerations, we examine the bill in detail, it is open to weighty objections.

In time of war it was eminently proper that we should provide for those who were passing suddenly from a condition of bondage to a state of freedom. But this bill proposes to make the Freedmen's Bureau, established by the act of 1865, as one of many great and extraordinary military measures to suppress a formidable rebellion, a permanent branch of the public administration, with its powers greatly enlarged. I have no reason to suppose, and I do not understand it to be alleged, that the act of March, 1865, has proved deficient for the purpose for which it was passed, although at that time, and for a considerable period thereafter, the government of the United States remained unacknowledged in most of the States whose inhabitants had been involved in the rebellion. The institution of slavery, for the military destruction of which the Freedmen's Bureau was called into existence as an auxiliary, has been already effectually and finally abrogated throughout the whole country by an amendment of the Constitution of the United States, and practically its eradication has received the assent and concurrence of most of those States in which it at any time had an existence. I am not, therefore, able to discern, in the condition of the country, anything to justify an apprehension that the powers and agencies of the Freedmen's Bureau, which were effective for the protection of freedmen and refugees during the actual continuance of hostilities and of African servitude, will now, in a time of peace,

and after the abolition of slavery, prove inadequate to the same proper ends. If I am correct in these views there can be no necessity for the enlargement of the powers of the bureau for which provision is made in the bill.

The third section of the bill authorizes a general and unlimited grant of support to the destitute and suffering refugees and freedmen, their wives and children. Succeeding sections make provision for the rent or purchase of landed estates for freedmen, and for the erection, for their benefit, of suitable buildings for asylums and schools—the expenses to be defrayed from the treasury of the whole people. The Congress of the United States has never heretofore thought itself empowered to establish asylums beyond the limits of the District of Columbia, except for the benefit of our disabled soldiers and sailors. It has never founded schools for any class of our own people; not even for the orphans of those who have fallen in the defence of the Union, but has left the care of education to the much more competent and efficient control of the States, of communities, of private associations, and of individuals. It has never deemed itself authorized to expend the public money for the rent or purchase of homes for the thousands, not to say millions of the white race, who are honestly toiling from day to day for their subsistence. A system for the support of indigent persons in the United States was never contemplated by the authors of the Constitution; nor can any good reason be advanced why, as a permanent establishment, it should be founded for one class or color of our people more than another. Pending the war many refugees and freedmen received support from the government, but it was never intended that they should thenceforth be fed, clothed, educated, and sheltered by the United States. The idea on which the slaves were assisted to freedom was that, on becoming free, they would be a self-sustaining population. Any legislation that shall imply that they are not expected to attain a self-sustaining condition must have a tendency injurious alike to their character and their prospects.

The appointment of an agent for every county and parish will create an immense patronage; and the expense of the numerous officers and their clerks, to be appointed by the President, will be great in the beginning, with a tendency steadily to increase. The appropriations asked by the Freedmen's Bureau, as now established for the year 1866, amount to $11,745,000. It may be safely estimated that the cost to be incurred under the pending bill will require double that amount—more than the entire sum expended in any one year under the administration of the second Adams. If the presence of agents in every parish and county is to be considered as a war measure, opposition, or even resistance might be provoked; so that, to give effect to their jurisdiction, troops would have to be stationed within reach of every one of them, and thus a large standing force be rendered necessary. Large appropriations would, therefore, be required to sustain and enforce military jurisdiction in every county or parish from the Potomac to the Rio Grande. The condition of our fiscal affairs is encouraging; but, in order to sustain the present measure of public confidence, it is necessary that we practice, not merely customary economy, but, as far as possible, severe retrenchment.

In addition to the objections already stated, the fifth section of the bill proposes to take away land from its former owners without any legal proceedings being first had, contrary to that provision of the Constitution which declares that no person shall "be deprived of life, liberty, or property without due process of law." It does not appear that a part of the lands to which this section refers may not be owned by minors, or persons of unsound mind, or by those who have been faithful to all their obligations as citizens of the United States. If any portion of the land is held by such persons, it is not competent for any authority to deprive them of it. If, on the other hand, it be found that the property is liable to confiscation, even then it cannot be appropriated to public purposes until, by due process of law, it shall have been declared forfeited to the government.

There is still further objection to the bill on grounds seriously affecting the class of persons to whom it is designed to bring relief. It will tend to keep the mind of the freedman in a state of uncertain expectation and restlessness, while to those among whom he lives it will be a source of constant and vague apprehension.

Undoubtedly the freedman should be protected, but he should be protected by the civil authorities, especially by the exercise of all the constitutional powers of the courts of the United States and of the States. His condition is not so exposed as may at first be imagined. He is in a portion of the country where his labor cannot well be spared. Competition for his services from planters, from those who are constructing or repairing railroads, and from capitalists in his vicinage or from other States, will enable him to command almost his own terms. He also possesses a perfect right to change his place of abode, and if, therefore, he does not find in one community or State a mode of life suited to his desires, or proper remuneration for his labor, he can move to another where that labor is more esteemed and better rewarded. In truth, however, each State, induced by its own wants and interests, will do what is necessary and proper to retain within its borders all the labor that is needed for the development of its resources. The laws that regulate supply and demand will maintain their force, and the wages of the laborer will be regulated thereby. There is no danger that the exceedingly great demand for labor will not operate in favor of the laborer.

Neither is sufficient consideration given to the ability of the freedmen to protect and take care of themselves. It is no more than justice to them to believe that as they have received their freedom with moderation and forbearance, so they will distinguish themselves by their industry and thrift, and soon show the world that in a condition of freedom they are self-sustaining, capable of selecting their own employment and their own places of abode, of insisting for themselves on a proper remuneration, and of establishing and maintaining their own asylumns and schools. It is earnestly hoped that, instead of wasting away, they will, by their own efforts, establish for themselves a condition of respectability and prosperity. It is certain that they can attain to that condition only through their own merits and exertions.

In this connexion the query presents itself whether the system proposed by the bill will not, when put into complete operation, practically transfer the entire care, support, and control of four millions of emancipated slaves to agents, overseers, or task-masters, who, appointed at Washington, are to be located in every county and parish throughout the United States containing freedmen and refugees? Such a system would inevitably tend to a concentration of power in the Executive, which would enable him, if so disposed, to control the action of this numerous class, and use them for the attainment of his own political ends.

I cannot but add another very grave objection to this bill. The Constitution imperatively declares, in connexion with taxation, that each State SHALL have at least one representative, and fixes the rule for the number to which, in future times, each State shall be entitled. It also provides that the Senate of the United States SHALL be composed of two senators from each State; and adds, with peculiar force, "that no State, without its consent, shall be deprived of its equal suffrage in the Senate." The original act was necessarily passed in the absence of the States chiefly to be affected, because their people were then contumaciously engaged in the rebellion. Now the case is changed, and some, at least, of those

States are attending Congress by loyal representatives, soliciting the allowance of the constitutional right of representation. At the time, however, of the consideration and the passing of this bill, there was no senator or representative in Congress from the eleven States which are to be mainly affected by its provisions. The very fact that reports were and are made against the good disposition of the people of that portion of the country is an additional reason why they need, and should have, representatives of their own in Congress, to explain their condition, reply to accusations, and assist, by their local knowledge, in the perfecting of measures immediately affecting themselves. While the liberty of deliberation would then be free, and Congress would have full power to decide according to its judgment, there could be no objection urged that the States most interested had not been permitted to be heard. The principle is firmly fixed in the minds of the American people, that there should be no taxation without representation. Great burdens have now to be borne by all the country, and we may best demand that they shall be borne without murmur when they are voted by a majority of the representatives of all the people. I would not interfere with the unquestionable right of Congress to judge, each house for itself, "of the elections, returns, and qualifications of its own members." But that authority cannot be construed as including the right to shut out, in time of peace, any State from the representation to which it is entitled by the Constitution. At present all the people of eleven States are excluded—those who were most faithful during the war not less than others. The State of Tennessee, for instance, whose authorities engaged in rebellion, was restored to all her constitutional relations to the Union by the patriotism and energy of her injured and betrayed people. Before the war was brought to a termination they had placed themselves in relations with the general government, had established a State government of their own, and, as they were not included in the emancipation proclamation, they, by their own act, had amended their constitution so as to abolish slavery within the limits of their State. I know no reason why the State of Tennessee, for example, should not fully enjoy "all her constitutional relations to the United States."

The President of the United States stands towards the country in a somewhat different attitude from that of any member of Congress. Each member of Congress is chosen from a single district or State; the President is chosen by the people of all the States. As eleven States are not at this time represented in either branch of Congress, it would seem to be

his duty, on all proper occasions to present their just claims to Congress. There always will be differences of opinion in the community, and individuals may be guilty of transgressions of the law, but these do not constitute valid objections against the right of a State to representation. I would in nowise interfere with the discretion of Congress with regard to the qualifications of members; but I hold it my duty to recommend to you, in the interests of peace and in the interests of Union, the admission of every State to its share in public legislation, when, however insubordinate, insurgent, or rebellious its people may have been, it presents itself not only in an attitude of loyalty and harmony, but in the persons of representatives whose loyalty cannot be questioned under any existing constitutional or legal test. It is plain that an indefinite or permanent exclusion of any part of the country from representation must be attended by a spirit of disquiet and complaint. It is unwise and dangerous to pursue a course of measures which will unite a very large section of the country against another section of the country, however much the latter may preponderate. The course of emigration, the development of industry and business, and natural causes, will raise up at the south men as devoted to the Union as those of any other part of the land. But if they are all excluded from Congress; if, in a permanent statute, they are declared not to be in full constitutional relations to the country, they may think they have cause to become a unit in feeling and sentiment against the government. Under the political education of the American people, the idea is inherent and ineradicable that the consent of the majority of the whole people is necessary to secure a willing acquiescence in legislation.

The bill under consideration refers to certain of the States as though they had not "been fully restored in all their constitutional relations to the United States." If they have not, let us at once act together to secure that desirable end at the earliest possible moment. It is hardly necessary for me to inform Congress that in my own judgment most of those States, so far at least as depends upon their own action, have already been fully restored, and are to be deemed as entitled to enjoy their constitutional rights as members of the Union. Reasoning from the Constitution itself, and from the actual situation of the country, I feel not only entitled but bound to assume, that with the federal courts restored, and those of the several States in the full exercise of their functions, the rights and interests of all classes of the people will, with the aid of the military in cases of resistance to the laws, be essentially protected against unconstitutional infringement or violation. Should this expectation unhappily fail, which I do not anticipate, then the Executive is already fully armed with the powers conferred by the act of March, 1865, establishing the Freedmen's Bureau, and hereafter, as heretofore, he can employ the land and naval forces of the country to suppress insurrection or to overcome obstructions to the laws.

In accordance with the Constitution I return the bill to the Senate, in the earnest hope that a measure involving questions and interests so important to the country will not become a law, unless upon deliberate consideration by the people it shall receive the sanction of an enlightened public judgment.

ANDREW JOHNSON.
Washington, *February* 19, 1866.

Civil Rights Act

April 9, 1866

An Act to protect all Persons in the United States in their Civil Rights, and furnish the Means of their Vindication.

Be it enacted by the Senate and House of Representatives of the United States of America in Congress assembled, That all persons born in the United States and not subject to any foreign power, excluding Indians not taxed, are hereby declared to be citizens of the United States; and such citizens, of every race and color, without regard to any previous condition of slavery or involuntary servitude, except as a punishment for crime whereof the party shall have been duly convicted, shall have the same right, in every State and Territory in the United States, to make and enforce contracts, to sue, be parties, and give evidence, to inherit, purchase, lease, sell, hold, and convey real and personal property, and to full and equal benefit of all laws and proceedings for the security of person and property, as is enjoyed by white citizens, and shall be subject to like punishment, pains, and penalties, and to none other, any law, statute, ordinance, regulation, or custom, to the contrary notwithstanding.

Sec. 2. *And be it further enacted,* That any person who, under color of any law, statute, ordinance, regulation, or custom, shall subject, or cause to be subjected, any inhabitant of any State or Territory to the deprivation of any right secured or protected by this act, or to different punishment, pains, or penalties on account of such person having at any time

been held in a condition of slavery or involuntary servitude, except as a punishment for crime whereof the party shall have been duly convicted, or by reason of his color or race, than is prescribed for the punishment of white persons, shall be deemed guilty of a misdemeanor, and, on conviction, shall be punished by fine not exceeding one thousand dollars, or imprisonment not exceeding one year, or both, in the discretion of the court.

Sec. 3. *And be it further enacted,* That the district courts of the United States, within their respective districts, shall have, exclusively of the courts of the several States, cognizance of all crimes and offences committed against the provisions of this act, and also, concurrently with the circuit courts of the United States, of all causes, civil and criminal, affecting persons who are denied or cannot enforce in the courts or judicial tribunals of the State or locality where they may be any of the rights secured to them by the first section of this act; and if any suit or prosecution, civil or criminal, has been or shall be commenced in any State court, against any such person, for any cause whatsoever, or against any officer, civil or military, or other person, for any arrest or imprisonment, trespasses, or wrongs done or committed by virtue or under color of authority derived from this act or the act establishing a Bureau for the relief of Freedmen and Refugees, and all acts amendatory thereof, or for refusing to do any act upon the ground that it would be inconsistent with this act, such defendant shall have the right to remove such cause for trial to the proper district or circuit court in the manner prescribed by the "Act relating to habeas corpus and regulating judicial proceedings in certain cases," approved March three, eighteen hundred and sixty-three, and all acts amendatory thereof. The jurisdiction in civil and criminal matters hereby conferred on the district and circuit courts of the United States shall be exercised and enforced in conformity with the laws of the United States, so far as such laws are suitable to carry the same into effect; but in all cases where such laws are not adapted to the object, or are deficient in the provisions necessary to furnish suitable remedies and punish offences against law, the common law, as modified and changed by the constitution and statutes of the State wherein the court having jurisdiction of the cause, civil or criminal, is held, so far as the same is not inconsistent with the Constitution and laws of the United States, shall be extended to and govern said courts in the trial and disposition of such cause, and, if of a criminal nature, in the infliction of punishment on the party found guilty.

Sec. 4. *And be it further enacted,* That the district attorneys, marshals, and deputy marshals of the United States, the commissioners appointed by the circuit and territorial courts of the United States, with powers of arresting, imprisoning, or bailing offenders against the laws of the United States, the officers and agents of the Freedmen's Bureau, and every other officer who may be specially empowered by the President of the United States, shall be, and they are hereby, specially authorized and required, at the expense of the United States, to institute proceedings against all and every person who shall violate the provisions of this act, and cause him or them to be arrested and imprisoned, or bailed, as the case may be, for trial before such court of the United States or territorial court as by this act has cognizance of the offence. And with a view to affording reasonable protection to all persons in their constitutional rights of equality before the law, without distinction of race or color, or previous condition of slavery or involuntary servitude, except as a punishment for crime, whereof the party shall have been duly convicted, and to the prompt discharge of the duties of this act, it shall be the duty of the circuit courts of the United States and the superior courts of the Territories of the United States, from time to time, to increase the number of commissioners, so as to afford a speedy and convenient means for the arrest and examination of persons charged with a violation of this act; and such commissioners are hereby authorized and required to exercise and discharge all the powers and duties conferred on them by this act, and the same duties with regard to offences created by this act, as they are authorized by law to exercise with regard to other offences against the laws of the United States.

SEC. 5. *And be it further enacted,* That it shall be the duty of all marshals and deputy marshals to obey and execute all warrants and precepts issued under the provisions of this act, when to them directed; and should any marshal or deputy marshal refuse to receive such warrant or other process when tendered, or to use all proper means diligently to execute the same, he shall, on conviction thereof, be fined in the sum of one thousand dollars, to the use of the person upon whom the accused is alleged to have committed the offence. And the better to enable the said commissioners to execute their duties faithfully and efficiently, in conformity with the Constitution of the United States and the requirements of this act, they are hereby authorized and empowered, within their counties respectively, to appoint, in writing, under their hands, any one or more suitable persons, from time to time, to execute all such warrants and other process as may be is-

sued by them in the lawful performance of their respective duties; and the persons so appointed to execute any warrant or process as aforesaid shall have authority to summon and call to their aid the bystanders or posse comitatus of the proper county, or such portion of the land or naval forces of the United States, or of the militia, as may be necessary to the performance of the duty with which they are charged, and to insure a faithful observance of the clause of the Constitution which prohibits slavery, in conformity with the provisions of this act; and said warrants shall run and be executed by said officers anywhere in the State or Territory within which they are issued.

SEC. 6. *And be it further enacted,* That any person who shall knowingly and wilfully obstruct, hinder, or prevent any officer, or other person charged with the execution of any warrant or process issued under the provisions of this act, or any person or persons lawfully assisting him or them, from arresting any person for whose apprehension such warrant or process may have been issued, or shall rescue or attempt to rescue such person from the custody of the officer, other person or persons, or those lawfully assisting as aforesaid, when so arrested pursuant to the authority herein given and declared, or shall aid, abet, or assist any person so arrested as aforesaid, directly or indirectly, to escape from the custody of the officer or other person legally authorized as aforesaid, or shall harbor or conceal any person for whose arrest a warrant or process shall have been issued as aforesaid, so as to prevent his discovery and arrest after notice or knowledge of the fact that a warrant has been issued for the apprehension of such person, shall, for either of said offences, be subject to a fine not exceeding one thousand dollars, and imprisonment not exceeding six months, by indictment and conviction before the district court of the United States for the district in which said offence may have been committed, or before the proper court of criminal jurisdiction, if committed within any one of the organized Territories of the United States.

SEC. 7. *And be it further enacted,* That the district attorneys, the marshals, their deputies, and the clerks of the said district and territorial courts shall be paid for their services the like fees as may be allowed to them for similar services in other cases; and in all cases where the proceedings are before a commissioner, he shall be entitled to a fee of ten dollars in full for his services in each case, inclusive of all services incident to such arrest and examination. The person or persons authorized to execute the process to be issued by such commissioners for the arrest of offenders against the provisions of this act shall be entitled to a fee of five dollars for each person he or they may arrest and take before any such commissioner as aforesaid, with such other fees as may be deemed reasonable by such commissioner for such other additional services as may be necessarily performed by him or them, such as attending at the examination, keeping the prisoner in custody, and providing him with food and lodging during his detention, and until the final determination of such commissioner, and in general for performing such other duties as may be required in the premises; such fees to be made up in conformity with the fees usually charged by the officers of the courts of justice within the proper district or county, as near as may be practicable, and paid out of the Treasury of the United States on the certificate of the judge of the district within which the arrest is made, and to be recoverable from the defendant as part of the judgment in case of conviction.

SEC. 8. *And be it further enacted,* That whenever the President of the United States shall have reason to believe that offences have been or are likely to be committed against the provisions of this act within any judicial district, it shall be lawful for him, in his discretion, to direct the judge, marshal, and district attorney of such district to attend at such place within the district, and for such time as he may designate, for the purpose of the more speedy arrest and trial of persons charged with a violation of this act; and it shall be the duty of every judge or other officer, when any such requisition shall be received by him, to attend at the place and for the time therein designated.

SEC. 9. *And be it further enacted,* That it shall be lawful for the President of the United States, or such person as he may empower for that purpose, to employ such part of the land or naval forces of the United States, or of the militia, as shall be necessary to prevent the violation and enforce the due execution of this act.

SEC. 10. *And be it further enacted,* That upon all questions of law arising in any cause under the provisions of this act a final appeal may be taken to the Supreme Court of the United States.

SCHUYLER COLFAX,
Speaker of the House of Representatives.
LA FAYETTE S. FOSTER,
President of the Senate, *pro tempore.*

In the Senate of the United States, April 6, 1866.

The President of the United States having returned to the Senate, in which it originated, the bill entitled "An act to protect all persons in the United States in their civil rights, and furnish the means of their vindication," with his objections thereto, the Senate proceeded, in pursuance of the Constitution, to reconsider the same; and,

Resolved, That the said bill do pass, two-thirds of the Senate agreeing to pass the same.

Attest: J. W. FORNEY,
                              Secretary of the Senate.

In the House of Representatives U.S. April 9th, 1866.

The House of Representatives having proceeded, in pursuance of the Constitution, to reconsider the bill entitled "An act to protect all persons in the United States in their civil rights, and furnish the means of their vindication," returned to the Senate by the President of the United States, with his objections, and sent by the Senate to the House of Representatives, with the message of the President returning the bill:

Resolved, That the bill do pass, two-thirds of the House of Representatives agreeing to pass the same.

Attest: EDWARD MCPHERSON, Clerk,
                         by CLINTON LLOYD, Chief Clerk.

First Reconstruction Act of 1867

Veto of the First Reconstruction Act, *Andrew Johnson,* 1867

First Supplements to First Reconstruction Act of 1867

Second Supplements to First Reconstruction Act of 1867

The Radical Republicans—a group committed to an extensive plan of Reconstruction— gained control over both houses of Congress in the elections of 1866. One result was the First Reconstruction Act of 1867, which divided ten former Confederate states into five military-run districts, demanded elections based on universal manhood suffrage, and conditioned readmittance to the Union on ratification of the Fourteenth Amendment. President Andrew Johnson vetoed the bill on the grounds that it overreached Congress's proper role of establishing peace and good order. Congress overrode the veto the same day. Congress also passed supplements to the Reconstruction Act intended to overcome Southern white opposition. These supplemental acts empowered Union military governors to impose election methods and other elemental constitutional reforms in former Confederate states.

First Reconstruction Act of 1867

March 2, 1867

An Act to provide for the more efficient Government of the Rebel States.

WHEREAS no legal State governments or adequate protection for life or property now exists in the rebel States of Virginia, North Carolina, South Carolina, Georgia, Mississippi, Alabama, Louisiana, Florida, Texas, and Arkansas; and whereas it is necessary that peace and good order should be enforced in said States until loyal and republican State governments can be legally established: Therefore,

Be it enacted by the Senate and House of Representatives of the United States of America in Congress assembled, That said rebel States shall be divided into military districts and made subject to the military authority of the United States as hereinafter prescribed, and for that purpose Virginia shall constitute the first district; North Carolina and South Carolina the second district; Georgia, Alabama, and Florida the third district; Mississippi and Arkansas the fourth district; and Louisiana and Texas the fifth district.

SEC. 2. *And be it further enacted,* That it shall be the duty of the President to assign to the command of each of said districts an officer of the army, not below the rank of brigadier-

general, and to detail a sufficient military force to enable such officer to perform his duties and enforce his authority within the district to which he is assigned.

SEC. 3. *And be it further enacted,* That it shall be the duty of each officer assigned as aforesaid, to protect all persons in their rights of person and property, to suppress insurrection, disorder, and violence, and to punish, or cause to be punished, all disturbers of the public peace and criminals; and to this end he may allow local civil tribunals to take jurisdiction of and to try offenders, or, when in his judgment it may be necessary for the trial of offenders, he shall have power to organize military commissions or tribunals for that purpose, and all interference under color of State authority with the exercise of military authority under this act, shall be null and void.

SEC. 4. *And be it further enacted,* That all persons put under military arrest by virtue of this act shall be tried without unnecessary delay, and no cruel or unusual punishment shall be inflicted, and no sentence of any military commission or tribunal hereby authorized, affecting the life or liberty of any person, shall be executed until it is approved by the officer in command of the district, and the laws and regulations for the government of the army shall not be affected by this act, except in so far as they conflict with its provisions: *Provided,* That no sentence of death under the provisions of this act shall be carried into effect without the approval of the President.

SEC. 5. *And be it further enacted,* That when the people of any one of said rebel States shall have formed a constitution of government in conformity with the Constitution of the United States in all respects, framed by a convention of delegates elected by the male citizens of said State, twenty-one years old and upward, of whatever race, color, or previous condition, who have been resident in said State for one year previous to the day of such election, except such as may be disfranchised for participation in the rebellion or for felony at common law, and when such constitution shall provide that the elective franchise shall be enjoyed by all such persons as have the qualifications herein stated for electors of delegates, and when such constitution shall be ratified by a majority of the persons voting on the question of ratification who are qualified as electors for delegates, and when such constitution shall have been submitted to Congress for examination and approval, and Congress shall have approved the same, and when said State, by a vote of its legislature elected under said constitution, shall have adopted the amendment to the Constitution of the United States, proposed by the Thirty-ninth Congress, and known as article fourteen, and when said article shall have become a part of the Constitution of the United States, said State shall be declared entitled to representation in Congress, and senators and representatives shall be admitted therefrom on their taking the oath prescribed by law, and then and thereafter the preceding sections of this act shall be inoperative in said State: *Provided,* That no person excluded from the privilege of holding office by said proposed amendment to the Constitution of the United States, shall be eligible to election as a member of the convention to frame a constitution for any of said rebel States, nor shall any such person vote for members of such convention.

SEC. 6. *And be it further enacted,* That, until the people of said rebel States shall be by law admitted to representation in the Congress of the United States, any civil governments which may exist therein shall be deemed provisional only, and in all respects subject to the paramount authority of the United States at any time to abolish, modify, control, or supersede the same; and in all elections to any office under such provisional governments all persons shall be entitled to vote, and none others, who are entitled to vote, under the provisions of the fifth section of this act; and no person shall be eligible to any office under any such provisional governments who would be disqualified from holding office under the provisions of the third *article* of said constitutional amendment.

SCHUYLER COLFAX,
Speaker of the House of Representatives.
LA FAYETTE S. FOSTER,
President of the Senate, pro tempore.

Veto of the First Reconstruction Act

March 2, 1867

Andrew Johnson

WASHINGTON, *March 2, 1867.*
To the House of Representatives:

I have examined the bill "to provide for the more efficient government of the rebel States" with the care and anxiety which its transcendent importance is calculated to awaken. I am unable to give it my assent, for reasons so grave that I hope a statement of them may have some influence on the minds of the patriotic and enlightened men with whom the decision must ultimately rest.

The bill places all the people of the ten States therein named under the absolute domination of military rulers; and the preamble undertakes to give the reason upon which the measure is based and the ground upon which it is justified. It declares that there exists in those States no legal governments and no adequate protection for life or property, and asserts the necessity of enforcing peace and good order within their limits. Is this true as matter of fact?

It is not denied that the States in question have each of them an actual government, with all the powers—executive, judicial, and legislative—which properly belong to a free state. They are organized like the other States of the Union, and, like them, they make, administer, and execute the laws which concern their domestic affairs. An existing *de facto* government, exercising such functions as these, is itself the law of the state upon all matters within its jurisdiction. To pronounce the supreme law-making power of an established state illegal is to say that law itself is unlawful.

The provisions which these governments have made for the preservation of order, the suppression of crime, and the redress of private injuries are in substance and principle the same as those which prevail in the Northern States and in other civilized countries. They certainly have not succeeded in preventing the commission of all crime, nor has this been accomplished anywhere in the world. There, as well as elsewhere, offenders sometimes escape for want of vigorous prosecution, and occasionally, perhaps, by the inefficiency of courts or the prejudice of jurors. It is undoubtedly true that these evils have been much increased and aggravated, North and South, by the demoralizing influences of civil war and by the rancorous passions which the contest has engendered. But that these people are maintaining local governments for themselves which habitually defeat the object of all government and render their own lives and property insecure is in itself utterly improbable, and the averment of the bill to that effect is not supported by any evidence which has come to my knowledge. All the information I have on the subject convinces me that the masses of the Southern people and those who control their public acts, while they entertain diverse opinions on questions of Federal policy, are completely united in the effort to reorganize their society on the basis of peace and to restore their mutual prosperity as rapidly and as completely as their circumstances will permit.

The bill, however, would seem to show upon its face that the establishment of peace and good order is not its real object. The fifth section declares that the preceding sections shall cease to operate in any State where certain events shall have happened. These events are, first, the selection of delegates to a State convention by an election at which negroes shall be allowed to vote; second, the formation of a State constitution by the convention so chosen; third, the insertion into the State constitution of a provision which will secure the right of voting at all elections to negroes and to such white men as may not be disfranchised for rebellion or felony; fourth, the submission of the constitution for ratification to negroes and white men not disfranchised, and its actual ratification by their vote; fifth, the submission of the State constitution to Congress for examination and approval, and the actual approval of it by that body; sixth, the adoption of a certain amendment to the Federal Constitution by a vote of the legislature elected under the new constitution; seventh, the adoption of said amendment by a sufficient number of other States to make it a part of the Constitution of the United States. All these conditions must be fulfilled before the people of any

of these States can be relieved from the bondage of military domination; but when they are fulfilled, then immediately the pains and penalties of the bill are to cease, no matter whether there be peace and order or not, and without any reference to the security of life or property. The excuse given for the bill in the preamble is admitted by the bill itself not to be real. The military rule which it establishes is plainly to be used, not for any purpose of order or for the prevention of crime, but solely as a means of coercing the people into the adoption of principles and measures to which it is known that they are opposed, and upon which they have an undeniable right to exercise their own judgment.

I submit to Congress whether this measure is not in its whole character, scope, and object without precedent and without authority, in palpable conflict with the plainest provisions of the Constitution, and utterly destructive to those great principles of liberty and humanity for which our ancestors on both sides of the Atlantic have shed so much blood and expended so much treasure.

The ten States named in the bill are divided into five districts. For each district an officer of the Army, not below the rank of a brigadier-general, is to be appointed to rule over the people; and he is to be supported with an efficient military force to enable him to perform his duties and enforce his authority. Those duties and that authority, as defined by the third section of the bill, are "to protect all persons in their rights of person and property, to suppress insurrection, disorder, and violence, and to punish or cause to be punished all disturbers of the public peace or criminals." The power thus given to the commanding officer over all the people of each district is that of an absolute monarch. His mere will is to take the place of all law. The law of the States is now the only rule applicable to the subjects placed under his control, and that is completely displaced by the clause which declares all interference of State authority to be null and void. He alone is permitted to determine what are rights of person or property, and he may protect them in such way as in his discretion may seem proper. It places at his free disposal all the lands and goods in his district, and he may distribute them without let or hindrance to whom he pleases. Being bound by no State law, and there being no other law to regulate the subject, he may make a criminal code of his own; and he can make it as bloody as any recorded in history, or he can reserve the privilege of acting upon the impulse of his private passions in each case that arises. He is bound by no rules of evidence; there is, indeed, no provision by which he is authorized or required to take any evidence at all. Everything is a crime which he chooses to call so, and all persons are condemned whom he pronounces to be guilty. He is not bound to keep any record or make any report of his proceedings. He may arrest his victims wherever he finds them, without warrant, accusation, or proof of probable cause. If he gives them a trial before he inflicts the punishment, he gives it of his grace and mercy, not because he is commanded so to do.

To a casual reader of the bill it might seem that some kind of trial was secured by it to persons accused of crime, but such is not the case. The officer "may allow local civil tribunals to try offenders," but of course this does not require that he shall do so. If any State or Federal court presumes to exercise its legal jurisdiction by the trial of a malefactor without his special permission, he can break it up and punish the judges and jurors as being themselves malefactors. He can save his friends from justice, and despoil his enemies contrary to justice.

It is also provided that "he shall have power to organize military commissions or tribunals"; but this power he is not commanded to exercise. It is merely permissive, and is to be used only "when in his judgment it may be necessary for the trial of offenders." Even if the sentence of a commission were made a prerequisite to the punishment of a party, it would be scarcely the slightest check upon the officer, who has authority to organize it as he pleases, prescribe its mode of proceeding, appoint its members from his own subordinates, and revise all its decisions. Instead of mitigating the harshness of his single rule, such a tribunal would be used much more probably to divide the responsibility of making it more cruel and unjust.

Several provisions dictated by the humanity of Congress have been inserted in the bill, apparently to restrain the power of the commanding officer; but it seems to me that they are of no avail for that purpose. The fourth section provides: First. That trials shall not be unnecessarily delayed; but I think I have shown that the power is given to punish without trial; and if so, this provision is practically inoperative. Second. Cruel or unusual punishment is not to be inflicted; but who is to decide what is cruel and what is unusual? The words have acquired a legal meaning by long use in the courts. Can it be expected that military officers will understand or follow a rule expressed in language so purely technical and not pertaining in the least degree to their profession? If not, then each officer may define cruelty according to his own temper, and if it is not usual he will make it usual. Corporal punishment, imprisonment, the gag, the ball and chain, and all the almost insupportable forms of torture invented for military punishment lie within the range of choice. Third. The sentence of a commission is not to be executed without being approved by the commander, if it affects life or liberty, and a sentence of death must be approved by the President. This applies to cases in which there has been a trial and sentence. I take it to be clear, under this bill, that the military commander may condemn to death without even the form of a trial by a military commission, so that the life of the condemned may depend upon the will of two men instead of one.

It is plain that the authority here given to the military officer amounts to absolute despotism. But to make it still more unendurable, the bill provides that it may be delegated to as many subordinates as he chooses to appoint, for it declares that he shall "punish or cause to be punished." Such a power has not been wielded by any monarch in England for more than five hundred years. In all that time no people who speak the English language have borne such servitude. It reduces the whole population of the ten States—all persons, of every color, sex, and condition, and every stranger within their limits—to the most abject and degrading slavery. No master ever had a control so absolute over the slaves as this bill gives to the military officers over both white and colored persons.

It may be answered to this that the officers of the Army are too magnanimous, just, and humane to oppress and trample upon a subjugated people. I do not doubt that army officers are as well entitled to this kind of confidence as any other class of men. But the history of the world has been written in vain if it does not teach us that unrestrained authority can never be safely trusted in human hands. It is almost sure to be more or less abused under any circumstances, and it has always resulted in gross tyranny where the rulers who exercise it are strangers to their subjects and come among them as the representatives of a distant power, and more especially when the power that sends them is unfriendly. Governments closely resembling that here proposed have been fairly tried in Hungary and Poland, and the suffering endured by those people roused the sympathies of the entire world. It was tried in Ireland, and, though tempered at first by principles of English law, it gave birth to cruelties so atrocious that they are never recounted without just indignation. The French Convention armed its deputies with this power and sent them to the southern departments of the Republic. The massacres, murders, and other atrocities which they committed show what the passions of the ablest men in the most civilized society will tempt them to do when wholly unrestrained by law.

The men of our race in every age have struggled to tie up the hands of their governments and keep them within the law, because their own experience of all mankind taught them that rulers could not be relied on to concede those rights which they were not legally bound to respect. The head of a great empire has sometimes governed it with a mild and paternal sway, but the kindness of an irresponsible deputy never yields what the law does not extort from him. Between such a master and the people subjected to his domination there can be nothing but enmity; he punishes them if they resist his authority, and if they submit to it he hates them for their servility.

I come now to a question which is, if possible, still more important. Have we the power to establish and carry into execution a measure like this? I answer, Certainly not, if we derive our authority from the Constitution and if we are bound by the limitations which it imposes.

This proposition is perfectly clear, that no branch of the Federal Government—executive, legislative, or judicial—can have any just powers except those which it derives through and exercises under the organic law of the Union. Outside of the Constitution we have no legal authority more than private citizens, and within it we have only so much as that instrument gives us. This broad principle limits all our functions and applies to all subjects. It protects not only the citizens of States which are within the Union, but it shields every human being who comes or is brought under our jurisdiction. We have no right to do in one place more than in another that which the Constitution says we shall not do at all. If, therefore, the Southern States were in truth out of the Union, we could not treat their people in a way which the fundamental law forbids.

Some persons assume that the success of our arms in crushing the opposition which was made in some of the States to the execution of the Federal laws reduced those States and all their people—the innocent as well as the guilty—to the condition of vassalage and gave us a power over them which the Constitution does not bestow or define or limit. No fallacy can be more transparent than this. Our victories subjected the insurgents to legal obedience, not to the yoke of an arbitrary despotism. When an absolute sovereign reduces his rebellious subjects, he may deal with them according to his pleasure, because he had that power before. But when a limited monarch puts down an insurrection, he must still govern according to law. If an insurrection should take place in one of our States against the authority of the State government and end in the

overthrow of those who planned it, would that take away the rights of all the people of the counties where it was favored by a part or a majority of the population? Could they for such a reason be wholly outlawed and deprived of their representation in the legislature? I have always contended that the Government of the United States was sovereign within its constitutional sphere; that it executed its laws, like the States themselves, by applying its coercive power directly to individuals, and that it could put down insurrection with the same effect as a State and no other. The opposite doctrine is the worst heresy of those who advocated secession, and can not be agreed to without admitting that heresy to be right.

Invasion, insurrection, rebellion, and domestic violence were anticipated when the Government was framed, and the means of repelling and suppressing them were wisely provided for in the Constitution; but it was not thought necessary to declare that the States in which they might occur should be expelled from the Union. Rebellions, which were invariably suppressed, occurred prior to that out of which these questions grow; but the States continued to exist and the Union remained unbroken. In Massachusetts, in Pennsylvania, in Rhode Island, and in New York, at different periods in our history, violent and armed opposition to the United States was carried on; but the relations of those States with the Federal Government were not supposed to be interrupted or changed thereby after the rebellious portions of their population were defeated and put down. It is true that in these earlier cases there was no formal expression of a determination to withdraw from the Union, but it is also true that in the Southern States the ordinances of secession were treated by all the friends of the Union as mere nullities and are now acknowledged to be so by the States themselves. If we admit that they had any force or validity or that they did in fact take the States in which they were passed out of the Union, we sweep from under our feet all the grounds upon which we stand in justifying the use of Federal force to maintain the integrity of the Government.

This is a bill passed by Congress in time of peace. There is not in any one of the States brought under its operation either war or insurrection. The laws of the States and of the Federal Government are all in undisturbed and harmonious operation. The courts, State and Federal, are open and in the full exercise of their proper authority. Over every State comprised in these five military districts, life, liberty, and property are secured by State laws and Federal laws, and the National Constitution is everywhere in force and everywhere obeyed.

What, then, is the ground on which this bill proceeds? The title of the bill announces that it is intended "for the more efficient government" of these ten States. It is recited by way of preamble that no legal State governments "nor adequate protection for life or property" exist in those States, and that peace and good order should be thus enforced. The first thing which arrests attention upon these recitals, which prepare the way for martial law, is this, that the only foundation upon which martial law can exist under our form of government is not stated or so much as pretended. Actual war, foreign invasion, domestic insurrection—none of these appear; and none of these, in fact, exist. It is not even recited that any sort of war or insurrection is threatened. Let us pause here to consider, upon this question of constitutional law and the power of Congress, a recent decision of the Supreme Court of the United States in *ex parte* Milligan.

I will first quote from the opinion of the majority of the court:

Martial law can not arise from a threatened invasion. The necessity must be actual and present, the invasion real, such as effectually closes the courts and deposes the civil administration.

We see that martial law comes in only when actual war closes the courts and deposes the civil authority; but this bill, in time of peace, makes martial law operate as though we were in actual war, and becomes the *cause* instead of the *consequence* of the abrogation of civil authority. One more quotation:

It follows from what has been said on this subject that there are occasions when martial law can be properly applied. If in foreign invasion or civil war the courts are actually closed, and it is impossible to administer criminal justice according to law, *then,* on the theater of active military operations, where war really prevails, there is a necessity to furnish a substitute for the civil authority thus overthrown, to preserve the safety of the army and society; and as no power is left but the military, it is allowed to govern by martial rule until the laws can have their free course.

I now quote from the opinion of the minority of the court, delivered by Chief Justice Chase:

We by no means assert that Congress can establish and apply the laws of war where no war has been declared or exists. Where peace exists, the laws of peace must prevail.

This is sufficiently explicit. Peace exists in all the territory to which this bill applies. It asserts a power in Congress in time of peace, to set aside the laws of peace and to substitute the laws of war. The minority, concurring with the majority, declares that Congress does not possess that power. Again, and, if possible, more emphatically, the Chief Justice, with remarkable clearness and condensation, sums up the whole matter as follows:

There are under the Constitution three kinds of military jurisdiction—one to be exercised both in peace and war; another to be exercised in time of foreign war without the boundaries of the United States, or in time of rebellion and civil war within States or districts occupied by rebels treated as belligerents; and a third to be exercised in time of invasion or insurrection within the limits of the United States, or during rebellion within the limits of the States maintaining adhesion to the National Government, when the public danger requires its exercise. The first of these may be called jurisdiction under military law, and is found in acts of Congress prescribing rules and articles of war or otherwise providing for the government of the national forces; the second may be distinguished as military government, superseding as far as may be deemed expedient the local law, and exercised by the military commander under the direction of the President, with the express or implied sanction of Congress; while the third may be denominated martial law proper, and is called into action by Congress, or temporarily, when the action of Congress can not be invited, and in the case of justifying or excusing peril, by the President, in times of insurrection or invasion or of civil or foreign war, within districts or localities where ordinary law no longer adequately secures public safety and private rights.

It will be observed that of the three kinds of military jurisdiction which can be exercised or created under our Constitution there is but one that can prevail in time of peace, and that is the code of laws enacted by Congress for the government of the national forces. That body of military law has no application to the citizen, nor even to the citizen soldier enrolled in the militia in time of peace. But this bill is not a part of that sort of military law, for that applies only to the soldier and not to the citizen, whilst, contrariwise, the military law provided by this bill applies only to the citizen and not to the solider.

I need not say to the representatives of the American people that their Constitution forbids the exercise of judicial power in any way but one—that is, by the ordained and established courts. It is equally well known that in all criminal cases a trial by jury is made indispensable by the express words of that instrument. I will not enlarge on the inestimable value of the right thus secured to every freeman or speak of the danger to public liberty in all parts of the country which must ensue from a denial of it anywhere or upon any pretense. A very recent decision of the Supreme Court has traced the history, vindicated the dignity, and made known the value of this great privilege so clearly that nothing more is needed. To what extent a violation of it might be excused in time of war or public danger may admit of discussion, but we are providing now for a time of profound peace, when there is not an armed soldier within our borders except those who are in the service of the Government. It is in such a condition of things that an act of Congress is proposed which if carried out, would deny a trial by the lawful courts and juries to 9,000,000 American citizens and to their posterity for an indefinite period. It seems to be scarcely possible that anyone should seriously believe this consistent with a Constitution which declares in simple, plain, and unambiguous language that all persons shall have that right and that no person shall ever in any case be deprived of it. The Constitution also forbids the arrest of the citizen without judicial warrant, founded on probable cause. This bill authorizes an arrest without warrant, at the pleasure of a military commander. The Constitution declares that "no person shall be held to answer for a capital or otherwise infamous crime unless on presentment by a grand jury." This bill holds every person not a soldier answerable for all crimes and all charges without any presentment. The Constitution declares that "no person shall be deprived of life, liberty, or property without due process of law." This bill sets aside all process of law, and makes the citizen answerable in his person and property to the will of one man, and as to his life to the will of two. Finally, the Constitution declares that "the privilege of the writ of *habeas corpus* shall not be suspended unless when, in case of rebellion or invasion, the public safety may require it"; whereas this bill declares martial law (which of itself suspends this great writ) in time of peace, and authorizes the military to make the arrest, and gives to the prisoner only one privilege, and that is a trial "without unnecessary delay." He has no hope of release from custody, except the hope, such as it is, of release by acquittal before a military commission.

The United States are bound to guarantee to each State a republican form of government. Can it be pretended that this obligation is not palpably broken if we carry out a measure like this, which wipes away every vestige of republican government in ten States and puts the life, property, liberty, and honor of all the people in each of them under the domination of a single person clothed with unlimited authority?

The Parliament of England, exercising the omnipotent power which it claimed, was accustomed to pass bills of attainder; that is to say, it would convict men of treason and other crimes by legislative enactment. The person accused had a hearing, sometimes a patient and fair one, but generally party prejudice prevailed instead of justice. It often became necessary for Parliament to acknowledge its error and reverse its own action. The fathers of our country determined that no such thing should occur here. They withheld the power from Congress, and thus forbade its exercise by that body, and they provided in the Constitution that no State should pass any bill of attainder. It is therefore impossible for any person in this country to be constitutionally convicted or punished for any crime by a legislative proceeding of any sort. Nevertheless, here is a bill of attainder against 9,000,000 people at once. It is based upon an accusation so vague as to be scarcely intelligible and found to be true upon no credible evidence. Not one of the 9,000,000 was heard in his own defense. The representatives of the doomed parties were excluded from all participation in the trial. The conviction is to be followed by the most ignominious punishment ever inflicted on large masses of men. It disfranchises them by hundreds of thousands and degrades them all, even those who are admitted to be guiltless, from the rank of freemen to the condition of slaves.

The purpose and object of the bill—the general intent which pervades it from beginning to end—is to change the entire structure and character of the State governments and to compel them by force to the adoption of organic laws and regulations which they are unwilling to accept if left to themselves. The negroes have not asked for the privilege of voting; the vast majority of them have no idea what it means. This bill not only thrusts it into their hands, but compels them, as well as the whites, to use it in a particular way. If they do not form a constitution with prescribed articles in it and afterwards elect a legislature which will act upon certain measures in a prescribed way, neither blacks nor whites can be relieved from the slavery which the bill imposes upon them. Without pausing here to consider the policy or impolicy of Africanizing the southern part of our territory, I would simply ask the attention of Congress to that manifest, well-known, and universally acknowledged rule of constitutional law which declares that the Federal Government has no jurisdiction, authority, or power to regulate such subjects for any State. To force the right of suffrage out of the hands of the white people and into the hands of the negroes is an arbitrary violation of this principle.

This bill imposes martial law at once, and its operations will begin so soon as the general and his troops can be put in place. The dread alternative between its harsh rule and compliance with the terms of this measure is not suspended, nor are the people afforded any time for free deliberation. The bill says to them, take martial law first, *then* deliberate. And when they have done all that this measure requires them to do other conditions and contingencies over which they have no control yet remain to be fulfilled before they can be relieved from martial law. Another Congress must first approve the Constitution made in conformity with the will of this Congress and must declare these States entitled to representation in both Houses. The whole question thus remains open and unsettled and must again occupy the attention of Congress; and in the meantime, the agitation which now prevails will continue to disturb all portions of the people.

The bill also denies the legality of the governments of ten of the States which participated in the ratification of the amendment to the Federal Constitution abolishing slavery forever within the jurisdiction of the United States and practically excludes them from the Union. If this assumption of the bill be correct, their concurrence can not be considered as having been legally given, and the important fact is made to appear that the consent of three-fourths of the States—the requisite number—has not been constitutionally obtained to the ratification of that amendment, thus leaving the question of slavery where it stood before the amendment was officially declared to have become a part of the Constitution.

That the measure proposed by this bill does violate the Constitution in the particulars mentioned and in many other ways which I forbear to enumerate is too clear to admit of the least doubt. It only remains to consider whether the injunctions of that instrument ought to be obeyed or not. I think they ought to be obeyed, for reasons which I will proceed to give as briefly as possible.

In the first place, it is the only system of free government which we can hope to have as a nation. When it ceases to be the rule of our conduct, we may perhaps take our choice between complete anarchy, a consolidated despotism, and a to-tal dissolution of the Union; but national liberty regulated by law will have passed beyond our reach.

It is the best frame of government the world ever saw. No other is or can be so well adapted to the genius, habits, or wants of the American people. Combining the strength of a great empire with unspeakable blessings of local self-government, having a central power to defend the general interests, and recognizing the authority of the States as the guardians of industrial rights, it is "the sheet anchor of our safety abroad and our peace at home." It was ordained "to form a more perfect union, establish justice, insure domestic tranquillity, promote the general welfare, provide for the common defense, and secure the blessings of liberty to ourselves and to our posterity." These great ends have been attained heretofore, and will be again by faithful obedience to it; but they are certain to be lost if we treat with disregard its sacred obligations.

It was to punish the gross crime of defying the Constitution and to vindicate its supreme authority that we carried on a bloody war of four years' duration. Shall we now acknowledge that we sacrificed a million of lives and expended billions of treasure to enforce a Constitution which is not worthy of respect and preservation?

Those who advocated the right of secession alleged in their own justification that we had no regard for law and that their rights of property, life, and liberty would not be safe under the Constitution as administered by us. If we now verify their assertion, we prove that they were in truth and in fact fighting for their liberty, and instead of branding their leaders with the dishonoring name of traitors against a righteous and legal government we elevate them in history to the rank of self-sacrificing patriots, consecrate them to the admiration of the world, and place them by the side of Washington, Hampden, and Sidney. No; let us leave them to the infamy they deserve, punish them as they should be punished, according to law, and take upon ourselves no share of the odium which they should bear alone.

It is a part of our public history which can never be forgotten that both Houses of Congress, in July, 1861, declared in the form of a solemn resolution that the war was and should be carried on for no purpose of subjugation, but solely to enforce the Constitution and laws, and that when this was yielded by the parties in rebellion the contest should cease, with the constitutional rights of the States and of individuals unimpaired. This resolution was adopted and sent forth to the world unanimously by the Senate and with only two dissenting voices in the House. It was accepted by the friends of the Union in the South as well as in the North as expressing honestly and truly the object of the war. On the faith of it many thousands of persons in both sections gave their lives and their fortunes to the cause. To repudiate it now by refusing to the States and to the individuals within them the rights which the Constitution and laws of the Union would secure to them is a breach of our plighted honor for which I can imagine no excuse and to which I can not voluntarily become a party.

The evils which spring from the unsettled state of our Government will be acknowledged by all. Commercial intercourse is impeded, capital is in constant peril, public securities fluctuate in value, peace itself is not secure, and the sense of moral and political duty is impaired. To avert these calamities from our country it is imperatively required that we should immediately decide upon some course of administration which can be steadfastly adhered to. I am thoroughly convinced that any settlement or compromise or plan of action which is inconsistent with the principles of the Constitution will not only be unavailing, but mischievous; that it will but multiply the present evils, instead of removing them. The Constitution, in its whole integrity and vigor, throughout the length and breadth of the land, is the best of all compromises. Besides, our duty does not, in my judgment, leave us a choice between that and any other. I believe that it contains the remedy that is so much needed, and that if the coordinate branches of the Government would unite upon its provisions they would be found broad enough and strong enough to sustain in time of peace the nation which they bore safely through the ordeal of a protracted civil war. Among the most sacred guaranties of that instrument are those which declare that "each State shall have at least one Representative," and that "no State, without its consent, shall be deprived of its equal suffrage in the Senate." Each House is made the "judge of the elections, returns, and qualifications of its own members," and may, "with the concurrence of two-thirds, expel a member." Thus, as heretofore urged, "in the admission of Senators and Representatives from any and all of the States there can be no just ground of apprehension that persons who are disloyal will be clothed with the powers of legislation, for this could not happen when the Constitution and the laws are enforced by a vigilant and faithful Congress." "When a Senator or Representative presents his certificate of election, he may at once be admitted or rejected; or, should there be any question as to his eligibility, his credentials may be referred for investigation to the appropriate committee. If admitted to a seat, it must be upon evidence satisfactory to the House of which he thus becomes a member that he possesses the requisite constitutional and legal qualifications. If refused admission as a member for want of due allegiance to the Government, and returned to his constituents, they are admonished that none but persons loyal to the United States will be allowed a voice in the legislative councils of the nation, and the political power and moral influence of Congress are thus effectively exerted in the interests of loyalty to the Government and fidelity to the Union." And is it not far better that the work of restoration should be accomplished by simple compliance with the plain requirements of the Constitution than by a recourse to measures which in effect destroy the States and threaten the subversion of the General Government? All that is necessary to settle this simple but important question without further agitation or delay is a willingness on the part of all to sustain the Constitution and carry its provisions into practical operation. If to-morrow either branch of Congress would declare that upon the presentation of their credentials members constitutionally elected and loyal to the General Government would be admitted to seats in Congress, while all others would be excluded and their places remain vacant until the selection by the people of loyal and qualified persons, and if at the same time assurance were given that this policy would be continued until all the States were represented in Congress, it would send a thrill of joy throughout the entire land, as indicating the inauguration of a system which must speedily bring tranquillity to the public mind.

While we are legislating upon subjects which are of great importance to the whole people, and which must affect all parts of the country, not only during the life of the present generation, but for ages to come, we should remember that all men are entitled at least to a hearing in the councils which decide upon the destiny of themselves and their children. At present ten States are denied representation, and when the Fortieth Congress assembles on the 4th day of the present month sixteen States will be without a voice in the House of Representatives. This grave fact, with the important questions before us, should induce us to pause in a course of legislation which, looking solely to the attainment of political ends, fails to consider the rights it transgresses, the law which it violates, or the institutions which it imperils.

ANDREW JOHNSON

First Supplement to the First Reconstruction Act of 1867

March 23, 1867

An Act supplementary to an Act entitled "An Act to provide for the more efficient Government of the Rebel States," passed March second, eighteen hundred and sixty-seven, and to facilitate Restoration.

Be it enacted by the Senate and House of Representatives of the United States of America in Congress assembled, That before the first day of September, eighteen hundred and sixty-seven, the commanding general in each district defined by an act entitled "An act to provide for the more efficient government of the rebel States," passed March second, eighteen hundred and sixty-seven, shall cause a registration to be made of the male citizens of the United States, twenty-one years of age and upwards, resident in each county or parish in the State or States included in his district, which registration shall include only those persons who are qualified to vote for delegates by the act aforesaid, and who shall have taken and subscribed the following oath or affirmation: "I, ———, do solemnly swear (or affirm), in the presence of Almighty God, that I am a citizen of the State of ———; that I have resided in said State for ——— months next preceding this day, and now reside in the county of ———, or the parish of ———, in said State (as the case may be); that I am twenty-one years old; that I have not been disfranchised for participation in any rebellion or civil war against the United States, nor for felony committed against the laws of any State or of the United States; that I have never been a member of any State legislature, nor held any executive or judicial office in any State and afterwards engaged in insurrection or rebellion against the United States, or given aid or comfort to the enemies thereof; that I have never taken an oath as a member of Congress of the United States, or as an officer of the United States, or as a member of any State legislature, or as an executive or judicial officer of any State, to support the Constitution of the United States, and afterwards engaged in insurrection or rebellion against the United States, or given aid or comfort to the enemies thereof; that I will faithfully support the Constitution and obey the laws of the United States, and will, to the best of my ability, encourage others so to do, so help me God"; which oath or affirmation may be administered by any registering officer.

SEC. 2. *And be it further enacted,* That after the completion of the registration hereby provided for in any State, at such time and places therein as the commanding general shall appoint and direct, of which at least thirty days' public notice shall be given, an election shall be held of delegates to a convention for the purpose of establishing a constitution and civil government for such State loyal to the Union, said convention in each State, except Virginia, to consist of the same number of members as the most numerous branch of the State legislature of such State in the year eighteen hundred and sixty, to be apportioned among the several districts, counties, or parishes of such State by the commanding general, giving to each representation in the ratio of voters registered as aforesaid as nearly as may be. The convention in Virginia shall consist of the same number of members as represented the territory now constituting Virginia in the most numerous branch of the legislature of said State in the year eighteen hundred and sixty, to be apportioned as aforesaid.

SEC. 3. *And be it further enacted,* That at said election the registered voters of each State shall vote for or against a convention to form a constitution therefor under this act. Those voting in favor of such a convention shall have written or printed on the ballots by which they vote for delegates, as aforesaid, the words "For a convention," and those voting against such a convention shall have written or printed on such ballots the words "Against a convention." The persons appointed to superintend said election, and to make return of the votes given thereat, as herein provided, shall count and make return of the votes given for and against a convention; and the commanding general to whom the same shall have been returned shall ascertain and declare the total vote in each State for and against a convention. If a majority of the votes given on that question shall be for a convention, then such convention shall be held as hereinafter provided; but if a majority of said votes shall be against a convention, then no such convention shall be held under this act: *Provided,* That such convention shall not be held unless a majority of all such registered voters shall have voted on the question of holding such convention.

SEC. 4. *And be it further enacted,* That the commanding general of each district shall appoint as many boards of registration as may be necessary, consisting of three loyal officers or persons, to make and complete the registration, superintend the election, and make return to him of the votes, list of voters, and of the persons elected as delegates by a plurality of the votes cast at said election; and upon receiving said returns he shall open the same, ascertain the persons elected as delegates, according to the returns of the officers who conducted said election, and make proclamation thereof; and if a majority of the votes given on that question shall be for a convention, the commanding general, within sixty days from the date of election, shall notify the delegates to assemble in convention, at a time and place to be mentioned in the notification, and said convention, when organized, shall proceed to frame a constitution and civil government according to the provisions of this act, and the act to which it is supplementary; and when the same shall have been so framed, said constitution shall be submitted by the convention for ratification to the persons registered under the provisions of this act at an election to be conducted by the officers or persons appointed or to be appointed by the commanding general, as hereinbefore provided, and to be held after the expiration of thirty days from the date of notice thereof, to be given by said convention; and the returns thereof shall be made to the commanding general of the district.

SEC. 5. *And be it further enacted,* That if, according to said returns, the constitution shall be ratified by a majority of the votes of the registered electors qualified as herein specified, cast at said election, at least one half of all the registered voters voting upon the question of such ratification, the president of the convention shall transmit a copy of the same, duly certified, to the President of the United States, who shall forthwith transmit the same to Congress, if then in session, and if not in session, then immediately upon its next assembling; and if it shall moreover appear to Congress that the election was one at which all the registered and qualified electors in the State had an opportunity to vote freely and without restraint, fear, or the influence of fraud, and if the Congress shall be satisfied that such constitution meets the approval of a majority of all the qualified electors in the State, and if the said constitution shall be declared by Congress to be in conformity with the provisions of the act to which this is supplementary, and the other provisions of said act shall have been complied with, and the said constitution shall be approved by Congress, the State shall be declared entitled to representation, and senators and representatives shall be admitted therefrom as therein provided.

SEC. 6. *And be it further enacted,* That all elections in the States mentioned in the said "Act to provide for the more efficient government of the rebel States," shall, during the operation of said act, be by ballot; and all officers making the said registration of voters and conducting said elections shall, before entering upon the discharge of their duties, take and subscribe the oath prescribed by the act approved July second, eighteen hundred and sixty-two, entitled "An act to prescribe an oath of office": *Provided,* That if any person shall knowingly and falsely take and subscribe any oath in this act prescribed, such person so offending and being thereof duly convicted shall be subject to the pains, penalties, and disabilities which by law are provided for the punishment of the crime of wilful and corrupt perjury.

SEC. 7. *And be it further enacted,* That all expenses incurred by the several commanding generals, or by virtue of any orders issued, or appointments made, by them, under or by virtue of this act, shall be paid out of any moneys in the treasury not otherwise appropriated.

SEC. 8. *And be it further enacted,* That the convention for each State shall prescribe the fees, salary, and compensation to be paid to all delegates and other officers and agents herein authorized or necessary to carry into effect the purposes of this act not herein otherwise provided for, and shall provide for the levy and collection of such taxes on the property in such State as may be necessary to pay the same.

SEC. 9. *And be it further enacted,* That the word "article," in the sixth section of the act to which this is supplementary, shall be construed to mean "section."

> SCHUYLER COLFAX,
> *Speaker of the House of Representatives.*
> B. F. WADE,
> *President of the Senate pro tempore.*

Second Supplement to the First Reconstruction Act of 1867

July 19, 1867

An Act supplementary to an Act entitled "An Act to provide for the more efficient Government of the Rebel States," passed on the second day of March, eighteen hundred and sixty-seven, and the Act supplementary thereto, passed on the twenty-third day of March, eighteen hundred and sixty-seven.

Be it enacted by the Senate and House of Representatives of the United States of America in Congress assembled, That it is hereby declared to have been the true intent and meaning of the act of the second day of March, one thousand eight hundred and sixty-seven, entitled "An act to provide for the more efficient government of the rebel States," and of the act supplementary thereto, passed on the twenty-third day of March, in the year one thousand eight hundred and sixty-seven, that the governments then existing in the rebel States of Virginia, North Carolina, South Carolina, Georgia, Mississippi, Alabama, Louisiana, Florida, Texas, and Arkansas were not legal State governments; and that thereafter said governments, if continued, were to be continued subject in all respects to the military commanders of the respective districts, and to the paramount authority of Congress.

SEC. 2. *And be it further enacted,* That the commander of any district named in said act shall have power, subject to the disapproval of the General of the army of the United States, and to have effect till disapproved, whenever in the opinion of such commander the proper administration of said act shall require it, to suspend or remove from office, or from the performance of official duties and the exercise of official powers, any officer or person holding or exercising, or professing to hold or exercise, any civil or military office or duty in such district under any power, election, appointment or authority derived from, or granted by, or claimed under, any so-called State or the government thereof, or any municipal or other division thereof, and upon such suspension or removal such commander, subject to the disapproval of the General as aforesaid, shall have power to provide from time to time for the performance of the said duties of such officer or person so suspended or removed, by the detail of some competent officer or soldier of the army, or by the appointment of some other person, to perform the same, and to fill vacancies occasioned by death, resignation, or otherwise.

SEC. 3. *And be it further enacted,* That the General of the army of the United States shall be invested with all the powers of suspension, removal, appointment, and detail granted in the preceding section to district commanders.

SEC. 4. *And be it further enacted,* That the acts of the officers of the army already done in removing in said districts persons exercising the functions of civil officers, and appointing others in their stead, are hereby confirmed: *Provided,* That any person heretofore or hereafter appointed by any district commander to exercise the functions of any civil office, may be removed either by the military officer in command of the district, or by the General of the army. And it shall be the duty of such commander to remove from office as aforesaid all persons who are disloyal to the government of the United

States, or who use their official influence in any manner to hinder, delay, prevent, or obstruct the due and proper administration of this act and the acts to which it is supplementary.

SEC. 5. *And be it further enacted,* That the boards of registration provided for in the act entitled "An act supplementary to an act entitled 'An act to provide for the more efficient government of the rebel States,' passed March two, eighteen hundred and sixty-seven, and to facilitate restoration," passed March twenty-three, eighteen hundred and sixty-seven, shall have power, and it shall be their duty before allowing the registration of any person, to ascertain, upon such facts or information as they can obtain, whether such person is entitled to be registered under said act, and the oath required by said act shall not be conclusive on such question, and no person shall be registered unless such board shall decide that he is entitled thereto; and such board shall also have power to examine, under oath, (to be administered by any member of such board,) any one touching the qualification of any person claiming registration; but in every case of refusal by the board to register an applicant, and in every case of striking his name from the list as hereinafter provided, the board shall make a note or memorandum, which shall be returned with the registration list to the commanding general of the district, setting forth the grounds of such refusal or such striking from the list: *Provided,* That no person shall be disqualified as member of any board of registration by reason of race or color.

SEC. 6. *And be it further enacted,* That the true intent and meaning of the oath prescribed in said supplementary act is, (among other things,) that no person who has been a member of the legislature of any State, or who has held any executive or judicial office in any State, whether he has taken an oath to support the Constitution of the United States or not, and whether he was holding such office at the commencement of the rebellion, or had held it before, and who has afterwards engaged in insurrection or rebellion against the United States, or given aid or comfort to the enemies thereof, is entitled to be registered or to vote; and the words "executive or judicial office in any State" in said oath mentioned shall be construed to include all civil offices created by law for the administration of any general law of a State, or for the administration of justice.

SEC. 7. *And be it further enacted,* That the time for completing the original registration provided for in said act may, in the discretion of the commander of any district be extended to the first day of October, eighteen hundred and sixty-seven; and the boards of registration shall have power, and it shall be their duty, commencing fourteen days prior to any election under said act, and upon reasonable public notice of the time and place thereof, to revise, for a period of five days, the registration lists, and upon being satisfied that any person not entitled thereto has been registered, to strike the name of such person from the list, and such person shall not be allowed to vote. And such board shall also, during the same period, add to such registry the names of all persons who at that time possess the qualifications required by said act who have not been already registered; and no person shall, at any time, be entitled to be registered or to vote by reason of any executive pardon or amnesty for any act or thing which, without such pardon or amnesty, would disqualify him from registration or voting.

SEC. 8. *And be it further enacted,* That section four of said last-named act shall be construed to authorize the commanding general named therein, whenever he shall deem it needful, to remove any member of a board of registration and to appoint another in his stead, and to fill any vacancy in such board.

SEC. 9. *And be it further enacted,* That all members of said boards of registration and all persons hereafter elected or appointed to office in said military districts, under any so-called State or municipal authority, or by detail or appointment of the district commanders, shall be required to take and to subscribe the oath of office prescribed by law for officers of the United States.

SEC. 10. *And be it further enacted,* That no district commander or member of the board of registration, or any of the officers or appointees acting under them, shall be bound in his action by any opinion of any civil officer of the United States.

SEC. 11. *And be it further enacted,* That all the provisions of this act and of the acts to which this is supplementary shall be construed liberally, to the end that all the intents thereof may be fully and perfectly carried out.

SCHUYLER COLFAX,
Speaker of the House of Representatives.
B. F. WADE,
President of the Senate pro tempore.

Articles of Impeachment of Andrew Johnson, 1868

Andrew Johnson was a slaveholder and former tailor's apprentice from Tennessee who rose to prominence in large measure because, when the Civil War began, he refused to resign his seat in the U.S. Senate, calling secessionists "traitors." Lincoln chose Johnson, a "War Democrat" as his running mate when he ran for reelection in 1864. Johnson originally was seen as a proponent of a reconstruction policy more strict than Lincoln's. But after Lincoln's assassination Johnson began opposing what he saw as Radical Republican attempts to punish former Confederate states. Unfortunately for Johnson, the Radical Republicans held overwhelming majorities in both houses of Congress, allowing them to override several presidential vetoes of their legislation (a rare occurrence until then). Among the overridden vetoes was that of the Tenure of Office Act, which required Senate approval before the president could dismiss any executive officer appointed with the advice and consent of the Senate. Johnson seemed to violate this law by attempting to eject the Radical Republican Edwin Stanton from his position as secretary of war. This act, along with Reconstruction policy disagreements, precipitated impeachment proceedings in the House, which in effect indicted Johnson for high crimes and misdemeanors. Johnson escaped removal from office when the Senate fell one vote short of the two-thirds majority required.

Articles of Impeachment of Andrew Johnson

February 21, 1868

ARTICLES

Exhibited by the House of Representatives of the United States, in the name of themselves and all the people of the United States, against Andrew Johnson, President of the United States, in maintenance and support of their impeachment against him for high crimes and misdemeanors in office.

ARTICLE I

That said Andrew Johnson, President of the United States, on the twenty-first day of February, in the year of our Lord one thousand eight hundred and sixty-eight, at Washington, in the District of Columbia, unmindful of the high duties of his office, of his oath of office, and of the requirement of the Constitution that he should take care that the laws be faithfully executed, did unlawfully, and in violation of the Constitution and laws of the United States, issue an order in writing for the removal of Edwin M. Stanton from the office of Secretary for the Department of War, said Edwin M. Stanton having been theretofore duly appointed and com-

missioned, by and with the advice and consent of the Senate of the United States, as such Secretary, and said Andrew Johnson, President of the United States, on the twelfth day of August, in the year of our Lord one thousand eight hundred and sixty-seven, and during the recess of said Senate, having suspended by his order Edwin M. Stanton from said office, and within twenty days after the first day of the next meeting of said Senate, that is to say, on the twelfth day of December in the year last aforesaid, having reported to said Senate such suspension with the evidence and reasons for his action in the case and the name of the person designated to perform the duties of such office temporarily until the next meeting of the Senate, and said Senate thereafterwards on the thirteenth day of January, in the year of our Lord one thousand eight hundred and sixty-eight, having duly considered the evidence and reasons reported by said Andrew Johnson for said suspension, and having refused to concur in said suspension, whereby and by force of the provisions of an act entitled "An act regulating the tenure of certain civil offices," passed

March second, eighteen hundred and sixty-seven, said Edwin M. Stanton did forthwith resume the functions of his office, whereof the said Andrew Johnson had then and there due notice, and said Edwin M. Stanton, by reason of the premises, on said twenty-first day of February, being lawfully entitled to hold said office of Secretary for the Department of War, which said order for the removal of said Edwin M. Stanton is in substance as follows, that is to say:

EXECUTIVE MANSION,
Washington, D.C., February 21, 1868.

SIR: By virtue of the power and authority vested in me as President by the Constitution and laws of the United States you are hereby removed from office as Secretary for the Department of War, and your functions as such will terminate upon receipt of this communication.

You will transfer to Brevet Major General, Lorenzo Thomas, Adjutant General of the army, who has this day been authorized and empowered to act as Secretary of War *ad interim,* all records, books, papers, and other public property now in your custody and charge.

Respectfully yours,

ANDREW JOHNSON.
To the Hon. EDWIN M. STANTON, *Washington, D.C.*

Which order was unlawfully issued with intent then and there to violate the act entitled "An act regulating the tenure of certain civil offices," passed March second, eighteen hundred and sixty-seven, and with the further intent, contrary to the provisions of said act, in violation thereof, and contrary to the provisions of the Constitution of the United States, and without the advice and consent of the Senate of the United States, the said Senate then and there being in session, to remove said Edwin M. Stanton from the office of Secretary for the Department of War, the said Edwin M. Stanton being then and there Secretary for the Department of War, and being then and there in the due and lawful execution and discharge of the duties of said office, whereby said Andrew Johnson, President of the United States, did then and there commit, and was guilty of a high misdemeanor in office.

ARTICLE II

That on said twenty-first day of February, in the year of our Lord one thousand eight hundred and sixty-eight, at Washington, in the District of Columbia, said Andrew Johnson, President of the United States, unmindful of the high du-

ties of his office, of his oath of office, and in violation of the Constitution of the United States, and contrary to the provisions of an act entitled "An act regulating the tenure of certain civil offices," passed March second, eighteen hundred and sixty-seven, without the advice and consent of the Senate of the United States, said Senate then and there being in session, and without authority of law, did, with intent to violate the Constitution of the United States, and the act aforesaid, issue and deliver to one Lorenzo Thomas a letter of authority in substance as follows, that is to say:

EXECUTIVE MANSION,
Washington, D.C., February 21, 1868.

SIR: The Hon. Edwin M. Stanton having been this day removed from office as Secretary for the Department of War, you are hereby authorized and empowered to act as Secretary of War *ad interim,* and will immediately enter upon the discharge of the duties pertaining to that office.

Mr. Stanton has been instructed to transfer to you all the records, books, papers, and other public property now in his custody and charge.

Respectfully, yours.

ANDREW JOHNSON.
To Brevet Major General LORENZO THOMAS,
Adjutant General U.S. Army, Washington, D.C.

Then and there being no vacancy in said office of Secretary for the Department of War, whereby said Andrew Johnson, President of the United States, did then and there commit, and was guilty of a high misdemeanor in office.

ARTICLE III

That said Andrew Johnson, President of the United States, on the twenty-first day of February, in the year of our Lord one thousand eight hundred and sixty-eight, at Washington, in the District of Columbia, did commit and was guilty of a high misdemeanor in office in this, that, without authority of law, while the Senate of the United States was then and there in session, he did appoint one Lorenzo Thomas to be Secretary for the Department of War *ad interim,* without the advice and consent of the Senate, and with intent to violate the Constitution of the United States, no vacancy having happened in said office of Secretary for the Department of War during the recess of the Senate, and no vacancy existing in said office at the time, and which said appointment, so made by said Andrew Johnson, of said Lorenzo Thomas, is in substance as follows, that is to say:

EXECUTIVE MANSION,
Washington, D.C., February 21, 1868.

SIR: The Hon. Edwin M. Stanton having been this day removed from office as Secretary for the Department of War, you are hereby authorized and empowered to act as Secretary of War *ad interim,* and will immediately enter upon the discharge of the duties pertaining to that office.

Mr. Stanton has been instructed to transfer to you all the records, books, papers, and other public property now in his custody and charge.

Respectfully yours,

ANDREW JOHNSON.

To Brevet Major General LORENZO THOMAS,
Adjutant General U.S. Army, Washington. D.C.

ARTICLE IV

That said Andrew Johnson, President of the United States, unmindful of the high duties of his office and of his oath of office, in violation of the Constitution and laws of the United States, on the twenty-first day of February, in the year of our Lord one thousand eight hundred and sixty-eight, at Washington, in the District of Columbia, did unlawfully conspire with one Lorenzo Thomas, and with other persons to the House of Representatives unknown, with intent, by intimidation and threats, unlawfully to hinder and prevent Edwin M. Stanton, then and there the Secretary for the Department of War, duly appointed under the laws of the United States, from holding said office of Secretary for the Department of War, contrary to and in violation of the Constitution of the United States and of the provisions of an act entitled "An act to define and punish certain conspiracies," approved July thirty-first, eighteen hundred and sixty-one, whereby said Andrew Johnson, President of the United States, did then and there commit and was guilty of a high crime in office.

ARTICLE V

That said Andrew Johnson, President of the United States, unmindful of the high duties of his office and of his oath of office, on the twenty-first day of February, in the year of our Lord one thousand eight hundred and sixty-eight, and on divers other days and times in said year, before the second day of March, in the year of our Lord one thousand eight hundred and sixty-eight, at Washington, in the District of Columbia, did unlawfully conspire with one Lorenzo Thomas, and with other persons to the House of Representatives unknown, to prevent and hinder the execution of an act entitled "An act regulating the tenure of certain civil offices," passed March second, eighteen hundred and sixty-seven, and in pursuance of said conspiracy, did unlawfully attempt to prevent Edwin M. Stanton, then and there being Secretary for the Department of War, duly appointed and commissioned under the laws of the United States, from holding said office, whereby the said Andrew Johnson, President of the United States, did then and there commit and was guilty of a high misdemeanor in office.

ARTICLE VI

That said Andrew Johnson, President of the United States, unmindful of the high duties of his office and of his oath of office, on the twenty-first day of February, in the year of our Lord one thousand eight hundred and sixty-eight, at Washington, in the District of Columbia, did unlawfully conspire with one Lorenzo Thomas, by force to seize, take, and possess the property of the United States in the Department of War, and then and there in the custody and charge of Edwin M. Stanton, Secretary for said department, contrary to the provisions of an act entitled "An act to define and punish certain conspiracies," approved July thirty-one, eighteen hundred and sixty-one, with intent to violate and disregard an act entitled "An act regulating the tenure of certain civil offices," passed March second, eighteen hundred and sixty-seven, whereby said Andrew Johnson, President of the United States, did then and there commit a high crime in office.

ARTICLE VII

That said Andrew Johnson, President of the United States, unmindful of the high duties of his office and of his oath of office, on the twenty-first day of February, in the year of our Lord one thousand eight hundred and sixty-eight, at Washington, in the District of Columbia, did unlawfully conspire with one Lorenzo Thomas with intent unlawfully to seize, take, and possess the property of the United States in the Department of War, in the custody and charge of Edwin M. Stanton, Secretary for said department, with intent to violate and disregard the act entitled "An act regulating the tenure of certain civil offices," passed March second, eighteen hundred and sixty-seven, whereby said Andrew Johnson, President of the United States, did then and there commit a high misdemeanor in office.

Article VIII

That said Andrew Johnson, President of the United States, unmindful of the high duties of his office, and of his oath of office, with intent unlawfully to control the disbursements of the moneys appropriated for the military service and for the Department of War, on the twenty-first day of February, in the year of our Lord one thousand eight hundred and sixty-eight, at Washington, in the District of Columbia, did unlawfully and contrary to the provisions of an act entitled "An act regulating the tenure of certain civil offices," passed March second, eighteen hundred and sixty-seven, and in violation of the Constitution of the United States, and without the advice and consent of the Senate of the United States, and while the Senate was then and there in session, there being no vacancy in the office of Secretary for the Department of War, and with intent to violate and disregard the act aforesaid, then and there issue and deliver to one Lorenzo Thomas a letter of authority in writing, in substance as follows, that is to say:

Executive Mansion,
Washington, D.C., February 21, 1868.
Sir: The Hon. Edwin M. Stanton having been this day removed from office as Secretary for the Department of War, you are hereby authorized and empowered to act as Secretary of War *ad interim* and will immediately enter upon the discharge of the duties pertaining to that office.

Mr. Stanton has been instructed to transfer to you all the records, books, papers, and other public property now in his custody and charge.

Respectfully yours,

ANDREW JOHNSON.
To Brevet Major General Lorenzo Thomas,
Adjutant General U.S. Army, Washington, D.C.

Whereby the said Andrew Johnson, President of the United States, did then and there commit and was guilty of a high misdemeanor in office.

Article IX

That said Andrew Johnson, President of the United States, on the twenty-second day of February, in the year of our Lord one thousand eight hundred and sixty-eight, at Washington, in the District of Columbia, in disregard of the Constitution and the laws of the United States duly enacted, as commander-in-chief of the army of the United States, did bring before himself then and there William H. Emory, a major general by brevet in the army of the United States, actually in command of the Department of Washington and the military forces thereof, and did then and there, as such commander-in-chief, declare to and instruct said Emory that part of a law of the United States, passed March second, eighteen hundred and sixty-seven, entitled "An act making appropriations for the support of the army for the year ending June thirtieth, eighteen hundred and sixty-eight, and for other purposes," especially the second section thereof, which provides, among other things, that "all orders and instructions relating to military operations issued by the President or Secretary of War shall be issued through the General of the army, and in case of his inability, through the next in rank," was unconstitutional and in contravention of the commission of said Emory, and which said provision of law had been theretofore duly and legally promulgated by General Order for the government and direction of the army of the United States, as the said Andrew Johnson then and there well knew, with intent thereby to induce said Emory, in his official capacity as commander of the Department of Washington, to violate the provisions of said act, and to take and receive, act upon and obey such orders as he, the said Andrew Johnson, might make and give, and which should not be issued through the General of the army of the United States, according to the provisions of said act, and with the further intent thereby to enable him, the said Andrew Johnson, to prevent the execution of the act entitled "An act regulating the tenure of certain civil offices," passed March second, eighteen hundred and sixty-seven, and to unlawfully prevent Edwin M. Stanton, then being Secretary for the Department of War, from holding said office and discharging the duties thereof, whereby said Andrew Johnson, President of the United States, did then and there commit and was guilty of a high misdemeanor in office.

And the House of Representatives, by protestation, saving to themselves the liberty of exhibiting at any time hereafter any further articles or other accusation or impeachment against the said Andrew Johnson, President of the United States, and also of replying to his answers which he shall make unto the articles herein preferred against him, and of offering proof to the same, and every part thereof, and to all and every other article, accusation, or impeachment which shall be exhibited by them, as the case shall require, DO DEMAND that the said Andrew Johnson may be put to answer the high crimes and misdemeanors in office herein charged against him, and that such proceedings, examinations, trials, and judgments may be thereupon had and given as may be agreeable to law and justice.

SCHUYLER COLFAX,
Speaker of the House of Representatives.

Attest:

EDWARD MCPHERSON,
Clerk of the House of Representatives.

IN THE HOUSE OF REPRESENTATIVES
UNITED STATES.
March 3, 1868.

The following additional articles of impeachment were agreed to, viz:

ARTICLE X

The said Andrew Johnson, President of the United States, unmindful of the high duties of his office and the dignity and proprieties thereof, and of the harmony and courtesies which ought to exist and be maintained between the executive and legislative branches of the government of the United States, designing and intending to set aside the rightful authority and powers of Congress, did attempt to bring into disgrace, ridicule, hatred, contempt and reproach the Congress of the United States, and the several branches thereof, to impair and destroy the regard and respect of all the good people of the United States for the Congress and legislative power thereof, (which all officers of the government ought inviolably to preserve and maintain,) and to excite the odium and resentment of all the good people of the United States against Congress and the laws by it duly and constitutionally enacted; and in pursuance of his said design and intent, openly and publicly, and before divers assemblages of the citizens of the United States convened in divers parts thereof to meet and receive said Andrew Johnson as the Chief Magistrate of the United States, did, on the eighteenth day of August, in the year of our Lord one thousand eight hundred and sixty-six, and on divers other days and times, as well before as afterward, make and deliver with a loud voice certain intemperate, inflammatory and scandalous harangues, and did therein utter loud threats and bitter menaces as well against Congress as the laws of the United States duly enacted thereby, amid the cries, jeers and laughter of the multitudes then assembled and in hearing, which are set forth in the several specifications hereinafter written, in substance and effect, that is to say:

SPECIFICATION FIRST. In this, that at Washington, in the District of Columbia, in the Executive Mansion, to a committee of citizens who called upon the President of the United States, speaking of and concerning the Congress of the United States, said Andrew Johnson, President of the United States, heretofore, to wit, on the eighteenth day of August, in the year of our Lord one thousand eight hundred and sixty-six, did, in a loud voice, declare in substance and effect, among other things, that is to say:

["]So far as the Executive Department of the government is concerned, the effort has been made to restore the Union, to heal the breach, to pour oil into the wounds which were consequent upon the struggle, and (to speak in common phrase) to prepare as the learned and wise physician would, a plaster healing in character and coextensive with the wound. We thought, and we think, that we had partially succeeded; but as the work progressed, as reconstruction seemed to be taking place, and the country was becoming reunited, we found a disturbing and marring element opposing us. In alluding to that element, I shall go no further than your convention and the distinguished gentleman who has delivered to me the report of its proceedings. I shall make no reference to it that I do not believe the time and the occasion justify.

"We have witnessed in one department of the government every endeavor to prevent the restoration of peace, harmony, and Union. We have seen hanging upon the verge of the government, as it were, a body called, or which assumes to be, the Congress of the United States, while in fact it is a Congress of only a part of the States. We have seen this Congress pretend to be for the Union, when its every step and act tended to perpetuate disunion and make a disruption of the States inevitable. . . . We have seen Congress gradually encroach step by step upon constitutional rights, and violate, day after day and month after month, fundamental principles of the government. We have seen a Congress that seemed to forget that there was a limit to the sphere and scope of legislation. We have seen a Congress in a minority assume to exercise power which, allowed to be consummated, would result in despotism or monarchy itself."

SPECIFICATION SECOND.—In this, that at Cleveland, in the State of Ohio, heretofore, to wit, on the third day of September, in the year of our Lord one thousand eight hundred and sixty-six, before a public assemblage of citizens and others, said Andrew Johnson, President of the United States, speaking of and concerning the Congress of the United States, did, in a loud voice, declare in substance and effect, among other things, that is to say:

"I will tell you what I did do. I called upon your Congress that is trying to break up the government. . . .

"In conclusion, beside that, Congress had taken much pains to poison their constituents against him. But what had Congress done? Have they done anything to restore the union of these States? No; on the contrary, they had done everything to prevent it; and because he stood now where he did when the rebellion commenced, he had been denounced as a traitor. Who had run greater risks or made greater sacrifices than himself? But Congress, factious and domineering, had undertaken to poison the minds of the American people."

SPECIFICATION THIRD—In this, that at St. Louis, in the State of Missouri, heretofore, to wit, on the eighth day of September, in the year of our Lord one thousand eight hundred and sixty-six, before a public assemblage of citizens and others, said Andrew Johnson, President of the United States, speaking of and concerning the Congress of the United States, did, in a loud voice, declare, in substance and effect, among other things, that is to say:

"Go on. Perhaps if you had a word or two on the subject of New Orleans you might understand more about it than you do. And if you will go back—if you will go back and ascertain the cause of the riot at New Orleans perhaps you will not be so prompt in calling out 'New Orleans.' If you will take up the riot at New Orleans, and trace it back to its source or its immediate cause, you will find out who was responsible for the blood that was shed there. If you will take up the riot at New Orleans and trace it back to the radical Congress, you will find that the riot at New Orleans was substantially planned. If you will take up the proceedings in their caucuses you will understand that they there knew that a convention was to be called which was extinct by its power having expired; that it was said that the intention was that a new government was to be organized, and on the organization of that government the intention was to enfranchise one portion of the population, called the colored population, who had just been emancipated, and at the same time disfranchise white men. When you design to talk about New Orleans you ought to understand what you are talking about. When you read

the speeches that were made, and take up the facts on the Friday and Saturday before that convention sat, you will there find that speeches were made incendiary in their character, exciting that portion of the population, the black population, to arm themselves and prepare for the shedding of blood. You will also find that that convention did assemble in violation of law, and the intention of that convention was to supersede the reorganized authorities in the State government of Louisiana, which had been recognized by the government of the United States; and every man engaged in that rebellion in that convention, with the intention of superseding and upturning the civil government which had been recognized by the government of the United States, I say that he was a traitor to the Constitution of the United States, and hence you find that another rebellion was commenced, *having its origin in the radical Congress*. . . .

"So much for the New Orleans riot. And there was the cause and the origin of the blood that was shed; and every drop of blood that was shed is upon their skirts, and they are responsible for it. I could test this thing a little closer, but will not do it here to-night. But when you talk about the causes and consequences that resulted from proceedings of that kind, perhaps, as I have been introduced here, and you have provoked questions of this kind, though it does not provoke me, I will tell you a few wholesome things that have been done by this radical Congress in connection with New Orleans and the extension of the elective franchise.

"I know that I have been traduced and abused. I know it has come in advance of me here as elsewhere—that I have attempted to exercise an arbitrary power in resisting laws that were intended to be forced upon the government; that I had exercised that power; that I had abandoned the party that elected me, and that I was a traitor, because I exercised the veto power in attempting, and did arrest for a time, a bill that was called a 'Freedmen's Bureau' bill; yes, that I was a traitor. And I have been traduced, I have been slandered, I have been maligned, I have been called Judas Iscariot and all that. Now, my countrymen here to-night, it is very easy to indulge in epithets; it is easy to call a man Judas and cry out traitor, but when he is called upon to give arguments and facts he is very often found wanting. Judas Iscariot—Judas. There was a Judas, and he was one of the twelve apostles. Oh! yes, the twelve apostles had a Christ. The twelve apostles had a Christ, and he never could have had a Judas unless he had had twelve apostles. If I have played the Judas, who has been my Christ that I have played the Judas with? Was it Thad. Stevens? Was it Wendell Phillips? Was it Charles Sumner? These are the men that stop and compare themselves with the Saviour; and everybody that differs with them in opinion, and to try to stay and arrest their diabolical and nefarious policy, is to be denounced as a Judas. . . .

"Well, let me say to you, if you will stand by me in this action, if you will stand by me in trying to give the people a fair chance—soldiers and citizens—to participate in these offices, God being willing, I will kick them out. I will kick them out just as fast as I can.

"Let me say to you, in concluding, that what I have said I intended to say. I was not provoked into this, and I care not for their menaces, the taunts, and the jeers. I care not for threats. I do not intend to be bullied by my enemies nor overawed by my friends. But, God willing, with your help, I will veto their measures whenever any of them come to me."

Which said utterances, declarations, threats, and harangues, highly censurable in any, are peculiarly indecent and unbecoming in the Chief Magistrate of the United States, by means whereof said Andrew Johnson has brought the high office of the President of the United States into contempt, ridicule, and disgrace, to the great scandal of all good citizens, whereby said Andrew Johnson, President of the United States, did commit, and was then and there guilty of a high misdemeanor in office.

Article XI

That said Andrew Johnson, President of the United States, unmindful of the high duties of his office, and of his oath of office, and in disregard of the Constitution and laws of the United States, did, heretofore, to wit, on the eighteenth day of August, A.D. eighteen hundred and sixty-six, at the city of Washington, and the District of Columbia, by public speech, declare and affirm, in substance, that the thirty-ninth Congress of the United States was not a Congress of the United States authorized by the Constitution to exercise legislative power under the same, but, on the contrary, was a Congress of only part of the States, thereby denying, and intending to deny, that the legislation of said Congress was valid or obligatory upon him, the said Andrew Johnson, except in so far as he saw fit to approve the same, and also thereby denying, and intending to deny, the power of the said thirty-ninth Congress to propose amendments to the Constitution of the United States; and, in pursuance of said declaration, the said Andrew Johnson, President of the United States, afterwards, to wit, on the twenty-first day of February, A.D. eighteen hundred and sixty-eight, at the city of Washington, in the District of Columbia, did, unlawfully, and in disregard of the requirement of the Constitution, that he should take care that the laws be faithfully executed, attempt to prevent the execution of an act entitled "An act regulating the tenure of certain civil offices," passed March second, eighteen hundred and sixty-seven, by unlawfully devising and contriving, and attempting to devise and contrive means by which he should prevent Edwin M. Stanton from forthwith resuming the functions of the office of Secretary for the Department of War, notwithstanding the refusal of the Senate to concur in the suspension theretofore made by said Andrew Johnson of said Edwin M. Stanton from said office of Secretary for the Department of War; and, also, by further unlawfully devising and contriving, and attempting to devise and contrive, means, then and there, to prevent the execution of an act entitled "An act making appropriations for the support of the army for the fiscal year ending June thirtieth, eighteen hundred and sixty-eight, and for other purposes," approved March second, eighteen hundred and sixty-seven; and, also, to prevent the execution of an act entitled "An act to provide for the more efficient government of the rebel States," passed March second, eighteen hundred and sixty-seven, whereby the said Andrew Johnson, President of the United States, did, then, to wit, on the twenty-first day of February, A.D. eighteen hundred and sixty-eight, at the city of Washington, commit, and was guilty of, a high misdemeanor in office.

SCHUYLER COLFAX,
Speaker of the House of Representatives.

Attest:

EDWARD MCPHERSON,
Clerk of the House of Representatives.

Debate on Proposed Fourteenth Amendment, 1866

U.S. Constitution, Fourteenth Amendment, 1868

U.S. Constitution, Fifteenth Amendment, 1870

When Congress passed the Civil Rights Act over President Johnson's veto, there remained questions concerning whether the act might be declared unconstitutional by the Supreme Court or altered fundamentally by a succeeding Congress not dominated by the Radical Republicans. Thus Congressional leaders sought to incorporate into the Constitution the Civil Rights Act's extension to African Americans of the privileges and immunities of citizenship, due process, and equal protection. Debate in Congress was extensive concerning how far the legislation ought to go in granting rights to African Americans, and how far it could successfully go and still gain ratification. The amendment, which gives Congress the power to enforce its provisions, was recommended to the states on June 13, 1866, but did not receive the required assent of twenty-eight state legislatures (out of thirty-seven states in the Union at that time) until July 9, 1868. Moreover, two states, Ohio and New Jersey, had "withdrawn" their assents before that date. On July 21, 1868, Congress passed a joint resolution declaring the amendment to be part of the Constitution. The secretary of state made the required certification on July 28; Alabama and Georgia in the meantime had assented to the amendment. In 1866 and 1867, respectively, Congress extended the right to vote to African Americans in the District of Columbia and required territories to guarantee that right to African Americans in order to secure admission to the Union as states. After the election of 1868, Congress recommended the Fifteenth Amendment to the states, forbidding denial of the right to vote on account of race, color, or previous condition of servitude and giving Congress the power to enforce the amendment's provisions.

Debate on Proposed Fourteenth Amendment

May 29, 1866

RECONSTRUCTION.

The SPEAKER. The morning hour having expired, the first business in order is House bill No. 543, which was made the special order for this day after the morning hour, being a bill to restore to the States lately in insurrection their full political rights.

Mr. ASHLEY, of Ohio. Unless the members of this Congress who represent the loyal people of this country approach the proposition before us, providing for the restoration of the late rebel States, in a proper spirit and with mutual concessions, I fear we shall fail to accomplish the great work committed to our hands. I desire to approach its consideration with charity for all and malice toward none. I know that I ap-

proach it in a forgiving spirit and with a thankful heart. With thankfulness, because the din of war has been hushed and the national conflagration extinguished. In a forgiving spirit, because I know how much there is to be forgiven if we would reunite dissevered and broken ties, secure the perpetual unity of the nation, and bind up its millions of bleeding and broken hearts.

In all the votes which I have given or may give on the propositions for reconstruction, in all I have said or may say, I shall keep steadily in view the one great desire of my heart, which outweighs and overshadows all others, and before which the petty schemes of parties and of men dwindle into insignificance and appear to me criminal. That desire is to see the

States recently in rebellion restored to all the rights, privileges and dignities of States of the American Union at the earliest day consistent with the national safety, and upon such terms as shall secure the power, unity, and glory of the Republic.

How can this most desirable result best be accomplished? In answering this interrogatory the first question which presents itself to every reflecting mind is this: has the Government of the United States as at present organized the constitutional power to demand or exact from the people in the late rebel States any conditions prior to the recognition of their recently reorganized State governments and the admission of their Senators and Representatives in Congress? If so, is it expedient to exact of them the terms or conditions proposed by the committee of fifteen, or such conditions of a like character as may finally be agreed upon by the two Houses of Congress, as conditions precedent to their resumption, as States, of all constitutional relations to the national Government which were severed by their acts of rebellion and war?

I claim that we have the power, and that it is not only our right but our duty to demand such conditions as the majority of the loyal representatives of this Congress may deem requisite for the safety and security of the nation. I believe we have the constitutional power, because I believe the States represented in this Hall during the war and now are the Government. If I did not believe this I could not vote for any of the propositions before the House or any proposition of a like character.

From the first I have held that when the people of the late rebel States abolished their constitutional State governments and confederated together in violation of the national Constitution and organized hostile State governments and a national confederate government, and maintained those governments by force of arms until the rebellion became so formidable as to claim the prerogatives of a national *de facto* government, and to have conceded to it by the United States and the great Powers of Europe belligerent rights, that from that hour constitutional State governments ceased in each of the States so confederated together, and until governments are reorganized in each of them in subordination to the national Constitution, and recognized by this Congress, there can be no constitutional State governments in such States.

Mr. RANDALL, of Pennsylvania. Will the gentleman allow me to ask him who he intends shall form the State governments—the people of the States, or who?

Mr. ASHLEY, of Ohio. I propose that the loyal people of these States shall reorganize these State governments and ad-

minister their governments under such rules and restrictions as the Congress of the United States, representing the people of the loyal States, shall require.

Mr. RANDALL, of Pennsylvania. Then I understand the gentleman to say that he is willing that the loyal people shall form State governments, or shall continue their State governments and protect and elect Congressmen as part of their duty. Do I understand him aright?

Mr. ASHLEY, of Ohio. Under such rules and restrictions as this Congress shall require.

Mr. RANDALL, of Pennsylvania. That is an after-clap.

Mr. ASHLEY, of Ohio. Now, Mr. Speaker, I hope I can go on without any more of these interruptions. From the outbreak of the rebellion I have sought to have all the Departments of the Government adopt and act upon this idea. I have held that the sovereignty of the nation was in the people who reside in the States which maintained constitutional State governments, recognizing the national Constitution as the supreme law of the land, and the Government which it created as the one to which all citizens owed a paramount allegiance. I have held that the sovereignty of the nation could not be impaired or destroyed within the territorial jurisdiction of the United States by the action, or the refusal to act, of any one or more States. In other words, that the people in the States which maintained their constitutional relations to the national Government were the only depositaries of the national sovereignty and the only constitutional governing power in the nation.

Holding these views, I insist that the people who maintained constitutional State governments, who, during the entire war, were represented here, and who are now represented here, the people who maintained this national Government and put down the rebellion, have a right under the laws of war as conquerors to prescribe such conditions as in the judgment of the majority of this Congress are necessary for the national safety and the national security. This is the right of the conqueror under every law, human and divine. If this be not the true theory, then, indeed, is our national Government a rope of sand.

Entertaining these ideas, at the extra session of Congress in July, 1861, I drew up a bill embodying them, but by the advice of friends I did not present it until the regular session in December. On the 12th of March following, by the direction of the Committee on Territories, I reported to this House "a bill to provide temporary provisional governments for the districts of country in rebellion against the United States."

That bill, on the motion of my then colleague, (Mr. Pendleton,) was laid upon the table by a vote of 65 to 56, a number of Republicans voting with the Opposition, and a still larger number not voting at all.

At the first session of the Thirty-Eighth Congress, upon consultation, it was thought best to have a committee on the rebellious States, and the late Henry Winter Davis offered a resolution for the appointment of such a committee. The committee was raised, and he was appointed its chairman.

After the committee was appointed, of which I was a member, I again introduced the old bill, with such modifications and additions as time had suggested. That bill which was reported passed both Houses of Congress, but did not receive the sanction of President Lincoln, and therefore failed to become a law.

At the second session of the Thirty-Eighth Congress I again introduced the same bill with some modifications, and by direction of the committee I reported it to this House. After a number of efforts to modify it so as to secure a majority vote, it was lost, and we were left at sea on this great question of reconstruction. And to-day we are reaping the fruits of our stupidity and folly. I allude to these facts to show how steadily the national mind has been marching up to this idea, that the men who remained loyal to this Government, who maintained constitutional State governments, and who during the war administered this Government are the Government.

Mr. WRIGHT. Will the gentleman from Ohio [Mr. ASHLEY] allow me to ask him a question?

Mr. ASHLEY, of Ohio. I would rather the gentleman would ask me his questions after I get through my argument.

Mr. WRIGHT. I wish simply to ask the gentleman to give us his definition of a loyal man.

Mr. ASHLEY, of Ohio. If the gentleman will ask me after I get through I will answer his question.

Mr. WRIGHT. Very well; I will ask the gentleman then.

Mr. ASHLEY, of Ohio. I was saying that I allude to those facts for the purpose of showing how steadily the national mind has been approaching this idea. And when this joint committee on reconstruction, composed of the ablest men in the nation, made their report the other day, they recognized the same idea, to wit, that the constitutional governments in all the rebel States were abolished; that during the war and now they were not in constitutional relations with the national Government. And the man, whoever he may be, who stands up and says they are now in constitutional relations

to the national Government utters that which he knows to be untrue. The man who stands up and says that during the entire war the rebel States were entitled to be represented here lays down a proposition which would undermine and sap the very foundations of the Government. If these rebel States had the right to be represented here and had been represented here during this war, this Government would have been bound hand and foot, and we would have been incapable of resistance.

This, then, being the idea adopted by the committee of fifteen, I can support this bill. I know that the proposition submitted by that committee falls far short of what I expected, far short of what the loyal men in the South had a right to expect, far short of what the men who sacrificed so much to preserve this nation had a right to expect. But if I can get nothing better I shall vote for their proposition, as I have already voted for the proposed constitutional amendment which was sent to the Senate the other day. When that proposition was up I desired to offer an amendment to it. But the honorable gentleman from Pennsylvania [Mr. STEVENS] who had charge of the measure had entered a motion to recommit, and would not allow the amendment to be offered. But I now send it to the Clerk's desk, as the amendment I then desired to offer. It may do no good to send it to the Senate now, as I learn since I got on my feet that the amendment which we sent over has received, with an amendment to the third section, the sanction of a majority of the true Union members of that body, and will, undoubtedly, pass that body.

The Clerk read as follows:

ARTICLE —.

SEC. 1. No State shall make or enforce any law which shall abridge the privileges and immunities of citizens of the United States; nor shall any State deprive any person of life, liberty, or property, without due process of law; nor deny to any person within its jurisdiction the equal protection of the laws.

SEC. 2. No State shall deny the elective franchise to any of its inhabitants, being citizens of the United States, above the age of twenty-one years because of race or color; but suffrage shall be impartial. And on the 4th day of July, A.D. 1876, all citizens of the United States above the age of twenty-one years, not convicted of crime or excluded from the right of the ballot by act of Congress or by the law of any State because of insurrection or rebellion against the

United States, shall be electors in each State and Territory of the United States; and on and after the 4th day of July, A.D. 1876, all natural-born citizens of the United States thereafter becoming twenty-one years of age, and all aliens who may thereafter be naturalized and are above the age of twenty-one years and can read and write the English language, shall be qualified to vote for electors of President and Vice President of the United States, for members of the Congress of the United States, and for Governors and members of State Legislatures.

SEC. 3. Representation shall be apportioned among the several States according to the respective number of inhabitants in each.

SEC. 4. No payment shall ever be made by the United States or any State for or on account of the emancipation of any slave or slaves, or for or on account of any debt contracted in aid of insurrection or rebellion against the United States.

SEC. 5. The Congress shall have power to enforce, by appropriate legislation, the provisions of this article.

Mr. ASHLEY, of Ohio. I do not desire to take up the time of the House in discussing this proposition, as I understand the Senate has practically agreed to sustain the proposition on representation which was sent them from this House a short time since. It will be noticed, that in prescribing the qualifications of electors, I omit the word "male" and use the words "all citizens of the United States above the age of twenty-one years." I did this purposely, as I am unwilling to prohibit any State from enfranchising its women if they desire to do so. The Senate having struck out the third clause and inserted another, this amendment will serve no other purpose than to show what I desired to offer the other day.

But, Mr. Speaker, I have an amendment which I desire to offer to this bill—an amendment upon which I shall ask a vote, and to which I desire the attention of the House. House bill No. 543, as reported by the committee, requires the adoption of the constitutional amendment proposed before any State, no matter when it may be ratified, shall be admitted here, thus putting it in the power of the northern States, if they desire to do so, to exclude States which in good faith ratified this constitutional amendment and amended their State constitutions and laws so as to comply with all the conditions we make. I desire, then, to have the bill reported by the committee so amended that whenever any State lately in insurrec-

tion and rebellion shall have ratified this amendment in good faith, and shall have modified its constitution and laws in conformity therewith, that its Senators and Representatives shall be admitted into Congress; that is, that the loyal men of Tennessee and Arkansas now elected shall be admitted; but that as to the other States, they shall, before being represented in Congress, after the adoption of this amendment and the modification of their constitution and laws, elect, or reëlect, if you will, Governors and all other State officers, members of the Legislature, Senators of the United States, and members of this House.

Why do I ask for this provision? Because these governments, set up by the President of the United States, set up over the heads of loyal men, have every one of them elected traitors to official positions in those States, have elected traitors to this House, have elected traitors to the Senate. I insist that this provision shall be applied to them, so that when their constitutions and their laws are modified in accordance with the proposition which we lay down, the loyal men of those States shall, under the amended Constitution and laws, vote for the officers which are to be recognized by the Government of the United States. I ask the Clerk to read the amendment which I propose to offer:

The Clerk read as follows:

That whenever any State lately in insurrection shall have ratified, in good faith and irrevocably, the above recited amendment, and shall have modified its constitution and laws in conformity therewith, and after such ratification and modification of its constitution and laws shall have elected a Governor and the State officers provided for in the constitution of such State, including the State Legislature and Senators and Representatives to the Congress of the United States, under such limitations and restrictions as may be imposed by the constitution and laws of such State when amended as herein prescribed, the Senators and Representatives from such State, if thus elected and qualified, may after having taken the oaths of office required by law, be admitted into Congress as such: *Provided,* That neither the State of Tennessee nor Arkansas shall be required to reëlect a Governor and State officers or a State Legislature or Senators or Representatives to the Congress of the United States; but whenever either of said States shall have ratified the above recited amendment, and shall have modified their constitutions and laws in conformity therewith, their Senators and Representatives now duly elected and qualified may be admitted into Congress on taking the oaths of office required by law.

Mr. ASHLEY, of Ohio. It will be observed, Mr. Speaker, that, by the adoption of this amendment, every State which adopts in good faith the proposed amendment to the Constitution and modifies its constitution and laws in conformity therewith, and after such modification elects a Governor and members of the Legislature and Senators and members of this House, it shall have its Representatives admitted here. An exception, however, is made in the case of Tennessee and Arkansas, which now have loyal Governors and other State officers and loyal Legislatures. Those States would not be required, under this amendment, to reëlect their officers, but the Senators and Representatives already elected, if they can take the oath, would be admitted to seats in Congress, and their present State officers would be allowed to continue in their present positions.

I think this modification a very necessary one. Let gentlemen look over the South and see the character of the men who have been elected as Senators. In almost every instance, where they are not out and out open-throated rebels, who ought to be incarcerated in prisons or exiled from the country instead of approaching this temple of liberty; in almost every instance, I say, where there has been any concessions made to loyal men the Legislatures have elected moderate men for the short term and the most malignant rebels for the long term. Sir, look at Georgia; they would not elect Joshua Hill, but elected Alexander H. Stephens; and so of nearly every rebel State. If the southern people are stupid enough to suppose that such men as Alexander H. Stephens will ever be admitted into the Senate or House of Representatives they might as well be undeceived now. Hence, I say that in view of the fact that the loyal men have had no voice in those reconstructed governments, have had no voice in their legislation, have been dumb and silent under the sway of these traitors who were placed in power over them by the Executive, the loyal men of those States should have a fair opportunity to select men who will truly represent them under the Constitution and laws when modified in accordance with the constitutional amendment proposed by Congress.

I also have an amendment which I intend to offer when the other bill comes up, but will not take up time by reading it now. I will send it to the reporter and he can insert it with my remarks.

Let us look, Mr. Speaker, at the condition in which we find the country. I hold in my hand the propositions reported by the committee of fifteen. I need not read them. They have been carefully examined by every member. All over the land, North and South, a cry is raised against the report of that committee. I ask gentlemen if they can put their hands on a single page of human history where, after a rebellion has been put down of the character of the one we had to deal with, they can find the conquerors making propositions so mild, so conciliatory, and so merciful as these made by the committee of fifteen—propositions as applicable to the conquerors as the conquered. Yet we find men in this Hall, men all over the South, men holding high positions in the Government before the rebellion, and high positions in the rebel government, who have the effrontery to tell the people of this country that they will not accept such conditions. If they will not and we permit them to dictate their own terms, is not this a practical surrender on the part of the conqueror to the conquered? Suppose our position had been reversed; suppose the anti-slavery men of this country had gone into a rebellion as the South did, without a pretext, without cause, when they had a majority in this and the other branch of Congress, simply because a pro-slavery man had been elected President. Suppose this to have been the case, that State after State had seceded, had captured the forts of the United States, and had made war on the Union for four years, destroying half a million of lives, as well as running up a debt of over $3,000,000,000 for posterity to pay. I say suppose this to have been the case, do you believe any such proposition would have been made by those men when they had conquered as have been made by this Government, nay, proposed by this very House? Do you suppose that leading anti-slavery men, like Garrison, Phillips, Beecher, Greeley, and Gerrit Smith, would have been sent for by a pro-slavery Executive to be counseled with and sent home as provisional governors to organize States over the heads of the only loyal men in those States? Do you think there would have been any such stupid performance if the North had been in rebellion? No, sir, we would have been stripped naked, as was said by Henry A. Wise the other evening at Alexandria.

My friend from Iowa in front of me [Mr. PRICE] hands the paper containing the extract I am quoting, and I will read it:

"If I had triumphed," said Governor Wise, "I should have favored stripping them naked. [Laughter.] Pardon! They might have appealed for pardon, but I would have seen them damned before I would have granted it. For myself, the boot being on the other leg, I take no oaths; I ask no pardons! [Prolonged cheers.] I give you that brigade—the old, the lasting, the enduring Wise brigade. [Cheers and applause.]"

Do you suppose if the rebellion in the North to which I have referred had been put down, any traitor would have been permitted to walk in Boston and utter such treason against the Government? No, sir; and yet we are denounced in this Congress as a rump Congress, as Jacobins, as sanguinary men. Why? Because we ask, in restoring the governments of the southern States, that our friends shall have a fair share in the administration of their State governments, and that the leading traitors shall be punished.

Sir, under the Administration, as matters are now going, not a single, solitary traitor will be punished. Rebel soldiers that were in prison have all been liberated, while the soldiers of the grand Union Army who are in prison for the slightest offenses remain, and you cannot get them pardoned out. These are unpleasant facts, but I could not pass them and do my duty without referring to them.

What do we ask? The loyal men of the nation ask that in the restoration of the rebel States the men who were our friends and allies during the rebellion—the loyal men—shall be clothed with the power of the local and State governments of the South. Is this asking too much? If this is not accorded to us, if these men are to come back here, the loyal oath to be repealed as is recommended, and no conditions are to be exacted; if these men are to come back here next year and take possession of the Government, so far from treason being punished and made odious it will only prove to have been a passport to favor and to power. . . .

Mr. Speaker, to me the only vital and living question growing out of this subject of reconstruction is whether the loyal men of the South, whether all citizens of the United States residing in the South, shall have the right of the ballot. And when I say all loyal citizens I mean all, black as well as white. I hold that every man born in the United States is a citizen of the United States, and that every citizen, native-born or naturalized, has the right to a voice in the Government under which he lives. It is a natural right, a divine right if you will, a right of which the Government cannot justly deprive any citizen except as a punishment for crime. Sir, every American citizen of the age of twenty-one years, not convicted of an infamous offense, has the right to vote for or against those who are to make and administer the laws under which he lives.

That is the high prerogative of every American citizen. Anything short of that is but a mockery.

I want this Congress, before it shall adjourn, to insist that every man who has been loyal to the Government in the South, whatever his race or color, shall have the right to the ballot. We now have the golden opportunity. If you do not guaranty these precious rights of the citizen now you leave the great work before us unfinished; and I warn you that agitation will follow your refusal to enact justice, and that there shall be no repose until every citizen of the Republic is enfranchised and stands equal before the law. Shall we falter, Mr. Speaker, in this sublime hour of victory which God has given us, or shall we finish the work which He has committed to our hands by securing the complete enfranchisement of all citizens of the United States?

The voice of every friend of this country in Europe, as it comes to us across the sea, cries out to us to enfranchise the men who in the late struggle were our friends and our allies. From Switzerland, the grand republic of the Old World, there come to us words of counsel and wisdom which we ought not to disregard. From every land beneath the sun, where liberty is loved and human hearts have been touched by our heroic struggle, there comes to us a plea that in reconstructing this Government we shall first of all see to it that justice is the basis upon which we build.

And better than all this, from the loyal men of the South, both white and black, there comes up to us the prayer that we will see to it that they have justice; that we will not falsify the pledges which the nation has made. Sir, do gentlemen expect that we can make the pledges we have made, and then turn these people over to the tender mercies of their enemies and ours without calling down upon us the execrations and denunciations of all right-thinking men? If they do, they are mistaken. Shall we hear and answer these words of counsel and wisdom and the prayer of our friends and allies, or shall we turn for counsel and advice to our late enemies?

We are as a nation either to go forward in the great work of progress or go backward; we cannot stand still. And I am desirous to know whether this Congress is going to attempt the work of staying the great anti-slavery revolution which has swept over the country and obliterated all the pro-slavery landmarks erected by parties and by men. Sir, I have faith to believe that neither President nor Cabinet nor Congress can long stay with their puny efforts the grand decree of the nation. He who attempts it, be he President, Cabinet minister, or statesman, will fall before its advancing power, and his political grave will be marked by the skeletons of those who for the past quarter of a century, having betrayed liberty, were wrecked along the political coast and to-day lie unburied and unhonored because there were none so base as to do them reverence.

Sir, I know that our hour of triumph may be delayed; but I have faith to believe that we cannot be defeated. Let the ballot be placed in the hands of every loyal man in the South, and this nation is safe—safe from rebellion, safe from repudiation, safe from a war of races, safe from the domination of traitors in its councils. Sir, without the ballot in the hands of every loyal man the nation is not safe. The ballot is the only sure weapon of protection and defense for the poor man, whether white or black. It is the sword and buckler and shield before which all oppressions, aristocracies, and special privileges bow. Sir, Mr. Lincoln, in a letter written to Governor Hahn, of Louisiana, pleading for the right of the black man to vote, said most beautifully and, as I believe, prophetically that "in some trying time the vote of the black man may serve to keep the jewel of liberty in the family of freedom."

I believe this most fully; and believing it, I would be false to myself and false to my country if I did not demand it. If I were a black man, with the chains just stricken from my limbs, without a home to shelter me or mine, and you should offer me the ballot, or a cabin and forty acres of cotton land, I would take the ballot, conscious that, with the ballot in my hand, rightly used, all else should be added unto me.

Sir, I would like to know whether there is one professedly loyal man in this nation who would rather confer the ballot upon a traitor to his country than upon a loyal black man who has fought to save the Republic. I should like to hear such a man speak out here or elsewhere. Sir, however much brazen-faced impudence there is in every public assembly, there is no man in this House so bold or so bad as to make such a declaration.

Mr. LE BLOND. With my colleague's permission, I wish to ask him a question. I infer from his remarks that he is in favor of negro suffrage. I wish to know whether he is in favor of negro suffrage in the States.

Mr. ASHLEY, of Ohio. Everywhere.

Mr. LE BLOND. In the State of Ohio?

Mr. ASHLEY, of Ohio. Everywhere.

Mr. LE BLOND. Then I wish to ask the gentleman another question: does he claim that Congress has the power to confer the right of suffrage upon negroes in the States?

Mr. ASHLEY, of Ohio. Well, sir, I do not intend to put myself on record against the right of Congress to do that. I am not prepared now to argue the point with my colleague; but I will say to him that when the time comes for the American Congress to take action on the question, I will be ready to speak. I will not say now whether I would vote for or against such a proposition.

Mr. LE BLOND. I wish to ask my colleague one more question: is he in favor of the report of the reconstruction committee?

Mr. ASHLEY, of Ohio. Well, sir, I am voting for it.

Mr. LE BLOND. Is my colleague in favor of keeping the States out until the conditions prescribed in that report are complied with?

Mr. ASHLEY, of Ohio. If my colleague had listened to my remarks and to the amendment which I presented, he would not have felt called upon to interrupt me to put this inquiry.

Mr. LE BLOND. I would like to inquire why the gentleman yields the question of suffrage, as he does, in supporting the proposition of the committee.

Mr. ASHLEY, of Ohio. Because I cannot get it. [Laughter.] Is not that a fair answer?

Mr. LE BLOND. That is honest.

Mr. ASHLEY, of Ohio. Now, sir, let us look at this question for a moment from the stand-point of the black man. And he who will not look at this question from the stand-point of the black man is unfit to sit in judgment on this question. Let me ask gentlemen on the other side, with whom I always deal fairly, suppose your ancestors had been in bondage for two hundred years, and that this nation—this nation of hypocrites and liars for more than eighty years—had enslaved and degraded you as no people were ever degraded before—making merchandise of your entire race, while professing Christianity and a love for liberty. I say suppose this to have been your condition when this war begun—a war inaugurated on the part of your masters to establish a government which should perpetuate your bondage—and after becoming satisfied that we could not conquer your masters without your aid, we had invited you in the hour of the nation's agony to join our army and help put down the rebellion, promising you your freedom, and that you had come two hundred thousand strong, and had stayed, if you did not turn, the tide of battle, thereby giving us the victory. I say suppose this to be the case, and after the rebellion had been crushed and your masters were put down by your aid, we had coolly and unblushingly turned you over to the control of local State governments administered by your late masters. I ask, what kind of justice would you call that?

Mr. ELDRIDGE. I wish to inquire—

Mr. ASHLEY, of Ohio. If you will answer that I will yield the floor.

Mr. ELDRIDGE. Was that so from the beginning?

Mr. ASHLEY, of Ohio. It was so with me. I do not know what issue the gentleman had. So far as his votes indicated, his position was on the other side.

Mr. ELDRIDGE. Was that the position of Mr. Lincoln and those who supported him from the beginning of the war?

Mr. ASHLEY, of Ohio. I do not think it was at the beginning.

Mr. ELDRIDGE. Was it at the end of the war?

Mr. ASHLEY, of Ohio. Yes, sir.

The SPEAKER. The gentleman's time has expired.

Mr. GARFIELD. I move that my colleague's time be extended.

Mr. LE BLOND. He is entitled to credit, and deserves extension. [Laughter.]

There was no objection, and it was ordered accordingly.

Mr. ASHLEY, of Ohio. Mr. Speaker. I want my friend from Ohio, or any one on that side of the House, to tell me, if after having fought to save the nation under the promise of freedom and the protection of his life and property, what would be his feelings toward those who committed the great crime of turning him over to the control of his enemies and ours? What would you say of such a Government? What would you say of the honor of its rulers? Sir, I know not what other men would say, but if I were a black man I would not submit. I would rather be the slave of one man who had a pecuniary interest in my health and life than to be the slave of a State whose government was controlled by my late masters. It is a terrible thing to be the slave of a State whose government is administered in the spirit of caste. Sir, if the members of this House could witness what I have often seen, free men made the slave of the State, they would know how intolerable is such a condition, and would not sleep soundly if by their vote they permitted four million people, who were our allies and friends in this late war, to become the slaves of a State whose government was in the hands of rebels.

Mr. HIGBY. They have reënacted the same laws.

Mr. ASHLEY, of Ohio. These laws have been reënacted in some of the so-called reconstructed States, as my friend from California remarks. Sir, I repeat, if this great injustice was done me I would not submit; and I tell you that these four million people, soon to increase to ten millions, will not submit to such monstrous legislation. If I were a black man I would rather go into rebellion and revolution than submit to such an intolerable wrong. I would take my children and go daily with them to the altar and swear eternal hostility to those who thus betrayed me. I would consecrate all the powers of mind and strength which I possessed to brand those with infamy who had been so false to my people, and to put them into history along with those who, in every generation, have disgraced the world as the betrayers of mankind and enemies of the human race.

Sir, nothing can give such security to the poor man as the ballot. The prejudice of caste is strong, but the ballot will soon banish its baneful spirit. If in the days of Know-Nothingism the Irishman had not had the protection which the ballot alone could give him his condition would have been intolerable. How much more intolerable the condition of the black man without the ballot when completely under the dominion of his late slave-master!

Mr. ELDRIDGE. Let me ask a question.

Mr. ASHLEY, of Ohio. Not now. When Richmond fell, when Lee surrendered, when the last rebel army surrendered, and the bells all over the North were ringing out their peals of joy, who were the men that stood up first in this Union and asked for mercy to a fallen foe? The men who had a right to speak, Garrison, Phillips, Beecher, Greeley, Bryant, and Gerrit Smith—the men of heart, of intellect, and of soul. While they demanded justice for black men and the loyal men of the South, they plead also for mercy to a fallen foe.

When I came here last spring to see the President he was talking about making treason odious, and declaring that traitors should take a back seat. I was more anxious to secure justice to our friends and allies than to execute vengeance on our enemies. All we asked then and all we ask now is justice— justice to our friends and mercy to a fallen foe. All we ask now for white men and black men in the South and in the North is justice; and I tell you, that by the blessing of God, we intend to have it. Be not deceived. You cannot always postpone the demands of justice. As a nation we have learned by sad experience that we cannot trample upon it with impunity. Neither laws nor customs nor despotism can silence its claim, because it is a principle implanted by the Creator in every human heart, and can never be wholly eradicated by the selfishness or tyranny of man. He who understands the simple teachings of the golden rule comprehends the application of justice alike by Governments and men.

It needs no learning or superior wisdom to interpret it. The ignorant black, so recently a slave, and the most scholarly white alike understand it. Justice demands liberty and equality before the law for all. It speaks in the heart of every man, wherever born, with an inspiration like unto that which spoke on the day of Pentecost with tongues of fire. Woe to the statesman or party or nation which tramples on this principle! Its complete recognition by our Government will bring us national grandeur and national glory, and secure unity, peace, prosperity, power. Its rejection will tarnish the fair fame of our country, and bring discord, dissension, adversity, war.

Let the corner-stone of each reconstructed State be justice and the cap-stone will be liberty. With liberty and justice as the fundamental law of our national and State governments there can be no war of races, no secession, no rebellion. It is injustice and oppression which bring dissension and war. The opposite will bring harmony and peace. He who votes injustice to-day will be held accountable by the people now, and in the great tribunal of human history will be justly chargeable with all the oppression, wrongs, and wars which must follow the enactment of injustice into law. The law-maker who demands nothing for himself which he will not concede to the humblest citizen is the only true statesman. Make the community of interests one by guarantying the equal rights of all men before the law, and the fidelity of every inhabitant of such a commonwealth becomes a necessity not only from interest but from a love of justice.

Sir, this Congress is writing a new chapter in American history. Let every man whose great privilege it is to record his name where it will stand forever, so record it as to secure the triumph of justice, and his name and memory shall have a life coequal with the Republic.

Sir, he who has comprehended the logic of the terrible conflict through which we have passed and studied with profit the lessons which it has taught, will have learned the point at which in our great march as a nation we have reached, and know something of the course which in the future it will travel.

Animated for many years by conflicting, sectional, hostile forces, I have lived to see since my entrance into Congress these antagonistic views so modified and melted into one that to-day the condition is accepted by all patriotic, right-thinking men, and the historian without confusion can make up the record. If this war has taught us any one lesson more clearly than another, it is that we are inseparably one people, that this continent can never again become the abode of human slavery, and that in all our future deliberations in these Halls old antagonisms will cease to divide us, and our hopes and aspirations become one, because our interests are one.

Let this measure, or those which the Senate may perfect, pass and go into the Constitution of the country; let the propositions before us become the law of the land, and you will have done something toward securing the triumph of justice. Pass these acts, and justice as a flaming sword will stand at the doors of the nation's council halls to guard its sanctuary from the presence of traitors. Pass them, and he who approaches this temple of liberty shall pause at the threshold before entering and swear eternal fidelity to the Republic.

Let these propositions pass and the proposed amendment of the Constitution become part of our fundamental law, and a generation shall not pass away before witnessing the complete enfranchisement of every freeman and the entire abolition of all class legislation.

In this faith and with this hope, believing that Providence in the future as in the past will overrule all for our good and supply where we have failed, I am prepared to give my voice and my vote for whatever measure a majority of the loyal members of the American Congress may adopt for the restoration of the States lately in rebellion. . . .

The SPEAKER. The gentleman from West Virginia [Mr. LATHAM] has the floor.

Mr. LATHAM. Mr. Speaker, we seem to have fallen upon an age of theories. We are told from day to day with much seeming sincerity and an air of the most profound political sagacity that the Union when restored must be restored upon a basis which will make it as permanent as the everlasting hills and as invulnerable as the throne of the Eternal, and with such safeguards that even treason will no longer be possible within its jurisdiction. I need not refer to particulars or quote authorities or precedents upon this point to show that I state the case fairly. To attempt to do so would be but to recite a hundred speeches made upon this floor during the present session, and the daily editorials of a thousand newspapers, made and published throughout the length and breadth of the land during the same period, and would be only an insipid reiteration of what everybody knows. The people have heard so much upon this subject; they have heard such declarations so often and so confidently made, and by those whom they have confidence will do what they themselves say ought to be done and must be done, that those of them who really love their country and are devoted to their Government are almost ready to believe that the long-looked for millennium will be ushered in with the reconstruction of the Union....

I now ask indulgence for a few moments while I explain as briefly as possible the difficulties which stand in the way of my support to this bill as a whole. Before, however, entering directly upon this discussion I will just here remark that I do not comprehend how or why the reconstruction or restoration of the States lately overrun by the rebellion involves the necessity of reconstructing the Constitution and Government of the United States. Was the Government of the United States overthrown, or were any of its parts or functions destroyed by the rebellion? If not, where or why the necessity of its reconstruction? Did the rebellion expose imperfection or weakness in any of its parts? Or did we, during its existence, feel the need of the exercise of any power which we did not at the same time feel we had the right to exercise? Did we experience during the rebellion that any change in the Constitution, or even in the form of our Government, could make us stronger than we were?

Sir, we had the right to use, and did use, all the means which God and nature had given us to preserve the life of the Republic. More men and more money were the only agencies which could have given us additional strength, and constitutional amendments could not supply these demands. Sir, even the success of the rebellion would have proved nothing against the wisdom of the provisions of our Constitution, the success of republican institutions, or the strength and permanence of our form of government which it would not have proved equally against that system called the laws of nations, and which we are informed supplanted the Constitution during the war. Much less does the mere fact of rebellion prove anything against either, for all the systems of which we have any information, from the most arbitrary and unjust on earth to that which was established by eternal wisdom for the government of angels in heaven, have been assailed by organized rebellion.

"Irreversible guarantees against rebellion" are a myth, a farce, a deception—mere clap-trap, coined for party purposes—the device of demagoguery, and not the dictate of statesmanship. Security against rebellion is in the administration rather than in the form of government. Place all political power securely in the hands of its friends, and then make it, by the manner of its administration, what the Almighty

intended civil government to be—"a terror to evil-doers, and a praise to them that do well"—by making the punishment of crime and the reward of virtue swift and certain, and you have the guarantees, and all the guarantees, against the renewal of the conflict here that the Almighty has in heaven against its renewal there.

There are two principles involved in the provisions of this bill which I desire to notice. First, that the approval of three fourths of the States now represented in Congress is sufficient to ratify the constitutional amendment. And second, that the ratification of the constitutional amendment recited in this bill shall be a condition-precedent to the right of representation in the States now unrepresented in Congress. These principles are necessarily based upon the presumption that these are not now States of the American Union. If this presumption be true, I ask gentlemen when and by what act they ceased to be States? Was it by the act of rebellion? That I admit was the design of the rebellion; but the rebellion failed in its purposes. Was it by the formal act or ordinance of secession? To state this proposition is now to answer it.

Am I told that the recognition of belligerent rights by the law of nations severed the connection? That the law of nations prevailed during the war and must prevail during the settlement growing out of it? I admit that the United States had the right to, and did, exercise and accord belligerent rights during the war to any extent justified either by policy or the dictates of humanity; but in so doing they never for a moment surrendered the rights of the sovereign; and that upon the submission of those in rebellion to the Constitution and laws the right to the exercise of belligerent powers under the law of nations ceased. Sovereignty alone prevailed—had triumphed; the Constitution and municipal law of the land attached, and the treatment to be accorded the offenders must be under the provisions of and in accordance with these instead of the law of nations, administered by the United States as sovereign and not as belligerent. Who, until at the present time, ever heard of a sovereign Power governing in time of peace any portion of its subjects as belligerents under the law of nations? Oh, what fools the wise men of past generations have been! How they must have desired to see the things that we see, to hear the things that we hear, to know the things that we know! How hard to die without seeing, hearing, and knowing them!

Sir, I assert, without fear of overreaching the principles of law governing the case, that loyal citizens, by being for a time overpowered by the rebellion, have lost none of the rights which attach or ever attached to them by virtue of the Constitution of the United States; and that consequently when they restore their State governments in harmony with that of the United States, they are entitled to exercise all the functions of a State, and to all the rights of a State in the Union. I say the "loyal citizens," for I believe the disloyal are entitled under the Constitution to no right except the right to be hung. When, however, an amnesty or pardon for past offenses is granted, the party having received it may then appeal for protection, and as of right in all matters affected or reached by such amnesty or pardon, to that law which, had it been enforced against him, might have demanded even his life. The law against which he had offended and by which he was condemned, which, while under condemnation, only thundered its anathemas against him, has, upon pardon and reconciliation, become his friend and the advocate of his rights which attach by virtue of such pardon. Now, in what do these rights consist? Do they consist solely of what we term "civil rights," or do they include "political rights" also? My own impression is that they include just what the sovereign granting the pardon may elect to have them include, nothing more, nothing less. And that if it is not yet safe to trust political power in the hands of the reconstructed, it should simply be withheld from them, and that those only who have been continuously loyal should be permitted to exercise it.

The committee, however, has failed to give us any information as to whether those State organizations are in the hands of the friends or the enemies of the Federal Government, or whether those recently in rebellion, but who have been pardoned, may yet be safely invested with "political rights." Where is the protection or encouragement they propose for the Union men of the South? Where, where are the recommendations of this committee upon the most vital question of the day, or involved in all the issues now upon us—the reward and encouragement of loyalty in the section lately overrun by rebellion? Echo answers, where! Gentlemen have labored hard to prove that the loyal are in like condemnation with the disloyal, because they were within rebel lines during the war; that all are "alien enemies" together; that the law of nations justifies us in treating them as such, and that we can make no discrimination between them. Let us see how this is. Allegiance and protection are reciprocal duties, binding, the one upon the citizen, the other upon the Government; and inseparably connected with the faithful observance of all the obligations of allegiance are all the rights which attach by virtue of citizenship. Now, when do these mutual obligations cease? Vattel, page 96, says:

"The natural subjects of a prince are bound to him without any other reserve than the fundamental laws; it is their duty to remain faithful to him, as it is his, on the other hand, to take care to govern them well. Both parties have but one common interest; the people and the prince together constitute but one complete whole, one and the same society. It is, then, an essential and necessary condition of political society that the subjects remain united to their prince as far as in their power."

Am I told that the late civil war dissevered all these bonds and relieved both parties from the observance of these reciprocal obligations and duties? Chitty, in his note to Vattel, page 97, says:

"No individual can shake off his natural allegiance until the part of country where he resides is absolutely conquered and the parent State has acknowledged the severance."

And in his Treatise on Commercial Law, page 129, he elaborates the same doctrine; and I assert, without fear of successful contradiction, that all the authorities on public law, where they touch upon this doctrine, confirm it.

The questions, how the subjects of a government who have been engaged in an unsuccessful rebellion may be treated, and how loyal citizens residing within the rebellious districts should be regarded, have never been considered questions legitimately belonging to the department of international law; because as subjects and citizens they are the objects of the local municipal regulations and laws of the country; the law of nations ceases to operate so soon as the state of war ceases to exist; and when we look to works of international law for authorities or precedents upon these points, we become bewildered because we are traveling out of the record. I have, however, some authorities which, though not bearing directly upon these points, go beyond and cover them. These authorities presuppose—necessarily, because wise men who have written upon these subjects never dreamed of the application of the principles of international law to a country subsequent to the overthrow of an unsuccessful rebellion. These authorities, then, presuppose the success of the rebellion and the permanent partition of the country. In the case of Respublica *vs.* Samuel Chapman, 1 Dallas, page 56, the court held that—

"None are subjects of the adopted government who have not freely assented thereto."

And in the case of Kelly vs. Harrison, 2 Johnson's Cases, page 29, the court held that—

"The division of an empire works no forfeiture of a right previously acquired, and as a consequence of it all the citizens of the United States who were born prior to our independence, and under the allegiance of the King of Great Britain, would be still entitled in Great Britain to the rights of British subjects."

This very language has been reaffirmed by the Supreme Court of the United States; and all these principles here contended for are as old as the law and are of universal acceptance, except with the new school of authorities, who have not yet published their works.

Does, then, the obligation of impartial justice on the part of the Government toward the subject or citizen cease, while that of fealty on his part remains; or does the obligation of fealty attach without carrying with it all the rights and privileges of citizenship? No, they both cease at one and the same time, the same instant, when the Government acknowledges its inability to extend its protection to him, and not until then. But am I told that the exercise and according of belligerent rights during the late civil war actually amounted, in contemplation of public law, to an acknowledgment of the severance by the United States? If so, then all, loyal and disloyal, "without distinction of race, color, or previous condition of slavery," within the limits of the late rebellion, are now aliens, foreigners, not citizens of the United States; and you have no more right, except as might makes right, to extend over them the provisions of your municipal law for the collection of taxes, and for other purposes, than you have to extend them over the people of Mexico, China, or the Russian empire. And why is Jeff. Davis to-day a state prisoner if you can deal with him only in accordance with the law of nations? The United States, sir, by the result of the late war, have acquired no right by conquest which does not legitimately belong to them as sovereign. It was simply a reassertion and triumphant vindication of their disputed sovereignty. The application of the law of nations works an extension or enlargement rather than a forfeiture or limitation of the rights of revolted subjects during the revolt, but all the rights and remedies of the sovereign, and all the pains and penalties which the law denounces against the offenders, an enlargement of power in the Government, and an abridgment of the rights of the offender, attach immediately upon the vindication of the national integrity.

I know that I am now trenching upon the doctrines of the distinguished gentleman from Pennsylvania, [Mr. STEVENS,] and I desire information from him upon the point I now make. Admit, for sake of argument, that all within the lines of the late rebellion were and are "alien enemies." By what principle or upon what authority would you define the limits of the late rebellion with sufficient certainty to ascertain who are "alien enemies"? When and by whom were they so defined? Was it by the President in his proclamation of August 16, 1861? The Government of Great Britain accorded "belligerent rights" to the rebels, by proclamation of the Queen, on the 13th day of May, 1861. The right to the exercise of "belligerent rights" by the United States has been recognized by the Supreme Court from the 15th day of May, 1861, and the President frequently changed the limits by proclamations of different dates, and on April 2, 1866, declared it without form and void—without "a local habitation or a name." As I remarked in this House, on the 8th day of January last, "the rebellion was never bounded by State lines, but its authority was extended wherever its power could carry it." The Supreme Court of the United States, upon this point, (2 Black, page 673, the decision being made during the existence of the rebellion,) say:

"It has a boundary marked by lines of bayonets and which can be crossed only by force; south of this line is enemy's territory, because it is claimed and held in possession by an organized, hostile, and belligerent power."

Now, who can define any fixed limits to the rebellion? To-day that "line of bayonets" is at Gettysburg, and all "south of that line is enemy's territory, because it is held by an organized hostile and belligerent power"; to-morrow that line is at Richmond, and then all between Gettysburg and Richmond is not enemy's territory, because it is not held by the enemy. To-day that "line of bayonets" bears hard upon Louisville, and "all south is enemy's territory"; to-morrow that line is at Chattanooga, Atlanta, Savannah, Columbia, Raleigh! To-day that line is at Jefferson City; to-morrow at Little Rock, at Shreveport, at Galveston, at the Rio Grande—nowhere! Now, who, I ask, ever has defined or ever shall or can define the limits of the rebellion, so as to determine that all were enemies within certain fixed geographical limits? How long occupancy by the enemy and peaceable acquiescence by the inhabitants, does it require to convert the citizen into a "public enemy"—a day, a month, or a year? I trust the gentleman from Pennsylvania never got south of that "line of bayonets," and thus became an "alien enemy," though it strikes me I have heard that the "line of bayonets" was at some time extended north of some of his property, which must now be liable to seizure by the Government as "enemy's property," because it was within "enemy's territory," "claimed and held in possession by an organized, hostile, and belligerent power."

What, sir, is the legitimate bearing of this doctrine upon the fundamental principles of our Government? This bill, sir, contains on its face, though somewhat veiled, and is so interpreted by its author, the monstrous doctrine the enormity of which I have been endeavoring to expose. Recognize this doctrine as a principle in our Government and rebellion will cease to be an individual crime and treason will be impossible, because the instant you engage in them you become an "alien enemy," entitled to "belligerent rights," and can be dealt with only in accordance with the law of nations as a "public enemy." In this way, sir, I admit that the committee has found the great panacea for all our troubles—the great and "irreversible guarantee against rebellion and treason"— by legalizing them. Wonderful discovery! Yet how plain, how simple! How is Columbus outstripped in teaching his wondering admirers how to set an egg on end!

> "The invention all admire, and each, how
> He to be the inventor missed; so easy it seems,
> Once found, which, yet unfound, most would have
>   thought
> Impossible."

What, think you, would our revolutionary fathers, who said that levying war against the United States was treason to be punished by the municipal law, think if they should rise from their graves to find what fools they are discovered to have been? "Angels and ministers of grace," spirits of Washington, Jefferson, Madison, and Hamilton, "defend us" from such heresy!

I, sir, am neither misrepresenting the principles of this bill nor placing a false construction upon this doctrine. It is the one leading idea which has been persistently pressed by the gentleman from Pennsylvania [Mr. Stevens] in connection with every measure which has been introduced looking to a restoration of the Union. It is the construction which he gives to this bill, of which he himself is the author. It is the principle further presented by him in the following section of the bill offered by him to the House on yesterday:

Sec. 6. All persons who held office, either civil or military, under the government called the "confederate States of America," or who swore allegiance to said government, are hereby declared to have forfeited their citizenship and to have renounced their allegiance to the United States, and shall not be entitled to exercise the elective franchise until five years after they shall have filed their intention or desire to be reinvested with the right of citizenship, and shall swear allegiance to the United States and renounce allegiance to all other governments or pretended governments, the said application to be filed and oath taken in the same courts that are authorized by law to naturalize foreigners.

"Forfeited their citizenship"; not citizens, then aliens. Citizens only can be punished for treason. Jeff. Davis "held office under and swore allegiance to the so-called confederate States of America"; hence Jeff. Davis is an alien, and hence he cannot be tried and punished for treason against the United States. Let us pause, sir, before we make this leap.

Sir, this is a subject which deserves the most careful and serious consideration of this Congress and of the country. It is a subject which should be approached and considered by all in no party spirit, but in the spirit of true and unbiased statesmanship and patriotism, and with a view to its bearing upon generations—millions of American citizens—yet unborn, and upon the future prosperity, security, and happiness of our entire common country. I have examined the plan (if plan it may be called) of reconstruction submitted by the committee, with a mind, I think, divested of prejudice and with the permanent welfare of my country only in view, and I am unable to give the plan my support, believing, for the reasons stated, that if adopted it would be productive of more evil than good. It is probably not my place to suggest or offer any plan further than has been indicated in the remarks I have made in opposition to the one proposed. I am prepared, however, to support any plan which promises a restoration of the Union upon principles which promise security to the country and do justice to the downtrodden and long overrun loyalists of the South, and which do not render treason impossible by simply legalizing it. I could even support this bill, not, however, as an *ultimatum*, if this monstrous doctrine was expunged from it; for though I would not make the reconstruction of the Government of the United States a condition for the restoration of the Union, I would be willing for restoration to take place either with or without the other conditions contained in this bill, the essentials of loyalty, properly organized constituency, &c., being complied with.

If the State governments, organized under the auspices of the President, are to be accepted as legitimate—and which is necessarily to be inferred from the action of the committee, because they do not, after six months' investigation, propose any change—then let us say so, and let the country so understand it. If they are not to be accepted as legitimate, then let the committee recommend what changes shall be made and how, and I venture it will be done. A stroke of his pen and a crack of his whip by the honorable gentleman from Pennsylvania, the chairman of the committee, are all that would be needed. If political power is in the hands of those who should not be its custodians, let us wrest it from them. If disloyalty to the United States is made honorable and loyalty made odious, let us reverse the order of things, and let us meet the issue fairly, and do it without any indirection, that the country and the world may know what we intend and why we intend it. If we have to appeal to the law of necessity to accomplish our purposes, let us do it. If those purposes are legitimate, are necessary for our present peace and future security and happiness, the country and the world will approve and justify it. I need not tell you, sir, that it is time Congress had a practicable policy before the country. The eyes of the world are on us, and the historian pauses with ink-dipped pen. What shall he write—that the virtue, intelligence, and patriotism of the American people have triumphed, or that a great people, powerful in war, united by disaster, have failed in the hour of triumph, have proved themselves incapable of securing the blessings and reaping the fruits of victory? Heaven save my country!

U.S. Constitution, Fourteenth Amendment

July 9, 1868

SECTION 1

All persons born or naturalized in the United States, and subject to the jurisdiction thereof, are citizens of the United States and of the State wherein they reside. No State shall make or enforce any law which shall abridge the privileges or immunities of citizens of the United States; nor shall any State deprive any person of life, liberty, or property, without due process of law; nor deny to any person within its jurisdiction the equal protection of the laws.

SECTION 2

Representatives shall be apportioned among the several States according to their respective numbers, counting the whole number of persons in each State, excluding Indians not taxed. But when the right to vote at any election for the choice of electors for President and Vice-President of the United States, Representatives in Congress, the Executive and Judicial officers of a State, or the members of the Legislature thereof, is denied to any of the male inhabitants of such State, being twenty-one years of age, and citizens of the United States, or in any way abridged, except for participation in rebellion, or other crime, the basis of representation therein shall be reduced in the proportion which the number of such male citizens shall bear to the whole number of male citizens twenty-one years of age in such State.

SECTION 3

No person shall be a Senator or Representative in Congress, or elector of President and Vice-President, or hold any office, civil or military, under the United States, or under any State, who, having previously taken an oath, as a member of Congress, or as an officer of the United States, or as a member of any State legislature, or as an executive or judicial officer of any State, to support the Constitution of the United States, shall have engaged in insurrection or rebellion against the same, or given aid or comfort to the enemies thereof. But Congress may by a vote of two-thirds of each House, remove such disability.

SECTION 4

The validity of the public debt of the United States, authorized by law, including debts incurred for payment of pensions and bounties for services in suppressing insurrection or rebellion, shall not be questioned. But neither the United States nor any State shall assume or pay any debt or obligation incurred in aid of insurrection or rebellion against the United States, or any claim for the loss or emancipation of any slave; but all such debts, obligations and claims shall be held illegal and void.

SECTION 5

The Congress shall have the power to enforce, by appropriate legislation, the provisions of this article.

U.S. Constitution, Fifteenth Amendment

February 3, 1870

SECTION 1

The right of citizens of the United States to vote shall not be denied or abridged by the United States or by any State on account of race, color, or previous condition of servitude—

SECTION 2

The Congress shall have the power to enforce this article by appropriate legislation.

Enforcement Act of 1870

Enforcement Act of 1871

Enforcement Act of 1875

Attempts to enforce provisions of the Fourteenth and Fifteenth Amendments in the South were met with opposition and violence. The Enforcement Act of 1870 sought to increase protection of African Americans and Republican voters by providing penalties for interference with these rights. Intimidation, riots, and murder of African Americans and white Republicans attempting to vote continued, most prominently through actions of the Ku Klux Klan. The Enforcement Act of 1871 (also called the Ku Klux Klan Act, the Force Act, and the Civil Rights Act of 1871) granted the president increased powers to act against conspiracies against, and actual denials of, constitutional rights. This included the right to suspend the writ of habeas corpus and to use federal troops to keep order and protect targeted individuals and groups. The Enforcement Act of 1875, generally referred to as the Civil Rights Act of 1875, extended to all persons full and equal enjoyment of public accommodations such as hotels, trains, and theaters. It also granted African Americans the right to sue for personal damages and to serve as jurors. This last act was, in essence, struck down by the U.S. Supreme Court in the Slaughter-House Cases *(1873).*

Enforcement Act of 1870

May 31, 1870

An Act to enforce the Right of Citizens of the United States to vote in the several States of this Union, and for other Purposes.

   Be it enacted by the Senate and House of Representatives of the United States of America in Congress assembled, That all citizens of the United States who are or shall be otherwise qualified by law to vote at any election by the people in any State, Territory, district, county, city, parish, township, school district, municipality, or other territorial subdivision, shall be entitled and allowed to vote at all such elections, without distinction of race, color, or previous condition of servitude; any constitution, law, custom, usage, or regulation of any State or Territory, or by or under its authority, to the contrary notwithstanding.

   Sec. 2. *And be it further enacted,* That if by or under the authority of the constitution or laws of any State, or the laws of any Territory, any act is or shall be required to be done as a prerequisite or qualification for voting, and by such constitution or laws persons or officers are or shall be charged with the performance of duties in furnishing to citizens an oppor-

tunity to perform such prerequisite, or to become qualified to vote, it shall be the duty of every such person and officer to give to all citizens of the United States the same and equal opportunity to perform such prerequisite, and to become qualified to vote without distinction of race, color, or previous condition of servitude; and if any such person or officer shall refuse or knowingly omit to give full effect to this section, he shall, for every such offence, forfeit and pay the sum of five hundred dollars to the person aggrieved thereby, to be recovered by an action on the case, with full costs, and such allowance for counsel fees as the court shall deem just, and shall also, for every such offence, be deemed guilty of a misdemeanor, and shall, on conviction thereof, be fined not less than five hundred dollars, or be imprisoned not less than one month and not more than one year, or both, at the discretion of the court.

   Sec. 3. *And be it further enacted,* That whenever, by or under the authority of the constitution or laws of any State, or the laws of any Territory, any act is or shall be required to [be] done by any citizen as a prerequisite to qualify or entitle him to vote, the offer of any such citizen to perform the act required to be done as aforesaid shall, if it fail to be carried into execution by reason of the wrongful act or omission aforesaid of the person or officer charged with the duty of receiving or permitting such performance or offer to perform, or acting thereon, be deemed and held as a performance in law of such act; and the person so offering and failing as aforesaid, and being otherwise qualified, shall be entitled to vote in the same manner and to the same extent as if he had in fact performed such act; and any judge, inspector, or other officer of election whose duty it is or shall be to receive, count, certify, register, report, or give effect to the vote of any such citizen who shall wrongfully refuse or omit to receive, count, certify, register, report, or give effect to the vote of such citizen upon the presentation by him of his affidavit stating such offer and the time and place thereof, and the name of the officer or person whose duty it was to act thereon, and that he was wrongfully prevented by such person or officer from performing such act, shall for every such offence forfeit and pay the sum of five hundred dollars to the person aggrieved thereby, to be recovered by an action on the case, with full costs, and such allowance for counsel fees as the court shall deem just, and shall also for every such offence be guilty of a misdemeanor, and shall, on conviction thereof, be fined not less than five hundred dollars, or be imprisoned not less than one month and not more than one year, or both, at the discretion of the court.

SEC. 4. *And be it further enacted,* That if any person, by force, bribery, threats, intimidation, or other unlawful means, shall hinder, delay, prevent, or obstruct, or shall combine and confederate with others to hinder, delay, prevent, or obstruct, any citizen from doing any act required to be done to qualify him to vote or from voting at any election as aforesaid, such person shall for every such offence forfeit and pay the sum of five hundred dollars to the person aggrieved thereby, to be recovered by an action on the case, with full costs, and such allowance for counsel fees as the court shall deem just, and shall also for every such offence be guilty of a misdemeanor, and shall, on conviction thereof, be fined not less than five hundred dollars, or be imprisoned not less than one month and not more than one year, or both, at the discretion of the court.

SEC. 5. *And be it further enacted,* That if any person shall prevent, hinder, control, or intimidate, or shall attempt to prevent, hinder, control, or intimidate, any person from exercising or in exercising the right of suffrage, to whom the right of suffrage is secured or guaranteed by the fifteenth amendment to the Constitution of the United States, by means of bribery, threats, or threats of depriving such person of employment or occupation, or of ejecting such person from rented house, lands, or other property, or by threats of refusing to renew leases or contracts for labor, or by threats of violence to himself or family, such person so offending shall be deemed guilty of a misdemeanor, and shall, on conviction thereof, be fined not less than five hundred dollars, or be imprisoned not less than one month and not more than one year, or both, at the discretion of the court.

SEC. 6. *And be it further enacted,* That if two or more persons shall band or conspire together, or go in disguise upon the public highway, or upon the premises of another, with intent to violate any provision of this act, or to injure, oppress, threaten, or intimidate any citizen with intent to prevent or hinder his free exercise and enjoyment of any right or privilege granted or secured to him by the Constitution or laws of the United States, or because of his having exercised the same, such persons shall be held guilty of felony, and, on conviction thereof, shall be fined or imprisoned, or both, at the discretion of the court,—the fine not to exceed five thousand dollars, and the imprisonment not to exceed ten years,—and shall, moreover, be thereafter ineligible to, and disabled from holding, any office or place of honor, profit, or trust created by the Constitution or laws of the United States.

SEC. 7. *And be it further enacted,* That if in the act of violating any provision in either of the two preceding sections, any other felony, crime, or misdemeanor shall be committed, the offender, on conviction of such violation of said sections, shall be punished for the same with such punishments as are attached to the said felonies, crimes, and misdemeanors by the laws of the State in which the offence may be committed.

SEC. 8. *And be it further enacted,* That the district courts of the United States, within their respective districts, shall have, exclusively of the courts of the several States, cognizance of all crimes and offences committed against the provisions of this act, and also, concurrently with the circuit courts of the United States, of all causes, civil and criminal, arising under this act, except as herein otherwise provided, and the jurisdiction hereby conferred shall be exercised in conformity with the laws and practice governing United States courts; and all crimes and offences committed against the provisions of this act may be prosecuted by the indictment of a grand jury, or, in cases of crimes and offences not infamous, the prosecution may be either by indictment or information filed by the district attorney in a court having jurisdiction.

SEC. 9. *And be it further enacted,* That the district attorneys, marshals, and deputy marshals of the United States, the commissioners appointed by the circuit and territorial courts of the United States, with powers of arresting, imprisoning, or bailing offenders against the laws of the United States, and every other officer who may be specially empowered by the President of the United States, shall be, and they are hereby, specially authorized and required, at the expense of the United States, to institute proceedings against all and every person who shall violate the provisions of this act, and cause him or them to be arrested and imprisoned, or bailed, as the case may be, for trial before such court of the United States or territorial court as has cognizance of the offense. And with a view to afford reasonable protection to all persons in their constitutional right to vote without distinction of race, color, or previous condition of servitude, and to the prompt discharge of the duties of this act, it shall be the duty of the circuit courts of the United States, and the superior courts of the Territories of the United States, from time to time, to increase the number of commissioners, so as to afford a speedy and convenient means for the arrest and examination of persons charged with a violation of this act; and such commissioners are hereby authorized and required to exercise and discharge all the powers and duties conferred on them by this act, and the same duties with regard to offences created by this act as they are authorized by law to exercise with regard to other offences against the laws of the United States.

SEC. 10. *And be it further enacted,* That it shall be the duty of all marshals and deputy marshals to obey and execute all warrants and precepts issued under the provisions of this act, when to them directed; and should any marshal or deputy marshal refuse to receive such warrant or other process when tendered, or to use all proper means diligently to execute the same, he shall, on conviction thereof, be fined in the sum of one thousand dollars, to the use of the person deprived of the rights conferred by this act. And the better to enable the said commissioners to execute their duties faithfully and efficiently, in conformity with the Constitution of the United States and the requirements of this act, they are hereby authorized and empowered, within their districts respectively, to appoint, in writing, under their hands, any one or more suitable persons, from time to time, to execute all such warrants and other process as may be issued by them in the lawful performance of their respective duties, and the persons so appointed to execute any warrant or process as aforesaid shall have authority to summon and call to their aid the bystanders or posse comitatus of the proper county, or such portion of the land or naval forces of the United States, or of the militia, as may be necessary to the performance of the duty with which they are charged, and to insure a faithful observance of the fifteenth amendment to the Constitution of the United States; and such warrants shall run and be executed by said officers anywhere in the State or Territory within which they are issued.

SEC. 11. *And be it further enacted,* That any person who shall knowingly and wilfully obstruct, hinder, or prevent any officer or other person charged with the execution of any warrant or process issued under the provisions of this act, or any person or persons lawfully assisting him or them from arresting any person for whose apprehension such warrant or process may have been issued, or shall rescue or attempt to rescue such person from the custody of the officer or other person or persons, or those lawfully assisting as aforesaid, when so arrested pursuant to the authority herein given and declared, or shall aid, abet, or assist any person so arrested as aforesaid, directly or indirectly, to escape from the custody of the officer or other person legally authorized as aforesaid, or shall harbor or conceal any person for whose arrest a warrant or process shall have been issued as aforesaid, so as to prevent his discovery and arrest after notice or knowledge of the fact that a warrant has been issued for the apprehension of such person, shall, for either of said offences, be subject to a fine not exceeding one thousand dollars, or imprisonment not exceeding six months, or both, at the discretion of the court, on conviction before the district or circuit court of the United States for the district or circuit in which said offence may have been committed; or before the proper court of criminal jurisdiction, if committed within any one of the organized Territories of the United States.

SEC. 12. *And be it further enacted,* That the commissioners, district attorneys, the marshals, their deputies, and the clerks of the said district, circuit, and territorial courts shall be paid for their services the like fees as may be allowed to them for similar services in other cases. The person or persons authorized to execute the process to be issued by such commissioners for the arrest of offenders against the provisions of this act shall be entitled to the usual fees allowed to the marshal for an arrest for each person he or they may arrest and take before any such commissioner as aforesaid, with such other fees as may be deemed reasonable by such commissioner for such other additional services as may be necessarily performed by him or them, such as attending at the examination, keeping the prisoner in custody, and providing him with food and lodging during his detention and until the final determination of such commissioner, and in general for performing such other duties as may be required in the premises; such fees to be made up in conformity with the fees usually charged by the officers of the courts of justice within the proper district or county as near as may be practicable, and paid out of the treasury of the United States on the certificate of the judge of the district within which the arrest is made, and to be recoverable from the defendant as part of the judgment in case of conviction.

SEC. 13. *And be it further enacted,* That it shall be lawful for the President of the United States to employ such part of the land or naval forces of the United States, or of the militia, as shall be necessary to aid in the execution of judicial process issued under this act.

SEC. 14. *And be it further enacted,* That whenever any person shall hold office, except as a member of Congress or of some State legislature, contrary to the provisions of the third section of the fourteenth article of amendment of the Constitution of the United States, it shall be the duty of the district attorney of the United States for the district in which such person shall hold office, as aforesaid, to proceed against such person, by writ of quo warranto, returnable to the circuit or district court of the United States in such district, and to prosecute the same to the removal of such person from office; and any writ of quo warranto so brought, as aforesaid, shall take precedence of all other cases on the docket of the court to which it is made returnable, and shall not be continued unless for cause proved to the satisfaction of the court.

SEC. 15. *And be it further enacted,* That any person who shall hereafter knowingly accept or hold any office under the United States, or any State to which he is ineligible under the third section of the fourteenth article of amendment of the Constitution of the United States, or who shall attempt to hold or exercise the duties of any such office, shall be deemed guilty of a misdemeanor against the United States, and, upon conviction thereof before the circuit or district court of the United States, shall be imprisoned not more than one year, or fined not exceeding one thousand dollars, or both, at the discretion of the court.

SEC. 16. *And be it further enacted,* That all persons within the jurisdiction of the United States shall have the same right in every State and Territory in the United States to make and enforce contracts, to sue, be parties, give evidence, and to the full and equal benefit of all laws and proceedings for the se-curity of person and property as is enjoyed by white citizens, and shall be subject to like punishment, pains, penalties, taxes, licenses, and exactions of every kind, and none other, any law, statute, ordinance, regulation, or custom to the contrary notwithstanding. No tax or charge shall be imposed or enforced by any State upon any person immigrating thereto from a foreign country which is not equally imposed and enforced upon every person immigrating to such State from any other foreign country; and any law of any State in conflict with this provision is hereby declared null and void.

SEC. 17. *And be it further enacted,* That any person who, under color of any law, statute, ordinance, regulation, or custom, shall subject, or cause to be subjected, any inhabitant of any State or Territory to the deprivation of any right secured or protected by the last preceding section of this act, or to different punishment, pains, or penalties on account of such person being an alien, or by reason of his color or race, than is prescribed for the punishment of citizens, shall be deemed guilty of a misdemeanor, and, on conviction, shall be punished by fine not exceeding one thousand dollars, or imprisonment not exceeding one year, or both, in the discretion of the court.

SEC. 18. *And be it further enacted,* That the act to protect all persons in the United States in their civil rights, and furnish the means of their vindication, passed April nine, eighteen hundred and sixty-six, is hereby re-enacted; and sections sixteen and seventeen hereof shall be enforced according to the provisions of said act.

SEC. 19. *And be it further enacted,* That if at any election for representative or delegate in the Congress of the United States any person shall knowingly personate and vote, or attempt to vote, in the name of any other person, whether living, dead, or fictitious; or vote more than once at the same election for any candidate for the same office; or vote at a place where he may not be lawfully entitled to vote; or vote without having a lawful right to vote; or do any unlawful act to secure a right or an opportunity to vote for himself or any other person; or by force, threat, menace, intimidation, bribery, reward, or offer, or promise thereof, or otherwise unlawfully prevent any qualified voter of any State of the United States of America, or of any Territory thereof, from freely exercising the right of suffrage, or by any such means induce any voter to refuse to exercise such right; or compel or induce by any such means, or otherwise, any officer of an election in any such State or Territory to receive a vote from a person not legally qualified or entitled to vote; or interfere in any manner with any officer of said elections in the discharge of his duties; or by any of such means, or other unlawful means, induce any officer of an election, or officer whose duty it is to ascertain, announce, or declare the result of any such election, or give or make any certificate, document, or evidence in relation thereto, to violate or refuse to comply with his duty, or any law regulating the same; or knowingly and wilfully receive the vote of any person not entitled to vote, or refuse to receive the vote of any person entitled to vote; or aid, counsel, procure, or advise any such voter, person, or officer to do any act hereby made a crime, or to omit to do any duty the omission of which is hereby made a crime, or attempt to do so, every such person shall be deemed guilty of a crime, and shall for such crime be liable to prosecution in any court of the United States of competent jurisdiction, and, on conviction thereof, shall be punished by a fine not exceeding five hundred dollars, or by imprisonment for a term not exceeding three years, or both, in the discretion of the court, and shall pay the costs of prosecution.

SEC. 20. *And be it further enacted,* That if, at any registration of voters for an election for representative or delegate in the Congress of the United States, any person shall knowingly personate and register, or attempt to register, in the name of any other person, whether living, dead, or fictitious, or fraudulently register, or fraudulently attempt to register, not having a lawful right so to do; or do any unlawful act to secure registration for himself or any other person; or by force, threat, menace, intimidation, bribery, reward, or offer, or promise thereof, or other unlawful means, prevent or hinder any person having a lawful right to register from duly exercising such right; or compel or induce, by any of such means, or other unlawful means, any officer of registration to admit to registration any person not legally entitled thereto, or interfere in any manner with any officer of registration in the discharge of his duties, or by any such means, or other unlawful means, induce any officer of registration to violate or refuse to comply with his duty, or any law regulating the same; or knowingly and wilfully receive the vote of any person not entitled to vote, or refuse to receive the vote of any person entitled to vote, or aid, counsel, procure, or advise any such voter, person, or officer to do any act hereby made a crime, or to omit any act, the omission of which is hereby made a crime, every such person shall be deemed guilty of a crime, and shall be liable to prosecution and punishment therefor, as provided in section nineteen of this act for persons guilty of any of the crimes therein specified: *Provided,* That every

registration made under the laws of any State or Territory, for any State or other election at which such representative or delegate in Congress shall be chosen, shall be deemed to be a registration within the meaning of this act, notwithstanding the same shall also be made for the purposes of any State, territorial, or municipal election.

SEC. 21. *And be it further enacted,* That whenever, by the laws of any State or Territory, the name of any candidate or person to be voted for as representative or delegate in Congress shall be required to be printed, written, or contained in any ticket or ballot with other candidates or persons to be voted for at the same election for State, territorial, municipal, or local officers, it shall be sufficient prima facie evidence, either for the purpose of indicting or convicting any person charged with voting, or attempting or offering to vote, unlawfully under the provisions of the preceding sections, or for committing either of the offenses thereby created, to prove that the person so charged or indicted, voted, or attempted or offered to vote, such ballot or ticket, or committed either of the offenses named in the preceding sections of this act with reference to such ballot. And the proof and establishment of such facts shall be taken, held, and deemed to be presumptive evidence that such person voted, or attempted or offered to vote, for such representative or delegate, as the case may be, or that such offense was committed with reference to the election of such representative or delegate, and shall be sufficient to warrant his conviction, unless it shall be shown that any such ballot, when cast, or attempted or offered to be cast, by him, did not contain the name of any candidate for the office of representative or delegate in the Congress of the United States, or that such offense was not committed with reference to the election of such representative or delegate.

SEC. 22. *And be it further enacted,* That any officer of any election at which any representative or delegate in the Congress of the United States shall be voted for, whether such officer of election be appointed or created by or under any law or authority of the United States, or by or under any State, territorial, district, or municipal law or authority, who shall neglect or refuse to perform any duty in regard to such election required of him by any law of the United States, or of any State or Territory thereof; or violate any duty so imposed, or knowingly do any act thereby unauthorized, with intent to affect any such election, or the result thereof; or fraudulently make any false certificate of the result of such election in regard to such representative or delegate; or withhold, conceal, or destroy any certificate of record so required by law respecting, concerning, or pertaining to the election of any such representative or delegate; or neglect or refuse to make and return the same as so required by law; or aid, counsel, procure, or advise any voter, person, or officer to do any act by this or any of the preceding sections made a crime; or to omit to do any duty the omission of which is by this or any of said sections made a crime, or attempt to do so, shall be deemed guilty of a crime and shall be liable to prosecution and punishment therefor, as provided in the nineteenth section of this act for persons guilty of any of the crimes therein specified.

SEC. 23. *And be it further enacted,* That whenever any person shall be defeated or deprived of his election to any office, except elector of President or Vice-President, representative or delegate in Congress, or member of a State legislature, by reason of the denial to any citizen or citizens who shall offer to vote, of the right to vote, on account of race, color, or previous condition of servitude, his right to hold and enjoy such office, and the emoluments thereof, shall not be impaired by such denial; and such person may bring any appropriate suit or proceeding to recover possession of such office, and in cases where it shall appear that the sole question touching the title to such office arises out of the denial of the right to vote to citizens who so offered to vote, on account of race, color, or previous condition of servitude, such suit or proceeding may be instituted in the circuit or district court of the United States of the circuit or district in which such person resides. And said circuit or district court shall have, concurrently with the State courts, jurisdiction thereof so far as to determine the rights of the parties to such office by reason of the denial of the right guaranteed by the fifteenth article of amendment to the Constitution of the United States, and secured by this act.

APPROVED, May 31, 1870

Enforcement Act of 1871

April 20, 1871

An Act to enforce the Provisions of the Fourteenth Amendment to the Constitution of the United States, and for other Purposes.

Be it enacted by the Senate and House of Representatives of the United States of America in Congress assembled, That any person who, under color of any law, statute, ordinance, regulation, custom, or usage of any State, shall subject, or cause to be subjected, any person within the jurisdiction of the United States to the deprivation of any rights, privileges, or immunities secured by the Constitution of the United States, shall, any such law, statute, ordinance, regulation, custom, or usage of the State to the contrary notwithstanding, be liable to the party injured in any action at law, suit in equity, or other proper proceeding for redress; such proceeding to be prosecuted in the several district or circuit courts of the United States, with and subject to the same rights of appeal, review upon error, and other remedies provided in like cases in such courts, under the provisions of the act of the ninth of April, eighteen hundred and sixty-six, entitled "An act to protect all persons in the United States in their civil rights, and to furnish the means of their vindication"; and the other remedial laws of the United States which are in their nature applicable in such cases.

SEC. 2. That if two or more persons within any State or Territory of the United States shall conspire together to overthrow, or to put down, or to destroy by force the government of the United States, or to levy war against the United States, or to oppose by force the authority of the government of the United States, or by force, intimidation, or threat to prevent, hinder, or delay the execution of any law of the United States, or by force to seize, take, or possess any property of the United States contrary to the authority thereof, or by force, intimidation, or threat to prevent any person from accepting or holding any office or trust or place of confidence under the United States, or from discharging the duties thereof, or by force, intimidation, or threat to induce any officer of the United States to leave any State, district, or place where his duties as such officer might lawfully be performed, or to injure him in his person or property on account of his lawful discharge of the duties of his office, or to injure his person while engaged in the lawful discharge of the duties of his office, or to injure his property so as to molest, interrupt, hinder, or impede him in the discharge of his official duty, or by force, intimidation, or threat to deter any party or witness in any court of the United States from attending such court, or from testifying in any matter pending in such court fully, freely, and truthfully, or to injure any such party or witness in his person or property on account of his having so attended or testified, or by force, intimidation, or threat to influence the verdict, presentment, or indictment, of any juror or grand juror in any court of the United States, or to injure such juror in his person or property on account of any verdict, presentment, or indictment lawfully assented to by him, or on account of his being or having been such juror, or shall conspire together, or go in disguise upon the public highway or upon the premises of another for the purpose, either directly or indirectly, of depriving any person or any class of persons of the equal protection of the laws, or of equal privileges or immunities under the laws, or for the purpose of preventing or hindering the constituted authorities of any State from giving or securing to all persons within such State the equal protection of the laws, or shall conspire together for the purpose of in any manner impeding, hindering, obstructing, or defeating the due course of justice in any State or Territory, with intent to deny to any citizen of the United States the due and equal protection of the laws, or to injure any person in his person or his property for lawfully enforcing the right of any person or class of persons to the equal protection of the laws, or by force, intimidation, or threat to prevent any citizen of the United States lawfully entitled to vote from giving his support or advocacy in a lawful manner towards or in favor of the election of any lawfully qualified person as an elector of President or Vice-President of the United States, or as a member of the Congress of the United States, or to injure any such citizen in his person or property on account of such support or advocacy, each and every person so offending shall be deemed guilty of a high crime, and, upon conviction thereof in any district or circuit court of the United States or district or supreme court of any Territory of the United States having jurisdiction of similar offences, shall be punished by a fine not less than five hundred nor more than five thousand dollars, or by imprisonment, with or without hard labor, as the court may determine, for a period of not less than six months nor more than six years, as the court may determine, or by both such fine and imprisonment as the court shall determine. And if any one or more persons engaged in any such conspiracy shall do, or cause to be done, any act in furtherance of the object of such conspiracy, whereby any person shall be injured in his person or property, or deprived of having and exercising any right or privilege of a citizen of the United States, the person so injured or deprived of such rights and privileges may have and maintain an action for the recovery of damages occasioned by such injury or deprivation of rights and privileges against any one or more of the persons engaged in such conspiracy, such action to be prosecuted in the proper district or circuit court of the United States, with and subject to the same rights of appeal, review upon error, and other remedies provided in like cases in such courts under the provisions of the act of April ninth, eighteen hundred and sixty-six, entitled "An act to protect all persons in the United States in their civil rights, and to furnish the means of their vindication."

SEC. 3. That in all cases where insurrection, domestic violence, unlawful combinations, or conspiracies in any State shall so obstruct or hinder the execution of the laws thereof, and of the United States, as to deprive any portion or class of the people of such State of any of the rights, privileges, or immunities, or protection, named in the Constitution and secured by this act, and the constituted authorities of such State shall either be unable to protect, or shall, from any cause, fail in or refuse protection of the people in such rights, such facts shall be deemed a denial by such State of the equal protection of the laws to which they are entitled under the Constitution of the United States; and in all such cases, or whenever any such insurrection, violence, unlawful combination, or conspiracy shall oppose or obstruct the laws of the United States or the due execution thereof, or impede or obstruct the due course of justice under the same, it shall be lawful for the President, and it shall be his duty to take such measures, by the employment of the militia or the land and naval forces of the United States, or of either, or by other means, as he may deem necessary for the suppression of such insurrection, domestic violence, or combinations; and any person who shall be arrested under the provisions of this and the preceding section shall be delivered to the marshal of the proper district, to be dealt with according to law.

SEC. 4. That whenever in any State or part of a State the unlawful combinations named in the preceding section of this act shall be organized and armed, and so numerous and powerful as to be able, by violence, to either overthrow or set at defiance the constituted authorities of such State, and of the United States within such State, or when the constituted authorities are in complicity with, or shall connive at the unlawful purposes of, such powerful and armed combinations; and whenever, by reason of either or all of the causes aforesaid, the conviction of such offenders and the preservation of the public safety shall become in such district impracticable, in every such case such combinations shall be deemed a rebellion against the government of the United States, and during the continuance of such rebellion, and within the limits of the district which shall be so under the sway thereof, such limits to be prescribed by proclamation, it shall be lawful for the President of the United States, when in his judgment the public safety shall require it, to suspend the privileges of the writ of habeas corpus, to the end that such rebellion may be overthrown: *Provided,* That all the provisions of the second section of an act entitled "An act relating to habeas corpus, and regulating judicial proceedings in certain cases," approved March third, eighteen hundred and sixty-three, which relate to the discharge of prisoners other than prisoners of war, and to the penalty for refusing to obey the order of the court, shall be in full force so far as the same are applicable to the provisions of this section: *Provided further,* That the President shall first have made proclamation, as now provided by law, commanding such insurgents to disperse: *And provided also,* That the provisions of this section shall not be in force after the end of the next regular session of Congress.

SEC. 5. That no person shall be a grand or petit juror in any court of the United States upon any inquiry, hearing, or trial of any suit, proceeding, or prosecution based upon or arising under the provisions of this act who shall, in the judgment of the court, be in complicity with any such combination or conspiracy; and every such juror shall, before entering upon any such inquiry, hearing, or trial, take and subscribe an oath in open court that he has never, directly or indirectly, counselled, advised, or voluntarily aided any such combination or conspiracy; and each and every person who shall take this oath, and shall therein swear falsely, shall be guilty of perjury, and shall be subject to the pains and penalties declared against that crime, and the first section of the act entitled "An act defining additional causes of challenge and prescribing an additional oath for grand and petit jurors in the United States courts," approved June seventeenth, eighteen hundred and sixty-two, be, and the same is hereby, repealed.

SEC. 6. That any person or persons, having knowledge that any of the wrongs conspired to be done and mentioned in the second section of this act are about to be committed, and having power to prevent or aid in preventing the same, shall neglect or refuse so to do, and such wrongful act shall be committed, such person or persons shall be liable to the person injured, or his legal representatives, for all damages caused by any such wrongful act which such first-named person or persons by reasonable diligence could have prevented; and such damages may be recovered in an action on the case in the proper circuit court of the United States, and any number of persons guilty of such wrongful neglect or refusal may be joined as defendants in such action: *Provided,* That such action shall be commenced within one year after such cause of action shall have accrued; and if the death of any person shall be caused by any such wrongful act and neglect, the le-

gal representatives of such deceased person shall have such action therefor, and may recover not exceeding five thousand dollars damages therein, for the benefit of the widow of such deceased person, if any there be, or if there be no widow, for the benefit of the next of kin of such deceased person.

SEC. 7. That nothing herein contained shall be construed to supersede or repeal any former act or law except so far as the same may be repugnant thereto; and any offences heretofore committed against the tenor of any former act shall be prosecuted, and any proceeding already commenced for the prosecution thereof shall be continued and completed, the same as if this act had not been passed, except so far as the provisions of this act may go to sustain and validate such proceedings.

APPROVED, April 20, 1871.

Enforcement Act of 1875

March 1, 1875

Be it enacted by the Senate and House of Representatives of the United States of America in Congress assembled, That all persons within the jurisdiction of the United States shall be entitled to the full and equal enjoyment of the accommodations, advantages, facilities, and privileges of inns, public conveyances on land or water, theaters, and other places of public amusement; subject only to the conditions and limitations established by law, and applicable alike to citizens of every race and color, regardless of any previous condition of servitude.

SEC. 2. That any person who shall violate the foregoing section by denying to any citizen, except for reasons by law applicable to citizens of every race and color, and regardless of any previous condition of servitude, the full enjoyment of any of the accommodations, advantages, facilities, or privileges in said section enumerated, or by aiding or inciting such denial, shall, for every such offense, forfeit and pay the sum of five hundred dollars to the person aggrieved thereby, to be recovered in an action of debt, with full costs; and shall also, for every such offense, be deemed guilty of a misdemeanor, and, upon conviction thereof, shall be fined not less than five hundred nor more than one thousand dollars, or shall be imprisoned not less than thirty days nor more than one year: *Provided,* That all persons may elect to sue for the penalty aforesaid or to proceed under their rights at common law and by State statutes; and having so elected to proceed in the one mode or the other, their right to proceed in the other jurisdiction shall be barred. But this proviso shall not apply to criminal proceedings, either under this act or the criminal law of any State: *And provided further,* That a judgment for the penalty in favor of the party aggrieved, or a judgment upon an indictment, shall be a bar to either prosecution respectively.

SEC. 3. That the district and circuit courts of the United States shall have, exclusively of the courts of the several States, cognizance of all crimes and offenses against, and violations of, the provisions of this act; and actions for the penalty given by the preceding section may be prosecuted in the territorial, district, or circuit courts of the United State[s] wherever the defendant may be found, without regard to the other party; and the district attorneys, marshals, and deputy marshals of the United States, and commissioners appointed by the circuit and territorial courts of the United States, with powers of arresting and imprisoning or bailing offenders against the laws of the United States, are hereby specially authorized and required to institute proceedings against every person who shall violate the provisions of this act, and cause him to be arrested and imprisoned or bailed, as the case may be, for trial before such court of the United States, or territorial court, as by law has cognizance of the offense, except in respect of the right of action accruing to the person aggrieved; and such district attorneys shall cause such proceedings to be prosecuted to their termination as in other cases: *Provided,* That nothing contained in this section shall be construed to deny or defeat any right of civil action accruing to any person, whether by

reason of this act or otherwise; and any district attorney who shall willfully fail to institute and prosecute the proceedings herein required, shall, for every such offense, forfeit and pay the sum of five hundred dollars to the person aggrieved thereby, to be recovered by an action of debt, with full costs, and shall, on conviction thereof, be deemed guilty of a misdemeanor, and be fined not less than one thousand nor more than five thousand dollars: *And provided further,* That a judgment for the penalty in favor of the party aggrieved against any such district attorney, or a judgment upon an indictment against any such district attorney, shall be a bar to either prosecution respectively.

SEC. 4. That no citizen possessing all other qualifications which are or may be prescribed by law shall be disqualified for service as grand or petit juror in any court of the United States, or of any State, on account of race, color, or previous condition of servitude; and any officer or other person charged with any duty in the selection or summoning of jurors who shall exclude or fail to summon any citizen for the cause aforesaid shall, on conviction thereof, be deemed guilty of a misdemeanor, and be fined not more than five thousand dollars.

SEC. 5. That all cases arising under the provisions of this act in the courts of the United States shall be reviewable by the Supreme Court of the United States, without regard to the sum in controversy, under the same provisions and regulations as are now provided by law for the review of other causes in said court.

Approved, March 1, 1875.

Constitution of the State of Mississippi, 1868

One result of congressional acts requiring that African American males be allowed to vote in the former Confederate states was election of a constitutional convention in Mississippi, among other states, that included African Americans (sixteen of ninety-four delegates). The resulting constitution not only extended the voting franchise to African Americans, but also established state-supported schools and disenfranchised the vast majority of white Mississippians who had supported the Confederacy. Amid fraud and violence, that constitution failed to be ratified by the people. However, once the section disenfranchising ex-Confederates was jettisoned, the constitution achieved ratification.

The Constitution of the State of Mississippi, as Adopted in Convention

May 15, 1868

Preamble

To the end that justice be established, public order maintained, and liberty perpetuated, we, the people of the State of Mississippi, grateful to Almighty God for the free exercise of the right to choose our own form of Government, do ordain this Constitution.

Article I

Bill of Rights

Section 1. All persons resident in this State, citizens of the United States, are hereby declared citizens of the State of Mississippi.

Sec. 2. No person shall be deprived of life, liberty, or property, except by due process of law.

Sec. 3. The privilege of the writ of *habeas corpus* shall not be suspended, unless when in case of rebellion or invasion, the public safety may require it.

Sec. 4. The freedom of speech and of the press shall be held sacred; and in all indictments for libel, the jury shall determine the law and the facts, under the direction of the court.

Sec. 5. No person's life or liberty shall be twice placed in jeopardy for the same offense.

Sec. 6. The right of the people peaceably to assemble and petition the government on any subject, shall never be impaired.

Sec. 7. In all criminal prosecutions, the accused shall have a right to be heard by himself or counsel, or both; to demand the nature and cause of the accusation; to be confronted by the witnesses against him; to have a compulsory process for obtaining witnesses in his favor, and in all prosecutions, by indictment or information, a speedy and public trial, by an impartial jury of the county where the offense was committed, and he shall not be compelled to give evidence against himself.

Sec. 8. Cruel or unusual punishment shall not be inflicted, nor shall excessive fines be imposed; excessive bail shall not be required, and all persons shall, before conviction, be bailable by sufficient securities, except for capital offenses, when the proof is evident, or presumption great.

Sec. 9. No *ex post facto* law or laws impairing the obligation of contracts, shall ever be passed.

Sec. 10. Private property shall not be taken for public use, except upon due compensation first being made to the owner or owners thereof, in a manner to be provided for by law.

Sec. 11. There shall be no imprisonment for debt.

Sec. 12. The right of trial by jury shall remain inviolate.

Sec. 13. No property qualification shall ever be required of any person to become a juror.

Sec. 14. The people shall be secure in their persons, houses, and possessions, from unreasonable seizure, or search, and no warrant shall be issued without probable cause, supported by oath or affirmation, specially designating the place to be searched, and the person or thing to be seized.

SEC. 15. All persons shall have a right to keep and bear arms for their defense.

SEC. 16. The rights of married women shall be protected by law, in property owned previous to marriage; and, also in all property acquired in good faith, by purchase, gift, devise, or bequest, after marriage; *Provided,* That nothing herein contained shall be so construed as to protect said property from being applied to the payment of their lawful debts.

SEC. 17. No property qualification for eligibility to office shall ever be required.

SEC. 18. No property or educational qualification shall ever be required for any person to become an elector.

SEC. 19. There shall be neither slavery nor involuntary servitude in this State, otherwise than in the punishment of crime, whereof the party shall have been duly convicted.

SEC. 20. The right to withdraw from the Federal Union, on account of any real or supposed grievances, shall never be assumed by this State, nor shall any law be passed in derogation of the paramount allegiance of the citizens of this State to the Government of the United States.

SEC. 21. No public money or moneys shall be appropriated for charitable or other public institution in this State, making any distinction among the citizens thereof; *Provided,* That nothing herein contained shall be so construed as to prevent the Legislature from appropriating the school fund in accordance with the article in this Constitution relating to public schools.

SEC. 22. No distinction shall ever be made by law between citizens and alien friends in reference to the possession, enjoyment or descent of property.

SEC. 23. No religious test as a qualification for office shall ever be required, and no preference shall ever be given by law to any religious sect or mode of worship, but the free enjoyment of all religious sentiments and the different modes of worship shall ever be held sacred; *Provided,* The rights hereby secured, shall not be construed to justify acts of licentiousness injurious to morals or dangerous to the peace and safety of the State.

SEC. 24. The right of all citizens to travel upon public conveyances shall not be infringed upon, nor in any manner abridged in this State.

SEC. 25. The military shall be in strict subordination to the civil power.

SEC. 26. Treason against the State shall consist only in levying war against the same, or in adhering to its enemies, giving them aid and comfort. No person shall be convicted of treason, unless on the testimony of two witnesses to the same overt act, or on confession in open court.

SEC. 27. No person's life shall be periled by the practice of dueling, and any person who shall hereafter fight a duel, or assist in the same, as second, or send, accept, or knowingly carry a challenge therefor, or go out of the State to fight a duel, shall be disqualified from holding any office under this Constitution, and shall forever be disfranchised in this State.

SEC. 28. All courts shall be open, and every person, for an injury done him in his lands, goods, person, or reputation, shall have remedy by due course of law, and right and justice administered without sale, denial or delay.

SEC. 29. No person shall ever be elected or appointed to any office in this State for life or during good behavior, but the term of all offices shall be for some specified period.

SEC. 30. No person shall be debarred from prosecuting or defending any civil cause for or against him or herself, before any tribunal in this State, by him or herself, or counsel or both.

SEC. 31. No person shall, for any indictable offense, be proceeded against criminally by information, except in cases arising in the land or naval forces, or the militia when in actual service, or by leave of the court, for misdemeanor in office; *Provided,* That the Legislature in cases of petit larceny, assaults, assault and battery, affray, riot, unlawful assembly, drunkenness, vagrancy, and other misdemeanors of like character, may dispense with an inquest of a grand jury and may authorize prosecutions before Justices of the Peace, or such other inferior court or courts as may be established by the Legislature, and the proceedings in such cases shall be regulated by law.

SEC. 32. The enumeration of rights in this Constitution shall not be construed to deny or impair others retained by and inherent in the people. . . .

ARTICLE VII

Franchise

SECTION 1. All elections by the people shall be by ballot.

SEC. 2. All male inhabitants of this State, except idiots and insane persons, and Indians, not taxed, citizens of the United States, or naturalized, twenty-one years old and upwards, who have resided in this State six months, and in the county one month next preceding the day of election, at which said inhabitant offers to vote, and who are duly registered according to the requirements of section 3 of this article, and who are not disqualified by reason of any crime, are declared to be qualified electors.

SEC. 3. The Legislature shall provide by law for the registration of all persons entitled to vote at any election, and all persons entitled to register shall take and subscribe the following oath or affirmation: "I ——, do solemnly swear (or affirm), in the presence of Almighty God, that I am twenty-one years old; that I have resided in this State six months, and in —— county one month; that I will faithfully support and obey the Constitution and laws of the United States, and of the State of Mississippi, and will bear true faith and allegiance to the same; that I am not disfranchised in any of the provisions of the acts known as the Reconstruction Acts of the 39th and 40th Congress; and that I admit the political and civil equality of all men; so help me God"; *Provided,* That if Congress shall, at any time, remove the disabilities of any persons disfranchised in the said Reconstruction Acts of the said 39th and 40th Congress (and the Legislature of this State shall concur therein), then so much of this oath, and so much only, as refers to the said Reconstruction Acts, shall not be required of such person, so pardoned, to entitle him to be registered.

SEC. 4. No person shall be eligible to any office of profit or trust, or to any office in the militia of this State, who is not a qualified elector.

SEC. 5. No person shall be eligible to any office of profit or trust, civil or military, in this State, who, as a member of the Legislature, voted for the call of the Convention that passed the Ordinance of Secession, or who, as a delegate to any Convention, voted for or signed any ordinance of secession, or who gave voluntary aid, countenance, counsel or encouragement to persons engaged in armed hostility to the United States, or who accepted or attempted to exercise the functions of any office, civil or military, under any authority or pretended government authority, power, or Constitution, within the United States, hostile or inimical thereto, except all persons who aided reconstruction by voting for this Convention, or who have continuously advocated the assembling of this Convention, and shall continuously and in good faith advocate the acts of the same; but the Legislature may remove such disability; *Provided,* That nothing in this section, except voting for or signing the Ordinance of Secession shall be so construed as to exclude from office the private soldier of the late so-called Confederate States army.

SEC. 6. In time of war, insurrection or rebellion, the right to vote at such place, and in such manner as shall be pre-

scribed by law, shall be enjoyed by all persons otherwise entitled thereto, who may be in the actual military or naval service of the United States or this State; *Provided,* Said votes be made to apply in the county or precinct wherein they reside.

ARTICLE VIII

School Fund, Education and Science

SECTION 1. As the stability of a Republican form of government depends mainly upon the intelligence and virtue of the people, it shall be the duty of the Legislature to encourage, by all suitable means, the promotion of intellectual, scientific, moral and agricultural improvement, by establishing a uniform system of free public schools, by taxation or otherwise, for all children between the ages of five and twenty-one years, and shall, as soon as practicable, establish schools of higher grade.

SEC. 2. There shall be a Superintendent of Public Education elected at the same time and in the same manner as the Governor, who shall have the qualification of the Secretary of State, and hold his office for four years, and until his successor shall be elected and qualified, whose duties shall be the general supervision of the common schools and the educational interests of the State, and who shall perform such other duties pertaining to his office, and receive such compensation as shall be prescribed by law; he shall report to the Legislature, for its adoption, within twenty days after the opening of its first session under this Constitution, a uniform system of free public schools.

SEC. 3. There shall be a Board of Education, consisting of the Secretary of State, the Attorney General, and the Superintendent of Public Education, for the management and investment of the school funds, under the general direction of the Legislature, and to perform such other duties as may be prescribed by law. The Superintendent and one other of said board shall constitute a quorum.

SEC. 4. There shall be a Superintendent of Public Education in each county, who shall be appointed by the Board of Education, by and with the advice and consent of the Senate, whose term of office shall be two years, and whose compensation and duties shall be prescribed by law; *Provided,* That the Legislature shall have power to make said office of County School Superintendent of the several counties elective, as other county officers are.

SEC. 5. A public school or schools shall be maintained in each school district at least four months in each year. Any school district neglecting to maintain such school or schools shall be deprived for that year of its proportion of the income of the free school fund and of all funds arising from taxes for the support of schools.

Sec. 6. There shall be established a common school fund, which shall consist of the proceeds of the lands now belonging to the State, heretofore granted by the United States, and of the lands known as "swamp lands," except the swamp lands lying and situated on Pearl river, in the counties of Hancock, Marion, Lawrence, Simpson, and Copiah, and of all lands now or hereafter vested in the State by escheat, or purchase, or forfeiture for taxes, and the clear proceeds of all fines collected in the several counties for any breach of the penal laws, and all moneys received for licenses granted under the general laws of the State, for the sale of intoxicating liquor, or keeping of dram shops; all moneys paid as an equivalent for persons exempt from military duty, and the funds arising from the consolidation of the Congressional township funds, and the lands belonging thereto, together with all moneys donated to the State for school purposes, which funds shall be securely invested in United States bonds, and remain a perpetual fund, which may be increased, but not diminished, the interest of which shall be inviolably appropriated for the support of free schools.

Sec. 7. The Legislature may levy a poll tax not to exceed two dollars a head, in aid of the school fund, and for no other purpose.

Sec. 8. The Legislature shall, as soon as practicable, provide for the establishment of an Agricultural College or Colleges, and shall appropriate the two hundred and ten thousand acres of land donated to the State for the support of such a college by the act of Congress passed July 2, A.D. 1865, or the money or scrip, as the case may be, arising from the sale of said lands or any lands which may hereafter be granted, or appropriated for such purpose.

Sec. 9. No religious sect or sects shall ever control any part of the school or university funds of this State.

Sec. 10. The Legislature shall, from time to time, as may be necessary, provide for the levy and collection of such other taxes as may be required to properly support the system of free schools herein adopted. And all school funds shall be divided *pro rata* among the children of school age.

Slaughter-House Cases, 1873

Only a few years after the Fourteenth Amendment was ratified, the nature of the protections it afforded and how they might restrict states' rights became the subject of intense debate. Critical to this debate was the decision in the Slaughter-House Cases, *actually a consolidation of several cases. These cases concerned a Louisiana law that enabled New Orleans to set up a monopoly centralizing and controlling the local slaughterhouse business. Butchers and others involved in the production of meat sued to overturn the law on the grounds that it infringed their Fourteenth Amendment right to pursue their legitimate occupations. In a 5–4 decision, the U.S. Supreme Court held that the Fourteenth Amendment extended no such general right. Instead, according to the Court, the Fourteenth Amendment merely protected the specific privileges and immunities of federal citizenship and would not interfere with legitimate exercise of each state's police powers. Because Louisiana passed the law with the stated aim of protecting the public health, it was seen to pass constitutional muster. This was only the beginning of a still-ongoing debate over the intent and effect of the Fourteenth Amendment.*

Slaughter-House Cases

April 14, 1873

The Butchers' Benevolent Association of New Orleans *v.* The Crescent City Live-Stock Landing and Slaughter-House Company.
Paul Esteben, L. Ruch, J. P. Rouede, W. Maylie, S. Firmberg, B. Beaubay, William Fagan, J. D. Broderick, N. Seibel, M. Lannes, J. Gitzinger, J. P. Aycock, D. Verges, The Live-Stock Dealers' and Butchers' Association of New Orleans, and Charles Cavaroc *v.* The State of Louisiana, *ex rel.* S. Belden, Attorney-General.
The Butchers' Benevolent Association of New Orleans *v.* The Crescent City Live-Stock Landing and Slaughter-House Company.

Mr. Justice MILLER, now, April 14th, 1873, delivered the opinion of the court.

These cases are brought here by writs of error to the Supreme Court of the State of Louisiana. They arise out of the efforts of the butchers of New Orleans to resist the Crescent City Live-Stock Landing and Slaughter-House Company in the exercise of certain powers conferred by the charter which created it, and which was granted by the legislature of that State.

The cases named on a preceding page, with others which have been brought here and dismissed by agreement, were all decided by the Supreme Court of Louisiana in favor of the Slaughter-House Company, as we shall hereafter call it for the sake of brevity, and these writs are brought to reverse those decisions. . . .

The records show that the plaintiffs in error relied upon, and asserted throughout the entire course of the litigation in the State courts, that the grant of privileges in the charter of defendant, which they were contesting, was a violation of the most important provisions of the thirteenth and fourteenth articles of amendment of the Constitution of the United States. The jurisdiction and the duty of this court to review the judgment of the State court on those questions is clear and is imperative.

The statute thus assailed as unconstitutional was passed March 8th, 1869, and is entitled "An act to protect the health of the city of New Orleans, to locate the stock-landings and slaughter-houses, and to incorporate the Crescent City Live-Stock Landing and Slaughter-House Company."

The first section forbids the landing or slaughtering of

animals whose flesh is intended for food, within the city of New Orleans and other parishes and boundaries named and defined, or the keeping or establishing any slaughter-houses or *abattoirs* within those limits except by the corporation thereby created, which is also limited to certain places afterwards mentioned. Suitable penalties are enacted for violations of this prohibition.

The second section designates the corporators, gives the name to the corporation, and confers on it the usual corporate powers.

The third and fourth sections authorize the company to establish and erect within certain territorial limits, therein defined, one or more stock-yards, stock-landings, and slaughter-houses, and imposes upon it the duty of erecting, on or before the first day of June, 1869, one grand slaughter-house of sufficient capacity for slaughtering five hundred animals per day.

It declares that the company, after it shall have prepared all the necessary buildings, yards, and other conveniences for that purpose, shall have the sole and exclusive privilege of conducting and carrying on the live-stock landing and slaughter-house business within the limits and privilege granted by the act, and that all such animals shall be landed at the stock-landings and slaughtered at the slaughter-houses of the company, and nowhere else. Penalties are enacted for infractions of this provision, and prices fixed for the maximum charges of the company for each steamboat and for each animal landed.

Section five orders the closing up of all other stock-landings and slaughter-houses after the first day of June, in the parishes of Orleans, Jefferson, and St. Bernard, and makes it the duty of the company to permit any person to slaughter animals in their slaughter-houses under a heavy penalty for each refusal. Another section fixes a limit to the charges to be made by the company for each animal so slaughtered in their building, and another provides for an inspection of all animals intended to be so slaughtered, by an officer appointed by the governor of the State for that purpose.

These are the principal features of the statute, and are all that have any bearing upon the questions to be decided by us.

This statute is denounced not only as creating a monopoly and conferring odious and exclusive privileges upon a small number of persons at the expense of the great body of the community of New Orleans, but it is asserted that it deprives a large and meritorious class of citizens—the whole of the butchers of the city—of the right to exercise their trade, the business to which they have been trained and on which they depend for the support of themselves and their families; and that the unrestricted exercise of the business of butchering is necessary to the daily subsistence of the population of the city.

But a critical examination of the act hardly justifies these assertions.

It is true that it grants, for a period of twenty-five years, exclusive privileges. And whether those privileges are at the expense of the community in the sense of a curtailment of any of their fundamental rights, or even in the sense of doing them an injury, is a question open to considerations to be hereafter stated. But it is not true that it deprives the butchers of the right to exercise their trade, or imposes upon them any restriction incompatible with its successful pursuit, or furnishing the people of the city with the necessary daily supply of animal food.

The act divides itself into two main grants of privilege, —the one in reference to stock-landings and stock-yards, and the other to slaughter-houses. That the landing of live-stock in large droves, from steamboats on the bank of the river, and from railroad trains, should, for the safety and comfort of the people and the care of the animals, be limited to proper places, and those not numerous, it needs no argument to prove. Nor can it be injurious to the general community that while the duty of making ample preparation for this is imposed upon a few men, or a corporation, they should, to enable them to do it successfully, have the exclusive right of providing such landing-places, and receiving a fair compensation for the service.

It is, however, the slaughter-house privilege, which is mainly relied on to justify the charges of gross injustice to the public, and invasion of private right.

It is not, and cannot be successfully controverted, that it is both the right and the duty of the legislative body—the supreme power of the State or municipality—to prescribe and determine the localities where the business of slaughtering for a great city may be conducted. To do this effectively it is indispensable that all persons who slaughter animals for food shall do it in those places *and nowhere else.*

The statute under consideration defines these localities and forbids slaughtering in any other. It does not, as has been asserted, prevent the butcher from doing his own slaughtering. On the contrary, the Slaughter-House Company is required, under a heavy penalty, to permit any person who wishes to do so, to slaughter in their houses; and they are bound to make ample provision for the convenience of all the slaughtering for the entire city. The butcher then is still permitted to slaughter, to prepare, and to sell his own meats; but he is required to slaughter at a specified place and to pay a reasonable compensation for the use of the accommodations furnished him at that place.

The wisdom of the monopoly granted by the legislature may be open to question, but it is difficult to see a justification for the assertion that the butchers are deprived of the right to labor in their occupation, or the people of their daily service in preparing food, or how this statute, with the duties and guards imposed upon the company, can be said to destroy the business of the butcher, or seriously interfere with its pursuit.

The power here exercised by the legislature of Louisiana is, in its essential nature, one which has been, up to the present period in the constitutional history of this country, always conceded to belong to the States, however it may *now* be questioned in some of its details.

"Unwholesome trades, slaughter-houses, operations offensive to the senses, the deposit of powder, the application of steam power to propel cars, the building with combustible materials, and the burial of the dead, may all," says Chancellor Kent,* "be interdicted by law, in the midst of dense masses of population, on the general and rational principle, that every person ought so to use his property as not to injure his neighbors; and that private interests must be made subservient to the general interests of the community." This is called the police power; and it is declared by Chief Justice Shaw† that it is much easier to perceive and realize the existence and sources of it than to mark its boundaries, or prescribe limits to its exercise.

This power is, and must be from its very nature, incapable of any very exact definition or limitation. Upon it depends the security of social order, the life and health of the citizen, the comfort of an existence in a thickly populated community, the enjoyment of private and social life, and the beneficial use of property. "It extends," says another eminent judge,‡ "to the protection of the lives, limbs, health, comfort, and quiet of all persons, and the protection of all property within the State; . . . and persons and property are subjected to all kinds of re-

straints and burdens in order to secure the general comfort, health, and prosperity of the State. Of the perfect right of the legislature to do this no question ever was, or, upon acknowledged general principles, ever can be made, so far as natural persons are concerned."

The regulation of the place and manner of conducting the slaughtering of animals, and the business of butchering within a city, and the inspection of the animals to be killed for meat, and of the meat afterwards, are among the most necessary and frequent exercises of this power. It is not, therefore, needed that we should seek for a comprehensive definition, but rather look for the proper source of its exercise.

In *Gibbons* v. *Ogden,** Chief Justice Marshall, speaking of inspection laws passed by the States, says: "They form a portion of that immense mass of legislation which controls everything within the territory of a State not surrendered to the General Government—all which can be most advantageously administered by the States themselves. Inspection laws, quarantine laws, health laws of every description, as well as laws for regulating the internal commerce of a State, and those which respect turnpike roads, ferries, &c., are component parts. No direct general power over these objects is granted to Congress; and consequently they remain subject to State legislation."

The exclusive authority of State legislation over this subject is strikingly illustrated in the case of the *City of New York* v. *Miln*.† In that case the defendant was prosecuted for failing to comply with a statute of New York which required of every master of a vessel arriving from a foreign port, in that of New York City, to report the names of all his passengers, with certain particulars of their age, occupation, last place of settlement, and place of their birth. It was argued that this act was an invasion of the exclusive right of Congress to regulate commerce. And it cannot be denied that such a statute operated at least indirectly upon the commercial intercourse between the citizens of the United States and of foreign countries. But notwithstanding this it was held to be an exercise of the police power properly within the control of the State, and unaffected by the clause of the Constitution which conferred on Congress the right to regulate commerce.

To the same purpose are the recent cases of *The License Tax*,‡ and *United States* v. *De Witt*.§ In the latter case an act

---

* 2 Commentaries, 340.

† Commonwealth *v.* Alger, 7 Cushing, 84.

‡ Thorpe *v.* Rutland and Burlington Railroad Co., 27 Vermont, 149.

* 9 Wheaton, 203.

† 11 Peters, 102.

‡ 5 Wallace, 471.

§ 9. Id. 41.

of Congress which undertook as a part of the internal revenue laws to make it a misdemeanor to mix for sale naphtha and illuminating oils, or to sell oil of petroleum inflammable at less than a prescribed temperature, was held to be void, because as a police regulation the power to make such a law belonged to the States, and did not belong to Congress.

It cannot be denied that the statute under consideration is aptly framed to remove from the more densely populated part of the city, the noxious slaughter-houses, and large and offensive collections of animals necessarily incident to the slaughtering business of a large city, and to locate them where the convenience, health, and comfort of the people require they shall be located. And it must be conceded that the means adopted by the act for this purpose are appropriate, are stringent, and effectual. But it is said that in creating a corporation for this purpose, and conferring upon it exclusive privileges—privileges which it is said constitute a monopoly—the legislature has exceeded its power. If this statute had imposed on the city of New Orleans precisely the same duties, accompanied by the same privileges, which it has on the corporation which it created, it is believed that no question would have been raised as to its constitutionality. In that case the effect on the butchers in pursuit of their occupation and on the public would have been the same as it is now. Why cannot the legislature confer the same powers on another corporation, created for a lawful and useful public object, that it can on the municipal corporation already existing? That wherever a legislature has the right to accomplish a certain result, and that result is best attained by means of a corporation, it has the right to create such a corporation, and to endow it with the powers necessary to effect the desired and lawful purpose, seems hardly to admit of debate. The proposition is ably discussed and affirmed in the case of *McCulloch* v. *The State of Maryland*,* in relation to the power of Congress to organize the Bank of the United States to aid in the fiscal operations of the government.

It can readily be seen that the interested vigilance of the corporation created by the Louisiana legislature will be more efficient in enforcing the limitation prescribed for the stock-landing and slaughtering business for the good of the city than the ordinary efforts of the officers of the law.

Unless, therefore, it can be maintained that the exclusive privilege granted by this charter to the corporation, is beyond the power of the legislature of Louisiana, there can be no just

* 4 Wheaton, 316.

exception to the validity of the statute. And in this respect we are not able to see that these privileges are especially odious or objectionable. The duty imposed as a consideration for the privilege is well defined, and its enforcement well guarded. The prices or charges to be made by the company are limited by the statute, and we are not advised that they are on the whole exorbitant or unjust.

The proposition is, therefore, reduced to these terms: Can any exclusive privileges be granted to any of its citizens, or to a corporation, by the legislature of a State?

The eminent and learned counsel who has twice argued the negative of this question, has displayed a research into the history of monopolies in England, and the European continent, only equalled by the eloquence with which they are denounced.

But it is to be observed, that all such references are to monopolies established by the monarch in derogation of the rights of his subjects, or arise out of transactions in which the people were unrepresented, and their interests uncared for. The great *Case of Monopolies,* reported by Coke, and so fully stated in the brief, was undoubtedly a contest of the commons against the monarch. The decision is based upon the ground that it was against common law, and the argument was aimed at the unlawful assumption of power by the crown; for whoever doubted the authority of Parliament to change or modify the common law? The discussion in the House of Commons cited from Macaulay clearly establishes that the contest was between the crown, and the people represented in Parliament.

But we think it may be safely affirmed, that the Parliament of Great Britain, representing the people in their legislative functions, and the legislative bodies of this country, have from time immemorial to the present day, continued to grant to persons and corporations exclusive privileges—privileges denied to other citizens—privileges which come within any just definition of the word monopoly, as much as those now under consideration; and that the power to do this has never been questioned or denied. Nor can it be truthfully denied, that some of the most useful and beneficial enterprises set on foot for the general good, have been made successful by means of these exclusive rights, and could only have been conducted to success in that way.

It may, therefore, be considered as established, that the authority of the legislature of Louisiana to pass the present statute is ample, unless some restraint in the exercise of that power be found in the constitution of that State or in the amendments to the Constitution of the United States, adopted since the date of the decisions we have already cited.

If any such restraint is supposed to exist in the constitution of the State, the Supreme Court of Louisiana having necessarily passed on that question, it would not be open to review in this court.

The plaintiffs in error accepting this issue, allege that the statute is a violation of the Constitution of the United States in these several particulars:

That it creates an involuntary servitude forbidden by the thirteenth article of amendment;

That it abridges the privileges and immunities of citizens of the United States;

That it denies to the plaintiffs the equal protection of the laws; and,

That it deprives them of their property without due process of law; contrary to the provisions of the first section of the fourteenth article of amendment.

This court is thus called upon for the first time to give construction to these articles.

We do not conceal from ourselves the great responsibility which this duty devolves upon us. No questions so far-reaching and pervading in their consequences, so profoundly interesting to the people of this country, and so important in their bearing upon the relations of the United States, and of the several States to each other and to the citizens of the States and of the United States, have been before this court during the official life of any of its present members. We have given every opportunity for a full hearing at the bar; we have discussed it freely and compared views among ourselves; we have taken ample time for careful deliberation, and we now propose to announce the judgments which we have formed in the construction of those articles, so far as we have found them necessary to the decision of the cases before us, and beyond that we have neither the inclination nor the right to go.

Twelve articles of amendment were added to the Federal Constitution soon after the original organization of the government under it in 1789. Of these all but the last were adopted so soon afterwards as to justify the statement that they were practically contemporaneous with the adoption of the original; and the twelfth, adopted in eighteen hundred and three, was so nearly so as to have become, like all the others, historical and of another age. But within the last eight years three other articles of amendment of vast importance have been added by the voice of the people to that now venerable instrument.

The most cursory glance at these articles discloses a unity of purpose, when taken in connection with the history of the times, which cannot fail to have an important bearing on any question of doubt concerning their true meaning. Nor can such doubts, when any reasonably exist, be safely and rationally solved without a reference to that history; for in it is found the occasion and the necessity for recurring again to the great source of power in this country, the people of the States, for additional guarantees of human rights; additional powers to the Federal government; additional restraints upon those of the States. Fortunately that history is fresh within the memory of us all, and its leading features, as they bear upon the matter before us, free from doubt.

The institution of African slavery, as it existed in about half the States of the Union, and the contests pervading the public mind for many years, between those who desired its curtailment and ultimate extinction and those who desired additional safeguards for its security and perpetuation, culminated in the effort, on the part of most of the States in which slavery existed, to separate from the Federal government, and to resist its authority. This constituted the war of the rebellion, and whatever auxiliary causes may have contributed to bring about this war, undoubtedly the overshadowing and efficient cause was African slavery.

In that struggle slavery, as a legalized social relation, perished. It perished as a necessity of the bitterness and force of the conflict. When the armies of freedom found themselves upon the soil of slavery they could do nothing less than free the poor victims whose enforced servitude was the foundation of the quarrel. And when hard pressed in the contest these men (for they proved themselves men in that terrible crisis) offered their services and were accepted by thousands to aid in suppressing the unlawful rebellion, slavery was at an end wherever the Federal government succeeded in that purpose. The proclamation of President Lincoln expressed an accomplished fact as to a large portion of the insurrectionary districts, when he declared slavery abolished in them all. But the war being over, those who had succeeded in re-establishing the authority of the Federal government were not content to permit this great act of emancipation to rest on the actual results of the contest or the proclamation of the Executive, both of which might have been questioned in after times, and they determined to place this main and most valuable result in the Constitution of the restored Union as one of its fundamental articles. Hence the thirteenth article of amendment of that instrument. Its two short sections seem hardly to admit of construction, so vigorous is their expression and so appropriate to the purpose we have indicated.

"1. Neither slavery nor involuntary servitude, except as a punishment for crime, whereof the party shall have been duly convicted, shall exist within the United States or any place subject to their jurisdiction.

"2. Congress shall have power to enforce this article by appropriate legislation."

To withdraw the mind from the contemplation of this grand yet simple declaration of the personal freedom of all the human race within the jurisdiction of this government—a declaration designed to establish the freedom of four millions of slaves—and with a microscopic search endeavor to find in it a reference to servitudes, which may have been attached to property in certain localities, requires an effort, to say the least of it.

That a personal servitude was meant is proved by the use of the word "involuntary," which can only apply to human beings. The exception of servitude as a punishment for crime gives an idea of the class of servitude that is meant. The word servitude is of larger meaning than slavery, as the latter is popularly understood in this country, and the obvious purpose was to forbid all shades and conditions of African slavery. It was very well understood that in the form of apprenticeship for long terms, as it had been practiced in the West India Islands, on the abolition of slavery by the English government, or by reducing the slaves to the condition of serfs attached to the plantation, the purpose of the article might have been evaded, if only the word slavery had been used. The case of the apprentice slave, held under a law of Maryland, liberated by Chief Justice Chase, on a writ of habeas corpus under this article, illustrates this course of observation.* And it is all that we deem necessary to say on the application of that article to the statute of Louisiana, now under consideration.

The process of restoring to their proper relations with the Federal government and with the other States those which had sided with the rebellion, undertaken under the proclamation of President Johnson in 1865, and before the assembling of Congress, developed the fact that, notwithstanding the formal recognition by those States of the abolition of slavery, the condition of the slave race would, without further protection of the Federal government, be almost as bad as it was before. Among the first acts of legislation adopted by several of the States in the legislative bodies which claimed to be

in their normal relations with the Federal government, were laws which imposed upon the colored race onerous disabilities and burdens, and curtailed their rights in the pursuit of life, liberty, and property to such an extent that their freedom was of little value, while they had lost the protection which they had received from their former owners from motives both of interest and humanity.

They were in some States forbidden to appear in the towns in any other character than menial servants. They were required to reside on and cultivate the soil without the right to purchase or own it. They were excluded from many occupations of gain, and were not permitted to give testimony in the courts in any case where a white man was a party. It was said that their lives were at the mercy of bad men, either because the laws for their protection were insufficient or were not enforced.

These circumstances, whatever of falsehood or misconception may have been mingled with their presentation, forced upon the statesmen who had conducted the Federal government in safety through the crisis of the rebellion, and who supposed that by the thirteenth article of amendment they had secured the result of their labors, the conviction that something more was necessary in the way of constitutional protection to the unfortunate race who had suffered so much. They accordingly passed through Congress the proposition for the fourteenth amendment, and they declined to treat as restored to their full participation in the government of the Union the States which had been in insurrection, until they ratified that article by a formal vote of their legislative bodies.

Before we proceed to examine more critically the provisions of this amendment, on which the plaintiffs in error rely, let us complete and dismiss the history of the recent amendments, as that history relates to the general purpose which pervades them all. A few years' experience satisfied the thoughtful men who had been the authors of the other two amendments that, notwithstanding the restraints of those articles on the States, and the laws passed under the additional powers granted to Congress, these were inadequate for the protection of life, liberty, and property, without which freedom to the slave was no boon. They were in all those States denied the right of suffrage. The laws were administered by the white man alone. It was urged that a race of men distinctively marked as was the negro, living in the midst of another and dominant race, could never be fully secured in their person and their property without the right of suffrage.

---

* Matter of Turner, 1 Abbott United States Reports, 84.

Hence the fifteenth amendment, which declares that "the right of a citizen of the United States to vote shall not be denied or abridged by any State on account of race, color, or previous condition of servitude." The negro having, by the fourteenth amendment, been declared to be a citizen of the United States, is thus made a voter in every State of the Union.

We repeat, then, in the light of this recapitulation of events, almost too recent to be called history, but which are familiar to us all; and on the most casual examination of the language of these amendments, no one can fail to be impressed with the one pervading purpose found in them all, lying at the foundation of each, and without which none of them would have been even suggested; we mean the freedom of the slave race, the security and firm establishment of that freedom, and the protection of the newly-made freeman and citizen from the oppressions of those who had formerly exercised unlimited dominion over him. It is true that only the fifteenth amendment, in terms, mentions the negro by speaking of his color and his slavery. But it is just as true that each of the other articles was addressed to the grievances of that race, and designed to remedy them as the fifteenth.

We do not say that no one else but the negro can share in this protection. Both the language and spirit of these articles are to have their fair and just weight in any question of construction. Undoubtedly while negro slavery alone was in the mind of the Congress which proposed the thirteenth article, it forbids any other kind of slavery, now or hereafter. If Mexican peonage or the Chinese coolie labor system shall develop slavery of the Mexican or Chinese race within our territory, this amendment may safely be trusted to make it void. And so if other rights are assailed by the States which properly and necessarily fall within the protection of these articles, that protection will apply; though the party interested may not be of African descent. But what we do say, and what we wish to be understood is, that in any fair and just construction of any section or phrase of these amendments, it is necessary to look to the purpose which we have said was the pervading spirit of them all, the evil which they were designed to remedy, and the process of continued addition to the Constitution, until that purpose was supposed to be accomplished, as far as constitutional law can accomplish it.

The first section of the fourteenth article, to which our attention is more specially invited, opens with a definition of citizenship—not only citizenship of the United States, but citizenship of the States. No such definition was previously found in the Constitution, nor had any attempt been made to define it by act of Congress. It had been the occasion of much discussion in the courts, by the executive departments, and in the public journals. It had been said by eminent judges that no man was a citizen of the United States, except as he was a citizen of one of the States composing the Union. Those, therefore, who had been born and resided always in the District of Columbia or in the Territories, though within the United States, were not citizens. Whether this proposition was sound or not had never been judicially decided. But it had been held by this court, in the celebrated Dred Scott case, only a few years before the outbreak of the civil war, that a man of African descent, whether a slave or not, was not and could not be a citizen of a State or of the United States. This decision, while it met the condemnation of some of the ablest statesmen and constitutional lawyers of the country, had never been overruled; and if it was to be accepted as a constitutional limitation of the right of citizenship, then all the negro race who had recently been made freemen, were still, not only not citizens, but were incapable of becoming so by anything short of an amendment to the Constitution.

To remove this difficulty primarily, and to establish a clear and comprehensive definition of citizenship which should declare what should constitute citizenship of the United States, and also citizenship of a State, the first clause of the first section was framed.

"All persons born or naturalized in the United States, and subject to the jurisdiction thereof, are citizens of the United States and of the State wherein they reside."

The first observation we have to make on this clause is, that it puts at rest both the questions which we stated to have been the subject of differences of opinion. It declares that persons may be citizens of the United States without regard to their citizenship of a particular State, and it overturns the Dred Scott decision by making *all persons* born within the United States and subject to its jurisdiction citizens of the United States. That its main purpose was to establish the citizenship of the negro can admit of no doubt. The phrase, "subject to its jurisdiction" was intended to exclude from its operation children of ministers, consuls, and citizens or subjects of foreign States born within the United States.

The next observation is more important in view of the arguments of counsel in the present case. It is, that the distinction between citizenship of the United States and citizenship of a State is clearly recognized and established. Not only may a man be a citizen of the United States without being a citizen of a State, but an important element is necessary to convert the former into the latter. He must reside within the State to make him a citizen of it, but it is only necessary that he should be born or naturalized in the United States to be a citizen of the Union.

It is quite clear, then, that there is a citizenship of the United States, and a citizenship of a State, which are distinct from each other, and which depend upon different characteristics or circumstances in the individual.

We think this distinction and its explicit recognition in this amendment of great weight in this argument, because the next paragraph of this same section, which is the one mainly relied on by the plaintiffs in error, speaks only of privileges and immunities of citizens of the United States, and does not speak of those of citizens of the several States. The argument, however, in favor of the plaintiffs rests wholly on the assumption that the citizenship is the same, and the privileges and immunities guaranteed by the clause are the same.

The language is, "No State shall make or enforce any law which shall abridge the privileges or immunities of citizens of *the United States.*" It is a little remarkable, if this clause was intended as a protection to the citizen of a State against the legislative power of his own State, that the word citizen of the State should be left out when it is so carefully used, and used in contradistinction to citizens of the United States, in the very sentence which precedes it. It is too clear for argument that the change in phraseology was adopted understandingly and with a purpose.

Of the privileges and immunities of the citizen of the United States, and of the privileges and immunities of the citizen of the State, and what they respectively are, we will presently consider; but we wish to state here that it is only the former which are placed by this clause under the protection of the Federal Constitution, and that the latter, whatever they may be, are not intended to have any additional protection by this paragraph of the amendment.

If, then, there is a difference between the privileges and immunities belonging to a citizen of the United States as such, and those belonging to the citizen of the State as such the latter must rest for their security and protection where they have heretofore rested; for they are not embraced by this paragraph of the amendment.

The first occurrence of the words "privileges and immunities" in our constitutional history, is to be found in the fourth of the articles of the old Confederation.

It declares "that the better to secure and perpetuate mu-

tual friendship and intercourse among the people of the different States in this Union, the free inhabitants of each of these States, paupers, vagabonds, and fugitives from justice excepted, shall be entitled to all the privileges and immunities of free citizens in the several States; and the people of each State shall have free ingress and regress to and from any other State, and shall enjoy therein all the privileges of trade and commerce, subject to the same duties, impositions and restrictions as the inhabitants thereof respectively."

In the Constitution of the United States, which superseded the Articles of Confederation, the corresponding provision is found in section two of the fourth article, in the following words: "The citizens of each State shall be entitled to all the privileges and immunities of citizens of the several States."

There can be but little question that the purpose of both these provisions is the same, and that the privileges and immunities intended are the same in each. In the article of the Confederation we have some of these specifically mentioned, and enough perhaps to give some general idea of the class of civil rights meant by the phrase.

Fortunately we are not without judicial construction of this clause of the Constitution. The first and the leading case on the subject is that of *Corfield* v. *Coryell,* decided by Mr. Justice Washington in the Circuit Court for the District of Pennsylvania in 1823.*

"The inquiry," he says, "is, what are the privileges and immunities of citizens of the several States? We feel no hesitation in confining these expressions to those privileges and immunities which are *fundamental;* which belong of right to the citizens of all free governments, and which have at all times been enjoyed by citizens of the several States which compose this Union, from the time of their becoming free, independent, and sovereign. What these fundamental principles are, it would be more tedious than difficult to enumerate. They may all, however, be comprehended under the following general heads: protection by the government, with the right to acquire and possess property of every kind, and to pursue and obtain happiness and safety, subject, nevertheless, to such restraints as the government may prescribe for the general good of the whole."

This definition of the privileges and immunities of citizens of the States is adopted in the main by this court in the recent case of *Ward* v. *The State of Maryland,*† while it declines to

---

* 4 Washington's Circuit Court, 371.
† 12 Wallace, 430.

undertake an authoritative definition beyond what was necessary to that decision. The description, when taken to include others not named, but which are of the same general character, embraces nearly every civil right for the establishment and protection of which organized government is instituted. They are, in the language of Judge Washington, those rights which are fundamental. Throughout his opinion, they are spoken of as rights belonging to the individual as a citizen of a State. They are so spoken of in the constitutional provision which he was construing. And they have always been held to be the class of rights which the State governments were created to establish and secure.

In the case of *Paul* v. *Virginia,** the court, in expounding this clause of the Constitution, says that "the privileges and immunities secured to citizens of each State in the several States, by the provision in question, are those privileges and immunities which are common to the citizens in the latter States under their constitution and laws by virtue of their being citizens."

The constitutional provision there alluded to did not create those rights, which it called privileges and immunities of citizens of the States. It threw around them in that clause no security for the citizen of the State in which they were claimed or exercised. Nor did it profess to control the power of the State governments over the rights of its own citizens.

Its sole purpose was to declare to the several States, that whatever those rights, as you grant or establish them to your own citizens, or as you limit or qualify, or impose restrictions on their exercise, the same, neither more nor less, shall be the measure of the rights of citizens of other States within your jurisdiction.

It would be the vainest show of learning to attempt to prove by citations of authority, that up to the adoption of the recent amendments, no claim or pretence was set up that those rights depended on the Federal government for their existence or protection, beyond the very few express limitations which the Federal Constitution imposed upon the States—such, for instance, as the prohibition against ex post facto laws, bills of attainder, and laws impairing the obligation of contracts. But with the exception of these and a few other restrictions, the entire domain of the privileges and immunities of citizens of the States, as above defined, lay within the constitutional and legislative power of the States, and without that of the Federal government. Was it the purpose of the fourteenth

* 8 Id. 180.

amendment, by the simple declaration that no State should make or enforce any law which shall abridge the privileges and immunities of *citizens of the United States,* to transfer the security and protection of all the civil rights which we have mentioned, from the States to the Federal government? And where it is declared that Congress shall have the power to enforce that article, was it intended to bring within the power of Congress the entire domain of civil rights heretofore belonging exclusively to the States?

All this and more must follow, if the proposition of the plaintiffs in error be sound. For not only are these rights subject to the control of Congress whenever in its discretion any of them are supposed to be abridged by State legislation, but that body may also pass laws in advance, limiting and restricting the exercise of legislative power by the States, in their most ordinary and usual functions, as in its judgment it may think proper on all such subjects. And still further, such a construction followed by the reversal of the judgments of the Supreme Court of Louisiana in these cases, would constitute this court a perpetual censor upon all legislation of the States, on the civil rights of their own citizens, with authority to nullify such as it did not approve as consistent with those rights, as they existed at the time of the adoption of this amendment. The argument we admit is not always the most conclusive which is drawn from the consequences urged against the adoption of a particular construction of an instrument. But when, as in the case before us, these consequences are so serious, so far-reaching and pervading, so great a departure from the structure and spirit of our institutions; when the effect is to fetter and degrade the State governments by subjecting them to the control of Congress, in the exercise of powers heretofore universally conceded to them of the most ordinary and fundamental character; when in fact it radically changes the whole theory of the relations of the State and Federal governments to each other and of both these governments to the people; the argument has a force that is irresistible, in the absence of language which expresses such a purpose too clearly to admit of doubt.

We are convinced that no such results were intended by the Congress which proposed these amendments, nor by the legislatures of the States which ratified them.

Having shown that the privileges and immunities relied on in the argument are those which belong to citizens of the States as such, and that they are left to the State governments for security and protection, and not by this article placed under the special care of the Federal government, we may hold ourselves excused from defining the privileges and immunities of citizens of the United States which no State can abridge, until some case involving those privileges may make it necessary to do so.

But lest it should be said that no such privileges and immunities are to be found if those we have been considering are excluded, we venture to suggest some which owe their existence to the Federal government, its National character, its Constitution, or its laws.

One of these is well described in the case of *Crandall* v. *Nevada.** It is said to be the right of the citizen of this great country, protected by implied guarantees of its Constitution, "to come to the seat of government to assert any claim he may have upon that government, to transact any business he may have with it, to seek its protection, to share its offices, to engage in administering its functions. He has the right of free access to its seaports, through which all operations of foreign commerce are conducted, to the subtreasuries, land offices, and courts of justice in the several States." And quoting from the language of Chief Justice Taney in another case, it is said "that *for all the great purposes for which the Federal government* was established, we are one people, with one common country, *we are all citizens of the United States*"; and it is, as such citizens, that their rights are supported in this court in *Crandall* v. *Nevada.*

Another privilege of a citizen of the United States is to demand the care and protection of the Federal government over his life, liberty, and property when on the high seas or within the jurisdiction of a foreign government. Of this there can be no doubt, nor that the right depends upon his character as a citizen of the United States. The right to peaceably assemble and petition for redress of grievances, the privilege of the writ of *habeas corpus,* are rights of the citizen guaranteed by the Federal Constitution. The right to use the navigable waters of the United States, however they may penetrate the territory of the several States, all rights secured to our citizens by treaties with foreign nations, are dependent upon citizenship of the United States, and not citizenship of a State. One of these privileges is conferred by the very article under consideration. It is that a citizen of the United States can, of his own volition, become a citizen of any State of the Union by a *bona fide* residence therein, with the same rights as other citizens of that State. To these may be added the rights secured by the thirteenth and fifteenth articles of amendment, and by the other clause of the fourteenth, next to be considered.

* 6 Wallace, 36.

But it is useless to pursue this branch of the inquiry, since we are of opinion that the rights claimed by these plaintiffs in error, if they have any existence, are not privileges and immunities of citizens of the United States within the meaning of the clause of the fourteenth amendment under consideration.

"All persons born or naturalized in the United States, and subject to the jurisdiction thereof, are citizens of the United States and of the State wherein they reside. No State shall make or enforce any law which shall abridge the privileges or immunities of citizens of the United States; nor shall any State deprive any person of life, liberty, or property without due process of law, nor deny to any person within its jurisdiction the equal protection of its laws."

The argument has not been much pressed in these cases that the defendant's charter deprives the plaintiffs of their property without due process of law, or that it denies to them the equal protection of the law. The first of these paragraphs has been in the Constitution since the adoption of the fifth amendment, as a restraint upon the Federal power. It is also to be found in some form of expression in the constitutions of nearly all the States, as a restraint upon the power of the States. This law then, has practically been the same as it now is during the existence of the government, except so far as the present amendment may place the restraining power over the States in this matter in the hands of the Federal government.

We are not without judicial interpretation, therefore, both State and National, of the meaning of this clause. And it is sufficient to say that under no construction of that provision that we have ever seen, or any that we deem admissible, can the restraint imposed by the State of Louisiana upon the exercise of their trade by the butchers of New Orleans be held to be a deprivation of property within the meaning of that provision.

"Nor shall any State deny to any person within its jurisdiction the equal protection of the laws."

In the light of the history of these amendments, and the pervading purpose of them, which we have already discussed, it is not difficult to give a meaning to this clause. The existence of laws in the States where the newly emancipated negroes resided, which discriminated with gross injustice and hardship against them as a class, was the evil to be remedied by this clause, and by it such laws are forbidden.

If, however, the States did not conform their laws to its requirements, then by the fifth section of the article of amendment Congress was authorized to enforce it by suitable legislation. We doubt very much whether any action of a State not directed by way of discrimination against the negroes as a class, or on account of their race, will ever be held to come within the purview of this provision. It is so clearly a provision for that race and that emergency, that a strong case would be necessary for its application to any other. But as it is a State that is to be dealt with, and not alone the validity of its laws, we may safely leave that matter until Congress shall have exercised its power, or some case of State oppression, by denial of equal justice in its courts, shall have claimed a decision at our hands. We find no such case in the one before us, and do not deem it necessary to go over the argument again, as it may have relation to this particular clause of the amendment.

In the early history of the organization of the government, its statesmen seem to have divided on the line which should separate the powers of the National government from those of the State governments, and though this line has never been very well defined in public opinion, such a division has continued from that day to this.

The adoption of the first eleven amendments to the Constitution so soon after the original instrument was accepted, shows a prevailing sense of danger at that time from the Federal power. And it cannot be denied that such a jealousy continued to exist with many patriotic men until the breaking out of the late civil war. It was then discovered that the true danger to the perpetuity of the Union was in the capacity of the State organizations to combine and concentrate all the powers of the State, and of contiguous States, for a determined resistance to the General Government.

Unquestionably this has given great force to the argument, and added largely to the number of those who believe in the necessity of a strong National government.

But, however pervading this sentiment, and however it may have contributed to the adoption of the amendments we have been considering, we do not see in those amendments any purpose to destroy the main features of the general system. Under the pressure of all the excited feeling growing out of the war, our statesmen have still believed that the existence of the States with powers for domestic and local government, including the regulation of civil rights—the rights of person and of property—was essential to the perfect working of our complex form of government, though they have thought proper to impose additional limitations on the States, and to confer additional power on that of the Nation.

But whatever fluctuations may be seen in the history of public opinion on this subject during the period of our national existence, we think it will be found that this court, so far as its functions required, has always held with a steady and an even hand the balance between State and Federal power, and we trust that such may continue to be the history of its relation to that subject so long as it shall have duties to perform which demand of it a construction of the Constitution, or of any of its parts.

The judgments of the Supreme Court of Louisiana in these cases are

AFFIRMED.

Mr. Justice FIELD, dissenting:

I am unable to agree with the majority of the court in these cases, and will proceed to state the reasons of my dissent from their judgment. . . .

The substance of the averments of the plaintiffs in error is this: That prior to the passage of the act in question they were engaged in the lawful and necessary business of procuring and bringing to the parishes of Orleans, Jefferson, and St. Bernard, animals suitable for human food, and in preparing such food for market; that in the prosecution of this business, they had provided in these parishes suitable establishments for landing, sheltering, keeping, and slaughtering cattle and the sale of meat; that with their association about four hundred persons were connected, and that in the parishes named about a thousand persons were thus engaged in procuring, preparing, and selling animal food. And they complain that the business of landing, yarding, and keeping, within the parishes named, cattle intended for sale or slaughter, which was lawful for them to pursue before the first day of June, 1869, is made by that act unlawful for any one except the corporation named; and that the business of slaughtering cattle and preparing animal food for market, which it was lawful for them to pursue in these parishes before that day, is made by that act unlawful for them to pursue afterwards, except in the buildings of the company, and upon payment of certain prescribed fees, and a surrender of a valuable portion of each animal slaughtered. And they contend that the lawful business of landing, yarding, sheltering, and keeping cattle intended for sale or slaughter, which they in common with every individual in the community of the three parishes had a right to follow, cannot be thus taken from them and given over for a period of twenty-five years to the sole and exclusive enjoyment of a corporation of seventeen persons or of anybody else. And they also contend that the lawful and necessary business of slaughtering cattle and preparing animal food for market, which they and all other individuals had a right to follow, cannot be thus restricted within this territory of 1154 square miles to the buildings of this corporation, or be subjected to tribute for the emolument of that body.

No one will deny the abstract justice which lies in the position of the plaintiffs in error; and I shall endeavor to show that the position has some support in the fundamental law of the country.

It is contended in justification for the act in question that it was adopted in the interest of the city, to promote its cleanliness and protect its health, and was the legitimate exercise of what is termed the police power of the State. That power undoubtedly extends to all regulations affecting the health, good order, morals, peace, and safety of society, and is exercised on a great variety of subjects, and in almost numberless ways. All sorts of restrictions and burdens are imposed under it, and when these are not in conflict with any constitutional prohibitions, or fundamental principles, they cannot be successfully assailed in a judicial tribunal. With this power of the State and its legitimate exercise I shall not differ from the majority of the court. But under the pretence of prescribing a police regulation the State cannot be permitted to encroach upon any of the just rights of the citizen, which the Constitution intended to secure against abridgment.

In the law in question there are only two provisions which can properly be called police regulations—the one which requires the landing and slaughtering of animals below the city of New Orleans, and the other which requires the inspection of the animals before they are slaughtered. When these requirements are complied with, the sanitary purposes of the act are accomplished. In all other particulars the act is a mere grant to a corporation created by it of special and exclusive privileges by which the health of the city is in no way promoted. It is plain that if the corporation can, without endangering the health of the public, carry on the business of landing, keeping, and slaughtering cattle within a district below the city embracing an area of over a thousand square miles, it would not endanger the public health if other persons were also permitted to carry on the same business within the same district under similar conditions as to the inspection of the animals. The health of the city might require the removal from its limits and suburbs of all buildings for keeping and slaughtering cattle, but no such object could possibly justify legislation removing such buildings from a large part of the State for the benefit of a single corporation. The

pretence of sanitary regulations for the grant of the exclusive privileges is a shallow one, which merits only this passing notice.

It is also sought to justify the act in question on the same principle that exclusive grants for ferries, bridges, and turnpikes are sanctioned. But it can find no support there. Those grants are of franchises of a public character appertaining to the government. Their use usually requires the exercise of the sovereign right of eminent domain. It is for the government to determine when one of them shall be granted, and the conditions upon which it shall be enjoyed. It is the duty of the government to provide suitable roads, bridges, and ferries for the convenience of the public, and if it chooses to devolve this duty to any extent, or in any locality, upon particular individuals or corporations, it may of course stipulate for such exclusive privileges connected with the franchise as it may deem proper, without encroaching upon the freedom or the just rights of others. The grant, with exclusive privileges, of a right thus appertaining to the government, is a very different thing from a grant, with exclusive privileges, of a right to pursue one of the ordinary trades or callings of life, which is a right appertaining solely to the individual.

Nor is there any analogy between this act of Louisiana and the legislation which confers upon the inventor of a new and useful improvement an exclusive right to make and sell to others his invention. The government in this way only secures to the inventor the temporary enjoyment of that which, without him, would not have existed. It thus only recognizes in the inventor a temporary property in the product of his own brain.

The act of Louisiana presents the naked case, unaccompanied by any public considerations, where a right to pursue a lawful and necessary calling, previously enjoyed by every citizen, and in connection with which a thousand persons were daily employed, is taken away and vested exclusively for twenty-five years, for an extensive district and a large population, in a single corporation, or its exercise is for that period restricted to the establishments of the corporation, and there allowed only upon onerous conditions.

If exclusive privileges of this character can be granted to a corporation of seventeen persons, they may, in the discretion of the legislature, be equally granted to a single individual. If they may be granted for twenty-five years they may be equally granted for a century, and in perpetuity. If they may be granted for the landing and keeping of animals intended for sale or slaughter they may be equally granted for the landing and storing of grain and other products of the earth, or for any article of commerce. If they may be granted for structures in which animal food is prepared for market they may be equally granted for structures in which farinaceous or vegetable food is prepared. They may be granted for any of the pursuits of human industry, even in its most simple and common forms. Indeed, upon the theory on which the exclusive privileges granted by the act in question are sustained, there is no monopoly, in the most odious form, which may not be upheld.

The question presented is, therefore, one of the gravest importance, not merely to the parties here, but to the whole country. It is nothing less than the question whether the recent amendments to the Federal Constitution protect the citizens of the United States against the deprivation of their common rights by State legislation. In my judgment the fourteenth amendment does afford such protection, and was so intended by the Congress which framed and the States which adopted it.

The counsel for the plaintiffs in error have contended, with great force, that the act in question is also inhibited by the thirteenth amendment.

That amendment prohibits slavery and involuntary servitude, except as a punishment for crime, but I have not supposed it was susceptible of a construction which would cover the enactment in question. I have been so accustomed to regard it as intended to meet that form of slavery which had previously prevailed in this country, and to which the recent civil war owed its existence, that I was not prepared, nor am I yet, to give to it the extent and force ascribed by counsel. Still it is evident that the language of the amendment is not used in a restrictive sense. It is not confined to African slavery alone. It is general and universal in its application. Slavery of white men as well as of black men is prohibited, and not merely slavery in the strict sense of the term, but involuntary servitude in every form.

The words "involuntary servitude" have not been the subject of any judicial or legislative exposition, that I am aware of, in this country, except that which is found in the Civil Rights Act, which will be hereafter noticed. It is, however, clear that they include something more than slavery in the strict sense of the term; they include also serfage, vassalage, villenage, peonage, and all other forms of compulsory service for the mere benefit or pleasure of others. Nor is this the full import of the terms. The abolition of slavery and involuntary servitude was intended to make every one born in this country a freeman, and as such to give to him the right to pursue the ordinary avo-

cations of life without other restraint than such as affects all others, and to enjoy equally with them the fruits of his labor. A prohibition to him to pursue certain callings, open to others of the same age, condition, and sex, or to reside in places where others are permitted to live, would so far deprive him of the rights of a freeman, and would place him, as respects others, in a condition of servitude. A person allowed to pursue only one trade or calling, and only in one locality of the country, would not be, in the strict sense of the term, in a condition of slavery, but probably none would deny that he would be in a condition of servitude. He certainly would not possess the liberties nor enjoy the privileges of a freeman. The compulsion which would force him to labor even for his own benefit only in one direction, or in one place, would be almost as oppressive and nearly as great an invasion of his liberty as the compulsion which would force him to labor for the benefit or pleasure of another, and would equally constitute an element of servitude. The counsel of the plaintiffs in error therefore contend that "wherever a law of a State, or a law of the United States, makes a discrimination between classes of persons, which deprives the one class of their freedom or their property, or which makes a caste of them to subserve the power, pride, avarice, vanity, or vengeance of others," there involuntary servitude exists within the meaning of the thirteenth amendment.

It is not necessary, in my judgment, for the disposition of the present case in favor of the plaintiffs in error, to accept as entirely correct this conclusion of counsel. It, however, finds support in the act of Congress known as the Civil Rights Act, which was framed and adopted upon a construction of the thirteenth amendment, giving to its language a similar breadth. That amendment was ratified on the eighteenth of December, 1865,* and in April of the following year the Civil Rights Act was passed.† Its first section declares that all persons born in the United States, and not subject to any foreign power, excluding Indians not taxed, are "citizens of the United States," and that "such citizens, of every race and color, without regard to any previous condition of slavery, or involuntary servitude, except as a punishment for crime, whereof the party shall have been duly convicted, shall have the same right in every State and Territory in the United States, to make and enforce contracts, to sue, be parties, and give evidence, to inherit, purchase, lease, sell, hold, and con-

---

* The proclamation of its ratification was made on that day (13 Stat. at Large, 774).
† 14 Id. 27.

vey real and personal property, and to full and equal benefit of all laws and proceedings for the security of person and property, as enjoyed by white citizens."

This legislation was supported upon the theory that citizens of the United States as such were entitled to the rights and privileges enumerated, and that to deny to any such citizen equality in these rights and privileges with others, was, to the extent of the denial, subjecting him to an involuntary servitude. Senator Trumbull, who drew the act and who was its earnest advocate in the Senate, stated, on opening the discussion upon it in that body, that the measure was intended to give effect to the declaration of the amendment, and to secure to all persons in the United States practical freedom. After referring to several statutes passed in some of the Southern States, discriminating between the freedmen and white citizens, and after citing the definition of civil liberty given by Blackstone, the Senator said: "I take it that any statute which is not equal to all, and which deprives any citizen of civil rights, which are secured to other citizens, is an unjust encroachment upon his liberty; and it is in fact a badge of servitude which by the Constitution is prohibited."*

By the act of Louisiana, within the three parishes named, a territory exceeding one thousand one hundred square miles, and embracing over two hundred thousand people, every man who pursues the business of preparing animal food for market must take his animals to the buildings of the favored company, and must perform his work in them, and for the use of the buildings must pay a prescribed tribute to the company, and leave with it a valuable portion of each animal slaughtered. Every man in these parishes who has a horse or other animal for sale, must carry him to the yards and stables of this company, and for their use pay a like tribute. He is not allowed to do his work in his own buildings, or to take his animals to his own stables or keep them in his own yards, even though they should be erected in the same district as the buildings, stables, and yards of the company, and that district embraces over eleven hundred square miles. The prohibitions imposed by this act upon butchers and dealers in cattle in these parishes, and the special privileges conferred upon the favored corporation, are similar in principle and as odious in character as the restrictions imposed in the last century upon the peasantry in some parts of France, where, as says a French writer, the peasant was prohibited "to hunt on his own lands, to fish in his own waters, to grind at his own mill, to cook at

his own oven, to dry his clothes on his own machines, to whet his instruments at his own grindstone, to make his own wine, his oil, and his cider at his own press, . . . or to sell his commodities at the public market." The exclusive right to all these privileges was vested in the lords of the vicinage. "The history of the most execrable tyranny of ancient times," says the same writer, "offers nothing like this. This category of oppressions cannot be applied to a free man, or to the peasant, except in violation of his rights."

But if the exclusive privileges conferred upon the Louisiana corporation can be sustained, it is not perceived why exclusive privileges for the construction and keeping of ovens, machines, grindstones, wine-presses, and for all the numerous trades and pursuits for the prosecution of which buildings are required, may not be equally bestowed upon other corporations or private individuals, and for periods of indefinite duration.

It is not necessary, however, as I have said, to rest my objections to the act in question upon the terms and meaning of the thirteenth amendment. The provisions of the fourteenth amendment, which is properly a supplement to the thirteenth, cover, in my judgment, the case before us, and inhibit any legislation which confers special and exclusive privileges like these under consideration. The amendment was adopted to obviate objections which had been raised and pressed with great force to the validity of the Civil Rights Act, and to place the common rights of American citizens under the protection of the National government. It first declares that "all persons born or naturalized in the United States, and subject to the jurisdiction thereof, are citizens of the United States and of the State wherein they reside." It then declares that "no State shall make or enforce any law which shall abridge the privileges or immunities of citizens of the United States, nor shall any State deprive any person of life, liberty, or property, without due process of law, nor deny to any person within its jurisdiction the equal protection of the laws."

The first clause of this amendment determines who are citizens of the United States, and how their citizenship is created. Before its enactment there was much diversity of opinion among jurists and statesmen whether there was any such citizenship independent of that of the State, and, if any existed, as to the manner in which it originated. With a great number the opinion prevailed that there was no such citizenship independent of the citizenship of the State. Such was the opinion of Mr. Calhoun and the class represented by him. In his celebrated speech in the Senate upon the Force Bill,

* Congressional Globe, 1st Session, 39th Congress, part 1, page 474.

in 1833, referring to the reliance expressed by a senator upon the fact that we are citizens of the United States, he said: "If by citizen of the United States he means a citizen at large, one whose citizenship extends to the entire geographical limits of the country without having a local citizenship in some State or Territory, a sort of citizen of the world, all I have to say is that such a citizen would be a perfect nondescript; that not a single individual of this description can be found in the entire mass of our population. Notwithstanding all the pomp and display of eloquence on the occasion, every citizen is a citizen of some State or Territory, and as such, under an express provision of the Constitution, is entitled to all privileges and immunities of citizens in the several States; and it is in this and no other sense that we are citizens of the United States."*

In the Dred Scott case this subject of citizenship of the United States was fully and elaborately discussed. The exposition in the opinion of Mr. Justice Curtis has been generally accepted by the profession of the country as the one containing the soundest views of constitutional law. And he held that, under the Constitution, citizenship of the United States in reference to natives was dependent upon citizenship in the several States, under their constitutions and laws.

The Chief Justice, in that case, and a majority of the court with him, held that the words "people of the United States" and "citizens" were synonymous terms; that the people of the respective States were the parties to the Constitution; that these people consisted of the free inhabitants of those States; that they had provided in their Constitution for the adoption of a uniform rule of naturalization; that they and their descendants and persons naturalized were the only persons who could be citizens of the United States, and that it was not in the power of any State to invest any other person with citizenship so that he could enjoy the privileges of a citizen under the Constitution, and that therefore the descendants of persons brought to this country and sold as slaves were not, and could not be citizens within the meaning of the Constitution.

The first clause of the fourteenth amendment changes this whole subject, and removes it from the region of discussion and doubt. It recognizes in express terms, if it does not create, citizens of the United States, and it makes their citizenship dependent upon the place of their birth, or the fact of their adoption, and not upon the constitution or laws of any State or the condition of their ancestry. A citizen of a State is now

* Calhoun's Works, vol. 2, p. 242.

only a citizen of the United States residing in that State. The fundamental rights, privileges, and immunities which belong to him as a free man and a free citizen, now belong to him as a citizen of the United States, and are not dependent upon his citizenship of any State. The exercise of these rights and privileges, and the degree of enjoyment received from such exercise, are always more or less affected by the condition and the local institutions of the State, or city, or town where he resides. They are thus affected in a State by the wisdom of its laws, the ability of its officers, the efficiency of its magistrates, the education and morals of its people, and by many other considerations. This is a result which follows from the constitution of society, and can never be avoided, but in no other way can they be affected by the action of the State, or by the residence of the citizen therein. They do not derive their existence from its legislation, and cannot be destroyed by its power.

The amendment does not attempt to confer any new privileges or immunities upon citizens, or to enumerate or define those already existing. It assumes that there are such privileges and immunities which belong of right to citizens as such, and ordains that they shall not be abridged by State legislation. If this inhibition has no reference to privileges and immunities of this character, but only refers, as held by the majority of the court in their opinion, to such privileges and immunities as were before its adoption specially designated in the Constitution or necessarily implied as belonging to citizens of the United States, it was a vain and idle enactment, which accomplished nothing, and most unnecessarily excited Congress and the people on its passage. With privileges and immunities thus designated or implied no State could ever have interfered by its laws, and no new constitutional provision was required to inhibit such interference. The supremacy of the Constitution and the laws of the United States always controlled any State legislation of that character. But if the amendment refers to the natural and inalienable rights which belong to all citizens, the inhibition has a profound significance and consequence.

What, then, are the privileges and immunities which are secured against abridgment by State legislation?

In the first section of the Civil Rights Act Congress has given its interpretation to these terms, or at least has stated some of the rights which, in its judgment, these terms include; it has there declared that they include the right "to make and enforce contracts, to sue, be parties and give evidence, to inherit, purchase, lease, sell, hold, and convey real and personal property, and to full and equal benefit of all laws and proceedings for the security of person and property." That act, it is true, was passed before the fourteenth amendment, but the amendment was adopted, as I have already said, to obviate objections to the act, or, speaking more accurately, I should say, to obviate objections to legislation of a similar character, extending the protection of the National government over the common rights of all citizens of the United States. Accordingly, after its ratification, Congress re-enacted the act under the belief that whatever doubts may have previously existed of its validity, they were removed by the amendment.*

The terms, privileges and immunities, are not new in the amendment; they were in the Constitution before the amendment was adopted. They are found in the second section of the fourth article, which declares that "the citizens of each State shall be entitled to all privileges and immunities of citizens in the several States," and they have been the subject of frequent consideration in judicial decisions. In *Corfield* v. *Coryell*,† Mr. Justice Washington said he had "no hesitation in confining these expressions to those privileges and immunities which were, in their nature, fundamental; which belong of right to citizens of all free governments, and which have at all times been enjoyed by the citizens of the several States which compose the Union, from the time of their becoming free, independent, and sovereign"; and, in considering what those fundamental privileges were, he said that perhaps it would be more tedious than difficult to enumerate them, but that they might be "all comprehended under the following general heads: protection by the government; the enjoyment of life and liberty, with the right to acquire and possess property of every kind, and to pursue and obtain happiness and safety, subject, nevertheless, to such restraints as the government may justly prescribe for the general good of the whole." This appears to me to be a sound construction of the clause in question. The privileges and immunities designated are those *which of right belong to the citizens of all free governments.* Clearly among these must be placed the right to pursue a lawful employment in a lawful manner, without other restraint than such as equally affects all persons. In the discussions in Congress upon the passage of the Civil Rights Act repeated reference was made to this language of Mr. Justice Washington. It was cited by Senator Trumbull with the observation that it enumerated the very rights belonging to a citizen of the United States set forth in the first section

of the act, and with the statement that all persons born in the United States, being declared by the act citizens of the United States, would thenceforth be entitled to the rights of citizens, and that these were the great fundamental rights set forth in the act; and that they were set forth "as appertaining to every freeman."

The privileges and immunities designated in the second section of the fourth article of the Constitution are, then, according to the decision cited, those which of right belong to the citizens of all free governments, and they can be enjoyed under that clause by the citizens of each State in the several States upon the same terms and conditions as they are enjoyed by the citizens of the latter States. No discrimination can be made by one State against the citizens of other States in their enjoyment, nor can any greater imposition be levied than such as is laid upon its own citizens. It is a clause which insures equality in the enjoyment of these rights between citizens of the several States whilst in the same State.

Nor is there anything in the opinion in the case of *Paul* v. *Virginia*,* which at all militates against these views, as is supposed by the majority of the court. The act of Virginia, of 1866, which was under consideration in that case, provided that no insurance company, not incorporated under the laws of the State, should carry on its business within the State without previously obtaining a license for that purpose; and that it should not receive such license until it had deposited with the treasurer of the State bonds of a specified character, to an amount varying from thirty to fifty thousand dollars. No such deposit was required of insurance companies incorporated by the State, for carrying on their business within the State; and in the case cited the validity of the discriminating provisions of the statute of Virginia between her own corporations and the corporations of other States, was assailed. It was contended that the statute in this particular was in conflict with that clause of the Constitution which declares that "the citizens of each State shall be entitled to all privileges and immunities of citizens in the several States." But the court answered, that corporations were not citizens within the meaning of this clause; that the term citizens as there used applied only to natural persons, members of the body politic owing allegiance to the State, not to artificial persons created by the legislature and possessing only the attributes which the legislature had prescribed; that though it had been held that where contracts or rights of property were

*May 31st, 1870; 16 Stat. at Large, 144.
† 4 Washington's Circuit Court, 380.

*8 Wallace, 168.

to be enforced by or against a corporation, the courts of the United States would, for the purpose of maintaining jurisdiction, consider the corporation as representing citizens of the State, under the laws of which it was created, and to this extent would treat a corporation as a citizen within the provision of the Constitution extending the judicial power of the United States to controversies between citizens of different States, it had never been held in any case which had come under its observation, either in the State or Federal courts, that a corporation was a citizen within the meaning of the clause in question, entitling the citizens of each State to the privileges and immunities of citizens in the several States. And the court observed, that the privileges and immunities secured by that provision were those privileges and immunities which were common to the citizens in the latter States, under their constitution and laws, by virtue of their being citizens; that special privileges enjoyed by citizens in their own States were not secured in other States by the provision; that it was not intended by it to give to the laws of one State any operation in other States; that they could have no such operation except by the permission, expressed or implied, of those States; and that the special privileges which they conferred must, therefore, be enjoyed at home unless the assent of other States to their enjoyment therein were given. And so the court held, that a corporation, being a grant of special privileges to the corporators, had no legal existence beyond the limits of the sovereignty where created, and that the recognition of its existence by other States, and the enforcement of its contracts made therein, depended purely upon the assent of those States, which could be granted upon such terms and conditions as those States might think proper to impose.

The whole purport of the decision was, that citizens of one State do not carry with them into other States any special privileges or immunities, conferred by the laws of their own States, of a corporate or other character. That decision has no pertinency to the questions involved in this case. The common privileges and immunities which of right belong to all citizens, stand on a very different footing. These the citizens of each State do carry with them into other States and are secured by the clause in question, in their enjoyment upon terms of equality with citizens of the latter States. This equality in one particular was enforced by this court in the recent case of *Ward* v. *The State of Maryland,* reported in the 12th of Wallace. A statute of that State required the payment of a larger sum from a non-resident trader for a license to enable him to sell his merchandise in the State, than it did of a resi-

dent trader, and the court held, that the statute in thus discriminating against the non-resident trader contravened the clause securing to the citizens of each State the privileges and immunities of citizens of the several States. The privilege of disposing of his property, which was an essential incident to his ownership, possessed by the non-resident, was subjected by the statute of Maryland to a greater burden than was imposed upon a like privilege of her own citizens. The privileges of the non-resident were in this particular abridged by that legislation.

What the clause in question did for the protection of the citizens of one State against hostile and discriminating legislation of other States, the fourteenth amendment does for the protection of every citizen of the United States against hostile and discriminating legislation against him in favor of others, whether they reside in the same or in different States. If under the fourth article of the Constitution equality of privileges and immunities is secured between citizens of different States, under the fourteenth amendment the same equality is secured between citizens of the United States.

It will not be pretended that under the fourth article of the Constitution any State could create a monopoly in any known trade or manufacture in favor of her own citizens, or any portion of them, which would exclude an equal participation in the trade or manufacture monopolized by citizens of other States. She could not confer, for example, upon any of her citizens the sole right to manufacture shoes, or boots, or silk, or the sole right to sell those articles in the State so as to exclude non-resident citizens from engaging in a similar manufacture or sale. The non-resident citizens could claim equality of privilege under the provisions of the fourth article with the citizens of the State exercising the monopoly as well as with others, and thus, as respects them, the monopoly would cease. If this were not so it would be in the power of the State to exclude at any time the citizens of other States from participation in particular branches of commerce or trade, and extend the exclusion from time to time so as effectually to prevent any traffic with them.

Now, what the clause in question does for the protection of citizens of one State against the creation of monopolies in favor of citizens of other States, the fourteenth amendment does for the protection of every citizen of the United States against the creation of any monopoly whatever. The privileges and immunities of citizens of the United States, of every one of them, is secured against abridgment in any form by any State. The fourteenth amendment places them under the guardianship of the National authority. All monopolies in any known trade or manufacture are an invasion of these privileges, for they encroach upon the liberty of citizens to acquire property and pursue happiness, and were held void at common law in the great *Case of Monopolies,* decided during the reign of Queen Elizabeth.

A monopoly is defined "to be an institution or allowance from the sovereign power of the State by grant, commission, or otherwise, to any person or corporation, for the sole buying, selling, making, working, or using of anything, whereby any person or persons, bodies politic or corporate, are sought to be restrained of any freedom or liberty they had before, or hindered in their lawful trade." All such grants relating to any known trade or manufacture have been held by all the judges of England, whenever they have come up for consideration, to be void at common law as destroying the freedom of trade, discouraging labor and industry, restraining persons from getting an honest livelihood, and putting it into the power of the grantees to enhance the price of commodities. The definition embraces, it will be observed, not merely the sole privilege of buying and selling particular articles, or of engaging in their manufacture, but also the sole privilege of using anything by which others may be restrained of the freedom or liberty they previously had in any lawful trade, or hindered in such trade. It thus covers in every particular the possession and use of suitable yards, stables, and buildings for keeping and protecting cattle and other animals, and for their slaughter. Such establishments are essential to the free and successful prosecution by any butcher of the lawful trade of preparing animal food for market. The exclusive privilege of supplying such yards, buildings, and other conveniences for the prosecution of this business in a large district of country, granted by the act of Louisiana to seventeen persons, is as much a monopoly as though the act had granted to the company the exclusive privilege of buying and selling the animals themselves. It equally restrains the butchers in the freedom and liberty they previously had, and hinders them in their lawful trade.

The reasons given for the judgment in the *Case of Monopolies* apply with equal force to the case at bar. In that case a patent had been granted to the plaintiff giving him the sole right to import playing-cards, and the entire traffic in them, and the sole right to make such cards within the realm. The defendant, in disregard of this patent, made and sold some gross of such cards and imported others, and was accordingly sued for infringing upon the exclusive privileges of the plaintiff. As to a portion of the cards made and sold within the realm, he pleaded that he was a haberdasher in London and a free citizen of that city, and as such had a right to make and sell them. The court held the plea good and the grant void, as against the common law and divers acts of Parliament. "All trades," said the court, "as well mechanical as others, which prevent idleness (the bane of the commonwealth) and exercise men and youth in labor for the maintenance of themselves and their families, and for the increase of their substance, to serve the queen when occasion shall require, are profitable for the commonwealth, and therefore the grant to the plaintiff to have the sole making of them is *against the common law and the benefit and liberty of the subject.*"* The case of Davenant and Hurdis was cited in support of this position. In that case a company of merchant tailors in London, having power by charter to make ordinances for the better rule and government of the company, so that they were consonant to law and reason, made an ordinance that any brother of the society who should have any cloth dressed by a cloth-worker, not being a brother of the society, should put one-half of his cloth to some brother of the same society who exercised the art of a cloth-worker, upon pain of forfeiting ten shillings, "and it was adjudged that the ordinance, although it had the countenance of a charter, was against the common law, *because it was against the liberty of the subject; for every subject, by the law, has freedom and liberty to put his cloth to be dressed by what cloth-worker he pleases, and cannot be restrained to certain persons, for that in effect would be a monopoly,* and, therefore, such ordinance, by color of a charter or any grant by charter or such effect, would be void."

Although the court, in its opinion, refers to the increase in prices and deterioration in quality of commodities which necessarily result from the grant of monopolies, the main ground of the decision was their interference with the liberty of the subject to pursue for his maintenance and that of his family any lawful trade or employment. This liberty is assumed to be the natural right of every Englishman.

The struggle of the English people against monopolies forms one of the most interesting and instructive chapters in their history. It finally ended in the passage of the statute of 21st James I, by which it was declared "that all monopolies and all commissions, grants, licenses, charters, and letters-patent, to any person or persons, bodies politic or corporate, whatsoever, of or for the sole buying, selling, making, work-

* Coke's Reports, part 11, page 86.

ing, or using of anything" within the realm or the dominion of Wales were altogether contrary to the laws of the realm and utterly void, with the exception of patents for new inventions for a limited period, and for printing, then supposed to belong to the prerogative of the king, and for the preparation and manufacture of certain articles and ordnance intended for the prosecution of war.

The common law of England, as is thus seen, condemned all monopolies in any known trade or manufacture, and declared void all grants of special privileges whereby others could be deprived of any liberty which they previously had, or be hindered in their lawful trade. The statute of James I, to which I have referred, only embodied the law as it had been previously declared by the courts of England, although frequently disregarded by the sovereigns of that country.

The common law of England is the basis of the jurisprudence of the United States. It was brought to this country by the colonists, together with the English statutes, and was established here so far as it was applicable to their condition. That law and the benefit of such of the English statutes as existed at the time of their colonization, and which they had by experience found to be applicable to their circumstances, were claimed by the Congress of the United Colonies in 1774 as a part of their "indubitable rights and liberties."* Of the statutes, the benefits of which was thus claimed, the statute of James I against monopolies was one of the most important. And when the Colonies separated from the mother country no privilege was more fully recognized or more completely incorporated into the fundamental law of the country than that every free subject in the British empire was entitled to pursue his happiness by following any of the known established trades and occupations of the country, subject only to such restraints as equally affected all others. The immortal document which proclaimed the independence of the country declared as self-evident truths that the Creator had endowed all men "with certain inalienable rights, and that among these are life, liberty, and the pursuit of happiness; and that to secure these rights governments are instituted among men."

If it be said that the civil law and not the common law is the basis of the jurisprudence of Louisiana, I answer that the decree of Louis XVI, in 1776, abolished all monopolies of trades and all special privileges of corporations, guilds, and trading companies, and authorized every person to exercise, without restraint, his art, trade, or profession, and such has

been the law of France and of her colonies ever since, and that law prevailed in Louisiana at the time of her cession to the United States. Since then, notwithstanding the existence in that State of the civil law as the basis of her jurisprudence, freedom of pursuit has been always recognized as the common right of her citizens. But were this otherwise, the fourteenth amendment secures the like protection to all citizens in that State against any abridgment of their common rights, as in other States. That amendment was intended to give practical effect to the declaration of 1776 of inalienable rights, rights which are the gift of the Creator, which the law does not confer, but only recognizes. If the trader in London could plead that he was a free citizen of that city against the enforcement to his injury of monopolies, surely under the fourteenth amendment every citizen of the United States should be able to plead his citizenship of the republic as a protection against any similar invasion of his privileges and immunities.

So fundamental has this privilege of every citizen to be free from disparaging and unequal enactments, in the pursuit of the ordinary avocations of life, been regarded, that few instances have arisen where the principle has been so far violated as to call for the interposition of the courts. But whenever this has occurred, with the exception of the present cases from Louisiana, which are the most barefaced and flagrant of all, the enactment interfering with the privilege of the citizen has been pronounced illegal and void. When a case under the same law, under which the present cases have arisen, came before the Circuit Court of the United States in the District of Louisiana, there was no hesitation on the part of the court in declaring the law, in its exclusive features, to be an invasion of one of the fundamental privileges of the citizen.* The presiding justice, in delivering the opinion of the court, observed that it might be difficult to enumerate or define what were the essential privileges of a citizen of the United States, which a State could not by its laws invade, but that so far as the question under consideration was concerned, it might be safely said that "it is one of the privileges of every American citizen to adopt and follow such lawful industrial pursuit, not injurious to the community, as he may see fit, without unreasonable regulation or molestation, and without being restricted by any of those unjust, oppressive, and odious monopolies or exclusive privileges which have been condemned by all free

* Journals of Congress, vol. i, pp. 28–30.

* Live-Stock, &c., Association v. The Crescent City, &c., Company (1 Abbott's United States Reports, 398).

governments." And again: "There is no more sacred right of citizenship than the right to pursue unmolested a lawful employment in a lawful manner. It is nothing more nor less than the sacred right of labor."

In the *City of Chicago* v. *Rumpff*,[*] which was before the Supreme Court of Illinois, we have a case similar in all its features to the one at bar. That city being authorized by its charter to regulate and license the slaughtering of animals within its corporate limits, the common council passed what was termed an ordinance in reference thereto, whereby a particular building was designated for the slaughtering of all animals intended for sale or consumption in the city, the owners of which were granted the exclusive right for a specified period to have all such animals slaughtered at their establishment, they to be paid a specific sum for the privilege of slaughtering there by all persons exercising it. The validity of this action of the corporate authorities was assailed on the ground of the grant of exclusive privileges, and the court said: "The charter authorizes the city authorities to license or regulate such establishments. Where that body has made the necessary regulations, required for the health or comfort of the inhabitants, all persons inclined to pursue such an occupation should have an opportunity of conforming to such regulations, otherwise the ordinance would be unreasonable and tend to oppression. Or, if they should regard it for the interest of the city that such establishments should be licensed, the ordinance should be so framed that all persons desiring it might obtain licenses by conforming to the prescribed terms and regulations for the government of such business. We regard it neither as a regulation nor a license of the business to confine it to one building or to give it to one individual. Such an action is oppressive, and creates a monopoly that never could have been contemplated by the General Assembly. It impairs the rights of all other persons, and cuts them off from a share in not only a legal, but a necessary business. Whether we consider this as an ordinance or a contract, it is equally unauthorized, as being opposed to the rules governing the adoption of municipal by-laws. The principle of equality of rights to the corporators is violated by this contract. If the common council may require all of the animals for the consumption of the city to be slaughtered in a single building, or on a particular lot, and the owner be paid a specific sum for the privilege, what would prevent the making a similar contract with some other person that all of the vegetables, or fruits, the flour, the gro-

ceries, the dry goods, or other commodities should be sold on his lot and he receive a compensation for the privilege? We can see no difference in principle."

It is true that the court in this opinion was speaking of a municipal ordinance and not of an act of the legislature of a State. But, as it is justly observed by counsel, a legislative body is no more entitled to destroy the equality of rights of citizens, nor to fetter the industry of a city, than a municipal government. These rights are protected from invasion by the fundamental law.

In the case of the *Norwich Gaslight Company* v. *The Norwich City Gas Company*,[*] which was before the Supreme Court of Connecticut, it appeared that the common council of the city of Norwich had passed a resolution purporting to grant to one Treadway, his heirs and assigns, for the period of fifteen years, the right to lay gas-pipes in the streets of that city, declaring that no other person or corporation should, by the consent of the common council, lay gas-pipes in the streets during that time. The plaintiffs having purchased of Treadway, undertook to assert an exclusive right to use the streets for their purposes, as against another company which was using the streets for the same purposes. And the court said: "As, then, no consideration whatever, either of a public or private character, was reserved for the grant; and as the business of manufacturing and selling gas is an ordinary business, like the manufacture of leather, or any other article of trade in respect to which the government has no exclusive prerogative, we think that so far as the restriction of other persons than the plaintiffs from using the streets for the purpose of distributing gas by means of pipes, can fairly be viewed as intended to operate as a restriction upon its free manufacture and sale, it comes directly within the definition and description of a monopoly; and although we have no direct constitutional provision against a monopoly, yet the whole theory of a free government is opposed to such grants, and it does not require even the aid which may be derived from the Bill of Rights, the first section of which declares 'that no man or set of men are entitled to exclusive public emoluments or privileges from the community,' to render them void."

In the *Mayor of the City of Hudson* v. *Thorne*,[†] an application was made to the chancellor of New York to dissolve an injunction restraining the defendants from erecting a building in the city of Hudson upon a vacant lot owned by them,

[*] 45 Illinois, 90.

[*] 25 Connecticut, 19.
[†] 7 Paige, 261.

intended to be used as a hay-press. The common council of the city had passed an ordinance directing that no person should erect, or construct, or cause to be erected or constructed, any wooden or frame barn, stable, or hay-press of certain dimensions, within certain specified limits in the city, without its permission. It appeared, however, that there were such buildings already in existence, not only in compact parts of the city, but also within the prohibited limits, the occupation of which for the storing and pressing of hay the common council did not intend to restrain. And the chancellor said: "If the manufacture of pressed hay within the compact parts of the city is dangerous in causing or promoting fires, the common council have the power expressly given by their charter to prevent the carrying on of such manufacture; but as all by-laws must be reasonable, the common council cannot make a by-law which shall permit one person to carry on the dangerous business and prohibit another who has an equal right from pursuing the same business."

In all these cases there is a recognition of the equality of right among citizens in the pursuit of the ordinary avocations of life, and a declaration that all grants of exclusive privileges, in contravention of this equality, are against common right, and void.

This equality of right, with exemption from all disparaging and partial enactments, in the lawful pursuits of life, throughout the whole country, is the distinguishing privilege of citizens of the United States. To them, everywhere, all pursuits, all professions, all avocations are open without other restrictions than such as are imposed equally upon all others of the same age, sex, and condition. The State may prescribe such regulations for every pursuit and calling of life as will promote the public health, secure the good order and advance the general prosperity of society, but when once prescribed, the pursuit or calling must be free to be followed by every citizen who is within the conditions designated, and will conform to the regulations. This is the fundamental idea upon which our institutions rest; and unless adhered to in the legislation of the country our government will be a republic only in name. The fourteenth amendment, in my judgment, makes it essential to the validity of the legislation of every State that this equality of right should be respected. How widely this equality has been departed from, how entirely rejected and

trampled upon by the act of Louisiana, I have already shown. And it is to me a matter of profound regret that its validity is recognized by a majority of this court, for by it the right of free labor, one of the most sacred and imprescriptible rights of man, is violated.* As stated by the Supreme Court of Connecticut, in the case cited, grants of exclusive privileges, such as is made by the act in question, are opposed to the whole theory of free government, and it requires no aid from any bill of rights to render them void. That only is a free government, in the American sense of the term, under which the inalienable right of every citizen to pursue his happiness is unrestrained, except by just, equal, and impartial laws.†

I am authorized by the CHIEF JUSTICE, Mr. Justice SWAYNE, and Mr. Justice BRADLEY, to state that they concur with me in this dissenting opinion.

* "The property which every man has in his own labor," says Adam Smith, "as it is the original foundation of all other property, so it is the most sacred and inviolable. The patrimony of the poor man lies in the strength and dexterity of his own hands; and to hinder him from employing this strength and dexterity in what manner he thinks proper, without injury to his neighbor, is a plain violation of this most sacred property. It is a manifest encroachment upon the just liberty both of the workman and of those who might be disposed to employ him. As it hinders the one from working at what he thinks proper, so it hinders the others from employing whom they think proper." (Smith's Wealth of Nations, b. 1, ch. 10, part 2.)

In the edict of Louis XVI, in 1776, giving freedom to trades and professions prepared by his minister, Turgot, he recites the contributions that had been made by the guilds and trade companies, and says: "It was the allurement of these fiscal advantages undoubtedly that prolonged the illusion and concealed the immense injury they did to industry and their infraction of natural right. This illusion had extended so far that some persons asserted that the right to work was a royal privilege which the king might sell, and that his subjects were bound to purchase from him. We hasten to correct this error and to repel the conclusion. God in giving to man wants and desires rendering labor necessary for their satisfaction, conferred the right to labor upon all men, and this property is the first, most sacred, and imprescriptible of all." . . . He, therefore, regards it "as the first duty of his justice, and the worthiest act of benevolence, to free his subjects from any restriction upon this inalienable right of humanity."

† "Civil liberty, the great end of all human society and government, is that state in which each individual has the power to pursue his own happiness according to his own views of his interest, and the dictates of his conscience, unrestrained, except by equal, just, and impartial laws." (1 Sharswood's Blackstone, 127, note 8.)

Inaugural Address, *Rutherford B. Hayes, 1877*

An ardent abolitionist from Ohio, Rutherford B. Hayes (1822–93) served in the Union Army during the Civil War, seeing extensive combat and reaching the rank of major general. Elected to Congress before the war's end, he later served as Ohio's governor. His election to the presidency in 1876 was marked by scandal and charges of corruption. His opponent, Samuel Tilden, a Democrat, won the popular vote and held more electoral votes than Hayes, one shy of a majority. Congress appointed an electoral commission to decide which candidate should receive the electoral votes from three Southern states whose electoral votes were in dispute. On a party-line vote, the commission awarded all the electoral votes to Hayes, giving him the presidency. Charges were made of a stolen election and also of a deal according to which Hayes would be given the presidency in exchange for an end to Reconstruction and provision of government aid to the South. No federal aid was forthcoming. But soon after his election, Hayes removed the final federal troops from former Confederate states, ending attempts at Reconstruction.

Inaugural Address

March 5, 1877

Rutherford B. Hayes

Fellow-Citizens:

We have assembled to repeat the public ceremonial, begun by Washington, observed by all my predecessors, and now a time-honored custom, which marks the commencement of a new term of the Presidential office. Called to the duties of this great trust, I proceed, in compliance with usage, to announce some of the leading principles, on the subjects that now chiefly engage the public attention, by which it is my desire to be guided in the discharge of those duties. I shall not undertake to lay down irrevocably principles or measures of administration, but rather to speak of the motives which should animate us, and to suggest certain important ends to be attained in accordance with our institutions and essential to the welfare of our country.

At the outset of the discussions which preceded the recent Presidential election it seemed to me fitting that I should fully make known my sentiments in regard to several of the important questions which then appeared to demand the consideration of the country. Following the example, and in part adopting the language, of one of my predecessors, I wish now, when every motive for misrepresentation has passed away, to repeat what was said before the election, trusting that my countrymen will candidly weigh and understand it, and that they will feel assured that the sentiments declared in accepting the nomination for the Presidency will be the standard of my conduct in the path before me, charged, as I now am, with the grave and difficult task of carrying them out in the practical administration of the Government so far as depends, under the Constitution and laws on the Chief Executive of the nation.

The permanent pacification of the country upon such principles and by such measures as will secure the complete protection of all its citizens in the free enjoyment of all their constitutional rights is now the one subject in our public affairs which all thoughtful and patriotic citizens regard as of supreme importance.

Many of the calamitous efforts of the tremendous revolution which has passed over the Southern States still remain. The immeasurable benefits which will surely follow, sooner or later, the hearty and generous acceptance of the legitimate results of that revolution have not yet been realized. Difficult and embarrassing questions meet us at the threshold of this subject. The people of those States are still impoverished, and the inestimable blessing of wise, honest, and peaceful local self-government is not fully enjoyed. Whatever difference of opinion may exist as to the cause of this condition of things, the fact is clear that in the progress of events the time has come when such government is the imperative necessity required by all the varied interests, public and private, of those States. But it must not be forgotten that only a local government which recognizes and maintains inviolate the rights of all is a true self-government.

With respect to the two distinct races whose peculiar relations to each other have brought upon us the deplorable complications and perplexities which exist in those States, it must be a government which guards the interests of both races carefully and equally. It must be a government which submits loyally and heartily to the Constitution and the laws—the laws of the nation and the laws of the States themselves—accepting and obeying faithfully the whole Constitution as it is.

Resting upon this sure and substantial foundation, the superstructure of beneficent local governments can be built up, and not otherwise. In furtherance of such obedience to the letter and the spirit of the Constitution, and in behalf of all that its attainment implies, all so-called party interests lose their apparent importance, and party lines may well be permitted to fade into insignificance. The question we have to consider for the immediate welfare of those States of the Union is the question of government or no government; of social order and all the peaceful industries and the happiness that belongs to it, or a return to barbarism. It is a question in which every citizen of the nation is deeply interested, and with respect to which we ought not to be, in a partisan sense, either Republicans or Democrats, but fellow-citizens and fellow-men, to whom the interests of a common country and a common humanity are dear.

The sweeping revolution of the entire labor system of a large portion of our country and the advance of 4,000,000 people from a condition of servitude to that of citizenship, upon an equal footing with their former masters, could not occur without presenting problems of the gravest moment, to be dealt with by the emancipated race, by their former masters, and by the General Government, the author of the act of emancipation. That it was a wise, just, and providential act, fraught with good for all concerned, is now generally conceded throughout the country. That a moral obligation rests upon the National Government to employ its constitutional power and influence to establish the rights of the people it has emancipated, and to protect them in the enjoyment of those rights when they are infringed or assailed, is also generally admitted.

The evils which afflict the Southern States can only be removed or remedied by the united and harmonious efforts of both races, actuated by motives of mutual sympathy and regard; and while in duty bound and fully determined to protect the rights of all by every constitutional means at the disposal of my Administration, I am sincerely anxious to use every legitimate influence in favor of honest and efficient local *self*-government as the true resource of those States for the promotion of the contentment and prosperity of their citizens. In the effort I shall make to accomplish this purpose I ask the cordial cooperation of all who cherish an interest in the welfare of the country, trusting that party ties and the prejudice of race will be freely surrendered in behalf of the great purpose to be accomplished. In the important work of restoring the South it is not the political situation alone that merits attention. The material development of that section of the country has been arrested by the social and political revolution through which it has passed, and now needs and deserves the considerate care of the National Government within the just limits prescribed by the Constitution and wise public economy.

But at the basis of all prosperity, for that as well as for every other part of the country, lies the improvement of the intellectual and moral condition of the people. Universal suffrage should rest upon universal education. To this end, liberal and permanent provision should be made for the support of free schools by the State governments, and, if need be, supplemented by legitimate aid from national authority.

Let me assure my countrymen of the Southern States that it is my earnest desire to regard and promote their truest interest—the interests of the white and of the colored people both and equally—and to put forth my best efforts in behalf of a civil policy which will forever wipe out in our political affairs the color line and the distinction between North and South, to the end that we may have not merely a united North or a united South, but a united country.

I ask the attention of the public to the paramount necessity of reform in our civil service—a reform not merely as to certain abuses and practices of so-called official patronage which have come to have the sanction of usage in the several Departments of our Government, but a change in the system of appointment itself; a reform that shall be thorough, radical, and complete; a return to the principles and practices of the founders of the Government. They neither expected nor desired from public officers any partisan service. They meant that public officers should owe their whole service to the Government and to the people. They meant that the officer should be secure in his tenure as long as his personal character remained untarnished and the performance of his duties satisfactory. They held that appointments to office were not to be made nor expected merely as rewards for partisan services, nor merely on the nomination of members of Congress, as being entitled in any respect to the control of such appointments.

The fact that both the great political parties of the country, in declaring their principles prior to the election, gave a prominent place to the subject of reform of our civil service, recognizing and strongly urging its necessity, in terms almost identical in their specific import with those I have here employed, must be accepted as a conclusive argument in behalf of these measures. It must be regarded as the expression of the united voice and will of the whole country upon this subject, and both political parties are virtually pledged to give it their unreserved support.

The President of the United States of necessity owes his election to office to the suffrage and zealous labors of a political party, the members of which cherish with ardor and regard as of essential importance the principles of their party organization; but he should strive to be always mindful of the fact that he serves his party best who serves the country best.

In furtherance of the reform we seek, and in other important respects a change of great importance, I recommend an amendment to the Constitution prescribing a term of six years for the Presidential office and forbidding a reelection.

With respect to the financial condition of the country, I shall not attempt an extended history of the embarrassment and prostration which we have suffered during the past three years. The depression in all our varied commercial and manufacturing interests throughout the country, which began in September, 1873, still continues. It is very gratifying, however, to be able to say that there are indications all around us of a coming change to prosperous times.

Upon the currency question, intimately connected, as it is, with this topic, I may be permitted to repeat here the statement made in my letter of acceptance, that in my judgment the feeling of uncertainty inseparable from an irredeemable paper currency, with its fluctuation of values, is one of the greatest obstacles to a return to prosperous times. The only safe paper currency is one which rests upon a coin basis and is at all times and promptly convertible into coin.

I adhere to the views heretofore expressed by me in favor of Congressional legislation in behalf of an early resumption of specie payments, and I am satisfied not only that this is wise, but that the interests, as well as the public sentiment, of the country imperatively demand it.

Passing from these remarks upon the condition of our own country to consider our relations with other lands, we are reminded by the international complications abroad, threatening the peace of Europe, that our traditional rule of noninterference in the affairs of foreign nations has proved of great value in past times and ought to be strictly observed.

The policy inaugurated by my honored predecessor, President Grant, of submitting to arbitration grave questions in dispute between ourselves and foreign powers points to a new, and incomparably the best, instrumentality for the preservation of peace, and will, as I believe, become a beneficent example of the course to be pursued in similar emergencies by other nations.

If, unhappily, questions of difference should at any time during the period of my Administration arise between the United States and any foreign government, it will certainly be my disposition and my hope to aid in their settlement in the same peaceful and honorable way, thus securing to our country the great blessings of peace and mutual good offices with all the nations of the world.

Fellow-citizens, we have reached the close of a political contest marked by the excitement which usually attends the contests between great political parties whose members espouse and advocate with earnest faith their respective creeds. The circumstances were, perhaps, in no respect extraordinary save in the closeness and the consequent uncertainty of the result.

For the first time in the history of the country it has been deemed best, in view of the peculiar circumstances of the case, that the objections and questions in dispute with reference to the counting of the electoral votes should be referred to the decision of a tribunal appointed for this purpose.

That tribunal—established by law for this sole purpose; its members, all of them, men of long-established reputation for integrity and intelligence, and, with the exception of those who are also members of the supreme judiciary, chosen equally from both political parties; its deliberations enlightened by the research and the arguments of able counsel—was entitled to the fullest confidence of the American people. Its decisions have been patiently waited for, and accepted as legally conclusive by the general judgment of the public. For the present, opinion will widely vary as to the wisdom of the several conclusions announced by that tribunal. This is to be anticipated in every instance where matters of dispute are made the subject of arbitration under the forms of law. Human judgment is never unerring, and is rarely regarded as otherwise than wrong by the unsuccessful party in the contest.

The fact that two great political parties have in this way settled a dispute in regard to which good men differ as to the facts and the law no less than as to the proper course to be pursued in solving the question in controversy is an occasion for general rejoicing.

Upon one point there is entire unanimity in public sentiment—that conflicting claims to the Presidency must be amicably and peaceably adjusted, and that when so adjusted the general acquiescence of the nation ought surely to follow.

It has been reserved for a government of the people, where the right of suffrage is universal, to give to the world the first example in history of a great nation, in the midst of the struggle of opposing parties for power, hushing its party tumults to yield the issue of the contest to adjustment according to the forms of law.

Looking for the guidance of that Divine Hand by which the destinies of nations and individuals are shaped, I call upon you, Senators, Representatives, judges, fellow-citizens, here and everywhere, to unite with me in an earnest effort to secure to our country the blessings, not only of material prosperity, but of justice, peace, and union—a union depending not upon the constraint of force, but upon the loving devotion of a free people; "and that all things may be so ordered and settled upon the best and surest foundations that peace and happiness, truth and justice, religion and piety, may be established among us for all generations."

Civil Rights Cases, 1883

The Civil Rights Act of 1875 gave private citizens the right to sue individuals and companies who refused them accommodations or admittance on the grounds of their race. The Civil Rights Cases consolidated five separate cases in which African Americans sued theaters, hotels, and transportation companies for excluding them from their premises or services. The Supreme Court declared the act unconstitutional, declaring that the Fourteenth Amendment forbade only state conduct denying equal protection to all citizens and that the Thirteenth Amendment forbade only the actual owning of slaves, not discriminatory conduct on the part of one private person toward another.

Civil Rights Cases

October 16, 1883

UNITED STATES *v.* STANLEY
ON CERTIFICATE OF DIVISION FROM THE CIRCUIT
COURT OF THE UNITED STATES FOR THE
DISTRICT OF KANSAS

UNITED STATES *v.* RYAN
IN ERROR TO THE CIRCUIT COURT OF THE UNITED
STATES FOR THE DISTRICT OF CALIFORNIA

UNITED STATES *v.* NICHOLS
ON CERTIFICATE OF DIVISION FROM THE CIRCUIT
COURT OF THE UNITED STATES FOR THE WESTERN
DISTRICT OF MISSOURI

UNITED STATES *v.* SINGLETON
ON CERTIFICATE OF DIVISION FROM THE CIRCUIT
COURT OF THE UNITED STATES FOR THE SOUTHERN
DISTRICT OF NEW YORK

ROBINSON & Wife *v.* MEMPHIS AND CHARLESTON RAILROAD COMPANY
IN ERROR TO THE CIRCUIT COURT OF THE UNITED
STATES FOR THE WESTERN DISTRICT OF TENNESSEE
Submitted October Term, 1882.—
Decided October 15th, 1883

These cases were all founded on the first and second sections of the Act of Congress, known as the Civil Rights Act, passed March 1st, 1875, entitled "An Act to protect all citizens in their civil and legal rights." 18 Stat. 335. Two of the cases, those against Stanley and Nichols, were indictments for de-

nying to persons of color the accommodations and privileges of an inn or hotel; two of them, those against Ryan and Singleton, were, one on information, the other an indictment, for denying to individuals the privileges and accommodations of a theatre, the information against Ryan being for refusing a colored person a seat in the dress circle of Maguire's theatre in San Francisco; and the indictment against Singleton was for denying to another person, whose color was not stated, the full enjoyment of the accommodations of the theatre known as the Grand Opera House in New York, "said denial not being made for any reasons by law applicable to citizens of every race and color, and regardless of any previous condition of servitude." The case of Robinson and wife against the Memphis & Charleston R. R. Company was an action brought in the Circuit Court of the United States for the Western District of Tennessee, to recover the penalty of five hundred dollars given by the second section of the act; and the gravamen was the refusal by the conductor of the railroad company to allow the wife to ride in the ladies' car, for the reason, as stated in one of the counts, that she was a person of African descent. The jury rendered a verdict for the defendants in this case upon the merits, under a charge of the court to which a bill of exceptions was taken by the plaintiffs. The case was tried on the assumption by both parties of the validity of the act of Congress; and the principal point made by the exceptions was, that the judge allowed evidence to go to the jury tending to show that the conductor had reason to suspect that the plaintiff, the wife, was an improper person, because she was in company with a young man whom he supposed to be a white man, and on that account inferred that there was some improper connection between them; and the judge charged the jury, in substance, that if this was the conductor's *bona fide* reason for excluding the woman from the car, they might take it into consideration on the question of the liability of the company. The case was brought here by writ of error at the suit of the plaintiffs. The cases of Stanley, Nichols, and Singleton, came up on certificates of division of opinion between the judges below as to the constitutionality of the first and second sections of the act referred to; and the case of Ryan, on a writ of error to the judgment of the Circuit Court for the District of California sustaining a demurrer to the information.

The Stanley, Ryan, Nichols, and Singleton cases were submitted together by the solicitor general at the last term of court, on the 7th day of November, 1882. There were no appearances and no briefs filed for the defendants.

The Robinson case was submitted on the briefs at the last term, on the 29th day of March, 1883.

MR. JUSTICE BRADLEY delivered the opinion of the court. After stating the facts in the above language he continued:

It is obvious that the primary and important question in all the cases is the constitutionality of the law: for if the law is unconstitutional none of the prosecutions can stand.

The sections of the law referred to provide as follows:

"SEC. 1. That all persons within the jurisdiction of the United States shall be entitled to the full and equal enjoyment of the accommodations, advantages, facilities, and privileges of inns, public conveyances on land or water, theatres, and other places of public amusement; subject only to the conditions and limitations established by law, and applicable alike to citizens of every race and color, regardless of any previous condition of servitude.

"SEC. 2. That any person who shall violate the foregoing section by denying to any citizen, except for reasons by law applicable to citizens of every race and color, and regardless of any previous condition of servitude, the full enjoyment of any of the accommodations, advantages, facilities, or privileges in said section enumerated, or by aiding or inciting such denial, shall for every such offence forfeit and pay the sum of five hundred dollars to the person aggrieved thereby, to be recovered in an action of

debt, with full costs; and shall also, for every such offence, be deemed guilty of a misdemeanor, and, upon conviction thereof, shall be fined not less than five hundred nor more than one thousand dollars, or shall be imprisoned not less than thirty days nor more than one year: *Provided,* That all persons may elect to sue for the penalty aforesaid, or to proceed under their rights at common law and by State statutes; and having so elected to proceed in the one mode or the other, their right to proceed in the other jurisdiction shall be barred. But this provision shall not apply to criminal proceedings, either under this act or the criminal law of any State: *And provided further,* That a judgment for the penalty in favor of the party aggrieved, or a judgment upon an indictment, shall be a bar to either prosecution respectively."

Are these sections constitutional? The first section, which is the principal one, cannot be fairly understood without attending to the last clause, which qualifies the preceding part.

The essence of the law is, not to declare broadly that all persons shall be entitled to the full and equal enjoyment of the accommodations, advantages, facilities, and privileges of inns, public conveyances, and theatres; but that such enjoyment shall not be subject to any conditions applicable only to citizens of a particular race or color, or who had been in a previous condition of servitude. In other words, it is the purpose of the law to declare that, in the enjoyment of the accommodations and privileges of inns, public conveyances, theatres, and other places of public amusement, no distinction shall be made between citizens of different race or color, or between those who have, and those who have not, been slaves. Its effect is to declare, that in all inns, public conveyances, and places of amusement, colored citizens, whether formerly slaves or not, and citizens of other races, shall have the same accommodations and privileges in all inns, public conveyances, and places of amusement as are enjoyed by white citizens; and *vice versa.* The second section makes it a penal offence in any person to deny to any citizen of any race or color, regardless of previous servitude, any of the accommodations or privileges mentioned in the first section.

Has Congress constitutional power to make such a law? Of course, no one will contend that the power to pass it was contained in the Constitution before the adoption of the last three amendments. The power is sought, first, in the Fourteenth Amendment, and the views and arguments of distinguished Senators, advanced whilst the law was under consideration, claiming authority to pass it by virtue of that amendment, are the principal arguments adduced in favor of the power. We have carefully considered those arguments, as was due to the eminent ability of those who put them forward, and have felt, in all its force, the weight of authority which always invests a law that Congress deems itself competent to pass. But the responsibility of an independent judgment is now thrown upon this court; and we are bound to exercise it according to the best lights we have.

The first section of the Fourteenth Amendment (which is the one relied on), after declaring who shall be citizens of the United States, and of the several States, is prohibitory in its character, and prohibitory upon the States. It declares that:

"No State shall make or enforce any law which shall abridge the privileges or immunities of citizens of the United States; nor shall any State deprive any person of life, liberty, or property without due process of law; nor deny to any person within its jurisdiction the equal protection of the laws."

It is State action of a particular character that is prohibited. Individual invasion of individual rights is not the subject-matter of the amendment. It has a deeper and broader scope. It nullifies and makes void all State legislation, and State action of every kind, which impairs the privileges and immunities of citizens of the United States, or which injures them in life, liberty or property without due process of law, or which denies to any of them the equal protection of the laws. It not only does this, but, in order that the national will, thus declared, may not be a mere *brutum fulmen,* the last section of the amendment invests Congress with power to enforce it by appropriate legislation. To enforce what? To enforce the prohibition. To adopt appropriate legislation for correcting the effects of such prohibited State laws and State acts, and thus to render them effectually null, void, and innocuous. This is the legislative power conferred upon Congress, and this is the whole of it. It does not invest Congress with power to legislate upon subjects which are within the domain of State legislation; but to provide modes of relief against State legislation, or State action, of the kind referred to. It does not authorize Congress to create a code of municipal law for the regulation of private rights; but to provide modes of redress against the operation of State laws, and the action of State officers executive or judicial, when these are subversive of the fundamental rights specified in the amendment. Positive rights and privileges are undoubtedly secured by the Four-

teenth Amendment; but they are secured by way of prohibition against State laws and State proceedings affecting those rights and privileges, and by power given to Congress to legislate for the purpose of carrying such prohibition into effect: and such legislation must necessarily be predicated upon such supposed State laws or State proceedings, and be directed to the correction of their operation and effect. A quite full discussion of this aspect of the amendment may be found in *United States* v. *Cruikshank,* 92 U.S. 542; *Virginia* v. *Rives,* 100 U.S. 313; and *Ex parte Virginia,* 100 U.S. 339.

An apt illustration of this distinction may be found in some of the provisions of the original Constitution. Take the subject of contracts, for example. The Constitution prohibited the States from passing any law impairing the obligation of contracts. This did not give to Congress power to provide laws for the general enforcement of contracts; nor power to invest the courts of the United States with jurisdiction over contracts, so as to enable parties to sue upon them in those courts. It did, however, give the power to provide remedies by which the impairment of contracts by State legislation might be counteracted and corrected: and this power was exercised. The remedy which Congress actually provided was that contained in the 25th section of the Judiciary Act of 1789, 1 Stat. 85, giving to the Supreme Court of the United States jurisdiction by writ of error to review the final decisions of State courts whenever they should sustain the validity of a State statute or authority alleged to be repugnant to the Constitution or laws of the United States. By this means, if a State law was passed impairing the obligation of a contract, and the State tribunals sustained the validity of the law, the mischief could be corrected in this court. The legislation of Congress, and the proceedings provided for under it, were corrective in their character. No attempt was made to draw into the United States courts the litigation of contracts generally; and no such attempt would have been sustained. We do not say that the remedy provided was the only one that might have been provided in that case. Probably Congress had power to pass a law giving to the courts of the United States direct jurisdiction over contracts alleged to be impaired by a State law; and under the broad provisions of the act of March 3d, 1875, ch. 137, 18 Stat. 470, giving to the circuit courts jurisdiction of all cases arising under the Constitution and laws of the United States, it is possible that such jurisdiction now exists. But under that, or any other law, it must appear as well by allegation, as proof at the trial, that the Constitution had been violated by the action of the State legislature. Some obnoxious State law passed, or that might be passed, is necessary to be assumed in order to lay the foundation of any federal remedy in the case; and for the very sufficient reason, that the constitutional prohibition is against *State laws* impairing the obligation of contracts.

And so in the present case, until some State law has been passed, or some State action through its officers or agents has been taken, adverse to the rights of citizens sought to be protected by the Fourteenth Amendment, no legislation of the United States under said amendment, nor any proceeding under such legislation, can be called into activity: for the prohibitions of the amendment are against State laws and acts done under State authority. Of course, legislation may, and should be, provided in advance to meet the exigency when it arises; but it should be adapted to the mischief and wrong which the amendment was intended to provide against; and that is, State laws, or State action of some kind, adverse to the rights of the citizen secured by the amendment. Such legislation cannot properly cover the whole domain of rights appertaining to life, liberty and property, defining them and providing for their vindication. That would be to establish a code of municipal law regulative of all private rights between man and man in society. It would be to make Congress take the place of the State legislatures and to supersede them. It is absurd to affirm that, because the rights of life, liberty and property (which include all civil rights that men have), are by the amendment sought to be protected against invasion on the part of the State without due process of law, Congress may therefore provide due process of law for their vindication in every case; and that, because the denial by a State to any persons, of the equal protection of the laws, is prohibited by the amendment, therefore Congress may establish laws for their equal protection. In fine, the legislation which Congress is authorized to adopt in this behalf is not general legislation upon the rights of the citizen, but corrective legislation, that is, such as may be necessary and proper for counteracting such laws as the States may adopt or enforce, and which, by the amendment, they are prohibited from making or enforcing, or such acts and proceedings as the States may commit or take, and which, by the amendment, they are prohibited from committing or taking. It is not necessary for us to state, if we could, what legislation would be proper for Congress to adopt. It is sufficient for us to examine whether the law in question is of that character.

An inspection of the law shows that it makes no reference whatever to any supposed or apprehended violation of the Fourteenth Amendment on the part of the States. It is not predicated on any such view. It proceeds *ex directo* to declare that certain acts committed by individuals shall be deemed offences, and shall be prosecuted and punished by proceedings in the courts of the United States. It does not profess to be corrective of any constitutional wrong committed by the States; it does not make its operation to depend upon any such wrong committed. It applies equally to cases arising in States which have the justest laws respecting the personal rights of citizens, and whose authorities are ever ready to enforce such laws, as to those which arise in States that may have violated the prohibition of the amendment. In other words, it steps into the domain of local jurisprudence, and lays down rules for the conduct of individuals in society towards each other, and imposes sanctions for the enforcement of those rules, without referring in any manner to any supposed action of the State or its authorities.

If this legislation is appropriate for enforcing the prohibitions of the amendment, it is difficult to see where it is to stop. Why may not Congress with equal show of authority enact a code of laws for the enforcement and vindication of all rights of life, liberty, and property? If it is supposable that the States may deprive persons of life, liberty, and property without due process of law (and the amendment itself does suppose this), why should not Congress proceed at once to prescribe due process of law for the protection of every one of these fundamental rights, in every possible case, as well as to prescribe equal privileges in inns, public conveyances, and theatres? The truth is, that the implication of a power to legislate in this manner is based upon the assumption that if the States are forbidden to legislate or act in a particular way on a particular subject, and power is conferred upon Congress to enforce the prohibition, this gives Congress power to legislate generally upon that subject, and not merely power to provide modes of redress against such State legislation or action. The assumption is certainly unsound. It is repugnant to the Tenth Amendment of the Constitution, which declares that powers not delegated to the United States by the Constitution, nor prohibited by it to the States, are reserved to the States respectively or to the people.

We have not overlooked the fact that the fourth section of the act now under consideration has been held by this court to be constitutional. That section declares "that no citizen, possessing all other qualifications which are or may be prescribed by law, shall be disqualified for service as grand or petit juror in any court of the United States, or of any State, on account of race, color, or previous condition of servitude; and any officer or other person charged with any duty in the selection or summoning of jurors who shall exclude or fail to summon any citizen for the cause aforesaid, shall, on conviction thereof, be deemed guilty of a misdemeanor, and be fined not more than five thousand dollars." In *Ex parte Virginia,* 100 U.S. 339, it was held that an indictment against a State officer under this section for excluding persons of color from the jury list is sustainable. But a moment's attention to its terms will show that the section is entirely corrective in its character. Disqualifications for service on juries are only created by the law, and the first part of the section is aimed at certain disqualifying laws, namely, those which make mere race or color a disqualification; and the second clause is directed against those who, assuming to use the authority of the State government, carry into effect such a rule of disqualification. In the Virginia case, the State, through its officer, enforced a rule of disqualification which the law was intended to abrogate and counteract. Whether the statute book of the State actually laid down any such rule of disqualification, or not, the State, through its officer, enforced such a rule: and it is against such State action, through its officers and agents, that the last clause of the section is directed. This aspect of the law was deemed sufficient to divest it of any unconstitutional character, and makes it differ widely from the first and second sections of the same act which we are now considering.

These sections, in the objectionable features before referred to, are different also from the law ordinarily called the "Civil Rights Bill," originally passed April 9th, 1866, 14 Stat. 27, ch. 31, and re-enacted with some modifications in sections 16, 17, 18, of the Enforcement Act, passed May 31st, 1870, 16 Stat. 140, ch. 114. That law, as re-enacted, after declaring that all persons within the jurisdiction of the United States shall have the same right in every State and Territory to make and enforce contracts, to sue, be parties, give evidence, and to the full and equal benefit of all laws and proceedings for the security of persons and property as is enjoyed by white citizens, and shall be subject to like punishment, pains, penalties, taxes, licenses and exactions of every kind, and none other, any law, statute, ordinance, regulation or custom to the contrary notwithstanding, proceeds to enact, that any person who, under color of any law, statute, ordinance, regulation or custom, shall subject, or cause to be subjected, any inhabitant of any State or Territory to the deprivation of any rights secured or protected by the preceding section (above quoted), or to different punishment, pains, or penalties, on account of such person being an alien, or by reason of his color or race, than is prescribed for the punishment of citizens, shall be deemed guilty of a misdemeanor, and subject to fine and imprisonment as specified in the act. This law is clearly corrective in its character, intended to counteract and furnish redress against State laws and proceedings, and customs having the force of law, which sanction the wrongful acts specified. In the Revised Statutes, it is true, a very important clause, to wit, the words "any law, statute, ordinance, regulation or custom to the contrary notwithstanding," which gave the declaratory section its point and effect, are omitted; but the penal part, by which the declaration is enforced, and which is really the effective part of the law, retains the reference to State laws, by making the penalty apply only to those who should subject parties to a deprivation of their rights under color of any statute, ordinance, custom, etc., of any State or Territory: thus preserving the corrective character of the legislation. Rev. St. §§ 1977, 1978, 1979, 5510. The Civil Rights Bill here referred to is analogous in its character to what a law would have been under the original Constitution, declaring that the validity of contracts should not be impaired, and that if any person bound by a contract should refuse to comply with it, under color or pretence that it had been rendered void or invalid by a State law, he should be liable to an action upon it in the courts of the United States, with the addition of a penalty for setting up such an unjust and unconstitutional defence.

In this connection it is proper to state that civil rights, such as are guaranteed by the Constitution against State aggression, cannot be impaired by the wrongful acts of individuals, unsupported by State authority in the shape of laws, customs, or judicial or executive proceedings. The wrongful act of an individual, unsupported by any such authority, is simply a private wrong, or a crime of that individual; an invasion of the rights of the injured party, it is true, whether they affect his person, his property, or his reputation; but if not sanctioned in some way by the State, or not done under State authority, his rights remain in full force, and may presumably be vindicated by resort to the laws of the State for redress. An individual cannot deprive a man of his right to vote, to hold property, to buy and sell, to sue in the courts, or to be a witness or a juror; he may, by force or fraud, interfere with the enjoyment of the right in a particular case; he may commit an assault against the person, or commit murder, or use ruffian violence at the polls, or slander the good name of a fellow citizen; but, unless protected in these wrongful acts by some shield of State law or State authority, he cannot destroy or injure the right; he will only render himself amenable to satisfaction or punishment; and amenable therefor to the laws of the State where the wrongful acts are committed. Hence, in all those cases where the Constitution seeks to protect the rights of the citizen against discriminative and unjust laws of the State by prohibiting such laws, it is not individual offences, but abrogation and denial of rights, which it denounces, and for which it clothes the Congress with power to provide a remedy. This abrogation and denial of rights, for which the States alone were or could be responsible, was the great seminal and fundamental wrong which was intended to be remedied. And the remedy to be provided must necessarily be predicated upon that wrong. It must assume that in the cases provided for, the evil or wrong actually committed rests upon some State law or State authority for its excuse and perpetration.

Of course, these remarks do not apply to those cases in which Congress is clothed with direct and plenary powers of legislation over the whole subject, accompanied with an express or implied denial of such power to the States, as in the regulation of commerce with foreign nations, among the several States, and with the Indian tribes, the coining of money, the establishment of post offices and post roads, the declaring of war, etc. In these cases Congress has power to pass laws for regulating the subjects specified in every detail, and the conduct and transactions of individuals in respect thereof. But where a subject is not submitted to the general legislative power of Congress, but is only submitted thereto for the purpose of rendering effective some prohibition against particular State legislation or State action in reference to that subject, the power given is limited by its object, and any legislation by Congress in the matter must necessarily be corrective in its character, adapted to counteract and redress the operation of such prohibited State laws or proceedings of State officers.

If the principles of interpretation which we have laid down are correct, as we deem them to be (and they are in accord with the principles laid down in the cases before referred to, as well as in the recent case of *United States* v. *Harris,* 106 U.S. 629), it is clear that the law in question cannot be sustained by any grant of legislative power made to Congress by the Fourteenth Amendment. That amendment prohibits the States from denying to any person the equal protection of the laws, and declares that Congress shall have power to enforce, by appropriate legislation, the provisions of the amendment. The law in question, without any reference to adverse State legislation on the subject, declares that all persons shall be en-

titled to equal accommodations and privileges of inns, public conveyances, and places of public amusement, and imposes a penalty upon any individual who shall deny to any citizen such equal accommodations and privileges. This is not corrective legislation; it is primary and direct; it takes immediate and absolute possession of the subject of the right of admission to inns, public conveyances, and places of amusement. It supersedes and displaces State legislation on the same subject, or only allows it permissive force. It ignores such legislation, and assumes that the matter is one that belongs to the domain of national regulation. Whether it would not have been a more effective protection of the rights of citizens to have clothed Congress with plenary power over the whole subject, is not now the question. What we have to decide is, whether such plenary power has been conferred upon Congress by the Fourteenth Amendment; and, in our judgment, it has not.

We have discussed the question presented by the law on the assumption that a right to enjoy equal accommodation and privileges in all inns, public conveyances, and places of public amusement, is one of the essential rights of the citizen which no State can abridge or interfere with. Whether it is such a right, or not, is a different question which, in the view we have taken of the validity of the law on the ground already stated, it is not necessary to examine.

We have also discussed the validity of the law in reference to cases arising in the States only; and not in reference to cases arising in the Territories or the District of Columbia, which are subject to the plenary legislation of Congress in every branch of municipal regulation. Whether the law would be a valid one as applied to the Territories and the District is not a question for consideration in the cases before us: they all being cases arising within the limits of States. And whether Congress, in the exercise of its power to regulate commerce amongst the several States, might or might not pass a law regulating rights in public conveyances passing from one State to another, is also a question which is not now before us, as the sections in question are not conceived in any such view.

But the power of Congress to adopt direct and primary, as distinguished from corrective legislation, on the subject in hand, is sought, in the second place, from the Thirteenth Amendment, which abolishes slavery. This amendment declares "that neither slavery, nor involuntary servitude, except as a punishment for crime, whereof the party shall have been duly convicted, shall exist within the United States, or any place subject to their jurisdiction"; and it gives Congress power to enforce the amendment by appropriate legislation.

This amendment, as well as the Fourteenth, is undoubtedly self-executing without any ancillary legislation, so far as its terms are applicable to any existing state of circumstances. By its own unaided force and effect it abolished slavery, and established universal freedom. Still, legislation may be necessary and proper to meet all the various cases and circumstances to be affected by it, and to prescribe proper modes of redress for its violation in letter or spirit. And such legislation may be primary and direct in its character; for the amendment is not a mere prohibition of State laws establishing or upholding slavery, but an absolute declaration that slavery or involuntary servitude shall not exist in any part of the United States.

It is true, that slavery cannot exist without law, any more than property in lands and goods can exist without law: and, therefore, the Thirteenth Amendment may be regarded as nullifying all State laws which establish or uphold slavery. But it has a reflex character also, establishing and decreeing universal civil and political freedom throughout the United States; and it is assumed, that the power vested in Congress to enforce the article by appropriate legislation, clothes Congress with power to pass all laws necessary and proper for abolishing all badges and incidents of slavery in the United States: and upon this assumption it is claimed, that this is sufficient authority for declaring by law that all persons shall have equal accommodations and privileges in all inns, public conveyances, and places of amusement; the argument being, that the denial of such equal accommodations and privileges is, in itself, a subjection to a species of servitude within the meaning of the amendment. Conceding the major proposition to be true, that Congress has a right to enact all necessary and proper laws for the obliteration and prevention of slavery with all its badges and incidents, is the minor proposition also true, that the denial to any person of admission to the accommodations and privileges of an inn, a public conveyance, or a theatre, does subject that person to any form of servitude, or tend to fasten upon him any badge of slavery? If it does not, then power to pass the law is not found in the Thirteenth Amendment.

In a very able and learned presentation of the cognate question as to the extent of the rights, privileges and immunities of citizens which cannot rightfully be abridged by state laws under the Fourteenth Amendment, made in a former case, a long list of burdens and disabilities of a servile character, incident to feudal vassalage in France, and which were abolished by the decrees of the National Assembly, was presented for the purpose of showing that all inequalities and observances exacted by one man from another were servitudes, or badges of slavery, which a great nation, in its effort to establish universal liberty, made haste to wipe out and destroy. But these were servitudes imposed by the old law, or by long custom, which had the force of law, and exacted by one man from another without the latter's consent. Should any such servitudes be imposed by a state law, there can be no doubt that the law would be repugnant to the Fourteenth, no less than to the Thirteenth Amendment; nor any greater doubt that Congress has adequate power to forbid any such servitude from being exacted.

But is there any similarity between such servitudes and a denial by the owner of an inn, a public conveyance, or a theatre, of its accommodations and privileges to an individual, even though the denial be founded on the race or color of that individual? Where does any slavery or servitude, or badge of either, arise from such an act of denial? Whether it might not be a denial of a right which, if sanctioned by the state law, would be obnoxious to the prohibitions of the Fourteenth Amendment, is another question. But what has it to do with the question of slavery?

It may be that by the Black Code (as it was called), in the times when slavery prevailed, the proprietors of inns and public conveyances were forbidden to receive persons of the African race, because it might assist slaves to escape from the control of their masters. This was merely a means of preventing such escapes, and was no part of the servitude itself. A law of that kind could not have any such object now, however justly it might be deemed an invasion of the party's legal right as a citizen, and amenable to the prohibitions of the Fourteenth Amendment.

The long existence of African slavery in this country gave us very distinct notions of what it was, and what were its necessary incidents. Compulsory service of the slave for the benefit of the master, restraint of his movements except by the master's will, disability to hold property, to make contracts, to have a standing in court, to be a witness against a white person, and such like burdens and incapacities, were the inseparable incidents of the institution. Severer punishments for crimes were imposed on the slave than on free persons guilty of the same offences. Congress, as we have seen, by the Civil Rights Bill of 1866, passed in view of the Thirteenth Amendment, before the Fourteenth was adopted, undertook to wipe out these burdens and disabilities, the necessary incidents of slavery, constituting its substance and visible form;

and to secure to all citizens of every race and color, and without regard to previous servitude, those fundamental rights which are the essence of civil freedom, namely, the same right to make and enforce contracts, to sue, be parties, give evidence, and to inherit, purchase, lease, sell and convey property, as is enjoyed by white citizens. Whether this legislation was fully authorized by the Thirteenth Amendment alone, without the support which it afterward received from the Fourteenth Amendment, after the adoption of which it was re-enacted with some additions, it is not necessary to inquire. It is referred to for the purpose of showing that at that time (in 1866) Congress did not assume, under the authority given by the Thirteenth Amendment, to adjust what may be called the social rights of men and races in the community; but only to declare and vindicate those fundamental rights which appertain to the essence of citizenship, and the enjoyment or deprivation of which constitutes the essential distinction between freedom and slavery.

We must not forget that the province and scope of the Thirteenth and Fourteenth amendments are different; the former simply abolished slavery: the latter prohibited the States from abridging the privileges or immunities of citizens of the United States; from depriving them of life, liberty, or property without due process of law, and from denying to any the equal protection of the laws. The amendments are different, and the powers of Congress under them are different. What Congress has power to do under one, it may not have power to do under the other. Under the Thirteenth Amendment, it has only to do with slavery and its incidents. Under the Fourteenth Amendment, it has power to counteract and render nugatory all State laws and proceedings which have the effect to abridge any of the privileges or immunities of citizens of the United States, or to deprive them of life, liberty or property without due process of law, or to deny to any of them the equal protection of the laws. Under the Thirteenth Amendment, the legislation, so far as necessary or proper to eradicate all forms and incidents of slavery and involuntary servitude, may be direct and primary, operating upon the acts of individuals, whether sanctioned by State legislation or not; under the Fourteenth, as we have already shown, it must necessarily be, and can only be, corrective in its character, addressed to counteract and afford relief against State regulations or proceedings.

The only question under the present head, therefore, is, whether the refusal to any persons of the accommodations of an inn, or a public conveyance, or a place of public amusement, by an individual, and without any sanction or support from any State law or regulation, does inflict upon such persons any manner of servitude, or form of slavery, as those terms are understood in this country? Many wrongs may be obnoxious to the prohibitions of the Fourteenth Amendment which are not, in any just sense, incidents or elements of slavery. Such, for example, would be the taking of private property without due process of law; or allowing persons who have committed certain crimes (horse stealing, for example) to be seized and hung by the *posse comitatus* without regular trial; or denying to any person, or class of persons, the right to pursue any peaceful avocations allowed to others. What is called class legislation would belong to this category, and would be obnoxious to the prohibitions of the Fourteenth Amendment, but would not necessarily be so to the Thirteenth, when not involving the idea of any subjection of one man to another. The Thirteenth Amendment has respect, not to distinctions of race, or class, or color, but to slavery. The Fourteenth Amendment extends its protection to races and classes, and prohibits any State legislation which has the effect of denying to any race or class, or to any individual, the equal protection of the laws.

Now, conceding, for the sake of the argument, that the admission to an inn, a public conveyance, or a place of public amusement, on equal terms with all other citizens, is the right of every man and all classes of men, is it any more than one of those rights which the states by the Fourteenth Amendment are forbidden to deny to any person? And is the Constitution violated until the denial of the right has some State sanction or authority? Can the act of a mere individual, the owner of the inn, the public conveyance or place of amusement, refusing the accommodation, be justly regarded as imposing any badge of slavery or servitude upon the applicant, or only as inflicting an ordinary civil injury, properly cognizable by the laws of the State, and presumably subject to redress by those laws until the contrary appears?

After giving to these questions all the consideration which their importance demands, we are forced to the conclusion that such an act of refusal has nothing to do with slavery or involuntary servitude, and that if it is violative of any right of the party, his redress is to be sought under the laws of the State; or if those laws are adverse to his rights and do not protect him, his remedy will be found in the corrective legislation which Congress has adopted, or may adopt, for counteracting the effect of State laws, or State action, prohibited by the Fourteenth Amendment. It would be running the slavery argument into the ground to make it apply to every act of discrimination which a person may see fit to make as to the guests he will entertain, or as to the people he will take into his coach or cab or car, or admit to his concert or theatre, or deal with in other matters of intercourse or business. Innkeepers and public carriers, by the laws of all the States, so far as we are aware, are bound, to the extent of their facilities, to furnish proper accommodation to all unobjectionable persons who in good faith apply for them. If the laws themselves make any unjust discrimination, amenable to the prohibitions of the Fourteenth Amendment, Congress has full power to afford a remedy under that amendment and in accordance with it.

When a man has emerged from slavery, and by the aid of beneficent legislation has shaken off the inseparable concomitants of that state, there must be some stage in the progress of his elevation when he takes the rank of a mere citizen, and ceases to be the special favorite of the laws, and when his rights as a citizen, or a man, are to be protected in the ordinary modes by which other men's rights are protected. There were thousands of free colored people in this country before the abolition of slavery, enjoying all the essential rights of life, liberty and property the same as white citizens; yet no one, at that time, thought that it was any invasion of his personal status as a freeman because he was not admitted to all the privileges enjoyed by white citizens, or because he was subjected to discriminations in the enjoyment of accommodations in inns, public conveyances and places of amusement. Mere discriminations on account of race or color were not regarded as badges of slavery. If, since that time, the enjoyment of equal rights in all these respects has become established by constitutional enactment, it is not by force of the Thirteenth Amendment (which merely abolishes slavery), but by force of the Fourteenth and Fifteenth Amendments.

On the whole we are of opinion, that no countenance of authority for the passage of the law in question can be found in either the Thirteenth or Fourteenth Amendment of the Constitution; and no other ground of authority for its passage being suggested, it must necessarily be declared void, at least so far as its operation in the several States is concerned.

This conclusion disposes of the cases now under consideration. In the cases of the *United States* v. *Michael Ryan,* and of *Richard A. Robinson and Wife* v. *The Memphis & Charleston Railroad Company,* the judgments must be affirmed. In the other cases, the answer to be given will be that the first and second sections of the act of Congress of March 1st, 1875,

entitled "An Act to protect all citizens in their civil and legal rights," are unconstitutional and void, and that judgment should be rendered upon the several indictments in those cases accordingly. *And it is so ordered.*

Mr. Justice Harlan dissenting. . . .

This court has always given a broad and liberal construction to the Constitution, so as to enable Congress, by legislation, to enforce rights secured by that instrument. The legislation which Congress may enact, in execution of its power to enforce the provisions of this amendment, is such as may be appropriate to protect the right granted. The word appropriate was undoubtedly used with reference to its meaning, as established by repeated decisions of this court. Under given circumstances, that which the court characterizes as corrective legislation might be deemed by Congress appropriate and entirely sufficient. Under other circumstances primary direct legislation may be required. But it is for Congress, not the judiciary, to say that legislation is appropriate—that is— best adapted to the end to be attained. The judiciary may not, with safety to our institutions, enter the domain of legislative discretion, and dictate the means which Congress shall employ in the exercise of its granted powers. That would be sheer usurpation of the functions of a co-ordinate department, which, if often repeated, and permanently acquiesced in, would work a radical change in our system of government. In *United States* v. *Fisher,* 2 Cr. 358, the court said that "Congress must possess the choice of means, and must be empowered to use any means which are in fact conducive to the exercise of a power granted by the Constitution." "The sound construction of the Constitution," said Chief Justice Marshall, "must allow to the national legislature that discretion, with respect to the means by which the powers it confers are to be carried into execution, which will enable that body to perform the high duties assigned to it in the manner most beneficial to the people. Let the end be legitimate, let it be within the scope of the Constitution, and all means which are appropriate, which are plainly adapted to that end, which are not prohibited, but consist with the letter and spirit of the Constitution, are constitutional." *McCulloch* v. *Maryland,* 4 Wh. 421.

Must these rules of construction be now abandoned? Are the powers of the national legislature to be restrained in proportion as the rights and privileges, derived from the nation, are valuable? Are constitutional provisions, enacted to secure the dearest rights of freemen and citizens, to be subjected to that rule of construction, applicable to private instruments, which requires that the words to be interpreted must be taken most strongly against those who employ them? Or, shall it be remembered that "a constitution of government, founded by the people for themselves and their posterity, and for objects of the most momentous nature—for perpetual union, for the establishment of justice, for the general welfare, and for a perpetuation of the blessings of liberty—necessarily requires that every interpretation of its powers should have a constant reference to these objects? No interpretation of the words in which those powers are granted can be a sound one, which narrows down their ordinary import so as to defeat those objects." 1 Story Const. § 422.

The opinion of the court, as I have said, proceeds upon the ground that the power of Congress to legislate for the protection of the rights and privileges secured by the Fourteenth Amendment cannot be brought into activity except with the view, and as it may become necessary, to correct and annul State laws and State proceedings in hostility to such rights and privileges. In the absence of State laws or State action adverse to such rights and privileges, the nation may not actively interfere for their protection and security, even against corporations and individuals exercising public or quasi public functions. Such I understand to be the position of my brethren. If the grant to colored citizens of the United States of citizenship in their respective States, imports exemption from race discrimination, in their States, in respect of such civil rights as belong to citizenship, then, to hold that the amendment remits that right to the States for their protection, primarily, and stays the hands of the nation, until it is assailed by State laws or State proceedings, is to adjudge that the amendment, so far from enlarging the powers of Congress—as we have heretofore said it did—not only curtails them, but reverses the policy which the general government has pursued from its very organization. Such an interpretation of the amendment is a denial to Congress of the power, by appropriate legislation, to enforce one of its provisions. In view of the circumstances under which the recent amendments were incorporated into the Constitution, and especially in view of the peculiar character of the new rights they created and secured, it ought not to be presumed that the general government has abdicated its authority, by national legislation, direct and primary in its character, to guard and protect privileges and immunities secured by that instrument. Such an interpretation of the Constitution ought not to be accepted if it be possible to avoid it. Its acceptance would lead to this anomalous result: that whereas, prior to the amendments, Congress, with the sanction of this court, passed the most stringent laws—operating directly and primarily upon States and their officers and agents, as well as upon individuals—in vindication of slavery and the right of the master, it may not now, by legislation of a like primary and direct character, guard, protect, and secure the freedom established, and the most essential right of the citizenship granted, by the constitutional amendments. With all respect for the opinion of others, I insist that the national legislature may, without transcending the limits of the Constitution, do for human liberty and the fundamental rights of American citizenship, what it did, with the sanction of this court, for the protection of slavery and the rights of the masters of fugitive slaves. If fugitive slave laws, providing modes and prescribing penalties, whereby the master could seize and recover his fugitive slave, were legitimate exercises of an implied power to protect and enforce a right recognized by the Constitution, why shall the hands of Congress be tied, so that—under an express power, by appropriate legislation, to enforce a constitutional provision granting citizenship—it may not, by means of direct legislation, bring the whole power of this nation to bear upon States and their officers, and upon such individuals and corporations exercising public functions as assume to abridge, impair, or deny rights confessedly secured by the supreme law of the land?

It does not seem to me that the fact that, by the second clause of the first section of the Fourteenth Amendment, the States are expressly prohibited from making or enforcing laws abridging the privileges and immunities of citizens of the United States, furnishes any sufficient reason for holding or maintaining that the amendment was intended to deny Congress the power, by general, primary, and direct legislation, of protecting citizens of the several States, being also citizens of the United States, against all discrimination, in respect of their rights as citizens, which is founded on race, color, or previous condition of servitude.

Such an interpretation of the amendment is plainly repugnant to its fifth section, conferring upon Congress power, by appropriate legislation, to enforce not merely the provisions containing prohibitions upon the States, but all of the provisions of the amendment, including the provisions, express and implied, in the first clause of the first section of the article granting citizenship. This alone is sufficient for holding that Congress is not restricted to the enactment of laws adapted to counteract and redress the operation of State legislation, or the action of State officers, of the character prohibited by the amendment. It was perfectly well known that the great danger to the equal enjoyment by citizens of their rights, as citizens, was to be apprehended not altogether from unfriendly State legislation, but from the hostile action of corporations and individuals in the States. And it is to be presumed that it was intended, by that section, to clothe Congress with power and authority to meet that danger. If the rights intended to be secured by the act of 1875 are such as belong to the citizen, in common or equally with other citizens in the same State, then it is not to be denied that such legislation is peculiarly appropriate to the end which Congress is authorized to accomplish, viz., to protect the citizen, in respect of such rights, against discrimination on account of his race. Recurring to the specific prohibition in the Fourteenth Amendment upon the making or enforcing of State laws abridging the privileges of citizens of the United States, I remark that if, as held in the *Slaughter-House Cases,* the privileges here referred to were those which belonged to citizenship of the United States, as distinguished from those belonging to State citizenship, it was impossible for any State prior to the adoption of that amendment to have enforced laws of that character. The judiciary could have annulled all such legislation under the provision that the Constitution shall be the supreme law of the land, anything in the constitution or laws of any State to the contrary notwithstanding. The States were already under an implied prohibition not to abridge any privilege or immunity belonging to citizens of the United States as such. Consequently, the prohibition upon State laws in hostility to rights belonging to citizens of the United States, was intended—in view of the introduction into the body of citizens of a race formerly denied the essential rights of citizenship—only as an express limitation on the powers of the States, and was not intended to diminish, in the slightest degree, the authority which the nation has always exercised, of protecting, by means of its own direct legislation, rights created or secured by the Constitution. Any purpose to diminish the national authority in respect of privileges derived from the nation is distinctly negatived by the express grant of power, by legislation, to enforce every provision of the amendment, including that which, by the grant of citizenship in the State, secures exemption from race discrimination in respect of the civil rights of citizens.

It is said that any interpretation of the Fourteenth Amendment different from that adopted by the majority of the court, would imply that Congress had authority to enact a municipal code for all the States, covering every matter affecting the life, liberty, and property of the citizens of the several States. Not so. Prior to the adoption of that amendment the constitutions of the several States, without perhaps an exception, secured all *persons* against deprivation of life, liberty, or property, otherwise than by due process of law, and, in some form, recognized the right of all *persons* to the equal protection of the laws. Those rights, therefore, existed before that amendment was proposed or adopted, and were not created by it. If, by reason of that fact, it be assumed that protection in these rights of persons still rests primarily with the States, and that Congress may not interfere except to enforce, by means of corrective legislation, the prohibitions upon State laws or State proceedings inconsistent with those rights, it does not at all follow, that privileges which have been *granted by the nation,* may not be protected by primary legislation upon the part of Congress. The personal rights and immunities recognized in the prohibitive clauses of the amendment were, prior to its adoption, under the protection, primarily, of the States, while rights, created by or derived from the United States, have always been, and, in the nature of things, should always be, primarily, under the protection of the general government. Exemption from race discrimination, in respect of the civil rights which are fundamental in *citizenship* in a republican government, is, as we have seen, a new right, created by the nation, with express power in Congress, by legislation, to enforce the constitutional provision from which it is derived. If, in some sense, such race discrimination is, within the letter of the last clause of the first section, a denial of that equal protection of the laws which is secured against State denial to all persons, whether citizens or not, it cannot be possible that a mere prohibition upon such State denial, or a prohibition upon State laws abridging the privileges and immunities of citizens of the United States, takes from the nation the power which it has uniformly exercised of protecting, by direct primary legislation, those privileges and immunities which existed under the Constitution before the adoption of the Fourteenth Amendment, or have been created by that amendment in behalf of those thereby made *citizens* of their respective States.

This construction does not in any degree intrench upon the just rights of the States in the control of their domestic affairs. It simply recognizes the enlarged powers conferred by the recent amendments upon the general government. In the view which I take of those amendments, the States possess the same authority which they have always had to define and regulate the civil rights which their own people, in virtue of

State citizenship, may enjoy within their respective limits; except that its exercise is now subject to the expressly granted power of Congress, by legislation, to enforce the provisions of such amendments—a power which necessarily carries with it authority, by national legislation, to protect and secure the privileges and immunities which are created by or are derived from those amendments. That exemption of citizens from discrimination based on race or color, in respect of civil rights, is one of those privileges or immunities, can no longer be deemed an open question in this court.

It was said of the case of *Dred Scott* v. *Sandford,* that this court, there overruled the action of two generations, virtually inserted a new clause in the Constitution, changed its character, and made a new departure in the workings of the federal government. I may be permitted to say that if the recent amendments are so construed that Congress may not, in its own discretion, and independently of the action or non-action of the States, provide, by legislation of a direct character, for the security of rights created by the national Constitution; if it be adjudged that the obligation to protect the fundamental privileges and immunities granted by the Fourteenth Amendment to citizens residing in the several States, rests primarily, not on the nation, but on the States; if it be further adjudged that individuals and corporations, exercising public functions, or wielding power under public authority, may, without liability to direct primary legislation on the part of Congress, make the race of citizens the ground for denying them that equality of civil rights which the Constitution ordains as a principle of republican citizenship; then, not only the foundations upon which the national supremacy has always securely rested will be materially disturbed, but we shall enter upon an era of constitutional law, when the rights of freedom and American citizenship cannot receive from the nation that efficient protection which heretofore was unhesitatingly accorded to slavery and the rights of the master.

But if it were conceded that the power of Congress could not be brought into activity until the rights specified in the act of 1875 had been abridged or denied by some State law or State action, I maintain that the decision of the court is erroneous. There has been adverse State action within the Fourteenth Amendment as heretofore interpreted by this court. I allude to *Ex parte Virginia supra*. It appears, in that case, that one Cole, judge of a county court, was charged with the duty, by the laws of Virginia, of selecting grand and petit jurors. The law of the State did not authorize or permit him, in making such selections, to discriminate against colored

citizens because of their race. But he was indicted in the federal court, under the act of 1875, for making such discriminations. The attorney-general of Virginia contended before us, that the State had done its duty, and had not authorized or directed that county judge to do what he was charged with having done; that the State had not denied to the colored race the equal protection of the laws; and that consequently the act of Cole must be deemed his individual act, in contravention of the will of the State. Plausible as this argument was, it failed to convince this court, and after saying that the Fourteenth Amendment had reference to the political body denominated a State, "by whatever instruments or in whatever modes that action may be taken," and that a State acts by its legislative, executive, and judicial authorities, and can act in no other way, we proceeded:

"The constitutional provision, therefore, must mean that no agency of the State, or of the officers or agents by whom its powers are exerted, shall deny to any person within its jurisdiction the equal protection of the laws. Whoever, by virtue of public position under a State government, deprives another of property, life, or liberty without due process of law, or denies or takes away the equal protection of the laws, violates the constitutional inhibition; and, as he acts under the name and for the State, and is clothed with the State's power, his act is that of the State. This must be so, or the constitutional prohibition has no meaning. Then the State has clothed one of its agents with power to annul or evade it. But the constitutional amendment was ordained for a purpose. It was to secure equal rights to all persons, and, to insure to all persons the enjoyment of such rights, power was given to Congress to enforce its provisions by appropriate legislation. Such legislation must act upon persons, not upon the abstract thing denominated a State, but upon the persons who are the agents of the State, in the denial of the rights which were intended to be secured." *Ex parte Virginia,* 100 U.S. 346–7.

In every material sense applicable to the practical enforcement of the Fourteenth Amendment, railroad corporations, keepers of inns, and managers of places of public amusement are agents or instrumentalities of the State, because they are charged with duties to the public, and are amenable, in respect of their duties and functions, to governmental regulation. It seems to me that, within the principle settled in *Ex parte Virginia,* a denial, by these instrumentalities of the

State, to the citizen, because of his race, of that equality of civil rights secured to him by law, is a denial by the State, within the meaning of the Fourteenth Amendment. If it be not, then that race is left, in respect of the civil rights in question, practically at the mercy of corporations and individuals wielding power under the States.

But the court says that Congress did not, in the act of 1866, assume, under the authority given by the Thirteenth Amendment, to adjust what may be called the social rights of men and races in the community. I agree that government has nothing to do with social, as distinguished from technically legal, rights of individuals. No government ever has brought, or ever can bring, its people into social intercourse against their wishes. Whether one person will permit or maintain social relations with another is a matter with which government has no concern. I agree that if one citizen chooses not to hold social intercourse with another, he is not and cannot be made amenable to the law for his conduct in that regard; for even upon grounds of race, no legal right of a citizen is violated by the refusal of others to maintain merely social relations with him. What I affirm is that no State, nor the officers of any State, nor any corporation or individual wielding power under State authority for the public benefit or the public convenience, can, consistently either with the freedom established by the fundamental law, or with that equality of civil rights which now belongs to every citizen, discriminate against freemen or citizens, in those rights, because of their race, or because they once labored under the disabilities of slavery imposed upon them as a race. The rights which Congress, by the act of 1875, endeavored to secure and protect are legal, not social rights. The right, for instance, of a colored citizen to use the accommodations of a public highway, upon the same terms as are permitted to white citizens, is no more a social right than his right, under the law, to use the public streets of a city or a town, or a turnpike road, or a public market, or a post office, or his right to sit in a public building with others, of whatever race, for the purpose of hearing the political questions of the day discussed. Scarcely a day passes without our seeing in this court-room citizens of the white and black races sitting side by side, watching the progress of our business. It would never occur to any one that the presence of a colored citizen in a court-house, or court-room, was an invasion of the social rights of white persons who may frequent such places. And yet, such a suggestion would be quite as sound in law—I say it with all respect—as is the suggestion that the claim of a colored citizen to use, upon the same terms as is permitted to white citizens, the accommodations of public highways, or public inns, or places of public amusement, established under the license of the law, is an invasion of the social rights of the white race.

The court, in its opinion, reserves the question whether Congress, in the exercise of its power to regulate commerce amongst the several States, might or might not pass a law regulating rights in public conveyances passing from one State to another. I beg to suggest that that precise question was substantially presented here in the only one of these cases relating to railroads—*Robinson and Wife* v. *Memphis & Charleston Railroad Company.* In that case it appears that Mrs. Robinson, a citizen of Mississippi, purchased a railroad ticket entitling her to be carried from Grand Junction, Tennessee, to Lynchburg, Virginia. Might not the act of 1875 be maintained in that case, as applicable at least to commerce between the States, notwithstanding it does not, upon its face, profess to have been passed in pursuance of the power of Congress to regulate commerce? Has it ever been held that the judiciary should overturn a statute, because the legislative department did not accurately recite therein the particular provision of the Constitution authorizing its enactment? We have often enforced municipal bonds in aid of railroad subscriptions, where they failed to recite the statute authorizing their issue, but recited one which did not sustain their validity. The inquiry in such cases has been, was there, in any statute, authority for the execution of the bonds? Upon this branch of the case, it may be remarked that the State of Louisiana, in 1869, passed a statute giving to passengers, without regard to race or color, equality of right in the accommodations of railroad and street cars, steamboats or other water crafts, stage coaches, omnibuses, or other vehicles. But in *Hall* v. *De Cuir,* 95 U.S. 487, that act was pronounced unconstitutional so far as it related to commerce between the States, this court saying that "if the public good requires such legislation it must come from Congress, and not from the States." I suggest, that it may become a pertinent inquiry whether Congress may, in the exertion of its power to regulate commerce among the States, enforce among passengers on public conveyances, equality of right, without regard to race, color or previous condition of servitude, if it be true—which I do not admit—that such legislation would be an interference by government with the social rights of the people.

My brethren say, that when a man has emerged from slavery, and by the aid of beneficent legislation has shaken off the inseparable concomitants of that state, there must be some stage in the progress of his elevation when he takes the rank of a mere citizen, and ceases to be the special favorite of the laws, and when his rights as a citizen, or a man, are to be protected in the ordinary modes by which other men's rights are protected. It is, I submit, scarcely just to say that the colored race has been the special favorite of the laws. The statute of 1875, now adjudged to be unconstitutional, is for the benefit of citizens of every race and color. What the nation, through Congress, has sought to accomplish in reference to that race, is—what had already been done in every State of the Union for the white race—to secure and protect rights belonging to them as freemen and citizens; nothing more. It was not deemed enough "to help the feeble up, but to support him after." The one underlying purpose of congressional legislation has been to enable the black race to take the rank of mere citizens. The difficulty has been to compel a recognition of the legal right of the black race to take the rank of citizens, and to secure the enjoyment of privileges belonging, under the law, to them as a component part of the people for whose welfare and happiness government is ordained. At every step, in this direction, the nation has been confronted with class tyranny, which a contemporary English historian says is, of all tyrannies, the most intolerable, "for it is ubiquitous in its operation, and weighs, perhaps, most heavily on those whose ob-

scurity or distance would withdraw them from the notice of a single despot." To-day, it is the colored race which is denied, by corporations and individuals wielding public authority, rights fundamental in their freedom and citizenship. At some future time, it may be that some other race will fall under the ban of race discrimination. If the constitutional amendments be enforced, according to the intent with which, as I conceive, they were adopted, there cannot be, in this republic, any class of human beings in practical subjection to another class, with power in the latter to dole out to the former just such privileges as they may choose to grant. The supreme law of the land has decreed that no authority shall be exercised in this country upon the basis of discrimination, in respect of civil rights, against freemen and citizens because of their race, color, or previous condition of servitude. To that decree—for the due enforcement of which, by appropriate legislation, Congress has been invested with express power—every one must bow, whatever may have been, or whatever now are, his individual views as to the wisdom or policy, either of the recent changes in the fundamental law, or of the legislation which has been enacted to give them effect.

For the reasons stated I feel constrained to withhold my assent to the opinion of the court.

Constitution of the State of Mississippi, 1890

The withdrawal of federal troops from the former Confederacy allowed white Democrats to wrest control over state governments from the combination of native Republicans (termed "scalawags"), transplanted northerners (termed "carpetbaggers"), and freed slaves that ruled after the Civil War. These states soon adopted so-called redeemer constitutions that instituted a variety of restrictions on voting rights, such as poll taxes and literacy tests, resulting in dramatic decreases in the number of voters—both white and African American. Race was not the only issue addressed in these constitutions passed during a time of economic hardship and instability. The increasing power of railroad corporations, often exercised through political bribery and local government issuance of stock, and public works projects such as river levees were also critical issues of the day.

Constitution of the State of Mississippi

November 1, 1890

We, the people of Mississippi, in Convention assembled, grateful to Almighty God, and invoking his blessing on our work, do ordain and establish this Constitution.

SEC. 183. No county, city, town or other municipal corporation shall hereafter become a subscriber to the capital stock of any railroad or other corporation or association, or make appropriation, or loan its credit in aid of such corporation or association. All authority heretofore conferred for any of the purposes aforesaid by the Legislature or by the charter of any corporation, is hereby repealed. Nothing in this section contained shall affect the right of any such corporation, municipality or county to make such subscription where the same has been authorized under laws existing at the time of the adoption of this Constitution, and by a vote of the people thereof, had prior to its adoption, and where the terms of submission and subscription have been or shall be complied with, or to prevent the issue of renewal bonds, or the use of such other means as are or may be prescribed by law for the payment or liquidation of such subscription, or of any existing indebtedness.

SEC. 184. All railroads which carry persons or property for hire, shall be public highways, and all railroad companies so engaged shall be common carriers. Any company organized for that purpose under the laws of the State, shall have the right to construct and operate a railroad between any points within this State, and to connect at the State line with roads of other States. Every railroad company shall have the right with its road to intersect, connect with, or cross any other railroad; and all railroad companies shall receive and transport each other's passengers, tonnage and cars, loaded or empty, without unnecessary delay or discrimination.

SEC. 185. The rolling stock, belonging to any railroad company or corporation in this State, shall be considered personal property and shall be liable to execution and sale as such.

SEC. 186. The Legislature shall pass laws to prevent abuses, unjust discrimination and extortion in all charges of express, telephone, sleeping car, telegraph and railroad companies, and shall enact laws for the supervision of railroads, express, telephone, telegraph, sleeping car companies and other common carriers in this State, by commission or otherwise, and shall provide adequate penalties, to the extent, if necessary for that purpose, of forfeiture of their franchises.

SEC. 187. No railroad hereafter constructed in this State, shall pass within three miles of any county seat without passing through the same, and establishing and maintaining a depot therein, unless prevented by natural obstacles; *Provided,* Such town or its citizens shall grant the right-of-way through its limits, and sufficient ground for ordinary depot purposes.

SEC. 188. No railroad or other transportation company shall grant free passes or tickets, or passes or tickets at a discount, to members of the Legislature, or any State, district, county or municipal officers, except Railroad Commissioners. The Legislature shall enact suitable laws for the detection, prevention and punishment of violations of this provision....

SEC. 190. The exercise of the right of eminent domain shall never be abridged, or so construed as to prevent the Legislature from taking the property and franchises of incorporated companies, and subjecting them to public use; and the exercise of the police powers of the State shall never be abridged, or so construed as to permit corporations to conduct their business in such manner as to infringe upon the rights of individuals, or the general well-being of the State.

SEC. 191. The Legislature shall provide for the protection of the employees of all corporations doing business in this State from interference with their social, civil, or political rights by said corporations, their agents or employees.

SEC. 192. Provision shall be made by general laws whereby cities and towns may be authorized to aid and encourage the establishment of manufactories, gas-works, water-works, and other enterprises of public utility other than railroads, within the limits of said cities or towns, by exempting all property used for such purposes, from municipal taxation for a period not longer than ten years.

SEC. 193. Every employee of any railroad corporation shall have the same right and remedies for any injury suffered by him from the act or omission of said corporation or its employees, as are allowed by law to other persons not employees, where the injury results from the negligence of a superior agent or officer, or of a person having the right to control or direct the services of the party injured, and also when the injury results from the negligence of a fellow-servant engaged in another department of labor from that of the party injured, or of a fellow servant on another train of cars, or one engaged about a different piece of work. Knowledge by any employee injured, of the defective or unsafe character or condition of any machinery, ways or appliances, shall be no defense to an action for injury caused thereby, except as to conductors or engineers in charge of dangerous or unsafe cars, or engines voluntarily operated by them. Where death ensues from any injury to employees, the legal or personal representatives of the person injured shall have the same right and remedies as are allowed by law to such representatives of other persons. Any contract or agreement, express or implied, made by any employee to waive the benefit of this section shall be null and void; and this section shall not be construed to deprive any employee of a corporation or his legal or personal representa-

tive, of any right or remedy that he now has by the law of the land. The Legislature may extend the remedies herein provided for to any other class of employees.

SEC. 194. The Legislature shall provide by law, that in all elections for directors or managers of incorporated companies, every stockholder shall have the right to vote in person or by proxy, for the number of shares of stock owned by him, for as many persons as there are directors or managers to be elected, or to cumulate said shares, so as to give one candidate as many votes as the number of directors multiplied by the number of his shares of stock shall equal, or to distribute them on the same principle among as many candidates as he shall see fit; and such directors or managers shall not be elected in any other manner; but no person who is engaged or interested in a competing business, either individually or as employee, or stockholder, shall serve on any board of directors of any corporation without the consent of a majority in interest of the stockholders thereof.

SEC. 195. Express, telegraph, telephone and sleeping car companies are declared common carriers in their respective lines of business and subject to liability as such.

SEC. 196. No transportation corporation shall issue stocks or bonds except for money, labor done, or in good faith agreed to be done, or money or property actually received; and all fictitious increase of stock or indebtedness shall be void.

SEC. 197. The Legislature shall not grant to any foreign corporation or association, a license to build, operate or lease any railroad in this State; but in all cases where a railroad is to be built or operated, and the same shall be partly in this State and partly in another State, or in other States, the owners or projectors thereof shall first become incorporated under the laws of this State; nor shall any foreign corporation or association lease or operate any railroad in this State or purchase the same, or any interest therein; consolidation of any railroad lines and corporations in this State with others shall be allowed only where the consolidated company shall become a domestic corporation of this State. No general or special law shall ever be passed for the benefit of any foreign corporation operating a railroad under an existing license from this State, or under an existing lease; and no grant of any right or privilege, and no exemption from any burden, shall be made to any such foreign corporation except upon the condition that the owners or stockholders thereof shall first organize a corporation in this State under the laws thereof, and shall thereafter operate and manage the same, and the business thereof under said domestic charter.

Sec. 198. The Legislature shall enact laws to prevent all trusts, combinations, contracts and agreements inimical to the public welfare.

Sec. 199. The term corporation used in this article shall include all associations and all joint stock companies for pecuniary gain, having privileges not possessed by individuals or partnerships.

Sec. 200. The Legislature shall enforce the provisions of this article by appropriate legislation.

Article VIII
Education

Sec. 201. It shall be the duty of the Legislature to encourage by all suitable means, the promotion of intellectual, scientific, moral and agricultural improvement, by establishing a uniform system of free public schools, by taxation, or otherwise, for all children between the ages of five and twenty-one years, and, as soon as practicable, to establish schools of higher grade.

Sec. 202. There shall be a Superintendent of Public Education elected at the same time and in the same manner as the Governor, who shall have the qualifications required of the Secretary of State, and hold his office for four years and until his successor shall be elected and qualified, who shall have the general supervision of the common schools, and of the educational interests of the State, and who shall perform such other duties and receive such compensation as shall be prescribed by law.

Sec. 203. There shall be a Board of Education, consisting of the Secretary of State, the Attorney-General, and the Superintendent of Public Education, for the management and investment of the school funds, according to law, and for the performance of such other duties as may be prescribed. The Superintendent and one other of said board shall constitute a quorum.

Sec. 204. There shall be a Superintendent of Public Education in each county, who shall be appointed by the Board of Education by and with the advice and consent of the Senate, whose term of office shall be four years, and whose qualifications, compensation and duties, shall be prescribed by law; *Provided,* That the Legislature shall have power to make the office of County School Superintendent of the several counties elective, or may otherwise provide for the discharge of the duties of County Superintendent, or abolish said office.

Sec. 205. A public school shall be maintained in each school district in the county at least four months during each scholastic year. A school district neglecting to maintain its school four months, shall be entitled to only such part of the free school fund as may be required to pay the teacher for the time actually taught.

Sec. 206. There shall be a common school fund which shall consist of the poll tax (to be retained in the counties where the same is collected) and an additional sum from the general fund in the State treasury which together shall be sufficient to maintain the common schools for the term of four months in each scholastic year. But any county or separate school district may levy an additional tax to maintain its schools for a longer time than the term of four months. The common school fund shall be distributed among the several counties and separate school districts, in proportion to the number of educable children in each, to be determined from data collected through the office of the State Superintendent of Education, in the manner to be prescribed by law.

Sec. 207. Separate schools shall be maintained for children of the white and colored races.

Sec. 208. No religious or other sect, or sects, shall ever control any part of the school or other educational funds of this State; nor shall any funds be appropriated towards the support of any sectarian school; or to any school that at the time of receiving such appropriation is not conducted as a free school....

Article XII
Franchise

Sec. 240. All elections by the people shall be by ballot.

Sec. 241. Every male inhabitant of this State, except idiots, insane persons and Indians not taxed, who is a citizen of the United States, twenty-one years old and upwards, who has resided in this State two years, and one year in the election district, or in the incorporated city or town, in which he offers to vote, and who is duly registered as provided in this article, and who has never been convicted of bribery, burglary, theft, arson, obtaining money or goods under false pretenses, perjury, forgery, embezzlement or bigamy, and who has paid, on or before the first day of February of the year in which he shall offer to vote, all taxes which may have been legally required of him, and which he has had an opportunity of paying according to law, for the two preceding years, and who shall produce to the officers holding the election satisfactory evidence that he has paid said taxes, is declared to be a qualified elector; but any minister of the gospel in charge of an organized church shall be entitled to vote after six months residence in the election district, if otherwise qualified.

SEC. 242. The Legislature shall provide by law for the registration of all persons entitled to vote at any election, and all persons offering to register shall take the following oath or affirmation: "I —— ——, do solemnly swear (or affirm) that I am twenty-one years old, (or I will be before the next election in this county) and that I will have resided in this State two years, and —— election district of —— county one year next preceding the ensuing election or (if it be stated in the oath that the person proposing to register is a minister of the gospel in charge of an organized church, then it will be sufficient to aver therein, two years residence in the State and six months in said election district), and am now in good faith a resident of the same, and that I am not disqualified from voting by reason of having been convicted of any crime named in the Constitution of this State as a disqualification to be an elector; that I will truly answer all questions propounded to me concerning my antecedents so far as they relate to my right to vote, and also as to my residence before my citizenship in this district; that I will faithfully support the Constitution of the United States and of the State of Mississippi, and will bear true faith and allegiance to the same. So help me God." In registering voters in cities and towns, not wholly in one election district, the name of such city or town may be substituted in the oath for the election district. Any wilful and corrupt false statement in said affidavit, or in answer to any material question propounded as herein authorized, shall be perjury.

SEC. 243. A uniform poll tax of two dollars, to be used in aid of the common schools, and for no other purpose, is hereby imposed on every male inhabitant of this State between the ages of twenty-one and sixty years, except persons who are deaf and dumb or blind, or who are maimed by loss of hand or foot; said tax to be a lien only upon taxable property. The Board of Supervisors of any county may, for the purpose of aiding the common schools in that county, increase the poll tax in said county, but in no case shall the entire poll tax exceed in any one year three dollars on each poll. No criminal proceedings shall be allowed to enforce the collection of the poll tax.

SEC. 244. On and after the first day of January, A.D., 1892, every elector shall, in addition to the foregoing qualifications, be able to read any section of the Constitution of this State; or he shall be able to understand the same when read to him, or give a reasonable interpretation thereof. A new registration shall be made before the next ensuing election after January the first, A.D., 1892.

SEC. 245. Electors in municipal elections shall possess all the qualifications herein prescribed, and such additional qualifications as may be provided by law.

SEC. 246. Prior to the first day of January, A.D., 1896, the elections by the people in this State shall be regulated by an ordinance of this Convention.

SEC. 247. The Legislature shall enact laws to secure fairness in party primary elections, conventions or other methods of naming party candidates.

SEC. 248. Suitable remedies by appeal or otherwise shall be provided by law, to correct illegal or improper registration and to secure the elective franchise to those who may be illegally or improperly denied the same.

SEC. 249. No one shall be allowed to vote for members of the Legislature or other officers who has not been duly registered under the Constitution and laws of this State, by an officer of this State, legally authorized to register the voters thereof. And registration under the Constitution and laws of this State by the proper officers of this State is hereby declared to be an essential and necessary qualification to vote at any and all elections.

SEC. 250. All qualified electors and no others shall be eligible to office except as otherwise provided in this Constitution. . . .

SEC. 263. The marriage of a white person with a negro or mulatto, or person who shall have one-eighth or more of negro blood, shall be unlawful and void.

SEC. 264. No person shall be a Grand or Petit Juror unless a qualified elector and able to read and write; but the want of any such qualification in any juror shall not vitiate any indictment or verdict. The Legislature shall provide by law for procuring a list of persons so qualified, and the drawing therefrom of Grand and Petit Jurors for each term of the Circuit Court. . . .

SEC. 269. Every devise or bequest of lands, tenements or hereditaments, or any interest therein, of freehold, or less than freehold, either present or future, vested or contingent, or of any money directed to be raised by the sale thereof, contained in any last will and testament, or codicil, or other testamentary writing, in favor of any religious or ecclesiastical corporation, sole or aggregate, or any religious or ecclesiastical society, or to any religious denomination, or association of persons, or to any person or body politic, in trust, either express or implied, secret or resulting, either for the use and benefit of such religious corporation, society, denomination or association, or for the purpose of being given or appropriated to charitable uses or purposes, shall be null and void, and the heir-at-law shall take the same property so devised or bequeathed, as though no testamentary disposition had been made.

Sec. 270. Every legacy, gift or bequest, of money or personal property, or of any interest, benefit or use therein, either direct, implied or otherwise, contained in any last will and testament or codocil, in favor of any religious or ecclesiastical corporation, sole or aggregate, or any religious or ecclesiastical society, or to any religious denomination or association, either for its own use or benefit, or for the purpose of being given or appropriated to charitable uses, shall be null and void, and the distributees shall take the same as though no such testamentary disposition had been made.

PART THREE Consolidating Markets

Daniel Freeman, c. 1904. He was the first homesteader in the United States and settled in Beatrice, Nebraska, in 1863. Library of Congress, Prints and Photographs Division, LC-USZC62-104167.

(below) Rhodes Manufacturing Co., Lincolnton, N.C. The girl on the left said she was ten years old and that she had been in the mill for more than a year. The spinner girl on the right said she was twelve years old. Library of Congress, Prints and Photographs Division, LC-DIG-nclc-01377.

The late nineteenth and early twentieth centuries were periods of vast expansion in the United States—from the extent of its borders, to the size of its population, to the size and wealth of its economy. But the settling of the United States' vast continental frontier, whether or not dictated by any manifest destiny, and the building of its industrial economy entailed great efforts, including on the part of government. These efforts, aimed at encouraging settlement, commerce, and domestic manufactures, were influenced by, even as they themselves influenced, conflicts among varying interests, cultural and occupational groups, and worldviews. The result would be a larger, richer America, and also one that was qualitatively different from what it had been before.

The Homestead Act, 1862

The disposition of unsettled public lands had been a political issue in America since before the War for Independence, as settlers looked for free land and the opportunities it could provide. These lands also played a significant role in arguments over slavery as Free Soil Party adherents called for homesteading to promote small farming and keep slavery out of the West. In 1862, after the Southern states had seceded, Congress passed the Homestead Act allowing Americans, including recent immigrants, to file for ownership of up to 160 acres of land and acquire title to it upon showing that they had farmed it, built a house on it, and lived on it for five years. Fraud and abuse were common problems as railroad companies and large ranchers misused the filing system to gain control of land and natural resources—especially water. Nonetheless, by 1900, six hundred thousand homestead claims had been filed, covering eighty million acres. The act remained in effect until 1976, with provisions allowing for homesteading in Alaska until 1986.

The Homestead Act

May 20, 1862

An Act to secure Homesteads to actual Settlers on the Public Domain.

Be it enacted by the Senate and House of Representatives of the United States of America in Congress assembled, That any person who is the head of a family, or who has arrived at the age of twenty-one years, and is a citizen of the United States, or who shall have filed his declaration of intention to become such, as required by the naturalization laws of the United States, and who has never borne arms against the United States Government or given aid and comfort to its enemies, shall, from and after the first January, eighteen hundred and sixty-three, be entitled to enter one quarter section or a less quantity of unappropriated public lands, upon which said person may have filed a preëmption claim, or which may, at the time the application is made, be subject to preëmption at one dollar and twenty-five cents, or less, per acre; or eighty acres or less of such unappropriated lands, at two dollars and fifty cents per acre, to be located in a body, in conformity to the legal subdivisions of the public lands, and after the same shall have been surveyed: *Provided,* That any person owning and residing on land may, under the provisions of this act, enter other land lying contiguous to his or her said land, which shall not, with the land so already owned and occupied, exceed in the aggregate one hundred and sixty acres.

SEC. 2. *And be it further enacted,* That the person applying for the benefit of this act shall, upon application to the register of the land office in which he or she is about to make such entry, make affidavit before the said register or receiver that he or she is the head of a family, or is twenty-one years or more of age, or shall have performed service in the army or navy of the United States, and that he has never borne arms against the Government of the United States or given aid and comfort to its enemies, and that such application is made for his or her exclusive use and benefit, and that said entry is made for the purpose of actual settlement and cultivation, and not either directly or indirectly for the use or benefit of any other person or persons whomsoever; and upon filing the said affidavit with the register or receiver, and on payment of ten dollars, he or she shall thereupon be permitted to enter the quantity of land specified: *Provided, however,* That no certificate shall be given or patent issued therefor until the expiration of five years from the date of such entry; and if, at the expiration of such time, or at any time within two years thereafter, the person making such entry; or, if he be dead, his widow; or in case of her death, his heirs or devisee; or in case of a widow making such entry, her heirs or devisee, in case of her death; shall prove by two credible witnesses that he, she, or they have resided upon or cultivated the same for the term of five years immediately succeeding the time of filing the affidavit aforesaid, and shall make affidavit that no part of said land has been alienated, and that he has borne true allegiance to the Government of the United States; then, in such case, he, she, or they, if at that time a citizen of the United States, shall be entitled to a patent, as in other cases provided for by law: *And provided, further,* That in case of the death of both father and mother, leaving an infant child, or children, under twenty-one years of age, the right and fee shall enure to the benefit of said infant child or children; and the executor, administrator, or guardian may, at any time within two years after the death of the surviving parent, and in accordance with the laws of the State in which such children for the time being have their domicil, sell said land for the benefit of said infants, but for no other purpose; and the purchaser shall acquire the absolute title by the purchase, and be entitled to a patent from the United States, on payment of the office fees and sum of money herein specified.

Sec. 3. *And be it further enacted,* That the register of the land office shall note all such applications on the tract books and plats of his office, and keep a register of all such entries, and make return thereof to the General Land Office, together with the proof upon which they have been founded.

Sec. 4. *And be it further enacted,* That no lands acquired under the provisions of this act shall in any event become liable to the satisfaction of any debt or debts contracted prior to the issuing of the patent therefor.

Sec. 5. *And be it further enacted,* That if, at any time after the filing of the affidavit, as required in the second section of this act, and before the expiration of the five years aforesaid, it shall be proven, after due notice to the settler, to the satisfaction of the register of the land office, that the person having filed such affidavit shall have actually changed his or her residence, or abandoned the said land for more than six months at any time, then and in that event the land so entered shall revert to the government.

Sec. 6. *And be it further enacted,* That no individual shall be permitted to acquire title to more than one quarter section under the provisions of this act; and that the Commissioner of the General Land Office is hereby required to prepare and issue such rules and regulations, consistent with this act, as shall be necessary and proper to carry its provisions into effect; and that the registers and receivers of the several land offices shall be entitled to receive the same compensation for any lands entered under the provisions of this act that they are now entitled to receive when the same quantity of land is entered with money, one half to be paid by the person making the application at the time of so doing, and the other half on the issue of the certificate by the person to whom it may be issued; but this shall not be construed to enlarge the maximum of compensation now prescribed by law for any register or receiver: *Provided,* That nothing contained in this act shall be so construed as to impair or interfere in any manner whatever with existing preëmption rights: *And provided, further,* That all persons who may have filed their applications for a preëmption right prior to the passage of this act, shall be entitled to all privileges of this act: *Provided, further,* That no person who has served, or may hereafter serve, for a period of not less than fourteen days in the army or navy of the United States, either regular or volunteer, under the laws thereof, during the existence of an actual war, domestic or foreign, shall be deprived of the benefits of this act on account of not having attained the age of twenty-one years.

Sec. 7. *And be it further enacted,* That the fifth section of the act entitled "An act in addition to an act more effectually to provide for the punishment of certain crimes against the United States, and for other purposes," approved the third of March, in the year eighteen hundred and fifty-seven, shall extend to all oaths, affirmations, and affidavits, required or authorized by this act.

Sec. 8. *And be it further enacted,* That nothing in this act shall be so construed as to prevent any person who has availed him or herself of the benefits of the first section of this act, from paying the minimum price, or the price to which the same may have graduated, for the quantity of land so entered at any time before the expiration of the five years, and obtaining a patent therefor from the government, as in other cases provided by law, on making proof of settlement and cultivation as provided by existing laws granting preëmption rights.

Approved, May 20, 1862.

The Pacific Railway Act, 1862

Internal improvements, including post roads, canals, and harbors, had been an issue of dispute since America's earliest days, raising questions of who should build them and how they should be funded. Perhaps the greatest internal improvement undertaken in the United States stemmed from the desire to link burgeoning settlements and economic activity in California to the rest of the nation. The Pacific Railway Act sought to spur construction of a transcontinental railroad by ensuring loans to specified railway companies and granting land on each side of these companies' railroad tracks, every other square mile for every mile of track laid outside urban areas. On May 10, 1869, the last rails were laid, completing the first transcontinental lines running between Omaha, Nebraska, and Sacramento, California. There were charges of massive corruption of corporate and government officials, but four additional transcontinental lines would be built by 1893.

The Pacific Railway Act

July 1, 1862

An Act to aid in the Construction of a Railroad and Telegraph Line from the Missouri River to the Pacific Ocean, and to secure to the Government the Use of the same for Postal, Military, and Other Purposes.

Be it enacted by the Senate and House of Representatives of the United States of America in Congress assembled, That Walter S. Burgess, William P. Blodget, Benjamin H. Cheever, Charles Fosdick Fletcher, of Rhode Island; Augustus Brewster, Henry P. Haven, Cornelius S. Bushnell, Henry Hammond, of Connecticut; Isaac Sherman, Dean Richmond, Royal Phelps, William H. Ferry, Henry A. Paddock, Lewis J. Stancliff, Charles A. Secor, Samuel R. Campbell, Alfred E. Tilton, John Anderson, Azariah Boody, John S. Kennedy, H. Carver, Joseph Field, Benjamin F. Camp, Orville W. Childs, Alexander J. Bergen, Ben. Holliday, D. N. Barney, S. De Witt Bloodgood, William H. Grant, Thomas W. Olcott, Samuel B. Ruggles, James B. Wilson, of New York; Ephraim Marsh, Charles M. Harker, of New Jersey; John Edgar Thompson, Benjamin Haywood, Joseph H. Scranton, Joseph Harrison, George W. Cass, John H. Bryant, Daniel J. Morell, Thomas M. Howe, William F. Johnson, Robert Finney, John A. Green, E. R. Myre, Charles F. Wells, junior, of Pennsylvania; Noah L. Wilson, Amasa Stone, William H. Clement, S. S. L'Hommedieu, John Brough, William Dennison, Jacob Blickinsderfer, of Ohio; William M. McPherson, R. W. Wells, Willard P. Hall, Armstrong Beatty, John Corby, of Missouri; S. J. Hensley, Peter Donahue, C. P. Huntington, T. D. Judah, James Bailey, James T. Ryan, Charles Hosmer, Charles Marsh, D. O. Mills, Samuel Bell, Louis McLane, George W. Mowe, Charles McLaughlin, Timothy Dame, John R. Robinson, of California; John Atchison and John D. Winters, of the Territory of Nevada; John D. Campbell, R. N. Rice, Charles A. Trowbridge, and Ransom Gardner, Charles W. Penny, Charles T. Gorham, William McConnell, of Michigan; William F. Coolbaugh, Lucius H. Langworthy, Hugh T. Reid, Hoyt Sherman, Lyman Cook, Samuel R. Curtis, Lewis A. Thomas, Platt Smith, of Iowa; William B. Ogden, Charles G. Hammond, Henry Farnum, Amos C. Babcock, W. Seldon Gale, Nehemiah Bushnell and Lorenzo Bull, of Illinois; William H. Swift, Samuel T. Dana, John Bertram, Franklin S. Stevens, Edward R. Tinker, of Massachusetts; Franklin Gorin, Laban J. Bradford, and John T. Levis, of Kentucky; James Dunning, John M. Wood, Edwin Noyes, Joseph Eaton, of Maine; Henry H. Baxter, George W. Collamer, Henry Keyes, Thomas H. Canfield, of Vermont; William S. Ladd, A. M. Berry, Benjamin F. Harding, of Oregon; William Bunn, junior, John Catlin, Levi Sterling, John Thompson, Elihu L. Phillips, Walter D. McIndoe, T. B. Stoddard, E. H. Brodhead, A. H. Virgin, of Wisconsin; Charles Paine, Thomas A. Morris, David C. Branham, Samuel Hanna, Jonas Votaw, Jesse L. Williams, Isaac C. Elston, of Indiana; Thomas Swan, Chauncey Brooks, Edward Wilkins, of Maryland; Francis R. E. Cornell, David Blakely, A. D. Seward, Henry A. Swift, Dwight Woodbury, John McKusick, John R. Jones, of Minnesota; Joseph A. Gilmore, Charles W. Woodman, of New Hampshire; W. H. Grimes, J. C. Stone, Chester Thomas, John Kerr, Werter R. Davis, Luther C. Challiss, Josiah Miller, of Kansas; Gilbert C. Monell and Augustus Kountz, T. M. Marquette, William H. Taylor, Alvin Saunders, of Nebraska; John Evans, of Colorado; together with five commissioners to be appointed by the Secretary of the Interior, and all persons who shall or may be associated with them, and their successors, are hereby created and erected into a body corporate and politic in deed and in law, by the name, style, and title of "The Union Pacific Railroad Company"; and by that name shall have perpetual succession, and shall be able to sue and to be sued, plead and be impleaded, defend and be defended, in all courts of law and equity within the United States, and may make and have a common seal; and the said corporation is hereby authorized and empowered to lay out, locate, construct, furnish, maintain, and enjoy a continuous railroad and telegraph, with the appurtenances, from a point on the one hundredth meridian of longitude west from Greenwich, between the south margin of the valley of the Republican River and the north margin of the valley of the Platte River, in the Territory of Nebraska, to the western boundary of Nevada Territory, upon the route and terms hereinafter provided, and is hereby vested with all the powers, privileges, and immunities necessary to carry into effect the purposes of this act as herein set forth. The capital stock of said company shall consist of one hundred thousand shares of one thousand dollars each, which shall be subscribed for and held in not more than two hundred shares by any one person, and shall be transferable in such manner as the by-laws of said corporation shall provide....

SEC. 2. *And be it further enacted,* That the right of way through the public lands be, and the same is hereby, granted to said company for the construction of said railroad and telegraph line; and the right, power, and authority is hereby given to said company to take from the public lands adjacent to the line of said road, earth, stone, timber, and other materials for the construction thereof; said right of way is granted to said railroad to the extent of two hundred feet in width on each side of said railroad where it may pass over the public lands, including all necessary grounds for stations, buildings, workshops, and depots, machine shops, switches, side tracks, turn-

tables, and water stations. The United States shall extinguish as rapidly as may be, the Indian titles to all lands falling under the operation of this act and required for the said right of way and grants hereinafter made.

SEC. 3. *And be it further enacted,* That there be, and is hereby, granted to the said company, for the purpose of aiding in the construction of said railroad and telegraph line, and to secure the safe and speedy transportation of the mails, troops, munitions of war, and public stores thereon, every alternate section of public land, designated by odd numbers, to the amount of five alternate sections per mile on each side of said railroad, on the line thereof, and within the limits of ten miles on each side of said road, not sold, reserved, or otherwise disposed of by the United States, and to which a preëmption or homestead claim may not have attached, at the time the line of said road is definitely fixed: *Provided,* That all mineral lands shall be excepted from the operation of this act; but where the same shall contain timber, the timber thereon is hereby granted to said company. And all such lands, so granted by this section, which shall not be sold or disposed of by said company within three years after the entire road shall have been completed, shall be subject to settlement and preëmption, like other lands, at a price not exceeding one dollar and twenty-five cents per acre, to be paid to said company.

SEC. 4. *And be it further enacted,* That whenever said company shall have completed forty consecutive miles of any portion of said railroad and telegraph line, ready for the service contemplated by this act, and supplied with all necessary drains, culverts, viaducts, crossings, sidings, bridges, turnouts, watering places, depots, equipments, furniture, and all other appurtenances of a first class railroad, the rails and all the other iron used in the construction and equipment of said road to be American manufacture of the best quality, the President of the United States shall appoint three commissioners to examine the same and report to him in relation thereto; and if it shall appear to him that forty consecutive miles of said railroad and telegraph line have been completed and equipped in all respects as required by this act, then, upon certificate of said commissioners to that effect, patents shall issue conveying the right and title to said lands to said company, on each side of the road as far as the same is completed, to the amount aforesaid; and patents shall in like manner issue as each forty miles of said railroad and telegraph line are completed, upon certificate of said commissioners. Any vacancies occurring in said board of commissioners by death, resignation, or otherwise, shall be filled by the President of the United States: *Provided, however,* That no such commissioners shall be appointed by the President of the United States unless there shall be presented to him a statement, verified on oath by the president of said company, that such forty miles have been completed, in the manner required by this act, and setting forth with certainty the points where such forty miles begin and where the same end; which oath shall be taken before a judge of a court of record.

Sec. 5. *And be it further enacted,* That for the purposes herein mentioned the Secretary of the Treasury shall, upon the certificate in writing of said commissioners of the completion and equipment of forty consecutive miles of said railroad and telegraph, in accordance with the provisions of this act, issue to said company bonds of the United States of one thousand dollars each, payable in thirty years after date, bearing six per centum per annum interest, (said interest payable semiannually,) which interest may be paid in United States treasury notes or any other money or currency which the United States have or shall declare lawful money and a legal tender, to the amount of sixteen of said bonds per mile for such section of forty miles; and to secure the repayment to the United States, as hereinafter provided, of the amount of said bonds so issued and delivered to said company, together with all interest thereon which shall have been paid by the United States, the issue of said bonds and delivery to the company shall ipso facto constitute a first mortgage on the whole line of the railroad and telegraph, together with the rolling stock, fixtures and property of every kind and description, and in consideration of which said bonds may be issued; and on the refusal or failure of said company to redeem said bonds, or any part of them, when required so to do by the Secretary of the Treasury, in accordance with the provisions of this act, the said road, with all the rights, functions, immunities, and appurtenances thereunto belonging, and also all lands granted to the said company by the United States, which, at the time of said default, shall remain in the ownership of the said company, may be taken possession of by the Secretary of the Treasury, for the use and benefit of the United States: *Provided,* This section shall not apply to that part of any road now constructed.

Sec. 6. *And be it further enacted,* That the grants aforesaid are made upon condition that said company shall pay said bonds at maturity, and shall keep said railroad and telegraph line in repair and use, and shall at all times transmit despatches over said telegraph line, and transport mails, troops, and munitions of war, supplies, and public stores upon said railroad, for the government, whenever required to do so by

any department thereof, and that the government shall at all times have the preference in the use of the same for all the purposes aforesaid, (at fair and reasonable rates of compensation, not to exceed the amounts paid by private parties for the same kind of service;) and all compensation for services rendered for the government shall be applied to the payment of said bonds and interest until the whole amount is fully paid. Said company may also pay the United States, wholly or in part, in the same or other bonds, treasury notes, or other evidences of debt against the United States, to be allowed at par; and after said road is completed, until said bonds and interest are paid, at least five per centum of the net earnings of said road shall also be annually applied to the payment thereof.

Sec. 7. *And be it further enacted,* That said company shall file their assent to this act, under the seal of said company, in the Department of the Interior, within one year after the passage of this act, and shall complete said railroad and telegraph from the point of beginning as herein provided, to the western boundary of Nevada Territory before the first day of July, one thousand eight hundred and seventy-four: *Provided,* That within two years after the passage of this act said company shall designate the general route of said road, as near as may be, and shall file a map of the same in the Department of the Interior, whereupon the Secretary of the Interior shall cause the lands within fifteen miles of said designated route or routes to be withdrawn from preëmption, private entry, and sale; and when any portion of said route shall be finally located, the Secretary of the Interior shall cause the said lands hereinbefore granted to be surveyed and set off as fast as may be necessary for the purposes herein named: *Provided,* That in fixing the point of connection of the main trunk with the eastern connections, it shall be fixed at the most practicable point for the construction of the Iowa and Missouri branches, as hereinafter provided.

Sec. 8. *And be it further enacted,* That the line of said railroad and telegraph shall commence at a point on the one hundredth meridian of longitude west from Greenwich, between the south margin of the valley of the Republican River and the north margin of the valley of the Platte River, in the Territory of Nebraska, at a point to be fixed by the President of the United States, after actual surveys; thence running westerly upon the most direct, central, and practicable route, through the territories of the United States, to the western boundary of the Territory of Nevada, there to meet and connect with the line of the Central Pacific Railroad Company of California.

SEC. 9. *And be it further enacted,* That the Leavenworth, Pawnee, and Western Railroad Company of Kansas are hereby authorized to construct a railroad and telegraph line, from the Missouri River, at the mouth of the Kansas River, on the south side thereof, so as to connect with the Pacific railroad of Missouri, to the aforesaid point, on the one hundredth meridian of longitude west from Greenwich, as herein provided, upon the same terms and conditions in all respects as are provided in this act for the construction of the railroad and telegraph line first mentioned, and to meet and connect with the same at the meridian of longitude aforesaid; and in case the general route or line of road from the Missouri River to the Rocky Mountains should be so located as to require a departure northwardly from the proposed line of said Kansas railroad before it reaches the meridian of longitude aforesaid, the location of said Kansas road shall be made so as to conform thereto; and said railroad through Kansas shall be so located between the mouth of the Kansas River, as aforesaid, and the aforesaid point, on the one hundredth meridian of longitude, that the several railroads from Missouri and Iowa, herein authorized to connect with the same, can make connection within the limits prescribed in this act, provided the same can be done without deviating from the general direction of the whole line to the Pacific coast. The route in Kansas, west of the meridian of Fort Riley, to the aforesaid point, on the one hundredth meridian of longitude, to be subject to the approval of the President of the United States, and to be determined by him on actual survey. And said Kansas company may proceed to build said railroad to the aforesaid point, on the one hundredth meridian of longitude west from Greenwich, in the territory of Nebraska. The Central Pacific Railroad Company of California, a corporation existing under the laws of the State of California, are hereby authorized to construct a railroad and telegraph line from the Pacific coast, at or near San Francisco, or the navigable waters of the Sacramento River, to the eastern boundary of California, upon the same terms and conditions, in all respects, as are contained in this act for the construction of said railroad and telegraph line first mentioned, and to meet and connect with the first mentioned railroad and telegraph line on the eastern boundary of California. Each of said companies shall file their acceptance of the conditions of this act in the Department of the Interior within six months after the passage of this act.

SEC. 10. *And be it further enacted,* That the said company chartered by the State of Kansas shall complete one hundred miles of their said road, commencing at the mouth of the Kansas River as aforesaid, within two years after filing their assent to the conditions of this act, as herein provided, and one hundred miles per year thereafter until the whole is completed; and the said Central Pacific Railroad Company of California shall complete fifty miles of their said road within two years after filing their assent to the provisions of this act, as herein provided, and fifty miles per year thereafter until the whole is completed; and after completing their roads, respectively, said companies, or either of them, may unite upon equal terms with the first-named company in constructing so much of said railroad and telegraph line and branch railroads and telegraph lines in this act hereinafter mentioned, through the Territories from the State of California to the Missouri River, as shall then remain to be constructed, on the same terms and conditions as provided in this act in relation to the said Union Pacific Railroad Company. And the Hannibal and St. Joseph Railroad, the Pacific Railroad Company of Missouri, and the first-named company, or either of them, on filing their assent to this act, as aforesaid, may unite upon equal terms, under this act, with the said Kansas company, in constructing said railroad and telegraph, to said meridian of longitude, with the consent of the said State of Kansas; and in case said first-named company shall complete their line to the eastern boundary of California before it is completed across said State by the Central Pacific Railroad Company of California, said first-named company is hereby authorized to continue in constructing the same through California, with the consent of said State, upon the terms mentioned in this act, until said roads shall meet and connect, and the whole line of said railroad and telegraph is completed; and the Central Pacific Railroad Company of California, after completing its road across said State, is authorized to continue the construction of said railroad and telegraph through the Territories of the United States to the Missouri River, including the branch roads specified in this act, upon the routes hereinbefore and hereinafter indicated, on the terms and conditions provided in this act in relation to the said Union Pacific Railroad Company, until said roads shall meet and connect, and the whole line of said railroad and branches and telegraph is completed.

SEC. 11. *And be it further enacted,* That for three hundred miles of said road most mountainous and difficult of construction, to wit: one hundred and fifty miles westwardly from the eastern base of the Rocky Mountains, and one hundred and fifty miles eastwardly from the western base of the

Sierra Nevada mountains, said points to be fixed by the President of the United States, the bonds to be issued to aid in the construction thereof shall be treble the number per mile hereinbefore provided, and the same shall be issued, and the lands herein granted be set apart, upon the construction of every twenty miles thereof, upon the certificate of the commissioners as aforesaid that twenty consecutive miles of the same are completed; and between the sections last named of one hundred and fifty miles each, the bonds to be issued to aid in the construction thereof shall be double the number per mile first mentioned, and the same shall be issued, and the lands herein granted be set apart, upon the construction of every twenty miles thereof, upon the certificate of the commissioners as aforesaid that twenty consecutive miles of the same are completed: *Provided,* That no more than fifty thousand of said bonds shall be issued under this act to aid in constructing the main line of said railroad and telegraph.

SEC. 12. *And be it further enacted,* That whenever the route of said railroad shall cross the boundary of any State or Territory, or said meridian of longitude, the two companies meeting or uniting there shall agree upon its location at that point, with reference to the most direct and practicable through route, and in case of difference between them as to said location the President of the United States shall determine the said location; the companies named in each State and Territory to locate the road across the same between the points so agreed upon, except as herein provided. The track upon the entire line of railroad and branches shall be of uniform width, to be determined by the President of the United States, so that, when completed, cars can be run from the Missouri River to the Pacific coast; the grades and curves shall not exceed the maximum grades and curves of the Baltimore and Ohio railroad; the whole line of said railroad and branches and telegraph shall be operated and used for all purposes of communication, travel, and transportation, so far as the public and government are concerned, as one connected, continuous line; and the companies herein named in Missouri, Kansas, and California, filing their assent to the provisions of this act, shall receive and transport all iron rails, chairs, spikes, ties, timber, and all materials required for constructing and furnishing said first-mentioned line between the aforesaid point, on the one hundredth meridian of longitude and western boundary of Nevada Territory, whenever the same is required by said, first-named company, at cost, over that portion of the roads of said companies constructed under the provisions of this act.

SEC. 13. *And be it further enacted,* That the Hannibal and Saint Joseph Railroad Company of Missouri may extend its roads from Saint Joseph, via Atchison, to connect and unite with the road through Kansas, upon filing its assent to the provisions of this act, upon the same terms and conditions, in all respects, for one hundred miles in length next to the Missouri River, as are provided in this act for the construction of the railroad and telegraph line first mentioned, and may for this purpose, use any railroad charter which has been or may be granted by the legislature of Kansas; *Provided,* That if actual survey shall render it desirable, the said company may construct their road, with the consent of the Kansas legislature, on the most direct and practicable route west from St. Joseph, Missouri, so as to connect and unite with the road leading from the western boundary of Iowa at any point east of the one hundredth meridian of west longitude, or with the main trunk road at said point; but in no event shall lands or bonds be given to said company, as herein directed, to aid in the construction of their said road for a greater distance than one hundred miles. And the Leavenworth, Pawnee, and Western Railroad Company of Kansas may construct their road from Leavenworth to unite with the road through Kansas.

SEC. 14. *And be it further enacted,* That the said Union Pacific Railroad Company is hereby authorized and required to construct a single line of railroad and telegraph from a point on the western boundary of the State of Iowa, to be fixed by the President of the United States, upon the most direct and practicable route, to be subject to his approval, so as to form a connection with the lines of said company at some point on the one hundredth meridian of longitude aforesaid, from the point of commencement on the western boundary of the State of Iowa, upon the same terms and conditions, in all respects, as are contained in this act for the construction of the said railroad and telegraph first mentioned; and the said Union Pacific Railroad Company shall complete one hundred miles of the road and telegraph in this section provided for, in two years after filing their assent to the conditions of this act, as by the terms of this act required, and at the rate of one hundred miles per year thereafter, until the whole is completed: *Provided,* That a failure upon the part of said company to make said connection in the time aforesaid, and to perform the obligations imposed on said company by this section and to operate said road in the same manner as the main line shall be operated, shall forfeit to the government of the United States all the rights, privileges, and franchises granted to and conferred upon said company by this act. And whenever there shall be a line of railroad completed through Minnesota or Iowa to Sioux City, then the said Pacific Railroad Company is hereby authorized and required to construct a railroad and telegraph from said Sioux City upon the most direct and practicable route to a point on, and so as to connect with, the branch railroad and telegraph in this section hereinbefore mentioned, or with the said Union Pacific Railroad, said point of junction to be fixed by the President of the United States, not further west than the one hundredth meridian of longitude aforesaid, and on the same terms and conditions as provided in this act for the construction of the Union Pacific Railroad as aforesaid, and to complete the same at the rate of one hundred miles per year; and should said company fail to comply with the requirements of this act in relation to the said Sioux City railroad and telegraph, the said company shall suffer the same forfeitures prescribed in relation to the Iowa branch railroad and telegraph hereinbefore mentioned.

SEC. 15. *And be it further enacted,* That any other railroad company now incorporated, or hereafter to be incorporated, shall have the right to connect their road with the road and branches provided for by this act, at such places and upon such just and equitable terms as the President of the United States may prescribe. Wherever the word company is used in this act it shall be construed to embrace the words their associates, successors, and assigns, the same as if the words had been properly added thereto.

SEC. 16. *And be it further enacted,* That at any time after the passage of this act all of the railroad companies named herein, and assenting hereto, or any two or more of them, are authorized to form themselves into one consolidated company; notice of such consolidation, in writing, shall be filed in the Department of the Interior, and such consolidated company shall thereafter proceed to construct said railroad and branches and telegraph line upon the terms and conditions provided in this act.

SEC. 17. *And be it further enacted,* That in case said company or companies shall fail to comply with the terms and conditions of this act, by not completing said road and telegraph and branches within a reasonable time, or by not keeping the same in repair and use, but shall permit the same, for an unreasonable time, to remain unfinished, or out of repair, and unfit for use, Congress may pass any act to insure the speedy completion of said road and branches, or put the same in repair and use, and may direct the income of said railroad

and telegraph line to be thereafter devoted to the use of the United States, to repay all such expenditures caused by the default and neglect of such company or companies: *Provided,* That if said roads are not completed, so as to form a continuous line of railroad, ready for use, from the Missouri River to the navigable waters of the Sacramento River, in California, by the first day of July, eighteen hundred and seventy-six, the whole of all of said railroads before mentioned and to be constructed under the provisions of this act, together with all their furniture, fixtures, rolling stock, machine shops, lands, tenements, and hereditaments, and property of every kind and character, shall be forfeited to and be taken possession of by the United States: *Provided,* That of the bonds of the United States in this act provided to be delivered for any and all parts of the roads to be constructed east of the one hundredth meridian of west longitude from Greenwich, and for any part of the road west of the west foot of the Sierra Nevada mountain, there shall be reserved of each part and instalment twenty-five per centum, to be and remain in the United States treasury, undelivered, until said road and all parts thereof provided for in this act are entirely completed; and of all the bonds provided to be delivered for the said road, between the two points aforesaid, there shall be reserved out of each instalment fifteen per centum, to be and remain in the treasury until the whole of the road provided for in this act is fully completed; and if the said road or any part thereof shall fail of completion at the time limited therefor in this act, then and in that case the said part of said bonds so reserved shall be forfeited to the United States.

SEC. 18. *And be it further enacted,* That whenever it appears that the net earnings of the entire road and telegraph, including the amount allowed for services rendered for the United States, after deducting all expenditures, including repairs, and the furnishing, running, and managing of said road, shall exceed ten per centum upon its cost, exclusive of the five per centum to be paid to the United States, Congress may reduce the rates of fare thereon, if unreasonable in amount, and may fix and establish the same by law. And the better to accomplish the object of this act, namely, to promote the public interest and welfare by the construction of said railroad and telegraph line, and keeping the same in working order, and to secure to the government at all times (but particularly in time of war) the use and benefits of the same for postal, military and other purposes, Congress may, at any time, having due regard for the rights of said companies named herein, add to, alter, amend, or repeal this act.

Sec. 19. *And be it further enacted,* That the several railroad companies herein named are authorized to enter into an arrangement with the Pacific Telegraph Company, the Overland Telegraph Company, and the California State Telegraph Company, so that the present line of telegraph between the Missouri River and San Francisco may be moved upon or along the line of said railroad and branches as fast as said roads and branches are built; and if said arrangement be entered into, and the transfer of said telegraph line be made in accordance therewith to the line of said railroad and branches, such transfer shall, for all purposes of this act, be held and considered a fulfilment on the part of said railroad companies of the provisions of this act in regard to the construction of said line of telegraph. And, in case of disagreement, said telegraph companies are authorized to remove their line of telegraph along and upon the line of railroad herein contemplated without prejudice to the rights of said railroad companies named herein.

Sec. 20. *And be it further enacted,* That the corporation hereby created and the roads connected therewith, under the provisions of this act, shall make to the Secretary of the Treasury an annual report wherein shall be set forth—

First. The names of the stockholders and their places of residence, so far as the same can be ascertained;

Second. The names and residences of the directors, and all other officers of the company;

Third. The amount of stock subscribed, and the amount thereof actually paid in;

Fourth. A description of the lines of road surveyed, of the lines thereof fixed upon for the construction of the road, and the cost of such surveys;

Fifth. The amount received from passengers on the road;

Sixth. The amount received for freight thereon;

Seventh. A statement of the expense of said road and its fixtures;

Eighth. A statement of the indebtedness of said company, setting forth the various kinds thereof. Which report shall be sworn to by the president of the said company, and shall be presented to the Secretary of the Treasury on or before the first day of July in each year.

Approved, July 1, 1862.

The Morrill Act, 1862

*Also known as the Land Grant Colleges Act, the Morrill Act had been blocked by South-
ern opposition until secession allowed for its enactment. The act provided for establishment of colleges to train Americans in engineering, agricultural, and other practical
sciences. It gave to each state that had remained in the Union a grant of thirty thousand
acres of public land for each member of its congressional delegation—a minimum of
ninety thousand acres per state—which the state was to sell to raise funds for the colleges.
A second Morrill Act, passed in 1890, extended the land grant provisions to the sixteen
Southern states and required that states either allow members of minority races to attend
the same land grant colleges as whites or "equitably" divide funds to establish separate,
racially segregated schools for the same purposes.*

The Morrill Act

July 2, 1862

*An Act donating Public Lands to the several States and
Territories which may provide Colleges for the Benefit of
Agriculture and the Mechanic Arts.*

*Be it enacted by the Senate and House of Representatives of
the United States of America in Congress assembled,* That there
be granted to the several States, for the purposes hereinafter
mentioned, an amount of public land, to be apportioned to
each State a quantity equal to thirty thousand acres for each
senator and representative in Congress to which the States
are respectively entitled by the apportionment under the census of eighteen hundred and sixty: *Provided,* That no mineral
lands shall be selected or purchased under the provisions of
this act.

SEC. 2. *And be it further enacted,* That the land aforesaid,
after being surveyed, shall be apportioned to the several States
in sections or subdivisions of sections, not less than one quarter of a section; and whenever there are public lands in a State
subject to sale at private entry at one dollar and twenty-five
cents per acre, the quantity to which said State shall be entitled shall be selected from such lands within the limits of
such State, and the Secretary of the Interior is hereby directed
to issue to each of the States in which there is not the quantity
of public lands subject to sale at private entry at one dollar and
twenty-five cents per acre, to which said State may be entitled
under the provisions of this act, land scrip to the amount in
acres for the deficiency of its distributive share: said scrip to
be sold by said States and the proceeds thereof applied to the

uses and purposes prescribed in this act, and for no other use
or purpose whatsoever: *Provided,* That in no case shall any
State to which land scrip may thus be issued be allowed to
locate the same within the limits of any other State, or of any
Territory of the United States, but their assignees may thus
locate said land scrip upon any of the unappropriated lands of
the United States subject to sale at private entry at one dollar
and twenty-five cents, or less, per acre: *And provided, further,*
That not more than one million acres shall be located by such
assignees in any one of the States: *And provided, further,* That
no such location shall be made before one year from the passage of this act.

SEC. 3. *And be it further enacted,* That all the expenses of
management, superintendence, and taxes from date of selection of said lands, previous to their sales, and all expenses incurred in the management and disbursement of the moneys
which may be received therefrom, shall be paid by the States
to which they may belong, out of the treasury of said States,
so that the entire proceeds of the sale of said lands shall be
applied without any diminution whatever to the purposes
hereinafter mentioned.

SEC. 4. *And be it further enacted,* That all moneys derived
from the sale of the lands aforesaid by the States to which the
lands are apportioned, and from the sales of land scrip hereinbefore provided for, shall be invested in stocks of the United
States, or of the States, or some other safe stocks, yielding not
less than five per centum upon the par value of said stocks;

and that the moneys so invested shall constitute a perpetual fund, the capital of which shall remain forever undiminished, (except so far as may be provided in section fifth of this act,) and the interest of which shall be inviolably appropriated, by each State which may take and claim the benefit of this act, to the endowment, support, and maintenance of at least one college where the leading object shall be, without excluding other scientific and classical studies, and including military tactics, to teach such branches of learning as are related to agriculture and the mechanic arts, in such manner as the legislatures of the States may respectively prescribe, in order to promote the liberal and practical education of the industrial classes in the several pursuits and professions in life.

SEC. 5. *And be it further enacted,* That the grant of land and land scrip hereby authorized shall be made on the following conditions, to which, as well as to the provisions hereinbefore contained, the previous assent of the several States shall be signified by legislative acts:

First. If any portion of the fund invested, as provided by the foregoing section, or any portion of the interest thereon, shall, by any action or contingency, be diminished or lost, it shall be replaced by the State to which it belongs, so that the capital of the fund shall remain forever undiminished; and the annual interest shall be regularly applied without diminution to the purposes mentioned in the fourth section of this act, except that a sum, not exceeding ten per centum upon the amount received by any State under the provisions of this act, may be expended for the purchase of lands for sites or experimental farms, whenever authorized by the respective legislatures of said States.

Second. No portion of said fund, nor the interest thereon, shall be applied, directly or indirectly, under any pretence whatever, to the purchase, erection, preservation, or repair of any building or buildings.

Third. Any State which may take and claim the benefit of the provisions of this act shall provide, within five years, at least not less than one college, as described in the fourth section of this act, or the grant to such State shall cease; and said State shall be bound to pay the United States the amount received of any lands previously sold, and that the title to purchasers under the State shall be valid.

Fourth. An annual report shall be made regarding the progress of each college, recording any improvements and experiments made, with their cost and results, and such other matters, including State industrial and economical statistics, as may be supposed useful; one copy of which shall be transmitted by mail free, by each, to all the other colleges which may be endowed under the provisions of this act, and also one copy to the Secretary of the Interior.

Fifth. When lands shall be selected from those which have been raised to double the minimum price, in consequence of railroad grants, they shall be computed to the States at the maximum price, and the number of acres proportionally diminished.

Sixth. No State while in a condition of rebellion or insurrection against the government of the United States shall be entitled to the benefit of this act.

Seventh. No State shall be entitled to the benefits of this act unless it shall express its acceptance thereof by its legislature within two years from the date of its approval by the President.

SEC. 6. *And be it further enacted,* That land scrip issued under the provisions of this act shall not be subject to location until after the first day of January, one thousand eight hundred and sixty-three.

SEC. 7. *And be it further enacted,* That the land officers shall receive the same fees for locating land scrip issued under the provisions of this act as is now allowed for the location of military bounty land warrants under existing laws; *Provided,* their maximum compensation shall not be thereby increased.

SEC. 8. *And be it further enacted,* That the Governors of the several States to which scrip shall be issued under this act shall be required to report annually to Congress all sales made of such scrip until the whole shall be disposed of, the amount received for the same, and what appropriation has been made of the proceeds.

APPROVED, July 2, 1862.

The Gospel of Wealth, *Andrew Carnegie, 1889*

Andrew Carnegie (1835–1919) was a Scottish immigrant who began working menial jobs at a young age and eventually became the owner of Carnegie Steel Company, later United States Steel. One of the richest men of his age, Carnegie argued for an ethic according to which people would pursue their own self-interest within unregulated markets for goods and labor. Those most successful in these markets would gain great wealth and be responsible for using that wealth to improve the ability of the less well-off to improve their own conditions. The essay reproduced here was originally published in the North American Review *as "Wealth." It was later published as a pamphlet, then renamed "The Gospel of Wealth" and included in a collection of essays.*

The Gospel of Wealth

1889

THE PROBLEM OF THE ADMINISTRATION OF WEALTH

The problem of our age is the proper administration of wealth, that the ties of brotherhood may still bind together the rich and poor in harmonious relationship. The conditions of human life have not only been changed, but revolutionized, within the past few hundred years. In former days there was little difference between the dwelling, dress, food, and environment of the chief and those of his retainers. The Indians are to-day where civilized man then was. When visiting the Sioux, I was led to the wigwam of the chief. It was like the others in external appearance, and even within the difference was trifling between it and those of the poorest of his braves. The contrast between the palace of the millionaire and the cottage of the laborer with us to-day measures the change which has come with civilization. This change, however, is not to be deplored, but welcomed as highly beneficial. It is well, nay, essential, for the progress of the race that the houses of some should be homes for all that is highest and best in literature and the arts, and for all the refinements of civilization, rather than that none should be so. Much better this great irregularity than universal squalor. Without wealth there can be no Maecenas. The "good old times" were not good old times. Neither master nor servant was as well situated then as to-day. A relapse to old conditions would be disastrous to both—not the least so to him who serves—and would sweep away civilization with it. But whether the change be for good or ill, it is upon us, beyond our power to alter, and, therefore, to be accepted and made the best of. It is a waste of time to criticize the inevitable.

It is easy to see how the change has come. One illustration will serve for almost every phase of the cause. In the manufacture of products we have the whole story. It applies to all combinations of human industry, as stimulated and enlarged by the inventions of this scientific age. Formerly, articles were manufactured at the domestic hearth, or in small shops which formed part of the household. The master and his apprentices worked side by side, the latter living with the master, and therefore subject to the same conditions. When these apprentices rose to be masters, there was little or no change in their mode of life, and they, in turn, educated succeeding apprentices in the same routine. There was, substantially, social equality, and even political equality, for those engaged in industrial pursuits had then little or no voice in the State.

The inevitable result of such a mode of manufacture was crude articles at high prices. To-day the world obtains commodities of excellent quality at prices which even the preceding generation would have deemed incredible. In the commercial world similar causes have produced similar results, and the race is benefited thereby. The poor enjoy what the rich could not before afford. What were the luxuries have become the necessaries of life. The laborer has now more comforts than the farmer had a few generations ago. The farmer has more luxuries than the landlord had, and is more richly clad and better housed. The landlord has books and pictures rarer and appointments more artistic than the king could then obtain.

The price we pay for this salutary change is, no doubt, great. We assemble thousands of operatives in the factory, and in the mine, of whom the employer can know little or nothing, and to whom he is little better than a myth. All intercourse between them is at an end. Rigid castes are formed, and, as usual, mutual ignorance breeds mutual distrust. Each caste is without sympathy with the other, and ready to credit anything disparaging in regard to it. Under the law of competition, the employer of thousands is forced into the strictest economies, among which the rates paid to labor figure prominently, and often there is friction between the employer and the employed, between capital and labor, between rich and poor. Human society loses homogeneity.

The price which society pays for the law of competition, like the price it pays for cheap comforts and luxuries, is also great; but the advantages of this law are also greater still than its cost—for it is to this law that we owe our wonderful material development, which brings improved conditions in its train. But, whether the law be benign or not, we must say of it, as we say of the change in the conditions of men to which we have referred: It is here; we cannot evade it; no substitutes for it have been found; and while the law may be sometimes hard for the individual, it is best for the race, because it insures the survival of the fittest in every department. We accept and welcome, therefore, as conditions to which we must accommodate ourselves, great inequality of environment; the concentration of business, industrial and commercial, in the hands of a few; and the law of competition between these, as being not only beneficial, but essential to the future progress of the race. Having accepted these, it follows that there must be great scope for the exercise of special ability in the merchant and in the manufacturer who has to conduct affairs upon a great scale. That this talent for organization and management is rare among men is proved by the fact that it invariably secures enormous rewards for its possessor, no matter where or under what laws or conditions. The experienced in affairs always rate the MAN whose services can be obtained as a partner as not only the first consideration, but such as render the question of his capital scarcely worth considering: for able men soon create capital; in the hands of those without the special talent required, capital soon takes wings. Such

men become interested in firms or corporations using millions; and, estimating only simple interest to be made upon the capital invested, it is inevitable that their income must exceed their expenditure and that they must, therefore, accumulate wealth. Nor is there any middle ground which such men can occupy, because the great manufacturing or commercial concern which does not earn at least interest upon its capital soon becomes bankrupt. It must either go forward or fall behind; to stand still is impossible. It is a condition essential to its successful operation that it should be thus far profitable, and even that, in addition to interest on capital, it should make profit. It is a law, as certain as any of the others named, that men possessed of this peculiar talent for affairs, under the free play of economic forces must, of necessity, soon be in receipt of more revenue than can be judiciously expended upon themselves; and this law is as beneficial for the race as the others.

Objections to the foundations upon which society is based are not in order, because the condition of the race is better with these than it has been with any other which has been tried. Of the effect of any new substitutes proposed we cannot be sure. The Socialist or Anarchist who seeks to overturn present conditions is to be regarded as attacking the foundation upon which civilization itself rests, for civilization took its start from the day when the capable, industrious workman said to his incompetent and lazy fellow, "If thou dost not sow, thou shalt not reap," and thus ended primitive Communism by separating the drones from the bees. One who studies this subject will soon be brought face to face with the conclusion that upon the sacredness of property civilization itself depends—the right of the laborer to his hundred dollars in the savings-bank, and equally the legal right of the millionaire to his millions. Every man must be allowed "to sit under his own vine and fig-tree, with none to make afraid," if human society is to advance, or even to remain so far advanced as it is. To those who propose to substitute Communism for this intense Individualism, the answer therefore is: The race has tried that. All progress from that barbarous day to the present time has resulted from its displacement. Not evil, but good, has come to the race from the accumulation of wealth by those who have had the ability and energy to produce it. But even if we admit for a moment that it might be better for the race to discard its present foundation, Individualism,— that it is a nobler ideal that man should labor, not for himself alone, but in and for a brotherhood of his fellows, and share with them all in common, realizing Swedenborg's idea of heaven, where, as he says, the angels derive their happiness, not from laboring for self, but for each other,—even admit all this, and a sufficient answer is, This is not evolution, but revolution. It necessitates the changing of human nature itself—a work of eons, even if it were good to change it, which we cannot know.

It is not practicable in our day or in our age. Even if desirable theoretically, it belongs to another and long-succeeding sociological stratum. Our duty is with what is practicable now—with the next step possible in our day and generation. It is criminal to waste our energies in endeavoring to uproot, when all we can profitably accomplish is to bend the universal tree of humanity a little in the direction most favorable to the production of good fruit under existing circumstances. We might as well urge the destruction of the highest existing type of man because he failed to reach our ideal as to favor the destruction of Individualism, Private Property, the Law of Accumulation of Wealth, and the Law of Competition; for these are the highest result of human experience, the soil in which society, so far, has produced the best fruit. Unequally or unjustly, perhaps, as these laws sometimes operate, and imperfect as they appear to the Idealist, they are, nevertheless, like the highest type of man, the best and most valuable of all that humanity has yet accomplished.

We start, then, with a condition of affairs under which the best interests of the race are promoted, but which inevitably gives wealth to the few. Thus far, accepting conditions as they exist, the situation can be surveyed and pronounced good. The question then arises,—and if the foregoing be correct, it is the only question with which we have to deal,—What is the proper mode of administering wealth after the laws upon which civilization is founded have thrown it into the hands of the few? And it is of this great question that I believe I offer the true solution. It will be understood that fortunes are here spoken of, not moderate sums saved by many years of effort, the returns from which are required for the comfortable maintenance and education of families. This is not wealth, but only competence, which it should be the aim of all to acquire, and which it is for the best interests of society should be acquired.

There are but three modes in which surplus wealth can be disposed of. It can be left to the families of the decedents; or it can be bequeathed for public purposes; or, finally, it can be administered by its possessors during their lives. Under the first and second modes most of the wealth of the world that has reached the few has hitherto been applied. Let us in turn consider each of these modes. The first is the most injudi-

cious. In monarchical countries, the estates and the greatest portion of the wealth are left to the first son, that the vanity of the parent may be gratified by the thought that his name and title are to descend unimpaired to succeeding generations. The condition of this class in Europe to-day teaches the failure of such hopes or ambitions. The successors have become impoverished through their follies, or from the fall in the value of land. Even in Great Britain the strict law of entail has been found inadequate to maintain an hereditary class. Its soil is rapidly passing into the hands of the stranger. Under republican institutions the division of property among the children is much fairer; but the question which forces itself upon thoughtful men in all lands is, Why should men leave great fortunes to their children? If this is done from affection, is it not misguided affection? Observation teaches that, generally speaking, it is not well for the children that they should be so burdened. Neither is it well for the State. Beyond providing for the wife and daughters moderate sources of income, and very moderate allowances indeed, if any, for the sons, men may well hesitate; for it is no longer questionable that great sums bequeathed often work more for the injury than for the good of the recipients. Wise men will soon conclude that, for the best interests of the members of their families, and of the State, such bequests are an improper use of their means.

It is not suggested that men who have failed to educate their sons to earn a livelihood shall cast them adrift in poverty. If any man has seen fit to rear his sons with a view to their living idle lives, or, what is highly commendable, has instilled in them the sentiment that they are in a position to labor for public ends without reference to pecuniary considerations, then, of course, the duty of the parent is to see that such are provided for in moderation. There are instances of millionaires' sons unspoiled by wealth, who, being rich, still perform great services to the community. Such are the very salt of the earth, as valuable as, unfortunately, they are rare. It is not the exception, however, but the rule, that men must regard; and, looking at the usual result of enormous sums conferred upon legatees, the thoughtful man must shortly say, "I would as soon leave to my son a curse as the almighty dollar," and admit to himself that it is not the welfare of the children, but family pride, which inspires these legacies.

As to the second mode, that of leaving wealth at death for public uses, it may be said that this is only a means for the disposal of wealth, provided a man is content to wait until he is dead before he becomes of much good in the world. Knowledge of the results of legacies bequeathed is not calculated to inspire the brightest hopes of much posthumous good being accomplished by them. The cases are not few in which the real object sought by the testator is not attained, nor are they few in which his real wishes are thwarted. In many cases the bequests are so used as to become only monuments of his folly. It is well to remember that it requires the exercise of not less ability than that which acquires it, to use wealth so as to be really beneficial to the community. Besides this, it may fairly be said that no man is to be extolled for doing what he cannot help doing, nor is he to be thanked by the community to which he only leaves wealth at death. Men who leave vast sums in this way may fairly be thought men who would not have left it at all had they been able to take it with them. The memories of such cannot be held in grateful remembrance, for there is no grace in their gifts. It is not to be wondered at that such bequests seem so generally to lack the blessing.

The growing disposition to tax more and more heavily large estates left at death is a cheering indication of the growth of a salutary change in public opinion. The State of Pennsylvania now takes—subject to some exceptions—one tenth of the property left by its citizens. The budget presented in the British Parliament the other day proposes to increase the death duties; and, most significant of all, the new tax is to be a graduated one. Of all forms of taxation this seems the wisest. Men who continue hoarding great sums all their lives, the proper use of which for public ends would work good to the community from which it chiefly came, should be made to feel that the community, in the form of the State, cannot thus be deprived of its proper share. By taxing estates heavily at death the State marks its condemnation of the self-ish millionaire's unworthy life.

It is desirable that nations should go much further in this direction. Indeed, it is difficult to set bounds to the share of a rich man's estate which should go at his death to the public through the agency of the State, and by all means such taxes should be graduated, beginning at nothing upon moderate sums to dependants, and increasing rapidly as the amounts swell, until of the millionaire's hoard, as of Shylock's, at least

The other half
Comes to the privy coffer of the State.

This policy would work powerfully to induce the rich man to attend to the administration of wealth during his life, which is the end that society should always have in view, as being by far the most fruitful for the people. Nor need it be feared that this policy would sap the root of enterprise and render men

less anxious to accumulate, for, to the class whose ambition it is to leave great fortunes and be talked about after their death, it will attract even more attention, and, indeed, be a some-what nobler ambition, to have enormous sums paid over to the State from their fortunes.

There remains, then, only one mode of using great fortunes; but in this we have the true antidote for the temporary unequal distribution of wealth, the reconciliation of the rich and the poor—a reign of harmony, another ideal, differing, indeed, from that of the Communist in requiring only the further evolution of existing conditions, not the total over-throw of our civilization. It is founded upon the present most intense Individualism, and the race is prepared to put it in practice by degrees whenever it pleases. Under its sway we shall have an ideal State, in which the surplus wealth of the few will become, in the best sense, the property of the many, because administered for the common good; and this wealth, passing through the hands of the few, can be made a much more potent force for the elevation of our race than if distributed in small sums to the people themselves. Even the poorest can be made to see this, and to agree that great sums gathered by some of their fellow-citizens and spent for public purposes, from which the masses reap the principal benefit, are more valuable to them than if scattered among themselves in trifling amounts through the course of many years.

If we consider the results which flow from the Cooper In-stitute, for instance, to the best portion of the race in New York not possessed of means, and compare these with those which would have ensued for the good of the masses from an equal sum distributed by Mr. Cooper in his lifetime in the form of wages, which is the highest form of distribution, being for work done and not for charity, we can form some estimate of the possibilities for the improvement of the race which lie embedded in the present law of the accumulation of wealth. Much of this sum, if distributed in small quanti-ties among the people, would have been wasted in the indul-gence of appetite, some of it in excess, and it may be doubted whether even the part put to the best use, that of adding to the comforts of the home, would have yielded results for the race, as a race, at all comparable to those which are flowing and are to flow from the Cooper Institute from generation to generation. Let the advocate of violent or radical change ponder well this thought.

We might even go so far as to take another instance—that of Mr. Tilden's bequest of five millions of dollars for a free library in the city of New York; but in referring to this one cannot help saying involuntarily: How much better if Mr. Tilden had devoted the last years of his own life to the proper administration of this immense sum; in which case neither legal contest nor any other cause of delay could have interfered with his aims. But let us assume that Mr. Tilden's millions finally become the means of giving to this city a noble public library, where the treasures of the world contained in books will be open to all forever, without money and without price. Considering the good of that part of the race which congregates in and around Manhattan Island, would its permanent benefit have been better promoted had these millions been allowed to circulate in small sums through the hands of the masses? Even the most strenuous advocate of Communism must entertain a doubt upon this subject. Most of those who think will probably entertain no doubt whatever.

Poor and restricted are our opportunities in this life, narrow our horizon, our best work most imperfect; but rich men should be thankful for one inestimable boon. They have it in their power during their lives to busy themselves in organizing benefactions from which the masses of their fellows will derive lasting advantage, and thus dignify their own lives. The highest life is probably to be reached, not by such imitation of the life of Christ as Count Tolstoi gives us, but, while animated by Christ's spirit, by recognizing the changed conditions of this age, and adopting modes of expressing this spirit suitable to the changed conditions under which we live, still laboring for the good of our fellows, which was the essence of his life and teaching, but laboring in a different manner.

This, then, is held to be the duty of the man of wealth: To set an example of modest, unostentatious living, shunning display or extravagance; to provide moderately for the legitimate wants of those dependent upon him; and, after doing so, to consider all surplus revenues which come to him simply as trust funds, which he is called upon to administer, and strictly bound as a matter of duty to administer in the manner which, in his judgment, is best calculated to produce the most beneficial results for the community—the man of wealth thus becoming the mere trustee and agent for his poorer brethren, bringing to their service his superior wisdom, experience, and ability to administer, doing for them better than they would or could do for themselves.

We are met here with the difficulty of determining what are moderate sums to leave to members of the family; what is modest, unostentatious living; what is the test of extravagance. There must be different standards for different conditions. The answer is that it is as impossible to name exact amounts or actions as it is to define good manners, good taste, or the rules of propriety; but, nevertheless, these are verities, well known, although indefinable. Public sentiment is quick to know and to feel what offends these. So in the case of wealth. The rule in regard to good taste in the dress of men or women applies here. Whatever makes one conspicuous offends the canon. If any family be chiefly known for display, for extravagance in home, table, or equipage, for enormous sums ostentatiously spent in any form upon itself—if these be its chief distinctions, we have no difficulty in estimating its nature or culture. So likewise in regard to the use or abuse of its surplus wealth, or to generous, free-handed coöperation in good public uses, or to unabated efforts to accumulate and hoard to the last, or whether they administer or bequeath. The verdict rests with the best and most enlightened public sentiment. The community will surely judge, and its judgments will not often be wrong.

The best uses to which surplus wealth can be put have already been indicated. Those who would administer wisely must, indeed, be wise; for one of the serious obstacles to the improvement of our race is indiscriminate charity. It were better for mankind that the millions of the rich were thrown into the sea than so spent as to encourage the slothful, the drunken, the unworthy. Of every thousand dollars spent in so-called charity to-day, it is probable that nine hundred and fifty dollars is unwisely spent—so spent, indeed, as to produce the very evils which it hopes to mitigate or cure. A well-known writer of philosophic books admitted the other day that he had given a quarter of a dollar to a man who approached him as he was coming to visit the house of his friend. He knew nothing of the habits of this beggar, knew not the use that would be made of this money, although he had every reason to suspect that it would be spent improperly. This man professed to be a disciple of Herbert Spencer; yet the quarter-dollar given that night will probably work more injury than all the money will do good which its thoughtless donor will ever be able to give in true charity. He only gratified his own feelings, saved himself from annoyance—and this was probably one of the most selfish and very worst actions of his life, for in all respects he is most worthy.

In bestowing charity, the main consideration should be to help those who will help themselves; to provide part of the means by which those who desire to improve may do so; to give those who desire to rise the aids by which they may rise; to assist, but rarely or never to do all. Neither the individual nor the race is improved by almsgiving. Those worthy of assistance, except in rare cases, seldom require assistance. The really valuable men of the race never do, except in case of accident or sudden change. Every one has, of course, cases of individuals brought to his own knowledge where temporary assistance can do genuine good, and these he will not overlook. But the amount which can be wisely given by the individual for individuals is necessarily limited by his lack of knowledge of the circumstances connected with each. He is the only true reformer who is as careful and as anxious not to aid the unworthy as he is to aid the worthy, and, perhaps, even more so, for in almsgiving more injury is probably done by rewarding vice than by relieving virtue.

The rich man is thus almost restricted to following the examples of Peter Cooper, Enoch Pratt of Baltimore, Mr. Pratt of Brooklyn, Senator Stanford, and others, who know that the best means of benefiting the community is to place within its reach the ladders upon which the aspiring can rise—free libraries, parks, and means of recreation, by which men are helped in body and mind; works of art, certain to give pleasure and improve the public taste; and public institutions of various kinds, which will improve the general condition of the people; in this manner returning their surplus wealth to the mass of their fellows in the forms best calculated to do them lasting good.

Thus is the problem of rich and poor to be solved. The laws of accumulation will be left free, the laws of distribution free. Individualism will continue, but the millionaire will be but a trustee for the poor, intrusted for a season with a great part of the increased wealth of the community, but administering it for the community far better than it could or would have done for itself. The best minds will thus have reached a stage in the development of the race in which it is clearly seen that there is no mode of disposing of surplus wealth creditable to thoughtful and earnest men into whose hands it flows, save by using it year by year for the general good. This day already dawns. Men may die without incurring the pity of their fellows, still sharers in great business enterprises from which their capital cannot be or has not been withdrawn, and which is left chiefly at death for public uses; yet the day is not far distant when the man who dies leaving behind him millions of available wealth, which was free for him to administer during life, will pass away "unwept, unhonored, and unsung," no matter to what uses he leaves the dross which he cannot take with him. Of such as these the public verdict will then be: "The man who dies thus rich dies disgraced."

Such, in my opinion, is the true gospel concerning wealth, obedience to which is destined some day to solve the problem of the rich and the poor, and to bring "Peace on earth, among men good will."

Cross of Gold Speech, *William Jennings Bryan, 1896*

First Inaugural Address, *William McKinley, 1897*

First Annual Message, *William McKinley, 1897*

The late nineteenth century was a period of rapid economic and industrial expansion in the United States. That expansion, and its consequences for industrialists, laborers, and farmers, brought two issues to the fore in American politics: the use of tariffs to raise revenue for the government and protect American manufacturers by making foreign goods more expensive, and the debate over whether the government should make its money redeemable in both gold and silver or in gold alone. William Jennings Bryan (1860–1925) opposed both high tariffs and the gold standard as attempts by monied interests to become yet richer on the backs of farmers and working people who would have to pay higher prices for goods while seeing the value of their land and labor diminish. His speech before the Democratic National Convention is one of the best known in American oratory. President William McKinley (1843–1901), a former congressman and governor from Ohio, supported both high tariffs and the gold standard. The election of 1896 proved a great victory for McKinley and the Republican Party. Soon after, McKinley called a special session of Congress to revise the tariff, then moved for a vigorous gold standard.

Cross of Gold Speech

July 9, 1896

William Jennings Bryan

Mr. Chairman and Gentlemen of the Convention: I would be presumptuous, indeed, to present myself against the distinguished gentlemen to whom you have listened if this were but a measuring of ability; but this is not a contest among persons. The humblest citizen in all the land, when clad in armor of a righteous cause, is stronger than all the whole hosts of error that they can bring. I come to speak to you in defense of a cause as holy as the cause of liberty—the cause of humanity. When this debate is concluded a motion will be made to lay upon the table the resolution offered in commendation of the Administration and also the resolution in condemnation of the Administration. I shall object to bringing this question down to a level of persons. The individual is but an atom; he is born, he acts, he dies but principles are eternal; and this has been a contest of principle.

Never before in the history of this country has there been witnessed such a contest as that through which we have passed. Never before in the history of American politics has a great issue been fought out, as this issue has been, by the voters themselves.

On the 4th of March, 1895, a few Democrats, most of them members of Congress, issued an address to the Democrats of the nation asserting that the money question was the paramount issue of the hour; asserting also the right of a majority of the Democratic party to control the position of the party on this paramount issue; concluding with the request that all believers in free coinage of silver in the Democratic party should organize and take charge of and control the policy of the Democratic party. Three months later, at Memphis, an organization was perfected, and the silver Democrats went forth openly and boldly and courageously proclaiming their belief and declaring that if successful they would crystallize in a platform the declaration [that] they had made; and then began the conflict with a zeal approaching the zeal which inspired the crusaders who followed PETER the Hermit. Our silver Democrats went forth from victory unto victory until they are assembled now, not to discuss, not to debate, but to enter up the judgment rendered by the plain people of this country.

But in this contest, brother has been arrayed against brother, and father against son. The warmest ties of love and acquaintance and association have been disregarded. Old leaders have been cast aside when they refused to give expression to the sentiments of those whom they would lead, and new leaders have sprung up to give direction to this cause of freedom. Thus has the contest been waged, and we have assembled here under as binding and solemn instructions as were ever fastened upon the representatives of a people.

We do not come as individuals. Why, as individuals we might have been glad to compliment the gentleman from New York (Senator HILL), but we knew that the people for whom we speak would never be willing to put him in a position where he could thwart the will of the Democratic party. I say it was not a question of persons; it was a question of principle, and it is not with gladness, my friends, that we find ourselves brought into conflict with those who are now arrayed on the other side. The gentleman who just preceded me (Governor RUSSELL) spoke of the old State of Massachusetts. Let me assure him that not one person in all this Convention entertains the least hostility to the people of the State of Massachusetts.

But we stand here representing people who are the equals before the law of the largest cities in the State of Massachusetts. When you come before us and tell us that we shall disturb your business interests, we reply that you have disturbed our business interests by your action. We say to you that you have made too limited in its application the definition of a business man. The man who is employed for wages is as much a business man as his employer. The attorney in a country town is as much a business man as the corporation counsel in a great metropolis. The merchant at the cross-roads store is as much a business man as the merchant of New York. The farmer who goes forth in the morning and toils all day, begins in the spring and toils all summer, and by the application of brain and muscle to the natural resources of this country creates wealth, is as much a business man as the man who goes upon the Board of Trade and bets upon the price of grain. The miners who go a thousand feet into the earth or climb 2,000 feet upon the cliffs and bring forth from their hiding places the precious metals to be poured in the channels of trade are as much business men as the few financial magnates who in a back room corner the money of the world.

We come to speak for this broader class of business men. Ah, my friends, we say not one word against those who live upon the Atlantic coast; but those hardy pioneers who braved all the dangers of the wilderness, who have made the desert to blossom as the rose—those pioneers away out there, rearing their children near to nature's heart, where they can mingle their voices with the voices of the birds—out there where they have erected school houses for the education of their children and churches where they praise their Creator, and the cemeteries where sleep the ashes of their dead—are as deserving of the consideration of this party as any people in this country.

It is for these that we speak. We do not come as aggressors. Our war is not a war of conquest. We are fighting in the defense of our homes, our families and posterity. We have petitioned, and our petitions have been scorned. We have entreated and our entreaties have been disregarded. We have begged, and they have mocked when our calamity came.

We beg no longer; we entreat no more; we petition no more. We defy them!

The gentleman from Wisconsin has said he fears a ROBESPIERRE. My friend, in this land of the free you need fear no tyrant who will spring up from among the people. What we need is an ANDREW JACKSON to stand as JACKSON stood, against the encroachments of aggregated wealth.

They tell us that this platform was made to catch votes. We reply to them that changing conditions make new issues; that the principles upon which rest Democracy are as everlasting as the hills; but that they must be applied to new conditions as they arise. Conditions have arisen and we are attempting to meet those conditions. They tell us that the income tax ought not to be brought in here; that is not a new idea. They criticise us for our criticism of the Supreme Court of the United States. My friends, we have made no criticism. We have simply called attention to what you know. If you want criticisms read the dissenting opinions of the Court. That will give you criticisms.

They say we passed an unconstitutional law. I deny it. The income tax was not unconstitutional when it was passed. It was not unconstitutional when it went before the Supreme Court for the first time. It did not become unconstitutional until one judge changed his mind; and we cannot be expected to know when a judge will change his mind.

The income tax is a just law. It simply intends to put the burdens of government justly upon the backs of the people. I am in favor of an income tax. When I find a man who is not willing to pay his share of the burden of the government which protects him I find a man who is unworthy to enjoy the blessings of a government like ours.

He says that we are opposing the national bank currency. It is true. If you will read what THOMAS BENTON said you will find that he said that in searching history he could find but one parallel to ANDREW JACKSON. That was CICERO, who destroyed the conspiracies of CATALINE and saved Rome. He did for Rome what JACKSON did when he destroyed the bank conspiracy and saved America.

We say in our platform that we believe that the right to coin money and issue money is a function of government. We believe it. We believe it is a part of sovereignty, and can no more with safety be delegated to private individuals than can the power to make penal statutes or levy laws for taxation.

Mr. JEFFERSON, who was once regarded as good Democratic authority, seems to have a different opinion from the gentleman who has addressed us on the part of the minority. Those who are opposed to this proposition tell us that the issue of paper money is a function of the bank, and that the Government ought to go out of the banking business. I stand with JEFFERSON, rather than with them, and tell them, as he did, that the issue of money is a function of the Government, and that the banks should go out of the governing business.

They complain about the plank which declares against the life tenure in office. They have tried to strain it to mean that which it does not mean. What we oppose in that plank is the life tenure that is being built up in Washington which establishes an office-holding class and excludes from participation in the benefits the humbler members of our society. I cannot dwell longer in my limited time upon these things.

Let me call attention to two or three great things. The gentleman from New York says that he will propose an amendment providing that this change in our law shall not affect contracts which, according to the present laws, are made payable in gold. But if he means to say that we cannot change our monetary system without protecting those who have loaned money before the change was made, I want to ask him where, in law or in morals, he can find authority for not protecting the debtors when the act of 1873 was passed, when he now insists that we must protect the creditor. He says he also wants to amend this platform so as to provide that if we fail to maintain the parity within a year that we will then suspend the coinage of silver. We reply that when we advocate a thing which we believe will be successful we are not compelled to raise a doubt as to our own sincerity by trying to show what

we will do if we are wrong. I ask him, if he will apply his logic to us, why he does not apply it to himself. He says that he wants this country to try to secure an international agreement. Why doesn't he tell us what he is going to do if they fail to secure an international agreement.

There is more reason for him to do that than for us to expect to fail to maintain the parity. They have tried for thirty years—thirty years—to secure an international agreement, and those are waiting for it most patiently who don't want it at all.

Now, my friends, let me come to the great paramount issue. If they ask us here why it is we say more on the money question than we say upon the tariff question, I reply that if protection has slain its thousands the gold standard has slain its tens of thousands. If they ask us why we did not embody all these things in our platform which we believe, we reply to them that when we have restored the money of the constitution all other necessary reforms will be possible, and that until that is done there is no reform that can be accomplished.

Why is it that within three months such a change has come over the sentiments of the country? Three months ago, when it was confidently asserted that those who believed in the gold standard would frame our platforms and nominate our candidates, even the advocates of the gold standard did not think that we could elect a President; but they had good reasons for the suspicion, because there is scarcely a State here to-day asking for the gold standard that is not within the absolute control of the Republican party. But note the change. Mr. McKINLEY was nominated at St. Louis upon a platform that declared for the maintenance of the gold standard until it should be changed into bimetallism by an international agreement. Mr. McKINLEY was the most popular man among the Republicans and everybody three months ago in the Republican party prophesied his election. How is it to-day? Why, that man who used to boast that he looked like NAPOLEON, that man shudders to-day when he thinks that he was nominated on the anniversary of the battle of Waterloo. Not only that, but as he listens he can hear with ever-increasing distinctness the sound of the waves as they beat upon the lonely shores of St. Helena.

Why this change? Ah, my friends, is not the change evident to anyone who will look at the matter? It is because no private character, however pure, no personal popularity, however great, can protect from the avenging wrath of an indignant people the man who will either declare that he is in favor of fastening the gold standard upon this people, or who is willing to surrender the right of self-government and place legislative control in the hands of foreign potentates and powers.

My friends, the prospect—

(The continued cheering made it impossible for the speaker to proceed. Finally Mr. BRYAN raising his hand, obtained silence, and said: I have only ten minutes left, and I ask you to let me occupy that time.)

We go forth confident that we shall win. Why? Because upon the paramount issue in this campaign there is not a spot of ground upon which the enemy will dare to challenge battle. Why, if they tell us that the gold standard is a good thing, we point to their platform and tell them that their platform pledges the party to get rid of a gold standard, and substitute bimetallism. If the gold standard is a good thing why try to get rid of it? If the gold standard, and I might call your attention to the fact that some of the very people who are in this convention to-day and who tell you that we ought to declare in favor of international bimetallism and thereby declare that the gold standard is wrong, and that the principles of bimetallism are better—these very people four months ago were open and avowed advocates of the gold standard and telling us that we could not legislate two metals together even with all the world.

I want to suggest this truth, that if the gold standard is a good thing we ought to declare in favor of its retention and not in favor of abandoning it; and if the gold standard is a bad thing why should we wait until some other nations are willing to help us to let it go?

Here is the line of battle. We care not upon which issue they force the fight. We are prepared to meet them on either issue or on both. If they tell us that the gold standard is the standard of civilization we reply to them that this, the most enlightened of all nations of the earth, has never declared for a gold standard, and both the parties this year are declaring against it. If the gold standard is the standard of civilization, why, my friends, should we not have it? So if they come to meet us on that we can present the history of our nation. More than that. We can tell them this, that they will search the pages of history in vain to find a single instance in which the common people of any land ever declared themselves in favor of a gold standard. They can find where the holders of fixed investments have.

Mr. CARLISLE said in 1878 that this was a struggle between the idle holders of idle capital and the struggling masses who produce the wealth and pay the taxes of the country; and my friends, it is simply a question that we shall decide upon which side shall the Democratic party fight? Upon the side of the idle holders of idle capital, or upon the side of the strug-

gling masses? That is the question that the party must answer first; and then it must be answered by each individual hereafter. The sympathies of the Democratic party, as described by the platform, are on the side of the struggling masses, who have ever been the foundation of the Democratic party.

There are two ideas of government. There are those who believe that if you just legislate to make the well-to-do prosperous that their prosperity will leak through on those below. The Democratic idea has been that if you legislate to make the masses prosperous their prosperity will find its way up and through every class that rests upon it.

You come to us and tell us that the great cities are in favor of the gold standard. I tell you that the great cities rest upon these broad and fertile prairies. Burn down your cities and leave our farms, and your cities will spring up again as if by magic. But destroy our farms and the grass will grow in the streets of every city in this country.

My friends, we shall declare that this nation is able to legislate for its own people on every question, without waiting for the aid or consent of any other nation on earth, and upon that issue we expect to carry every single State in this Union.

I shall not slander the fair State of Massachusetts nor the State of New York by saying that when its citizens are confronted with the proposition, "Is this nation able to attend to its own business?"—I will not slander either one by saying that the people of those States will declare our helpless impotency as a nation to attend to our own business. It is the issue of 1776 over again. Our ancestors, when but 3,000,000, had the courage to declare their political independence of every other nation upon earth. Shall we, their descendants, when we have grown to 70,000,000, declare that we are less independent than our forefathers? No, my friends, it will never be the judgment of this people. Therefore, we care not upon what lines the battle is fought. If they say bimetallism is good, but we cannot have it till some nation helps us, we reply that, instead of having a gold standard because England has, we shall restore bimetallism, and then let England have bimetallism because the United States have.

If they dare to come out and in the open defend the gold standard as a good thing, we shall fight them to the uttermost, having behind us the producing masses of the Nation and the world. Having behind us the commercial interests and the laboring interests and all the toiling masses, we shall answer their demands for a gold standard by saying to them, you shall not press down upon the brow of labor this crown of thorns. You shall not crucify mankind upon a cross of gold.

First Inaugural Address

March 4, 1897

William McKinley

Fellow-Citizens:

In obedience to the will of the people, and in their presence, by the authority vested in me by this oath, I assume the arduous and responsible duties of President of the United States, relying upon the support of my countrymen and invoking the guidance of Almighty God. Our faith teaches that there is no safer reliance than upon the God of our fathers, who has so singularly favored the American people in every national trial, and who will not forsake us so long as we obey His commandments and walk humbly in His footsteps.

The responsibilities of the high trust to which I have been called—always of grave importance—are augmented by the prevailing business conditions entailing idleness upon willing labor and loss to useful enterprises. The country is suffering from industrial disturbances from which speedy relief must be had. Our financial system needs some revision; our money is all good now, but its value must not further be threatened. It should all be put upon an enduring basis, not subject to easy attack, nor its stability to doubt or dispute. Our currency should continue under the supervision of the Government. The several forms of our paper money offer, in my judgment, a constant embarrassment to the Government and a safe balance in the Treasury. Therefore I believe it necessary to devise a system which, without diminishing the circulating medium or offering a premium for its contraction, will present a remedy for those arrangements which, temporary in their nature, might well in the years of our prosperity have been displaced by wiser provisions. With adequate revenue secured, but not until then, we can enter upon such changes in our fiscal laws as will, while insuring safety and volume to our money, no longer impose upon the Government the necessity of maintaining so large a gold reserve, with its attendant and inevitable temptations to speculation. Most of our financial laws are the outgrowth of experience and trial, and should not be amended without investigation and demonstration of the wisdom of the proposed changes. We must be both "sure we are right" and "make haste slowly." If, therefore, Congress, in its wisdom, shall deem it expedient to create a commission to take under early consideration the revision of our coinage, banking and currency laws, and give them that exhaustive, careful and dispassionate examination that their importance demands, I shall cordially concur in such action. If such power is vested in the President, it is my purpose to appoint a commission of prominent, well-informed citizens of different parties, who will command public confidence, both on account of their ability and special fitness for the work. Business experience and public training may thus be combined, and the patriotic zeal of the friends of the country be so directed that such a report will be made as to receive the support of all parties, and our finances cease to be the subject of mere partisan contention. The experiment is, at all events, worth a trial, and, in my opinion, it can but prove beneficial to the entire country.

The question of international bimetallism will have early and earnest attention. It will be my constant endeavor to secure it by co-operation with the other great commercial powers of the world. Until that condition is realized when the parity between our gold and silver money springs from and is supported by the relative value of the two metals, the value of the silver already coined and of that which may hereafter be coined, must be kept constantly at par with gold by every resource at our command. The credit of the Government, the integrity of its currency, and the inviolability of its obligations must be preserved. This was the commanding verdict of the people, and it will not be unheeded.

Economy is demanded in every branch of the Government at all times, but especially in periods, like the present, of depression in business and distress among the people. The severest economy must be observed in all public expenditures, and extravagance stopped wherever it is found, and prevented wherever in the future it may be developed. If the revenues are to remain as now, the only relief that can come must be from decreased expenditures. But the present must not become the permanent condition of the Government. It has been our uniform practice to retire, not increase our outstanding obligations, and this policy must again be resumed and vigorously enforced. Our revenues should always be large enough to meet with ease and promptness not only our current needs and the principal and interest of the public debt, but to make proper and liberal provision for that most deserving body of public creditors, the soldiers and sailors and the widows and orphans who are the pensioners of the United States.

The Government should not be permitted to run behind or increase its debt in times like the present. Suitably to provide against this is the mandate of duty—the certain and easy remedy for most of our financial difficulties. A deficiency is inevitable so long as the expenditure of the Government exceed its receipts. It can only be met by loans or an increased revenue. While a large annual surplus of revenue may invite waste and extravagance, inadequate revenue creates distrust and undermines public and private credit. Neither should be encouraged. Between more loans and more revenue there ought to be but one opinion. We should have more revenue, and that without delay, hindrance, or postponement. A surplus in the Treasury created by loans is not a permanent or safe reliance. It will suffice while it lasts, but it can not last long while the outlays of the Government are greater than its receipts, as has been the case during the past two years. Nor must it be forgotten that however much such loans may temporarily relieve the situation, the Government is still indebted for the amount of the surplus thus accrued, which it must ultimately pay, while its ability to pay is not strengthened, but weakened by a continued deficit. Loans are imperative in great emergencies to preserve the Government or its credit, but a failure to supply needed revenue in time of peace for the maintenance of either has no justification.

The best way for the Government to maintain its credit is to pay as it goes—not by resorting to loans, but by keeping out of debt—through an adequate income secured by a system of taxation, external or internal, or both. It is the settled policy of the Government, pursued from the beginning and practised by all parties and Administrations, to raise the bulk of our revenue from taxes upon foreign productions entering the United States for sale and consumption, and avoiding, for the most part, every form of direct taxation, except in time of war. The country is clearly opposed to any needless additions to the subject of internal taxation, and is committed by its latest popular utterance to the system of tariff taxation. There can be no misunderstanding, either, about the principle upon which this tariff taxation shall be levied. Nothing has ever been made plainer at a general election than that the controlling principle in the raising of revenue from duties on imports is zealous care for American interests and American labor. The people have declared that such legislation should be had as will give ample protection and encouragement to the industries and the development of our country. It is, therefore, earnestly hoped and expected that Congress will, at the earliest practicable moment, enact revenue legislation that shall be fair, reasonable, conservative, and just, and which, while supplying sufficient revenue for public purposes, will still be signally beneficial and helpful to every section and every enterprise of the people. To this policy we are all, of whatever

party, firmly bound by the voice of the people—a power vastly more potential than the expression of any political platform. The paramount duty of Congress is to stop deficiencies by the restoration of that protective legislation which has always been the firmest prop of the Treasury. The passage of such a law or laws would strengthen the credit of the Government both at home and abroad, and go far toward stopping the drain upon the gold reserve held for the redemption of our currency, which has been heavy and well-nigh constant for several years.

In the revision of the tariff especial attention should be given to the re-enactment and extension of the reciprocity principle of the law of 1890, under which so great a stimulus was given to our foreign trade in new and advantageous markets for our surplus agricultural and manufactured products. The brief trial given this legislation amply justifies a further experiment and additional discretionary power in the making of commercial treaties, the end in view always to be the opening up of new markets for the products of our country, by granting concessions to the products of other lands that we need and cannot produce ourselves, and which do not involve any loss of labor to our own people, but tend to increase their employment.

The depression of the past four years has fallen with especial severity upon the great body of toilers of the country, and upon none more than the holders of small farms. Agriculture has languished and labour suffered. The revival of manufacturing will be a relief to both. No portion of our population is more devoted to the institution of free government nor more loyal in their support, while none bears more cheerfully or fully its proper share in the maintenance of the Government or is better entitled to its wise and liberal care and protection. Legislation helpful to producers is beneficial to all. The depressed condition of industry on the farm and in the mine and factory has lessened the ability of the people to meet the demands upon them, and they rightfully expect that not only a system of revenue shall be established that will secure the largest income with the least burden, but that every means will be taken to decrease, rather than increase, our public expenditures. Business conditions are not the most promising. It will take time to restore the prosperity of former years. If we cannot promptly attain it, we can resolutely turn our faces in that direction and aid its return by friendly legislation. However troublesome the situation may appear, Congress will not, I am sure, be found lacking in disposition or ability to relieve it as far as legislation can do so. The restoration of confidence and the revival of business, which men of all parties so much desire, depend more largely upon the prompt, energetic, and intelligent action of Congress than upon any other single agency affecting the situation.

It is inspiring, too, to remember that no great emergency in the one hundred and eight years of our eventful national life has ever arisen that has not been met with wisdom and courage by the American people, with fidelity to their best interests and highest destiny, and to the honor of the American name. These years of glorious history have exalted mankind and advanced the cause of freedom throughout the world, and immeasurably strengthened the precious free institutions which we enjoy. The people love and will sustain these institutions. The great essential to our happiness and prosperity is that we adhere to the principles upon which the Government was established and insist upon their faithful observance. Equality of rights must prevail, and our laws be always and everywhere respected and obeyed. We may have failed in the discharge of our full duty as citizens of the great Republic, but it is consoling and encouraging to realize that free speech, a free press, free thought, free schools, the free and unmolested right of religious liberty and worship, and free and fair elections are dearer and more universally enjoyed to-day than ever before. These guaranties must be sacredly preserved and wisely strengthened. The constituted authorities must be cheerfully and vigorously upheld. Lynchings must not be tolerated in a great and civilized country like the United States; courts, not mobs, must execute the penalties of the law. The preservation of public order, the right of discussion, the integrity of courts, and the orderly administration of justice must continue forever the rock of safety upon which our Government securely rests.

One of the lessons taught by the late election, which all can rejoice in, is that the citizens of the United States are both law-respecting and law-abiding people, not easily swerved from the path of patriotism and honor. This is in entire accord with the genius of our institutions, and but emphasizes the advantages of inculcating even a greater love for law and order in the future. Immunity should be granted to none who violate the laws, whether individuals, corporations, or communities; and as the Constitution imposes upon the President the duty of both its own execution, and of the statutes enacted in pursuance of its provisions, I shall endeavor carefully to carry them into effect. The declaration of the party now restored to power has been in the past that of "opposition to all combinations of capital organized in trusts, or otherwise, to control arbitrarily the condition of trade among our citi-

zens," and it has supported "such legislation as will prevent the execution of all schemes to oppress the people by undue charges on their supplies, or by unjust rates for the transportation of their products to the market." This purpose will be steadily pursued, both by the enforcement of the laws now in existence and the recommendation and support of such new statutes as may be necessary to carry it into effect.

Our naturalization and immigration laws should be further improved to the constant promotion of a safer, a better, and a higher citizenship. A grave peril to the Republic would be a citizenship too ignorant to understand or too vicious to appreciate the great value and beneficence of our institutions and laws, and against all who come here to make war upon them our gates must be promptly and tightly closed. Nor must we be unmindful of the need of improvement among our own citizens, but with the zeal of our forefathers encourage the spread of knowledge and free education. Illiteracy must be banished from the land if we shall attain that high destiny as the foremost of the enlightened nations of the world which, under Providence, we ought to achieve.

Reforms in the civil service must go on; but the changes should be real and genuine, not perfunctory, or prompted by a zeal in behalf of any party simply because it happens to be in power. As a member of Congress I voted and spoke in favor of the present law, and I shall attempt its enforcement in the spirit in which it was enacted. The purpose in view was to secure the most efficient service of the best men who would accept appointment under the Government, retaining faithful and devoted public servants in office, but shielding none, under the authority of any rule or custom, who are inefficient, incompetent, or unworthy. The best interests of the country demand this, and the people heartily approve the law wherever and whenever it has been thus administrated.

Congress should give prompt attention to the restoration of our American merchant marine, once the pride of the seas in all the great ocean highways of commerce. To my mind, few more important subjects so imperatively demand its intelligent consideration. The United States has progressed with marvelous rapidity in every field of enterprise and endeavor until we have become foremost in nearly all the great lines of inland trade, commerce, and industry. Yet, while this is true, our American merchant marine has been steadily declining until it is now lower, both in the percentage of tonnage and the number of vessels employed, than it was prior to the Civil War. Commendable progress has been made of late years in the upbuilding of the American Navy, but we must supplement these efforts by providing as a proper consort for it a merchant marine amply sufficient for our own carrying trade to foreign countries. The question is one that appeals both to our business necessities and the patriotic aspirations of a great people.

It has been the policy of the United States since the foundation of the Government to cultivate relations of peace and amity with all the nations of the world, and this accords with my conception of our duty now. We have cherished the policy of non-interference with affairs of foreign governments wisely inaugurated by Washington, keeping ourselves free from entanglement, either as allies or foes, content to leave undisturbed with them the settlement of their own domestic concerns. It will be our aim to pursue a firm and dignified foreign policy, which shall be just, impartial, ever watchful of our national honor, and always insisting upon the enforcement of the lawful rights of American citizens everywhere. Our diplomacy should seek nothing more and accept nothing less than is due us. We want no wars of conquest; we must avoid the temptation of territorial aggression. War should never be entered upon until every agency of peace has failed; peace is preferable to war in almost every contingency. Arbitration is the true method of settlement of international as well as local or individual differences. It was recognized as the best means of adjustment of differences between employers and employees by the Forty-ninth Congress, in 1886, and its application was extended to our diplomatic relations by the unanimous concurrence of the Senate and House of the Fifty-first Congress in 1890. The latter resolution was accepted as the basis of negotiations with us by the British House of Commons in 1893, and upon our invitation a treaty of arbitration between the United States and Great Britain was signed at Washington and transmitted to the Senate for its ratification in January last. Since this treaty is clearly the result of our own initiative: since it has been recognized as the leading feature of our foreign policy throughout our entire national history—the adjustment of difficulties by judicial methods rather than force of arms—and since it presents to the world the glorious example of reason and peace, not passion and war, controlling the relations between two of the greatest nations in the world, an example certain to be followed by others, I respectfully urge the early action of the Senate thereon, not merely as a matter of policy, but as a duty to mankind. The importance and moral influence of the ratification of such a treaty can hardly be overestimated in the cause of advancing civilization. It may well engage the best thought of the statesmen and people of every country, and I cannot but consider it fortunate that it was reserved to the United States to have the leadership in so grand a work.

It has been the uniform practice of each President to avoid, as far as possible, the convening of Congress in extraordinary session. It is an example which, under ordinary circumstances and in the absence of a public necessity, is to be commended. But a failure to convene the representatives of the people in Congress in extra session when it involves neglect of a public duty places the responsibility of such neglect upon the Executive himself. The condition of the public Treasury, as has been indicated, demands the immediate consideration of Congress. It alone has the power to provide revenues for the Government. Not to convene it under such circumstances I can view in no other sense than the neglect of a plain duty. I do not sympathize with the sentiment that Congress in session is dangerous to our general business interests. Its members are the agents of the people, and their presence at the seat of Government in the execution of the sovereign will should not operate as an injury, but a benefit. There could be no better time to put the Government upon a sound financial and economic basis than now. The people have only recently voted that this should be done, and nothing is more binding upon the agents of their will than the obligation of immediate action. It has always seemed to me that the postponement of the meeting of Congress until more than a year after it has been chosen deprived Congress too often of the inspiration of the popular will and the country of the corresponding benefits. It is evident, therefore, that to postpone action in the presence of so great a necessity would be unwise on the part of the Executive because unjust to the interests of the people. Our action now will be freer from mere partisan consideration than if the question of tariff revision was postponed until the regular session of Congress. We are nearly two years from a Congressional election, and politics cannot so greatly distract us as if such contest was immediately pending. We can approach the problem calmly and patriotically, without fearing its effect upon an early election.

Our fellow-citizens who may disagree with us upon the character of this legislation prefer to have the question settled now, even against their preconceived views, and perhaps settled so reasonably, as I trust and believe it will be, as to insure great permanence, than to have further uncertainty menacing the vast and varied business interests of the United States. Again, whatever action Congress may take will be given a fair opportunity for trial before the people are called to pass judgment upon it, and this I consider a great essential to the rightful and lasting settlement of the question. In view of these considerations, I shall deem it my duty as President to convene Congress in extraordinary session on Monday, the 15th day of March, 1897.

In conclusion, I congratulate the country upon the fraternal spirit of the people and the manifestations of good will everywhere so apparent. The recent election not only most fortunately demonstrated the obliteration of sectional or geographical lines, but to some extent also the prejudices which for years have distracted our councils and marred our true greatness as a nation. The triumph of the people, whose verdict is carried into effect today, is not the triumph of one section, nor wholly of one party, but of all sections and all the people. The North and the South no longer divide on the old lines, but upon principles and policies; and in this fact surely every lover of the country can find cause for true felicitation. Let us rejoice in and cultivate this spirit; it is ennobling and will be both a gain and a blessing to our beloved country. It will be my constant aim to do nothing, and permit nothing to be done, that will arrest or disturb this growing sentiment of unity and co-operation, this revival of esteem and affiliation which now animates so many thousands in both the old antagonistic sections, but I shall cheerfully do everything possible to promote and increase it.

Let me again repeat the words of the oath administered by the Chief Justice which, in their respective spheres, so far as applicable, I would have all my countrymen observe: "I will faithfully execute the office of President of the United States, and will, to the best of my ability, preserve, protect, and defend the Constitution of the United States." This is the obligation I have reverently taken before the Lord Most High. To keep it will be my single purpose, my constant prayer; and I shall confidently rely upon the forbearance and assistance of all the people in the discharge of my solemn responsibilities.

First Annual Message

December 6, 1897

William McKinley

To the Senate and House of Representatives:

It gives me pleasure to extend greeting to the Fifty-fifth Congress, assembled in regular session at the seat of Government, with many of whose Senators and Representatives I have been associated in the legislative service. Their meeting occurs under felicitous conditions, justifying sincere congratulation and calling for our grateful acknowledgment to a beneficent Providence which has so signally blessed and prospered us as a nation. Peace and good will with all the nations of the earth continue unbroken.

A matter of genuine satisfaction is the growing feeling of fraternal regard and unification of all sections of our country, the incompleteness of which has too long delayed realization of the highest blessings of the Union. The spirit of patriotism is universal and is ever increasing in fervor. The public questions which now must engross us are lifted far above either partisanship, prejudice, or former sectional differences. They affect every part of our common country alike and permit of no division on ancient lines. Questions of foreign policy, of revenue, the soundness of the currency, the inviolability of national obligations, the improvement of the public service, appeal to the individual conscience of every earnest citizen to whatever party he belongs or in whatever section of the country he may reside.

The extra session of this Congress which closed during July last enacted important legislation, and while its full effect has not yet been realized, what it has already accomplished assures us of its timeliness and wisdom. To test its permanent value, further time will be required, and the people, satisfied with its operation and results [thus] far, are in no mind to withhold from it a fair trial.

Tariff legislation having been settled by the extra session of Congress, the question next pressing for consideration is that of the currency.

The work of putting our finances upon a sound basis, difficult as it may seem, will appear easier when we recall the financial operations of the Government since 1866. On the 30th day of June of that year we had outstanding demand liabilities in the sum of $728,808,447.41. On the 1st of January, 1870, these liabilities had been reduced to $143,880,495.88.

Of our interest-bearing obligations, the figures are even more striking. On July 1, 1866, the principal of the interest-bearing debt of the Government was $2,332,331,208. On the 1st day of July, 1893, this sum had been reduced to $585,037,100, or an aggregate reduction of $1,747,294,108. The interest-bearing debt of the United States on the 1st day of December, 1897, was $847,365,620. The Government money now outstanding (December 1) consists of $346,681,016 of United States notes, $107,793,280 of Treasury notes issued by authority of the law of 1890, $384,963,504 of silver certificates, and $61,280,761 of standard silver dollars.

With the great resources of the Government, and with the honorable example of the past before us, we ought not to hesitate to enter upon a currency revision which will make our demand obligations less onerous to the Government and relieve our financial laws from ambiguity and doubt.

The brief review of what was accomplished from the close of the war to 1893 makes unreasonable and groundless any distrust either of our financial ability or soundness; while the situation from 1893 to 1897 must admonish Congress of the immediate necessity of so legislating as to make the return of the conditions then prevailing impossible.

There are many plans proposed as a remedy for the evil. Before we can find the true remedy we must appreciate the real evil. It is not that our currency of every kind is not good, for every dollar of it is good; good because the Government's pledge is out to keep it so, and that pledge will not be broken. However, the guaranty of our purpose to keep the pledge will be best shown by advancing toward its fulfillment.

The evil of the present system is found in the great cost to the Government of maintaining the parity of our different forms of money, that is, keeping all of them at par with gold. We surely can not be longer heedless of the burden this imposes upon the people, even under fairly prosperous conditions, while the past four years have demonstrated that it is not only an expensive charge upon the Government, but a dangerous menace to the national credit.

It is manifest that we must devise some plan to protect the Government against bond issues for repeated redemptions. We must either curtail the opportunity for speculation, made easy by the multiplied redemptions of our demand obligations, or increase the gold reserve for their redemption. We have $900,000,000 of currency which the Government by solemn enactment has undertaken to keep at par with gold. Nobody is obliged to redeem in gold but the Government. The banks are not required to redeem in gold. The Govern-ment is obliged to keep equal with gold all its outstanding currency and coin obligations, while its receipts are not required to be paid in gold. They are paid in every kind of money but gold, and the only means by which the Government can with certainty get gold is by borrowing. It can get it in no other way when it most needs it. The Government, without any fixed gold revenue, is pledged to maintain gold redemption, which it has steadily and faithfully done, and which under the authority now given it will continue to do.

The law which requires the Government after having redeemed its United States notes to pay them out again as current funds demands a constant replenishment of the gold reserve. This is especially so in times of business panic and when the revenues are insufficient to meet the expenses of the Government. At such times the Government has no other way to supply its deficit and maintain redemption but through the increase of its bonded debt, as during the Administration of my predecessor, when $262,315,400 of 4½ per cent bonds were issued and sold and the proceeds used to pay the expenses of the Government in excess of the revenues and sustain the gold reserve. While it is true that the greater part of the proceeds of these bonds were used to supply deficient revenues, a considerable portion was required to maintain the gold reserve.

With our revenues equal to our expenses, there would be no deficit requiring the issuance of bonds. But if the gold reserve falls below $100,000,000, how will it be replenished except by selling more bonds? Is there any other way practicable under existing law? The serious question then is, Shall we continue the policy that has been pursued in the past; that is, when the gold reserve reaches the point of danger, issue more bonds and supply the needed gold, or shall we provide other means to prevent these recurring drains upon the gold reserve? If no further legislation is had and the policy of selling bonds is to be continued, then Congress should give the Secretary of the Treasury authority to sell bonds at long or short periods, bearing a less rate of interest than is now authorized by law.

I earnestly recommend, as soon as the receipts of the Government are quite sufficient to pay all the expenses of the Government, that when any of the United States notes are presented for redemption in gold and are redeemed in gold, such notes shall be kept and set apart, and only paid out in exchange for gold. This is an obvious duty. If the holder of the United States note prefers the gold and gets it from the Government, he should not receive back from the Government a United States note without paying gold in exchange for it. The reason for this is made all the more apparent when the Government issues an interest-bearing debt to provide gold for the redemption of United States notes—a non-interest-bearing debt. Surely it should not pay them out again except on demand and for gold. If they are put out in any other way, they may return again to be followed by another bond issue to redeem them—another interest-bearing debt to redeem a non-interest-bearing debt.

In my view, it is of the utmost importance that the Government should be relieved from the burden of providing all the gold required for exchanges and export. This responsibility is alone borne by the Government without any of the usual and necessary banking powers to help itself. The banks do not feel the strain of gold redemption. The whole strain rests upon the Government, and the size of the gold reserve in the Treasury has come to be, with or without reason, the signal of danger or of security. This ought to be stopped.

If we are to have an era of prosperity in the country, with sufficient receipts for the expenses of the Government, we may feel no immediate embarrassment from our present currency; but the danger still exists and will be ever present, menacing us so long as the existing system continues. And besides, it is in times of adequate revenues and business tranquillity that the Government should prepare for the worst. We can not avoid without serious consequences the wise consideration and prompt solution of this question.

The Secretary of the Treasury has outlined a plan in great detail for the purpose of removing the threatened recurrence of a depleted gold reserve and save us from future embarrassment on that account. To this plan I invite your careful consideration.

I concur with the Secretary of the Treasury in his recommendation that national banks be allowed to issue notes to the face value of the bonds which they have deposited for circulation, and that the tax on circulating notes secured by deposit of such bonds be reduced to one-half of 1 per cent per annum. I also join him in recommending that authority be given for the establishment of national banks with a minimum capital of $25,000. This will enable the smaller villages and agricultural regions of the country to be supplied with currency to meet their needs.

I recommend that the issue of national-bank notes be restricted to the denomination of $10 and upwards. If the suggestions I have herein made shall have the approval of Congress, then I would recommend that national banks be required to redeem their notes in gold.

In the Slaughter-House *and* Civil Rights *cases the Supreme Court had given a very narrow reading of the privileges and immunities provided by the Fourteenth Amendment. In the* Lochner *case the Court provided a much wider, substantive reading of the due process clause of that same amendment. In invalidating a New York law limiting the work hours of bakers (a law instituted with the stated intention of protecting workers' health), the Court argued that such legislation unduly interfered with the workers' freedom to contract with employers regarding pay and working conditions. The case spawned strong dissents from justices in the minority, who argued that it in essence imposed the majority's philosophical and policy preferences onto the Constitution. This case would not be formally overturned, but its impact would be lessened repeatedly over the years, until 1955 when, in the case of* Williamson v. Lee Optical of Oklahoma, *the Supreme Court opined that "the day is gone when this Court uses the due process clause of the Fourteenth Amendment to strike down state laws, regulatory of business and industrial conditions, because they may be unwise, improvident, or out of harmony with a particular school of thought."*

Lochner v. New York

April 17, 1905

ERROR TO THE COUNTY COURT OF ONEIDA COUNTY, STATE OF NEW YORK

Argued February 23, 24, 1905.—Decided April 17, 1905.

MR. JUSTICE PECKHAM,
            delivered the opinion of the court.

The indictment, it will be seen, charges that the plaintiff in error violated the one hundred and tenth section of article 8, chapter 415, of the Laws of 1897, known as the labor law of the State of New York, in that he wrongfully and unlawfully required and permitted an employé working for him to work more than sixty hours in one week. There is nothing in any of the opinions delivered in this case, either in the Supreme Court or the Court of Appeals of the State, which construes the section, in using the word "required," as referring to any physical force being used to obtain the labor of the employé. It is assumed that the word means nothing more than the requirement arising from voluntary contract for such labor in excess of the number of hours specified in the statute. There is no pretense in any of the opinions that the statute was intended to meet a case of involuntary labor in any form. All the opinions assume that there is no real distinction, so far as this question is concerned, between the words "required" and

"permitted." The mandate of the statute that "no employé shall be required or permitted to work," is the substantial equivalent of an enactment that "no employé shall contract or agree to work," more than ten hours per day, and as there is no provision for special emergencies the statute is mandatory in all cases. It is not an act merely fixing the number of hours which shall constitute a legal day's work, but an absolute prohibition upon the employer, permitting, under any circumstances, more than ten hours work to be done in his establishment. The employé may desire to earn the extra money, which would arise from his working more than the prescribed time, but this statute forbids the employer from permitting the employé to earn it.

The statute necessarily interferes with the right of contract between the employer and employés, concerning the number of hours in which the latter may labor in the bakery of the employer. The general right to make a contract in relation to his business is part of the liberty of the individual protected by the Fourteenth Amendment of the Federal Constitution. *Allgeyer* v. *Louisiana,* 165 U.S. 578. Under the provision no State can deprive any person of life, liberty or property without due process of law. The right to purchase or to sell labor is part of the liberty protected by this amendment, unless there are circumstances which exclude the right. There are, however, certain powers, existing in the sovereignty of each State in the Union, somewhat vaguely termed police powers, the exact description and limitation of which have not been attempted by the courts. Those powers, broadly stated and without, at present, any attempt at a more specific limitation, relate to the safety, health, morals and general welfare of the public. Both property and liberty are held on such reasonable conditions as may be imposed by the governing power of the State in the exercise of those powers, and with such conditions the Fourteenth Amendment was not designed to interfere. *Mugler* v. *Kansas,* 123 U.S. 623; *In re Kemmler,* 136 U.S. 436; *Crowley* v. *Christensen,* 137 U.S. 86; *In re Converse,* 137 U.S. 624.

The State, therefore, has power to prevent the individual from making certain kinds of contracts, and in regard to them the Federal Constitution offers no protection. If the contract be one which the State, in the legitimate exercise of its police power, has the right to prohibit, it is not prevented from prohibiting it by the Fourteenth Amendment. Contracts in violation of a statute, either of the Federal or state government, or a contract to let one's property for immoral purposes, or to do any other unlawful act, could obtain no protection from the Federal Constitution, as coming under the liberty of person or of free contract. Therefore, when the State, by its legislature, in the assumed exercise of its police powers, has passed an act which seriously limits the right to labor or the right of contract in regard to their means of livelihood between persons who are *sui juris* (both employer and employé), it becomes of great importance to determine which shall prevail—the right of the individual to labor for such time as he may choose, or the right of the State to prevent the individual from laboring or from entering into any contract to labor, beyond a certain time prescribed by the State.

This court has recognized the existence and upheld the exercise of the police powers of the States in many cases which might fairly be considered as border ones, and it has, in the course of its determination of questions regarding the asserted invalidity of such statutes, on the ground of their violation of the rights secured by the Federal Constitution, been guided by rules of a very liberal nature, the application of which has resulted, in numerous instances, in upholding the validity of state statutes thus assailed. Among the latter cases where the state law has been upheld by this court is that of *Holden* v. *Hardy,* 169 U.S. 366. A provision in the act of the legislature of Utah was there under consideration, the act limiting the employment of workmen in all underground mines or workings, to eight hours per day, "except in cases of emergency, where life or property is in imminent danger." It also limited the hours of labor in smelting and other institutions for the reduction or refining of ores or metals to eight hours per day, except in like cases of emergency. The act was held to be a valid exercise of the police powers of the State. A review of many of the cases on the subject, decided by this and other courts, is given in the opinion. It was held that the kind of employment, mining, smelting, etc., and the character of the employés in such kinds of labor, were such as to make it reasonable and proper for the State to interfere to prevent the employés from being constrained by the rules laid down by the proprietors in regard to labor. The following citation from the observations of the Supreme Court of Utah in that case was made by the judge writing the opinion of this court, and approved: "The law in question is confined to the protection of that class of people engaged in labor in underground mines, and in smelters and other works wherein ores are reduced and refined. This law applies only to the classes subjected by their employment to the peculiar conditions and effects attending underground mining and work in smelters, and other works for the reduction and refining of ores. Therefore it is not necessary to discuss or decide whether the legislature can fix the hours of labor in other employments."

It will be observed that, even with regard to that class of labor, the Utah statute provided for cases of emergency wherein the provisions of the statute would not apply. The statute now before this court has no emergency clause in it, and, if the statute is valid, there are no circumstances and no emergencies under which the slightest violation of the provisions of the act would be innocent. There is nothing in *Holden* v. *Hardy* which covers the case now before us. Nor does *Atkin* v. *Kansas,* 191 U.S. 207, touch the case at bar. The *Atkin case* was decided upon the right of the State to control its municipal corporations and to prescribe the conditions upon which it will permit work of a public character to be done for a municipality. *Knoxville Iron Co. v. Harbison,* 183 U.S. 13, is equally far from an authority for this legislation. The employés in that case were held to be at a disadvantage with the employer in matters of wages, they being miners and coal workers, and the act simply provided for the cashing of coal orders when presented by the miner to the employer. . . .

The question whether this act is valid as a labor law, pure and simple, may be dismissed in a few words. There is no reasonable ground for interfering with the liberty of person or the right of free contract, by determining the hours of labor, in the occupation of a baker. There is no contention that bakers as a class are not equal in intelligence and capacity to men in other trades or manual occupations, or that they are not able to assert their rights and care for themselves without the protecting arm of the State, interfering with their independence of judgment and of action. They are in no sense wards of the State. Viewed in the light of a purely labor law, with no reference whatever to the question of health, we think that a law like the one before us involves neither the safety, the morals nor the welfare of the public, and that the interest of the public is not in the slightest degree affected by such an act. The law must be upheld, if at all, as a law pertaining to the health of the individual engaged in the occupation of a baker. It does not affect any other portion of the public than those who are engaged in that occupation. Clean and wholesome bread does not depend upon whether the baker works but ten hours per day or only sixty hours a week. The limitation of the hours of labor does not come within the police power on that ground.

It is a question of which of two powers or rights shall prevail—the power of the State to legislate or the right of the individual to liberty of person and freedom of contract. The mere assertion that the subject relates though but in a remote degree to the public health does not necessarily render the enactment valid. The act must have a more direct relation, as a means to an end, and the end itself must be appropriate and legitimate, before an act can be held to be valid which interferes with the general right of an individual to be free in his person and in his power to contract in relation to his own labor.

This case has caused much diversity of opinion in the state courts. In the Supreme Court two of the five judges composing the Appellate Division dissented from the judgment affirming the validity of the act. In the Court of Appeals three of the seven judges also dissented from the judgment upholding the statute. Although found in what is called a labor law of the State, the Court of Appeals has upheld the

act as one relating to the public health—in other words, as a health law. One of the judges of the Court of Appeals, in upholding the law, stated that, in his opinion, the regulation in question could not be sustained unless they were able to say, from common knowledge, that working in a bakery and candy factory was an unhealthy employment. The judge held that, while the evidence was not uniform, it still led him to the conclusion that the occupation of a baker or confectioner was unhealthy and tended to result in diseases of the respiratory organs. Three of the judges dissented from that view, and they thought the occupation of a baker was not to such an extent unhealthy as to warrant the interference of the legislature with the liberty of the individual.

We think the limit of the police power has been reached and passed in this case. There is, in our judgment, no reasonable foundation for holding this to be necessary or appropriate as a health law to safeguard the public health or the health of the individuals who are following the trade of a baker. If this statute be valid, and if, therefore, a proper case is made out in which to deny the right of an individual, *sui juris,* as employer or employé, to make contracts for the labor of the latter under the protection of the provisions of the Federal Constitution, there would seem to be no length to which legislation of this nature might not go. The case differs widely, as we have already stated, from the expressions of this court in regard to laws of this nature, as stated in *Holden* v. *Hardy* and *Jacobson* v. *Massachusetts, supra.*

We think that there can be no fair doubt that the trade of a baker, in and of itself, is not an unhealthy one to that degree which would authorize the legislature to interfere with the right to labor, and with the right of free contract on the part of the individual, either as employer or employé. In looking through statistics regarding all trades and occupations, it may be true that the trade of a baker does not appear to be as healthy as some other trades, and is also vastly more healthy than still others. To the common understanding the trade of a baker has never been regarded as an unhealthy one. Very likely physicians would not recommend the exercise of that or of any other trade as a remedy for ill health. Some occupations are more healthy than others, but we think there are none which might not come under the power of the legislature to supervise and control the hours of working therein, if the mere fact that the occupation is not absolutely and perfectly healthy is to confer that right upon the legislative department of the Government. It might be safely affirmed that almost all occupations more or less affect the health.

There must be more than the mere fact of the possible existence of some small amount of unhealthiness to warrant legislative interference with liberty. It is unfortunately true that labor, even in any department, may possibly carry with it the seeds of unhealthiness. But are we all, on that account, at the mercy of legislative majorities? A printer, a tinsmith, a locksmith, a carpenter, a cabinetmaker, a dry goods clerk, a bank's, a lawyer's or a physician's clerk, or a clerk in almost any kind of business, would all come under the power of the legislature, on this assumption. No trade, no occupation, no mode of earning one's living, could escape this all-pervading power, and the acts of the legislature in limiting the hours of labor in all employments would be valid, although such limitation might seriously cripple the ability of the laborer to support himself and his family. In our large cities there are many buildings into which the sun penetrates for but a short time in each day, and these buildings are occupied by people carrying on the business of bankers, brokers, lawyers, real estate, and many other kinds of business, aided by many clerks, messengers, and other employés. Upon the assumption of the validity of this act under review, it is not possible to say that an act, prohibiting lawyers' or bank clerks, or others, from contracting to labor for their employers more than eight hours a day, would be invalid. It might be said that it is unhealthy to work more than that number of hours in an apartment lighted by artificial light during the working hours of the day; that the occupation of the bank clerk, the lawyer's clerk, the real estate clerk, or the broker's clerk in such offices is therefore unhealthy, and the legislature in its paternal wisdom must, therefore, have the right to legislate on the subject of and to limit the hours for such labor, and if it exercises that power and its validity be questioned it is sufficient to say, it has reference to the public health; it has reference to the health of the employés condemned to labor day after day in buildings where the sun never shines; it is a health law, and therefore it is valid, and cannot be questioned by the courts.

It is also urged, pursuing the same line of argument, that it is to the interest of the State that its population should be strong and robust, and therefore any legislation which may be said to tend to make people healthy must be valid as health laws, enacted under the police power. If this be a valid argument and a justification for this kind of legislation, it follows that the protection of the Federal Constitution from undue interference with liberty of person and freedom of contract is visionary, wherever the law is sought to be justified as a valid exercise of the police power. Scarcely any law but might find

shelter under such assumptions, and conduct, properly so called, as well as contract, would come under the restrictive sway of the legislature. Not only the hours of employés but the hours of employers, could be regulated, and doctors, lawyers, scientists, all professional men, as well as athletes and artisans, could be forbidden to fatigue their brains and bodies by prolonged hours of exercise, lest the fighting strength of the State be impaired. We mention these extreme cases because the contention is extreme. We do not believe in the soundness of the views which uphold this law. On the contrary, we think that such a law as this, although passed in the assumed exercise of the police power, and as relating to the public health, or the health of the employés named, is not within that power, and is invalid. The act is not, within any fair meaning of the term, a health law, but is an illegal interference with the rights of individuals, both employers and employés, to make contracts regarding labor upon such terms as they may think best, or which they may agree upon with the other parties to such contracts. Statutes of the nature of that under review, limiting the hours in which grown and intelligent men may labor to earn their living, are mere meddlesome interferences with the rights of the individual, and they are not saved from condemnation by the claim that they are passed in the exercise of the police power and upon the subject of the health of the individual whose rights are interfered with, unless there be some fair ground, reasonable in and of itself, to say that there is material danger to the public health or to the health of the employés, if the hours of labor are not curtailed. If this be not clearly the case the individuals, whose rights are thus made the subject of legislative interference, are under the protection of the Federal Constitution regarding their liberty of contract as well as of person; and the legislature of the State has no power to limit their right as proposed in this statute. All that it could properly do has been done by it with regard to the conduct of bakeries, as provided for in the other sections of the act, above set forth. These several sections provide for the inspection of the premises where the bakery is carried on, with regard to furnishing proper wash-rooms and water-closets, apart from the bake-room, also with regard to providing proper drainage, plumbing and painting; the sections, in addition, provide for the height of the ceiling, the cementing or tiling of floors, where necessary in the opinion of the factory inspector, and for other things of that nature; alterations are also provided for and are to be made where necessary in the opinion of the inspector, in order to comply with the provisions of the statute. These various sections may be wise and valid regulations, and they certainly go to the full extent of providing for the cleanliness and the healthiness, so far as possible, of the quarters in which bakeries are to be conducted. Adding to all these requirements, a prohibition to enter into any contract of labor in a bakery for more than a certain number of hours a week is, in our judgment, so wholly beside the matter of a proper, reasonable and fair provision, as to run counter to that liberty of person and of free contract provided for in the Federal Constitution. . . .

It is manifest to us that the limitation of the hours of labor as provided for in this section of the statute under which the indictment was found, and the plaintiff in error convicted, has no such direct relation to and no such substantial effect upon the health of the employé, as to justify us in regarding the section as really a health law. It seems to us that the real object and purpose were simply to regulate the hours of labor between the master and his employés (all being men, *sui juris*), in a private business, not dangerous in any degree to morals or in any real and substantial degree, to the health of the employés. Under such circumstances the freedom of master and employé to contract with each other in relation to their employment, and in defining the same, cannot be prohibited or interfered with, without violating the Federal Constitution.

The judgment of the Court of Appeals of New York as well as that of the Supreme Court and of the County Court of Oneida County must be reversed and the case remanded to the County Court for further proceedings not inconsistent with this opinion.

Reversed.

Mr. Justice Harlan, with whom Mr. Justice White and Mr. Justice Day concurred, dissenting.

While this court has not attempted to mark the precise boundaries of what is called the police power of the State, the existence of the power has been uniformly recognized, both by the Federal and state courts.

All the cases agree that this power extends at least to the protection of the lives, the health and the safety of the public against the injurious exercise by any citizen of his own rights.

In *Patterson* v. *Kentucky*, 97 U.S. 501, after referring to the general principle that rights given by the Constitution cannot be impaired by state legislation of any kind, this court said: "It [this court] has, nevertheless, with marked distinctness and uniformity, recognized the necessity, growing out of the fundamental conditions of civil society, of upholding state police regulations which were enacted in good faith, and had appropriate and direct connection with that protection to life, health, and property which each State owes to her citizens." So in *Barbier* v. *Connolly*, 113 U.S. 27: "But neither the [14th] Amendment—broad and comprehensive as it is—nor any other Amendment, was designed to interfere with the power of the State, sometimes termed its police power, to prescribe regulations to promote the health, peace, morals, education, and good order of the people."

Speaking generally, the State in the exercise of its powers may not unduly interfere with the right of the citizen to enter into contracts that may be necessary and essential in the enjoyment of the inherent rights belonging to every one, among which rights is the right "to be free in the enjoyment of all his faculties; to be free to use them in all lawful ways; to live and work where he will; to earn his livelihood by any lawful calling; to pursue any livelihood or avocation." This was declared in *Allgeyer* v. *Louisiana,* 165 U.S. 578, 589. But in the same case it was conceded that the right to contract in relation to persons and property or to do business, within a State, may be "regulated and sometimes prohibited, when the contracts or business conflict with the policy of the State as contained in its statutes" (p. 591). . . .

Granting then that there is a liberty of contract which cannot be violated even under the sanction of direct legislative enactment, but assuming, as according to settled law we may assume, that such liberty of contract is subject to such regulations as the State may reasonably prescribe for the common good and the well-being of society, what are the conditions under which the judiciary may declare such regulations to be in excess of legislative authority and void? Upon this point there is no room for dispute; for the rule is universal that a legislative enactment, Federal or state, is never to be disregarded or held invalid unless it be, beyond question, plainly and palpably in excess of legislative power. In *Jacobson* v. *Massachusetts, supra,* we said that the power of the courts to review legislative action in respect of a matter affecting the general welfare exists *only* "when that which the legislature has done comes within the rule that if a statute purporting to have been enacted to protect the public health, the public morals or the public safety, has no real or substantial relation to those objects, or is, beyond all question, a plain, palpable invasion of rights secured by the fundamental law"—citing *Mugler* v. *Kansas,* 123 U.S. 623, 661; *Minnesota* v. *Barber,* 136 U.S. 313, 320; *Atkin* v. *Kansas,* 191 U.S. 207, 223. If there be doubt as to the validity of the statute, that doubt must therefore be resolved in favor of its validity, and the courts must keep their hands off, leaving the legislature to meet the responsibility for unwise legislation. If the end which the legislature seeks to accomplish be one to which its power extends, and if the means employed to that end, although not the wisest or best, are yet not plainly and palpably unauthorized by law, then the court cannot interfere. In other words, when the validity of a statute is questioned, the burden of proof, so to speak, is upon those who assert it to be unconstitutional. *McCulloch* v. *Maryland,* 4 Wheat. 316, 421.

Let these principles be applied to the present case. By the statute in question it is provided that, "No employé shall be required or permitted to work in a biscuit, bread or cake bakery or confectionery establishment more than sixty hours in any one week, or more than ten hours in any one day, unless for the purpose of making a shorter work day on the last day of the week; nor more hours in any one week than will make an average of ten hours per day for the number of days during such week in which such employé shall work."

It is plain that this statute was enacted in order to protect the physical well-being of those who work in bakery and confectionery establishments. It may be that the statute had its origin, in part, in the belief that employers and employés in such establishments were not upon an equal footing, and that the necessities of the latter often compelled them to submit to such exactions as unduly taxed their strength. Be this as it may, the statute must be taken as expressing the belief of the people of New York that, as a general rule, and in the case of the average man, labor in excess of sixty hours during a week in such establishments may endanger the health of those who thus labor. Whether or not this be wise legislation it is not the province of the court to inquire. Under our systems of government the courts are not concerned with the wisdom or policy of legislation. So that in determining the question of power to interfere with liberty of contract, the court may inquire whether the means devised by the State are germane to an end which may be lawfully accomplished and have a real or substantial relation to the protection of health, as involved in the daily work of the persons, male and female, engaged in bakery and confectionery establishments. But when this inquiry is entered upon I find it impossible, in view of common experience, to say that there is here no real or substantial relation between the means employed by the State and the end sought to be accomplished by its legislation. *Mugler* v. *Kansas, supra.* Nor can I say that the statute has no appropriate or direct connection with that protection to health which

each state owes to her citizens, *Patterson* v. *Kentucky, supra;* or that it is not promotive of the health of the employés in question, *Holden* v. *Hardy, Lawton* v. *Steele, supra;* or that the regulation prescribed by the State is utterly unreasonable and extravagant or wholly arbitrary, *Gundling* v. *Chicago, supra.* Still less can I say that the statute is, beyond question, a plain, palpable invasion of rights secured by the fundamental law. *Jacobson* v. *Massachusetts, supra.* Therefore I submit that this court will transcend its functions if it assumes to annul the statute of New York. It must be remembered that this statute does not apply to all kinds of business. It applies only to work in bakery and confectionery establishments, in which, as all know, the air constantly breathed by workmen is not as pure and healthful as that to be found in some other establishments or out of doors.

Professor Hirt in his treatise on the "Diseases of the Workers" has said: "The labor of the bakers is among the hardest and most laborious imaginable, because it has to be performed under conditions injurious to the health of those engaged in it. It is hard, very hard work, not only because it requires a great deal of physical exertion in an overheated workshop and during unreasonably long hours, but more so because of the erratic demands of the public, compelling the baker to perform the greater part of his work at night, thus depriving him of an opportunity to enjoy the necessary rest and sleep, a fact which is highly injurious to his health." Another writer says: "The constant inhaling of flour dust causes inflammation of the lungs and of the bronchial tubes. The eyes also suffer through this dust, which is responsible for the many cases of running eyes among the bakers. The long hours of toil to which all bakers are subjected produce rheumatism, cramps and swollen legs. The intense heat in the workshops induces the workers to resort to cooling drinks, which together with their habit of exposing the greater part of their bodies to the change in the atmosphere, is another source of a number of diseases of various organs. Nearly all bakers are pale-faced and of more delicate health than the workers of other crafts, which is chiefly due to their hard work and their irregular and unnatural mode of living, whereby the power of resistance against disease is greatly diminished. The average age of a baker is below that of other workmen; they seldom live over their fiftieth year, most of them dying between the ages of forty and fifty. During periods of epidemic diseases the bakers are generally the first to succumb to the disease, and the number swept away during such periods far exceeds the number of other crafts in comparison to the men employed in the respective industries. When, in 1720, the plague visited the city of Marseilles, France, every baker in the city succumbed to the epidemic, which caused considerable excitement in the neighboring cities and resulted in measures for the sanitary protection of the bakers."

In the Eighteenth Annual Report by the New York Bureau of Statistics of Labor it is stated that among the occupations involving exposure to conditions that interfere with nutrition is that of a baker (p. 52). In that Report it is also stated that "from a social point of view, production will be increased by any change in industrial organization which diminishes the number of idlers, paupers and criminals. Shorter hours of work, by allowing higher standards of comfort and purer family life, promise to enhance the industrial efficiency of the wage-working class—improved health, longer life, more content and greater intelligence and inventiveness" (p. 82).

Statistics show that the average daily working time among workingmen in different countries is, in Australia, 8 hours; in Great Britain, 9; in the United States, 9¾; in Denmark, 9¾; in Norway, 10; Sweden, France and Switzerland, 10½; Germany, 10¼; Belgium, Italy and Austria, 11; and in Russia, 12 hours.

We judicially know that the question of the number of hours during which a workman should continuously labor has been, for a long period, and is yet, a subject of serious consideration among civilized peoples, and by those having special knowledge of the laws of health. Suppose the statute prohibited labor in bakery and confectionery establishments in excess of eighteen hours each day. No one, I take it, could dispute the power of the State to enact such a statute. But the statute before us does not embrace extreme or exceptional cases. It may be said to occupy a middle ground in respect of the hours of labor. What is the true ground for the State to take between legitimate protection, by legislation, of the public health and liberty of contract is not a question easily solved, nor one in respect of which there is or can be absolute certainty. There are very few, if any, questions in political economy about which entire certainty may be predicated. One writer on relation of the State to labor has well said: "The manner, occasion, and degree in which the State may interfere with the industrial freedom of its citizens is one of the most debatable and difficult questions of social science." Jevons, 33.

We also judicially know that the number of hours that should constitute a day's labor in particular occupations involving the physical strength and safety of workmen has been the subject of enactments by Congress and by nearly all of the

States. Many, if not most, of those enactments fix eight hours as the proper basis of a day's labor.

I do not stop to consider whether any particular view of this economic question presents the sounder theory. What the precise facts are it may be difficult to say. It is enough for the determination of this case, and it is enough for this court to know, that the question is one about which there is room for debate and for an honest difference of opinion. There are many reasons of a weighty, substantial character, based upon the experience of mankind, in support of the theory that, all things considered, more than ten hours' steady work each day, from week to week, in a bakery or confectionery establishment, may endanger the health, and shorten the lives of the workmen, thereby diminishing their physical and mental capacity to serve the State, and to provide for those dependent upon them.

If such reasons exist that ought to be the end of this case, for the State is not amenable to the judiciary, in respect of its legislative enactments, unless such enactments are plainly, palpably, beyond all question, inconsistent with the Constitution of the United States. We are not to presume that the state of New York has acted in bad faith. Nor can we assume that its legislature acted without due deliberation, or that it did not determine this question upon the fullest attainable information, and for the common good. We cannot say that the State has acted without reason nor ought we to proceed upon the theory that its action is a mere sham. Our duty, I submit, is to sustain the statute as not being in conflict with the Federal Constitution, for the reason—and such is an all-sufficient reason—it is not shown to be plainly and palpably inconsistent with that instrument. Let the State alone in the management of its purely domestic affairs, so long as it does not appear beyond all question that it has violated the Federal Constitution. This view necessarily results from the principle that the health and safety of the people of a State are primarily for the State to guard and protect.

I take leave to say that the New York statute, in the particulars here involved, cannot be held to be in conflict with the Fourteenth Amendment, without enlarging the scope of the Amendment far beyond its original purpose and without bringing under the supervision of this court matters which have been supposed to belong exclusively to the legislative departments of the several States when exerting their conceded power to guard the health and safety of their citizens by such regulations as they in their wisdom deem best. Health laws of every description constitute, said Chief Justice Marshall, a part of that mass of legislation which "embraces everything within the territory of a State, not surrendered to the General Government; all which can be most advantageously exercised by the States themselves." *Gibbons* v. *Ogden,* 9 Wheat. 1, 203. A decision that the New York statute is void under the Fourteenth Amendment will, in my opinion, involve consequences of a far-reaching and mischievous character; for such a decision would seriously cripple the inherent power of the States to care for the lives, health and well-being of their citizens. Those are matters which can be best controlled by the States. The preservation of the just powers of the States is quite as vital as the preservation of the powers of the General Government.

When this court had before it the question of the constitutionality of a statute of Kansas making it a criminal offense for a contractor for public work to permit or require his employés to perform labor upon such work in excess of eight hours each day, it was contended that the statute was in derogation of the liberty both of employés and employer. It was further contended that the Kansas statute was mischievous in its tendencies. This court, while disposing of the question only as it affected public work, held that the Kansas statute was not void under the Fourteenth Amendment. But it took occasion to say what may well be here repeated: "The responsibility therefor rests upon legislators, not upon the courts. No evils arising from such legislation could be more far-reaching than those that might come to our system of government if the judiciary, abandoning the sphere assigned to it by the fundamental law, should enter the domain of legislation, and upon grounds merely of justice or reason or wisdom annul statutes that had received the sanction of the people's representatives. We are reminded by counsel that it is the solemn duty of the courts in cases before them to guard the constitutional rights of the citizen against merely arbitrary power. That is unquestionably true. But it is equally true—indeed, the public interests imperatively demand—that legislative enactments should be recognized and enforced by the courts as embodying the will of the people, unless they are plainly and palpably, beyond all question, in violation of the fundamental law of the Constitution." *Atkin* v. *Kansas,* 191 U.S. 207, 223.

The judgment in my opinion should be affirmed.

Mr. Justice Holmes dissenting.

I regret sincerely that I am unable to agree with the judgment in this case, and that I think it my duty to express my dissent.

This case is decided upon an economic theory which a large part of the country does not entertain. If it were a question whether I agreed with that theory I should desire to study it further and long before making up my mind. But I do not conceive that to be my duty, because I strongly believe that my agreement or disagreement has nothing to do with the right of a majority to embody their opinions in law. It is settled by various decisions of this court that state constitutions and state laws may regulate life in many ways which we as legislators might think as injudicious or if you like as tyrannical as this, and which equally with this interfere with the liberty to contract. Sunday laws and usury laws are ancient examples. A more modern one is the prohibition of lotteries. The liberty of the citizen to do as he likes so long as he does not interfere with the liberty of others to do the same, which has been a shibboleth for some well-known writers, is interfered with by school laws, by the Post Office, by every state or municipal institution which takes his money for purposes thought desirable, whether he likes it or not. The Fourteenth Amendment does not enact Mr. Herbert Spencer's Social Statics. The other day we sustained the Massachusetts vaccination law. *Jacobson* v. *Massachusetts,* 197 U.S. 11. United States and state statutes and decisions cutting down the liberty to contract by way of combination are familiar to this court. *Northern Securities Co.* v. *United States,* 193 U.S. 197. Two years ago we upheld the prohibition of sales of stock on margins or for future delivery in the constitution of California. *Otis* v. *Parker,* 187 U.S. 606. The decision sustaining an eight hour law for miners is still recent. *Holden* v. *Hardy,* 169 U.S. 366. Some of these laws embody convictions or prejudices which judges are likely to share. Some may not. But a constitution is not intended to embody a particular economic theory, whether of paternalism and the organic relation of the citizen to the State or of *laissez faire.* It is made for people of fundamentally differing views, and the accident of our finding certain opinions natural and familiar or novel and even shocking ought not to conclude our judgment upon the question whether statutes embodying them conflict with the Constitution of the United States.

General propositions do not decide concrete cases. The decision will depend on a judgment or intuition more subtle than any articulate major premise. But I think that the proposition just stated, if it is accepted, will carry us far toward the end. Every opinion tends to become a law. I think that the word liberty in the Fourteenth Amendment is perverted when it is held to prevent the natural outcome of a dominant opinion, unless it can be said that a rational and fair man necessarily would admit that the statute proposed would infringe fundamental principles as they have been understood by the traditions of our people and our law. It does not need research to show that no such sweeping condemnation can be passed upon the statute before us. A reasonable man might think it a proper measure on the score of health. Men whom I certainly could not pronounce unreasonable would uphold it as a first instalment of a general regulation of the hours of work. Whether in the latter aspect it would be open to the charge of inequality I think it unnecessary to discuss.

PART FOUR　Consolidating Culture?

Dr. W. E. B. DuBois. Library of Congress, Prints and Photographs Division, LC-DIG-ggbain-07435.

Booker T. Washington. Library of Congress, Prints and Photographs Division, LC-USZ62-119898.

DURING THE LATE nineteenth and early twentieth centuries, increases in immigration, particularly from countries outside Great Britain and northern Europe, combined with urbanization and greater geographical mobility to bring pressure in the United States for greater cultural assimilation. Increased diversity and increased, and more frequent, contact among diverse groups, coupled with the inherent stresses of changing economic and social relations, caused social tension. Moreover, the emancipation of African Americans in the South, along with the conflict between land-hungry settlers and Native Americans, brought fear and resentment throughout the United States. Public responses varied from increased emphasis on ideological conformity to overt racial segregation. These public responses would help spawn and shape reform movements as well as attempts to resist changes in traditional cultural arrangements.

Twelfth Annual Report of the Massachusetts State School Board,
   Horace Mann, 1848

*Horace Mann (1796–1859) was largely self-educated as a youth but achieved distinction in
a college career at Brown University, in the practice of law, as secretary to the Massachusetts state board of education, and as president of Antioch College. Mann served in both
the Massachusetts and federal legislatures. While secretary to the Massachusetts board
of education he wrote a series of annual reports arguing for and defending establishment
of government supported "common schools," as well as other educational reforms. Mann
particularly argued for nonsectarian schools that would teach a common morality and
train young people in the habits he believed necessary for maintenance of a democratic
republic.*

Twelfth Annual Report of the Massachusetts State School Board

Horace Mann

MORAL EDUCATION

Moral education is a primal necessity of social existence. The unrestrained passions of men are not only homicidal, but suicidal; and a community without a conscience would soon extinguish itself. Even with a natural conscience, how often has Evil triumphed over Good! From the beginning of time, Wrong has followed Right, as the shadow the substance. As the relations of men became more complex, and the business of the world more extended, new opportunities and new temptations for wrong-doing have been created. With the endearing relations of parent and child, came also the possibility of infanticide and parricide; and the first domestic altar that brothers ever reared was stained with fratricidal blood. Following close upon the obligations to truth, came falsehood and perjury, and closer still upon the duty of obedience to the Divine law, came disobedience. With the existence of private relations between men, came fraud; and with the existence of public relations between nations, came aggression, war, and slavery. And so, just in proportion as the relations of life became more numerous, and the interests of society more various and manifold, the range of possible and of actual offences has been continually enlarging. As for every new substance there may be a new shadow, so for every new law there may be a new transgression. No form of the precious metals has ever been used which dishonest men have not counterfeited; and no kind of artificial currency has ever been legalized which

rogues have not forged. The government sees the evils that come from the use of intoxicating drinks, and prohibits their sale; but unprincipled men pander to depraved appetites, and gather a harvest of dishonest profits. Instead of licensing lotteries, and deriving a revenue from the sale of tickets, the State forbids the mischievous traffic; but while law-abiding men disdain to practise an illicit trade, knavish brokers, by means of the prohibition itself, secure a monopoly of the sales, and pocket the infamous gain. The government imposes duties on imported goods; smugglers evade the law, and bring goods into the country clandestinely; or perjurers swear to false invoices, and escape the payment of duty, and thus secure to themselves the double advantage of increased sales, and enhanced profits upon what is sold. Science prepares a new medicine to heal or alleviate the diseases of men; crime adulterates it, or prepares, as a substitute, some cheap poison that resembles it, and can be sold instead of it. A benefactor of the race discovers an agent which has the marvellous power to suspend consciousness, and take away the susceptibility of pain; a villain uses it to rob men or pollute women. Houses are built; the incendiary burns them, that he may purloin the smallest portion of their goods. The press is invented to spread intelligence; but libellers use it to give wings to slander. And, so, throughout all the infinitely complex and ramified relations of society, wherever there is a right there may be a wrong; and wherever a law is made to repress the wrong, it may be evaded by artifice or overborne by violence. In fine, all means and laws designed to repress injustice and crime, give occasion to new injustice and crime. For every lock that is made, a false key is made to pick it; and for every Paradise that is created, there is a Satan who would scale its walls.

Nor does this view of the subject exhibit the scope and multitude of the transgressions that may be committed. To represent the range and compass of possible violations, every law that exists must be multiplied by a high power. When the whole family of mankind consisted of but two persons, there could be only two offenders. But, now, when the race has increased to millions and hundreds of millions, the laws may be broken by millions and hundreds of millions,—an increased number of transgressors of an increased number of laws. The multitude, then, of possible violations of law, is terrific to the imagination; even the actual violations are sufficient to make our best civilization look but little better than barbarism.

But the above outline, whose vast circumference may be filled up by the commission of crimes against positive law, embraces not a tithe of possible transgressions. Every law in the statute-book might be obeyed, so as to leave no penalty to be awarded by the courts, or inflicted by executive officers, and yet myriads of private vices, too subtle and intangible for legislative enactments, and too undefinable to be dealt with by the tribunals of justice, might still embitter all domestic and social relations, and leave nothing in life worth living for. Were the greater plagues of public crime and open violence to be stayed, still the lesser ones might remain;—like the plagues of Egypt, they might invade every house, penetrate to every chamber, corrupt the water in the fountains, and the bread in the kneading-troughs, and turn the dust into loathsome life, so that the plague of hail, and the plague of darkness, might seem to be blessings in the comparison. In offences, against what are usually called the "minor morals,"—against propriety, against decency, against the domestic relations, and against good neighborhood, as they are illustrated and enjoined by the example of Christ, the precepts of the Gospel, and the perfect law of love;—here is a vast region where offences may grow, and where they do grow, thick-standing and rankly luxuriant.

Against these social vices, in all ages of the world, the admonitions of good men have been directed. The moralist has exposed their deformity in his didactic page; the satirist has chastised them in his pungent verse; the dramatist has held them up to ridicule on the mimic stage; and, to some extent, the Christian minister has exhibited their gross repugnancy to the character of a disciple of Jesus. Still they continue to exist; and,—to say nothing of heathen nations,—the moral condition of all Christendom is, in this respect, like the physical condition of one of the nations that compose it;—that extraordinary people, I mean, whose dwellings, whose flocks, whose agriculture, whose merchandise, and who, themselves, are below the level of the ocean; and against them, at all times, this ocean rages, and lifts itself up; and whenever or wherever it can find a breach, or make one, it rushes in, and overwhelms men and their possessions in one common inundation. Even so, like a weltering flood, do immoralities and crimes break over all moral barriers, destroying and profaning the securities and the sanctities of life. Now, how best shall this deluge be repelled? What mighty power, or combination of powers, can prevent its inrushing, or narrow the sweep of its ravages?

The race has existed long enough to try many experiments for the solution of this greatest problem ever submitted to its hands; and the race has experimented, without stint of time or circumscription of space, to mar or modify legitimate results. Mankind have tried despotisms, monarchies, and republican forms of government. They have tried the extremes of anarchy and of autocracy. They have tried Draconian codes of law; and, for the lightest offences, have extinguished the life of the offender. They have established theological standards, claiming for them the sanction of Divine authority, and the attributes of a perfect and infallible law; and then they have imprisoned, burnt, massacred, not individuals only, but whole communities at a time, for not bowing down to idols which ecclesiastical authority had set up. These and other great systems of measures have been adopted as barriers against error and guilt; they have been extended over empires, prolonged through centuries, and administered with terrible energy; and yet the great ocean of vice and crime overleaps every embankment, pours down upon our heads, saps the foundations under our feet, and sweeps away the securities of social order, of property, liberty, and life.

At length, these experiments have been so numerous, and all of them have terminated so disastrously, that a body of men has risen up, in later times, powerful in influence, and not inconsiderable in numbers, who, if I may use a mercantile phrase, would abandon the world as a total loss;—who mock at the idea of its having a benevolent or even an intelligent Author or Governor; and who, therefore, would give over the race to the dominion of chance, or to that of their own licentious passions, whose rule would be more fatal than chance.

But to all doubters, disbelievers, or despairers, in human progress, it may still be said, there is one experiment which has never yet been tried. It is an experiment which, even before its inception, offers the highest authority for its ultimate success. Its formula is intelligible to all; and it is as legible as though written in starry letters on an azure sky. It is expressed in these few and simple words:— *"Train up a child in the way he should go, and when he is old he will not depart from it."* This declaration is positive. If the conditions are complied with, it makes no provision for a failure. Though pertaining to morals, yet, if the terms of the direction are observed, there is no more reason to doubt the result, than there would be in an optical or a chemical experiment.

But this experiment has never yet been tried. Education has never yet been brought to bear with one hundredth part of its potential force, upon the natures of children, and, through them, upon the character of men, and of the race. In all the attempts to reform mankind which have hitherto been made, whether by changing the frame of government, by aggravating or softening the severity of the penal code, or by substituting a government-created, for a God-created religion;—in all these attempts, the infantile and youthful mind, its amenability to influences, and the enduring and self-operating character of the influences it receives, have been almost wholly unrecognized. Here, then, is a new agency, whose powers are but just beginning to be understood, and whose mighty energies, hitherto, have been but feebly invoked; and yet, from our experience, limited and imperfect as it is, we do know that, far beyond any other earthly instrumentality, it is comprehensive and decisive.

Reformatory efforts, hitherto made, have been mainly expended upon the oaken-fibred hardihood and incorrigibleness of adult offenders; and not upon the flexibleness and ductility of youthful tendencies. Rulers have forgotten that, though a giant's arm cannot bend a tree of a century's growth, yet the finger of an infant could have given direction to its germ. When a man has invested fifty thousand dollars in the business of importing ardent spirits into the country, it often does little more than to enrage him, to point out the different results between such an investment, and the investment of the same sum in whale ships; where, besides its own permanent value, it will soon add fifty thousand dollars more to the actual wealth of the community. Show the distiller how he changes the life-sustaining fruits of the earth into a physical and moral poison, and what a deluge of destruc-

tion he is sending forth over society, and his blood will boil hardly less fiercely than his accursed caldrons; but who will be rash enough to say of any child in the land;—who will be rash enough to say of any man now engaged in the business of promoting and spreading intemperance, and visiting another generation with all its calamities;—who will dare say, of any of them, that the nature and consequences of this direful occupation might not have been so vividly depicted to the imagination, and so clearly explained to the conscience, during the years of childhood, that any child would sooner think of getting a living by counterfeiting money than by engaging in the traffic? Would any child, on whose heart the horrors and atrocities of the slave-trade had made their natural impression, before his arrival at the age of fourteen years, ever connect himself with slavery afterwards? Were a child taught the dignity, the healthfulness, and the advantages of voluntary labor, and the meanness of living upon the unrequited services of the weak and defenceless, could he ever bear to live a life of pampered indolence, secured to him by a hundred lives,—each as precious and as sacred, in the sight of Heaven, as his own,—of unpaid toil and irredeemable debasement? Did genius pour out its heart as fervently to depict the calamities of war, as it has done to blazon forth what is called military glory, would not children be led to abhor all unnecessary wars as much more than they abhor murder, as the destruction of an army is greater than that of a single murderer? If the schools were earnestly to teach children that office and honor are not synonymous terms, and that the only value of any office consists in its opening a wider sphere for useful exertion, should we find so many men renouncing usefulness and forfeiting honor for the acquisition of office? If wealth were not forever talked of before children as among the chief prizes of life, should we see such throngs making haste to be rich, with all the attendant consequences of fraud and dishonor? Indeed, so decisive is the effect of early training upon adult habits and character, that numbers of the most able and experienced teachers,—those who have had the best opportunities to become acquainted with the errors and the excellences of children, their waywardness and their docility,—have unanimously declared it to be their belief, that, if all the children in the community, from the age of four years to that of sixteen, could be brought within the reformatory and elevating influences of good schools, the dark host of private vices and public crimes, which now embitter domestic peace and stain the civilization of the age, might, in ninety-nine cases in every hundred, be banished from the world.* When Christ taught his disciples to pray, "Thy kingdom come, thy will be done, *on earth* as it is done in heaven," did he teach them to pray for what shall never come to pass[?] And if this consummation is ever to be realized, is it to be by some mighty, sudden, instantaneous revolution, effected by a miracle; or is it to be produced gradually by that Providence which uses human agents as its instruments?

Were we to hear that some far-off land had been discovered, over which the tempest of war had never swept; where institutions of learning and religion were reverenced, and their ministers held in the foremost rank of honor; where falsehood, detraction, and perjury were never uttered; where neither intemperance, nor the guilty knowledge how to prepare its means, nor the guilty agents to diffuse them, were ever known; where all the obligations, growing out of the domestic relations, were sacredly kept; where office always sought the wisest and best men for incumbents, and never failed to find them; where witnesses were true, and jurors just, (for we can hardly conceive of a state of society upon earth so perfect as to exclude all differences of opinion about rights;) in fine, where all men were honest in their dealings, and exemplary in their lives,—with the exception of here and there an individual, who, from the rareness of his appearance, would be regarded almost as a monster;—were we to hear of such a realm, who, that loves peace and the happiness that comes from security and order, would not wish to escape from the turmoil and the violence, the rancor and the mean ambitions, of our present sphere, and go there to dwell and to die? And yet, it is the opinion of our most intelligent, dispassionate, and experienced teachers, that we can, in the course of two or three generations, and through the instrumentality of good teachers and good schools, superinduce, substantially, such a state of society upon the present one; and this, too, without any miracle, without any extraordinary sacrifices, or costly effort; but only by working our existing Common School system with such a degree of vigor as can easily be put forth, and at such an expense as even the poorest community can easily bear. If the leaders of society,—those whose law-giving eloquence determines what statutes shall be enacted by the Legislature, or those who speak for the common heart in self-constituted

* As authority for this assertion, see Eleventh Annual Report of the Secretary of the Board of Education, where the letters of distinguished and experienced teachers, residing in different parts of the country, and acquainted with all classes of children, are published.

assemblies, or those who shape popular opinion through the public press, or in the private intercourse of life,—if these are not yet prepared to have faith in the reformatory power of an early and wise training for the young, the fact only shows and measures the extent of the work which teachers and educationists have yet to perform. If men decline to coöperate with us, because uninspired by our living faith, then the arguments, the labors, and the results, which will create this faith, are a preliminary step in our noble work.

Is any high-minded, exemplary, and conscientious man disposed to believe that this substantial extirpation of social vices and crimes, (according to the testimony of the witnesses above referred to,) is a utopian idea,—is more than we have any reason to expect while human nature remains as it is, let me use the *ad hominem* argument to refute him. Let me refer him to himself, and ask him why the same influences which have saved him from gaming, intemperance, dissoluteness, falsehood, dishonesty, violence, and their kindred offences, and have made him a man of sobriety, frugality, and probity;— why the same influences which have saved him from ruin, might not, if brought to bear upon others, save them also? So far as human instrumentalities are concerned, we have abundant means for surrounding every child in the State with preservative and moral influences, as extensive and as efficient as those under which the present industrious, worthy, and virtuous members of the community were reared. And, as to all those things, in regard to which we are directly dependent upon the Divine favor, have we not the promise, explicit and unconditional, that the men SHALL NOT depart from the way in which they should go, if the children are trained up in it? It has been overlooked, that this promise is not restricted to parents; but seems to be addressed indiscriminately to all,—whether parents, communities, states, or mankind.

RELIGIOUS EDUCATION

But, it will be said that this grand result, in Practical Morals, is a consummation of blessedness that can never be attained without Religion; and that no community will ever be religious, without a Religious Education. Both these propositions, I regard as eternal and immutable truths. Devoid of religious principles and religious affections, the race can never fall so low but that it may sink still lower; animated and sanctified by them, it can never rise so high but that it may ascend still higher. And is it not at least as presumptuous to expect that mankind will attain to the knowledge of truth, without being instructed in truth, and without that general expansion and development of faculty which will enable them to recognize and comprehend truth, in any other department of human interest, as in the department of religion? No creature of God, of whom we have any knowledge, has such a range of moral oscillation as a human being. He may despise privileges, and turn a deaf ear to warnings and instructions, such as evil spirits may never have known, and therefore be more guilty than they; or, ascending through temptation and conflict, along the radiant pathway of duty, he may reach the sublimest heights of happiness, and may there experience the joys of a contrast, such as ever-perfect beings can never feel. And can it be that our nature, in this respect, is taken out of the law that governs it in every other respect;—the law, namely, that the teachings which supply it with new views, and the training that leads it to act in conformity with those views, are ineffective and nugatory?

Indeed, the whole frame and constitution of the human soul show, that if man be not a religious being, he is among the most deformed and monstrous of all possible existences. His propensities and passions need the fear of God, as a restraint from evil; and his sentiments and affections need the love of God, as a condition and preliminary to every thing worthy of the name of happiness. Without a capability or susceptibility, therefore, of knowing and reverencing his Maker and Preserver, his whole nature is a contradiction and a solecism;—it is a moral absurdity,—as strictly so, as a triangle with but two sides, or a circle without a circumference, is a mathematical absurdity. The man, indeed, of whatever denomination, or kindred, or tongue, he may be, who believes that the human race, or any nation, or any individual in it, can attain to happiness, or avoid misery, without religious principle and religious affections, must be ignorant of the capacities of the human soul, and of the highest attributes in the nature of man. We know, from the very structure and functions of our physical organization, that all the delights of the appetites and of the grosser instincts are evanescent and perishing. All bodily pleasures over-indulged, become pains. Abstemiousness is the stern condition of prolonged enjoyment,—a condition that balks desire at the very moment when it is most craving. Did the fields teem, and the forests bend, and the streams flow, with the most exquisite delicacies, how small the proportion of our time in which we could luxuriate in their sweets, without satiety and disgust! Unchastened by temperance, the richest earthly banquets stimulate, only to end in loathing. Perpetual self-restraint, on the one side, or intolerable

pains, on the other, is the law of all our animal desires; and it may well be questioned, which are the sharper sufferings,—the fiercest pangs of hunger and of thirst, or the agonizing diseases that form the fearful retinue of epicurism and Bacchanalian indulgence. Were the pleasures of sense the only pleasures we could enjoy, immortality might well be scoffed at as worthless, and annihilation welcomed; for, if another Eden were created around us, filled with all that could gratify the appetite, or regale the sense, and were the whole range and command of its embowering shades and clustering fruits bestowed upon us, still, with our present natures, we should feel intellectual longings, which not all the objects of sight and of sense could appease; and luxuries would sate the palate, and beauties pall upon the eye, in the absence of objects to quicken and stimulate the sterner energies of the mind.

The delights of the intellect are of a far nobler order than those of the senses; but even these have no power to fill up the capacities of an immortal mind. The strongest intellect tires. It cannot sustain an ever-upward wing. Even in minds of Olympian vastness and vigor, there must be seasons for relaxation and repose;—intervals, when the wearied faculties, mounted upon the topmost of all their achievements, must stop in their ascending career, to review the distance they have traversed, and to replenish their energies for an onward flight. And, although, in the far-off cycles of eternity, the stature of the intellect should become lofty as an archangel's; although its powers of comprehension should become so vast, and its intuitions so penetrating, that it could learn the history of a planet in a day, and master, at a single lesson, all the sciences that belong to a system of stars; still, I repeat, that, with our present nature, we should be conscious of faculties unoccupied, and restless, yea, tormented with a sense of privation and loss,—like lungs in a vacuum gasping vainly for breath, or like the eye in darkness straining to catch some glimmering of light. Without sympathy, without spiritual companionship with other beings, without some Being, all-glorious in his perfections, whom the spirit could commune with and adore, it would be a mourner and a wanderer amid all the splendors of the universe. Through the lone realms of immensity would it fly, calling for love, as a mother calls for her departed first-born, but its voice would return to it in echoes of mockery. Nay, though the intellect of man should become as effulgent as the stars amid which he might walk, yet sympathetic and devout affections alone can fertilize the desolations of the heart. Love is as necessary to the human heart as knowledge is to the mind; and infinite knowledge can never supply the place of infinite good. The universe, grand, glorious, and beautiful as it is, can be truly enjoyed only through the worship as well as the knowledge of the great Being that created it. Among people, where there is no true knowledge of God, the errors, superstitions, and sufferings of a false religion, always rush in to fill the vacuum.

There is not a faculty nor a susceptibility in the nature of man, from the lightning-like intuitions that make him akin to the cherubim, or the fire and fervor of affection that assimilate him to seraphic beings, down to the lowest appetites and desires by which he holds brotherhood with beast and reptile and worm;—there is not one of them all, that will ever be governed by its proper law, or enjoy a full measure of the gratification it was adapted to feel, without a knowledge of the true God, without a sense of acting in harmony with His will, and without spontaneous effusions of gratitude for His goodness. Convictions and sentiments, such as these, can alone supply the vacuity in the soul of man, and fill with significance and loveliness what would otherwise be a blank and hollow universe.

How limited and meagre, too, would be the knowledge which should know all things else, but still be ignorant of the self-existent Author of all! What is the exquisite beauty of flowers, of foliage, or of plumage, if we know nothing of the Great Limner who has painted them, and blended their colors with such marvellous skill? So the profundity of all science is shallowness, if we know nothing of the Eternal Mind that projected all sciences, and made their laws so exact and harmonious, that all the objects in an immensity can move onward throughout an eternity, without deviation or error. Even the visible architecture of the heavens, majestic and refulgent as it is, dwindles and glooms into littleness and darkness, in the presence of the Great Builder, who "of old laid the foundation of the earth," and "meted out heaven with a span." Among all the objects of knowledge, the Author of knowledge is infinitely the greatest; and the microscopic animalcule, which, by a life of perseverance, has circumnavigated a drop of water, or the tiny insect which has toiled and climbed, until it has at last reached the highest peak of a grain of sand, knows proportionally more of the height and depth and compass of planetary spaces, than the philosopher who has circuited all other knowledge, but is still ignorant of God. In the acquisition of whatever art, or in the pursuit of whatever science, there is a painful sense of incompleteness and imperfection, while we remain untaught in any great department known to belong to it. And so, in the development

and culture of the human soul, we are conscious not merely of the want of symmetry, but of gross disfigurement and mutilation, when the noblest and most enduring part of an appropriate development and culture is wanting. In merely an artistical point of view, to be presented with the torso of Hercules, or with the truncated body of Minerva, when we were expecting to behold the fulness of their majestic proportions, would be less painful and shocking, than a system of human culture from which religious culture should be omitted.

So, too, if the subject be viewed in relation to all the purer and loftier affections and susceptibilities of the human soul, the results are the same. If, in surveying the highest states of perfection which the character of man has ever yet reached upon earth, we select, from among the whole circle of our personal or historical acquaintance, those who are adorned with the purest quality and the greatest number of excellences, as the objects of our most joyful admiration and love; why should not the soul be lifted into sublimer exstasies, and into raptures proportionately more exalted and enduring, if it could be raised to the contemplation of Him, whose "name alone is excellent"? If we delight in exhibitions of power, why should we pass heedlessly by the All-powerful? If human hearts are touched with deeds of mercy, there is One whose tender mercies are over all His works. If we reverence wisdom, there is such perfect wisdom on high, that that of angels becomes "folly" in its presence. If we love the sentiment of love, has not the Apostle told us that God is Love? There are many endearing objects upon earth from which the heart of man may be sundered; but he only is bereaved of all things who is bereaved of his Father in heaven.

I here place the argument, in favor of a religious education for the young, upon the most broad and general grounds; purposely leaving it to every individual to add, for himself, those auxiliary arguments which may result from his own peculiar views of religious truth. But such is the force of the conviction to which my own mind is brought by these general considerations, that I could not avoid regarding the man, who should oppose the religious education of the young, as an insane man; and were it proposed to debate the question between us, I should desire to restore him to his reason, before entering upon the discussion. If, suddenly summoned to eternity, I were able to give but one parting word of advice to my own children, or to the children of others;—if I were sinking beneath the wave, and had time to utter but one articulate breath, or were wasting away upon the death-bed, and had strength to make but one exhortation more,—that dying legacy should be, "Remember thy Creator in the days of thy youth."

I can, then, confess myself second to no one in the depth and sincerity of my convictions and desires, respecting the necessity and universality, both on abstract and on practical grounds, of a religious education for the young; and if I had stronger words at command, in which to embody these views, I would not fail to use them. But the question still remains, How shall so momentous an object be pursued? In the measures we adopt to give a religious education to others, shall we ourselves abide by the dictates of religion; or shall we do, as has almost universally been done, ever since the unhallowed union between church and state, under Constantine,—shall we seek to educate the community religiously, through the use of the most irreligious means?

On this subject, I propose to speak with freedom and plainness, and more at length than I should feel required to do, but for the peculiar circumstances in which I have been placed. It is matter of notoriety, that the views of the Board of Education,—and my own, perhaps still more than those of the Board,—on the subject of religious instruction in our Public Schools, have been subjected to animadversion. Grave charges have been made against us, that our purpose was to exclude religion; and to exclude that, too, which is the common exponent of religion,—the Bible,—from the Common Schools of the State; or, at least, to derogate from its authority, and destroy its influence in them. Whatever prevalence a suspicion of the truth of these imputations may have heretofore had, I have reason to believe that further inquiry and examination have done much to disabuse the too credulous recipients of so groundless a charge. Still, amongst a people so commendably sensitive on the subject of religion, as are the people of Massachusetts, any suspicion of irreligious tendencies, will greatly prejudice any cause, and, so far as any cause may otherwise have the power of doing good, will greatly impair that power.

It is known, too, that our noble system of Free Schools for the whole people, is strenuously opposed;—by a few persons in our own State, and by no inconsiderable numbers in some of the other states of this Union;—and that a rival system of "Parochial" or "Sectarian Schools," is now urged upon the public by a numerous, a powerful, and a well-organized body of men. It has pleased the advocates of this rival system, in various public addresses, in reports, and through periodicals devoted to their cause, to denounce our system as irreligious

and anti-Christian. They do not trouble themselves to describe what our system is, but adopt a more summary way to forestall public opinion against it, by using general epithets of reproach, and signals of alarm.

In this age of the world, it seems to me that no student of history, or observer of mankind, can be hostile to the precepts and the doctrines of the Christian religion, or opposed to any institutions which expound and exemplify them; and no man who thinks, as I cannot but think, respecting the enduring elements of character, whether public or private, can be willing to have his name mentioned while he is living, or remembered when he is dead, as opposed to religious instruction, and Bible instruction for the young. In making this final Report, therefore, I desire to vindicate my conduct from the charges that have been made against it; and, so far as the Board has been implicated in these charges, to leave my testimony on record for their exculpation. Indeed, on this point, the Board and myself must be justified or condemned together; for I do not believe they would have enabled me, by their annual reëlections, to carry forward any plan for excluding either the Bible or religious instruction from the schools; and had the Board required me to execute such a purpose, I certainly should have given them the earliest opportunity to appoint my successor. I desire, also, to vindicate the system with which I have been so long and so intimately connected, not only from the aspersion, but from the suspicion, of being an irreligious, or anti-Christian, or an un-Christian system. I know, full well, that it is unlike the systems which prevail in Great Britain, and in many of the continental nations of Europe, where the Established Church controls the education of the young, in order to keep itself established. But this is presumptive evidence in its favor, rather than against it.

All the schemes ever devised by governments, to secure the prevalence and permanence of religion among the people, however variant in form they may have been, are substantially resolvable into two systems. One of these systems holds the regulation and control of the religious belief of the people to be one of the functions of government, like the command of the army or the navy, or the establishment of courts, or the collection of revenues. According to the other system, religious belief is a matter of individual and parental concern; and, while the government furnishes all practicable facilities for the independent formation of that belief, it exercises no authority to prescribe, or coercion to enforce it. The former is the system, which, with very few exceptions, has prevailed throughout Christendom, for fifteen hundred years. Our own government is almost a solitary example among the nations of the earth, where freedom of opinion, and the inviolability of conscience, have been even theoretically recognized by the law.

The argument in behalf of a government-established religion, at the time when it was first used, was not without its plausibility; but the principle, once admitted, drew after it a train of the most appalling consequences. If religion is absolutely essential to the stability of the State, as well as to the present and future happiness of the subject; why, it was naturally asked, should not the government enforce it? And, if government is to enforce religion, it follows, as a necessary consequence, that it must define it?—for how can it enforce a duty which, being undefined, is uncertain? And, again, if government begins to define religion, it must define what it is not, as well as what it is; and while it upholds whatever is included in the definition, it must suppress and abolish whatever is excluded from it. The definition, too, must keep pace with speculation, and must take cognizance of all outward forms and observances; for, if speculation is allowed to run riot, and ceremonies and observances to spring up unrestrained, religion will soon elude control, emerge into new forms, and exercise, if it does not arrogate, a substantial independence. Both in regard to matters of form and of substance, all recusancy must be subdued, either by the deprivation of civil rights, or by positive inflictions; for the laws of man, not possessing, like the laws of God, a self-executing power, must be accompanied by some effective sanction, or they will not be obeyed. If a light penalty proves inadequate, a heavier one must follow,—the loss of civil privileges by disfranchisement, or of religious hopes by excommunication. If the non-conformist feels himself, by the aid of a higher power, to be secure against threats of future perdition, the civil magistrate has terrible resources at command, in this life,—imprisonment, scourging, the rack, the fagot, death. Should it ever be said that these are excessive punishments for exercising freedom of thought, and for allowing the heart to pour forth those sentiments of adoration to God, with which it believes God himself has inspired it?—the answer is always ready, that nothing is so terrible as the heresy that draws after it the endless wrath of the Omnipotent; and, therefore, that Smithfield fires, and Inquisitorial tortures, and *auto-de-fes*, and St. Bartholomews, are cheap offerings at the shrine of Truth;—nay, compared with the awful and endless consequences of a false faith, they are of less moment than the

slightest puncture of a nerve. And, assuming the truth of the theory, and the right of the government to secure faith by force, it surely would be better, infinitely better, that every hill-top should be lighted with the fires of Smithfield, and every day in the calendar should be a St. Bartholomew's, than that errors so fatal should go un-abolished.

In the council-hall of the Inquisition at Avignon, there still is, or lately was, to be seen, a picture of the good Samaritan painted upon the wall. The deed of mercy commemorated by this picture, was supposed to be the appropriate emblem of the Inquisitor's work. The humanity of pouring oil and wine into the wounds of the bleeding wayfarer who had fallen among thieves; the kindness of dismounting from his own beast, and setting the half-dead victim of violence upon it; and the generosity of purchasing comfort and restoration for him at an inn, were held to be copied and imitated, upon an ampler and a nobler scale, by the arrest of the heretic, by the violence that tore him from home and friends, and by the excruciating tortures that at last wrenched soul and body asunder. The priests who sentenced, and the familiars that turned the wheel, or lighted the fagot; or, with red-hot pincers, tore the living flesh from the quivering limbs, were but imitators of the good Samaritan, binding up moral wounds, and seeking to take a lost traveller to a place of recovery and eternal repose. So when the news of the massacre of St. Bartholomew's,—on which occasion, thirty thousand men, women, and children, were butchered at the stroke of a signal-bell,—reached Rome, the Pope and his cardinals ordained a Thanksgiving, that all true believers might rejoice together at so glorious an event, and that God might be honored for the pious hearts that designed and the benevolent hands that executed so Christian a deed. And, admitting their premises, surely they were right. Could communities, or even individuals, be rescued from endless perdition, at the price of a massacre or an *auto-de-fe,* the men who would wield the sword, or kindle the flame, would be only nobler Samaritans; and the picture upon the Inquisition walls at Avignon would be but an inadequate emblem of their soul-saving beneficence.

But in all the persecutions and oppressions ever committed in the name of religion, one point has been unwarrantably assumed;—namely, *that the faith of their authors was certainly and infallibly the true faith*. With the fewest exceptions, the advocates of all the myriad conflicting creeds that have ever been promulgated have held substantially the same language: *"Our"* faith we know to be true. For its truth, we have the evidence of our reason and our conscience; we have the Word of God in our hands, and we have the Spirit of God in our hearts, testifying to its truth."* The answer to this claim is almost too obvious to be mentioned. The advocates of hundreds and thousands of hostile creeds have placed themselves upon the same ground. Each has claimed the same proof from reason and conscience, the same external revelation from God, and the same inward light of His spirit. But if truth be *one,* and hence necessarily harmonious; if God be its author; and if the voice of God be not more dissonant than the tongues of Babel; then, at least all but one of the different forms of faith ever promulgated by human authority, so far as these forms conflict with each other, cannot have emanated from the Fountain of all truth. These faiths must have been more or less erroneous. The believers in them must have been more or less mistaken. Who, on an impartial survey of the whole, and a recollection of the confidence with which each one has been claimed to be infallibly true, shall dare to affirm that any one of them all is a perfect transcript of the perfect law, as it exists in the Divine Mind, *and that that one is his?*

But here arises a practical distinction, which the world has lost sight of. It is this: After seeking all possible light from within, from without, and from above, each man's belief is his own standard of truth; *but it is not the standard for any other man.* The believer is bound to live by his belief under all circumstances, in the face of all perils, and at the cost of any sacrifice. But his standard of truth is the standard for himself alone; *never for his neighbor.* That neighbor must have his own standard, which to him must be supreme. And the fact that each man is bound to follow his own best light and guidance is an express negation of any other man's right, and of any government's right, of forcible interference. Here is the dividing line. On one side, lie personal freedom and the recognition of freedom in others; on the other side, are intolerance, oppression, and all the wrongs and woes of persecution for conscience' sake. The hierarchs of the world have generally reversed this rule of duty. They have been more rigid in demanding that others should live according to their faith, than in living in accordance with it themselves.

Did the history of mankind show that there has been the most of virtue and piety in those nations where religion has been most rigorously enforced by law, the advocates of ecclesiastical domination would have a powerful argument

in favor of their measures of coercion. But the united and universal voice of history, observation, and experience, gives the argument to the other side. Nor is this surprising. Weak and fallible as human reason is, it was too much to expect that any mere man, even though aided by the light of a written revelation, would ever fathom the whole counsels of the Omnipotent and the Eternal. But the limitations and short-sightedness of men's reason did not constitute the only obstacle to their discovery of truth. All the passions and perversities of human nature conspired to prevent so glorious an achievement. The easily-acquired but awful power possessed by those who were acknowledged to be the chosen expounders of the Divine will, tempted men to set up a false claim to be the depositaries of God's purposes towards men, and the selected medium of his communication with them; and to this temptation erring mortals were fain to yield. Those who were supposed able to determine the destiny of the soul in the next world, came easily to control opinion, conduct, and fortune, in this. Hence they established themselves as a third power,—a power between the creature and the Creator,—not to facilitate the direct communion between man and his Maker, but to supersede it. They claimed to carry on the intercourse between heaven and earth, as merchants carry on commerce between distant nations, where the parties to the interchange never meet each other. The consequence soon was, that this celestial commerce degenerated into the basest and most mercenary traffic. The favors of heaven were bought and sold, like goods in the marketplace. Robbery purchased pardon and impunity by bribing the judge with a portion of the wealth it had plundered. The assassin bought permission to murder, and the incendiary to burn. A Price-Current of crime was established, in which sins were so graduated, as to meet the pecuniary ability of both rich and poor offenders. Licenses to violate the laws of God and man became luxuries, for which customers paid according to their several ability. Gold was the representative of all virtues as well as of all values. Under such a system, men lost their conscience, and women their virtue; for the right to commit all enormities was purchasable by money, and pardonable by grace;—save only the guilt of heresy; and the worst of all heresies consisted in men's worshipping the God of their fathers according to the dictates of their consciences.

Those religious exercises which consist in a communion of the soul with its Father in heaven, have been beautifully compared to telegraphic communications between distant friends; where, silent as thought, and swift as the lightning,

---

* Or, as I once heard the same sentiment expressed in the pulpit, from the lips of an eminent divine: "I am right, and I know I am right, and I know I know it."

each makes known to the other his joys and his desires, his affection and his fidelity, while the busy world around may know nought of their sacred communings. But as soon as hierarchies obtained control over men, they changed the channel of these communications between heaven and earth. An ecclesiastical bureau was established; and it was decreed that all the telegraphic wires should centre in that;—so that all the communications between man and his Maker should be subject to the inspection of its chiefs, and carried on through their agency alone. Thus, whether the soul had gratitude or repentance to offer to its God, or light or forgiveness to receive from on high, the whole intercourse, in both directions, must go through the government office, and there be subject to take such form; to be added to or subtracted from, as the ministers or managers, in possession of power, might deem to be expedient. Considering the nature of man, one may well suppose that many of the most precious of the messages were never forwarded; that others were perverted, or forged ones put in their place; and that, in some instances at least, the reception of fees was the main inducement to keep the machinery in operation.

Among the infinite errors and enormities, resulting from systems of religion devised by man, and enforced by the terrors of human government, have been those dreadful reactions, which have abjured all religion, spurned its obligations, and voted the Deity into non-existence. This extreme is, if possible, more fatal than that by which it was produced. Between these extremes, philanthropic and godly men have sought to find a medium which should avoid both the evils of ecclesiastical tyranny, and the greater evils of atheism. And this medium has at length been supposed to be found. It is promulgated in the great principle, that government should do all that it can to facilitate the acquisition of religious truth; but shall leave the decision of the question, what religious truth is, to the arbitrament, without human appeal, of each man's reason and conscience;—in other words, that government shall never, by the infliction of pains and penalties, or by the privation of rights or immunities, call such decision either into pre-judgment or into review. The formula in which the Constitution of Massachusetts expresses it, is in these words: "All religious sects and denominations, demeaning themselves peaceably and as good citizens, shall be equally under the protection of law; and no subordination of one sect or denomination to another shall ever be established by law."

The great truth recognized and expressed in these few words of our Constitution, is one which it has cost centuries of struggle and of suffering, and the shedding of rivers of blood, to attain; and he who would relinquish or forfeit it, virtually impetrates upon his fellow-men other centuries of suffering and the shedding of other rivers of blood. Nor are we as yet entirely removed from all danger of relapse. The universal interference of government in matters of religion, for so many centuries, has hardened the public mind to its usurpations. Men have become tolerant of intolerance; and among many nations of Christendom the common idea of Religious Freedom is satisfied by an exemption from fine and imprisonment for religious belief. They have not yet reached the conception of equal privileges and franchises for all. Doubtless the time will come when any interference, either by positive infliction or by legal disability, with another man's conscience in religious concernments, so long as he molests no one by the exercise of his faith, will be regarded as the crowning and supereminent act of guilt, which one human being can perpetrate against another. But this time is far from having yet arrived, and nations, otherwise equally enlightened, are at very different distances from this moral goal. The oppressed, on succeeding to power, are prone to become oppressors, in their turn; and to forget, as victors, the lessons, which, as victims, they had learned.

The Colonial, Provincial, and State history of Massachusetts shows by what slow degrees the rigor of our own laws was relaxed, as the day-star of religious freedom slowly arose after the long, black midnight of the Past. It was not, indeed, until a very recent period, that all vestige of legal penalty or coercion was obliterated from our statute book, and all sects and denominations were placed upon a footing of absolute equality in the eye of the law. Until the ninth day of April, 1821, no person, in Massachusetts, was eligible to the office of Governor, Lieutenant Governor, or Counsellor, or to that of senator or representative in the General Court, unless he would make oath to a belief in the particular form of religion adopted and sanctioned by the State. And until the eleventh day of November, 1833, every citizen was taxable, by the constitution and laws of the State, for the support of the *Protestant* religion, whether he were a Protestant, a Catholic, or a believer in any other faith. Nor was it until the tenth day of March, 1827 (St. 1826, ch. 143, § 7,) that it was made unlawful to use the Common Schools of the State as the means of proselyting children to a belief in the doctrines of particular sects, whether their parents believed in those doctrines or not.

All know the energetic tendency of men's minds to continue in a course to which long habit has accustomed them.

The same law is as true in regard to institutions administered by bodies of men, as in regard to individual minds. The doctrine of momentum, or head-way, belongs to metaphysics, as much as to mechanics. A statute may be enacted, and may even be executed by the courts, long before it is ratified and enforced by public opinion. Within the last few years, how many examples of this truth has the cause of temperance furnished! And such was the case, in regard to the law of 1827, prohibiting sectarian instruction in our Public Schools. It was not easy for committees, at once, to withdraw or to exclude the books, nor for teachers to renounce the habits, by which this kind of instruction had been given. Hence, more than ten years subsequent to the passage of that law, at the time when I made my first educational and official circuits over the State, I found books in the schools, as strictly and exclusively *doctrinal* as any on the shelves of a theological library. I heard teachers giving oral instruction, as strictly and purely *doctrinal,* as any ever heard from the pulpit, or from the professor's chair. And more than this: I have now in my possession, printed directions, given by committee men to teachers, enjoining upon them the use of a catechism, in school, which is wholly devoted to an exposition of the doctrines of one of the denominations amongst us. These directions bear date a dozen years subsequent to the prohibitory law, above referred to. I purposely forbear to intimate what doctrine or what denomination was *"favored,"* in the language of the law, by these means; because I desire to have this statement as impersonal as it can be.

After years of endurance, after suffering under misconstructions of conduct, and the imputation of motives, whose edge is sharper than a knife, it was, at my suggestion, and by making use of materials which I had laboriously collected, that the Board made its Eighth Annual Report;—a document said to be the ablest argument in favor of the use of the Bible in Schools, any where to be found. This Report had my full concurrence. Since its appearance, I have always referred to it, as explanatory of the views of the Board, and as setting forth the law of a wise Commonwealth and the policy of a Christian people. Officially and unofficially, publicly and privately, in theory and in practice, my course has always been in conformity with its doctrines. And I avail myself of this, the last opportunity which I may ever have, to say, in regard to all affirmations or intimations, that I have ever attempted to exclude religious instruction from school, or to exclude the Bible from school, or to impair the force of that volume, arising out of itself, are now, and always have been, without substance or semblance of truth.

But it may still be said, and it is said, that, however sincere, or however religiously disposed, the advocates of our school system may be, still the character of the system is not to be determined by the number, nor by the sincerity of its defenders, but by its own inherent attributes; and that, if judged by these attributes, it is, in fact and in truth, an irreligious, an un-Christian, and an anti-Christian system. Having devoted the best part of my life to the promotion of this system, and believing it to be the only system which ought to prevail, or can permanently prevail, in any free country; I am not content to see it suffer, unrelieved, beneath the weight of imputations so grievous; nor is it right that any hostile system should be built up by so gross a misrepresentation of ours. That our Public Schools are not Theological Seminaries, is admitted. That they are debarred by law from inculcating the peculiar and distinctive doctrines of any one religious denomination amongst us, is claimed; and that they are also prohibited from ever teaching that what they do teach, is the whole of religion, or all that is essential to religion or to salvation, is equally certain. But our system earnestly inculcates all Christian morals; it founds its morals on the basis of religion; it welcomes the religion of the Bible; and, in receiving the Bible, it allows it to do what it is allowed to do in no other system,— *to speak for itself.* But here it stops, not because it claims to have compassed all truth; but because it disclaims to act as an umpire between hostile religious opinions.

The very terms, *Public School,* and *Common School,* bear upon their face, that they are schools which the children of the entire community may attend. Every man, not on the pauper list, is taxed for their support. But he is not taxed to support them as special religious institutions; if he were, it would satisfy, at once, the largest definition of a Religious Establishment. But he is taxed to support them, as a *preventive* means against dishonesty, against fraud, and against violence; on the same principle that he is taxed to support criminal courts as a *punitive* means against the same offences. He is taxed to support schools, on the same principle that he is taxed to support paupers; because a child without education is poorer and more wretched than a man without bread. He is taxed to support schools, on the same principle that he would be taxed to defend the nation against foreign invasion, or against rapine committed by a foreign foe; because the general prevalence of ignorance, superstition, and vice, will breed Goth and Vandal at home, more fatal to the public well-being, than any Goth or Vandal from abroad. And, finally, he is taxed to support schools, because they are the most effective means of developing and training those powers and faculties in a child, by which, when he becomes a man, he may understand what his highest interests and his highest duties are; and may be, in fact, and not in name only, a free agent. The elements of a political education are not bestowed upon any school child, for the purpose of making him vote with this or that political party, when he becomes of age; but for the purpose of enabling him to choose for himself, with which party he will vote. So the religious education which a child receives at school, is not imparted to him, for the purpose of making him join this or that denomination, when he arrives at years of discretion, but for the purpose of enabling him to judge for himself, according to the dictates of his own reason and conscience, what his religious obligations are, and whither they lead. But if a man is taxed to support a school, where religious doctrines are inculcated which he believes to be false, and which he believes that God condemns; then he is excluded from the school by the Divine law, at the same time that he is compelled to support it by the human law. This is a double wrong. It is politically wrong, because, if such a man educates his children at all, he must educate them elsewhere, and thus pay two taxes, while some of his neighbors pay less than their due proportion of one; and it is religiously wrong, because he is constrained, by human power, to promote what he believes the Divine Power forbids. The principle involved in such a course is pregnant with all tyrannical consequences. It is broad enough to sustain any claim of ecclesiastical domination, ever made in the darkest ages of the world. Every religious persecution, since the time of Constantine, may find its warrant in it, and can be legitimately defended upon it. If a man's estate may be taken from him to pay for teaching a creed which he believes to be false, his children can be taken from him to be taught the same creed; and he, too, may be punished to any extent, for not voluntarily surrendering both his estate and his offspring. If his children can be compulsorily taken and taught to believe a creed which the parent disbelieves, then the parent can be compulsorily taken and made to subscribe the same creed. And, in regard to the extent of the penalties which may be invoked to compel conformity, there is no stopping-place between taking a penny and inflicting perdition. It is only necessary to call a man's reason and conscience and religious faith, by the name of recusancy, or contumacy, or heresy, and so to inscribe them on the statute book; and then the non-conformist or dissenter may be subdued by steel, or cord, or fire; by anathema and excommunication in this life, and the terrors of endless perdition in the next. Surely, that system cannot be an irreligious, an anti-Christian, or an un-Christian one, whose first and cardinal principle it is, to recognize and protect the highest and dearest of all human interests, and of all human rights.

Again; it seems almost too clear for exposition, that our system, *in one of its most essential features,* is not only, not an irreligious one, but that it is more strictly religious than any other which has ever yet been adopted. Every intelligent man understands what is meant by the term "Jurisdiction." It is the rightful authority which one person, or one body of men, exercises over another person, or persons. Every intelligent man understands, that there are some things which are within the jurisdiction of government, and other things which are not within it. As Americans, we understand that there is a line, dividing the jurisdiction of the State Governments from the jurisdiction of the Federal Government; and that it is a violation of the constitutions of both, for either to invade the legitimate sphere of action which belongs to the other. We all understand, that neither any State in this Union, nor the Union itself, has any right of interference between the British sovereign and a British subject, or between the French government and a citizen of France. Let this doctrine be applied to the relations which our fellow-citizens bear to the rulers who have authority over them. Primarily, religious rights embrace the relations between the creature and the Creator, just as political rights embrace the relations between subject and sovereign, or between a free citizen and the government of his choice; and just as parental rights embrace the relation between parent and child. Rights, therefore, which are strictly religious, lie out of, and beyond the jurisdiction of civil governments. They belong, exclusively, to the jurisdiction of the Divine government. If, then, the State of Massachusetts has no right of forcible interference between an Englishman, or a Frenchman, and the English or French government; still less, far less, has it any right of forcible interference, between the soul of man, and the King and Lord to whom that soul owes undivided and supreme allegiance. Civil society may exist, or it may cease to exist. Civil government may continue for centuries in the hands of the same dynasty, or it may change hands, by revolution, with every new moon. The man, outcast and outlawed to-day, and to whom, therefore, we owe no obedience, may be rightfully installed in office tomorrow, and may then require submission to his legitimate authority. The civil governor may resign, or be deposed; the frame-work of the government may be changed, or its laws altered; so that the duty of allegiance to a temporal sovereign may have a succession of new objects, or a succession of new definitions. But the relation of man to his Maker never changes. Its object and its obligations are immutable. The jurisdiction which God exercises over the religious obligations which his rational and accountable offspring owe to Him, excludes human jurisdiction. And, hence it is, that religious rights are inalienable rights. Hence, also, it is, that it is an infinitely greater offence to invade the special and exclusive jurisdiction which the Creator claims over the consciences and hearts of men, than it would be to invade the jurisdiction which any foreign nation rightfully possesses over its own subjects or citizens. The latter would be only an offence against international law; the former is treason against the majesty of Heaven. The one violates secular and temporal rights only; the other violates sacred and eternal ones. When the British Government passed its various statutes of *praemunire,* as they were called,—statutes to prevent the Roman Pontiff from interfering between the British sovereign and the British subject,—it was itself constantly enacting and enforcing laws which interfered between the Sovereign of the universe and His subjects upon earth, far more directly and aggressively, than any edict of the Roman See ever interfered with any allegiance due from a British subject to the self-styled Defender of the Faith.

It was in consequence of laws that invaded the direct and exclusive jurisdiction which our Father in heaven exercises over his children upon earth, that the Pilgrims fled from their native land, to that which is the land of our nativity. They sought a residence so remote and so inaccessible, in the hope that the prerogatives of the Divine Magistrate might no longer be set at nought by the usurpations of the civil power. Was it not an irreligious and an impious act, on the part of the British government, to pursue our ancestors with such cruel penalties and privations, as to drive them into banishment? Was it not a religious and a pious act in the Pilgrim Fathers to seek a place of refuge, where the arm of earthly power could neither restrain them from worshipping God in the manner which they believed to be most acceptable to Him, nor command their worship in a manner believed to be unacceptable? And if it was irreligious in the British government to violate freedom of conscience in the case of our forefathers, two centuries ago, then it is more flagrantly irreligious to repeat the oppression, in this more enlightened age of the world. If it was a religious act in our forefathers to escape from ecclesiastical tyranny, then it must be in the strictest conformity to religion for us to abstain from all religious oppression over others; and to oppose it wherever it is threatened. And this

abstinence from religious oppression, this acknowledgement of the rights of others, this explicit recognition and avowal of the supreme and exclusive jurisdiction of Heaven, and this denial of the right of any earthly power to encroach upon that jurisdiction, is precisely what the Massachusetts school system purports to do in theory, and what it does actually in practice. Hence I infer that our system is not an irreligious one, but is in the strictest accordance with religion and its obligations.

It is still easier to prove that the Massachusetts school system is not anti-Christian nor un-Christian. The Bible is the acknowledged expositor of Christianity. In strictness, Christianity has no other authoritative expounder. This Bible is in our Common Schools, by common consent. Twelve years ago, it was not in all the schools. Contrary to the genius of our government, if not contrary to the express letter of the law, it had been used for sectarian purposes,—to prove one sect to be right, and others to be wrong. Hence, it had been excluded from the schools of some towns, by an express vote. But since the law and the reasons on which it is founded, have been more fully explained and better understood; and since sectarian instruction has, to a great extent, ceased to be given, the Bible has been restored. I am not aware of the existence of a single town in the State, in whose schools it is not now introduced, either by a direct vote of the school committee, or by such general desire and acquiescence, as supersede the necessity of a vote. In all my intercourse, for twelve years, whether personal or by letter, with all the school officers in the State, and with tens of thousands of individuals in it, I have never heard an objection made to the use of the Bible in school except in one or two instances; and, in those cases, the objection was put upon the ground, that daily familiarity with the book, in school, would tend to impair a reverence for it.

If the Bible, then, is the exponent of Christianity; if the Bible contains the communications, precepts, and doctrines, which make up the religious system, called and known as Christianity; if the Bible makes known those truths, which, according to the faith of Christians, are able to make men wise unto salvation; and if this Bible is in the schools, how can it be said that Christianity is excluded from the schools; or how can it be said that the school system, which adopts and uses the Bible, is an anti-Christian, or an un-Christian system? If that which is the acknowledged exponent and basis of Christianity is in the schools, by what tergiversation in language, or paralogism in logic, can Christianity be said to be shut out from the schools? If the Old Testament were in the schools, could a Jew complain, that Judaism was excluded from them? If the Koran were read regularly and reverently in the schools, could a Mahomedan say that Mahomedanism was excluded? Or, if the Mormon Bible were in the schools, could it be said that Mormonism was excluded from them?

And further; our law explicitly and solemnly enjoins it upon all teachers, without any exception, "to exert their best endeavors, to impress on the minds of children and youth committed to their care and instruction, the principles of piety, justice, and a sacred regard to truth, love to their country, humanity and universal benevolence, sobriety, industry, and frugality, chastity, moderation, and temperance, and those other virtues which are the ornament of human society, and the basis upon which a republican constitution is founded." Are not these virtues and graces part and parcel of Christianity? In other words, can there be Christianity without them? While these virtues and these duties towards God and man, are inculcated in our schools, any one who says that the schools are anti-Christian or un-Christian, expressly affirms that his own system of Christianity does not embrace any one of this radiant catalogue; that it rejects them all; that it embraces their opposites!

And further still; our system makes it the express duty of all the "resident ministers of the Gospel" to bring all the children within the moral and Christian inculcations above enumerated; so that he who avers that our system is an anti-Christian or an un-Christian one, avers that it is both anti-Christian and un-Christian for a "minister OF THE GOSPEL to promote, or labor to diffuse, the moral attributes and excellences, which the statute so earnestly enjoins. . . .

I know of but one argument, having the semblance of plausibility, that can be urged against this feature of our system. It may be said, that if questions of doctrinal religion are left to be decided by men, for themselves, or by parents for their children, numerous and grievous errors will be mingled with the instruction. Doubtless, the fact is so. If truth be one, and if many contradictory dogmas are taught as truth, then it is mathematically certain, that all the alleged truths, but one, is a falsity. But, though the statement is correct, the inference which is drawn from it, in favor of a government standard of faith, is not legitimate; for all the religious errors which are believed in by the free mind of man, or which are taught by free parents to their children, are tolerable and covetable, compared with those which the patronage and the seductions of government can suborn men to adopt, and which the ter-

rors of government can compel them to perpetuate. The errors of free minds are so numerous and so various, that they prevent any monster-error from acquiring the ascendancy; and, therefore, Truth has a chance to struggle forward amid the strifes of the combatants; but if the monster-error can usurp the throne of the civil Power, fortify itself by prescription, defend its infallibility with all the forces of the State, sanctify its enormities under sacred names, and plead the express command of God for all its atrocities;—against such an antagonist, Truth must struggle for centuries, bleed at every pore, be wounded in every vital part, and can triumph at last, only after thousands and tens of thousands of her holiest disciples shall have fallen in the conflict.

If, then, a government would recognize and protect the rights of religious freedom, it must abstain from subjugating the capacities of its children to any legal standard of religious faith, with as great fidelity as it abstains from controlling the opinions of men. It must meet the unquestionable fact, that the old spirit of religious domination is adopting new measures to accomplish its work,—measures, which, if successful, will be as fatal to the liberties of mankind, as those which were practised in by-gone days of violence and terror. These new measures are aimed at children instead of men. They propose to supersede the necessity of subduing free thought, *in the mind of the adult,* by forestalling the development of any capacity of free thought, *in the mind of the child.* They expect to find it easier to subdue the free agency of children, by binding them in fetters of bigotry, than to subdue the free agency of men, by binding them in fetters of iron. For this purpose, some are attempting to deprive children of their right to labor, and, of course, of their daily bread, unless they will attend a government school, and receive its sectarian instruction. Some are attempting to withhold all means, even of secular education, from the poor, and thus punish them with ignorance, unless, with the secular knowledge which they desire, they will accept theological knowledge which they condemn. Others, still, are striving to break down all free Public School systems, where they exist, and to prevent their establishment, where they do not exist, in the hope, that on the downfall of these, their system will succeed. The sovereign antidote against these machinations, is, Free Schools for all, and the right of every parent to determine the religious education of his children.

Without undervaluing any other human agency, it may be safely affirmed that the Common School, improved and energized, as it can easily be, may become the most effective and benignant of all the forces of civilization. Two reasons sustain this position. In the first place, there is a universality in its operation, which can be affirmed of no other institution whatever. If administered in the spirit of justice and conciliation, all the rising generation may be brought within the circle of its reformatory and elevating influences. And, in the second place, the materials upon which it operates are so pliant and ductile as to be susceptible of assuming a greater variety of forms than any other earthly work of the Creator. The inflexibility and ruggedness of the oak, when compared with the lithe sapling or the tender germ, are but feeble emblems to typify the docility of childhood, when contrasted with the obduracy and intractableness of man. It is these inherent advantages of the Common School, which, in our own State, have produced results so striking, from a system so imperfect, and an administration so feeble. In teaching the blind, and the deaf and dumb, in kindling the latent spark of intelligence that lurks in an idiot's mind, and in the more holy work of reforming abandoned and outcast children, education has proved what it can do, by glorious experiments. These wonders, it has done in its infancy, and with the lights of a limited experience; but, when its faculties shall be fully developed, when it shall be trained to wield its mighty energies for the protection of society against the giant vices which now invade and torment it;—against intemperance, avarice, war, slavery, bigotry, the woes of want and the wickedness of waste,—then, there will not be a height to which these enemies of the race can escape, which it will not scale, nor a Titan among them all, whom it will not slay.

I proceed, then, in endeavoring to show how the true business of the schoolroom connects itself, and becomes identical, with the great interests of society. The former is the infant, immature state of those interests; the latter, their developed, adult state. As "the child is father to the man," so may the training of the schoolroom expand into the institutions and fortunes of the State.

Address on Colonization, *Abraham Lincoln*, 1862

Legal disabilities faced free African Americans during the time of slavery, up to and including provisions of state constitutions forbidding their settled presence. This hostility was rooted in the conviction that racial differences made peaceful coexistence impossible in the United States. One response to this perceived situation was the foundation of the American Colonization Society in 1817. This society worked to relocate freed slaves and their descendants to Africa (it took the lead in founding the African nation of Liberia as a homeland for freed slaves). Abraham Lincoln was a longtime supporter of such resettlement efforts, though he opposed forced resettlement, particularly in light of African American service in the Civil War.

Address on Colonization to a Deputation of Negroes

Abraham Lincoln

August 14, 1862

This afternoon the President of the United States gave audience to a Committee of colored men at the White House. They were introduced by the Rev. J. Mitchell, Commissioner of Emigration. E. M. Thomas, the Chairman, remarked that they were there by invitation to hear what the Executive had to say to them. Having all been seated, the President, after a few preliminary observations, informed them that a sum of money had been appropriated by Congress, and placed at his disposition for the purpose of aiding the colonization in some country of the people, or a portion of them, of African descent, thereby making it his duty, as it had for a long time been his inclination, to favor that cause; and why, he asked, should the people of your race be colonized, and where? Why should they leave this country? This is, perhaps, the first question for proper consideration. You and we are different races. We have between us a broader difference than exists between almost any other two races. Whether it is right or wrong I need not discuss, but this physical difference is a great disadvantage to us both, as I think your race suffer very greatly, many of them by living among us, while ours suffer from your presence. In a word we suffer on each side. If this is admitted, it affords a reason at least why we should be separated. You here are freemen I suppose.

A Voice: Yes, sir.

The President—Perhaps you have long been free, or all

your lives. Your race are suffering, in my judgment, the greatest wrong inflicted on any people. But even when you cease to be slaves, you are yet far removed from being placed on an equality with the white race. You are cut off from many of the advantages which the other race enjoy. The aspiration of men is to enjoy equality with the best when free, but on this broad continent, not a single man of your race is made the equal of a single man of ours. Go where you are treated the best, and the ban is still upon you.

I do not propose to discuss this, but to present it as a fact with which we have to deal. I cannot alter it if I would. It is a fact, about which we all think and feel alike, I and you. We look to our condition, owing to the existence of the two races on this continent. I need not recount to you the effects upon white men, growing out of the institution of Slavery. I believe in its general evil effects on the white race. See our present condition—the country engaged in war!—our white men cutting one another's throats, none knowing how far it will extend; and then consider what we know to be the truth. But for your race among us there could not be war, although many men engaged on either side do not care for you one way or the other. Nevertheless, I repeat, without the institution of Slavery and the colored race as a basis, the war could not have an existence.

It is better for us both, therefore, to be separated. I know that there are free men among you, who even if they could better their condition are not as much inclined to go out of the country as those, who being slaves could obtain their freedom on this condition. I suppose one of the principal difficulties in the way of colonization is that the free colored man cannot see that his comfort would be advanced by it. You may believe you can live in Washington or elsewhere in the United States the remainder of your life [as easily], perhaps more so than you can in any foreign country, and hence you may come to the conclusion that you have nothing to do with the idea of going to a foreign country. This is (I speak in no unkind sense) an extremely selfish view of the case.

But you ought to do something to help those who are not so fortunate as yourselves. There is an unwillingness on the part of our people, harsh as it may be, for you free colored people to remain with us. Now, if you could give a start to white people, you would open a wide door for many to be made free. If we deal with those who are not free at the beginning, and whose intellects are clouded by Slavery, we have very poor materials to start with. If intelligent colored men, such as are before me, would move in this matter, much might be accomplished. It is exceedingly important that we have men at the beginning capable of thinking as white men, and not those who have been systematically oppressed.

There is much to encourage you. For the sake of your race you should sacrifice something of your present comfort for the purpose of being as grand in that respect as the white people. It is a cheering thought throughout life that something can be done to ameliorate the condition of those who have been subject to the hard usage of the world. It is difficult to make a man miserable while he feels he is worthy of himself, and claims kindred to the great God who made him. In the American Revolutionary war sacrifices were made by men engaged in it; but they were cheered by the future. Gen. Washington himself endured greater physical hardships than if he had remained a British subject. Yet he was a happy man, because he was engaged in benefiting his race—something for the children of his neighbors, having none of his own.

The colony of Liberia has been in existence a long time. In a certain sense it is a success. The old President of Liberia, Roberts, has just been with me—the first time I ever saw him. He says they have within the bounds of that colony between 300,000 and 400,000 people, or more than in some of our old States, such as Rhode Island or Delaware, or in some of our newer States, and less than in some of our larger ones.

They are not all American colonists, or their descendants. Something less than 12,000 have been sent thither from this country. Many of the original settlers have died, yet, like people elsewhere, their offspring outnumber those deceased.

The question is if the colored people are persuaded to go anywhere, why not there? One reason for an unwillingness to do so is that some of you would rather remain within reach of the country of your nativity. I do not know how much attachment you may have toward our race. It does not strike me that you have the greatest reason to love them. But still you are attached to them at all events.

The place I am thinking about having for a colony is in Central America. It is nearer to us than Liberia—not much more than one-fourth as far as Liberia, and within seven days' run by steamers. Unlike Liberia it is on a great line of travel—it is a highway. The country is a very excellent one for any people, and with great natural resources and advantages, and especially because of the similarity of climate with your native land—thus being suited to your physical condition.

The particular place I have in view is to be a great highway from the Atlantic or Caribbean Sea to the Pacific Ocean, and this particular place has all the advantages for a colony. On both sides there are harbors among the finest in the world. Again, there is evidence of very rich coal mines. A certain amount of coal is valuable in any country, and there may be more than enough for the wants of the country. Why I attach so much importance to coal is, it will afford an opportunity to the inhabitants for immediate employment till they get ready to settle permanently in their homes.

If you take colonists where there is no good landing, there is a bad show; and so where there is nothing to cultivate, and of which to make a farm. But if something is started so that you can get your daily bread as soon as you reach there, it is a great advantage. Coal land is the best thing I know of with which to commence an enterprise.

To return, you have been talked to upon this subject, and told that a speculation is intended by gentlemen, who have an interest in the country, including the coal mines. We have been mistaken all our lives if we do not know whites as well as blacks look to their self-interest. Unless among those deficient of intellect everybody you trade with makes something. You meet with these things here as elsewhere.

If such persons have what will be an advantage to them, the question is whether it cannot be made of advantage to you. You are intelligent, and know that success does not as much depend on external help as on self-reliance. Much, therefore, depends upon yourselves. As to the coal mines, I think I see the means available for your self-reliance.

I shall, if I get a sufficient number of you engaged, have provisions made that you shall not be wronged. If you will engage in the enterprise I will spend some of the money intrusted to me. I am not sure you will succeed. The Government may lose the money, but we cannot succeed unless we try; but we think, with care, we can succeed.

The political affairs in Central America are not in quite as satisfactory condition as I wish. There are contending factions in that quarter; but it is true all the factions are agreed alike on the subject of colonization, and want it, and are more generous than we are here. To your colored race they have no objection. Besides, I would endeavor to have you made equals, and have the best assurance that you should be the equals of the best.

The practical thing I want to ascertain is whether I can get a number of able-bodied men, with their wives and children, who are willing to go, when I present evidence of encouragement and protection. Could I get a hundred tolerably intelligent men, with their wives and children, to "cut their own fodder," so to speak? Can I have fifty? If I could find twenty-five able-bodied men, with a mixture of women and children, good things in the family relation, I think I could make a successful commencement.

I want you to let me know whether this can be done or not. This is the practical part of my wish to see you. These are subjects of very great importance, worthy of a month's study, [instead] of a speech delivered in an hour. I ask you then to consider seriously not pertaining to yourselves merely, nor for your race, and ours, for the present time, but as one of the things, if successfully managed, for the good of mankind—not confined to the present generation, but as

"From age to age descends the lay,
    To millions yet to be,
Till far its echoes roll away,
    Into eternity."

The above is merely given as the substance of the President's remarks.

The Chairman of the delegation briefly replied that "they would hold a consultation and in a short time give an answer." The President said: "Take your full time—no hurry at all."

The delegation then withdrew.

Atlanta Exposition Speech, *Booker T. Washington*, 1895

Booker T. Washington (1856–1915) was born into slavery in Virginia. Once emancipated he began working menial jobs while striving to educate himself. Having graduated from the Hampton Normal and Agricultural Institute (now Hampton University), Washington, at the age of twenty-five, became the first principal of what was then called the Tuskegee Negro Normal Institute, a teachers' college that also taught agricultural and mechanic arts and came to be known as Tuskegee Institute and, later, Tuskegee University. Washington argued, and operated on the assumption that African Americans would have to persuade whites to grant them full civil rights by mastering mechanical professions and proving their upstanding character. He was the only African American to deliver a speech before the 1895 Atlanta Cotton States and International Exposition. Sometimes criticized as an accommodationist, Washington cultivated contacts with a variety of rich and powerful Americans to raise funds and establish teachers' colleges and other institutions to improve African American education.

Address of Booker T. Washington, Principal Tuskegee Normal and Industrial Institute, Tuskegee, Ala., at the Opening of the Exposition

September 18, 1895

Mr. President and Gentlemen of the Board of Directors and Citizens:

One-third of the population of the South is of the negro race. No enterprise seeking the material, civil or moral welfare of this section, can disregard this element of our population and reach the highest success. I but convey to you, Mr. President and Directors, the sentiment of the masses of my race, when I say that in no way have the value and manhood of the American negro been more fittingly and generously recognized than by the managers of this magnificent Exposition at every stage of its progress. It is a recognition that will do more to cement the friendship of the two races than any occurrence since the dawn of our freedom.

Not only this, but the opportunity here afforded will awaken among us a new era of industrial progress. Ignorant and inexperienced, it is not strange that in the first years of our new life we began at the top instead of at the bottom, that a seat in Congress or the State Legislature was more sought than real estate or industrial skill, that the political convention or stump speaking had more attractions than starting a dairy farm or truck garden.

A ship lost at sea for many days suddenly sighted a friendly vessel. From the mast of the unfortunate vessel was seen the signal: "Water, water; we die of thirst." The answer from the friendly vessel at once came back: "Cast down your bucket where you are." A second time the signal, "Water, water; send us water!" ran up from the distressed vessel, and was answered, "Cast down your bucket where you are." And a third and fourth signal for water was answered: "Cast down your bucket where you are." The captain of the distressed vessel, at last heeding the injunction, cast down his bucket, and it came up full of fresh sparkling water from the mouth of the Amazon river. To those of my race who depend on bettering their condition in a foreign land, or who underestimate the importance of cultivating friendly relations with the Southern white man, who is their next-door neighbor, I would say, "Cast down your bucket where you are,"—cast it down in making friends in every manly way of the people of all races by whom we are surrounded.

Cast it down in agriculture, mechanics, in commerce, in domestic service, and in the professions. And in this connection it is well to bear in mind that, whatever other sins the South may be called to bear, when it comes to business, pure and simple, it is in the South that the negro is given a man's chance in the commercial world; and in nothing is this Exposition more eloquent than in emphasizing this chance. Our greatest danger is that, in the great leap from slavery to freedom, we may overlook the fact that the masses of us are to live by the productions of our hands, and fail to keep in mind that we shall prosper in proportion as we learn to dignify and glorify common labor and put brains and skill into common occupations of life; shall prosper in proportion as we learn to draw the line between the superficial and the substantial, the ornamental gewgaws of life and the useful. No race can prosper until it learns that there is as much dignity in tilling a field as in writing a poem. It is at the bottom of life we must begin, and not at the top. Nor should we permit our grievances to overshadow our opportunities.

To those of the white race who look to the incoming of those of foreign birth and strange tongue and habits for the prosperity of the South, were I permitted, I would repeat what I say to my own race: "Cast down your bucket where you are." Cast it down among the 8,000,000 negroes whose habits you know, whose fidelity and love you have tested in days when to have proved treacherous meant the ruin of your firesides. Cast down your bucket among these people, who have, without strikes and labor wars, tilled your fields, cleared your forests, builded your railroads and cities, and brought forth treasures from the bowels of the earth, and helped make possible this magnificent representation of the progress of the South. Casting down your bucket among my people, helping them and encouraging them, as you are doing on these grounds, and to education of head, hand and heart, you will find that they will buy your surplus land, make blossom the waste places in your fields and run your factories. While doing this, you can be sure in the future, as in the past, that you and your families will be surrounded by the most patient, faithful, law-abiding and unresentful people that the world has seen. As we have proved our loyalty to you in the past, in nursing your children, watching by the sick bed of your mothers and fathers, and often following them with tear-dimmed eyes to their graves, so in the future, in our humble way, we shall stand by you with a devotion that no foreigner can approach, ready to lay down our lives, if need be, in defense of yours, interlacing our industrial, commercial, civil and religious life with yours in a way that shall make the interests of both races one. In all things that are purely social, we can be as separate as the fingers, yet one as the hand in all things essential to mutual progress.

There is no defense of security for any of us except in the highest intelligence and development of all. If anywhere there are efforts tending to curtail the fullest growth of the negro, let these efforts be turned into stimulating, encouraging and making him the most useful and intelligent citizen. Effort or means so invested will pay a thousand per cent interest. These efforts will be twice-blessed—"blessing him that gives and him that takes."

There is no escape, through law of God, from the inevitable:

> "The laws of changeless justice bind,
>   Oppressor with oppressed;
> And close as sin and suffering joined,
>   We march to fate abreast."

Nearly sixteen millions of hands will aid you in pulling the load upward, or they will pull against you the load downward. We shall constitute one-third, and more, of the ignorance and crime of the South, or one-third its intelligence and progress; we shall contribute one-third to the business or industrial prosperity of the South, or we shall prove a veritable body of death, stagnating, depressing, retarding every effort to advance the body politic.

Gentlemen of the Exposition, as we present to you our humble effort at an exhibition of our progress, you must not expect over much. Starting thirty years ago with ownership here and there in a few quilts and pumpkins and chickens (gathered from miscellaneous sources), remember the path that has led from these to the inventions and production of agricultural implements, buggies, steam engines, newspapers, books, statuary, carving, paintings, the management of drug stores and banks, has not been trodden without contact with thorns and thistles. While we take pride in what we exhibit as a result of our independent efforts, we do not for a moment forget that our part in this Exhibition would fall far short of your expectations but for the constant help that has come to our educational life, not only from the Southern States, but especially from Northern philanthropists, who have made their gifts a constant stream of blessing and encouragement.

The wisest among my race understand that the agitation of questions of social equality is the extremest folly, and that progress in the enjoyment of all the privileges that will come to us must be the result of severe and constant struggle rather than of artificial forcing. No race that has anything to contribute to the markets of the world is long in any degree ostracized. It is important and right that all the privileges of the law be ours, but it is vastly more important that we be prepared for the exercise of these privileges. The opportunity to earn a dollar in a factory, just now, is worth infinitely more than the opportunity to spend a dollar in an opera house.

In conclusion, may I repeat that nothing in thirty years has given us more hope and encouragement, and drawn us so near to you of the white race as this opportunity offered by the Exposition, and here, bending, as it were, over the altar that represents the results of the struggles of your race and mine, both starting practically empty-handed three decades ago, I pledge that in your effort to work out the great and intricate problem which God has laid at the doors of the South, you shall have, at all times, the patient, sympathetic help of my race; only let this be constantly in mind, that, while from representations in these buildings of the product of field, of forest, of mine, of factory, letters and art, much good will come, yet far above and beyond material benefits will be that higher good, that, let us pray God, will come in a blotting out of sectional differences and racial animosities and suspicions, in a determination to administer absolute justice, in a willing obedience among all classes to the mandates of the law. This, this, coupled with our material prosperity, will bring into our beloved South a new Heaven and a new earth.

Plessy v. Ferguson, 1896

Homer Plessy, a shoemaker with one-eighth African American heritage, was chosen by a civil rights group in Louisiana to challenge that state's law requiring separate train cars for whites and African Americans on train lines running only within the state. Federal law prevented such segregation on interstate lines. Plessy purchased a first-class ticket and was subsequently arrested for refusing to move to a third-class car (there were no first-class cars for African Americans). The Supreme Court held that state laws requiring separate facilities based on race did not deprive African Americans of their Thirteenth and Fourteenth Amendment rights. The decision did not use the phrase "separate but equal" but did assert that laws mandating separate facilities pass constitutional muster so long as they did not make those facilities inferior.

Plessy v. Ferguson

ERROR TO THE SUPREME COURT OF THE
STATE OF LOUISIANA

No. 210. Argued April 18, 1896.—Decided May 18, 1896

MR. JUSTICE BROWN, after stating the case, delivered the opinion of the court.

This case turns upon the constitutionality of an act of the General Assembly of the State of Louisiana, passed in 1890, providing for separate railway carriages for the white and colored races. Acts 1890, No. 111, p. 152.

The first section of the statute enacts "that all railway companies carrying passengers in their coaches in this State, shall provide equal but separate accommodations for the white, and colored races, by providing two or more passenger coaches for each passenger train, or by dividing the passenger coaches by a partition so as to secure separate accommodations: *Provided,* That this section shall not be construed to apply to street railroads. No person or persons, shall be admitted to occupy seats in coaches, other than the ones assigned to them on account of the race they belong to."

By the second section it was enacted "that the officers of such passenger trains shall have power and are hereby required to assign each passenger to the coach or compartment used for the race to which such passenger belongs; any passenger insisting on going into a coach or compartment to which by race he does not belong, shall be liable to a fine of twenty-five dollars, or in lieu thereof to imprisonment for a period of not more than twenty days in the parish prison, and any officer of any railroad insisting on assigning a passenger to a coach or compartment other than the one set aside for the race to which said passenger belongs, shall be liable to a fine of twenty-five dollars, or in lieu thereof to imprisonment for a period of not more than twenty days in the parish prison; and should any passenger refuse to occupy the coach or compartment to which he or she is assigned by the officer of such railway, said officer shall have power to refuse to carry such passenger on his train, and for such refusal neither he nor the railway company which he represents shall be liable for damages in any of the courts of this State."

The third section provides penalties for the refusal or neglect of the officers, directors, conductors and employés of railway companies to comply with the act, with a proviso that "nothing in this act shall be construed as applying to nurses attending children of the other race." The fourth section is immaterial.

The information filed in the criminal District Court charged in substance that Plessy, being a passenger between two stations within the State of Louisiana, was assigned by officers of the company to the coach used for the race to which he belonged, but he insisted upon going into a coach used by the race to which he did not belong. Neither in the information nor plea was his particular race or color averred.

The petition for the writ of prohibition averred that petitioner was seven eighths Caucasian and one eighth African blood; that the mixture of colored blood was not discernible in him, and that he was entitled to every right, privilege and immunity secured to citizens of the United States of the white race; and that, upon such theory, he took possession of a vacant seat in a coach where passengers of the white race were accommodated, and was ordered by the conductor to vacate said coach and take a seat in another assigned to persons of the colored race, and having refused to comply with such demand he was forcibly ejected with the aid of a police officer, and imprisoned in the parish jail to answer a charge of having violated the above act.

The constitutionality of this act is attacked upon the ground that it conflicts both with the Thirteenth Amendment of the Constitution, abolishing slavery, and the Fourteenth Amendment, which prohibits certain restrictive legislation on the part of the States.

1. That it does not conflict with the Thirteenth Amendment, which abolished slavery and involuntary servitude, except as a punishment for crime, is too clear for argument. Slavery implies involuntary servitude—a state of bondage; the ownership of mankind as a chattel, or at least the control of the labor and services of one man for the benefit of another, and the absence of a legal right to the disposal of his own person, property and services. This amendment was said in the *Slaughter-house cases*, 16 Wall. 36, to have been intended primarily to abolish slavery, as it had been previously known in this country, and that it equally forbade Mexican peonage or the Chinese coolie trade, when they amounted to slavery or involuntary servitude, and that the use of the word "servitude" was intended to prohibit the use of all forms of involuntary slavery, of whatever class or name. It was intimated, however, in that case that this amendment was regarded by the statesmen of that day as insufficient to protect the colored race from certain laws which had been enacted in the Southern States, imposing upon the colored race onerous disabilities and burdens, and curtailing their rights in the pursuit of life, liberty and property to such an extent that their freedom was of little value; and that the Fourteenth Amendment was devised to meet this exigency.

So, too, in the *Civil Rights cases*, 109 U.S. 3, 24, it was said that the act of a mere individual, the owner of an inn, a public conveyance or place of amusement, refusing accommodations to colored people, cannot be justly regarded as imposing any badge of slavery or servitude upon the applicant, but only as involving an ordinary civil injury, properly cognizable by the laws of the State, and presumably subject to redress by those laws until the contrary appears. "It would be running the slavery argument into the ground," said Mr. Justice Bradley, "to make it apply to every act of discrimination which a person may see fit to make as to the guests he will entertain, or as to the people he will take into his coach or cab or car, or admit to his concert or theatre, or deal with in other matters of intercourse or business."

A statute which implies merely a legal distinction between the white and colored races—a distinction which is founded in the color of the two races, and which must always exist so long as white men are distinguished from the other race by color—has no tendency to destroy the legal equality of the two races, or reëstablish a state of involuntary servitude. Indeed, we do not understand that the Thirteenth Amendment is strenuously relied upon by the plaintiff in error in this connection.

2. By the Fourteenth Amendment, all persons born or naturalized in the United States, and subject to the jurisdiction thereof, are made citizens of the United States and of the State wherein they reside; and the States are forbidden from making or enforcing any law which shall abridge the privileges or immunities of citizens of the United States, or shall deprive any person of life, liberty or property without due process of law, or deny to any person within their jurisdiction the equal protection of the laws.

The proper construction of this amendment was first called to the attention of this court in the *Slaughter-house cases*, 16 Wall. 36, which involved, however, not a question of race, but one of exclusive privileges. The case did not call for any expression of opinion as to the exact rights it was intended to secure to the colored race, but it was said generally that its main purpose was to establish the citizenship of the negro; to give definitions of citizenship of the United States and of the States, and to protect from the hostile legislation of the States the privileges and immunities of citizens of the United States, as distinguished from those of citizens of the States.

The object of the amendment was undoubtedly to enforce the absolute equality of the two races before the law, but in the nature of things it could not have been intended to abolish distinctions based upon color, or to enforce social, as distinguished from political equality, or a commingling of the two races upon terms unsatisfactory to either. Laws permitting, and even requiring, their separation in places where they are liable to be brought into contact do not necessarily imply the inferiority of either race to the other, and have been generally, if not universally, recognized as within the competency of the state legislatures in the exercise of their police power. The most common instance of this is connected with the establishment of separate schools for white and colored children, which has been held to be a valid exercise of the legislative power even by courts of States where the political rights of the colored race have been longest and most earnestly enforced.

One of the earliest of these cases is that of *Roberts* v. *City of Boston,* 5 Cush. 198, in which the Supreme Judicial Court of Massachusetts held that the general school committee of Boston had power to make provision for the instruction of colored children in separate schools established exclusively for them, and to prohibit their attendance upon the other schools. "The great principle," said Chief Justice Shaw, p. 206, "advanced by the learned and eloquent advocate for the plaintiff" (Mr. Charles Sumner) "is, that by the constitution and laws of Massachusetts, all persons without distinction of age or sex, birth or color, origin or condition, are equal before the law.... But, when this great principle comes to be applied to the actual and various conditions of persons in society, it will not warrant the assertion, that men and women are legally clothed with the same civil and political powers, and that children and adults are legally to have the same functions and be subject to the same treatment; but only that the rights of all, as they are settled and regulated by law, are equally entitled to the paternal consideration and protection of the law for their maintenance and security." It was held that the powers of the committee extended to the establishment of separate schools for children of different ages, sexes and colors, and that they might also establish special schools for poor and neglected children, who have become too old to attend the primary school, and yet have not acquired the rudiments of learning, to enable them to enter the ordinary schools. Similar laws have been enacted by Congress under its general power of legislation over the District of Columbia, Rev. Stat. D.C. §§ 281, 282, 283, 310, 319, as well as by the legislatures of many of the States, and have been generally, if not uniformly, sustained by the courts. *State* v. *McCann,* 21 Ohio St. 198; *Lehew* v. *Brummell,* 15 S. W. Rep. 765; *Ward* v. *Flood,* 48 California, 36; *Bertonneau* v. *School Directors,* 3 Woods, 177; *People* v. *Gallagher,* 93 N.Y. 438; *Cory* v. *Carter,* 48 Indiana, 327; *Dawson* v. *Lee,* 83 Kentucky, 49.

Laws forbidding the intermarriage of the two races may be said in a technical sense to interfere with the freedom of con-

tract, and yet have been universally recognized as within the police power of the State. *State* v. *Gibson,* 36 Indiana, 389.

The distinction between laws interfering with the political equality of the negro and those requiring the separation of the two races in schools, theatres and railway carriages has been frequently drawn by this court. Thus in *Strauder* v. *West Virginia,* 100 U.S. 303, it was held that a law of West Virginia limiting to white male persons, 21 years of age and citizens of the State, the right to sit upon juries, was a discrimination which implied a legal inferiority in civil society, which lessened the security of the right of the colored race, and was a step toward reducing them to a condition of servility. Indeed, the right of a colored man that, in the selection of jurors to pass upon his life, liberty and property, there shall be no exclusion of his race, and no discrimination against them because of color, has been asserted in a number of cases. *Virginia* v. *Rives,* 100 U.S. 313; *Neal* v. *Delaware,* 103 U.S. 370; *Bush* v. *Kentucky,* 107 U.S. 110; *Gibson* v. *Mississippi,* 162 U.S. 565. So, where the laws of a particular locality or the charter of a particular railway corporation has provided that no person shall be excluded from the cars on account of color, we have held that this meant that persons of color should travel in the same car as white ones, and that the enactment was not satisfied by the company's providing cars assigned exclusively to people of color, though they were as good as those which they assigned exclusively to white persons. *Railroad Company* v. *Brown,* 17 Wall. 445.

Upon the other hand, where a statute of Louisiana required those engaged in the transportation of passengers among the States to give to all persons travelling within that State, upon vessels employed in that business, equal rights and privileges in all parts of the vessel, without distinction on account of race or color, and subjected to an action for damages the owner of such a vessel, who excluded colored passengers on account of their color from the cabin set aside by him for the use of whites, it was held to be so far as it applied to interstate commerce, unconstitutional and void. *Hall* v. *De Cuir,* 95 U.S. 485. The court in this case, however, expressly disclaimed that it had anything whatever to do with the statute as a regulation of internal commerce, or affecting anything else than commerce among the States.

In the *Civil Rights case,* 109 U.S. 3, it was held that an act of Congress, entitling all persons within the jurisdiction of the United States to the full and equal enjoyment of the accommodations, advantages, facilities and privileges of inns, public conveyances, on land or water, theatres and other places of public amusement, and made applicable to citizens of every race and color, regardless of any previous condition of servitude, was unconstitutional and void, upon the ground that the Fourteenth Amendment was prohibitory upon the States only, and the legislation authorized to be adopted by Congress for enforcing it was not direct legislation on matters respecting which the States were prohibited from making or enforcing certain laws, or doing certain acts, but was corrective legislation, such as might be necessary or proper for counteracting and redressing the effect of such laws or acts. In delivering the opinion of the court Mr. Justice Bradley observed that the Fourteenth Amendment "does not invest Congress with power to legislate upon subjects that are within the domain of state legislation; but to provide modes of relief against state legislation, or state action, of the kind referred to. It does not authorize Congress to create a code of municipal law for the regulation of private rights; but to provide modes of redress against the operation of state laws, and the action of state officers, executive or judicial, when these are subversive of the fundamental rights specified in the amendment. Positive rights and privileges are undoubtedly secured by the Fourteenth Amendment; but they are secured by way of prohibition against state laws and state proceedings affecting those rights and privileges, and by power given to Congress to legislate for the purpose of carrying such prohibition into effect; and such legislation must necessarily be predicated upon such supposed state laws or state proceedings, and be directed to the correction of their operation and effect."

Much nearer, and, indeed, almost directly in point, is the case of the *Louisville, New Orleans &c. Railway* v. *Mississippi,* 133 U.S. 587, wherein the railway company was indicted for a violation of a statute of Mississippi, enacting that all railroads carrying passengers should provide equal, but separate, accommodations for the white and colored races, by providing two or more passenger cars for each passenger train, or by dividing the passenger cars by a partition, so as to secure separate accommodations. The case was presented in a different aspect from the one under consideration, inasmuch as it was an indictment against the railway company for failing to provide the separate accommodations, but the question considered was the constitutionality of the law. In that case, the Supreme Court of Mississippi, 66 Mississippi, 662, had held that the statute applied solely to commerce within the State, and, that being the construction of the state statute by its highest court, was accepted as conclusive. "If it be a matter,"

said the court, p. 591, "respecting commerce wholly within a State, and not interfering with commerce between the States, then, obviously, there is no violation of the commerce clause of the Federal Constitution.... No question arises under this section, as to the power of the State to separate in different compartments interstate passengers, or affect, in any manner, the privileges and rights of such passengers. All that we can consider is, whether the State has the power to require that railroad trains within her limits shall have separate accommodations for the two races; that affecting only commerce within the State is no invasion of the power given to Congress by the commerce clause."

A like course of reasoning applies to the case under consideration, since the Supreme Court of Louisiana in the case of the *State ex rel. Abbott* v. *Hicks, Judge, et al.,* 44 La. Ann. 770, held that the statute in question did not apply to interstate passengers, but was confined in its application to passengers travelling exclusively within the borders of the State. The case was decided largely upon the authority of *Railway Co.* v. *State,* 66 Mississippi, 662, and affirmed by this court in 133 U.S. 587. In the present case no question of interference with interstate commerce can possibly arise, since the East Louisiana Railway appears to have been purely a local line, with both its termini within the State of Louisiana. Similar statutes for the separation of the two races upon public conveyances were held to be constitutional in *West Chester &c. Railroad* v. *Miles,* 55 Penn. St. 209; *Day* v. *Owen,* 5 Michigan, 520; *Chicago &c. Railway* v. *Williams,* 55 Illinois, 185; *Chesapeake &c. Railroad* v. *Wells,* 85 Tennessee, 613; *Memphis &c. Railroad* v. *Benson,* 85 Tennessee, 627; *The Sue,* 22 Fed. Rep. 843; *Logwood* v. *Memphis &c. Railroad,* 23 Fed. Rep. 318; *McGuinn* v. *Forbes,* 37 Fed. Rep. 639; *People* v. *King,* 18 N. E. Rep. 245; *Houck* v. *South Pac. Railway,* 38 Fed. Rep. 226; *Heard* v. *Georgia Railroad Co.,* 3 Int. Com. Com'n, 111; *S.C.,* 1 Ibid. 428.

While we think the enforced separation of the races, as applied to the internal commerce of the State, neither abridges the privileges or immunities of the colored man, deprives him of his property without due process of law, nor denies him the equal protection of the laws, within the meaning of the Fourteenth Amendment, we are not prepared to say that the conductor, in assigning passengers to the coaches according to their race, does not act at his peril, or that the provision of the second section of the act, that denies to the passenger compensation in damages for a refusal to receive him into the coach in which he properly belongs, is a valid exercise of the legislative power. Indeed, we understand it to be conceded by the State's attorney, that such part of the act as exempts from liability the railway company and its officers is unconstitutional. The power to assign to a particular coach obviously implies the power to determine to which race the passenger belongs, as well as the power to determine who, under the laws of the particular State, is to be deemed a white, and who a colored person. This question, though indicated in the brief of the plaintiff in error, does not properly arise upon the record in this case, since the only issue made is as to the unconstitutionality of the act, so far as it requires the railway to provide separate accommodations, and the conductor to assign passengers according to their race.

It is claimed by the plaintiff in error that, in any mixed community, the reputation of belonging to the dominant race, in this instance the white race, is *property,* in the same sense that a right of action, or of inheritance, is property. Conceding this to be so, for the purposes of this case, we are unable to see how this statute deprives him of, or in any way affects his right to, such property. If he be a white man and assigned to a colored coach, he may have his action for damages against the company for being deprived of his so called property. Upon the other hand, if he be a colored man and be so assigned, he has been deprived of no property, since he is not lawfully entitled to the reputation of being a white man.

In this connection, it is also suggested by the learned counsel for the plaintiff in error that the same argument that will justify the state legislature in requiring railways to provide separate accommodations for the two races will also authorize them to require separate cars to be provided for people whose hair is of a certain color, or who are aliens, or who belong to certain nationalities, or to enact laws requiring colored people to walk upon one side of the street, and white people upon the other, or requiring white men's houses to be painted white, and colored men's black, or their vehicles or business signs to be of different colors, upon the theory that one side of the street is as good as the other, or that a house or vehicle of one color is as good as one of another color. The reply to all this is that every exercise of the police power must be reasonable, and extend only to such laws as are enacted in good faith for the promotion for the public good, and not for the annoyance or oppression of a particular class. Thus in *Yick Wo* v. *Hopkins,* 118 U.S. 356, it was held by this court that a municipal ordinance of the city of San Francisco, to regulate the carrying on of public laundries within the limits of the municipality, violated the provisions of the Constitution of the United States, if it conferred upon the municipal

authorities arbitrary power, at their own will, and without regard to discretion, in the legal sense of the term, to give or withhold consent as to persons or places, without regard to the competency of the persons applying, or the propriety of the places selected for the carrying on of the business. It was held to be a covert attempt on the part of the municipality to make an arbitrary and unjust discrimination against the Chinese race. While this was the case of a municipal ordinance, a like principle has been held to apply to acts of a state legislature passed in the exercise of the police power. *Railroad Company* v. *Husen,* 95 U.S. 465; *Louisville & Nashville Railroad* v. *Kentucky,* 161 U.S. 677, and cases cited on p. 700; *Daggett* v. *Hudson,* 43 Ohio St. 548; *Capen* v. *Foster,* 12 Pick. 485; *State ex rel. Wood* v. *Baker,* 38 Wisconsin, 71; *Monroe* v. *Collins,* 17 Ohio St. 665; *Hulseman* v. *Rems,* 41 Penn. St. 396; *Orman* v. *Riley,* 15 California, 48.

So far, then, as a conflict with the Fourteenth Amendment is concerned, the case reduces itself to the question whether the statute of Louisiana is a reasonable regulation, and with respect to this there must necessarily be a large discretion on the part of the legislature. In determining the question of reasonableness it is at liberty to act with reference to the established usages, customs and traditions of the people, and with a view to the promotion of their comfort, and the preservation of the public peace and good order. Gauged by this standard, we cannot say that a law which authorizes or even requires the separation of the two races in public conveyances is unreasonable, or more obnoxious to the Fourteenth Amendment than the acts of Congress requiring separate schools for colored children in the District of Columbia, the constitutionality of which does not seem to have been questioned, or the corresponding acts of state legislatures.

We consider the underlying fallacy of the plaintiff's argument to consist in the assumption that the enforced separation of the two races stamps the colored race with a badge of inferiority. If this be so, it is not by reason of anything found in the act, but solely because the colored race chooses to put that construction upon it. The argument necessarily assumes that if, as has been more than once the case, and is not unlikely to be so again, the colored race should become the dominant power in the state legislature, and should enact a law in precisely similar terms, it would thereby relegate the white race to an inferior position. We imagine that the white race, at least, would not acquiesce in this assumption. The argument also assumes that social prejudices may be overcome by legislation, and that equal rights cannot be secured to the negro except by an enforced commingling of the two races. We cannot accept this proposition. If the two races are to meet upon terms of social equality, it must be the result of natural affinities, a mutual appreciation of each other's merits and a voluntary consent of individuals. As was said by the Court of Appeals of New York in *People* v. *Gallagher,* 93 N.Y. 438, 448, "this end can neither be accomplished nor promoted by laws which conflict with the general sentiment of the community upon whom they are designed to operate. When the government, therefore, has secured to each of its citizens equal rights before the law and equal opportunities for improvement and progress, it has accomplished the end for which it was organized and performed all of the functions respecting social advantages with which it is endowed." Legislation is powerless to eradicate racial instincts or to abolish distinctions based upon physical differences, and the attempt to do so can only result in accentuating the difficulties of the present situation. If the civil and political rights of both races be equal one cannot be inferior to the other civilly or politically. If one race be inferior to the other socially, the Constitution of the United States cannot put them upon the same plane.

It is true that the question of the proportion of colored blood necessary to constitute a colored person, as distinguished from a white person, is one upon which there is a difference of opinion in the different States, some holding that any visible admixture of black blood stamps the person as belonging to the colored race, (*State* v. *Chavers,* 5 Jones, [N.C.] 1, p. 11); others that it depends upon the preponderance of blood, (*Gray* v. *State,* 4 Ohio, 354; *Monroe* v. *Collins,* 17 Ohio St. 665); and still others that the predominance of white blood must only be in the proportion of three fourths. (*People* v. *Dean,* 14 Michigan, 406; *Jones* v. *Commonwealth,* 80 Virginia, 538.) But these are questions to be determined under the laws of each State and are not properly put in issue in this case. Under the allegations of his petition it may undoubtedly become a question of importance whether, under the laws of Louisiana, the petitioner belongs to the white or colored race.

The judgment of the court below is, therefore,

Affirmed.

MR. JUSTICE HARLAN dissenting.

By the Louisiana statute, the validity of which is here involved, all railway companies (other than street railroad companies) carrying passengers in that State are required to have separate but equal accommodations for white and colored persons, "by providing two or more passenger coaches for each passenger train, *or* by dividing the passenger coaches by a *partition* so as to secure separate accommodations." Under this statute, no colored person is permitted to occupy a seat in a coach assigned to white persons; nor any white person, to occupy a seat in a coach assigned to colored persons. The managers of the railroad are not allowed to exercise any discretion in the premises, but are required to assign each passenger to some coach or compartment set apart for the exclusive use of his race. If a passenger insists upon going into a coach or compartment not set apart for persons of his race, he is subject to be fined, or to be imprisoned in the parish jail. Penalties are prescribed for the refusal or neglect of the officers, directors, conductors and employés of railroad companies to comply with the provisions of the act.

Only "nurses attending children of the other race" are excepted from the operation of the statute. No exception is made of colored attendants travelling with adults. A white man is not permitted to have his colored servant with him in the same coach, even if his condition of health requires the constant, personal assistance of such servant. If a colored maid insists upon riding in the same coach with a white woman whom she has been employed to serve, and who may need her personal attention while travelling, she is subject to be fined or imprisoned for such an exhibition of zeal in the discharge of duty.

While there may be in Louisiana persons of different races who are not citizens of the United States, the words in the act, "white and colored races," necessarily include all citizens of the United States of both races residing in that State. So that we have before us a state enactment that compels, under penalties, the separation of the two races in railroad passenger coaches, and makes it a crime for a citizen of either race to enter a coach that has been assigned to citizens of the other race.

Thus the State regulates the use of a public highway by citizens of the United States solely upon the basis of race.

However apparent the injustice of such legislation may be, we have only to consider whether it is consistent with the Constitution of the United States.

That a railroad is a public highway, and that the corporation which owns or operates it is in the exercise of public functions, is not, at this day, to be disputed. Mr. Justice Nelson, speaking for this court in *New Jersey Steam Navigation Co.* v. *Merchants' Bank,* 6 How. 344, 382, said that a common carrier was in the exercise "of a sort of public office, and has public duties to perform, from which he should not be permitted to exonerate himself without the assent of the parties concerned." Mr. Justice Strong, delivering the judgment of this court in *Olcott* v. *The Supervisors,* 16 Wall. 678, 694, said: "That railroads, though constructed by private corporations and owned by them, are public highways, has been the doctrine of nearly all the courts ever since such conveniences for passage and transportation have had any existence. Very early the question arose whether a State's right of eminent domain could be exercised by a private corporation created for the purpose of constructing a railroad. Clearly it could not, unless taking land for such a purpose by such an agency is taking land for public use. The right of eminent domain nowhere justifies taking property for a private use. Yet it is a doctrine universally accepted that a state legislature may authorize a private corporation to take land for the construction of such a road, making compensation to the owner. What else does this doctrine mean if not that building a railroad, though it be built by a private corporation, is an act done for a public use?" So, in *Township of Pine Grove* v. *Talcott,* 19 Wall. 666, 676: "Though the corporation [a railroad company] was private, its work was public, as much so as if it were to be constructed by the State." So, in *Inhabitants of Worcester* v. *Western Railroad Corporation,* 4 Met. 564: "The establishment of that great thoroughfare is regarded as a public work, established by public authority, intended for the public use and benefit, the use of which is secured to the whole community, and constitutes, therefore, like a canal, turnpike or highway, a public easement." It is true that the real and personal property, necessary to the establishment and management of the railroad, is vested in the corporation; but it is in trust for the public.

In respect of civil rights, common to all citizens, the Constitution of the United States does not, I think, permit any public authority to know the race of those entitled to be protected in the enjoyment of such rights. Every true man has pride of race, and under appropriate circumstances when the rights of others, his equals before the law, are not to be affected, it is his privilege to express such pride and to take such action based upon it as to him seems proper. But I deny that any legislative body or judicial tribunal may have regard to the race of citizens when the civil rights of those citizens are involved. Indeed, such legislation, as that here in question, is inconsistent not only with that equality of rights which pertains to citizenship, National and State, but with the personal liberty enjoyed by every one within the United States.

The Thirteenth Amendment does not permit the with-

holding or the deprivation of any right necessarily inhering in freedom. It not only struck down the institution of slavery as previously existing in the United States, but it prevents the imposition of any burdens or disabilities that constitute badges of slavery or servitude. It decreed universal civil freedom in this country. This court has so adjudged. But that amendment having been found inadequate to the protection of the rights of those who had been in slavery, it was followed by the Fourteenth Amendment, which added greatly to the dignity and glory of American citizenship, and to the security of personal liberty, by declaring that "all persons born or naturalized in the United States, and subject to the jurisdiction thereof, are citizens of the United States and of the State wherein they reside," and that "no State shall make or enforce any law which shall abridge the privileges or immunities of citizens of the United States; nor shall any State deprive any person of life, liberty or property without due process of law, nor deny to any person within its jurisdiction the equal protection of the laws." These two amendments, if enforced according to their true intent and meaning, will protect all the civil rights that pertain to freedom and citizenship. Finally, and to the end that no citizen should be denied, on account of his race, the privilege of participating in the political control of his country, it was declared by the Fifteenth Amendment that "the right of citizens of the United States to vote shall not be denied or abridged by the United States or by any State on account of race, color or previous condition of servitude."

These notable additions to the fundamental law were welcomed by the friends of liberty throughout the world. They removed the race line from our governmental systems. They had, as this court has said, a common purpose, namely, to secure "to a race recently emancipated, a race that through many generations have been held in slavery, all the civil rights that the superior race enjoy." They declared, in legal effect, this court has further said, "that the law in the States shall be the same for the black as for the white; that all persons, whether colored or white, shall stand equal before the laws of the States, and, in regard to the colored race, for whose protection the amendment was primarily designed, that no discrimination shall be made against them by law because of their color." We also said: "The words of the amendment, it is true, are prohibitory, but they contain a necessary implication of a positive immunity, or right, most valuable to the colored race—the right to exemption from unfriendly legislation against them distinctively as colored—exemption from legal discriminations, implying inferiority in civil society, lessening the security of their enjoyment of the rights which others enjoy, and discriminations which are steps towards reducing them to the condition of a subject race." It was, consequently, adjudged that a state law that excluded citizens of the colored race from juries, because of their race and however well qualified in other respects to discharge the duties of jurymen, was repugnant to the Fourteenth Amendment. *Strauder* v. *West Virginia,* 100 U.S. 303, 306, 307; *Virginia* v. *Rives,* 100 U.S. 313; *Ex parte Virginia,* 100 U.S. 339; *Neal* v. *Delaware,* 103 U.S. 370, 386; *Bush* v. *Kentucky,* 107 U.S. 110, 116. At the present term, referring to the previous adjudications, this court declared that "underlying all of those decisions is the principle that the Constitution of the United States, in its present form, forbids, so far as civil and political rights are concerned, discrimination by the General Government or the States against any citizen because of his race. All citizens are equal before the law." *Gibson* v. *Mississippi,* 162 U.S. 565.

The decisions referred to show the scope of the recent amendments of the Constitution. They also show that it is not within the power of a State to prohibit colored citizens, because of their race, from participating as jurors in the administration of justice.

It was said in argument that the statute of Louisiana does not discriminate against either race, but prescribes a rule applicable alike to white and colored citizens. But this argument does not meet the difficulty. Every one knows that the statute in question had its origin in the purpose, not so much to exclude white persons from railroad cars occupied by blacks, as to exclude colored people from coaches occupied by or assigned to white persons. Railroad corporations of Louisiana did not make discrimination among whites in the matter of accommodation for travellers. The thing to accomplish was, under the guise of giving equal accommodation for whites and blacks, to compel the latter to keep to themselves while travelling in railroad passenger coaches. No one would be so wanting in candor as to assert the contrary. The fundamental objection, therefore, to the statute is that it interferes with the personal freedom of citizens. "Personal liberty," it has been well said, "consists in the power of locomotion, of changing situation, or removing one's person to whatsoever places one's own inclination may direct, without imprisonment or restraint, unless by due course of law." 1 Bl. Com. *134. If a white man and a black man choose to occupy the same public conveyance on a public highway, it is their right to do so, and no government, proceeding alone on grounds of race, can prevent it without infringing the personal liberty of each.

It is one thing for railroad carriers to furnish, or to be required by law to furnish, equal accommodations for all whom they are under a legal duty to carry. It is quite another thing for government to forbid citizens of the white and black races from travelling in the same public conveyance, and to punish officers of railroad companies for permitting persons of the two races to occupy the same passenger coach. If a State can prescribe, as a rule of civil conduct, that whites and blacks shall not travel as passengers in the same railroad coach, why may it not so regulate the use of the streets of its cities and towns as to compel white citizens to keep on one side of a street and black citizens to keep on the other? Why may it not, upon like grounds, punish whites and blacks who ride together in street cars or in open vehicles on a public road or street? Why may it not require sheriffs to assign whites to one side of a court-room and blacks to the other? And why may it not also prohibit the commingling of the two races in the galleries of legislative halls or in public assemblages convened for the consideration of the political questions of the day? Further, if this statute of Louisiana is consistent with the personal liberty of citizens, why may not the State require the separation in railroad coaches of native and naturalized citizens of the United States, or of Protestants and Roman Catholics?

The answer given at the argument to these questions was that regulations of the kind they suggest would be unreasonable, and could not, therefore, stand before the law. Is it meant that the determination of questions of legislative power depends upon the inquiry whether the statute whose validity is questioned is, in the judgment of the courts, a reasonable one, taking all the circumstances into consideration? A statute may be unreasonable merely because a sound public policy forbade its enactment. But I do not understand that the courts have anything to do with the policy or expediency of legislation. A statute may be valid, and yet, upon grounds of public policy, may well be characterized as unreasonable. Mr. Sedgwick correctly states the rule when he says that the legislative intention being clearly ascertained, "the courts have no other duty to perform than to execute the legislative will, without any regard to their views as to the wisdom or justice of the particular enactment." Stat. & Const. Constr. 324. There is a dangerous tendency in these latter days to enlarge the functions of the courts, by means of judicial interference with the will of the people as expressed by the legislature. Our institutions have the distinguishing characteristic that the three departments of government are coördinate and separate. Each must keep within the limits defined by the Constitution. And the courts best discharge their duty by executing the will of the law-making power, constitutionally expressed, leaving the results of legislation to be dealt with by the people through their representatives. Statutes must always have a reasonable construction. Sometimes they are to be construed strictly; sometimes, liberally, in order to carry out the legislative will. But however construed, the intent of the legislature is to be respected, if the particular statute in question is valid, although the courts, looking at the public interests, may conceive the statute to be both unreasonable and impolitic. If the power exists to enact a statute, that ends the matter so far as the courts are concerned. The adjudged cases in which statutes have been held to be void, because unreasonable, are those in which the means employed by the legislature were not at all germane to the end to which the legislature was competent.

The white race deems itself to be the dominant race in this country. And so it is, in prestige, in achievements, in education, in wealth and in power. So, I doubt not, it will continue to be for all time, if it remains true to its great heritage and holds fast to the principles of constitutional liberty. But in view of the Constitution, in the eye of the law, there is in this country no superior, dominant, ruling class of citizens. There is no caste here. Our Constitution is color-blind, and neither knows nor tolerates classes among citizens. In respect of civil rights, all citizens are equal before the law. The humblest is the peer of the most powerful. The law regards man as man, and takes no account of his surroundings or of his color when his civil rights as guaranteed by the supreme law of the land are involved. It is, therefore, to be regretted that this high tribunal, the final expositor of the fundamental law of the land, has reached the conclusion that it is competent for a State to regulate the enjoyment by citizens of their civil rights solely upon the basis of race.

In my opinion, the judgment this day rendered will, in time, prove to be quite as pernicious as the decision made by this tribunal in the *Dred Scott case.* It was adjudged in that case that the descendants of Africans who were imported into this country and sold as slaves were not included nor intended to be included under the word "citizens" in the Constitution, and could not claim any of the rights and privileges which that instrument provided for and secured to citizens of the United States; that at the time of the adoption of the Constitution they were "considered as a subordinate and inferior class of beings, who had been subjugated by the dominant race, and, whether emancipated or not, yet remained subject to their authority, and had no rights or privileges but such as those who held the power and the government might choose to grant them." The recent amendments of the Constitution, it was supposed, had eradicated these principles from our institutions. But it seems that we have yet, in some of the States, a dominant race—a superior class of citizens, which assumes to regulate the enjoyment of civil rights, common to all citizens, upon the basis of race. The present decision, it may well be apprehended, will not only stimulate aggressions, more or less brutal and irritating, upon the admitted rights of colored citizens, but will encourage the belief that it is possible, by means of state enactments, to defeat the beneficent purposes which the people of the United States had in view when they adopted the recent amendments of the Constitution, by one of which the blacks of this country were made citizens of the United States and of the States in which they respectively reside, and whose privileges and immunities, as citizens, the States are forbidden to abridge. Sixty millions of whites are in no danger from the presence here of eight millions of blacks. The destinies of the two races, in this country, are indissolubly linked together, and the interests of both require that the common government of all shall not permit the seeds of race hate to be planted under the sanction of law. What can more certainly arouse race hate, what more certainly create and perpetuate a feeling of distrust between these races, than state enactments, which, in fact, proceed on the ground that colored citizens are so inferior and degraded that they cannot be allowed to sit in public coaches occupied by white citizens? That, as all will admit, is the real meaning of such legislation as was enacted in Louisiana.

The sure guarantee of the peace and security of each race is the clear, distinct, unconditional recognition by our governments, National and State, of every right that inheres in civil freedom, and of the equality before the law of all citizens of the United States without regard to race. State enactments, regulating the enjoyment of civil rights, upon the basis of race, and cunningly devised to defeat legitimate results of the war, under the pretence of recognizing equality of rights, can have no other result than to render permanent peace impossible, and to keep alive a conflict of races, the continuance of which must do harm to all concerned. This question is not met by the suggestion that social equality cannot exist between the white and black races in this country. That argument, if it can be properly regarded as one, is scarcely worthy of consideration; for social equality no more exists between two races when travelling in a passenger coach or a public highway than when members of the same races sit by each other in a street car or in the jury box, or stand or sit with each other in a political assembly, or when they use in common the streets of a city or town, or when they are in the same room for the purpose of having their names placed on the registry of voters, or when they approach the ballot-box in order to exercise the high privilege of voting.

There is a race so different from our own that we do not permit those belonging to it to become citizens of the United States. Persons belonging to it are, with few exceptions, absolutely excluded from our country. I allude to the Chinese race. But by the statute in question, a Chinaman can ride in the same passenger coach with white citizens of the United States, while citizens of the black race in Louisiana, many of whom, perhaps, risked their lives for the preservation of the Union, who are entitled, by law, to participate in the political control of the State and nation, who are not excluded, by law or by reason of their race, from public stations of any kind, and who have all the legal rights that belong to white citizens, are yet declared to be criminals, liable to imprisonment, if they ride in a public coach occupied by citizens of the white race. It is scarcely just to say that a colored citizen should not object to occupying a public coach assigned to his own race. He does not object, nor, perhaps, would he object to separate coaches for his race, if his rights under the law were recognized. But he objects, and ought never to cease objecting to the proposition, that citizens of the white and black races can be adjudged criminals because they sit, or claim the right to sit, in the same public coach on a public highway.

The arbitrary separation of citizens, on the basis of race, while they are on a public highway, is a badge of servitude wholly inconsistent with the civil freedom and the equality before the law established by the Constitution. It cannot be justified upon any legal grounds.

If evils will result from the commingling of the two races upon public highways established for the benefit of all, they will be infinitely less than those that will surely come from state legislation regulating the enjoyment of civil rights upon the basis of race. We boast of the freedom enjoyed by our people above all other peoples. But it is difficult to reconcile that boast with a state of the law which, practically, puts the brand of servitude and degradation upon a large class of our fellow-citizens, our equals before the law. The thin disguise of "equal" accommodations for passengers in railroad

coaches will not mislead any one, nor atone for the wrong this day done.

The result of the whole matter is, that while this court has frequently adjudged, and at the present term has recognized the doctrine, that a State cannot, consistently with the Constitution of the United States, prevent white and black citizens, having the required qualifications for jury service, from sitting in the same jury box, it is now solemnly held that a State may prohibit white and black citizens from sitting in the same passenger coach on a public highway, or may require that they be separated by a "partition," when in the same passenger coach. May it not now be reasonably expected that astute men of the dominant race, who affect to be disturbed at the possibility that the integrity of the white race may be corrupted, or that its supremacy will be imperilled, by contact on public highways with black people, will endeavor to procure statutes requiring white and black jurors to be separated in the jury box by a "partition," and that, upon retiring from the court room to consult as to their verdict, such partition, if it be a moveable one, shall be taken to their consultation room, and set up in such way as to prevent black jurors from coming too close to their brother jurors of the white race. If the "partition" used in the court room happens to be stationary, provision could be made for screens with openings through which jurors of the two races could confer as to their verdict without coming into personal contact with each other. I cannot see but that, according to the principles this day announced, such state legislation, although conceived in hostility to, and enacted for the purpose of humiliating citizens of the United States of a particular race, would be held to be consistent with the Constitution.

I do not deem it necessary to review the decisions of state courts to which reference was made in argument. Some, and the most important, of them are wholly inapplicable, because rendered prior to the adoption of the last amendments of the Constitution, when colored people had very few rights which the dominant race felt obliged to respect. Others were made at a time when public opinion, in many localities, was dominated by the institution of slavery; when it would not have been safe to do justice to the black man; and when, so far as the rights of blacks were concerned, race prejudice was, practically, the supreme law of the land. Those decisions cannot be guides in the era introduced by the recent amendments of the supreme law, which established universal civil freedom, gave citizenship to all born or naturalized in the United States and residing here, obliterated the race line from our systems of governments, National and State, and placed our free institutions upon the broad and sure foundation of the equality of all men before the law.

I am of opinion that the statute of Louisiana is inconsistent with the personal liberty of citizens, white and black, in that State, and hostile to both the spirit and letter of the Constitution of the United States. If laws of like character should be enacted in the several States of the Union, the effect would be in the highest degree mischievous. Slavery, as an institution tolerated by law would, it is true, have disappeared from our country, but there would remain a power in the States, by sinister legislation, to interfere with the full enjoyment of the blessings of freedom; to regulate civil rights, common to all citizens, upon the basis of race; and to place in a condition of legal inferiority a large body of American citizens, now constituting a part of the political community called the People of the United States, for whom, and by whom through representatives, our government is administered. Such a system is inconsistent with the guarantee given by the Constitution to each State of a republican form of government, and may be stricken down by Congressional action, or by the courts in the discharge of their solemn duty to maintain the supreme law of the land, anything in the constitution or laws of any State to the contrary notwithstanding.

For the reasons stated, I am constrained to withhold my assent from the opinion and judgment of the majority.

Mr. Justice Brewer did not hear the argument or participate in the decision of this case.

The Talented Tenth, *W. E. B. DuBois,* 1903

W. E. B. DuBois (1868–1963) was born in Massachusetts and educated at Fisk College (now University), the University of Berlin, and Harvard, from which he received his Ph.D. A prominent sociologist and author of a number of books, DuBois was also a founder of the National Association for the Advancement of Colored People (NAACP) and leader in a variety of movements, including those working for African American civil rights and those promoting international socialism and pan-African solidarity. He engaged in a long-running debate with Booker T. Washington over whether African Americans should forgo political agitation in favor of economic improvement and stability. The essay reproduced here argues for greater emphasis on development of higher education for the "most talented" African Americans. This contrasted pointedly with Washington's emphasis on education in trades and mechanical arts.

The Talented Tenth

W. E. B. DuBois

The Negro race, like all races, is going to be saved by its exceptional men. The problem of education, then, among Negroes must first of all deal with the Talented Tenth; it is the problem of developing the Best of this race that they may guide the Mass away from the contamination and death of the Worst, in their own and other races. Now the training of men is a difficult and intricate task. Its technique is a matter for educational experts, but its object is for the vision of seers. If we make money the object of man-training, we shall develop money-makers but not necessarily men; if we make technical skill the object of education, we may possess artisans but not, in nature, men. Men we shall have only as we make manhood the object of the work of the schools—intelligence, broad sympathy, knowledge of the world that was and is, and of the relation of men to it—this is the curriculum of that Higher Education which must underlie true life. On this foundation we may build bread winning, skill of hand and quickness of brain, with never a fear lest the child and man mistake the means of living for the object of life.

If this be true—and who can deny it—three tasks lay before me; first to show from the past that the Talented Tenth as they have risen among American Negroes have been worthy of leadership; secondly, to show how these men may be educated and developed; and thirdly, to show their relation to the Negro problem.

You misjudge us because you do not know us. From the very first it has been the educated and intelligent of the Negro people that have led and elevated the mass, and the sole obstacles that nullified and retarded their efforts were slavery and race prejudice; for what is slavery but the legalized survival of the unfit and the nullification of the work of natural internal leadership? Negro leadership, therefore, sought from the first to rid the race of this awful incubus that it might make way for natural selection and the survival of the fittest. In colonial days came Phillis Wheatley and Paul Cuffe striving against the bars of prejudice; and Benjamin Banneker, the almanac maker, voiced their longings when he said to Thomas Jefferson, "I freely and cheerfully acknowledge that I am of the African race, and in colour which is natural to them, of the deepest dye; and it is under a sense of the most profound gratitude to the Supreme Ruler of the Universe, that I now confess to you that I am not under that state of tyrannical thraldom and inhuman captivity to which too many of my brethren are doomed, but that I have abundantly tasted of the fruition of those blessings which proceed from that free and unequalled liberty with which you are favored, and which I hope you will willingly allow, you have mercifully received from the immediate hand of that Being from whom proceedeth every good and perfect gift.

"Suffer me to recall to your mind that time, in which the arms of the British crown were exerted with every powerful effort, in order to reduce you to a state of servitude; look back, I entreat you, on the variety of dangers to which you were exposed; reflect on that period in which every human aid appeared unavailable, and in which even hope and fortitude wore the aspect of inability to the conflict, and you cannot but be led to a serious and grateful sense of your miraculous and providential preservation, you cannot but acknowledge, that the present freedom and tranquility which you enjoy, you have mercifully received, and that a peculiar blessing of heaven.

"This, sir, was a time when you clearly saw into the injustice of a state of Slavery, and in which you had just apprehensions of the horrors of its condition. It was then that your abhorrence thereof was so excited, that you publicly held forth this true and invaluable doctrine, which is worthy to be recorded and remembered in all succeeding ages: 'We hold these truths to be self evident, that all men are created equal; that they are endowed with certain inalienable rights, and that among these are life, liberty and the pursuit of happiness.'"

Then came Dr. James Derham, who could tell even the learned Dr. Rush something of medicine, and Lemuel Haynes, to whom Middlebury College gave an honorary A.M. in 1804. These and others we may call the Revolutionary group of distinguished Negroes—they were persons of marked ability, leaders of a Talented Tenth, standing conspicuously among the best of their time. They strove by word and deed to save the color line from becoming the line between the bond and free, but all they could do was nullified by Eli Whitney and the Curse of Gold. So they passed into forgetfulness.

But their spirit did not wholly die; here and there in the early part of the century came other exceptional men. Some were natural sons of unnatural fathers and were given often a liberal training and thus a race of educated mulattoes sprang up to plead for black men's rights. There was Ira Aldridge, whom all Europe loved to honor; there was that Voice crying in the Wilderness, David Walker, and saying:

"I declare it does appear to me as though some nations think God is asleep, or that he made the Africans for nothing else but to dig their mines and work their farms, or they cannot believe history, sacred or profane. I ask every man who has a heart, and is blessed with the privilege of believing—Is not God a God of justice to all his creatures? Do you say he is? Then if he gives peace and tranquility to tyrants and permits them to keep our fathers, our mothers, ourselves and our children in eternal ignorance and wretchedness to sup-

port them and their families, would he be to us a God of Justice? I ask, O, ye Christians, who hold us and our children in the most abject ignorance and degradation that ever a people were afflicted with since the world began—I say if God gives you peace and tranquility, and suffers you thus to go on afflicting us, and our children, who have never given you the least provocation—would He be to us a God of Justice? If you will allow that we are men, who feel for each other, does not the blood of our fathers and of us, their children, cry aloud to the Lord of Sabaoth against you for the cruelties and murders with which you have and do continue to afflict us?"

This was the wild voice that first aroused Southern legislators in 1829 to the terrors of abolitionism.

In 1831 there met that first Negro convention in Philadelphia, at which the world gaped curiously but which bravely attacked the problems of race and slavery, crying out against persecution and declaring that "Laws as cruel in themselves as they were unconstitutional and unjust, have in many places been enacted against our poor, unfriended and unoffending brethren (without a shadow of provocation on our part), at whose bare recital the very savage draws himself up for fear of contagion—looks noble and prides himself because he bears not the name of Christian." Side by side this free Negro movement, and the movement for abolition, strove until they merged into one strong stream. Too little notice has been taken of the work which the Talented Tenth among Negroes took in the great abolition crusade. From the very day that a Philadelphia colored man became the first subscriber to Garrison's "Liberator," to the day when Negro soldiers made the Emancipation Proclamation possible, black leaders worked shoulder to shoulder with white men in a movement, the success of which would have been impossible without them. There was Purvis and Remond, Pennington and Highland Garnett, Sojourner Truth and Alexander Crummel, and above all, Frederick Douglass—what would the abolition movement have been without them? They stood as living examples of the possibilities of the Negro race, their own hard experiences and well wrought culture said silently more than all the drawn periods of orators—they were the men who made American slavery impossible. As Maria Weston Chapman once said, from the school of anti-slavery agitation "a throng of authors, editors, lawyers, orators and accomplished gentlemen of color have taken their degree! It has equally implanted hopes and aspirations, noble thoughts, and sublime purposes, in the hearts of both races. It has prepared the white man for the freedom of the black man, and it has made the black man scorn the thought of enslavement, as does a white man, as far as its influence has extended. Strengthen that noble influence! Before its organization, the country only saw here and there in slavery some faithful Cudjoe or Dinah, whose strong natures blossomed even in bondage, like a fine plant beneath a heavy stone. Now, under the elevating and cherishing influence of the American Anti-slavery Society, the colored race, like the white, furnishes Corinthian capitals for the noblest temples."

Where were these black abolitionists trained? Some, like Frederick Douglass, were self-trained, but yet trained liberally; others, like Alexander Crummell and McCune Smith, graduated from famous foreign universities. Most of them rose up through the colored schools of New York and Philadelphia and Boston, taught by college-bred men like Russworm, of Dartmouth, and college-bred white men like Neau and Benezet.

After emancipation came a new group of educated and gifted leaders: Langston, Bruce and Elliot. Greener, Williams and Payne. Through political organization, historical and polemic writing and moral regeneration, these men strove to uplift their people. It is the fashion of to-day to sneer at them and to say that with freedom Negro leadership should have begun at the plow and not in the Senate—a foolish and mischievous lie; two hundred and fifty years that black serf toiled at the plow and yet that toiling was in vain till the Senate passed the war amendments; and two hundred and fifty years more the half-free serf of to-day may toil at his plow, but unless he have political rights and righteously guarded civic status, he will still remain the poverty-stricken and ignorant plaything of rascals, that he now is. This all sane men know even if they dare not say it.

And so we come to the present—a day of cowardice and vacillation, of strident wide-voiced wrong and faint hearted compromise; of double-faced dallying with Truth and Right. Who are to-day guiding the work of the Negro people? The "exceptions" of course. And yet so sure as this Talented Tenth is pointed out, the blind worshippers of the Average cry out in alarm: "These are exceptions, look here at death, disease and crime—these are the happy rule." Of course they are the rule, because a silly nation made them the rule: Because for three long centuries this people lynched Negroes who dared to be brave, raped black women who dared to be virtuous, crushed dark-hued youth who dared to be ambitious, and encouraged and made to flourish servility and lewdness and apathy. But not even this was able to crush all manhood and chastity and

aspiration from black folk. A saving remnant continually survives and persists, continually aspires, continually shows itself in thrift and ability and character. Exceptional it is to be sure, but this is its chiefest promise; it shows the capability of Negro blood, the promise of black men. Do Americans ever stop to reflect that there are in this land a million men of Negro blood, well-educated, owners of homes, against the honor of whose womanhood no breath was ever raised, whose men occupy positions of trust and usefulness, and who, judged by any standard, have reached the full measure of the best type of modern European culture? Is it fair, is it decent, is it Christian to ignore these facts of the Negro problem, to belittle such aspiration, to nullify such leadership and seek to crush these people back into the mass out of which by toil and travail, they and their fathers have raised themselves?

Can the masses of the Negro people be in any possible way more quickly raised than by the effort and example of this aristocracy of talent and character? Was there ever a nation on God's fair earth civilized from the bottom upward? Never; it is, ever was and ever will be from the top downward that culture filters. The Talented Tenth rises and pulls all that are worth the saving up to their vantage ground. This is the history of human progress; and the two historic mistakes which have hindered that progress were the thinking first that no more could ever rise save the few already risen; or second, that it would better the unrisen to pull the risen down.

How then shall the leaders of a struggling people be trained and the hands of the risen few strengthened? There can be but one answer: The best and most capable of their youth must be schooled in the colleges and universities of the land. We will not quarrel as to just what the university of the Negro should teach or how it should teach it—I willingly admit that each soul and each race-soul needs its own peculiar curriculum. But this is true: A university is a human invention for the transmission of knowledge and culture from generation to generation, through the training of quick minds and pure hearts, and for this work no other human invention will suffice, not even trade and industrial schools.

All men cannot go to college but some men must; every isolated group or nation must have its yeast, must have for the talented few centers of training where men are not so mystified and befuddled by the hard and necessary toil of earning a living, as to have no aims higher than their bellies, and no God greater than Gold. This is true training, and thus in the beginning were the favored sons of the freedmen trained. Out of the colleges of the North came, after the blood of war,

Ware, Cravath, Chase, Andrews, Bumstead and Spence to build the foundations of knowledge and civilization in the black South. Where ought they to have begun to build? At the bottom, of course, quibbles the mole with his eyes in the earth. Aye! truly at the bottom, at the very bottom; at the bottom of knowledge, down in the very depths of knowledge there where the roots of justice strike into the lowest soil of Truth. And so they did begin; they founded colleges, and up from the colleges shot normal schools, and out from the normal schools went teachers, and around the normal teachers clustered other teachers to teach the public schools; the college trained in Greek and Latin and mathematics, 2,000 men; and these men trained full 50,000 others in morals and manners, and they in turn taught thrift and the alphabet to nine millions of men, who to-day hold $300,000,000 of property. It was a miracle—the most wonderful peace-battle of the 19th century, and yet to-day men smile at it, and in fine superiority tell us that it was all a strange mistake; that a proper way to found a system of education is first to gather the children and buy them spelling books and hoes; afterward men may look about for teachers, if haply they may find them; or again they would teach men Work, but as for Life—why, what has Work to do with Life, they ask vacantly.

Was the work of these college founders successful; did it stand the test of time? Did the college graduates, with all their fine theories of life, really live? Are they useful men helping to civilize and elevate their less fortunate fellows? Let us see. Omitting all institutions which have not actually graduated students from a college course, there are to-day in the United States thirty-four institutions giving something above high school training to Negroes and designed especially for this race.

Three of these were established in border States before the War; thirteen were planted by the Freedmen's Bureau in the years 1864–1869; nine were established between 1870 and 1880 by various church bodies; five were established after 1881 by Negro churches, and four are state institutions supported by United States' agricultural funds. In most cases the college departments are small adjuncts to high and common school work. As a matter of fact six institutions—Atlanta, Fisk, Howard, Shaw, Wilberforce and Leland, are the important Negro colleges so far as actual work and number of students are concerned. In all these institutions, seven hundred and fifty Negro college students are enrolled. In grade the best of these colleges are about a year behind the smaller New England colleges and a typical curriculum is that of Atlanta Uni-

versity. Here students from the grammar grades, after a three years' high school course, take a college course of 136 weeks. One-fourth of this time is given to Latin and Greek; one-fifth, to English and modern languages; one-sixth, to history and social science; one-seventh, to natural science; one-eighth to mathematics, and one-eighth to philosophy and pedagogy.

In addition to these students in the South, Negroes have attended Northern colleges for many years. As early as 1826 one was graduated from Bowdoin College, and from that time till to-day nearly every year has seen elsewhere, other such graduates. They have, of course, met much color prejudice. Fifty years ago very few colleges would admit them at all. Even to-day no Negro has ever been admitted to Princeton, and at some other leading institutions they are rather endured than encouraged. Oberlin was the great pioneer in the work of blotting out the color line in colleges, and has more Negro graduates by far than any other Northern college.

The total number of Negro college graduates up to 1899 (several of the graduates of that year not being reported) was as follows:

	Negro Colleges	White Colleges
Before '76	137	75
'75–80	143	22
'80–85	250	31
'85–90	413	43
'90–95	465	66
'95–99	475	88
Class Unknown	57	64
TOTAL	1,914	390

Of these graduates 2,079 were men and 252 were women; 50 per cent. of Northern-born college men come South to work among the masses of their people, at a sacrifice which few people realize; nearly 90 per cent. of the Southern-born graduates instead of seeking that personal freedom and broader intellectual atmosphere which their training has led them, in some degree, to conceive, stay and labor and wait in the midst of their black neighbors and relatives.

The most interesting question, and in many respects the crucial question, to be asked concerning college-bred Negroes, is: Do they earn a living? It has been intimated more than once that the higher training of Negroes has resulted in sending into the world of work, men who could find nothing to do suitable to their talents. Now and then there comes a rumor of a colored college man working at menial service, etc. Fortunately, returns as to occupations of college-bred Negroes, gathered by the Atlanta conference, are quite full—nearly sixty per cent. of the total number of graduates.

This enables us to reach fairly certain conclusions as to the occupations of all college-bred Negroes. Of 1,312 persons reported, there were:

	Per Cent.
Teachers	53.4
Clergymen	16.8
Physicians, etc.	6.3
Students	5.6
Lawyers	4.7
In Govt. Service	4.0
In Business	3.6
Farmers and Artisans	2.7
Editors, Secretaries and Clerks	2.4
Miscellaneous	.5

Over half are teachers, a sixth are preachers, another sixth are students and professional men; over 6 per cent. are farmers, artisans and merchants, and 4 per cent. are in government service. In detail the occupations are as follows:

Occupations of College-Bred Men

Teachers:

Presidents and Deans	19	
Teacher of Music	7	
Professors, Principals and Teachers	675	Total 701

Clergymen:

Bishop	1	
Chaplains U.S. Army	2	
Missionaries	9	
Presiding Elders	12	
Preachers	197	Total 221

Physicians:

Doctors of Medicine	76	
Druggists	4	
Dentists	3	Total 83
Students		74
Lawyers		62

Civil Service:

U.S. Minister Plenipotentiary	1	
U.S. Consul	1	
U.S. Deputy Collector	1	
U.S. Gauger	1	
U.S. Postmasters	2	
U.S. Clerks	44	
State Civil Service	2	
City Civil Service	1	Total 53

Business Men:

Merchants, etc.	30	
Managers	13	
Real Estate Dealers	4	Total 47
Farmers		26

Clerks and Secretaries:

Secretary of National Societies	7	
Clerks, etc.	15	Total 22
Artisans		9
Editors		9
Miscellaneous		5

These figures illustrate vividly the function of the college-bred Negro. He is, as he ought to be, the group leader, the man who sets the ideals of the community where he lives, directs its thoughts and heads its social movements. It need hardly be argued that the Negro people need social leadership more than most groups; that they have no traditions to fall back upon, no long established customs, no strong family ties, no well defined social classes. All these things must be slowly and painfully evolved. The preacher was, even before the war, the group leader of the Negroes, and the church their greatest social institution. Naturally this preacher was ignorant and often immoral, and the problem of replacing the older type by better educated men has been a difficult one. Both by direct work and by direct influence on other preachers, and on congregations, the college-bred preacher has an opportunity for reformatory work and moral inspiration, the value of which cannot be overestimated.

It has, however, been in the furnishing of teachers that the Negro college has found its peculiar function. Few persons realize how vast a work, how mighty a revolution has been thus accomplished. To furnish five millions and more of ignorant people with teachers of their own race and blood, in one generation, was not only a very difficult undertaking, but a very important one, in that, it placed before the eyes of almost every Negro child an attainable ideal. It brought the masses of the blacks in contact with modern civilization, made black men the leaders of their communities and trainers of the new generation. In this work college-bred Negroes were first teachers, and then teachers of teachers. And here it is that the broad culture of college work has been of peculiar value. Knowledge of life and its wider meaning, has been the point of the Negro's deepest ignorance, and the sending out of teachers whose training has not been simply for bread winning, but also for human culture, has been of inestimable value in the training of these men.

In earlier years the two occupations of preacher and teacher were practically the only ones open to the black college graduate. Of later years a larger diversity of life among his people, has opened new avenues of employment. Nor have these college men been paupers and spendthrifts; 557 college-bred Negroes owned in 1899, $1,342,862.50 worth of real estate, (assessed value) or $2,411 per family. The real value of the total accumulations of the whole group is perhaps about $10,000,000, or $5,000 a piece. Pitiful, is it not, beside the fortunes of oil kings and steel trusts, but after all is the fortune of the millionaire the only stamp of true and successful living? Alas! it is, with many, and there's the rub.

The problem of training the Negro is to-day immensely complicated by the fact that the whole question of the efficiency and appropriateness of our present systems of education, for any kind of child, is a matter of active debate, in which final settlement seems still afar off. Consequently it often happens that persons arguing for or against certain systems of education for Negroes, have these controversies in mind and miss the real question at issue. The main question, so far as the Southern Negro is concerned, is: What under the present circumstance, must a system of education do in order to raise the Negro as quickly as possible in the scale of civilization? The answer to this question seems to me clear: It must strengthen the Negro's character, increase his knowledge and teach him to earn a living. Now it goes without saying, that it is hard to do all these things simultaneously or suddenly, and that at the same time it will not do to give all the attention to one and neglect the others: we could give black boys trades, but that alone will not civilize a race of ex-slaves; we might simply increase their knowledge of the world, but this would not necessarily make them wish to use this knowledge honestly; we might seek to strengthen character and purpose, but to what end if this people have nothing to eat or to wear? A system of education is not one thing, nor does it have a single definite object, nor is it a mere matter of schools. Education is that whole system of human training within and without the school house walls, which molds and develops men. If then we start out to train an ignorant and unskilled

people with a heritage of bad habits, our system of training must set before itself two great aims—the one dealing with knowledge and character, the other part seeking to give the child the technical knowledge necessary for him to earn a living under the present circumstances. These objects are accomplished in part by the opening of the common schools on the one, and of the industrial schools on the other. But only in part, for there must also be trained those who are to teach these schools—men and women of knowledge and culture and technical skill who understand modern civilization, and have the training and aptitude to impart it to the children under them. There must be teachers, and teachers of teachers, and to attempt to establish any sort of a system of common and industrial school training, without *first* (and I say *first* advisedly) without *first* providing for the higher training of the very best teachers, is simply throwing your money to the winds. School houses do not teach themselves—piles of brick and mortar and machinery do not send out *men*. It is the trained, living human soul, cultivated and strengthened by long study and thought, that breathes the real breath of life into boys and girls and makes them human, whether they be black or white, Greek, Russian or American. Nothing, in these latter days, has so dampened the faith of thinking Negroes in recent educational movements, as the fact that such movements have been accompanied by ridicule and denouncement and decrying of those very institutions of higher training which made the Negro public school possible, and make Negro industrial schools thinkable. It was Fisk, Atlanta, Howard and Straight, those colleges born of the faith and sacrifice of the abolitionists, that placed in the black schools of the South the 30,000 teachers and more, which some, who depreciate the work of these higher schools, are using to teach their own new experiments. If Hampton, Tuskegee and the hundred other industrial schools prove in the future to be as successful as they deserve to be, then their success in training black artisans for the South, will be due primarily to the white colleges of the North and the black colleges of the South, which trained the teachers who to-day conduct these institutions. There was a time when the American people believed pretty devoutly that a log of wood with a boy at one end and Mark Hopkins at the other, represented the highest ideal of human training. But in these eager days it would seem that we have changed all that and think it necessary to add a couple of saw-mills and a hammer to this outfit, and, at a pinch, to dispense with the services of Mark Hopkins.

I would not deny, or for a moment seem to deny, the paramount necessity of teaching the Negro to work, and to work steadily and skillfully; or seem to depreciate in the slightest degree the important part industrial schools must play in the accomplishment of these ends, but I *do* say, and insist upon it, that it is industrialism drunk with its vision of success, to imagine that its own work can be accomplished without providing for the training of broadly cultured men and women to teach its own teachers, and to teach the teachers of the public schools.

But I have already said that human education is not simply a matter of schools; it is much more a matter of family and group life—the training of one's home, of one's daily companions, of one's social class. Now the black boy of the South moves in a black world—a world with its own leaders, its own thoughts, its own ideals. In this world he gets by far the larger part of his life training, and through the eyes of this dark world he peers into the veiled world beyond. Who guides and determines the education which he receives in his world? His teachers here are the group-leaders of the Negro people—the physicians and clergymen, the trained fathers and mothers, the influential and forceful men about him of all kinds; here it is, if at all, that the culture of the surrounding world trickles through and is handed on by the graduates of the higher schools. Can such culture training of group leaders be neglected? Can we afford to ignore it? Do you think that if the leaders of thought among Negroes are not trained and educated thinkers, that they will have no leaders? On the contrary a hundred half-trained demagogues will still hold the places they so largely occupy now, and hundreds of vociferous busy-bodies will multiply. You have no choice; either you must help furnish this race from within its own ranks with thoughtful men of trained leadership, or you must suffer the evil consequences of a headless misguided rabble.

I am an earnest advocate of manual training and trade teaching for black boys, and for white boys, too. I believe that next to the founding of Negro colleges the most valuable addition to Negro education since the war, has been industrial training for black boys. Nevertheless, I insist that the object of all true education is not to make men carpenters, it is to make carpenters men; there are two means of making the carpenter a man, each equally important: the first is to give the group and community in which he works, liberally trained teachers and leaders to teach him and his family what life means; the second is to give him sufficient intelligence and technical skill to make him an efficient workman; the first object demands

the Negro college and college-bred men—not a quantity of such colleges, but a few of excellent quality; not too many college-bred men, but enough to leaven the lump, to inspire the masses, to raise the Talented Tenth to leadership; the second object demands a good system of common schools, well-taught, conveniently located and properly equipped.

The Sixth Atlanta Conference truly said in 1901:

"We call the attention of the Nation to the fact that less than one million of the three million Negro children of school age, are at present regularly attending school, and these attend a session which lasts only a few months.

"We are to-day deliberately rearing millions of our citizens in ignorance, and at the same time limiting the rights of citizenship by educational qualifications. This is unjust. Half the black youth of the land have no opportunities open to them for learning to read, write and cipher. In the discussion as to the proper training of Negro children after they leave the public schools, we have forgotten that they are not yet decently provided with public schools.

"Propositions are beginning to be made in the South to reduce the already meagre school facilities of Negroes. We congratulate the South on resisting, as much as it has, this pressure, and on the many millions it has spent on Negro education. But it is only fair to point out that Negro taxes and the Negroes' share of the income from indirect taxes and endowments have fully repaid this expenditure, so that the Negro public school system has not in all probability cost the white taxpayers a single cent since the war.

"This is not fair. Negro schools should be a public burden, since they are a public benefit. The Negro has a right to demand good common school training at the hands of the States and the Nation since by their fault he is not in position to pay for this himself."

What is the chief need for the building up of the Negro public school in the South? The Negro race in the South needs teachers to-day above all else. This is the concurrent testimony of all who know the situation. For the supply of this great demand two things are needed—institutions of higher education and money for school houses and salaries. It is usually assumed that a hundred or more institutions for Negro training are to-day turning out so many teachers and college-bred men that the race is threatened with an oversupply. This is sheer nonsense. There are to-day less than 3,000 living Negro college graduates in the United States, and less than 1,000 Negroes in college. Moreover, in the 164 schools for Negroes, 95 per cent. of their students are doing elementary and secondary work, work which should be done in the public schools. Over half the remaining 2,157 students are taking high school studies. The mass of so-called "normal" schools for the Negro, are simply doing elementary common school work, or, at most, high school work, with a little instruction in methods. The Negro colleges and the postgraduate courses at other institutions are the only agencies for the broader and more careful training of teachers. The work of these institutions is hampered for lack of funds. It is getting increasingly difficult to get funds for training teachers in the best modern methods, and yet all over the South, from State Superintendents, county officials, city boards and school principals comes the wail, "We need TEACHERS!" and teachers must be trained. As the fairest minded of all white Southerners, Atticus G. Haygood, once said: "The defects of colored teachers are so great as to create an urgent necessity for training better ones. Their excellencies and their successes are sufficient to justify the best hopes of success in the effort, and to vindicate the judgment of those who make large investments of money and service, to give to colored students opportunity for thoroughly preparing themselves for the work of teaching children of their people."

The truth of this has been strikingly shown in the marked improvement of white teachers in the South. Twenty years ago the rank and file of white public school teachers were not as good as the Negro teachers. But they, by scholarships and good salaries, have been encouraged to thorough normal and collegiate preparation, while the Negro teachers have been discouraged by starvation wages and the idea that any training will do for a black teacher. If carpenters are needed it is well and good to train men as carpenters. But to train men as carpenters, and then set them to teaching is wasteful and criminal; and to train men as teachers and then refuse them living wages, unless they become carpenters, is rank nonsense.

The United States Commissioner of Education says in his report for 1900: "For comparison between the white and colored enrollment in secondary and higher education, I have added together the enrollment in high schools and secondary schools, with the attendance on colleges and universities, not being sure of the actual grade of work done in the colleges and universities. The work done in the secondary schools is reported in such detail in this office, that there can be no doubt of its grade."

He then makes the following comparisons of persons in every million enrolled in secondary and higher education:

	Whole Country	Negroes
1880	4,362	1,289
1900	10,743	2,061

And he concludes: "While the number in colored high schools and colleges had increased somewhat faster than the population, it had not kept pace with the average of the whole country, for it had fallen from 30 per cent. to 24 per cent. of the average quota. Of all colored pupils, one (1) in one hundred was engaged in secondary and higher work, and that ratio has continued substantially for the past twenty years. If the ratio of colored population in secondary and higher education is to be equal to the average for the whole country, it must be increased to five times its present average." And if this be true of the secondary and higher education, it is safe to say that the Negro has not one-tenth his quota in college studies. How baseless, therefore, is the charge of too much training! We need Negro teachers for the Negro common schools, and we need first-class normal schools and colleges to train them. This is the work of higher Negro education and it must be done.

Further than this, after being provided with group leaders of civilization, and a foundation of intelligence in the public schools, the carpenter, in order to be a man, needs technical skill. This calls for trade schools. Now trade schools are not nearly such simple things as people once thought. The original idea was that the "Industrial" school was to furnish education, practically free, to those willing to work for it; it was to "do" things—i.e.: become a center of productive industry, it was to be partially, if not wholly, self-supporting, and it was to teach trades. Admirable as were some of the ideas underlying this scheme, the whole thing simply would not work in practice; it was found that if you were to use time and material to teach trades thoroughly, you could not at the same time keep the industries on a commercial basis and make them pay. Many schools started out to do this on a large scale and went into virtual bankruptcy. Moreover, it was found also that it was possible to teach a boy a trade mechanically, without giving him the full educative benefit of the process, and, vice versa, that there was a distinctive educative value in teaching a boy to use his hands and eyes in carrying out certain physical processes, even though he did not actually learn a trade. It has happened, therefore, in the last decade, that a noticeable change has come over the industrial schools. In the first place the idea of commercially remunerative industry in a school is being pushed rapidly to the background. There are still schools with shops and farms that bring an income, and schools that use student labor partially for the erection of their buildings and the furnishing of equipment. It is coming to be seen, however, in the education of the Negro, as clearly as it has been seen in the education of the youths the world over, that it is the *boy* and not the material product, that is the true object of education. Consequently the object of the industrial school came to be the thorough training of boys regardless of the cost of the training, so long as it was thoroughly well done.

Even at this point, however, the difficulties were not surmounted. In the first place modern industry has taken great strides since the war, and the teaching of trades is no longer a simple matter. Machinery and long processes of work have greatly changed the work of the carpenter, the ironworker and the shoemaker. A really efficient workman must be to-day an intelligent man who has had good technical training in addition to thorough common school, and perhaps even higher training. To meet this situation the industrial schools began a further development; they established distinct Trade Schools for the thorough training of better class artisans, and at the same time they sought to preserve for the purposes of general education, such of the simpler processes of elementary trade learning as were best suited therefor. In this differentiation of the Trade School and manual training, the best of the industrial schools simply followed the plain trend of the present educational epoch. A prominent educator tells us that, in Sweden, "In the beginning the economic conception was generally adopted, and everywhere manual training was looked upon as a means of preparing the children of the common people to earn their living. But gradually it came to be recognized that manual training has a more elevated purpose, and one, indeed, more useful in the deeper meaning of the term. It came to be considered as an educative process for the complete moral, physical and intellectual development of the child."

Thus, again, in the manning of trade schools and manual training schools we are thrown back upon the higher training as its source and chief support. There was a time when any aged and wornout carpenter could teach in a trade school. But not so to-day. Indeed the demand for college-bred men by a school like Tuskegee, ought to make Mr. Booker T. Washington the firmest friend of higher training. Here he has as helpers the son of a Negro senator, trained in Greek and the humanities, and graduated at Harvard; the son of a Negro congressman and lawyer, trained in Latin and mathematics, and graduated at Oberlin; he has as his wife, a woman who read Virgil and Homer in the same class room with me; he has as college chaplain, a classical graduate of Atlanta University; as teacher of science, a graduate of Fisk; as teacher of history, a graduate of Smith,—indeed some thirty of his chief teachers are college graduates, and instead of studying French grammars in the midst of weeds, or buying pianos for dirty cabins, they are at Mr. Washington's right hand helping him in a noble work. And yet one of the effects of Mr. Washington's propaganda has been to throw doubt upon the expediency of such training for Negroes, as these persons have had.

Men of America, the problem is plain before you. Here is a race transplanted through the criminal foolishness of your fathers. Whether you like it or not the millions are here, and here they will remain. If you do not lift them up, they will pull you down. Education and work are the levers to uplift a people. Work alone will not do it unless inspired by the right ideals and guided by intelligence. Education must not simply teach work—it must teach Life. The Talented Tenth of the Negro race must be made leaders of thought and missionaries of culture among their people. No others can do this work and Negro colleges must train men for it. The Negro race, like all other races, is going to be saved by its exceptional men.

Navajo Treaty, 1868

The "Treaty between the United States of America and the Navajo Tribe of Indians" was concluded on June 1, 1868, between General William Tecumseh Sherman and leaders of the Navajo (or Diné) tribe and proclaimed by President Andrew Johnson on August 12 of the same year. The Navajo had been captured by scout and Indian fighter Kit Carson through a scorched-earth campaign and forced to take a three-hundred-mile Long Walk to Bosque Redondo. Bosque Redondo was a forty-square-mile area set aside as a reservation. The Navajo, along with a number of Apache, their traditional enemies, were to be taught to farm the land and become self-sufficient. But the land was poor, as was the water in the area, and there was very little firewood. After much suffering by the Navajo (many of the Apache escaped) and the expenditure of much government money by the U.S. Army in its attempt to force Navajo settlement, General Sherman negotiated a treaty by which the Navajo would return to a portion of their ancestral lands. In addition to providing for resettlement and peace, the treaty provided for distribution of land and buildings to encourage farming and "civilization" of the tribe. The bulk of promised supplies and other assistance was never received by the Navajo.

Treaty between the United States of America and the Navajo Tribe of Indians; Concluded June 1, 1868; Ratification advised July 25, 1868; Proclaimed August 12, 1868.

ANDREW JOHNSON,
PRESIDENT OF THE UNITED STATES OF AMERICA,
TO ALL AND SINGULAR TO WHOM THESE PRESENTS
SHALL COME, GREETING:

WHEREAS a treaty was made and concluded at Fort Sumner, in the Territory of New Mexico, on the first day of June, in the year of our Lord one thousand eight hundred and sixty-eight, by and between Lieutenant-General W. T. Sherman and Samuel F. Tappan, commissioners, on the part of the United States, and Barboncito, Armijo, and other chiefs and headmen of the Navajo tribe of Indians, on the part of said Indians, and duly authorized thereto by them, which treaty is in the words and figures following, to wit:—

Articles of a treaty and agreement made and entered into at Fort Sumner, New Mexico, on the first day of June, one thousand eight hundred and sixty-eight, by and between the United States, represented by its commissioners, Lieutenant-General W. T. Sherman and Colonel Samuel F. Tappan, of the one part, and the Navajo nation or tribe of Indians, represented by their chiefs and headmen, duly authorized and empowered to act for the whole people of said nation or tribe, (the names of said chiefs and headmen being hereto subscribed,) of the other part, witness:—

ARTICLE I. From this day forward all war between the parties to this agreement shall forever cease. The government of the United States desires peace, and its honor is hereby pledged to keep it. The Indians desire peace, and they now pledge their honor to keep it.

If bad men among the whites, or among other people subject to the authority of the United States, shall commit any wrong upon the person or property of the Indians, the United States will, upon proof made to the agent and forwarded to the Commissioner of Indian Affairs at Washington city, proceed at once to cause the offender to be arrested and punished according to the laws of the United States, and also to reimburse the injured persons for the loss sustained.

If bad men among the Indians shall commit a wrong or depredation upon the person or property of any one, white, black, or Indian, subject to the authority of the United States and at peace therewith, the Navajo tribe agree that they will, on proof made to their agent, and on notice by him, deliver up the wrongdoer to the United States, to be tried and punished according to its laws; and in case they wilfully refuse so to do, the person injured shall be reimbursed for his loss from the annuities or other moneys due or to become due to them under this treaty, or any others that may be made with the United States. And the President may prescribe such rules and regulations for ascertaining damages under this article as in his judgment may be proper; but no such damage shall be adjusted and paid until examined and passed upon by the Commissioner of Indian Affairs, and no one sustaining loss whilst violating, or because of his violating, the provisions of this treaty or the laws of the United States, shall be reimbursed therefor.

ARTICLE II. The United States agrees that the following district of country, to wit: bounded on the north by the 37th degree of north latitude, south by an east and west line passing through the site of old Fort Defiance, in Cañon Bonito, east by the parallel of longitude which, if prolonged south, would pass through old Fort Lyon, or the Ojo-de-oso, Bear Spring, and west by a parallel of longitude about 109° 30′ west of Greenwich, provided it embraces the outlet of the Cañon-de-Chilly, which cañon is to be all included in this reservation, shall be, and the same is hereby, set apart for the use and occupation of the Navajo tribe of Indians, and for such other friendly tribes or individual Indians as from time to time they may be willing, with the consent of the United States, to admit among them; and the United States agrees that no persons except those herein so authorized to do, and except such officers, soldiers, agents, and employés of the government, or of the Indians, as may be authorized to enter upon Indian reservations in discharge of duties imposed by law, or the orders of the President, shall ever be permitted to pass over, settle upon, or reside in, the territory described in this article.

ARTICLE III. The United States agrees to cause to be built, at some point within said reservation, where timber and water may be convenient, the following buildings: a warehouse, to cost not exceeding twenty-five hundred dollars; an agency building for the residence of the agent, not to cost exceeding three thousand dollars; a carpenter shop and blacksmith shop, not to cost exceeding one thousand dollars each; and a school-house and chapel, so soon as a sufficient number of children can be induced to attend school, which shall not cost to exceed five thousand dollars.

ARTICLE IV. The United States agrees that the agent for the Navajos shall make his home at the agency building; that he shall reside among them, and shall keep an office open at all times for the purpose of prompt and diligent inquiry into such matters of complaint by or against the Indians as may be presented for investigation, as also for the faithful discharge of other duties enjoined by law. In all cases of depredation on person or property he shall cause the evidence to be taken in writing and forwarded, together with his finding, to the Commissioner of Indian Affairs, whose decision shall be binding on the parties to this treaty.

ARTICLE V. If any individual belonging to said tribe, or legally incorporated with it, being the head of a family, shall desire to commence farming, he shall have the privilege to select, in the presence and with the assistance of the agent then in charge, a tract of land within said reservation, not exceeding one hundred and sixty acres in extent, which tract, when so selected, certified, and recorded in the "land book" as herein described, shall cease to be held in common, but the same may be occupied and held in the exclusive possession of the person selecting it, and of his family, so long as he or they may continue to cultivate it.

Any person over eighteen years of age, not being the head of a family, may in like manner select, and cause to be certified to him or her for purposes of cultivation, a quantity of land, not exceeding eighty acres in extent, and thereupon be entitled to the exclusive possession of the same as above directed.

For each tract of land so selected a certificate containing a description thereof, and the name of the person selecting it, with a certificate endorsed thereon, that the same has been recorded, shall be delivered to the party entitled to it by the agent, after the same shall have been recorded by him in a book to be kept in his office, subject to inspection, which said book shall be known as the "Navajo Land Book."

The President may at any time order a survey of the reservation, and when so surveyed, Congress shall provide for protecting the rights of said settlers in their improvements, and may fix the character of the title held by each.

The United States may pass such laws on the subject of alienation and descent of property between the Indians and their descendants as may be thought proper.

ARTICLE VI. In order to insure the civilization of the Indians entering into this treaty, the necessity of education is admitted, especially of such of them as may be settled on said agricultural parts of this reservation, and they therefore pledge themselves to compel their children, male and female, between the ages of six and sixteen years, to attend school; and it is hereby made the duty of the agent for said Indians to see that this stipulation is strictly complied with; and the United States agrees that, for every thirty children between said ages who can be induced or compelled to attend school, a house shall be provided, and a teacher competent to teach the elementary branches of an English education shall be furnished, who will reside among said Indians, and faithfully discharge his or her duties as a teacher.

The provisions of this article to continue for not less than ten years.

ARTICLE VII. When the head of a family shall have selected lands and received his certificate as above directed, and the agent shall be satisfied that he intends in good faith to commence cultivating the soil for a living, he shall be entitled to receive seeds and agricultural implements for the first year, not exceeding in value one hundred dollars, and for each succeeding year he shall continue to farm, for a period of two years, he shall be entitled to receive seeds and implements to the value of twenty-five dollars.

ARTICLE VIII. In lieu of all sums of money or other annuities provided to be paid to the Indians herein named under any treaty or treaties heretofore made, the United States agrees to deliver at the agency house on the reservation herein named, on the first day of September of each year for ten years, the following articles, to wit:

Such articles of clothing, goods, or raw materials in lieu thereof, as the agent may make his estimate for, not exceeding in value five dollars per Indian—each Indian being encouraged to manufacture their own clothing, blankets, &c.; to be furnished with no article which they can manufacture themselves. And, in order that the Commissioner of Indian Affairs may be able to estimate properly for the articles herein named, it shall be the duty of the agent each year to forward to him a full and exact census of the Indians, on which the estimate from year to year can be based.

And in addition to the articles herein named, the sum of ten dollars for each person entitled to the beneficial effects of this treaty shall be annually appropriated for a period of ten years, for each person who engages in farming or mechanical pursuits, to be used by the Commissioner of Indian Affairs in the purchase of such articles as from time to time the condition and necessities of the Indians may indicate to be proper; and if within the ten years at any time it shall appear that the amount of money needed for clothing, under the article, can be appropriated to better uses for the Indians named herein, the Commissioner of Indian Affairs may change the appropriation to other purposes, but in no event shall the amount of this appropriation be withdrawn or discontinued for the period named, provided they remain at peace. And the President shall annually detail an officer of the army to be present and attest the delivery of all the goods herein named to the Indians, and he shall inspect and report on the quantity and quality of the goods and the manner of their delivery.

ARTICLE IX. In consideration of the advantages and benefits conferred by this treaty, and the many pledges of friendship by the United States, the tribes who are parties to this agreement hereby stipulate that they will relinquish all right to occupy any territory outside their reservation, as herein defined, but retain the right to hunt on any unoccupied lands contiguous to their reservation, so long as the large game may range thereon in such numbers as to justify the chase; and they, the said Indians, further expressly agree:

1st. That they will make no opposition to the construction of railroads now being built or hereafter to be built across the continent.

2nd. That they will not interfere with the peaceful construction of any railroad not passing over their reservation as herein defined.

3rd. That they will not attack any persons at home or travelling, nor molest or disturb any wagon trains, coaches, mules or cattle belonging to the people of the United States, or to persons friendly therewith.

4th. That they will never capture or carry off from the settlements women or children.

5th. They will never kill or scalp white men, nor attempt to do them harm.

6th. They will not in future oppose the construction of railroads, wagon roads, mail stations, or other works of utility or necessity which may be ordered or permitted by the laws of the United States; but should such roads or other works be constructed on the lands of their reservation, the government will pay the tribe whatever amount of damage may be assessed by three disinterested commissioners to be appointed by the President for that purpose, one of said commissioners to be a chief or head man of the tribe.

7th. They will make no opposition to the military posts or roads now established, or that may be established, not in violation of treaties heretofore made or hereafter to be made with any of the Indian tribes.

ARTICLE X. No future treaty for the cession of any portion or part of the reservation herein described, which may be held in common, shall be of any validity or force against said Indians unless agreed to and executed by at least three fourths of all the adult male Indians occupying or interested in the same; and no cession by the tribe shall be understood or construed in such manner as to deprive, without his consent, any individual member of the tribe of his rights to any tract of land selected by him as provided in article —— of this treaty.

ARTICLE XI. The Navajos also hereby agree that at any time after the signing of these presents they will proceed in such manner as may be required of them by the agent, or by the officer charged with their removal, to the reservation herein provided for, the United States paying for their subsistence en route, and providing a reasonable amount of transportation for the sick and feeble.

ARTICLE XII. It is further agreed by and between the parties to this agreement that the sum of one hundred and fifty thousand dollars appropriated or to be appropriated shall be disbursed as follows, subject to any conditions provided in the law, to wit:

1st. The actual cost of the removal of the tribe from the Bosque Redondo reservation to the reservation, say fifty thousand dollars.

2nd. The purchase of fifteen thousand sheep and goats, at a cost not to exceed thirty thousand dollars.

3rd. The purchase of five hundred beef cattle and a million pounds of corn, to be collected and held at the military post nearest the reservation, subject to the orders of the agent, for the relief of the needy during the coming winter.

4th. The balance, if any, of the appropriation to be invested for the maintenance of the Indians pending their removal, in such manner as the agent who is with them may determine.

5th. The removal of this tribe to be made under the supreme control and direction of the military commander of the Territory of New Mexico, and when completed, the management of the tribe to revert to the proper agent.

ARTICLE XIII. The tribe herein named, by their representatives, parties to this treaty, agree to make the reservation herein described their permanent home, and they will not as a tribe make any permanent settlement elsewhere, reserving the right to hunt on the lands adjoining the said reservation formerly called theirs, subject to the modifications named in this treaty and the orders of the commander of the department in which said reservation may be for the time being; and it is further agreed and understood by the parties to this treaty, that if any Navajo Indian or Indians shall leave the reservation herein described to settle elsewhere, he or they shall forfeit all the rights, privileges, and annuities conferred by the terms of this treaty; and it is further agreed by the parties to this treaty, that they will do all they can to induce Indians now away from reservations set apart for the exclusive use and occupation of the Indians, leading a nomadic life, or engaged in war against the people of the United States, to abandon such a life and settle permanently in one of the territorial reservations set apart for the exclusive use and occupation of the Indians.

In testimony of all which the said parties have hereunto, on this the first day of June, one thousand eight hundred and sixty-eight, at Fort Sumner, in the Territory of New Mexico, set their hands and seals.

W. T. SHERMAN,
Lt. Gen'l, Indian Peace Commissioner.
S. F. TAPPAN,
Indian Peace Commissioner.

BARBONCITO, Chief.	his x mark.
ARMIJO.	his x mark.
DELGADO.	
MANUELITO.	his x mark.
LARGO.	his x mark.
HERRERO.	his x mark.
CHIQUETO.	his x mark.
MUERTO DE HOMBRE.	his x mark.
HOMBRO.	his x mark.
NARBONO.	his x mark.
NARBONO SEGUNDO.	his x mark.
GAÑADO MUCHO.	his x mark.

Council.

RIQUO.	his x mark.
JUAN MARTIN.	his x mark.
SERGINTO.	his x mark.
GRANDE.	his x mark.
INOETENITO.	his x mark.
MUCHACHOS MUCHO.	his x mark.

CHIQUETO SEGUNDO: his x mark.
CABELLO AMARILLO.   his x mark.
FRANCISCO.   his x mark.
TORIVIO.   his x mark.
DESDENDADO.   his x mark.
JUAN.   his x mark.
GUERO.   his x mark.
GUGADORE.   his x mark.
CABASON.   his x mark.
BARBON SEGUNDO.   his x mark.
CABARES COLORADOS.   his x mark.

Attest:

GEO. W. G. GETTY,
    Col. 37th Inf'y, Bt. Maj. Gen'l U.S.A.
B. S. ROBERTS,
    Bt. Brg. Gen'l U.S.A., Lt. Col. 3d Cav'y.
J. COOPER MCKEE,
    Bt. Lt. Col. Surgeon U.S.A.
THEO. H. DODD,
    U.S. Indian Ag't for Navajos.
CHAS. MCCLURE,
    Bt. Maj. and C.S. U.S.A
JAMES F. WEEDS,
    Bt. Maj. and Asst. Surg. U.S.A.
J. C. SUTHERLAND,
    Interpreter.
WILLIAM VAUX,
    Chaplain U.S.A.

And whereas, the said treaty having been submitted to the Senate of the United States for its constitutional action thereon, the Senate did, on the twenty-fifth day of July, one thousand eight hundred and sixty-eight, advise and consent to the ratification of the same, by a resolution in the words and figures following, to wit:—

IN EXECUTIVE SESSION, SENATE OF THE
               UNITED STATES,
                      July 25, 1868.

Resolved, (two-thirds of the senators present concurring,) That the Senate advise and consent to the ratification of the treaty between the United States and the Navajo Indians, concluded at Fort Sumner, New Mexico, on the first day of June, 1868.

Attest: GEO. C. GORHAM,
                          Secretary,
                  By W. J. McDONALD,
                        Chief Clerk.

Now, therefore, be it known that I, ANDREW JOHNSON, President of the United States of America, do, in pursuance of the advice and consent of the Senate, as expressed in its resolution of the twenty-fifth of July, one thousand eight hundred and sixty-eight, accept, ratify, and confirm the said treaty.

In testimony whereof, I have hereto signed my name, and caused the seal of the United States to be affixed.

Done at the City of Washington, this twelfth day of August, in the year of our Lord one thousand eight hundred and sixty-eight, and of the Independence of the United States of America the ninety-third.

[SEAL]   ANDREW JOHNSON.

By the President:

W. HUNTER,
    Acting Secretary of State.

Dawes (Indian Lands) Act, 1887

Named after its congressional sponsor, U.S. senator Henry L. Dawes, of Massachusetts, the "General Allotment Act of 1887" responded to the failure of attempts to force various Indian tribes to settle into Western-style agricultural lives on reservations. Because of the lack of good arable land, the severe strain on tribal culture posed by Western economic and social structures, and the combination of white settler encroachment and Indian raiding and reprisals, the original system of reservations had brought decades of bloody conflict. The Dawes Act both broke up the reservation system and further undermined traditional economic arrangements by splitting reservations into specific parcels of land assigned to individual Indians and heads of households. Much land not formally assigned to individuals was given to white settlers. Not all tribes or reservations were covered by this act. For example, the "Five Civilized Tribes" of more assimilated Indians forcibly resettled to Oklahoma initially were excluded, though the pattern of splitting up communal lands into discrete household settlements and leaving unassigned lands open for white settlers quickly became dominant.

Dawes Act

February 8, 1887

An act to provide for the allotment of lands in severalty to Indians on the various reservations, and to extend the protection of the laws of the United States and the Territories over the Indians, and for other purposes.

Be it enacted by the Senate and House of Representatives of the United States of America in Congress assembled, That in all cases where any tribe or band of Indians has been, or shall hereafter be, located upon any reservation created for their use, either by treaty stipulation or by virtue of an act of Congress or executive order setting apart the same for their use, the President of the United States be, and he hereby is, authorized, whenever in his opinion any reservation or any part thereof of such Indians is advantageous for agricultural and grazing purposes, to cause said reservation, or any part thereof, to be surveyed, or resurveyed if necessary, and to allot the lands in said reservation in severalty to any Indian located thereon in quantities as follows:

To each head of a family, one-quarter of a section;

To each single person over eighteen years of age, one-eighth of a section;

To each orphan child under eighteen years of age, one-eighth of a section; and

To each other single person under eighteen years now liv-

ing, or who may be born prior to the date of the order of the President directing an allotment of the lands embraced in any reservation, one-sixteenth of a section: *Provided,* That in case there is not sufficient land in any of said reservations to allot lands to each individual of the classes above named in quantities as above provided, the lands embraced in such reservation or reservations shall be allotted to each individual of each of said classes pro rata in accordance with the provisions of this act: *And provided further,* That where the treaty or act of Congress setting apart such reservation provides for the allotment of lands in severalty in quantities in excess of those herein provided, the President, in making allotments upon such reservation, shall allot the lands to each individual Indian belonging thereon in quantity as specified in such treaty or act: *And provided further,* That when the lands allotted are only valuable for grazing purposes, an additional allotment of such grazing lands, in quantities as above provided, shall be made to each individual.

SEC. 2. That all allotments set apart under the provisions of this act shall be selected by the Indians, heads of families selecting for their minor children, and the agents shall select for each orphan child, and in such manner as to embrace the improvements of the Indians making the selection. Where the improvements of two or more Indians have been made on the same legal subdivision of land, unless they shall otherwise agree, a provisional line may be run dividing said lands between them, and the amount to which each is entitled shall be equalized in the assignment of the remainder of the land to which they are entitled under this act: *Provided,* That if any one entitled to an allotment shall fail to make a selection within four years after the President shall direct that allotments may be made on a particular reservation, the Secretary of the Interior may direct the agent of such tribe or band, if such there be, and if there be no agent, then a special agent appointed for that purpose, to make a selection for such Indian, which election shall be allotted as in cases where selections are made by the Indians, and patents shall issue in like manner.

Sec. 3. That the allotments provided for in this act shall be made by special agents appointed by the President for such purpose, and the agents in charge of the respective reservations on which the allotments are directed to be made, under such rules and regulations as the Secretary of the Interior may from time to time prescribe, and shall be certified by such agents to the Commissioner of Indian Affairs, in duplicate, one copy to be retained in the Indian Office and the other to be transmitted to the Secretary of the Interior for his action, and to be deposited in the General Land Office.

Sec. 4. That where any Indian not residing upon a reservation, or for whose tribe no reservation has been provided by treaty, act of Congress, or executive order, shall make settlement upon any surveyed or unsurveyed lands of the United States not otherwise appropriated, he or she shall be entitled, upon application to the local land office for the district in which the lands are located, to have the same allotted to him or her, and to his or her children, in quantities and manner as provided in this act for Indians residing upon reservations; and when such settlement is made upon unsurveyed lands, the grant to such Indians shall be adjusted upon the survey of the lands so as to conform thereto; and patents shall be issued to them for such lands in the manner and with the restrictions as herein provided. And the fees to which the officers of such local land office would have been entitled had such lands been entered under the general laws for the disposition of the public lands shall be paid to them, from any moneys in the Treasury of the United States not otherwise appropriated, upon a statement of an account in their behalf for such fees by the Commissioner of the General Land Office, and a certification of such account to the Secretary of the Treasury by the Secretary of the Interior.

Sec. 5. That upon the approval of the allotments provided for in this act by the Secretary of the Interior, he shall cause patents to issue therefor in the name of the allottees, which patents shall be of the legal effect, and declare that the United States does and will hold the land thus allotted, for the period of twenty-five years, in trust for the sole use and benefit of the Indian to whom such allotment shall have been made, or, in case of his decease, of his heirs according to the laws of the State or Territory where such land is located, and that at the expiration of said period the United States will convey the same by patent to said Indian, or his heirs as aforesaid, in fee, discharged of said trust and free of all charge or incumbrance whatsoever: *Provided,* That the President of the United States may in any case in his discretion extend the period. And if any conveyance shall be made of the lands set apart and allotted as herein provided, or any contract made touching the same, before the expiration of the time above mentioned, such conveyance or contract shall be absolutely null and void: *Provided,* That the law of descent and partition in force in the State or Territory where such lands are situate shall apply thereto after patents therefor have been executed and delivered, except as herein otherwise provided; and the laws of the State of Kansas regulating the descent and partition of real estate shall, so far as practicable, apply to all lands in the Indian Territory which may be allotted in severalty under the provisions of this act: *And provided further,* That at any time after lands have been allotted to all the Indians of any tribe as herein provided, or sooner if in the opinion of the President it shall be for the best interests of said tribe, it shall be lawful for the Secretary of the Interior to negotiate with such Indian tribe for the purchase and release by said tribe, in conformity with the treaty or statute under which such reservation is held, of such portions of its reservation not allotted as such tribe shall, from time to time, consent to sell, on such terms and conditions as shall be considered just and equitable between the United States and said tribe of Indians, which purchase shall not be complete until ratified by Congress, and the form and manner of executing such release shall also be prescribed by Congress: *Provided however,* That all lands adapted to agriculture, with or without irrigation so sold or released to the United States by any Indian tribe shall be held by the United States for the sole purpose of securing homes to actual settlers and shall be disposed of by the United States to actual and bona fide settlers only in tracts not exceeding one hundred and sixty acres to any one person, on such terms as Congress shall prescribe, subject to grants which Congress may make in aid of education: *And provided further,* That no patents shall issue therefor except to the person so taking the same as and for a homestead, or his heirs, and after the expiration of five years occupancy thereof as such homestead; and any conveyance of said lands so taken as a homestead, or any contract touching the same, or lien thereon, created prior to the date of such patent, shall be null and void. And the sums agreed to be paid by the United States as purchase money for any portion of any such reservation shall be held in the Treasury of the United States for the sole use of the tribe or tribes of Indians; to whom such reservations belonged; and the same, with interest thereon at three per cent per annum, shall be at all times subject to appropriation by Congress for the education and civilization of such tribe or tribes of Indians or the members thereof. The patents aforesaid shall be recorded in the General Land Office, and afterward delivered, free of charge, to the allottee entitled thereto. And if any religious society or other organization is now occupying any of the public lands to which this act is applicable, for religious or educational work among the Indians, the Secretary of the Interior is hereby authorized to confirm such occupation to such society or organization, in quantity not exceeding one hundred and sixty acres in any one tract, so long as the same shall be so occupied, on such terms as he shall deem just; but nothing herein contained shall change or alter any claim of such society for religious or educational purposes heretofore granted by law. And hereafter in the employment of Indian police, or any other employes in the public service among any of the Indian tribes or bands affected by this act, and where Indians can perform the duties required, those Indians who have availed themselves of the provisions of this act and become citizens of the United States shall be preferred.

SEC. 6. That upon the completion of said allotments and the patenting of the lands to said allottees, each and every member of the respective bands or tribes of Indians to whom allotments have been made shall have the benefit of and be subject to the laws, both civil and criminal, of the State or Territory in which they may reside; and no Territory shall pass or enforce any law denying any such Indian within its jurisdiction the equal protection of the law. And every Indian born within the territorial limits of the United States to whom allotments shall have been made under the provisions of this act, or under any law or treaty, and every Indian born within the territorial limits of the United States who has voluntarily taken up, within said limits, his residence separate

and apart from any tribe of Indians therein, and has adopted the habits of civilized life, is hereby declared to be a citizen of the United States, and is entitled to all the rights, privileges, and immunities of such citizens, whether said Indian has been or not, by birth or otherwise, a member of any tribe of Indians within the territorial limits of the United States without in any manner impairing or otherwise affecting the right of any such Indian to tribal or other property.

SEC. 7. That in cases where the use of water for irrigation is necessary to render the lands within any Indian reservation available for agricultural purposes, the Secretary of the Interior be, and he is hereby, authorized to prescribe such rules and regulations as he may deem necessary to secure a just and equal distribution thereof among the Indians residing upon any such reservations; and no other appropriation or grant of water by any riparian proprietor shall be authorized or permitted to the damage of any other riparian proprietor.

SEC. 8. That the provision of this act shall not extend to the territory occupied by the Cherokees, Creeks, Choctaws, Chickasaws, Seminoles, and Osage, Miamies and Peorias, and Sacs and Foxes, in the Indian Territory, nor to any of the reservations of the Seneca Nation of New York Indians in the State of New York, nor to that strip of territory in the State of Nebraska adjoining the Sioux Nation on the south added by executive order.

SEC. 9. That for the purpose of making the surveys and resurveys mentioned in section two of this act, there be, and hereby is, appropriated, out of any moneys in the Treasury not otherwise appropriated, the sum of one hundred thousand dollars, to be repaid proportionately out of the proceeds of the sales of such land as may be acquired from the Indians under the provisions of this act.

SEC. 10. That nothing in this act contained shall be so construed as to affect the right and power of Congress to grant the right of way through any lands granted to an Indian, or a tribe of Indians, for railroads or other highways, or telegraph lines, for the public use, or to condemn such lands to public uses, upon making just compensation.

SEC 11. That nothing in this act shall be so construed as to prevent the removal of the Southern Ute Indians from their present reservation in Southwestern Colorado to a new reservation by and with the consent of a majority of the adult male members of said tribe.

Approved, February 8, 1887.

Proposed Constitutional Amendment Regarding Religious
  Establishment, 1876

Massachusetts Constitutional Provision, 1855

*In December of 1875 Congressman James G. Blaine, with the support of the president,
Ulysses S. Grant, sought adoption of a constitutional amendment banning funds intended
for public education from being "under the control of any religious sect." The intent was
to end public support for schools run by the Catholic Church (seen as a religious establishment) without interfering with the teaching of the King James Bible in public schools. In
1876 the measure passed by a margin of 180 to 7 in the House, but failed to garner the necessary two-thirds majority in the Senate. At least nine so-called Blaine Amendments, including that of Massachusetts, actually predate Blaine's measure. But Blaine's attempt is
credited with giving momentum to the adoption of numerous strikingly similar state constitutional amendments, along with federal provisions requiring that territories include
Blaine amendments in their constitutions in order to achieve statehood. Today thirty-
seven states have some version of the Blaine amendment as part of their constitutions.*

Proposed Constitutional Amendment

Mr. BLAINE introduced a joint resolution, H.R. No. 1; which was read a first and second time, and referred to the Committee on the Judiciary:

Resolved by the Senate and House of Representatives, That the following be proposed to the several States of the Union as an amendment to the Constitution:

ARTICLE XVI

No State shall make any law respecting an establishment of religion or prohibiting the free exercise thereof; and no money raised by taxation in any State for the support of public schools, or derived from any public fund therefor, nor any public lands devoted thereto, shall ever be under the control of any religious sect, nor shall any money so raised or lands so devoted be divided between religious sects or denominations.

Massachusetts Constitutional Provision

ART. XVIII. All moneys raised by taxation in the towns and cities for the support of public schools, and all moneys which may be appropriated by the State for the support of common schools, shall be applied to, and expended in, no other schools than those which are conducted according to law, under the order and superintendence of the authorities of the town or city in which the money is to be expended; and such moneys shall never be appropriated to any religious sect for the maintenance, exclusively, of its own schools.

Reynolds v. United States, 1879

The Late Corporation of the Church of Jesus Christ of Latter-day Saints v. United States, 1890

The Utah territory had been settled largely by members of the Church of Jesus Christ of Latter-day Saints (Mormon). The Mormon Church at that time held that those males able to do so should marry more than one woman. The Morrill Anti-Bigamy Act of 1862, specifically aimed at the Mormons, outlawed this practice. George Reynolds, a Mormon, was convicted of marrying a woman while married to another. Reynolds argued that because he was a Mormon it was his religious duty to practice polygamy, and therefore it would be a violation of his constitutional right of religious free exercise to convict him of a criminal act for so doing. In Reynolds v. United States, *the Supreme Court argued that polygamy was hostile to American democratic institutions and culture and that religious conduct, as opposed to belief, was liable to generally applicable criminal laws. This decision was part of a sustained campaign according to which members of the Mormon Church were denied various rights, including those to vote and sit on juries, on account of the church's position on polygamy. This campaign culminated in the 1887 Edmunds-Tucker Act, which revoked the corporate legal status of the church and provided for confiscation of the bulk of its property. In upholding this act, the Supreme Court, in* The Late Corporation of the Church of Jesus Christ of Latter-day Saints v. United States, *held the practice "abhorrent to the sentiments and feelings of the civilized world." Federal action against the Mormon Church ended after the 1890 Manifesto, according to which the Morman Church president, Wilford Woodruff, declared that he had received a revelation from God directing that polygamy be prohibited among church members.*

Reynolds v. United States

January 4, 1879

Mr. Chief Justice Waite delivered the opinion of the court.

The assignments of error, when grouped, present the following questions:—

1. Was the indictment bad because found by a grand jury of less than sixteen persons?

2. Were the challenges of certain petit jurors by the accused improperly overruled?

3. Were the challenges of certain other jurors by the government improperly sustained?

4. Was the testimony of Amelia Jane Schofield, given at a former trial for the same offence, but under another indictment, improperly admitted in evidence?

5. Should the accused have been acquitted if he married the second time, because he believed it to be his religious duty?

6. Did the court err in that part of the charge which directed the attention of the jury to the consequences of polygamy?

These questions will be considered in their order. . . .

5. As to the defence of religious belief or duty.

On the trial, the plaintiff in error, the accused, proved that at the time of his alleged second marriage he was, and for many years before had been, a member of the Church of Jesus Christ of Latter-Day Saints, commonly called the Mormon Church, and a believer in its doctrines; that it was an accepted doctrine of that church "that it was the duty of male members of said church, circumstances permitting, to practise polygamy; . . . that this duty was enjoined by different books which the members of said church believed to be of divine origin, and among others the Holy Bible, and also that the members of the church believed that the practice of polygamy was directly enjoined upon the male members thereof by the Almighty God, in a revelation to Joseph Smith, the founder and prophet of said church; that the failing or refusing to practise polygamy by such male members of said church, when circumstances would admit, would be punished, and that the penalty for such failure and refusal would be damnation in the life to come." He also proved "that he had received permission from the recognized authorities in said church to enter into polygamous marriage; . . . that Daniel H. Wells, one having authority in said church to perform the marriage ceremony, married the said defendant on or about the time the crime is alleged to have been committed, to some woman by the name of Schofield, and that such marriage ceremony was performed under and pursuant to the doctrines of said church."

Upon this proof he asked the court to instruct the jury that if they found from the evidence that he "was married as charged—if he was married—in pursuance of and in conformity with what he believed at the time to be a religious duty, that the verdict must be 'not guilty.'" This request was refused, and the court did charge "that there must have been a criminal intent, but that if the defendant, under the influence of a religious belief that it was right,—under an inspiration, if you please, that it was right,—deliberately married a second time, having a first wife living, the want of consciousness of evil intent—the want of understanding on his part that he was committing a crime—did not excuse him; but the law inexorably in such case implies the criminal intent."

Upon this charge and refusal to charge the question is raised, whether religious belief can be accepted as a justification of an overt act made criminal by the law of the land. The inquiry is not as to the power of Congress to prescribe criminal laws for the Territories, but as to the guilt of one who knowingly violates a law which has been properly enacted, if he entertains a religious belief that the law is wrong.

Congress cannot pass a law for the government of the Territories which shall prohibit the free exercise of religion. The first amendment to the Constitution expressly forbids such legislation. Religious freedom is guaranteed everywhere throughout the United States, so far as congressional in-

terference is concerned. The question to be determined is, whether the law now under consideration comes within this prohibition.

The word "religion" is not defined in the Constitution. We must go elsewhere, therefore, to ascertain its meaning, and nowhere more appropriately, we think, than to the history of the times in the midst of which the provision was adopted. The precise point of the inquiry is, what is the religious freedom which has been guaranteed.

Before the adoption of the Constitution, attempts were made in some of the colonies and States to legislate not only in respect to the establishment of religion, but in respect to its doctrines and precepts as well. The people were taxed, against their will, for the support of religion, and sometimes for the support of particular sects to whose tenets they could not and did not subscribe. Punishments were prescribed for a failure to attend upon public worship, and sometimes for entertaining heretical opinions. The controversy upon this general subject was animated in many of the States, but seemed at last to culminate in Virginia. In 1784, the House of Delegates of that State having under consideration "a bill establishing provision for teachers of the Christian religion," postponed it until the next session, and directed that the bill should be published and distributed, and that the people be requested "to signify their opinion respecting the adoption of such a bill at the next session of assembly."

This brought out a determined opposition. Amongst others, Mr. Madison prepared a "Memorial and Remonstrance," which was widely circulated and signed, and in which he demonstrated "that religion, or the duty we owe the Creator," was not within the cognizance of civil government. Semple's Virginia Baptists, Appendix. At the next session the proposed bill was not only defeated, but another, "for establishing religious freedom," drafted by Mr. Jefferson, was passed. 1 Jeff. Works, 45; 2 Howison, Hist. of Va. 298. In the preamble of this act (12 Hening's Stat. 84) religious freedom is defined; and after a recital "that to suffer the civil magistrate to intrude his powers into the field of opinion, and to restrain the profession or propagation of principles on supposition of their ill tendency, is a dangerous fallacy which at once destroys all religious liberty," it is declared "that it is time enough for the rightful purposes of civil government for its officers to interfere when principles break out into overt acts against peace and good order." In these two sentences is found the true distinction between what properly belongs to the church and what to the State.

In a little more than a year after the passage of this statute the convention met which prepared the Constitution of the United States. Of this convention Mr. Jefferson was not a member, he being then absent as minister to France. As soon as he saw the draft of the Constitution proposed for adoption, he, in a letter to a friend, expressed his disappointment at the absence of an express declaration insuring the freedom of religion (2 Jeff. Works, 355), but was willing to accept it as it was, trusting that the good sense and honest intentions of the people would bring about the necessary alterations. 1 Jeff. Works, 79. Five of the States, while adopting the Constitution, proposed amendments. Three—New Hampshire, New York, and Virginia—included in one form or another a declaration of religious freedom in the changes they desired to have made, as did also North Carolina, where the convention at first declined to ratify the Constitution until the proposed amendments were acted upon. Accordingly, at the first session of the first Congress the amendment now under consideration was proposed with others by Mr. Madison. It met the views of the advocates of religious freedom, and was adopted. Mr. Jefferson afterwards, in reply to an address to him by a committee of the Danbury Baptist Association (8 id. 113), took occasion to say: "Believing with you that religion is a matter which lies solely between man and his God; that he owes account to none other [for] his faith or his worship; that the legislative powers of the government reach actions only, and not opinions,—I contemplate with sovereign reverence that act of the whole American people which declared that their legislature should 'make no law respecting an establishment of religion or prohibiting the free exercise thereof,' thus building a wall of separation between church and State. Adhering to this expression of the supreme will of the nation in behalf of the rights of conscience, I shall see with sincere satisfaction the progress of those sentiments which tend to restore man to all his natural rights, convinced he has no natural right in opposition to his social duties." Coming as this does from an acknowledged leader of the advocates of the measure, it may be accepted almost as an authoritative declaration of the scope and effect of the amendment thus secured. Congress was deprived of all legislative power over mere opinion, but was left free to reach actions which were in violation of social duties or subversive of good order.

Polygamy has always been odious among the northern and western nations of Europe, and, until the establishment of the Mormon Church, was almost exclusively a feature of the life of Asiatic and of African people. At common law, the second marriage was always void (2 Kent, Com. 79), and from the earliest history of England polygamy has been treated as an offence against society. After the establishment of the ecclesiastical courts, and until the time of James I., it was punished through the instrumentality of those tribunals, not merely because ecclesiastical rights had been violated, but because upon the separation of the ecclesiastical courts from the civil the ecclesiastical were supposed to be the most appropriate for the trial of matrimonial causes and offences against the rights of marriage, just as they were for testamentary causes and the settlement of the estates of deceased persons.

By the statute of 1 James I. (c. 11), the offence, if committed in England or Wales, was made punishable in the civil courts, and the penalty was death. As this statute was limited in its operation to England and Wales, it was at a very early period re-enacted, generally with some modifications, in all the colonies. In connection with the case we are now considering, it is a significant fact that on the 8th of December, 1788, after the passage of the act establishing religious freedom, and after the convention of Virginia had recommended as an amendment to the Constitution of the United States the declaration in a bill of rights that "all men have an equal, natural, and unalienable right to the free exercise of religion, according to the dictates of conscience," the legislature of that State substantially enacted the statute of James I., death penalty included, because, as recited in the preamble, "it hath been doubted whether bigamy or poligamy be punishable by the laws of this Commonwealth." 12 Hening's Stat. 691. From that day to this we think it may safely be said there never has been a time in any State of the Union when polygamy has not been an offence against society, cognizable by the civil courts and punishable with more or less severity. In the face of all this evidence, it is impossible to believe that the constitutional guaranty of religious freedom was intended to prohibit legislation in respect to this most important feature of social life. Marriage, while from its very nature a sacred obligation, is nevertheless, in most civilized nations, a civil contract, and usually regulated by law. Upon it society may be said to be built, and out of its fruits spring social relations and social obligations and duties, with which government is necessarily required to deal. In fact, according as monogamous or polygamous marriages are allowed, do we find the principles on which the government of the people, to a greater or less extent, rests. Professor Lieber says, polygamy leads to the patriarchal principle, and which, when applied to large communities, fetters the people in stationary despotism, while that principle cannot long exist in connection with monogamy. Chancellor Kent observes that this remark is equally striking and profound. 2 Kent, Com. 81, note (*e*). An exceptional colony of polygamists under an exceptional leadership may sometimes exist for a time without appearing to disturb the social condition of the people who surround it; but there cannot be a doubt that, unless restricted by some form of constitution, it is within the legitimate scope of the power of every civil government to determine whether polygamy or monogamy shall be the law of social life under its dominion.

In our opinion, the statute immediately under consideration is within the legislative power of Congress. It is constitutional and valid as prescribing a rule of action for all those residing in the Territories, and in places over which the United States have exclusive control. This being so, the only question which remains is, whether those who make polygamy a part of their religion are excepted from the operation of the statute. If they are, then those who do not make polygamy a part of their religious belief may be found guilty and punished, while those who do, must be acquitted and go free. This would be introducing a new element into criminal law. Laws are made for the government of actions, and while they cannot interfere with mere religious belief and opinions, they may with practices. Suppose one believed that human sacrifices were a necessary part of religious worship, would it be seriously contended that the civil government under which he lived could not interfere to prevent a sacrifice? Or if a wife religiously believed it was her duty to burn herself upon the funeral pile of her dead husband, would it be beyond the power of the civil government to prevent her carrying her belief into practice?

So here, as a law of the organization of society under the exclusive dominion of the United States, it is provided that plural marriages shall not be allowed. Can a man excuse his practices to the contrary because of his religious belief? To permit this would be to make the professed doctrines of religious belief superior to the law of the land, and in effect to permit every citizen to become a law unto himself. Government could exist only in name under such circumstances.

A criminal intent is generally an element of crime, but every man is presumed to intend the necessary and legitimate consequences of what he knowingly does. Here the accused knew he had been once married, and that his first wife was living. He also knew that his second marriage was forbidden by law. When, therefore, he married the second time, he is presumed to have intended to break the law. And the break-

ing of the law is the crime. Every act necessary to constitute the crime was knowingly done, and the crime was therefore knowingly committed. Ignorance of a fact may sometimes be taken as evidence of a want of criminal intent, but not ignorance of the law. The only defence of the accused in this case is his belief that the law ought not to have been enacted. It matters not that his belief was a part of his professed religion: it was still belief, and belief only.

In *Regina* v. *Wagstaff* (10 Cox Crim. Cases, 531), the parents of a sick child, who omitted to call in medical attendance because of their religious belief that what they did for its cure would be effective, were held not to be guilty of manslaughter, while it was said the contrary would have been the result if the child had actually been starved to death by the parents, under the notion that it was their religious duty to abstain from giving it food. But when the offence consists of a positive act which is knowingly done, it would be dangerous to hold that the offender might escape punishment because he religiously believed the law which he had broken ought never to have been made. No case, we believe, can be found that has gone so far.

6. As to that part of the charge which directed the attention of the jury to the consequences of polygamy.

The passage complained of is as follows: "I think it not improper, in the discharge of your duties in this case, that you should consider what are to be the consequences to the innocent victims of this delusion. As this contest goes on, they multiply, and there are pure-minded women and there are innocent children,—innocent in a sense even beyond the degree of the innocence of childhood itself. These are to be the sufferers; and as jurors fail to do their duty, and as these cases come up in the Territory of Utah, just so do these victims multiply and spread themselves over the land."

While every appeal by the court to the passions or the prejudices of a jury should be promptly rebuked, and while it is the imperative duty of a reviewing court to take care that wrong is not done in this way, we see no just cause for complaint in this case. Congress, in 1862 (12 Stat. 501), saw fit to make bigamy a crime in the Territories. This was done because of the evil consequences that were supposed to flow from plural marriages. All the court did was to call the attention of the jury to the peculiar character of the crime for which the accused was on trial, and to remind them of the duty they had to perform. There was no appeal to the passions, no instigation of prejudice. Upon the showing made by the accused himself, he was guilty of a violation of the law under which he had been indicted: and the effort of the court seems to have been not to withdraw the minds of the jury from the issue to be tried, but to bring them to it; not to make them partial, but to keep them impartial.

Upon a careful consideration of the whole case, we are satisfied that no error was committed by the court below.

Judgment affirmed.

The Late Corporation of the Church of Jesus Christ of Latter-Day Saints et al. *v.* United States

May 19, 1890

Mr. Justice Bradley delivered the opinion of the Court:

This case originated under and in pursuance of the Act of Congress, entitled "An Act to Amend an Act Entitled 'An Act to Amend Section 5352 of the Revised Statutes of the United States, in Reference to Bigamy, and for Other Purposes, Approved March 22, 1882,'" which Act was passed February 19, 1887, and became a law by not being returned by the President. This Act, besides making additional provision with regard to the prosecution of polygamy in the Territories, and other matters concerning the Territory of Utah, provided, in the 13th, 17th and 26th sections, as follows:

"Sec. 13. That it shall be the duty of the Attorney-General of the United States to institute and prosecute proceedings to forfeit and escheat to the United States the property of corporations obtained or held in violation of section three of the Act of Congress approved the first day of July, eighteen hundred and sixty-two, entitled 'An Act to Punish and Prevent the Practice of Polygamy in the Territories of the United States and Other Places, and Disapproving and Annulling Certain Acts of the Legislative Assembly of the Territory of Utah,' or in violation of section eighteen hundred and ninety of the Revised Statutes of the United States; and all such property so forfeited and escheated to the United States shall be disposed of by the Secretary of the Interior, and the proceeds thereof applied to the use and benefit of the common schools in the Territory in which such property may

be: *Provided,* That no building, or the grounds appurtenant thereto, which is held and occupied exclusively for purposes of the worship of God, or parsonage connected therewith, or burial ground, shall be forfeited."

"Sec. 17. That the Acts of the Legislative Assembly of the Territory of Utah incorporating, continuing or providing for the Corporation known as the Church of Jesus Christ of Latter-Day Saints, and the ordinance of the so-called 'General Assembly of the State of Deseret' incorporating the Church of Jesus Christ of Latter-Day Saints, so far as the same may now have legal force and validity, are hereby disapproved and annulled, and the said Corporation, in so far as it may now have, or pretend to have, any legal existence, is hereby dissolved; that it shall be the duty of the Attorney-General of the United States to cause such proceedings to be taken in the Supreme Court of the Territory of Utah as shall be proper to execute the foregoing provisions of this section and to wind up the affairs of said Corporation conformably to law; and in such proceedings the court shall have power, and it shall be its duty, to make such decree or decrees as shall be proper to effectuate the transfer of the title to real property now held and used by said Corporation for places of worship, and parsonages connected therewith, and burial grounds, and of the description mentioned in the proviso to section thirteen of this Act and in section twenty-six of this Act, to the respective trustees mentioned in section twenty-six of this Act; and for the purposes of this section said court shall have all the powers of a court of equity."

"Sec. 26. That all religious societies, sects and congregations shall have the right to have and to hold, through trustees appointed by any court exercising probate powers in a Territory, only on the nomination of the authorities of such society, sect or congregation, so much real property for the erection or use of houses of worship, and for such parsonages and burial grounds as shall be necessary for the convenience and use of the several congregations of such religious society, sect or congregation." (24 U.S. Stat. 637, 638, and 641.)

In pursuance of the 13th section above recited, proceedings were instituted by information on behalf of the United States in the Third District Court of the Territory of Utah, for the purpose of having declared forfeited and escheated to the government the real estate of the Corporation called the Church of Jesus Christ of Latter-Day Saints, except a certain block in Salt Lake City used exclusively for public worship. On the 30th of September, 1887, the bill in the present case was filed in the Supreme Court of the Territory, under the

17th section of the Act, for the appointment of a receiver to collect the debts due to said Corporation and the rents, issues and profits of its real estate; and to take possession of and manage the same for the time being; and for a decree of dissolution and annulment of the charter of said Corporation, and other incidental relief. . . .

The Act of Congress of July 1, 1862, referred to in the pleadings, is entitled "An Act to Punish and Prevent the Practice of Polygamy in the Territories of the United States, and Other Places, and Disapproving and Annulling Certain Acts of the Legislative Assembly of the Territory of Utah," and provides as follows:

"Be it enacted by the Senate and House of Representatives of the United States of America in Congress assembled: That every person having a husband or wife living, who shall marry any other person, whether married or single, in a Territory of the United States, or other place over which the United States have exclusive jurisdiction, shall, except in the cases specified in the proviso to this section, be adjudged guilty of bigamy, and, upon conviction thereof, shall be punished by a fine not exceeding five hundred dollars, and by imprisonment for a term not exceeding five years: *Provided, nevertheless,* That this section shall not extend to any person by reason of any former marriage whose husband or wife by such marriage shall have been absent for five successive years without being known to such person within that time to be living; nor to any person by reason of any former marriage which shall have been dissolved by the decree of a competent court; nor to any person by reason of any former marriage which shall have been annulled or pronounced void by the sentence or decree of a competent court on the ground of the nullity of the marriage contract.

"Sec. 2. *And be it further enacted:* That the following ordinance of the provisional government of the 'State of Deseret,' so-called, namely, 'An Ordinance Incorporating the Church of Jesus Christ of Latter-Day Saints,' passed February eight, in the year eighteen hundred and fifty-one, and adopted, re-enacted and made valid by the governor and Legislative Assembly of the Territory of Utah by an Act passed January nineteen, in the year eighteen hundred and fifty-five, entitled 'An Act in Relation to the Compilation and Revision of the Laws and Resolutions in Force in Utah Territory, Their Publication and Distribution,' and all other Acts and parts of Acts heretofore passed by the said Legislative Assembly of the

Territory of Utah, which establish, support, maintain, shield or countenance polygamy, be, and the same hereby are, disapproved and annulled: *Provided,* That this Act shall be so limited and construed as not to affect or interfere with the right of property legally acquired under the ordinance heretofore mentioned, nor with the right 'to worship God according to the dictates of conscience,' but only to annul all Acts and laws which establish, maintain, protect or countenance the practice of polygamy, evasively called spiritual marriage, however disguised by legal or ecclesiastical solemnities, sacraments, ceremonies, consecrations or other contrivances.

"Sec. 3. *And be it further enacted:* That it shall not be lawful for any corporation or association for religious or charitable purposes to acquire or hold real estate in any Territory of the United States during the existence of the territorial government, of a greater value than fifty thousand dollars; and all real estate acquired or held by any such corporation or association contrary to the provisions of this Act shall be forfeited and escheat to the United States: *Provided,* That existing vested rights in real estate shall not be impaired by the provisions of this section." (12 U.S. Stat. 501.)

Another Act, known as the Edmunds Act, was approved March 22, 1882, entitled "An Act to Amend Section 5352 of the Revised Statutes of the United States in Reference to Bigamy, and for Other Purposes." This Act contained stringent provisions against the crime of polygamy, and has frequently come under the consideration of this court, and need not be recited in detail. . . .

The principal questions raised are, first, as to the power of Congress to repeal the charter of the Church of Jesus Christ of Latter-Day Saints; and, secondly, as to the power of Congress and the courts to seize the property of said Corporation and to hold the same for the purposes mentioned in the decree.

The power of Congress over the Territories of the United States is general and plenary, arising from and incidental to the right to acquire the territory itself, and from the power given by the Constitution to make all needful rules and regulations respecting the territory or other property belonging to the United States. It would be absurd to hold that the United States has power to acquire territory, and no power to govern it when acquired. The power to acquire territory, other than the territory northwest of the Ohio River (which belonged to the United States at the adoption of the Constitution), is derived from the treaty-making power and the power to declare and carry on war. The incidents of these powers are those of national sovereignty, and belong to all independent governments. The power to make acquisitions of territory by conquest, by treaty and by cession is an incident of national sovereignty. The Territory of Louisiana, when acquired from France, and the Territories west of the Rocky Mountains, when acquired from Mexico, became the absolute property and domain of the United States, subject to such conditions as the government, in its diplomatic negotiations, had seen fit to accept relating to the rights of the people then inhabiting those Territories. Having rightfully acquired said Territories, the United States government was the only one which could impose laws upon them, and its sovereignty over them was complete. No State of the Union had any such right of sovereignty over them; no other country or government had any such right. These propositions are so elementary, and so necessarily follow from the condition of things arising upon the acquisition of new territory, that they need no argument to support them. They are self-evident. *Chief Justice* Marshall, in the case of the *American & O. Ins. Cos.* v. *356 Bales of Cotton*, 26 U.S. 1 Pet. 511, 542 [7: 242, 255], well said: "Perhaps the power of governing a Territory belonging to the United States, which has not, by becoming a State, acquired the means of self-government, may result necessarily from the facts, that it is not within the jurisdiction of any particular State, and is within the power and jurisdiction of the United States. The right to govern may be the inevitable consequence of the right to acquire territory. Whichever may be the source whence the power is derived, the possession of it is unquestioned." And *Mr. Justice* Nelson, delivering the opinion of the court in *Benner* v. *Porter*, 50 U.S. 9 How. 235, 242 [13: 119, 122], speaking of the territorial governments established by Congress, says: "They are legislative governments, and their courts legislative courts, Congress, in the exercise of its powers in the organization and government of the Territories, combining the powers of both the federal and state authorities." *Chief Justice* Waite, in the case of *First Nat. Bank* v. *Yankton County*, 101 U.S. 129, 133 [25: 1046, 1047], said: "In the Organic Act of Dakota there was not an express reservation of power in Congress to amend the Acts of the Territorial Legislature, nor was it necessary. Such a power is an incident of sovereignty, and continues until granted away. Congress may not only abrogate laws of the Territorial Legislatures, but it may itself legislate directly for the local government. It may make a void Act of the Territorial Legislature valid, and a valid Act

void. In other words, it has full and complete legislative authority over the people of the Territories and all the departments of the territorial governments. It may do for the Territories what the people, under the Constitution of the United States, may do for the States." In a still more recent case, and one relating to the legislation of Congress over the Territory of Utah itself, *Murphy* v. *Ramsey*, 114 U.S. 15, 44 [29: 47, 57], *Mr. Justice* Matthews said: "The counsel for the appellants in argument seem to question the constitutional power of Congress to pass the Act of March 22, 1882, so far as it abridges the rights of electors in the Territory under previous laws. But that question is, we think, no longer open to discussion. It has passed beyond the stage of controversy into final judgment. The people of the United States, as sovereign owners of the National Territories, have supreme power over them and their inhabitants. In the exercise of this sovereign dominion, they are represented by the government of the United States, to whom all the powers of government over that subject have been delegated, subject only to such restrictions as are expressed in the Constitution, or are necessarily implied in its terms." Doubtless Congress, in legislating for the Territories, would be subject to those fundamental limitations in favor of personal rights which are formulated in the Constitution and its Amendments; but these limitations would exist rather by inference and the general spirit of the Constitution from which Congress derives all its powers, than by any express and direct application of its provisions.

The supreme power of Congress over the Territories, and over the Acts of the Territorial Legislatures established therein, is generally expressly reserved in the Organic Acts establishing governments in said Territories. This is true of the Territory of Utah. In the 6th section of the Act establishing a territorial government in Utah, approved September 9, 1850, it is declared "that the legislative powers of said Territory shall extend to all rightful subjects of legislation, consistent with the Constitution of the United States and the provisions of this Act. . . . All the laws passed by the Legislative Assembly and governor shall be submitted to the Congress of the United States, and if disapproved shall be null and of no effect." (9 Stat. 454.)

This brings us directly to the question of the power of Congress to revoke the charter of the Church of Jesus Christ of Latter-Day Saints. That Corporation, when the Territory of Utah was organized, was a corporation *de facto*, existing under an ordinance of the so-called "State of Deseret," approved February 8, 1851. This ordinance had no validity except in the voluntary acquiescence of the people of Utah then residing there. Deseret, or Utah, had ceased to belong to the Mexican government by the Treaty of Guadalupe Hidalgo, and in 1851 it belonged to the United States, and no government without authority from the United States, express or implied, had any legal right to exist there. The assembly of Deseret had no power to make any valid law. Congress had already passed the law for organizing the Territory of Utah into a government, and no other government was lawful within the bounds of that Territory. But after the organization of the territorial government of Utah under the Act of Congress, the Legislative Assembly of the Territory passed the following resolution: "*Resolved by the Legislative Assembly of the Territory of Utah,* That the laws heretofore passed by the provisional government of the State of Deseret, and which do not conflict with the Organic Act of said Territory, be and the same are hereby declared to be legal and in full force and virtue, and shall so remain until superseded by the action of the Legislative Assembly of the Territory of Utah." This resolution was approved October 4, 1851. The confirmation was repeated on the 19th of January, 1855, by the Act of the Legislative Assembly entitled "An Act in Relation to the Compilation and Revision of the Laws and Resolutions in Force in Utah Territory, Their Publication and Distribution." From the time of these confirmatory Acts, therefore, the said Corporation had a legal existence under its charter. But it is too plain for argument that this charter, or enactment, was subject to revocation and repeal by Congress whenever it should see fit to exercise its power for that purpose. Like any other Act of the Territorial Legislature, it was subject to this condition. Not only so, but the power of Congress could be exercised in modifying or limiting the powers and privileges granted by such charter; for if it could repeal, it could modify; the greater includes the less. Hence there can be no question that the Act of July 1, 1862, already recited, was a valid exercise of congressional power. Whatever may be the effect or true construction of this Act, we have no doubt of its validity. As far as it went it was effective. If it did not absolutely repeal the charter of the Corporation, it certainly took away all right or power which may have been claimed under it to establish, protect or foster the practice of polygamy, under whatever disguise it might be carried on; and it also limited the amount of property which might be acquired by the Church of Jesus Christ of Latter-Day Saints; not interfering, however, with vested rights in real estate existing at that time. If the Act of July 1, 1862, had but a partial effect, Congress had still the power

to make the abrogation of its charter absolute and complete. This was done by the Act of 1887. By the 17th section of that Act it is expressly declared that "the Acts of the Legislative Assembly of the Territory of Utah, incorporating, continuing or providing for the Corporation known as the Church of Jesus Christ of Latter-Day Saints, and the ordinance of the so-called 'General Assembly of the State of Deseret,' incorporating the said Church, so far as the same may now have legal force and validity, are hereby disapproved and annulled, and the said Corporation, so far as it may now have or pretend to have any legal existence, is hereby dissolved." This absolute annulment of the laws which gave the said Corporation a legal existence has dissipated all doubt on the subject, and the said Corporation has ceased to have any existence as a civil body, whether for the purpose of holding property or of doing any other corporate act. It was not necessary to resort to the condition imposed by the Act of 1862, limiting the amount of real estate which any corporation or association for religious or charitable purposes was authorized to acquire or hold; although it is apparent from the findings of the court that this condition was violated by the Corporation before the passage of the Act of 1887. Congress, for good and sufficient reasons of its own, independent of that limitation, and of any violation of it, had a full and perfect right to repeal its charter and abrogate its corporate existence, which of course depended upon its charter.

The next question is, whether Congress or the court had the power to cause the property of the said Corporation to be seized and taken possession of, as was done in this case.

When a business corporation, instituted for the purpose of gain or private interest, is dissolved, the modern doctrine is, that its property, after payment of its debts, equitably belongs to its stockholders. But this doctrine has never been extended to public or charitable corporations. As to these, the ancient and established rule prevails, namely: that when a corporation is dissolved, its personal property, like that of a man dying without heirs, ceases to be the subject of private ownership, and becomes subject to the disposal of the sovereign authority; whilst its real estate reverts or escheats to the grantor or donor, unless some other course of devolution has been directed by positive law, though still subject, as we shall hereafter see, to the charitable use. To this rule the Corporation in question was undoubtedly subject. But the grantor of all, or the principal part, of the real estate of the Church of Jesus Christ of Latter-Day Saints was really the United States, from whom the property was derived by the Church, or its trustees, through the operation of the Town-Site Act. Besides, as we have seen, the Act of 1862 expressly declared that all real estate acquired or held by any of the corporations or associations therein mentioned (of which the Church of Jesus Christ of Latter-Day Saints was one), contrary to the provisions of that Act, should be forfeited and escheat to the United States, with a saving of existing vested rights. The Act prohibited the acquiring or holding of real estate of greater value than $50,000 in a Territory, and no legal title had vested in any of the lands in Salt Lake City at that time, as the Town-Site Act was not passed until March 2, 1867. There can be no doubt, therefore, that the real estate of the Corporation in question could not, on its dissolution, revert or pass to any other person or persons than the United States.

If it be urged that the real estate did not stand in the name of the Corporation, but in the name of a trustee or trustees, and therefore was not subject to the rules relating to corporate property, the substance of the difficulty still remains. It cannot be contended that the prohibition of the Act of 1862 could have been so easily evaded as by putting the property of the Corporation into the hands of trustees. The equitable or trust estate was vested in the Corporation. The trustee held it for no other purpose; and the Corporation being dissolved, that purpose was at an end. The trust estate devolved to the United States in the same manner as the legal estate would have done had it been in the hands of the Corporation. The trustee became trustee for the United States instead of trustee for the Corporation. We do not now speak of the religious and charitable uses for which the Corporation, through its trustee, held and managed the property. That aspect of the subject is one which places the power of the government and of the court over the property on a distinct ground.

Where a charitable corporation is dissolved, and no private donor or founder appears to be entitled to its real estate (its personal property not being subject to such reclamation), the government, or sovereign authority, as the chief and common guardian of the state, either through its judicial tribunals or otherwise, necessarily has the disposition of the funds of such corporation, to be exercised, however, with due regard to the objects and purposes of the charitable uses to which the property was originally devoted, so far as they are lawful and not repugnant to public policy. This is the general principle, which will be more fully discussed further on. In this direction, it will be pertinent, in the mean time, to examine into the character of the Corporation of the Church of Jesus Christ of Latter-Day Saints, and the objects which,

by its constitution and principles, it promoted and had in view.

It is distinctly stated in the pleadings and findings of fact that the property of the said Corporation was held for the purpose of religious and charitable uses. But it is also stated in the findings of fact, and is a matter of public notoriety, that the religious and charitable uses intended to be subserved and promoted are the inculcation and spread of the doctrines and usages of the Mormon Church, or Church of Latter-Day Saints, one of the distinguishing features of which is the practice of polygamy—a crime against the laws, and abhorrent to the sentiments and feelings of the civilized world. Notwithstanding the stringent laws which have been passed by Congress—notwithstanding all the efforts made to suppress this barbarous practice—the sect or community composing the Church of Jesus Christ of Latter-Day Saints perseveres, in defiance of law, in preaching, upholding, promoting and defending it. It is a matter of public notoriety that its emissaries are engaged in many countries in propagating this nefarious doctrine, and urging its converts to join the community in Utah. The existence of such a propaganda is a blot on our civilization. The organization of a community for the spread and practice of polygamy is, in a measure, a return to barbarism. It is contrary to the spirit of Christianity and of the civilization which Christianity has produced in the Western World. The question therefore is whether the promotion of such a nefarious system and practice, so repugnant to our laws and to the principles of our civilization, is to be allowed to continue by the sanction of the government itself; and whether the funds accumulated for that purpose shall be restored to the same unlawful uses as heretofore to the detriment of the true interests of civil society.

It is unnecessary here to refer to the past history of the sect, to their defiance of the government authorities, to their attempt to establish an independent community, to their efforts to drive from the Territory all who were not connected with them in communion and sympathy. The tale is one of patience on the part of the American government and people, and of contempt of authority and resistance to law on the part of the Mormons. Whatever persecutions they may have suffered in the early part of their history, in Missouri and Illinois, they have no excuse for their persistent defiance of law under the government of the United States.

One pretense for this obstinate course is, that their belief in the practice of polygamy, or in the right to indulge in it, is a religious belief, and therefore under the protection of the constitutional guaranty of religious freedom. This is altogether a sophistical plea. No doubt the Thugs of India imagined that their belief in the right of assassination was a religious belief; but their thinking so did not make it so. The practice of suttee by the Hindu widows may have sprung from a supposed religious conviction. The offering of human sacrifices by our own ancestors in Britain was no doubt sanctioned by an equally conscientious impulse. But no one, on that account, would hesitate to brand these practices, now, as crimes against society, and obnoxious to condemnation and punishment by the civil authority.

The state has a perfect right to prohibit polygamy, and all other open offenses against the enlightened sentiment of mankind, notwithstanding the pretense of religious conviction by which they may be advocated and practised. *Davis* v. *Benson,* 133 U.S. 333 [33: 637]. And since polygamy has been forbidden by the laws of the United States, under severe penalties, and since the Church of Jesus Christ of Latter-Day Saints has persistently used, and claimed the right to use, and the unincorporated community still claims the same right to use, the funds with which the Late Corporation was endowed for the purpose of promoting and propagating the unlawful practice as an integral part of their religious usages, the question arises, whether the government, finding these funds without legal ownership, has or has not the right, through its courts, and in due course of administration, to cause them to be seized and devoted to objects of undoubted charity and usefulness—such for example as the maintenance of schools—for the benefit of the community whose leaders are now misusing them in the unlawful manner above described; setting apart, however, for the exclusive possession and use of the Church, sufficient and suitable portions of the property for the purposes of public worship, parsonage buildings and burying grounds, as provided in the Law.

The property in question has been dedicated to public and charitable uses. It matters not whether it is the product of private contributions, made during the course of half a century, or of taxes imposed upon the people, or of gains arising from fortunate operations in business, or appreciation in values, the charitable uses for which it is held are stamped upon it by charter, by ordinance, by regulation and by usage, in such an indelible manner that there can be no mistake as to their character, purpose or object.

The law respecting property held for charitable uses of course depends upon the legislation and jurisprudence of the country in which the property is situated and the uses are carried out; and when the positive law affords no specific provision for actual cases that arise, the subject must necessarily be governed by those principles of reason and public policy which prevail in all civilized and enlightened communities.

The principles of the law of charities are not confined to a particular people or nation, but prevail in all civilized countries pervaded by the spirit of Christianity. They are found embedded in the civil law of Rome, in the laws of European nations, and especially in the laws of that nation from which our institutions are derived. A leading and prominent principle prevailing in them all is, that property devoted to a charitable and worthy object, promotive of the public good, shall be applied to the purposes of its dedication, and protected from spoliation and from diversion to other objects. Though devoted to a particular use, it is considered as given to the public, and is therefore taken under the guardianship of the laws. If it cannot be applied to the particular use for which it was intended, either because the objects to be subserved have failed, or because they have become unlawful and repugnant to the public policy of the State, it will be applied to some object of kindred character so as to fulfill in substance, if not in manner and form, the purpose of its consecration. . . .

The attempt made, after the passage of the Act of February 19, 1887, and whilst it was in the President's hands for his approval or rejection, to transfer the property from the trustee then holding it to other persons, and for the benefit of different associations, was so evidently intended as an evasion of the Law that the court below justly regarded it as void and without force or effect.

We have carefully examined the decree, and do not find anything in it that calls for a reversal. It may perhaps require modification in some matters of detail, and for that purpose only *the case is reserved for further consideration.*

Immigration Act of 1882

Immigration Act of 1921

Immigration Act of 1924

The United States has been the object of waves of immigrants since before its inception. Many of these waves, particularly those that brought people from countries outside the traditional settler homelands of the British Isles and Protestant Northern Europe brought calls for restrictions on immigration. The first substantive legislation enacting such restrictions was the so-called Chinese Exclusion Act of 1882, which sought, as its name implies, to exclude Chinese people completely from becoming permanent United States residents. While this act all but ended immigration from that part of the world, the United States nonetheless received an unprecedented number of immigrants at the beginning of the twentieth century (eight million total between 1901 and 1910). Fears ranging from lower wages owing to competition for jobs, to strains on political, economic, and social infrastructure, to communist and anarchist subversion, to "racial impurity" spurred a drive to place limits on immigration. In 1921 an immigration act was passed, often called the "Emergency Immigration Act" or the "Emergency Quota Act" that included the first quota system for immigrants. It restricted immigration from any one country in the Eastern Hemisphere to no more than 3 percent of the number of people from the country of origin already in the United States in 1910 and established an overall cap of 350,000 immigrants per year. No restrictions were placed on immigration from the Western Hemisphere. The act was seen as a temporary measure, with more comprehensive legislation to follow. That legislation was the National Origins Quota Act of 1924. This legislation capped immigration at 150,000 per year, plus wives and children. It also capped the number of immigrants from any one country at 2 percent of the resident population in 1890—a baseline twenty years earlier than that set by the 1921 act. This act resulted in dramatic decreases in immigration from Eastern Europe, Southern Europe, Asia, and the Indian subcontinent (barring the latter outright). Its provisions remained in effect until passage of the Immigration and Nationality Act of 1965.

Immigration Act

May 6, 1882

An act to execute certain treaty stipulations relating to Chinese.

Whereas, in the opinion of the Government of the United States the coming of Chinese laborers to this country endangers the good order of certain localities within the territory thereof: Therefore,

Be it enacted by the Senate and House of Representatives of the United States of America in Congress assembled, That from and after the expiration of ninety days next after the passage of this act, and until the expiration of ten years next after the passage of this act, the coming of Chinese laborers to the United States be, and the same is hereby, suspended; and during such suspension it shall not be lawful for any Chinese laborer to come, or, having so come after the expiration of said ninety days, to remain within the United States.

SEC. 2. That the master of any vessel who shall knowingly bring within the United States on such vessel, and land or permit to be landed, any Chinese laborer, from any foreign port or place, shall be deemed guilty of a misdemeanor, and on conviction thereof shall be punished by a fine of not more than five hundred dollars for each and every such Chinese laborer so brought, and may be also imprisoned for a term not exceeding one year.

SEC. 3. That the two foregoing sections shall not apply to Chinese laborers who were in the United States on the seventeenth day of November, eighteen hundred and eighty, or who shall have come into the same before the expiration of ninety days next after the passage of this act, and who shall produce to such master before going on board such vessel, and shall produce to the collector of the port in the United States at which such vessel shall arrive, the evidence hereinafter in this act required of his being one of the laborers in this section mentioned; nor shall the two foregoing sections apply to the case of any master whose vessel, being bound to a port not within the United States, shall come within the jurisdiction of the United States by reason of being in distress or in stress of weather, or touching at any port of the United States on its voyage to any foreign port or place: *Provided,* That all Chinese laborers brought on such vessel shall depart with the vessel on leaving port.

SEC. 4. That for the purpose of properly identifying Chinese laborers who were in the United States on the seventeenth day of November, eighteen hundred and eighty, or who shall have come into the same before the expiration of ninety days next after the passage of this act, and in order to furnish them with the proper evidence of their right to go from and come to the United States of their free will and accord, as provided by the treaty between the United States and China dated November seventeenth, eighteen hundred and eighty, the collector of customs of the district from which any such Chinese laborer shall depart from the United States shall, in person or by deputy, go on board each vessel having on board any such Chinese laborer and cleared or about to sail from his district for a foreign port, and on such vessel make a list of all such Chinese laborers, which shall be entered in registry-books to be kept for that purpose, in which shall be stated the name, age, occupation, last place of residence, physical marks or peculiarities, and all facts necessary for the identification of each of such Chinese laborers, which books shall be safely kept in the custom-house; and every such Chinese laborer so departing from the United States shall be entitled to,

and shall receive, free of any charge or cost upon application therefor, from the collector or his deputy, at the time such list is taken, a certificate, signed by the collector or his deputy and attested by his seal of office, in such form as the Secretary of the Treasury shall prescribe, which certificate shall contain a statement of the name, age, occupation, last place of residence, personal description, and facts of identification of the Chinese laborer to whom the certificate is issued, corresponding with the said list and registry in all particulars. In case any Chinese laborer after having received such certificate shall leave such vessel before her departure he shall deliver his certificate to the master of the vessel, and if such Chinese laborer shall fail to return to such vessel before her departure from port the certificate shall be delivered by the master to the collector of customs for cancellation. The certificate herein provided for shall entitle the Chinese laborer to whom the same is issued to return to and re-enter the United States upon producing and delivering the same to the collector of customs of the district at which such Chinese laborer shall seek to re-enter; and upon delivery of such certificate by such Chinese laborer to the collector of customs at the time of re-entry in the United States, said collector shall cause the same to be filed in the custom-house and duly canceled.

SEC. 5. That any Chinese laborer mentioned in section four of this act being in the United States, and desiring to depart from the United States by land, shall have the right to demand and receive, free of charge or cost, a certificate of identification similar to that provided for in section four of this act to be issued to such Chinese laborers as may desire to leave the United States by water; and it is hereby made the duty of the collector of customs of the district next adjoining the foreign country to which said Chinese laborer desires to go to issue such certificate, free of charge or cost, upon application by such Chinese laborer, and to enter the same upon registry-books to be kept by him for the purpose, as provided for in section four of this act.

SEC. 6. That in order to the faithful execution of articles one and two of the treaty in this act before mentioned, every Chinese person other than a laborer who may be entitled by said treaty and this act to come within the United States, and who shall be about to come to the United States, shall be identified as so entitled by the Chinese Government in each case, such identity to be evidenced by a certificate issued under the authority of said government, which certificate shall be in the English language or (if not in the English language) accompanied by a translation into English, stating such right to come, and which certificate shall state the name, title, or official rank, if any, the age, height, and all physical peculiarities, former and present occupation or profession, and place of residence in China of the person to whom the certificate is issued and that such person is entitled conformably to the treaty in this act mentioned to come within the United States. Such certificate shall be prima-facie evidence of the fact set forth therein, and shall be produced to the collector of customs, or his deputy, of the port in the district in the United States at which the person named therein shall arrive.

SEC. 7. That any person who shall knowingly and falsely alter or substitute any name for the name written in such certificate or forge any such certificate, or knowingly utter any forged or fraudulent certificate, or falsely personate any person named in any such certificate, shall be deemed guilty of a misdemeanor; and upon conviction thereof shall be fined in a sum not exceeding one thousand dollars, and imprisoned in a penitentiary for a term of not more than five years.

SEC. 8. That the master of any vessel arriving in the United States from any foreign port or place shall, at the same time he delivers a manifest of the cargo, and if there be no cargo, then at the time of making a report of the entry of the vessel pursuant to law, in addition to the other matter required to be reported, and before landing, or permitting to land, any Chinese passengers, deliver and report to the collector of customs of the district in which such vessels shall have arrived a separate list of all Chinese passengers taken on board his vessel at any foreign port or place, and all such passengers on board the vessel at that time. Such list shall show the names of such passengers (and if accredited officers of the Chinese Government traveling on the business of that government, or their servants, with a note of such facts), and the names and other particulars, as shown by their respective certificates; and such list shall be sworn to by the master in the manner required by law in relation to the manifest of the cargo. Any willful refusal or neglect of any such master to comply with the provisions of this section shall incur the same penalties and forfeiture as are provided for a refusal or neglect to report and deliver a manifest of the cargo.

SEC. 9. That before any Chinese passengers are landed from any such vessel, the collector, or his deputy, shall proceed to examine such passengers, comparing the certificates with the list and with the passengers; and no passenger shall be allowed to land in the United States from such vessel in violation of law.

SEC. 10. That every vessel whose master shall knowingly violate any of the provisions of this act shall be deemed forfeited to the United States, and shall be liable to seizure and condemnation in any district of the United States into which such vessel may enter or in which she may be found.

SEC. 11. That any person who shall knowingly bring into or cause to be brought into the United States by land, or who shall knowingly aid or abet the same, or aid or abet the landing in the United States from any vessel of any Chinese person not lawfully entitled to enter the United States, shall be deemed guilty of a misdemeanor, and shall, on conviction thereof, be fined in a sum not exceeding one thousand dollars, and imprisoned for a term not exceeding one year.

SEC. 12. That no Chinese person shall be permitted to enter the United States by land without producing to the proper officer of customs the certificate in this act required of Chinese persons seeking to land from a vessel. And any Chinese person found unlawfully within the United States shall be caused to be removed therefrom to the country from whence he came, by direction of the President of the United States, and at the cost of the United States, after being brought before some justice, judge, or commissioner of a court of the United States and found to be one not lawfully entitled to be or remain in the United States.

SEC. 13. That this act shall not apply to diplomatic and other officers of the Chinese Government traveling upon the business of that government, whose credentials shall be taken as equivalent to the certificate in this act mentioned, and shall exempt them and their body and household servants from the provisions of this act as to other Chinese persons.

SEC. 14. That hereafter no State court or court of the United States shall admit Chinese to citizenship; and all laws in conflict with this act are hereby repealed.

SEC. 15. That the words "Chinese laborers," wherever used in this act, shall be construed to mean both skilled and unskilled laborers and Chinese employed in mining.

Approved, May 6, 1882.

Immigration Act

May 19, 1921

An Act To limit the immigration of aliens into the United
 States.

*Be it enacted by the Senate and House of Representatives
of the United States of America in Congress assembled,* That as
used in this Act—

The term "United States" means the United States, and
any waters, territory, or other place subject to the jurisdiction
thereof except the Canal Zone and the Philippine Islands; but
if any alien leaves the Canal Zone or any insular possession of
the United States and attempts to enter any other place under
the jurisdiction of the United States nothing contained in
this Act shall be construed as permitting him to enter under
any other conditions than those applicable to all aliens.

The word "alien" includes any person not a native-born or
naturalized citizen of the United States, but this definition
shall not be held to include Indians of the United States not
taxed nor citizens of the islands under the jurisdiction of the
United States.

The term "Immigration Act" means the Act of February
5, 1917, entitled "An Act to regulate the immigration of aliens
to, and the residence of aliens in, the United States"; and the
term "immigration laws" includes such Act and all laws, conventions, and treaties of the United States relating to the immigration, exclusion, or expulsion of aliens.

SEC. 2. (a) That the number of aliens of any nationality
who may be admitted under the immigration laws to the
United States in any fiscal year shall be limited to 3 per centum of the number of foreign-born persons of such nationality resident in the United States as determined by the United
States census of 1910. This provision shall not apply to the
following, and they shall not be counted in reckoning any of
the percentage limits provided in this Act: (1) Government
officials, their families, attendants, servants, and employees;
(2) aliens in continuous transit through the United States; (3)
aliens lawfully admitted to the United States who later go in
transit from one part of the United States to another through
foreign contiguous territory; (4) aliens visiting the United
States as tourists or temporarily for business or pleasure; (5)
aliens from countries immigration from which is regulated in
accordance with treaties or agreements relating solely to immigration; (6) aliens from the so-called Asiatic barred zone, as

described in section 3 of the Immigration Act; (7) aliens who
have resided continuously for at least one year immediately
preceding the time of their admission to the United States in
the Dominion of Canada, Newfoundland, the Republic of
Cuba, the Republic of Mexico, countries of Central or South
America, or adjacent islands; or (8) aliens under the age of
eighteen who are children of citizens of the United States.

(b) For the purposes of this Act nationality shall be determined by country of birth, treating as separate countries the
colonies or dependencies for which separate enumeration was
made in the United States census of 1910.

(c) The Secretary of State, the Secretary of Commerce, and
the Secretary of Labor, jointly, shall, as soon as feasible after
the enactment of this Act, prepare a statement showing the
number of persons of the various nationalities resident in the
United States as determined by the United States census of
1910, which statement shall be the population basis for the
purposes of this Act. In case of changes in political boundaries in foreign countries occurring subsequent to 1910 and
resulting (1) in the creation of new countries, the Governments of which are recognized by the United States, or (2)
in the transfer of territory from one country to another, such
transfer being recognized by the United States, such officials,
jointly, shall estimate the number of persons resident in the
United States in 1910 who were born within the area included
in such new countries or in such territory so transferred, and
revise the population basis as to each country involved in
such change of political boundary. For the purpose of such
revision and for the purposes of this Act generally aliens born
in the area included in any such new country shall be considered as having been born in such country, and aliens born in
any territory so transferred shall be considered as having been
born in the country to which such territory was transferred.

(d) When the maximum number of aliens of any nationality who may be admitted in any fiscal year under this Act
shall have been admitted all other aliens of such nationality, except as otherwise provided in this Act, who may apply
for admission during the same fiscal year shall be excluded:
Provided, That the number of aliens of any nationality who
may be admitted in any month shall not exceed 20 per centum of the total number of aliens of such nationality who are
admissible in that fiscal year: *Provided further,* That aliens
returning from a temporary visit abroad, aliens who are professional actors, artists, lecturers, singers, nurses, ministers of
any religious denomination, professors for colleges or seminaries, aliens belonging to any recognized learned profession,

or aliens employed as domestic servants, may, if otherwise admissible, be admitted notwithstanding the maximum number of aliens of the same nationality admissible in the same month or fiscal year, as the case may be, shall have entered the United States; but aliens of the classes included in this proviso who enter the United States before such maximum number shall have entered shall (unless excluded by subdivision (a) from being counted) be counted in reckoning the percentage limits provided in this Act: *Provided further,* That in the enforcement of this Act preference shall be given so far as possible to the wives, parents, brothers, sisters, children under eighteen years of age, and fiancées, (1) of citizens of the United States, (2) of aliens now in the United States who have applied for citizenship in the manner provided by law, or (3) of persons eligible to United States citizenship who served in the military or naval forces of the United States at any time between April 6, 1917, and November 11, 1918, both dates inclusive, and have been separated from such forces under honorable conditions.

SEC. 3. That the Commissioner General of Immigration, with the approval of the Secretary of Labor, shall, as soon as feasible after the enactment of this Act, and from time to time thereafter, prescribe rules and regulations necessary to carry the provisions of this Act into effect. He shall, as soon as feasible after the enactment of this Act, publish a statement showing the number of aliens of the various nationalities who may be admitted to the United States between the date this Act becomes effective and the end of the current fiscal year, and on June 30 thereafter he shall publish a statement showing the number of aliens of the various nationalities who may be admitted during the ensuing fiscal year. He shall also publish monthly statements during the time this Act remains in force showing the number of aliens of each nationality already admitted during the then current fiscal year and the number who may be admitted under the provisions of this Act during the remainder of such year, but when 75 per centum of the maximum number of any nationality admissible during the fiscal year shall have been admitted such statements shall be issued weekly thereafter. All statements shall be made available for general publication and shall be mailed to all transportation companies bringing aliens to the United States who shall request the same and shall file with the Department of Labor the address to which such statements shall be sent. The Secretary of Labor shall also submit such statements to the Secretary of State, who shall transmit the information contained therein to the proper diplomatic and consular officials of the United States, which officials shall make the same available to persons intending to emigrate to the United States and to others who may apply.

SEC. 4. That the provisions of this Act are in addition to and not in substitution for the provisions of the immigration laws.

SEC. 5. That this Act shall take effect and be enforced 15 days after its enactment (except sections 1 and 3 and subdivisions (b) and (c) of section 2, which shall take effect immediately upon the enactment of this Act), and shall continue in force until June 30, 1922, and the number of aliens of any nationality who may be admitted during the remaining period of the current fiscal year, from the date when this Act becomes effective to June 30, shall be limited in proportion to the number admissible during the fiscal year 1922.

Approved, May 19, 1921.

Immigration Act

May 29, 1924

An Act To limit the immigration of aliens into the United States, and for other purposes.

Be it enacted by the Senate and House of Representatives of the United States of America in Congress assembled, That this Act may be cited as the "Immigration Act of 1924."

NON-QUOTA IMMIGRANTS

SEC. 4. When used in this Act the term "non-quota immigrant" means—

(a) An immigrant who is the unmarried child under 18 years of age, or the wife, of a citizen of the United States who resides therein at the time of the filing of a petition under section 9;

(b) An immigrant previously lawfully admitted to the United States, who is returning from a temporary visit abroad;

(c) An immigrant who was born in the Dominion of Canada, Newfoundland, the Republic of Mexico, the Republic of Cuba, the Republic of Haiti, the Dominican Republic, the Canal Zone, or an independent country of Central or South America, and his wife, and his unmarried children under 18 years of age, if accompanying or following to join him;

(d) An immigrant who continuously for at least two years immediately preceding the time of his application for admission to the United States has been, and who seeks to enter the United States solely for the purpose of, carrying on the vocation of minister of any religious denomination, or professor of a college, academy, seminary, or university; and his wife, and his unmarried children under 18 years of age, if accompanying or following to join him; or

(e) An immigrant who is a bona fide student at least 15 years of age and who seeks to enter the United States solely for the purpose of study at an accredited school, college, academy, seminary, or university, particularly designated by him and approved by the Secretary of Labor, which shall have agreed to report to the Secretary of Labor the termination of attendance of each immigrant student, and if any such institution of learning fails to make such reports promptly the approval shall be withdrawn.

QUOTA IMMIGRANTS

SEC. 5. When used in this Act the term "quota immigrant" means any immigrant who is not a non-quota immigrant. An alien who is not particularly specified in this Act as a non-quota immigrant or a non-immigrant shall not be admitted as a non-quota immigrant or a non-immigrant by reason of relationship to any individual who is so specified or by reason of being excepted from the operation of any other law regulating or forbidding immigration.

PREFERENCES WITHIN QUOTAS

SEC. 6. (a) In the issuance of immigration visas to quota immigrants preference shall be given—

(1) To a quota immigrant who is the unmarried child under 21 years of age, the father, the mother, the husband, or the wife, of a citizen of the United States who is 21 years of age or over; and

(2) To a quota immigrant who is skilled in agriculture, and his wife, and his dependent children under the age of 16 years, if accompanying or following to join him. The preference provided in this paragraph shall not apply to immigrants of any nationality the annual quota for which is less than 300.

(b) The preference provided in subdivision (a) shall not in the case of quota immigrants of any nationality exceed 50 per centum of the annual quota for such nationality. Nothing in this section shall be construed to grant to the class of immigrants specified in paragraph (1) of subdivision (a) a priority in preference over the class specified in paragraph (2).

(c) The preference provided in this section shall, in the case of quota immigrants of any nationality, be given in the calendar month in which the right to preference is established, if the number of immigration visas which may be issued in such month to quota immigrants of such nationality has not already been issued; otherwise in the next calendar month.

NUMERICAL LIMITATIONS

SEC. 11. (a) The annual quota of any nationality shall be 2 per centum of the number of foreign-born individuals of such nationality resident in continental United States as determined by the United States census of 1890, but the minimum quota of any nationality shall be 100.

(b) The annual quota of any nationality for the fiscal year beginning July 1, 1927, and for each fiscal year thereafter, shall be a number which bears the same ratio to 150,000 as the number of inhabitants in continental United States in 1920 having that national origin (ascertained as hereinafter provided in this section) bears to the number of inhabitants in continental United States in 1920, but the minimum quota of any nationality shall be 100.

(c) For the purpose of subdivision (b) national origin shall be ascertained by determining as nearly as may be, in respect of each geographical area which under section 12 is to be treated as a separate country (except the geographical areas specified in subdivision (c) of section 4) the number of inhabitants in continental United States in 1920 whose origin by birth or ancestry is attributable to such geographical area. Such determination shall not be made by tracing the ancestors or descendants of particular individuals, but shall be based upon statistics of immigration and emigration, together with rates of increase of population as shown by successive decennial United States censuses, and such other data as may be found to be reliable.

(d) For the purpose of subdivisions (b) and (c) the term "inhabitants in continental United States in 1920" does not include (1) immigrants from the geographical areas specified in subdivision (c) of section 4 or their descendants, (2) aliens ineligible to citizenship or their descendants, (3) the descendants of slave immigrants, or (4) the descendants of American aborigines.

(e) The determination provided for in subdivision (c) of this section shall be made by the Secretary of State, the Secretary of Commerce, and the Secretary of Labor, jointly. In making such determination such officials may call for information and expert assistance from the Bureau of the Census.

Such officials shall, jointly, report to the President the quota of each nationality, determined as provided in subdivision (b), and the President shall proclaim and make known the quotas so reported. Such proclamation shall be made on or before April 1, 1927. If the proclamation is not made on or before such date, quotas proclaimed therein shall not be in effect for any fiscal year beginning before the expiration of 90 days after the date of the proclamation. After the making of a proclamation under this subdivision the quotas proclaimed therein shall continue with the same effect as if specifically stated herein, and shall be final and conclusive for every purpose except (1) in so far as it is made to appear to the satisfaction of such officials and proclaimed by the President, that an error of fact has occurred in such determination or in such proclamation, or (2) in the case provided for in subdivision (c) of section 12. If for any reason quotas proclaimed under this subdivision are not in effect for any fiscal year, quotas for such year shall be determined under subdivision (a) of this section.

(f) There shall be issued to quota immigrants of any nationality (1) no more immigration visas in any fiscal year than the quota for such nationality, and (2) in any calendar month of any fiscal year no more immigration visas than 10 per centum of the quota for such nationality, except that if such quota is less than 300 the number to be issued in any calendar month shall be prescribed by the Commissioner General, with the approval of the Secretary of Labor, but the total number to be issued during the fiscal year shall not be in excess of the quota for such nationality.

(g) Nothing in this Act shall prevent the issuance (without increasing the total number of immigration visas which may be issued) of an immigration visa to an immigrant as a quota immigrant even though he is a non-quota immigrant.

NATIONALITY

SEC. 12. (a) For the purposes of this Act nationality shall be determined by country of birth, treating as separate countries the colonies, dependencies, or self-governing dominions, for which separate enumeration was made in the United States census of 1890; except that (1) the nationality of a child under twenty-one years of age not born in the United States, accompanied by its alien parent not born in the United States, shall be determined by the country of birth of such parent if such parent is entitled to an immigration visa, and the nationality of a child under twenty-one years of age not born in the United States, accompanied by both alien parents not born

in the United States, shall be determined by the country of birth of the father if the father is entitled to an immigration visa; and (2) if a wife is of a different nationality from her alien husband and the entire number of immigration visas which may be issued to quota immigrants of her nationality for the calendar month has already been issued, her nationality may be determined by the country of birth of her husband if she is accompanying him and he is entitled to an immigration visa, unless the total number of immigration visas which may be issued to quota immigrants of the nationality of the husband for the calendar month has already been issued. An immigrant born in the United States who has lost his United States citizenship shall be considered as having been born in the country of which he is a citizen or subject, or if he is not a citizen or subject of any country, then in the country from which he comes.

(b) The Secretary of State, the Secretary of Commerce, and the Secretary of Labor, jointly, shall, as soon as feasible after the enactment of this Act, prepare a statement showing the number of individuals of the various nationalities resident in continental United States as determined by the United States census of 1890, which statement shall be the population basis for the purposes of subdivision (a) of section 11. In the case of a country recognized by the United States, but for which a separate enumeration was not made in the census of 1890, the number of individuals born in such country and resident in continental United States in 1890, as estimated by such officials jointly, shall be considered for the purposes of subdivision (a) of section 11 as having been determined by the United States census of 1890. In the case of a colony or dependency existing before 1890, but for which a separate enumeration was not made in the census of 1890 and which was not included in the enumeration for the country to which such colony or dependency belonged, or in the case of territory administered under a protectorate, the number of individuals born in such colony, dependency, or territory, and resident in continental United States in 1890, as estimated by such officials jointly, shall be considered for the purposes of subdivision (a) of section 11 as having been determined by the United States census of 1890 to have been born in the country to which such colony or dependency belonged or which administers such protectorate.

(c) In case of changes in political boundaries in foreign countries occurring subsequent to 1890 and resulting in the creation of new countries, the Governments of which are recognized by the United States, or in the establishment of self-governing dominions, or in the transfer of territory from one country to another, such transfer being recognized by the United States, or in the surrender by one country of territory, the transfer of which to another country has not been recognized by the United States, or in the administration of territories under mandates, (1) such officials, jointly, shall estimate the number of individuals resident in continental United States in 1890 who were born within the area included in such new countries or self-governing dominions or in such territory so transferred or surrendered or administered under a mandate, and revise (for the purposes of subdivision (a) of section 11) the population basis as to each country involved in such change of political boundary, and (2) if such changes in political boundaries occur after the determination provided for in subdivision (c) of section 11 has been proclaimed, such officials, jointly, shall revise such determination, but only so far as necessary to allot the quotas among the countries involved in such change of political boundary. For the purpose of such revision and for the purpose of determining the nationality of an immigrant, (A) aliens born in the area included in any such new country or self-governing dominion shall be considered as having been born in such country or dominion, and aliens born in any territory so transferred shall be considered as having been born in the country to which such territory was transferred, and (B) territory so surrendered or administered under a mandate shall be treated as a separate country. Such treatment of territory administered under a mandate shall not constitute consent by the United States to the proposed mandate where the United States has not consented in a treaty to the administration of the territory by a mandatory power.

(d) The statements, estimates, and revisions provided in this section shall be made annually, but for any fiscal year for which quotas are in effect as proclaimed under subdivision (e) of section 11, shall be made only (1) for the purpose of determining the nationality of immigrants seeking admission to the United States during such year, or (2) for the purposes of clause (2) of subdivision (c) of this section.

(e) Such officials shall, jointly, report annually to the President the quota of each nationality under subdivision (a) of section 11, together with the statements, estimates, and revisions provided for in this section. The President shall proclaim and make known the quotas so reported and thereafter such quotas shall continue, with the same effect as if specifically stated herein, for all fiscal years except those years for which quotas are in effect as proclaimed under subdivision (e) of section 11, and shall be final and conclusive for every purpose.

The Principles of Scientific Management, *Frederick Winslow Taylor*, 1911

A former industrial apprentice, Frederick Winslow Taylor (1856–1915) became an industrial engineer and eventually a professor at the business school of Dartmouth College and president of the American Society of Mechanical Engineers. Sometimes called the "father of scientific management," Taylor was influential in formulating time and motion studies by which industrial tasks were broken down into their smallest and simplest component parts in order to determine how each could be completed most quickly and efficiently. A principal roadblock to his methods was the traditional craft-union tradition of apprenticeship and quality for its own sake. Taylor and his followers argued that such methods were inefficient and that trade unions would be made unnecessary once appropriate methods of cooperation between management and labor were established.

The Principles of Scientific Management

Frederick Winslow Taylor

INTRODUCTION

President Roosevelt, in his address to the Governors at the White House, prophetically remarked that "The conservation of our national resources is only preliminary to the larger question of national efficiency."

The whole country at once recognized the importance of conserving our material resources and a large movement has been started which will be effective in accomplishing this object. As yet, however, we have but vaguely appreciated the importance of "the larger question of increasing our national efficiency."

We can see our forests vanishing, our water-powers going to waste, our soil being carried by floods into the sea; and the end of our coal and our iron is in sight. But our larger wastes of human effort, which go on every day through such of our acts as are blundering, ill-directed, or inefficient, and which Mr. Roosevelt refers to as a lack of "national efficiency," are less visible, less tangible, and are but vaguely appreciated.

We can see and feel the waste of material things. Awkward, inefficient, or ill-directed movements of men, however, leave nothing visible or tangible behind them. Their appreciation calls for an act of memory, an effort of the imagination. And for this reason, even though our daily loss from this source is greater than from our waste of material things, the one has stirred us deeply, while the other has moved us but little.

As yet there has been no public agitation for "greater national efficiency," no meetings have been called to consider how this is to be brought about. And still there are signs that the need for greater efficiency is widely felt.

The search for better, for more competent men, from the presidents of our great companies down to our household servants, was never more vigorous than it is now. And more than ever before is the demand for competent men in excess of the supply.

What we are all looking for, however, is the ready-made, competent man; the man whom some one else has trained. It is only when we fully realize that our duty, as well as our opportunity, lies in systematically cooperating to train and to make this competent man, instead of in hunting for a man whom some one else has trained, that we shall be on the road to national efficiency.

In the past the prevailing idea has been well expressed in the saying that "Captains of industry are born, not made"; and the theory has been that if one could get the right man, methods could be safely left to him. In the future it will be appreciated that our leaders must be trained right as well as born right, and that no great man can (with the old system of personal management) hope to compete with a number of ordinary men who have been properly organized so as efficiently to cooperate.

In the past the man has been first; in the future the system must be first. This in no sense, however, implies that great men are not needed. On the contrary, the first object of any good system must be that of developing first-class men; and under systematic management the best man rises to the top more certainly and more rapidly than ever before.

This paper has been written:

First. To point out, through a series of simple illustrations, the great loss which the whole country is suffering through inefficiency in almost all of our daily acts.

Second. To try to convince the reader that the remedy for this inefficiency lies in systematic management, rather than in searching for some unusual or extraordinary man.

Third. To prove that the best management is a true science, resting upon clearly defined laws, rules, and principles, as a foundation. And further to show that the fundamental principles of scientific management are applicable to all kinds of human activities, from our simplest individual acts to the work of our great corporations, which call for the most elaborate cooperation. And, briefly, through a series of illustrations, to convince the reader that whenever these principles are correctly applied, results must follow which are truly astounding.

This paper was originally prepared for presentation to The American Society of Mechanical Engineers. The illustrations chosen are such as, it is believed, will especially appeal to engineers and to managers of industrial and manufacturing establishments, and also quite as much to all of the men who are working in these establishments. It is hoped, however, that it will be clear to other readers that the same principles can be applied with equal force to all social activities: to the management of our homes; the management of our farms; the management of the business of our tradesmen, large and small; of our churches, our philanthropic institutions, our universities, and our governmental departments.

Chapter I
Fundamentals of Scientific Management
The principal object of management should be to secure the maximum prosperity for the employer, coupled with the maximum prosperity for each employé.

The words "maximum prosperity" are used, in their broad sense, to mean not only large dividends for the company or owner, but the development of every branch of the business to its highest state of excellence, so that the prosperity may be permanent.

In the same way maximum prosperity for each employé means not only higher wages than are usually received by men of his class, but, of more importance still, it also means the development of each man to his state of maximum efficiency, so that he may be able to do, generally speaking, the highest grade of work for which his natural abilities fit him, and it further means giving him, when possible, this class of work to do.

It would seem to be so self-evident that maximum prosperity for the employer, coupled with maximum prosperity for the employé, ought to be the two leading objects of management, that even to state this fact should be unnecessary. And yet there is no question that, throughout the industrial world, a large part of the organization of employers, as well as employés, is for war rather than for peace, and that perhaps the majority on either side do not believe that it is possible so to arrange their mutual relations that their interests become identical.

The majority of these men believe that the fundamental interests of employés and employers are necessarily antagonistic. Scientific management, on the contrary, has for its very foundation the firm conviction that the true interests of the two are one and the same; that prosperity for the employer cannot exist through a long term of years unless it is accompanied by prosperity for the employé, and *vice versa;* and that it is possible to give the workman what he most wants—high wages—and the employer what he wants—a low labor cost—for his manufactures.

It is hoped that some at least of those who do not sympathize with each of these objects may be led to modify their views; that some employers, whose attitude toward their workmen has been that of trying to get the largest amount of work out of them for the smallest possible wages, may be led to see that a more liberal policy toward their men will pay them better; and that some of those workmen who begrudge a fair and even a large profit to their employers, and who feel that all of the fruits of their labor should belong to them, and that those for whom they work and the capital invested in the business are entitled to little or nothing, may be led to modify these views.

No one can be found who will deny that in the case of any single individual the greatest prosperity can exist only when that individual has reached his highest state of efficiency; that is, when he is turning out his largest daily output.

The truth of this fact is also perfectly clear in the case of two men working together. To illustrate: if you and your workman have become so skilful that you and he together are making two pairs of shoes in a day, while your competitor and his workman are making only one pair, it is clear that after selling your two pairs of shoes you can pay your workman much higher wages than your competitor who produces only one pair of shoes is able to pay his man, and that there will still be enough money left over for you to have a larger profit than your competitor.

In the case of a more complicated manufacturing establishment, it should also be perfectly clear that the greatest permanent prosperity for the workman, coupled with the greatest prosperity for the employer, can be brought about only when the work of the establishment is done with the smallest combined expenditure of human effort, plus nature's resources, plus the cost for the use of capital in the shape of machines, buildings, etc. Or, to state the same thing in a different way: that the greatest prosperity can exist only as the result of the greatest possible productivity of the men and machines of the establishment—that is, when each man and each machine are turning out the largest possible output; because unless your men and your machines are daily turning out more work than others around you, it is clear that competition will prevent your paying higher wages to your workmen than are paid to those of your competitor. And what is true as to the possibility of paying high wages in the case of two companies competing close beside one another is also true as to whole districts of the country and even as to nations which are in competition. In a word, that maximum prosperity can exist only as the result of maximum productivity. Later in this paper illustrations will be given of several companies which are earning large dividends and at the same time paying from 30 per cent. to 100 per cent. higher wages to their men than are paid to similar men immediately around them, and with whose employers they are in competition. These illustrations will cover different types of work, from the most elementary to the most complicated.

If the above reasoning is correct, it follows that the most important object of both the workmen and the management should be the training and development of each individual in the establishment, so that he can do (at his fastest pace and with the maximum of efficiency) the highest class of work for which his natural abilities fit him.

These principles appear to be so self-evident that many men may think it almost childish to state them. Let us, however, turn to the facts, as they actually exist in this country and in England. The English and American peoples are the greatest sportsmen in the world. Whenever an American workman plays baseball, or an English workman plays cricket, it is safe to say that he strains every nerve to secure victory for his side. He does his very best to make the largest possible number of runs. The universal sentiment is so strong that any man who fails to give out all there is in him in sport is branded as a "quitter," and treated with contempt by those who are around him.

When the same workman returns to work on the following day, instead of using every effort to turn out the largest possible amount of work, in a majority of the cases this man deliberately plans to do as little as he safely can—to turn out far less work than he is well able to do—in many instances to do not more than one-third to one-half of a proper day's work. And in fact if he were to do his best to turn out his largest possible day's work, he would be abused by his fellow-workers for so doing, even more than if he had proved himself a "quitter" in sport. Underworking, that is, deliberately working slowly so as to avoid doing a full day's work, "soldiering," as it is called in this country, "hanging it out," as it is called in England, "ca canae," as it is called in Scotland, is almost universal in industrial establishments, and prevails also to a large extent in the building trades; and the writer asserts without fear of contradiction that this constitutes the greatest evil with which the working-people of both England and America are now afflicted.

It will be shown later in this paper that doing away with slow working and "soldiering" in all its forms and so arranging the relations between employer and employé that each workman will work to his very best advantage and at his best speed, accompanied by the intimate cooperation with the management and the help (which the workman should receive) from the management, would result on the average in nearly doubling the output of each man and each machine. What other reforms, among those which are being discussed by these two nations, could do as much toward promoting prosperity, toward the diminution of poverty, and the alleviation of suffering? America and England have been recently agitated over such subjects as the tariff, the control of the large corporations on the one hand, and of hereditary power on the other hand, and over various more or less socialistic proposals for taxation, etc. On these subjects both peoples have been profoundly stirred, and yet hardly a voice has been raised to call attention to this vastly greater and more important subject of "soldiering," which directly and powerfully affects the wages, the prosperity, and the life of almost every working-man, and also quite as much the prosperity of every industrial establishment in the nation.

The elimination of "soldiering" and of the several causes of slow working would so lower the cost of production that both our home and foreign markets would be greatly enlarged, and we could compete on more than even terms with our rivals. It would remove one of the fundamental causes for dull times, for lack of employment, and for poverty, and therefore would have a more permanent and far-reaching effect upon these misfortunes than any of the curative remedies that are now being used to soften their consequences. It would insure higher wages and make shorter working hours and better working and home conditions possible.

Why is it, then, in the face of the self-evident fact that maximum prosperity can exist only as the result of the determined effort of each workman to turn out each day his largest possible day's work, that the great majority of our men are deliberately doing just the opposite, and that even when the men have the best of intentions their work is in most cases far from efficient?

There are three causes for this condition, which may be briefly summarized as:

First. The fallacy, which has from time immemorial been almost universal among workmen, that a material increase in the output of each man or each machine in the trade would result in the end in throwing a large number of men out of work.

Second. The defective systems of management which are in common use, and which make it necessary for each workman to soldier, or work slowly, in order that he may protect his own best interests.

Third. The inefficient rule-of-thumb methods, which are still almost universal in all trades, and in practising which our workmen waste a large part of their effort.

This paper will attempt to show the enormous gains which would result from the substitution by our workmen of scientific for rule-of-thumb methods.

To explain a little more fully these three causes:

First. The great majority of workmen still believe that if they were to work at their best speed they would be doing a great injustice to the whole trade by throwing a lot of men out of work, and yet the history of the development of each trade shows that each improvement, whether it be the invention of a new machine or the introduction of a better method, which results in increasing the productive capacity of the men in the trade and cheapening the costs, instead of throwing men out of work make[s] in the end work for more men.

The cheapening of any article in common use almost immediately results in a largely increased demand for that article. Take the case of shoes, for instance. The introduction of machinery for doing every element of the work which was formerly done by hand has resulted in making shoes at a fraction of their former labor cost, and in selling them so cheap that now almost every man, woman, and child in the working-classes buys one or two pairs of shoes per year, and wears shoes all the time, whereas formerly each workman bought perhaps one pair of shoes every five years, and went barefoot most of the time, wearing shoes only as a luxury or as a matter of the sternest necessity. In spite of the enormously increased output of shoes per workman, which has come with shoe machinery, the demand for shoes has so increased that there are relatively more men working in the shoe industry now than ever before.

The workmen in almost every trade have before them an object lesson of this kind, and yet, because they are ignorant of the history of their own trade even, they still firmly believe, as their fathers did before them, that it is against their best interests for each man to turn out each day as much work as possible.

Under this fallacious idea a large proportion of the workmen of both countries each day deliberately work slowly so as to curtail the output. Almost every labor union has made, or is contemplating making, rules which have for their object curtailing the output of their members, and those men who have the greatest influence with the working-people, the labor leaders as well as many people with philanthropic feelings who are helping them, are daily spreading this fallacy and at the same time telling them that they are overworked.

A great deal has been and is being constantly said about "sweat-shop" work and conditions. The writer has great sympathy with those who are overworked, but on the whole a greater sympathy for those who are *under paid*. For every individual, however, who is overworked, there are a hundred who intentionally underwork—greatly underwork—every day of their lives, and who for this reason deliberately aid in establishing those conditions which in the end inevitably result in low wages. And yet hardly a single voice is being raised in an endeavor to correct this evil.

As engineers and managers, we are more intimately acquainted with these facts than any other class in the community, and are therefore best fitted to lead in a movement to combat this fallacious idea by educating not only the workmen but the whole of the country as to the true facts.

And yet we are practically doing nothing in this direction, and are leaving this field entirely in the hands of the labor agitators (many of whom are misinformed and misguided), and of sentimentalists who are ignorant as to actual working conditions.

Second. As to the second cause for soldiering—the relations which exist between employers and employés under almost all of the systems of management which are in common use—it is impossible in a few words to make it clear to one not familiar with this problem why it is that the *ignorance of employers* as to the proper time in which work of various kinds should be done makes it for the interest of the workman to "soldier."

The writer therefore quotes herewith from a paper read before The American Society of Mechanical Engineers, in June, 1903, entitled "Shop Management," which it is hoped will explain fully this cause for soldiering:

"This loafing or soldiering proceeds from two causes. First, from the natural instinct and tendency of men to take it easy, which may be called natural soldiering. Second, from more intricate second thought and reasoning caused by their relations with other men, which may be called systematic soldiering.

"There is no question that the tendency of the average man (in all walks of life) is toward working at a slow, easy gait, and that it is only after a good deal of thought and observation on his part or as a result of example, conscience, or external pressure that he takes a more rapid pace.

"There are, of course, men of unusual energy, vitality, and ambition who naturally choose the fastest gait, who set up their own standards, and who work hard, even though it may be against their best interests. But these few uncommon men only serve by forming a contrast to emphasize the tendency of the average.

"This common tendency to 'take it easy' is greatly increased by bringing a number of men together on similar work and at a uniform standard rate of pay by the day.

"Under this plan the better men gradually but surely slow down their gait to that of the poorest and least efficient. When a naturally energetic man works for a few days beside a lazy one, the logic of the situation is unanswerable. 'Why should I work hard when that lazy fellow gets the same pay that I do and does only half as much work?'

"A careful time study of men working under these conditions will disclose facts which are ludicrous as well as pitiable.

"To illustrate: The writer has timed a naturally energetic workman who, while going and coming from work, would walk at a speed of from three to four miles per hour, and not infrequently trot home after a day's work. On arriving at his work he would immediately slow down to a speed of about one mile an hour. When, for example, wheeling a loaded wheelbarrow, he would go at a good fast pace even up hill in order to be as short a time as possible under load, and immediately on the return walk slow down to a mile an hour, improving every opportunity for delay short of actually sitting down. In order to be sure not to do more than his lazy neighbor, he would actually tire himself in his effort to go slow.

"These men were working under a foreman of good reputation and highly thought of by his employer, who, when his attention was called to this state of things, answered: 'Well, I can keep them from sitting down, but the devil can't make them get a move on while they are at work.'

"The natural laziness of men is serious, but by far the greatest evil from which both workmen and employers are suffering is the *systematic soldiering* which is almost universal under all of the ordinary schemes of management and which results from a careful study on the part of the workmen of what will promote their best interests.

"The writer was much interested recently in hearing one small but experienced golf caddy boy of twelve explaining to a green caddy, who had shown special energy and interest, the necessity of going slow and lagging behind his man when he came up to the ball, showing him that since they were paid by the hour, the faster they went the less money they got, and finally telling him that if he went too fast the other boys would give him a licking.

"This represents a type of *systematic soldiering* which is not, however, very serious, since it is done with the knowledge of the employer, who can quite easily break it up if he wishes.

"The greater part of the *systematic soldiering,* however, is done by the men with the deliberate object of keeping their employers ignorant of how fast work can be done.

"So universal is soldiering for this purpose that hardly a competent workman can be found in a large establishment, whether he works by the day or on piece work, contract work, or under any of the ordinary systems, who does not devote a considerable part of his time to studying just how slow he can work and still convince his employer that he is going at a good pace.

"The causes for this are, briefly, that practically all employers determine upon a maximum sum which they feel it is right for each of their classes of employees to earn per day, whether their men work by the day or piece.

"Each workman soon finds out about what this figure is for his particular case, and he also realizes that when his employer is convinced that a man is capable of doing more work than he has done, he will find sooner or later some way of compelling him to do it with little or no increase of pay.

"Employers derive their knowledge of how much of a given class of work can be done in a day from either their own experience, which has frequently grown hazy with age, from casual and unsystematic observation of their men, or at best from records which are kept, showing the quickest time in which each job has been done. In many cases the employer will feel almost certain that a given job can be done faster than it has been, but he rarely cares to take the drastic measures necessary to force men to do it in the quickest time, unless he has an actual record proving conclusively how fast the work can be done.

"It evidently becomes for each man's interest, then, to see that no job is done faster than it has been in the past. The younger and less experienced men are taught this by their elders, and all possible persuasion and social pressure is brought to bear upon the greedy and selfish men to keep them from making new records which result in temporarily increasing their wages, while all those who come after them are made to work harder for the same old pay.

"Under the best day work of the ordinary type, when accurate records are kept of the amount of work done by each man and of his efficiency, and when each man's wages are raised as he improves, and those who fail to rise to a certain standard are discharged and a fresh supply of carefully selected men are given work in their places, both the natural loafing and systematic soldiering can be largely broken up. This can only be done, however, when the men are thoroughly convinced that there is no intention of establishing piece work even in the remote future, and it is next to impossible to make men believe this when the work is of such a nature that they believe piece work to be practicable. In most cases their fear of making a record which will be used as a basis for piece work will cause them to soldier as much as they dare.

"It is, however, under piece work that the art of systematic soldiering is thoroughly developed; after a workman has had the price per piece of the work he is doing lowered two or three times as a result of his having worked harder and increased his output, he is likely entirely to lose sight of his employer's side of the case and become imbued with a grim determination to have no more cuts if soldiering can prevent it. Unfortunately for the character of the workman, soldiering involves a deliberate attempt to mislead and deceive his employer, and thus upright and straightforward workmen are compelled to become more or less hypocritical. The employer is soon looked upon as an antagonist, if not an enemy, and the mutual confidence which should exist between a leader and his men, the enthusiasm, the feeling that they are all working for the same end and will share in the results is entirely lacking.

"The feeling of antagonism under the ordinary piece-work system becomes in many cases so marked on the part of the men that any proposition made by their employers, however reasonable, is looked upon with suspicion, and soldiering becomes such a fixed habit that men will frequently take pains to restrict the product of machines which they are running when even a large increase in output would involve no more work on their part."

Third. As to the third cause for slow work, considerable space will later in this paper be devoted to illustrating the great gain, both to employers and employés, which results from the substitution of scientific for rule-of-thumb methods in even the smallest details of the work of every trade. The enormous saving of time and therefore increase in the output which it is possible to effect through eliminating unnecessary motions and substituting fast for slow and inefficient motions for the men working in any of our trades can be fully realized only after one has personally seen the improvement which results from a thorough motion and time study, made by a competent man.

To explain briefly: owing to the fact that the workmen in all of our trades have been taught the details of their work by observation of those immediately around them, there are many different ways in common use for doing the same thing, perhaps forty, fifty, or a hundred ways of doing each act in each trade, and for the same reason there is a great variety in the implements used for each class of work. Now, among the various methods and implements used in each element of each trade there is always one method and one implement which is quicker and better than any of the rest. And this one best method and best implement can only be discovered or developed through a scientific study and analysis of all of the methods and implements in use, together with accurate, minute, motion and time study. This involves the gradual substitution of science for rule of thumb throughout the mechanic arts.

This paper will show that the underlying philosophy of all of the old systems of management in common use makes it imperative that each workman shall be left with the final responsibility for doing his job practically as he thinks best, with comparatively little help and advice from the management. And it will also show that because of this isolation of workmen, it is in most cases impossible for the men working under these systems to do their work in accordance with the rules and laws of a science or art, even where one exists.

The writer asserts as a general principle (and he proposes to give illustrations tending to prove the fact later in this paper) that in almost all of the mechanic arts the science which underlies each act of each workman is so great and amounts to so much that the workman who is best suited to actually doing the work is incapable of fully understanding this science, without the guidance and help of those who are working with him or over him, either through lack of education or through insufficient mental capacity. In order that the work may be done in accordance with scientific laws, it is necessary that there shall be a far more equal division of the responsibility between the management and the workmen than exists under any of the ordinary types of management. Those in the management whose duty it is to develop this science should also guide and help the workman in working under it, and should assume a much larger share of the responsibility for results than under usual conditions is assumed by the management.

The body of this paper will make it clear that, to work according to scientific laws, the management must take over and perform much of the work which is now left to the men; almost every act of the workman should be preceded by one or more preparatory acts of the management which enable him to do his work better and quicker than he otherwise could. And each man should daily be taught by and receive the most friendly help from those who are over him, instead of being, at the one extreme, driven or coerced by his bosses, and at the other left to his own unaided devices.

This close, intimate, personal cooperation between the management and the men is of the essence of modern scientific or task management.

It will be shown by a series of practical illustrations that, through this friendly cooperation, namely, through sharing equally in every day's burden, all of the great obstacles (above described) to obtaining the maximum output for each man and each machine in the establishment are swept away. The 30 per cent. to 100 per cent. increase in wages which the workmen are able to earn beyond what they receive under the old type of management, coupled with the daily intimate shoulder to shoulder contact with the management, entirely removes all cause for soldiering. And in a few years, under this system, the workmen have before them the object lesson of seeing that a great increase in the output per man results in giving employment to more men, instead of throwing men out of work, thus completely eradicating the fallacy that a larger output for each man will throw other men out of work.

It is the writer's judgment, then, that while much can be done and should be done by writing and talking toward educating not only workmen, but all classes in the community, as to the importance of obtaining the maximum output of each man and each machine, it is only through the adoption of modern scientific management that this great problem can be finally solved. Probably most of the readers of this paper will say that all of this is mere theory. On the contrary, the theory, or philosophy, of scientific management is just beginning to be understood, whereas the management itself has been a gradual evolution, extending over a period of nearly thirty years. And during this time the employés of one company after another, including a large range and diversity of industries, have gradually changed from the ordinary to the scientific type of management. At least 50,000 workmen in the United States are now employed under this system; and they are receiving from 30 per cent. to 100 per cent. higher wages daily than are paid to men of similar caliber with whom they are surrounded, while the companies employing them are more prosperous than ever before. In these companies the output, per man and per machine, has on an average been doubled. During all these years there has never been a single strike among the men working under this system. In place of the suspicious watchfulness and the more or less open warfare which characterizes the ordinary types of management, there is universally friendly cooperation between the management and the men.

Several papers have been written, describing the expedients which have been adopted and the details which have been developed under scientific management and the steps to be taken in changing from the ordinary to the scientific type. But unfortunately most of the readers of these papers have mistaken the mechanism for the true essence. Scientific management fundamentally consists of certain broad general principles, a certain philosophy, which can be applied in many ways, and a description of what any one man or men may believe to be the best mechanism for applying these general principles should in no way be confused with the principles themselves.

It is not here claimed that any single panacea exists for all of the troubles of the working-people or of employers. As long as some people are born lazy or inefficient, and others are born greedy and brutal, as long as vice and crime are with us, just so long will a certain amount of poverty, misery, and unhappiness be with us also. No system of management, no single expedient within the control of any man or any set of men can insure continuous prosperity to either workmen or employers. Prosperity depends upon so many factors entirely beyond the control of any one set of men, any state, or even any one country, that certain periods will inevitably come when both sides must suffer, more or less. It is claimed, however, that under scientific management the intermediate periods will be far more prosperous, far happier, and more free from discord and dissension. And also, that the periods will be fewer, shorter and the suffering less. And this will be particularly true in any one town, any one section of the country, or any one state which first substitutes the principles of scientific management for the rule of thumb.

That these principles are certain to come into general use practically throughout the civilized world, sooner or later, the writer is profoundly convinced, and the sooner they come the better for all the people.

Buck v. Bell, 1927

*Carrie Buck was an inmate at Virginia's State Colony for Epileptics and Feeble Minded—
an institution for those deemed to be mentally disabled. Virginia law at the time provided
for the forced sterilization of inmates in state institutions when it was determined to be in
the best interests of the patient and society. Buck was the natural daughter of a woman,
deemed "feeble-minded," who had been found prone to prostitution. Her adoptive parents
had Buck committed after she became pregnant. Buck's guardian argued that sterilizing
her against her will would violate her Fourteenth Amendment rights to due process and
equal protection. In his opinion for the Supreme Court, Justice Oliver Wendell Holmes Jr.
held that the hearing procedures outlined in the Virginia law provided sufficient protections and that the state's interests would be served best by sterilizing Buck, because "three
generations of imbeciles are enough." State eugenics laws aimed at preventing "mentally
deficient" people from having children (deemed dangerous to public safety and genetic
progress) multiplied after the decision in this case.*

Carrie Buck, by R. G. Shelton, Her Guardian and Next Friend, Plff. in Err., v. J. H. Bell, Superintendent of the State Colony for Epileptics and Feeble Minded

Argued April 22, 1927. Decided May 2, 1927.

Mr. Justice Holmes delivered the opinion of the court:

This is a writ of error to review a judgment of the supreme court of appeals of the state of Virginia, affirming a judgment of the circuit court of Amherst county, by which the defendant in error, the superintendent of the State Colony for Epileptics and Feeble Minded, was ordered to perform the operation of salpingectomy upon Carrie Buck, the plaintiff in error, for the purpose of making her sterile. 143 Va. 310, 51 A.L.R. 855, 130 S. E. 516. The case comes here upon the contention that the statute authorizing the judgment is void under the 14th Amendment as denying to the plaintiff in error due process of law and the equal protection of the laws.

Carrie Buck is a feeble minded white woman who was committed to the State Colony above mentioned in due form. She is the daughter of a feeble minded mother in the same institution, and the mother of an illegitimate feeble minded child. She was eighteen years old at the time of the trial of her case in the circuit court, in the latter part of 1924. An Act of Virginia approved March 20, 1924, recites that the health of the patient and the welfare of society may be promoted in certain cases by the sterilization of mental defectives, under careful safeguard, etc.; that the sterilization may be effected in males by vasectomy and in females by salpingectomy, without serious pain or substantial danger to life; that the Commonwealth is supporting in various institutions many defective persons who if now discharged would become a menace but if incapable of procreating might be discharged with safety and become self-supporting with benefit to themselves and to society; and that experience has shown that heredity plays an important part in the transmission of insanity, imbecility, etc. The statute then enacts that whenever the superintendent of certain institutions including the above named State Colony shall be of opinion that it is for the best interests of the patients and of society that an inmate under his care should be sexually sterilized, he may have the operation performed upon any patient afflicted with hereditary forms of insanity, imbecility, etc., on complying with the very careful provisions by which the act protects the patients from possible abuse.

The superintendent first presents a petition to the special

board of directors of his hospital or colony, stating the facts and the grounds for his opinion, verified by affidavit. Notice of the petition and of the time and place of the hearing in the institution is to be served upon the inmate, and also upon his guardian, and if there is no guardian the superintendent is to apply to the circuit court of the county to appoint one. If the inmate is a minor notice also is to be given to his parents if any with a copy of the petition. The board is to see to it that the inmate may attend the hearings if desired by him or his guardian. The evidence is all to be reduced to writing, and after the board has made its order for or against the operation, the superintendent, or the inmate, or his guardian, may appeal to the circuit court of the county. The circuit court may consider the record of the board and the evidence before it and such other admissible evidence as may be offered, and may affirm, revise, or reverse the order of the board and enter such order as it deems just. Finally any party may apply to the supreme court of appeals, which, if it grants the appeal, is to hear the case upon the record of the trial in the circuit court and may enter such order as it thinks the circuit court should have entered. There can be no doubt that so far as procedure is concerned the rights of the patient are most carefully considered, and as every step in this case was taken in scrupulous compliance with the statute and after months of observation, there is no doubt that in that respect the plaintiff in error has had due process of law.

The attack is not upon the procedure but upon the substantive law. It seems to be contended that in no circumstances could such an order be justified. It certainly is contended that the order cannot be justified upon the existing grounds. The judgment finds the facts that have been recited and that Carrie Buck "is the probable potential parent of socially inadequate offspring, likewise afflicted, that she may be sexually sterilized without detriment to her general health

and that her welfare and that of society will be promoted by her sterilization," and thereupon makes the order. In view of the general declarations of the legislature and the specific findings of the court obviously we cannot say as matter of law that the grounds do not exist, and if they exist they justify the result. We have seen more than once that the public welfare may call upon the best citizens for their lives. It would be strange if it could not call upon those who already sap the strength of the state for these lesser sacrifices, often not felt to be such by those concerned, in order to prevent our being swamped with incompetence. It is better for all the world, if instead of waiting to execute degenerate offspring for crime, or to let them starve for their imbecility, society can prevent those who are manifestly unfit from continuing their kind. The principle that sustains compulsory vaccination is broad enough to cover cutting the Fallopian tubes. Jacobson v. Massachusetts, 197 U.S. 11, 49 L. ed. 643, 25 Sup. Ct. Rep. 358, 3 Ann. Cas. 765. Three generations of imbeciles are enough.

But, it is said, however it might be if this reasoning were applied generally, it fails when it is confined to the small number who are in the institutions named and is not applied to the multitudes outside. It is the usual last resort of constitutional arguments to point out shortcomings of this sort. But the answer is that the law does all that is needed when it does all that it can, indicates a policy, applies it to all within the lines, and seeks to bring within the lines all similarly situated so far and so fast as its means allow. Of course so far as the operations enable those who otherwise must be kept confined to be returned to the world, and thus open the asylum to others, the equality aimed at will be more nearly reached.

Judgment affirmed.

Mr. Justice Butler dissents.

I'll Take My Stand, *Twelve Southerners, 1930*

A collection of essays by twelve prominent writers sometimes called the Nashville Agrarians, I'll Take My Stand *describes and defends the agricultural way of life dominant in the American South but increasingly embattled by industrialization after the Civil War. Its contributors (several of whom, including John Crowe Ransom and Allen Tate, would achieve prominence in literary circles) rejected the materialistic habits and values they saw infecting industrial economics and culture. They called for a return to smaller scale, more personal and humane relations not dominated by mass institutions and the profit motive.*

Introduction to *I'll Take My Stand*

Twelve Southerners

A STATEMENT OF PRINCIPLES

THE authors contributing to this book are Southerners, well acquainted with one another and of similar tastes, though not necessarily living in the same physical community, and perhaps only at this moment aware of themselves as a single group of men. By conversation and exchange of letters over a number of years it had developed that they entertained many convictions in common, and it was decided to make a volume in which each one should furnish his views upon a chosen topic. This was the general background. But background and consultation as to the various topics were enough; there was to be no further collaboration. And so no single author is responsible for any view outside his own article. It was through the good fortune of some deeper agreement that the book was expected to achieve its unity. All the articles bear in the same sense upon the book's title-subject: all tend to support a Southern way of life against what may be called the American or prevailing way; and all as much as agree that the best terms in which to represent the distinction are contained in the phrase, Agrarian *versus* Industrial.

But after the book was under way it seemed a pity if the contributors, limited as they were within their special subjects, should stop short of showing how close their agreements really were. On the contrary, it seemed that they ought to go on and make themselves known as a group already consolidated by a set of principles which could be stated with a good deal of particularity. This might prove useful for the sake of future reference, if they should undertake any further joint publication. It was then decided to prepare a general introduction for the book which would state briefly the common

convictions of the group. This is the statement. To it every one of the contributors in this book has subscribed.

Nobody now proposes for the South, or for any other community in this country, an independent political destiny. That idea is thought to have been finished in 1865. But how far shall the South surrender its moral, social, and economic autonomy to the victorious principle of Union? That question remains open. The South is a minority section that has hitherto been jealous of its minority right to live its own kind of life. The South scarcely hopes to determine the other sections, but it does propose to determine itself, within the utmost limits of legal action. Of late, however, there is the melancholy fact that the South itself has wavered a little and shown signs of wanting to join up behind the common or American industrial ideal. It is against that tendency that this book is written. The younger Southerners, who are being converted frequently to the industrial gospel, must come back to the support of the Southern tradition. They must be persuaded to look very critically at the advantages of becoming a "new South" which will be only an undistinguished replica of the usual industrial community.

But there are many other minority communities opposed to industrialism, and wanting a much simpler economy to live by. The communities and private persons sharing the agrarian tastes are to be found widely within the Union. Proper living is a matter of the intelligence and the will, does not depend on the local climate or geography, and is capable of a definition which is general and not Southern at all. Southerners have a filial duty to discharge to their own section. But their cause is precarious and they must seek alliances with sympathetic communities everywhere. The members of the present group would be happy to be counted as members of a national agrarian movement.

Industrialism is the economic organization of the collective American society. It means the decision of society to invest its economic resources in the applied sciences. But the word science has acquired a certain sanctitude. It is out of order to quarrel with science in the abstract, or even with the applied sciences when their applications are made subject to criticism and intelligence. The capitalization of the applied sciences has now become extravagant and uncritical; it has enslaved our human energies to a degree now clearly felt to be burdensome. The apologists of industrialism do not like to meet this charge directly; so they often take refuge in saying that they are devoted simply to science! They are really devoted to the applied sciences and to practical production. Therefore it is necessary to employ a certain skepticism even at the expense of the Cult of Science, and to say, It is an Americanism, which looks innocent and disinterested, but really is not either.

The contribution that science can make to a labor is to render it easier by the help of a tool or a process, and to assure the laborer of his perfect economic security while he is engaged upon it. Then it can be performed with leisure and enjoyment. But the modern laborer has not exactly received this benefit under the industrial regime. His labor is hard, its tempo is fierce, and his employment is insecure. The first principle of a good labor is that it must be effective, but the second principle is that it must be enjoyed. Labor is one of the largest items in the human career; it is a modest demand to ask that it may partake of happiness.

The regular act of applied science is to introduce into labor a labor-saving device or a machine. Whether this is a benefit depends on how far it is advisable to save the labor. The philosophy of applied science is generally quite sure that the saving of labor is a pure gain, and that the more of it the better. This is to assume that labor is an evil, that only the end of labor or the material product is good. On this assumption labor becomes mercenary and servile, and it is no wonder if many forms of modern labor are accepted without resentment though they are evidently brutalizing. The act of labor as one of the happy functions of human life has been in effect abandoned, and is practiced solely for its rewards.

Even the apologists of industrialism have been obliged to admit that some economic evils follow in the wake of the machines. These are such as overproduction, unemployment, and a growing inequality in the distribution of wealth. But the remedies proposed by the apologists are always homeopathic. They expect the evils to disappear when we have bigger and better machines, and more of them. Their remedial programs, therefore, look forward to more industrialism. Sometimes they see the system righting itself spontaneously and without direction: they are Optimists. Sometimes they rely on the benevolence of capital, or the militancy of labor, to bring about a fairer division of the spoils: they are Coöperationists or Socialists. And sometimes they expect to find super-engineers, in the shape of Boards of Control, who will adapt production to consumption and regulate prices and guarantee business against fluctuations: they are Sovietists. With respect to these last it must be insisted that the true Sovietists or Communists—if the term may be used here in the European sense—are the Industrialists themselves. They would have the government set up an economic superorganization, which in turn would become the government. We therefore look upon the Communist menace as a menace indeed, but not as a Red one; because it is simply according to the blind drift of our industrial development to expect in America at last much the same economic system as that imposed by violence upon Russia in 1917.

Turning to consumption, as the grand end which justifies the evil of modern labor, we find that we have been deceived. We have more time in which to consume, and many more products to be consumed. But the tempo of our labors communicates itself to our satisfactions, and these also become brutal and hurried. The constitution of the natural man probably does not permit him to shorten his labor-time and enlarge his consuming-time indefinitely. He has to pay the penalty in satiety and aimlessness. The modern man has lost his sense of vocation.

Religion can hardly expect to flourish in an industrial society. Religion is our submission to the general intention of a nature that is fairly inscrutable; it is the sense of our rôle as creatures within it. But nature industrialized, transformed into cities and artificial habitations, manufactured into commodities, is no longer nature but a highly simplified picture of nature. We receive the illusion of having power over nature, and lose the sense of nature as something mysterious and contingent. The God of nature under these conditions is merely an amiable expression, a superfluity, and the philosophical understanding ordinarily carried in the religious experience is not there for us to have.

Nor do the arts have a proper life under industrialism, with the general decay of sensibility which attends it. Art depends, in general, like religion, on a right attitude to nature; and in particular on a free and disinterested observation of nature that occurs only in leisure. Neither the creation nor the understanding of works of art is possible in an industrial age except by some local and unlikely suspension of the industrial drive.

The amenities of life also suffer under the curse of a strictly-business or industrial civilization. They consist in such practices as manners, conversation, hospitality, sympathy, family life, romantic love—in the social exchanges which reveal and develop sensibility in human affairs. If religion and the arts are founded on right relations of man-to-nature, these are founded on right relations of man-to-man.

Apologists of industrialism are even inclined to admit that its actual processes may have upon its victims the spiritual effects just described. But they think that all can be made right by extraordinary educational efforts, by all sorts of cultural institutions and endowments. They would cure the poverty of the contemporary spirit by hiring experts to instruct it in spite of itself in the historic culture. But salvation is hardly to be encountered on that road. The trouble with the life-pattern is to be located at its economic base, and we cannot rebuild it by pouring in soft materials from the top. The young men and women in colleges, for example, if they are already placed in a false way of life, cannot make more than an inconsequential acquaintance with the arts and humanities transmitted to them. Or else the understanding of these arts and humanities will but make them the more wretched in their own destitution.

The "Humanists" are too abstract. Humanism, properly speaking, is not an abstract system, but a culture, the whole way in which we live, act, think, and feel. It is a kind of imaginatively balanced life lived out in a definite social tradition. And, in the concrete, we believe that this, the genuine humanism, was rooted in the agrarian life of the older South and of other parts of the country that shared in such a tradition. It was not an abstract moral "check" derived from the classics—it was not soft material poured in from the top. It was deeply founded in the way of life itself—in its tables, chairs, portraits, festivals, laws, marriage customs. We cannot recover our native humanism by adopting some standard of taste that is critical enough to question the contemporary arts but not critical enough to question the social and economic life which is their ground.

The tempo of the industrial life is fast, but that is not the worst of it; it is accelerating. The ideal is not merely some set form of industrialism, with so many stable industries, but industrial progress, or an incessant extension of industrialization. It never proposes a specific goal; it initiates the infinite series. We have not merely capitalized certain industries; we have capitalized the laboratories and inventors, and undertaken to employ all the labor-saving devices that come out of them. But a fresh labor-saving device introduced into an industry does not emancipate the laborers in that industry so much as it evicts them. Applied at the expense of agriculture, for example, the new processes have reduced the part of the population supporting itself upon the soil to a smaller and smaller fraction. Of course no single labor-saving process is fatal; it brings on a period of unemployed labor and unemployed capital, but soon a new industry is devised which will put them both to work again, and a new commodity is thrown upon the market. The laborers were sufficiently embarrassed in the meantime, but, according to the theory, they will eventually be taken care of. It is now the public which is embarrassed; it feels obligated to purchase a commodity for which it had expressed no desire, but it is invited to make its budget equal to the strain. All might yet be well, and stability and comfort might again obtain, but for this: partly because of industrial ambitions and partly because the repressed creative impulse must break out somewhere, there will be a stream of further labor-saving devices in all industries, and the cycle will have to be repeated over and over. The result is an increasing disadjustment and instability.

It is an inevitable consequence of industrial progress that production greatly outruns the rate of natural consumption. To overcome the disparity, the producers, disguised as the pure idealists of progress, must coerce and wheedle the public into being loyal and steady consumers, in order to keep the machines running. So the rise of modern advertising—along with its twin, personal salesmanship—is the most significant development of our industrialism. Advertising means to persuade the consumers to want exactly what the applied sciences are able to furnish them. It consults the happiness of the consumer no more than it consulted the happiness of the laborer. It is the great effort of a false economy of life to approve itself. But its task grows more difficult every day.

It is strange, of course, that a majority of men anywhere could ever as with one mind become enamored of industrialism: a system that has so little regard for individual wants. There is evidently a kind of thinking that rejoices in setting up a social objective which has no relation to the individual. Men are prepared to sacrifice their private dignity and happiness to an abstract social ideal, and without asking whether the social ideal produces the welfare of any individual man whatsoever. But this is absurd. The responsibility of men is for their own welfare and that of their neighbors; not for the hypothetical welfare of some fabulous creature called society.

Opposed to the industrial society is the agrarian, which does not stand in particular need of definition. An agrarian society is hardly one that has no use at all for industries, for professional vocations, for scholars and artists, and for the life of cities. Technically, perhaps, an agrarian society is one in which agriculture is the leading vocation, whether for wealth, for pleasure, or for prestige—a form of labor that is pursued with intelligence and leisure, and that becomes the model to which the other forms approach as well as they may. But an agrarian regime will be secured readily enough where the superfluous industries are not allowed to rise against it. The theory of agrarianism is that the culture of the soil is the best and most sensitive of vocations, and that therefore it should have the economic preference and enlist the maximum number of workers.

These principles do not intend to be very specific in proposing any practical measures. How may the little agrarian community resist the Chamber of Commerce of its county seat, which is always trying to import some foreign industry that cannot be assimilated to the life-pattern of the community? Just what must the Southern leaders do to defend the traditional Southern life? How may the Southern and the Western agrarians unite for effective action? Should the agrarian forces try to capture the Democratic party, which historically is so closely affiliated with the defense of individualism, the small community, the state, the South? Or must the agrarians—even the Southern ones—abandon the Democratic party to its fate and try a new one? What legislation could most profitably be championed by the powerful agrarians in the Senate of the United States? What anti-industrial measures might promise to stop the advances of industrialism, or even undo some of them, with the least harm to those concerned? What policy should be pursued by the educators who have a tradition at heart? These and many other questions are of the greatest importance, but they cannot be answered here.

For, in conclusion, this much is clear: If a community, or a section, or a race, or an age, is groaning under industrialism, and well aware that it is an evil dispensation, it must find the way to throw it off. To think that this cannot be done is pusillanimous. And if the whole community, section, race, or age thinks it cannot be done, then it has simply lost its political genius and doomed itself to impotence.

PART FIVE Reform Movements

WHY AMERICA WENT DRY

LESS DRINK
MORE HOMES

Henry living in a wet State, found it easy to spend a dollar a week for beer. After 25 years all there was to show for his money was a pile of empty beer kegs—and he did not own those.

John, living in a dry State, found it easy to put a dollar a week into the Building Loan Association. After 25 years he owned a *good home*.

Sobriety Fosters the Clear Brain, the Steady Hand, the Thrift Habit

COPYRIGHTED 1920
BY SCIENTIFIC TEMPERANCE FEDERATION
BOSTON, MASS.

THE AMERICAN ISSUE PUBLISHING CO.
WESTERVILLE, OHIO

PRINTED IN U. S. A.

No. 75

Archbishop Ireland
Says:

The Great Cause of Crime is

DRINK

The Great Cause of Poverty is

DRINK

When I Hear of a Family Broken Up
I Ask the Cause

DRINK

If I go to the Gallows and ask its Victims
the Cause, the Answer is

DRINK

Then I Ask Myself in Perfect Wonderment

Why do not Men put a Stop to this thing?

Anti-saloon flier. Anti-Saloon League Museum, Westerville Public Library, Westerville, Ohio.

Anti-saloon flier. Anti-Saloon League Museum, Westerville Public Library, Westerville, Ohio.

THIS SECTION INCLUDES documents related to a variety of reform movements—some centered on particular issues, such as women's suffrage, and some advocating a more general program of reform, such as Populism, seen as necessary to protect fundamental values and interests endangered by self-interested groups. Most of these movements had their real legal and constitutional impact after the start of the twentieth century. But their roots lay at the beginnings of the republic, and beyond. Moreover, throughout the nineteenth and early twentieth centuries there were deep connections among those seeking reform, and the reforms they sought. Those seeking the abolition of slavery, the prohibition of intoxicating spirits, the extension of greater rights to women, and economic reforms intended to care for the poor often were the same people. At times there were conflicts, as when some former abolitionists split with those seeking voting rights for African Americans in order to argue that white women should have those rights. Moreover, there were substantial differences among those seeking reforms of the American system and those who brought into public discourse theories and assumptions regarding economic class and industrialism originally more connected with European radicalism. But the results—particularly as measured by constitutional reforms—changed the very structure of American public life.

Populist Party Platform, 1892

*American farmers and ranchers repeatedly formed movements aimed at protecting them-
selves against powerful interests they believed were profiting from corrupt policies that
hurt people who worked the land. These interests varied, depending on the era and the
agrarians involved, but generally included bankers and large industrial corporations—
especially railroad companies. In 1892 agrarian forces coalesced to form the People's Party,
more generally referred to as the Populist Party. At its first national convention, the party
nominated James K. Weaver for president and adopted the platform reproduced here.
Many of its proposals, aimed at fighting concentrations of wealth and power, found their
way into later reform movements.*

National People's Party Platform, adopted at Omaha, Neb., July 4, 1892

Assembled upon the 116th anniversary of the Declaration of Independence, the People's Party of America, in their first national convention, invoking upon their action the blessing of Almighty God, put forth in the name and on behalf of the people of this country, the following preamble and declaration of principles:

PREAMBLE

The conditions which surround us best justify our co-operation; we meet in the midst of a nation brought to the verge of moral, political, and material ruin. Corruption dominates the ballot-box, the Legislatures, the Congress, and touches even the ermine of the bench. The people are demoralized; most of the States have been compelled to isolate the voters at the polling places to prevent universal intimidation and bribery. The newspapers are largely subsidized or muzzled, public opinion silenced, business prostrated, homes covered with mortgages, labor impoverished, and the land concentrating in the hands of capitalists. The urban workmen are denied the right to organize for self-protection, imported pauperized labor beats down their wages, a hireling standing army, unrecognized by our laws, is established to shoot them down, and they are rapidly degenerating into European conditions. The fruits of the toil of millions are boldly stolen to build up colossal fortunes for a few, unprecedented in the history of mankind; and the possessors of those, in turn, despise the Republic and endanger liberty. From the same prolific womb of governmental injustice we breed the two great classes—tramps and millionaires.

The national power to create money is appropriated to enrich bondholders; a vast public debt payable in legal tender currency has been funded into gold-bearing bonds, thereby adding millions to the burdens of the people.

Silver, which has been accepted as coin since the dawn of history, has been demonetized to add to the purchasing power of gold by decreasing the value of all forms of property as well as human labor, and the supply of currency is purposely abridged to fatten usurers, bankrupt enterprise, and enslave industry. A vast conspiracy against mankind has been organized on two continents, and it is rapidly taking possession of the world. If not met and overthrown at once it forebodes terrible social convulsions, the destruction of civilization, or the establishment of an absolute despotism.

We have witnessed for more than a quarter of a century the struggles of the two great political parties for power and plunder, while grievous wrongs have been inflicted upon the suffering people. We charge that the controlling influences dominating both these parties have permitted the existing dreadful conditions to develop without serious effort to prevent or restrain them. Neither do they now promise us any substantial reform. They have agreed together to ignore, in the coming campaign, every issue but one. They propose to drown the outcries of a plundered people with the uproar of a sham battle over the tariff, so that capitalists, corporations, national banks, rings, trusts, watered stock, the demonetization of silver and the oppressions of the usurers may all be lost sight of. They propose to sacrifice our homes, lives, and children on the altar of mammon; to destroy the multitude in order to secure corruption funds from the millionaires.

Assembled on the anniversary of the birthday of the nation, and filled with the spirit of the grand general and chief who established our independence, we seek to restore the government of the Republic to the hands of "the plain people," with which class it originated. We assert our purposes to be identical with the purposes of the National Constitution; to form a more perfect union and establish justice, insure domestic tranquillity, provide for the common defence, promote the general welfare, and secure the blessings of liberty for ourselves and our posterity.

We declare that this Republic can only endure as a free government while built upon the love of the whole people for each other and for the nation; that it cannot be pinned together by bayonets; that the civil war is over, and that every passion and resentment which grew out of it must die with it, and that we must be in fact, as we are in name, one united brotherhood of free men.

Our country finds itself confronted by conditions for which there is no precedent in the history of the world; our annual agricultural productions amount to billions of dollars in value, which must, within a few weeks or months, be exchanged for billions of dollars' worth of commodities consumed in their production; the existing currency supply is wholly inadequate to make this exchange; the results are falling prices, the formation of combines and rings, the impoverishment of the producing class. We pledge ourselves that if given power we will labor to correct these evils by wise and reasonable legislation, in accordance with the terms of our platform.

We believe that the power of government—in other words, of the people—should be expanded (as in the case of the postal service) as rapidly and as far as the good sense of an intelligent people and the teachings of experience shall justify, to the end that oppression, injustice, and poverty shall eventually cease in the land.

While our sympathies as a party of reform are naturally upon the side of every proposition which will tend to make men intelligent, virtuous, and temperate, we nevertheless regard these questions, important as they are, as secondary to the great issues now pressing for solution, and upon which not only our individual prosperity but the very existence of free institutions depend; and we ask all men to first help us to determine whether we are to have a republic to administer before we differ as to the conditions upon which it is to be administered, believing that the forces of reform this day organized will never cease to move forward until every wrong is remedied and equal rights and equal privileges securely established for all the men and women of this country.

PLATFORM

We declare, therefore—

First.—That the union of the labor forces of the United States this day consummated shall be permanent and perpetual; may its spirit enter into all hearts for the salvation of the Republic and the uplifting of mankind.

Second.—Wealth belongs to him who creates it, and every dollar taken from industry without an equivalent is robbery. "If any will not work, neither shall he eat." The interests of rural and civic labor are the same; their enemies are identical.

Third.—We believe that the time has come when the railroad corporations will either own the people or the people must own the railroads, and should the government enter upon the work of owning and managing all railroads, we should favor an amendment to the Constitution by which all persons engaged in the government service shall be placed under a civil-service regulation of the most rigid character, so as to prevent the increase of the power of the national administration by the use of such additional government employés.

FINANCE.—We demand a national currency, safe, sound, and flexible, issued by the general government only, a full legal lender for all debts, public and private, and that without the use of banking corporations, a just, equitable, and efficient means of distribution direct to the people, at a tax not to exceed 2 per cent. per annum, to be provided as set forth in the sub-treasury plan of the Farmers' Alliance, or a better system; also by payments in discharge of its obligations for public improvements.

1. We demand free and unlimited coinage of silver and gold at the present legal ratio of 16 to 1.

2. We demand that the amount of circulating medium be speedily increased to not less than $50 per capita.

3. We demand a graduated income tax.

4. We believe that the money of the country should be kept as much as possible in the hands of the people, and hence we demand that all State and national revenues shall be limited to the necessary expenses of the government, economically and honestly administered.

5. We demand that postal savings banks be established by the government for the safe deposit of the earnings of the people and to facilitate exchange.

TRANSPORTATION.—Transportation being a means of exchange and a public necessity, the government should own and operate the railroads in the interest of the people. The telegraph, telephone, like the post-office system, being a necessity for the transmission of news, should be owned and operated by the government in the interest of the people.

LAND.—The land, including all the natural sources of wealth, is the heritage of the people, and should not be monopolized for speculative purposes, and alien ownership of land should be prohibited. All land now held by railroads and other corporations in excess of their actual needs, and all lands now owned by aliens should be reclaimed by the government and held for actual settlers only.

EXPRESSION OF SENTIMENTS

Your Committee on Platform and Resolutions beg leave unanimously to report the following:

Whereas, Other questions have been presented for our consideration, we hereby submit the following, not as a part of the Platform of the People's Party, but as resolutions expressive of the sentiment of this Convention:

1. RESOLVED, That we demand a free ballot and a fair count in all elections, and pledge ourselves to secure it to every legal voter without Federal intervention, through the adoption by the States of the unperverted Australian or secret ballot system.

2. RESOLVED, That the revenue derived from a graduated income tax should be applied to the reduction of the burden of taxation now levied upon the domestic industries of this country.

3. RESOLVED, That we pledge our support to fair and liberal pensions to ex-Union soldiers and sailors.

4. RESOLVED, That we condemn the fallacy of protecting American labor under the present system, which opens our ports to the pauper and criminal classes of the world and crowds out our wage-earners; and we denounce the present ineffective laws against contract labor, and demand the further restriction of undesirable emigration.

5. RESOLVED, That we cordially sympathize with the efforts of organized workingmen to shorten the hours of labor, and demand a rigid enforcement of the existing eight-hour law on Government work, and ask that a penalty clause be added to the said law.

6. RESOLVED, That we regard the maintenance of a large standing army of mercenaries, known as the Pinkerton system, as a menace to our liberties, and we demand its abolition; and we condemn the recent invasion of the Territory of Wyoming by the hired assassins of plutocracy, assisted by Federal officers.

7. RESOLVED, That we commend to the favorable consideration of the people and the reform press the legislative system known as the initiative and referendum.

8. RESOLVED, That we favor a constitutional provision limiting the office of President and Vice-President to one term, and providing for the election of Senators of the United States by a direct vote of the people.

9. RESOLVED, That we oppose any subsidy or national aid to any private corporation for any purpose.

10. RESOLVED, That this convention sympathizes with the Knights of Labor and their righteous contest with the tyrannical combine of clothing manufacturers of Rochester, and declare it to be a duty of all who hate tyranny and oppression to refuse to purchase the goods made by the said manufacturers, or to patronize any merchants who sell such goods.

Coin's Financial School, *William H. Harvey*, 1894

Few issues fostered more debate and rancor during the last quarter of the nineteenth century than the popular demand to remonetize silver. Supporters of the gold standard, mostly from the business class and centered in the Northeast, adamantly opposed this drive to restore silver to its former role as the standard by which the value of the nation's currency would be determined. But remonetization, aimed at increasing the supply of money, gained wide support among farmers primarily in the South and West. In 1894 William Hope Harvey (1851–1936) published Coin's Financial School, *calling for the free and unlimited coinage of silver. Harvey had held numerous jobs, including lawyer, real estate salesman, and silver-mine operator, before opening a publishing business linked to his campaign for free silver. Published during the worst depression in American history, Harvey's book sold nearly one million copies. It showcased Professor "Coin," who argued that London businessmen had worked in the shadows to orchestrate the "Crime of '73" in the U.S. Congress—the demonetization of silver. The result, Coin argued, was deflation, which impoverished American farmers and workers. Coin's references to the English House of Rothschild's complicity in demonetization hinted at Jewish conspiracy.*

Coin's Financial School

William H. Harvey

The Money Unit

"In money there must be a unit. In arithmetic, as you are aware, you are taught what a unit is. Thus, I make here on the blackboard the figure 1. That, in arithmetic, is a unit. All countings are sums or multiples of that unit. A unit, therefore, in mathematics, was a necessity as a basis to start from. In making money it was equally as necessary to establish a unit. The constitution gave the power to Congress to 'coin money and regulate the value thereof.' Congress adopted silver and gold as money. It then proceeded to fix the unit.

"That is, it then fixed what should constitute one dollar, the same thing that the mathematician did when he fixed one figure from which all others should be counted. Congress fixed the monetary unit to consist of 371¼ grains of pure silver, and provided for a certain amount of alloy (baser metals) to be mixed with it to give it greater hardness and durability. This was in 1792, in the days of Washington and Jefferson and our revolutionary forefathers, who had a hatred of England, and an intimate knowledge of her designs on this country.

"They had fought eight long years for their independence from British domination in this country, and when they had seen the last red-coat leave our shores, they settled down to establish a permanent government, and among the first things

they did was to make 371¼ grains of silver the unit of values. That much silver was to constitute a dollar. And each dollar was a unit. They then provided for all other money to be counted from this unit of a silver dollar. Hence, dimes, quarters and half-dollars were exact fractional parts of the dollar so fixed.

"Gold was made money, but its value was counted from these silver units or dollars. The ratio between silver and gold was fixed at 15 to 1, and afterward at 16 to 1. So that in making gold coins their relative weight was regulated by this ratio.

"This continued to be the law up to 1873. During that long period, the unit of values was never changed and always contained 371¼ grains of pure silver. While that was the law it was impossible for any one to say that the silver in a silver dollar was only worth 47 cents, or any other number of cents less than 100 cents, or a dollar. For it was itself the unit of values. While that was the law it would have been as absurd to say that the silver in a silver dollar was only worth 47 cents, as it would be to say that this figure 1 which I have on the blackboard is only forty-seven one-hundredths of one.

"When the ratio was changed from 15 to 1 to 16 to 1 the silver dollar or unit was left the same size and the gold dollar was made smaller. The latter was changed from 24.7 grains to 23.2 grains pure gold, thus making it smaller. This occurred in 1834. The silver dollar still remained the unit and continued so until 1873.

"Both were legal tender in the payment of all debts, and the mints were open to the coinage of all that came. So that up to 1873, we were on what was known as a bimetallic basis, but what was in fact a silver basis, with gold as a companion metal enjoying the same privileges as silver, except that silver fixed the unit, and the value of gold was regulated by it. This was bimetallism.

"Our forefathers showed much wisdom in selecting silver, of the two metals, out of which to make the unit. Much depended on this decision. For the one selected to represent the unit would thereafter be unchangeable in value. That is, the metal in it could never be worth less than a dollar, for it would be the unit of value itself. The demand for silver in the arts or for money by other nations might make the quantity of silver in a silver dollar sell for more than a dollar, but it could never be worth less than a dollar. Less than itself.

"In considering which of these two metals they would thus favor by making it the unit, they were led to adopt silver because it was the most reliable. It was the most favored as money by the people. It was scattered among all the people. Men having a design to injure business by making money scarce, could not so easily get hold of all the silver and hide it away, as they could gold. This was the principal reason that led them to the conclusion to select silver, the more stable of the two metals, upon which to fix the unit. It was so much handled by the people and preferred by them, that it was called the people's money.

"Gold was considered the money of the rich. It was owned principally by that class of people, and the poor people seldom handled it, and the very poor people seldom ever saw any of it."

THE CRIME OF 1873

"We now come to the act of 1873," continued COIN. "On February 12, 1873, Congress passed an act purporting to be a revision of the coinage laws. This law covers 15 pages of our statutes. It repealed the *unit* clause in the law of 1792, and in its place substituted a law in the following language:

"That the gold coins of the United States shall be a one-dollar piece which at the standard weight of twenty-five and eight-tenths grains *shall be the unit of value.*

"It then deprived silver of its right to unrestricted free coinage, and destroyed it as legal tender money in the payment of debts, except to the amount of five dollars.

"At that time we were all using paper money. No one was handling silver and gold coins. It was when specie payments were about to be resumed that the country appeared to realize what had been done. The newspapers on the morning of February 13, 1873, and at no time in the vicinity of that period, had any account of the change. General Grant, who was President of the United States at that time, said afterwards, that he had no idea of it, and would not have signed the bill if he had known that it demonetized silver.

"In the language of Senator Daniel of Virginia, it seems to have gone through Congress 'like the silent tread of a cat.'

"An army of a half million of men invading our shores, the warships of the world bombarding our coasts, could not have made us surrender the money of the people and substitute in its place the money of the rich. A few words embraced in fifteen pages of statutes put through Congress in the rush of bills did it. The pen was mightier than the sword.

"But we are not here to deal with sentiment. We are here to learn facts. Plain, blunt facts.

"The law of 1873 made gold the *unit* of values. And that is the law to-day. When silver was the unit of value, gold enjoyed *free coinage,* and was legal tender in the payment of all debts. Now things have changed. Gold is the unit and silver does not enjoy free coinage. It is refused at the mints. We might get along with gold as the *unit,* if silver enjoyed the same right gold did prior to 1873. But that right is now denied to silver. When silver was the unit, the unlimited demand for gold to coin into money, made the demand as great as the supply, and this held up the value of gold bullion."

Here Victor F. Lawson, Jr., of the Chicago *Evening News,* interrupted the little financier with the statement that his paper, the *News,* had stated time and again that silver had become so plentiful it had ceased to be a precious metal. And that this statement believed by him to be a fact had more to do with his prejudice to silver than anything else. And he would like to know if that was not a fact?

"There is no truth in the statement," replied COIN. "On page 21 of my Handbook you will find a table on this subject, compiled by Mulhall, the London statistician. It gives the quantity of gold and silver in the world both coined and uncoined at six periods—at the years 1600, 1700, 1800, 1848, 1880, and 1890. It shows that in 1600 there were 27 tons of silver to one ton of gold. In 1700, 34 tons of silver to one ton of gold. In 1800, 32 tons of silver to one ton of gold. In 1848, 31 tons of silver to one ton of gold. In 1880, 18 tons of silver to one ton of gold. In 1890, 18 tons of silver to one ton of gold.

"The United States is producing more silver than it ever did, or was until recently. But the balance of the world is producing much less. They are fixing the price on our silver and taking it away from us, at their price. The report of the Director of the Mint shows that since 1850 the world has produced less silver than gold, while during the first fifty years of the century the world produced 78 per cent more silver than gold. Instead of becoming more plentiful, it is less plentiful. So it is less, instead of more.

"Any one can get the official statistics by writing to the treasurer at Washington, and asking for his official book of statistics. Also write to the Director of the Mint and ask him for his report. If you get no answer write to your Congressman. These books are furnished free and you will get them.

"At the time the United States demonetized silver in February, 1873, silver as measured in gold was worth $1.02. The argument of depreciated silver could not then be made. Not one of the arguments that are now made against silver was then possible. They are all the bastard children of the crime of 1873.

"It was demonetized secretly, and since then a powerful money trust has used deception and misrepresentations that have led tens of thousands of honest minds astray."

William Henry Smith, Jr., of the Associated Press, wanted to know if the size of the gold dollar was ever changed more than the one time mentioned by COIN, viz., in 1834.

"Yes," said COIN. "In 1837 it was changed from 23.2 to 23.22. This change of $\frac{2}{100}$ths was for convenience in calculation, but the change was made in the gold coin—never in the silver dollar (the *unit*) till 1873.

"We have seen," replied COIN, "how the commercial value of the two metals were parted. By the same laws that produced this result, silver was made redeemable in gold, and ceased to be redemption money. Silver now circulates like paper money, both redeemable in gold. It is now subsidary coin or token money.

"Strictly speaking, nothing is money but redemption money—all other forms of so called money are money only in the sense that certified checks are money.

"In the sense in which *you* say silver is money, nickel and copper are money, but they form no part of our stock of redemption money. Gold now takes the place formerly oc-cupied by both gold and silver, and is our only redemption money. Silver, as now treated, cuts no figure in our currency that could not be substituted by paper or other metals. What is meant by demonetization is, that silver has been destroyed as primary money.

"We are now on a single gold standard, and have come to it through a period of limping bimetallism."

ANOTHER ILLUSTRATION

"We express values in dollars, the unit of our monetary system. That unit is now the gold dollar of twenty-three and two-tenths grains of pure gold, or twenty-five and eight-tenths grains of standard gold. If we were to cut this amount in two and make eleven and six-tenths grains pure gold a *unit* or dollar, we would thereby double the value of all the property in the United States, except debts.

"If we were to double the weight of the *unit* or dollar by putting forty-six and four-tenths grains in it, we would thus reduce the value of all the property in the world, as expressed in dollars, except debts, as they call for so many dollars.

"If you don't understand this proposition as I have stated it, you will by enlarging the scale. Keep on adding gold to the dollar, till it takes one hundred grains—five hundred grains—one thousand grains—to make a legal *unit* or dollar. Go on making it larger till you have all of the gold in the world in one thousand *units,* or dollar pieces.

"Who could give up property enough to buy one of them? To buy a single dollar? Suppose you owed a note calling for $100.00 payable in gold, one-tenth the gold of the world—how could you pay it? Think of the property that would have to be slaughtered to get it.

"Carry the illustration still further and put all the gold in the world in one dollar. A note for one dollar would require all the gold to pay it. When you reduce the number of primary dollars, you reduce the value of property as expressed in dollars accordingly, and make it that much more difficult for debtors to pay their debts.

"And yet this is the kind of injustice that was committed when silver was demonetized. It struck down one-half the number of dollars that made up our primary money and standard of values for measuring the values of all property. It reduced the average value of silver and all other property one-half, except debts.

"It is commonly known as the *crime of 1873*. A crime, because it has confiscated millions of dollars worth of property. A crime, because it has made thousands of paupers.

A crime, because it has made tens of thousands of tramps. A crime, because it has made thousands of suicides. A crime, because it has brought tears to strong men's eyes, and hunger and pinching want to widows and orphans. A crime, because it is destroying the honest yeomanry of the land, the bulwark of the nation. A crime, because it has brought this once great republic to the verge of ruin, where it is now in imminent danger of tottering to its fall. [Applause.]

"Pardon me for an expression of feeling. We are not here to comment on the effects of demonetization, but "I now think we understand," said COIN, "what to learn what money is, and wherein our financial system has been changed."

The little speaker, without intending it, through a feeling of honest indignation, had burst forth in a recital of this catalogue of crimes. It had a perceptible effect on the audience. His earnest eloquence was melting hearts that never before had thawed to the presentation of the subject.

It is one of the wonders of the world—how the people have been so slow in grasping the financial problem—in learning what it is that measures values, and that the lesson should have to be learned through an experience so bitter.

What Pragmatism Means, *William James*, 1907

A physician, psychologist, and self-trained philosopher, William James (1842–1910) is best known as the principal founder and exponent of the philosophical school of Pragmatism. This school was highly influential in the United States for several decades and helped shape the Progressive tradition in politics. It quickly became known as a particularly American philosophy because of its emphasis on analyzing particular concepts by look- ing at their concrete, practical consequences or "cash value." James also published highly influential works on human psychology and the nature of religious experience. The essay reprinted here is one of eight lectures dedicated to the English utilitarian John Stuart Mill and published in Pragmatism: A New Name for Some Old Ways of Thinking.

Lecture II: What Pragmatism Means

William James

Some years ago, being with a camping party in the mountains, I returned from a solitary ramble to find every one engaged in a ferocious metaphysical dispute. The *corpus* of the dispute was a squirrel—a live squirrel supposed to be clinging to one side of a tree-trunk; while over against the tree's opposite side a human being was imagined to stand. This human witness tries to get sight of the squirrel by moving rapidly round the tree, but no matter how fast he goes, the squirrel moves as fast in the opposite direction, and always keeps the tree between himself and the man, so that never a glimpse of him is caught. The resultant metaphysical problem now is this: *Does the man go round the squirrel or not?* He goes round the tree, sure enough, and the squirrel is on the tree; but does he go round the squirrel? In the unlimited leisure of the wilderness, dis- cussion had been worn threadbare. Every one had taken sides, and was obstinate; and the numbers on both sides were even. Each side, when I appeared therefore appealed to me to make it a majority. Mindful of the scholastic adage that whenever you meet a contradiction you must make a distinction, I im- mediately sought and found one, as follows: "Which party is right," I said, "depends on what you *practically mean* by 'go- ing round' the squirrel. If you mean passing from the north of him to the east, then to the south, then to the west, and then . to the north of him again, obviously the man does go round him, for he occupies these successive positions. But if on the contrary you mean being first in front of him, then on the right of him, then behind him, then on his left, and finally

in front again, it is quite as obvious that the man fails to go round him, for by the compensating movements the squirrel makes, he keeps his belly turned towards the man all the time, and his back turned away. Make the distinction, and there is no occasion for any farther dispute. You are both right and both wrong according as you conceive the verb 'to go round' in one practical fashion or the other."

Although one or two of the hotter disputants called my speech a shuffling evasion, saying they wanted no quibbling or scholastic hair-splitting, but meant just plain honest Eng- lish 'round,' the majority seemed to think that the distinction had assuaged the dispute.

I tell this trivial anecdote because it is a peculiarly simple ex- ample of what I wish now to speak of as *the pragmatic method.* The pragmatic method is primarily a method of settling meta- physical disputes that otherwise might be interminable. Is the world one or many?—fated or free?—material or spiritual?— here are notions either of which may or may not hold good of the world; and disputes over such notions are unending. The pragmatic method in such cases is to try to interpret each notion by tracing its respective practical consequences. What difference would it practically make to any one if this notion rather than that notion were true? If no practical difference whatever can be traced, then the alternatives mean practically the same thing, and all dispute is idle. Whenever a dispute is serious, we ought to be able to show some practical differ- ence that must follow from one side or the other's being right.

A glance at the history of the idea will show you still better what pragmatism means. The term is derived from the same Greek word πράγμα, meaning action, from which our words 'practice' and 'practical' come. It was first introduced into philosophy by Mr. Charles Peirce in 1878. In an article entitled 'How to Make Our Ideas Clear,' in the 'Popular Science Monthly' for January of that year[1] Mr. Peirce, after pointing out that our beliefs are really rules for action, said that, to develop a thought's meaning, we need only determine what conduct it is fitted to produce: that conduct is for us its sole significance. And the tangible fact at the root of all our thought-distinctions, however subtle, is that there is no one of them so fine as to consist in anything but a possible difference of practice. To attain perfect clearness in our thoughts of an object, then, we need only consider what conceivable effects of a practical kind the object may involve—what sensations we are to expect from it, and what reactions we must prepare. Our conception of these effects, whether immediate or remote, is then for us the whole of our conception of the object, so far as that conception has positive significance at all.

This is the principle of Peirce, the principle of pragmatism. It lay entirely unnoticed by any one for twenty years, until I, in an address before Professor Howison's philosophical union at the university of California, brought it forward again and made a special application of it to religion. By that date (1898) the times seemed ripe for its reception. The word 'pragmatism' spread, and at present it fairly spots the pages of the philosophic journals. On all hands we find the 'pragmatic movement' spoken of, sometimes with respect, sometimes with contumely, seldom with clear understanding. It is evident that the term applies itself conveniently to a number of tendencies that hitherto have lacked a collective name, and that it has 'come to stay.'

To take in the importance of Peirce's principle, one must get accustomed to applying it to concrete cases. I found a few years ago that Ostwald, the illustrious Leipzig chemist, had been making perfectly distinct use of the principle of pragmatism in his lectures on the philosophy of science, though he had not called it by that name.

"All realities influence our practice," he wrote me, "and that influence is their meaning for us. I am accustomed to put questions to my classes in this way: In what respects would the world be different if this alternative or that were true? If I

can find nothing that would become different, then the alternative has no sense."

That is, the rival views mean practically the same thing, and meaning, other than practical, there is for us none. Ostwald in a published lecture gives this example of what he means. Chemists have long wrangled over the inner constitution of certain bodies called 'tautomerous.' Their properties seemed equally consistent with the notion that an instable hydrogen atom oscillates inside of them, or that they are instable mixtures of two bodies. Controversy raged, but never was decided. "It would never have begun," says Ostwald, "if the combatants had asked themselves what particular experimental fact could have been made different by one or the other view being correct. For it would then have appeared that no difference of fact could possibly ensue; and the quarrel was as unreal as if, theorizing in primitive times about the raising of dough by yeast, one party should have invoked a 'brownie,' while another insisted on an 'elf' as the true cause of the phenomenon."[2]

It is astonishing to see how many philosophical disputes collapse into insignificance the moment you subject them to this simple test of tracing a concrete consequence. There can *be* no difference anywhere that doesn't *make* a difference elsewhere—no difference in abstract truth that doesn't express itself in a difference in concrete fact and in conduct consequent upon that fact, imposed on somebody, somehow, somewhere, and somewhen. The whole function of philosophy ought to be to find out what definite difference it will make to you and me, at definite instants of our life, if this world-formula or that world-formula be the true one.

There is absolutely nothing new in the pragmatic method. Socrates was an adept at it. Aristotle used it methodically. Locke, Berkeley, and Hume made momentous contributions to truth by its means. Shadworth Hodgson keeps insisting that realities are only what they are 'known as.' But these forerunners of pragmatism used it in fragments: they were preluders only. Not until in our time has it generalized itself, become conscious of a universal mission, pretended to a con-

---

1. Translated in the *Revue Philosophique* for January, 1879 (vol. vii).

2. 'Theorie und Praxis,' *Zeitsch. des Oesterreichischen Ingenieur u. Architecten-Vereines*, 1905, Nr. 4 u. 6. I find a still more radical pragmatism than Ostwald's in an address by Professor W. S. Franklin: "I think that the sickliest notion of physics, even if a student gets it, is that it is 'the science of masses, molecules, and the ether.' And I think that the healthiest notion, even if a student does not wholly get it, is that physics is the science of the ways of taking hold of bodies and pushing them!" (*Science*, January 2, 1903.)

quering destiny. I believe in that destiny, and I hope I may end by inspiring you with my belief.

Pragmatism represents a perfectly familiar attitude in philosophy, the empiricist attitude, but it represents it, as it seems to me, both in a more radical and in a less objectionable form than it has ever yet assumed. A pragmatist turns his back resolutely and once for all upon a lot of inveterate habits dear to professional philosophers. He turns away from abstraction and insufficiency, from verbal solutions, from bad *a priori* reasons, from fixed principles, closed systems, and pretended absolutes and origins. He turns towards concreteness and adequacy, towards facts, towards action and towards power. That means the empiricist temper regnant and the rationalist temper sincerely given up. It means the open air and possibilities of nature, as against dogma, artificiality, and the pretence of finality in truth.

At the same time it does not stand for any special results. It is a method only. But the general triumph of that method would mean an enormous change in what I called in my last lecture the 'temperament' of philosophy. Teachers of the ultra-rationalistic type would be frozen out, much as the courtier type is frozen out in republics, as the ultramontane type of priest is frozen out in protestant lands. Science and metaphysics would come much nearer together, would in fact work absolutely hand in hand.

Metaphysics has usually followed a very primitive kind of quest. You know how men have always hankered after unlawful magic, and you know what a great part in magic *words* have always played. If you have his name, or the formula of incantation that binds him, you can control the spirit, genie, afrite, or whatever the power may be. Solomon knew the names of all the spirits, and having their names, he held them subject to his will. So the universe has always appeared to the natural mind as a kind of enigma, of which the key must be sought in the shape of some illuminating or power-bringing word or name. That word names the universe's *principle,* and to possess it is after a fashion to possess the universe itself. 'God,' 'Matter,' 'Reason,' 'the Absolute,' 'Energy,' are so many solving names. You can rest when you have them. You are at the end of your metaphysical quest.

But if you follow the pragmatic method, you cannot look on any such word as closing your quest. You must bring out of each word its practical cash-value, set it at work within the stream of your experience. It appears less as a solution, then, than as a program for more work, and more particularly as an indication of the ways in which existing realities may be *changed.*

Theories thus become instruments, not answers to enigmas, in which we can rest. We don't lie back upon them, we move forward, and, on occasion, make nature over again by their aid. Pragmatism unstiffens all our theories, limbers them up and sets each one at work. Being nothing essentially new, it harmonizes with many ancient philosophic tendencies. It agrees with nominalism for instance, in always appealing to particulars; with utilitarianism in emphasizing practical aspects; with positivism in its disdain for verbal solutions, useless questions and metaphysical abstractions.

All these, you see, are *anti-intellectualist* tendencies. Against rationalism as a pretension and a method pragmatism is fully armed and militant. But, at the outset, at least, it stands for no particular results. It has no dogmas, and no doctrines save its method. As the young Italian pragmatist Papini has well said, it lies in the midst of our theories, like a corridor in a hotel. Innumerable chambers open out of it. In one you may find a man writing an atheistic volume; in the next some one on his knees praying for faith and strength; in a third a chemist investigating a body's properties. In a fourth a system of idealistic metaphysics is being excogitated; in a fifth the impossibility of metaphysics is being shown. But they all own the corridor, and all must pass through it if they want a practicable way of getting into or out of their respective rooms.

No particular results then, so far, but only an attitude of orientation, is what the pragmatic method means. *The attitude of looking away from first things, principles, 'categories,' supposed necessities; and of looking towards last things, fruits, consequences, facts.*

So much for the pragmatic method! You may say that I have been praising it rather than explaining it to you, but I shall presently explain it abundantly enough by showing how it works on some familiar problems. Meanwhile the word pragmatism has come to be used in a still wider sense, as meaning also a certain *theory of truth*. I mean to give a whole lecture to the statement of that theory, after first paving the way, so I can be very brief now. But brevity is hard to follow, so I ask for your redoubled attention for a quarter of an hour. If much remains obscure, I hope to make it clearer in the later lectures.

One of the most successfully cultivated branches of philosophy in our time is what is called inductive logic, the study of the conditions under which our sciences have evolved. Writers on this subject have begun to show a singular unanimity as to what the laws of nature and elements of fact mean, when formulated by mathematicians, physicists and chemists. When the first mathematical, logical, and natural uniformities, the first *laws,* were discovered, men were so carried away by the clearness, beauty and simplification that resulted, that they believed themselves to have deciphered authentically the eternal thoughts of the Almighty. His mind also thundered and reverberated in syllogisms. He also thought in conic sections, squares and roots and ratios, and geometrized like Euclid. He made Kepler's laws for the planets to follow; he made velocity increase proportionally to the time in falling bodies; he made the law of the sines for light to obey when refracted; he established the classes, orders, families and genera of plants and animals, and fixed the distances between them. He thought the archetypes of all things, and devised their variations; and when we rediscover any one of these his wondrous institutions, we seize his mind in its very literal intention.

But as the sciences have developed farther, the notion has gained ground that most, perhaps all, of our laws are only approximations. The laws themselves, moreover, have grown so numerous that there is no counting them; and so many rival formulations are proposed in all the branches of science that investigators have become accustomed to the notion that no theory is absolutely a transcript of reality, but that any one of them may from some point of view be useful. Their great use is to summarize old facts and to lead to new ones. They are only a man-made language, a conceptual shorthand, as some one calls them, in which we write our reports of nature; and languages, as is well known, tolerate much choice of expression and many dialects.

Thus human arbitrariness has driven divine necessity from scientific logic. If I mention the names of Sigwart, Mach, Ostwald, Pearson, Milhaud, Poincaré, Duhem, Ruyssen, those of you who are students will easily identify the tendency I speak of, and will think of additional names.

Riding now on the front of this wave of scientific logic Messrs. Schiller and Dewey appear with their pragmatistic account of what truth everywhere signifies. Everywhere, these teachers say, 'truth' in our ideas and beliefs means the same thing that it means in science. It means, they say, nothing but this, *that ideas (which themselves are but parts of our experience) become true just in so far as they help us to get into satisfactory relation with other parts of our experience,* to summarize them and get about among them by conceptual short-cuts instead of following the interminable succession of particular phenomena. Any idea upon which we can ride, so to speak; any idea that will carry us prosperously from any one part of our experience to any other part, linking things satisfactorily,

working securely, simplifying, saving labor; is true for just so much, true in so far forth, true *instrumentally.* This is the 'instrumental' view of truth taught so successfully at Chicago, the view that truth in our ideas means their power to 'work,' promulgated so brilliantly at Oxford.

Messrs. Dewey, Schiller and their allies, in reaching this general conception of all truth, have only followed the example of geologists, biologists and philologists. In the establishment of these other sciences, the successful stroke was always to take some simple process actually observable in operation—as denudation by weather, say, or variation from parental type, or change of dialect by incorporation of new words and pronunciations—and then to generalize it, making it apply to all times, and produce great results by summating its effects through the ages.

The observable process which Schiller and Dewey particularly singled out for generalization is the familiar one by which any individual settles into *new opinions.* The process here is always the same. The individual has a stock of old opinions already, but he meets a new experience that puts them to a strain. Somebody contradicts them; or in a reflective moment he discovers that they contradict each other; or he hears of facts with which they are incompatible; or desires arise in him which they cease to satisfy. The result is an inward trouble to which his mind till then had been a stranger, and from which he seeks to escape by modifying his previous mass of opinions. He saves as much of it as he can, for in this matter of belief we are all extreme conservatives. So he tries to change first this opinion, and then that (for they resist change very variously), until at last some new idea comes up which he can graft upon the ancient stock with a minimum of disturbance of the latter, some idea that mediates between the stock and the new experience and runs them into one another most felicitously and expediently.

This new idea is then adopted as the true one. It preserves the older stock of truths with a minimum of modification, stretching them just enough to make them admit the novelty, but conceiving that in ways as familiar as the case leaves possible. An *outrée* explanation, violating all our preconceptions, would never pass for a true account of a novelty. We should scratch round industriously till we found something less eccentric. The most violent revolutions in an individual's beliefs leave most of his old order standing. Time and space, cause and effect, nature and history, and one's own biography remain untouched. New truth is always a go-between, a smoother-over of transitions. It marries old opinion to new fact so as ever to show a minimum of jolt, a maximum of continuity. We hold a theory true just in proportion to its success in solving this 'problem of maxima and minima.' But success in solving this problem is eminently a matter of approximation. We say this theory solves it on the whole more satisfactorily than that theory; but that means more satisfactorily to ourselves, and individuals will emphasize their points of satisfaction differently. To a certain degree, therefore, everything here is plastic.

The point I now urge you to observe particularly is the part played by the older truths. Failure to take account of it is the source of much of the unjust criticism levelled against pragmatism. Their influence is absolutely controlling. Loyalty to them is the first principle—in most cases it is the only principle; for by far the most usual way of handling phenomena so novel that they would make for a serious rearrangement of our preconception is to ignore them altogether, or to abuse those who bear witness for them.

You doubtless wish examples of this process of truth's growth, and the only trouble is their superabundance. The simplest case of new truth is of course the mere numerical addition of new kinds of facts, or of new single facts of old kinds, to our experience—an addition that involves no alteration in the old beliefs. Day follows day, and its contents are simply added. The new contents themselves are not true, they simply *come* and *are*. Truth is *what we say about* them, and when we say that they have come, truth is satisfied by the plain additive formula.

But often the day's contents oblige a rearrangement. If I should now utter piercing shrieks and act like a maniac on this platform, it would make many of you revise your ideas as to the probable worth of my philosophy. 'Radium' came the other day as part of the day's content, and seemed for a moment to contradict our ideas of the whole order of nature, that order having come to be identified with what is called the conservation of energy. The mere sight of radium paying heat away indefinitely out of its own pocket seemed to violate that conservation. What to think? If the radiations from it were nothing but an escape of unsuspected 'potential' energy, pre-existent inside of the atoms, the principle of conservation would be saved. The discovery of 'helium' as the radiation's outcome, opened a way to this belief. So Ramsay's view is generally held to be true, because, although it extends our old ideas of energy, it causes a minimum of alteration in their nature.

I need not multiply instances. A new opinion counts as 'true' just in proportion as it gratifies the individual's desire to assimilate the novel in his experience to his beliefs in stock. It must both lean on old truth and grasp new fact; and its success (as I said a moment ago) in doing this, is a matter for the individual's appreciation. When old truth grows, then, by new truth's addition, it is for subjective reasons. We are in the process and obey the reasons. That new idea is truest which performs most felicitously its function of satisfying our double urgency. It makes itself true, gets itself classed as true, by the way it works; grafting itself then upon the ancient body of truth, which thus grows much as a tree grows by the activity of a new layer of cambium.

Now Dewey and Schiller proceed to generalize this observation and to apply it to the most ancient parts of truth. They also once were plastic. They also were called true for human reasons. They also mediated between still earlier truths and what in those days were novel observations. Purely objective truth, truth in whose establishment the function of giving human satisfaction in marrying previous parts of experience with newer parts played no rôle whatever, is nowhere to be found. The reasons why we call things true is the reason why they *are* true, for 'to be true' *means* only to perform this marriage-function.

The trail of the human serpent is thus over everything. Truth independent; truth that we *find* merely; truth no longer malleable to human need; truth incorrigible, in a word; such truth exists indeed superabundantly—or is supposed to exist by rationalistically minded thinkers; but then it means only the dead heart of the living tree, and its being there means only that truth also has its paleontology, and its 'prescription,' and may grow stiff with years of veteran service and petrified in men's regard by sheer antiquity. But how plastic even the oldest truths nevertheless really are has been vividly shown in our day by the transformation of logical and mathematical ideas, a transformation which seems even to be invading physics. The ancient formulas are reinterpreted as special expressions of much wider principles, principles that our ancestors never got a glimpse of in their present shape and formulation.

Mr. Schiller still gives to all this view of truth the name of 'Humanism,' but, for this doctrine too, the name of pragmatism seems fairly to be in the ascendant, so I will treat it under the name of pragmatism in these lectures.

Such then would be the scope of pragmatism—first, a method; and second, a genetic theory of what is meant by truth. And these two things must be our future topics.

What I have said of the theory of truth will, I am sure, have appeared obscure and unsatisfactory to most of you by reason of its brevity. I shall make amends for that hereafter. In a lecture on 'common sense' I shall try to show what I mean by truths grown petrified by antiquity. In another lecture I shall expatiate on the idea that our thoughts become true in proportion as they successfully exert their go-between function. In a third I shall show how hard it is to discriminate subjective from objective factors in Truth's development. You may not follow me wholly in these lectures; and if you do, you may not wholly agree with me. But you will, I know, regard me at least as serious, and treat my effort with respectful consideration.

You will probably be surprised to learn, then, that Messrs. Schiller's and Dewey's theories have suffered a hailstorm of contempt and ridicule. All rationalism has risen against them. In influential quarters Mr. Schiller, in particular, has been treated like an impudent schoolboy who deserves a spanking. I should not mention this, but for the fact that it throws so much sidelight upon that rationalistic temper to which I have opposed the temper of pragmatism. Pragmatism is uncomfortable away from facts. Rationalism is comfortable only in the presence of abstractions. This pragmatist talk about truths in the plural, about their utility and satisfactoriness, about the success with which they 'work,' etc., suggests to the typical intellectualist mind a sort of coarse lame second-rate makeshift article of truth. Such truths are not real truth. Such tests are merely subjective. As against this, objective truth must be something non-utilitarian, haughty, refined, remote, august, exalted. It must be an absolute correspondence of our thoughts with an equally absolute reality. It must be what we *ought* to think unconditionally. The conditioned ways in which we *do* think are so much irrelevance and matter for psychology. Down with psychology, up with logic, in all this question!

See the exquisite contrast of the types of mind! The pragmatist clings to facts and concreteness, observes truth at its work in particular cases, and generalizes. Truth, for him, becomes a class-name for all sorts of definite working-values in experience. For the rationalist it remains a pure abstraction, to the bare name of which we must defer. When the pragmatist undertakes to show in detail just *why* we must defer, the rationalist is unable to recognize the concretes from which his own abstraction is taken. He accuses us of *denying* truth; whereas we have only sought to trace exactly why people follow it and always ought to follow it. Your typical ultra-abstractionist fairly shudders at concreteness: other things equal, he positively prefers the pale and spectral. If the two universes were offered, he would always choose the skinny outline rather than the rich thicket of reality. It is so much purer, clearer, nobler.

I hope that as these lectures go on, the concreteness and closeness to facts of the pragmatism which they advocate may be what approves itself to you as its most satisfactory peculiarity. It only follows here the example of the sister-sciences, interpreting the unobserved by the observed. It brings old and new harmoniously together. It converts the absolutely empty notion of a static relation of 'correspondence' (what that may mean we must ask later) between our minds and reality, into that of a rich and active commerce (that any one may follow in detail and understand) between particular thoughts of ours, and the great universe of other experiences in which they play their parts and have their uses.

But enough of this at present! The justification of what I say must be postponed. I wish now to add a word in further explanation of the claim I made at our last meeting, that pragmatism may be a happy harmonizer of empiricist ways of thinking with the more religious demands of human beings.

Men who are strongly of the fact-loving temperament, you may remember me to have said, are liable to be kept at a distance by the small sympathy with facts which that philosophy from the present-day fashion of idealism offers them. It is far too intellectualistic. Old fashioned theism was bad enough, with its notion of God as an exalted monarch, made up of a lot of unintelligible or preposterous 'attributes'; but, so long as it held strongly by the argument from design, it kept some touch with concrete realities. Since, however, darwinism has once for all displaced design from the minds of the 'scientific,' theism has lost that foothold; and some kind of an immanent or pantheistic deity working *in* things rather than above them is, if any, the kind recommended to our contemporary imagination. Aspirants to a philosophic religion turn, as a rule, more hopefully nowadays towards idealistic pantheism than towards the older dualistic theism, in spite of the fact that the latter still counts able defenders.

But, as I said in my first lecture, the brand of pantheism offered is hard for them to assimilate if they are lovers of facts, or empirically minded. It is the absolutistic brand, spurning the dust and reared upon pure logic. It keeps no connexion whatever with concreteness. Affirming the Absolute Mind, which is its substitute for God, to be the rational presupposition of all particulars of fact, whatever they may be, it remains supremely indifferent to what the particular facts in our world actually are. Be they what they may, the Absolute will father them. Like the sick lion in Esop's fable, all footprints lead into his den, but *nulla vestigia retrorsum.* You cannot re-descend into the world of particulars by the Absolute's aid, or deduce any necessary consequences of detail important for your life from your idea of his nature. He gives you indeed the assurance that all is well with *Him,* and for his eternal way of thinking; but thereupon he leaves you to be finitely saved by your own temporal devices.

Far be it from me to deny the majesty of this conception, or its capacity to yield religious comfort to a most respectable class of minds. But from the human point of view, no one can pretend that it doesn't suffer from the faults of remoteness and abstractness. It is eminently a product of what I have ventured to call the rationalistic temper. It disdains empiricism's needs. It substitutes a pallid outline for the real world's richness. It is dapper, it is noble in the bad sense, in the sense in which to be noble is to be inapt for humble service. In this real world of sweat and dirt, it seems to me that when a view of things is 'noble,' that ought to count as a presumption against its truth, and as a philosophic disqualification. The prince of darkness may be a gentleman, as we are told he is, but whatever the God of earth and heaven is, he can surely be no gentleman. His menial services are needed in the dust of our human trials, even more than his dignity is needed in the empyrean.

Now pragmatism, devoted though she be to facts, has no such materialistic bias as ordinary empiricism labors under. Moreover, she has no objection whatever to the realizing of abstractions, so long as you get about among particulars with their aid and they actually carry you somewhere. Interested in no conclusions but those which our minds and our experiences work out together, she has no *a priori* prejudices against theology. *If theological ideas prove to have a value for concrete life, they will be true, for pragmatism, in the sense of being good for so much. For how much more they are true, will depend entirely on their relations to the other truths that also have to be acknowledged.*

What I said just now about the Absolute, of transcendental idealism, is a case in point. First, I called it majestic and said it yielded religious comfort to a class of minds, and then I accused it of remoteness and sterility. But so far as it affords such comfort, it surely is not sterile; it has that amount of value; it performs a concrete function. As a good pragmatist, I myself ought to call the Absolute true 'in so far forth,' then; and I unhesitatingly now do so.

But what does *true in so far forth* mean in this case? To answer, we need only apply the pragmatic method. What do believers in the Absolute mean by saying that their belief affords them comfort? They mean that since, in the Absolute finite evil is 'overruled' already, we may, therefore, whenever we wish, treat the temporal as if it were potentially the eternal, be sure that we can trust its outcome, and, without sin, dismiss our fear and drop the worry of our finite responsibility. In short, they mean that we have a right ever and anon to take a moral holiday, to let the world wag in its own way, feeling that its issues are in better hands than ours and are none of our business.

The universe is a system of which the individual members may relax their anxieties occasionally, in which the don't-care mood is also right for men, and moral holidays in order,— that, if I mistake not, is part, at least, of what the Absolute is 'known-as,' that is the great difference in our particular experiences which his being true makes, for us, that is his cash-value when he is pragmatically interpreted. Farther than that the ordinary lay-reader in philosophy who thinks favorably of absolute idealism does not venture to sharpen his conceptions. He can use the Absolute for so much, and so much is very precious. He is pained at hearing you speak incredulously of the Absolute, therefore, and disregards your criticisms because they deal with aspects of the conception that he fails to follow.

If the Absolute means this, and means no more than this, who can possibly deny the truth of it? To deny it would be to insist that men should never relax, and that holidays are never in order.

I am well aware how odd it must seem to some of you to hear me say that an idea is 'true' so long as to believe it is profitable to our lives. That it is *good,* for as much as it profits, you will gladly admit. If what we do by its aid is good, you will allow the idea itself to be good in so far forth, for we are the better for possessing it. But is it not a strange misuse of the word 'truth,' you will say, to call ideas also 'true' for this reason?

To answer this difficulty fully is impossible at this stage of my account. You touch here upon the very central point of Messrs. Schiller's, Dewey's and my own doctrine of truth, which I can not discuss with detail until my sixth lecture. Let me now say only this, that truth is *one species of good,* and not, as is usually supposed, a category distinct from good, and co-ordinate with it. *The true is the name of whatever proves itself to be good in the way of belief, and good, too, for definite, assignable reasons.* Surely you must admit this, that if there were *no* good for life in true ideas, or if the knowledge of them were positively disadvantageous and false ideas the only useful ones, then the current notion that truth is divine and precious, and its pursuit a duty, could never have grown up or become a dogma. In a world like that, our duty would be to *shun* truth, rather. But in this world, just as certain foods are not only agreeable to our taste, but good for our teeth, our stomach, and our tissues; so certain ideas are not only agreeable to think about, or agreeable as supporting other ideas that we are fond of, but they are also helpful in life's practical struggles. If there be any life that it is really better we should lead, and if there be any idea which, if believed in, would help us to lead that life, then it would be really *better for us* to believe in that idea, *unless, indeed, belief in it incidentally clashed with other greater vital benefits.*

'What would be better for us to believe'! This sounds very like a definition of truth. It comes very near to saying 'what we *ought* to believe': and in *that* definition none of you would find any oddity. Ought we ever not to believe what it is *better for us* to believe? And can we then keep the notion of what is better for us, and what is true for us, permanently apart?

Pragmatism says no, and I fully agree with her. Probably you also agree, so far as the abstract statement goes, but with a suspicion that if we practically did believe everything that made for good in our own personal lives, we should be found indulging all kinds of fancies about this world's affairs, and all kinds of sentimental superstitions about a world hereafter. Your suspicion here is undoubtedly well founded, and it is evident that something happens when you pass from the abstract to the concrete that complicates the situation.

I said just now that what is better for us to believe is true *unless the belief incidentally clashes with some other vital benefit.* Now in real life what vital benefits is any particular belief of ours most liable to clash with? What indeed except the vital benefits yielded by *other beliefs* when these prove incompatible with the first ones? In other words, the greatest enemy of any one of our truths may be the rest of our truths. Truths have once for all this desperate instinct of self-preservation and of desire to extinguish whatever contradicts them. My belief in the Absolute, based on the good it does me, must run the gauntlet of all my other beliefs. Grant that it may be true in giving me a moral holiday. Nevertheless, as I conceive it,— and let me speak now confidentially, as it were, and merely in my own private person,—it clashes with other truths of mine whose benefits I hate to give up on its account. It happens to be associated with a kind of logic of which I am the

enemy, I find that it entangles me in metaphysical paradoxes that are inacceptable, etc., etc. But as I have enough trouble in life already without adding the trouble of carrying these intellectual inconsistencies, I personally just give up the Absolute. I just *take* my moral holidays; or else as a professional philosopher, I try to justify them by some other principle.

If I could restrict my notion of the Absolute to its bare holiday-giving value, it wouldn't clash with my other truths. But we can not easily thus restrict our hypotheses. They carry supernumerary features, and these it is that clash so. My disbelief in the Absolute means then disbelief in those other supernumerary features, for I fully believe in the legitimacy of taking moral holidays.

You see by this what I meant when I called pragmatism a mediator and reconciler and said, borrowing the word from Papini, that she 'unstiffens' our theories. She has in fact no prejudices whatever, no obstructive dogmas, no rigid canons of what shall count as proof. She is completely genial. She will entertain any hypothesis, she will consider any evidence. It follows that in the religious field she is at a great advantage both over positivistic empiricism, with its anti-theological bias, and over religious rationalism, with its exclusive interest in the remote, the noble, the simple, and the abstract in the way of conception.

In short, she widens the field of search for God. Rationalism sticks to logic and the empyrean. Empiricism sticks to the external senses. Pragmatism is willing to take anything, to follow either logic or the senses and to count the humblest and most personal experiences. She will count mystical experiences if they have practical consequences. She will take a God who lives in the very dirt of private fact—if that should seem a likely place to find him.

Her only test of probable truth is what works best in the way of leading us, what fits every part of life best and combines with the collectivity of experience's demands, nothing being omitted. If theological ideas should do this, if the notion of God, in particular, should prove to do it, how could pragmatism possibly deny God's existence? She could see no meaning in treating as 'not true' a notion that was pragmatically so successful. What other kind of truth could there be, for her, than all this agreement with concrete reality?

In my last lecture I shall return again to the relations of pragmatism with religion. But you see already how democratic she is. Her manners are as various and flexible, her resources as rich and endless, and her conclusions as friendly as those of mother nature.

The Socialist Party and the Working Class, *Eugene V. Debs, 1904*

A prominent union organizer and five-time presidential candidate of the Socialist Party of America, Eugene V. Debs (1855–1926) was twice jailed for his activities—the first time for his American Railway Union's role in the bloody Pullman strike of 1894 (Debs was convicted of interfering with delivery of the U.S. mail), and the second time for speaking against American involvement in World War I. In 1920 Debs, while still in prison, ran for president for the fifth time, receiving 913,664 votes, 3.4 percent of the total. The speech reproduced here was delivered by Debs during his first run for the presidency. It presents Debs's views of the Republican and Democratic parties as well as the role of voting in fostering solidarity among workers.

The Socialist Party and the Working Class

Eugene V. Debs

Opening Speech Delivered as Candidate of the Socialist Party for President, at Indianapolis, Ind., September 1, 1904

Mr. Chairman, Citizens and Comrades:

There has never been a free people, a civilized nation, a real republic on this earth. Human society has always consisted of masters and slaves, and the slaves have always been and are today, the foundation stones of the social fabric.

Wage-labor is but a name; wage-slavery is the fact.

The twenty-five millions of wage-workers in the United States are twenty-five millions of twentieth century slaves.

This is the plain meaning of what is known as

THE LABOR MARKET

And the labor market follows the capitalist flag.

The most barbarous fact in all Christendom is the labor market. The mere term sufficiently expresses the animalism of commercial civilization.

They who buy and they who sell in the labor market are alike dehumanized by the inhuman traffic in the brains and blood and bones of human beings.

The labor market is the foundation of so-called civilized society. Without these shambles, without this commerce in human life, this sacrifice of manhood and womanhood, this barter of babes, this sales of souls, the capitalist civilizations of all lands and all climes would crumble to ruin and perish from the earth.

Twenty-five millions of wage-slaves are bought and sold daily at prevailing prices in the American Labor Market.

This is the

PARAMOUNT ISSUE

in the present national campaign.

Let me say at the very threshold of this discussion that the workers have but the one issue in this campaign, the overthrow of the capitalist system and the emancipation of the working class from wage-slavery.

The capitalists may have the tariff, finance, imperialism and other dust-covered and moth-eaten issues entirely to themselves.

The rattle of these relics no longer deceives workingmen whose heads are on their own shoulders.

They know by experience and observation that the gold standard, free silver, fiat money, protective tariff, free trade, imperialism and anti-imperialism all mean capitalist rule and wage-slavery.

Their eyes are open and they can see; their brains are in operation and they can think.

The very moment a workingman begins to do his own thinking he understands the paramount issue, parts company with the capitalist politician and falls in line with his own class on the political battlefield.

The political solidarity of the working class means the death of despotism, the birth of freedom, the sunrise of civilization.

Having said this much by way of introduction I will now enter upon the actualities of my theme.

THE CLASS STRUGGLE

We are entering tonight upon a momentous campaign. The struggle for political supremacy is not between political parties merely, as appears upon the surface, but at bottom it is a life and death struggle between two hostile economic classes, the one the capitalist, and the other the working class.

The capitalist class is represented by the Republican, Democratic, Populist and Prohibition parties, all of which stand for private ownership of the means of production, and the triumph of any one of which will mean continued wage-slavery to the working class.

As the Populist and Prohibition sections of the capitalist party represent minority elements which propose to reform the capitalist system without disturbing wage-slavery, a vain and impossible task, they will be omitted from this discussion with all the credit due the rank and file for their good intentions.

The Republican and Democratic parties, or, to be more exact, the Republican-Democratic party, represent the capitalist class in the class struggle. They are the political wings of the capitalist system and such differences as arise between them relate to spoils and not to principles.

With either of these parties in power one thing is always certain and that is that the capitalist class is in the saddle and the working class under the saddle.

Under the administration of both these parties the means of production are private property, production is carried forward for capitalist profit purely, markets are glutted and industry paralyzed, workingmen become tramps and criminals while injunctions, soldiers and riot guns are brought into action to preserve "law and order" in the chaotic carnival of capitalistic anarchy.

Deny it as may the cunning capitalists who are clear-sighted enough to perceive it, or ignore it as may the torpid workers who are too blind and unthinking to see it, the struggle in which we are engaged today is a class struggle, and as the toiling millions come to see and understand it and rally to the political standard of their class, they will drive all capitalist parties of whatever name into the same party, and the class

struggle will then be so clearly revealed that the hosts of labor will find their true place in the conflict and strike the united and decisive blow that will destroy slavery and achieve their full and final emancipation.

In this struggle the workingmen and women and children are represented by the Socialist party and it is my privilege to address you in the name of that revolutionary and uncompromising party of the working class.

ATTITUDE OF THE WORKERS

What shall be the attitude of the workers of the United States in the present campaign? What part shall they take in it? What party and what principles shall they support by their ballots? And why?

These are questions the importance of which are not sufficiently recognized by workingmen or they would not be the prey of parasites and the service tools of scheming politicians who use them only at election time to renew their masters' lease of power and perpetuate their own ignorance, poverty and shame.

In answering these questions I propose to be as frank and candid as plain-meaning words will allow, for I have but one object in this discussion and that object is not office, but the truth, and I shall state it as I see it, if I have to stand alone.

But I shall not stand alone, for the party that has my allegiance and may have my life, the Socialist party, the party of the working class, the party of emancipation, is made up of men and women who know their rights and scorn to compromise with their oppressors; who want no votes that can be bought and no support under any false pretense whatsoever.

The Socialist party stands squarely upon its proletarian principles and relies wholly upon the forces of industrial progress and the education of the working class.

The Socialist party buys no votes and promises no offices. Not a farthing is spent for whiskey or cigars. Every penny in the campaign fund is the voluntary offerings of workers and their sympathizers and every penny is used for education.

What other parties can say the same?

Ignorance alone stands in the way of socialist success. The capitalist parties understand this and use their resources to prevent the workers from seeing the light.

Intellectual darkness is essential to industrial slavery.

Capitalist parties stand for Slavery and Night.

The Socialist party is the herald of Freedom and Light.

Capitalist parties cunningly contrive to divide the workers upon dead issues.

The Socialist party is uniting them upon the living issue: Death to Wage Slavery!

When industrial slavery is as dead as the issues of the Siamese capitalist parties the Socialist party will have fulfilled its mission and enriched history.

And now to our questions:

First, all workingmen and women owe it to themselves, their class and their country to take an active and intelligent interest in political affairs.

THE BALLOT

The ballot of united labor expresses the people's will and the people's will is the supreme law of a free nation.

The ballot means that labor is no longer dumb, that at last it has a voice, that it may be heard and if united shall be heeded.

Centuries of struggle and sacrifice were required to wrest this symbol of freedom from the mailed clutch of tyranny and place it in the hand of labor as the shield and lance of attack and defense.

The abuse and not the use of it is responsible for its evils.

The divided vote of labor is the abuse of the ballot and the penalty is slavery and death.

The united vote of those who toil and have not will vanquish those who have and toil not, and solve forever the problem of democracy.

THE HISTORIC STRUGGLE OF CLASSES

Since the race was young there have been class struggles. In every state of society, ancient and modern, labor has been exploited, degraded and in subjection.

Civilization has done little for labor except to modify the forms of its exploitation.

Labor has always been the mudsill of the social fabric—is so now and will be until the class struggle ends in class extinction and free society.

Society has always been and is now built upon exploitation—the exploitation of a class—the working class, whether slaves, serfs or wage-laborers, and the exploited working class in subjection have always been, instinctively or consciously, in revolt against their oppressors.

Through all the centuries the enslaved toilers have moved slowly but surely toward their final freedom.

The call of the Socialist party is to the exploited class, the workers in all useful trades and professions, all honest occupations, from the most menial service to the highest skill, to rally beneath their own standard and put an end to the last of the barbarous class struggles by conquering the capitalist government, taking possession of the means of production and making them the common property of all, abolishing wage-slavery and establishing the co-operative commonwealth.

The first step in this direction is to sever all relations with

CAPITALIST PARTIES

They are precisely alike and I challenge their most discriminating partisans to tell them apart in relation to labor.

The Republican and Democratic parties are alike capitalist parties—differing only in being committed to different sets of capitalist interests—they have the same principles under varying colors, are equally corrupt and are one in their subservience to capital and their hostility to labor.

The ignorant workingman who supports either of these parties forges his own fetters and is the unconscious author of his own misery. He can and must be made to see and think and act with his fellows in supporting the party of his class and this work of education is the crowning virtue of the socialist movement.

THE REPUBLICAN PARTY

Let us briefly consider the Republican party from the worker's standpoint. It is capitalist to the core. It has not and can not have the slightest interest in labor except to exploit it.

Why should a workingman support the Republican party?

Why should a millionaire support the Socialist party?

For precisely the same reason that all the millionaires are opposed to the Socialist party, all the workers should be opposed to the Republican party. It is a capitalist party, is loyal to capitalist interests and entitled to the support of capitalist voters on election day.

All it has for workingmen is its "glorious past" and a "glad hand" when it wants their votes.

The Republican party is now and has been for several years, in complete control of government.

What has it done for labor? What has it not done for capital?

Not one of the crying abuses of capital has been curbed under Republican rule.

Not one of the petitions of labor has been granted.

The eight hour and anti-injunction bills, upon which organized labor is a unit, were again ruthlessly slain by the last congress in obedience to the capitalist masters.

David M. Parry has greater influence at Washington than all the millions of organized workers.

Read the national platform of the Republican party and see if there is in all its bombast a crumb of comfort for labor. The convention that adopted it was a capitalist convention and the only thought it had of labor was how to abstract its vote without waking it up.

In the only reference it made to labor it had to speak easy so as to avoid offense to the capitalists who own it and furnish the boodle to keep it in power.

The labor platforms of the Republican and Democratic parties are interchangeable and non-redeemable. They both favor "justice to capital and justice to labor." This hoary old platitude is worse than meaningless. It is false and misleading and so intended. Justice to labor means that labor shall have what it produces. This leaves nothing for capital.

Justice to labor means the end of capital.

The old parties intend nothing of the kind. It is false pretense and false promise. It has served well in the past. Will it continue to catch the votes of unthinking and deluded workers?

What workingmen had part in the Republican national convention or were honored by it?

The grand coliseum swarmed with trust magnates, corporation barons, money lords, stock gamblers, professional politicians, lawyers, lobbyists and other plutocratic tools and mercenaries, but there was no room for the horny-handed and horny-headed sons of toil. They built it, but were not in it.

Compare that convention with the convention of the Socialist party, composed almost wholly of working men and women and controlled wholly in the interest of their class.

But a party is still better known by its chosen representatives than by its platform declarations.

Who are the nominees of the Republican party for the highest offices in the gift of the nation and what is their relation to the working class?

First of all, Theodore Roosevelt and Charles W. Fairbanks, candidates for President and Vice-President, respectively, deny the class struggle and this almost infallibly fixes their status as friends of capital and enemies of labor. They insist that they can serve both; but the fact is obvious that only one can be served and that one at the expense of the other. Mr. Roosevelt's whole political career proves it.

The capitalists made no mistake in nominating Mr. Roosevelt. They know him well and he has served them well. They know that his instincts, associations, tastes and desires are with them, that he is in fact one of them and that he has nothing in common with the working class.

The only evidence to the contrary is his membership in the Brotherhood of Locomotive Firemen which seems to have come to him co-incident with his ambition to succeed himself in the presidential chair. He is a full fledged member of the union, has the grip, signs and passwords; but it is not reported that he is attending meetings, doing picket duty, supporting strikes and boycotts and performing such other duties as his union obligation imposes.

When Ex-President Grover Cleveland violated the constitution and outraged justice by seizing the state of Illinois by the throat and handcuffing her civil administration at the behest of the crime-stained trusts and corporations, Theodore Roosevelt was among his most ardent admirers and enthusiastic supporters. He wrote in hearty commendation of the atrocious act, pronounced it most exalted patriotism and said he would have done the same himself had he been president.

And so he would and so he will!

How impressive to see the Rough Rider embrace the Smooth Statesman! Oyster Bay and Buzzard's Bay! "Two souls with but a single thought, two hearts that beat as one."

There is also the highest authority for the statement charging Mr. Roosevelt with declaring about the same time he was lauding Cleveland that if he was in command he would have such as Altgeld, Debs and other traitors lined up against a dead wall and shot. The brutal remark was not for publication but found its way into print and Mr. Roosevelt, after he became a candidate, attempted to make denial, but the words themselves sound like Roosevelt and bear the impress of his savage visage.

Following the Pullman strike in 1894 there was an indignant and emphatic popular protest against "government by injunction," which has not yet by any means subsided.

Organized labor was, and is, a unit against this insidious form of judicial usurpation as a means of abrogating constitutional restraints of despotic power.

Mr. Roosevelt with his usual zeal to serve the ruling class and keep their slaves in subjection, vaulted into the arena and launched his tirade upon the "mob" that dared oppose the divine rule of a corporation judge.

"Men who object to what they style 'government by injunction,'" said he, "are, as regards the essential principles of government, in hearty sympathy with their remote skin-clad ancestors, who lived in caves, fought one another with stone-headed axes and ate the mammoth and woolly rhinoceros. They are dangerous whenever there is the least danger of their making the principles of this ages-buried past living factors in our present life. They are not in sympathy with men of good minds and good civic morality."

In direct terms and plain words Mr. Roosevelt denounces all those who oppose "Government by Injunction" as cannibals, barbarians and anarchists, and this violent and sweeping stigma embraces the whole organized movement of labor, every man, woman and child that wears the badge of union labor in the United States.

It is not strange in the light of these facts that the national congress, under President Roosevelt's administration, suppresses anti-injunction and eight-hour bills and all other measures favored by labor and resisted by capital.

No stronger or more convincing proof is required of Mr. Roosevelt's allegiance to capital and opposition to labor, nor of the class struggle and class rule which he so vehemently denies; and the workingman who in the face of these words and acts, can still support Mr. Roosevelt, must feel himself flattered in being publicly proclaimed a barbarian, and sheer gratitude, doubtless, impels him to crown his benefactor with the highest honors.

If the working class are barbarians, according to Mr. Roosevelt, this may account for his esteeming himself as having the very qualities necessary to make himself Chief of the Tribe.

But it must be noted that Mr. Roosevelt denounced organized labor as savages long before he was a candidate for president. After he became a candidate he joined the tribe and is today, himself, according to his own dictum, a barbarian and the enemy of civic morality.

The labor union to which President Roosevelt belongs and which he is solemnly obligated to support, is unanimously opposed to "Government by Injunction." President Roosevelt knew it when he joined it and he also knew that those who oppose injunction rule have the instincts of cannibals and are a menace to morality, but his proud nature succumbed to political ambition, and his ethical ideas vanished as he struck the trail that led to the tribe and, after a most dramatic scene and impressive ceremony, was decorated with the honorary badge of international barbarism.

How Theodore Roosevelt, the trade-unionist, can support the presidential candidate who denounced him as an immoral and dangerous barbarian, he may decide at his leisure, and so may all other union men in the United States who are branded with the same vulgar stigma, and their ballots will determine if they have the manhood to resent insult and rebuke its author, or if they have been fitly characterized and deserve humiliation and contempt.

The appointment of Judge Taft to a cabinet position is corroborative evidence, if any be required, of President Roosevelt's fervent faith in Government by Injunction. Judge Taft first came into national notoriety when, some years ago, sitting with Judge Ricks, who was later tried for malfeasance, they issued the celebrated injunction during the Toledo, Ann Arbor & North Michigan railroad strike that paralyzed the Brotherhoods of Locomotive Engineers and Firemen and won for them the gratitude and esteem of every corporation in the land. They were hauled to Toledo, the headquarters of the railroad, in a special car, pulled by a special engine, on special time, and after hastily consulting the railroad magnates and receiving instructions, let go the judicial lightning that shivered the unions to splinters and ended the strike in total defeat. Judge Taft is a special favorite with the trust barons and his elevation to the cabinet was ratified with joy at the court of St. Plutus.

Still again did President Roosevelt drive home his archenmity to labor and his implacable hostility to the trade-union movement when he made Paul Morton, the notorious union hater and union wrecker, his secretary of the navy. That appointment was an open insult to every trade-unionist in the country and they who lack the self-respect to resent it at the polls may wear the badge, but they are lacking wholly in the spirit and principles of union labor.

Go ask the brotherhood men who were driven from the C. B. & Q. and the striking union machinists on the Santa Fe to give you the pedigree of Mr. Morton and you will learn that his hate for union men is equalled only by his love for the scabs who take their places.

Such a man and such another as Sherman Bell, the military ferret of the Colorado mine owners, are the ideal patriots and personal chums of Mr. Roosevelt, and by honoring these he dishonors himself and should be repudiated by the ballot of every working man in the nation.

Mr. Fairbanks, the Republican candidate for Vice-President, is a corporation attorney of the first class and a plutocrat in good and regular standing. He is in every respect a fit and proper representative of his party and every millionaire in the land may safely support him.

The Democratic Party

In referring to the Democratic party in this discussion we may save time by simply saying that since it was born again at the St. Louis convention it is near enough like its Republican ally to pass for a twin brother.

The former party of the "common people" is no longer under the boycott of the plutocracy since it has adopted the Wall street label and renounced its middle class heresies.

The radical and progressive element of the former Democracy have been evicted and must seek other quarters. They were an unmitigated nuisance in the conservative counsels of the old party. They were for the "common people" and the trusts have no use for such a party.

Where but to the Socialist party can these progressive people turn? They are now without a party and the only genuine Democratic party in the field is the Socialist party, and every true Democrat should thank Wall street for driving him out of a party that is democratic in name only and into one that is democratic in fact.

The St. Louis convention was a trust jubilee. The Wall street reorganizers made short work of the free silver element. From first to last it was a capitalistic convocation. Labor was totally ignored. As an incident, two thousand choice chairs were reserved for the Business Men's League of St. Louis, an organization hostile to organized labor, but not a chair was tendered to those whose labor had built the convention hall, had clothed, transported, fed and wined the delegates and whose votes are counted on as if they were so many dumb driven cattle, to pull the ticket through in November.

As another incident, when Lieutenant Richmond Hobson dramatically declared that President Cleveland had been the only president who had ever been patriotic enough to use the federal troops to crush union labor, the trust agents, lobbyists, tools and clackers screamed with delight and the convention shook with applause.

The platform is precisely the same as the Republican platform in relation to labor. It says nothing and means the same. A plank was proposed condemning the outrages in Colorado under Republican administration, but upon order from the Parryites it was promptly thrown aside.

The editor of *American Industries,* organ of the Manufacturers' Association, commented at length in its issue of July 15 on the triumph of capital and the defeat of labor at both Republican and Democratic national conventions. Among other things he said: "The two labor lobbies, partly similar in make-up, were, to put it bluntly, thrown out bodily in both places." And that is the simple fact and is known of all men who read the papers. The capitalist organs exult because labor, to use their own brutal expression, was kicked bodily out of both the Republican and Democratic national conventions.

What more than this is needed to open the eyes of work-ingmen to the fact that neither of these parties is their party and that they are as strangely out of place in them as Rockefeller and Vanderbilt would be in the Socialist party?

And how many more times are they to be "kicked out bodily" before they stay out and join the party of their class in which labor is not only honored but is supreme, a party that is clean, that has conscience and convictions, a party that will one day sweep the old parties from the field like chaff and issue the Proclamation of Labor's Emancipation?

Judge Alton B. Parker corresponds precisely to the Democratic platform. It was made to order for him. His famous telegram in the expiring hour removed the last wrinkle and left it a perfect fit.

Thomas W. Lawson, the Boston millionaire, charges that Senator Patrick McCarren, who brought out Judge Parker for the nomination, is on the pay roll of the Standard Oil Company as political master mechanic at twenty thousand dollars a year, and that Parker is the chosen tool of Standard Oil. Mr. Lawson offers Senator McCarren one hundred thousand dollars if he will disprove the charge.

William Jennings Bryan denounced Judge Parker as a tool of Wall street before he was nominated and declared that no self-respecting Democrat could vote for him, and after his nomination he charged that it had been dictated by the trusts and secured by "crooked and indefensible methods." Mr. Bryan also said that labor had been betrayed in the convention and need look for nothing from the Democratic party. He made many other damaging charges against his party and its candidates, but when the supreme test came he was not equal to it, and instead of denouncing the betrayers of the "common people" and repudiating their made-to-order Wall street program, he compromised with the pirates that scuttled his ship and promised with his lips the support his heart refused and his conscience condemned.

The Democratic nominee for President was one of the Supreme Judges of the State of New York who declared the eight-hour law unconstitutional and this is an index of his political character.

In his address accepting the nomination he makes but a single allusion to labor and in this he takes occasion to say that labor is charged with having recently used dynamite in destroying property and that the perpetrators should be subjected to "the most rigorous punishment known to the law." This cruel intimation amounts to conviction in advance of trial and indicates clearly the trend of his capitalistically trained judicial mind. He made no such reference to capital, nor to those ermined rascals who use judicial dynamite in blowing up the constitution while labor is looted and starved by capitalistic freebooters who trample all law in the mire and leer and mock at their despoiled and helpless victims.

It is hardly necessary to make more than passing reference to Henry G. Davis, Democratic candidate for Vice-President. He is a coal baron, railroad owner and, of course, an enemy to union labor. He has amassed a great fortune exploiting his wage-slaves and has always strenuously resisted every attempt to organize them for the betterment of their condition. Mr. Davis is a staunch believer in the virtue of the injunction as applied to union labor. As a young man he was in charge of a slave plantation and his conviction is that wage-slaves should be kept free from the contaminating influence of the labor agitator and render cheerful obedience to their master.

Mr. Davis is as well qualified to serve his party as is Senator Fairbanks to serve the Republican party and wage-workers should have no trouble in making their choice between this pernicious pair of plutocrats, and certainly no intelligent workingman will hesitate an instant to discard them both and cast his vote for Ben Hanford, their working class competitor, who is as loyally devoted to labor as Fairbanks and Davis are to capital.

The Socialist Party

In what has been said of other parties I have tried to show why they should not be supported by the common people, least of all by workingmen, and I think I have shown clearly enough that such workers as do support them are guilty, consciously or unconsciously, of treason to their class. They are voting into power the enemies of labor and are morally responsible for the crimes thus perpetrated upon their fellow-workers and sooner or later they will have to suffer the consequences of their miserable acts.

The Socialist party is not, and does not pretend to be, a capitalist party. It does not ask, nor does it expect the votes of the capitalist class. Such capitalists as do support it do so seeing the approaching doom of the capitalist system and with a full understanding that the Socialist party is not a capitalist party, nor a middle class party, but a revolutionary working class party, whose historic mission it is to conquer capitalism on the political battle-field, take control of government and through the public powers take possession of the means of wealth production, abolish wage-slavery and emancipate all workers and all humanity.

The people are as capable of achieving their industrial freedom as they were to secure their political liberty, and both are necessary to a free nation.

The capitalist system is no longer adapted to the needs of modern society. It is outgrown and fetters the forces of progress. Industrial and commercial competition are largely of the past. The handwriting blazes on the wall. Centralization and combination are the modern forces in industrial and commercial life. Competition is breaking down and co-operation is supplanting it.

The hand tools of early times are used no more. Mammoth machines have taken their places. A few thousand capitalists own them and many millions of workingmen use them.

All the wealth the vast army of labor produces above its subsistence is taken by the machine owning capitalists, who also own the land and the mills, the factories, railroads and mines, the forests and fields and all other means of production and transportation.

Hence wealth and poverty, millionaires and beggars, castles and caves, luxury and squalor, painted parasites on the boulevard and painted poverty among the red lights.

Hence strikes, boycotts, riots, murder, suicide, insanity, prostitution on a fearful and increasing scale.

The capitalist parties can do nothing. They are a part, an iniquitous part, of the foul and decaying system.

There is no remedy for the ravages of death.

Capitalism is dying and its extremities are already decomposing. The blotches upon the surface show that the blood no longer circulates. The time is near when the cadaver will have to be removed and the atmosphere purified.

In contrast with the Republican and Democratic conventions, where politicians were the puppets of plutocrats, the convention of the Socialist party consisted of workingmen and women fresh from their labors, strong, clean, wholesome, self-reliant, ready to do and dare for the cause of labor, the cause of humanity.

Proud indeed am I to have been chosen by such a body of men and women to bear aloft the proletarian standard in this campaign, and heartily do I endorse the clear and cogent platform of the party which appeals with increasing force and eloquence to the whole working class of the country.

To my associate upon the national ticket I give my hand with all my heart. Ben Hanford typifies the working class and fitly represents the historic mission and revolutionary character of the Socialist party.

Closing Words

These are stirring days for living men. The day of crisis is drawing near and Socialists are exerting all their power to prepare the people for it.

The old order of society can survive but little longer. Socialism is next in order. The swelling minority sounds warning of the impending change. Soon that minority will be the majority and then will come the co-operative commonwealth.

Every workingman should rally to the standard of his class and hasten the full-orbed day of freedom.

Every progressive Democrat must find his way in our direction and if he will but free himself from prejudice and study the principles of Socialism he will soon be a sturdy supporter of our party.

Every sympathizer with labor, every friend of justice, every lover of humanity should support the Socialist party as the only party that is organized to abolish industrial slavery, the prolific source of the giant evils that afflict the people.

Who with a heart in his breast can look upon Colorado without keenly feeling the cruelties and crimes of capitalism! Repression will not help her. Brutality will only brutalize her. Private ownership and wage-slavery are the curse of Colorado. Only Socialism will save Colorado and the nation.

The overthrow of capitalism is the object of the Socialist party. It will not fuse with any other party and it would rather die than compromise.

The Socialist party comprehends the magnitude of its task and has the patience of preliminary defeat and the faith of ultimate victory.

The working class must be emancipated by the working class.

Woman must be given her true place in society by the working class.

Child labor must be abolished by the working class.

Society must be reconstructed by the working class.

The working class must be employed by the working class.

The fruits of labor must be enjoyed by the working class.

War, bloody war, must be ended by the working class.

These are the principles and objects of the Socialist party and we fearlessly proclaim them to our fellowmen.

We know our cause is just and that it must prevail.

With faith and hope and courage we hold our heads erect and with dauntless spirit marshal the working class for the march from Capitalism to Socialism, from Slavery to Freedom, from Barbarism to Civilization.

Preamble to the Constitution and By-Laws of the Industrial Workers
  of the World, 1908

*The Industrial Workers of the World (IWW), or "Wobblies," were formed in Chicago
in 1905 at a convention of radical trade unionists. These unionists sought a worldwide
union that would abolish all wage and class systems and implement a form of democracy
in every workplace. The IWW sought "direct action" through strikes and boycotts to
overthrow the capitalist system, eschewing the methods of Eugene Debs and other socialist
political leaders. It also rejected collective bargaining contracts on the grounds that they
would hobble rank-and-file attempts to further workers' interests through unannounced
work stoppages. At its height during the 1910s and early 1920s IWW membership reached
the tens of thousands, and the organization was involved in numerous strikes and other
industrial actions. A series of confrontations with police, the military, and local citizens
eventually brought membership down, and a series of legal actions aimed at foreign-born
radicals and Communist party influence left the IWW a shadow of its former self.*

Preamble

The working class and the employing class have nothing in common. There can be no peace so long as hunger and want are found among millions of working people and the few, who make up the employing class, have all the good things of life.

Between these two classes a struggle must go on until all the toilers come together on the political, as well as on the industrial field, and take and hold that which they produce by their labor through an economic organization of the working class without affiliation with any political party.

The rapid gathering of wealth and the centering of the management of industries into fewer and fewer hands make the trades unions unable to cope with the ever-growing power of the employing class, because the trades unions foster a state of things which allows one set of workers to be pitted against another set of workers in the same industry, thereby helping defeat one another in wage wars. The trades unions aid the employing class to mislead the workers into the belief that the working class have interests in common with their employers.

These sad conditions can be changed and the interests of the working class upheld only by an organization formed in such a way that all its members in any one industry, or in all industries, if necessary, cease work whenever a strike or lock-out is on in any department thereof, thus making an injury to one an injury to all.

The Subjective Necessity for Social Settlements, *Jane Addams*, 1892

Pacifist, labor advocate, child welfare reformer, and social worker, Jane Addams (1860–1935) centered her activities on Hull House, a "settlement" in a Chicago immigrant neighborhood. A prolific writer and organizer, she headed what became known as the "settlement house movement" through which numerous local programs were established to provide medical care, education, daycare, training, employment services, and other forms of support, particularly for immigrants and working mothers. Recipient of the Nobel Peace Prize for her pacifist activism, Addams secured state laws regulating child labor and was active in the women's suffrage movement. The material reproduced here originally was delivered as a lecture to various philanthropic societies. In it Addams emphasizes the need for comprehensive local involvement on the part of social workers— living among rather than simply serving those in need.

The Subjective Necessity for Social Settlements

Jane Addams

HULL HOUSE, which was Chicago's first Settlement, was established in September, 1889. It represented no association, but was opened by two women, backed by many friends, in the belief that the mere foothold of a house, easily accessible, ample in space, hospitable and tolerant in spirit, situated in the midst of the large foreign colonies which so easily isolate themselves in American cities, would be in itself a serviceable thing for Chicago. Hull House endeavors to make social intercourse express the growing sense of the economic unity of society. It is an effort to add the social function to democracy. It was opened on the theory that the dependence of classes on each other is reciprocal; and that as "the social relation is essentially a reciprocal relation, it gave a form of expression that has peculiar value."

This paper is an attempt to treat of the subjective necessity for Social Settlements, to analyze the motives which underlie a movement based not only upon conviction, but genuine emotion. Hull House of Chicago is used as an illustration, but so far as the analysis is faithful, it obtains wherever educated young people are seeking an outlet for that sentiment of universal brotherhood which the best spirit of our times is forcing from an emotion into a motive.

I have divided the motives which constitute the subjective pressure toward Social Settlements into three great lines: the first contains the desire to make the entire social organism democratic, to extend democracy beyond its political expression; the second is the impulse to share the race life, and to bring as much as possible of social energy and the accumulation of civilization to those portions of the race which have little; the third springs from a certain *renaissance* of Christianity, a movement toward its early humanitarian aspects.

It is not difficult to see that although America is pledged to the democratic ideal, the view of democracy has been partial, and that its best achievement thus far has been pushed along the line of the franchise. Democracy has made little attempt to assert itself in social affairs. We have refused to move beyond the position of its eighteenth-century leaders, who believed that political equality alone would secure all good to all men. We conscientiously followed the gift of the ballot hard upon the gift of freedom to the negro, but we are quite unmoved by the fact that he lives among us in a practical social ostracism. We hasten to give the franchise to the immigrant from a sense of justice, from a tradition that he ought to have it, while we dub him with epithets deriding his past life or present occupation, and feel no duty to invite him to our houses. We are forced to acknowledge that it is only in our local and national politics that we try very hard for the ideal so dear to those who were enthusiasts when the century was young. We have almost given it up as our ideal in social intercourse. There are city wards in which many of the votes are sold for drinks and dollars; still there is a remote pretence, at least a fiction current, that a man's vote is his own. The judgment of the voter is consulted and an opportunity for remedy given. There is not even a theory in the social order, not a shadow answering to the polls in politics. The time may come when the politician who sells one by one to the highest bidder all the offices in his grasp, will not be considered more base in his code of morals, more hardened in his practice, than the woman who constantly invites to her receptions those alone who bring her an equal social return, who shares her beautiful surroundings only with those who minister to a liking she has for successful social events. In doing this is she not just as unmindful of the common weal, as unscrupulous in her use of power, as is any city "boss" who consults only the interests of the "ring"?

In politics "bossism" arouses a scandal. It goes on in society constantly and is only beginning to be challenged. Our consciences are becoming tender in regard to the lack of democracy in social affairs. We are perhaps entering upon the second phase of democracy, as the French philosophers entered upon the first, somewhat bewildered by its logical conclusions. The social organism has broken down through large districts of our great cities. Many of the people living there are very poor, the majority of them without leisure or energy for anything but the gain of subsistence. They move often from one wretched lodging to another. They live for the moment side by side, many of them without knowledge of each other, without fellowship, without local tradition or public spirit, without social organization of any kind. Practically nothing is done to remedy this. The people who might do it, who have the social tact and training, the large houses, and the traditions and custom of hospitality, live in other parts of the city. The club-houses, libraries, galleries, and semi-public conveniences for social life are also blocks away. We find working-men organized into armies of producers because men of executive ability and business sagacity have found it to their interests thus to organize them. But these working-men are not organized socially; although living in crowded tenement-houses, they are living without a corresponding social contact. The chaos is as great as it would be were they working in huge factories without foreman or superintendent. Their ideas and resources are cramped. The desire for higher social pleasure is extinct. They have no share in the traditions and social energy which make for progress.

Too often their only place of meeting is a saloon, their only host a bartender; a local demagogue forms their public opinion. Men of ability and refinement, of social power and university cultivation, stay away from them. Personally, I believe the men who lose most are those who thus stay away. But the paradox is here: when cultivated people do stay away from a certain portion of the population, when all social advantages are persistently withheld, it may be for years, the result itself is pointed at as a reason, is used as an argument, for the continued withholding.

It is constantly said that because the masses have never had social advantages they do not want them, that they are heavy and dull, and that it will take political or philanthropic machinery to change them. This divides a city into rich and poor; into the favored, who express their sense of the social obligation by gifts of money, and into the unfavored, who express it by clamoring for a "share"—both of them actuated by a vague sense of justice. This division of the city would be more justifiable, however, if the people who thus isolate themselves on certain streets and use their social ability for each other gained enough thereby and added sufficient to the sum total of social progress to justify the withholding of the pleasures and results of that progress from so many people who ought to have them. But they cannot accomplish this. "The social spirit discharges itself in many forms, and no one form is adequate to its total expression." We are all uncomfortable in regard to the sincerity of our best phrases, because we hesitate to translate our philosophy into the deed.

It is inevitable that those who feel most keenly this insincerity and partial living should be our young people, our so-called educated young people who accomplish little toward the solution of this social problem, and who bear the brunt of being cultivated into unnourished, over-sensitive lives. They have been shut off from the common labor by which they live and which is a great source of moral and physical health. They feel a fatal want of harmony between their theory and their lives, a lack of co-ordination between thought and action. I think it is hard for us to realize how seriously many of them are taking to the notion of human brotherhood, how eagerly they long to give tangible expression to the democratic ideal. These young men and women, longing to socialize their democracy, are animated by certain hopes.

These hopes may be loosely formulated thus: that if in a democratic country nothing can be permanently achieved save through the masses of the people, it will be impossible to establish a higher political life than the people themselves crave; that it is difficult to see how the notion of a higher civic life can be fostered save through common intercourse; that the blessings which we associate with a life of refinement and cultivation can be made universal and must be made universal if they are to be permanent; that the good we secure for ourselves is precarious and uncertain, is floating in mid-air, until it is secured for all of us and incorporated into our common life.

These hopes are responsible for results in various directions, pre-eminently in the extension of educational advantages. We find that all educational matters are more democratic in their political than in their social aspects. The public schools in the poorest and most crowded wards of the city are inadequate to the number of children, and many of the teachers are ill-prepared and overworked; but in each ward there is an effort to secure public education. The schoolhouse itself stands as a pledge that the city recognizes and endeavors to fulfil the duty of educating its children. But what becomes of these children when they are no longer in public schools? Many of them never come under the influence of a professional teacher nor a cultivated friend after they are twelve. Society at large does little for their intellectual development. The dream of transcendentalists that each New England village would be a university, that every child taken from the common school would be put into definite lines of study and mental development, had its unfulfilled beginning in the village lyceum and lecture courses, and has its feeble representative now in the multitude of clubs for study which are so sadly restricted to educators, to the leisure class, or only to the advanced and progressive wage-workers.

The University Extension movement—certainly when it is closely identified with Settlements—would not confine learning to those who already want it, or to those who, by making an effort, can gain it, or to those among whom professional educators are already at work, but would take it to the tailors of East London and the dock-laborers of the Thames. It requires tact and training, love of learning, and the conviction of the justice of its diffusion to give it to people whose intellectual faculties are untrained and disused. But men in England are found who do it successfully, and it is believed there are men and women in America who can do it. I also believe that the best work in University Extension can be done in Settlements, where the teaching will be further socialized, where the teacher will grapple his students, not only by formal lectures, but by every hook possible to the fuller intellectual life which he represents. This teaching requires distinct

methods, for it is true of people who have been allowed to remain undeveloped and whose faculties are inert and sterile, that they cannot take their learning heavily. It has to be diffused in a social atmosphere. Information held in solution, a medium of fellowship and goodwill can be assimilated by the dullest.

If education is, as Froebel defined it, "deliverance," deliverance of the forces of the body and mind, then the untrained must first be delivered from all constraint and rigidity before their faculties can be used. Possibly one of the most pitiful periods in the drama of the much-praised young American who attempts to rise in life is the time when his educational requirements seem to have locked him up and made him rigid. He fancies himself shut off from his uneducated family and misunderstood by his friends. He is bowed down by his mental accumulations and often gets no farther than to carry them through life as a great burden. Not once has he had a glimpse of the delights of knowledge. Intellectual life requires for its expansion and manifestation the influence and assimilation of the interests and affections of others. Mazzini, that greatest of all democrats, who broke his heart over the condition of the South European peasantry, said: "Education is not merely a necessity of true life by which the individual renews his vital force in the vital force of humanity; it is a Holy Communion with generations dead and living, by which he fecundates all his faculties. When he is withheld from this Communion for generations, as the Italian peasant has been, we point our finger at him and say, 'He is like a beast of the field; he must be controlled by force.'" Even to this it is sometimes added that it is absurd to educate him, immoral to disturb his content. We stupidly use again the effect as an argument for a continuance of the cause. It is needless to say that a Settlement is a protest against a restricted view of education, and makes it possible for every educated man or woman with a teaching faculty to find out those who are ready to be taught. The social and educational activities of a Settlement are but differing manifestations of the attempt to socialize democracy, as is the existence of the settlement itself.

I find it somewhat difficult to formulate the second line of motives which I believe to constitute the trend of the subjective pressure toward the Settlement. There is something primordial about these motives, but I am perhaps over-bold in designating them as a great desire to share the race life. We all bear traces of the starvation struggle which for so long made up the life of the race. Our very organism holds memories and glimpses of that long life of our ancestors which still goes on among so many of our contemporaries. Nothing so deadens the sympathies and shrivels the power of enjoyment as the persistent keeping away from the great opportunities for helpfulness and a continual ignoring of the starvation struggle which makes up the life of at least half the race. To shut one's self away from that half of the race life is to shut one's self away from the most vital part of it; it is to live out but half the humanity which we have been born heir to and to use but half our faculties. We have all had longings for a fuller life which should include the use of these faculties. These longings are the physical complement of the "Intimations of Immortality" on which no ode has yet been written. To portray these would be the work of a poet, and it is hazardous for any but a poet to attempt it.

You may remember the forlorn feeling which occasionally seizes you when you arrive early in the morning a stranger in a great city. The stream of laboring people goes past you as you gaze through the plate-glass window of your hotel. You see hard-working men lifting great burdens; you hear the driving and jostling of huge carts. Your heart sinks with a sudden sense of futility. The door opens behind you and you turn to the man who brings you in your breakfast with a quick sense of human fellowship. You find yourself praying that you may never lose your hold on it all. A more poetic prayer would be that the great mother breasts of our common humanity, with its labor and suffering and its homely comforts, may never be withheld from you. You turn helplessly to the waiter. You feel that it would be almost grotesque to claim from him the sympathy you crave. Civilization has placed you far apart, but you resent your position with a sudden sense of snobbery. Literature is full of portrayals of these glimpses. They come to shipwrecked men on rafts; they overcome the differences of an incongruous multitude when in the presence of a great danger or when moved by a common enthusiasm. They are not, however, confined to such moments, and if we were in the habit of telling them to each other, the recital would be as long as the tales of children are, when they sit down on the green grass and confide to each other how many times they have remembered that they lived once before. If these tales are the stirring of inherited impressions, just so surely is the other the striving of inherited powers.

"There is nothing after disease, indigence, and a sense of guilt so fatal to health and to life itself as the want of a proper outlet for active faculties." I have seen young girls suffer and grow sensibly lowered in vitality in the first years after they leave school. In our attempt then to give a girl pleasure and freedom from care we succeed, for the most part, in making her pitifully miserable. She finds "life" so different from what she expected it to be. She is besotted with innocent little ambitions, and does not understand this apparent waste of herself, this elaborate preparation, if no work is provided for her. There is a heritage of noble obligation which young people accept and long to perpetuate. The desire for action, the wish to right wrong and alleviate suffering, haunts them daily. Society smiles at it indulgently instead of making it of value to itself. The wrong to them begins even farther back, when we restrain the first childish desires for "doing good" and tell them that they must wait until they are older and better fitted. We intimate that social obligation begins at a fixed date, forgetting that it begins with birth itself. We treat them as children who, with strong-growing limbs, are allowed to use their legs but not their arms, or whose legs are daily carefully exercised that after awhile their arms may be put to high use. We do this in spite of the protest of the best educators, Locke and Pestalozzi. We are fortunate in the mean time if their unused members do not weaken and disappear. They do sometimes. There are a few girls who, by the time they are "educated," forget their old childish desires to help the world and to play with poor little girls "who haven't playthings." Parents are often inconsistent. They deliberately expose their daughters to knowledge of the distress in the world. They send them to hear missionary addresses on famines in India and China; they accompany them to lectures on the suffering in Siberia; they agitate together over the forgotten region of East London. In addition to this, from babyhood the altruistic tendencies of these daughters are persistently cultivated. They are taught to be self-forgetting and self-sacrificing, to consider the good of the Whole before the good of the Ego. But when all this information and culture show results, when the daughter comes back from college and begins to recognize her social claim to the "submerged tenth," and to evince a disposition to fulfil it, the family claim is strenuously asserted; she is told that she is unjustified, ill-advised in her efforts. If she persists the family too often are injured and unhappy, unless the efforts are called missionary, and the religious zeal of the family carry them over their sense of abuse. When this zeal does not exist the result is perplexing. It is a curious violation of what we would fain believe a fundamental law—that the final return of the Deed is upon the head of the Doer. The Deed is that of exclusiveness and caution, but the return instead of falling upon the head of the exclusive and cautious, falls upon a young head full of generous and unselfish plans.

The girl loses something vital out of her life which she is entitled to. She is restricted and unhappy; her elders, meanwhile, are unconscious of the situation, and we have all the elements of a tragedy.

We have in America a fast-growing number of cultivated young people who have no recognized outlet for their active faculties. They hear constantly of the great social maladjustment, but no way is provided for them to change it, and their uselessness hangs about them heavily. Huxley declares that the sense of uselessness is the severest shock which the human system can sustain, and that, if persistently sustained, it results in atrophy of function. These young people have had advantages of college, of European travel and economic study, but they are sustaining this shock of inaction. They have pet phrases, and they tell you that the things that make us all alike are stronger than the things that make us different. They say that all men are united by needs and sympathies far more permanent and radical than anything that temporarily divides them and sets them in opposition to each other. If they affect art, they say that the decay in artistic expression is due to the decay in ethics, that art when shut away from the human interests and from the great mass of humanity is self-destructive. They tell their elders with all the bitterness of youth that if they expect success from them in business, or politics, or in whatever lines their ambition for them has run, they must let them consult all of humanity; that they must let them find out what the people want and how they want it. It is only the stronger young people, however, who formulate this. Many of them dissipate their energies in so-called enjoyment. Others, not content with that, go on studying and go back to college for their second degrees, not that they are especially fond of study, but because they want something definite to do, and their powers have been trained in the direction of mental accumulation. Many are buried beneath mere mental accumulation with lowered vitality and discontent. Walter Besant says they have had the vision that Peter had when he saw the great sheet let down from heaven, wherein was neither clean nor unclean. He calls it the sense of humanity. It is not philanthropy nor benevolence. It is a thing fuller and wider than either of these. This young life, so sincere in its emotion and good phrases and yet so undirected, seems to me as pitiful as the other great mass of destitute lives. One is supplementary to the other, and some method of communication can surely be devised. Mr. Barnett, who urged the first Settlement,—Toynbee Hall, in East London,—recognized this need of outlet for the young men of Oxford and Cambridge, and hoped that the Settlement would supply the communication. It is easy to see why the Settlement movement originated in England, where the years of education are more constrained and definite than they are here, where class distinctions are more rigid. The necessity of it was greater there, but we are fast feeling the pressure of the need and meeting the necessity for Settlements in America. Our young people feel nervously the need of putting theory into action, and respond quickly to the Settlement form of activity.

The third division of motives which I believe make toward the Settlement is the result of a certain *renaissance* going forward in Christianity. The impulse to share the lives of the poor, the desire to make social service, irrespective of propaganda, express the spirit of Christ, is as old as Christianity itself. We have no proof from the records themselves that the early Roman Christians, who strained their simple art to the point of grotesqueness in their eagerness to record a "good news" on the walls of the catacombs, considered this "good news" a religion. Jesus had no set of truths labelled "Religious." On the contrary, his doctrine was that all truth is one, that the appropriation of it is freedom. His teaching had no dogma to mark it off from truth and action in general. He himself called it a revelation—a life. These early Roman Christians received the Gospel message, a command to love all men, with a certain joyous simplicity. The image of the Good Shepherd is blithe and gay beyond the gentlest shepherd of Greek mythology; the hart no longer pants, but rushes to the water brooks. The Christians looked for the continuous revelation, but believed what Jesus said, that this revelation to be held and made manifest must be put into terms of action; that action is the only medium man has for receiving and appropriating truth. "If any man will do His will, he shall know of the doctrine."

That Christianity has to be revealed and embodied in the line of social progress is a corollary to the simple proposition that man's action is found in his social relationships in the way in which he connects with his fellows, that his motives for action are the zeal and affection with which he regards his fellows. By this simple process was created a deep enthusiasm for humanity, which regarded man as at once the organ and object of revelation; and by this process came about that wonderful fellowship, that true democracy of the early Church, that so captivates the imagination. The early Christians were pre-eminently non-resistant. They believed in love as a cosmic force. There was no iconoclasm during the minor peace of the Church. They did not yet denounce, nor tear down temples, nor preach the end of the world. They grew to a mighty number, but it never occurred to them, either in their weakness or their strength, to regard other men for an instant as their foes or as aliens. The spectacle of the Christians loving all men was the most astounding Rome had ever seen. They were eager to sacrifice themselves for the weak, for children and the aged. They identified themselves with slaves and did not avoid the plague. They longed to share the common lot that they might receive the constant revelation. It was a new treasure which the early Christians added to the sum of all treasures, a joy hitherto unknown in the world—the joy of finding the Christ which lieth in each man, but which no man can unfold save in fellowship. A happiness ranging from the heroic to the pastoral enveloped them. They were to possess a revelation as long as life had new meaning to unfold, new action to propose.

I believe that there is a distinct turning among many young men and women toward this simple acceptance of Christ's message. They resent the assumption that Christianity is a set of ideas which belong to the religious consciousness, whatever that may be, that it is a thing to be proclaimed and instituted apart from the social life of the community. They insist that it shall seek a simple and natural expression in the social organism itself. The Settlement movement is only one manifestation of that wider humanitarian movement which throughout Christendom, but pre-eminently in England, is endeavoring to embody itself, not in a sect, but in society itself. Tolstoï has reminded us all very forcibly of Christ's principle of non-resistance. His formulation has been startling and his expression has deviated from the general movement, but there is little doubt that he has many adherents, men and women who are philosophically convinced of the futility of opposition, who believe that evil can be overcome only with good and cannot be opposed. If love is the creative force of the universe, the principle which binds men together, and by their interdependence on each other makes them human, just so surely is anger and the spirit of opposition the destructive principle of the universe, that which tears down, thrusts men apart, and makes them isolated and brutal.

I cannot, of course, speak for other Settlements, but it would, I think, be unfair to Hull House not to emphasize the conviction with which the first residents went there, that it would simply be a foolish and an unwarrantable expenditure of force to oppose or to antagonize any individual or set of people in the neighborhood; that whatever of good the House had to offer should be put into positive terms; that its

residents should live with opposition to no man, with recognition of the good in every man, even the meanest. I believe that this turning, this *renaissance* of the early Christian humanitarianism, is going on in America, in Chicago, if you please, without leaders who write or philosophize, without much speaking, but with a bent to express in social service, in terms of action, the spirit of Christ. Certain it is that spiritual force is found in the Settlement movement, and it is also true that this force must be evoked and must be called into play before the success of any Settlement is assured. There must be the over-mastering belief that all that is noblest in life is common to men as men, in order to accentuate the likenesses and ignore the differences which are found among the people whom the Settlement constantly brings into juxtaposition. It may be true, as Frederic Harrison insists, that the very religious fervor of man can be turned into love for his race and his desire for a future life into content to live in the echo of his deeds. How far the Positivists' formula of the high ardor for humanity can carry the Settlement movement, Mrs. Humphry Ward's house in London may in course of time illustrate. Paul's formula of seeking for the Christ which lieth in each man and founding our likenesses on him seems a simpler formula to many of us.

If you have heard a thousand voices singing in the Hallelujah Chorus in Handel's "Messiah," you have found that the leading voices could still be distinguished, but that the differences of training and cultivation between them and the voices of the chorus were lost in the unity of purpose and the fact that they were all human voices lifted by a high motive. This is a weak illustration of what a Settlement attempts to do. It aims, in a measure, to lead whatever of social life its neighborhood may afford, to focus and give form to that life, to bring to bear upon it the results of cultivation and training; but it receives in exchange for the music of isolated voices the volume and strength of the chorus. It is quite impossible for me to say in what proportion or degree the subjective necessity which led to the opening of Hull House combined the three trends: first the desire to interpret democracy in social terms; secondly, the impulse beating at the very source of our lives urging us to aid in the race progress; and, thirdly, the Christian movement toward Humanitarianism. It is difficult to analyze a living thing; the analysis is at best imperfect. Many more motives may blend with the three trends; possibly the desire for a new form of social success due to the nicety of imagination, which refuses worldly pleasures unmixed with the joys of self-sacrifice; possibly a love of approbation, so vast that it is not content with the treble clapping of delicate hands, but wishes also to hear the bass notes from toughened palms, may mingle with these.

The Settlement, then, is an experimental effort to aid in the solution of the social and industrial problems which are engendered by the modern conditions of life in a great city. It insists that these problems are not confined to any one portion of a city. It is an attempt to relieve, at the same time, the over-accumulation at one end of society and the destitution at the other; but it assumes that this over-accumulation and destitution is most sorely felt in the things that pertain to social and educational advantage. From its very nature it can stand for no political or social *propaganda*. It must, in a sense, give the warm welcome of an inn to all such *propaganda,* if perchance one of them be found an angel. The one thing to be dreaded in the Settlement is that it lose its flexibility, its power of quick adaptation, its readiness to change its methods as its environment may demand. It must be open to conviction and must have a deep and abiding sense of tolerance. It must be hospitable and ready for experiment. It should demand from its residents a scientific patience in the accumulation of facts and the steady holding of their sympathies as one of the best instruments for that accumulation. It must be grounded in a philosophy whose foundation is on the solidarity of the human race, a philosophy which will not waver when the race happens to be represented by a drunken woman or an idiot boy. Its residents must be emptied of all conceit of opinion and all self-assertion, and ready to arouse and interpret the public opinion of their neighborhood. They must be content to live quietly side by side with their neighbors until they grow into a sense of relationship and mutual interests. Their neighbors are held apart by differences of race and language which the residents can more easily overcome. They are bound to see the needs of their neighborhood as a whole, to furnish data for legislation, and use their influence to secure it. In short, residents are pledged to devote themselves to the duties of good citizenship and to the arousing of the social energies which too largely lie dormant in every neighborhood given over to industrialism. They are bound to regard the entire life of their city as organic, to make an effort to unify it, and to protest against its over-differentiation.

Our philanthropies of all sorts are growing so expensive and institutional that it is to be hoped the Settlement movement will keep itself facile and unincumbered. From its very nature it needs no endowment, no roll of salaried officials. Many residents must always come in the attitude of students,

assuming that the best teacher of life is life itself, and regarding the Settlement as a classroom. Hull House from the outside may appear to be a cumbrous plant of manifold industries, with its round of clubs and classes, its day nursery, diet kitchen, library, art exhibits, lectures, statistical work and polyglot demands for information, a thousand people coming and going in an average week. But viewed as a business enterprise it is not costly, for from this industry are eliminated two great items of expense—the cost of superintendence and the cost of distribution. All the management and teaching are voluntary and unpaid, and the consumers—to continue the commercial phraseology—are at the door and deliver the goods themselves. In the instance of Hull House, rent is also largely eliminated through the courtesy of the owner.

Life is manifold and Hull House attempts to respond to as many sides as possible. It does this fearlessly, feeling sure that among the able people of Chicago are those who will come to do the work when once the outline is indicated. It pursues much the same policy in regard to money. It seems to me an advantage—this obligation to appeal to business men for their judgment and their money, to the educated for their effort and enthusiasm, to the neighborhood for their response and co-operation. It tests the sanity of an idea, and we enter upon a new line of activity with a feeling of support and confidence. We have always been perfectly frank with our neighbors. I have never tried so earnestly to set forth the gist of the Settlement movement, to make clear its reciprocity, as I have to them. At first we were often asked why we came to live there when we could afford to live somewhere else. I remember one man who used to shake his head and say it was "the strangest thing he had met in his experience," but who was finally convinced that it was not strange but natural. I trust that now it seems natural to all of us that the Settlement should be there. If it is natural to feed the hungry and care for the sick, it is certainly natural to give pleasure to the young and to minister to the deep-seated craving for social intercourse that all men feel. Whoever does it is rewarded by something which, if not gratitude, is at least spontaneous and vital and lacks that irksome sense of obligation with which a substantial benefit is too often acknowledged. The man who looks back to the person who first put him in the way of good literature has no alloy in his gratitude.

I remember when the statement seemed to me very radical that the salvation of East London was the destruction of West London; but I believe now that there will be no wretched quarters in our cities at all when the conscience of each man is so touched that he prefers to live with the poorest of his brethren, and not with the richest of them that his income will allow. It is to be hoped that this moving and living will at length be universal and need no name. The Settlement movement is from its nature a provisional one. It is easy in writing a paper to make all philosophy point one particular moral and all history adorn one particular tale; but I hope you forgive me for reminding you that the best speculative philosophy sets forth the solidarity of the human race; that the highest moralists have taught that without the advance and improvement of the whole no man can hope for any lasting improvement in his own moral or material individual condition. The subjective necessity for Social Settlements is identical with that necessity which urges us on toward social and individual salvation.

Why the Ward Boss Rules, *Jane Addams, 1898*

One of the central features of the Progressive movement in America was opposition to "machine politics." These "machines" were organizations of immigrant leaders who took control of neighborhood and city government. "Boss Tweed" in New York City was merely the most infamous head of a citywide organization that received votes in exchange for favors like help in securing work. Efficient city government was not a goal of such bosses, and violence was a part of maintaining discipline in the organization. Here Addams illustrates the source of "boss" power in carefully nurtured patron-client relationships.

Why the Ward Boss Rules

Jane Addams

Primitive people, such as the South Italian peasants who live in the Nineteenth Ward, deep down in their hearts admire nothing so much as the good man. The successful candidate must be a good man according to the standards of his constituents. He must not attempt to hold up a morality beyond them, nor must he attempt to reform or change the standard. If he believes what they believe, and does what they are all cherishing a secret ambition to do, he will dazzle them by his success and win their confidence. Any one who has lived among poorer people cannot fail to be impressed with their constant kindness to each other; that unfailing response to the needs and distresses of their neighbors, even when in danger of bankruptcy themselves. This is their reward for living in the midst of poverty. They have constant opportunities for self-sacrifice and generosity, to which, as a rule, they respond. A man stands by his friend when he gets too drunk to take care of himself, when he loses his wife or child, when he is evicted for non-payment of rent, when he is arrested for a petty crime. It seems to such a man entirely fitting that his Alderman should do the same thing on a larger scale—that he should help a constituent out of trouble just because he is in trouble, irrespective of the justice involved.

The Alderman, therefore, bails out his constituents when they are arrested, or says a good word to the police justice when they appear before him for trial; uses his "pull" with the magistrate when they are likely to be fined for a civil misdemeanor, or sees what he can do to "fix up matters" with the State's attorney when the charge is really a serious one.

Because of simple friendliness, the Alderman is expected to pay rent for the hard-pressed tenant when no rent is forthcoming, to find jobs when work is hard to get, to procure and divide among his constituents all the places which he can seize from the City Hall. The Alderman of the Nineteenth Ward at one time made the proud boast that he had two thousand six hundred people in his ward upon the public pay-roll. This, of course, included day-laborers, but each one felt under distinct obligations to him for getting the job.

If we recollect, further, that the franchise-seeking companies pay respectful heed to the applicants backed by the Alderman, the question of voting for the successful man becomes as much an industrial as a political one. An Italian laborer wants a job more than anything else, and quite simply votes for the man who promises him one.

The Alderman may himself be quite sincere in his acts of kindness. In certain stages of moral evolution, a man is incapable of unselfish action the results of which will not benefit some one of his acquaintances; still more, of conduct that does not aim to assist any individual whatsoever; and it is a long step in moral progress to appreciate the work done by the individual for the community.

The Alderman gives presents at weddings and christenings. He seizes these days of family festivities for making friends. It is easiest to reach people in the holiday mood of expansive good will, but on their side it seems natural and kindly that he should do it. The Alderman procures passes from the railroads when his constituents wish to visit friends or to attend the funerals of distant relatives; he buys tickets galore for benefit entertainments given for a widow or a consumptive in peculiar distress; he contributes to prizes which are awarded to the handsomest lady or the most popular man.

At a church bazaar, for instance, the Alderman finds the stage all set for his dramatic performance. When others are spending pennies he is spending dollars. Where anxious relatives are canvassing to secure votes for the two most beautiful children who are being voted upon, he recklessly buys votes from both sides, and laughingly declines to say which one he likes the best, buying off the young lady who is persistently determined to find out, with five dollars for the flower bazaar, the posies, of course, to be sent to the sick of the parish. The moral atmosphere of a bazaar suits him exactly. He murmurs many times, "Never mind; the money all goes to the poor," or, "It is all straight enough if the church gets it."

There is something archaic in a community of simple people in their attitude towards death and burial. Nothing so easy to collect money for as a funeral. If the Alderman seizes upon festivities for expressions of his good will, much more does he seize upon periods of sorrow. At a funeral he has the double advantage of ministering to a genuine craving for comfort and solace, and at the same time of assisting at an important social function.

In addition to this, there is among the poor, who have few social occasions, a great desire for a well-arranged funeral, the grade of which almost determines their social standing in the neighborhood. The Alderman saves the very poorest of his constituents from that awful horror of burial by the county; he provides carriages for the poor, who otherwise could not have them; for the more prosperous he sends extra carriages, so that they may invite more friends and have a longer procession; for the most prosperous of all there will be probably only a large "flower-piece." It may be too much to say that all the relatives and friends who ride in the carriages provided by the Alderman's bounty vote for him, but they are certainly influenced by his kindness, and talk of his virtues during the long hours of the ride back and forth from the suburban cemetery. A man who would ask at such a time where all this money comes from would be considered sinister. Many a man at such a time has formulated a lenient judgment of political corruption and has heard kindly speeches which he has remembered on election day. "Ah, well, he has a big Irish heart. He is good to the widow and the fatherless." "He knows the poor better than the big guns who are always about talking civil service and reform."

Indeed, what headway can the notion of civic purity, of honesty of administration, make against this big manifestation of human friendliness, this stalking survival of village kindness? The notions of the civic reformer are negative and impotent before it. The reformers give themselves over largely to criticisms of the present state of affairs, to writing and talking of what the future must be; but their goodness is not dramatic; it is not even concrete and human.

Such an Alderman will keep a standing account with an undertaker, and telephone every week, and sometimes more than once, the kind of outfit he wishes provided for a bereaved constituent, until the sum may roll up into hundreds a year. Such a man understands what the people want, and ministers just as truly to a great human need as the musician or the artist does. I recall an attempt to substitute what we might call a later standard.

A delicate little child was deserted in the Hull House nursery. An investigation showed that it had been born ten days previously in the Cook County Hospital, but no trace could be found of the unfortunate mother. The little thing lived for several weeks, and then, in spite of every care, died. We decided to have it buried by the county, and the wagon was to arrive by eleven o'clock. About nine o'clock in the morning the rumor of this awful deed reached the neighbors. A half-dozen of them came, in a very excited state of mind, to protest. They took up a collection out of their poverty with which to defray a funeral. We were then comparatively new in the neighborhood. We did not realize that we were really shocking a genuine moral sentiment of the community. In our crudeness, we instanced the care and tenderness which had been expended upon the little creature while it was alive; that it had had every attention from a skilled physician and trained nurse; we even intimated that the excited members of the group had not taken part in this, and that it now lay with us to decide that the child should be buried, as it had been born, at the county's expense. It is doubtful whether Hull House has ever done anything which injured it so deeply in the minds of some of its neighbors. We were only forgiven by the most indulgent on the ground that we were spinsters and could not know a mother's heart. No one born and reared in the community could possibly have made a mistake like that. No one who had studied the ethical standards with any care could have bungled so completely.

Last Christmas our Alderman distributed six tons of turkeys, and four or more tons of ducks and geese; but each luckless biped was handed out either by himself or one of his friends with a "Merry Christmas." Inevitably, some families got three or four apiece, but what of that? He had none of the nagging rules of the charitable societies, nor was he ready to declare that, because a man wanted two turkeys for

Christmas, he was a scoundrel, who should never be allowed to eat turkey again.

The Alderman's wisdom was again displayed in procuring from down-town friends the sum of three thousand dollars wherewith to uniform and equip a boys' temperance brigade which had been formed in the ward a few months before his campaign. Is it strange that the good leader, whose heart was filled with innocent pride as he looked upon these promising young scions of virtue, should decline to enter into a reform campaign?

The question does, of course, occur to many minds, Where does the money come from with which to dramatize so successfully? The more primitive people accept the truthful statement of its sources without any shock to their moral sense. To their simple minds he gets it "from the rich," and so long as he again gives it out to the poor, as a true Robin Hood, with open hand, they have no objections to offer. Their ethics are quite honestly those of the merry-making foresters. The next less primitive people of the vicinage are quite willing to admit that he leads "the gang" in the City Council, and sells out the city franchises; that he makes deals with the franchise-seeking companies; that he guarantees to steer dubious measures through the Council, for which he demands liberal pay; that he is, in short, a successful boodler. But when there is intellect enough to get this point of view, there is also enough to make the contention that this is universally done; that all the Aldermen do it more or less successfully, but that the Alderman of the Nineteenth Ward is unique in being so generous; that such a state of affairs is to be deplored, of course, but that that is the way business is run, and we are fortunate when a kind-hearted man who is close to the people gets a large share of the boodle; that he serves these franchised companies who employ men in the building and construction of their enterprises, and that they are bound in return to give jobs to his constituency. Even when they are intelligent enough to complete the circle, and to see that the money comes, not from the pockets of the companies' agents, but from the street-car fares of people like themselves, it almost seems as if they would rather pay two cents more each time they ride than give up the consciousness that they have a big, warm-hearted friend at court who will stand by them in an emergency. The sense of just dealing comes apparently much later than the desire for protection and kindness. The Alderman is really elected because he is a good friend and neighbor.

During a campaign a year and a half ago, when a reform league put up a candidate against our corrupt Alderman, and

when Hull House worked hard to rally the moral sentiment of the ward in favor of the new man, we encountered another and unexpected difficulty. Finding that it was hard to secure enough local speakers of the moral tone which we desired, we imported orators from other parts of the town, from the "better element," so to speak. Suddenly we heard it rumored on all sides that, while the money and speakers for the reform candidate were coming from the swells, the money which was backing our corrupt Alderman also came from a swell source; it was rumored that the president of a street-car combination, for whom he performed constant offices in the City Council, was ready to back him to the extent of fifty thousand dollars; that he, too, was a good man, and sat in high places; that he had recently given a large sum of money to an educational institution, and was, therefore, as philanthropic, not to say good and upright, as any man in town; that our Alderman had the sanction of the highest authorities, and that the lecturers who were talking against corruption, and the selling and buying of franchises, were only the cranks, and not the solid business men who had developed and built up Chicago.

All parts of the community are bound together in ethical development. If the so-called more enlightened members of the community accept public gifts from the man who buys up the Council, and the so-called less enlightened members accept individual gifts from the man who sells out the Council, we surely must take our punishment together.

Another curious experience during that campaign was the difference of standards between the imported speakers and the audience. One man, high in the council of the "better element," one evening used as an example of the philanthropic politician an Alderman of the vicinity, recently dead, who was devotedly loved and mourned by his constituents. When the audience caught the familiar name in the midst of the platitudes, they brightened up wonderfully. But, as the speaker went on, they first looked puzzled, then astounded, and gradually their astonishment turned to indignation. The speaker, all unconscious of the situation, went on, imagining, perhaps, that he was addressing his usual audience, and totally unaware that he was perpetrating an outrage upon the finest feelings of the people who were sitting before him. He certainly succeeded in irrevocably injuring the chances of the candidate for whom he was speaking. The speaker's standard of ethics was upright dealing in positions of public trust. The standard of ethics held by his audience was, being good to the poor and speaking gently of the dead. If he considered them corrupt and illiterate voters, they quite honestly held him a blackguard.

If we would hold to our political democracy, some pains must be taken to keep on common ground in our human experiences, and to some solidarity in our ethical conceptions. And if we discover that men of low ideals and corrupt practice are forming popular political standards simply because such men stand by and for and with the people, then nothing remains but to obtain a like sense of identification before we can hope to modify ethical standards.

JANE ADDAMS.

Hull House, Chicago.

Declaration of Principles of the Progressive Party, *Theodore Roosevelt*, 1912

Theodore Roosevelt (1858–1919) was central to the Progressive movement as president and, afterwards, as a political activist and, in 1912, a third-party candidate for the presidency. Roosevelt, who served as president from 1901 to 1909, had sought increased federal regulation of large corporations and had brought suits aimed at breaking up various corporate trusts. Dissatisfied with the policies of his less activist successor, William Howard Taft, Roosevelt eventually determined to oppose Taft's nomination for a second term. Taft, however, controlled the party machinery. And the modern primary system, with its emphasis on popular votes, did not yet exist. Defeated for the nomination, Roosevelt formed his own, the Progressive Party. The platform of that party embodied the reformist impulses and policies of the era. Industrial regulation, women's suffrage, popular election of U.S. senators, child labor regulations, and a series of other reforms aimed at more direct citizen participation in mass political action all were set forth as needed policies. Roosevelt lost to the Democratic candidate, Woodrow Wilson (who also termed himself a Progressive) but outpolled Taft.

Declaration of Principles of the Progressive Party

August 7, 1912

Theodore Roosevelt

The conscience of the people, in a time of grave national problems, has called into being a new party, born of the nation's awakened sense of justice. We of the Progressive party here dedicate ourselves to the fulfillment of the duty laid upon us by our fathers to maintain that government of the people, by the people and for the people whose foundations they laid.

We hold with Thomas Jefferson and Abraham Lincoln that the people are the masters of their constitution, to fulfill its purposes and to safeguard it from those who, by perversion of its intent, would convert it into an instrument of injustice. In accordance with the needs of each generation the people must use their sovereign powers to establish and maintain equal opportunity and industrial justice, to secure which this government was founded and without which no republic can endure.

This country belongs to the people who inhabit it. Its resources, its business, its institutions and its laws should be utilized, maintained or altered in whatever manner will best promote the general interest.

It is time to set the public welfare in the first place.

THE OLD PARTIES

Political parties exist to secure responsible government and to execute the will of the people.

From these great tasks both of the old parties have turned aside. Instead of instruments to promote the general welfare, they have become the tools of corrupt interests which use them impartially to serve their selfish purposes. *Behind the ostensible government sits enthroned an invisible government, owing no allegiance and acknowledging no responsibility to the people.*

To destroy this invisible government, to dissolve the unholy alliance between corrupt business and corrupt politics is the first task of the statesmanship of the day.

The deliberate betrayal of its trust by the Republican party, and the fatal incapacity of the Democratic party to deal with the new issues of the new time, have compelled the people to forge a new instrument of government through which to give effect to their will in laws and institutions.

Unhampered by tradition, uncorrupted by power, undismayed by the magnitude of the task, the new party offers itself as the instrument of the people to sweep away old abuses, to build a new and nobler commonwealth.

A Covenant with the People

This declaration is our covenant with the people, and we hereby bind the party and its candidates in state and nation to the pledges made herein.

The Rule of the People

The Progressive party, committed to the principle of government by a self-controlled democracy expressing its will through representatives of the people, pledges itself to secure such alterations in the fundamental law of the several states and of the United States as shall insure the representative character of the government.

In particular, the party declares for direct primaries for the nomination of state and national officers, for nation-wide preferential primaries for candidates for the presidency, for the direct election of United States senators by the people; and we urge on the states the policy of the short ballot, with responsibility to the people secured by the initiative, referendum and recall.

Amendment of Constitution

The Progressive party, believing that a free people should have the power from time to time to amend their fundamental law so as to adapt it progressively to the changing needs of the people, pledges itself to provide a more easy and expeditious method of amending the federal constitution.

Nation and State

Up to the limit of the constitution, and later by amendment of the constitution, if found necessary, we advocate bringing under effective national jurisdiction those problems which have expanded beyond reach of the individual states.

It is as grotesque as it is intolerable that the several states should by unequal laws in matter of common concern become competing commercial agencies, barter the lives of their children, the health of their women and the safety and well-being of their working people for the profit of their financial interests.

The extreme insistence on states' rights by the Democratic party in the Baltimore platform demonstrates anew its inability to understand the world into which it has survived or to administer the affairs of a union of states which have in all essential respects become one people.

Social and Industrial Justice

The supreme duty of the nation is the conservation of human resources through an enlightened measure of social and industrial justice. We pledge ourselves to work unceasingly in state and nation for:

Effective legislation looking to the prevention of industrial accidents, occupational diseases, overwork, involuntary unemployment, and other injurious effects incident to modern industry;

The fixing of minimum safety and health standards for the various occupations, and the exercise of the public authority of state and nation, including the federal control over interstate commerce and the taxing power, to maintain such standards;

The prohibition of child labor;

Minimum wage standards for working women, to provide a living scale in all industrial occupations;

The prohibition of night work for women and the establishment of an eight-hour day for women and young persons;

One day's rest in seven for all wage-workers;

The eight-hour day in continuous twenty-four-hour industries;

The abolition of the convict contract labor system; substituting a system of prison production for governmental consumption only; and the application of prisoners' earnings to the support of their dependent families;

Publicity as to wages, hours and conditions of labor; full reports upon industrial accidents and diseases, and the opening to public inspection of all tallies, weights, measures and check systems on labor products;

Standards of compensation for death by industrial accident and injury and trade diseases which will transfer the burden of lost earnings from the families of working people to the industry, and thus to the community;

The protection of home life against the hazards of sickness, irregular employment and old age through the adoption of a system of social insurance adapted to American use;

The development of the creative labor power of America by lifting the last load of illiteracy from American youth and establishing continuation schools for industrial education under public control and encouraging agricultural education and demonstration in rural schools;

The establishment of industrial research laboratories to put the methods and discoveries of science at the service of American producers.

We favor the organization of the workers, men and women, as a means of protecting their interests and of promoting their progress.

BUSINESS

We believe that true popular government, justice and prosperity go hand in hand, and, so believing, it is our purpose to secure that large measure of general prosperity which is the fruit of legitimate and honest business, fostered by equal justice and by sound progressive laws.

We demand that the test of true prosperity shall be the benefits conferred thereby on all the citizens not confined to individuals or classes and that the test of corporate efficiency shall be the ability better to serve the public; that those who profit by control of business affairs shall justify that profit and that control by sharing with the public the fruits thereof.

We therefore demand a strong national regulation of interstate corporations. The corporation is an essential part of modern business. The concentration of modern business, in some degree, is both inevitable and necessary for national and international business efficiency. But the existing concentration of vast wealth under a corporate system, unguarded and uncontrolled by the nation, has placed in the hands of a few men enormous, secret, irresponsible power over the daily life of the citizen—a power insufferable in a free government and certain of abuse.

This power has been abused, in monopoly of national resources, in stock watering, in unfair competition and unfair privileges, and finally in sinister influences on the public agencies of state and nation. We do not fear commercial power, but we insist that it shall be exercised openly, under publicity, supervision and regulation of the most efficient sort, which will preserve its good while eradicating and preventing its evils.

To that end we urge the establishment of a strong federal administrative commission of high standing, which shall maintain permanent active supervision over industrial corporations engaged in interstate commerce, or such of them as are of public importance, doing for them what the govern-ment now does for the national banks, and what is now done for the railroads by the Interstate Commerce Commission.

Such a commission must enforce the complete publicity of those corporation transactions which are of public interest; must attack unfair competition, false capitalization and special privilege, and by continuous trained watchfulness guard and keep open equally to all the highways of American commerce.

Thus the business man will have certain knowledge of the law, and will be able to conduct his business easily in conformity therewith; the investor will find security for his capital; dividends will be rendered more certain, and the savings of the people will be drawn naturally and safely into the channels of trade.

Under such a system of constructive regulation, legitimate business, freed from confusion, uncertainty and fruitless litigation, will develop normally in response to the energy and enterprise of the American business man.

COMMERCIAL DEVELOPMENT

The time has come when the federal government should co-operate with manufacturers and producers in extending our foreign commerce. To this end we demand adequate appropriations by Congress, and the appointment of diplomatic and consular officers solely with a view to their special fitness and worth, and not in consideration of political expediency.

It is imperative to the welfare of our people that we enlarge and extend our foreign commerce. We are preeminently fitted to do this because as a people we have developed high skill in the art of manufacturing; our business men are strong executives, strong organizers. In every way possible our Federal Government should co-operate in this important matter. Anyone who has had opportunity to study and observe first-hand Germany's course in this respect must realize that their policy of co-operation between Government and business has in comparatively few years made them a leading competitor for the commerce of the world. It should be remembered that they are doing this on a national scale and with large units of business, while the Democrats would have us believe that we should do it with small units of business, which would be controlled not by the National Government but by forty-nine conflicting sovereignties. Such a policy is utterly out of keeping with the progress of the times and gives our great commercial rivals in Europe—hungry for international markets—golden opportunities of which they are rapidly taking advantage.

Tariff

We believe in a protective tariff which shall equalize conditions of competition between the United States and foreign countries, both for the farmer and the manufacturer and which shall maintain for labor an adequate standard of living.

Primarily the benefit of any tariff should be disclosed in the pay envelope of the laborer. We declare that no industry deserves protection which is unfair to labor or which is operating in violation of federal law. We believe that the presumption is always in favor of the consuming public.

We demand tariff revision because the present tariff is unjust to the people of the United States. Fair-dealing toward the people requires an immediate downward revision of those schedules wherein duties are shown to be unjust or excessive.

We pledge ourselves to the establishment of a non-partisan scientific tariff commission, reporting both to the President and to either branch of Congress, which shall report, first, as to the costs of production, efficiency of labor, capitalization, industrial organization and efficiency and the general competitive position in this country and abroad of industries seeking protection from Congress; second, as to the revenue-producing power of the tariff and its relation to the resources of government; and, third, as to the effect of the tariff on prices, operations of middlemen, and on the purchasing power of the consumer.

We believe that this commission should have plenary power to elicit information, and for this purpose to prescribe a uniform system of accounting for the great protected industries. The work of the commission should not prevent the immediate adoption of acts reducing those schedules generally recognized as excessive.

We condemn the Payne-Aldrich bill as unjust to the people. The Republican organization is in the hands of those who have broken, and cannot again be trusted to keep, the promise of necessary downward revision. The Democratic party is committed to the destruction of the protective system through a tariff for revenue only—a policy which would inevitably produce widespread industrial and commercial disaster.

We demand the immediate repeal of the Canadian reciprocity act.

High Cost of Living

The high cost of living is due partly to world-wide and partly to local causes; partly to natural and partly to artificial causes. The measures proposed in this platform on various subjects such as the tariff, the trusts and conservation, will of themselves tend to remove the artificial causes.

There will remain other elements such as the tendency to leave the country for the city, waste, extravagance, bad system of taxation, poor methods of raising crops and bad business methods in marketing crops.

To remedy these conditions requires the fullest information and based on this information, effective government supervision and control to remove all the artificial causes. We pledge ourselves to such full and immediate inquiry and to immediate action to deal with every need such inquiry discloses.

Currency

We believe there exists imperative need for prompt legislation for the improvement of our national currency system. We believe the present method of issuing notes through private agencies is harmful and unscientific.

The issue of currency is fundamentally a government function and the system should have as basic principles soundness and elasticity. The control should be lodged with the government and should be protected from domination or manipulation by Wall Street or any special interests.

We are opposed to the so-called Aldrich currency bill, because its provisions would place our currency and credit system in private hands, not subject to effective public control.

Conservation

The natural resources of the nation must be promptly developed and generously used to supply the people's needs, but we cannot safely allow them to be wasted, exploited, monopolized, or controlled against the general good. We heartily favor the policy of conservation, and we pledge our party to protect the national forests without hindering their legitimate use for the benefit of all the people.

Agricultural lands in the national forests are, and should remain, open to the genuine settler. Conservation will not retard legitimate development. The honest settler must receive his patent promptly, without needless restrictions or delays.

We believe that the remaining forests, coal and oil lands, water powers and other natural resources still in state or national control (except agricultural lands) are more likely to be wisely conserved and utilized for the general welfare if held in the public hands.

In order that consumers and producers, managers and

workmen, now and hereafter, need not pay toll to private monopolies of power and raw material, we demand that such resources shall be retained by the state or nation, and opened to immediate use under laws which will encourage development and make to the people a moderate return for benefits conferred.

In particular we pledge our party to require reasonable compensation to the public for water-power rights hereafter granted by the public.

We pledge legislation to lease the public grazing lands under equitable provisions now pending which will increase the production of food for the people and thoroughly safeguard the rights of the actual homemaker. Natural resources, whose conservation is necessary for the national welfare, should be owned or controlled by the nation.

WATERWAYS

The rivers of the United States are the natural arteries of this continent. We demand that they shall be opened to traffic as indispensable parts of a great nation-wide system of transportation in which the Panama canal will be the central link, thus enabling the whole interior of the United States to share with the Atlantic and Pacific seaboards in the benefit derived from the canal.

It is a national obligation to develop our rivers, and especially the Mississippi and its tributaries, without delay, under a comprehensive general plan covering each river system from its source to its mouth, designed to secure its highest usefulness for navigation, irrigation, domestic supply, water power and the prevention of floods.

We pledge our party to the immediate preparation of such a plan, which should be made and carried out in close and friendly co-operation between the nation, the states and the cities affected.

Under such a plan, the destructive floods of the Mississippi and other streams, which represent a vast and needless loss to the nation, would be controlled by forest conservation and water storage at the headwaters, and by levees below; land sufficient to support millions of people would be reclaimed from the deserts and the swamps, water power enough to transform the industrial standing of whole states would be developed, adequate water terminals would be provided, transportation by river would revive, and the railroads would be compelled to co-operate as freely with the boat lines as with each other.

The equipment, organization and experience acquired in constructing the Panama canal soon will be available for the Lakes-to-the-Gulf deep waterway and other portions of this great work, and should be utilized by the nation in co-operation with the various states, at the lowest net cost to the people.

PANAMA CANAL

The Panama canal, built and paid for by the American people, must be used primarily for their benefit.

We demand that the canal shall be so operated as to break the transportation monopoly now held and misused by the trans-continental railroads by maintaining sea competition with them; that ships directly or indirectly owned or controlled by American railroad corporations shall not be permitted to use the canal, and that American ships engaged in coastwise trade shall pay no tolls.

The Progressive party will favor legislation having for its aim the development of friendship and commerce between the United States and Latin-American nations.

ALASKA

The coal and other natural resources of Alaska should be opened to development at once. They are owned by the people of the United States, and are safe from monopoly, waste or destruction only while so owned.

We demand that they shall neither be sold nor given away, except under the homestead law, but while held in government ownership shall be opened to use promptly upon liberal terms requiring immediate development.

Thus the benefit of cheap fuel will accrue to the government of the United States and to the people of Alaska and the Pacific coast; the settlement of extensive agricultural lands will be hastened; the extermination of the salmon will be prevented, and the just and wise development of Alaskan resources will take the place of private extortion or monopoly.

We demand also that extortion or monopoly in transportation shall be prevented by the prompt acquisition, construction, or improvement by the government of such railroads, harbor and other facilities for transportation as the welfare of the people may demand.

We promise the people of the territory of Alaska the same measure of local self-government that was given to other American territories, and that federal officials appointed there shall be qualified by previous bona-fide residence in the territory.

EQUAL SUFFRAGE

The Progressive party, believing that no people can justly claim to be a true democracy which denies political rights on account of sex, pledges itself to the task of securing equal suffrage to men and women alike.

CORRUPT PRACTICES

We pledge our party to legislation that will compel strict limitation on all campaign contributions and expenditures, and detailed publicity of both before as well as after primaries and elections.

PUBLICITY AND PUBLIC SERVICE

We pledge our party to legislation compelling the registration of lobbyists; publicity of committee hearings except on foreign affairs, and recording of all votes in committee; and forbidding federal appointees from holding office in state or national political organizations, or taking part as officers or delegates in political conventions for the nomination of elective state or national officials.

THE COURTS

The Progressive party demands such restriction of the power of the courts as shall leave to the people the ultimate authority to determine fundamental questions of social welfare and public policy. To secure this end, it pledges itself to provide:

1. That when an act, passed under the police power of the state, is held unconstitutional under the state constitution, by the courts, the people, after an ample interval for deliberation, shall have an opportunity to vote on the question whether they desire the act to become a law, notwithstanding such decision.

2. That every decision of the highest appellate court of a state declaring an act of the legislature unconstitutional on the ground of its violation of the federal constitution shall be subject to the same review by the Supreme Court of the United States as is now accorded to decisions sustaining such legislation.

ADMINISTRATION OF JUSTICE

The Progressive party, in order to secure to the people a better administration of justice and by that means to bring about a more general respect for the law and the courts, pledges itself to work unceasingly for the reform of legal procedure and judicial methods.

We believe that the issuance of injunctions in cases arising out of labor disputes should be prohibited when such injunctions would not apply when no labor disputes existed.

We also believe that a person cited for contempt in labor disputes, except when such contempt was committed in the actual presence of the court or so near thereto as to interfere with the proper administration of justice, should have a right to trial by jury.

DEPARTMENT OF LABOR

We pledge our party to establish a Department of Labor with a seat in the cabinet, and with wide jurisdiction over matters affecting the conditions of labor and living.

COUNTRY LIFE

The development and prosperity of country life are as important to the people who live in the cities as they are to the farmers. Increase of prosperity on the farm will favorably affect the cost of living and promote the interests of all who dwell in the country, and all who depend upon its products for clothing, shelter and food.

We pledge our party to foster the development of agricultural credit and co-operation, the teaching of agriculture in schools, agricultural college extension, the use of mechanical power on the farm, and to re-establish the Country Life Commission, thus directly promoting the welfare of the farmers, and bringing the benefits of better farming, better business and better living within their reach.

HEALTH

We favor the union of all the existing agencies of the federal government dealing with the public health into a single national health service without discrimination against or for any one set of therapeutic methods, school of medicine, or school of healing with such additional powers as may be necessary to enable it to perform efficiently such duties in the protection of the public from preventable diseases as may be properly undertaken by the federal authorities; including the executing of existing laws regarding pure food; quarantine and cognate subjects; the promotion of appropriate action for the improvement of vital statistics and the extension of the registration area of such statistics, and co-operation with the health activities of the various states and cities of the nation.

PATENTS

We pledge ourselves to the enactment of a patent law which will make it impossible for patents to be suppressed or used against the public welfare in the interests of injurious monopolies.

INTERSTATE COMMERCE COMMISSION

We pledge our party to secure to the Interstate Commerce Commission the power to value the physical property of railroads. In order that the power of the commission to protect the people may not be impaired or destroyed, we demand the abolition of the Commerce Court.

GOOD ROADS

We recognize the vital importance of good roads and we pledge our party to foster their extension in every proper way, and we favor the early construction of national highways. We also favor the extension of the rural free delivery service.

INHERITANCE AND INCOME TAX

We believe in a graduated inheritance tax as a national means of equalizing the obligations of holders of property to government, and we hereby pledge our party to enact such a federal law as will tax large inheritances, returning to the states an equitable percentage of all amounts collected.

We favor the ratification of the pending amendment to the constitution giving the government power to levy an income tax.

PEACE AND NATIONAL DEFENSE

The Progressive party deplores the survival in our civilization of the barbaric system of warfare among nations with its enormous waste of resources even in time of peace, and the consequent impoverishment of the life of the toiling masses. We pledge the party to use its best endeavors to substitute judicial and other peaceful means of settling international differences.

We favor an international agreement for the limitation of naval forces. Pending such an agreement, and as the best means of preserving peace, we pledge ourselves to maintain for the present the policy of building two battleships a year.

TREATY RIGHTS

We pledge our party to protect the rights of American citizenship at home and abroad. No treaty should receive the sanction of our government which discriminates between American citizens because of birthplace, race, or religion, or that does not recognize the absolute right of expatriation.

THE IMMIGRANT

Through the establishment of industrial standards we propose to secure to the able-bodied immigrant and to his native fellow workers a larger share of American opportunity.

We denounce the fatal policy of indifference and neglect which has left our enormous immigrant population to become the prey of chance and cupidity.

We favor governmental action to encourage the distribution of immigrants away from the congested cities, to rigidly supervise all private agencies dealing with them and to promote their assimilation, education and advancement.

PENSIONS

We pledge ourselves to a wise and just policy of pensioning American soldiers and sailors and their widows and children by the federal government. And we approve the policy of the southern states in granting pensions to the ex-Confederate soldiers and sailors and their widows and children.

PARCELS POST

We pledge our party to the immediate creation of a parcels post, with rates proportionate to distance and service.

CIVIL SERVICE

We condemn the violations of the civil service law under the present administration, including the coercion and assessment of subordinate employees, and the President's refusal to punish such violation after a finding of guilty by his own commission; his distribution of patronage among subservient congressmen, while withholding it from those who refuse support of administration measures; his withdrawal of nominations from the Senate until political support for himself was secured, and his open use of the offices to reward those who voted for his renomination.

To eradicate these abuses, we demand not only the enforcement of the civil service act in letter and spirit, but also legislation which will bring under the competitive system postmasters, collectors, marshals and all other non-political officers, as well as the enactment of an equitable retirement law, and we also insist upon continuous service during good behavior and efficiency.

GOVERNMENT BUSINESS ORGANIZATION

We pledge our party to readjustment of the business methods of the national government and a proper co-ordination of the federal bureaus, which will increase the economy and efficiency of the government service, prevent duplications and secure better results to the taxpayers for every dollar expended.

Government Supervision Over Investments

The people of the United States are swindled out of many millions of dollars every year, through worthless investments. The plain people, the wage-earner and the men and women with small savings, have no way of knowing the merit of concerns sending out highly colored prospectuses offering stock for sale, prospectuses that make big returns seem certain and fortunes easily within grasp.

We hold it to be the duty of the government to protect its people from this kind of piracy. We, therefore, demand wise, carefully thought out legislation that will give us such governmental supervision over this matter as will furnish to the people of the United States this much-needed protection, and we pledge ourselves thereto.

Conclusion

On these principles and on the recognized desirability of uniting the Progressive forces of the nation into an organization which shall unequivocally represent the Progressive spirit and policy we appeal for the support of all American citizens, without regard to previous political affiliations.

Speech on Constitutionality of an Income Tax, *William Howard Taft*, 1909

U.S. Constitution, Sixteenth Amendment, 1913

Congress enacted the first federal income tax in 1861, as a means of securing funding for the Civil War. That tax was repealed ten years later. In 1894 Congress enacted a new income tax. But this tax was ruled unconstitutional by the Supreme Court because it taxed people directly, without the amount collected being apportioned according to the population of each state. As with many issues, President William Howard Taft sought a moderate position, arguing for the income tax's constitutionality, but eschewing more radical calls for a tax that would seek to combat the concentration of wealth by imposing increasingly higher rates as incomes increased. Principled opposition to the income tax soon dissipated. By the end of 1913 Congress had passed the first tax on individual incomes, imposing a rate of 1 percent on incomes over $3,000 per year ($4,000 for married couples) with a surtax ranging from 1 to 6 percent on higher incomes.

Speech on Constitutionality of an Income Tax

June 16, 1909

William Howard Taft

To the Senate and House of Representatives:

It is the constitutional duty of the President from time to time to recommend to the consideration of Congress such measures as he shall judge necessary and expedient. In my inaugural address, immediately preceding this present extraordinary session of Congress, I invited attention to the necessity for a revision of the tariff at this session, and stated the principles upon which I thought the revision should be effected. I referred to the then rapidly increasing deficit and pointed out the obligation on the part of the framers of the tariff bill to arrange the duty so as to secure an adequate income, and suggested that if it was not possible to do so by import duties, new kinds of taxation must be adopted, and among them I recommended a graduated inheritance tax as correct in principle and as certain and easy of collection. The House of Representatives has adopted the suggestion, and has provided in the bill it passed for the collection of such a tax. In the Senate the action of its Finance Committee and the course of the debate indicate that it may not agree to this provision, and it is now proposed to make up the deficit by the imposition of a general income tax, in form and substance of almost exactly the same character as that which in the case of Pollock *v.* Farmers' Loan and Trust Company (157 U.S., 429) was held by the Supreme Court to be a direct tax, and therefore not within the power of the Federal Government to impose unless apportioned among the several States according to population. This new proposal, which I did not discuss in my inaugural address or in my message at the opening of the present session, makes it appropriate for me to submit to the Congress certain additional recommendations.

The decision of the Supreme Court in the income-tax cases deprived the National Government of a power which, by reason of previous decisions of the court, it was generally supposed that Government had. It is undoubtedly a power the National Government ought to have. It might be indispensable to the Nation's life in great crises. Although I have not considered a constitutional amendment as necessary to the exercise of certain phases of this power, a mature consideration has satisfied me that an amendment is the only proper course for its establishment to its full extent. I therefore recommend to the Congress that both Houses, by a two-thirds vote, shall propose an amendment to the Constitution conferring the power to levy an income tax upon the National Government without apportionment among the States in proportion to population.

This course is much to be preferred to the one proposed of reenacting a law once judicially declared to be unconstitutional. For the Congress to assume that the court will reverse itself, and to enact legislation on such an assumption, will not strengthen popular confidence in the stability of judicial construction of the Constitution. It is much wiser policy to accept the decision and remedy the defect by amendment in due and regular course.

Again, it is clear that by the enactment of the proposed law the Congress will not be bringing money into the Treasury to meet the present deficiency, but by putting on the statute book a law already there and never repealed will simply be suggesting to the executive officers of the Government their possible duty to invoke litigation. If the court should maintain its former view, no tax would be collected at all. If it should ultimately reverse itself, still no taxes would have been collected until after protracted delay.

It is said the difficulty and delay in securing the approval of three-fourths of the States will destroy all chance of adopting the amendment. Of course, no one can speak with certainty upon this point, but I have become convinced that a great majority of the people of this country are in favor of vesting the National Government with power to levy an income tax, and that they will secure the adoption of the amendment in the States, if proposed to them.

Second, the decision in the Pollock case left power in the National Government to levy an excise tax, which accomplishes the same purpose as a corporation income tax and is free from certain objections urged to the proposed income-tax measure.

I therefore recommend an amendment to the tariff bill imposing upon all corporations and joint stock companies for profit, except national banks (otherwise taxed), savings banks, and building and loan associations, an excise tax measured by 2 per cent on the net income of such corporations. This is an excise tax upon the privilege of doing business as an artificial entity and of freedom from a general partnership liability enjoyed by those who own the stock.

I am informed that a 2 per cent tax of this character would bring into the Treasury of the United States not less than $25,000,000.

The decision of the Supreme Court in the case of Spreckels Sugar Refining Company against McClain (192 U.S., 397) seems clearly to establish the principle that such a tax as this is an excise tax upon privilege and not a direct tax on property, and is within the federal power without apportionment according to population. The tax on net income is preferable to one proportionate to a percentage of the gross receipts, because it is a tax upon success and not failure. It imposes a burden at the source of the income at a time when the corporation is well able to pay and when collection is easy.

Another merit of this tax is the federal supervision which must be exercised in order to make the law effective over the annual accounts and business transactions of all corporations. While the faculty of assuming a corporate form has been of the utmost utility in the business world, it is also true that substantially all of the abuses and all of the evils which have aroused the public to the necessity of reform were made possible by the use of this very faculty. If now, by a perfectly legitimate and effective system of taxation, we are incidentally able to possess the Government and the stockholders and the public of the knowledge of the real business transactions and the gains and profits of every corporation in the country, we have made a long step toward that supervisory control of corporations which may prevent a further abuse of power.

I recommend, then, first, the adoption of a joint resolution by two-thirds of both Houses, proposing to the States an amendment to the Constitution granting to the Federal Government the right to levy and collect an income tax without apportionment among the States according to population; and, second, the enactment, as part of the pending revenue measure, either as a substitute for, or in addition to, the inheritance tax, of an excise tax upon all corporations, measured by 2 per cent of their net income.

WM. H. TAFT.

THE WHITE HOUSE, *June 16, 1909.*

U.S. Constitution, Sixteenth Amendment

February 3, 1913

The Congress shall have power to lay and collect taxes on incomes, from whatever source derived, without apportionment among the several States, and without regard to any census or enumeration.

Resolution Opposing Direct Election of Senators, 1893

U.S. Constitution, Seventeenth Amendment, 1913

The American Constitution originally required that U.S. senators be appointed by their state legislatures. This provision was intended to protect the rights of states and the independence of senators from electoral pressures. Beginning in the 1850s there were a number of instances of legislative deadlock resulting in vacant Senate seats, as well as a number of bribery scandals related to the choosing of senators. While proposals for direct election had been made as early as 1826, they made little headway until the late nineteenth century, and resistance among senators remained especially fierce. In 1893 the House of Representatives passed a resolution favoring direct election of senators. Senator George Hoar of Massachusetts successfully led opposition to the resolution. After federal reforms failed, states began enacting laws providing for increasing participation of the general public in the election of senators, as well as petitioning Congress for reform. Over time the focus of resistance shifted from direct election itself to the question of whether the federal government should be allowed to control the means of senators' selection; Southern senators in particular protested the possibility of federal troops at the polls enforcing federal regulations. A version of the amendment was passed by the Senate in April 1912 and sent to the states for ratification, which was achieved the next year, with Delaware and Utah the only states refusing to ratify.

Resolution Opposing Direct Election of Senators

IN THE SENATE OF THE UNITED STATES

April 3, 1893.—Laid on the table and ordered to be printed.

Mr. Hoar submitted the following
RESOLUTION:

Resolved, That it is inexpedient that the resolution sent to the Senate by the House of Representatives during the last Congress providing for an amendment of the Constitution securing the election of Senators by the people of the several States be adopted;

Such a method of election would essentially change the character of the Senate as conceived by the convention that framed the Constitution and the people who adopted it;

It would transfer, practically, the selection of the members of this body from the legislatures, who are intrusted with all legislative powers of the States, to bodies having no other responsibilities, whose election can not be regulated by law, whose members act by proxy, whose tenure of office is for a single day, whose votes and proceedings are not recorded, who act under no personal responsibility, whose mistakes, ordinarily, can only be corrected by the choice of Senators who do not represent the opinions concerning public measures and policies of the people who choose them;

It requires the substitution of pluralities for majorities in the election;

It will transfer the seat of political power in great States, now distributed evenly over their territory, to the great cities and masses of population;

It will create new temptation to fraud, corruption, and

other illegal practices, and, in close cases, will give rise to numerous election contests, which must tend seriously to weaken the confidence of the people in the Senate;

It will absolve the larger States from the constitutional obligation which secures the equal representation of all the States in the Senate by providing that no State shall be deprived of that equality without its consent;

It implies what the whole current of our history shows to be untrue, that the Senate has during the past century failed to meet the just expectations of the people, and that the State legislatures have proved themselves unfit to be the depositaries of the power of electing Senators;

The reasons which require this change, if acted upon and carried to their logical result, will lead to the election by the direct popular vote, and by popular majorities, of the President and of the Judiciary, and will compel the placing of these elections under complete national control;

It will result in the overthrow of the whole scheme of the Senate and, in the end, of the whole scheme of the National Constitution as designed and established by the framers of the Constitution and the people who adopted it.

U.S. Constitution, Seventeenth Amendment

May 31, 1913

The Senate of the United States shall be composed of two Senators from each State, elected by the people thereof, for six years; and each Senator shall have one vote. The electors in each State shall have the qualifications requisite for electors of the most numerous branch of the State legislatures.

When vacancies happen in the representation of any State in the Senate, the executive authority of such State shall issue writs of election to fill such vacancies: *Provided,* That the legislature of any State may empower the executive thereof to make temporary appointments until the people fill the vacancies by election as the legislature may direct.

This amendment shall not be so construed as to affect the election or term of any Senator chosen before it becomes valid as part of the Constitution.

Address to Woman's State Temperance Society, *Elizabeth Cady Stanton*, 1853

Prohibition Debate, 1917

U.S. Constitution, Eighteenth Amendment, 1919

U.S. Constitution, Twenty-first Amendment, 1933

The demand for alcohol on the frontier, where there was little by way of law or material comforts, conflicted with the self-denying Calvinist roots of American religious life. Temperance societies, committed to the closing of saloons and the outlawing of strong drink, were powerful by early in the nineteenth century. Elizabeth Cady Stanton (1815–1902) was for decades a leader in the women's temperance movement, as well as in movements for women's rights and the abolition of slavery. Stanton, who worked closely with the suffragist Susan B. Anthony for decades, consistently argued that social and political progress required temperance and that the banning of alcoholic beverages would reduce crime, poverty, and the costs of government. Opponents of prohibition had been painted as enemies of progress, and their statements tended to question the wisdom, not of prohibition itself, but rather of the placement of prohibition in a federal constitutional amendment. States' rights arguments failed, and the Eighteenth Amendment was ratified. Within a few years, however, even former supporters were calling for the repeal of prohibition on the grounds that the "noble experiment" had not yielded the desired results—indeed, had produced increased crime, poverty, and government expense. It should be noted that repeal of the Eighteenth Amendment merely undid the national policy of prohibition, leaving the states to decide what policy to take in regard to alcoholic beverages.

First Annual Meeting of the Woman's State Temperance Society

Rochester, June 1 and 2, 1853

Elizabeth Cady Stanton

MRS. STANTON'S ADDRESS

A little more than one year ago, in this same hall, we formed the first Woman's State Temperance Society. We believed that the time had come for woman to speak on this question, and to insist on her right to be heard in the councils of Church and State. It was proposed at that time that we, instead of forming a society, should go *en masse* into the Men's State Temperance Society. We were assured that in becoming members by paying the sum of $1, we should thereby secure the right to speak and vote in their meetings.

We who had watched the jealousy with which man had ever eyed the slow aggressions of woman, warned you against the insidious proposition made by agents from that Society. We told you they would no doubt gladly receive the dollar, but that you would never be allowed to speak or vote in their meetings. Many of you thought us suspicious and unjust toward the temperance men of the Empire State. The fact that Abby Kelly had been permitted to speak in one of their public meetings, was brought up as an argument by some agent of that Society to prove our fears unfounded. We suggested that she spoke by favor and not right, and our right there as equals to speak and vote, we well knew would never be acknowledged. A long debate saved you from that false step, and our predictions have been fully realized in the treatment our delegates received at the annual meeting held at Syracuse last July, and at the recent Brick Church meeting in New York.

In forming our Society, the mass of us being radical and liberal, we left our platform free; we are no respecters of persons, all are alike welcome here without regard to sect, sex, color, or caste. There have been, however, many objections made to one feature in our Constitution, and that is, that although we admit men as members with equal right to speak in our meetings, we claim the offices for women alone. We felt, in starting, the necessity of throwing all the responsibility on woman, which we knew she never would take, if there were any men at hand to think, act, and plan for her. The result has shown the wisdom of what seemed so objectionable to many. It was, however, a temporary expedient, and as that seeming violation of man's rights prevents some true friends of the cause from becoming members of our Society, and as the officers are now well skilled in the practical business of getting up meetings, raising funds, etc., and have fairly learned how to stand and walk alone, it may perhaps be safe to raise man to an entire equality with ourselves, hoping, however, that he will modestly permit the women to continue the work they have so successfully begun. I would suggest, therefore, that after the business of the past year be disposed of, this objectionable feature of our Constitution be brought under consideration.

Our experience thus far as a Society has been most encouraging. We number over two thousand members. We have four agents who have traveled in various parts of the State, and I need not say what is well known to all present, that their labors thus far have given entire satisfaction to the Society and the public. I was surprised and rejoiced to find that women, without the least preparation or experience, who had never raised their voices in public one year ago, should with so much self-reliance, dignity, and force, enter at once such a field of labor, and so ably perform the work. In the metropolis of our country, in the capital of our State, before our Legislature, and in the country school-house, they have been alike earnest and faithful to the truth. In behalf of our Society, I thank you for your unwearied labors during the past year. In the name of humanity, I bid you go on and devote yourselves humbly to the cause you have espoused. The noble of your sex everywhere rejoice in your success, and feel in themselves a new impulse to struggle upward and onward; and the deep, though silent gratitude that ascends to Heaven from the wretched outcast, the wives, the mothers, and the daughters of brutal drunkards, is well known to all who have listened to their tales of woe, their bitter experience, the dark, sad passages of their tragic lives.

I hope this, our first year, is prophetic of a happy future of strong, united, and energetic action among the women of our State. If we are sincere and earnest in our love of this cause, in our devotion to truth, in our desire for the happiness of the race, we shall ever lose sight of self; each soul will, in a measure, forget its own individual interests in proclaiming great principles of justice and right. It is only a true, a deep, and abiding love of truth, that can swallow up all petty jealousies, envies, discords, and dissensions, and make us truly magnanimous and self-sacrificing. We have every reason to think, from reports we hear on all sides, that our Society has given this cause a new impulse, and if the condition of our treasury is a test, we have abundant reason to believe that in the hearts of the people we are approved, and that by their purses we shall be sustained.

It has been objected to our Society that we do not confine ourselves to the subject of temperance, but talk too much about woman's rights, divorce, and the Church. It could be easily shown how the consideration of this great question carries us legitimately into the discussion of these various subjects. One class of minds would deal with effects alone; another would inquire into causes; the work of the former is easily perceived and quickly done; that of the latter requires deep thought, great patience, much time, and a wise self-denial. Our physicians of the present day are a good type of the mass of our reformers. They take out cancers, cut off tonsils, drive the poison which nature has wisely thrown to the surface, back again, quiet unsteady nerves with valerian, and by means of ether infuse an artificial courage into a patient that he may bravely endure some painful operation. It requires but little thought to feel that the wise physician who shall trace out the true causes of suffering; who shall teach us the great, immutable laws of life and health; who shall show us how and where in our every-day life, we are violating these laws, and the true point to begin the reform, is doing a much higher, broader, and deeper work than he who shall bend all his energies to the temporary relief of suffering. Those temperance men or women whose whole work consists in denouncing rum-sellers, appealing to legislatures, eulogizing Neal Dow, and shouting Maine Law, are superficial reformers, mere surface-workers. True, this outside work is well, and must be done; let those who see no other do this, but let them lay no hindrances in the way of that class of mind, who, seeing in our present false social relations the causes of the moral deformities of the race, would fain declare the immutable laws that govern mind as well as matter, and point out the true causes of the evils we see about us, whether lurking under the shadow of the altar, the sacredness of the marriage institution, or the assumed superiority of man.

1. We have been obliged to preach woman's rights, because many, instead of listening to what we had to say on temperance, have questioned the right of a woman to speak on any subject. In courts of justice and legislative assemblies, if the right of the speaker to be there is questioned, all business waits until that point is settled. Now, it is not settled in the mass of minds that woman has any rights on this footstool, and much less a right to stand on an even pedestal with man, look him in the face as an equal, and rebuke the sins of her day and generation. Let it be clearly understood, then, that we are a woman's rights Society; that we believe it is woman's duty to speak whenever she feels the impression to do so; that it is her right to be present in all the councils of Church and State. The fact that our agents are women, settles the question of our character on this point.

Again, in discussing the question of temperance, all lecturers, from the beginning, have made mention of the drunkards' wives and children, of widows' groans and orphans' tears; shall these classes of sufferers be introduced but as themes for rhetorical flourish, as pathetic touches of the speaker's eloquence; shall we passively shed tears over their condition, or by giving them their rights, bravely open to them the doors of escape from a wretched and degraded life? Is it not legitimate in this to discuss the social degradation, the legal disabilities of the drunkard's wife? If in showing her wrongs, we prove the right of all womankind to the elective franchise; to a fair representation in the government; to the right in criminal cases to be tried by peers of her own choosing, shall it be said that we transcend the bounds of our subject? If in pointing out her social degradation, we show you how the present laws outrage the sacredness of the marriage institution; if in proving to you that justice and mercy demand a legal separation from drunkards, we grasp the higher idea that a unity of soul alone constitutes and sanctifies true marriage, and that any law or public sentiment that forces two immortal, high-born souls to live together as husband and wife, unless held there by love, is false to God and humanity; who shall say that the discussion of this question does not lead us legitimately into the consideration of the important subject of divorce?

But why attack the Church? We do not attack the Church; we defend ourselves merely against its attacks. It is true that the Church and reformers have always been in an antagonistic position from the time of Luther down to our own day, and will continue to be until the devotional and practical types of Christianity shall be united in one harmonious whole. To those who see the philosophy of this position, there seems to be no cause for fearful forebodings or helpless regret. By the light of reason and truth, in good time, all these seeming differences will pass away. I have no special fault to find with that part of humanity that gathers into our churches; to me, human nature seems to manifest itself in very much the same way in the Church and out of it. Go through any community you please—into the nursery, kitchen, the parlor, the places of merchandise, the market-place, and exchange, and who can tell the church member from the outsider? I see no reason why we should expect more of them than other men. Why, say you, they lay claim to greater holiness; to more rigid creeds; to a belief in a sterner God; to a closer observance of forms. The Bible, with them, is the rule of life, the foundation of faith, and why should we not look to them for patterns of purity, goodness, and truth above all other men? I deny the assumption. Reformers on all sides claim for themselves a higher position than the Church. Our God is a God of justice, mercy, and truth. Their God sanctions violence, oppression, and wine-bibbing, and winks at gross moral delinquencies. Our Bible commands us to love our enemies; to resist not evil; to break every yoke and let the oppressed go free; and makes a noble life of more importance than a stern faith. Their Bible permits war, slavery, capital punishment, and makes salvation depend on faith and ordinances. In their creed it is a sin to dance, to pick up sticks on the Sabbath day, to go to the theater, or large parties during Lent, to read a notice of any reform meeting from the altar, or permit a woman to speak in the church. In our creed it is a sin to hold a slave; to hang a man on the gallows; to make war on defenseless nations, or to sell rum to a weak brother, and rob the widow and the orphan of a protector and a home. Thus may we write out some of our differences, but from the similarity in the conduct of the human family, it is fair to infer that our differences are more intellectual than spiritual, and the great truths we hear so clearly uttered on all sides, have been incorporated as vital principles into the inner life of but few indeed.

We must not expect the Church to leap *en masse* to a higher position. She sends forth her missionaries of truth one by one. All of our reformers have, in a measure, been developed in the Church, and all our reforms have started there.

The advocates and opposers of the reforms of our day, have grown up side by side, partaking of the same ordinances and officiating at the same altars; but one, by applying more fully his Christian principles to life, and pursuing an admitted truth to its legitimate results, has unwittingly found himself in antagonism with his brother.

Belief is not voluntary, and change is the natural result of growth and development. We would fain have all church members sons and daughters of temperance; but if the Church, in her wisdom, has made her platform so broad that wine-bibbers and rum-sellers may repose in ease thereon, we who are always preaching liberality ought to be the last to complain. Having thus briefly noticed some of the objections to our movement, I will not detain the audience longer at this time.

PETERBORO, *May 7,* 1853.

Prohibition Debate

Mr. Webb.

Mr. Speaker, government is but the organized forces of the union formed for strengthening its power and advancing its life. Its highest aim is to suppress those agencies which have a tendency to sap and weaken the nation's strength, to suppress vice and crime in order that the nation may, unrestrained by these evils, go forward in its efforts for greater liberty, freedom, and achievement; that it may raise itself into a higher civilization more nearly approaching our ideal of a perfect government.

The use of intoxicating liquors for beverage purposes has long attracted the attention of our leading statesmen, and with great unanimity has been condemned as one of the greatest agencies for evil and crime that is now retarding our national growth.

The right to make and use intoxicating beverages has so long been enjoyed, and this right so long licensed and sanctioned by Federal taxing laws, that the ignorant have come to the conclusion that it is one of the inalienable rights of man which the Government should not interfere with. Those with broader mental horizons insist that the long-continued toleration of this evil has given those who claim it a vested right to carry on their business or enjoy their beverage; a kind of immunity from any interference by the Government to aid humanity. The one is as fallacious as the other. Either would deprive the Government of one of its chief reasons to exist.

The resolution now under consideration would submit to the States of the Union the one question, whether the Federal Government shall prohibit "the manufacture, sale, or transportation of intoxicating liquors within, the importation thereof into, or the exportation thereof from the United States and all territory subject to the jurisdiction thereof for beverage purposes."

The submission and ratification of the proposed amendment by the required number of States would be no invasion of States' rights. It would be but the orderly and legal granting of this power to the Federal Government by the legislatures of the several States in the way the sovereign people of the States have provided for amending their constitution.

The people of the United States, when they ordained and established the Constitution for the United States of America, stating in the preamble that it was "to promote the general welfare" and other objects, realized that in order to accomplish their aims it would become necessary to add to the powers granted, from time to time, as the nation grew in wealth and population, and as the Government from necessity became more complex, that unforeseen conditions and problems would arise and require solution.

In order to meet such conditions and problems the framers of the Constitution wisely provided in Article V:

That Congress, whenever two-thirds of both Houses shall deem it necessary, shall propose amendments to this Constitution . . . which . . . shall be valid to all intents and purposes as part of this Constitution, when ratified by the legislatures of three-fourths of the several States.

The adoption of the amendment here proposed would not be a move to tear down or weaken this ancient landmark, but would be in keeping with the plan of its framers to add to it a power for "the general welfare" of the people.

If we should hold it too sacred to be changed, we make of it a dead monument to its fathers. Like the "Old Ironsides" that now floats in Boston Harbor, it would still be revered for the splendid service it has performed, but it would not be equipped to meet the modern problems.

If we give it a liberal construction which will afford a reasonable opportunity to amend it as provided for in the fifth article, then like the trees of the forest which add new cells to their structure each recurring season to perpetuate their life and strength, you will make of the Constitution a viral power adapted to this and succeeding generations.

Senator Blair, in a favorable report made to the Senate

on a similar resolution in 1888, is authority for the statement that:

It is well known that but for the belief in the conventions of the States that the opportunity to amend the Constitution would be most liberally afforded by Congress in accordance with the forms provided in that instrument, the original ratification never would have been obtained.

The question of the expediency of passing this resolution is primarily addressed to the Members of Congress. It is only after it has been favorably acted upon by Congress that it is passed out to the States for their ratification.

In passing upon this question I think Congress should view it from two angles: First, whether there is such a public sentiment back of it as to justify Congress in submitting it to the States; and, second, whether we, in our wisdom, approve this grant of power.

I do not believe it is the duty of Congress to submit every proposition that might be offered to the States for their ratification. Aside from the merits which the proposition might possess, such a course, would result in a continuous agitation in the States which could not be justified by Congress.

On the other hand, any great question vitally affecting the life of the people that the wisdom of Congress might approve which has found sufficient public favor to lead Congress to believe might be adopted by the requisite number of States should be submitted in order that the sovereign people might pass upon it.

Senator Blair, in 1880, in favorably reporting to the Senate a resolution to amend the Constitution and provide for national prohibition, similar to the one under consideration, says:

When any considerable and respectable portion of the American people desire to plead their cause in the great tribunal of sovereigns, who, in a free country, decide every fundamental issue [in the last] (sic) resort, it is the duty of Congress to enact such preliminary legislation as is here proposed, so that under the forms of the Constitution they can be heard on the question of its own amendment. To deny this is of the very essence of despotism, and for Congress unreasonably to refuse the hearing is just cause of revolution. The people will demand a hearing for every large and respectable minority, and to grant this opportunity is the purpose of this resolution. Whatever may be the

result, all must abide by it. But there can be no justification of a denial of the right to be heard.

In 1800 Senator Blair, in making a favorable report to the Senate upon a similar resolution, sums up the duty of Congress as he sees it in the following extract from his report:

It being the fact that a very large proportion of the American people are anxious that the National Constitution be amended in accordance with the resolution, we believe that they have a right to be heard in the forum of the State legislatures, where alone the question can be decided whether the National Constitution shall be amended. That Constitution points out definitely the manner in which a change in its provisions may be effected. The Constitution of the country must be amended from time to time to correspond with the evolution of the Nation itself, for it is impossible to fetter the growth of the Nation in any direction. It will grow, peacefully or otherwise. The Constitution must yield here and there, corresponding to the necessities of the times and of the people, and the necessary changes be peacefully made, in accordance with the methods of amendment pointed out in the Constitution itself, or revolution and bloodshed will perform their work. The Constitution and the spirit of the age must be one. Whenever any considerable and respectable portion of the American people (and no considerable number can fail to be respectable) desire change in the fundamental law and ask respectful consideration of their propositions by the Nation at large, we hold it to be the duty of Congress to give them a status in the court provided by the Constitution for its own amendment.

I do not think this Congress can fail to find, beyond question, that this proposition is backed by a public sentiment of such strength and character as to not only justify, but require us to submit it to the States for ratification.

This movement is not of a temporary, spasmodic character, which may pass away with the summer, but has received the careful thought and approval of the moral and commercial forces of the Nation.

This and preceding Congresses have been overwhelmed by letters and petitions asking and pleading with Congress to submit this question to the States. These requests come from our highest type of law-abiding Christian men and women, who have their country's welfare closest to their hearts.

As further proof of the strength of this sentiment, it is not improper for me to call attention to the fact that during this Congress the Senate, on the 1st day of August, by a vote of 65 to 20, passed this resolution.

In 1907 only Kansas, North Dakota, and Maine had prohibition laws. Up to September 1, 1914, six additional States had been added. To-day we have legislative prohibition in 27 States of the Union, comprising a population of 61,000,000. Of the [2,597] counties in the United States, 2,238 are dry and only 355 counties in the entire Nation are wet. Over half of the world to-day is dry territory.

In my opinion the time has come when Congress can not fail to recognize the overwhelming demands that are being made from every section of this Nation and from all classes of her people to submit this proposition to the States for their ratification. The aim of the prohibition advocates is that the leaven that has been at work and brought good to the local districts, townships, counties, and finally States, may be permitted to leaven the whole Nation. With such an overwhelming sentiment, making new conquests at each new encounter, is it not reasonable to suppose that this sentiment would be reflected in the action which the several legislatures would take, and that this amendment would be ratified by them?

I appeal to the Members of this House to follow the lead of the Senate and give this proposed amendment your hearty approval as a wise and beneficial policy for this Government to pursue.

The use of alcoholic liquors for beverage purposes has long been regarded as a great national evil, which physically, mentally, and morally unfits man for his greatest usefulness.

The fact has been established by carefully compiled statistics that intemperate use of alcoholic beverages by parents weakens the vitality of their offspring, increases their death rate, increases the number of feeble-minded and defective children, and renders them more susceptible and less able to resist disease.

Alcoholic beverages impair the skill, lessen the power of endurance, increase accidents, and shorten the life of those addicted to its use. Alcoholism claims more victims than does either typhoid fever or smallpox. Drink is one cause of over 66,000 deaths every year in the United States. One insane person out of every four owes his affliction to its use, and it is given credit for breaking up over 9,000 happy homes each year.

The religious world has found it undermines the morals of the Nation. The business world has found that it weakens the intellect and has set the stamp of disapproval upon the use of such beverage by men it employs. The courts of the country find it the cause of crime, and justify this conclusion by the records of their criminal courts.

Such being its established reputation, it is not surprising to find the moral and religious forces of the Nation up in arms against it and trying to crush it by whatever means they have.

Is it not time for us to become aroused to the necessity of using the strong arm of the National Government to help suppress this great source of national weakness? This Government can be no stronger than the combined strength and vitality of the people. The Government can not serve its people better than by helping to preserve its people's strength and life.

It would be hard to understand why a National Government that has, with a lavish hand, reached out into the domain of the State and for the sake of protecting property smote down upon the cattle tick and the boll weevil and stopped the ravages of the foot-and-mouth disease, or that strained its power to regulate the commerce from the great manufacturing industries of the Nation in order to cure a practice that might weaken the vitality of the people, would then hesitate to lend its helping hand to meet and blot out the greatest agency for the destruction of property, life, and morals known to man.

The problem of suppressing the use of alcohol as a beverage is bigger than a county or a State. It is a national problem. Local regulations have been of great help in curbing the evil but they are not adequate. It has been demonstrated by an honest effort to regulate the traffic that one wet county in a State will inflict this evil upon the rest of the State. The same is true of a wet State in relation to the other States of the Union. You can not, by regulations, localize the bad effects that flow from this national evil.

Aside from the great difficulty in preventing the transportation of alcoholic beverages from a place where they can be legally made and sold into the dry territory, there would be no local boundary line to stop the degenerates, inebriates, weak-minded criminals, and diseased persons whom it had produced, and keep them within the political division of the country that had permitted the manufacture and sale of the poison that had caused their sad condition. These would travel faster and with less restraint than the cattle tick, the boll weevil, or the cattle disease, and would become a menace to the health and morals of, and perhaps a public charge upon, some community that maybe had pleaded for an opportunity to help blot out these sore spots in our body politic.

Those engaged in fighting this great national evil think that this Government should cease to be a partner of the liquor manufacturer and seller by licensing such business in return for the tax which such a policy is made to pay. It is estimated that for every dollar collected by the Government in the shape of a tax $20 is paid into the pockets of the men carrying on this business by the poor, diseased slaves of drink. The Government can not afford to pursue this policy for the sake of the revenue it derives, when by doing so it puts it within the power of the liquor interests to collect for their own pockets many times this tax, and often from those who deprive their families of comforts and necessities to pay it. There is no way to accurately estimate the cost to the Government of accidents, crimes, and diseases caused by the traffic, but it must be appalling, and if it could be accurately stated in figures, I feel safe in predicting that no man, in opposition to this resolution would ever have the temerity to speak or vote against its adoption on account of the incidental loss of taxes that might result from its ratification by the States.

Other solutions have been attempted to solve this liquor problem, but with only partial success. Opponents of the prohibition cause tell us our fight is all wrong; that it is a moral issue and we should appeal to the individual to restrain himself.

This disease of alcoholism is of stealthy character. It stimulates its victim into hilarity while it creeps upon him and binds him as its slave before he feels its grasp, even while the poor victim still boasts of his strength and power to resist it. They are to be pitied, for they need help to free themselves from its bondage. These victims should be able to look to their Government for protection against so dangerous an enemy.

We have already tried moral suasion. Godly men for all these years have preached temperance to the people and have saved many a poor soul from a drunkard's grave, but they still find that their weaker wards stumble on their journey through life and succumb to this frailty of humanity when faced by the alluring invitation of an open bar room, licensed, protected, and taxed, if not encouraged, by this Government of ours. Since we have not been successful in keeping our weaker brother from whisky, let us try keeping whisky from our weaker brother.

Here is a note I have just received from Miss Gordon:

CONGRESSMAN WEBB: It is an honor to present to you, and through you, to the House of Representatives, the appeal of 500,000 members of the Woman's Christian Temperance Union, praying for the passage of the joint resolution providing for a referendum to the States on national constitutional prohibition. This appeal comes from a host of home-loving women who with untiring energy and unstinted devotion have wrought marvelously for the moral and spiritual advancement of our country. This appeal comes from half a million patriots who answered promptly the call to the colors. The nobility of woman's sacrifice, the fine quality of her patriotic service, her keen discernment in the adjustment of industrial conditions for women and children, her tender ministrations at home and on the battlefield should entitle her to the granting by the Congress of this appeal.

In addition to the petition of women members of the National Woman's Christian Temperance Union, I beg to present a huge petition of the indorsers of the joint resolution for a referendum to the States on national constitutional prohibition secured through the efforts of the Woman's Christian Temperance Union and representing 8,000,000 men and women of our Republic. Adding to these the petitions sent directly to Members of Congress it is safe to say that our appeal is backed by more than 11,000,000 people. If these petitioners could be massed in solid phalanx in our Capital City you would see more than thirty times the population of the District of Columbia. Unquestionably it is an appeal for an act of true democracy, an appeal for a patriotic measure. Autocracy and alcohol must both be overthrown. "Speed up" is the urgent cry echoing back to us from the awful battle fronts of Europe. Speed up on the prohibition legislation is the respectful appeal of the Woman's Christian Temperance Union to the Congress of the United States. We pray that in this crucial time of a stupendous world crisis the House of Representatives will rise to this exalted opportunity and give to the legislatures of the various States the chance to deal with a question so enormously vital to the economic and moral interests of our Republic. When the war is over and a righteous peace has been secured, only the clear brain of a sober Nation can be intrusted with the solution of the mighty problems that will then confront the greatest democracy on earth—the United States of America.

ANNA A. GORDON
President National W.C.T.U.

MR. SMALL. Mr. Speaker, this resolution proposes an amendment to the Federal Constitution which prohibits the manufacture, sale, and transportation of intoxicating liquors, or the importation thereof, into the United States. I am constrained upon my conscience and in the exercise of my best judgment to vote against this proposed amendment. I shall not discuss the merits or demerits of prohibition. The attitude of a citizen or a Member of the House upon that question should not determine his vote upon this resolution. There are those who gravely doubt whether the attempt to enforce throughout the country total abstinence is the best solution. Many believe that the discouragement of the manufacture and use of distilled liquors and the encouragement of the use of light beers and wines would best subserve the interests of genuine temperance and good citizenship. But, as I have just stated, total prohibition, or partial prohibition, is not the issue before us. We are called upon to determine whether we will propose an amendment to the Constitution depriving the States of their present exclusive jurisdiction to regulate and control intoxicating liquors and transfer the same in whole or in part to the Federal Government.

I am opposed to this resolution because it proposes to incorporate into our organic law a proposition which is distinctly legislative. There have been 17 amendments to our Constitution and not one of them invaded the field of legislative action. They all relate to the Bill of Rights or the instruments of government itself, or, in other words, they relate to the form of government or the powers of Congress. If the Constitution is to forbid the manufacture and sale of intoxicating liquors there is no reason why in the future, in response to reformers, it should not forbid the manufacture and consumption of other products which may be deemed deleterious to humanity. The Constitution has been the great charter of our liberties. It describes the powers of our Federal Government and fixes the fine balance between the States and the Central Government. It has been the cohesive bond which has bound together the sovereign States into one indestructible union. We should not mar this great instrument by making it the receptacle of prohibitive or permissive legislation and thus mar this fine structure and bring it into disrepute.

I am opposed to this amendment because it proposes to take away from the States an essential right of local self-government. It proposes to impair the police power of the States. This is concededly true, else this amendment would not be proposed. If Congress had jurisdiction to regulate or prohibit the manufacture and sale of intoxicating liquors it would not be necessary to incorporate this legislative provision into the Constitution. The perpetuity of this Republic is based on the maintenance of the right of local self-government in each of the States of the Union. If the time ever comes when the States are shorn of the right to govern themselves in all local matters and are deprived of the right to exercise their untrammeled police powers in the enforcement of the same we will see the beginning of the end of this Republic. When all government is centralized at Washington there will come local and State disaffection, loyalty to the Central Government will be impaired, and ultimately revolution will stalk abroad throughout the land. It may be said that this invasion of the right of the States constitutes only one instance and that other invasions will not necessarily follow. In a matter of such supreme import even one invasion of local self-government may not be justified, but unfortunately this is only one of a number which are now being pressed by zealous reformers. The first error will make easier subsequent efforts. When we have once weakened the fine balance of powers between the States and the Federal Government we will have endangered the stability of the entire structure.

The Constitution was framed to protect the States in the right of local self-government. It was particularly intended to protect the small States. All the early efforts to amend the Constitution were prohibitions against the Federal Government and in favor of the integrity of the States. In the first 10 amendments which were adopted soon after the original Constitution, their provisions were so basic and fundamental that they have been universally denominated as the "Bill of Rights." So jealous were our fathers that some of the reserved and essential rights of the States might be impaired that in the tenth amendment it was provided that—

The powers not delegated to the United States by the Constitution, nor prohibited by it to the States, are reserved to the States respectively, or to the people.

They thought they had settled for all time any possibility that the right of local self-government reserved to the States should ever be successfully attacked.

This amendment is not necessary to enable any State to control or prohibit the manufacture, sale, consumption, or importation into such State of intoxicating liquors. Each State has the power, to use a familiar expression, to make itself "bone dry." Not only may each State pass laws prohibiting within its borders the manufacture, sale, or consumption of intoxicating liquors in any form, but under the Webb law, as interpreted by the Supreme Court of the United States, it may prevent the importation of any intoxicating liquors into such State. Through its administrative officers and by its own courts each State may literally enforce such laws. The statement may be emphasized that each State now has the exclusive power over intoxicating liquors.

It may be asked, then, What is the necessity of this amendment to the Constitution? Is it to enable one State in combination with others to exercise power over another State? To express it baldly, the purpose of this amendment is to enable the legislature of one State to join with the legislatures of 36 other States and impose absolute prohibition over the remaining 12 unwilling States. If the subject of prohibition is now a matter of local self-government with each State, which will be admitted, then it may be stated with equal force that it was never intended in our scheme of government that three-quarters of the States should take away from the remaining one-quarter any reserved right of local self-government. My own State of North Carolina, which is dry, can not consistently claim the right to join with 36 other States and impose prohibition upon the States of New York or Massachusetts or Wisconsin against the will of the people of those States. Such a result would be resented by the people of those States who are not yet ready to adopt prohibition. Let me give a concrete illustration. In 1881 there was a referendum in North Carolina upon the question of State-wide prohibition. There were cast for Prohibition 48,000 votes and against prohibition 166,000 votes, an adverse majority of 118,000 votes. So long as the majority of the people of North Carolina were opposed to prohibition, I ask in all good faith what impression would have been made on the people of that State if 36 other States in a proposition to amend the Federal Constitution had decreed that North Carolina should be dry, contrary to the solemn vote of the electorate of the State? The question answers itself. There would have followed resentment, and the people of the State would have felt that they had been deprived of a sovereign right to settle this question for themselves. In 1908, 27 years later, North Carolina had another referendum upon prohibition, at which time a majority was recorded in its favor. May I ask if this change in the attitude of the people of the State toward a sumptuary law necessarily changes the fundamental proposition involved? If the people of North Carolina would have resented in 1882 the action of 36 other States in imposing upon them prohibition against

their will, are the people of that State justified in 1917 in trying to impose prohibition upon the people of an unwilling State simply because the people of North Carolina have reversed themselves upon this question? The query answers itself.

It is contended that national prohibition is necessary in the interest of good morals. The leaders of the Anti-Saloon League say that they can not await the slow process of adopting prohibition State by State, and that they prefer the summary method of imposing it upon all of the States without having to undergo the trouble of discussion and education, in order to effect a change of public opinion in each of the States. I submit that the maintenance of the basis and the fundamentals of our Government is superior to the virtues of prohibition, even if we concede all its blessings by the most enthusiastic advocates. I confess that I deem it of more importance to defend the integrity of the States and to assume the perpetuity of our Republic than to anticipate the will of the people and to attempt to force prohibition by this summary process upon unwilling States.

There have been 17 amendments to our Constitution. Each one of these amendments dealt with the fundamentals of government and did not attempt to invade the reserved right of local self-government in the States except the fifteenth amendment. This amendment forbade any State to deny the right of suffrage to any citizen on account of race or color. It was intended to compel the Southern States to give to the negro equal rights of franchise with the whites. I shall not combat the righteous motives which actuated the advocates of that amendment. But I do submit these comments. Until the fifteenth amendment the right of the States to fix and regulate the qualifications of the franchise was not denied. It has always been conceded that the right to vote comes as a privilege from the States and not from the Federal Government. This amendment was an attempt to control this right of the States in so far as the negro was concerned by giving him equality of suffrage. It was contended by the white citizens of the South that the negroes as a whole were not qualified for the suffrage, and that to give literal effect to this amendment would imperil their civilization and make possible bad government. It is unnecessary to describe the results of the amendment. Reconstruction followed in its wake, racial disturbances were frequent, progress was checked, and evil government prevailed. The fifteenth amendment still remains, but by common consent in all sections of the country, the intelligence and the civic virtues of those who are qualified to ordain and preserve good government are left in the several States to settle this matter in the light of their consciences and their responsibilities.

In the face of the result of this attempt to invade the rights of the States to fix the qualifications of suffrage, I am left to inquire, What ought to be the attitude of the Members of this House from the Southern States in the consideration of this proposed amendment? Simply because most of the Southern States have adopted prohibition, shall they favor an amendment which would deprive other States of settling for themselves this question of prohibition? If they vote for this amendment, they will be doing an act which they would openly resent if an attempt was made by other States to invade their rights of local self-government. Very soon this House may be called upon to vote for another amendment to the Federal Constitution for woman suffrage. It so happens that in most of the Southern States public opinion does not yet favor equal suffrage, and they will vote against such an amendment. Why not be consistent? As a great fundamental of government, is the right of local self-government upon any one question to be determined by the attitude of the voters of a particular State upon that question?

The very fact that an amendment proposed by Congress is to be ratified by the legislatures of the several States rather than by the popular vote throughout the country indicates the firm attitude of the fathers in preserving the rights of the small States against the encroachments of the large States. It never occurred to the framers of the Constitution that Delaware and Rhode Island, or Nevada, would join in depriving the people of the State of New York of any essential and reserved right of local self-government. The fear was that New York and Pennsylvania and Virginia might unite with other large States and deprive Delaware and Rhode Island of some essential local power. Therefore, they provided in the ratification of an amendment that the vote of Delaware and of Rhode Island should count just as much as the vote of New York and Pennsylvania.

What is the duty of a Member of this House? A high official of the Anti-Saloon League recently made this statement:

The Anti-Saloon League is not asking any Member of Congress to declare that he is in favor of national prohibition, but simply that he shall not become an avowed exponent and protector of the liquor traffic by refusing to vote to allow the people of the Nation, by States, through their

representatives, to determine this question in the manner provided therefor by the framers of the Constitution.

This has been a familiar form of expression by some of the advocates of this amendment. In other words, they contend it is the duty of a Member of Congress to vote for any proposed amendment if a considerable number of the voters of the country appear to favor same. There can be no more solemn duty imposed upon a Member than in determining his attitude toward a proposition to amend the Federal Constitution. Congress must initiate the amendment, and each Member must consider it in the light of his intelligence and patriotic judgment. We are not mere automatons to register the will of the Anti-Saloon League or any other organization of reformers. We are sworn to defend the Constitution as it stands, and it is our solemn duty to avoid any action which will impair or imperil the foundations of our Government. Any Member who votes for or against this amendment solely actuated by fear of his political fortunes has little comprehension of the fundamentals of our Government and is elevating his political preferment above the preservation of the essentials of sound democracy. There has already been too much of intimidation and coercion. The highest ideal is to discharge one's duty, and if one is to adopt the personal view it is also the best politics.

We are engaged in a great war. The President, in his recent epochal address before Congress, invoked unity upon the part of all the people. He declared that we should mobilize every resource, material and spiritual, in the successful prosecution of this war. The adoption of this amendment will thrust before the people a mooted question upon which there are strong differences. In the famous "Shannon" letter of the President in 1911, while he was governor of New Jersey, he referred to the acute divisions in public sentiment which followed the injection of the liquor question into any party organization. This proposition ought not to have been brought into Congress at this supreme moment in the national life. Congress has heretofore enacted all necessary legislation regarding intoxicating liquors for the period of the war. The further production of distilled liquors has been forbidden. The President, under the authority of law, has decreased the production of beer and the percentage of alcoholic contents. The great body of the people are satisfied. For patriotic reasons alone we would be justified in defeating this measure at this inopportune time. [Applause.]

U.S. Constitution, Eighteenth Amendment

January 16, 1919

SECTION 1
After one year from the ratification of this article the manufacture, sale, or transportation of intoxicating liquors within, the importation thereof into, or the exportation thereof from the United States and all territory subject to the jurisdiction thereof for beverage purposes is hereby prohibited.

SECTION 2
The Congress and the several States shall have concurrent power to enforce this article by appropriate legislation.

SECTION 3
This article shall be inoperative unless it shall have been ratified as an amendment to the Constitution by the legislatures of the several States, as provided in the Constitution, within seven years from the date of the submission hereof to the States by the Congress.

U.S. Constitution, Twenty-first Amendment

December 5, 1933

SECTION 1
The eighteenth article of amendment to the Constitution of the United States is hereby repealed.

SECTION 2
The transportation or importation into any State, Territory, or Possession of the United States for delivery or use therein of intoxicating liquors, in violation of the laws thereof, is hereby prohibited.

SECTION 3
This article shall be inoperative unless it shall have been ratified as an amendment to the Constitution by conventions in the several States, as provided in the Constitution, within seven years from the date of the submission hereof to the States by the Congress.

The Fundamental Principle of a Republic, *Anna Howard Shaw*, 1915

Debate on Women's Suffrage, 1919

U.S. Constitution, Nineteenth Amendment, 1920

The right of women to vote was a contentious issue in the United States from its very beginnings. Immediately following independence from Great Britain a number of states allowed women to vote, then, beginning in 1777, rescinded that right. Movements to establish women's rights, and the right to vote in particular, grew steadily over the course of the nineteenth century. In 1869 the Wyoming Territory granted women suffrage. A number of states, especially in the West, followed. Such victories were the result of decades of organizing and campaigning on the part of women such as Susan B. Anthony, Elizabeth Cady Stanton, and Anna Howard Shaw—all of them also active in peace and temperance movements. Shaw (1847–1919) was a Methodist minister, physician, and, for fifteen years, the president of the National American Woman Suffrage Association. Her speech reproduced here insists on the inconsistency of a democracy, supposedly founded on the rule of the people, refusing to recognize the right to vote of one-half its population. Opponents, as shown by the congressional debate reproduced here, focused on two issues: perceived differences between the sexes and their proper duties, and the need to maintain state control over issues as important as the franchise. By the time of World War I, with women already working in jobs and industries once reserved for men, President Woodrow Wilson proposed, as a "war measure," an amendment by which the federal government would recognize women's right to vote. Passed by the House of Representatives, the amendment was defeated by the Senate in 1918, achieving passage by both houses only in June 1919.

The Fundamental Principle of a Republic

June 21, 1915

Anna Howard Shaw

When I came into your hall tonight, I thought of the last time I was in your city. Twenty-one years ago I came here with Susan B. Anthony, and we came for exactly the same purpose as that for which we are here tonight. Boys have been born since that time and have become voters, and the women are still trying to persuade American men to believe in the fundamental principles of democracy, and I never quite feel as if it was a fair field to argue this question with men, because in doing it you have to assume that a man who professes to believe in a Republican form of government does not believe in a Republican form of government, for the only thing that woman's enfranchisement means at all is that a government which claims to be a Republic should be a Republic, and not an aristocracy. The difficulty with discussing this question with those who oppose us is that they make any number of arguments but none of them have anything to do with Woman's Suffrage; they always have something to do with something else, therefore the arguments which we have to make rarely ever have anything to do with the subject, because we have to answer our opponents who always escape the subject as far as possible in order to have any sort of reason in connection with what they say.

Now one of two things is true: either a Republic is a desirable form of government, or else it is not. If it is, then we should have it, if it is not then we ought not to pretend that we have it. We ought at least to be true to our ideals, and the men of New York have, for the first time in their lives, the rare opportunity, on the second day of next November, of making the state truly a part of a Republic. It is the greatest opportunity which has ever come to the men of the state. They have never had so serious a problem to solve before, they will never have a more serious problem to solve in any future year of our Nation's life, and the thing that disturbs me more than anything else in connection with it is that so few people realize what a profound problem they have to solve on November 2. It is not merely a trifling matter; it is not a little thing that does not concern the state, it is the most vital problem that we could have, and any man who goes to the polls on the second day of next November without thoroughly informing himself in regard to this subject is unworthy to be a citizen of this state, and unfit to cast a ballot.

If Woman's Suffrage is wrong, it is a great wrong; if it is right, it is a profound and fundamental principle, and we all know, if we know what a Republic is, that it is the fundamental principle upon which a Republic must rise. Let us see where we are as a people; how we act here and what we think we are. The difficulty with the men of this country is that they are so consistent in their inconsistency that they are not aware of having been inconsistent; because their consistency has been so continuous and their inconsistency so consecutive that it has never been broken, from the beginning of our Nation's life to the present time. If we trace our history back we will find that from the very dawn of our existence as a people, men have been imbued with a spirit and a vision more lofty than they have been able to live; they have been led by visions of the sublimest truth, both in regard to religion and in regard to government that ever inspired the souls of men from the time the Puritans left the old world to come to this country, led by the Divine ideal which is the sublimest and supremest ideal in religious freedom which men have ever known, the theory that a man has a right to worship God according to the dictates of his own conscience, without the intervention of any other man or any other group of men. And it was this theory, this vision of the right of the human soul which led men first to the shores of this country.

Now, nobody can deny that they are sincere, honest and earnest men. No one can deny that the Puritans were men of profound conviction, and yet these men who gave up everything in behalf of an ideal, hardly established their communities in this new country before they began to practice exactly the same sort of persecutions on other men which had been practiced upon them. They settled in their communities on the New England shores and when they formed their compacts by which they governed their local societies, they permitted no man to have a voice in the affairs unless he was a member of the church, and not a member of any church, but a member of the particular church which dominated the particular community in which he happened to be. In Massachusetts they drove the Baptists down to Rhode Island; in Connecticut they drove the Presbyterians over to New Jersey; they burned the Quakers in Massachusetts and ducked the witches, and no colony, either Catholic or Protestant allowed a Jew to have a voice. And so a man must worship God according to the conscience of the particular community in which he was located, and yet they called that religious freedom, they were not able to live the ideal of religious liberty, and from that time to this the men of this government have been following along the same line of inconsistency, while they too have been following a vision of equal grandeur and power.

Never in the history of the world did it dawn upon the human mind as it dawned upon your ancestors, what it would mean for men to be free. They got the vision of a government in which the people would be the supreme power, and so inspired by this vision men wrote such documents as were sent from the Massachusetts legislature, from the New York legislature and from the Pennsylvania group over to the Parliament of Great Britain, which rang with the profoundest measures of freedom and justice. They did not equivocate in a single word when they wrote the Declaration of Independence; no one can dream that these men had not got the sublimest ideal of democracy which had ever dawned upon the souls of men. But as soon as the war was over and our government was formed, instead of asking the question, who shall be the governing force in this great new Republic, when they brought those thirteen little territories together, they began to eliminate instead of include the men who should be the great governing forces, and they said, who shall have the voice in this great new Republic, and you would have supposed that such men as fought the Revolutionary war would have been able to answer that every man who has fought, every one who has given up all he has and all he has been able to accumulate shall be free, it never entered their minds. These excellent ancestors of yours had not been away from the old world long enough to realize that man is of more value than his purse, so they said every man who has an estate in the government shall have a voice; and they said what shall that estate be? And they answered that a man who had property valued at two hundred and fifty dollars will be able to cast a vote, and so they sang "The land of the free and the home of the brave." And they wrote into their Constitution, "All males who pay taxes on $250 shall cast a vote," and they called themselves a Republic, and we call ourselves a Republic, and they were not quite so much of a Republic as we are and we are not quite so much of a Republic that we should be called a Republic yet. We might call ourselves angels, but that wouldn't make us angels, you have got to be an angel before you are an angel, and you have got to be a Republic before you are a Republic. Now what did we do? Before the word "male" in the local compacts they wrote the word "church-members"; and they wrote in the word "tax-payer." Then there arose a great Democrat, Thomas Jefferson, who looked down into the day when you and I are living and saw that the rapidly accumulated wealth in the hands of a few men would endanger the liberties of the people, and he knew what you and I know, that no power under heaven or among men is known in a Republic by which men can defend their liberties except by the power of the ballot, and so the Democratic party took another step in the evolution of a Republic out of a monarchy and they rubbed out the word "tax-payer" and wrote in the word "white," and then the Democrats thought the millenium had come, and they sang "The land of the free and the home of the brave" as lustily as the Republicans had sung it before them and spoke of the divine right of motherhood with the same thrill in their voices and at the same time they were selling mother's babies by the pound on the auction block, and mothers apart from their babies. Another arose who said a man is not a good citizen because he is white, he is a good citizen because he is a man, and the Republican party took out that progressive evolutionary eraser and rubbed out the word "white" from before the word "male" and could not think of another word to put in there—they were all in, black and white, rich and poor, wise and otherwise, drunk and sober; not a man left out to be put in, and so the Republicans could not write anything before the word "male," and they had to let that little word "male" stay alone by itself.

And God said in the beginning, "It is not good for man to stand alone." That is why we are here tonight, and that is all that woman's suffrage means; just to repeat again and again that first declaration of the Divine, "It is not good for

man to stand alone," and so the women of this state are asking that the word "male" shall be stricken out of the constitution altogether and that the constitution stand as it ought to have stood in the beginning and as it must before this state is any part of a Republic. Every citizen possessing the necessary qualifications shall be entitled to cast one vote at every election, and have that vote counted. We are not asking, as our Anti-Suffrage friends think we are, for any of the awful things that we hear will happen if we are allowed to vote: we are simply asking that that government which professes to be a Republic shall be a Republic and not pretend to be what it is not.

Now what is a Republic? Take your dictionary, encyclopedia, lexicon or anything else you like and look up the definition and you will find that a Republic is a form of government in which the laws are enacted by representatives elected by the people. Now when did the people of New York ever elect their representatives? Never in the world. The men of New York have, and I grant you that men are people, admirable people, as far as they go, but they only go half way. There is still another half of the people who have not elected representatives, and you never read a definition of a Republic in which half of the people elect representatives to govern the whole of the people. That is an aristocracy and that is just what we are. We have been many kinds of aristocracies. We have been a hierarchy of church members, [then] an oligarchy of sex.

There are two old theories which are dying today. Dying hard but dying. One of them is dying on the plains of Flanders and the Mountains of Galicia and Austria, and that is the theory of the divine right of kings. The other is dying here in the state of New York and Massachusetts and New Jersey and Pennsylvania and that is the divine right of sex. Neither of them had a foundation in reason, or justice or common sense.

Now I want to make this proposition, and I believe every man will accept it. Of course he will if he is intelligent. Whenever a Republic prescribes the qualifications as applying equally to all the citizens of the Republic, when the Republic says in order to vote, a citizen must be twenty-one years of age, it applies to all alike, there is no discrimination against any race or sex. When the government says that a citizen must be a native born citizen or a naturalized citizen, that applies to all; we are either born or naturalized, somehow or other we are here. Whenever the government says that a citizen, in order to vote, must be a resident of a community a certain length of time, and of the state a certain length of time and of the nation a certain length of time, that applies to all equally. There is no discrimination. We might go further and we might say that in order to vote the citizen must be able to read his ballot. We have not gone that far yet. We have been very careful of male ignorance in these United States. I was much interested, as perhaps many of you, in reading the Congressional Record this last winter over the debate over the immigration bill, and when that illiteracy clause was introduced into the immigration bill, what fear there was in the souls of men for fear we would do injustice to some of the people who might want to come to our shores, and I was much interested in the language in which the President vetoed the bill, when he declared that by inserting the clause we would keep out of our shores a large body of very excellent people. I could not help wondering then how it happens that male ignorance is so much less ignorant than female ignorance. When I hear people say that if women were permitted to vote a large body of ignorant people would vote, and therefore because an ignorant woman would vote, no intelligent women should be allowed to vote. I wonder why we have made it so easy for male ignorance and so hard for female ignorance.

When I was a girl, years ago, I lived in the back woods and there the number of votes cast at each election depended entirely upon the size of the ballot box. We had what was known as the old tissue ballots and the man who got the most tissue in was the man elected. Now the best part of our community was very much disturbed by this method, . . . but they did not know what to do in order to get a ballot both safe and secret; but they heard that over in Australia, where the women voted, they had a ballot which was both safe and secret, so we went over there and we got the Australian ballot and brought it here. But when we got it over we found it was not adapted to this country, because in Australia they have to be able to read their ballot. Now the question was how could we adapt it to our conditions? Someone discovered that if you should put a symbol at the head of each column, like a rooster, or an eagle, or a hand holding a hammer, that if a man has intelligence to know the difference between a rooster and an eagle he will know which political party to vote for, and when the ballot was adapted it was a very beautiful ballot, it looked like a page from Life.

Now almost any American woman could vote that ballot, or if she had not that intelligence to know the difference between an eagle and a rooster, we could take the eagle out and put in the hen. Now when we take so much pains to adapt the ballot to the male intelligence of the United States, we should

be very humble when we talk about female ignorance. Now if we should take a vote and the men had to read their ballot in order to vote it, more women could vote than men. But when the government says not only that you must be twenty-one years of age, a resident of the community and native born or naturalized, those are qualifications, but when it says that an elector must be a male, that is not a qualification for citizenship; that is an insurmountable barrier between one half of the people and the other half of the citizens and their rights as citizens. No such nation can call itself a Republic. It is only an aristocracy. That barrier must be removed before that government can become a Republic, and that is exactly what we are asking now, that the last step in this evolutionary process shall be taken on November 2d, and that this great state of New York shall become in fact, as it is in theory, a part of a government of the people, by the people and for the people.

Men know the inconsistencies themselves; they realize it in one way while they do not realize it in another, because you never heard a man make a political speech when he did not speak of this country as a whole as though the thing existed which does not exist and that is that the people were equally free, because you hear them declare over and over again on the Fourth of July "Under God, the people rule." They know it is not true but they say it with a great hurrah, and they repeat over and over again that clause from the Declaration of Independence, "Governments derive their just powers from the consent of the governed," and then they see how they can prevent half of us from giving our consent to anything, and then they give it to us on the Fourth of July in two languages, so if it is not true in one it will be in the other, "vox [populi], vox Dei." "The voice of the people is the voice of God," and the orator forgets that in the people's voice there is a soprano as well as a bass. If the voice of the people is the voice of God, how are we ever going to know what God's voice is when we are content to listen to a bass solo. Now if it is true that the voice of the people is the voice of God, we will never know what the Deity's voice in government is until the bass and soprano are mingled together, the result of which will be the divine harmony. Take any of the magnificent appeals for freedom which men make, and rob them of their universal application and you take the very life and soul out of them.

Where is the difficulty? Just in one thing and one thing only, that men are so sentimental. We used to believe that women were the sentimental sex, but they cannot hold a tallow candle compared with the arc light of the men. Men are so sentimental in their attitude about women that they cannot reason about them. Now men are usually very fair to each other. I think the average man recognizes that he has no more right to anything at the hands of the government than has every other man. He has no right at all to anything to which every other man has not an equal right with himself. He says why have I a right to certain things in the government; why have I a right to life and liberty; why have I a right to this or this? Does he say because I am a man? Not at all, because I am human, and being human I have a right to everything which belongs to humanity, and every right which any other human being has, I have. And then he says of his neighbor, and my neighbor he also is human, therefore every right which belongs to me as a human being, belongs to him as a human being, and I have no right to anything under the government to which he is not equally entitled. And then up comes a woman, and then they say now she's a woman; she is not quite human, but she is my wife, or my sister, or my daughter or an aunt, or my cousin. She is not quite human, she is only related to a human, and being related to a human a human will take care of her. So we have had that care taking human being to look after us and they have not recognized that women too are equally human with men. Now if men could forget for a minute—I believe the anti-suffragists say that we want men to forget that we are related to them, they don't know me—if for a minute they could forget our relationship and remember that we are equally human with themselves, then they would say—yes, and this human being, not because she is a woman, but because she is human is entitled to every privilege and every right under the government which I, as a human being am entitled to. The only reason men do not see as fairly in regard to women as they do in regard to each other is because they have looked upon us from an altogether different plane than what they have looked at men; that is because women have been the homemakers while men have been the so-called protectors, in the period of the world's civilization when people needed to be protected. I know that they say that men protect us now and when we ask them what they are protecting us from the only answer they can give is from themselves. I do not think that men need any very great credit for protecting us from themselves. They are not protecting us from any special thing from which we could not protect ourselves except themselves. Now this old time idea of protection was all right when the world needed this protection, but today the protection in civilization comes from within and not from without.

What are the arguments which our good Antis friends give us? We know that lately they have stopped to argue and call suffragettes all sorts of creatures. If there is anything we believe that we do not believe, we have not heard about them, so the cry goes out of this; the cry of the infant's mind; the cry of a little child. The anti-suffragists' cries are all the cries of little children who are afraid of the unborn and are forever crying, "The goblins will catch you if you don't watch out." So that anything that has not been should not be and all that is is right, when as a matter of fact if the world believed that we would be in a statical condition and never move, except back like a crab. And so the cries go on.

When suffragettes are feminists, and when I ask what that is no one is able to tell me. I would give anything to know what a feminist is. They say, would you like to be a feminist? If I could find out I would, you either have to be masculine or feminine and I prefer feminine. Then they cry that we are socialists, and anarchists. Just how a human can be both at the same time, I really do not know. If I know what socialism means it means absolute government and anarchism means no government at all. So we are feminists, socialists, anarchists and mormons or spinsters. Now that is about the list. I have not heard the last speech. Now as a matter of fact, as a unit we are nothing, as individuals we are like all other individuals.

We have our theories, our beliefs, but as suffragettes we have but one belief, but one principle, but one theory and this is the right of a human being to have a voice in the government under which he or she lives, on that we agree, if on nothing else. Whether we agree or not on religion or politics we are not concerned. A clergyman asked me the other day, "By the way, what church does your official board belong to," I said I don't know. He said, "Don't you know what religion your official board believes." I said, "Really it never occurred to me, but I will hunt them up and see, they are not elected to my board because they believe in any particular church.["] We had no concern either as to what we believe as religionists or as to what we believe as women in regard to theories of government, except that one fundamental theory in the right of democracy. We do not believe in this fad or the other, but whenever any question is to be settled in any community, then the people of that community shall settle that question, the women people equally with the men people. That is all there is to it, and yet when it comes to arguing our case they bring up all sorts of arguments, and the beauty of it is they always answer all their own arguments. They never make an argument but they answer it. When I was asked to answer one of their debates I said, "What is the use? Divide up their literature and let them destroy themselves." . . .

I remember hearing Rev. Dr. Abbot speak before the anti-suffrage meeting in Brooklyn and he stated that if women were permitted to vote we would not have so much time for charity and philanthropy, and I would like to say, "Thank God, there will not be so much need of charity and philanthropy." The end and aim of the suffrage is not to furnish an opportunity for excellent old ladies to be charitable. There are two words that we ought to be able to get along without, and they are charity and philanthropy. They are not needed in a Republic. If we put in the word "opportunity" instead, that is what Republics stand for. Our doctrine is not to extend the length of our bread lines or the size of our soup kitchens, what we need is the opportunity for men to buy their own bread and eat their own soup. We women have used up our lives and strength in fool charities, and we have made more paupers than we have ever helped by the folly of our charities and philanthropies; the unorganized methods by which we deal with the conditions of society, and instead of giving people charity we must learn to give them an opportunity to develop and make themselves capable of earning the bread; no human being has the right to live without toil; toil of some kind, and that old theory that we used to hear "The world owes a man a living" never was true and never will be true. This world does not owe anybody a living, what it does owe to every human being is the opportunity to earn a living. We have a right to the opportunity and then the right to the living thereafter. We want it. No woman, any more than a man, has the right to live an idle life in this world, we must learn to give back something for the space occupied and we must do our duty wherever duty calls, and the woman herself must decide where her duty calls, just as a man does.

Now they tell us we should not vote because we have not the time, we are so burdened that we should not have any more burdens. Then, if that is so, I think we ought to allow the women to vote instead of the men, since we pay a man anywhere from a third to a half more than we do women it would be better to use up the cheap time of the women instead of the dear time of the men. And talking about time you would think it took about a week to vote. . . .

Now what does it matter whether the women will vote as their husbands do or will not vote; whether they have time or have not; or whether they will vote for prohibition or not. What has that to do with the fundamental question of democracy, no one has yet discovered. But they cannot argue on that; they cannot argue on the fundamental basis of our existence so that they have to get off on all these side tricks to get anything approaching an argument. So they tell you that democracy is a form of government. It is not. It was before governments were; it will prevail when governments cease to be; it is more than a form of government; it is a great spiritual force emanating from the heart of the Infinite, transforming human character until some day, some day in the distant future, man by the power of the spirit of democracy, will be able to look back into the face of the Infinite and answer, as man cannot answer today, "One is our Father, even God, and all we people are the children of one family." And when democracy has taken possession of human lives no man will ask for him to grant to his neighbor, whether that neighbor be a man or a woman; no man will then be willing to allow another man to rise to power on his shoulders, nor will he be willing to rise to power on the shoulders of another prostrate human being. But that has not yet taken possession of us, but some day we will be free, and we are getting nearer and nearer to it all the time; and never in the history of our country had the men and women of this nation a better right to approach it than they have today; never in the history of the nation did it stand out so splendidly as it stands today, and never ought we men and women to be more grateful for anything than that there presides in the White House today a man of peace.

And so our good friends go on with one thing after another and they say if women should vote they will have to sit on the jury and they ask whether we will like to see a woman sitting on a jury. I have seen some juries that ought to be sat on and I have seen some women that would be glad to sit on anything. When a woman stands up all day behind a counter, or when she stands all day doing a washing she is glad enough to sit; and when she stands for seventy-five cents she would like to sit for two dollars a day. But don't you think we need some women on juries in this country? You read your paper and you read that one day last week or the week before or the week before a little girl went out to school and never came back; another little girl was sent on an errand and never came back; another little girl was left in charge of a little sister and her mother went out to work and when she returned the little girl was not there, and you read it over and over again, and the horror of it strikes you. You read that in these United States five thousand young girls go out and never come back, don't you think that the men and women, the vampires of our country who fatten and grow rich on the ignorance and innocence of children would rather face Satan himself than a jury of mothers. I would like to see some juries of mothers. I lived in the slums of Boston for three years and I know the need of juries of mothers.

Then they tell us that if women were permitted to vote that they would take office, and you would suppose that we just took office in this country. There is a difference of getting an office in this country and in Europe. In England a man stands for Parliament and in this country he runs for Congress, and so long as it is a question of running for office I don't think women have much chance, especially with our present hobbles. There are some women who want to hold office and I may as well own up, I am one of them. I have been wanting to hold office for more than thirty-five years. Thirty-five years ago I lived in the slums of Boston and ever since then I have wanted to hold office. I have applied to the mayor to be made an officer; I wanted to be the greatest office holder in the world, I wanted the position of the man I think is to be the most envied, as far as ability to do good is concerned, and that is a policeman. I have always wanted to be a policeman and I have applied to be appointed policeman and the very first question that was asked me was, "Could you knock a man down and take him to jail?" That is some people's idea of the highest service that a policeman can render a community. Knock somebody down and take him to jail. My idea is not so much to arrest criminals as it is to prevent crime. That is what is needed in the police force of every community. When I lived for three years in the back alleys of Boston, I saw there that it was needed to prevent crime and from that day to this I believe there is no great public gathering of any sort whatever where we do not need women on the police force; we need them at every moving picture show, every dance house, every restaurant, every hotel and every great store with a great bargain counter and every park and every resort where the vampires who fatten on the crimes and vices of men and women gather. We need women on the police force and we will have them there some day.

If women vote will they go to war? They are great on having us fight. They tell you that the government rests on force, but there are a great many kinds of force in this world, and never in the history of man were the words of the Scriptures proved to the extent that they are today, that the men of the nation that lives by the sword shall die by the sword. When I was speaking in North Dakota from an automobile with a great crowd and a great number of men gathered around a man who had been sitting in front of a store whittling a stick called out to another man and asked if women get the vote

will they go over to Germany and fight the Germans? I said, "Why no, why should we go over to Germany and fight Germans?" "If Germans come over here would you fight?" I said, "Why should we women fight men, but if Germany should send an army of women over here, then we would show you what we would do.["] We would go down and meet them and say, "Come on, let's go up to the opera house and talk this matter over." It might grow wearisome but it would not be death.

Would it not be better if the heads of the governments in Europe had talked things over? What might have happened to the world if a dozen men had gotten together in Europe and settled the awful controversy which is today decimating the nations of Europe? We women got together over there last year, over in Rome, the delegates from twenty-eight different nations of women, and for two weeks we discussed problems which had like interests to us all. They were all kinds of Protestants, both kinds of Catholics, Roman and Greek, three were Jews and Mohamedans, but we were not there to discuss our different religious beliefs, but we were there to discuss the things that were of vital importance to us all, and at the end of the two weeks, after the discussions were over we passed a great number of resolutions. We discussed white slavery, the immigration laws, we discussed the spread of contagious and infectious diseases; we discussed various forms of education, and various forms of juvenile criminals, every question which every nation has to meet, and at the end of two weeks we passed many resolutions, but two of them were passed unanimously. One was presented by myself as Chairman on the Committee on Suffrage and on that resolution we called upon all civilizations of the world to give to women equal rights with men and there was not a dissenting vote.

The other resolution was on peace. We believed then and many of us believe today, notwithstanding all the discussion that is going on, we believe and we will continue to believe that preparedness for war is an incentive to war, and the only hope of permanent peace is the systematic and scientific disarmament of all the nations of the world, and we passed a resolution and passed it unanimously to that effect. A few days afterward I attended a large reception given by the American Ambassador and there was an Italian diplomat there and he spoke rather superciliously and said, "You women think you have been having a very remarkable convention, and I understand that a resolution on peace was offered by the Germans, the French women seconded it, and the British presiding officer presented it and it was carried unanimously." We none of us dreamed what was taking place at that time, but he knew and we learned it before we arrived home, that awful, awful thing that was about to sweep over the nations of the world. The American ambassador replied to the Italian diplomat and said, "Yes Prince, it was a remarkable convention, and it is a remarkable thing that the only people who can get together internationally and discuss their various problems without acrimony and without a sword at their side are the women of the world, but we men, even when we go to The Hague to discuss peace, we go with a sword dangling at our side." It is remarkable that even at this age men cannot discuss international problems and discuss them in peace.

When I turned away from that place up in North Dakota that man in the crowd called out again, just as we were leaving, and said, "Well, what does a woman know about war anyway?" I had read my paper that morning and I knew what the awful headline was, and I saw a gentleman standing in the crowd with a paper in his pocket, and I said, "Will that gentleman hold the paper up," and he held it up, and the headline read, "250,000 Men Killed Since the War Began." I said, "You ask me what a woman knows about war? No woman can read that line and comprehend the awful horror; no woman knows the significance of 250,000 dead men, but you tell me that one man lay dead and I might be able to tell you something of its awful meaning to one woman.["] I would know that years before a woman whose heart beat in unison with her love and her desire for motherhood walked day by day with her face to an open grave, with courage, which no man has ever surpassed, and if she did not fill that grave, if she lived and if there was laid in her arms a tiny little bit of helpless humanity, I would know that there went out from her soul such a cry of thankfulness as none save a mother could know. And then I would know, what men have not yet learned, that women are human; that they have human hopes and human passions, aspirations and desires as men have, and I would know that that mother had laid aside all those hopes and aspirations for herself, laid them aside for her boy, and if after years had passed by she forgot her nights of sleeplessness and her days of fatiguing toil in her care of her growing boy, and when at last he became a man and she stood looking up into his eyes and beheld him, bone of her bone and flesh of her flesh, for out of her woman's life she had carved twenty beautiful years that went into the making of a man; and there he stands, the most wonderful thing in all the world; for in all the Universe of God there is nothing more sublimely wonderful than a strong limbed clean hearted, keen brained, aggressive young man, standing as he does on the border line of life, ready to reach out and grapple with its problems. O, how wonderful he is, and he is her's. She gave her life for him, and in an hour this country calls him out and in an hour he lies dead; that wonderful, wonderful thing lies dead; and sitting by his side, that mother looking into the dark years to come knows that when her son died her life's hope died with him, and in the face of that wretched motherhood, what man dare ask what a woman knows of war. And that is not all. Read your papers, you cannot read it because it is not printable; you cannot tell it because it is not speakable, you cannot even think it because it is not thinkable, the horrible crimes perpetrated against women by the blood drunken men of the war.

You read your paper again and the second headline reads, "It Costs Twenty Millions of Dollars a Day," for what? To buy the material to slaughter the splendid results of civilization of the centuries. Men whom it has taken centuries to build up and make into great scientific forces of brain, the flower of the manhood of the great nations of Europe, and we spend twenty millions of dollars a day to blot out all the results of civilization of hundreds and hundreds of years. And what do we do? We lay a mortgage on every unborn child for a hundred and more years to come. Mortgage his brain, his brawn, every pulse of his heart in order to pay the debt, to buy the material to slaughter the men of our country. And that is not all, the greatest crime of war is the crime against the unborn. Read what they are doing. They are calling out every man, every young man, every virile man from seventeen to forty-five or fifty years old, they are calling them out. All the splendid scientific force and energy of the splendid virile manhood are being called out to be food for the cannon, and they are leaving behind the degenerate, defective imbecile, the unfit, the criminals, the diseased to be the fathers of the children yet to be born. The crime of crimes of the war is the crime against the unborn children, and in the face of the fact that women are driven out of the home shall men ask if women shall fight if they are permitted to vote.

No we women do not want the ballot in order that we may fight, but we do want the ballot in order that we may help men to keep from fighting, whether it is in the home or in the state, just as the home is not without the man, so the state is not without the woman, and you can no more build up homes without men than you can build up the state without women. We are needed everywhere where human life is. We are needed everywhere where human problems are to be solved. Men and women must go through this world together from the cradle to the grave, it is God's way and it is the fundamental principle of a Republican form of government.

Debate on Women's Suffrage

May 21, 1919

MR. LITTLE. Mr. Speaker, the gentleman from Pennsylvania [Mr. MOORE] suggests that the ladies who are not in favor of woman suffrage are taken unawares. To register surprise at the appearance of propositions of a certain welcome, friendly, complimentary, and anticipated tenor is one of the most highly valued privileges of that charming sex, which no gentleman, even in the heat of debate, would ask them to surrender for any political right, however important. The ladies are certainly no more surprised than I am, because it is scarce 30 minutes since notification from the gentleman from Illinois [Mr. MANN], chairman of the Woman Suffrage Committee and author of the resolution at issue, whose rare parliamentary sagacity and unrivaled parliamentary leadership made this day's work possible, that I was to open this debate. This is a good time to bring it up.

Five years ago Julius Caesar, after 19 centuries, challenged Jesus Christ to a final contest. The Kaiser threw down the gantlet and the friends of Christian civilization took it up. The tide of war turned in favor of the Son of Bethlehem and against the Prussian; and, if anything has been decided, it has been decided that now right, not might, shall rule the world. [Applause.] Unless our sons and our billions have been sacrificed in vain, the world is about ready to substitute the rule of reason for the rule of force in the government of reasoning creatures. What better expression of that could there be than to say now that the mothers who risked their lives to bring into the world the four millions of soldiers we mustered shall have some word to say about the destinies of their sons? [Applause.] The British House of Commons voted, I think, 7 to 1, and recently, I believe, the French Chamber of Deputies voted 7 to 1, for woman suffrage. The time is opportune for marking an era's close. Civilization has reached a state, a period, a moment, when we can ring the liberty bell again and announce that this great step forward has been taken.

They tell us that woman should not vote merely because she is a female. No other reason has been advanced except that form which says that she can not bear arms. Every mother who bears a son to fight for the Republic takes the same chance of death that a son takes when he goes to arms. The fact that she is a woman is a reason for, not against, the utilization of every force for the advancement of society. Ninety-nine per cent of the murderers in the world are men. Ninety-nine per cent of the burglars are men. Ninety-nine per cent of the gamblers are men. Ninety-nine per cent of counterfeiters are men. Ninety-nine per cent of all the thieves, outlaws, forgers, pickpockets, bank robbers, train robbers, pirates, and drunkards in the world are men. Ninety-nine per cent of all criminals are men.

Ninety-nine per cent of all diseases inherited by reason of evil lives of parents come down from the male side. For every courtesan there is a seducer and panderer and a thousand customers. When one considers the character of the two sexes, he better appreciates the power of the instinct of race preservation which nature has planted in the human kind, which certainly is all that has induced women to remain on the same continent with man for 60 centuries. If the world were open and the best character of votes were the dominating factor, women would control the ballot entirely. If good character were the basis for the franchise, most of the voters would probably have been women long ago.

In the last analysis those who oppose woman suffrage simply ignore everything except brute force. They discard brains, scholarship, character, and simply seek to enforce the law of the herd, that the biggest bull is the boss. Under their theories Napoleon Bonaparte was a greater man than Abraham Lincoln; John L. Sullivan a more useful citizen than Thomas Edison. I challenge all such claims as unworthy of the citizens of a Christian and cultured land. Carried to their logical conclusion those theories have dominated and guided and wrecked and ruined the great Empire of Germany perhaps for centuries to come, and at the very moment when they had attained the rounded summit of a successful, brutal, despotic development of brute force. If during the last 40 years the women had held absolute control of Germany, that mighty State would now be rich, happy, contented, and yet there are still those who will tell you woman should not rule because she can not fight.

They told us last year the determination of this issue should be relegated to the States. One of the fundamental privileges under the Constitution is to amend it. If three-fourths of the States wish it, there is no authority under the Constitution that endows any State with the privilege of denying. They suggest they wanted a referendum vote. The Constitution prescribes, orders, another method. When the women come here and ask for the ballot, they simply invoke the methods by which the Constitution has always been amended. Any other system would be illegal. If you say to them that you are not willing to abide by those rules under which every amendment has been made, you simply plead the baby act; and when the mother of a soldier comes here to demand the privilege of the ballot you should not do that.

Men have argued here for 50 years that woman suffrage would break up the home. But in the Western States, where we have had woman suffrage in one form and another for years, we know of no family that has ever been disrupted by quarrel over politics. We know of no fireside that has burned more dimly because of any difference of opinion about the use of the ballot. To permit the mothers of this country to express their views on important issues will not injure the homes. As I reflect now I realize that every time I followed my mother's advice I did well. Generally when I did not list to her I lived to regret it. She was a thoughtful and prudent woman. The long and short of the whole matter is that for centuries you have treated woman as a slave, dragged her over the pages of history by the hair, and then you pretend to think she is an angel, too good to interfere in the affairs of men. Give her now a fixed, reasonable status, as becomes a rational human being like yourself.

I wish there were a home for every woman. But our civilization has developed in another direction. During this great war it has been determined that women are to take part in every vocation of human life. There is no place they have not filled with ability. The increase in population, the complex demands of a complicated civilization, have made it absolutely essential that many women shall come away from the fireside and go to work for a living and fight and struggle with men.

In the streets of Strasburg I have myself seen women assisted by dogs hitched in harness pulling carts and selling milk at the homes along the streets. My friends and I traveling the path through an Egyptian field were suddenly accosted by a woman, who rose with her sickle from among the wheat to cry in Arabic, "In your great country, sir, women do not thus toil in the field." But now, in my great country, women throng the shops, the offices, the factories, in their strife with men to earn a living. In uncivilized nations they still treat her as a slave and as an angel. Your great civilization gives woman the glorious privilege that man has to battle for a livelihood if she will do so for small wages, but denies her the use of the

ballot in her struggle. What are you afraid of? The Burmese women handle all the business of that country. Is this, then, a Burmese peril which menaces you?

The gentleman who leads the opposition to-day said once that she could not have the rights of a man and the privileges of a woman. Why can she not? That can not be true. If we are going to be the gentlemen we assume to be, why should she not have the rights of a man and the privileges of a woman? Men retained all the male privileges of drinking whisky, playing poker, and racing horses when they cast the ballot. Why can not she still retain the privilege of being treated like a lady, a wife, a mother, even if she votes? God Almighty placed upon her certain duties from which you escape, and you are wonderfully fortunate that you do, and every time you think of it you should blush for shame that you would deny any rights you have because of the responsibility that God has placed upon her.

It has been a source of profound regret to me this morning that I did not have some notice that would enable me to present this subject more thoroughly. The women of the Republic come here and say to you that they want the ballot. Gentlemen, God Almighty has made you strong; they have made your Republic great and made you statesmen of this great Republic. They have given you infinite powers, mighty responsibilities. Now, the mother who bore you, the wife who brought your son into the world, and those who have gone before reach out and ask that you apply to them the rules of common sense, and no more, no less.

If you should throw 200 people upon an island, why should any particular member or set of members there for any reason have the power to say what should be done? Why should not a sensible, God-fearing, intelligent woman have just as good a right to have her say about what goes on in any nation as any man that walks the earth?

As I have said to you, she takes the same risk that every soldier did. Which of you is there who has taken the same chance on any battle field that a mother has taken every time a child comes into the world? Who are you that you should say to the mothers of America that they can not vote as you do?

The world must progress according to the methods of Julius Caesar or the theories of Jesus Christ. During the last five years that ancient contest came to a head and the cross of Christ must henceforth and forever be made the standard of civilization instead of the crown of Julius Caesar. For the second time in this House I appeal from the rule of force to the rule of reason. The conquering armies camped on the Rhine have fought to establish the fact that civilization is better civilized than barbarism. If common sense is more potent than the sword, if men have determined that that is their sober intention and their law, woman should now be accorded the same opportunity to take part in the life that men have always had.

When I am laid away on the hillside, Bert Berry, my orderly in the Philippines, will bring the bugle he blew for me at Marilao, Guiguinto, and San Fernando and sound taps above my last earthly resting place, and I trust I shall hear no more of wars for all eternity. I hope, as my dear wife holds my hand for the last time as I pass out into the starlight, and as my dear mother extends her sainted hand to me as the trumpets sound the reveille on the other side, both will know that the sons for whom they went down into the valley of the shadow have granted to the mothers of this most august and stateliest Republic of all time the same power, authority, and opportunity to fashion and preserve the lives of their sons that is possessed by their fathers. [Applause.] . . .

Mr. MacCRATE. Mr. Speaker and gentlemen, I realize thoroughly that a man only three days in Congress should hold his tongue, but coming as I do from a district which has equal suffrage, and being a member of the Committee on Woman Suffrage, I felt it obligatory to say why we from our section believe this national resolution or amendment should be submitted to the States for the States to decide in the constitutional way whether it shall be adopted. Now, whether you consider the franchise a right or a privilege, the women of America deserve the right, or they have earned the privilege. Everywhere you went during the past two years you saw women in uniform. You saw them in the Salvation Army, the Red Cross, the Knights of Columbus, the Young Men's Christian Association, Young Men's Hebrew Association, and other allied war activities. Whether you were at home or whether you were abroad, and like myself had the privilege of seeing the streets of London and Liverpool in January of this year, you realized that American womanhood had met the last argument that men have given for denying them the suffrage privilege, namely, that no one who is not a potential soldier is entitled to the franchise. I submit to your fairness and judgment that the women of America have been as potential soldiers during the past war as have been the men of America. [Applause.] And if potentiality for military service is the last objection, then certainly with the men who avoided the draft, or with the slackers, the women of America ought

never be compared; and more certainly if men who continued in agricultural pursuits to win the war, if men who continued in shipyards to win the war, if men who continued in other branches of activities to win the war are entitled to the franchise, the women who maintained equal industrial and agricultural burdens and high moral burdens to win the war are entitled to the franchise. [Applause.] Not only that, but this resolution seems to me to be in perfect harmony with the Constitution itself. The preamble of the Constitution declares its purpose to be "to form a more perfect Union." This amendment will help us perfect the Union. It does not go into the homes of the country and tell the people what they shall put on or what they shall eat or what they shall drink. It does not say to the men and women of America they shall not do this or they shall not do that, but it does recognize a fundamental of our Government that rights and privileges shall be equal, and declares that sex alone shall not deprive women of the right or privilege of voting. I submit to you that this resolution is in harmony with the spirit of the Constitution itself. [Applause.]

Mr. MANN. Mr. Speaker, I now renew my request that all Members have leave to extend their remarks in the RECORD on this subject for five legislative days.

The SPEAKER. The gentleman from Illinois asks unanimous consent that all Members may be permitted to extend their remarks in the RECORD on this subject—

Mr. RAGSDALE. I object, Mr. Speaker.

The SPEAKER. The gentleman from South Carolina objects.

Mr. CLARK of Florida. Mr. Speaker, I yield five minutes to the gentleman from Pennsylvania. [Mr. FOCHT.]

Mr. FOCHT. Mr. Speaker, I desire to ask unanimous consent to extend by remarks in the RECORD.

The SPEAKER. Is there an objection?

Mr. FERRIS. Mr. Speaker, reserving the right to object, I do not think it fair to let in any more extensions unless we let in those who did not have a chance to speak, and so I object—of course, without any discourtesy whatever to the gentleman.

Mr. FOCHT. Mr. Speaker, we all realize that this is a transcendent and far-reaching question. It has been decided in Pennsylvania more than once what the people there think about it. It has been decided in many, many States what they think about it there. It has been brought to Congress for decision. In Pennsylvania the last time the test was made the amendment was defeated by 50,000 majority, and it is conceded it would have been 250,000 majority or 300,000 majority had the question been voted on separately instead of in connection with four other amendments.

In my own district in Pennsylvania, comprised of eight counties, which are typical of the Christianity, civilization, and the chivalry of America, every last county went against it after a full discussion of the question. I dare say, if it were submitted again, yes or no on its merits, it would go double what it was the last time against it. I appreciate the tribute that has been paid here, very tenderly and, I might say, patriotically, to womanhood. How could any of us do otherwise than pay high tribute to the mother or wife or daughter? These gentlemen say that those of us who are opposed to this amendment are denying the women something; that we are defeating them in a high and laudable purpose. I challenge that statement and that argument. My proposition is that those mothers of the soldier boys do not ask for this thing. I need not dwell upon the greatness of Pennsylvania, or her glory, or the soldiers she sent to the front, or the money she gave to back them up, but it is well that you be reminded that Pennsylvania's only vote of record is against woman suffrage. In the time I have here I want to enter the protest of one Member from Pennsylvania against going too far afield at this particular time in this uncharted matter, simply because a few States out West have adopted the suffrage program. And with all respect for the Members who come from those States where they have had woman suffrage, I do not believe many appeals come to them or much concern is felt for the franchise by most women. I do not believe a vast majority of women want the vote, nor do they need it for their protection.

Furthermore, let me say that in the State of Pennsylvania 20 years ago we had better laws for the protection of womanhood than they have in the States where they have had woman suffrage for 25 years, and we have better laws there now; hence it is to be seen that it is not necessary for women to engage in the conflict and asperities of politics to secure more than equality of protection with men. Formerly it was contended that the vote for women was necessary to win the war and to further prohibition, but the fallacy of these arguments was made manifest by subsequent events.

Mr. HICKS. Will the gentleman yield for a moment?

Mr. FOCHT. I can not, having but a few minutes' time. I know where your heart is. You are really not for this. [Laughter.] There is no Member here, either from the States of New York, Pennsylvania, or Ohio, who down in his heart is for this sort of thing.

Another reason why women in their good sense are not here appealing for the vote and sphere of political activity may be that they have a better conception of the biological and physiological laws than some gentlemen who will vote in the affirmative on account of coming from States where women now vote—laws ordained by God, and which the vote of Congress nor an amendment to the Constitution can not change or set aside. [Applause.]

In conclusion I will submit a letter I received this morning from Mrs. Horace Brock, president of the Pennsylvania Association Opposed to Woman Suffrage, and which includes some salient points on this question:

By the submission of the question of woman suffrage to the voters of the State in 1915 Pennsylvania declared against Federal interference and for the right of the electorate to decide this question. There is a bill now before the State senate, which has passed the house, providing for a resubmission to the people. We opposed this bill in the house, for, while we agree a referendum to the people is the only democratic and just way of deciding this issue, we know there is no increased demand for woman suffrage, but rather increased opposition to it. Since the passage of the bill in the house, however, we have made no further opposition and are making our opposition to the passage of an amendment to the Federal Constitution, which would deprive the State of the right to decide its own electorate.

A Federal amendment to the Constitution is a serious matter, because it is irrevocable. The voters of New York State, men and women, finding double suffrage increases taxes and the socialist vote, are planning a resubmission of this question to the voters before long. If the Federal amendment is not passed, this will certainly be done.

A noisy minority are demanding votes for women as a reward for their war work, but the majority of women war workers, who have been largely antisuffragists desiring no reward, object to being penalized and given this added burden because of their work. Moreover, because a woman is efficient in Red Cross and industrial work, it does not follow she would be efficient in Congress. Also, it is not advisable to legislate for normal times extraordinary measures that may be useful and necessary in abnormal times.

I therefore ask you, in justice to your State and its electorate, to vote against the Federal woman-suffrage amendment. [Applause.]

The SPEAKER pro tempore (Mr. FESS). The time of the gentleman from North Carolina has again expired.

Mr. CLARK of Florida. Mr. Speaker, I yield five minutes to the gentleman from Texas [Mr. BLACK].

The SPEAKER pro tempore. The gentleman from Texas is recognized for five minutes.

Mr. BLACK. Mr. Speaker, of course there is no dispute upon the proposition that Congress by a two-thirds vote of both Houses may submit any amendment which it sees fit, and when such amendment is ratified by three-fourths of the legislatures of the several States it would become a part of the Constitution and binding upon all the States. There is no controversy upon that point. And since the right of a State to peaceably secede from the Union has forever been settled in the negative, there can no longer be any sound contention that any amendment which is adopted in the constitutional manner violates any of the rights of the other States. The minority States must, of course, yield to the will of the majority.

But this very fact makes all the more important that Congress should be careful in submitting amendments, and the States should be slow in ratifying those which delegate power to the Federal Government hitherto reserved to the States and exercised by their own legislative machinery.

Article I, section 2, of our Federal Constitution provides—

The House of Representatives shall be composed of Members chosen every second year by the people of the several States. . . . And the electors in each State shall have the qualifications requisite for electors of the most numerous branch of the State legislature.

Thus it will be seen that the framers of our Constitution, recognizing the State as the sovereign unit of government, deemed it wise to reserve to the States the right to regulate their own suffrage and provided in affirmative terms that the House of Representatives should be chosen by electors having the same qualifications as those who should choose the most numerous branch of the State legislatures.

And when 123 years later the seventeenth amendment was adopted, which provided for the election of United States Senators by direct vote of the people, this same provision was carried which prescribed that the electors should have the same qualifications as those required for electing the most numerous branch of the State legislatures.

Now, the amendment which we have under consideration proposes to change all of this and turn over to the Federal Government one of the most essential elements of State sovereignty; that is, to limit and control the States in their right to determine and prescribe the qualifications of their own electors.

And while I concede that the method by which it is proposed to be done is a perfectly legal one, the question is, Should it be done as a matter of wise government policy?

Is suffrage such a question as should be snatched from the control of the States and lodged in a rapidly centralizing government? That is a question which I consider myself called upon to answer as the elected Representative of the people from the district which I have the honor to represent in this body.

When I consider the principles which underlie the structure of our republican form of government, with its "indissoluble Union of indestructible States"; when I consider the fact that I am a Democratic Representative and owe at least some allegiance to the historic principles of the party and some degree of obedience to its most recent national platform, then I am not in doubt as to how I should vote.

I should vote against the submission of the amendment and leave each State free to regulate and control the matter of its own suffrage.

Therefore I will vote that way I think and believe.

If my own State—Texas—for instance, wants to grant full suffrage to women, it has a perfectly simple method of doing it. On next Saturday, May 24, the people of our State will vote upon a constitutional amendment which has for its object this very purpose.

In the submission of this State amendment the voters get a real referendum. If they adopt it, they will have no need of this Federal amendment. If they do not adopt it, then why should I vote for a Federal amendment which would impose it upon them against their own will.

The committee at the last session of Congress who reported this resolution made this remarkable statement on page 4 of their report. I would not refer to it now except for the fact that it is illustrative of much of the logic used by the proponents of this amendment. The language was:

To deny the States the opportunity to establish woman suffrage if they wish to do so is an act of autocratic injustice which would certainly be misunderstood abroad and would deeply incense the millions of women who are voters, as well as the millions more who are petitioning for the vote.

That is a very remarkable statement. I would like to inquire what provision there is in the Federal Constitution which in the slightest degree prohibits the States from granting full suffrage to their women whenever they desire to do so? And if there is no such prohibition, then what possible power is there anywhere which can prevent a State from doing so?

Every schoolboy knows that all the powers not delegated to the United States by the Constitution nor prohibited by it to the States are reserved to the States, respectively, or to the people. If that report had said, instead of the language which I have quoted, that "To deny the States the opportunity to control their own suffrage, if they wish to do so, is an act of autocratic injustice," then it would have been a statement, as I understand it, of the doctrine which the Democratic Party has championed for more than a hundred years and which has been so ably defended by many of the party's greatest leaders. I do not think that the matter has been more clearly stated anywhere than by President Wilson in a statement to a delegation of suffragists January 6, 1917:

I am tied to a conviction which I have had all my life, that changes of this sort ought to be brought State by State. It is a deeply matured conviction on my part, and therefore I would be without excuse to my own constitutional principles if I lent my support to this very important movement for an amendment to the Constitution of the United States.

Of course it will be conceded that the President has expressed some contrary opinions since then, but the newest is not always the best. The date or luster of the coin does not determine its true value, and "he who chooses without a proper test may perish, both a pauper and a fool."

When we put these different statements of the President to the test of Democratic principles, as interpreted throughout the history of our party and by our recent Democratic platforms, I am compelled to choose his option, as expressed on January 6, 1917, as the soundest and wisest one, rather than that of these more recent days.

Our platform at St. Louis in 1916 contained this declaration:

We recommend the extension of the franchise to the women of the country by the States on the same terms as to men.

If the party had intended to take the position that woman suffrage is a Federal and not a State matter, then the platform would have recommended that Congress take action on the question instead of making its recommendation to the several States of the Union. There is no declaration in the platform anywhere for the submission of a national woman suffrage amendment, and no Democratic national convention in the history of the party has ever declared for it.

On the contrary, it is perfectly well known that the attitude of the party has long been that the regulation of suffrage belongs to the States, and that as a matter of proper public policy it should be left there.

It is for these reasons, and not because I am opposed to woman suffrage by State action, that I will vote against the submission of this amendment. [Applause.]

U.S. Constitution, Nineteenth Amendment

August 26, 1920

The right of citizens of the United States to vote shall not be denied or abridged by the United States or by any State on account of sex.

Congress shall have power to enforce this article by appropriate legislation.

PART SIX

Consolidating Government

Political cartoon opposing Franklin D. Roosevelt's 1937 Supreme Court–packing plan. Illustration by J. N. "Ding" Darling. © Bettman/CORBIS.

(*below*) Men waiting outside Al Capone soup kitchen, 1930. © Bettman/CORBIS.

GOVERNMENT HAD PLAYED a significant role in Americans' lives from the earliest settlements. The Puritans and other early settlers had to look to their local governments for protection from attack, disease, and hunger in their isolated state. Moreover, there had been a perfectionist streak in the settlers that demanded laws aimed at improving and guarding the people's morals. But such laws always had been local in character. It was during the late nineteenth century that mass movements began forming on the conviction that new economic and social forces required a national response. While the earliest reformers sought to eliminate large combinations of wealth and power, the call soon came for the federal government to regulate such interests as the railroads and large industrial enterprises. With the coming of the Great Depression and its consequent economic hardships, the call became more sustained for a federal system of economic insurance. At all times these calls came in conflict with the view that Americans' virtue and well-being depended on habits of self-help and charity that would be undermined by public programs of assistance—the more so as these programs began to come from a federal government many believed was not authorized to take on the role of social insurer.

The Pendleton Act, 1883

The assassination of President James A. Garfield by a man who sought, but failed to secure, a government job brought to a head decades of increasing discontent with the federal "spoils system." This system was instituted by President Andrew Jackson, who served from 1829 to 1837. It rested on the assumption that government jobs should go to those loyal to the victorious political party. The policy encouraged loyalty to the ruling party's policies and personnel. It also brought widespread bribery, incompetence, and use of public employees for political purposes. The Pendleton Act established the Civil Service Commission to oversee competitive examinations for some 10 percent of federal jobs (the number grew steadily, eventually topping 90 percent of the total). Hiring, raises, and promotions were now to be based on a test-based merit system, with campaign activities banned for persons in these positions.

The Pendleton Act

January 16, 1883

An act to regulate and improve the civil service of the
    United States.

Be it enacted by the Senate and House of Representatives of the United States of America in Congress assembled, That the President is authorized to appoint, by and with the advice and consent of the Senate, three persons, not more than two of whom shall be adherents of the same party, as Civil Service Commissioners, and said three commissioners shall constitute the United States Civil Service Commission. Said commissioners shall hold no other official place under the United States.

The President may remove any commissioner; and any vacancy in the position of commissioner shall be so filled by the President, by and with the advice and consent of the Senate, as to conform to said conditions for the first selection of commissioners.

The commissioners shall each receive a salary of three thousand five hundred dollars a year. And each of said commissioners shall be paid his necessary traveling expenses incurred in the discharge of his duty as a commissioner.

SEC. 2. That it shall be the duty of said commissioners:

FIRST. To aid the President, as he may request, in preparing suitable rules for carrying this act into effect, and when said rules shall have been promulgated it shall be the duty of all officers of the United States in the departments and offices to which any such rules may relate to aid, in all proper ways, in carrying said rules, and any modifications thereof, into effect.

SECOND. And, among other things, said rules shall provide and declare, as nearly as the conditions of good administration will warrant, as follows:

First, for open, competitive examinations for testing the fitness of applicants for the public service now classified or to be classified hereunder. Such examinations shall be practical in their character, and so far as may be shall relate to those matters which will fairly test the relative capacity and fitness of the persons examined to discharge the duties of the service into which they seek to be appointed.

Second, that all the offices, places, and employments so arranged or to be arranged in classes shall be filled by selections according to grade from among those graded highest as the results of such competitive examinations.

Third, appointments to the public service aforesaid in the departments at Washington shall be apportioned among the several States and Territories and the District of Columbia upon the basis of population as ascertained at the last preceding census. Every application for an examination shall contain, among other things, a statement, under oath, setting forth his or her actual bona fide residence at the time of making the application, as well as how long he or she has been a resident of such place.

Fourth, that there shall be a period of probation before any absolute appointment or employment aforesaid.

Fifth, that no person in the public service is for that reason under any obligations to contribute to any political fund, or to render any political service, and that he will not be removed or otherwise prejudiced for refusing to do so.

Sixth, that no person in said service has any right to use his official authority or influence to coerce the political action of any person or body.

Seventh, there shall be non-competitive examinations in all proper cases before the commission, when competent persons do not compete, after notice has been given of the existence of the vacancy, under such rules as may be prescribed by the commissioners as to the manner of giving notice.

Eighth, that notice shall be given in writing by the appointing power to said commission of the persons selected for appointment or employment from among those who have been examined, of the place of residence of such persons, of the rejection of any such persons after probation, of transfers, resignations, and removals, and of the date thereof, and a record of the same shall be kept by said commission. And any necessary exceptions from said eight fundamental provisions of the rules shall be set forth in connection with such rules, and the reasons therefor shall be stated in the annual reports of the commission.

THIRD. Said commission shall, subject to the rules that may be made by the President, make regulations for, and have control of, such examinations, and, through its members or the examiners, it shall supervise and preserve the records of the same; and said commission shall keep minutes of its own proceedings.

FOURTH. Said commission may make investigations concerning the facts, and may report upon all matters touching the enforcement and effects of said rules and regulations, and concerning the action of any examiner or board of examiners hereinafter provided for, and its own subordinates, and those in the public service, in respect to the execution of this act.

FIFTH. Said commission shall make an annual report to the President for transmission to Congress, showing its own action, the rules and regulations and the exceptions thereto in force, the practical effects thereof, and any suggestions it may approve for the more effectual accomplishment of the purposes of this act.

SEC. 3. That said commission is authorized to employ a chief examiner, a part of whose duty it shall be, under its direction, to act with the examining boards, so far as practicable, whether at Washington or elsewhere, and to secure accuracy, uniformity, and justice in all their proceedings, which shall be at all times open to him. The chief examiner shall be entitled to receive a salary at the rate of three thousand dollars a year, and he shall be paid his necessary traveling expenses incurred in the discharge of his duty. The commission shall have a secretary, to be appointed by the President, who shall receive a salary of one thousand six hundred dollars per annum. It may, when necessary, employ a stenographer, and a messenger, who shall be paid, when employed, the former at the rate of one thousand six hundred dollars a year, and the latter at the rate of six hundred dollars a year. The commission shall, at Washington, and in one or more places in each State and Territory where examinations are to take place, designate and select a suitable number of persons, not less than three, in the official service of the United States, residing in said State or Territory, after consulting the head of the department or office in which such persons serve, to be members of boards of examiners, and may at any time substitute any other person in said service living in such State or Territory in the place of any one so selected. Such boards of examiners shall be so located as to make it reasonably convenient and inexpensive for applicants to attend before them; and where there are persons to be examined in any State or Territory, examinations shall be held therein at least twice in each year. It shall be the duty of the collector, postmaster, and other officers of the United States, at any place outside of the District of Columbia where examinations are directed by the President or by said board to be held, to allow the reasonable use of the public buildings for holding such examinations, and in all proper ways to facilitate the same.

SEC. 4. That it shall be the duty of the Secretary of the Interior to cause suitable and convenient rooms and accommodations to be assigned or provided, and to be furnished, heated, and lighted, at the city of Washington, for carrying on the work of said commission and said examinations, and to cause the necessary stationery and other articles to be supplied, and the necessary printing to be done for said commission.

SEC. 5. That any said commissioner, examiner, copyist, or messenger, or any person in the public service who shall willfully and corruptly, by himself or in co-operation with one or more other persons, defeat, deceive, or obstruct any person in respect of his or her right of examination according to any such rules or regulations, or who shall willfully, corruptly, and falsely mark, grade, estimate, or report upon the examination or proper standing of any person examined hereunder, or aid in so doing, or who shall willfully and corruptly make any false representations concerning the same or concerning the person examined, or who shall willfully and corruptly furnish to any person any special or secret information for the purpose of either improving or injuring the prospects or chances of any person so examined, or to be examined, being appointed, employed, or promoted, shall for each such offense be deemed guilty of a misdemeanor, and upon conviction thereof, shall be punished by a fine of not less than one hundred dollars, nor more than one thousand dollars, or by imprisonment not less than ten days, nor more than one year, or by both such fine and imprisonment.

SEC. 6. That within sixty days after the passage of this act it shall be the duty of the Secretary of the Treasury, in as near conformity as may be to the classification of certain clerks now existing under the one hundred and sixty-third section of the Revised Statutes, to arrange in classes the several clerks and persons employed by the collector, naval officer, surveyor, and appraisers, or either of them, or being in the public service, at their respective offices in each customs district where the whole number of said clerks and persons shall be all together as many as fifty. And thereafter, from time to time, on the direction of the President, said Secretary shall make the like classification or arrangement of clerks and persons so employed, in connection with any said office or offices, in any other customs district. And, upon like request, and for the purposes of this act, said Secretary shall arrange in one or more of said classes, or of existing classes, any other clerks, agents, or persons employed under his department in any said district not now classified; and every such arrangement and classification upon being made shall be reported to the President.

Second. Within said sixty days it shall be the duty of the Postmaster-General, in general conformity to said one hundred and sixty-third section, to separately arrange in classes the several clerks and persons employed, or in the public service, at each post-office, or under any postmaster of the United States, where the whole number of said clerks and persons shall together amount to as many as fifty. And thereafter, from time to time, on the direction of the President, it shall be the duty of the Postmaster-General to arrange in like classes the clerks and persons so employed in the postal service in connection with any other post-office; and every such arrangement and classification upon being made shall be reported to the President.

Third. That from time to time said Secretary, the Postmaster-General, and each of the heads of departments mentioned in the one hundred and fifty-eighth section of the Revised Statutes, and each head of an office, shall, on the direction of the President, and for facilitating the execution of this act, respectively revise any then existing classification or arrangement of those in their respective departments and offices, and shall, for the purposes of the examination herein provided for, include in one or more of such classes, so far as practicable, subordinate places, clerks, and officers in the public service pertaining to their respective departments not before classified for examination.

SEC. 7. That after the expiration of six months from the passage of this act no officer or clerk shall be appointed, and no person shall be employed to enter or be promoted in either of the said classes now existing, or that may be arranged hereunder pursuant to said rules, until he has passed an examination, or is shown to be specially exempted from such examination in conformity herewith. But nothing herein contained shall be construed to take from those honorably discharged from the military or naval service any preference conferred by the seventeen hundred and fifty-fourth section of the Revised Statutes, nor to take from the President any authority not inconsistent with this act conferred by the seventeen hundred and fifty-third section of said statutes; nor shall any officer not in the executive branch of the government, or any person merely employed as a laborer or workman, be required to be classified hereunder; nor, unless by direction of the Senate, shall any person who has been nominated for confirmation by the Senate be required to be classified or to pass an examination.

SEC. 8. That no person habitually using intoxicating beverages to excess shall be appointed to, or retained in, any office, appointment, or employment to which the provisions of this act are applicable.

SEC. 9. That whenever there are already two or more members of a family in the public service in the grades covered by this act, no other member of such family shall be eligible to appointment to any of said grades.

SEC. 10. That no recommendation of any person who shall apply for office or place under the provisions of this act which may be given by any Senator or member of the House of Representatives, except as to the character or residence of the applicant, shall be received or considered by any person concerned in making any examination or appointment under this act.

Sec. 11. That no Senator, or Representative, or Territorial Delegate of the Congress, or Senator, Representative, or Delegate elect, or any officer or employee of either of said houses, and no executive, judicial, military, or naval officer of the United States, and no clerk or employee of any department, branch or bureau of the executive, judicial, or military or naval service of the United States, shall, directly or indirectly, solicit or receive, or be in any manner concerned in soliciting or receiving, any assessment, subscription, or contribution for any political purpose whatever, from any officer, clerk, or employee of the United States, or any department, branch, or bureau thereof, or from any person receiving any salary or compensation from moneys derived from the Treasury of the United States.

Sec. 12. That no person shall, in any room or building occupied in the discharge of official duties by any officer or employee of the United States mentioned in this act, or in any navy-yard, fort, or arsenal, solicit in any manner whatever, or receive any contribution of money or any other thing of value for any political purpose whatever.

Sec. 13. No officer or employee of the United States mentioned in this act shall discharge, or promote, or degrade, or in manner change the official rank or compensation of any other officer or employee, or promise or threaten so to do, for giving or withholding or neglecting to make any contribution of money or other valuable thing for any political purpose.

Sec. 14. That no officer, clerk, or other person in the service of the United States shall, directly or indirectly, give or hand over to any other officer, clerk, or person in the service of the United States, or to any Senator or Member of the House of Representatives, or Territorial Delegate, any money or other valuable thing on account of or to be applied to the promotion of any political object whatever.

Sec. 15. That any person who shall be guilty of violating any provision of the four foregoing sections shall be deemed guilty of a misdemeanor, and shall, on conviction thereof, be punished by a fine not exceeding five thousand dollars, or by imprisonment for a term not exceeding three years, or by such fine and imprisonment or both, in the discretion of the court.

Approved, January sixteenth, 1883.

The Interstate Commerce Act, 1887

Railroads were a central feature of economic life and political debate in late nineteenth-century America. Charges of bribery, corruption, and price fixing against the railroads began before most of them had begun laying track. Western agrarians felt especially aggrieved because they depended on railroads to get their goods to market. A series of state measures intended to regulate railroads' conduct were struck down during this era by the Supreme Court. Responding to calls for reform, the Interstate Commerce Act set up the first true federal commission—the Interstate Commerce Commission. The commission was empowered to investigate abuses under the law, which required that rates be published and be "reasonable and just," that secret rebates be discontinued, and that rates no longer discriminate against small markets.

Interstate Commerce Act

February 4, 1887

An act to regulate commerce.

Be it enacted by the Senate and House of Representatives of the United States of America in Congress assembled, That the provisions of this act shall apply to any common carrier or carriers engaged in the transportation of passengers or property wholly by railroad, or partly by railroad and partly by water when both are used, under a common control, management, or arrangement, for a continuous carriage or shipment, from one State or Territory of the United States, or the District of Columbia, to any other State or Territory of the United States, or the District of Columbia, or from any place in the United States to an adjacent foreign country, or from any place in the United States through a foreign country to any other place in the United States, and also to the transportation in like manner of property shipped from any place in the United States to a foreign country and carried from such place to a port of transshipment, or shipped from a foreign country to any place in the United States and carried to such place from a port of entry either in the United States or an adjacent foreign country: *Provided, however,* That the provisions of this act shall not apply to the transportation of passengers or property, or to the receiving, delivering, storage, or handling of property, wholly within one State, and not shipped to or from a foreign country from or to any State or Territory as aforesaid.

The term "railroad" as used in this act shall include all bridges and ferries used or operated in connection with any railroad, and also all the road in use by any corporation operating a railroad, whether owned or operated under a contract, agreement, or lease; and the term "transportation" shall include all instrumentalities of shipment or carriage.

All charges made for any service rendered or to be rendered in the transportation of passengers or property as aforesaid, or in connection therewith, or for the receiving, delivering, storage, or handling of such property, shall be reasonable and just; and every unjust and unreasonable charge for such service is prohibited and declared to be unlawful.

SEC. 2. That if any common carrier subject to the provisions of this act shall, directly or indirectly, by any special rate, rebate, drawback, or other device, charge, demand, collect, or receive from any person or persons a greater or less compensation for any service rendered, or to be rendered, in the transportation of passengers or property, subject to the provisions of this act, than it charges, demands, collects, or receives from any other person or persons for doing for him or them a like and contemporaneous service in the transportation of a like kind of traffic under substantially similar circumstances and conditions, such common carrier shall be deemed guilty of unjust discrimination, which is hereby prohibited and declared to be unlawful.

SEC. 3. That it shall be unlawful for any common carrier subject to the provisions of this act to make or give any undue or unreasonable preference or advantage to any particular person, company, firm, corporation, or locality, or any particular description of traffic, in any respect whatsoever, or to subject any particular person, company, firm, corporation, or locality, or any particular description of traffic, to any undue or unreasonable prejudice or disadvantage in any respect whatsoever.

Every common carrier subject to the provisions of this act shall, according to their respective powers, afford all reasonable, proper, and equal facilities for the interchange of traffic between their respective lines, and for the receiving, forwarding, and delivering of passengers and property to and from their several lines and those connecting therewith, and shall not discriminate in their rates and charges between such connecting lines; but this shall not be construed as requiring any such common carrier to give the use of its tracks or terminal facilities to another carrier engaged in like business.

Sec. 4. That it shall be unlawful for any common carrier subject to the provisions of this act to charge or receive any greater compensation in the aggregate for the transportation of passengers or of like kind of property, under substantially similar circumstances and conditions, for a shorter than for a longer distance over the same line, in the same direction, the shorter being included within the longer distance; but this shall not be construed as authorizing any common carrier within the terms of this act to charge and receive as great compensation for a shorter as for a longer distance: *Provided, however,* That upon application to the Commission appointed under the provisions of this act, such common carrier may, in special cases, after investigation by the Commission, be authorized to charge less for a longer than for shorter distances for the transportation of passengers or property; and the Commission may from time to time prescribe the extent to which such designated common carrier may be relieved from the operation of this section of this act.

Sec. 5. That it shall be unlawful for any common carrier subject to the provisions of this act to enter into any contract, agreement, or combination with any other common carrier or carriers for the pooling of freights of different and competing railroads, or to divide between them the aggregate or net proceeds of the earnings of such railroads, or any portion thereof; and in any case of an agreement for the pooling of freights as aforesaid, each day of its continuance shall be deemed a separate offense.

Sec. 6. That every common carrier subject to the provisions of this act shall print and keep for public inspection schedules showing the rates and fares and charges for the transportation of passengers and property which any such common carrier has established and which are in force at the time upon its railroad, as defined by the first section of this act. The schedules printed as aforesaid by any such common carrier shall plainly state the places upon its railroad between which property and passengers will be carried, and shall contain the classification of freight in force upon such railroad, and shall also state separately the terminal charges and any rules or regulations which in any wise change, affect, or determine any part or the aggregate of such aforesaid rates and fares and charges. Such schedules shall be plainly printed in large type, of at least the size of ordinary pica, and copies for the use of the public shall be kept in every depot or station upon any such railroad, in such places and in such form that they can be conveniently inspected. . . .

And when any such common carrier shall have established and published its rates, fares, and charges in compliance with the provisions of this section, it shall be unlawful for such common carrier to charge, demand, collect, or receive from any person or persons a greater or less compensation for the transportation of passengers or property, or for any services in connection therewith, than is specified in such published schedule of rates, fares, and charges as may at the time be in force.

Every common carrier subject to the provisions of this act shall file with the Commission hereinafter provided for copies of its schedules of rates, fares, and charges which have been established and published in compliance with the requirements of this section, and shall promptly notify said Commission of all changes made in the same. Every such common carrier shall also file with said Commission copies of all contracts, agreements, or arrangements with other common carriers in relation to any traffic affected by the provisions of this act to which it may be a party. And in cases where passengers and freight pass over continuous lines or routes operated by more than one common carrier, and the several common carriers operating such lines or routes establish joint tariffs of rates or fares or charges for such continuous lines or routes, copies of such joint tariffs shall also, in like manner, be filed with said Commission. Such joint rates, fares, and charges on such continuous lines so filed as aforesaid shall be made public by such common carriers when directed by said Commission, in so far as may, in the judgment of the Commission, be deemed practicable; and said Commission shall from time to time prescribe the measure of publicity which shall be given to such rates, fares, and charges, or to such part of them as it may deem it practicable for such common carriers to publish, and the places in which they shall be published; but no common carrier party to any such joint tariff shall be liable for the failure of any other common carrier party thereto to observe and adhere to the rates, fares, or charges thus made and published.

If any such common carrier shall neglect or refuse to file or publish its schedules or tariffs of rates, fares, and charges as provided in this section, or any part of the same, such common carrier shall, in addition to other penalties herein prescribed, be subject to a writ of mandamus, to be issued by any circuit court of the United States in the judicial district wherein the principal office of said common carrier is situated or wherein such offense may be committed, and if such common carrier be a foreign corporation, in the judicial circuit wherein such common carrier accepts traffic and has an agent to perform such service, to compel compliance with the aforesaid provisions of this section; and such writ shall issue in the name of the people of the United States, at the relation of the Commissioners appointed under the provisions of this act; and failure to comply with its requirements shall be punishable as and for a contempt; and the said Commissioners, as complainants, may also apply, in any such circuit court of the United States, for a writ of injunction against such common carrier, to restrain such common carrier from receiving or transporting property among the several States and Territories of the United States, or between the United States and adjacent foreign countries, or between ports of transshipment and of entry and the several States and Territories of the United States, as mentioned in the first section of this act, until such common carrier shall have complied with the aforesaid provisions of this section of this act.

Sec. 7. That it shall be unlawful for any common carrier subject to the provisions of this act to enter into any combination, contract, or agreement, expressed or implied, to prevent, by change of time schedule, carriage in different cars, or by other means or devices, the carriage of freights from being continuous from the place of shipment to the place of destination; and no break of bulk, stoppage, or interruption made by such common carrier shall prevent the carriage of freights from being and being treated as one continuous carriage from the place of shipment to the place of destination, unless such break, stoppage, or interruption was made in good faith for some necessary purpose, and without any intent to avoid or unnecessarily interrupt such continuous carriage or to evade any of the provisions of this act.

Sec. 8. That in case any common carrier subject to the provisions of this act shall do, cause to be done, or permit to be done any act, matter, or thing in this act prohibited or declared to be unlawful, or shall omit to do any act, matter, or thing in this act required to be done, such common carrier shall be liable to the person or persons injured thereby for the full amount of damages sustained in consequence of any such violation of the provisions of this act, together with a reasonable counsel or attorney's fee, to be fixed by the court in every case of recovery, which attorney's fee shall be taxed and collected as part of the costs in the case.

Sec. 9. That any person or persons claiming to be damaged by any common carrier subject to the provisions of this act may either make complaint to the Commission as hereinafter provided for, or may bring suit in his or their own behalf for the recovery of the damages for which such common carrier may be liable under the provisions of this act, in any district or circuit court of the United States of competent jurisdiction; but such person or persons shall not have the right to pursue both of said remedies, and must in each case elect which one of the two methods of procedure herein provided for he or they will adopt. In any such action brought for the recovery of damages the court before which the same shall be pending may compel any director, officer, receiver, trustee, or agent of the corporation or company defendant in such suit to attend, appear, and testify in such case, and may compel the production of the books and papers of such corporation or company party to any such suit; the claim that any such testimony or evidence may tend to criminate the person giving such evidence shall not excuse such witness from testifying, but such evidence or testimony shall not be used against such person on the trial of any criminal proceeding.

Sec. 10. That any common carrier subject to the provisions of this act, or, whenever such common carrier is a corporation, any director or officer thereof, or any receiver, trustee, lessee, agent, or person acting for or employed by such corporation, who, alone or with any other corporation, company, person, or party, shall willfully do or cause to be done, or shall willingly suffer or permit to be done, any act, matter, or thing in this act prohibited or declared to be unlawful, or who shall aid or abet therein, or shall willfully omit or fail to do any act, matter, or thing in this act required to be done, or shall cause or willingly suffer or permit any act, matter, or thing so directed or required by this act to be done not to be so done, or shall aid or abet any such omission or failure, or shall be guilty of any infraction of this act, or shall aid or abet therein, shall be deemed guilty of a misdemeanor, and shall, upon conviction thereof in any district court of the United States within the jurisdiction of which such offense was committed, be subject to a fine of not to exceed five thousand dollars for each offense.

Sec. 11. That a Commission is hereby created and established to be known as the Inter-State Commerce Commission, which shall be composed of five Commissioners, who shall be appointed by the President, by and with the advice and consent of the Senate. The Commissioners first appointed under this act shall continue in office for the term of two, three, four, five, and six years, respectively, from the first day of January, anno Domini eighteen hundred and eighty-seven, the term of each to be designated by the President; but their successors shall be appointed for terms of six years, except that any person chosen to fill a vacancy shall be appointed only for the unexpired term of the Commissioner whom he shall succeed. Any Commissioner may be removed by the President for inefficiency, neglect of duty, or malfeasance in office. Not more than three of the Commissioners shall be appointed from the same political party. No person in the employ of or holding any official relation to any common carrier subject to the provisions of this act, or owning stock or bonds thereof, or who is in any manner pecuniarily interested therein, shall enter upon the duties of or hold such office. Said Commissioners shall not engage in any other business, vocation, or employment. No vacancy in the Commission shall impair the right of the remaining Commissioners to exercise all the powers of the Commission.

Sec. 12. That the Commission hereby created shall have authority to inquire into the management of the business of all common carriers subject to the provisions of this act, and shall keep itself informed as to the manner and method in which the same is conducted, and shall have the right to obtain from such common carriers full and complete information necessary to enable the Commission to perform the duties and carry out the objects for which it was created; and for the purposes of this act the Commission shall have power to require the attendance and testimony of witnesses and the production of all books, papers, tariffs, contracts, agreements, and documents relating to any matter under investigation, and to that end may invoke the aid of any court of the United States in requiring the attendance and testimony of witnesses and the production of books, papers, and documents under the provisions of this section.

And any of the circuit courts of the United States within

the jurisdiction of which such inquiry is carried on may, in case of contumacy or refusal to obey a subpoena issued to any common carrier subject to the provisions of this act, or other person, issue an order requiring such common carrier or other person to appear before said Commission (and produce books and papers if so ordered) and give evidence touching the matter in question; and any failure to obey such order of the court may be punished by such court as a contempt thereof. The claim that any such testimony or evidence may tend to criminate the person giving such evidence shall not excuse such witness from testifying; but such evidence or testimony shall not be used against such person on the trial of any criminal proceeding.

Sec. 13. That any person, firm, corporation, or association, or any mercantile, agricultural, or manufacturing society, or any body politic or municipal organization complaining of anything done or omitted to be done by any common carrier subject to the provisions of this act in contravention of the provisions thereof, may apply to said Commission by petition, which shall briefly state the facts; whereupon a statement of the charges thus made shall be forwarded by the Commission to such common carrier, who shall be called upon to satisfy the complaint or to answer the same in writing within a reasonable time, to be specified by the Commission. If such common carrier, within the time specified, shall make reparation for the injury alleged to have been done, said carrier shall be relieved of liability to the complainant only for the particular violation of law thus complained of. If such carrier shall not satisfy the complaint within the time specified, or there shall appear to be any reasonable ground for investigating said complaint, it shall be the duty of the Commission to investigate the matters complained of in such manner and by such means as it shall deem proper.

Said Commission shall in like manner investigate any complaint forwarded by the railroad commissioner or railroad commission of any State or Territory, at the request of such commissioner or commission, and may institute any inquiry on its own motion in the same manner and to the same effect as though complaint had been made.

No complaint shall at any time be dismissed because of the absence of direct damage to the complainant.

Sec. 14. That whenever an investigation shall be made by said Commission, it shall be its duty to make a report in writing in respect thereto, which shall include the findings of fact upon which the conclusions of the Commission are based, together with its recommendation as to what reparation, if any, should be made by the common carrier to any party or parties who may be found to have been injured; and such findings so made shall thereafter, in all judicial proceedings, be deemed prima facie evidence as to each and every fact found.

All reports of investigations made by the Commission shall be entered of record, and a copy thereof shall be furnished to the party who may have complained, and to any common carrier that may have been complained of.

Sec. 15. That if in any case in which an investigation shall be made by said Commission it shall be made to appear to the satisfaction of the Commission, either by the testimony of witnesses or other evidence, that anything has been done or omitted to be done in violation of the provisions of this act, or of any law cognizable by said Commission, by any common carrier, or that any injury or damage has been sustained by the party or parties complaining, or by other parties aggrieved in consequence of any such violation, it shall be the duty of the Commission to forthwith cause a copy of its report in respect thereto to be delivered to such common carrier, together with a notice to said common carrier to cease and desist from such violation, or to make reparation for the injury so found to have been done, or both, within a reasonable time, to be specified by the Commission; and if, within the time specified, it shall be made to appear to the Commission that such common carrier has ceased from such violation of law, and has made reparation for the injury found to have been done, in compliance with the report and notice of the Commission, or to the satisfaction of the party complaining, a statement to that effect shall be entered of record by the Commission, and the said common carrier shall thereupon be relieved from further liability or penalty for such particular violation of law.

Sec. 16. That whenever any common carrier, as defined in and subject to the provisions of this act, shall violate or refuse or neglect to obey any lawful order or requirement of the Commission in this act named, it shall be the duty of the Commission, and lawful for any company or person interested in such order or requirement, to apply, in a summary way, by petition, to the circuit court of the United States sitting in equity in the judicial district in which the common carrier complained of has its principal office, or in which the violation or disobedience of such order or requirement shall happen, alleging such violation or disobedience, as the case may be; and the said court shall have power to hear and determine the matter, on such short notice to the common carrier complained of as the court shall deem reasonable; and such notice may be served on such common carrier, his or its officers, agents, or servants in such manner as the court shall direct; and said court shall proceed to hear and determine the matter speedily as a court of equity, and without the formal pleadings and proceedings applicable to ordinary suits in equity, but in such manner as to do justice in the premises; and to this end such court shall have power, if it think fit, to direct and prosecute, in such mode and by such persons as it may appoint, all such inquiries as the court may think needful to enable it to form a just judgment in the matter of such petition; and on such hearing the report of said Commission shall be prima facie evidence of the matters therein stated; and if it be made to appear to such court, on such hearing or on report of any such person or persons, that the lawful order or requirement of said Commission drawn in question has been violated or disobeyed, it shall be lawful for such court to issue a writ of injunction or other proper process, mandatory or otherwise, to restrain such common carrier from further continuing such violation or disobedience of such order or requirement of said Commission, and enjoining obedience to the same; and in case of any disobedience of any such writ of injunction or other proper process, mandatory or otherwise, it shall be lawful for such court to issue writs of attachment, or any other process of said court incident or applicable to writs of injunction or other proper process, mandatory or otherwise, against such common carrier, and if a corporation, against one or more of the directors, officers, or agents of the same, or against any owner, lessee, trustee, receiver, or other person failing to obey such writ of injunction or other proper process, mandatory or otherwise; and said court may, if it shall think fit, make an order directing such common carrier or other person so disobeying such writ of injunction or other proper process, mandatory or otherwise, to pay such sum of money not exceeding for each carrier or person in default the sum of five hundred dollars for every day after a day to be named in the order that such carrier or other person shall fail to obey such injunction or other proper process, mandatory or otherwise; and such moneys shall be payable as the court shall direct, either to the party complaining, or into court to abide the ultimate decision of the court, or into the Treasury; and payment thereof may, without prejudice to any other mode of recovering the same, be enforced by attachment or order in the nature of a writ of execution, in like manner as if the same had been recovered by a final decree in personam in such court. When the subject in dispute shall be of the value of two thousand dollars or more, either party to such proceeding before said court may appeal to the Supreme Court of the United States, under the same regulations now provided by law in respect of security for such appeal; but such appeal shall not operate to stay or supersede the order of the court or the execution of any writ or process thereon; and such court may, in every such matter, order the payment of such costs and counsel fees as shall be deemed reasonable. Whenever any such petition shall be filed or presented by the Commission it shall be the duty of the district attorney, under the direction of the Attorney-General of the United States, to prosecute the same; and the costs and expenses of such prosecution shall be paid out of the appropriation for the expenses of the courts of the United States. For the purposes of this act, excepting its penal provisions, the circuit courts of the United States shall be deemed to be always in session. . . .

SEC. 22. That nothing in this act shall apply to the carriage, storage, or handling of property free or at reduced rates for the United States, State, or municipal governments, or for charitable purposes, or to or from fairs and expositions for exhibition thereat, or the issuance of mileage, excursion, or commutation passenger tickets; nothing in this act shall be construed to prohibit any common carrier from giving reduced rates to ministers of religion; nothing in this act shall he construed to prevent railroads from giving free carriage to their own officers and employees, or to prevent the principal officers of any railroad company or companies from exchanging passes or tickets with other railroad companies for their officers and employees; and nothing in this act contained shall in any way abridge or alter the remedies now existing at common law or by statute, but the provisions of this act are in addition to such remedies: *Provided,* That no pending litigation shall in any way be affected by this act.

SEC. 23. That the sum of one hundred thousand dollars is hereby appropriated for the use and purposes of this act for the fiscal year ending June thirtieth, anno Domini eighteen hundred and eighty-eight, and the intervening time anterior thereto.

SEC. 24. That the provisions of sections eleven and eighteen of this act, relating to the appointment and organization of the Commission herein provided for, shall take effect immediately, and the remaining provisions of this act shall take effect sixty days after its passage.

Approved, February 4, 1887.

Veto of Texas Seed Bill, *Grover Cleveland*, 1887

During 1886, a severe drought in Texas destroyed the bulk, not just of the corn crop, but also of the seed needed to plant crops for the next season. At this time the federal government did not usually provide direct relief to its citizens. Relief bills generally took the form of pensions awarded to specific citizens on the basis of public service. Grover Cleveland (1837–1908) was president from 1885 to 1889 and again from 1893 to 1897. A Democrat, he consistently argued for fiscal restraint, small government, and free markets. His veto message expresses the concern that such assistance, though small in amount ($10,000), was not warranted by the Constitution and would undermine both self-help and charity by encouraging reliance on a paternal federal government.

Veto Message—Distribution of Seeds

February 16, 1887

Grover Cleveland

The SPEAKER laid before the House the following message from the President of the United States; which was read:

To the House of Representatives:

I return without my approval House bill No. 10203, entitled "An act to enable the Commissioner of Agriculture to make a special distribution of seeds in the drought-stricken counties of Texas, and making an appropriation therefor."

It is represented that a long-continued and extensive drought has existed in certain portions of the State of Texas, resulting in a failure of crops and consequent distress and destitution.

Though there has been some difference in statements concerning the extent of the people's needs in the localities thus affected, there seems to be no doubt that there has existed a condition calling for relief; and I am willing to believe that, notwithstanding the aid already furnished, a donation of seed grain to the farmers located in this region to enable them to put in new crops would serve to avert a continuance or return of an unfortunate blight.

And yet I feel obliged to withhold my approval of the plan as proposed by this bill to indulge a benevolent and charitable sentiment through the appropriation of public funds for that purpose.

I can find no warrant for such an appropriation in the Constitution; and I do not believe that the power and duty of the General Government ought to be extended to the relief of individual suffering which is in no manner properly related to the public service or benefit. A prevalent tendency to disregard the limited mission of this power and duty should, I think, be steadfastly resisted, to the end that the lesson should be constantly enforced that, though the people support the Government, the Government should not support the people.

The friendliness and charity of our countrymen can always be relied upon to relieve their fellow-citizens in misfortune. This has been respeatedly and quite lately demonstrated. Federal aid in such cases encourages the expectation of paternal care on the part of the Government and weakens the sturdiness of our national character, while it prevents the indulgence among out people of that kindly sentiment and conduct which strengthens the bonds of a common brotherhood.

It is within my personal knowledge that individual aid has to some extent already been extended to the sufferers mentioned in this bill. The failure of the proposed appropriation of $10,000 additional to meet their remaining wants will not necessarily result in continued distress if the emergency is fully made known to the people of the country.

It is here suggested that the Commissioner of Agriculture is annually directed to expend a large sum of money for the purchase, propagation, and distribution of seeds and other things of this description, two-thirds of which are, upon the request of Senators, Representatives, and Delegates in Congress, supplied to them for distribution among their constituents. The appropriation of the current year for this purpose is $100,000, and it will probably be no less in the appropriation for the ensuing year. I understand that a large quantity of grain is furnished for such distribution, and it is supposed that this free apportionment among their neighbors is a privilege which may be waived by our Senators and Representatives. If sufficient of them should request the Commissioner of Agriculture to send their shares of the grain thus allowed them to the suffering farmers of Texas, they might be enabled to sow their crops, the constituents for whom in theory this grain is intended could well bear thus temporary deprivation, and the donors would experience the satisfaction attending deeds of charity.

GROVER CLEVELAND.

Executive Mansion,
Washington, February 16, 1887.

Sherman Antitrust Act, 1890

Opposition to powerful corporations and combinations of corporations grew substantially during the period after the Civil War. Farmers and ranchers were particularly concerned, but merchants and political activists also sought to defeat what they saw as unjustly powerful economic concerns and to stop unfair trade practices intended to artificially increase prices. These practices included lowering prices so as to drive the competition out of business, buying out competitors, and otherwise gaining monopoly control, then forcing customers to sign long-term contracts or contracts for unwanted goods in exchange for the goods desired. Passed in 1890, the Sherman Antitrust Act authorized the Justice Department to sue companies they found to be acting in these ways. Sanctions included fines, imprisonment, and the dissolving of corporate combinations. The act was little used until the "trust busting" presidency of Theodore Roosevelt. Several major combinations were dissolved under the act, including that of the Standard Oil Company and the American Tobacco Company. The act also was used to break up labor unions as restraints on trade until this practice ceased under the terms of the Clayton Antitrust Act (1914).

Sherman Antitrust Act

July 2, 1890

An act to protect trade and commerce against unlawful restraints and monopolies.

Be it enacted by the Senate and House of Representatives of the United States of America in Congress assembled,

SEC. 1. Every contract, combination in the form of trust or otherwise, or conspiracy, in restraint of trade or commerce among the several States, or with foreign nations, is hereby declared to be illegal. Every person who shall make any such contract or engage in any such combination or conspiracy, shall be deemed guilty of a misdemeanor, and, on conviction thereof, shall be punished by fine not exceeding five thousand dollars, or by imprisonment not exceeding one year, or by both said punishments, in the discretion of the court.

SEC. 2. Every person who shall monopolize, or attempt to monopolize, or combine or conspire with any other person or persons, to monopolize any part of the trade or commerce among the several States, or with foreign nations, shall be deemed guilty of a misdemeanor, and, on conviction thereof, shall be punished by fine not exceeding five thousand dollars, or by imprisonment not exceeding one year, or by both said punishments, in the discretion of the court.

SEC. 3. Every contract, combination in form of trust or otherwise, or conspiracy, in restraint of trade or commerce in any Territory of the United States or of the District of Columbia, or in restraint of trade or commerce between any such Territory and another, or between any such Territory or Territories and any State or States or the District of Columbia, or with foreign nations, or between the District of Columbia and any State or States or foreign nations, is hereby declared illegal. Every person who shall make any such contract or engage in any such combination or conspiracy, shall be deemed guilty of a misdemeanor, and, on conviction thereof, shall be punished by fine not exceeding five thousand dollars, or by imprisonment not exceeding one year, or by both said punishments, in the discretion of the court.

SEC. 4. The several circuit courts of the United States are hereby invested with jurisdiction to prevent and restrain violations of this act; and it shall be the duty of the several district attorneys of the United States, in their respective districts, under the direction of the Attorney-General, to institute proceedings in equity to prevent and restrain such violations. Such proceedings may be by way of petition setting forth the case and praying that such violation shall be enjoined or otherwise prohibited. When the parties complained of shall have been duly notified of such petition the court shall proceed, as soon as may be, to the hearing and determination of the case; and pending such petition and before final decree, the court may at any time make such temporary restraining order or prohibition as shall be deemed just in the premises.

SEC. 5. Whenever it shall appear to the court before which any proceeding under section four of this act may be pending, that the ends of justice require that other parties should be brought before the court, the court may cause them to be summoned, whether they reside in the district in which the court is held or not; and subpoenas to that end may be served in any district by the marshal thereof.

SEC. 6. Any property owned under any contract or by any combination, or pursuant to any conspiracy (and being the subject thereof) mentioned in section one of this act, and being in the course of transportation from one State to another, or to a foreign country, shall be forfeited to the United States, and may be seized and condemned by like proceedings as those provided by law for the forfeiture, seizure, and condemnation of property imported into the United States contrary to law.

SEC. 7. Any person who shall be injured in his business or property by any other person or corporation by reason of anything forbidden or declared to be unlawful by this act, may sue therefor in any circuit court of the United States in the district in which the defendant resides or is found, without respect to the amount in controversy, and shall recover three fold the damages by him sustained, and the costs of suit, including a reasonable attorney's fee.

SEC. 8. That the word "person," or "persons," wherever used in this act shall be deemed to include corporations and associations existing under or authorized by the laws of either the United States, the laws of any of the Territories, the laws of any State, or the laws of any foreign country.

Approved, July 2, 1890.

First Message to Congress, *Theodore Roosevelt*, 1901

Theodore Roosevelt became the youngest president in American history when President McKinley was assassinated by an anarchist and Roosevelt, his vice president, succeeded him in office. Though not yet elected in his own right to the presidency, Roosevelt immediately asserted his public, rhetorical leadership. Having promised Republican Party leaders that he would follow in the cautious ways of McKinley, Roosevelt nonetheless called for broad policies aimed at bringing large economic and industrial organizations under the regulatory control of the federal government.

President's Message to the Senate and House of Representatives

December 3, 1901

Theodore Roosevelt

During the last five years business confidence has been restored, and the Nation is to be congratulated because of its present abounding prosperity. Such prosperity can never be created by law alone, although it is easy enough to destroy it by mischievous laws. If the hand of the Lord is heavy upon any country, if flood or drought comes, human wisdom is powerless to avert the calamity. Moreover, no law can guard us against the consequences of our own folly. The men who are idle or credulous, the men who seek gains not by genuine work with head or hand, but by gambling in any form, are always a source of menace not only to themselves, but to others. If the business world loses its head, it loses what legislation cannot supply. Fundamentally the welfare of each citizen, and therefore the welfare of the aggregate of citizens which makes the Nation, must rest upon individual thrift and energy, resolution and intelligence. Nothing can take the place of this individual capacity; but wise legislation and honest and intelligent administration can give it the fullest scope, the largest opportunity to work to good effect.

The tremendous and highly complex industrial development which went on with ever accelerated rapidity during the latter half of the nineteenth century brings us face to face, at the beginning of the twentieth, with very serious social problems. The old laws, and the old customs which had almost the binding force of law, were once quite sufficient to regulate the accumulation and distribution of wealth. Since the industrial changes which have so enormously increased the productive power of mankind, they are no longer sufficient.

The growth of cities has gone on beyond comparison faster than the growth of the country, and the upbuilding of the great industrial centers has meant a startling increase, not merely in the aggregate of wealth, but in the number of very large individual, and especially of very large corporate, fortunes. The creation of these great corporate fortunes has not been due to the tariff nor to any other governmental action, but to natural causes in the business world, operating in other countries as they operate in our own.

The process has aroused much antagonism, a great part of which is wholly without warrant. It is not true that as the rich have grown richer the poor have grown poorer. On the contrary, never before has the average man, the wage-worker, the farmer, the small trader, been so well off as in this country and at the present time. There have been abuses connected with the accumulation of wealth; yet it remains true that a fortune accumulated in legitimate business can be accumulated by the person specially benefited only on condition of conferring immense incidental benefits upon others. Successful enterprise, of the type which benefits all mankind, can only exist if the conditions are such as to offer great prizes as the rewards of success.

The captains of industry, who have driven the railway systems across this continent, who have built up our commerce, who have developed our manufactures, have on the whole done great good to our people. Without them the material development of which we are so justly proud could never have taken place. Moreover we should recognize the immense importance to this material development of leaving as unhampered as is compatible with the public good the strong and forceful men upon whom the success of business operations inevitably rests. The slightest study of business conditions will satisfy anyone capable of forming a judgment that the personal equation is the most important factor in a business operation; that the business ability of the man at the head of any business concern, big or little, is usually the factor which fixes the gulf between striking success and hopeless failure.

An additional reason for caution in dealing with corporations is to be found in the international commercial conditions of to-day. The same business conditions which have produced the great aggregations of corporate and individual wealth have made them very potent factors in international commercial competition. Business concerns which have the largest means at their disposal and are managed by the ablest men are naturally those which take the lead in the strife for commercial supremacy among the nations of the world. America has only just begun to assume that commanding position in the international business world which we believe will more and more be hers. It is of the utmost importance that this position be not jeopardized, especially at a time when the overflowing abundance of our own natural resources and the skill, business energy, and mechanical aptitude of our people make foreign markets essential. Under such conditions it would be most unwise to cramp or to fetter the youthful strength of our nation.

Moreover, it cannot too often be pointed out that to strike with ignorant violence at the interests of one set of men almost inevitably endangers the interests of all. The fundamental rule in our national life—the rule which underlies all others—is that, on the whole, and in the long run, we shall go up or down together. There are exceptions; and in times of prosperity some will prosper far more, and in times of adversity some will suffer far more, than others; but speaking generally, a period of good times means that all share more or less in them, and in a period of hard times all feel the stress to a greater or less degree. It surely ought not to be necessary to enter into any proof of this statement; the memory of the lean years which began in 1893 is still vivid, and we can contrast them with the conditions in this very year which is now closing. Disaster to great business enterprises can never have its effects limited to the men at the top. It spreads throughout, and while it is bad for everybody, it is worst for those farthest down. The capitalist may be shorn of his luxuries; but the wage-worker may be deprived of even bare necessities.

The mechanism of modern business is so delicate that extreme care must be taken not to interfere with it in a spirit of rashness or ignorance. Many of those who have made it their vocation to denounce the great industrial combinations which are popularly, although with technical inaccuracy, known as "trusts," appeal especially to hatred and fear. These are precisely the two emotions, particularly when combined with ignorance, which unfit men for the exercise of cool and steady judgment. In facing new industrial conditions, the whole history of the world shows that legislation will generally be both unwise and ineffective unless undertaken after calm inquiry and with sober self-restraint. Much of the legislation directed at the trusts would have been exceedingly mischievous had it not also been entirely ineffective. In accordance with a well-known sociological law, the ignorant or reckless agitator has been the really effective friend of the evils which he has been nominally opposing. In dealing with business interests, for the Government to undertake by crude and ill-considered legislation to do what may turn out to be bad, would be to incur the risk of such far-reaching national disaster that it would be preferable to undertake nothing at all. The men who demand the impossible or the undesirable serve as the allies of the forces with which they are nominally at war, for they hamper those who would endeavor to find out in rational fashion what the wrongs really are and to what extent and in what manner it is practicable to apply remedies.

All this is true; and yet it is also true that there are real and grave evils, one of the chief being over-capitalization because of its many baleful consequences; and a resolute and practical effort must be made to correct these evils.

There is a widespread conviction in the minds of the American people that the great corporations known as trusts are in certain of their features and tendencies hurtful to the general welfare. This springs from no spirit of envy or uncharitableness, nor lack of pride in the great industrial achievements that have placed this country at the head of the nations struggling for commercial supremacy. It does not rest upon a lack of intelligent appreciation of the necessity of meeting changing and changed conditions of trade with new methods, nor upon ignorance of the fact that combination of capital in the effort to accomplish great things is necessary when the world's progress demands that great things be done. It is based upon sincere conviction that combination and concentration should be, not prohibited, but supervised and within reasonable limits controlled; and in my judgment this conviction is right.

It is no limitation upon property rights or freedom of contract to require that when men receive from Government the privilege of doing business under corporate form, which frees them from individual responsibility, and enables them to call into their enterprises the capital of the public, they shall do so upon absolutely truthful representations as to the value of the property in which the capital is to be invested. Corporations engaged in interstate commerce should be regulated if they are found to exercise a license working to the public injury. It should be as much the aim of those who seek for social betterment to rid the business world of crimes of cunning as to rid the entire body politic of crimes of violence. Great corporations exist only because they are created and safeguarded by our institutions; and it is therefore our right and our duty to see that they work in harmony with these institutions.

The first essential in determining how to deal with the great industrial combinations is knowledge of the facts—publicity. In the interest of the public, the Government should have the right to inspect and examine the workings of the great corporations engaged in interstate business. Publicity is the only sure remedy which we can now invoke. What further remedies are needed in the way of governmental regulation, or taxation, can only be determined after publicity has been obtained, by process of law, and in the course of administration. The first requisite is knowledge, full and complete—knowledge which may be made public to the world.

Artificial bodies, such as corporations and joint stock or other associations, depending upon any statutory law for their existence or privileges, should be subject to proper governmental supervision, and full and accurate information as to their operations should be made public regularly at reasonable intervals.

The large corporations, commonly called trusts, though organized in one State, always do business in many States, often doing very little business in the State where they are incorporated. There is utter lack of uniformity in the State laws about them; and as no State has any exclusive interest in or power over their acts, it has in practice proved impossible to get adequate regulation through State action. Therefore, in the interest of the whole people, the Nation should, without interfering with the power of the States in the matter itself, also assume power of supervision and regulation over all corporations doing an interstate business. This is especially true where the corporation derives a portion of its wealth from the existence of some monopolistic element or tendency in its business. There would be no hardship in such supervision;

banks are subject to it, and in their case it is now accepted as a simple matter of course. Indeed, it is probable that supervision of corporations by the National Government need not go so far as is now the case with the supervision exercised over them by so conservative a State as Massachusetts, in order to produce excellent results.

When the Constitution was adopted, at the end of the eighteenth century, no human wisdom could foretell the sweeping changes, alike in industrial and political conditions, which were to take place by the beginning of the twentieth century. At that time it was accepted as a matter of course that the several States were the proper authorities to regulate, so far as was then necessary, the comparatively insignificant and strictly localized corporate bodies of the day. The conditions are now wholly different and wholly different action is called for. I believe that a law can be framed which will enable the National Government to exercise control along the lines above indicated; profiting by the experience gained through the passage and administration of the Interstate-Commerce Act. If, however, the judgment of the Congress is that it lacks the constitutional power to pass such an act, then a constitutional amendment should be submitted to confer the power.

There should be created a Cabinet officer, to be known as Secretary of Commerce and Industries, as provided in the bill introduced at the last session of the Congress. It should be his province to deal with commerce in its broadest sense: including among many other things whatever concerns labor and all matters affecting the great business corporations and our merchant marine.

The course proposed is one phase of what should be a comprehensive and far-reaching scheme of constructive statesmanship for the purpose of broadening our markets, securing our business interests on a safe basis, and making firm our new position in the international industrial world; while scrupulously safeguarding the rights of wage-worker and capitalist, of investor and private citizen, so as to secure equity as between man and man in this Republic.

With the sole exception of the farming interest, no one matter is of such vital moment to our whole people as the welfare of the wage-workers. If the farmer and the wage-worker are well off, it is absolutely certain that all others will be well off, too. It is therefore a matter for hearty congratulation that on the whole wages are higher to-day in the United States than ever before in our history, and far higher than in any other country. The standard of living is also higher than ever before. Every effort of legislator and administrator should be bent to secure the permanency of this condition of things and its improvement wherever possible. Not only must our labor be protected by the tariff, but it should also be protected so far as it is possible from the presence in this country of any laborers brought over by contract, or of those who, coming freely, yet represent a standard of living so depressed that they can undersell our men in the labor market and drag them to a lower level. I regard it as necessary, with this end in view, to re-enact immediately the law excluding Chinese laborers and to strengthen it wherever necessary in order to make its enforcement entirely effective.

The National Government should demand the highest quality of service from its employees; and in return it should be a good employer. If possible legislation should be passed, in connection with the Interstate Commerce Law, which will render effective the efforts of different States to do away with the competition of convict contract labor in the open labor market. So far as practicable under the conditions of Government work, provision should be made to render the enforcement of the eight-hour law easy and certain. In all industries carried on directly or indirectly for the United States Government women and children should be protected from excessive hours of labor, from night work, and from work under unsanitary conditions. The Government should provide in its contracts that all work should be done under "fair" conditions, and in addition to setting a high standard should uphold it by proper inspection, extending if necessary to the subcontractors. The Government should forbid all night work for women and children, as well as excessive overtime. For the District of Columbia a good factory law should be passed; and, as a powerful indirect aid to such laws, provision should be made to turn the inhabited alleys, the existence of which is a reproach to our Capital City, into minor streets, where the inhabitants can live under conditions favorable to health and morals.

American wage-workers work with their heads as well as their hands. Moreover, they take a keen pride in what they are doing; so that, independent of the reward, they wish to turn out a perfect job. This is the great secret of our success in competition with the labor of foreign countries.

The most vital problem with which this country, and for that matter the whole civilized world, has to deal, is the problem which has for one side the betterment of social conditions, moral and physical, in large cities, and for another side the effort to deal with that tangle of far-reaching questions which we group together when we speak of "labor." The chief factor in the success of each man—wage-worker, farmer, and capitalist alike—must ever be the sum total of his own individual qualities and abilities. Second only to this comes the power of acting in combination or association with others. Very great good has been and will be accomplished by associations or unions of wage-workers, when managed with forethought, and when they combine insistence upon their own rights with law-abiding respect for the rights of others. The display of these qualities in such bodies is a duty to the Nation no less than to the associations themselves. Finally, there must also in many cases be action by the Government in order to safeguard the rights and interests of all. Under our Constitution there is much more scope for such action by the State and the municipality than by the Nation. But on points such as those touched on above the National Government can act.

When all is said and done, the rule of brotherhood remains as the indispensable prerequisite to success in the kind of national life for which we strive. Each man must work for himself, and unless he so works no outside help can avail him; but each man must remember also that he is indeed his brother's keeper, and that while no man who refuses to walk can be carried with advantage to himself or anyone else, yet that each at times stumbles or halts, that each at times needs to have the helping hand outstretched to him. To be permanently effective, aid must always take the form of helping a man to help himself; and we can all best help ourselves by joining together in the work that is of common interest to all.

Federal Trade Commission Act, 1914

Before establishment of the Federal Trade Commission (FTC), federal action against anticompetitive practices generally took the form of lawsuits filed against particular corporations for specific conduct. This was the form of Theodore Roosevelt's "trust busting," carried forward by his successor, William Howard Taft. When Woodrow Wilson became president, he sought institutionalization of regulations protecting consumers from unfair trade practices. The FTC was empowered to investigate, hold hearings, and issue orders against corporations it found to be violating provisions of relevant federal legislation.

Federal Trade Commission Act

September 26, 1914

An Act To create a Federal Trade Commission, to define its powers and duties, and for other purposes.

Be it enacted by the Senate and House of Representatives of the United States of America in Congress assembled, That a commission is hereby created and established, to be known as the Federal Trade Commission (hereinafter referred to as the commission), which shall be composed of five commissioners, who shall be appointed by the President, by and with the advice and consent of the Senate. Not more than three of the commissioners shall be members of the same political party. The first commissioners appointed shall continue in office for terms of three, four, five, six, and seven years, respectively, from the date of the taking effect of this Act, the term of each to be designated by the President, but their successors shall be appointed for terms of seven years, except that any person chosen to fill a vacancy shall be appointed only for the unexpired term of the commissioner whom he shall succeed. The commission shall choose a chairman from its own membership. No commissioner shall engage in any other business, vocation, or employment. Any commissioner may be removed by the President for inefficiency, neglect of duty, or malfeasance in office. A vacancy in the commission shall not impair the right of the remaining commissioners to exercise all the powers of the commission.

The commission shall have an official seal, which shall be judicially noticed. . . .

SEC. 5. That unfair methods of competition in commerce are hereby declared unlawful.

The commission is hereby empowered and directed to prevent persons, partnerships, or corporations, except banks, and common carriers subject to the Acts to regulate commerce, from using unfair methods of competition in commerce.

Whenever the commission shall have reason to believe that any such person, partnership, or corporation has been or is using any unfair method of competition in commerce, and if it shall appear to the commission that a proceeding by it in respect thereof would be to the interest of the public, it shall issue and serve upon such person, partnership, or corporation a complaint stating its charges in that respect, and containing a notice of a hearing upon a day and at a place therein fixed at least thirty days after the service of said complaint. The person, partnership, or corporation so complained of shall have the right to appear at the place and time so fixed and show cause why an order should not be entered by the commission requiring such person, partnership, or corporation to cease and desist from the violation of the law so charged in said complaint. Any person, partnership, or corporation may make application, and upon good cause shown may be allowed by the commission, to intervene and appear in said proceeding by counsel or in person. The testimony in any such proceeding shall be reduced to writing and filed in the office of the commission. If upon such hearing the commission shall be of the opinion that the method of competition in question is prohibited by this Act, it shall make a report in writing in which it shall state its findings as to the facts, and shall issue and cause to be served on such person, partnership, or corporation an order requiring such person, partnership, or corporation to cease and desist from using such method of competition. Until a transcript of the record in such hearing shall have been filed in a circuit court of appeals of the United States, as hereinafter provided, the commission may at any time, upon such notice and in such manner as it shall deem proper, modify or set aside, in whole or in part, any report or any order made or issued by it under this section.

If such person, partnership, or corporation fails or neglects to obey such order of the commission while the same is in effect, the commission may apply to the circuit court of appeals of the United States, within any circuit where the method of competition in question was used or where such person, partnership, or corporation resides or carries on business, for the enforcement of its order, and shall certify and file with its application a transcript of the entire record in the proceeding, including all the testimony taken and the report and order of the commission. Upon such filing of the application and transcript the court shall cause notice thereof to be served upon such person, partnership, or corporation and thereupon shall have jurisdiction of the proceeding and of the question determined therein, and shall have power to make and enter upon the pleadings, testimony, and proceedings set forth in such transcript a decree affirming, modifying, or setting aside the order of the commission. The findings of the commission as to the facts, if supported by testimony, shall be conclusive. If either party shall apply to the court for leave to adduce additional evidence, and shall show to the satisfaction of the court that such additional evidence is material and that there were reasonable grounds for the failure to adduce such evidence in the proceeding before the commission, the court may order such additional evidence to be taken before the commission and to be adduced upon the hearing in such manner and upon such terms and conditions as to the court may seem proper. The commission may modify its findings as to the facts, or make new findings, by reason of the additional evidence so taken, and it shall file such modified or new findings, which, if supported by testimony, shall be conclusive, and its recommendation, if any, for the modification or setting aside of its original order, with the return of such additional evidence. The judgment and decree of the court shall be final, except that the same shall be subject to review by the Supreme Court upon certiorari as provided in section two hundred and forty of the Judicial Code.

Any party required by such order of the commission to cease and desist from using such method of competition may obtain a review of such order in said circuit court of appeals by filing in the court a written petition praying that the order of the commission be set aside. A copy of such petition shall be forthwith served upon the commission, and thereupon the commission forthwith shall certify and file in the court a transcript of the record as hereinbefore provided. Upon the filing of the transcript the court shall have the same jurisdiction to affirm, set aside, or modify the order of the commission as in the case of an application by the commission for the enforcement of its order, and the findings of the commission as to the facts, if supported by testimony, shall in like manner be conclusive.

The jurisdiction of the circuit court of appeals of the United States to enforce, set aside, or modify orders of the commission shall be exclusive.

Such proceedings in the circuit court of appeals shall be given precedence over other cases pending therein, and shall be in every way expedited. No order of the commission or judgment of the court to enforce the same shall in any wise relieve or absolve any person, partnership, or corporation from any liability under the antitrust acts.

Complaints, orders, and other processes of the commission under this section may be served by anyone duly authorized by the commission, either (a) by delivering a copy thereof to the person to be served, or to a member of the partnership to be served, or to the president, secretary, or other executive officer or a director of the corporation to be served; or (b) by leaving a copy thereof at the principal office or place of business of such person, partnership, or corporation; or (c) by registering and mailing a copy thereof addressed to such person, partnership, or corporation at his or its principal office or place of business. The verified return by the person so serving said complaint, order, or other process setting forth the manner of said service shall be proof of the same, and the return post-office receipt for said complaint, order, or other process registered and mailed as aforesaid shall be proof of the service of the same.

SEC. 6. That the commission shall also have power—

(a) To gather and compile information concerning, and to investigate from time to time the organization, business, conduct, practices, and management of any corporation engaged in commerce, excepting banks and common carriers subject to the Act to regulate commerce, and its relation to other corporations and to individuals, associations, and partnerships.

(b) To require, by general or special orders, corporations engaged in commerce, excepting banks, and common carriers subject to the Act to regulate commerce, or any class of them, or any of them, respectively, to file with the commission in such form as the commission may prescribe annual or special, or both annual and special, reports or answers in writing to specific questions, furnishing to the commission such information as it may require as to the organization, business, conduct, practices, management, and relation to other corporations, partnerships, and individuals of the respective corporations filing such reports or answers in writing. Such reports and answers shall be made under oath, or otherwise, as the commission may prescribe, and shall be filed with the commission within such reasonable period as the commission may prescribe, unless additional time be granted in any case by the commission.

(c) Whenever a final decree has been entered against any defendant corporation in any suit brought by the United States to prevent and restrain any violation of the antitrust Acts, to make investigation, upon its own initiative, of the manner in which the decree has been or is being carried out, and upon the application of the Attorney General it shall be its duty to make such investigation. It shall transmit to the Attorney General a report embodying its findings and recommendations as a result of any such investigation, and the report shall be made public in the discretion of the commission.

(d) Upon the direction of the President or either House of Congress to investigate and report the facts relating to any alleged violations of the antitrust Acts by any corporation.

(e) Upon the application of the Attorney General to investigate and make recommendations for the readjustment of the business of any corporation alleged to be violating the antitrust Acts in order that the corporation may thereafter maintain its organization, management, and conduct of business in accordance with law.

(f) To make public from time to time such portions of the information obtained by it hereunder, except trade secrets and names of customers, as it shall deem expedient in the public interest; and to make annual and special reports to the Congress and to submit therewith recommendations for additional legislation; and to provide for the publication of its reports and decisions in such form and manner as may be best adapted for public information and use.

(g) From time to time to classify corporations and to make rules and regulations for the purpose of carrying out the provisions of this Act.

(h) To investigate, from time to time, trade conditions in and with foreign countries where associations, combinations, or practices of manufacturers, merchants, or traders, or other conditions, may affect the foreign trade of the United States, and to report to Congress thereon, with such recommendations as it deems advisable.

SEC. 7. That in any suit in equity brought by or under the direction of the Attorney General as provided in the antitrust Acts, the court may, upon the conclusion of the testimony therein, if it shall be then of opinion that the complainant is entitled to relief, refer said suit to the commission, as a master in chancery, to ascertain and report an appropriate form of decree therein. The commission shall proceed upon such notice to the parties and under such rules of procedure as the court may prescribe, and upon the coming in of such report such exceptions may be filed and such proceedings had in relation thereto as upon the report of a master in other equity causes, but the court may adopt or reject such report, in whole or in part, and enter such decree as the nature of the case may in its judgment require.

SEC. 8. That the several departments and bureaus of the Government when directed by the President shall furnish the commission, upon its request, all records, papers, and information in their possession relating to any corporation subject to any of the provisions of this Act, and shall detail from time to time such officials and employees to the commission as he may direct.

SEC. 9. That for the purposes of this Act the commission, or its duly authorized agent or agents, shall at all reasonable times have access to, for the purpose of examination, and the right to copy any documentary evidence of any corporation being investigated or proceeded against; and the commission shall have power to require by subpoena the attendance and testimony of witnesses and the production of all such documentary evidence relating to any matter under investigation. Any member of the commission may sign subpoenas, and members and examiners of the commission may administer oaths and affirmations, examine witnesses, and receive evidence.

Such attendance of witnesses, and the production of such documentary evidence, may be required from any place in the United States, at any designated place of hearing. And in case of disobedience to a subpoena the commission may invoke the aid of any court of the United States in requiring the attendance and testimony of witnesses and the production of documentary evidence.

Any of the district courts of the United States within the jurisdiction of which such inquiry is carried on may, in case of contumacy or refusal to obey a subpoena issued to any corporation or other person, issue an order requiring such corporation or other person to appear before the commissioner, or to produce documentary evidence if so ordered, or to give evidence touching the matter in question; and any failure to obey such order of the court may be punished by such court as a contempt thereof.

Upon the application of the Attorney General of the United States, at the request of the commission, the district courts of the United States shall have jurisdiction to issue writs of mandamus commanding any person or corporation to comply with the provisions of this Act or any order of the commission made in pursuance thereof.

The commission may order testimony to be taken by deposition in any proceeding or investigation pending under this Act at any stage of such proceeding or investigation. Such depositions may be taken before any person designated by the commission and having power to administer oaths. Such testimony shall be reduced to writing by the person taking the deposition, or under his direction, and shall then be subscribed by the deponent. Any person may be compelled to appear and depose and to produce documentary evidence in the same manner as witnesses may be compelled to appear and testify and produce documentary evidence before the commission as hereinbefore provided.

Witnesses summoned before the commission shall be paid the same fees and mileage that are paid witnesses in the courts of the United States, and witnesses whose depositions are taken and the persons taking the same shall severally be entitled to the same fees as are paid for like services in the courts of the United States.

No person shall be excused from attending and testifying or from producing documentary evidence before the commission or in obedience to the subpoena of the commission on the ground or for the reason that the testimony or evidence, documentary or otherwise, required of him may tend to criminate him or subject him to a penalty or forfeiture. But no natural person shall be prosecuted or subjected to any penalty or forfeiture for or on account of any transaction, matter, or thing concerning which he may testify, or produce evidence, documentary or otherwise, before the commission in obedience to a subpoena issued by it: *Provided,* That no natural person so testifying shall be exempt from prosecution and punishment for perjury committed in so testifying.

SEC. 10. That any person who shall neglect or refuse to attend and testify, or to answer any lawful inquiry, or to produce documentary evidence, if in his power to do so, in obedience to the subpoena or lawful requirement of the commission, shall be guilty of an offense and upon conviction thereof by a court of competent jurisdiction shall be punished by a fine of not less than $1,000 nor more than $5,000, or by imprisonment for not more than one year, or by both such fine and imprisonment.

Any person who shall willfully make, or cause to be made, any false entry or statement of fact in any report required to be made under this Act, or who shall willfully make, or cause to be made, any false entry in any account, record, or memorandum kept by any corporation subject to this Act, or who shall willfully neglect or fail to make, or to cause to be made, full, true, and correct entries in such accounts, records, or memoranda of all facts and transactions appertaining to the business of such corporation, or who shall willfully remove out of the jurisdiction of the United States, or willfully mutilate, alter, or by any other means falsify any documentary evidence of such corporation, or who shall willfully refuse to submit to the commission or to any of its authorized agents, for the purpose of inspection and taking copies, any documentary evidence of such corporation in his possession or within his control, shall be deemed guilty of an offense against the United States, and shall be subject, upon conviction in any court of the United States of competent jurisdiction, to a fine not less than $1,000 nor more than $5,000, or to imprisonment for a term of not more than three years, or to both such fine and imprisonment.

If any corporation required by this Act to file any annual or special report shall fail so to do within the time fixed by the commission for filing the same, and such failure shall continue for thirty days after notice of such default, the corporation shall forfeit to the United States the sum of $100 for each and every day of the continuance of such failure, which forfeiture shall be payable into the Treasury of the United States, and shall be recoverable in a civil suit in the name of the United States brought in the district where the corporation has its principal office or in any district in which it shall do business. It shall be the duty of the various district attorneys, under the direction of the Attorney General of the United States, to prosecute for the recovery of forfeitures. The costs and expenses of such prosecution shall be paid out of the appropriation for the expenses of the courts of the United States.

Any officer or employee of the commission who shall make public any information obtained by the commission without its authority, unless directed by a court, shall be deemed guilty of a misdemeanor, and, upon conviction thereof, shall be punished by a fine not exceeding $5,000, or by imprisonment not exceeding one year, or by fine and imprisonment, in the discretion of the court.

Sec. 11. Nothing contained in this Act shall be construed to prevent or interfere with the enforcement of the provisions of the antitrust Acts or the Acts to regulate commerce, nor shall anything contained in the Act be construed to alter, modify, or repeal the said antitrust Acts or the Acts to regulate commerce or any part or parts thereof.

Approved, September 26, 1914.

The Place of the Independent Commission, *Joseph B. Eastman,* 1928

Joseph Eastman (1882–1944) spent his professional life working for government agencies and nonprofit organizations in various capacities, including as chairman of the Interstate Commerce Commission. A determined political independent, he was appointed to a variety of positions by presidents of both parties and saw himself as an advocate for the public good, as opposed to the interests of either business or labor. The essay reproduced here sets forth the rationale for government commissions intended to be independent of all political parties and branches of government.

The Place of the Independent Commission

Joseph B. Eastman

The subject which I am to discuss has roots which run deep into the past. It invites historical research, and discussion will be illuminated thereby. To my regret I have not been able to undertake such research. On the independent commission of which I am a member, namely, the Interstate Commerce Commission, it is a constant struggle to keep abreast of current work. My observations will, therefore, be the product chiefly of such experience as I have had as a member of one particular independent commission, and I shall perforce use that commission by way of illustration in the course of my remarks.

The Federal Government is supposed, popularly at least, to be divided into three separate and quite distinct branches—the executive or administrative, the legislative, and the judicial. To what branch does an independent commission belong? That question is not so simple as it may sound. The best answer that I can give is that the work of such a commission may, and usually does, combine aspects of all three branches. Let me, by way of illustration, cite expressions of the Supreme Court of the United States upon the duties of the Interstate Commerce Commission:

The Interstate Commerce Commission is purely an administrative body. It is true that it may exercise and must exercise *quasi* judicial duties, but its functions are defined, and, in the main, explicitly directed by the act creating it (*Int. Com. Comm. v. Humboldt Steamship Co.,* 224 U.S. 474, 484).

But awarding reparation for the past and fixing rates for the future involve the determination of matters essentially different. One is in its nature private and the other public. One is made by the Commission in its *quasi*-judicial capacity to measure past injuries sustained by a private shipper; the other in its *quasi*-legislative capacity to prevent future injury to the public (*Baer Bros. v. Denver & R. G. R. R.,* 233 U.S. 479, 486).

The Congress may not delegate its purely legislative power to a commission, but, having laid down the general rules of action under which a commission shall proceed, it may require of that commission the application of such rules to particular situations and the investigation of facts, with a view to making orders in a particular matter within the rules laid down by the Congress (*Int. Com. Comm. v. Goodrich Transit Co.,* 224 U.S. 194, 214).

The making of rates is a legislative and not a judicial function. . . . The division of joint rates is also legislative in character (*Terminal R. R. Asso. v. U.S.,* 266 U.S. 17, 30).

In the case at bar, the function exercised by the Commission is wholly legislative. Its authority to legislate is limited to establishing a reasonable rule. But in establishing a rule of general application, it is not a condition of its validity that there be adduced evidence of its appropriateness in respect to every railroad to which it will be applicable. In this connection, the Commission, like other legislators, may reason from the particular to the general (*Assigned Car Cases,* decided May 31, 1927).

These expressions may seem, perhaps, not altogether consistent. In one case, for example, the Commission is described as "purely an administrative body"; in another case it is pointed out that "Congress may not delegate its purely legislative power to a commission"; but in the most recent case cited a function exercised by the Commission is described as "wholly legislative," it is stated that its "authority to legislate is limited to establishing a reasonable rule," and the Commission is classed with "other legislators." These apparent inconsistencies can, I think, be reconciled, but before I attempt such reconciliation, let us consider for a moment the degree of control which the three branches of the Government exercise over an independent commission.

The commission is created by, and in that sense is the creature of, the Congress. Its powers and duties are determined in the first instance by the Congress. The manner in which those duties are performed, however, depends upon the mental characteristics of the commissioners, and they are selected by the President, although the Senate has a negative power of disapproval. Moreover, the ultimate interpretation of the powers of the commission and the constitutionality of their exercise rest with the courts, and the results are not always such as were anticipated by the Congress. Thus it will be seen that the functioning of an independent commission is to some extent controlled by all three branches of the Government. It may be that this is the reason why these commissions, after they have been created by the Congress, are not always regarded by that body in a wholly paternal light.

Returning to the essential character of the duties of the Interstate Commerce Commission, it is important to bear in mind that prior to the creation of the Commission the public regulation of interstate common carriers lay partly with the courts and partly with the Congress. The powers of the courts, which were far from clear and definite, were apparently limited to the redressing of past wrongs. With the Congress lay the power of protecting the public interest through the control of future conditions. In exercising jurisdiction over what has been done in the past, the Commission is, therefore, doing what the courts used to do and what they may yet do to some extent; but in prescribing rates and rules for the future the Commission is exercising a power which has always been regarded as of a distinctly legislative nature. Strictly speaking its duties of this latter class are administrative, for the general rule or standard is established by the Congress and the Commission's function is merely to apply that general rule to particular cases. As a practical matter, however, the general rules which the Congress lays down are often so exceedingly broad and general as to afford wide latitude of action, and thus the Commission's function, while administrative in theory, bor-

ders closely in reality upon the legislative. This is, I presume, what the Supreme Court meant when it recently classed the Commission with "legislators." When I say that the rules laid down by the Congress are broad and general, I have in mind the fact that the standard prescribed is often defined only by such expressions as "just and reasonable," "consistent with the public interest," and the like. In addition to these quasi-judicial and quasi-legislative functions, it is also true that the Commission has various duties which may without qualification be described as administrative. Such, for example, are its duties in enforcing various penal provisions of the statutes.

But to my mind the cataloging of the duties of an independent commission by tags representing the three traditional subdivisions of the Government is little more than an interesting mental exercise. It may have legal significance, but for the most part the legal questions which have arisen in that connection are in the realm of decided issues. As a matter of fact the outlines of the three governmental branches are considerably blurred, and there is much merging of functions. It has been intimated, indeed, that even the courts sometimes legislate, and I am not prepared to contest that intimation. The independent commissions are the evolutionary product of public need. The important question is whether they meet that public need in the best practicable way.

The need for a commission arises, it seems to me, when the legislative body finds that particular conditions call for continual and very frequent acts of legislation, based on a uniform and consistent policy, which in themselves require intimate and expert knowledge of numerous and complex facts, a knowledge which can only be obtained by processes of patient, impartial and continued investigation. This may be illustrated by the subject of railroad rates. As we have seen, the fixing of common carrier charges for the future is a legislative function. State legislatures have in the past undertaken to fix such charges directly, without the agency of a commission. But trial and experience demonstrated that the task could not wisely be performed in this way, even within a single State, and the fixing of interstate railroad rates is a far larger and more involved undertaking. It is particularly complicated by the fact that the railroad industry is not wholly monopolistic but is subject to the influence of competition to a very considerable extent. There are a myriad of diverse circumstances and conditions to be taken into consideration, and these circumstances and conditions continually fluctuate. The task of regulating rates is not, therefore, one which can be performed in a single, mighty effort, but rather it is a continuous performance which must be accompanied by continual inquiry and investigation.

Obviously a legislative body like the Congress, with all the other numerous and important duties which it must perform, can not itself undertake the vast and painful detail of railroad rate regulation. Obviously, also, the answer to the problem is the creation of a special agency or tribunal which shall devote its energies to this particular task under the control of general rules laid down by the Congress. Such a device has two other important advantages which should be mentioned.

In the first place this agency or tribunal can be utilized by the Congress as an expert advisory body from which it can from time to time obtain the information necessary to determine what addition to or changes in the general rules of regulation should be made, and which it can direct, if need be, to make special investigations in new but related fields of inquiry. One of the important provisions of the interstate commerce act is that which authorizes the Commission "to inquire into the management of the business of all common carriers" subject to the act and directs it to "keep itself informed as to the manner and method in which the same is conducted." Another is the provision which requires the Commission in its annual report to Congress to transmit "such information and data collected by the Commission as may be considered of value in the determination of questions connected with the regulation of commerce, together with such recommendations as to additional legislation relating thereto as the Commission may deem necessary."

In the second place it is possible to provide, and in fact it is provided, that the Commission shall exercise its power, in general, only after investigation conducted with the thoroughness and impartiality of judicial proceedings. This has been done quite simply, as the following quotation from the opinion of the Supreme Court will show:

> Congress by using the phrase "whenever the Commission is of opinion, after hearing," prescribed quasi-judicial action.... The provision for a hearing implies both the privilege of introducing evidence and the duty of deciding in accordance with it. To refuse to consider evidence introduced or to make an essential finding without supporting evidence is arbitrary action (*Chicago Junction Case,* 264 U.S. 258, 265).

No such restriction, of course, circumscribes the acts of the Congress. The Supreme Court, however, has said as to these hearings:

The inquiry of a board of the character of the Interstate Commerce Commission should not be too narrowly constrained by technical rules as to the admissibility of proof. Its function is largely one of investigation and it should not be hampered in making inquiry pertaining to interstate commerce by those narrow rules which prevail in trials at common law where a strict correspondence is required between allegation and proof (*Int. Com. Comm. v. Baird,* 194 U.S., 25, 44).

The Commission has more freedom than a court in other ways. Thus it can institute an investigation upon its own motion, and even in proceedings which arise upon complaint or petition it can introduce evidence which is not proffered by the parties, and utilize the services of its own staff of employees in this connection. In the more important proceedings the Commission is at times represented by counsel to aid in the development of the facts.

The reasons which impel the Congress to create a commission for the purpose of administering certain general legislative rules are by logical extension the reasons which impel it to impose various duties of a strictly executive or judicial nature upon such commissions. Reverting again to the subject of railroad rates, by way of illustration, the determination of reasonable rates in the past is closely associated with the determination of reasonable rates for the future, notwithstanding that the one may be termed a judicial and the other a legislative act. It follows that if an expert body is to be created for the determination of future rates, it is both logical and appropriate that it be given jurisdiction over past rates; and this has been done, although the courts have to some extent been permitted to retain concurrent jurisdiction in the latter case. And where it is necessary for the Congress to impose upon some agency duties of a strictly executive character, it is both logical and appropriate that an independent commission should be selected as the agency when such duties relate to its sphere of activity. With its expert knowledge and trained staff of employees, the commission can perform these executive duties with maximum economy and efficiency, and in the process it will gain valuable additions to its store of knowledge and experience. Thus the Interstate Commerce Commission, in cooperation with the Department of Justice, can enforce the railroad safety appliance statutes with greater efficiency than would be possible if the Department were obliged to rely wholly upon a staff of local district attorneys and other agents dealing with innumerable other matters, and in the process of enforcement the Commission acquires a knowledge of railroad operating conditions which is of material value in other branches of its work.

It remains to consider whether independent commissions are the best practicable means of meeting the public needs which have led to their creation. Obviously some special agencies or tribunals are necessary, and the only alternative to *independent* commissions, as I see it, is some form of *dependent* commissions. Strictly speaking there is, of course, no such thing as an independent commission, for I have already shown that the Congress, the President, and the courts all have some measure of control over their functioning. However, it is quite possible to increase the degree of dependency, and suggestions have from time to time been made to that end.

In general the courts may not now review the acts of the Interstate Commerce Commission except to determine whether there has been a violation of the Constitution, or a failure to conform to statutory authority, or an exercise of power so arbitrary that it virtually transcends the authority conferred, although it may not technically do so. The courts have no concern with the correctness of the Commission's reasoning, nor with the soundness or wisdom of its conclusions, nor with the consistency or inconsistency of its findings in various cases. In short, they will not consider the facts further than to determine whether there was evidence to support the order. There is a partial exception to this rule in suits to enforce orders of the Commission awarding money damages, where its findings are only *prima facie* evidence of the facts. Originally the duty of the courts to determine whether an order of the Commission should or should not be enforced carried with it the obligation to consider both the facts and the law. Experience demonstrated the wisdom of the present rule and there are few who are now disposed to question it.

A moment's reflection will suffice to realize that if the courts were given broad powers of review over the Commission's findings of fact, the result would be to transfer the duties of common carrier regulation from the Commission to the courts. All proceedings could upon appeal be retried *de novo,* thus prolonging litigation beyond endurable limits. There would be substituted for the judgment upon complex facts of a special tribunal expert through daily experience with and concentration upon such facts and aided by a trained staff of technicians, the conflicting judgments of district courts throughout the country not equipped for the task in any comparable way and having a multitude of other and diverse duties to perform. No one has more clearly rec-

ognized the evils of such a superimposed authority than the Supreme Court itself. In *Proctor & Gamble v. United States* (225 U.S. 282, 296), it pointed out that the regulations and consequent duties imposed upon carriers by the act to regulate commerce

required, first, for their compulsory enforcement the exercise of official functions of an administrative nature, and, second, for their harmonious development an official unity of action which could only be brought about by a single administrative initiative and primary control.

And later in that opinion it stated that the recognition of a right of complete court review "would of necessity amount to a substitution of the court for the Commission, or at all events would be to create a divided authority on a matter where from the beginning primary singleness of action and unity was deemed to be imperative," with the result that there would be brought about "contradiction and the confusion which it had been the inflexible purpose of the lawmaker from the beginning to guard against."

Any suggestion that the so-called independent commissions should be made more dependent upon the judicial branch of the Federal Government may, I think, be dismissed without further discussion.

It has been suggested, however, although I think rather faintly, that these commissions might well be made more dependent upon the executive branch of the Government. One way in which this suggestion is sometimes phrased is that they should be made a "part of the administration." In considering it, we must start, I think, by appraising again the essential characteristics of these commissions. They are creatures of the Congress sworn to the faithful performance of certain specific duties by impartial, judicial methods. The Supreme Court has said that their powers are "expected to be exercised in the coldest neutrality." They are clearly nonpartisan in their makeup, and party policies do not enter into their activities except to the extent that such policies may be definitely registered in the statutes which they are sworn to enforce. No more than a majority of the members of the Interstate Commerce Commission may belong to any one political party, but I presume that the purpose of this provision is to emphasize the nonpartisan character of the body. Certainly, when once the members are selected their political affiliations cease to be of the slightest consequence, and so far as my knowledge runs the Commission has never divided in its decisions along political lines.

What purpose, then, would be served by bringing an independent commission within the jurisdiction of some executive department or cabinet officer? I can conceive of no purpose except to influence in some way the judgment of the commission or to bring it within the sway of some administration policy. But plainly, it seems to me, the cold neutrality of the commission, to use the expression of the Supreme Court, ought rather to be safeguarded jealously against precisely such extraneous influences. They are as out of place in the case of a commission as they would be in the case of a court. The great majority of those who appear before the Interstate Commerce Commission—I can not, of course, speak for the other independent commissions—appreciate this fact quite clearly. Now and then some litigant forgets the properties and seeks resort in some fashion to "pull" and so-called political influence, but in my judgment he gains nothing from such tactics. And even if this were not the fact, manifestly the remedy is not to make the Commission dependent in any way upon some cabinet officer necessarily influenced by considerations of party politics. I speak, of course, without any disrespect whatsoever, for such political considerations have a very proper place in national affairs. But, as I see it, they have no place so far as the independent commissions are concerned.

Summing up the discussion, the place of the independent commissions in the Federal Government in my judgment is the place which they now occupy. I would not increase their dependence upon any branch of the Government. In this respect, at least, I am a standpatter. As I stated at the outset, they are the evolutionary product of experience in meeting very genuine public needs, and I know of no other way in which such needs can be met. This is not to say that the functioning of these commissions can not be improved. On the contrary, I believe that the functioning of the particular commission of which I am a member can be improved, and in important respects. We are endeavoring to the best of our ability to effect such improvements, and welcome advice and aid to that end. But confining attention to essential characteristics and place in the structure of Government I have no improvements to suggest.

Permit me to say in conclusion that there appears to be some sentiment throughout the country against the multiplication of what are termed "government bureaucracies," and I presume that the independent commissions are included in that category. Catch-phrases and slogans such as this are dangerous, inflammable substances to be handled with caution, and they are often used for ulterior purposes. Independent commissions ought not to be created without a real public need, and any that are not serving such a need ought clearly to be abolished. But there can not be too many to the extent that they are demanded and required by the public interest. I ask only that before the bureaucracy slogan is accepted at face value, there be some careful consideration of the vital underlying question of public need.

Herbert Hoover (1874–1964) was a mining engineer, self-made millionaire, and leader of a variety of international humanitarian efforts. He served as the secretary of commerce during the administrations of Presidents Warren G. Harding and Calvin Coolidge, whom he succeeded in 1928. A constant proponent of cooperation between government and business in the interests of efficiency, he faced, soon after his inauguration, the worst depression in American history. Brought on by a stock market crash and a sudden, drastic constriction of the supply of money, among other factors, the Great Depression put millions out of work, brought mass foreclosures and bank collapses, and made hunger and homelessness national issues. Hoover responded with a series of actions aimed at increasing public works projects, protecting American businesses from foreign competition, and spurring voluntary relief. Hoover opposed any attempt at direct federal aid for individuals, arguing that such paternalism would deaden individual initiative and private charity. The speech reproduced here announced a nationwide campaign using federal resources to coordinate the raising of local relief funds to maintain the "spirit of mutual help through voluntary giving."

Radio Address on Unemployment Relief

October 18, 1931

Herbert Hoover

This broadcast to-night marks the beginning of the mobilization of the Nation for a great undertaking to provide security for those of our citizens and their families who, through no fault of their own, face unemployment and privation during the coming winter. Its success depends upon the sympathetic and generous action of every man and woman in our country. No one with a spark of human sympathy can contemplate unmoved the possibilities of suffering that can crush many of our unfortunate fellow Americans if we fail them.

The depression has been deepened by events from abroad which are beyond the control either of our citizens or our Government. Although it is a passing incident in our national life, we must meet the consequences in unemployment which arise from it with that completeness of effort and that courage and spirit for which citizenship in this Nation always has and always must stand.

As an important part of our plans for national unity of action in this emergency I have created a national organiza-

tion under the leadership of Mr. Walter Gifford to cooperate with the governors, the State and local agencies, and with the many national organizations of business, labor, and welfare, with the churches and other societies so that the countless streams of human helpfulness which have been the mainstay of our country in all emergencies may be directed wisely and effectively.

Over a thousand towns and cities have well-organized and experienced unemployment relief committees, community chests, or other agencies for the efficient administration of this relief. With this occasion begins the nation-wide movement to aid each of these volunteer organizations in securing the funds to meet their task over the forthcoming winter.

This organized effort is our opportunity to express our sympathy, to lighten the burden of the heavy laden, and to cast sunshine into the habitation of despair.

The amounts being sought by the committee in your town or city are in part to provide work, for it is through work that we wish to give help in keeping with the dignity of American manhood and womanhood. But much of their funds are necessary to provide direct relief to those families where circumstances and ill fortune can only be met by direct assistance. Included in many community appeals are the sums necessary to vital measures of health and character building, the maintenance of which were never more necessary than in these times.

The Federal Government is taking its part in aid to unemployment through the advancement and enlargement of public works in all parts of the Nation. All immigration has been stopped in order that our burdens should not be increased by unemployed emigrants from abroad. Measures have been adopted which will assure normal credits and thus stimulate employment in industry, commerce, and agriculture. The employers in national industries have spread work amongst their employees so that the maximum number may participate in the wages that are available. Our States, counties, and municipalities, through the expansion of their public works and through tax-supported relief activities, are doing their part. Yet, beyond all this, there is a margin of relief which must be provided by voluntary action. Through these agencies Americans must meet the demands of national conscience that there be no hunger or cold amongst our people.

Similar organization and generous support were provided during the past winter in localities where it was necessary. We succeeded in the task of that time. We demonstrated that it could be done. But in many localities our need will be greater this winter than a year ago. While many are affected by the depression the number who are threatened with privation is a minor percentage of our whole people.

This task is not beyond the ability of these thousands of community organizations to solve. Each local organization from its experience last winter and summer has formulated careful plans and made estimates completely to meet the need of that community. I am confident that the generosity of each community will fully support these estimates. The sum of these budgets will meet the needs of the Nation as a whole.

To solve this problem in this way accords with the fundamental sense of responsibility, neighbor to neighbor, community to community, upon which our Nation is founded.

The possible misery of helpless people gives me more concern than any other trouble this depression has brought us. It is with these convictions in mind that I have the responsibility of opening this nation-wide appeal to citizens of each community that they provide the funds with which, community by community, this task shall be met.

The maintenance of a spirit of mutual self-help through voluntary giving, through the responsibility of local government, is of infinite importance to the future of America. Everyone who from a sympathetic heart gives to these services is giving hope and courage to some deserving family. Everyone who aids in this service will have lighted a beacon of help on the stormy coast of human adversity.

The success and the character of nations are to be judged by the ideals and the spirit of its people. Time and again the American people have demonstrated a spiritual quality, a capacity for unity of action, of generosity, a certainty of results in time of emergency that have made them great in the annals of the history of all nations. This is the time and this is the occasion when we must arouse that idealism, that spirit, that determination, that unity of action, from which there can be no failure in this primary obligation of every man to his neighbor and of a nation to its citizens, that none who deserve shall suffer.

I would that I possessed the art of words to fix the real issue with which the troubled world is faced into the mind and heart of every American man and woman. Our country and the world are to-day involved in more than a financial crisis. We are faced with the primary question of human relations, which reaches to the very depth of organized society and to the very depth of human conscience. This civilization and this great complex, which we call American life, is builded and can alone survive upon the translation into individual action of that fundamental philosophy announced by the Savior nineteen centuries ago. Part of our national suffering to-day is from failure to observe these primary yet inexorable laws of human relationship. Modern society can not survive with the defense of Cain, "Am I my brother's keeper?"

No governmental action, no economic doctrine, no economic plan or project can replace that God-imposed responsibility of the individual man and woman to their neighbors. That is a vital part of the very soul of the people. If we shall gain in this spirit from this painful time, we shall have created a greater and more glorious America. The trial of it is here now. It is a trial of the heart and conscience, of individual men and women.

In a little over a month we shall celebrate our time-honored festival of Thanksgiving. I appeal to the American people to make November 26 next the outstanding Thanksgiving Day in the history of the United States; that we may say on that day that America has again demonstrated her ideals; that we have each of us contributed our full part; that we in each of our communities have given full assurance against hunger and cold among our people; that upon this Thanksgiving Day we have removed the fear of the forthcoming winter from the hearts of all who are suffering and in distress—that we are our brother's keeper.

I am on my way to participate in the commemoration of the victory of Yorktown. It is a name which brings a glow of pride to every American. It recalls the final victory of our people after years of sacrifice and privation. This Nation passed through Valley Forge and came to Yorktown.

A cousin of Theodore Roosevelt and the son of wealthy, aristocratic parents, Franklin Delano Roosevelt (1882–1945) followed Theodore into public service as state legislator, assistant secretary of the Navy, governor of New York, and, beginning in 1932, president. The 1932 campaign against President Herbert Hoover centered on the Great Depression and what the federal government should do about it. The speech reproduced here, received with great reserve by the audience of businessmen to whom it was delivered, provided no blueprint for Roosevelt's eventual New Deal policies, but rather a more general call for a more "equitable" distribution of wealth and opportunity. Roosevelt defeated Hoover in a landslide, garnering 57 percent of the popular vote.

Commonwealth Club Address

September 23, 1932

Franklin Delano Roosevelt

I count it a privilege to be invited to address the Commonwealth Club. It has stood in the life of this city and State, and, it is perhaps accurate to add, the nation, as a group of citizen leaders interested in fundamental problems of government and chiefly concerned with achievement of progress in government through non-partisan means.

The privilege of addressing you, therefore, in the heat of a political campaign, is great. I want to respond to your courtesy in terms consistent with your policy.

I want to speak not of politics but of government. I want to speak not of parties but of universal principles. They are not political except in that large sense in which a great American once expressed a definition of politics—that nothing in all of human life is foreign to the science of politics.

I do want to give you, however, a recollection of a long life spent, for a large part, in public office. Some of my conclusions and observations have been deeply accentuated in these past few weeks.

I have traveled far—from Albany to the Golden Gate. I have seen many people, and heard many things, and today, when, in a sense, my journey has reached the halfway mark, I am glad of the opportunity to discuss with you what it all means to me.

Sometimes, my friends, particularly in years such as these, the hand of discouragement falls upon us. It seems that things are in a rut, fixed, settled, that the world has grown old and tired and very much out of joint. This is the mood of depression, of dire and weary depression.

But then we look around us in America, and everything tells us that we are wrong. America is new. It is in the process of change and development. It has the great potentialities of youth, and particularly is this true of the great West and of this coast and of California.

I would not have you feel that I regard this in any sense a new community. I have traveled in many parts of the world, but never have I felt more the arresting thought of the change and development more than here, where the old, mystic East would seem to be near to us, where the currents of life and thought and commerce of the whole world meet us. This factor alone is sufficient to cause man to stop and think of the deeper meaning of things when he stands in this community.

But, more than that, I appreciate that the membership of this club consists of men who are thinking in terms beyond the immediate present, beyond their own immediate tasks, beyond their own individual interest.

I want to invite you, therefore, to consider with me in the large some of the relationships of government and economic life that go deep into our daily lives, our happiness, our future and our security.

The issue of government has always been whether individual men and women will have to serve some system of government or economics or whether a system of government and economics exists to serve individual men and women.

This question has persistently dominated the discussions of government for many generations. On questions relating to these things men have differed, and for time immemorial it is probable that honest men will continue to differ.

The final word belongs to no man; yet we can still believe in change and in progress. Democracy, as a dear old friend of mine in Indiana, Meredith Nicholson, has called it, is a quest, a never-ending seeking for better things, and in the seeking for these things and the striving for them there are many roads to follow.

But if we map the course of these roads, we find that there are only two general directions.

When we look about us we are likely to forget how hard people have worked to win the privilege of government.

The growth of the national governments of Europe was a struggle for the development of a centralized force in the nation, strong enough to impose peace upon ruling barons. In many instances the victory of the central government, the creation of a strong central government, was a haven of refuge to the individual. The people preferred the master far away to the exploitation and cruelty of the smaller master near at hand.

But the creators of national government were perforce ruthless men. They were often cruel in their methods, but they did strive steadily toward something that society needed and very much wanted—a strong central State, able to keep the peace, to stamp out civil war, to put the unruly nobleman in his place and to permit the bulk of individuals to live safely.

The man of ruthless force had his place in developing a pioneer country, just as he did in fixing the power of the central government in the development of the nations. Society paid him well for his services and its development. When the development among the nations of Europe, however, had been completed, ambition and ruthlessness, having served its term, tended to overstep its mark.

There came a growing feeling that government was conducted for the benefit of a few who thrived unduly at the expense of all. The people sought a balancing—a limiting force. There came gradually, through town councils, trade guilds, national parliaments, by constitutions and by popular participation and control, limitations on arbitrary power.

Another factor that tended to limit the power of those who ruled was the rise of the ethical conception that a ruler bore a responsibility for the welfare of his subjects.

The American colonies were born in this struggle. The American Revolution was a turning point in it. After the Revolution the struggle continued and shaped itself in the public life of the country.

There were those who, because they had seen the confusion which attended the years of war for American independence, surrendered to the belief that popular government was essentially dangerous and essentially unworkable.

They were honest people, my friends, and we cannot deny that their experience had warranted some measure of fear.

The most brilliant, honest and able exponent of this point of view was Hamilton. He was too impatient of slow-moving methods.

Fundamentally he believed that the safety of the Republic lay in the autocratic strength of its government, that the destiny of individuals was to serve that government and that fundamentally a great and strong group of central institutions, guided by a small group of able and public-spirited citizens, could best direct all government.

But Mr. Jefferson, in the Summer of 1776, after drafting the Declaration of Independence, turned his mind to the same problem and took a different view.

He did not deceive himself with outward forms. Government to him was a means to an end, not an end in itself; it might be either a refuge and a help or a threat and a danger, depending on the circumstances.

We find him carefully analyzing the society for which he was to organize a government:

"We have no paupers—the great mass of our population is of laborers, our rich who cannot live without labor, either manual or professional, being few and of moderate wealth. Most of the laboring class possess property, cultivate their own lands, have families and from the demands for their labor are enabled to exact from the rich and the competent such prices as enable them to feed abundantly, clothe above mere decency, to labor moderately and raise their families."

These people, he considered, had two sets of rights, those of "personal competency" and those involved in acquiring and possessing property.

By "personal competency" he meant the right of free thinking, freedom of forming and expressing opinions and freedom of personal living, each man according to his own lights.

To insure the first set of rights a government must so order its functions as not to interfere with the individual.

But even Jefferson realized that the exercise of the property rights might so interfere with the rights of the individual that the government, without whose assistance the property rights could not exist, must intervene, not to destroy individualism but to protect it.

You are familiar with the great political duel which followed; and how Hamilton and his friends, building toward a dominant, centralized power, were at length defeated in the great election of 1800 by Mr. Jefferson's party. Out of that duel came the two parties, Republican and Democratic, as we know them today.

So began, in American political life, the new day, the day of the individual against the system, the day in which individualism was made the great watchword of American life.

The happiest of economic conditions made that day long and splendid. On the western frontier land was substantially free. No one who did not shirk the task of earning a living was entirely without opportunity to do so. Depressions could, and did, come and go; but they could not alter the fundamental fact that most of the people lived partly by selling their labor and partly by extracting their livelihood from the soil, so that starvation and dislocation were practically impossible.

At the very worst there was always the possibility of climbing into a covered wagon and moving West, where the untilled prairies afforded a haven for men to whom the East did not provide a place.

So great were our natural resources that we could offer this relief not only to our own people but to the distressed of all the world. We could invite immigration from Europe and welcome it with open arms.

Traditionally, when a depression came a new section of land was opened in the West. And even our temporary misfortune served our manifest destiny.

It was in the middle of the nineteenth century that a new force was released and a new dream created. The force was what is called the industrial revolution, the advance of steam and machinery and the rise of the forerunners of the modern industrial plant.

The dream was the dream of an economic machine, able to raise the standard of living for every one; to bring luxury within the reach of the humblest; to annihilate distance by steam power and later by electricity, and to release every one from the drudgery of the heaviest manual toil.

It was to be expected that this would necessarily affect government. Heretofore, government had merely been called upon to produce conditions within which people could live happily, labor peacefully and rest secure. Now it was called upon to aid in the consummation of this new dream.

There was, however, a shadow over the dream. To be made real it required use of the talents of men of tremendous will and tremendous ambition, since by no other force could the problems of financing and engineering and new developments be brought to a consummation.

So manifest were the advantages of the machine age, however, that the United States fearlessly, cheerfully and, I think, rightly accepted the bitter with the sweet.

It was thought that no price was too high to pay for the advantages which we could draw from a finished industrial system.

The history of the last half century is accordingly in large measure a history of a group of financial titans, whose methods were not scrutinized with too much care and who were honored in proportion as they produced the results, irrespective of the means they used.

The financiers who pushed the railroads to the Pacific were always ruthless, often wasteful and frequently corrupt, but they did build railroads and we have them today.

It has been estimated that the American investor paid for the American railway system more than three times over in the process, but despite this fact the net advantage was to the United States.

As long as we had free land, as long as population was growing by leaps and bounds, as long as our industrial plants were insufficient to supply our own needs, society chose to give the ambitious man free play and unlimited reward, provided only that he produced the economic plant so much desired.

During this period of expansion there was equal opportunity for all, and the business of government was not to interfere but to assist in the development of industry.

This was done at the request of business men themselves. The tariff was originally imposed for the purpose of "fostering our infant industry," a phrase I think the older among you will remember as a political issue not so long ago.

The railroads were subsidized, sometimes by grants of money, oftener by grants of land. Some of the most valuable oil lands in the United States were granted to assist the financing of the railroad which pushed through the Southwest.

A nascent merchant marine was assisted by grants of money or by mail subsidies, so that our steam shipping might ply the seven seas.

Some of my friends tell me that they do not want the government in business. With this I agree, but I wonder whether they realize the implications of the past.

For while it has been American doctrine that the government must not go into business in competition with private enterprises, still it has been traditional, particularly in Republican administrations, for business urgently to ask the government to put at private disposal all kinds of government assistance.

The same man who tells you that he does not want to see the government interfere in business—and he means it and has plenty of good reasons for saying so—is the first to go to Washington and ask the government for a prohibitory tariff on his product.

When things get just bad enough—as they did two years ago—he will go with equal speed to the United States Government and ask for a loan. And the Reconstruction Finance Corporation is the outcome of it.

Each group has sought protection from the government for its own special interests without realizing that the function of government must be to favor no small group at the expense of its duty to protect the rights of personal freedom and of private property of all its citizens.

In retrospect we can now see that the turn of the tide came with the turn of the century. We were reaching our last frontier; there was no more free land and our industrial combinations had become great uncontrolled and irresponsible units of power within the State.

Clear-sighted men saw with fear the danger that opportunity would no longer be equal; that the growing corporation, like the feudal baron of old, might threaten the economic freedom of individuals to earn a living. In that hour our anti-trust laws were born.

The cry was raised against the great corporations. Theodore Roosevelt, the first great Republican Progressive, fought a Presidential campaign on the issue of "trust busting" and talked freely about malefactors of great wealth. If the government had a policy it was rather to turn the clock back, to destroy the large combinations and to return to the time when every man owned his individual small business.

This was impossible. Theodore Roosevelt, abandoning the idea of "trust busting," was forced to work out a difference between "good" trusts and "bad" trusts.

The Supreme Court set forth the famous "rule of reason" by which it seems to have meant that a concentration of industrial power was permissible if the method by which it got its power, and the use it made of that power, was reasonable.

Woodrow Wilson, elected in 1912, saw the situation more clearly. Where Jefferson had feared the encroachment of political power on the lives of individuals, Wilson knew that the new power was financial. He saw, in the highly centralized economic system, the despot of the twentieth century, on whom great masses of individuals relied for their safety and their livelihood, and whose irresponsibility and greed (if it were not controlled) would reduce them to starvation and penury.

The concentration of financial power had not proceeded as far in 1912 as it has today, but it had grown far enough for Mr. Wilson to realize fully its implications.

It is interesting, now, to read his speeches. What is called "radical" today (and I have reason to know whereof I speak) is mild compared to the campaign of Mr. Wilson.

"No man can deny," he said, "that the lines of endeavor have more and more narrowed and stiffened; no man who knows anything about the development of industry in this country can have failed to observe the larger kinds of credit are more and more difficult to obtain unless you obtain them upon terms of uniting your efforts with those who already control the industry of the country, and nobody can fail to observe that every man who tries to set himself up in competition with any process of manufacture which has taken place under the control of large combinations of capital will presently find himself either squeezed out or obliged to sell and allow himself to be absorbed."

Had there been no World War—had Mr. Wilson been able to devote eight years to domestic instead of to international affairs—we might have had a wholly different situation at the present time.

However, the then distant roar of European cannon, growing ever louder, forced him to abandon the study of this issue.

The problem he saw so clearly is left with us as a legacy; and no one of us on either side of the political controversy can deny that it is a matter of grave concern to the government.

A glance at the situation today only too clearly indicates that equality of opportunity as we have known it no longer exists. Our industrial plant is built. The problem just now is whether, under existing conditions, it is not overbuilt.

Our last frontier has long since been reached, and there is practically no more free land. More than half of our people do not live on the farms or on lands and cannot derive a living by cultivating their own property.

There is no safety valve in the form of a Western prairie to which those thrown out of work by the Eastern economic machines can go for a new start. We are not able to invite the immigration from Europe to share our endless plenty. We are now providing a drab living for our own people.

Our system of constantly rising tariffs has at last reacted against us to the point of closing our Canadian frontier on the north, our European markets on the east, many of our Latin-American markets to the south and a goodly proportion of our Pacific markets on the west through the retaliatory tariffs of those countries.

It has forced many of our great industrial institutions, who exported their surplus production to such countries, to establish plants in such countries, within the tariff walls.

This has resulted in the reduction of the operation of their American plants and opportunity for employment.

Just as freedom to farm has ceased, so also the opportunity in business has narrowed. It still is true that men can start small enterprises, trusting to native shrewdness and ability to keep abreast of competitors; but area after area has been preempted altogether by the great corporations, and even in the fields which still have no great concerns the small man starts under a handicap.

The unfeeling statistics of the past three decades show that the independent business man is running a losing race. Perhaps he is forced to the wall; perhaps he cannot command credit; perhaps he is "squeezed out," in Mr. Wilson's words, by highly organized corporate competitors, as your corner grocery man can tell you.

Recently a careful study was made of the concentration of business in the United States.

It showed that our economic life was dominated by some 600-odd corporations who controlled two-thirds of American industry. Ten million small business men divided the other third.

More striking still, it appeared that, if the process of concentration goes on at the same rate, at the end of another century we shall have all American industry controlled by a dozen corporations and run by perhaps a hundred men.

Put plainly, we are steering a steady course toward economic oligarchy, if we are not there already.

Clearly, all this calls for a reappraisal of values. A mere builder of more industrial plants, a creator of more railroad systems, an organizer of more corporations, is as likely to be a danger as a help.

The day of the great promoter or the financial titan, to whom we granted anything if only he would build or develop, is over. Our task now is not discovery or exploitation of natural resources or necessarily producing more goods.

It is the soberer, less dramatic business of administering resources and plants already in hand, of seeking to re-establish foreign markets for our surplus production, of meeting the problem of under-consumption, of adjusting production to consumption, of distributing wealth and products more equitably, of adapting existing economic organizations to the service of the people.

The day of enlightened administration has come.

Just as in older times the central government was first a haven of refuge and then a threat, so now in a closer economic system the central and ambitious financial unit is no longer a servant of national desire but a danger. I would draw the parallel one step further. We did not think because national government had become a threat in the eighteenth century that therefore we should abandon the principle of national government.

Nor today should we abandon the principle of strong economic units called corporations merely because their power is susceptible of easy abuse.

In other times we dealt with the problem of an unduly ambitious central government by modifying it gradually into a constitutional democratic government. So today we are modifying and controlling our economic units.

As I see it, the task of government in its relation to business is to assist the development of an economic declaration of rights, an economic constitutional order. This is the common task of statesman and business man. It is the minimum requirement of a more permanently safe order of things.

Happily, the times indicate that to create such an order not only is the proper policy of government but it is the only line of safety for our economic structures as well.

We know now that these economic units cannot exist unless prosperity is uniform—that is, unless purchasing power is well distributed throughout every group in the nation.

That is why even the most selfish of corporations for its own interest would be glad to see wages restored and unemployment aided and to bring the Western farmer back to his accustomed level of prosperity and to assure a permanent safety to both groups.

That is why some enlightened industries themselves endeavor to limit the freedom of action of each man and business group within the industry in the common interest of all; why business men everywhere are asking a form of organization which will bring the scheme of things into balance, even though it may in some measure qualify the freedom of action of individual units within the business.

The exposition need not further be elaborated. It is brief and incomplete, but you will be able to expand it in terms of your own business or occupation without difficulty.

I think every one who has actually entered the economic struggle—which means every one who was not born to safe wealth—knows in his own experience and his own life that we have now to apply the earlier concepts of American government to the conditions of today.

The Declaration of Independence discusses the problem of government in terms of a contract. Government is a relation of give and take—a contract, perforce, if we would follow the thinking out of which it grew.

Under such a contract rulers were accorded power, and the people consented to that power on consideration that they be accorded certain rights.

The task of statesmanship has always been the redefinition of these rights in terms of a changing and growing social order. New conditions impose new requirements upon government and those who conduct government.

I held, for example, in proceedings before me as Governor the purpose of which was the removal of the Sheriff of New York, that under modern conditions it was not enough for a public official merely to evade the legal terms of official wrongdoing. He owed a positive duty as well.

I said, in substance, that if he had acquired large sums of money, he was, when accused, required to explain the sources of such wealth. To that extent this wealth was colored with a public interest.

I said that public servants should, even beyond private citizens, in financial matters be held to a stern and uncompromising rectitude.

I feel that we are coming to a view, through the drift of our legislation and our public thinking in the past quarter century, that private economic power is, to enlarge an old phrase, a public trust as well.

I hold that continued enjoyment of that power by any individual or group must depend upon the fulfillment of that trust. The men who have reached the summit of American business life know this best; happily, many of these urge the binding quality of this greater social contract.

The terms of that contract are as old as the Republic and as new as the new economic order.

Every man has a right to life, and this means that he has also a right to make a comfortable living. He may by sloth or crime decline to exercise that right, but it may not be denied him.

We have no actual famine or dearth; our industrial and agricultural mechanism can produce enough and to spare.

Our government, formal and informal, political and economic, owes to every one an avenue to possess himself of a portion of that plenty, sufficient for his needs through his own work.

Every man has a right to his own property, which means a right to be assured to the fullest extent attainable, in the safety of his savings. By no other means can men carry the burdens of those parts of life which in the nature of things afford no chance of labor—childhood, sickness, old age.

In all thought of property, this right is paramount; all other property rights must yield to it.

If, in accord with this principle, we must restrict the operations of the speculator, the manipulator, even the financier, I believe we must accept the restriction as needful not to hamper individualism but to protect it.

These two requirements must be satisfied, in the main, by the individuals who claim and hold control of the great industrial and financial combinations which dominate so large a part of our industrial life. They have undertaken to be not business men but princes—princes of property.

I am not prepared to say that the system which produces them is wrong. I am very clear that they must fearlessly and competently assume the responsibility which goes with the power. So many enlightened business men know this that the statement would be little more than a platitude were it not for an added implication.

This implication is, briefly, that the responsible heads of finance and industry, instead of acting each for himself, must work together to achieve the common end.

They must, where necessary, sacrifice this or that private advantage, and in reciprocal self-denial must seek a general advantage. It is here that formal government—political government, if you choose—comes in.

Whenever in the pursuit of this objective the lone wolf, the unethical competitor, the reckless promoter, the Ishmael or Insull, whose hand is against every man's, declines to join in achieving an end recognized as being for the public welfare, and threatens to drag the industry back to a state of anarchy, the government may properly be asked to apply restraint.

Likewise, should the group ever use its collective power contrary to the public welfare, the government must be swift to enter and protect the public interest.

The government should assume the function of economic regulation only as a last resort, to be tried only when private initiative, inspired by high responsibility, with such assistance and balance as government can give, has finally failed.

As yet there has been no final failure, because there has been no attempt; and I decline to assume that this nation is unable to meet the situation.

The final term of the high contract was for liberty and the pursuit of happiness.

We have learned a great deal of both in the past century. We know that individual liberty and individual happiness mean nothing unless both are ordered in the sense that one man's meat is not another man's poison.

We know that the old "rights of personal competency"—the right to read, to think, to speak, to choose and live a mode of life—must be respected at all hazards.

We know that liberty to do anything which deprives others of those elemental rights is outside the protection of any compact, and that government in this regard is the maintenance of a balance within which every individual may have a place if he will take it, in which every individual may find safety if he wishes it, in which every individual may attain such power as his ability permits, consistent with his assuming the accompanying responsibility.

All this is a long, slow task. Nothing is more striking than the simple innocence of the men who insist, whenever an objective is present, on the prompt production of a patent scheme guaranteed to produce a result.

Human endeavor is not so simple as that. Government includes the art of formulating a policy and using the political technique to attain so much of that policy as will receive general support; persuading, leading, sacrificing, teaching always, because the greatest duty of a statesman is to educate.

But in the matters of which I have spoken we are learning rapidly in a severe school. The lessons so learned must not be forgotten even in the mental lethargy of a speculative upturn.

We must build toward the time when a major depression cannot occur again; and if this means sacrificing the easy profits of inflationist booms, then let them go; and good riddance.

Faith in America, faith in our tradition of personal responsibility, faith in our institutions, faith in ourselves demands that we recognize the new terms of the old social contact.

We shall fulfill them, as we fulfilled the obligation of the apparent utopia which Jefferson imagined for us in 1776 and which Jefferson, Roosevelt and Wilson sought to bring to realization.

We must do so lest a rising tide of misery, engendered by our common failure, engulf us all.

But failure is not an American habit, and in the strength of great hope we must all shoulder our common load.

First Inaugural Address, *Franklin Delano Roosevelt*, 1933

FDR's landslide victory in the election of 1932 was clearly linked to the fact that the nation was in the grips of a massive economic depression, affecting all aspects of its people's lives. More than ten thousand banks had failed, wiping out their depositors' savings. Millions were out of work, with millions more working for subsistence wages. Farmers could not afford to get their produce to market. During the presidential campaign, Roosevelt had not provided specifics on how he would meet the situation. In his first address as president, reproduced here, he presented the broad outlines of his approach, calling for vastly increased federal powers, and increased presidential authority in particular, to "wage a war" against the Depression, a war in which Americans would "have nothing to fear but fear itself."

Inaugural Address

March 4, 1933

Franklin Delano Roosevelt

I am certain that my fellow Americans expect that on my induction into the Presidency I will address them with a candor and a decision which the present situation of our Nation impels. This is preeminently the time to speak the truth, the whole truth, frankly and boldly. Nor need we shrink from honestly facing conditions in our country to-day. This great Nation will endure as it has endured, will revive and will prosper. So, first of all, let me assert my firm belief that the only thing we have to fear is fear itself—nameless, unreasoning, unjustified terror which paralyzes needed efforts to convert retreat into advance. In every dark hour of our national life a leadership of frankness and vigor has met with that understanding and support of the people themselves which is essential to victory. I am convinced that you will again give that support to leadership in these critical days.

In such a spirit on my part and on yours we face our common difficulties. They concern, thank God, only material things. Values have shrunken to fantastic levels; taxes have risen; our ability to pay has fallen; government of all kinds is faced by serious curtailment of income; the means of exchange are frozen in the currents of trade; the withered leaves of industrial enterprise lie on every side; farmers find no markets for their produce; the savings of many years in thousands of families are gone.

More important, a host of unemployed citizens face the grim problem of existence, and an equally great number toil with little return. Only a foolish optimist can deny the dark realities of the moment.

Yet our distress comes from no failure of substance. We are stricken by no plague of locusts. Compared with the perils which our forefathers conquered because they believed and were not afraid, we have still much to be thankful for. Nature still offers her bounty and human efforts have multiplied it. Plenty is at our doorstep, but a generous use of it languishes in the very sight of the supply. Primarily this is because the rulers of the exchange of mankind's goods have failed, through their own stubbornness and their own incompetence, have admitted their failure, and abdicated. Practices of the unscrupulous money changers stand indicted in the court of public opinion, rejected by the hearts and minds of men.

True they have tried, but their efforts have been cast in the pattern of an outworn tradition. Faced by failure of credit they have proposed only the lending of more money. Stripped of the lure of profit by which to induce our people to follow their false leadership, they have resorted to exhortations, pleading tearfully for restored confidence. They know only the rules of a generation of self-seekers. They have no vision, and when there is no vision the people perish.

The money changers have fled from their high seats in the temple of our civilization. We may now restore that temple to the ancient truths. The measure of the restoration lies in the extent to which we apply social values more noble than mere monetary profit.

Happiness lies not in the mere possession of money; it lies in the joy of achievement, in the thrill of creative effort. The joy and moral stimulation of work no longer must be forgotten in the mad chase of evanescent profits. These dark days will be worth all they cost us if they teach us that our true destiny is not to be ministered unto but to minister to ourselves and to our fellow men.

Recognition of the falsity of material wealth as the standard of success goes hand in hand with the abandonment of the false belief that public office and high political position are to be valued only by the standards of pride of place and personal profit; and there must be an end to a conduct in banking and in business which too often has given to a sacred trust the likeness of callous and selfish wrongdoing. Small wonder that confidence languishes, for it thrives only on honesty, on honor, on the sacredness of obligations, on faithful protection, on unselfish performance; without them it can not live.

Restoration calls, however, not for changes in ethics alone. This Nation asks for action, and action now.

Our greatest primary task is to put people to work. This is no unsolvable problem if we face it wisely and courageously. It can be accomplished in part by direct recruiting by the Government itself, treating the task as we would treat the emergency of a war, but at the same time, through this employment, accomplishing greatly needed projects to stimulate and reorganize the use of our natural resources.

Hand in hand with this we must frankly recognize the overbalance of population in our industrial centers and, by engaging on a national scale in a redistribution, endeavor to provide a better use of the land for those best fitted for the land. The task can be helped by definite efforts to raise the values of agricultural products and with this the power to purchase the output of our cities. It can be helped by preventing realistically the tragedy of the growing loss through foreclosure of our small homes and our farms. It can be helped by insistence that the Federal, State, and local governments act forthwith on the demand that their cost be drastically reduced. It can be helped by the unifying of relief activities which to-day are often scattered, uneconomical, and unequal. It can be helped by national planning for and supervision of all forms of transportation and of communications and other utilities which have a definitely public character. There are many ways in which it can be helped, but it can never be helped merely by talking about it. We must act and act quickly.

Finally, in our progress toward a resumption of work we require two safeguards against a return of the evils of the old order; there must be a strict supervision of all banking and credits and investments; there must be an end to speculation with other people's money, and there must be provision for an adequate but sound currency.

There are the lines of attack. I shall presently urge upon a new Congress in special session detailed measures for their fulfillment, and I shall seek the immediate assistance of the several States.

Through this program of action we address ourselves to putting our own national house in order and making income balance outgo. Our international trade relations, though vastly important, are in point of time and necessity secondary to the establishment of a sound national economy. I favor as a practical policy the putting of first things first. I shall spare no effort to restore world trade by international economic readjustment, but the emergency at home cannot wait on that accomplishment.

The basic thought that guides these specific means of national recovery is not narrowly nationalistic. It is the insistence, as a first consideration, upon the interdependence of the various elements in all parts of the United States—a recognition of the old and permanently important manifestation of the American spirit of the pioneer. It is the way to recovery. It is the immediate way. It is the strongest assurance that the recovery will endure.

In the field of world policy I would dedicate this Nation to the policy of the good neighbor—the neighbor who resolutely respects himself and, because he does so, respects the rights of others—the neighbor who respects his obligations and respects the sanctity of his agreements in and with a world of neighbors.

If I read the temper of our people correctly, we now realize as we have never realized before our interdependence on each other; that we can not merely take but we must give as well; that if we are to go forward, we must move as a trained and loyal army willing to sacrifice for the good of a common discipline, because without such discipline no progress is made, no leadership becomes effective. We are, I know, ready and willing to submit our lives and property to such discipline, because it makes possible a leadership which aims at a larger good. This I propose to offer, pledging that the larger purposes will bind upon us all as a sacred obligation with a unity of duty hitherto evoked only in time of armed strife.

With this pledge taken, I assume unhesitatingly the leadership of this great army of our people dedicated to a disciplined attack upon our common problems.

Action in this image and to this end is feasible under the form of government which we have inherited from our ancestors. Our Constitution is so simple and practical that it is possible always to meet extraordinary needs by changes in emphasis and arrangement without loss of essential form. That is why our constitutional system has proved itself the most superbly enduring political mechanism the modern world has produced. It has met every stress of vast expansion of territory, of foreign wars, of bitter internal strife, of world relations.

It is to be hoped that the normal balance of executive and legislative authority may be wholly adequate to meet the unprecedented task before us. But it may be that an unprecedented demand and need for undelayed action may call for temporary departure from that normal balance of public procedure.

I am prepared under my constitutional duty to recommend the measures that a stricken nation in the midst of a stricken world may require. These measures, or such other measures as the Congress may build out of its experience and wisdom, I shall seek, within my constitutional authority, to bring to speedy adoption.

But in the event that the Congress shall fail to take one of these two courses, and in the event that the national emergency is still critical, I shall not evade the clear course of duty that will then confront me. I shall ask the Congress for the one remaining instrument to meet the crisis—broad Executive power to wage a war against the emergency, as great as the power that would be given to me if we were in fact invaded by a foreign foe.

For the trust reposed in me I will return the courage and the devotion that befit the time. I can do no less.

We face the arduous days that lie before us in the warm courage of the national unity; with the clear consciousness of seeking old and precious moral values; with the clean satisfaction that comes from the stern performance of duty by old and young alike. We aim at the assurance of a rounded and permanent national life.

We do not distrust the future of essential democracy. The people of the United States have not failed. In their need they have registered a mandate that they want direct, vigorous action. They have asked for discipline and direction under leadership. They have made me the present instrument of their wishes. In the spirit of the gift I take it.

In this dedication of a Nation we humbly ask the blessing of God. May He protect each and every one of us. May He guide me in the days to come.

The first one hundred days of the Roosevelt administration brought a flurry of legislative activity. The Federal Emergency Relief Act, one of the first pieces of New Deal legislation, set up the Federal Emergency Relief Administration (FERA) to distribute money to the needy. In actuality, building on the Emergency Relief Administration formed in 1932 under Herbert Hoover, FERA funneled money through state agencies for the unemployed and public work projects. Between 1933 and 1935 FERA distributed three billion dollars. In 1935 FERA's work was taken over by the Works Progress Administration and the Social Security Board.

Federal Emergency Relief Act

May 12, 1933

AN ACT

To provide for cooperation by the Federal Government with the several States and Territories and the District of Columbia in relieving the hardship and suffering caused by unemployment, and for other purposes.

Be it enacted by the Senate and House of Representatives of the United States of America in Congress assembled, That the Congress hereby declares that the present economic depression has created a serious emergency, due to widespread unemployment and increasing inadequacy of State and local relief funds, resulting in the existing or threatened deprivation of a considerable number of families and individuals of the necessities of life, and making it imperative that the Federal Government cooperate more effectively with the several States and Territories and the District of Columbia in furnishing relief to their needy and distressed people.

SEC. 2. (a) The Reconstruction Finance Corporation is authorized and directed to make available out of the funds of the Corporation not to exceed $500,000,000, in addition to the funds authorized under title I of the Emergency Relief and Construction Act of 1932, for expenditure under the provisions of this Act upon certification by the Federal Emergency Relief Administrator provided for in section 3.

(b) The amount of notes, debentures, bonds, or other such obligations which the Reconstruction Finance Corporation is authorized and empowered under section 9 of the Reconstruction Finance Corporation Act, as amended, to have outstanding at any one time is increased by $500,000,000: *Provided,* That no such additional notes, debentures, bonds, or other such obligations authorized by this subsection shall be issued except at such times and in such amounts as the President shall approve.

(c) After the expiration of ten days after the date upon which the Federal Emergency Relief Administrator has qualified and has taken office, no application shall be approved by the Reconstruction Finance Corporation under the provisions of title I of the Emergency Relief and Construction Act of 1932, and the Federal Emergency Relief Administrator shall have access to all files and records of the Reconstruction Finance Corporation relating to the administration of funds under title I of such Act. At the expiration of such ten-day period, the unexpended and unobligated balance of the funds authorized under title I of such Act shall be available for the purposes of this Act.

SEC. 3. (a) There is hereby created a Federal Emergency Relief Administration, all the powers of which shall be exercised by a Federal Emergency Relief Administrator (referred to in this Act as the "Administrator") to be appointed by the President, by and with the advice and consent of the Senate. The Administrator shall receive a salary to be fixed by the President at not to exceed $10,000, and necessary traveling and subsistence expenses within the limitations prescribed by law for civilian employees in the executive branch of the

Government. The Federal Emergency Relief Administration and the office of Federal Emergency Relief Administrator shall cease to exist upon the expiration of two years after the date of enactment of this Act, and the unexpended balance on such date of any funds made available under the provisions of this Act shall be disposed of as the Congress may by law provide.

(b) The Administrator may appoint and fix the compensation of such experts and their appointment may be made and compensation fixed without regard to the civil service laws, or the Classification Act of 1923, as amended, and the Administrator may, in the same manner, appoint and fix the compensation of such other officers and employees as are necessary to carry out the provisions of this Act, but such compensation shall not exceed in any case the sum of $8,000; and may make such expenditures (including expenditures for personal services and rent at the seat of government and elsewhere and for printing and binding), not to exceed $350,000, as are necessary to carry out the provisions of this Act, to be paid by the Reconstruction Finance Corporation out of funds made available by this Act upon presentation of vouchers approved by the Administrator or by an officer of the Administration designated by him for that purpose. The Administrator may, under rules and regulations prescribed by the President, assume control of the administration in any State or States where, in his judgment, more effective and efficient cooperation between the State and Federal authorities may thereby be secured in carrying out the purposes of this Act.

(c) In executing any of the provisions of this Act, the Administrator, and any person duly authorized or designated by him, may conduct any investigation pertinent or material to the furtherance of the purposes of this Act and, at the request of the President, shall make such further investigations and studies as the President may deem necessary in dealing with problems of unemployment relief.

(d) The Administrator shall print monthly, and shall submit to the President and to the Senate and the House of Representatives (or to the Secretary of the Senate and the Clerk of the House of Representatives, if those bodies are not in session), a report of his activities and expenditures under this Act. Such reports shall, when submitted, be printed as public documents.

Sec. 4. (a) Out of the funds of the Reconstruction Finance Corporation made available by this Act, the Administrator is authorized to make grants to the several States to aid in meeting the costs of furnishing relief and work relief and in relieving the hardship and suffering caused by unemployment in the form of money, service, materials, and/or commodities to provide the necessities of life to persons in need as a result of the present emergency, and/or to their dependents, whether resident, transient, or homeless.

(b) Of the amounts made available by this Act not to exceed $250,000,000 shall be granted to the several States applying therefor, in the following manner: Each State shall be entitled to receive grants equal to one third of the amount expended by such State, including the civil subdivisions thereof, out of public moneys from all sources for the purposes set forth in subsection (a) of this section; and such grants shall be made quarterly, beginning with the second quarter in the calendar year 1933, and shall be made during any quarter upon the basis of such expenditures certified by the States to have been made during the preceding quarter.

(c) The balance of the amounts made available by this Act, except the amount required for administrative expenditures under section 3, shall be used for grants to be made whenever, from an application presented by a State, the Administrator finds that the combined moneys which can be made available within the State from all sources, supplemented by any moneys, available under subsection (b) of this section, will fall below the estimated needs within the State for the purposes specified in subsection (a) of this section: *Provided,* That the Administrator may certify out of the funds made available by this subsection additional grants to States applying therefor to aid needy persons who have no legal settlement in any one State or community, and to aid in assisting cooperative and self-help associations for the barter of goods and services.

(d) After October 1, 1933, notwithstanding the provisions of subsection (b), the unexpended balance of the amounts available for the purposes of subsection (b) may, in the discretion of the Administrator and with the approval of the President, be available for grants under subsection (c).

(e) The decision of the Administrator as to the purpose of any expenditure shall be final.

(f) The amount available to any one State under subsections (b) and (c) of this section shall not exceed 15 per centum of the total amount made available by such subsections.

Sec. 5. Any State desiring to obtain funds under this Act shall through its Governor make application therefor from time to time to the Administrator. Each application so made shall present in the manner requested by the Administrator information showing (1) the amounts necessary to meet relief needs in the State during the period covered by such application and the amounts available from public or private sources within the State, its political subdivisions, and private agencies, to meet the relief needs of the State, (2) the provision made to assure adequate administrative supervision, (3) the provision made for suitable standards of relief, and (4) the purposes for which the funds requested will be used.

SEC. 6. The Administrator upon approving a grant to any State shall so certify to the Reconstruction Finance Corporation which shall, except upon revocation of a certificate by the Administrator, make payments without delay to the State in such amounts and at such times as may be prescribed in the certificate. The Governor of each State receiving grants under this Act shall file monthly with the Administrator, and in the form required by him, a report of the disbursements made under such grants.

SEC. 7. As used in the foregoing provisions of this Act, the term "State" shall include the District of Columbia, Alaska, Hawaii, the Virgin Islands, and Puerto Rico; and the term "Governor" shall include the Commissioners of the District of Columbia.

SEC. 8. This Act may be cited as the "Federal Emergency Relief Act of 1933."

Approved, May 12, 1933

National Industrial Recovery Act, 1933

Central to FDR's program to end the Depression were federal efforts to increase wages and prices. To this end the National Industrial Recovery Act created an executive agency, the National Recovery Administration (NRA). The NRA set up codes of "fair competition" dictating specific levels of wages, production, and hours of work. Compliance was gained in part by allowing cooperating businesses to display the administration's blue eagle, warding off boycotts. After the act was struck down by the Supreme Court in Schechter Poultry Co. v. U.S., *many of its labor provisions were incorporated into the Wagner Act, which set up the National Labor Relations Board.*

National Industrial Recovery Act

June 16, 1933

AN ACT

To encourage national industrial recovery, to foster fair competition, and to provide for the construction of certain useful public works, and for other purposes.

Be it enacted by the Senate and House of Representatives of the United States of America in Congress assembled,

TITLE I—INDUSTRIAL RECOVERY

Declaration of Policy

SECTION 1. A national emergency productive of widespread unemployment and disorganization of industry, which burdens interstate and foreign commerce, affects the public welfare, and undermines the standards of living of the American people, is hereby declared to exist. It is hereby declared to be the policy of Congress to remove obstructions to the free flow of interstate and foreign commerce which tend to diminish the amount thereof; and to provide for the general welfare by promoting the organization of industry for the purpose of cooperative action among trade groups, to induce and maintain united action of labor and management under adequate governmental sanctions and supervision, to eliminate unfair competitive practices, to promote the fullest possible utilization of the present productive capacity of industries, to avoid undue restriction of production (except as may be temporarily required), to increase the consumption of industrial and agricultural products by increasing purchasing power, to reduce and relieve unemployment, to improve

standards of labor, and otherwise to rehabilitate industry and to conserve natural resources.

Administrative Agencies

SEC. 2. (a) To effectuate the policy of this title, the President is hereby authorized to establish such agencies, to accept and utilize such voluntary and uncompensated services, to appoint, without regard to the provisions of the civil service laws, such officers and employees, and to utilize such Federal officers and employees, and, with the consent of the State, such State and local officers and employees, as he may find necessary, to prescribe their authorities, duties, responsibilities, and tenure, and, without regard to the Classification Act of 1923, as amended, to fix the compensation of any officers and employees so appointed.

(b) The President may delegate any of his functions and powers under this title to such officers, agents, and employees as he may designate or appoint, and may establish an industrial planning and research agency to aid in carrying out his functions under this title.

(c) This title shall cease to be in effect and any agencies established hereunder shall cease to exist at the expiration of two years after the date of enactment of this Act, or sooner if the President shall by proclamation or the Congress shall by joint resolution declare that the emergency recognized by section 1 has ended.

Codes of Fair Competition

SEC. 3. (a) Upon the application to the President by one or more trade or industrial associations or groups, the President may approve a code or codes of fair competition for the trade or industry or subdivision thereof, represented by the applicant or applicants, if the President finds (1) that such associations or groups impose no inequitable restrictions on admission to membership therein and are truly representative of such trades or industries or subdivisions thereof, and (2) that such code or codes are not designed to promote monopolies or to eliminate or oppress small enterprises and will not operate to discriminate against them, and will tend to effectuate the policy of this title: *Provided,* That such code or codes shall not permit monopolies or monopolistic practices: *Provided further,* That where such code or codes affect the services and welfare of persons engaged in other steps of the economic process, nothing in this section shall deprive such persons of the right to be heard prior to approval by the President of such code or codes. The President may, as a condition of his approval of any such code, impose such conditions (including requirements for the making of reports and the keeping of accounts) for the protection of consumers, competitors, employees, and others, and in furtherance of the public interest, and may provide such exceptions to and exemptions from the provisions of such code, as the President in his discretion deems necessary to effectuate the policy herein declared.

(b) After the President shall have approved any such code, the provisions of such code shall be the standards of fair competition for such trade or industry or subdivision thereof. Any violation of such standards in any transaction in or affecting interstate or foreign commerce shall be deemed an unfair method of competition in commerce within the meaning of the Federal Trade Commission Act, as amended; but nothing in this title shall be construed to impair the powers of the Federal Trade Commission under such Act, as amended.

(c) The several district courts of the United States are hereby invested with jurisdiction to prevent and restrain violations of any code of fair competition approved under this title; and it shall be the duty of the several district attorneys of the United States, in their respective districts, under the direction of the Attorney General, to institute proceedings in equity to prevent and restrain such violations.

(d) Upon his own motion, or if complaint is made to the President that abuses inimical to the public interest and contrary to the policy herein declared are prevalent in any trade or industry or subdivision thereof, and if no code of fair competition therefor has theretofore been approved by the President, the President, after such public notice and hearing as he shall specify, may prescribe and approve a code of fair competition for such trade or industry or subdivision thereof, which shall have the same effect as a code of fair competition approved by the President under subsection (a) of this section.

(e) On his own motion, or if any labor organization, or any trade or industrial organization, association, or group, which has complied with the provisions of this title, shall make complaint to the President that any article or articles are being imported into the United States in substantial quantities or increasing ratio to domestic production of any competitive article or articles and on such terms or under such conditions as to render ineffective or seriously to endanger the maintenance of any code or agreement under this title, the President may cause an immediate investigation to be made by the United States Tariff Commission, which shall give precedence to investigations under this subsection, and if, after such investigation and such public notice and hearing as he shall specify, the President shall find the existence of such facts, he shall, in order to effectuate the policy of this title, direct that the article or articles concerned shall be permitted entry into the United States only upon such terms and conditions and subject to the payment of such fees and to such limitations in the total quantity which may be imported (in the course of any specified period or periods) as he shall find it necessary to prescribe in order that the entry thereof shall not render or tend to render ineffective any code or agreement made under this title. In order to enforce any limitations imposed on the total quantity of imports, in any specified period or periods, of any article or articles under this subsection, the President may forbid the importation of such article or articles unless the importer shall have first obtained from the Secretary of the Treasury a license pursuant to such regulations as the President may prescribe. Upon information of any action by the President under this subsection the Secretary of the Treasury shall, through the proper officers, permit entry of the article or articles specified only upon such terms and conditions and subject to such fees, to such limitations in the quantity which may be imported, and to such requirements of license, as the President shall have directed. The decision of the President as to facts shall be conclusive. Any condition or limitation of entry under this subsection shall continue in effect until the President shall find and inform the Secretary of the Treasury that the conditions which led to the imposition of such condition or limitation upon entry no longer exists.

(f) When a code of fair competition has been approved or prescribed by the President under this title, any violation of any provision thereof in any transaction in or affecting interstate or foreign commerce shall be a misdemeanor and upon conviction thereof an offender shall be fined not more than $500 for each offense, and each day such violation continues shall be deemed a separate offense.

Agreements and Licenses

SEC. 4. (a) The President is authorized to enter into agreements with, and to approve voluntary agreements between and among, persons engaged in a trade or industry, labor organizations, and trade or industrial organizations, associations, or groups, relating to any trade or industry, if in his judgment such agreements will aid in effectuating the policy of this title with respect to transactions in or affecting interstate or foreign commerce, and will be consistent with the requirements of clause (2) of subsection (a) of section 3 for a code of fair competition.

(b) Whenever the President shall find that destructive wage or price cutting or other activities contrary to the policy of this title are being practiced in any trade or industry or any subdivision thereof, and, after such public notice and hearing as he shall specify, shall find it essential to license business enterprises in order to make effective a code of fair competition or an agreement under this title or otherwise to effectuate the policy of this title, and shall publicly so announce, no person shall, after a date fixed in such announcement, engage in or carry on any business, in or affecting interstate or foreign commerce, specified in such announcement, unless he shall have first obtained a license issued pursuant to such regulations as the President shall prescribe. The President may suspend or revoke any such license, after due notice and opportunity for hearing, for violations of the terms or conditions thereof. Any order of the President suspending or revoking any such license shall be final if in accordance with law. Any person who, without such a license or in violation of any condition thereof, carries on any such business for which a license is so required, shall, upon conviction thereof, be fined not more than $500, or imprisoned not more than six months, or both, and each day such violation continues shall be deemed a separate offense. Notwithstanding the provisions of section 2 (c),

this subsection shall cease to be in effect at the expiration of one year after the date of enactment of this Act or sooner if the President shall by proclamation or the Congress shall by joint resolution declare that the emergency recognized by section 1 has ended.

SEC. 5. While this title is in effect (or in the case of a license, while section 4 (a) is in effect) and for sixty days thereafter, any code, agreement, or license approved, prescribed, or issued and in effect under this title, and any action complying with the provisions thereof taken during such period, shall be exempt from the provisions of the antitrust laws of the United States.

Nothing in this Act, and no regulation thereunder, shall prevent an individual from pursuing the vocation of manual labor and selling or trading the products thereof; nor shall anything in this Act, or regulation thereunder, prevent anyone from marketing or trading the produce of his farm.

Limitations Upon Application of Title

SEC. 6. (a) No trade or industrial association or group shall be eligible to receive the benefit of the provisions of this title until it files with the President a statement containing such information relating to the activities of the association or group as the President shall by regulation prescribe.

(b) The President is authorized to prescribe rules and regulations designed to insure that any organization availing itself of the benefits of this title shall be truly representative of the trade or industry or subdivision thereof represented by such organization. Any organization violating any such rule or regulation shall cease to be entitled to the benefits of this title.

(c) Upon the request of the President, the Federal Trade Commission shall make such investigations as may be necessary to enable the President to carry out the provisions of this title, and for such purposes the Commission shall have all the powers vested in it with respect of investigations under the Federal Trade Commission Act, as amended.

SEC. 7. (a) Every code of fair competition, agreement, and license approved, prescribed, or issued under this title shall contain the following conditions: (1) That employees shall have the right to organize and bargain collectively through representatives of their own choosing, and shall be free from the interference, restraint, or coercion of employers of labor, or their agents, in the designation of such representatives or in self-organization or in other concerted activities for the purpose of collective bargaining or other mutual aid or protection; (2) that no employee and no one seeking employment shall be required as a condition of employment to join any company union or to refrain from joining, organizing, or assisting a labor organization of his own choosing; and (3) that employers shall comply with the maximum hours of labor, minimum rates of pay, and other conditions of employment, approved or prescribed by the President.

(b) The President shall, so far as practicable, afford every opportunity to employers and employees in any trade or industry or subdivision thereof with respect to which the conditions referred to in clauses (1) and (2) of subsection (a) prevail, to establish by mutual agreement, the standards as to the maximum hours of labor, minimum rates of pay, and such other conditions of employment as may be necessary in such trade or industry or subdivision thereof to effectuate the policy of this title; and the standards established in such agreements, when approved by the President, shall have the same effect as a code of fair competition, approved by the President under subsection (a) of section 3.

(c) Where no such mutual agreement has been approved by the President he may investigate the labor practices, policies, wages, hours of labor, and conditions of employment in such trade or industry or subdivision thereof; and upon the basis of such investigations, and after such hearings as the President finds advisable, he is authorized to prescribe a limited code of fair competition fixing such maximum hours of labor, minimum rates of pay, and other conditions of employment in the trade or industry or subdivision thereof investigated as he finds to be necessary to effectuate the policy of this title, which shall have the same effect as a code of fair competition approved by the President under subsection (a) of section 3. The President may differentiate according to experience and skill of the employees affected and according to the locality of employment; but no attempt shall be made to introduce any classification according to the nature of the work involved which might tend to set a maximum as well as a minimum wage.

(d) As used in this title, the term "person" includes any individual, partnership, association, trust, or corporation; and the terms "interstate and foreign commerce" and "interstate or foreign commerce" include, except where otherwise indicated, trade or commerce among the several States and with foreign nations, or between the District of Columbia or any Territory of the United States and any State, Territory, or foreign nation, or between any insular possessions or other places under the jurisdiction of the United States, or between

any such possession or place and any State or Territory of the United States or the District of Columbia or any foreign nation, or within the District of Columbia or any Territory or any insular possession or other place under the jurisdiction of the United States.

TITLE II—PUBLIC WORKS AND CONSTRUCTION PROJECTS

Federal Emergency Administration of Public Works

SECTION 201. (a) To effectuate the purposes of this title, the President is hereby authorized to create a Federal Emergency Administration of Public Works, all the powers of which shall be exercised by a Federal Emergency Administrator of Public Works (hereafter referred to as the "Administrator"), and to establish such agencies, to accept and utilize such voluntary and uncompensated services, to appoint, without regard to the civil service laws, such officers and employees, and to utilize such Federal officers and employees, and, with the consent of the State, such State and local officers and employees as he may find necessary, to prescribe their authorities, duties, responsibilities, and tenure, and, without regard to the Classification Act of 1923, as amended, to fix the compensation of any officers and employees so appointed. The President may delegate any of his functions and powers under this title to such officers, agents, and employees as he may designate or appoint.

(b) The Administrator may, without regard to the civil service laws or the Classification Act of 1923, as amended, appoint and fix the compensation of such experts and such other officers and employees as are necessary to carry out the provisions of this title; and may make such expenditures (including expenditures for personal services and rent at the seat of government and elsewhere, for law books and books of reference, and for paper, printing and binding) as are necessary to carry out the provisions of this title.

(c) All such compensation, expenses, and allowances shall be paid out of funds made available by this Act.

(d) After the expiration of two years after the date of the enactment of this Act, or sooner if the President shall by proclamation or the Congress shall by joint resolution declare that the emergency recognized by section 1 has ended, the President shall not make any further loans or grants or enter upon any new construction under this title, and any agencies established hereunder shall cease to exist and any of their remaining functions shall be transferred to such departments of the Government as the President shall designate:

Provided, That he may issue funds to a borrower under this title prior to January 23, 1939, under the terms of any agreement, or any commitment to bid upon or purchase bonds, entered into with such borrower prior to the date of termination, under this section, of the power of the President to make loans.

SEC. 202. The Administrator, under the direction of the President, shall prepare a comprehensive program of public works, which shall include among other things the following: (a) Construction, repair, and improvement of public highways and park ways, public buildings, and any publicly owned instrumentalities and facilities; (b) conservation and development of natural resources, including control, utilization, and purification of waters, prevention of soil or coastal erosion, development of water power, transmission of electrical energy, and construction of river and harbor improvements and flood control and also the construction of any river or drainage improvement required to perform or satisfy any obligation incurred by the United States through a treaty with a foreign Government heretofore ratified and to restore or develop for the use of any State or its citizens water taken from or denied to them by performance on the part of the United States of treaty obligations heretofore assumed: *Provided,* That no river or harbor improvements shall be carried out unless they shall have heretofore or hereafter been adopted by the Congress or are recommended by the Chief of Engineers of the United States Army; (c) any projects of the character heretofore constructed or carried on either directly by public authority or with public aid to serve the interests of the general public; (d) construction, reconstruction, alteration, or repair under public regulation or control of low-cost housing and slum-clearance projects; (e) any project (other than those included in the foregoing classes) of any character heretofore eligible for loans under subsection (a) of section 201 of the Emergency Relief and Construction Act of 1932, as amended, and paragraph (3) of such subsection (a) shall for such purposes be held to include loans for the construction or completion of hospitals the operation of which is partly financed from public funds, and of reservoirs and pumping plants and for the construction of dry docks; and if in the opinion of the President it seems desirable, the construction of naval vessels within the terms and/or limits established by the London Naval Treaty of 1930 and of aircraft required therefor and construction of heavier-than-air aircraft and technical construction for the Army Air Corps and such Army housing projects as the President may approve, and provision of original equipment for the mechanization or motorization of such Army tactical units as he may designate: *Provided, however,* That in the event of an international agreement for the further limitation of armament, to which the United States is signatory, the President is hereby authorized and empowered to suspend, in whole or in part, any such naval or military construction or mechanization and motorization of Army units: *Provided further,* That this title shall not be applicable to public works under the jurisdiction or control of the Architect of the Capitol or of any commission or committee for which such Architect is the contracting and/or executive officer.

SEC. 203. (a) With a view to increasing employment quickly (while reasonably securing any loans made by the United States) the President is authorized and empowered, through the Administrator or through such other agencies as he may designate or create, (1) to construct, finance, or aid in the construction or financing of any public-works project included in the program prepared pursuant to section 202; (2) upon such terms as the President shall prescribe, to make grants to States, municipalities, or other public bodies for the construction, repair, or improvement of any such project, but no such grant shall be in excess of 30 per centum of the cost of the labor and materials employed upon such project; (3) to acquire by purchase, or by exercise of the power of eminent domain, any real or personal property in connection with the construction of any such project, and to sell any security acquired or any property so constructed or acquired or to lease any such property with or without the privilege of purchase: *Provided,* That all moneys received from any such sale or lease or the repayment of any loan shall be used to retire obligations issued pursuant to section 209 of this Act, in addition to any other moneys required to be used for such purpose; (4) to aid in the financing of such railroad maintenance and equipment as may be approved by the Interstate Commerce Commission as desirable for the improvement of transportation facilities; and (5) to advance, upon request of the Commission having jurisdiction of the project, the unappropriated balance of the sum authorized for carrying out the provisions of the Act entitled "An Act to provide for the construction and equipment of an annex to the Library of Congress," approved June 13, 1930 (46 Stat. 583); such advance to be expended under the direction of such Commission and in accordance with such Act: *Provided,* That in deciding to extend any aid or grant hereunder to any State, county, or municipality the President may consider whether action is in process or in good faith assured therein reasonably designed to bring the ordinary current expenditures thereof within the prudently estimated revenues thereof. The provisions of this section and section 202 shall extend to public works in the several States, Hawaii, Alaska, the District of Columbia, Puerto Rico, the Canal Zone, and the Virgin Islands.

(b) All expenditures for authorized travel by officers and employees, including subsistence, required on account of any Federal public-works projects, shall be charged to the amounts allocated to such projects, notwithstanding any other provisions of law; and there is authorized to be employed such personal services in the District of Columbia and elsewhere as may be required to be engaged upon such work and to be in addition to employees otherwise provided for, the compensation of such additional personal services to be a charge against the funds made available for such construction work.

(c) In the acquisition of any land or site for the purposes of Federal public buildings and in the construction of such buildings provided for in this title, the provisions contained in sections 305 and 306 of the Emergency Relief and Construction Act of 1932, as amended, shall apply.

(d) The President, in his discretion, and under such terms as he may prescribe, may extend any of the benefits of this title to any State, county, or municipality notwithstanding any constitutional or legal restriction or limitation on the right or power of such State, county, or municipality to borrow money or incur indebtedness.

SEC. 204. (a) For the purpose of providing for emergency construction of public highways and related projects, the President is authorized to make grants to the highway departments of the several States in an amount not less than $400,000,000, to be expended by such departments in accordance with the provisions of the Federal Highway Act, approved November 9, 1921, as amended and supplemented, except as provided in this title, as follows:

(1) For expenditure in emergency construction on the Federal aid highway system and extensions thereof into and through municipalities. The amount apportioned to any State under this paragraph may be used to pay all or any part of the cost of surveys, plans, and of highway and bridge construction including the elimination of hazards to highway traffic, such as the separation of grades at crossing, the reconstruction of existing railroad grade crossing structures, the relocation of highways to eliminate railroad crossings, the widening of narrow bridges and roadways, the building of footpaths, the replacement of unsafe bridges, the construction of routes

to avoid congested areas, the construction of facilities to improve accessibility and the free flow of traffic, and the cost of any other construction that will provide safer traffic facilities or definitely eliminate existing hazards to pedestrian or vehicular traffic. No funds made available by this title shall be used for the acquisition of any land, right of way, or easement in connection with any railroad grade elimination project.

(2) For expenditure in emergency construction on secondary or feeder roads to be agreed upon by the State highway departments and the Secretary of Agriculture: *Provided,* That the State or responsible political subdivision shall provide for the proper maintenance of said roads. Such grants shall be available for payment of the full cost of surveys, plans, improvement, and construction of secondary or feeder roads, on which projects shall be submitted by the State highway department and approved by the Secretary of Agriculture.

(b) Any amounts allocated by the President for grants under subsection (a) of this section shall be apportioned among the several States seven-eighths in accordance with the provisions of section 21 of the Federal Highway Act, approved November 9, 1921, as amended and supplemented (which Act is hereby further amended for the purposes of this title to include the District of Columbia), and one-eighth in the ratio which the population of each State bears to the total population of the United States, according to the latest decennial census and shall be available on July 1, 1933, and shall remain available until expended; but no part of the funds apportioned to any State need be matched by the State, and such funds may also be used in lieu of State funds to match unobligated balances of previous apportionments of regular Federal-aid appropriations.

(c) All contracts involving the expenditure of such grants shall contain provisions establishing minimum rates of wages, to be predetermined by the State highway department, which contractors shall pay to skilled and unskilled labor, and such minimum rates shall be stated in the invitation for bids and shall be included in proposals for bids for the work.

(d) In the expenditure of such amounts, the limitations in the Federal Highway Act, approved November 9, 1921, as amended and supplemented, upon highway construction, reconstruction, and bridges within municipalities and upon payments per mile which may be made from Federal funds, shall not apply.

(e) As used in this section the term "State" includes the Territory of Hawaii and the District of Columbia. The term "highway" as defined in the Federal Highway Act approved

November 9, 1921, as amended and supplemented, for the purposes of this section, shall be deemed to include such main parkways as may be designated by the State and approved by the Secretary of Agriculture as part of the Federal-aid highway system.

(f) Whenever, in connection with the construction of any highway project under this section or section 202 of this Act, it is necessary to acquire rights of way over or through any property or tracts of land owned and controlled by the Government of the United States, it shall be the duty of the proper official of the Government of the United States having control of such property or tracts of land with the approval of the President and the Attorney General of the United States, and without any expense whatsoever to the United States, to perform any acts and to execute any agreements necessary to grant the rights of way so required, but if at any time the land or the property the subject of the agreement shall cease to be used for the purposes of the highway, the title in and the jurisdiction over the land or property shall automatically revert to the Government of the United States and the agreement shall so provide.

(g) Hereafter in the administration of the Federal Highway Act, and Acts amendatory thereof or supplementary thereto, the first paragraph of section 9 of said Act shall not apply to publicly owned toll bridges or approaches thereto, operated by the highway department of any State, subject, however, to the condition that all tolls received from the operation of any such bridge, less the actual cost of operation and maintenance, shall be applied to the repayment of the cost of its construction or acquisition, and when the cost of its construction or acquisition shall have been repaid in full, such bridge thereafter shall be maintained and operated as a free bridge.

SEC. 205. (a) Not less than $50,000,000 of the amount made available by this Act shall be allotted for (A) national forest highways, (B) national forest roads, trails, bridges, and related projects, (C) national park roads and trails in national parks owned or authorized, (D) roads on Indian reservations, and (E) roads through public lands, to be expended in the same manner as provided in paragraph (2) of section 301 of the Emergency Relief and Construction Act of 1932, in the case of appropriations allocated for such purposes, respectively, in such section 301, to remain available until expended.

(b) The President may also allot funds made available by this Act for the construction, repair, and improvement of public highways in Alaska, the Canal Zone, Puerto Rico, and the Virgin Islands.

SEC. 206. All contracts let for construction projects and all loans and grants pursuant to this title shall contain such provisions as are necessary to insure (1) that no convict labor shall be employed on any such project; (2) that (except in executive, administrative, and supervisory positions), so far as practicable and feasible, no individual directly employed on any such project shall be permitted to work more than thirty hours in any one week; (3) that all employees shall be paid just and reasonable wages which shall be compensation sufficient to provide, for the hours of labor as limited, a standard of living in decency and comfort; (4) that in the employment of labor in connection with any such project, preference shall be given, where they are qualified, to ex-service men with dependents, and then in the following order: (A) To citizens of the United States and aliens who have declared their intention of becoming citizens, who are bona fide residents of the political subdivision and/or county in which the work is to be performed, and (B) to citizens of the United States and aliens who have declared their intention of becoming citizens, who are bona fide residents of the State, Territory, or district in which the work is to be performed: *Provided,* That these preferences shall apply only where such labor is available and qualified to perform the work to which the employment relates; and (5) that the maximum of human labor shall be used in lieu of machinery wherever practicable and consistent with sound economy and public advantage.

SEC. 207. (a) For the purpose of expediting the actual construction of public works contemplated by this title and to provide a means of financial assistance to persons under contract with the United States to perform such construction, the President is authorized and empowered, through the Administrator or through such other agencies as he may designate or create, to approve any assignment executed by any such contractor, with the written consent of the surety or sureties upon the penal bond executed in connection with his contract, to any national or State bank, or his claim against the United States, or any part of such claim, under such contract; and any assignment so approved shall be valid for all purposes, notwithstanding the provisions of sections 3737 and 3477 of the Revised Statutes, as amended.

(b) The funds received by a contractor under any advances made in consideration of any such assignment are hereby declared to be trust funds in the hands of such contractor to be first applied to the payment of claims of subcontractors, architects, engineers, surveyors, laborers, and material men in connection with the project, to the payment of premiums on the penal bond or bonds, and premiums accruing during the construction of such project on insurance policies taken in connection therewith. Any contractor and any officer, director, or agent of any such contractor, who applies, or consents to the application of, such funds for any other purpose and fails to pay any claim or premium hereinbefore mentioned, shall be deemed guilty of a misdemeanor and shall be punished by a fine of not more than $1,000 or by imprisonment for not more than one year, or by both such fine and imprisonment.

(c) Nothing in this section shall be considered as imposing upon the assignee any obligation to see to the proper application of the funds advanced by the assignee in consideration of such assignment.

Subsistence Homesteads

SEC. 208. To provide for aiding the redistribution of the overbalance of population in industrial centers $25,000,000 is hereby made available to the President, to be used by him through such agencies as he may establish and under such regulations as he may make, for making loans for and otherwise aiding in the purchase of subsistence homesteads. The moneys collected as repayment of said loans shall constitute a revolving fund to be administered as directed by the President for the purposes of this section.

Redistribution of Wealth, *Huey Long*, 1935

"Kingfish" Huey Long (1893–1935) served as governor of Louisiana (1928–32) and as a U.S. senator from 1932 until his death by gunshot in 1935. An outspoken opponent of large corporations, Long instituted social welfare programs and massive public works projects in Louisiana. An early supporter of FDR, by 1933 Long had become one of the New Deal's harshest critics, arguing that it could not succeed, because it failed to institute a radical redistribution of the country's wealth. Long then assembled a nationwide "Share our Wealth" organization that had more than seven million members by 1935. Long's program would cap personal wealth, income, and inheritances and use the money to guarantee a minimum income to all Americans and to fund social welfare and public works programs. Often accused of political corruption, and unabashedly partisan in his use of state patronage jobs, Long became a symbol of radical populism in America.

Redistribution of Wealth

January 14, 1935

Huey Long

Mr. LONG. Mr. President, I send to the desk a radio address and a letter by myself which I ask to have inserted in the RECORD.

There being no objection, the address and the letter were ordered to be printed in the RECORD, as follows:

Ladies and gentlemen, there is a verse which says that the
> "Saddest words of tongue or pen
> Are these: 'It might have been.'"

I must tell you good people of our beloved United States that the saddest words I have to say are:
> "I told you so!"

In January 1932 I stood on the floor of the United States Senate and told what would happen in 1933. It all came to pass.

In March 1933, a few days after Mr. Roosevelt had become President and had made a few of his moves, I said what to expect in 1934. That came to pass.

As the Congress met in the early months of 1934 and I had a chance to see the course of events for that year, I again gave my belief on what would happen by the time we met again this January 1935. I am grieved to say to you that this week I had to say on the floor of the United States Senate, "I told you so!"

How I wish tonight that I might say to you that all my fears and beliefs of last year proved untrue! But here are the facts—

1. We have 1,000,000 more men out of work now than 1 year ago.

2. We have had to put 5,000,000 more families on the dole than we had there a year ago.

3. The newspapers report from the Government statistics that this past year we had an increase in the money made by the big men, but a decrease in the money made by the people of average and small means. In other words, still "the rich getting richer and the poor getting poorer."

4. The United States Government's Federal Deposit Insurance Corporation reports that it has investigated to see who owns the money in the banks, and they wind up by showing that two-thirds of 1 percent of the people own 67 percent of all the money in the banks, showing again that the average man and the poor man have less than ever of what we have left in this country and that the big man has more of it.

So, without going into more figures, the situation finally presents to us once more the fact that a million more people are out of work; 5,000,000 more are on the dole, and that many more are crying to get on it; the rich earn more, the common people earn less; more and more the rich get hold of what there is in the country, and, in general, America travels on toward its route to ——.

Now what is there to comfort us on this situation? In other words, is there a silver lining? Let's see if there is. I read the following newspaper clipping on what our President of the United States is supposed to think about it. It reads as follows:

{From the New Orleans Morning Tribune, Dec. 18, 1934}
"PRESIDENT FORBIDS MORE TAXES ON RICH
—TELLS CONGRESSMEN DECREASES
MIGHT MAKE BUSINESS STAMPEDE
By the United Press

"WASHINGTON, December 17.—The administration is determined to prevent any considerable increase in taxes on the very rich, many of whom pay no taxes at all, on the ground that such a plan would cause another 'stampede' by business. Word has been sent up to Democratic congressional leaders that it is essential nothing be done to injure confidence. The less said about distribution of wealth, limitation of earned income, and taxes on capital, 'new dealers' feel, the better.

"Repeatedly since the Democrats won a two-thirds majority in both Houses in the congressional elections last month the administration has sought to assure the worker, the taxpayer, and the manufacturer that they had nothing to fear.

"Meantime reports reached the Capital that fear of potential increases in inheritance taxes and gift levies at the coming Congress was in part responsible for the failure of private capital to take up a greater share of the recovery burden."

That ends the news article on what President Roosevelt has had to say.

President Roosevelt was elected on November 8, 1932. People look upon an elected President as the President. This is January 1935. We are in our third year of the Roosevelt depression, with the conditions growing worse. That says nothing about the state of our national finances. I do not even bring that in for important mention, except to give the figures:

Our national debt of today has risen to $28,500,000,000. When the World War ended we shuddered in our boots because the national debt had climbed to $26,000,000,000. But we consoled ourselves by saying that the foreign countries owed us $11,000,000,000 and that in reality the United

States national debt was only $15,000,000,000. But say that it was all of the $26,000,000,000 today. Without a war our national debt under Mr. Roosevelt has climbed up to $28,500,000,000, or more than we owed when the World War ended by 2½ billions of dollars. And in the Budget message of the President he admits that next year the public debt of the United States will go up to $34,000,000,000, or 5½ billion dollars more than we now owe.

Now this big debt would not be so bad if we had something to show for it. If we had ended this depression once and for all we could say that it is worth it all, but at the end of this rainbow of the greatest national debt in all history that must get bigger and bigger, what do we find?

One million more unemployed; 5,000,000 more families on the dole, and another 5,000,000 trying to get there; the fortunes of the rich becoming bigger and the fortunes of the average and little men getting less and less; the money in the banks nearly all owned by a mere handful of people, and the President of the United States quoted as saying: "Don't touch the rich!"

I begged, I pleaded, and did everything else under the sun for over 2 years to try to get Mr. Roosevelt to keep his word that he gave to us; I hoped against hope that sooner or later he would see the light and come back to his promises on which he was made President. I warned what would happen last year and for this year if he did not keep these promises made to the people.

But going into this third year of Roosevelt's administration, I can hope for nothing further from the Roosevelt policies. And I call back to mind that whatever we have been able to do to try to hold the situation together during the past 3 years has been forced down the throat of the national administration. I held the floor in the Senate for days until they allowed the bank laws to be amended that permitted the banks in the small cities and towns to reopen. The bank deposit guaranty law and the Frazier-Lemke farm debt moratorium law had to be passed in spite of the Roosevelt administration. I helped to pass them both.

All the time we have pointed to the rising cloud of debt, the increases in unemployment, the gradual slipping away of what money the middle man and the poor man have into the hands of the big masters, all the time we have prayed and shouted, begged and pleaded, and now we hear the message once again from Roosevelt that he cannot touch the big fortunes.

Hope for more through Roosevelt? He has promised and promised, smiled and bowed; he has read fine speeches and told anyone in need to get in touch with him. What has it meant?

We must now become awakened! We must know the truth and speak the truth. There is no use to wait 3 more years. It is not Roosevelt or ruin; it is Roosevelt's ruin.

Now, my friends, it makes no difference who is President or who is Senator. America is for 125,000,000 people and the unborn to come. We ran Mr. Roosevelt for the Presidency of the United States because he promised to us by word of mouth and in writing:

1. That the size of the big man's fortune would be reduced so as to give the masses at the bottom enough to wipe out all poverty; and

2. That the hours of labor would be so reduced that all would share in the work to be done and in consuming the abundance mankind produced.

Hundreds of words were used by Mr. Roosevelt to make these promises to the people, but they were made over and over again. He reiterated these pledges even after he took his oath as President. Summed up, what these promises meant was: "Share our wealth."

When I saw him spending all his time of ease and recreation with the business partners of Mr. John D. Rockefeller, Jr., with such men as the Astors, etc. maybe I ought to have had better sense than to have believed he would ever break down their big fortunes to give enough to the masses to end poverty—maybe some will think me weak for ever believing it all, but millions of other people were fooled the same as myself. I was like a drowning man grabbing at a straw, I guess. The face and eyes, the hungry forms of mothers and children, the aching hearts of students denied education were before our eyes, and when Roosevelt promised, we jumped for that ray of hope.

So therefore I call upon the men and women of America to immediately join our work and movement to share our wealth.

There are thousands of share-our-wealth societies organized in the United States now. We want a hundred thousand such societies formed for every nook and corner of the country, societies that will meet, talk, and work, all for the purpose that the great wealth and abundance of this great land that belongs to us may be shared and enjoyed by all of us.

We have nothing more for which we should ask the Lord. He has allowed this land to have too much of everything that humanity needs.

So in this land of God's abundance we propose laws, viz:

1. The fortunes of the multimillionaires and billionaires shall be reduced so that no one person shall own more than a few million dollars to the person. We would do this by a capital levy tax. On the first million that a man was worth we would not impose any tax. We would say, "All right for your first million dollars, but after you get that rich you will have to start helping the balance of us." So we would not levy any capital levy tax on the first million one owned. But on the second million a man owns we would tax that 1 percent, so that every year the man owned the second million dollars he would be taxed $10,000. On the third million we would impose a tax of 2 percent. On the fourth million we would impose a tax of 4 percent. On the fifth million we would impose a tax of 8 percent. On the sixth million we would impose a tax of 16 percent. On the seventh million we would impose a tax of 32 percent. On the eighth million we would impose a tax of 64 percent; and on all over the eighth million we would impose a tax of 100 percent. What this would mean is that the annual tax would bring the biggest fortune down to three or four million dollars to the person because no one could pay taxes very long in the higher brackets. But three to four million dollars is enough for any one person and his children and his children's children. We cannot allow one to have more than that because it would not leave enough for the balance to have something.

2. We propose to limit the amount any one man can earn in 1 year or inherit to $1,000,000 to the person.

3. Now, by limiting the size of the fortunes and incomes of the big men we will throw into the Government Treasury the money and property from which we will care for the millions of people who have nothing; and with this money we will provide a home and the comforts of home, with such common conveniences as radio and automobile, for every family in America, free of debt.

4. We guarantee food and clothing and employment for everyone who should work by shortening the hours of labor to 30 hours per week, maybe less, and to 11 months per year, maybe less. We would have the hours shortened just so much as would give work to everybody to produce enough for everybody; and if we were to get them down to where they were too short, then we would lengthen them again. As long as all the people working can produce enough of automobiles, radios, homes, schools, and theaters for everyone to have that kind of comfort and convenience, then let us all have work to do and have that much of heaven on earth.

5. We would provide education at the expense of the States

and the United States for every child, not only through grammar school and high school but through to a college and vocational education. We would simply extend the Louisiana plan to apply to colleges and all people. Yes; we would have to build thousands of more colleges and employ a hundred thousand more teachers; but we have materials, men, and women who are ready and available for the work. Why have the right to a college education depend upon whether the father or mother is so well to do as to send a boy or girl to college? We would give every child the right to education and a living at birth.

6. We would give a pension to all persons above 60 years of age in an amount sufficient to support them in comfortable circumstances, excepting those who earn $1,000 per year or who are worth $10,000.

7. Until we could straighten things out—and we can straighten things out in 2 months under our program—we would grant a moratorium on all debts which people owe that they cannot pay.

And now you have our program, none too big, none too little, but every man a king.

We owe debts in America today, public and private, amounting to $252,000,000,000. That means that every child is born with a $2,000 debt tied around his neck to hold him down before he gets started. Then, on top of that, the wealth is locked in a vice owned by a few people. We propose that children shall be born in a land of opportunity, guaranteed a home, food, clothes, and the other things that make for living, including the right to education.

Our plan would injure no one. It would not stop us from having millionaires—it would increase them tenfold, because so many more people could make a million dollars if they had the chance our plan gives them. Our plan would not break up big concerns. The only difference would be that maybe 10,000 people would own a concern instead of 10 people owning it.

But my friends, unless we do share our wealth, unless we limit the size of the big man so as to give something to the little man, we can never have a happy or free people. God said so! He ordered it.

We have everything our people need. Too much of food, clothes, and houses—why not let all have their fill and lie down in the ease and comfort God has given us? Why not? Because a few own everything—the masses own nothing.

I wonder if any of you people who are listening to me were ever at a barbecue! We used to go there—sometimes a thousand people or more. If there were 1,000 people we would put enough meat and bread and everything else on the table for 1,000 people. Then everybody would be called and everyone would eat all they wanted. But suppose at one of these barbecues for 1,000 people that one man took 90 percent of the food and ran off with it and ate until he got sick and let the balance rot. Then 999 people would have only enough for 100 to eat and there would be many to starve because of the greed of just one person for something he couldn't eat himself.

Well, ladies and gentlemen, America, all the people of America, have been invited to a barbecue. God invited us all to come and eat and drink all we wanted. He smiled on our land and we grew crops of plenty to eat and wear. He showed us in the earth the iron and other things to make everything we wanted. He unfolded to us the secrets of science so that our work might be easy. God called: "Come to my feast."

Then what happened? Rockefeller, Morgan, and their crowd stepped up and took enough for 120,000,000 people and left only enough for 5,000,000 for all the other 125,000,000 to eat. And so many millions must go hungry and without these good things God gave us unless we call on them to put some of it back.

I call on you to organize share-our-wealth societies. Write to me in Washington if you will help.

Let us dry the eyes of those who suffer; let us lift the hearts of the sad. There is plenty. There is more. Why should we not secure laws to do justice—laws that were promised to us— never should we have quibbled over the soldiers' bonus. We need that money circulating among our people. That is why I offered the amendment to pay it last year. I will do so again this year.

Why weep or slumber, America?
   Land of brave and true,
With castles, clothing, and food for all
   All belongs to you.

Ev'ry man a king, ev'ry man a king,
   For you can be a millionaire;
But there's something belonging to others,
There's enough for all people to share.
When it's sunny June and December, too,
Or in the wintertime or spring,
There'll be peace without end,
Ev'ry neighbor a friend,
   With ev'ry man a king.

UNITED STATES SENATE,
Washington, D.C.

DEAR FRIEND: Two reports are repeatedly published in the newspapers and announced in programs rendered by the big interests in their radio programs. The first report is that I am a man of great means. If I could sell everything I own, which is not much, I could not pay one-half of my debts.

The other report repeatedly printed and circulated is that the speeches and literature which I send out are printed at Government expense. That statement is also false. With the exception of Government bulletins, etc., everything we sent out, including the enclosed document, must be paid for by us. We are frequently unable to pay some of our printing ac-counts, and, therefore, have to delay sending out articles requested of us until we can find money with which to do so. That fact can be verified by the accounts we have owed to the Government Printing Office.

We do not make any solicitation of you for any help, and are glad of the privilege to send anything we can on request absolutely free in the hope that those who feel that our cause is just will make known to their neighbors some of the facts which we furnish.

Yours sincerely,

HUEY P. LONG,
United States Senator.

The National Recovery Administration (NRA), established under the National Indus-trial Recovery Act, in effect brought unions and large companies together to set wages, prices, working conditions, and the like. It also gave the president the power to declare the resulting codes to be the law of the land. Many small companies resisted the NRA. Among these was the Schechter Poultry Corporation, a wholesaler of chickens in New York City. Convicted of a number of offenses, including selling a sick chicken, Schechter argued before the Supreme Court that the National Industrial Recovery Act was unconstitutional because it entailed federal regulation of commerce that was conducted entirely within one state, and because, through it, Congress had abdicated its responsibility to pass only laws that specifically stated what conduct was mandated or forbidden. The NRA was already generally regarded as a failure by this time, but the Court's decision, siding with Schech-ter, set up a historic confrontation between the president and the Court regarding the constitutionality of federal regulation.

A. L. A. Schechter Poultry Corp. et al. v. United States

May 27, 1935

MR. CHIEF JUSTICE HUGHES delivered the opinion of the Court.*

Petitioners in No. 854 were convicted in the District Court of the United States for the Eastern District of New York on eighteen counts of an indictment charging violations of what is known as the "Live Poultry Code," and on an additional count for conspiracy to commit such violations. By demurrer to the indictment and appropriate motions on the trial, the defendants contended (1) that the Code had been adopted pursuant to an unconstitutional delegation by Congress of legislative power; (2) that it attempted to regulate intrastate transactions which lay outside the authority of Congress; and (3) that in certain provisions it was repugnant to the due pro-cess clause of the Fifth Amendment.

The Circuit Court of Appeals sustained the conviction on the conspiracy count and on sixteen counts for violation of the Code, but reversed the conviction on two counts which charged violation of requirements as to minimum wages and maximum hours of labor, as these were not deemed to be within the congressional power of regulation. On the re-

spective applications of the defendants (No. 854) and of the Government (No. 864) this Court granted writs of certiorari, April 15, 1935.

New York City is the largest live-poultry market in the United States. Ninety-six per cent. of the live poultry there marketed comes from other States. Three-fourths of this amount arrives by rail and is consigned to commission men or receivers. Most of these freight shipments (about 75 per cent.) come in at the Manhattan Terminal of the New York Central Railroad, and the remainder at one of the four termi-nals in New Jersey serving New York City. The commission men transact by far the greater part of the business on a com-mission basis, representing the shippers as agents, and remit-ting to them the proceeds of sale, less commissions, freight and handling charges. Otherwise, they buy for their own account. They sell to slaughterhouse operators who are also called market-men.

The defendants are slaughterhouse operators of the latter class. A. L. A. Schechter Poultry Corporation and Schechter Live Poultry Market are corporations conducting wholesale poultry slaughterhouse markets in Brooklyn, New York City. Joseph Schechter operated the latter corporation and also guaranteed the credits of the former corporation which was

---

* Internal citations have been omitted.—B. F.

operated by Martin, Alex and Aaron Schechter. Defendants ordinarily purchase their live poultry from commission men at the West Washington Market in New York City or at the railroad terminals serving the City, but occasionally they purchase from commission men in Philadelphia. They buy the poultry for slaughter and resale. After the poultry is trucked to their slaughterhouse markets in Brooklyn, it is there sold, usually within twenty-four hours, to retail poultry dealers and butchers who sell directly to consumers. The poultry purchased from defendants is immediately slaughtered, prior to delivery, by shochtim in defendants' employ. Defendants do not sell poultry in interstate commerce. . . .

Of the eighteen counts of the indictment upon which the defendants were convicted, aside from the count for conspiracy, two counts charged violation of the minimum wage and maximum hour provisions of the Code, and ten counts were for violation of the requirement (found in the "trade practice provisions") of "straight killing." This requirement was really one of "straight" selling. The term "straight killing" was defined in the Code as "the practice of requiring persons purchasing poultry for resale to accept the run of any half coop, coop, or coops, as purchased by slaughterhouse operators, except for culls." The charges in the ten counts, respectively, were that the defendants in selling to retail dealers and butchers had permitted "selections of individual chickens taken from particular coops and half coops."

Of the other six counts, one charged the sale to a butcher of an unfit chicken; two counts charged the making of sales without having the poultry inspected or approved in accordance with regulations or ordinances of the City of New York; two counts charged the making of false reports or the failure to make reports relating to the range of daily prices and volume of sales for certain periods; and the remaining count was for sales to slaughterers or dealers who were without licenses required by the ordinances and regulations of the city of New York.

First. Two preliminary points are stressed by the Government with respect to the appropriate approach to the important questions presented. We are told that the provision of the statute authorizing the adoption of codes must be viewed in the light of the grave national crisis with which Congress was confronted. Undoubtedly, the conditions to which power is addressed are always to be considered when the exercise of power is challenged. Extraordinary conditions may call for extraordinary remedies. But the argument necessarily stops short of an attempt to justify action which lies outside the sphere of constitutional authority. Extraordinary conditions do not create or enlarge constitutional power. The Constitution established a national government with powers deemed to be adequate, as they have proved to be both in war and peace, but these powers of the national government are limited by the constitutional grants. Those who act under these grants are not at liberty to transcend the imposed limits because they believe that more or different power is necessary. Such assertions of extra-constitutional authority were anticipated and precluded by the explicit terms of the Tenth Amendment,—"The powers not delegated to the United States by the Constitution, nor prohibited by it to the States, are reserved to the States respectively, or to the people."

The further point is urged that the national crisis demanded a broad and intensive coöperative effort by those engaged in trade and industry, and that this necessary coöperation was sought to be fostered by permitting them to initiate the adoption of codes. But the statutory plan is not simply one for voluntary effort. It does not seek merely to endow voluntary trade or industrial associations or groups with privileges or immunities. It involves the coercive exercise of the law-making power. The codes of fair competition which the statute attempts to authorize are codes of laws. If valid, they place all persons within their reach under the obligation of positive law, binding equally those who assent and those who do not assent. Violations of the provisions of the codes are punishable as crimes.

Second. The question of the delegation of legislative power. We recently had occasion to review the pertinent decisions and the general principles which govern the determination of this question. *Panama Refining Co.* v. *Ryan,* 293 U.S. 388. The Constitution provides that "All legislative powers herein granted shall be vested in a Congress of the United States, which shall consist of a Senate and House of Representatives." Art. I, § 1. And the Congress is authorized "To make all laws which shall be necessary and proper for carrying into execution" its general powers. Art. I, § 8, par. 18. The Congress is not permitted to abdicate or to transfer to others the essential legislative functions with which it is thus vested. We have repeatedly recognized the necessity of adapting legislation to complex conditions involving a host of details with which the national legislature cannot deal directly. We pointed out in the *Panama Company* case that the Constitution has never been regarded as denying to Congress the necessary resources of flexibility and practicality, which will enable it to perform its function in laying down policies and establishing standards, while leaving to selected instrumentalities the making of subordinate rules within prescribed limits and the determination of facts to which the policy as declared by the legislature is to apply. But we said that the constant recognition of the necessity and validity of such provisions, and the wide range of administrative authority which has been developed by means of them, cannot be allowed to obscure the limitations of the authority to delegate, if our constitutional system is to be maintained.

Accordingly, we look to the statute to see whether Congress has overstepped these limitations,—whether Congress in authorizing "codes of fair competition" has itself established the standards of legal obligation, thus performing its essential legislative function, or, by the failure to enact such standards, has attempted to transfer that function to others.

The aspect in which the question is now presented is distinct from that which was before us in the case of the *Panama Company*. There, the subject of the statutory prohibition was defined. National Industrial Recovery Act, § 9 (c). That subject was the transportation in interstate and foreign commerce of petroleum and petroleum products which are produced or withdrawn from storage in excess of the amount permitted by state authority. The question was with respect to the range of discretion given to the President in prohibiting that transportation. As to the "codes of fair competition," under § 3 of the Act, the question is more fundamental. It is whether there is any adequate definition of the subject to which the codes are to be addressed.

What is meant by "fair competition" as the term is used in the Act? Does it refer to a category established in the law, and is the authority to make codes limited accordingly? Or is it used as a convenient designation for whatever set of laws the formulators of a code for a particular trade or industry may propose and the President may approve (subject to certain restrictions), or the President may himself prescribe, as being wise and beneficent provisions for the government of the trade or industry in order to accomplish the broad purposes of rehabilitation, correction and expansion which are stated in the first section of Title I?

The Act does not define "fair competition." "Unfair competition," as known to the common law, is a limited concept. Primarily, and strictly, it relates to the palming off of one's goods as those of a rival trader. In recent years, its scope has been extended. It has been held to apply to misappropriation as well as misrepresentation, to the selling of another's goods as one's own,—to misappropriation of what equita-

bly belongs to a competitor. Unfairness in competition has been predicated of acts which lie outside the ordinary course of business and are tainted by fraud, or coercion, or conduct otherwise prohibited by law. But it is evident that in its widest range, "unfair competition," as it has been understood in the law, does not reach the objectives of the codes which are authorized by the National Industrial Recovery Act. The codes may, indeed, cover conduct which existing law condemns, but they are not limited to conduct of that sort. The Government does not contend that the Act contemplates such a limitation. It would be opposed both to the declared purposes of the Act and to its administrative construction.

The Federal Trade Commission Act (§ 5) introduced the expression "unfair methods of competition," which were declared to be unlawful. That was an expression new in the law. Debate apparently convinced the sponsors of the legislation that the words "unfair competition," in the light of their meaning at common law, were too narrow. We have said that the substituted phrase has a broader meaning, that it does not admit of precise definition, its scope being left to judicial determination as controversies arise. What are "unfair methods of competition" are thus to be determined in particular instances, upon evidence, in the light of particular competitive conditions and of what is found to be a specific and substantial public interest. To make this possible, Congress set up a special procedure. A Commission, a quasi-judicial body, was created. Provision was made for formal complaint, for notice and hearing, for appropriate findings of fact supported by adequate evidence, and for judicial review to give assurance that the action of the Commission is taken within its statutory authority.

In providing for codes, the National Industrial Recovery Act dispenses with this administrative procedure and with any administrative procedure of an analogous character. But the difference between the code plan of the Recovery Act and the scheme of the Federal Trade Commission Act lies not only in procedure but in subject matter. We cannot regard the "fair competition" of the codes as antithetical to the "unfair methods of competition" of the Federal Trade Commission Act. The "fair competition" of the codes has a much broader range and a new significance. The Recovery Act provides that it shall not be construed to impair the powers of the Federal Trade Commission, but, when a code is approved, its provisions are to be the "standards of fair competition" for the trade or industry concerned, and any violation of such standards in any transaction in or affecting interstate or foreign commerce is to be deemed "an unfair method of competition" within the meaning of the Federal Trade Commission Act. § 3 (b).

For a statement of the authorized objectives and content of the "codes of fair competition" we are referred repeatedly to the "Declaration of Policy" in section one of Title I of the Recovery Act. Thus, the approval of a code by the President is conditioned on his finding that it "will tend to effectuate the policy of this title." § 3 (a). The President is authorized to impose such conditions "for the protection of consumers, competitors, employees, and others, and in furtherance of the public interest, and may provide such exceptions to and exemptions from the provisions of such code as the President in his discretion deems necessary to effectuate the policy herein declared." The "policy herein declared" is manifestly that set forth in section one. That declaration embraces a broad range of objectives. Among them we find the elimination of "unfair competitive practices." But even if this clause were to be taken to relate to practices which fall under the ban of existing law, either common law or statute, it is still only one of the authorized aims described in section one. It is there declared to be "the policy of Congress"—

"to remove obstructions to the free flow of interstate and foreign commerce which tend to diminish the amount thereof; and to provide for the general welfare by promoting the organization of industry for the purpose of coöperative action among trade groups, to induce and maintain united action of labor and management under adequate governmental sanctions and supervision, to eliminate unfair competitive practices, to promote the fullest possible utilization of the present productive capacity of industries, to avoid undue restriction of production (except as may be temporarily required), to increase the consumption of industrial and agricultural products by increasing purchasing power, to reduce and relieve unemployment, to improve standards of labor, and otherwise to rehabilitate industry and to conserve natural resources."

Under § 3, whatever "may tend to effectuate" these general purposes may be included in the "codes of fair competition." We think the conclusion is inescapable that the authority sought to be conferred by § 3 was not merely to deal with "unfair competitive practices" which offend against existing law, and could be the subject of judicial condemnation without further legislation, or to create administrative machinery for the application of established principles of law to particular instances of violation. Rather, the purpose is clearly disclosed to authorize new and controlling prohibitions through codes of laws which would embrace what the formulators would propose, and what the President would approve, or prescribe, as wise and beneficent measures for the government of trades and industries in order to bring about their rehabilitation, correction and development, according to the general declaration of policy in section one. Codes of laws of this sort are styled "codes of fair competition."

We find no real controversy upon this point and we must determine the validity of the Code in question in this aspect. As the Government candidly says in its brief: "The words 'policy of this title' clearly refer to the 'policy' which Congress declared in the section entitled 'Declaration of Policy'—§ 1. All of the policies there set forth point toward a single goal— the rehabilitation of industry and the industrial recovery which unquestionably was the major policy of Congress in adopting the National Industrial Recovery Act." And that this is the controlling purpose of the Code now before us appears both from its repeated declarations to that effect and from the scope of its requirements. It will be observed that its provisions as to the hours and wages of employees and its "general labor provisions" were placed in separate articles, and these were not included in the article on "trade practice provisions" declaring what should be deemed to constitute "unfair methods of competition." The Secretary of Agriculture thus stated the objectives of the Live Poultry Code in his report to the President, which was recited in the executive order of approval:

"That said code will tend to effectuate the declared policy of title I of the National Industrial Recovery Act as set forth in section 1 of said act in that the terms and provisions of such code tend to: (a) Remove obstructions to the free flow of interstate and foreign commerce which tend to diminish the amount thereof; (b) to provide for the general welfare by promoting the organization of industry for the purpose of coöperative action among trade groups; (c) to eliminate unfair competitive practices; (d) to promote the fullest possible utilization of the present productive capacity of industries; (e) to avoid undue restriction of production (except as may be temporarily required); (f) to increase the consumption of industrial and agricultural products by increasing purchasing power; and (g) otherwise to rehabilitate industry and to conserve natural resources."

The Government urges that the codes will "consist of rules of competition deemed fair for each industry by representative members of that industry—by the persons most vitally concerned and most familiar with its problems." Instances are cited in which Congress has availed itself of such assistance; as *e.g.,* in the exercise of its authority over the public domain, with respect to the recognition of local customs or rules of miners as to mining claims, or, in matters of a more or less technical nature, as in designating the standard height of drawbars. But would it be seriously contended that Congress could delegate its legislative authority to trade or industrial associations or groups so as to empower them to enact the laws they deem to be wise and beneficent for the rehabilitation and expansion of their trade or industries? Could trade or industrial associations or groups be constituted legislative bodies for that purpose because such associations or groups are familiar with the problems of their enterprises? And, could an effort of that sort be made valid by such a preface of generalities as to permissible aims as we find in section 1 of title I? The answer is obvious. Such a delegation of legislative power is unknown to our law and is utterly inconsistent with the constitutional prerogatives and duties of Congress.

The question, then, turns upon the authority which § 3 of the Recovery Act vests in the President to approve or prescribe. If the codes have standing as penal statutes, this must be due to the effect of the executive action. But Congress cannot delegate legislative power to the President to exercise an unfettered discretion to make whatever laws he thinks may be needed or advisable for the rehabilitation and expansion of trade or industry.

Accordingly we turn to the Recovery Act to ascertain what limits have been set to the exercise of the President's discretion. *First,* the President, as a condition of approval, is required to find that the trade or industrial associations or groups which propose a code, "impose no inequitable restrictions on admission to membership" and are "truly representative." That condition, however, relates only to the status of the initiators of the new laws and not to the permissible scope of such laws. *Second,* the President is required to find that the code is not "designed to promote monopolies or to eliminate or oppress small enterprises and will not operate to discriminate against them." And, to this is added a proviso that the code "shall not permit monopolies or monopolistic practices." But these restrictions leave virtually untouched the field of policy envisaged by section one, and, in that wide field of legislative possibilities, the proponents of a code, refraining from monopolistic designs, may roam at will and the President may approve or disapprove their proposals as he may see fit. That is the precise effect of the further finding that the President is to make—that the code "will tend to ef-

fectuate the policy of this title." While this is called a finding, it is really but a statement of an opinion as to the general effect upon the promotion of trade or industry of a scheme of laws. These are the only findings which Congress has made essential in order to put into operation a legislative code having the aims described in the "Declaration of Policy."

Nor is the breadth of the President's discretion left to the necessary implications of this limited requirement as to his findings. As already noted, the President in approving a code may impose his own conditions, adding to or taking from what is proposed, as "in his discretion" he thinks necessary "to effectuate the policy" declared by the Act. Of course, he has no less liberty when he prescribes a code on his own motion or on complaint, and he is free to prescribe one if a code has not been approved. The Act provides for the creation by the President of administrative agencies to assist him, but the action or reports of such agencies, or of his other assistants,—their recommendations and findings in relation to the making of codes—have no sanction beyond the will of the President, who may accept, modify or reject them as he pleases. Such recommendations or findings in no way limit the authority which § 3 undertakes to vest in the President with no other conditions than those there specified. And this authority relates to a host of different trades and industries, thus extending the President's discretion to all the varieties of laws which he may deem to be beneficial in dealing with the vast array of commercial and industrial activities throughout the country.

Such a sweeping delegation of legislative power finds no support in the decisions upon which the Government especially relies. By the Interstate Commerce Act, Congress has itself provided a code of laws regulating the activities of the common carriers subject to the Act, in order to assure the performance of their services upon just and reasonable terms, with adequate facilities and without unjust discrimination. Congress from time to time has elaborated its requirements, as needs have been disclosed. To facilitate the application of the standards prescribed by the Act, Congress has provided an expert body. That administrative agency, in dealing with particular cases, is required to act upon notice and hearing, and its orders must be supported by findings of fact which in turn are sustained by evidence.

When the Commission is authorized to issue, for the construction, extension or abandonment of lines, a certificate of "public convenience and necessity," or to permit the acquisition by one carrier of the control of another, if that is found to be "in the public interest," we have pointed out that these provisions are not left without standards to guide determination. The authority conferred has direct relation to the standards prescribed for the service of common carriers and can be exercised only upon findings, based upon evidence, with respect to particular conditions of transportation.

Similarly, we have held that the Radio Act of 1927 established standards to govern radio communications and, in view of the limited number of available broadcasting frequencies, Congress authorized allocation and licenses. The Federal Radio Commission was created as the licensing authority, in order to secure a reasonable equality of opportunity in radio transmission and reception. The authority of the Commission to grant licenses "as public convenience, interest or necessity requires" was limited by the nature of radio communications, and by the scope, character and quality of the services to be rendered and the relative advantages to be derived through distribution of facilities. These standards established by Congress were to be enforced upon hearing, and evidence, by an administrative body acting under statutory restrictions adapted to the particular activity. . . .

To summarize and conclude upon this point: Section 3 of the Recovery Act is without precedent. It supplies no standards for any trade, industry or activity. It does not undertake to prescribe rules of conduct to be applied to particular states of fact determined by appropriate administrative procedure. Instead of prescribing rules of conduct, it authorizes the making of codes to prescribe them. For that legislative undertaking, § 3 sets up no standards, aside from the statement of the general aims of rehabilitation, correction and expansion described in section one. In view of the scope of that broad declaration, and of the nature of the few restrictions that are imposed, the discretion of the President in approving or prescribing codes, and thus enacting laws for the government of trade and industry throughout the country, is virtually unfettered. We think that the code-making authority thus conferred is an unconstitutional delegation of legislative power.

Third. The question of the application of the provisions of the Live Poultry Code to intrastate transactions. Although the validity of the codes (apart from the question of delegation) rests upon the commerce clause of the Constitution, § 3 (a) is not in terms limited to interstate and foreign commerce. From the generality of its terms, and from the argument of the Government at the bar, it would appear that § 3 (a) was designed to authorize codes without that limitation. But under § 3 (f) penalties are confined to violations of a code provision "in any transaction in or affecting interstate or foreign commerce." This aspect of the case presents the question whether the particular provisions of the Live Poultry Code, which the defendants were convicted for violating and for having conspired to violate, were within the regulating power of Congress.

These provisions relate to the hours and wages of those employed by defendants in their slaughterhouses in Brooklyn and to the sales there made to retail dealers and butchers.

(1) Were these transactions "*in*" interstate commerce? Much is made of the fact that almost all the poultry coming to New York is sent there from other States. But the code provisions, as here applied, do not concern the transportation of the poultry from other States to New York, or the transactions of the commission men or others to whom it is consigned, or the sales made by such consignees to defendants. When defendants had made their purchases, whether at the West Washington Market in New York City or at the railroad terminals serving the City, or elsewhere, the poultry was trucked to their slaughterhouses in Brooklyn for local disposition. The interstate transactions in relation to that poultry then ended. Defendants held the poultry at their slaughterhouse markets for slaughter and local sale to retail dealers and butchers who in turn sold directly to consumers. Neither the slaughtering nor the sales by defendants were transactions in interstate commerce.

The undisputed facts thus afford no warrant for the argument that the poultry handled by defendants at their slaughterhouse markets was in a "*current*" or "*flow*" of interstate commerce and was thus subject to congressional regulation. The mere fact that there may be a constant flow of commodities into a State does not mean that the flow continues after the property has arrived and has become commingled with the mass of property within the State and is there held solely for local disposition and use. So far as the poultry here in question is concerned, the flow in interstate commerce had ceased. The poultry had come to a permanent rest within the State. It was not held, used, or sold by defendants in relation to any further transactions in interstate commerce and was not destined for transportation to other States. Hence, decisions which deal with a stream of interstate commerce—where goods come to rest within a State temporarily and are later to go forward in interstate commerce—and with the regulation of transactions involved in that practical continuity of movement, are not applicable here.

(2) Did the defendants' transactions directly "*affect*" interstate commerce so as to be subject to federal regulation? The power of Congress extends not only to the regulation of transactions which are part of interstate commerce, but to the protection of that commerce from injury. It matters not that the injury may be due to the conduct of those engaged in intrastate operations. Thus, Congress may protect the safety of those employed in interstate transportation "no matter what may be the source of the dangers which threaten it." We said in *Second Employers' Liability Cases,* 223 U.S. 1, 51, that it is the "effect upon interstate commerce," not "the source of the injury," which is "the criterion of congressional power." We have held that, in dealing with common carriers engaged in both interstate and intrastate commerce, the dominant authority of Congress necessarily embraces the right to control their intrastate operations in all matters having such a close and substantial relation to interstate traffic that the control is essential or appropriate to secure the freedom of that traffic from interference or unjust discrimination and to promote the efficiency of the interstate service. And combinations and conspiracies to restrain interstate commerce, or to monopolize any part of it, are none the less within the reach of the Anti-Trust Act because the conspirators seek to attain their end by means of intrastate activities.

We recently had occasion, in *Local 167* v. *United States,* 291 U.S. 293, to apply this principle in connection with the live poultry industry. That was a suit to enjoin a conspiracy to restrain and monopolize interstate commerce in violation of the Anti-Trust Act. It was shown that marketmen, teamsters and slaughterers (shochtim) had conspired to burden the free movement of live poultry into the metropolitan area in and about New York City. Marketmen had organized an association, had allocated retailers among themselves, and had agreed to increase prices. To accomplish their objects, large amounts of money were raised by levies upon poultry sold, men were hired to obstruct the business of dealers who resisted, wholesalers and retailers were spied upon and by violence and other forms of intimidation were prevented from freely purchasing live poultry. Teamsters refused to handle poultry for recalcitrant marketmen and members of the shochtim union refused to slaughter. In view of the proof of that conspiracy, we said that it was unnecessary to decide when interstate commerce ended and when intrastate commerce began. We found that the proved interference by the conspirators "with the unloading, the transportation, the sales by marketmen to retailers, the prices charged and the amount of profits exacted" operated "substantially and directly to restrain and burden the untrammeled shipment and movement of the poultry" while unquestionably it was in interstate commerce. The intrastate acts of the conspirators were included in the injunction because that was found to be necessary for the protection of interstate commerce against the attempted and illegal restraint.

The instant case is not of that sort. This is not a prosecution for a conspiracy to restrain or monopolize interstate commerce in violation of the Anti-Trust Act. Defendants have been convicted, not upon direct charges of injury to interstate commerce or of interference with persons engaged in that commerce, but of violations of certain provisions of the Live Poultry Code and of conspiracy to commit these violations. Interstate commerce is brought in only upon the charge that violations of these provisions—as to hours and wages of employees and local sales—"*affected*" interstate commerce.

In determining how far the federal government may go in controlling intrastate transactions upon the ground that they "affect" interstate commerce, there is a necessary and well-established distinction between direct and indirect effects. The precise line can be drawn only as individual cases arise, but the distinction is clear in principle. Direct effects are illustrated by the railroad cases we have cited, as *e.g.,* the effect of failure to use prescribed safety appliances on railroads which are the highways of both interstate and intrastate commerce, injury to an employee engaged in interstate transportation by the negligence of an employee engaged in an intrastate movement, the fixing of rates for intrastate transportation which unjustly discriminate against interstate commerce. But where the effect of intrastate transactions upon interstate commerce is merely indirect, such transactions remain within the domain of state power. If the commerce clause were construed to reach all enterprises and transactions which could be said to have an indirect effect upon interstate commerce, the federal authority would embrace practically all the activities of the people and the authority of the State over its domestic concerns would exist only by sufferance of the federal government. Indeed, on such a theory, even the development of the State's commercial facilities would be subject to federal control. As we said in the *Minnesota Rate Cases,* 230 U.S. 352, 410: "In the intimacy of commercial relations, much that is done in the superintendence of local matters may have an indirect bearing upon interstate commerce. The development of local resources and the extension of local facilities may have a very important effect upon communities less favored and to an appreciable degree alter the course of trade. The freedom of local trade may stimulate interstate commerce, while restrictive measures within the police power of the State enacted exclusively with respect to internal business, as distinguished from interstate traffic, may in their reflex or indirect influence diminish the latter and reduce the volume of articles transported into or out of the State."

The distinction between direct and indirect effects has been clearly recognized in the application of the Anti-Trust Act. Where a combination or conspiracy is formed, with the intent to restrain interstate commerce or to monopolize any part of it, the violation of the statute is clear. But where that intent is absent, and the objectives are limited to intrastate activities, the fact that there may be an indirect effect upon interstate commerce does not subject the parties to the federal statute, notwithstanding its broad provisions. This principle has frequently been applied in litigation growing out of labor disputes. In the case last cited we quoted with approval the rule that had been stated and applied in *Industrial Association* v. *United States, supra,* after review of the decisions, as follows: "The alleged conspiracy and the acts here complained of, spent their intended and direct force upon a local situation,—for building is as essentially local as mining, manufacturing or growing crops,—and if, by a resulting diminution of the commercial demand, interstate trade was curtailed either generally or in specific instances, that was a fortuitous consequence so remote and indirect as plainly to cause it to fall outside the reach of the Sherman Act."

While these decisions related to the application of the federal statute, and not to its constitutional validity, the distinction between direct and indirect effects of intrastate transactions upon interstate commerce must be recognized as a fundamental one, essential to the maintenance of our constitutional system. Otherwise, as we have said, there would be virtually no limit to the federal power and for all practical purposes we should have a completely centralized government. We must consider the provisions here in question in the light of this distinction.

The question of chief importance relates to the provisions of the Code as to the hours and wages of those employed in defendants' slaughterhouse markets. It is plain that these requirements are imposed in order to govern the details of defendants' management of their local business. The persons employed in slaughtering and selling in local trade are not employed in interstate commerce. Their hours and wages have no direct relation to interstate commerce. The question of how many hours these employees should work and what they should be paid differs in no essential respect from similar questions in other local businesses which handle commodities brought into a State and there dealt in as a part of its internal commerce. This appears from an examination of the considerations urged by the Government with respect to conditions in the poultry trade. Thus, the Government argues that hours and wages affect prices; that slaughterhouse men sell at a small margin above operating costs; that labor represents 50 to 60 per cent. of these costs; that a slaughterhouse operator paying lower wages or reducing his cost by exacting long hours of work, translates his saving into lower prices; that this results in demands for a cheaper grade of goods; and that the cutting of prices brings about a demoralization of the price structure. Similar conditions may be adduced in relation to other businesses. The argument of the Government proves too much. If the federal government may determine the wages and hours of employees in the internal commerce of a State, because of their relation to cost and prices and their indirect effect upon interstate commerce, it would seem that a similar control might be exerted over other elements of cost, also affecting prices, such as the number of employees, rents, advertising, methods of doing business, etc. All the processes of production and distribution that enter into cost could likewise be controlled. If the cost of doing an intrastate business is in itself the permitted object of federal control, the extent of the regulation of cost would be a question of discretion and not of power.

The Government also makes the point that efforts to enact state legislation establishing high labor standards have been impeded by the belief that unless similar action is taken generally, commerce will be diverted from the States adopting such standards, and that this fear of diversion has led to demands for federal legislation on the subject of wages and hours. The apparent implication is that the federal authority under the commerce clause should be deemed to extend to the establishment of rules to govern wages and hours in intrastate trade and industry generally throughout the country, thus overriding the authority of the States to deal with domestic problems arising from labor conditions in their internal commerce.

It is not the province of the Court to consider the economic advantages or disadvantages of such a centralized system. It is sufficient to say that the Federal Constitution does not provide for it. Our growth and development have called for wide use of the commerce power of the federal government in its control over the expanded activities of interstate commerce, and in protecting that commerce from burdens, interferences, and conspiracies to restrain and monopolize it. But the authority of the federal government may not be pushed to such an extreme as to destroy the distinction, which the commerce clause itself establishes, between commerce "among the several States" and the internal concerns of a State. The same answer must be made to the contention that is based upon the serious economic situation which led to the passage of the Recovery Act,—the fall in prices, the decline in wages and employment, and the curtailment of the market for commodities. Stress is laid upon the great importance of maintaining wage distributions which would provide the necessary stimulus in starting "the cumulative forces making for expanding commercial activity." Without in any way disparaging this motive, it is enough to say that the recuperative efforts of the federal government must be made in a manner consistent with the authority granted by the Constitution.

We are of the opinion that the attempt through the provisions of the Code to fix the hours and wages of employees of defendants in their intrastate business was not a valid exercise of federal power.

The other violations for which defendants were convicted related to the making of local sales. Ten counts, for violation of the provision as to "straight killing," were for permitting customers to make "selections of individual chickens taken from particular coops and half coops." Whether or not this practice is good or bad for the local trade, its effect, if any, upon interstate commerce was only indirect. The same may be said of violations of the Code by intrastate transactions consisting of the sale "of an unfit chicken" and of sales which were not in accord with the ordinances of the City of New York. The requirement of reports as to prices and volumes of defendants' sales was incident to the effort to control their intrastate business.

In view of these conclusions, we find it unnecessary to discuss other questions which have been raised as to the validity of certain provisions of the Code under the due process clause of the Fifth Amendment.

On both the grounds we have discussed, the attempted delegation of legislative power, and the attempted regulation of intrastate transactions which affect interstate commerce only indirectly, we hold the code provisions here in question to be invalid and that the judgment of conviction must be reversed.

No. 854—reversed.
No. 864—affirmed.

Fireside Chat on the Reorganization of the Judiciary, *Franklin Delano Roosevelt, 1937*

The ninth in a series of radio addresses to the nation, the "fireside chat" reproduced here lays out FDR's plan to overcome Supreme Court opposition to New Deal legislation. A number of programs FDR deemed central to his program to bring the nation out of the Great Depression had been struck down by the Court on the grounds that they overstepped the federal government's constitutional powers. FDR consistently criticized these decisions as unwarranted by the language of the Constitution and inappropriate, given the extent of the national crisis. But, despite the fact that most of these decisions were handed down on votes of 5–4, FDR saw no immediate prospect for changes in personnel that might break the interbranch deadlock. As a result FDR proposed what came to be known as his "court-packing plan." Arguing that elderly judges were not capable of keeping up with their workload and understanding "modern conditions," he proposed a bill allowing the president to appoint one new Supreme Court justice for every justice who was over the age of seventy years and six months. Even leaders in FDR's own party opposed the bill as extraconstitutional and dangerous, and it failed to achieve passage.

Fireside Chat on the Reorganization of the Judiciary

March 9, 1937

Franklin Delano Roosevelt

Last Thursday I described in detail certain economic problems which everyone admits now face the Nation. For the many messages which have come to me after that speech, and which it is physically impossible to answer individually, I take this means of saying "thank you."

Tonight, sitting at my desk in the White House, I make my first radio report to the people in my second term of office.

I am reminded of that evening in March, four years ago, when I made my first radio report to you. We were then in the midst of the great banking crisis.

Soon after, with the authority of the Congress, we asked the Nation to turn over all of its privately held gold, dollar for dollar, to the Government of the United States.

Today's recovery proves how right that policy was.

But when, almost two years later, it came before the Supreme Court its constitutionality was upheld only by a five-to-four vote. The change of one vote would have thrown all the affairs of this great Nation back into hopeless chaos. In effect, four Justices ruled that the right under a private contract to exact a pound of flesh was more sacred than the main objectives of the Constitution to establish an enduring Nation.

In 1933 you and I knew that we must never let our economic system get completely out of joint again—that we could not afford to take the risk of another great depression.

We also became convinced that the only way to avoid a repetition of those dark days was to have a government with power to prevent and to cure the abuses and the inequalities which had thrown that system out of joint.

We then began a program of remedying those abuses and inequalities—to give balance and stability to our economic system—to make it bomb-proof against the causes of 1929.

Today we are only part-way through that program—and recovery is speeding up to a point where the dangers of 1929 are again becoming possible, not this week or month perhaps, but within a year or two.

National laws are needed to complete that program. Individual or local or state effort alone cannot protect us in 1937 any better than ten years ago.

It will take time—and plenty of time—to work out our remedies administratively even after legislation is passed. To complete our program of protection in time, therefore, we cannot delay one moment in making certain that our National Government has power to carry through.

Four years ago action did not come until the eleventh hour. It was almost too late.

If we learned anything from the depression we will not allow ourselves to run around in new circles of futile discussion and debate, always postponing the day of decision.

The American people have learned from the depression. For in the last three national elections an overwhelming majority of them voted a mandate that the Congress and the President begin the task of providing that protection—not after long years of debate, but now.

The Courts, however, have cast doubts on the ability of the elected Congress to protect us against catastrophe by meeting squarely our modern social and economic conditions.

We are at a crisis in our ability to proceed with that protection. It is a quiet crisis. There are no lines of depositors outside closed banks. But to the far-sighted it is far-reaching in its possibilities of injury to America.

I want to talk with you very simply about the need for present action in this crisis—the need to meet the unanswered challenge of one-third of a Nation ill-nourished, ill-clad, ill-housed.

Last Thursday I described the American form of Government as a three horse team provided by the Constitution to the American people so that their field might be plowed. The three horses are, of course, the three branches of government—the Congress, the Executive and the Courts. Two of the horses are pulling in unison today; the third is not. Those who have intimated that the President of the United States is trying to drive that team, overlook the simple fact that the President, as Chief Executive, is himself one of the three horses.

It is the American people themselves who are in the driver's seat.

It is the American people themselves who want the furrow plowed.

It is the American people themselves who expect the third horse to pull in unison with the other two.

I hope that you have re-read the Constitution of the United States in these past few weeks. Like the Bible, it ought to be read again and again.

It is an easy document to understand when you remem-ber that it was called into being because the Articles of Confederation under which the original thirteen States tried to operate after the Revolution showed the need of a National Government with power enough to handle national problems. In its Preamble, the Constitution states that it was intended to form a more perfect Union and promote the general welfare; and the powers given to the Congress to carry out those purposes can be best described by saying that they were all the powers needed to meet each and every problem which then had a national character and which could not be met by merely local action.

But the framers went further. Having in mind that in succeeding generations many other problems then undreamed of would become national problems, they gave to the Congress the ample broad powers "to levy taxes . . . and provide for the common defense and general welfare of the United States."

That, my friends, is what I honestly believe to have been the clear and underlying purpose of the patriots who wrote a Federal Constitution to create a National Government with national power, intended as they said, "to form a more perfect union . . . for ourselves and our posterity."

For nearly twenty years there was no conflict between the Congress and the Court. Then Congress passed a statute which, in 1803, the Court said violated an express provision of the Constitution. The Court claimed the power to declare it unconstitutional and did so declare it. But a little later the Court itself admitted that it was an extraordinary power to exercise and through Mr. Justice Washington laid down this limitation upon it: "It is but a decent respect due to the wisdom, the integrity and the patriotism of the legislative body, by which any law is passed, to presume in favor of its validity until its violation of the Constitution is proved beyond all reasonable doubt."

But since the rise of the modern movement for social and economic progress through legislation, the Court has more and more often and more and more boldly asserted a power to veto laws passed by the Congress and State Legislatures in complete disregard of this original limitation.

In the last four years the sound rule of giving statutes the benefit of all reasonable doubt has been cast aside. The Court has been acting not as a judicial body, but as a policy-making body.

When the Congress has sought to stabilize national agriculture, to improve the conditions of labor, to safeguard business against unfair competition, to protect our national resources, and in many other ways, to serve our clearly national needs, the majority of the Court has been assuming the power to pass on the wisdom of these Acts of the Congress—and to approve or disapprove the public policy written into these laws.

That is not only my accusation. It is the accusation of most distinguished Justices of the present Supreme Court. I have not the time to quote to you all the language used by dissenting Justices in many of these cases. But in the case holding the Railroad Retirement Act unconstitutional, for instance, Chief Justice Hughes said in a dissenting opinion that the majority opinion was "a departure from sound principles," and placed "an unwarranted limitation upon the commerce clause." And three other Justices agreed with him.

In the case holding the A.A.A. unconstitutional, Justice Stone said of the majority opinion that it was a "tortured construction of the Constitution." And two other Justices agreed with him.

In the case holding the New York Minimum Wage Law unconstitutional, Justice Stone said that the majority were actually reading into the Constitution their own "personal economic predilections," and that if the legislative power is not left free to choose the methods of solving the problems of poverty, subsistence and health of large numbers in the community, then "government is to be rendered impotent." And two other Justices agreed with him.

In the face of these dissenting opinions, there is no basis for the claim made by some members of the Court that something in the Constitution has compelled them regretfully to thwart the will of the people.

In the face of such dissenting opinions, it is perfectly clear, that as Chief Justice Hughes has said: "We are under a Constitution, but the Constitution is what the Judges say it is."

The Court in addition to the proper use of its judicial functions has improperly set itself up as a third House of the Congress—a super-legislature, as one of the justices has called it—reading into the Constitution words and implications which are not there, and which were never intended to be there.

We have, therefore, reached the point as a Nation where we must take action to save the Constitution from the Court and the Court from itself. We must find a way to take an appeal from the Supreme Court to the Constitution itself. We want a Supreme Court which will do justice under the Constitution—not over it. In our Courts we want a government of laws and not of men.

I want—as all Americans want—an independent judi-

ciary as proposed by the framers of the Constitution. That means a Supreme Court that will enforce the Constitution as written—that will refuse to amend the Constitution by the arbitrary exercise of judicial power—amendment by judicial say-so. It does not mean a judiciary so independent that it can deny the existence of facts universally recognized.

How then could we proceed to perform the mandate given us? It was said in last year's Democratic platform, "If these problems cannot be effectively solved within the Constitution, we shall seek such clarifying amendment as will assure the power to enact those laws, adequately to regulate commerce, protect public health and safety, and safeguard economic security." In other words, we said we would seek an amendment only if every other possible means by legislation were to fail.

When I commenced to review the situation with the problem squarely before me, I came by a process of elimination to the conclusion that, short of amendments, the only method which was clearly constitutional, and would at the same time carry out other much needed reforms, was to infuse new blood into all our Courts. We must have men worthy and equipped to carry out impartial justice. But, at the same time, we must have Judges who will bring to the Courts a present-day sense of the Constitution—Judges who will retain in the Courts the judicial functions of a court, and reject the legislative powers which the courts have today assumed.

In forty-five out of the forty-eight States of the Union, Judges are chosen not for life but for a period of years. In many States Judges must retire at the age of seventy. Congress has provided financial security by offering life pensions at full pay for Federal Judges on all Courts who are willing to retire at seventy. In the case of Supreme Court Justices, that pension is $20,000 a year. But all Federal Judges, once appointed, can, if they choose, hold office for life, no matter how old they may get to be.

What is my proposal? It is simply this: whenever a Judge or Justice of any Federal Court has reached the age of seventy and does not avail himself of the opportunity to retire on a pension, a new member shall be appointed by the President then in office, with the approval, as required by the Constitution, of the Senate of the United States.

That plan has two chief purposes. By bringing into the judicial system a steady and continuing stream of new and younger blood, I hope, first, to make the administration of all Federal justice speedier and, therefore, less costly; secondly, to bring to the decision of social and economic problems younger men who have had personal experience and contact with modern facts and circumstances under which average men have to live and work. This plan will save our national Constitution from hardening of the judicial arteries.

The number of Judges to be appointed would depend wholly on the decision of present Judges now over seventy, or those who would subsequently reach the age of seventy.

If, for instance, any one of the six Justices of the Supreme Court now over the age of seventy should retire as provided under the plan, no additional place would be created. Consequently, although there never can be more than fifteen, there may be only fourteen, or thirteen, or twelve. And there may be only nine.

There is nothing novel or radical about this idea. It seeks to maintain the Federal bench in full vigor. It has been discussed and approved by many persons of high authority ever since a similar proposal passed the House of Representatives in 1869.

Why was the age fixed at seventy? Because the laws of many States, the practice of the Civil Service, the regulations of the Army and Navy, and the rules of many of our Universities and of almost every great private business enterprise, commonly fix the retirement age at seventy years or less.

The statute would apply to all the courts in the Federal system. There is general approval so far as the lower Federal courts are concerned. The plan has met opposition only so far as the Supreme Court of the United States itself is concerned. If such a plan is good for the lower courts it certainly ought to be equally good for the highest Court from which there is no appeal.

Those opposing this plan have sought to arouse prejudice and fear by crying that I am seeking to "pack" the Supreme Court and that a baneful precedent will be established.

What do they mean by the words "packing the Court"?

Let me answer this question with a bluntness that will end all *honest* misunderstanding of my purposes.

If by that phrase "packing the Court" it is charged that I wish to place on the bench spineless puppets who would disregard the law and would decide specific cases as I wished them to be decided, I make this answer: that no President fit for his office would appoint, and no Senate of honorable men fit for their office would confirm, that kind of appointees to the Supreme Court.

But if by that phrase the charge is made that I would appoint and the Senate would confirm Justices worthy to sit beside present members of the Court who understand those modern conditions, that I will appoint Justices who will not undertake to override the judgment of the Congress on legislative policy, that I will appoint Justices who will act as Justices and not as legislators—if the appointment of such Justices can be called "packing the Courts," then I say that I and with me the vast majority of the American people favor doing just that thing—now.

Is it a dangerous precedent for the Congress to change the number of the Justices? The Congress has always had, and will have, that power. The number of Justices has been changed several times before, in the Administrations of John Adams and Thomas Jefferson—both signers of the Declaration of Independence—Andrew Jackson, Abraham Lincoln and Ulysses S. Grant.

I suggest only the addition of Justices to the bench in accordance with a clearly defined principle relating to a clearly defined age limit. Fundamentally, if in the future, America cannot trust the Congress it elects to refrain from abuse of our Constitutional usages, democracy will have failed far beyond the importance to it of any kind of precedent concerning the Judiciary.

We think it so much in the public interest to maintain a vigorous judiciary that we encourage the retirement of elderly Judges by offering them a life pension at full salary. Why then should we leave the fulfillment of this public policy to chance or make it dependent upon the desire or prejudice of any individual Justice?

It is the clear intention of our public policy to provide for a constant flow of new and younger blood into the Judiciary. Normally every President appoints a large number of District and Circuit Judges and a few members of the Supreme Court. Until my first term practically every President of the United States had appointed at least one member of the Supreme Court. President Taft appointed five members and named a Chief Justice; President Wilson, three; President Harding, four, including a Chief Justice; President Coolidge, one; President Hoover, three, including a Chief Justice.

Such a succession of appointments should have provided a Court well-balanced as to age. But chance and the disinclination of individuals to leave the Supreme bench have now given us a Court in which five Justices will be over seventy-five years of age before next June and one over seventy. Thus a sound public policy has been defeated.

I now propose that we establish by law an assurance against any such ill-balanced Court in the future. I propose that hereafter, when a Judge reaches the age of seventy, a new and younger Judge shall be added to the Court automatically. In this way I propose to enforce a sound public policy by law instead of leaving the composition of our Federal Courts, including the highest, to be determined by chance or the personal decision of individuals.

If such a law as I propose is regarded as establishing a new precedent, is it not a most desirable precedent?

Like all lawyers, like all Americans, I regret the necessity of this controversy. But the welfare of the United States, and indeed of the Constitution itself, is what we all must think about first. Our difficulty with the Court today rises not from the Court as an institution but from human beings within it. But we cannot yield our constitutional destiny to the personal judgment of a few men who, being fearful of the future, would deny us the necessary means of dealing with the present.

This plan of mine is no attack on the Court; it seeks to restore the Court to its rightful and historic place in our system of Constitutional Government and to have it resume its high task of building anew on the Constitution "a system of living law." The Court itself can best undo what the Court has done.

I have thus explained to you the reasons that lie behind our efforts to secure results by legislation within the Constitution. I hope that thereby the difficult process of constitutional amendment may be rendered unnecessary. But let us examine that process.

There are many types of amendment proposed. Each one is radically different from the other. There is no substantial group within the Congress or outside it who are agreed on any single amendment.

It would take months or years to get substantial agreement upon the type and language of an amendment. It would take months and years thereafter to get a two-thirds majority in favor of that amendment in *both* Houses of the Congress.

Then would come the long course of ratification by three-fourths of all the States. No amendment which any powerful economic interests or the leaders of any powerful political party have had reason to oppose has ever been ratified within anything like a reasonable time. And thirteen States which contain only five percent of the voting population can block ratification even though the thirty-five States with ninety-five percent of the population are in favor of it.

A very large percentage of newspaper publishers, Chambers of Commerce, Bar Associations, Manufacturers' Associations, who are trying to give the impression that they really do want a constitutional amendment would be the first to exclaim as soon as an amendment was proposed, "Oh! I was for an amendment all right, but this amendment that you have proposed is not the kind of an amendment that I was thinking about. I am, therefore, going to spend my time, my efforts and my money to block that amendment, although I would be awfully glad to help get some other kind of amendment ratified."

Two groups oppose my plan on the ground that they favor a constitutional amendment. The first includes those who fundamentally object to social and economic legislation along modern lines. This is the same group who during the campaign last Fall tried to block the mandate of the people.

Now they are making a last stand. And the strategy of that last stand is to suggest the time-consuming process of amendment in order to kill off by delay the legislation demanded by the mandate.

To them I say: I do not think you will be able long to fool the American people as to your purposes.

The other group is composed of those who honestly believe the amendment process is the best and who would be willing to support a reasonable amendment if they could agree on one.

To them I say: we cannot rely on an amendment as the immediate or only answer to our present difficulties. When the time comes for action, you will find that many of those who pretend to support you will sabotage any constructive amendment which is proposed. Look at these strange bed-fellows of yours. When before have you found them really at your side in your fights for progress?

And remember one thing more. Even if an amendment were passed, and even if in the years to come it were to be ratified, its meaning would depend upon the kind of Justices who would be sitting on the Supreme Court bench. An amendment, like the rest of the Constitution, is what the Justices say it is rather than what its framers or you might hope it is.

This proposal of mine will not infringe in the slightest upon the civil or religious liberties so dear to every American.

My record as Governor and as President proves my devotion to those liberties. You who know me can have no fear that I would tolerate the destruction by any branch of government of any part of our heritage of freedom.

The present attempt by those opposed to progress to play upon the fears of danger to personal liberty brings again to mind that crude and cruel strategy tried by the same opposition to frighten the workers of America in a pay-envelope propaganda against the Social Security Law. The workers were not fooled by that propaganda then. The people of America will not be fooled by such propaganda now.

I am in favor of action through legislation:

First, because I believe that it can be passed at this session of the Congress.

Second, because it will provide a reinvigorated, liberal-minded Judiciary necessary to furnish quicker and cheaper justice from bottom to top.

Third, because it will provide a series of Federal Courts willing to enforce the Constitution as written, and unwilling to assert legislative powers by writing into it their own political and economic policies.

During the past half century the balance of power between the three great branches of the Federal Government, has been tipped out of balance by the Courts in direct contradiction of the high purposes of the framers of the Constitution. It is my purpose to restore that balance. You who know me will accept my solemn assurance that in a world in which democracy is under attack, I seek to make American democracy succeed. You and I will do our part.

National Labor Relations Board v. Jones & Laughlin Steel, 1937

The Roosevelt administration's string of defeats in the Supreme Court ended with the case reproduced here. Here the Court held that the National Labor Relations (or Wagner) Act, which established the National Labor Relations Board (NLRB), was, in fact, constitutional. That board was empowered to investigate charges of unfair labor practices and to conduct elections in which workers would choose whether to unionize. Jones & Laughlin Steel had fired employees seeking to unionize one of its plants. The NLRB had ordered their reinstatement, but Jones & Laughlin refused to comply, on the grounds that the Wagner Act was unconstitutional because it overstepped the federal government's powers under the Commerce Clause. The Court found that while particular labor activities may not affect commerce crossing state lines, Congress has the power to control activities, such as labor relations, that are closely and substantially related to interstate commerce such that, for example, labor unrest could interrupt the flow of goods in commerce. Many observers at the time credited this decision with scuttling FDR's Court-packing plan.

National Labor Relations Board v. Jones & Laughlin Steel

April 12, 1937

MR. CHIEF JUSTICE HUGHES delivered the opinion of the Court.*

In a proceeding under the National Labor Relations Act of 1935, the National Labor Relations Board found that the respondent, Jones & Laughlin Steel Corporation, had violated the Act by engaging in unfair labor practices affecting commerce. The proceeding was instituted by the Beaver Valley Lodge No. 200, affiliated with the Amalgamated Association of Iron, Steel and Tin Workers of America, a labor organization. The unfair labor practices charged were that the corporation was discriminating against members of the union with regard to hire and tenure of employment, and was coercing and intimidating its employees in order to interfere with their self-organization. The discriminatory and coercive action alleged was the discharge of certain employees.

The National Labor Relations Board, sustaining the charge, ordered the corporation to cease and desist from such discrimination and coercion, to offer reinstatement to ten of the employees named, to make good their losses in pay, and to post for thirty days notices that the corporation would not discharge or discriminate against members, or those desiring to become members, of the labor union. As the corporation

failed to comply, the Board petitioned the Circuit Court of Appeals to enforce the order. The court denied the petition, holding that the order lay beyond the range of federal power. 83 F. (2d) 998. We granted certiorari. . . .

Contesting the ruling of the Board, the respondent argues (1) that the Act is in reality a regulation of labor relations and not of interstate commerce; (2) that the Act can have no application to the respondent's relations with its production employees because they are not subject to regulation by the federal government; and (3) that the provisions of the Act violate § 2 of Article III and the Fifth and Seventh Amendments of the Constitution of the United States. . . .

Practically all the factual evidence in the case, except that which dealt with the nature of respondent's business, concerned its relations with the employees in the Aliquippa plant whose discharge was the subject of the complaint. These employees were active leaders in the labor union. Several were officers and others were leaders of particular groups. Two of the employees were motor inspectors; one was a tractor driver; three were crane operators; one was a washer in the coke plant; and three were laborers. Three other employees were mentioned in the complaint but it was withdrawn as to one of them and no evidence was heard on the action taken with respect to the other two.

---

* Internal citations have been omitted.—B.F.

While respondent criticises the evidence and the attitude of the Board, which is described as being hostile toward employers and particularly toward those who insisted upon their constitutional rights, respondent did not take advantage of its opportunity to present evidence to refute that which was offered to show discrimination and coercion. In this situation, the record presents no ground for setting aside the order of the Board so far as the facts pertaining to the circumstances and purpose of the discharge of the employees are concerned. Upon that point it is sufficient to say that the evidence supports the findings of the Board that respondent discharged these men "because of their union activity and for the purpose of discouraging membership in the union." We turn to the questions of law which respondent urges in contesting the validity and application of the Act.

First. The scope of the Act.—The Act is challenged in its entirety as an attempt to regulate all industry, thus invading the reserved powers of the States over their local concerns. It is asserted that the references in the Act to interstate and foreign commerce are colorable at best; that the Act is not a true regulation of such commerce or of matters which directly affect it but on the contrary has the fundamental object of placing under the compulsory supervision of the federal government all industrial labor relations within the nation. The argument seeks support in the broad words of the preamble (section one) and in the sweep of the provisions of the Act, and it is further insisted that its legislative history shows an essential universal purpose in the light of which its scope cannot be limited by either construction or by the application of the separability clause.

If this conception of terms, intent and consequent inseparability were sound, the Act would necessarily fall by reason of the limitation upon the federal power which inheres in the constitutional grant, as well as because of the explicit reservation of the Tenth Amendment. The authority of the federal government may not be pushed to such an extreme as to destroy the distinction, which the commerce clause itself establishes, between commerce "among the several States" and the internal concerns of a State. That distinction between what is national and what is local in the activities of commerce is vital to the maintenance of our federal system. *Id.*

But we are not at liberty to deny effect to specific provisions, which Congress has constitutional power to enact, by superimposing upon them inferences from general legislative declarations of an ambiguous character, even if found in the same statute. The cardinal principle of statutory construc-

tion is to save and not to destroy. We have repeatedly held that as between two possible interpretations of a statute, by one of which it would be unconstitutional and by the other valid, our plain duty is to adopt that which will save the act. Even to avoid a serious doubt the rule is the same.

We think it clear that the National Labor Relations Act may be construed so as to operate within the sphere of constitutional authority. The jurisdiction conferred upon the Board, and invoked in this instance, is found in § 10 (a), which provides:

"SEC. 10 (a). The Board is empowered, as hereinafter provided, to prevent any person from engaging in any unfair labor practice (listed in section 8) affecting commerce."

The critical words of this provision, prescribing the limits of the Board's authority in dealing with the labor practices, are "affecting commerce." The Act specifically defines the "commerce" to which it refers (§ 2 (6)):

"The term 'commerce' means trade, traffic, commerce, transportation, or communication among the several States, or between the District of Columbia or any Territory of the United States and any State or other Territory, or between any foreign country and any State, Territory, or the District of Columbia, or within the District of Columbia or any Territory, or between points in the same State but through any other State or any Territory or the District of Columbia or any foreign country."

There can be no question that the commerce thus contemplated by the Act (aside from that within a Territory or the District of Columbia) is interstate and foreign commerce in the constitutional sense. The Act also defines the term "affecting commerce" (§ 2 (7)):

"The term 'affecting commerce' means in commerce, or burdening or obstructing commerce or the free flow of commerce, or having led or tending to lead to a labor dispute burdening or obstructing commerce or the free flow of commerce."

This definition is one of exclusion as well as inclusion. The grant of authority to the Board does not purport to extend to the relationship between all industrial employees and employers. Its terms do not impose collective bargaining upon all industry regardless of effects upon interstate or foreign commerce. It purports to reach only what may be deemed to burden or obstruct that commerce and, thus qualified, it must be construed as contemplating the exercise of control within constitutional bounds. It is a familiar principle that acts which directly burden or obstruct interstate or foreign commerce, or its free flow, are within the reach of the congressional power. Acts having that effect are not rendered immune because they grow out of labor disputes. It is the effect upon commerce, not the source of the injury, which is the criterion. Whether or not particular action does affect commerce in such a close and intimate fashion as to be subject to federal control, and hence to lie within the authority conferred upon the Board, is left by the statute to be determined as individual cases arise. We are thus to inquire whether in the instant case the constitutional boundary has been passed.

Second. The unfair labor practices in question.—The unfair labor practices found by the Board are those defined in § 8, subdivisions (1) and (3). These provide:

Sec. 8. It shall be an unfair labor practice for an employer—

"(1) To interfere with, restrain, or coerce employees in the exercise of the rights guaranteed in section 7."

"(3) By discrimination in regard to hire or tenure of employment or any term or condition of employment to encourage or discourage membership in any labor organization: . . ."

Section 8, subdivision (1), refers to § 7, which is as follows:

"Sec. 7. Employees shall have the right to self-organization, to form, join, or assist labor organizations, to bargain collectively through representatives of their own choosing, and to engage in concerted activities, for the purpose of collective bargaining or other mutual aid or protection."

Thus, in its present application, the statute goes no further than to safeguard the right of employees to self-organization and to select representatives of their own choosing for collective bargaining or other mutual protection without restraint or coercion by their employer.

That is a fundamental right. Employees have as clear a right to organize and select their representatives for lawful purposes as the respondent has to organize its business and select its own officers and agents. Discrimination and coercion to prevent the free exercise of the right of employees to self-organization and representation is a proper subject for condemnation by competent legislative authority. Long ago we stated the reason for labor organizations. We said that they were organized out of the necessities of the situation; that a single employee was helpless in dealing with an employer; that he was dependent ordinarily on his daily wage for the maintenance of himself and family; that if the employer refused to pay him the wages that he thought fair, he was nevertheless unable to leave the employ and resist arbitrary and unfair treatment; that union was essential to give labor-

ers opportunity to deal on an equality with their employer. We reiterated these views when we had under consideration the Railway Labor Act of 1926. Fully recognizing the legality of collective action on the part of employees in order to safeguard their proper interests, we said that Congress was not required to ignore this right but could safeguard it. Congress could seek to make appropriate collective action of employees an instrument of peace rather than of strife. We said that such collective action would be a mockery if representation were made futile by interference with freedom of choice. Hence the prohibition by Congress of interference with the selection of representatives for the purpose of negotiation and conference between employers and employees, "instead of being an invasion of the constitutional right of either, was based on the recognition of the rights of both." We have reasserted the same principle in sustaining the application of the Railway Labor Act as amended in 1934.

Third. The application of the Act to employees engaged in production.—The principle involved.—Respondent says that whatever may be said of employees engaged in interstate commerce, the industrial relations and activities in the manufacturing department of respondent's enterprise are not subject to federal regulation. The argument rests upon the proposition that manufacturing in itself is not commerce.

The Government distinguishes these cases. The various parts of respondent's enterprise are described as interdependent and as thus involving "a great movement of iron ore, coal and limestone along well-defined paths to the steel mills, thence through them, and thence in the form of steel products into the consuming centers of the country—a definite and well-understood course of business." It is urged that these activities constitute a "stream" or "flow" of commerce, of which the Aliquippa manufacturing plant is the focal point, and that industrial strife at that point would cripple the entire movement. Reference is made to our decision sustaining the Packers and Stockyards Act. The Court found that the stockyards were but a "throat" through which the current of commerce flowed and the transactions which there occurred could not be separated from that movement. Hence the sales at the stockyards were not regarded as merely local transactions, for while they created "a local change of title" they did not "stop the flow," but merely changed the private interests in the subject of the current. Distinguishing the cases which upheld the power of the State to impose a non-discriminatory tax upon property which the owner intended to transport to another State, but which was not in actual transit and was held within the State subject to the disposition of the owner, the Court remarked: "The question, it should be observed, is not with respect to the extent of the power of Congress to regulate interstate commerce, but whether a particular exercise of state power in view of its nature and operation must be deemed to be in conflict with this paramount authority." Applying the doctrine of *Stafford* v. *Wallace, supra,* the Court sustained the Grain Futures Act of 1922 with respect to transactions on the Chicago Board of Trade, although these transactions were "not in and of themselves interstate commerce." Congress had found that they had become "a constantly recurring burden and obstruction to that commerce."

Respondent contends that the instant case presents material distinctions. Respondent says that the Aliquippa plant is extensive in size and represents a large investment in buildings, machinery and equipment. The raw materials which are brought to the plant are delayed for long periods and, after being subjected to manufacturing processes, "are changed substantially as to character, utility and value." The finished products which emerge "are to a large extent manufactured without reference to pre-existing orders and contracts and are entirely different from the raw materials which enter at the other end." Hence respondent argues that "If importation and exportation in interstate commerce do not singly transfer purely local activities into the field of congressional regulation, it should follow that their combination would not alter the local situation."

We do not find it necessary to determine whether these features of defendant's business dispose of the asserted analogy to the "stream of commerce" cases. The instances in which that metaphor has been used are but particular, and not exclusive, illustrations of the protective power which the Government invokes in support of the present Act. The congressional authority to protect interstate commerce from burdens and obstructions is not limited to transactions which can be deemed to be an essential part of a "flow" of interstate or foreign commerce. Burdens and obstructions may be due to injurious action springing from other sources. The fundamental principle is that the power to regulate commerce is the power to enact "all appropriate legislation" for "its protection and advancement"; to adopt measures "to promote its growth and insure its safety"; "to foster, protect, control and restrain." That power is plenary and may be exerted to protect interstate commerce "no matter what the source of the dangers which threaten it." Although activities may be intrastate in character when separately considered, if they have

such a close and substantial relation to interstate commerce that their control is essential or appropriate to protect that commerce from burdens and obstructions, Congress cannot be denied the power to exercise that control. Undoubtedly the scope of this power must be considered in the light of our dual system of government and may not be extended so as to embrace effects upon interstate commerce so indirect and remote that to embrace them, in view of our complex society, would effectually obliterate the distinction between what is national and what is local and create a completely centralized government. The question is necessarily one of degree. As the Court said in *Chicago Board of Trade* v. *Olsen, supra,* p. 37, repeating what had been said in *Stafford* v. *Wallace, supra:* "Whatever amounts to more or less constant practice, and threatens to obstruct or unduly to burden the freedom of interstate commerce is within the regulatory power of Congress under the commerce clause and it is primarily for Congress to consider and decide the fact of the danger and meet it."

That intrastate activities, by reason of close and intimate relation to interstate commerce, may fall within federal control is demonstrated in the case of carriers who are engaged in both interstate and intrastate transportation. There federal control has been found essential to secure the freedom of interstate traffic from interference or unjust discrimination and to promote the efficiency of the interstate service. It is manifest that intrastate rates deal *primarily* with a local activity. But in rate-making they bear such a close relation to interstate rates that effective control of the one must embrace some control over the other. Under the Transportation Act, 1920, Congress went so far as to authorize the Interstate Commerce Commission to establish a state-wide level of intrastate rates in order to prevent an unjust discrimination against interstate commerce. Other illustrations are found in the broad requirements of the Safety Appliance Act and the Hours of Service Act. It is said that this exercise of federal power has relation to the maintenance of adequate instrumentalities of interstate commerce. But the agency is not superior to the commerce which uses it. The protective power extends to the former because it exists as to the latter. . . .

It is thus apparent that the fact that the employees here concerned were engaged in production is not determinative. The question remains as to the effect upon interstate commerce of the labor practice involved. In the *Schechter* case, *supra,* we found that the effect there was so remote as to be beyond the federal power. To find "immediacy or directness" there was to find it "almost everywhere," a result inconsistent with the maintenance of our federal system. In the *Carter* case, *supra,* the Court was of the opinion that the provisions of the statute relating to production were invalid upon several grounds,—that there was improper delegation of legislative power, and that the requirements not only went beyond any sustainable measure of protection of interstate commerce but were also inconsistent with due process. These cases are not controlling here.

Fourth. Effects of the unfair labor practice in respondent's enterprise.—Giving full weight to respondent's contention with respect to a break in the complete continuity of the "stream of commerce" by reason of respondent's manufacturing operations, the fact remains that the stoppage of those operations by industrial strife would have a most serious effect upon interstate commerce. In view of respondent's far-flung activities, it is idle to say that the effect would be indirect or remote. It is obvious that it would be immediate and might be catastrophic. We are asked to shut our eyes to the plainest facts of our national life and to deal with the question of direct and indirect effects in an intellectual vacuum. Because there may be but indirect and remote effects upon interstate commerce in connection with a host of local enterprises throughout the country, it does not follow that other industrial activities do not have such a close and intimate relation to interstate commerce as to make the presence of industrial strife a matter of the most urgent national concern. When industries organize themselves on a national scale, making their relation to interstate commerce the dominant factor in their activities, how can it be maintained that their industrial labor relations constitute a forbidden field into which Congress may not enter when it is necessary to protect interstate commerce from the paralyzing consequences of industrial war? We have often said that interstate commerce itself is a practical conception. It is equally true that interferences with that commerce must be appraised by a judgment that does not ignore actual experience.

Experience has abundantly demonstrated that the recognition of the right of employees to self-organization and to have representatives of their own choosing for the purpose of collective bargaining is often an essential condition of industrial peace. Refusal to confer and negotiate has been one of the most prolific causes of strife. This is such an outstanding fact in the history of labor disturbances that it is a proper subject of judicial notice and requires no citation of instances. The opinion in the case of *Virginian Railway Co.* v. *System Federation, No. 40, supra,* points out that, in the case of car-

riers, experience has shown that before the amendment, of 1934, of the Railway Labor Act "when there was no dispute as to the organizations authorized to represent the employees and when there was a willingness of the employer to meet such representative for a discussion of their grievances, amicable adjustment of differences had generally followed and strikes had been avoided." That, on the other hand, "a prolific source of dispute had been the maintenance by the railroad of company unions and the denial by railway management of the authority of representatives chosen by their employees." The opinion in that case also points to the large measure of success of the labor policy embodied in the Railway Labor Act. But with respect to the appropriateness of the recognition of self-organization and representation in the promotion of peace, the question is not essentially different in the case of employees in industries of such a character that interstate commerce is put in jeopardy from the case of employees of transportation companies. And of what avail is it to protect the facility of transportation, if interstate commerce is throttled with respect to the commodities to be transported!

These questions have frequently engaged the attention of Congress and have been the subject of many inquiries. The steel industry is one of the great basic industries of the United States, with ramifying activities affecting interstate commerce at every point. The Government aptly refers to the steel strike of 1919–1920 with its far-reaching consequences. The fact that there appears to have been no major disturbance in that industry in the more recent period did not dispose of the possibilities of future and like dangers to interstate commerce which Congress was entitled to foresee and to exercise its protective power to forestall. It is not necessary again to detail the facts as to respondent's enterprise. Instead of being beyond the pale, we think that it presents in a most striking way the close and intimate relation which a manufacturing industry may have to interstate commerce and we have no doubt that Congress had constitutional authority to safeguard the right of respondent's employees to self-organization and freedom in the choice of representatives for collective bargaining.

Fifth. The means which the Act employs.—*Questions under the due process clause and other constitutional restrictions.*— Respondent asserts its right to conduct its business in an orderly manner without being subjected to arbitrary restraints. What we have said points to the fallacy in the argument. Employees have their correlative right to organize for the purpose of securing the redress of grievances and to promote agreements with employers relating to rates of pay and conditions of work. Restraint for the purpose of preventing an unjust interference with that right cannot be considered arbitrary or capricious. The provision of § 9 (a) that representatives, for the purpose of collective bargaining, of the majority of the employees in an appropriate unit shall be the exclusive representatives of all the employees in that unit, imposes upon the respondent only the duty of conferring and negotiating with the authorized representatives of its employees for the purpose of settling a labor dispute. This provision has its analogue in § 2, Ninth, of the Railway Labor Act which was under consideration in *Virginian Railway Co.* v. *System Federation, No. 40, supra.* The decree which we affirmed in that case required the Railway Company to treat with the representative chosen by the employees and also to refrain from entering into collective labor agreements with anyone other than their true representative as ascertained in accordance with the provisions of the Act. We said that the obligation to treat with the true representative was exclusive and hence imposed the negative duty to treat with no other. We also pointed out that, as conceded by the Government, the injunction against the Company's entering into any contract concerning rules, rates of pay and working conditions except with a chosen representative was "designed only to prevent collective bargaining with anyone purporting to represent employees" other than the representative they had selected. It was taken "to prohibit the negotiation of labor contracts generally applicable to employees" in the described unit with any other representative than the one so chosen, "but not as precluding such individual contracts" as the Company might "elect to make directly with individual employees." We think this construction also applies to § 9 (a) of the National Labor Relations Act.

The Act does not compel agreements between employers and employees. It does not compel any agreement whatever. It does not prevent the employer "from refusing to make a collective contract and hiring individuals on whatever terms" the employer "may by unilateral action determine." The Act expressly provides in § 9 (a) that any individual employee or a group of employees shall have the right at any time to present grievances to their employer. The theory of the Act is that free opportunity for negotiation with accredited representatives of employees is likely to promote industrial peace and may bring about the adjustments and agreements which the Act in itself does not attempt to compel. As we said in *Texas & N. O. R. Co.* v. *Railway Clerks, supra,* and repeated in *Virginian Railway Co.* v. *System Federation, No. 40, supra,* the cases of *Adair* v. *United States,* 208 U.S. 161, and *Coppage* v. *Kansas,* 236 U.S. 1, are inapplicable to legislation of this character. The Act does not interfere with the normal exercise of the right of the employer to select its employees or to discharge them. The employer may not, under cover of that right, intimidate or coerce its employees with respect to their self-organization and representation, and, on the other hand, the Board is not entitled to make its authority a pretext for interference with the right of discharge when that right is exercised for other reasons than such intimidation and coercion. The true purpose is the subject of investigation with full opportunity to show the facts. It would seem that when employers freely recognize the right of their employees to their own organizations and their unrestricted right of representation there will be much less occasion for controversy in respect to the free and appropriate exercise of the right of selection and discharge.

The Act has been criticised as one-sided in its application; that it subjects the employer to supervision and restraint and leaves untouched the abuses for which employees may be responsible; that it fails to provide a more comprehensive plan,—with better assurances of fairness to both sides and with increased chances of success in bringing about, if not compelling, equitable solutions of industrial disputes affecting interstate commerce. But we are dealing with the power of Congress, not with a particular policy or with the extent to which policy should go. We have frequently said that the legislative authority, exerted within its proper field, need not embrace all the evils within its reach. The Constitution does not forbid "cautious advance, step by step," in dealing with the evils which are exhibited in activities within the range of legislative power. The question in such cases is whether the legislature, in what it does prescribe, has gone beyond constitutional limits.

The procedural provisions of the Act are assailed. But these provisions, as we construe them, do not offend against the constitutional requirements governing the creation and action of administrative bodies. The Act establishes standards to which the Board must conform. There must be complaint, notice and hearing. The Board must receive evidence and make findings. The findings as to the facts are to be conclusive, but only if supported by evidence. The order of the Board is subject to review by the designated court, and only when sustained by the court may the order be enforced. Upon that review all questions of the jurisdiction of the Board and the regularity of its proceedings, all questions of constitutional right or statutory authority, are open to examination by the court. We construe the procedural provisions as affording adequate opportunity to secure judicial protection against arbitrary action in accordance with the well-settled rules applicable to administrative agencies set up by Congress to aid in the enforcement of valid legislation. It is not necessary to repeat these rules which have frequently been declared. None of them appears to have been transgressed in the instant case. Respondent was notified and heard. It had opportunity to meet the charge of unfair labor practices upon the merits, and by withdrawing from the hearing it declined to avail itself of that opportunity. The facts found by the Board support its order and the evidence supports the findings. Respondent has no just ground for complaint on this score.

The order of the Board required the reinstatement of the employees who were found to have been discharged because of their "union activity" and for the purpose of "discouraging membership in the union." That requirement was authorized by the Act. § 10 (c). In *Texas & N. O. B. Co.* v. *Railway Clerks, supra,* a similar order for restoration to service was made by the court in contempt proceedings for the violation of an injunction issued by the court to restrain an interference with the right of employees as guaranteed by the Railway Labor Act of 1926. The requirement of restoration to service, of employees discharged in violation of the provisions of that Act, was thus a sanction imposed in the enforcement of a judicial decree. We do not doubt that Congress could impose a like sanction for the enforcement of its valid regulation. The fact that in the one case it was a judicial sanction, and in the other a legislative one, is not an essential difference in determining its propriety.

Respondent complains that the Board not only ordered reinstatement but directed the payment of wages for the time lost by the discharge, less amounts earned by the employee during that period. This part of the order was also authorized by the Act. § 10 (c). It is argued that the requirement is equivalent to a money judgment and hence contravenes the Seventh Amendment with respect to trial by jury. The Seventh Amendment provides that "In suits at common law, where the value in controversy shall exceed twenty dollars, the right of trial by jury shall be preserved." The Amendment thus preserves the right which existed under the common law when the Amendment was adopted. Thus it has no application to cases where recovery of money damages is an incident to equitable relief even though damages might have been recovered in an action at law. It does not apply where the proceeding is not in the nature of a suit at common law.

The instant case is not a suit at common law or in the nature of such a suit. The proceeding is one unknown to the common law. It is a statutory proceeding. Reinstatement of the employee and payment for time lost are requirements imposed for violation of the statute and are remedies appropriate to its enforcement. The contention under the Seventh Amendment is without merit.

Our conclusion is that the order of the Board was within its competency and that the Act is valid as here applied. The judgment of the Circuit Court of Appeals is reversed and the cause is remanded for further proceedings in conformity with this opinion.

Reversed.

PART SEVEN   America in the World

Charles Lindbergh speaking to an overflow crowd at the 1941 America First Rally in the Chicago Arena. The famous flyer, who joined the organization, urged the huge audience to "unite and stay out of the war," by joining forces with the America First Committee. © Bettmann/CORBIS.

President Franklin D. Roosevelt signing H.R. 1776, the Lend-Lease Bill to give aid to Great Britain, China, and Greece. Library of Congress, New York World-Telegram and Sun Newspaper Photograph Collection, LC-USZ62-128765.

HAVING BEEN SETTLED by people of faith fleeing into the wilderness in order to lead a more godly communal life, America often has been defined essentially in opposition to the Old World of Europe. And American public pronouncements concerning their nation's proper role in international affairs has repeatedly returned to this theme. This section begins with an early document, President James Monroe's "Monroe Doctrine," setting out the argument for American influence in the Western hemisphere, and isolation from European conflicts in particular. Changes in technology, warfare, and the size and power of the United States would bring this conception into question. Debate would ensue concerning whether America had a duty to maintain its status as an aloof "city on a hill" serving as an example to others or become involved in international affairs, for reasons of self-interest, to secure peace, democracy, and justice throughout the world, or, perhaps, both.

Monroe Doctrine, *James Monroe, 1823*

Since its first proclamation as part of President James Monroe's (1758–1831) seventh annual message to Congress, the Monroe Doctrine has been central to American foreign policy. Proclaimed during a time of increasing decolonization of former colonies in Central and South America, the Monroe Doctrine made clear the United States' opposition to further acts of colonizing (or recolonizing) in the New World by any European power. At a time when the United States was not a major power, the Monroe Doctrine nonetheless asserted that the U.S. government would view European interference in the affairs of the various countries of Central and South America as dangers to its own safety. The doctrine also stated America's intention to stay out of any European conflict not directly affecting the rights of the United States.

Monroe Doctrine—Seventh Annual Message

James Monroe

WASHINGTON, *December 2, 1823.*

Follow-Citizens of the Senate and House of Representatives:

Many important subjects will claim your attention during the present session, of which I shall endeavor to give, in aid of your deliberations, a just idea in this communication. I undertake this duty with diffidence, from the vast extent of the interests on which I have to treat and of their great importance to every portion of our Union. I enter on it with zeal from a thorough conviction that there never was a period since the establishment of our Revolution when, regarding the condition of the civilized world and its bearing on us, there was greater necessity for devotion in the public servants to their respective duties, or for virtue, patriotism, and union in our constituents.

Meeting in you a new Congress, I deem it proper to present this view of public affairs in greater detail than might otherwise be necessary. I do it, however, with peculiar satisfaction, from a knowledge that in this respect I shall comply more fully with the sound principles of our Government. The people being with us exclusively the sovereign, it is indispensable that full information be laid before them on all important subjects, to enable them to exercise that high power with complete effect. If kept in the dark, they must be incompetent to it. We are all liable to error, and those who are engaged in the management of public affairs are more subject to excitement and to be led astray by their particular interests and passions than the great body of our constituents, who, living at home in the pursuit of their ordinary avocations, are calm but deeply interested spectators of events and of the conduct of those who are parties to them. To the people every department of the Government and every individual in each are responsible, and the more full their information the better they can judge of the wisdom of the policy pursued and of the conduct of each in regard to it. From their dispassionate judgment much aid may always be obtained, while their approbation will form the greatest incentive and most gratifying reward for virtuous actions, and the dread of their censure the best security against the abuse of their confidence. Their interests in all vital questions are the same, and the bond, by sentiment as well as by interest, will be proportionably strengthened as they are better informed of the real state of public affairs, especially in difficult conjunctures. It is by such knowledge that local prejudices and jealousies are surmounted, and that a national policy, extending its fostering care and protection to all the great interests of our Union, is formed and steadily adhered to.

A precise knowledge of our relations with foreign powers as respects our negotiations and transactions with each is thought to be particularly necessary. Equally necessary is it that we should form a just estimate of our resources, revenue, and progress in every kind of improvement connected with the national prosperity and public defense. It is by rendering justice to other nations that we may expect it from them. It is by our ability to resent injuries and redress wrongs that we may avoid them.

The commissioners under the fifth article of the treaty of Ghent, having disagreed in their opinions respecting that portion of the boundary between the Territories of the United States and of Great Britain the establishment of which had been submitted to them, have made their respective reports in compliance with that article, that the same might be referred to the decision of a friendly power. It being manifest, however, that it would be difficult, if not impossible, for any power to perform that office without great delay and much inconvenience to itself, a proposal has been made by this Government, and acceded to by that of Great Britain, to endeavor to establish that boundary by amicable negotiation. It appearing from long experience that no satisfactory arrangement could be formed of the commercial intercourse between the United States and the British colonies in this hemisphere by legislative acts while each party pursued its own course without agreement or concert with the other, a proposal has been made to the British Government to regulate this commerce by treaty, as it has been to arrange in like manner the just claim of the citizens of the United States inhabiting the States and Territories bordering on the lakes and rivers which empty into the St. Lawrence to the navigation of that river to the ocean. For these and other objects of high importance to the interests of both parties a negotiation has been opened with the British Government which it is hoped will have a satisfactory result.

The commissioners under the sixth and seventh articles of the treaty of Ghent having successfully closed their labors in relation to the sixth, have proceeded to the discharge of those relating to the seventh. Their progress in the extensive survey required for the performance of their duties justifies the presumption that it will be completed in the ensuing year.

The negotiation which had been long depending with the French Government on several important subjects, and particularly for a just indemnity for losses sustained in the late wars by the citizens of the United States under unjustifiable seizures and confiscations of their property, has not as yet had the desired effect. As this claim rests on the same principle with others which have been admitted by the French Government, it is not perceived on what just ground it can be rejected. A minister will be immediately appointed to proceed to France and resume the negotiation on this and other subjects which may arise between the two nations.

At the proposal of the Russian Imperial Government, made through the minister of the Emperor residing here, a full power and instructions have been transmitted to the minister of the United States at St. Petersburg to arrange by amicable negotiation the respective rights and interests of the two nations on the northwest coast of this continent. A similar proposal had been made by His Imperial Majesty to the Government of Great Britain, which has likewise been acceded to. The Government of the United States has been desirous by this friendly proceeding of manifesting the great value which they have invariably attached to the friendship of the Emperor and their solicitude to cultivate the best understanding with his Government. In the discussions to which this interest has given rise and in the arrangements by which they may terminate the occasion has been judged proper for asserting, as a principle in which the rights and interests of the United States are involved, that the American continents, by the free and independent condition which they have assumed and maintain, are henceforth not to be considered as subjects for future colonization by any European powers.

Since the close of the last session of Congress the commissioners and arbitrators for ascertaining and determining the amount of indemnification which may be due to citizens of the United States under the decision of His Imperial Majesty the Emperor of Russia, in conformity to the convention concluded at St. Petersburg on the 12th of July, 1822, have assembled in this city, and organized themselves as a board for the performance of the duties assigned to them by that treaty. The commission constituted under the eleventh article of the treaty of the 22d of February, 1819, between the United States and Spain is also in session here, and as the term of three years limited by the treaty for the execution of the trust will expire before the period of the next regular meeting of Congress, the attention of the Legislature will be drawn to the measures which may be necessary to accomplish the objects for which the commission was instituted.

In compliance with a resolution of the House of Representatives adopted at their last session, instructions have been given to all the ministers of the United States accredited to the powers of Europe and America to propose the proscription of the African slave trade by classing it under the denomination, and inflicting on its perpetrators the punishment, of piracy. Should this proposal be acceded to, it is not doubted that this odious and criminal practice will be promptly and entirely suppressed. It is earnestly hoped that it will be acceded to, from the firm belief that it is the most effectual expedient that can be adopted for the purpose.

At the commencement of the recent war between France and Spain it was declared by the French Government that it would grant no commissions to privateers, and that neither the commerce of Spain herself nor of neutral nations should be molested by the naval force of France, except in the breach of a lawful blockade. This declaration, which appears to have been faithfully carried into effect, concurring with principles proclaimed and cherished by the United States from the first establishment of their independence, suggested the hope that the time had arrived when the proposal for adopting it as a permanent and invariable rule in all future maritime wars might meet the favorable consideration of the great European powers. Instructions have accordingly been given to our ministers with France, Russia, and Great Britain to make those proposals to their respective Governments, and when the friends of humanity reflect on the essential amelioration to the condition of the human race which would result from the abolition of private war on the sea and on the great facility by which it might be accomplished, requiring only the consent of a few sovereigns, an earnest hope is indulged that these overtures will meet with an attention animated by the spirit in which they were made, and that they will ultimately be successful.

The ministers who were appointed to the Republics of Colombia and Buenos Ayres during the last session of Congress proceeded shortly afterwards to their destinations. Of their arrival there official intelligence has not yet been received. The minister appointed to the Republic of Chile will sail in a few days. An early appointment will also be made to Mexico. A minister has been received from Colombia, and the other Governments have been informed that ministers, or diplomatic agents of inferior grade, would be received from each, accordingly as they might prefer the one or the other.

The minister appointed to Spain proceeded soon after his appointment for Cadiz, the residence of the Sovereign to whom he was accredited. In approaching that port the frigate which conveyed him was warned off by the commander of the French squadron by which it was blockaded and not permitted to enter, although apprised by the captain of the frigate of the public character of the person whom he had on board, the landing of whom was the sole object of his proposed entry. This act, being considered an infringement of the rights of ambassadors and of nations, will form a just cause of complaint to the Government of France against the officer by whom it was committed. . . .

It was stated at the commencement of the last session that a great effort was then making in Spain and Portugal to improve the condition of the people of those countries, and that it appeared to be conducted with extraordinary moderation. It need scarcely be remarked that the result has been so far very different from what was then anticipated. Of events in that quarter of the globe, with which we have so much intercourse and from which we derive our origin, we have always been anxious and interested spectators. The citizens of the United States cherish sentiments the most friendly in favor of the liberty and happiness of their fellow-men on that side of the Atlantic. In the wars of the European powers in matters relating to themselves we have never taken any part, nor does it comport with our policy so to do. It is only when our rights are invaded or seriously menaced that we resent injuries or make preparation for our defense. With the movements in this hemisphere we are of necessity more immediately connected, and by causes which must be obvious to all enlightened and impartial observers. The political system of the allied powers is essentially different in this respect from that of America. This difference proceeds from that which exists in their respective Governments; and to the defense of our own, which has been achieved by the loss of so much blood and treasure, and matured by the wisdom of their most enlightened citizens, and under which we have enjoyed unexampled felicity, this whole nation is devoted. We owe it, therefore, to candor and to the amicable relations existing between the United States and those powers to declare that we should consider any attempt on their part to extend their system to any portion of this hemisphere as dangerous to our peace and safety. With the existing colonies or dependencies of any European power we have not interfered and shall not interfere. But with the Governments who have declared their independence and maintained it, and whose independence we have, on great consideration and on just principles, acknowledged, we could not view any interposition for the purpose of oppressing them, or controlling in any other manner their destiny, by any European power in any other light than as the manifestation of an unfriendly disposition toward the United States. In the war between those new Governments and Spain we declared our neutrality at the time of their recognition, and to this we have adhered, and shall continue to adhere, provided no change shall occur which, in the judgment of the competent authorities of this Government, shall make a corresponding change on the part of the United States indispensable to their security.

The late events in Spain and Portugal shew that Europe is still unsettled. Of this important fact no stronger proof can be adduced than that the allied powers should have thought it proper, on any principle satisfactory to themselves, to have interposed by force in the internal concerns of Spain. To what extent such interposition may be carried, on the same principle, is a question in which all independent powers whose governments differ from theirs are interested, even those most remote, and surely none more so than the United States. Our policy in regard to Europe, which was adopted at an early stage of the wars which have so long agitated that quarter of the globe, nevertheless remains the same, which is, not to interfere in the internal concerns of any of its powers; to consider the government *de facto* as the legitimate government for us; to cultivate friendly relations with it, and to preserve those relations by a frank, firm, and manly policy, meeting in all instances the just claims of every power, submitting to injuries from none. But in regard to those continents circumstances are eminently and conspicuously different. It is impossible that the allied powers should extend their political system to any portion of either continent without endangering our peace and happiness; nor can anyone believe that our southern brethren, if left to themselves, would adopt it of their own accord. It is equally impossible, therefore, that we should behold such interposition in any form with indifference. If we look to the comparative strength and resources of Spain and those new Governments, and their distance from each other, it must be obvious that she can never subdue them. It is still the true policy of the United States to leave the parties to themselves, in the hope that other powers will pursue the same course.

If we compare the present condition of our Union with its actual state at the close of our Revolution, the history of the world furnishes no example of a progress in improvement in all the important circumstances which constitute the happiness of a nation which bears any resemblance to it. At the first epoch our population did not exceed 3,000,000. By the last census it amounted to about 10,000,000, and, what is more extraordinary, it is almost altogether native, for the immigration from other countries has been inconsiderable. At the first epoch half the territory within our acknowledged limits was uninhabited and a wilderness. Since then new territory has been acquired of vast extent, comprising within it many rivers, particularly the Mississippi, the navigation of which to the ocean was of the highest importance to the original States. Over this territory our population has expanded in every direction, and new States have been established almost equal in number to those which formed the first bond of our Union. This expansion of our population and accession of new States to our Union have had the happiest effect on all its highest interests. That it has eminently augmented our resources and added to our strength and respectability as a power is admitted by all. But it is not in these important circumstances only that this happy effect is felt. It is manifest that by enlarging the basis of our system and increasing the number of States the system itself has been greatly strengthened in both its branches. Consolidation and disunion have thereby been rendered equally impracticable. Each Government, confiding in its own strength, has less to apprehend from the other, and in consequence each, enjoying a greater freedom of action, is rendered more efficient for all the purposes for which it was instituted. It is unnecessary to treat here of the vast improvement made in the system itself by the adoption of this Constitution and of its happy effect in elevating the character and in protecting the rights of the nation as well as of individuals. To what, then, do we owe these blessings? It is known to all that we derive them from the excellence of our institutions. Ought we not, then, to adopt every measure which may be necessary to perpetuate them?

JAMES MONROE.

First stated in May 1904 in response to fears that European nations might invade the Dominican Republic because that country had repudiated its debts, the Roosevelt Corollary to the Monroe Doctrine was fully laid out in Theodore Roosevelt's fifth annual message to Congress. In his extension of the Monroe Doctrine, Roosevelt asserted the United States' responsibility to maintain peace and order in the Western Hemisphere. The United States denied the right of any European government to intervene in Latin America but would itself intervene "in flagrant cases" of "wrongdoing or impotence" threatening the rights of the United States and international creditors and to protect "the entire body of American nations" from foreign aggression. Various American presidents would point to the Roosevelt Corollary as justification for interventions in a number of Latin American nations. The administration of Roosevelt's cousin, Franklin Delano Roosevelt, later promoted a "good neighbor policy," pledging military nonintervention in Latin America as a means of promoting greater cooperation in the face of potential common enemies.

Roosevelt Corollary to Monroe Doctrine

December 6, 1904

Theodore Roosevelt

FOREIGN POLICY

In treating of our foreign policy and of the attitude that this great Nation should assume in the world at large, it is absolutely necessary to consider the Army and the Navy, and the Congress, through which the thought of the Nation finds its expression, should keep ever vividly in mind the fundamental fact that it is impossible to treat our foreign policy, whether this policy takes shape in the effort to secure justice for others or justice for ourselves, save as conditioned upon the attitude we are willing to take toward our Army, and especially toward our Navy. It is not merely unwise, it is contemptible, for a nation, as for an individual, to use high-sounding language to proclaim its purposes, or to take positions which are ridiculous if unsupported by potential force, and then to refuse to provide this force. If there is no intention of providing and of keeping the force necessary to back up a strong attitude, then it is far better not to assume such an attitude.

The steady aim of this Nation, as of all enlightened nations, should be to strive to bring ever nearer the day when there shall prevail throughout the world the peace of justice. There are kinds of peace which are highly undesirable, which are in the long run as destructive as any war. Tyrants and oppressors have many times made a wilderness and called it peace. Many times peoples who were slothful or timid or shortsighted, who had been enervated by ease or by luxury, or misled by false teachings, have shrunk in unmanly fashion from doing duty that was stern and that needed self-sacrifice, and have sought to hide from their own minds their shortcomings, their ignoble motives, by calling them love of peace. The peace of tyrannous terror, the peace of craven weakness, the peace of injustice, all these should be shunned as we shun unrighteous war. The goal to set before us as a nation, the goal which should be set before all mankind, is the attainment of the peace of justice, of the peace which comes when each nation is not merely safe-guarded in its own rights, but scrupulously recognizes and performs its duty toward others. Generally peace tells for righteousness; but if there is conflict between the two, then our fealty is due first to the cause of righteousness. Unrighteous wars are common, and unrighteous peace is rare; but both should be shunned. The right of freedom and the responsibility for the exercise of that right can not be divorced. One of our great poets has well and finely said that freedom is not a gift that tarries long in the hands of cowards. Neither does it tarry long in the hands of those too slothful, too dishonest, or too unintelligent to exercise it. The eternal vigilance which is the price of liberty must be exercised, sometimes to guard against outside foes; although of course far more often to guard against our own selfish or thoughtless shortcomings.

If these self-evident truths are kept before us, and only if they are so kept before us, we shall have a clear idea of what our foreign policy in its larger aspects should be. It is our duty to remember that a nation has no more right to do injustice to another nation, strong or weak, than an individual has to do injustice to another individual; that the same moral law applies in one case as in the other. But we must also remember that it is as much the duty of the Nation to guard its own rights and its own interests as it is the duty of the individual so to do. Within the Nation the individual has now delegated this right to the State, that is, to the representative of all the individuals, and it is a maxim of the law that for every wrong there is a remedy. But in international law we have not advanced by any means as far as we have advanced in municipal law. There is as yet no judicial way of enforcing a right in international law. When one nation wrongs another or wrongs many others, there is no tribunal before which the wrongdoer can be brought. Either it is necessary supinely to acquiesce in the wrong, and thus put a premium upon brutality and aggression, or else it is necessary for the aggrieved nation valiantly to stand up for its rights. Until some method is devised by which there shall be a degree of international control over offending nations, it would be a wicked thing for the most civilized powers, for those with most sense of international obligations and with keenest and most generous appreciation of the difference between right and wrong, to disarm. If the great civilized nations of the present day should completely disarm, the result would mean an immediate recrudescence of barbarism in one form or another. Under any circumstances a sufficient armament would have to be kept up to serve the purposes of international police; and until international cohesion and the sense of international duties and rights are far more advanced than at present, a nation desirous both of securing respect for itself and of doing good to others must have a force adequate for the work which it feels is allotted to it as its part of the general world duty. Therefore it follows that a self-respecting, just, and far-seeing nation should on the one hand endeavor by every means to aid in the development of the various movements which tend to provide substitutes for war, which tend to render nations in their actions toward one another, and indeed toward their own peoples, more responsive to the general sentiment of humane and civilized mankind; and on the other hand that it should keep prepared, while scrupulously avoiding wrongdoing itself, to repel any wrong, and in exceptional cases to take action which in a more advanced stage of international relations would come under the head of the exercise of the international police. A great free people owes it to itself and to all mankind not to sink into helplessness before the powers of evil.

ARBITRATION TREATIES—SECOND HAGUE CONFERENCE

We are in every way endeavoring to help on, with cordial good will, every movement which will tend to bring us into more friendly relations with the rest of mankind. In pursuance of this policy I shall shortly lay before the Senate treaties of arbitration with all powers which are willing to enter into these treaties with us. It is not possible at this period of the world's development to agree to arbitrate all matters, but there are many matters of possible difference between us and other nations which can be thus arbitrated. Furthermore, at the request of the Interparliamentary Union, an eminent body composed of practical statesmen from all countries, I have asked the Powers to join with this Government in a second Hague conference, at which it is hoped that the work already so happily begun at The Hague may be carried some steps further toward completion. This carries out the desire expressed by the first Hague conference itself.

POLICY TOWARD OTHER NATIONS OF WESTERN HEMISPHERE

It is not true that the United States feels any land hunger or entertains any projects as regards the other nations of the Western Hemisphere save such as are for their welfare. All that this country desires is to see the neighboring countries stable, orderly, and prosperous. Any country whose people conduct themselves well can count upon our hearty friendship. If a nation shows that it knows how to act with reasonable efficiency and decency in social and political matters, if it keeps order and pays its obligations, it need fear no interference from the United States. Chronic wrongdoing, or an impotence which results in a general loosening of the ties of civilized society, may in America, as elsewhere, ultimately require intervention by some civilized nation, and in the Western Hemisphere the adherence of the United States to the Monroe Doctrine may force the United States, however reluctantly, in flagrant cases of such wrongdoing or impotence, to the exercise of an international police power. If every country washed by the Caribbean Sea would show the progress in stable and just civilization which with the aid of the Platt amendment Cuba has shown since our troops left the island, and which so many of the republics in both Americas are constantly and brilliantly showing, all question of interference by this Nation with their affairs would be at an end. Our interests and those of our southern neighbors are in reality identical. They have great natural riches, and if within their borders the reign of law and justice obtains, prosperity is sure to come to them. While they thus obey the primary laws of civilized society they may rest assured that they will be treated by us in a spirit of cordial and helpful sympathy. We would interfere with them only in the last resort, and then only if it became evident that their inability or unwillingness to do justice at home and abroad had violated the rights of the United States or had invited foreign aggression to the detriment of the entire body of American nations. It is a mere truism to say that every nation, whether in America or anywhere else, which desires to maintain its freedom, its independence, must ultimately realize that the right of such independence can not be separated from the responsibility of making good use of it.

In asserting the Monroe Doctrine, in taking such steps as we have taken in regard to Cuba, Venezuela, and Panama, and in endeavoring to circumscribe the theater of war in the Far East, and to secure the open door in China, we have acted in our own interest as well as in the interest of humanity at large. There are, however, cases in which, while our own interests are not greatly involved, strong appeal is made to our sympathies. Ordinarily it is very much wiser and more useful for us to concern ourselves with striving for our own moral and material betterment here at home than to concern ourselves with trying to better the condition of things in other nations. We have plenty of sins of our own to war against, and under ordinary circumstances we can do more for the general uplifting of humanity by striving with heart and soul to put a stop to civic corruption, to brutal lawlessness and violent race prejudices here at home than by passing resolutions about wrongdoing elsewhere. Nevertheless there are occasional crimes committed on so vast a scale and of such peculiar horror as to make us doubt whether it is not our manifest duty to endeavor at least to show our disapproval of the deed and our sympathy with those who have suffered by it. The cases must be extreme in which such a course is justifiable. There must

be no effort made to remove the mote from our brother's eye if we refuse to remove the beam from our own. But in extreme cases action may be justifiable and proper. What form the action shall take must depend upon the circumstances of the case; that is, upon the degree of the atrocity and upon our power to remedy it. The cases in which we could interfere by force of arms as we interfered to put a stop to intolerable conditions in Cuba are necessarily very few. Yet it is not to be expected that a people like ours, which in spite of certain very obvious shortcomings, nevertheless as a whole shows by its consistent practice its belief in the principles of civil and religious liberty and of orderly freedom, a people among whom even the worst crime, like the crime of lynching, is never more than sporadic, so that individuals and not classes are molested in their fundamental rights—it is inevitable that such a nation should desire eagerly to give expression to its horror on an occasion like that of the massacre of the Jews in Kishenef, or when it witnesses such systematic and long-extended cruelty and oppression as the cruelty and oppression of which the Armenians have been the victims, and which have won for them the indignant pity of the civilized world.

RIGHTS OF AMERICAN CITIZENS ABROAD

Even where it is not possible to secure in other nations the observance of the principles which we accept as axiomatic, it is necessary for us firmly to insist upon the rights of our own citizens without regard to their creed or race; without regard to whether they were born here or born abroad. It has proved very difficult to secure from Russia the right for our Jewish fellow-citizens to receive passports and travel through Russian territory. Such conduct is not only unjust and irritating toward us, but it is difficult to see its wisdom from Russia's standpoint. No conceivable good is accomplished by it. If an American Jew or an American Christian misbehaves himself in Russia he can at once be driven out; but the ordinary American Jew, like the ordinary American Christian, would behave just about as he behaves here, that is, behave as any good citizen ought to behave; and where this is the case it is a wrong against which we are entitled to protest to refuse him his passport without regard to his conduct and character, merely on racial and religious grounds. In Turkey our difficulties arise less from the way in which our citizens are sometimes treated than from the indignation inevitably excited in seeing such fearful misrule as has been witnessed both in Armenia and Macedonia.

THE NAVY

The strong arm of the Government in enforcing respect for its just rights in international matters is the Navy of the United States. I most earnestly recommend that there be no halt in the work of upbuilding the American Navy. There is no more patriotic duty before us as a people than to keep the Navy adequate to the needs of this country's position. We have undertaken to build the Isthmian Canal. We have undertaken to secure for ourselves our just share in the trade of the Orient. We have undertaken to protect our citizens from improper treatment in foreign lands. We continue steadily to insist on the application of the Monroe Doctrine to the Western Hemisphere. Unless our attitude in these and all similar matters is to be a mere boastful sham we can not afford to abandon our naval programme. Our voice is now potent for peace, and is so potent because we are not afraid of war. But our protestations upon behalf of peace would neither receive nor deserve the slightest attention if we were impotent to make them good.

The war which now unfortunately rages in the far East has emphasized in striking fashion the new possibilities of naval warfare. The lessons taught are both strategic and tactical, and are political as well as military. The experiences of the war have shown in conclusive fashion that while sea-going and sea-keeping torpedo destroyers are indispensable, and fast lightly armed and armored cruisers very useful, yet that the main reliance, the main standby, in any navy worthy the name must be the great battle ships, heavily armored and heavily gunned. Not a Russian or Japanese battle ship has been sunk by a torpedo boat, or by gunfire, while among the less protected ships, cruiser after cruiser has been destroyed whenever the hostile squadrons have gotten within range of one another's weapons. There will always be a large field of usefulness for cruisers, especially of the more formidable type. We need to increase the number of torpedo-boat destroyers, paying less heed to their having a knot or two extra speed than to their capacity to keep the seas for weeks, and, if necessary, for months at a time. It is wise to build submarine torpedo boats, as under certain circumstances they might be very useful. But most of all we need to continue building our fleet of battle ships, or ships so powerfully armed that they can inflict the maximum of damage upon our opponents, and so well protected that they can suffer a severe hammering in return without fatal impairment of their ability to fight and maneuver. Of course ample means must be provided for enabling the personnel of the Navy to be brought to the highest point of efficiency. Our great fighting ships and torpedo boats must be ceaselessly trained and maneuvered in squadrons. The officers and men can only learn their trade thoroughly by ceaseless practice on the high seas. In the event of war it would be far better to have no ships at all than to have ships of a poor and ineffective type, or ships which, however good, were yet manned by untrained and unskillful crews. The best officers and men in a poor ship could do nothing against fairly good opponents; and on the other hand a modern war ship is useless unless the officers and men aboard her have become adepts in their duties. The marksmanship in our Navy has improved in an extraordinary degree during the last three years, and on the whole the types of our battle ships are improving; but much remains to be done. Sooner or later we shall have to provide for some method by which there will be promotions for merit as well as for seniority, or else retirement of all those who after a certain age have not advanced beyond a certain grade; while no effort must be spared to make the service attractive to the enlisted men in order that they may be kept as long as possible in it. Reservation public schools should be provided wherever there are navy-yards.

THE ARMY

Within the last three years the United States has set an example in disarmament where disarmament was proper. By law our Army is fixed at a maximum of one hundred thousand and a minimum of sixty thousand men. When there was insurrection in the Philippines we kept the Army at the maximum. Peace came in the Philippines, and now our Army has been reduced to the minimum at which it is possible to keep it with due regard to its efficiency. The guns now mounted require twenty-eight thousand men, if the coast fortifications are to be adequately manned. Relatively to the Nation, it is not now so large as the police force of New York or Chicago relatively to the population of either city. We need more officers; there are not enough to perform the regular army work. It is very important that the officers of the Army should be accustomed to handle their men in masses, as it is also important that the National Guard of the several States should be accustomed to actual field maneuvering, especially in connection with the regulars. For this reason we are to be congratulated upon the success of the field maneuvers at Manassas last fall, maneuvers in which a larger number of Regulars and National Guard took part than was ever before assembled together in time of peace. No other civilized nation has, relatively to its population, such a diminutive Army as ours; and while the Army is so small we are not to be excused if we fail to keep it at a very high grade of proficiency. It must be incessantly practiced; the standard for the enlisted men should be kept very high, while at the same time the service should be made as attractive as possible; and the standard for the officers should be kept even higher—which, as regards the upper ranks, can best be done by introducing some system of selection and rejection into the promotions. We should be able, in the event of some sudden emergency, to put into the field one first-class army corps, which should be, as a whole, at least the equal of any body of troops of like number belonging to any other nation.

Great progress has been made in protecting our coasts by adequate fortifications with sufficient guns. We should, however, pay much more heed than at present to the development of an extensive system of floating mines for use in all our more important harbors. These mines have been proved to be a most formidable safeguard against hostile fleets.

MEDALS OF HONOR IN THE NAVY

I earnestly call the attention of the Congress to the need of amending the existing law relating to the award of Congressional medals of honor in the Navy so as to provide that they may be awarded to commissioned officers and warrant officers as well as to enlisted men. These justly prized medals are given in the Army alike to the officers and the enlisted men, and it is most unjust that the commissioned officers and warrant officers of the Navy should not in this respect have the same rights as their brethren in the Army and as the enlisted men of the Navy.

THE PHILIPPINES

In the Philippine Islands there has been during the past year a continuation of the steady progress which has obtained ever since our troops definitely got the upper hand of the insurgents. The Philippine people, or, to speak more accurately, the many tribes, and even races, sundered from one another more or less sharply, who go to make up the people of the Philippine Islands, contain many elements of good, and some elements which we have a right to hope stand for progress. At present they are utterly incapable of existing in independence at all or of building up a civilization of their own. I firmly believe that we can help them to rise higher and higher in the scale of civilization and of capacity for self-government, and I most earnestly hope that in the end they will be able to stand, if not entirely alone, yet in some such relation to

the United States as Cuba now stands. This end is not yet in sight, and it may be indefinitely postponed if our people are foolish enough to turn the attention of the Filipinos away from the problems of achieving moral and material prosperity, of working for a stable, orderly, and just government, and toward foolish and dangerous intrigues for a complete independence for which they are as yet totally unfit.

On the other hand our people must keep steadily before their minds the fact that the justification for our stay in the Philippines must ultimately rest chiefly upon the good we are able to do in the islands. I do not overlook the fact that in the development of our interests in the Pacific Ocean and along its coasts, the Philippines have played and will play an important part, and that our interests have been served in more than one way by the possession of the islands. But our chief reason for continuing to hold them must be that we ought in good faith to try to do our share of the world's work, and this particular piece of work has been imposed upon us by the results of the war with Spain. The problem presented to us in the Philippine Islands is akin to, but not exactly like, the problems presented to the other great civilized powers which have possessions in the Orient. There are points of resemblance in our work to the work which is being done by the British in India and Egypt, by the French in Algiers, by the Dutch in Java, by the Russians in Turkestan, by the Japanese in Formosa; but more distinctly than any of these powers we are endeavoring to develop the natives themselves so that they shall take an ever-increasing share in their own government, and as far as is prudent we are already admitting their representatives to a governmental equality with our own. There are commissioners, judges, and governors in the islands who are Filipinos and who have exactly the same share in the government of the islands as have their colleagues who are Americans, while in the lower ranks, of course, the great majority of the public servants are Filipinos. Within two years we shall be trying the experiment of an elective lower house in the Philippine legislature. It may be that the Filipinos will misuse this legislature, and they certainly will misuse it if they are misled by foolish persons here at home into starting an agitation for their own independence or into any factious or improper action. In such case they will do themselves no good and will stop for the time being all further effort to advance them and give them a greater share in their own government. But if they act with wisdom and self-restraint, if they show that they are capable of electing a legislature which in its turn is capable of taking a sane and efficient part in the actual work of government, they can rest assured that a full and increasing measure of recognition will be given them. Above all they should remember that their prime needs are moral and industrial, not political. It is a good thing to try the experiment of giving them a legislature; but it is a far better thing to give them schools, good roads, railroads which will enable them to get their products to market, honest courts, an honest and efficient constabulary, and all that tends to produce order, peace, fair dealing as between man and man, and habits of intelligent industry and thrift. If they are safeguarded against oppression, and if their real wants, material and spiritual, are studied intelligently and in a spirit of friendly sympathy, much more good will be done them than by any effort to give them political power, though this effort may in its own proper time and place be proper enough.

Meanwhile our own people should remember that there is need for the highest standard of conduct among the Americans sent to the Philippine Islands, not only among the public servants but among the private individuals who go to them. It is because I feel this so deeply that in the administration of these islands I have positively refused to permit any discrimination whatsoever for political reasons and have insisted that in choosing the public servants consideration should be paid solely to the worth of the men chosen and to the needs of the islands. There is no higher body of men in our public service than we have in the Philippine Islands under Governor Wright and his associates. So far as possible these men should be given a free hand, and their suggestions should receive the hearty backing both of the Executive and of the Congress. There is need of a vigilant and disinterested support of our public servants in the Philippines by good citizens here in the United States. Unfortunately hitherto those of our people here at home who have specially claimed to be the champions of the Filipinos have in reality been their worst enemies. This will continue to be the case as long as they strive to make the Filipinos independent, and stop all industrial development of the islands by crying out against the laws which would bring it on the ground that capitalists must not "exploit" the islands. Such proceedings are not only unwise, but are most harmful to the Filipinos, who do not need independence at all, but who do need good laws, good public servants, and the industrial development that can only come if the investment of American and foreign capital in the islands is favored in all legitimate ways.

Every measure taken concerning the islands should be taken primarily with a view to their advantage. We should certainly give them lower tariff rates on their exports to the United States; if this is not done it will be a wrong to extend our shipping laws to them. I earnestly hope for the immediate enactment into law of the legislation now pending to encourage American capital to seek investment in the islands in railroads, in factories, in plantations, and in lumbering and mining.

THEODORE ROOSEVELT.

THE WHITE HOUSE, *December 6, 1904.*

The Fallacy of Territorial Extension, *William Graham Sumner,* 1896

William Graham Sumner (1840–1910) was a prominent sociologist at Yale University and leader of movements for free markets and free trade and against American territorial expansion, including that produced by the Spanish-American War. Often linked to the ideas of the British theorist of social evolution Herbert Spencer, Sumner's work focused on the importance of ethnic ties and folkways, the limits of the government's ability to produce progress, and the dangers of concentrations of economic and political power. It was their tendency to produce such concentrations of power to which Sumner pointed in arguing against territorial conquest and expansion.

The Fallacy of Territorial Extension

William Graham Sumner

The traditional belief is that a state aggrandizes itself by territorial extension, so that winning new land is gaining in wealth and prosperity, just as an individual would gain if he increased his land possessions. It is undoubtedly true that a state may be so small in territory and population that it cannot serve the true purposes of a state for its citizens, especially in international relations with neighboring states which control a large aggregate of men and capital. There is, therefore, under given circumstances, a size of territory and population which is at the maximum of advantage for the civil unit. The unification of Germany and Italy was apparently advantageous for the people affected. In the nineteenth century there has been a tendency to create national states, and nationality has been advocated as the true basis of state unity. The cases show, however, that the national unit does not necessarily coincide with the most advantageous state unit, and that the principle of nationality cannot override the historical accidents which have made the states. Sweden and Norway, possessing unity, threaten to separate. Austro-Hungary, a conglomerate of nationalities largely hostile to each other, will probably he held together by political necessity. The question of expedient size will always be one for the judgment and good sense of statesmen. The opinion may be risked that Russia has carried out a policy of territorial extension which has been harmful to its internal integration. For three hundred years it has been reaching out after more territory and has sought the grandeur and glory of conquest and size. To this it has sacrificed the elements of social and industrial strength. The autocracy has been confirmed and established because it is the only institution which symbolizes and maintains the unity of the great mass, and the military and tax burdens have distorted the growth of the society to such an extent as to produce disease and weakness.

Territorial aggrandizement enhances the glory and personal importance of the man who is the head of a dynastic state. The fallacy of confusing this with the greatness and strength of the state itself is an open pitfall close at hand. It might seem that a republic, one of whose chief claims to superiority over a monarchy lies in avoiding the danger of confusing the king with the state, ought to be free from this fallacy of national greatness, but we have plenty of examples to prove that the traditional notions are not cut off by changing names and forms.

The notion that gain of territory is gain of wealth and strength for the state, after the expedient size has been won, is a delusion. In the Middle Ages the beneficial interest in land and the jurisdiction over the people who lived on it were united in one person. The modern great states, upon their formation, took to themselves the jurisdiction, and the beneficial interest turned into full property in land. The confusion of the two often reappears now, and it is one of the most fruitful causes of fallacy in public questions. It is often said that the United States owns silver-mines, and it is inferred that the policy of the state in regard to money and currency ought to be controlled in some way by this fact. The "United States," as a subject of property rights and of monetary claims and obligations, may be best defined by calling it the "Fiscus." This legal person owns no silver-mines. If it did, it could operate them by farming them or by royalties. The revenue thus received would lower taxes. The gain would inure to all the people in the United States. The body politic named the United States has nothing to do with the silver-mines except that it exercises jurisdiction over the territory in which they lie. If it levies taxes on them it also incurs expenses for them, and as it wins no profits on its total income and outgo, these must be taken to be equal. It renders services for which it exacts only the cost thereof. The beneficial and property interest in the mines belongs to individuals, and they win profits only by conducting the exploitation of the mines with an expenditure of labor and capital. These individuals are of many nationalities. They alone own the product and have the use and enjoyment of it. No other individuals, American or others, have any interest, right, duty, or responsibility in the matter. The United States has simply provided the protection of its laws and institutions for the mine-workers while they were carrying on their enterprise. Its jurisdiction was only a burden to it, not a profitable good. Its jurisdiction was a boon to the mine-workers and certainly did not entail further obligation.

It is said that the boundary between Alaska and British America runs through a gold field, and some people are in great anxiety as to who will "grab it." If an American can go over to the English side and mine gold there for his profit, under English laws and jurisdiction, and an Englishman can come over to the American side and mine gold there for his profit, under American laws and jurisdiction, what difference does it make where the line falls? The only case in which it would make any difference is where the laws and institutions of the two states were not on equal stages of enlightenment.

This case serves to bring out distinctly a reason for the old notion of territorial extension which is no longer valid. In the old colonial system, states conquered territories or founded colonies in order to shut them against all other states and to exploit them on principles of subjugation and monopoly. It is only under this system that the jurisdiction is anything but a burden.

If the United States should admit Hawaii to the Union, the Fiscus of the former state would collect more taxes and incur more expenses. The circumstances are such that the latter would probably be the greater. The United States would not acquire a square foot of land in property unless it paid for it. Individual Americans would get no land to till without paying for it and would win no products from it except by wisely expending their labor and capital on it. All that they can do now. So long as there is a government on the islands, native or other, which is competent to guarantee peace, order, and security, no more is necessary, and for any outside power to seize the jurisdiction is an unjustifiable aggression. That jurisdiction would be the best founded which was the most liberal and enlightened, and would give the best security to all persons who sought the islands upon their lawful occasions. The jurisdiction would, in any case, be a burden, and any state might be glad to see any other state assume the burden, provided that it was one which could be relied upon to execute the charge on enlightened principles for the good of all. The best case is, therefore, always that in which the resident population produce their own state by the institutions of self-government.

What private individuals want is free access, under order and security, to any part of the earth's surface, in order that they may avail themselves of its natural resources for their use, either by investment or commerce. If, therefore, we could have free trade with Hawaii while somebody else had the jurisdiction, we should gain all the advantages and escape all the burdens. The Constitution of the United States establishes absolute free trade between all parts of the territory under its jurisdiction. A large part of our population was thrown into indignant passion because the Administration rejected the annexation of Hawaii, regarding it like the act of a man who refuses the gift of a farm. These persons were generally those who are thrown into excitement by any proposition of free trade. They will not, therefore, accept free trade with the islands while somebody else has the trouble and burden of the jurisdiction, but they would accept free trade with the islands eagerly if they could get the burden of the jurisdiction too.

Canada has to deal with a race war and a religious war, each of great virulence, which render governmental jurisdiction in the Dominion difficult and hazardous. If we could go to Canada and trade there our products for those of that country, we could win all for our private interests which that country is able to contribute to the welfare of mankind, and we should have nothing to do with the civil and political difficulties which harass the government. We refuse to have free trade with Canada. Our newspaper and congressional economists prove to their own satisfaction that it would be a great harm to us to have free trade with her now, while she is outside the jurisdiction under which we live, but, within a few months, we have seen an eager impulse of public opinion toward a war of conquest against Canada. If, then, we could force her to come under the same jurisdiction, by a cruel and unprovoked war, thus bringing on ourselves the responsibility for all her civil discords and problems, it appears to be believed that free trade with her would be a good thing.

The case of Cuba is somewhat different. If we could go to the island and trade with the same freedom with which we can go to Louisiana, we could make all the gains, by investment and commerce, which the island offers to industry and enterprise, provided that either Spain or a local government would give the necessary security, and we should have no share in political struggles there. It may be that the proviso is not satisfied, or soon will not be. Here is a case, then, which illustrates the fact that states are often forced to extend their jurisdiction whether they want to do so or not. Civilized states are forced to supersede the local jurisdiction of uncivilized or half-civilized states, in order to police the territory and establish the necessary guarantees of industry and commerce. It is idle to set up absolute doctrines of national ownership in the soil which would justify a group of population in spoiling a part of the earth's surface for themselves and everybody else. The island of Cuba may fall into anarchy. If it does, the civilized world may look to the United States to take the jurisdiction and establish order and security there. We might be compelled to do it. It would, however, be a great burden, and possibly a fatal calamity to us. Probably any proposition that England should take it would call out a burst of jingo passion against which all reasoning would be powerless. We ought to pray that England would take it. She would govern it well, and everybody would have free access to it for the purposes of private interest, while our Government would be free from all complications with the politics of the island. If we take the jurisdiction of the island, we shall find ourselves in a political dilemma, each horn of which is as disastrous as the other: either we must govern it as a subject province, or we must admit it into the Union as a state or group of states. Our system is unfit for the government of subject provinces. They have no place in it. They would become seats of corruption, which would react on our own body politic. If we admitted the island as a state or group of states, we should have to let it help govern us. The prospect of adding to the present senate a number of Cuban senators, either native or carpet-bag, is one whose terrors it is not necessary to unfold. Nevertheless it appears that there is a large party which would not listen to free trade with the island while any other nation has the jurisdiction of it, but who are ready to grab it at any cost and to take free trade with it, provided that they can get the political burdens too.

This confederated state of ours was never planned for indefinite expansion or for an imperial policy. We boast of it a great deal, but we must know that its advantages are won at the cost of limitations, as is the case with most things in this world. The fathers of the Republic planned a confederation of free and peaceful industrial commonwealths, shielded by their geographical position from the jealousies, rivalries, and traditional policies of the Old World and bringing all the resources of civilization to bear for the domestic happiness of the population only. They meant to have no grand statecraft or "high politics," no "balance of power" or "reasons of state," which had cost the human race so much. They meant to offer no field for what Benjamin Franklin called the "pest of glory." It is the limitation of this scheme of the state that the state created under it must forego a great number of the grand functions of European states; especially that it contains no methods and apparatus of conquest, extension, domination, and imperialism. The plan of the fathers would have no controlling authority for us if it had been proved by experience that that plan was narrow, inadequate, and mistaken. Are we prepared to vote that it has proved so? For our territorial extension has reached limits which are complete for all purposes and leave no necessity for "rectification of boundaries." Any extension will open questions, not close them. Any extension will not make us more secure where we are, but will force us to take new measures to secure our new acquisitions. The preservation of acquisitions will force us to reorganize our internal resources, so as to make it possible to prepare them in advance and to mobilize them with promptitude. This will lessen liberty and require discipline. It will increase taxation and all the pressure of government. It will divert the national energy from the provision of self-maintenance and comfort for the people, and will necessitate stronger and more elaborate governmental machinery. All this will be disastrous to republican institutions and to democracy. Moreover, all extension puts a new strain on the internal cohesion of the pre-existing mass, threatening a new cleavage within. If we had never taken Texas and Northern Mexico we should never have had secession.

The sum of the matter is that colonization and territorial extension are burdens, not gains. Great civilized states cannot avoid these burdens. They are the penalty of greatness because they are the duties of it. No state can successfully undertake to extend its jurisdiction unless its internal vitality is high, so that it has surplus energy to dispose of. Russia, as already mentioned, is a state which has taken upon itself tasks of this kind beyond its strength, and for which it is in no way competent. Italy offers at this moment the strongest instance of a state which is imperiling its domestic welfare for a colonial policy which is beyond its strength, is undertaken arbitrarily, and has no proper motive. Germany has taken up a colonial policy with great eagerness, apparently from a notion that it is one of the attributes of a great state. To maintain it she must add a great navy to her great military establishment and increase the burdens of a population which is poor and heavily taxed and which has not in its territory any great natural resources from which to draw the strength to bear its burdens. Spain is exhausting her last strength to keep Cuba, which can never repay the cost unless it is treated on the old colonial plan as a subject province to be exploited for the benefit of the mother-country. If that is done, however, the only consequence will be another rebellion and greater expenditure. England, as a penalty of her greatness, finds herself in all parts of the world face to face with the necessity of maintaining her jurisdiction and of extending it in order to maintain it. When she does so she finds herself only extending law and order for the benefit of everybody. It is only in circumstances like hers that the burdens have any compensation.

The Star of Empire, *Alfred J. Beveridge*, 1900

Both a trained historian and a United States senator, Alfred J. Beveridge (1862–1927) was one of the most powerful supporters of American territorial expansion. Closely identified with Theodore Roosevelt and progressivism (he was a Progressive Party nominee for both the United States Senate and the governorship of Indiana), Beveridge sought the extension of American control over foreign territories, deeming it best for the United States and for the people of countries like the Philippines, whom he deemed inferior to European peoples and in need of political, social, and cultural guidance to prepare them for constitutional government.

The Star of Empire

September 25, 1900

Alfred J. Beveridge

"Westward the Star of Empire takes its Way." Not the star of kingly power, for kingdoms are everywhere dissolving in the increasing rights of men; not the star of autocratic oppression, for civilization is brightening and the liberties of the people are broadening under every flag. But the star of empire, as Washington used the word, when he called this Republic an "empire"; as Jefferson understood it, when he declared our form of government ideal for extending "our empire"; as Marshall understood it, when he closed a noble period of an immortal constitutional opinion by naming the domain of the American people "our empire."

This is the "empire" of which the prophetic voice declared "Westward the Star of Empire takes its Way"—the star of the empire of liberty and law, of commerce and communication, of social order and the Gospel of our Lord—the star of the empire of the civilization of the world. Westward *that* star of empire takes its course. And to-day it illumines our path of duty across the Pacific into the islands and lands where Providence has called us.

In that path the American government is marching forward, opposed at every step by those who deny the right of the Republic to plant the institutions of the Flag where events have planted that Flag itself. For this is our purpose, to perform which the Opposition declares that the Republic has no warrant in the Constitution, in morals or in the rights of man. And I mean to examine to-night every argument they advance for their policy of reaction and retreat.

It is not true, as the Opposition asserts, that every race without instruction and guidance is naturally self-governing. If so, the Indians were capable of self-government. America belonged to them whether they were or were not capable of self-government. If they were capable of self-government it was not only wrong, but it was a crime to set up our independent government on their land without their consent. If this is true, the Puritans, instead of being noble, are despicable characters; and the patriots of 1776, to whom the Opposition compares the Filipinos, were only a swarm of land pirates. If the Opposition is right, the Zulus who owned the Transvaal were capable of self-government; and the Boers who expelled them, according to the Opposition, deserve the abhorrence of righteous men.

But while the Boers took the lands they occupy from the natives who peopled them; while we peopled this country in spite of the Indian who owned it; and while this may be justified by the welfare of the world which those events advanced, that is not what is to be done in the Philippines. The American government, as a government, will not appropriate the Filipinos' land or permit Americans as individuals to seize it. It will protect the Filipinos in their possessions. If any American secures real estate in the Philippines, it will be because he buys it from the owner. Under American administration the Filipino who owns his little plot of ground will experience a security in the possession of his property that he has never known before.

The English in Egypt and India have not taken the land from its owners; they have confirmed the occupants in their ownership. In Hawaii we have not taken the land from its owners; we have secured its owners in their peaceable possession. And our administration in the Philippines will also establish there that same security of property and life which is the very beginning of civilization itself.

If it be said that tropical countries can not be peopled by the Caucasian race, I answer that, even if true, it is no reason why they should not be governed by the Caucasian race. India is a tropical country. India is ruled by England to the advantage of India and England alike. Who denies that India's 300,000,000 are better off under English administration than under the bestial tyranny of native rulers, to whom the agony of their subjects was the highest form of amusement?

Dare Mr. Bryan say that he would have India back to its condition before England took it? If he dare not, he is answered. Dare he say that he would withdraw English rule now? If he dare not, he is answered. Dare he say that he would take the English "residents" from the Malay States and turn them back again to the rule of their brutal lords? If he dare not, he is answered. Dare he say that the Boers should restore the Transvaal to its original owners? If he dare not, he is answered. Dare he deny that the greatest progress shown upon the map of earth to-day is the progress of Egypt during the last twenty years under English rule? If he dare not, he is answered. And he dare not. If he proclaims his faith in the Filipino people, who know not the meaning of self-government, I declare my faith in the American people, who have developed the realities of liberty.

Grant, for the purposes of argument, the Opposition's premise that the white man can not people the Philippines. Grant, also, that the Malays of those islands can not, unaided, establish civilization there; build roads, open mines, erect schools, maintain social order, repress piracy and administer safe government throughout the archipelago. And this must be granted; for they are the same race which inhabits the Malay Peninsula. What, then, is the conclusion demanded by the general welfare of the world?

Surely not that this land, rich in all that civilized man requires, and these people needing the very blessings they ignorantly repel, should be remanded to savagery and the wilderness! If you say this, you say that barbarism and undeveloped resources are better than civilization and the earth's resources developed. What is the conclusion, then, which the logic of civilization compels from these admitted premises? It is that the reign of law must be established throughout these islands, their resources developed and their people civilized by those in whose blood resides the genius of administration.

Such are all Teutonic and Celtic peoples. Such are the Dutch; behold their work in Java. Such are the English; behold their work all around the world. Such the German; behold his advance into the fields of world-regeneration and administration. Such were the French before Napoleon diverted their energies; behold their work in Canada, Louisiana and our great Northwest. And such, more than any people who ever lived, are the Americans, into whose hands God has given the antipodes to develop their resources, to regenerate their people and to establish there the civilization of law-born liberty and liberty-born law.

If the Opposition declares that we ought to set up a separate government over the Philippines because we are setting up a separate government over Cuba, I answer that such an error in Cuba does not justify the same error in the Philippines. I am speaking for myself alone, but speaking thus, I say, that for the good of Cuba more even than for the good of the United States, a separate government over Cuba, uncontrolled by the American Republic, *never should have been promised*.

Cuba is a mere extension of our Atlantic coast-line. It commands the ocean entrances to the Mississippi and the Isthmian Canal. Jefferson's dearest dream was that Cuba should belong to the United States. To possess this extension of American soil has been the wish of every far-seeing statesman from Jefferson to Blaine. Annexation to the greatest nation the world has ever seen is a prouder Cuban destiny than separate nationality. As an American possession, Cuba might possibly have been fitted for statehood in a period not much longer than that in which Louisiana was prepared for statehood.

Even now the work of regeneration—of cleansing cities, building roads, establishing posts, erecting a system of universal education and the action of all the forces that make up our civilization—is speeding forward faster than at any time or place in human history—American administration! But yesterday there were less than ten thousand Cuban children in school; to-day there are nearly one hundred and fifty thousand Cuban children in school—American administration! But yesterday Havana was the source of our yellow-fever plagues; to-day it is nearly as healthy as New Orleans—American administration!

When we stop this work and withdraw our restraint, revolution will succeed revolution in Cuba, as in the Central and South American countries; Havana again fester with the yellow death; systematic education again degenerate into sporadic instances; and Cuba, which under our control should be a source of profit, power and glory to the Republic and herself, will be a source of irritation and of loss, of danger and disease to both. The United States needs Cuba for our protection; *but Cuba needs the United States for Cuba's salvation.*

The resolution for Cuban independence, hastily passed by all parties in Congress, at an excited hour, was an error which years of time, propinquity of location, common commerce, mutual interests and similar dangers surely will correct. The President, jealous of American honor, considers that resolution a promise. And American promise means performance. And so the unnatural experiment is to be tried. What war and nature—aye, what God hath joined together—is to be put asunder.

I speak for myself alone, but speaking thus, I say that it will be an evil day for Cuba when the Stars and Stripes come down from Morro Castle. I speak for myself alone, but I believe that in this my voice is the voice of the American millions, as it is the voice of the ultimate future, when I say that Porto Rico is ours and ours for ever; the Philippines are ours and ours for ever; and Cuba ought to have been ours, and by the free choice of her people some day will be ours, and ours for ever.

We have a foreign nation on our north; another on our southwest; and now to permit another foreign nation within cannon shot of our southeast coast, will indeed create conditions which will require that militarism which the Opposition to the Government pretends to fear. Think of Cuba in alliance with England or Germany or France! Think of Cuba a naval station and ally of one of the great foreign powers, every one of whom is a rival of America! And so my answer to Mr. Bryan's comparison is that, if we have made a mistake in Cuba, we ought not to make the same mistake in the Philippines.

I predict that within ten years we shall again be forced to assume the government of Cuba, but only after our commerce has again been paralyzed by revolution, after internal dissension has again spilled Cuban blood, after the yellow fever has threatened our southern coast from its hot-bed in Havana harbor. Cuba independent! Impossible! I predict that at the very next session of Congress we shall pass some kind of law giving this Republic control of Cuba's destiny. If we do not we fail in our duty.

Consider, now, the Opposition's proposed method of procedure in the Philippines: It is to establish a stable government there, turn that government over to the Filipinos, and protect them and their government from molestation by any other nation.

Suppose the Opposition's plan in operation. Suppose a satisfactory government is established, turned over to the Filipinos and American troops withdrawn. The new government must experience feuds, factions and revolution. This is the history of every new government. It was so even with the American people. Witness Shays' Rebellion against the National Government, almost shaking its foundations; witness the Whiskey Rebellion in Pennsylvania, which required the first exercise of armed national power to maintain order with a state of the Union. And we were of a self-governing race—at that period we were almost wholly Anglo-Saxon.

How can we expect the Philippine Malays to escape this common fate of all new governments? Remember that as a race they have not that civil cohesion which binds a people into a nation. Remember that every island is envious of every other one; and that in each island every officer is a "general," jealous of his dignity, intriguing for advancement.

How long would this stable government, which the Opposition asks us to "establish," *remain* "stable," if we withdrew our forces? And if resistance broke out in the Visayas, if revolt sprang into flame among the murderous Moros, what would be our duty? It would be to reënter where we had withdrawn and restore the stability of the government which the Opposition declares that we shall establish before we withdraw. And so the Opposition program constantly defeats itself and compels us to do over and over again the work which we must perform at the beginning. And all this without benefit to the Philippine people, without improvement to their lands and with immeasurable loss to ourselves recouped not from a single source of profit. But the American flag floating there for ever means not only established liberty, but permanent stability.

Again governments must have money. That is their first necessity; money for salaries, money for the army, money for public buildings, money for improvements. Before the revenues are established, the government must have money. If the revenues are inadequate, nevertheless the government must have money. Therefore, all governments are borrowers. Even the government of the American people—the richest people of history—is a borrower. Even the government of the British people, who for centuries have been accumulating wealth, must borrow; its bonds are in our own bank vaults. Much more, then, must little governments borrow money.

If, then, we "establish a stable government," as the Opposition demands, and turn that government over to the Filipinos, they also must borrow money. But suppose the Philippine government can not pay its debt when it falls due, as has been the case in many instances on our own continent within the last quarter of a century; as is the case to-day with one of the governments of Central America. If that loan is an English loan, England would seize the revenues of the Philippines for the payment of her debt, as she has done before and is doing now. So would France or Germany or whoever was the creditor nation. Should we have a right to interfere? Of course not, unless we were willing to guarantee the Philippine debt. If, then, the first purpose of the Opposition candidate is carried out, we must:

Keep "stable" the government which we first *"establish,"* or the very purpose of the establishment of that government is defeated.

If the second proposition of the Opposition is performed, we must:

First: Control the finances of the Philippines perpetually; or,

Second: Guarantee the loans the Philippine government makes with other nations; or,

Third: Go to war with those nations to defeat their collection of their just debts.

Is this sound policy? Is it profitable? Is it moral? Is it just to the Filipinos, to the world, to ourselves? Is it humane to the masses of those children who need first of all, and more than all, order, law and peace? Is it prudent, wise, far-seeing statesmanship? *And does the adoption of a similar course in Cuba justify it in the Philippines?*

No. Here is the program of reason and righteousness, and Time and Events will make it the program of the Republic:

First: We have given Porto Rico such a civil government as her situation demands, under the Stars and Stripes.

Second: We will put down the rebellion and then give the Philippines such a civil government as the situation demands, under the Stars and Stripes.

Third: We are regenerating Cuba, and when our preparatory work is done, we should have given Cuba such a civil government as her situation may demand, under the Stars and Stripes.

The sovereignty of the Stars and Stripes can be nothing but a blessing to any people and to any land.

I do not advocate this course for commercial reasons, though these have their weight. All men who understand production and exchange, understand the commercial advantage resulting from our ownership of these rich possessions. But I waive this large consideration as insignificant, compared with the master argument of the progress of civilization, which under God, the American people are henceforth to lead until our day is done. For henceforward in the trooping of the colors of the nations they shall cluster around and follow the Republic's banner.

The mercantile argument is mighty with Americans in merely mercantile times, and it should be so; but the argument of destiny is the master argument in the hour of destiny, and it should be so. The American people never yet entered on a great movement for merely mercantile reasons. Sentiment and duty have started and controlled every noble current of American history. And at this historic hour, destiny is the controlling consideration in the prophetic statesmanship which conditions require of the American people.

It is destiny that the world shall be rescued from its natural wilderness and from savage men. Civilization is no less an evolution than the changing forms of animal and vegetable life. Surely and steadily the reign of law, which is the very spirit of liberty, takes the place of arbitrary caprice. Surely and steadily the methods of social order are bringing the whole earth under their subjection. And to deny that this is right, is to deny that civilization should increase. In this great work the American people must have their part. They are fitted for the work as no people have ever been fitted; and their work lies before them.

If the Opposition say that they grant this, but that the higher considerations of abstract human rights demand that the Philippines shall have such a government as they wish, regardless of the remainder of the world, I answer that the desire of the Filipinos is not the only factor in determining their government, just as the desire of no individual man is the only factor determining his conduct. It is written in the moral law of individuals that "No man liveth to himself alone"; and it is no less written in the moral law of peoples that "No people liveth to itself alone."

The world is interested in the Philippines, and it has a right to be. The world is interested in India, and it has a right to be. Civilization is interested in China and its government, and that is the duty of civilization. You can not take the Philippines out of the operation of those forces which are binding all mankind into one vast and united intelligence. When Circumstance has raised our flag above them, we dare not turn these misguided children over to destruction by themselves or spoliation by others, and then make answer when the God of nations requires them at our hands, "Am I my brother's keeper?"

If you admit that it is the purpose of that Intelligence that rules the universe to civilize and unify mankind, how is this to be accomplished? If you say that it is by leaving each people to themselves to work out their own salvation, I answer that history shows that civilization has been preserved only by the most superior nations extending it. And the method of extending civilization is by colonization where the superior nation can establish itself among the inferior races; or in place of them, if the inferior races can not exist under civilization, as in New Zealand, Australia and the like. The method is by administration where the superior nation can not, because of climatic conditions, establish itself among or supplant the inferior races, as in Java, India, and the like. And finally that method is by creating and developing commerce among all the peoples of the world.

It is thus that America itself was discovered; thus that this Republic was builded; thus that South Africa was reclaimed; thus that Australia was recovered from the Bushman and made the home of civilization; thus that Ceylon was taken from wild men and tangled jungle and brought beneath the rule of religion, law and industry. It is thus that Egypt is being redeemed, her deserts fertilized, her starving millions fed, her fellahs made men and the blessings of just government bestowed upon the land of the Pharaohs. It is thus that the regeneration of India has progressed, her cities been cleansed, the reign of hygiene and health gradually established in the very kingdom of pestilence and disease; and the arbitrary and infamous tyranny of petty princes, holding power of life and death over miserable subjects, reduced to the orderly administration of equal and unpurchased justice under equal and impartial laws.

History establishes these propositions:

First: Every people who have become great, have become colonizers or administrators;

Second: Coincident with this colonization and administration, their material and political greatness develops;

Third: Their decline is coincident with the abandonment of the policy of possession and administration, or departure from the true principles thereof.

And as a corollary to these propositions is this self-evident and contemporaneous truth:

Every progressive nation of Europe to-day is seeking lands to colonize and governments to administer.

And can this common instinct of the most progressive peoples of the world—this common conclusion of the ablest statesmen of other nations—be baseless?

If the Opposition asks why this is the mission of the American people now more than heretofore, I answer that before any people assumes these great tasks it goes through a process of consolidation and unification, just as a man achieves maturity before he assumes the tasks of a man. Great Britain never became a colonizing and administering power until the separate peoples of England, Scotland, Ireland and Wales, welded into a single indivisible people, were ready to go forth as a national unit and do the great work to which the world was calling it.

The German people did not embark upon this natural policy until separate duchies, principalities and kingdoms were finally welded by a common war, common blood, and common interests into a great single and indivisible people ready to go forth as a national unit to the great work to which the world was calling it.

The French became colonizers of lands and administrators of governments only when her great statesmen, from Richelieu to Colbert, had knit the separate and divided French people into a national unit and sent it forth to the work to which the world was calling it; and France declined only when she abandoned that natural law of national power and progress, and Napoleon diverted her energies to the internal strifes of Europe. Then her decline began. She lost Canada. The Corsican sold Louisiana to us. And to-day French statesmen at last realize the fatal operation of this law when once disobeyed, and so again are seeking to become one of the colonizing and administering powers of earth.

The American Republic has been going through the process of fitting it for the execution of this natural law of civilization. Hitherto we have had local divisions. The proposition that we were a single people, a national unit, and not a sum of segregated factions, was denied. And it required war and commerce and time—the shedding of blood, the uniting of communities by railroads and telegraphs, the knitting together of the fabric of Nationality by that wonderful loom of human intelligence called the post; and finally, the common and united effort of a foreign war, to bring us to a consciousness of our power *as a people*. And there is never in nature a power without a corresponding purpose. Shall we now stop this process of nature?

We are this at last, a great national unit ready to carry out that universal law of civilization which requires of every people who have reached our high estate to become colonizers of new lands, administrators of orderly government over savage and senile peoples. And being thus prepared, the lands and peoples needing our administration are delivered to our keeping, not by our design, but by occurrence beyond our control. In the astronomy of Destiny, American Opportunity, American Duty and American Preparedness are in conjunction. Who shall oppose their progress?

These are the laws which history advises are the laws of civilization's growth. These, therefore, are the high ordinances of universal and racial morality which has for its ultimate object "that far-off divine event towards which civilization tends." And it is to this divine order of progress that I appeal in answer to the misapplied individual moralities that would give Australia back to its Bushmen, the United States to its Indians, Ceylon to its natives, and the whole world back to barbarism and night.

If the Opposition says that this program, written not in the statutes of man, but in the nature of things, will smother our institutions with a myriad of soldiers, I answer that the world to-day demonstrates that it will result in the reverse. If they point to Germany, and other nations with vast military establishments, to prove that colonization and administration over lands held as possessions and dependencies result in the supremacy of the soldiery over the common people, I answer that the examples do not sustain, but destroy the proposition.

Consider Germany. Her standing army in times of peace is 562,000 men. Does colonization cause or require them? No; because she maintained that mighty multitude before the present Emperor and his counsellors developed Germany's progressive colonial and administrative policy. No, again; because, of Germany's standing army of 562,000 men, less than 4,000 are in her possessions, the remainder of her mighty host being stationed within the Empire itself. No, again; because Austria, with no colonies at all, has a standing army in times of peace of over 361,000 men, none of whom is employed in the care of possessions. No, again; because France, a republic, has a standing army in times of peace of 616,000 men, of which less than 10,000 are employed in her colonies and possessions except in Algeria and Tunis, which are considered an immediate part of France. No, again; because Italy, with hardly a colonial possession, maintains a standing army in times of peace of nearly 325,000 men. No, again; because

Spain, the world's second largest holder of possessions before we won them, maintained a standing army of less than 100,000 men, of whom less than 10,000 were kept in her misruled and oppressed possessions. No, again; because the greatest colonial power that the world has ever seen, the Empire of Great Britain, has a smaller standing army in times of peace than any power of Europe—less than half as many as Germany, almost two-thirds less than the soldiers of France, nearly one-third less than Italy, and one-third less than the soldiers maintained by Austria, an absolutely non-colonizing power.

Great Britain's entire standing army of English, Scotch, Welsh and Irish soldiers throughout the entire Empire is only 231,351, of which Ceylon, with a population of 3,500,000, has only one battalion of English infantry and two companies of English artillery. Egypt, with nearly 10,000,000, has less than 6,000 English officers and men; and India, with 300,000,000 population, has less than 75,000 English soldiers. The other soldiers upholding the English flag throughout England's possessions are native soldiers. England has learned the statesmanship of sentiment; and so the people England rules supply the soldiers who defend her flag.

What is it that establishes militarism in Germany? On the west, the immediate proximity of France, her hereditary foe; on the east, the immediate proximity of Russia, her hereditary foe; on the south, the immediate proximity of an heterogenous empire. What is it that establishes militarism in France? The immediate proximity of Germany on the East, her hereditary foe; the immediate proximity of England on the north, an historic enemy; the immediate proximity of Italy on the south, the third of the Anti-French Dreibund. These are the things which establish militarism in Europe—not colonization, not possessions, not obedience to the great natural law of expansion and growth.

If France, Germany, Italy, Austria, would devote themselves to the world's great work of rescuing the wilderness, of planting civilization, of extending their institutions as England has done, as Germany is beginning to do, as the American Republic, under God, is going to lead the world in doing, the armaments of these European military powers would necessarily dissolve, because there would be no longer occasion for them; and because all their energies would be required in the nobler work to which they would thus set their hands.

To produce the same militarism in America that curses Europe, it would be necessary for Canada on the north to be an equal power with us, hostile with present rivalry and centuries of inherited hatred; and for Mexico to be the same thing on the south. And even then we should have only half the conditions that produce militarism in any European nation. Separate government in Cuba is the only proposed step that creates conditions of militarism in America. Militarism in extending American authority! No! No! The wider the dominion of the Stars and Stripes, the broader the reign of peace.

If we do our duty in the Philippines, it is admitted that we ought not to govern the Filipinos as fellow-citizens of the Republic. The Platform of the Opposition says that "to make the Filipinos citizens would endanger our civilization." To force upon Malays, who three hundred years ago were savages and who since that time have been schooled only in oppression, that form of self-government exercised by the citizens of the United States, would be to clothe an infant in the apparel of a giant and require of it a giant's strength and tasks. If we govern them, we must govern them with common sense. They must first be made familiar with the simplest principles of liberty—equal obedience to equal laws, impartial justice by unpurchasable courts, protection of property and of the right to labor—in short, with the *substance* of liberty which civilized government will establish among them.

The Filipinos must begin at the beginning and grow in the knowledge of free institutions, and, if possible, into the ultimate practice of free government by observing the operation of those institutions among them and by experiencing their benefits. They have experienced unjust, unequal and arbitrary taxation; this is the result of the institutions of tyranny. They must experience equal, just and scientific taxation; this is the result of free institutions. They have experienced arrest without cause, imprisonment without a hearing, and beheld justice bought and sold; these are the results of the institutions of tyranny. They must experience arrest only for cause publicly made known, conviction only after trial publicly conducted and justice impartial, unpurchasable and speedily administered; these are the results of free institutions.

They have experienced the violation of the home and robbery by public officers; these are the results of the institutions of tyranny. They must experience the sanctity of the fireside, the separation of Church and State, the punishment of soldier or public official practising outrage or extortion upon them; these are the results of free institutions. And these are the results which they will experience under the government of the American Republic. For these are the results of American Institutions, and our *institutions* follow the flag.

The institutions of every nation follow its flag. German institutions follow the flag of the Fatherland. English institutions follow the banner of St. George. French institutions follow the tricolor of France. And just so, American institutions follow the emblem of the Republic. Nay! Our institutions not only follow the flag, *they accompany it.* They troop beneath its fold. Wherever an American citizen goes, he carries the spirit of our institutions. On whatever soil his blood is shed to establish the sovereignty of our flag, there are planted the imperishable seeds of the institutions of our Nation; and there those institutions flourish in proportion as the soil where they are planted is prepared for them.

Free institutions are as definite, certain and concrete as our Constitution itself. Free speech is an institution of liberty. Free schools are an institution of liberty. Freedom of worship is an institution of liberty. Any American schoolboy can catalogue free institutions. And as fast as the simplest of these institutions prepares these children Providence has given into our keeping for higher grades, just so fast more complex forms of our institutions will follow as naturally as childhood succeeds infancy, youth succeeds childhood and manhood crowns maturity. Our flag! Our institutions! Our Constitution! This is the immortal order in which American civilization marches.

And so the answer to the politician's battle-cry that "our Constitution follows the flag" is this great truth of popular liberty, OUR INSTITUTIONS FOLLOW THE FLAG.

We are a Nation. We can acquire territory. If we can acquire territory, we can govern it. If we can govern it, we can govern it as its situation may demand. If the Opposition says that power so broad is dangerous to the liberties of the American people, I answer that the American people's liberties can never be endangered at the hands of the American people; and, therefore, that their liberties can not be endangered by the exercise of this power, because this power is power exercised by the American people themselves.

"Congress shall have power to dispose of and make all needful rules and regulations respecting territory belonging to the United States," says the Constitution.

And what is Congress? The agent of the American people. The Constitution created Congress. But who created the Constitution? "We, the people," declares the Constitution itself.

The American people created the Constitution; it is their method. The American people established Congress; it is their instrument. The American people elect the members of Congress; they are the people's servants. Their laws are the people's laws. Their power is the people's power. And if you fear this power, you fear the people. If you want their power restricted, it is because you want the power of the people restricted; and a restriction of their power is a restriction of their liberty. So that the end of the logic of the Opposition is limitation upon the liberties of the American people, for fear that the liberties of the American people will suffer at the hands of the American people—which is absurd.

If the Opposition asserts that the powers which the Constitution gives to the legislative agents of the American people will not be exercised in righteousness, I answer that that can only be because the American people themselves are not righteous. It is the American people, through their agents, who exercise the power; and if those agents do not act as the people would have them, they will discharge those agents and annul their acts. The heart of the whole argument on the constitutional power of the government is faith in the wisdom and virtue of the people; and in that virtue and wisdom I believe, as every man must, who believes in a republic. In the end, the judgment of the masses is right. If this were not so, progress would be impossible, since only through the people is progress achieved. . . .

The Opposition says that American liberties will be lost if we administer the substance of liberty to those children. Does any man believe that the American institution of free schools will be destroyed or impaired because we plant free schools throughout the Philippines? Does any man believe that equal rights will be impaired here, because we establish equal rights there?

The individual rights of Englishmen have not declined since England became an administrator of external governments; on the contrary, as England has extended her colonies, the individual rights of individual Englishmen have increased. The rights of the Crown have not enlarged as England's empire has extended; on the contrary, they have diminished. The period of England's great activity in external government has been precisely the period of the extension of the suffrage in England itself, of the enactment of laws for the protection of labor and the amelioration of all the conditions of life among the common people of England.

The period of England's most active extension of empire has not been the period of her most violent oppression of Ireland; the contrary is true. Ireland's bitterest hour was in Cromwell's day and at Cromwell's hands; and yet England had no definite plan of empire then. Ireland's most progressive period has been within the last quarter of a century, when land laws were enacted by the British Parliament compelling Irish landlords to sell their lands to Irish tenants, and permitting the tenant to purchase his landlord's land by the payment of his rent at a price, fixed not by the landlord, but by the courts and commissions.

Ireland's brightest day has been within the last ten years, in which her people have deposited more money in savings banks than in a century before. And yet the last quarter of a century has been England's most imperial period. The last ten years have witnessed the most systematic work by England in empire building in all her history. And England's experience is not an isolated instance. It would not be isolated even if it were confined to England, since her sway is as wide as the world. But the experience of her people is the experience of every other people who have embarked upon the same great voyage.

This is no unprecedented struggle. It is the ever-old and yet the ever-new, because the ever-elemental contest between the forces of a growing nationality and those who resist it; between the forces of extending dominion and those who oppose it; between the forces that are making us the master people of the world and those who think that our activities should be confined to this continent for ever. It is the eternal duel between the forces of progress and reaction, of construction and disintegration, of growth and of decay.

Both sides are and always have been sincere. Washington was sincere when he advocated the adoption of the Constitution; Patrick Henry was sincere when he resisted it as the death-blow to our liberties. Jefferson was sincere when he acquired the empire of Louisiana; Josiah Quincy was sincere when he declared in Congress that the Louisiana acquisition meant the dissolution of the Union.

Webster was sincere when he asserted the sovereignty of the Nation, the indestructibility of the Union, and declared that the Constitution could not follow the flag until the American people so decreed; and Calhoun was sincere when he pronounced the doctrine of state sovereignty, the right of nullification, and announced that the Constitution, carrying slavery, followed the flag in spite of the will of the American people. Lincoln was sincere when he proclaimed that the Union was older than the Constitution, that nationality was the indestructible destiny of the American people, and that he would maintain that nationality by arms; and those mistaken ones were sincere who sought to divide the American people and on the field of battle poured out their blood fighting for their faith.

But their sincerity did not make them *right*. Their earnestness, ability, courage could not give them victory. They were struggling against the Fates. They were resisting the onward forces which were making of the American people the master Nation of the world—the forces that established us first as a separate political body, then welded us into a national unit, indivisible; then extended our dominion from ocean to ocean over unexplored wilderness; and now in the ripeness of time fling our authority and unfurl our flag almost around the globe. It is the "divine event" of American principles among the governments of men for which these forces have been working since the Pilgrims landed on the red man's soil. Men—patriotic, brave and wise—have sought to stay that tremendous purpose of destiny, but their opposition was as the feeble finger of a babe against the resistless pour of the Gulf Stream's mighty current.

For God's hand was in it all. His plans were working out their glorious results. And just as futile is resistance to the continuance to-day of the eternal movement of the American people toward the mastery of the world. This is a destiny neither vague nor undesirable. It is definite, splendid and holy.

When nations shall war no more without the consent of the American Republic: what American heart thrills not with pride at that prospect? And yet our interests are weaving themselves so rapidly around the world that that time is almost here.

When governments stay the slaughter of human beings, because the American Republic demands it: what American heart thrills not with pride at that prospect? And yet to-night there sits in Constantinople a sovereign who knows that time is nearly here.

When the commerce of the world on which the world's peace hangs, traveling every ocean highway of earth, shall pass beneath the guns of the great Republic: what American heart thrills not at that prospect? Yet that time will be here before the first quarter of the twentieth century closes.

When any changing of the map of earth requires a conference of the Powers, and when, at any Congress of the Nations, the American Republic will preside as the most powerful of powers and most righteous of judges: what American heart thrills not at that prospect? And yet, that prospect is in sight, even as I speak.

It is the high and holy destiny of the American people, and from that destiny the American bugles will never sound retreat. "Westward the Star of Empire takes its way!" AMERICAN INSTITUTIONS FOLLOW THE AMERICAN FLAG.

Open Door Note, *John Hay, 1899*

The letter reproduced here was written by U.S. Secretary of State John Hay (1838–1905) for distribution to the governments of Germany, Russia, Great Britain, France, Japan, and Italy. It sets forth a proposal by the American government to maintain free trade in and among the various sections of China. At this time China was under the domination of various foreign powers, which had carved out spheres of influence within which their nations' interests enjoyed special privileges. The United States, which recently had taken over control of the Philippines in the Spanish-American War, did not have any sphere of influence of its own in China. The resulting "open door policy" gained little substantive support from the other powers in China but became central to American policy in the Far East.

Open Door Note

John Hay

Mr. Hay to Mr. White
DEPARTMENT OF STATE,
Washington, September 6, 1899.

SIR: At the time when the Government of the United States was informed by that of Germany that it had leased from His Majesty the Emperor of China the port of Kiao-chao and the adjacent territory in the province of Shantung, assurances were given to the ambassador of the United States at Berlin by the Imperial German minister for foreign affairs that the rights and privileges insured by treaties with China to citizens of the United States would not thereby suffer or be in anywise impaired within the area over which Germany had thus obtained control.

More recently, however, the British Government recognized by a formal agreement with Germany the exclusive right of the latter country to enjoy in said leased area and the contiguous "sphere of influence or interest" certain privileges, more especially those relating to railroads and mining enterprises; but as the exact nature and extent of the rights thus recognized have not been clearly defined, it is possible that serious conflicts of interest may at any time arise not only between British and German subjects within said area, but that the interests of our citizens may also be jeopardized thereby.

Earnestly desirous to remove any cause of irritation and to insure at the same time to the commerce of all nations in China the undoubted benefits which should accrue from a formal recognition by the various powers claiming "spheres of interest" that they shall enjoy perfect equality of treatment for their commerce and navigation within such "spheres," the Government of the United States would be pleased to see His German Majesty's Government give formal assurances, and lend its cooperation in securing like assurances from the other interested powers, that each, within its respective sphere of whatever influence—

First. Will in no way interfere with any treaty port or any vested interest within any so-called "sphere of interest" or leased territory it may have in China.

Second. That the Chinese treaty tariff of the time being shall apply to all merchandise landed or shipped to all such ports as are within said "sphere of interest" (unless they be "free ports"), no matter to what nationality it may belong, and that duties so leviable shall be collected by the Chinese Government.

Third. That it will levy no higher harbor dues on vessels of another nationality frequenting any port in such "sphere" than shall be levied on vessels of its own nationality, and no higher railroad charges over lines built, controlled, or operated within its "sphere" on merchandise belonging to citizens or subjects of other nationalities transported through such "sphere" than shall be levied on similar merchandise belonging to its own nationals transported over equal distances.

The liberal policy pursued by His Imperial German Majesty in declaring Kiao-chao a free port and in aiding the

Chinese Government in the establishment there of a custom-house are so clearly in line with the proposition which this Government is anxious to see recognized that it entertains the strongest hope that Germany will give its acceptance and hearty support.

The recent ukase of His Majesty the Emperor of Russia declaring the port of Ta-lien-wan open during the whole of the lease under which it is held from China to the merchant ships of all nations, coupled with the categorical assurances made to this Government by His Imperial Majesty's representative at this capital at the time and since repeated to me by the present Russian ambassador, seem to insure the support of the Emperor to the proposed measure. Our ambassador at the Court of St. Petersburg has in consequence been instructed to submit it to the Russian Government and to request their early consideration of it. A copy of my instruction on the subject to Mr. Tower is herewith inclosed for your confidential information.

The commercial interests of Great Britain and Japan will be so clearly served by the desired declaration of intentions, and the views of the Governments of these countries as to the desirability of the adoption of measures insuring the benefits of equality of treatment of all foreign trade throughout China are so similar to those entertained by the United States, that their acceptance of the propositions herein outlined and their cooperation in advocating their adoption by the other powers can be confidently expected. I inclose herewith copy of the instruction which I have sent to Mr. Choate on the subject.

In view of the present favorable conditions, you are instructed to submit the above considerations to His Imperial German Majesty's Minister for Foreign Affairs, and to request his early consideration of the subject.

Copy of this instruction is sent to our ambassadors at London and at St. Petersburg for their information.

I have, etc.,

JOHN HAY.

Statement on American Neutrality, 1914

Address to the Senate Calling for Declaration of War, 1917

When World War I broke out in Europe, President Woodrow Wilson made clear his desire that the United States remain officially neutral in the conflict. He also argued strenuously for the rights of noncombatant nations to continue trading with nations involved in the war. The result was increasing conflict with Germany, which had responded to the blockading of its ports by Allied navies by launching a campaign of submarine warfare aimed at producing the same shortages of food, medicines, and other goods it was experiencing. By 1917, when Germany announced resumption of unrestricted submarine warfare after a lull, Wilson was calling for a declaration of war. It should be noted that Wilson, including in the speech reproduced here, portrayed America's goal as the vindication of human rights and international law, even "to end all wars," rather than solely the protection of American lives and interests. Congress declared war on Germany on April 6, 1917.

Statement on American Neutrality

August 19, 1914

Woodrow Wilson

STATEMENT OF THE PRESIDENT

MY FELLOW COUNTRYMEN:

I suppose that every thoughtful man in America has asked himself, during these last troubled weeks, what influence the European war may exert upon the United States, and I take the liberty of addressing a few words to you in order to point out that it is entirely within our own choice what its effects upon us will be and to urge very earnestly upon you the sort of speech and conduct which will best safeguard the Nation against distress and disaster.

The effect of the war upon the United States will depend upon what American citizens say and do. Every man who really loves America will act and speak in the true spirit of neutrality, which is the spirit of impartiality and fairness and friendliness to all concerned. The spirit of the Nation in this critical matter will be determined largely by what individuals and society and those gathered in public meetings do and say, upon what newspapers and magazines contain, upon what ministers utter in their pulpits, and men proclaim as their opinions on the street.

The people of the United States are drawn from many na-

tions, and chiefly from the nations now at war. It is natural and inevitable that there should be the utmost variety of sympathy and desire among them with regard to the issues and circumstances of the conflict. Some will wish one nation, others another, to succeed in the momentous struggle. It will be easy to excite passion and difficult to allay it. Those responsible for exciting it will assume a heavy responsibility, responsibility for no less a thing than that the people of the United States, whose love of their country and whose loyalty to its Government should unite them as Americans all, bound in honor and affection to think first of her and her interests, may be divided in camps of hostile opinion, hot against each other, involved in the war itself in impulse and opinion if not in action.

Such divisions among us would be fatal to our peace of mind and might seriously stand in the way of the proper performance of our duty as the one great nation at peace, the one people holding itself ready to play a part of impartial mediation and speak the counsels of peace and accommodation, not as a partisan, but as a friend.

I venture, therefore, my fellow countrymen, to speak a solemn word of warning to you against that deepest, most subtle, most essential breach of neutrality which may spring out of partisanship, out of passionately taking sides. The United States must be neutral in fact as well as in name during these days that are to try men's souls. We must be impartial in thought as well as in action, must put a curb upon our sentiments as well as upon every transaction that might be construed as a preference of one party to the struggle before another.

My thought is of America. I am speaking, I feel sure, the earnest wish and purpose of every thoughtful American that this great country of ours, which is, of course, the first in our thoughts and in our hearts, should show herself in this time of peculiar trial a Nation fit beyond others to exhibit the fine poise of undisturbed judgment, the dignity of self-control, the efficiency of dispassionate action; a Nation that neither sits in judgment upon others nor is disturbed in her own counsels and which keeps herself fit and free to do what is honest and disinterested and truly serviceable for the peace of the world.

Shall we not resolve to put upon ourselves the restraints which will bring to our people the happiness and the great and lasting influence for peace we covet for them?

Address to the Senate

April 2, 1917

Woodrow Wilson

ADDRESS BY THE PRESIDENT OF THE UNITED STATES (S. DOC. NO. 5.)
The address of the President of the United States this day delivered at a joint session of the two Houses of Congress is as follows:

GENTLEMEN OF THE CONGRESS: I have called the Congress into extraordinary session because there are serious, very serious, choices of policy to be made, and made immediately, which it was neither right nor constitutionally permissible that I should assume the responsibility of making.

On the third of February last I officially laid before you the extraordinary announcement of the Imperial German Government that on and after the first day of February it was its purpose to put aside all restraints of law or of humanity and use its submarines to sink every vessel that sought to approach either the ports of Great Britain and Ireland or the western coasts of Europe or any of the ports controlled by the enemies of Germany within the Mediterranean. That had seemed to be the object of the German submarine warfare earlier in the war, but since April of last year the Imperial Government had somewhat restrained the commanders of its undersea craft in conformity with its promise then given to us that passenger boats should not be sunk and that due warning would be given to all other vessels which its submarines might seek to destroy, when no resistance was offered or escape attempted, and care taken that their crews were given at least a fair chance to save their lives in their open boats. The precautions taken were meagre and haphazard enough, as was proved in distressing instance after instance in the progress of the cruel and unmanly business, but a certain degree of restraint was observed. The new policy has swept every restriction aside. Vessels of every kind, whatever their flag, their character, their cargo, their destination, their errand, have been ruthlessly sent to the bottom without warning and without thought of help or mercy for those on board, the vessels of friendly neutrals along with those of belligerents. Even hospital ships and ships carrying relief to the sorely bereaved and stricken people of Belgium, though the latter were provided with safe conduct through the proscribed areas by the German Government itself and were distinguished by unmistakable marks of identity, have been sunk with the same reckless lack of compassion or of principle.

I was for a little while unable to believe that such things would in fact be done by any government that had hitherto subscribed to the humane practices of civilized nations. International law had its origin in the attempt to set up some law which would be respected and observed upon the seas, where no nation had right of dominion and where lay the free highways of the world. By painful stage after stage has that law been built up, with meagre enough results, indeed, after all was accomplished that could be accomplished, but always with a clear view, at least, of what the heart and conscience of mankind demanded. This minimum of right the German Government has swept aside under the plea of retaliation and necessity and because it had no weapons which it could use at sea except these which it is impossible to employ as it is employing them without throwing to the winds all scruples of humanity or the respect for the understandings that were supposed to underlie the intercourse of the world. I am not now thinking of the loss of property involved, immense and serious as that is, but only of the wanton and wholesale destruction of the lives of noncombatants, men, women, and children, engaged in pursuits which have always, even in the darkest periods of modern history, been deemed innocent and legitimate. Property can be paid for; the lives of peaceful and innocent people cannot be. The present German submarine warfare against commerce is a warfare against mankind.

It is a war against all nations. American ships have been sunk, American lives taken, in ways which it has stirred us very deeply to learn of, but these ships and people of other neutral and friendly nations have been sunk and overwhelmed in the waters in the same way. There has been no discrimination. The challenge is to all mankind. Each nation must decide for itself how it will meet it. The choice we make for ourselves must be made with moderation of counsel and a temperateness of judgment befitting our character and our motives as a nation. We must put excited feeling away. Our motive will not be revenge or the victorious assertion of the physical might of the nation, but only the vindication of right, of human right, of which we are only a single champion.

When I addressed the Congress on the twenty-sixth of February last I thought that it would suffice to assert our neutral rights with arms, our right to use the seas against unlawful interference, our right to keep our people safe against unlawful violence. But armed neutrality, it now appears, is impracticable. Because submarines are in effect outlaws when used as the German submarines have been used against merchant shipping, it is impossible to defend ships against their attacks as the law of nations has assumed that merchantmen would defend themselves against privateers or cruisers, visible craft giving chase upon the open sea. It is common prudence in such circumstances, grim necessity indeed, to endeavour to destroy them before they have shown their own intention. They must be dealt with upon sight, if dealt with at all. The German Government denies the right of neutrals to use arms at all within the areas of the sea which it has proscribed, even in the defense of rights which no modern publicist has ever before questioned their right to defend. The intimation is conveyed that the armed guards which we have placed on our merchant ships will be treated as beyond the pale of law and subject to be dealt with as pirates would be. Armed neutrality is ineffectual enough at best; in such circumstances and in the face of such pretensions it is worse than ineffectual: it is likely only to produce what it was meant to prevent; it is practically certain to draw us into the war without either the rights or the effectiveness of belligerents. There is one choice we cannot make, we are incapable of making: we will not choose the path of submission and suffer the most sacred rights of our nation and our people to be ignored or violated. The wrongs against which we now array ourselves are no common wrongs; they cut to the very roots of human life.

With a profound sense of the solemn and even tragical character of the step I am taking and of the grave responsibilities which it involves, but in unhesitating obedience to what I deem my constitutional duty, I advise that the Congress declare the recent course of the Imperial German Government to be in fact nothing less than war against the government and people of the United States; that it formally accept the status of belligerent which has thus been thrust upon it; and that it take immediate steps not only to put the country in a more thorough state of defense but also to exert all its power and employ all its resources to bring the Government of the German Empire to terms and end the war.

What this will involve is clear. It will involve the utmost practicable cooperation in counsel and action with the governments now at war with Germany, and, as incident to that, the extension to those governments of the most liberal financial credits, in order that our resources may so far as possible be added to theirs. It will involve the organization and mobilization of all the material resources of the country to supply the materials of war and serve the incidental needs of the nation in the most abundant and yet the most economical and efficient way possible. It will involve the immediate full equipment of the navy in all respects but particularly in supplying it with the best means of dealing with the enemy's submarines. It will involve the immediate addition to the armed forces of the United States already provided for by law in case of war at least five hundred thousand men, who should, in my opinion, be chosen upon the principle of universal liability to service, and also the authorization of subsequent additional increments of equal force so soon as they may be needed and can be handled in training. It will involve also, of course, the granting of adequate credits to the Government, sustained, I hope, so far as they can equitably be sustained by the present generation, by well conceived taxation.

I say sustained so far as may be equitable by taxation because it seems to me that it would be most unwise to base the credits which will now be necessary entirely on money borrowed. It is our duty, I most respectfully urge, to protect our people so far as we may against the very serious hardships and evils which would be likely to arise out of the inflation which would be produced by vast loans.

In carrying out the measures by which these things are

to be accomplished we should keep constantly in mind the wisdom of interfering as little as possible in our own preparation and in the equipment of our own military forces with the duty—for it will be a very practical duty,—of supplying the nations already at war with Germany with the materials which they can obtain only from us or by our assistance. They are in the field and we should help them in every way to be effective there.

I shall take the liberty of suggesting, through the several executive departments of the Government, for the consideration of your committees, measures for the accomplishment of the several objects I have mentioned. I hope that it will be your pleasure to deal with them as having been framed after very careful thought by the branch of the Government upon which the responsibility of conducting the war and safeguarding the nation will most directly fall.

While we do these things, these deeply momentous things, let us be very clear, and make very clear to all the world what our motives and our objects are. My own thought has not been driven from its habitual and normal course by the unhappy events of the last two months, and I do not believe that the thought of the nation has been altered or clouded by them. I have exactly the same things in mind now that I had in mind when I addressed the Senate on the twenty-second of January last; the same that I had in mind when I addressed the Congress on the third of February and on the twenty-sixth of February. Our object now, as then, is to vindicate the principles of peace and justice in the life of the world as against selfish and autocratic power and to set up amongst the really free and self-governed peoples of the world such a concert of purpose and of action as will henceforth ensure the observance of those principles. Neutrality is no longer feasible or desirable where the peace of the world is involved and the freedom of its peoples, and the menace to that peace and freedom lies in the existence of autocratic governments backed by organized force which is controlled wholly by their will, not by the will of their people. We have seen the last of neutrality in such circumstances. We are at the beginning of an age in which it will be insisted that the same standards of conduct and of responsibility for wrong done shall be observed among nations and their governments that are observed among the individual citizens of civilized states.

We have no quarrel with the German people. We have no feeling towards them but one of sympathy and friendship. It was not upon their impulse that their government acted in entering this war. It was not with their previous knowledge or approval. It was a war determined upon as wars used to be determined upon in the old, unhappy days when peoples were nowhere consulted by their rulers and wars were provoked and waged in the interest of dynasties or of little groups of ambitious men who were accustomed to use their fellow men as pawns and tools. Self-governed nations do not fill their neighbour states with spies or set the course of intrigue to bring about some critical posture of affairs which will give them an opportunity to strike and make conquest. Such designs can be successfully worked out only under cover and where no one has the right to ask questions. Cunningly contrived plans of deception or aggression, carried, it may be, from generation to generation, can be worked out and kept from the light only within the privacy of courts or behind the carefully guarded confidences of a narrow and privileged class. They are happily impossible where public opinion commands and insists upon full information concerning all the nation's affairs.

A steadfast concert for peace can never be maintained except by a partnership of democratic nations. No autocratic government could be trusted to keep faith within it or observe its covenants. It must be a league of honour, a partnership of opinion. Intrigue would eat its vitals away; the plottings of inner circles who could plan what they would and render account to no one would be a corruption seated at its very heart. Only free peoples can hold their purpose and their honour steady to a common end and prefer the interests of mankind to any narrow interest of their own.

Does not every American feel that assurance has been added to our hope for the future peace of the world by the wonderful and heartening things that have been happening within the last few weeks in Russia? Russia was known by those who knew it best to have been always in fact democratic at heart, in all the vital habits of her thought, in all the intimate relationships of her people that spoke their natural instinct, their habitual attitude towards life. The autocracy that crowned the summit of her political structure, long as it had stood and terrible as was the reality of its power, was not in fact Russian in origin, character, or purpose; and now it has been shaken off and the great, generous Russian people have been added in all their naive majesty and might to the forces that are fighting for freedom in the world, for justice, and for peace. Here is a fit partner for a League of Honour.

One of the things that has served to convince us that the Prussian autocracy was not and could never be our friend is that from the very outset of the present war it has filled our unsuspecting communities and even our offices of government with spies and set criminal intrigues everywhere afoot against our national unity of counsel, our peace within and without, our industries and our commerce. Indeed it is now evident that its spies were here even before the war began; and it is unhappily not a matter of conjecture but a fact proved in our courts of justice that the intrigues which have more than once come perilously near to disturbing the peace and dislocating the industries of the country have been carried on at the instigation, with the support, and even under the personal direction of official agents of the Imperial Government accredited to the Government of the United States. Even in checking these things and trying to extirpate them we have sought to put the most generous interpretation possible upon them because we knew that their source lay, not in any hostile feeling or purpose of the German people towards us (who were no doubt as ignorant of them as we ourselves were), but only in the selfish designs of a Government that did what it pleased and told its people nothing. But they have played their part in serving to convince us at last that that Government entertains no real friendship for us and means to act against our peace and security at its convenience. That it means to stir up enemies against us at our very doors the intercepted note to the German Minister at Mexico City is eloquent evidence.

We are accepting this challenge of hostile purpose because we know that in such a government, following such methods, we can never have a friend; and that in the presence of its organized power, always lying in wait to accomplish we know not what purpose, there can be no assured security for the democratic governments of the world. We are now about to accept gauge of battle with this natural foe to liberty and shall, if necessary, spend the whole force of the nation to check and nullify its pretensions and its power. We are glad, now that we see the facts with no veil of false pretence about them, to fight thus for the ultimate peace of the world and for the liberation of its peoples, the German peoples included: for the rights of nations great and small and the privilege of men everywhere to choose their way of life and of obedience. The world must be made safe for democracy. Its peace must be planted upon the tested foundations of political liberty. We have no selfish ends to serve. We desire no conquest, no dominion. We seek no indemnities for ourselves, no material compensation for the sacrifices we shall freely make. We are but one of the champions of the rights of mankind. We shall be satisfied when those rights have been made as secure as the faith and the freedom of nations can make them.

Just because we fight without rancour and without selfish object, seeking nothing for ourselves but what we shall wish to share with all free peoples, we shall, I feel confident, conduct our operations as belligerents without passion and ourselves observe with proud punctilio the principles of right and of fair play we profess to be fighting for.

I have said nothing of the governments allied with the Imperial Government of Germany because they have not made war upon us or challenged us to defend our right and our honour. The Austro-Hungarian Government has, indeed, avowed its unqualified endorsement and acceptance of the reckless and lawless submarine warfare adopted now without the disguise by the Imperial German Government, and it has therefore not been possible for this Government to receive Count Tarnowski, the Ambassador recently accredited to this Government by the Imperial and Royal Government of Austria-Hungary; but that Government has not actually engaged in warfare against citizens of the United States on the seas, and I take the liberty, for the present at least, of postponing a discussion of our relations with the authorities at Vienna. We enter this war only where we are clearly forced into it because there are no other means of defending our rights.

It will be all the easier for us to conduct ourselves as belligerents in a high spirit of right and fairness because we act without animus, not in enmity towards a people or with the desire to bring any injury or disadvantage upon them, but only in armed opposition to an irresponsible government which has thrown aside all considerations of humanity and of right and is running amuck. We are, let me say again, the sincere friends of the German people, and shall desire nothing so much as the early re-establishment of intimate relations of mutual advantage between us—however hard it may be for them, for the time being, to believe that this is spoken from our hearts. We have borne with their present government through all these bitter months because of that friendship—exercising a patience and forbearance which would otherwise have been impossible. We shall, happily, still have an opportunity to prove that friendship in our daily attitude and actions towards the millions of men and women of German birth and native sympathy who live amongst us and share our life, and we shall be proud to prove it towards all who are in fact loyal to their neighbors and to the Government in the hour of test. They are, most of them, as true and loyal Americans as if they had never known any other fealty or allegiance. They will be prompt to stand with us in rebuking and restraining the few who may be of a different mind and purpose. If there should be disloyalty, it will be dealt with with a firm hand of stern repression; but, if it lifts its head at all, it will lift it only here and there and without countenance except from a lawless and malignant few.

It is a distressing oppressive duty, Gentlemen of the Congress, which I have performed in thus addressing you. There are, it may be, many months of fiery trial and sacrifice ahead of us. It is a fearful thing to lead this great peaceful people into war, into the most terrible and disastrous of all wars, civilization itself seeming to be in the balance. But the right is more precious than peace, and we shall fight for democracy, for the right of those who submit to authority to have a voice in their own governments, for the rights and liberties of small nations, for a universal dominion of right by such a concert of free peoples as shall bring peace and safety to all nations and make the world itself at last free. To such a task we can dedicate our lives and our fortunes, everything that we are and everything that we have, with the pride of those who know that the day has come when America is privileged to spend her blood and her might for the principles that gave her birth and happiness and the peace which she has treasured. God helping her, she can do no other.

Espionage Act, 1917

Free Speech in Wartime, *Robert La Follette,* 1917

Sedition Act, 1918

Schenck v. United States, 1919

Fearful lest internal dissent undermine the war effort, President Wilson urged Congress to pass legislation making it a crime to obtain or communicate information intended to harm the United States or assist its enemies. The resulting Espionage Act empowered the postmaster general to refuse to mail newspapers and magazines deemed illegal under its provisions, including various socialist and communist periodicals and numerous political and nonpolitical periodicals written in German. Among the strongest opponents of Wilson's internal policies was Wisconsin senator Robert M. La Follette (1855–1925), an opponent of the war and future Progressive Party candidate for president. In the speech reproduced here La Follette opposes public prosecution and intimidation of the war's opponents. Wilson responded to dissent by calling for stronger measures; the result was the Sedition Act. This legislation amended the Espionage Act to ban "disloyal, profane, scurrilous, or abusive language" about the U.S. government, Constitution, or armed forces. Hundreds of antiwar speakers, protesters, and writers were jailed. Among those jailed was Charles Schenck, a socialist who had distributed leaflets to recent draftees into the Army, urging them to peacefully seek an end to military conscription. The U.S. Supreme Court upheld Schenck's conviction on the grounds that handing out leaflets opposing conscription during time of war presented a clear and present danger that the war effort would be undermined.

Espionage Act

June 15, 1917

An Act To punish acts of interference with the foreign relations, the neutrality, and the foreign commerce of the United States, to punish espionage, and better to enforce the criminal laws of the United States, and for other purposes.

Be it enacted by the Senate and House of Representatives of the United States of America in Congress assembled:

TITLE I

Espionage

SECTION 1. That (a) whoever, for the purpose of obtaining information respecting the national defense with intent or reason to believe that the information to be obtained is to be used to the injury of the United States, or to the advantage of any foreign nation, goes upon, enters, flies over, or otherwise obtains information concerning any vessel, aircraft, work of defense, navy yard, naval station, submarine base, coaling station, fort, battery, torpedo station, dockyard, canal, railroad, arsenal, camp, factory, mine, telegraph, telephone, wireless, or signal station, building, office, or other place connected with the national defense, owned or constructed, or in progress of construction by the United States or under the control of the United States, or of any of its officers or agents, or within the exclusive jurisdiction of the United States, or any place in which any vessel, aircraft, arms, munitions, or other materials or instruments for use in time of war are being made, prepared, repaired, or stored, under any contract or agreement with the United States, or with any person on behalf of the United States, or otherwise on behalf of the United States, or any prohibited place within the meaning of section six of this title; or (b) whoever for the purpose aforesaid, and with like intent or reason to believe, copies, takes, makes, or obtains, or attempts, or induces or aids another to copy, take, make, or obtain, any sketch, photograph, photographic negative, blue print, plan, map, model, instrument, appliance, document, writing, or note of anything connected with the national defense; or (c) whoever, for the purpose aforesaid, receives or obtains or agrees or attempts or induces or aids another to receive or obtain from any person, or from any source whatever, any document, writing, code book, signal book, sketch, photograph, photographic negative, blue print, plan, map, model, instrument, appliance, or note, of anything connected with the national defense, knowing or having reason to believe, at the time he receives or obtains, or agrees or attempts or induces or aids another to receive or obtain it, that it has been or will be obtained, taken, made or disposed of by any person contrary to the provisions of this title; or (d) whoever, lawfully or unlawfully having possession of, access to, control over, or being intrusted with any document, writing, code book, signal book, sketch, photograph, photographic negative, blue print, plan, map, model, instrument, appliance, or note relating to the national defense, willfully communicates or transmits or attempts to communicate or transmit the same to any person not entitled to receive it, or willfully retains the same and fails to deliver it on demand to the officer or employee of the United States entitled to receive it; or (e) whoever, being intrusted with or having lawful possession or control of any document, writing, code book, signal book, sketch, photograph, photographic negative, blue print, plan, map, model, note, or information, relating to the national defense, through gross negligence permits the same to be removed from its proper place of custody or delivered to anyone in violation of his trust, or to be lost, stolen, abstracted, or destroyed, shall be punished by a fine of not more than $10,000, or by imprisonment for not more than two years, or both.

SEC. 2. (a) Whoever, with intent or reason to believe that it is to be used to the injury of the United States or to the advantage of a foreign nation, communicates, delivers, or transmits, or attempts to, or aids or induces another to, communicate, deliver, or transmit, to any foreign government, or to any faction or party or military or naval force within a foreign country, whether recognized or unrecognized by the United States, or to any representative, officer, agent, employee, subject, or citizen thereof, either directly or indirectly, any document, writing, code book, signal book, sketch, photograph, photographic negative, blue print, plan, map, model, note, instrument, appliance, or information relating to the national defense, shall be punished by imprisonment for not more than twenty years: *Provided,* That whoever shall violate the provisions of subsection (a) of this section in time of war shall be punished by death or by imprisonment for not more than thirty years; and (b) whoever, in time of war, with intent that the same shall be communicated to the enemy, shall collect, record, publish, or communicate, or attempt to elicit any information with respect to the movement, numbers, description, condition, or disposition of any of the armed forces, ships, aircraft, or war materials of the United States, or with respect to the plans or conduct, or supposed plans or conduct of any naval or military operations, or with respect to any works or measures undertaken for or connected with, or intended for the fortification or defense of any place, or any other information relating to the public defense, which might be useful to the enemy, shall be punished by death or by imprisonment for not more than thirty years.

SEC. 3. Whoever, when the United States is at war, shall willfully make or convey false reports or false statements with intent to interfere with the operation or success of the military or naval forces of the United States or to promote the success of its enemies and whoever, when the United States is at war, shall willfully cause or attempt to cause insubordination, disloyalty, mutiny, or refusal of duty, in the military or naval forces of the United States, or shall willfully obstruct the recruiting or enlistment service of the United States, to the injury of the service or of the United States, shall be punished by a fine of not more than $10,000 or imprisonment for not more than twenty years, or both.

SEC. 4. If two or more persons conspire to violate the provisions of sections two or three of this title, and one or more of such persons does any act to effect the object of the conspiracy, each of the parties to such conspiracy shall be punished as in said sections provided in the case of the doing of the act the accomplishment of which is the object of such conspiracy. Except as above provided conspiracies to commit offenses under this title shall be punished as provided by section thirty-seven of the Act to codify, revise, and amend the penal laws of the United States approved March fourth, nineteen hundred and nine.

SEC. 5. Whoever harbors or conceals any person who he knows, or has reasonable grounds to believe or suspect, has committed, or is about to commit, an offense under this title shall be punished by a fine of not more than $10,000 or by imprisonment for not more than two years, or both.

SEC. 6. The President in time of war or in case of national emergency may by proclamation designate any place other than those set forth in subsection (a) of section one hereof in which anything for the use of the Army or Navy is being prepared or constructed or stored as a prohibited place for the purposes of this title: *Provided,* That he shall determine that information with respect thereto would be prejudicial to the national defense.

SEC. 7. Nothing contained in this title shall be deemed to limit the jurisdiction of the general courts-martial, military commissions, or naval courts-martial under sections thirteen hundred and forty-two, thirteen hundred and forty-three, and sixteen hundred and twenty-four of the Revised Statutes as amended.

SEC. 8. The provisions of this title shall extend to all Territories, possessions, and places subject to the jurisdiction of the United States whether or not contiguous thereto, and offenses under this title when committed upon the high seas or elsewhere within the admiralty and maritime jurisdiction of the United States and outside the territorial limits thereof shall be punishable hereunder.

SEC. 9. The Act entitled "An Act to prevent the disclosure of national defense secrets," approved March third, nineteen hundred and eleven, is hereby repealed.

Free Speech in Wartime

Free Speech and the Right of Congress to Declare the Objects of War

Mr. LA FOLLETTE. Mr. President, I rise to a question of personal privilege.

I have no intention of taking the time of the Senate with a review of the events which led to our entrance into the war except in so far as they bear upon the question of personal privilege to which I am addressing myself.

Six Members of the Senate and 50 Members of the House voted against the declaration of war. Immediately there was let loose upon those Senators and Representatives a flood of invective and abuse from newspapers and individuals who

had been clamoring for war, unequaled, I believe, in the history of civilized society.

Prior to the declaration of war every man who has ventured to oppose our entrance into it had been condemned as a coward or worse, and even the President had by no means been immune from those attacks.

Since the declaration of war the triumphant war press has pursued those Senators and Representatives who voted against war with malicious falsehood and recklessly libelous attacks, going to the extreme limit of charging them with treason against their country.

This campaign of libel and character assassination directed against the Members of Congress who opposed our entrance into the war has been continued down to the present hour, and I have upon my desk newspaper clippings, some of them libels upon me alone, some directed as well against other Senators who voted in opposition to the declaration of war.

One of these newspaper reports most widely circulated represents a Federal judge in the State of Texas as saying, in a charge to a grand jury—I read the article as it appeared in the newspaper and the headline with which it was introduced:

DISTRICT JUDGE WOULD LIKE TO TAKE SHOT AT TRAITORS IN CONGRESS.

[By Associated Press leased wire.]

HOUSTON, TEX., *October 1, 1917.*

Judge Waller T. Burns of the United States district court, in charging a Federal grand jury at the beginning of the October term to-day, after calling by name Senators STONE of Missouri, HARDWICK of Georgia, VARDAMAN of Mississippi, GRONNA of North Dakota, GORE of Oklahoma, and LA FOLLETTE of Wisconsin, said:

"If I had a wish, I would wish that you men had jurisdiction to return bills of indictment against these men. They ought to be tried promptly and fairly, and I believe this court could administer the law fairly; but I have a conviction as strong as life, that this country should stand them up against an adobe wall to-morrow and give them what they deserve. If any man deserves death, it is a traitor. I wish that I could pay for the ammunition. I would like to attend the execution, and if I were in the firing squad I would not want to be the marksman who had the blank shell.

The above clipping, Mr. President, was sent to me by another Federal judge, who wrote upon the margin of the clipping that it occurred to him that the conduct of the judge might very properly be the subject of investigation. He inclosed with the clipping a letter, from which I quote the following:

> I have been greatly depressed by the brutal and unjust attacks that great business interests have organized against you. It is a time when all the spirits of evil are turned loose. The Kaisers of high finance, who have been developing hatred of you for a generation because you have fought against them and for the common good, see this opportunity to turn the war patriotism into an engine of attack. They are using it everywhere, and it is a day when lovers of democracy, not only in the world, but here in the United States, need to go apart on the mountain and spend the night in fasting and prayer. I still have faith that the forces of good on this earth will be found to be greater than the forces of evil, but we all need resolution. I hope you will have the grace to keep your center of gravity on the inside of you and to keep a spirit that is unclouded by hatred. It is a time for the words "with malice toward none and charity for all." It is the office of great service to be a shield to the good man's character against malice. Before this fight is over you will have a new revelation that such a shield is yours.

If this newspaper clipping were a single or exceptional instance of lawless defamation, I should not trouble the Senate with a reference to it. But, Mr. President, it is not.

In this mass of newspaper clippings which I have here upon my desk, and which I shall not trouble the Senate to read unless it is desired, and which represent but a small part of the accumulation clipped from the daily press of the country in the last three months, I find other Senators, as well as myself, accused of the highest crimes of which any man can be guilty—treason and disloyalty—and, sir, accused not only with no evidence to support the accusation, but without the suggestion that such evidence anywhere exists. It is not claimed that Senators who opposed the declaration of war have since that time acted with any concerted purpose either regarding war measures or any others. They have voted according to their individual opinions, have often been opposed to each other on bills which have come before the Senate since the declaration of war, and, according to my recollection, have never all voted together since that time upon any single proposition upon which the Senate has been divided.

I am aware, Mr. President, that in pursuance of this general campaign of villification and attempted intimidation, requests from various individuals and certain organizations have been submitted to the Senate for my expulsion from this body, and that such requests have been referred to and considered by one of the committees of the Senate.

If I alone had been made the victim of these attacks, I should not take one moment of the Senate's time for their consideration, and I believe that other Senators who have been unjustly and unfairly assailed, as I have been, hold the same attitude upon this that I do. *Neither the clamor of the mob nor the voice of power will ever turn me by the breadth of a hair from the course I mark out for myself, guided by such knowledge as I can obtain and controlled and directed by a solemn conviction of right and duty.*

But, sir, it is not alone Members of Congress that the war party in this country has sought to intimidate. The mandate seems to have gone forth to the sovereign people of this country that they must be silent while those things are being done by their Government which most vitally concern their well-being, their happiness, and their lives. To-day and for weeks past, honest and law-abiding citizens of this country are being terrorized and outraged in their rights by those sworn to uphold the laws and protect the rights of the people. I have in my possession numerous affidavits establishing the fact that people are being unlawfully arrested, thrown into jail, held incommunicado for days, only to be eventually discharged without ever having been taken into court, because they have committed no crime. Private residences are being invaded, loyal citizens of undoubted integrity and probity arrested, cross-examined, and the most sacred constitutional rights guaranteed to every American citizen are being violated.

It appears to be the purpose of those conducting this campaign to throw the country into a state of terror, to coerce public opinion, to stifle criticism, and suppress discussion of the great issues involved in this war.

I think all men recognize that in time of war the citizen must surrender some rights for the common good which he is entitled to enjoy in time of peace. *But, sir, the right to control their own Government according to constitutional forms is not one of the rights that the citizens of this country are called upon to surrender in time of war.*

Rather in time of war the citizen must be more alert to the preservation of his right to control his Government. He must be most watchful of the encroachment of the military upon the civil power. He must beware of those precedents in support of arbitrary action by administrative officials, which excused on the plea of necessity in war time, become the fixed rule when the necessity has passed and normal conditions have been restored.

More than all, the citizen and his representative in Congress in time of war must maintain his right of free speech. More than in times of peace it is necessary that the channels for free public discussion of governmental policies shall be open and unclogged. I believe, Mr. President, that I am now touching upon the most important question in this country to-day—and that is the right of the citizens of this country and their representatives in Congress to discuss in an orderly way frankly and publicly and without fear, from the platform and through the press, every important phase of this war; its causes, the manner in which it should be conducted, and the terms upon which peace should be made. The belief which is becoming widespread in this land that this most fundamental right is being denied to the citizens of this country is a fact the tremendous significance of which, those in authority have not yet begun to appreciate.

I am contending, Mr. President, for the great fundamental right of the sovereign people of this country to make their voice heard and have that voice heeded upon the great questions arising out of this war, including not only how the war shall be prosecuted but the conditions upon which it may be terminated with a due regard for the rights and the honor of this Nation and the interests of humanity.

I am contending for this right because the exercise of it is necessary to the welfare, to the existence, of this Government, to the successful conduct of this war, and to a peace which shall be enduring and for the best interest of this country.

Suppose success attends the attempt to stifle all discussion of the issues of the war, all discussion of the terms upon which it should be concluded, all discussion of the objects and purpose to be accomplished by it, and concede the demand of the war-mad press and war extremists that they monopolize the right of public utterance upon those questions unchallenged, what think you would be the consequence to this country not only during the war but after the war?

Right of People to Discuss War Issues

Mr. President, our Government, above all others, is founded on the right of the people freely to discuss all matters pertaining to their Government in war not less than in peace, for in this Government the people are the rulers in war no less than in peace. It is true, sir, that Members of the House of Representatives are elected for two years, the President for four years, and the Members of the Senate for six years, and during their temporary official terms these officers constitute what is called the Government. But back of them always is the controlling sovereign power of the people, and when the people can make their will known, the faithful officer will obey that will. Though the right of the people to express their will by ballot is suspended during the term of office of the elected official, nevertheless the duty of the official to obey the popular will continues throughout his entire term of office. How can that popular will express itself between elections except by meetings, by speeches, by publications, by petitions, and by addresses to the representatives of the people? Any man who seeks to set a limit upon those rights, whether in war or peace, aims a blow at the most vital part of our Government. And then as the time for election approaches and the official is called to account for his stewardship—not a day, not a week, not a month, before the election, but a year or more before it, if the people choose—they must have the right to the freest possible discussion of every question upon which their representative has acted, of the merits of every measure he has supported or opposed, of every vote he has cast and every speech that he has made. And before this great fundamental right every other must, if necessary, give way, for in no other manner can representative government be preserved.

Mr. President, what I am saying has been exemplified in the lives and public discussion of the ablest statesmen of this country, whose memories we must revere and whose deeds we most justly commemorate. I shall presently ask the attention of the Senate to the views of some of these men upon the subject we are now considering.

Closely related to this subject of the right of the citizen to discuss war is that of the constitutional power and duty of the Congress to declare the purposes and objects of any war in which our country may be engaged. The authorities which I shall cite cover both the right of the people to discuss the war in all its phases and the right and the duty of the people's representatives in Congress to declare the purposes and objects of the war. For the sake of brevity I shall present these quotations together at this point instead of submitting them separately.

Discussion by American Statesmen

Henry Clay, in a memorable address at Lexington, Ky., on the 18th day of November, 1847, during the Mexican War, took a strong position in behalf of the right of the people to freely discuss every question relating to the war, even though the discussion involved a strong condemnation of the war policy of the Executive. He also declared it to be not only the right but the duty of the Congress to declare the objects of the war. As a part of that address he presented certain resolutions embodying his views on these subjects. These resolutions were adopted at that meeting by the people present, and were adopted at many other mass meetings throughout the country during the continuance of the Mexican War.

For introducing in this body some time ago a resolution asserting the right of Congress to declare the purposes of the present war, I have, as the newspaper clippings here will show, been denounced as a traitor and my conduct characterized as treasonable.

As bearing directly upon the conduct for which I have been so criticized and condemned, I invite your attention to the language of Henry Clay in the address I have mentioned. He said:

But the havoc of war is in progress and the no less deplorable havoc of an inhospitable and pestilential climate. Without indulging in an unnecessary retrospect and useless reproaches on the past, all hearts and heads should unite in the patriotic endeavor to bring it to a satisfactory close. Is there no way that this can be done? Must we blindly continue the conflict without any visible object or any prospect of a definite termination? This is the important subject upon which I desire to consult and to commune with you. Who in this free Government is to decide upon the subjects of a war at its commencement or at any time during its existence? Does the power belong to collective wisdom of the Nation in Congress assembled, or is it vested solely in a single functionary of the Government? . . .

I quote further:

The Constitution provides that Congress shall have power to declare war and grant letters of marque and reprisal, to make rules concerning captures on land and water, to raise and support armies, and provide and maintain a navy, and to make rules for the government of the land and naval forces. Thus we perceive that the principal power, in regard to war, with all its auxiliary attendants, is granted to Congress. Whenever called upon to determine upon the solemn question of peace or war, Congress must consider and deliberate and decide upon the motives, objects, and causes of the war.

If that be true, is it treason for a Senator upon this floor to offer a resolution dealing with that question? . . .

Abraham Lincoln was a Member of Congress at the time

of the Mexican War. He strongly opposed the war while it was in progress and severely criticized President Polk on the floor of the House because he did not state in his message when peace might be expected.

In the course of his speech Lincoln said:

At its beginning, Gen. Scott was by this same President driven into disfavor, if not disgrace, for intimating that peace could not be conquered in less than three or four months. But now, at the end of 20 months . . . this same President gives a long message, without showing us that as to the end he himself has even an imaginary conception. As I have said, he knows not where he is. He is a bewildered, confounded, and miserably perplexed man. God grant he may be able to show there is not something about his conscience more painful than his mental perplexity.

Writing to a friend who had objected to his opposition to Polk in relation to this power of the President in war, Lincoln said:

The provision of the Constitution giving the war-making power to Congress was dictated, as I understand it, by the following reasons: Kings had always been involving and impoverishing their people in wars, pretending generally, if not always, that the good of the people was the object. This our convention understood to be the most oppressive of all kingly oppressions, and they resolved to so frame the Constitution that no man should hold the power of bringing this oppression upon us. But your view destroys the whole matter and places our President where kings have always stood.

I now quote from the speech of Charles Sumner, delivered at Tremont Temple, Boston, November 5, 1846.

John A. Andrew, who was the great war governor of Massachusetts, as I remember, presided at this public meeting, which was in support of the independent nomination of Dr. I. G. Howe as Representative in Congress. Mr. Sumner was followed by Hon. Charles Francis Adams, who also delivered an address at this meeting.

This is the view of Mr. Sumner on the Mexican War, which was then in progress, as expressed by him on this occasion:

The Mexican War is an enormity born of slavery. . . . Base in object, atrocious in beginning, immoral in all its influences, vainly prodigal of treasure and life, it is a war of infamy, which must blot the pages of our history.

In closing his eloquent and powerful address, he said:

Even if we seem to fail in this election we shall not fail in reality. The influence of this effort will help to awaken and organize that powerful public opinion by which this war will at last be arrested. Hang out, fellow citizens, the white banner of peace; let the citizens of Boston rally about it: and may it be borne forward by an enlightened, conscientious people, aroused to condemnation of this murderous war, until Mexico, now wet with blood unjustly shed, shall repose undisturbed beneath its folds.

Contrast this position taken by Charles Sumner at Tremont Temple with that of the Secretary of the Treasury, Mr. McAdoo. He is now touring the country with all the prestige of his great financial mission and the authority of his high place in the administration. I quote the language of the authorized report of his speech before the Bankers' Association of West Virginia, September 21, 1917. According to daily press reports he is making substantially the same denunciation in all his addresses:

America intends that those well-meaning but misguided people who talk inopportunely of peace when there can be no peace until the cancer which has rotted civilization in Europe is extinguished and destroyed forever shall be silenced. I want to say here and now and with due deliberation that every pacifist speech in this country made at this inopportune and improper time is in effect traitorous.

In these times we had better turn the marble bust of Charles Sumner to the wall. It ill becomes those who tamely surrender the right of free speech to look upon that strong, noble, patriotic face.

Mr. President, Daniel Webster, then in the zenith of his power, and with the experience and knowledge of his long life and great public service in many capacities to add weight to his words, spoke at Faneuil Hall, November 6, 1846, in opposition to the Mexican War. He said:

Mr. Chairman, I wish to speak with all soberness in this respect, and I would say nothing here to-night which I would not say in my place in Congress or before the whole world. The question now is, *For what purposes and to what ends is this present war to be prosecuted!*

What will you say to the stature of the statesmanship that imputes treason to his country to a Member of this body who introduces a resolution having no other import than that?

Webster saw no reason why the purposes of the war in which his country was engaged should not be discussed in Congress or out of Congress by the people's representatives or by the people themselves.

After referring to Mexico as a weak and distracted country he proceeded:

It is time for us to know what are the objects and designs of our Government.

It is not the habit of the American people, nor natural to their character, to consider the expense of a war which they deem just and necessary—

Not only just, but necessary—

but it is their habit and belongs to their character to inquire into the justice and necessity of a war in which it is proposed to involve them.

Mr. Webster discussed the Mexican War at Springfield, Mass., September 29, 1847, and again, while the war was in progress, he did not hesitate to express his disapproval in plain language.

Many battles had been fought and won, and our victorious armies were in the field, on foreign soil.

Sir, free speech had not been suppressed. The right of the people to assemble and to state their grievances was still an attribute of American freedom. Mr. Webster said:

We are, in my opinion, in a most unnecessary and therefore a most unjustifiable war.

Whoever expects to whip men, free men, in this country into a position where they are to be denied the right to exercise the same freedom of speech and discussion that Webster exercised in that speech little understand the value which the average citizen of this country places upon the liberty guaranteed to him by the Constitution. Sir, until the sacrifices of every battle field consecrated to the establishment of representative government and of constitutional freedom shall be obliterated from the pages of history and forgotten of men, the plain citizenship of this country will jealously guard that liberty and that freedom and will not surrender it.

To return to my text. Mr. Webster said:

We are, in my opinion, in a most unnecessary and therefore a must unjustifiable war. I hope we are nearing the close of it. I attend carefully and anxiously to every rumor and every breeze that brings to us any report that the effusion of blood, caused, in my judgment, by a rash and unjustifiable proceeding on the part of the Government, may cease.

He makes the charge that the war was begun under false pretexts, as follows:

Now, sir, the law of nations instructs us that there are wars of pretexts. The history of the world proves that there have been, and we are not now without proof that there are, wars waged on pretexts; that is, on pretenses, where the cause assigned is not the true cause. That I believe on my conscience is the true character of the war now waged against Mexico. I believe it to be a war of pretexts; a war in which the true motive is not distinctly avowed, but in which pretenses, afterthoughts, evasions, and other methods are employed to put a case before the community which is not the true case.

Think you Mr. Webster was not within his constitutional rights in thus criticizing the character of the war, its origin, and the reasons which were given from time to time in justification of it?

Mr. Webster discusses at length what he considers some of the false pretexts of the war. Later on he says:

Sir, men there are whom we see, and whom we hear speak of the duty of extending our free institutions over the whole world if possible. We owe it to benevolence, they think, to confer the blessings we enjoy on every other people. But while I trust that liberty and free civil institutions, as we have experienced them, may ultimately spread over the globe, I am by no means sure that all people are fit for them: nor am I desirous of imposing, or forcing, our peculiar forms upon any nation that does not wish to embrace them.

Taking up the subject that war does now exist, Mr. Webster asks:

What is our duty? I say for one, that I suppose it to be true—I hope it to be true—that a majority of the next House of Representatives will be Whigs: will be opposed to the war. I think we have heard from the East and the West, the North and the South, some things that make that pretty clear. Suppose it to be so. What then? Well, sir, I say for one, and at once, that unless the President of the United States shall make out a case which shall show to Congress that the aim and object for which the war is now prosecuted is no purpose not connected with the safety of the Union and the just rights of the American people, then Congress ought to pass resolutions against the prosecution of the war, and grant no further supplies. I would speak here with caution and all just limitation. It must be admitted to be the clear intent of the Constitution that no foreign war should exist without the assent of Congress. This was meant as a restraint on the Executive power. But, if, when a war has once begun, the President may continue it as long as he pleases, free of all control of Congress, then it is clear that the war power is substantially in his own single hand. Nothing will be done by a wise Congress hastily or rashly, nothing that partakes of the nature of violence or recklessness; a high and delicate regard must, of course, be had for the honor and credit of the Nation but, after all, if the war should become odious to the people, if they shall disapprove the objects for which it appears to be prosecuted, then it will be the bounden duty of their Representatives in Congress to demand of the President a full statement of his objects and purposes. And if these purposes shall appear to them not to be founded in the public good, or not consistent with the honor and character of the country, then it will be their duty to put an end to it by the exercise of their constitutional authority. If this be not so, then the whole balance of the Constitution is overthrown, and all just restraint on the Executive power, in a matter of the highest concern to the peace and happiness of the country, entirely destroyed. If we do not maintain this doctrine; if it is not so—if Congress, in whom the war-making power is expressly made to reside, is to have no voice in the declaration or continuance of war; if it is not to judge of the propriety of beginning or carrying it on—then we depart at once, and broadly, from the Constitution.

Mr. Webster concluded his speech in these memorable words:

We may be tossed upon an ocean where we can see no land—nor perhaps, the sun or stars. But there is a chart and a compass for us to study, to consult, and to obey. That chart is the Constitution of the country. That compass is an honest, single-eyed purpose to preserve the institutions and the liberty with which God has blessed us.

In 1847 Senator Tom Corwin made a memorable speech in the Senate on the Mexican War. It was one of the ablest addresses made by that very able statesman, and one of the great contributions to the discussion of the subject we are now considering. At the time of Senator Corwin's address the majority in Congress were supporting the President. The people up to that time had had no chance to express their views at an election. After referring to the doctrine then preached by the dominant faction of the Senate, that after war is declared it must be prosecuted to the bitter end as the President may direct, until one side or the other is hopelessly beaten and devastated by the conflict, with one man—the President—in sole command of the destinies of the Nation. Mr. Corwin said:

> With these doctrines for our guide, I will thank any Senator to furnish me with any means of escaping from the prosecution of this or any other war, for an hundred years to come. If it please the President who shall be, to continue it so long. Tell me, ye who contend that, being in war, duty demands of Congress for its prosecution all the money and every able-bodied man in America to carry it on if need be, who also contend that it is the right of the President, without the control of Congress, to march your embodied hosts to Monterey, to Yucatan, to Mexico, to Panama, to China, and that under penalty of death to the officer who disobeys him—tell me, I demand it of you—tell me, tell the American people, tell the nations of Christendom, what is the difference between your democracy and the most odious, most hateful despotism that a merciful God has ever allowed a nation to be afflicted with since government on earth began? You may call this free government, but it is such freedom, and no other, as of old was established at Babylon, at Susa, at Bactrina, or Persepolis. Its parallel is scarcely to be found when thus falsely understood, in any, even the worst, forms of civil polity in modern times. Sir, it is not so; such is not your Constitution; it is something else, something other and better than this.

Lincoln, Webster, Clay, Sumner—what a galaxy of names in American history! They all believed and asserted and advocated in the midst of war that it was the right—the constitutional right—and the patriotic duty of American citizens, after the declaration of war and while the war was in progress, to discuss the issues of the war and to criticize the policies employed in its prosecution and to work for the election of representatives opposed to prolonging war.

The right of Lincoln, Webster, Clay, Sumner to oppose the Mexican War, criticize its conduct, advocate its conclusion on a just basis, is exactly the same right and privilege as that possessed by every Representative in Congress and by each and every American citizen in our land to-day in respect to the war in which we are now engaged. Their arguments as to the power of Congress to shape the war policy and their opposition to what they believed to be the usurpation of power on the part of the Executive are potent so long as the Constitution remains the law of the land....

Mr. President, while we were struggling for our independence the Duke of Grafton, in the House of Lords, October 28, 1775, speaking against voting thanks to British officers and soldiers, after the battles of Lexington and Bunker Hill, declared:

> I pledge myself to your lordships and my country that if necessity should require it and my health otherwise permit it, I mean to come down to this House in a litter in order to express my full and hearty disapproval of the measures now pursued, and, as I understand from the noble lords in office, meant to be pursued.

On the same occasion, Mr. Fox said:

> I could not consent to the bloody consequences of so silly a contest, about so silly an object, conducted in the silliest manner that history or observation had ever furnished an instance of, and from which we are likely to derive poverty, misery, disgrace, defeat, and ruin.

In the House of Commons, May 14, 1777, Mr. Burke is reported in the parliamentary debates against the war on the American Colonies, as saying he was, and ever would be, ready to support a just war, whether against subjects or alien enemies, but where justice or color of justice was wanting he would ever be the first to oppose it.

Lord Chatham, November 18, 1777, spoke as follows regarding the war between England and the American Colonies:

> I would sell my shirt off my back to assist in proper measures, properly and wisely conducted, but I would not part with a single shilling to the present ministers. Their plans are founded in destruction and disgrace. It is, my lords, a ruinous and destructive war; it is full of danger; it teems with disgrace and must end in ruin ... if I were an American, as I am an Englishman, while a foreign troop was landed in my country I never would lay down my arms! Never! Never! Never!

Mr. President, I have made these quotations from some of the leading statesmen of England to show that the principle of free speech was no new doctrine born of the Constitution of the United States. Our Constitution merely declared the principle. It did not create it. It is a heritage of English-speaking peoples, which has been won by incalculable sacrifice, and which they must preserve so long as they hope to live as free men. I say without fear of contradiction that there has never been a time for more than a century and a half when the right of free speech and free press and the right of the people to peaceably assemble for public discussion have been so violated among English-speaking people as they are violated to-day throughout the United States. To-day, in the land we have been wont to call the free United States, governors, mayors, and policemen are preventing or breaking up peaceable meetings called to discuss the questions growing out of this war, and judges and courts, with some notable and worthy exceptions, are failing to protect the citizens in their rights.

It is no answer to say that when the war is over the citizen may once more resume his rights and feel some security in his liberty and his person. As I have already tried to point out, now is precisely the time when the country needs the counsel of all its citizens. In time of war even more than in time of peace, whether citizens happen to agree with the ruling administration or not, these precious fundamental personal rights—free speech, free press, and right of assemblage so explicitly and emphatically guaranteed by the Constitution should be maintained inviolable. There is no rebellion in the land, no martial law, no courts are closed, no legal processes suspended, and there is no threat even of invasion.

But more than this, if every preparation for war can be made the excuse for destroying free speech and a free press and the right of the people to assemble together for peaceful discussion, then we may well despair of ever again finding ourselves for a long period in a state of peace. With the possessions we already have in remote parts of the world, with the obligations we seem almost certain to assume as a result of the present war, a war can be made any time overnight and the destruction of personal rights now occurring will be pointed to then as precedents for a still further invasion of the rights of the citizen. This is the road which all free governments have heretofore traveled to their destruction, and how far we have progressed along it is shown when we compare the standard of liberty of Lincoln, Clay, and Webster with the standard of the present day.

This leads me, Mr. President, to the next thought to which I desire to invite the attention of the Senate, and that is the power of Congress to declare the purpose and objects of the war, and the failure of Congress to exercise that power in the present crisis.

Power of Congress to Declare Objects of War

For the mere assertion of that right, in the form of a resolution to be considered and discussed—which I introduced August 11, 1917—I have been denounced throughout this broad land as a traitor to my country.

Mr. President, we are in a war the awful consequences of which no man can foresee, which, in my judgment, could have been avoided if the Congress had exercised its constitutional power to influence and direct the foreign policy of this country.

On the 8th day of February, 1915, I introduced in the Senate a resolution authorizing the President to invite the representatives of the neutral nations of the world to assemble and consider, among other things, whether it would not be possible to lay out lanes of travel upon the high seas and through proper negotiation with the belligerent powers have those lanes recognized as neutral territory, through which the commerce of neutral nations might pass. This, together with other provisions, constituted a resolution, as I shall always regard it, of most vital and supreme importance in the world crisis, and one that should have been considered and acted upon by Congress.

I believe, sir, that had some such action been taken the history of the world would not be written at this hour in the blood of more than one-half of the nations of the earth, with the remaining nations in danger of becoming involved.

I believe that had Congress exercised the power in this respect, which I contend it possesses, we could and probably would have avoided the present war.

Mr. President, I believe that if we are to extricate ourselves from this war and restore this country to an honorable and lasting peace, the Congress must exercise in full the war powers intrusted to it by the Constitution. I have already called your attention sufficiently, no doubt, to the opinions upon this subject expressed by some of the greatest lawyers and statesmen of the country, and I now venture to ask your attention to a little closer examination of the subject viewed in the light of distinctly legal authorities and principles.

Constitutional Provisions Involved

Section 8, Article I, of the Constitution provides:

The Congress shall have power to lay and collect taxes, duties, imposts, and excises to pay the debts and provide for the common defense and general welfare of the United States.

In this first sentence we find that no war can be prosecuted without the consent of the Congress. No war can be prosecuted without money. There is no power to raise the money for war except the power of Congress. From this provision alone it must follow absolutely and without qualification that the duty of determining whether a war shall be prosecuted or not, whether the people's money shall be expended for the purpose of war or not rests upon the Congress, and with that power goes necessarily the power to determine the purposes of the war, for if the Congress does not approve the purposes of the war, it may refuse to lay the tax upon the people to prosecute it.

Again, section 8 further provides that Congress shall have power—

To declare war, grant letters of marque and reprisal, and make rules concerning captures on land and water;

To raise and support armies, but no appropriation of money to that use shall be for a longer term than two years;

To provide and maintain a Navy;

To make rules for the government and regulation of the land and naval forces;

To provide for calling forth the militia to execute the laws of the Union, suppress insurrection, and repel invasion;

To provide for organizing, arming, and disciplining the militia, and for governing such part of them as may be employed in the service of the United States, reserving to the States, respectively, the appointment of the officers and the authority of training the militia according to the discipline prescribed by Congress.

In the foregoing grants of power, which are as complete as language can make them, there is no mention of the President. Nothing is omitted from the powers conferred upon the Congress. Even the power to make the rules for the government and the regulation of all the national forces, both on land and on the sea, is vested in the Congress.

Then, not content with this, to make certain that no question could possibly arise, the framers of the Constitution declared that Congress shall have power—

To make all laws which shall be necessary and proper for carrying into execution the foregoing powers, and all other powers vested by this Constitution in the Government of the United States, or in any department or officer thereof.

We all know from the debates which took place in the constitutional convention why it was that the Constitution was so framed as to vest in the Congress the entire war-making power. The framers of the Constitution knew that to give to one man that power meant danger to the rights and liberties of the people. They knew that it mattered not whether you call the man king or emperor, czar or president, to put into his hands the power of making war or peace meant despotism. It meant that the people would be called upon to wage wars in which they had no interest or to which they might even be opposed. It meant secret diplomacy and secret treaties. It meant that in those things most vital to the lives and welfare of the people, they would have nothing to say. The framers of the Constitution believed that they had guarded against this in the language I have quoted. They placed the entire control of this subject in the hands of the Congress. And it was assumed that debate would be free and open, that many men representing all the sections of the country would freely, frankly, and calmly exchange their views, unafraid of the power of the Executive, uninfluenced by anything except their own convictions, and a desire to obey the will of the people expressed in a constitutional manner.

Another reason for giving this power to the Congress was that the Congress, particularly the House of Representatives, was assumed to be directly responsible to the people and would most nearly represent their views. The term of office for a Representative was fixed at only two years. One-third of the Senate would be elected each two years. It was believed that this close relation to the people would insure a fair representation of the popular will in the action which the Congress might take. Moreover, if the Congress for any reason was unfaithful to its trust and declared a war which the people did not desire to support or to continue, they could in two years at most retire from office their unfaithful Representatives and return others who would terminate the war. It is true that within two years much harm could be done by an unwise declaration of war, especially a war of aggression, where men were sent abroad. The framers of the Constitution made no provision for such a condition, for they apparently never contemplated that such a condition would arise.

Moreover, under the system of voluntary enlistment, which was the only system of raising an army for use outside the country of which the framers of the Constitution had any idea, the people could force a settlement of any war to which they were opposed by the simple means of not volunteering to fight it.

The only power relating to war with which the Executive

was intrusted was that of acting as Commander in Chief of the Army and Navy and of the militia when called into actual service. This provision is found in section 2 of Article II, and is as follows:

The President shall be Commander in Chief of the Army and Navy of the United States and of the militia of the several States when called into the actual service of the United States.

Here is found the sum total of the President's war powers. After the Army is raised he becomes the General in Command. His function is purely military. He is the General in Command of the entire Army, just as there is a general in command of a certain field of operation. The authority of each is confined strictly to the field of military service. The Congress must raise and support and equip and maintain the Army which the President is to command. Until the Army is raised the President has no military authority over any of the persons that may compose it. He can not enlist a man, or provide a uniform, or a single gun, or pound of powder. The country may be invaded from all sides and except for the command of the Regular Army, the President, as Commander in Chief of the Army, is as powerless as any citizen to stem the tide of the invasion. In such case his only resort would be to the militia, as provided in the Constitution. Thus completely did the fathers of the Constitution strip the Executive of military power.

It may be said that the duty of the President to enforce the laws of the country carries with it by implication control over the military forces for that purpose, and that the decision as to when the laws are violated, and the manner in which they should be redressed, rests with the President. This whole matter was considered in the famous case of Ex parte Milligan. The question of enforcing the laws of the United States, however, does not arise in the present discussion. *The laws of the United States have no effect outside the territory of the United States.* Our Army in France or our Navy on the high seas may be engaged in worthy enterprises, but they are not enforcing the laws of the United States, and the President derives from his constitutional obligation to enforce the laws of the country no power to determine the purposes of the present war.

The only remaining provision of the Constitution to be considered on the subject is that provision of Article II, section 2, which provides that the President—

Shall have power by and with the consent of the Senate to make treaties, *providing two-thirds of the Senate present concur.*

This is the same section of the Constitution which provides that the President "shall nominate, and by and with the advice and consent of the Senate, shall appoint ambassadors, other public ministers, consuls, judges of the Supreme Court," and so forth.

Observe, the President under this constitutional provision gets no authority to declare the purposes and objects of any war in which the country may be engaged. It is true that a treaty of peace can not be executed except the President and the Senate concur in its execution. If a President should refuse to agree to terms of peace which were proposed, for instance, by a resolution of Congress, and accepted by the parliament of an enemy nation against the will, we will say, of an emperor, the war would simply stop. If the two parliaments agreed and exercised their powers respectively to withhold supplies; and the formal execution of a treaty of peace would be postponed until the people could select another President. It is devoutly to be hoped that such a situation will never arise, and it is hardly conceivable that it should arise with both an Executive and a Senate anxious, respectively, to discharge the constitutional duties of their office. But if it should arise, under the Constitution, the final authority and the power to ultimately control is vested by the Constitution in the Congress. The President can no more make a treaty of peace without the approval not only of the Senate but of two-thirds of the Senators present than he can appoint a judge of the Supreme Court without the concurrence of the Senate. A decent regard for the duties of the President, as well as the duties of the Senators, and the consideration of the interests of the people, whose servants both the Senators and the President are, requires that the negotiations which lead up to the making of peace should be participated in equally by the Senators and by the President. For Senators to take any other position is to shirk a plain duty; is to avoid an obligation imposed upon them by the spirit and letter of the Constitution and by the solemn oath of office each has taken. . . .

Since the Constitution vests in Congress the supreme power to determine when and for what purpose the country will engage in war and the objects to attain which the war will be prosecuted, it seems to me to be an evasion of a solemn duty on the part of the Congress not to exercise that power at this critical time in the Nation's affairs. The Congress can no more avoid its responsibility in this matter than it can in any other. As the Nation's purposes in conducting this war are of supreme importance to the country, it is the supreme duty of Congress to exercise the function conferred upon it by the Constitution of guiding the foreign policy of the Nation in the present crisis.

A minor duty may be evaded by Congress, a minor responsibility avoided without disaster resulting, but on this momentous question there can be no evasion, no shirking of duty of the Congress, without subverting our form of government. If our Constitution is to be changed so as to give the President the power to determine the purposes for which this Nation will engage in war, and the conditions on which it will make peace, then let that change be made deliberately by an amendment to the Constitution proposed and adopted in a constitutional manner. It would be bad enough if the Constitution clothed the President with any such power, but to exercise such power without constitutional authority can not long be tolerated if even the forms of free government are to remain. We all know that no amendment to the Constitution giving the President the powers suggested would be adopted by the people. We know that if such an amendment were to be proposed it would be overwhelmingly defeated.

The universal conviction of those who yet believe in the rights of the people is that the first step toward the prevention of war and the establishment of peace, permanent peace, is to give the people who must bear the brunt of war's awful burden more to say about it. The masses will understand that it was the evil of a one-man power exercised in a half dozen nations through the malevolent influences of a system of secret diplomacy that plunged the helpless peoples of Europe into the awful war that has been raging with increasing horror and fury ever since it began and that now threatens to engulf the world before it stops.

No conviction is stronger with the people to-day than that there should be no future wars except in case of actual invasion, unless supported by a referendum, a plebiscite, a vote of ratification upon the declaration of war before it shall become effective.

And because there is no clearness of understanding, no unity of opinion in this country on the part of the people as to the conditions upon which we are prosecuting this war or what the specific objects are upon the attainment of which the present administration would be willing to conclude a peace, it becomes still more imperative each day that Congress should assert its constitutional power to define

and declare the objects of this war which will afford the basis for a conference and for the establishment of permanent peace. The President has asked the German people to speak for themselves on this great world issue; why should not the American people voice their convictions through their chosen representatives in Congress?

Ever since new Russia appeared upon the map she has been holding out her hands to free America to come to her support in declaring for a clear understanding of the objects to be attained to secure peace. Shall we let this most remarkable revolution the world has ever witnessed appeal to us in vain?

We have been six months at war. We have incurred financial obligations and made expenditures of money in amounts already so large that the human mind can not comprehend them. The Government has drafted from the peaceful occupations of civil life a million of our finest young men—and more will be taken if necessary—to be transported 4,000 miles over the sea, with their equipment and supplies, to the trenches of Europe.

The first chill winds of autumn remind us that another winter is at hand. The imagination is paralyzed at the thought of the human misery, the indescribable suffering, which the winter months, with their cold and sleet and ice and snow, must bring to the war-swept lands, not alone to the soldiers at the front but to the noncombatants at home.

To such excesses of cruelty has this war descended that each nation is now, as a part of its strategy, planning to starve the women and children of the enemy countries. Each warring nation is carrying out the unspeakable plan of starving noncombatants. Each nurses the hope that it may break the spirit of the men of the enemy country at the front by starving the wives and babes at home, and woe be it that we have become partners in this awful business and are even cutting off food shipments from neutral countries in order to force them to help starve women and children of the country against whom we have declared war.

There may be some necessity overpowering enough to justify these things, but the people of America should demand to know what results are expected to satisfy the sacrifice of all that civilization holds dear upon the bloody altar of a conflict which employs such desperate methods of warfare.

The question is, Are we to sacrifice millions of our young men—the very promise of the land—and spend billions and more billions, and pile up the cost of living until we starve—and for what? Shall the fearfully overburdened people of this country continue to bear the brunt of a prolonged war for any objects not openly stated and defined?

The answer, sir, rests, in my judgment, with the Congress, whose duty it is to declare our specific purposes in the present war and to state the objects upon the attainment of which we will make peace.

CAMPAIGN SHOULD BE MADE ON CONSTITUTIONAL LINES

And, sir, this is the ground on which I stand. I maintain that Congress has the right and the duty to declare the objects of the war and the people have the right and the obligation to discuss it.

American citizens may hold all shades of opinion as to the war; one citizen may glory in it, another may deplore it, each has the same right to voice his judgment. An American citizen may think and say that we are not justified in prosecuting this war for the purpose of dictating the form of government which shall be maintained by our enemy or our ally, and not be subject to punishment at law. He may pray aloud that our boys shall not be sent to fight and die on European battle fields for the annexation of territory or the maintenance of trade agreements and be within his legal rights. He may express the hope that an early peace may be secured on the terms set forth by the new Russia and by President Wilson in his speech of January 22, 1917, and he can not lawfully be sent to jail for the expression of his convictions.

It is the citizen's duty to obey the law until it is repealed or declared unconstitutional. But he has the inalienable right to fight what he deems an obnoxious law or a wrong policy in the courts and at the ballot box.

It is the suppressed emotion of the masses that breeds revolution.

If the American people are to carry on this great war, if public opinion is to be enlightened and intelligent, there must be free discussion.

Congress, as well as the people of the United States, entered the war in great confusion of mind and under feverish excitement. The President's leadership was followed in the faith that he had some big, unrevealed plan by which peace that would exalt him before all the world would soon be achieved.

Gradually, reluctantly, Congress and the country are beginning to perceive that we are in this terrific world conflict not only to *right* our wrongs, not only to *aid* the allies, not only to *share* its awful death toll and its fearful tax burden, but, perhaps, to *bear the brunt* of the war.

And so I say, if we are to forestall the danger of being drawn into years of war, perhaps finally to maintain imperialism and exploitation, the people must unite in a campaign along constitutional lines for free discussion of the policy of the war and its conclusion on a just basis.

Permit me, sir, this word in conclusion. It is said by many persons for whose opinions I have profound respect and whose motives I know to be sincere that "we are in this war and must go through to the end." That is true. But it is not true that we must go through to the end to *accomplish an undisclosed purpose, or to reach an unknown goal.*

I believe that whatever there is of honest difference of opinion concerning this war, arises precisely at this point.

There is, and of course can be, no real difference of opinion concerning the duty of the citizen to discharge to the last limit whatever obligation the war lays upon him.

Our young men are being taken by the hundreds of thousands for the purpose of waging this war on the Continent of Europe, possibly Asia or Africa, or anywhere else that they may be ordered. Nothing must be left undone for their protection. They must have the best army, ammunition, and equipment that money can buy. They must have the best training and the best officers which this great country can provide. The dependents and relatives they leave at home must be provided for, not meagerly, but generously so far as money can provide for them.

I have done some of the hardest work of my life during the last few weeks on the revenue bill to raise the largest possible amount of money from surplus incomes and war profits for this war and upon other measures to provide for the protection of the soldiers and their families. That I was not able to accomplish more along this line is a great disappointment to me. I did all that I could, and I shall continue to fight with all the power at my command until wealth is made to bear more of the burden of this war than has been laid upon it by the present Congress. Concerning these matters there can be no difference of opinion. We have not yet been able to muster the forces to conscript wealth, as we have conscripted men, but no one has ever been able to advance even a plausible argument for not doing so.

No, Mr. President; it is on the other point suggested where honest differences of opinion may arise. Shall we ask the people of this country to shut their eyes and take the entire war program on faith? There are no doubt many honest and well-meaning persons who are willing to answer that question in the affirmative rather than risk the dissensions which they fear may follow a free discussion of the issues of this war. With that position I do not—I can not agree. Have the people no intelligent contribution to make to the solution of the problems of this war? I believe that they have, and that in this matter, as in so many others, they may be wiser than their leaders, and that if left free to discuss the issues of the war they will find the correct settlement of these issues.

But it is said that Germany will fight with greater determination if her people believe that we are not in perfect agreement. Mr. President, that is the same worn-out pretext which has been used for three years to keep the plain people of Europe engaged in killing each other in this war. And, sir, as applied to this country, at least, it is a pretext with nothing to support it.

The way to paralyze the German arm, to weaken the German military force, in my opinion, is to declare our objects in this war, and show by that declaration to the German people that we are not seeking to dictate a form of government to Germany or to render more secure England's domination of the seas.

A declaration of our purposes in this war, so far from strengthening our enemy, I believe would immeasurably weaken her, for it would no longer be possible to misrepresent our purposes to the German people. Such a course on our part, so far from endangering the life of a single one of our boys, I believe would result in saving the lives of hundreds of thousands of them by bringing about an earlier and more lasting peace by intelligent negotiation, instead of securing a peace by the complete exhaustion of one or the other of the belligerents.

Such a course would also immeasurably, I believe, strengthen our military force in this country, because when the objects of this war are clearly stated and the people approve of those objects they will give to the war a popular support it will never otherwise receive.

Then, again, honest dealing with the entente allies, as well as with our own people, requires a clear statement of our objects in this war. If we do not expect to support the entente allies in the dreams of conquest we know some of them entertain, then in all fairness to them that fact should be stated now. If we do expect to support them in their plans for conquest and aggrandizement, then our people are entitled to know that vitally important fact before this war proceeds further. Common honesty and fair dealing with the people of this country and with the nations by whose side we are fighting, as well as a sound military policy at home, requires the

fullest and freest discussion before the people of every issue involved in this great war and that a plain and specific declaration of our purposes in the war be speedily made by the Congress of the United States.

Sedition Act

May 16, 1918

An Act To amend section three, title one, of the Act entitled "An Act to punish acts of interference with the foreign relations, the neutrality, and the foreign commerce of the United States, to punish espionage, and better to enforce the criminal laws of the United States, and for other purposes," approved June fifteenth, nineteen hundred and seventeen, and for other purposes.

Be it enacted by the Senate and House of Representatives of the United States of America in Congress assembled, That section three of title one of the Act entitled "An Act to punish acts of interference with the foreign relations, the neutrality, and the foreign commerce of the United States, to punish espionage, and better to enforce the criminal laws of the United States, and for other purposes," approved June fifteenth, nineteen hundred and seventeen, be, and the same is hereby, amended so as to read as follows:

"Sec. 3. Whoever, when the United States is at war, shall willfully make or convey false reports or false statements with intent to interfere with the operation or success of the military or naval forces of the United States, or to promote the success of its enemies, or shall willfully make or convey false reports or false statements, or say or do anything except by way of bona fide and not disloyal advice to an investor or investors, with intent to obstruct the sale by the United States of bonds or other securities of the United States or the making of loans by or to the United States, and whoever, when the United States is at war, shall willfully cause or attempt to cause, or incite or attempt to incite, insubordination, disloyalty, mutiny, or refusal of duty, in the military or naval forces of the United States, or shall willfully obstruct or attempt to obstruct the recruiting or enlistment service of the United States, and whoever, when the United States is at war, shall willfully utter, print, write, or publish any disloyal, profane, scurrilous, or abusive language about the form of government of the United States, or the Constitution of the

United States, or the military or naval forces of the United States, or the flag of the United States, or the uniform of the Army or Navy of the United States, or any language intended to bring the form of government of the United States, or the Constitution of the United States, or the military or naval forces of the United States, or the flag of the United States, or the uniform of the Army or Navy of the United States into contempt, scorn, contumely, or disrepute, or shall willfully utter, print, write, or publish any language intended to incite, provoke, or encourage resistance to the United States, or to promote the cause of its enemies, or shall willfully display the flag of any foreign enemy, or shall willfully by utterance, writing, printing, publication, or language spoken, urge, incite, or advocate any curtailment of production in this country of any thing or things, product or products, necessary or essential to the prosecution of the war in which the United States may be engaged, with intent by such curtailment to cripple or hinder the United States in the prosecution of the war, and whoever shall willfully advocate, teach, defend, or suggest the doing of any of the acts or things in this section enumerated, and whoever shall by word or act support or favor the cause of any country with which the United States is at war or by word or act oppose the cause of the United States therein, shall be punished by a fine of not more than $10,000 or imprisonment for not more than twenty years, or both: *Provided,* That any employee or official of the United States Government who commits any disloyal act or utters any unpatriotic or disloyal language, or who, in an abusive and violent manner criticizes the Army or Navy or the flag of the United States shall be at once dismissed from the service. Any such employee shall be dismissed by the head of the department in which the employee may be engaged, and any such official shall be dismissed by the authority having power to appoint a successor to the dismissed official."

Sec. 2. That section one of Title XII and all other provisions of the Act entitled "An Act to punish acts of interference with the foreign relations, the neutrality, and the foreign commerce of the United States, to punish espionage, and better to enforce the criminal laws of the United States, and for other purposes," approved June fifteenth, nineteen hundred and seventeen, which apply to section three of Title I thereof shall apply with equal force and effect to said section three as amended.

Title XII of the said Act of June fifteenth, nineteen hundred and seventeen, be, and the same is hereby, amended by adding thereto the following section:

"Sec. 4. When the United States is at war, the Postmaster General may, upon evidence satisfactory to him that any person or concern is using the mails in violation of any of the provisions of this Act, instruct the postmaster at any post office at which mail is received addressed to such person or concern to return to the postmaster at the office at which they were originally mailed all letters or other matter so addressed, with the words 'Mail to this address undeliverable under Espionage Act' plainly written or stamped upon the outside thereof, and all such letters or other matter so returned to such postmasters shall be by them returned to the senders thereof under such regulations as the Postmaster General may prescribe."

Approved, May 16, 1918.

Schenck v. United States

Mr. Justice Holmes delivered the opinion of the court.

This is an indictment in three counts. The first charges a conspiracy to violate the Espionage Act of June 15, 1917, c. 30, § 3, 40 Stat. 217, 219, by causing and attempting to cause insubordination, &c., in the military and naval forces of the United States, and to obstruct the recruiting and enlistment service of the United States, when the United States was at war with the German Empire, to-wit, that the defendants wilfully conspired to have printed and circulated to men who had been called and accepted for military service under the Act of May 18, 1917, a document set forth and alleged to be calculated to cause such insubordination and obstruction. The count alleges overt acts in pursuance of the conspiracy, ending in the distribution of the document set forth. The second count alleges a conspiracy to commit an offence against the United States, to-wit, to use the mails for the transmission of matter declared to be non-mailable by Title XII, § 2 of the Act of June 15, 1917, to-wit, the above mentioned document, with an averment of the same overt acts. The third count charges an unlawful use of the mails for the transmission of the same matter and otherwise as above. The defendants were found guilty on all the counts. They set up the First Amendment to the Constitution forbidding Congress to make any law abridging the freedom of speech, or of the press, and bringing the case here on that ground have argued some other points also of which we must dispose.

It is argued that the evidence, if admissible, was not sufficient to prove that the defendant Schenck was concerned in sending the documents. According to the testimony Schenck said he was general secretary of the Socialist party and had charge of the Socialist headquarters from which the documents were sent. He identified a book found there as the minutes of the Executive Committee of the party. The book showed a resolution of August 13, 1917, that 15,000 leaflets should be printed on the other side of one of them in use, to be mailed to men who had passed exemption boards, and for distribution. Schenck personally attended to the printing. On August 20 the general secretary's report said "Obtained new leaflets from printer and started work addressing envelopes" &c.; and there was a resolve that Comrade Schenck be allowed $125 for sending leaflets through the mail. He said that he had about fifteen or sixteen thousand printed. There were files of the circular in question in the inner office which he said were printed on the other side of the one sided circular and were there for distribution. Other copies were proved to have been sent through the mails to drafted men. Without going into confirmatory details that were proved, no reasonable man could doubt that the defendant Schenck was largely instrumental in sending the circulars about. As to the defendant Baer there was evidence that she was a member of the Executive Board and that the minutes of its transactions were hers. The argument as to the sufficiency of the evidence that the defendants conspired to send the documents only impairs the seriousness of the real defence.

It is objected that the documentary evidence was not admissible because obtained upon a search warrant, valid so far as appears. The contrary is established. *Adams* v. *New York,* 192 U.S. 585; *Weeks* v. *United States,* 232 U.S. 383, 395, 396. The search warrant did not issue against the defendant but against the Socialist headquarters at 1326 Arch Street and it would seem that the documents technically were not even in the defendants' possession. See *Johnson* v. *United States,* 228 U.S. 457. Notwithstanding some protest in argument the notion that evidence even directly proceeding from the defendant in a criminal proceeding is excluded in all cases by the Fifth Amendment is plainly unsound. *Holt* v. *United States,* 218 U.S. 245, 252, 253.

The document in question upon its first printed side recited the first section of the Thirteenth Amendment, said that the idea embodied in it was violated by the Conscription Act and that a conscript is little better than a convict. In impassioned language it intimated that conscription was despotism in its worst form and a monstrous wrong against humanity in the interest of Wall Street's chosen few. It said "Do not submit to intimidation," but in form at least confined itself to peaceful measures such as a petition for the repeal of the act. The other and later printed side of the sheet was headed "Assert Your Rights." It stated reasons for alleging that any one violated the Constitution when he refused to recognize "your right to assert your opposition to the draft," and went on "If you do not assert and support your rights, you are helping to deny or disparage rights which it is the solemn duty of all citizens and residents of the United States to retain." It described the arguments on the other side as coming from cunning politicians and a mercenary capitalist press, and even silent consent to the conscription law as helping to support an infamous conspiracy. It denied the power to send our citizens away to foreign shores to shoot up the people of other lands, and added that words could not express the condemnation such cold-blooded ruthlessness deserves, &c., &c., winding up "You must do your share to maintain, support and uphold the rights of the people of this country." Of course the document would not have been sent unless it had been intended to have some effect, and we do not see what effect it could be expected to have upon persons subject to the draft except to influence them to obstruct the carrying of it out. The defendants do not deny that the jury might find against them on this point.

But it is said, suppose that that was the tendency of this circular, it is protected by the First Amendment to the Constitution. Two of the strongest expressions are said to be quoted respectively from well-known public men. It well may be that the prohibition of laws abridging the freedom of speech is not confined to previous restraints, although to prevent them may have been the main purpose, as intimated in *Patterson* v. *Colorado,* 205 U.S. 454, 462. We admit that in many places and in ordinary times the defendants in saying all that was said in the circular would have been within their constitutional rights. But the character of every act depends upon the circumstances in which it is done. *Aikens* v. *Wisconsin,* 195 U.S. 194, 205, 206. The most stringent protection of free speech would not protect a man in falsely shouting fire in a theatre and causing a panic. It does not even protect a man from an injunction against uttering words that may have all the effect of force. *Gompers* v. *Bucks Stove & Range Co.,* 221 U.S. 418, 439. The question in every case is whether the words used are used in such circumstances and are of such a nature as to create a clear and present danger that they will bring about the substantive evils that Congress has a right to prevent. It is a question of proximity and degree. When a nation is at war many things that might be said in time of peace are such a hindrance to its effort that their utterance will not be endured so long as men fight and that no Court could regard them as protected by any constitutional right. It seems to be admitted that if an actual obstruction of the recruiting service were proved, liability for words that produced that effect might be enforced. The statute of 1917 in § 4 punishes conspiracies to obstruct as well as actual obstruction. If the act, (speaking, or circulating a paper,) its tendency and the intent with which it is done are the same, we perceive no ground for saying that success alone warrants making the act a crime. *Goldman* v. *United States,* 245 U.S. 474, 477. Indeed that case might be said to dispose of the present contention if the precedent covers all *media concludendi.* But as the right to free speech was not referred to specially, we have thought fit to add a few words.

It was not argued that a conspiracy to obstruct the draft was not within the words of the Act of 1917. The words are "obstruct the recruiting or enlistment service," and it might be suggested that they refer only to making it hard to get volunteers. Recruiting heretofore usually having been accomplished by getting volunteers the word is apt to call up that method only in our minds. But recruiting is gaining fresh supplies for the forces, as well by draft as otherwise. It is put as an alternative to enlistment or voluntary enrollment in this act. The fact that the Act of 1917 was enlarged by the amending Act of May 16, 1918, c. 75, 40 Stat. 553, of course, does not affect the present indictment and would not, even if the former act had been repealed. Rev. Stats., § 13.

Judgments affirmed.

Fourteen Points Speech, *Woodrow Wilson*, 1918

*Delivered to a joint session of Congress while World War I still raged, the speech repro-
duced here sets forth Wilson's view of the principles and specific actions necessary to secure
a just and lasting peace in Europe and throughout the world. Many of Wilson's points
attempted to address deep-seated geographical and cultural problems and the results of the
war itself. Other, more general, points sought the vindication of Wilsonian principles of
international human rights, including free trade, the elimination of secret treaties, and
the redrawing of national borders to reflect people's cultural and other ties. Once the war
ended, Wilson sought to enshrine his Fourteen Points in the Versailles Treaty. His partial
success was further limited by the United States' refusal to ratify that treaty.*

Fourteen Points Speech

January 8, 1918

Woodrow Wilson

ADDRESS BY THE PRESIDENT OF THE UNITED STATES.

The address of the President of the United States, this day
delivered at a joint session of the two Houses of Congress, is
as follows:

Gentlemen of the Congress, once more, as repeatedly before, the spokesmen of the Central Empires have indicated
their desire to discuss the objects of the war and the possible
bases of a general peace. Parleys have been in progress at Brest-
Litovsk between Russian representatives and representatives
of the Central Powers, in which the attention of all the belligerents has been invited for the purpose of ascertaining whether
it may be possible to extend these parleys into a general conference with regard to terms of peace and settlement. The
Russian representatives presented not only a perfectly definite
statement of the principles upon which they would be willing
to conclude peace, but also an equally definite programme of
the concrete application of those principles. The representatives of the Central Powers, on their part, presented an outline of settlement which, if much less definite, seemed suscep
tible of liberal interpretation until their specific programme
of practical terms was added. That programme proposed no
concessions at all either to the sovereignty of Russia or to the
preferences of the populations with whose fortunes it dealt,
but meant, in a word, that the Central Empires were to keep

every foot of territory their armed forces had occupied,—
every province, every city, every point of vantage,—as a permanent addition to their territories and their power. It is a reasonable conjecture that the general principles of settlement
which they at first suggested originated with the more liberal
statesmen of Germany and Austria, the men who have begun
to feel the force of their own peoples' thought and purpose,
while the concrete terms of actual settlement came from the
military leaders who have no thought but to keep what they
have got. The negotiations have been broken off. The Russian representatives were sincere and in earnest. They cannot
entertain such proposals of conquest and domination.

The whole incident is full of significance. It is also full of
perplexity. With whom are the Russian representatives dealing? For whom are the representatives of the Central Empires
speaking? Are they speaking for the majorities of their respective parliaments or for the minority parties, that military
and imperialistic minority which has so far dominated their
whole policy and controlled the affairs of Turkey and of the
Balkan states which have felt obliged to become their associates in the war? The Russian representatives have insisted,
very justly, very wisely, and in the true spirit of modern democracy, that the conferences they have been holding with

the Teutonic and Turkish statesmen should be held within open, not closed, doors, and all the world has been audience, as was desired. To whom have we been listening, then? To those who speak the spirit and intention of the Resolutions of the German Reichstag of the ninth of July last, the spirit and intention of the liberal leaders and parties of Germany, or to those who resist and defy that spirit and intention and insist upon conquest and subjugation? Or are we listening, in fact, to both, unreconciled and in open and hopeless contradiction? These are very serious and pregnant questions. Upon the answer to them depends the peace of the world.

But, whatever the results of the parleys at Brest-Litovsk, whatever the confusions of counsel and of purpose in the utterances of the spokesmen of the Central Empires, they have again attempted to acquaint the world with their objects in the war and have again challenged their adversaries to say what their objects are and what sort of settlement they would deem just and satisfactory. There is no good reason why that challenge should not be responded to, and responded to with the utmost candor. We did not wait for it. Not once, but again and again, we have laid our whole thought and purpose before the world, not in general terms only, but each time with sufficient definition to make it clear what sort of definitive terms of settlement must necessarily spring out of them. Within the last week Mr. Lloyd George has spoken with admirable candor and in admirable spirit for the people and Government of Great Britain. There is no confusion of counsel among the adversaries of the Central Powers, no uncertainty of principle, no vagueness of detail. The only secrecy of counsel, the only lack of fearless frankness, the only failure to make definite statement of the objects of the war, lies with Germany and her Allies. The issues of life and death hang upon these definitions. No statesman who has the least conception of his responsibility ought for a moment to permit himself to continue this tragical and appalling outpouring of blood and treasure unless he is sure beyond a peradventure that the objects of the vital sacrifice are part and parcel of the very life of Society and that the people for whom he speaks think them right and imperative as he does.

There is, moreover, a voice calling for these definitions of principle and of purpose which is, it seems to me, more thrilling and more compelling than any of the many moving voices with which the troubled air of the world is filled. It is the voice of the Russian people. They are prostrate and all but helpless, it would seem, before the grim power of Germany, which has hitherto known no relenting and no pity. Their

power, apparently, is shattered. And yet their soul is not subservient. They will not yield either in principle or in action. Their conception of what is right, of what it is humane and honorable for them to accept, has been stated with a frankness, a largeness of view, a generosity of spirit, and a universal human sympathy which must challenge the admiration of every friend of mankind; and they have refused to compound their ideals or desert others that they themselves may be safe. They call to us to say what it is that we desire, in what, if in anything, our purpose and our spirit differ from theirs: and I believe that the people of the United States would wish me to respond, with utter simplicity and frankness. Whether their present leaders believe it or not, it is our heartfelt desire and hope that some way may be opened whereby we may be privileged to assist the people of Russia to attain their utmost hope of liberty and ordered peace.

It will be our wish and purpose that the processes of peace, when they are begun, shall be absolutely open and that they shall involve and permit henceforth no secret understandings of any kind. The day of conquest and aggrandizement is gone by; so is also the day of secret covenants entered into in the interest of particular governments and likely at some unlooked-for moment to upset the peace of the world. It is this happy fact, now clear to the view of every public man whose thoughts do not still linger in an age that is dead and gone, which makes it possible for every nation whose purposes are consistent with justice and the peace of the world to avow now or at any other time the objects it has in view.

We entered this war because violations of right had occurred which touched us to the quick and made the life of our own people impossible unless they were corrected and the world secured once for all against their recurrence. What we demand in this war, therefore, is nothing peculiar to ourselves. It is that the world be made fit and safe to live in; and particularly that it be made safe for every peace-loving nation which, like our own, wishes to live its own life, determine its own institutions, be assured of justice and fair dealing by the other peoples of the world as against force and selfish aggression. All the peoples of the world are in effect partners in this interest, and for our own part we see very clearly that unless justice be done to others it will not be done to us. The programme of the world's peace, therefore, is our programme; and that programme, the only possible programme, as we see it, is this:

I. Open covenants of peace openly arrived at, after which there shall be no private international understandings of any kind but diplomacy shall proceed always frankly and in the public view.

II. Absolute freedom of navigation upon the seas, outside territorial waters, alike in peace and in war, except as the seas may be closed in whole or in part by international action for the enforcement of international covenants.

III. The removal, so far as possible, of all economic barriers and the establishment of an equality of trade conditions among all the nations consenting to the peace and associating themselves for its maintenance.

IV. Adequate guarantees given and taken that national armaments will be reduced to the lowest point consistent with domestic safety.

V. A free, open-minded, and absolutely impartial adjustment of all colonial claims, based upon a strict observance of the principle that in determining all such questions of sovereignty the interests of the populations concerned must have equal weight with the equitable claims of the government where this is to be determined.

VI. The evacuation of all Russian territory and such a settlement of all questions affecting Russia as will secure the best and freest cooperation of the other nations of the world in obtaining for her an unhampered and unembarrassed opportunity for the independent determination of her own political development and national policy and assure her of a sincere welcome into the society of free nations under institutions of her own choosing and, more than a welcome, assistance also of every kind that she may need and may herself desire. The treatment accorded Russia by her sister nations in the months to come will be the acid test of their good will, of their comprehension of her needs, as distinguished from their own interests, and of their intelligent and unselfish sympathy.

VII. Belgium, the whole world will agree, must be evacuated and restored, without any attempt to limit the sovereignty which she enjoys in common with all other free nations. No other single act will serve as this will serve to restore confidence among the nations in the laws which they have themselves set and determined for the government of their relations with one another. Without this healing act the whole structure and validity of international law is forever impaired.

VIII. All French territory should be freed and the invaded portions restored, and the wrong done to France by Prussia in 1871 in the matter of Alsace-Lorraine, which has unsettled the peace of the world for nearly fifty years, should be righted, in order that peace may once more be made secure in the interest of all.

IX. A readjustment of the frontiers of Italy should be effected along clearly recognizable lines of nationality.

X. The peoples of Austria-Hungary, whose place among the nations we wish to see safeguarded and assured, should be accorded the freest opportunity of autonomous development.

XI. Rumania, Serbia, and Montenegro should be evacuated; occupied territories restored; Serbia accorded free and secure access to the sea; and the relations of the several Balkan states to one another determined by friendly counsel along historically established lines of allegiance and nationality; and international guarantees of the political and economic independence and territorial integrity of the several Balkan states should be entered into.

XII. The Turkish portions of the present Ottoman Empire should be assured a secure sovereignty, but the other nationalities which are now under Turkish rule should be assured an undoubted security of life and an absolutely unmolested opportunity of autonomous development, and the Dardanelles should be permanently opened as a free passage to the ships and commerce of all nations under international guarantees.

XIII. An independent Polish state should be erected which should include the territories inhabited by indisputably Polish populations, which should be assured a free and secure access to the sea, and whose political and economic independence and territorial integrity should be guaranteed by international covenant.

XIV. A general association of nations must be formed under specific covenants for the purpose of affording mutual guarantees of political independence and territorial integrity to great and small states alike.

In regard to these essential rectifications of wrong and assertions of right we feel ourselves to be intimate partners of all the governments and peoples associated together against the Imperialists. We cannot be separate in interest or divided in purpose. We stand together until the end.

For such arrangements and covenants we are willing to fight and to continue to fight until they are achieved; but only because we wish the right to prevail and desire a just and stable peace such as can be secured only by removing the chief provocations to war, which this programme does remove. We have no jealousy of German greatness, and there is nothing in this programme that impairs it. We grudge her no achievement or distinction of learning or of pacific enterprise such as have made her record very bright and very enviable. We do not wish to injure her or to block in any way her legitimate influence or power. We do not wish to fight her either with arms or with hostile arrangements of trade if she is willing to associate herself with us and the other peace-loving nations of the world in covenants of justice and law and fair dealing. We wish her only to accept a place of equality among the peoples of the world,—the new world in which we now live,—instead of a place of mastery.

Neither do we presume to suggest to her any alteration or modification of her institutions. But it is necessary, we must frankly say, and necessary as a preliminary to any intelligent dealings with her on our part, that we should know whom her spokesmen speak for when they speak to us, whether for the Reichstag majority or for the military party and the men whose creed is imperial domination.

We have spoken now, surely, in terms too concrete to admit of any further doubt or question. An evident principle runs through the whole programme I have outlined. It is the principle of justice to all peoples and nationalities, and their right to live on equal terms of liberty and safety with one another, whether they be strong or weak. Unless this principle be made its foundation no part of the structure of international justice can stand. The people of the United States could act upon no other principle; and to the vindication of this principle they are ready to devote their lives, their honor, and everything they possess. The moral climax of this the culminating and final war for human liberty has come, and they are ready to put their own strength, their own highest purpose, their own integrity and devotion to the test.

Covenant of the League of Nations, 1919

Speech against the League of Nations, *Henry Cabot Lodge,* 1919

The last "point" in President Wilson's Fourteen Points speech declared the need for an international body that would guarantee the independence and territorial integrity of all nations. Wilson successfully made this same proposal to other Allied leaders as part of the peace process. The resulting covenant, or agreement, established a League of Nations, originally encompassing forty-two countries. The covenant, included in the Versailles Treaty, which officially ended World War I, includes provisions for international organizations to assist in the League's goal of world peace through measures aimed at assisting refugees, moving colonies to independence, promoting health, and combating slavery and other public ills. The League's primary diplomatic role involved it in numerous conflicts and potential conflicts until the eventual beginning of World War II. It was supplanted by the United Nations after the end of that war. U.S. senator Henry Cabot Lodge (1850–1924) was a leading opponent of the League. In the speech reproduced here he argues against the practicality of any institution aiming at perpetual peace, as well as any international body that would impinge on the sovereignty of the United States. Wilson campaigned around the nation in favor of the League but refused any compromise with his opponents in the Senate (which must ratify any treaty). In the end, the Senate refused to ratify the Versailles Treaty or join the League.

Covenant of the League of Nations

February 14, 1919

The High Contracting Parties, in order to promote international co-operation and to achieve international peace and security by the acceptance of obligations not to resort to war, by the prescription of open, just and honourable relations between nations, by the firm establishment of the understandings of international law as the actual rule of conduct among Governments, and by the maintenance of justice and a scrupulous respect for all treaty obligations in the dealings of organised peoples with one another, agree to this Covenant of the League of Nations.

ARTICLE I

The original Members of the League shall be those of the Signatories which are named in the Annex to this Covenant and also such of those other States named in the Annex as shall accede without reservation to this Covenant. Such accession shall be effected by a Declaration deposited with the Secretariat within two months of the coming into force of the Covenant. Notice thereof shall be sent to all other Members of the League.

Any fully self-governing State, Dominion or Colony not named in the Annex, may become a Member of the League if its admission is agreed to by two-thirds of the Assembly, provided that it shall give effective guarantees of its sincere intention to observe its international obligations, and shall accept such regulations as may be prescribed by the League in regard to its military, naval and air forces and armaments.

Any Member of the League may, after two years' notice of its intention so to do, withdraw from the League, provided that all its international obligations and all its obligations under this Covenant shall have been fulfilled at the time of its withdrawal.

ARTICLE II

The action of the League under this Covenant shall be effected through the instrumentality of an Assembly and of a Council, with a permanent Secretariat.

ARTICLE III

The Assembly shall consist of Representatives of the Members of the League.

The Assembly shall meet at stated intervals and from time

to time as occasion may require, at the Seat of the League or at such other place as may be decided upon.

The Assembly may deal at its meetings with any matter within the sphere of action of the League or affecting the peace of the world.

At meetings of the Assembly each Member of the League shall have one vote, and may have not more than three Representatives.

ARTICLE IV

The Council shall consist of Representatives of the Principal Allied and Associated Powers, together with Representatives of four other Members of the League. These four Members of the League shall be selected by the Assembly from time to time in its discretion. Until the appointment of the Representatives of the four Members of the League first selected by the Assembly, Representatives of Belgium, Brazil, Greece, and Spain shall be members of the Council.

With the approval of the majority of the Assembly, the Council may name additional Members of the League whose Representatives shall always be members of the Council; the Council with like approval may increase the number of Members of the League to be selected by the Assembly for representation on the Council.

The Council shall meet from time to time as occasion may require, and at least once a year, at the Seat of the League, or at such other place as may be decided upon.

The Council may deal at its meetings with any matter within the sphere of action of the League or affecting the peace of the world.

Any Member of the League not represented on the Council shall be invited to send a Representative to sit as a member at any meeting of the Council during the consideration of matters specially affecting the interests of that Member of the League.

At meetings of the Council each Member of the League represented on the Council shall have one vote, and may have not more than one Representative.

ARTICLE V

Except where otherwise expressly provided in this Covenant or by the terms of the present Treaty, decisions at any meeting of the Assembly or of the Council shall require the agreement of all the Members of the League represented at the meeting.

All matters of procedure at meetings of the Assembly or of the Council, including the appointment of committees to investigate particular matters, shall be regulated by the Assembly or by the Council, and may be decided by a majority of the Members of the League represented at the meeting.

The first meeting of the Assembly and the first meeting of the Council shall be summoned by the President of the United States of America.

ARTICLE VI

The permanent Secretariat shall be established at the Seat of the League. The Secretariat shall comprise a Secretary-General and such secretaries and staff as may be required.

The first Secretary-General shall be the person named in the Annex; thereafter the Secretary-General shall be appointed by the Council with the approval of the majority of the Assembly.

The secretaries and staff of the Secretariat shall be appointed by the Secretary-General with the approval of the Council.

The Secretary-General shall act in that capacity at all meetings of the Assembly and of the Council.

The expenses of the Secretariat shall be borne by the Members of the League in accordance with the apportionment of the expenses of the International Bureau of the Universal Postal Union.

ARTICLE VII

The Seat of the League is established at Geneva.

The Council may at any time decide that the Seat of the League shall be established elsewhere.

All positions under or in connection with the League, including the Secretariat, shall be open equally to men and women.

Representatives of the Members of the League and officials of the League when engaged on the business of the League shall enjoy diplomatic privileges and immunities.

The buildings and other property occupied by the League or its officials or by Representatives attending its meetings shall be inviolable.

ARTICLE VIII

The Members of the League recognise that the maintenance of peace requires the reduction of national armaments to the lowest point consistent with national safety and the enforcement by common action of international obligations.

The Council, taking account of the geographical situation

and circumstances of each State, shall formulate plans for such reduction for the consideration and action of the several Governments.

Such plans shall be subject to reconsideration and revision at least every ten years.

After these plans shall have been adopted by the several Governments, the limits of armaments therein fixed shall not be exceeded without the concurrence of the Council.

The Members of the League agree that the manufacture by private enterprise of munitions and implements of war is open to grave objections. The Council shall advise how the evil effects attendant upon such manufacture can be prevented, due regard being had to the necessities of those Members of the League which are not able to manufacture the munitions and implements of war necessary for their safety.

The Members of the League undertake to interchange full and frank information as to the scale of their armaments, their military, naval and air programmes and the condition of such of their industries as are adaptable to war-like purposes.

ARTICLE IX

A permanent Commission shall be constituted to advise the Council on the execution of the provisions of Articles I and VIII, and on military, naval and air questions generally.

ARTICLE X

The Members of the League undertake to respect and preserve as against external aggression the territorial integrity and existing political independence of all Members of the League. In case of any such aggression or in case of any threat or danger of such aggression the Council shall advise upon the means by which this obligation shall be fulfilled.

ARTICLE XI

Any war or threat of war, whether immediately affecting any of the Members of the League or not, is hereby declared a matter of concern to the whole League, and the League shall take any action that may be deemed wise and effectual to safeguard the peace of nations. In case any such emergency should arise the Secretary-General shall on the request of any Member of the League forthwith summon a meeting of the Council.

It is also declared to be the friendly right of each Member of the League to bring to the attention of the Assembly or of the Council any circumstance whatever affecting international relations which threatens to disturb international peace or the good understanding between nations upon which peace depends.

ARTICLE XII

The Members of the League agree that if there should arise between them any dispute likely to lead to a rupture, they will submit the matter either to arbitration or to inquiry by the Council, and they agree in no case to resort to war until three months after the award by the arbitrators or the report by the Council.

In any case under this Article the award of the arbitrators shall be made within a reasonable time, and the report of the Council shall be made within six months after the submission of the dispute.

ARTICLE XIII

The Members of the League agree that whenever any dispute shall arise between them which they recognise to be suitable for submission to arbitration and which cannot be satisfactorily settled by diplomacy, they will submit the whole subject-matter to arbitration.

Disputes as to the interpretation of a treaty, as to any question of international law, as to the existence of any fact which if established would constitute a breach of any international obligation, or as to the extent and nature of the reparation to be made for any such breach, are declared to be among those which are generally suitable for submission to arbitration.

For the consideration of any such dispute the court of arbitration to which the case is referred shall be the court agreed on by the parties to the dispute or stipulated in any convention existing between them.

The Members of the League agree that they will carry out in full good faith any award that may be rendered and that they will not resort to war against a Member of the League which complies therewith. In the event of any failure to carry out such an award, the Council shall propose what steps should be taken to give effect thereto.

ARTICLE XIV

The Council shall formulate and submit to the Members of the League for adoption plans for the establishment of a Permanent Court of International Justice. The Court shall be competent to hear and determine any dispute of an international character which the parties thereto submit to it. The Court may also give an advisory opinion upon any dispute or question referred to it by the Council or by the Assembly.

Article XV

If there should arise between Members of the League any dispute likely to lead to a rupture, which is not submitted to arbitration as above, the Members of the League agree that they will submit the matter to the Council. Any party to the dispute may effect such submission by giving notice of the existence of the dispute to the Secretary-General who will make all necessary arrangements for a full investigation and consideration thereof.

For this purpose the parties to the dispute will communicate to the Secretary-General, as promptly as possible, statements of their case with all the relevant facts and papers, and the Council may forthwith direct the publication thereof.

The Council shall endeavour to effect a settlement of the dispute, and if such efforts are successful, a statement shall be made public giving such facts and explanations regarding the dispute and the terms of settlement thereof as the Council may deem appropriate.

If the dispute is not thus settled, the Council, either unanimously or by a majority vote, shall make and publish a report containing a statement of the facts of the dispute and the recommendations which are deemed just and proper in regard thereto.

Any Member of the League represented on the Council may make public a statement of the facts of the dispute and of its conclusions regarding the same.

If a report by the Council is unanimously agreed to by the members thereof other than the Representatives of one or more of the parties to the dispute, the Members of the League agree that they will not go to war with any party to the dispute which complies with the recommendations of the report.

If the Council fails to reach a report which is unanimously agreed to by the members thereof, other than the Representatives of one or more of the parties to the dispute, the Members of the League reserve to themselves the right to take such action as they shall consider necessary for the maintenance of right and justice.

If the dispute between the parties is claimed by one of them, and is found by the Council to arise out of a matter which by international law is solely within the domestic jurisdiction of that party, the Council shall so report, and shall make no recommendation as to its settlement.

The Council may in any case under this Article refer the dispute to the Assembly. The dispute shall be so referred at the request of either party to the dispute, provided that such request be made within fourteen days after the submission of the dispute to the Council.

In any case referred to the Assembly, all the provisions of this Article and of Article XII relating to the action and powers of the Council shall apply to the action and powers of the Assembly, provided that a report made by the Assembly, if concurred in by the Representatives of those Members of the League represented on the Council and of a majority of the other Members of the League, exclusive in each case of the Representatives of the parties to the dispute, shall have the same force as a report by the Council concurred in by all the members thereof other than the Representatives of one or more of the parties to the dispute.

Article XVI

Should any Member of the League resort to war in disregard of its covenants under Articles XII, XIII, or XV, it shall *ipso facto* be deemed to have committed an act of war against all other Members of the League, which hereby undertake immediately to subject it to the severance of all trade or financial relations, the prohibition of all intercourse between their nationals and the nationals of the covenant-breaking State, and the prevention of all financial, commercial, or personal intercourse between the nationals of the covenant-breaking State and the nationals of any other State, whether a Member of the League or not.

It shall be the duty of the Council in such case to recommend to the several Governments concerned what effective military, naval or air force the Members of the League shall severally contribute to the armed forces to be used to protect the covenants of the League.

The Members of the League agree, further, that they will mutually support one another in the financial and economic measures which are taken under this article, in order to minimise the loss and inconvenience resulting from the above measures, and that they will mutually support one another in resisting any special measures aimed at one of their number by the covenant-breaking State, and that they will take the necessary steps to afford passage through their territory to the forces of any of the Members of the League which are co-operating to protect the covenants of the League.

Any member of the League which has violated any covenant of the League may be declared to be no longer a Member of the League by a vote of the Council concurred in by the Representatives of all the other Members of the League represented thereon.

ARTICLE XVII

In the event of a dispute between a Member of the League and a State which is not a Member of the League, or between States not Members of the League, the State or States not Members of the League shall be invited to accept the obligations of membership in the League for the purposes of such dispute, upon such conditions as the Council may deem just. If such invitation is accepted, the provisions of Articles XII to XVI inclusive shall be applied with such modifications as may be deemed necessary by the Council.

Upon such invitation being given the Council shall immediately institute an inquiry into the circumstances of the dispute and recommend such action as may seem best and most effectual in the circumstances.

If a State so invited shall refuse to accept the obligations of membership in the League for the purposes of such dispute, and shall resort to war against a Member of the League, the provisions of Article XVI shall be applicable as against the State taking such action.

If both parties to the dispute when so invited refuse to accept the obligations of membership in the League for the purposes of such dispute, the Council may take such measures and make such recommendations as will prevent hostilities and will result in the settlement of the dispute.

ARTICLE XVIII

Every treaty or international engagement entered into hereafter by any Member of the League shall be forthwith registered with the Secretariat and shall as soon as possible be published by it. No such treaty or international engagement shall be binding until so registered.

ARTICLE XIX

The Assembly may from time to time advise the reconsideration by Members of the League of treaties which have become inapplicable and the consideration of international conditions whose continuance might endanger the peace of the world.

ARTICLE XX

The Members of the League severally agree that this Covenant is accepted as abrogating all obligations or understandings *inter se* which are inconsistent with the terms thereof, and solemnly undertake that they will not hereafter enter into any engagements inconsistent with the terms thereof.

In case any Member of the League shall, before becoming a Member of the League, have undertaken any obligations inconsistent with the terms of this Covenant, it shall be the duty of such Member to take immediate steps to procure its release from such obligations.

ARTICLE XXI

Nothing in this Covenant shall be deemed to affect the validity of international engagements such as treaties of arbitration or regional understandings like the Monroe Doctrine for securing the maintenance of peace.

ARTICLE XXII

To those colonies and territories which as a consequence of the late war have ceased to be under the sovereignty of the States which formerly governed them and which are inhabited by peoples not yet able to stand by themselves under the strenuous conditions of the modern world, there should be applied the principle that the well-being and development of such peoples form a sacred trust of civilisation and that securities for the performance of this trust should be embodied in this Covenant.

The best method of giving practical effect to this principle is that the tutelage of such peoples should be entrusted to advanced nations who by reason of their resources, their experience or their geographical position, can best undertake this responsibility, and who are willing to accept it, and that this tutelage should be exercised by them as Mandatories on behalf of the League.

The character of the mandate must differ according to the stage of the development of the people, the geographical situation of the territory, its economic conditions and other similar circumstances.

Certain communities formerly belonging to the Turkish Empire have reached a stage of development where their existence as independent nations can be provisionally recognised subject to the rendering of administrative advice and assistance by a Mandatory until such time as they are able to stand alone. The wishes of these communities must be a principal consideration in the selection of the Mandatory.

Other peoples, especially those of Central Africa, are at such a stage that the Mandatory must be responsible for the administration of the territory under conditions which will guarantee freedom of conscience or religion, subject only to the maintenance of public order and morals, the prohibition of abuses such as the slave trade, the arms traffic and the liquor traffic, and the prevention of the establishment of fortifications or military and naval bases and of military training of the natives for other than police purposes and the defence of territory, and will also secure equal opportunities for the trade and commerce of other Members of the League.

There are territories, such as South-West Africa and certain of the South Pacific Islands, which, owing to the sparseness of their population, or their small size, or their remoteness from the centres of civilisation, or their geographical contiguity to the territory of the Mandatory, and other circumstances, can be best administered under the laws of the Mandatory as integral portions of its territory, subject to the safeguards above mentioned in the interests of the indigenous population.

In every case of mandate, the Mandatory shall render to the Council an annual report in reference to the territory committed to its charge.

The degree of authority, control, or administration to be exercised by the Mandatory shall, if not previously agreed upon by the Members of the League, be explicitly defined in each case by the Council.

A permanent Commission shall be constituted to receive and examine the annual reports of the Mandatories and to advise the Council on all matters relating to the observance of the mandates.

ARTICLE XXIII

Subject to and in accordance with the provisions of international conventions existing or hereafter to be agreed upon, the Members of the League—

(a) will endeavour to secure and maintain fair and humane conditions of labour for men, women, and children, both in their own countries and in all countries to which their commercial and industrial relations extend, and for that purpose will establish and maintain the necessary international organisations;

(b) undertake to secure just treatment of the native inhabitants of territories under their control;

(c) will entrust the League with the general supervision over the execution of agreements with regard to the traffic in women and children, and the traffic in opium and other dangerous drugs;

(d) will entrust the League with the general supervision of the trade in arms and ammunition with the countries in which the control of this traffic is necessary in the common interest;

(e) will make provision to secure and maintain freedom of communications and of transit and equitable treatment for the commerce of all Members of the League. In this connection, the special necessities of the regions devastated during the war of 1914–1918 shall be borne in mind;

(f) will endeavour to take steps in matters of international concern for the prevention and control of disease.

ARTICLE XXIV

There shall be placed under the direction of the League all international bureaux already established by general treaties if the parties to such treaties consent. All such international bureaux and all commissions for the regulation of matters of international interest hereafter constituted shall be placed under the direction of the League.

In all matters of international interest which are regulated by general conventions but which are not placed under the control of international bureaux or commissions, the Secretariat of the League shall, subject to the consent of the Council and if desired by the parties, collect and distribute all relevant information and shall render any other assistance which may be necessary or desirable.

The Council may include as part of the expenses of the Secretariat the expenses of any bureau or commission which is placed under the direction of the League.

ARTICLE XXV

The Members of the League agree to encourage and promote the establishment and co-operation of duly authorised voluntary national Red Cross organisations having as purposes the improvement of health, the prevention of disease and the mitigation of suffering throughout the world.

ARTICLE XXVI

Amendments to this Covenant will take effect when ratified by the Members of the League whose Representatives compose the Council and by a majority of the Members of the League whose Representatives compose the Assembly.

No such amendment shall bind any Member of the League which signifies its dissent therefrom, but in that case it shall cease to be a Member of the League.

Speech against the League of Nations

August 12, 1919

Henry Cabot Lodge

LEAGUE OF NATIONS.

Mr. LODGE. Mr. President, in the Essays of Elia, one of the most delightful is that entitled "Popular Fallacies." There is one very popular fallacy, however, which Lamb did not include in his list and that is the common saying that history repeats itself. Universal negatives are always dangerous, but if there is anything which is fairly certain, it is that history never exactly repeats itself. Popular fallacies, nevertheless, generally have some basis, and this saying springs from the undoubted truth that mankind from generation to generation is constantly repeating itself. We have an excellent illustration of this fact in the proposed experiment now before us, of making arrangements to secure the permanent peace of the world. To assure the peace of the world by a combination of the nations is no new idea. Leaving out the leagues of antiquity and of mediaeval times and going back no further than the treaty of Utrecht at the beginning of the eighteenth century, we find that at that period a project of a treaty to establish perpetual peace was brought forward in 1713 by the Abbé de Saint-Pierre. The treaty of Utrecht was to be the basis of an international system. A European league or Christian republic was to be set up, under which the members were to renounce the right of making war against each other and submit their disputes for arbitration to a central tribunal of the allies, the decisions of which were to be enforced by a common armament. I need not point out the resemblance between this theory and that which underlies the present league of nations. It was widely discussed during the eighteenth century, receiving much support in public opinion; and Voltaire said that the nations of Europe, united by ties of religion, institutions, and culture, were really but a single family. The idea remained in an academic condition until 1791, when under the pressure of the French Revolution Count Kaunitz sent out a circular letter in the name of Leopold of Austria, urging that it was the duty of all the powers to make common cause for the purpose of "preserving public peace, tranquillity of States, the inviolability of possessions, and the faith of treaties," which has a very familiar sound. Napoleon had a scheme of his own for consolidating the great European peoples and establishing a central assembly, but the Napoleonic idea differed from that of the eighteenth century, as one would expect. A single great personality dominated and hovered over all. In 1804 the Emperor Alexander took up the question, and urged a general treaty for the formation of a European confederation. "Why could one not submit to it," the Emperor asked, "the positive rights of nations, assure the privilege of neutrality, insert the obligation of never beginning war until all the resources which the mediation of a third party could offer have been exhausted, until the grievances have by this means been brought to light, and an effort to remove them has been made? On principles such as these one could proceed to a general pacification, and give birth to a league of which the stipulations would form, so to speak, a new code of the law of nations, while those who should try to infringe it would risk bringing upon themselves the forces of the new union."

The Emperor, moved by more immediately alluring visions, put aside this scheme at the treaty of Tilsit and then decided that peace could best be restored to the world by having two all-powerful emperors, one of the east and one of the west. After the Moscow campaign, however, he returned to his early dream. Under the influence of the Baroness von Krudener he became a devotee of a certain mystic pietism which for some time guided his public acts, and I think it may be fairly said that his liberal and popular ideas of that period, however vague and uncertain, were sufficiently genuine. Based upon the treaties of alliance against France, those of Chaumont and of Vienna, was the final treaty of Paris, of November 20, 1815. In the preamble the signatories, who were Great Britain, Austria, Russia, and Prussia, stated that it is the purpose of the ensuing treaty and their desire "to employ all their means to prevent the general tranquillity—the object of the wishes of mankind and the constant end of their efforts—from being again disturbed; desirous, moreover, to draw closer the ties which unite them for the common interests of their people, have resolved to give to the principles solemnly laid down in the treaties of Chaumont of March 1, 1814, and of Vienna of March 25, 1815, the application the most analogous to the present state of affairs, and to fix beforehand by a solemn treaty the principles which they propose to follow, in order to guarantee Europe from dangers by which she may still be menaced."

Then follow five articles which are devoted to an agreement to hold France in control and check, based largely on other more detailed agreements. But in article 6 it is said:

> To facilitate and to secure the execution of the present treaty, and to consolidate the connections which at the present moment so closely unite the four sovereigns for the happiness of the world, the high contracting parties have agreed to renew their meeting at fixed periods, either under the immediate auspices of the sovereigns themselves, or by their respective ministers, for the purpose of consulting upon their common interests, and for the consideration of the measures which at each of those periods shall be considered the most salutary for the repose and prosperity of nations and for the maintenance of the peace of Europe.

Certainly nothing could be more ingenuous or more praiseworthy than the purposes of the alliance being formed, and yet it was this very combination of powers which was destined to grow into what has been known, and we might add cursed, throughout history as the Holy Alliance.

As early as 1818 it had become apparent that upon this innocent statement might be built an alliance which was to be used to suppress the rights of nationalities and every attempt of any oppressed people to secure their freedom. Lord Castlereagh was a Tory of the Tories, but at that time, only three years after the treaty of Paris when the representatives of the alliance met at Aix-la-Chapelle he began to suspect that this new European system was wholly inconsistent with the liberties to which Englishmen of all types were devoted. At the succeeding meetings, at Troppau and Laibach, his suspicion was confirmed and England began to draw away from her partners. He had indeed determined to break with the alliance before the Congress of Verona, but his death threw the question into the hands of George Canning, who stands forth as the man who separated Great Britain from the combination of the continental powers. The attitude of England, which was defined in a memorandum where it was said that nothing could be more injurious to the idea of government generally than the belief that their force was collectively to be prostituted to the support of an established power without any consideration of the extent to which it was to be abused, led to a compromise in 1818 in which it was declared that it was the intention of the five powers, France being invited to adhere, "to maintain the intimate union, strengthened by the ties of Christian brotherhood, contracted by the sovereigns; to pronounce the object of this union to be the preservation of peace on the basis of respect for treaties." Admirable and gentle words these, setting forth purposes which all men must approve.

In 1820 the British Government stated that they were prepared to fulfill all treaty obligations, but that if it was desired "to extend the alliance so as to include all objects, present and future, foreseen and unforeseen, it would change its character to such an extent and carry us so far that we should see in it an additional motive for adhering to our course at the risk of seeing the alliance move away from us, without our having quitted it." The Czar Alexander abandoned his Liberal theories and threw himself into the arms of Metternich, as mean a tyrant as history can show, whose sinister designs probably caused as much misery and oppression in the years which followed as have ever been evolved by one man of second-rate abilities. The three powers, Russia, Austria, and Prussia, then put out a famous protocol in which it was said that the "States which have undergone a change of government due to revolution, the results of which threaten other States, ipso facto cease to be members of the European alliance, and remain excluded from it until their situation gives guaranties for legal order and stability. If, owing to such alterations, immediate danger threatens other States, the powers bind themselves, by peaceful means, or if need be by arms, to bring back the guilty State into the bosom of the great alliance." To this point had the innocent and laudable declarations of the treaty of Paris already developed. In 1822 England broke away and Canning made no secret of his pleasure at the breach. In a letter to the British minister at St. Petersburg he said:

So things are getting back to a wholesome state again. Every nation for itself, and God for us all. The time for Areopagus, and the like of that, is gone by.

He also said, in the same year, 1823: "What is the influence we have had in the counsels of the alliance, and which Prince Metternich exhorts us to be so careful not to throw away? We protested at Laibach; we remonstrated at Verona. Our protest was treated as waste paper; our remonstrances mingled with the air. Our influence, if it is to be maintained abroad, must be secure in the source of strength at home; and the sources of that strength are in the sympathy between the people and the Government; in the union of the public sentiment with the public counsels; in the reciprocal confidence and cooperation of the House of Commons and the Crown." These words of Canning are as applicable and as weighty now as when they were uttered and as worthy of consideration.

The Holy Alliance, thus developed by the three continental powers and accepted by France under the Bourbons, proceeded to restore the inquisition in Spain, to establish the Neapolitan Bourbons, who for 40 years were to subject the people of southern Italy to one of the most detestable tyrannies ever known, and proposed further to interfere against the colonies in South America which had revolted from Spain and to have their case submitted to a congress of the powers. It was then that Canning made his famous statement, "We have called a new world into existence to redress the balance of the old." It was at this point also that the United States intervened. The famous message of Monroe, sent to Congress on December 2, 1823, put an end to any danger of European influence in the American Continents. A distinguished English historian, Mr. William Alison Phillips, says:

The attitude of the United States effectually prevented the attempt to extend the dictatorship of the alliance beyond the bounds of Europe, in itself a great service to mankind.

In 1825 Great Britain recognized the South American Republics. So far as the New World was concerned the Holy Alliance had failed. It was deprived of the support of France by the revolution of 1830, but it continued to exist under the guidance of Metternich and its last exploit was in 1849, when the Emperor Nicholas sent a Russian army into Hungary to crush out the struggle of Kossuth for freedom and independence.

I have taken the trouble to trace in the merest outline the development of the Holy Alliance, so hostile and dangerous to human freedom, because I think it carries with it a lesson for us at the present moment, showing as it does what may come from general propositions and declarations of purposes in which all the world agrees. Turn to the preamble of the covenant of the league of nations now before us, which states the objects of the league. It is formed "in order to promote international cooperation and to achieve international peace and security by the acceptance of obligations not to resort to war, by the prescription of open, just, and honorable relations between nations, by the firm establishment of the understandings of international laws as the actual rule of conduct among governments, and by the maintenance of justice and a scrupulous respect for all treaty obligations in the dealings of organized peoples with one another."

No one would contest the loftiness or the benevolence of these purposes. Brave words, indeed! They do not differ essentially from the preamble of the treaty of Paris, from which sprang the Holy Alliance. But the covenant of this league contains a provision which I do not find in the treaty of Paris, and which is as follows:

The assembly may deal at its meetings with any matter within the sphere of action of the league or affecting the peace of the world.

There is no such sweeping or far-reaching provision as that in the treaty of Paris, and yet able men developed from that treaty the Holy Alliance, which England, and later France, were forced to abandon and which, for 35 years, was an unmitigated curse to the world. England broke from the Holy Alliance and the breach began three years after it was formed, because English statesmen saw that it was intended to turn the alliance—and this league is an alliance—into a means of repressing internal revolutions or insurrections. There was nothing in the treaty of Paris which warranted such action, but in this covenant of the league of nations the authority is clearly given in the third paragraph of article 3, where it is said:

The assembly may deal at its meetings with any matter within the sphere of action of the league or affecting the peace of the world.

No revolutionary movement, no internal conflict, of any magnitude can fail to affect the peace of the world. The

French Revolution, which was wholly internal at the beginning, affected the peace of the world to such an extent that it brought on a world war which lasted some 25 years. Can anyone say that our Civil War did not affect the peace of the world? At this very moment, who would deny that the condition of Russia, with internal conflicts raging in all parts of that great Empire, does not affect the peace of the world and therefore come properly within the jurisdiction of the league? "Any matter affecting the peace of the world" is a very broad statement which could be made to justify almost any interference on the part of the league with the internal affairs of other countries. That this fair and obvious interpretation is the one given to it abroad is made perfectly apparent in the direct and vigorous statement of M. Clemenceau in his letter to Mr. Paderewski, in which he takes the ground in behalf of the Jews and other nationalities in Poland that they should be protected, and where he says that the associated powers would feel themselves bound to secure guaranties in Poland "of certain essential rights which will afford to the inhabitants the necessary protection, whatever changes may take place in the internal constitution of the Polish Republic," he contemplates and defends interference with the internal affairs of Poland—among other things—in behalf of a complete religious freedom, a purpose with which we all deeply sympathize. These promises of the French prime minister are embodied in effective clauses in the treaties with Germany and with Poland and deal with the internal affairs of nations, and their execution is intrusted to the "principal allied and associated powers"; that is, to the United States, Great Britain, France, Italy, and Japan. This is a practical demonstration of what can be done under article 3 and under article 11 of the league covenant, and the authority which permits interference in behalf of religious freedom—an admirable object—is easily extended to the repression of internal disturbances, which may well prove a less admirable purpose. If Europe desires such an alliance or league with a power of this kind, so be it. I have no objection, provided they do not interfere with the American Continents or force us against our will but bound by a moral obligation into all the quarrels of Europe. If England, abandoning the policy of Canning, desires to be a member of a league which has such powers as this, I have not a word to say. But I object in the strongest possible way to having the United States agree, directly or indirectly, to be controlled by a league which may at any time, and perfectly lawfully and in accordance with the terms of the covenant, be drawn in to deal with internal conflicts in other countries, no

matter what those conflicts may be. We should never permit the United States to be involved in any internal conflict in another country, except by the will of her people expressed through the Congress which represents them.

With regard to wars of external aggression on a member of the league, the case is perfectly clear. There can be no genuine dispute whatever about the meaning of the first clause of article 10. In the first place, it differs from every other obligation in being individual and placed upon each nation without the intervention of the league. Each nation for itself promises to respect and preserve as against external aggression the boundaries and the political independence of every member of the league. Of the right of the United States to give such a guaranty I have never had the slightest doubt, and the elaborate arguments which have been made here and the learning which has been displayed about our treaty with Granada, now Colombia, and with Panama, were not necessary for me, because, I repeat, there can be no doubt of our right to give a guaranty to another nation that we will protect its boundaries and independence. The point I wish to make is that the pledge is an individual pledge. We have, for example, given guaranties to Panama and for obvious and sufficient reasons. The application of that guaranty would not be in the slightest degree affected by ten or twenty other nations giving the same pledge, if Panama, when in danger, appealed to us to fulfill our obligation. We should be bound to do so without the slightest reference to the other guarantors. In article 10 the United States is bound on the appeal of any member of the league not only to respect but to preserve its independence and its boundaries, and that pledge, if we give it, must be fulfilled.

There is to me no distinction whatever in a treaty between what some persons are pleased to call legal and moral obligation. A treaty rests and must rest, except where it is imposed under duress and securities and hostages are taken for its fulfillment, upon moral obligations. No doubt a great power impossible of coercion can cast aside a moral obligation if it sees fit and escape from the performance of the duty which it promises. The pathway of dishonor is always open. I for one, however, can not conceive of voting for a clause of which I disapprove because I know it can be escaped in that way. Whatever the United States agrees to, by that agreement she must abide. Nothing could so surely destroy all prospects of the world's peace as to have any powerful nation refuse to carry out an obligation, direct or indirect, because it rests only on moral grounds. Whatever we promise we must carry out to the full, "without mental reservation or purpose of evasion." To me any other attitude is inconceivable. Without the most absolute and minute good faith in carrying out a treaty to which we have agreed, without ever resorting to doubtful interpretations or to the plea that it is only a moral obligation, treaties are worthless. The greatest foundation of peace is the scrupulous observance of every promise, express or implied, of every pledge, whether it can be described as legal or moral. No vote should be given to any clause in any treaty or to any treaty except in this spirit and with this understanding.

I return, then, to the first clause of article 10. It is, I repeat, an individual obligation. It requires no action on the part of the league, except that in the second sentence the authorities of the league are to have the power to advise as to the means to be employed in order to fulfill the purpose of the first sentence. But that is a detail of execution, and I consider that we are morally and in honor bound to accept and act upon that advice. The broad fact remains that if any member of the league suffering from external aggression should appeal directly to the United States for support the United States would be bound to give that support in its own capacity and without reference to the action of other powers, because the United States itself is bound, and I hope the day will never come when the United States will not carry out its promises. If that day should come, and the United States or any other great country should refuse, no matter how specious the reasons, to fulfill both in letter and spirit every obligation in this covenant, the United States would be dishonored and the league would crumble into dust, leaving behind it a legacy of wars. If China should rise up and attack Japan in an effort to undo the great wrong of the cession of the control of Shantung to that power, we should be bound under the terms of article 10 to sustain Japan against China, and a guaranty of that sort is never invoked except when the question has passed beyond the stage of negotiation and has become a question for the application of force. I do not like the prospect. It shall not come into existence by any vote of mine.

Article 11 carries this danger still further, for it says:

Any war or threat of war, whether immediately affecting any of the members of the league or not, is hereby declared a matter of concern to the whole league and the league shall take any action that shall be deemed wise and effectual to safeguard the peace of nations.

"Any war or threat of war" means both external aggression and internal disturbance, as I have already pointed out in dealing with article 3. "Any action" covers military action, because it covers action of any sort or kind. Let me take an example, not an imaginary case, but one which may have been overlooked, because most people have not the slightest idea where or what a King of the Hejaz is. The following dispatch appeared recently in the newspapers:

HEJAZ AGAINST BEDOUINS

The forces of Emir Abdullah recently suffered a grave defeat, the Wahabis attacking and capturing Kurma, east of Mecca. Ibn Savond is believed to be working in harmony with the Wahabis. A squadron of the royal air force was ordered recently to go to the assistance of King Hussein.

Hussein I take to be the Sultan of Hejaz. He is being attacked by the Bedouins, as they are known to us, although I fancy the general knowledge about the Wahabis and Ibn Savond and Emir Abdullah is slight and the names mean but little to the American people. Nevertheless, here is a case of a member of the league—for the King of the Hejaz is such a member in good and regular standing and signed the treaty by his representatives, Mr. Rustem Haidar and Mr. Abdul Havi Aouni.

Under article 10, if King Hussein appealed to us for aid and protection against external aggression affecting his independence and the boundaries of his kingdom, we should be bound to give that aid and protection and to send American soldiers to Arabia. It is not relevant to say that this is unlikely to occur; that Great Britain is quite able to take care of King Hussein, who is her fair creation, reminding one a little of the Mosquito King, a monarch once developed by Great Britain on the Mosquito Coast of Central America. The fact that we should not be called upon does not alter the right which the King of Hejaz possesses to demand the sending of American troops to Arabia in order to preserve his independence against the assaults of the Wahabis or Bedouins. I am unwilling to give that right to King Hussein, and this illustrates the point which is to me the most objectionable in the league as it stands—the right of other powers to call out American troops and American ships to go to any part of the world, an obligation we are bound to fulfill under the terms of this treaty. I know the answer well—that of course they could not be sent without action by Congress. Congress would have no choice if acting in good faith, and if under article 10 any member of the league summoned us, or if under article 11 the league itself summoned us, we should be bound in honor and morally to obey. There would be no escape except by a breach of faith, and legislation by Congress under those circumstances would be a mockery of independent action. Is it too much to ask that provision should be made that American troops and American ships should never be sent anywhere or ordered to take part in any conflict except after the deliberate action of the American people, expressed according to the Constitution through their chosen representatives in Congress?

Let me now briefly point out the insuperable difficulty which I find in article 15. It begins: "If there should arise between members of the league any dispute likely to lead to a rupture." "Any dispute" covers every possible dispute. It therefore covers a dispute over tariff duties and over immigration. Suppose we have a dispute with Japan or with some European country as to immigration. I put aside tariff duties as less important than immigration. This is not an imaginary case. Of late years there has probably been more international discussion and negotiation about questions growing out of immigration laws than any other one subject. It comes within the definition of "any dispute" at the beginning of article 15. In the eighth paragraph of that article it is said that "if the dispute between the parties is claimed by one of them, and is found by the council to arise out of a matter which, by international law, is solely within the domestic jurisdic[t]ion of that party, the council shall so report and shall make no recommendation as to its settlement." That is one of the statements, of which there are several in this treaty where words are used which it is difficult to believe their authors could have written down in seriousness. They seem to have been put in for the same purpose as what is known in natural history as protective coloring. Protective coloring is intended so to merge the animal, the bird, or the insect in its background that it will be indistinguishable from its surroundings and difficult, if not impossible, to find the elusive and hidden bird, animal, or insect. Protective coloring here is used in the form of words to give an impression that we are perfectly safe upon immigration and tariffs, for example, because questions which international law holds to be solely within domestic jurisdiction are not to have any recommendation from the council, but the dangers are there just the same, like the cunningly colored insect on the tree or the young bird crouching motionless upon the sand. The words and the coloring are alike intended to deceive. I wish somebody would point out to me those provisions of international law which make a list of questions which are hard and fast within the domestic jurisdiction. No such distinction can be applied to tariff duties or immigra-

tion nor indeed finally and conclusively to any subject. Have we not seen the school laws of California, most domestic of subjects, rise to the dignity of a grave international dispute? No doubt both import duties and immigration are primarily domestic questions, but they both constantly involve and will continue to involve international effects. Like the protective coloration, this paragraph is wholly worthless unless it is successful in screening from the observer the existence of the animal, insect, or bird which it is desired to conceal. It fails to do so and the real object is detected. But even if this bit of deception was omitted—and so far as the question of immigration or tariff questions are concerned it might as well be—the ninth paragraph brings the important point clearly to the front. Immigration, which is the example I took, can not escape the action of the league by any claim of domestic jurisdiction; it has too many international aspects.

Article 9 says:

The council may, in any case under this article, refer the dispute to the assembly.

We have our dispute as to immigration with Japan or with one of the Balkan States, let us say. The council has the power to refer the dispute to the assembly. Moreover, the dispute shall be so referred at the request of either party to the dispute, provided that such request be made within 14 days after the submission of the dispute to the council. So that Japan or the Balkan States, for example, with which we may easily have the dispute, ask that it be referred to the assembly, and the immigration question between the United States and Jugoslavia or Japan, as the case may be, goes to the assembly. The United States and Japan or Jugoslavia are excluded from voting, and the provisions of article 12, relating to the action and powers of the council, apply to the action and powers of the assembly, provided, as set forth in article 15, that a report made by the assembly, "if concurred in by the representatives of those members of the league represented on the council and of a majority of the other members of the league, exclusive in each case of the representatives of the parties to the dispute, shall have the same force as a report by the council concurred in by all the members thereof other than the representatives of one or more of the parties to the dispute." This course of procedure having been pursued, we find the question of immigration between the United States and Japan is before the assembly for decision. The representatives of the council, except the delegates of the United States and of Japan or Jugoslavia, must all vote unanimously upon it, as I understand it, but a majority of the entire assembly, where the council will have only seven votes, will decide. Can anyone say beforehand what the decision of that assembly will be, in which the United States and Jugoslavia or Japan will have no vote? The question in one case may affect immigration from every country in Europe, although the dispute exists only for one, and in the other the whole matter of Asiatic immigration is involved. Is it too fanciful to think that it might be decided against us? For my purpose it matters not whether it is decided for or against us. An immigration dispute or a dispute over tariff duties, met by the procedure set forth in article 15, comes before the assembly of delegates for a decision by what is practically a majority vote of the entire assembly. That is something to which I do not find myself able to give my assent. So far as immigration is concerned, and also so far as tariff duties, although less important, are concerned, I deny the jurisdiction. There should be no possibility of other nations deciding who shall come into the United States or under what conditions they shall enter. The right to say who shall come into a country is one of the very highest attributes of sovereignty. If a nation can not say without appeal who shall come within its gates and become a part of its citizenship it has ceased to be a sovereign nation. It has become a tributary and a subject nation, and it makes no difference whether it is subject to a league or to a conqueror.

If other nations are willing to subject themselves to such a domination, the United States, to which many immigrants have come and many more will come, ought never to submit to it for a moment. They tell us that so far as Asiatic emigration is concerned there is not the slightest danger that that will ever be forced upon us by the league, because Australia and Canada and New Zealand are equally opposed to it. I think it highly improbable that it would be forced upon us under those conditions, but it is by no means impossible. It is true the United States has one vote, and that England, if you count the King of the Hejaz, has seven—in all eight—votes; yet it might not be impossible for Japan and China and Siam to rally enough other votes to defeat us; but whether we are protected in that way or not does not matter. The very offering of that explanation accepts the jurisdiction of the league, and personally I can not consent to putting the protection of my country and of her workingmen against undesirable immigration out of our own hands. We and we alone must say who shall come into the United States and become citizens of this Republic, and no one else should have any power to utter one word in regard to it.

Article 21 says:

Nothing in this covenant shall be deemed to affect the validity of international engagements, such as treaties of arbitration or regional understandings like the Monroe doctrine for securing the maintenance of peace.

This provision did not appear in the first draft of the covenant, and when the President explained the second draft of the convention to the peace conference he said:

Article 21 is new.

And that was all he said. No one can question the truth of the remark, but I trust I shall not be considered disrespectful if I say that it was not an illuminating statement. The article was new, but the fact of its novelty, which the President declared, was known to everyone who had taken the trouble to read the two documents. We were not left, however, without a fitting explanation. The British delegation took it upon themselves to explain article 21 at some length, and this is what they said:

Article 21 makes it clear that the covenant is not intended to abrogate or weaken any other agreements, so long as they are consistent with its own terms, into which members of the league may have entered or may hereafter enter for the assurance of peace. Such agreements would include special treaties for compulsory arbitration and military conventions that are genuinely defensive.

The Monroe doctrine and similar understandings are put in the same category. They have shown themselves in history to be not instruments of national ambition, but guarantees of peace. The origin of the Monroe doctrine is well known. It was proclaimed in 1823 to prevent America from becoming a theater for intrigues of European absolutism. At first a principle of American foreign policy, it has become an international understanding, and it is not illegitimate for the people of the United States to say that the covenant should recognize that fact.

In its essence it is consistent with the spirit of the covenant, and indeed, the principles of the league, as expressed in article 10, represent the extension to the whole world of the principles of the doctrine while, should any dispute as to the meaning of the latter ever arise between the American and European powers, the league is there to settle it.

The explanation of Great Britain received the assent of France.

It seems to me monumentally paradoxical and a trifle infantile—

Says M. Lausanne, solicitor of the "Treaties" and a chief spokesman for M. Clemenceau—

to pretend the contrary.

When the executive council of the league of nations fixes the "reasonable limits of the armament of Peru": when it shall demand information concerning the naval program of Brazil (art. 7 of the covenant); when it shall tell Argentina what shall [be] the measure of the "contribution to the armed forces to protect the signature of the social covenant" (art. 16); when it shall demand the immediate registration of the treaty between the United States and Canada at the seat of the league, it will control, whether it wills or not, the destinies of America.

And when the American States shall be obliged to take a hand in every war or menace of war in Europe (art. 11), they will necessarily fall afoul of the fundamental principle laid down by Monroe.

. . . If the league takes in the world, then Europe must mix in the affairs of America: if only Europe is included, then America will violate of necessity her own doctrine by intermixing in the affairs of Europe.

It has seemed to me that the British delegation travelled a little out of the precincts of the peace conference when they undertook to explain the Monroe doctrine and tell the United States what it was and what it was not proposed to do with it under the new article. That, however, is merely a matter of taste and judgment. Their statement that the Monroe doctrine under this article, if any question arose in regard to it, would be passed upon and interpreted by the league of nations is absolutely correct. There is no doubt that this is what the article means. Great Britain so stated it, and no American authority, whether friendly or unfriendly to the league, has dared to question it. I have wondered a little why it was left to the British delegation to explain that article, which so nearly concerns the United States, but that was merely a fugitive thought upon which I will not dwell. The statement of M. Lausanne is equally explicit and truthful, but he makes

one mistake. He says in substance that if we are to meddle in Europe, Europe can not be excluded from the Americas. He overlooks the fact that the Monroe doctrine also says:

Our policy in regard to Europe, which was adopted at an early stage of the wars which have so long agitated that corner of the globe, nevertheless remains the same, which is not to interfere in the internal concerns of any of the powers.

The Monroe doctrine was the corollary of Washington's neutrality policy and of his injunction against permanent alliances. It reiterates and reaffirms the principle. We do not seek to meddle in the affairs of Europe and keep Europe out of the Americas. It is as important to keep the United States out of European affairs as to keep Europe out of the American Continents. Let us maintain the Monroe doctrine, then, in its entirety, and not only preserve our own safety, but in this way best promote the real peace of the world. Whenever the preservation of freedom and civilization and the overthrow of a menacing world conqueror summon us we shall respond fully and nobly, as we did in 1917. He who doubts that we should do so has little faith in America. But let it be our own act, and not done reluctantly by the coercion of other nations, at the bidding or by the permission of other countries.

Let me now deal with the article itself. We have here some protective coloration again. The Monroe doctrine is described as a "regional understanding," whatever that may mean. The boundaries between the States of the Union, I suppose, are "regional understandings," if anyone chooses to apply to them that somewhat swollen phraseology. But the Monroe doctrine is no more a regional understanding than it is an "international engagement." The Monroe doctrine was a policy declared by President Monroe. Its immediate purpose was to shut out Europe from interfering with the South American Republics, which the Holy Alliance designed to do. It was stated broadly, however, as we all know, and went much further than that. It was, as I have just said, the corollary of Washington's declaration against our interfering in European questions. It was so regarded by Jefferson at the time, and by John Quincy Adams, who formulated it, and by President Monroe, who declared it. It rested firmly on the great law of self-preservation, which is the basic principle of every independent State. It is not necessary to trace its history, or to point out the extensions which it has received, or its universal acceptance by all American statesmen without regard to party. All Americans have always been for it. They may not have known its details, or read all the many discussions in regard to it, but they knew that it was an American doctrine, and that, broadly stated, it meant the exclusion of Europe from interference with American affairs and from any attempt to colonize or set up new States within the boundaries of the American Continent. I repeat, it was purely an American doctrine, a purely American policy, designed and wisely designed for our defense. It has never been an "international engagement." No nation has ever formally recognized it. It has been the subject of reservation at international conventions by American delegates. It has never been a "regional understanding," or an understanding of any kind with anybody. It was the declaration of the United States of America, in their own behalf, supported by their own power. They brought it into being, and its life was predicated on the force which the United States could place behind it. Unless the United States could sustain it, it would die. The United States has supported it. It has lived—strong, efficient, respected. It is now proposed to kill it by a provision in a treaty for a league of nations.

The instant that the United States, who declared, interpreted, and sustained the doctrine, ceases to be the sole judge of what it means, that instant the Monroe doctrine ceases and disappears from history and from the face of the earth. I think it is just as undesirable to have Europe interfere in American affairs now as Mr. Monroe thought it was in 1823, and equally undesirable that we should be compelled to involve ourselves in all the wars and brawls of Europe. The Monroe doctrine has made for peace. Without the Monroe doctrine we should have had many a struggle with European powers to save ourselves from possible assault and certainly from the necessity of becoming a great military power, always under arms and always ready to resist invasion from States in our near neighborhood. In the interests of the peace of the world it is now proposed to wipe away this American policy, which has been a bulwark and a barrier for peace. With one exception it has always been successful, and then success was only delayed. When we were torn by civil war France saw fit to enter Mexico and endeavored to establish an empire there. When our hands were once free the empire perished, and with it the unhappy tool of the third Napoleon. If the United States had not been rent by civil war no such attempt would have been made, and nothing better illustrates the value to the cause of peace of the Monroe doctrine. Why, in the name of peace, should we extinguish it? Why, in the name of peace, should we be called upon to leave the interpretation of the Monroe doctrine to other nations? It is an American policy.

It is our own. It has guarded us well, and I for one can never find consent in my heart to destroy it by a clause in a treaty and hand over its body for dissection to the nations of Europe. If we need authority to demonstrate what the Monroe doctrine has meant to the United States we can not do better than quote the words of Grover Cleveland, who directed Mr. Olney to notify the world that "to-day the United States is practically sovereign on this continent, and its fiat is law to which it confines its interposition." Theodore Roosevelt, in the last article written before his death, warned us, his countrymen, that we are "in honor bound to keep ourselves so prepared that the Monroe doctrine shall be accepted as immutable international law." Grover Cleveland was a Democrat and Theodore Roosevelt was a Republican, but they were both Americans, and it is the American spirit which has carried this country always to victory and which should govern us to-day, and not the international spirit, which would in the name of peace hand the United States over bound hand and foot to obey the fiat of other powers.

Another point in this covenant where change must be made in order to protect the safety of the United States in the future is in article 1, where withdrawal is provided for. This provision was an attempt to meet the very general objection to the first draft of the league, that there was no means of getting out of it without denouncing the treaty; that is, there was no arrangement for the withdrawal of any nation. As it now stands it reads that—

> Any member of the league may, after two years' notice of its intention to do so, withdraw from the league, provided that all its international obligations and all its obligations under this covenant shall have been fulfilled at the time of its withdrawal.

The right of withdrawal is given by this clause, although the time for notice, two years, is altogether too long. Six months or a year would be found, I think, in most treaties to be the normal period fixed for notice of withdrawal. But whatever virtue there may be in the right thus conferred is completely nullified by the proviso. The right of withdrawal can not be exercised until all the international obligations and all the obligations of the withdrawing nations have been fulfilled. The league alone can decide whether "all international obligations and all obligations under this covenant" have been fulfilled, and this would require, under the provisions of the league, a unanimous vote, so that any nation desiring to withdraw could not do so, even on the two years' notice, if one nation voted that the obligations had not been fulfilled. Remember that this gives the league not only power to review all our obligations under the covenant but all our treaties with all nations, for every one of those is an "international obligation."

Are we deliberately to put ourselves in fetters and be examined by the league of nations as to whether we have kept faith with Cuba or Panama before we can be permitted to leave the league? This seems to me humiliating, to say the least. The right of withdrawal, if it is to be of any value whatever, must be absolute, because otherwise a nation desiring to withdraw could be held in the league by objections from other nations until the very act which induces the nation to withdraw had been completed, until the withdrawing nation had been forced to send troops to take part in a war with which it had no concern and upon which it did not desire to enter. It seems to me vital to the safety of the United States not only that this provision should be eliminated and the right to withdraw made absolute but that the period of withdrawal should be much reduced. As it stands it is practically no better in this respect than the first league draft, which contained no provision for withdrawal at all, because the proviso here inserted so encumbers it that every nation to all intents and purposes must remain a member of the league indefinitely unless all the other members are willing that it should retire. Such a provision as this, ostensibly framed to meet the objection, has the defect which other similar gestures to give an impression of meeting objections have, that it apparently keeps the promise to the ear but most certainly breaks it to the hope.

I have dwelt only upon those points which seem to me most dangerous. There are, of course, many others, but these points, in the interest not only of the safety of the United States but of the maintenance of the treaty and the peace of the world, should be dealt with here before it is too late. Once in the league the chance of amendment is so slight that it is not worth considering. Any analysis of the provisions of this league covenant, however, brings out in startling relief one great fact. Whatever may be said, it is not a league of peace; it is an alliance, dominated at the present moment by five great powers, really by three, and it has all the marks of an alliance. The development of international law is neglected. The court which is to decide disputes brought before it fills but a small place. The conditions for which this league really provides with the utmost care are political conditions, not judicial questions, to be reached by the executive council and the assembly, purely political bodies without any trace of a judicial character about them. Such being its machinery, the control being in the hands of political appointees whose votes will be controlled by interest and expediency, it exhibits that most marked characteristic of an alliance—that its decisions are to be carried out by force. Those articles upon which the whole structure rests are articles which provide for the use of force; that is, for war. This league to enforce peace does a great deal for enforcement and very little for peace. It makes more essential provisions looking to war than to peace for the settlement of disputes.

Article 10 I have already discussed. There is no question that the preservation of a State against external aggression can contemplate nothing but war. In article 11, again, the league is authorized to take any action which may be necessary to safeguard the peace of the world. "Any action" includes war. We also have specific provisions for a boycott, which is a form of economic warfare. The use of troops might be avoided, but the enforcement of a boycott would require blockades in all probability, and certainly a boycott in its essence is simply an effort to starve a people into submission, to ruin their trade, and, in the case of nations which are not self-supporting, to cut off their food supply. The misery and suffering caused by such a measure as this may easily rival that caused by actual war. Article 16 embodies the boycott and also, in the last paragraph, provides explicitly for war. We are told that the word "recommend" has no binding force; it constitutes a moral obligation; that is all. But it means that if we, for example, should refuse to accept the recommendation we should nullify the operation of article 16 and, to that extent, of the league. It seems to me that to attempt to relieve us of clearly imposed duties by saying that the word "recommend" is not binding is an escape of which no nation regarding the sanctity of treaties and its own honor would care to avail itself. The provisions of article 16 are extended to States outside the league who refuse to obey its command to come in and submit themselves to its jurisdiction—another provision for war.

Taken altogether, these provisions for war present what to my mind is the gravest objection to this league in its present form. We are told that of course nothing will be done in the way of warlike acts without the assent of Congress. If that is true let us say so in the covenant. But as it stands there is no doubt whatever in my mind that American troops and American ships may be ordered to any part of the world by nations other than the United States, and that is a proposition to which I for one can never assent. It must be made perfectly clear that no American soldiers, not even a corporal's guard, that no American sailors, not even the crew of a submarine, can ever be engaged in war or ordered anywhere except by the constitutional authorities of the United States. To Congress is granted by the Constitution the right to declare war, and nothing that would take the troops out of the country at the bidding or demand of other nations should ever be permitted except through congressional action. The lives of Americans must never be sacrificed except by the will of the American people expressed through their chosen Representatives in Congress. This is a point upon which no doubt can be permitted. American soldiers and American sailors have never failed the country when the country called upon them. They went in their hundreds of thousands into the war just closed. They went to die for the great cause of freedom and of civilization. They went at their service. We were late in entering the war. We made no preparation, as we ought to have done, for the ordeal which was clearly coming upon us; but we went and we turned the wavering scale. It was done by the American soldier, the American sailor, and the spirit and energy of the American people. They overrode all obstacles and all short-comings on the part of the administration or of Congress and gave to their country a great place in the great victory. It was the first time we had been called upon to rescue the civilized world. Did we fail? On the contrary, we succeeded, succeeded largely and nobly, and we did it without any command from any league of nations. When the emergency came we met it, and we were able to meet it because we had built up on this continent the greatest and most powerful Nation in the world, built it up under our own policies, in our own way, and one great element of our strength was the fact that we had held aloof and had not thrust ourselves into European quarrels; that we had no selfish interest to serve. We made great sacrifices. We have done splendid work. I believe that we do not require to be told by foreign nations when we shall do work which freedom and civilization require. I think we can move to victory much better under our own command than under the command of others. Let us unite with the world to promote the peaceable settlement of all international disputes. Let us try to develop international law. Let us associate ourselves with the other nations for these purposes. But let us retain in our own hands and in our own control the lives of the youth of the land. Let no American be sent into battle except by the constituted authorities of his own country and by the will of the people of the United States.

Those of us, Mr. President, who are either wholly opposed to the league, or who are trying to preserve the independence and the safety of the United States by changing the terms of the league, and who are endeavoring to make the league, if we are to be a member of it, less certain to promote war instead of peace have been reproached with selfishness in our outlook and with a desire to keep our country in a state of isolation. So far as the question of isolation goes, it is impossible to isolate the United States. I well remember the time, 20 years ago, when eminent Senators and other distinguished gentlemen who were opposing the Philippines and shrieking about imperialism sneered at the statement made by some of us, that the United States had become a world power. I think no one now would question that the Spanish war marked the entrance of the United States into world affairs to a degree which had never obtained before. It was both an inevitable and an irrevocable step, and our entrance into the war with Germany certainly showed once and for all that the United States was not unmindful of its world responsibilities. We may set aside all this empty talk about isolation. Nobody expects to isolate the United States or to make it a hermit Nation, which is a sheer absurdity. But there is a wide difference between taking a suitable part and bearing a due responsibility in world affairs and plunging the United States into every controversy and conflict on the face of the globe. By meddling in all the differences which may arise among any portion or fragment of humankind we simply fritter away our influence and injure ourselves to no good purpose. We shall be of far more value to the world and its peace by occupying, so far as possible, the situation which we have occupied for the last 20 years and by adhering to the policy of Washington and Hamilton, of Jefferson and Monroe, under which we have risen to our present greatness and prosperity. The fact that we have been separated by our geographical situation and by our consistent policy from the broils of Europe has made us more than any one thing capable of performing the great work which we performed in the war against Germany, and our disinterestedness is of far more value to the world than our eternal meddling in every possible dispute could ever be.

Now as to our selfishness. I have no desire to boast that we are better than our neighbors, but the fact remains that this Nation in making peace with Germany had not a single selfish or individual interest to serve. All we asked was that

Germany should be rendered incapable of again breaking forth, with all the horrors incident to German warfare, upon an unoffending world, and that demand was shared by every free nation and indeed by humanity itself. For ourselves we asked absolutely nothing. We have not asked any government or governments to guarantee our boundaries or our political independence. We have no fear in regard to either. We have sought no territory, no privileges, no advantages for ourselves. That is the fact. It is apparent on the face of the treaty. I do not mean to reflect upon a single one of the powers with which we have been associated in the war against Germany, but there is not one of them which has not sought individual advantages for their own national benefit. I do not criticize their desires at all. The services and sacrifices of England and France and Belgium and Italy are beyond estimate and beyond praise. I am glad they should have what they desire for their own welfare and safety. But they all receive under the peace territorial and commercial benefits. We are asked to give, and we in no way seek to take. Surely it is not too much to insist that when we are offered nothing but the opportunity to give and to aid others we should have the right to say what sacrifices we shall make and what the magnitude of our gifts shall be. In the prosecution of the war we gave unstintedly American lives and American treasure. When the war closed we had 3,000,000 men under arms. We were turning the country into a vast workshop for war. We advanced ten billions to our allies. We refused no assistance that we could possibly render. All the great energy and power of the Republic were put at the service of the good cause. We have not been ungenerous. We have been devoted to the cause of freedom, humanity, and civilization everywhere. Now we are asked, in the making of peace, to sacrifice our sovereignty in important respects, to involve ourselves almost without limit in the affairs of other nations and to yield up policies and rights which we have maintained throughout our history. We are asked to incur liabilities to an unlimited extent and furnish assets at the same time which no man can measure. I think it is not only our right but our duty to determine how far we shall go. Not only must we look carefully to see where we are being led into endless disputes and entanglements, but we must not forget that we have in this country millions of people of foreign birth and parentage.

Our one great object is to make all these people Americans so that we may call on them to place America first and serve America as they have done in the war just closed. We can not Americanize them if we are continually thrusting them back into the quarrels and difficulties of the countries from which they came to us. We shall fill this land with political disputes about the troubles and quarrels of other countries. We shall have a large portion of our people voting not on American questions and not on what concerns the United States but dividing on issues which concern foreign countries alone. That is an unwholesome and perilous condition to force upon this country. We must avoid it. We ought to reduce to the lowest possible point the foreign questions in which we involve ourselves. Never forget that this league is primarily—I might say overwhelmingly—a political organization, and I object strongly to having the politics of the United States turn upon disputes where deep feeling is aroused but in which we have no direct interest. It will all tend to delay the Americanization of our great population, and it is more important not only to the United States but to the peace of the world to make all these people good Americans than it is to determine that some piece of territory should belong to one European country rather than to another. For this reason I wish to limit strictly our interference in the affairs of Europe and of Africa. We have interests of our own in Asia and in the Pacific which we must guard upon our own account, but the less we undertake to play the part of umpire and thrust ourselves into European conflicts the better for the United States and for the world.

It has been reiterated here on this floor, and reiterated to the point of weariness, that in every treaty there is some sacrifice of sovereignty. That is not a universal truth by any means, but it is true of some treaties and it is a platitude which does not require reiteration. The question and the only question before us here is how much of our sovereignty we are justified in sacrificing. In what I have already said about other nations putting us into war I have covered one point of sovereignty which ought never to be yielded—the power to send American soldiers and sailors everywhere, which ought never to be taken from the American people or impaired in the slightest degree. Let us beware how we palter with our independence. We have not reached the great position from which we were able to come down into the field of battle and help to save the world from tyranny by being guided by others. Our vast power has all been built up and gathered together by ourselves alone. We forced our way upward from the days of the Revolution, through a world often hostile and always indifferent. We owe no debt to anyone except to France in that Revolution, and those policies and those rights on which our power has been founded should never be lessened or weakened. It will be no service to the world to do so and it will be of intolerable injury to the United States. We will do our share. We are ready and anxious to help in all ways to preserve the world's peace. But we can do it best by not crippling ourselves.

I am as anxious as any human being can be to have the United States render every possible service to the civilization and the peace of mankind, but I am certain we can do it best by not putting ourselves in leading strings or subjecting our policies and our sovereignty to other nations. The independence of the United States is not only more precious to ourselves but to the world than any single possession. Look at the United States to-day. We have made mistakes in the past. We have had shortcomings. We shall make mistakes in the future and fall short of our own best hopes. But none the less is there any country to-day on the face of the earth which can compare with this in ordered liberty, in peace, and in the largest freedom? I feel that I can say this without being accused of undue boastfulness, for it is the simple fact, and in making this treaty and taking on these obligations all that we do is in a spirit of unselfishness and in a desire for the good of mankind. But it is well to remember that we are dealing with nations every one of which has a direct individual interest to serve, and there is grave danger in an unshared idealism. Contrast the United States with any country on the face of the earth to-day and ask yourself whether the situation of the United States is not the best to be found. I will go as far as anyone in world service, but the first step to world service is the maintenance of the United States. You may call me selfish, if you will, conservative or reactionary, or use any other harsh adjective you see fit to apply, but an American I was born, an American I have remained all my life. I can never be anything else but an American, and I must think of the United States first, and when I think of the United States first in an arrangement like this I am thinking of what is best for the world, for if the United States falls the best hopes of mankind fall with it. I have never had but one allegiance—I can not divide it now. I have loved but one flag and I can not share that devotion and give affection to the mongrel banner invented for a league. Internationalism, illustrated by the Bolshevik and by the men to whom all countries are alike provided they can make money out of them, is to me repulsive. National I must remain, and in that way I like all other Americans can render the amplest service to the world. The United States is the world's best hope, but if you fetter her in the interests and quarrels of other nations, if you tangle her in the intrigues of Europe, you will destroy her power for good and endanger her very existence. Leave her to march freely through the centuries to come as in the years that have gone. Strong, generous, and confident, she has nobly served mankind. Beware how you trifle with your marvelous inheritance, this great land of ordered liberty, for if we stumble and fall freedom and civilization everywhere will go down in ruin.

We are told that we shall "break the heart of the world" if we do not take this league just as it stands. I fear that the hearts of the vast majority of mankind would beat on strongly and steadily and without any quickening if the league were to perish altogether. If it should be effectively and beneficently changed the people who would lie awake in sorrow for a single night could be easily gathered in one not very large room but those who would draw a long breath of relief would reach to millions.

We hear much of visions and I trust we shall continue to have visions and dream dreams of a fairer future for the race. But visions are one thing and visionaries are another, and the mechanical appliances of the rhetorician designed to give a picture of a present which does not exist and of a future which no man can predict are as unreal and short lived as the steam or canvas clouds, the angels suspended on wires and the artificial lights of the stage. They pass with the moment of effect and are shabby and tawdry in the daylight. Let us at least be real. Washington's entire honesty of mind and his fearless look into the face of all facts are qualities which can never go out of fashion and which we should all do well to imitate.

Ideals have been thrust upon us as an argument for the league until the healthy mind which rejects cant revolts from them. Are ideals confined to this deformed experiment upon a noble purpose, tainted, as it is, with bargains and tied to a peace treaty which might have been disposed of long ago to the great benefit of the world if it had not been compelled to carry this rider on its back? "Post equitem sedet atra cura," Horace tells us, but no blacker care ever sat behind any rider than we shall find in this covenant of doubtful and disputed interpretation as it now perches upon the treaty of peace.

No doubt many excellent and patriotic people see a coming fulfillment of noble ideals in the words "League for Peace." We all respect and share these aspirations and desires, but some of us see no hope, but rather defeat, for them in this murky covenant. For we, too, have our ideals, even if we differ from those who have tried to establish a monopoly of idealism. Our first ideal is our country, and we see her in the future, as in the past, giving service to all her people and to the world. Our ideal of the future is that she should continue to render that service of her own free will. She has great problems of her own to solve, very grim and perilous problems, and a right solution, if we can attain to it, would largely benefit mankind. We would have our country strong to resist a peril from the West, as she has flung back the German menace from the East. We would not have our politics distracted and embittered by the dissensions of other lands. We would not have our country's vigor exhausted, or her moral force abated, by everlasting meddling and muddling in every quarrel, great and small, which afflicts the world. Our ideal is to make her ever stronger and better and finer, because in that way alone, so we believe, can she be of the greatest service to the world's peace and to the welfare of mankind. [Prolonged applause in the galleries.]

Kellogg-Briand Pact, 1929

Named for its drafters, the American secretary of state, Frank B. Kellogg, and the French foreign minister, Aristide Briand, the Kellogg-Briand Pact began as a proposal by Briand for a treaty between the United States and France. The administration of President Calvin Coolidge responded to the idea, and to significant pressure from the American press and a variety of public and private organizations, by calling on nations around the world to join in a treaty banning war as an instrument of national policy. Coolidge's successor, Herbert Hoover, signed the resulting pact. The U.S. Senate ratified the pact by an overwhelming margin but added two caveats: the United States would not renounce its right to self-defense, and it would not be bound to use military action to enforce the pact. Originally signed by fifteen nations, and eventually by sixty-two nations, it did not prevent the variety of military actions that culminated in World War II.

Kellogg-Briand Pact

July 24, 1929

BY THE PRESIDENT OF THE UNITED STATES
OF AMERICA
A PROCLAMATION

WHEREAS a Treaty between the President of the United States of America, the President of the German Reich, His Majesty the King of the Belgians, the President of the French Republic, His Majesty the King of Great Britain, Ireland and the British Dominions beyond the Seas, Emperor of India, His Majesty the King of Italy, His Majesty the Emperor of Japan, the President of the Republic of Poland, and the President of the Czechoslovak Republic, providing for the renunciation of war as an instrument of national policy, was concluded and signed by their respective Plenipotentiaries at Paris on the twenty-seventh day of August, one thousand nine hundred and twenty-eight, the original of which Treaty, being in the English and French languages, is word for word as follows:

THE PRESIDENT OF THE GERMAN REICH, THE PRESIDENT OF THE UNITED STATES OF AMERICA, HIS MAJESTY THE KING OF THE BELGIANS, THE PRESIDENT OF THE FRENCH REPUBLIC, HIS MAJESTY THE KING OF GREAT BRITAIN, IRELAND AND THE BRITISH DOMINIONS BEYOND THE SEAS, EMPEROR OF INDIA, HIS MAJESTY THE KING OF ITALY, HIS MAJESTY THE EMPEROR OF JAPAN, THE PRESIDENT OF THE REPUBLIC OF POLAND, THE PRESIDENT OF THE CZECHOSLOVAK REPUBLIC,

Deeply sensible of their solemn duty to promote the welfare of mankind;

Persuaded that the time has come when a frank renunciation of war as an instrument of national policy should be made to the end that the peaceful and friendly relations now existing between their peoples may be perpetuated;

Convinced that all changes in their relations with one another should be sought only by pacific means and be the result of a peaceful and orderly process, and that any signatory Power which shall hereafter seek to promote its national interests by resort to war should be denied the benefits furnished by this Treaty;

Hopeful that, encouraged by their example, all the other nations of the world will join in this humane endeavor and by adhering to the present Treaty as soon as it comes into force bring their peoples within the scope of its beneficent provisions, thus uniting the civilized nations of the world in a common renunciation of war as an instrument of their national policy;

Have decided to conclude a Treaty and for that purpose have appointed as their respective Plenipotentiaries:

THE PRESIDENT OF THE GERMAN REICH:
Dʳ Gustav STRESEMANN, Minister for Foreign Affairs;

THE PRESIDENT OF THE UNITED STATES OF AMERICA:
The Honorable Frank B. KELLOGG, Secretary of State;

HIS MAJESTY THE KING OF THE BELGIANS:
Mr. Paul HYMANS, Minister for Foreign Affairs, Minister of State;

THE PRESIDENT OF THE FRENCH REPUBLIC:
Mr. Aristide BRIAND, Minister for Foreign Affairs;

HIS MAJESTY THE KING OF GREAT BRITAIN, IRELAND AND THE BRITISH DOMINIONS BEYOND THE SEAS, EMPEROR OF INDIA:
For GREAT BRITAIN and NORTHERN IRELAND and all parts of the British Empire which are not separate Members of the League of Nations:
The Right Honourable Lord CUSHENDUN, Chancellor of the Duchy of Lancaster, Acting Secretary of State for Foreign Affairs;

For the DOMINION OF CANADA:
The Right Honourable William Lyon MACKENZIE KING, Prime Minister and Minister for External Affairs;

For the COMMONWEALTH OF AUSTRALIA:
The Honourable Alexander John McLACHLAN, Member of the Executive Federal Council;

For the DOMINION OF NEW ZEALAND:
The Honourable Sir Christopher James PARR, High Commissioner for New Zealand in Great Britain;

For the UNION OF SOUTH AFRICA:
The Honourable Jacobus Stephanus SMIT, High Commissioner for the Union of South Africa in Great Britain;

For the IRISH FREE STATE:
Mr. William Thomas COSGRAVE, President of the Executive Council;

For INDIA:
The Right Honourable Lord CUSHENDUN, Chancellor of the Duchy of Lancaster, Acting Secretary of State for Foreign Affairs;

HIS MAJESTY THE KING OF ITALY:
Count Gaetano MANZONI, his Ambassador Extraordinary and Plenipotentiary at Paris.

HIS MAJESTY THE EMPEROR OF JAPAN:
Count UCHIDA, Privy Councillor;

THE PRESIDENT OF THE REPUBLIC OF POLAND:
Mr. A. ZALESKI, Minister for Foreign Affairs;

THE PRESIDENT OF THE CZECHOSLOVAK REPUBLIC:
Dʳ Eduard BENÈS, Minister for Foreign Affairs;

who, having communicated to one another their full powers found in good and due form have agreed upon the following articles:

ARTICLE I

The High Contracting Parties solemnly declare in the names of their respective peoples that they condemn recourse to war for the solution of international controversies, and renounce it as an instrument of national policy in their relations with one another.

ARTICLE II

The High Contracting Parties agree that the settlement or solution of all disputes or conflicts of whatever nature or of whatever origin they may be, which may arise among them, shall never be sought except by pacific means.

ARTICLE III

The present Treaty shall be ratified by the High Contracting Parties named in the Preamble in accordance with their respective constitutional requirements, and shall take effect as between them as soon as all their several instruments of ratification shall have been deposited at Washington.

This Treaty shall, when it has come into effect as prescribed in the preceding paragraph, remain open as long as may be necessary for adherence by all the other Powers of the world. Every instrument evidencing the adherence of a Power shall be deposited at Washington and the Treaty shall immediately upon such deposit become effective as between the Power thus adhering and the other Powers parties hereto.

It shall be the duty of the Government of the United States to furnish each Government named in the Preamble and every Government subsequently adhering to this Treaty with a certified copy of the Treaty and of every instrument of ratification or adherence. It shall also be the duty of the Government of the United States telegraphically to notify such Governments immediately upon the deposit with it of each instrument of ratification or adherence.

IN FAITH WHEREOF the respective Plenipotentiaries have signed this Treaty in the French and English languages both texts having equal force, and hereunto affix their seals.

DONE at Paris, the twenty-seventh day of August in the year one thousand nine hundred and twenty-eight.

[SEAL]	GUSTAV STRESEMANN
[SEAL]	FRANK B KELLOGG
[SEAL]	PAUL HYMANS
[SEAL]	ARI BRIAND
[SEAL]	CUSHENDUN
[SEAL]	W. L. MACKENZIE KING
[SEAL]	A J MCLACHLAN
[SEAL]	C. J. PARR
[SEAL]	J S. SMIT
[SEAL]	LIAM T. MACCOSGAIR
[SEAL]	CUSHENDUN
[SEAL]	G. MANZONI
[SEAL]	UCHIDA
[SEAL]	AUGUST ZALESKI
[SEAL]	DR EDUARD BENES

Certified to be a true copy of the signed original deposited with the Government of the United States of America.

FRANK B. KELLOGG
Secretary of State of the United States of America

AND WHEREAS it is stipulated in the said Treaty that it shall take effect as between the High Contracting Parties as soon as all the several instruments of ratification shall have been deposited at Washington;

AND WHEREAS the said Treaty has been duly ratified on the parts of all the High Contracting Parties and their several instruments of ratification have been deposited with the Government of the United States of America, the last on July 24, 1929;

NOW, THEREFORE, be it known that I, Herbert Hoover, President of the United States of America, have caused the said Treaty to be made public, to the end that the same and every article and clause thereof may be observed and fulfilled with good faith by the United States and the citizens thereof.

IN TESTIMONY WHEREOF, I have hereunto set my hand and caused the seal of the United States to be affixed.

DONE at the city of Washington this twenty-fourth day of July in the year of our Lord one thousand nine hundred and twenty-nine, and of the Independence of the United States of America the one hundred and fifty-fourth.

[SEAL]   HERBERT HOOVER

By the President:

HENRY L STIMSON
Secretary of State

NOTE BY THE DEPARTMENT OF STATE
ADHERING COUNTRIES

When this Treaty became effective on July 24, 1929, the instruments of ratification of all of the signatory powers having been deposited at Washington, the following countries, having deposited instruments of definitive adherence, became parties to it:

Afghanistan	Finland	Peru
Albania	Guatemala	Portugal
Austria	Hungary	Rumania
Bulgaria	Iceland	Russia
China	Latvia	Kingdom of the Serbs,
Cuba	Liberia	Croats and Slovenes
Denmark	Lithuania	Siam
Dominican Republic	Netherlands	Spain
Egypt	Nicaragua	Sweden
Estonia	Norway	Turkey
Ethiopia	Panama	

Additional adhesions deposited subsequent to July 24, 1929.

Persia, July 2, 1929; Greece, August 3, 1929; Honduras, August 5, 1929; Chile, August 12, 1929; Luxemburg, August 14, 1929; Danzig, September 11, 1929; Costa Rica, October 1, 1929; Venezuela, October 24, 1929.

Note on Chinchow, *Henry L. Stimson, 1932*

Japan was among the signatories to, and most flagrant violators of, the Kellogg-Briand Pact. Its continued military actions in China had brought condemnation by the League of Nations but little action. Among those refusing to act was the U.S. president Herbert Hoover, who, facing the Great Depression and a public clearly opposed to any intervention in the Far East, did not desire to risk inviting further aggression from Japan by taking a strong stand against its incursions in the region of China then called Manchuria. By 1932 Japan had secured control over the region and established Manchukuo—a separate state under a puppet government. Hoover's secretary of state, Henry L. Stimson, sought to salvage America's Open Door Policy regarding China through the note reproduced here, which was forwarded to both the Chinese and the Japanese governments. Stimson's statement of America's refusal to recognize changes brought about through violations of the Kellogg-Briand Pact was met by Japan with diplomatic demurrers and further military action in China. There was no substantive American response, until the eventual outbreak of World War II.

Note on Chinchow

January 7, 1932

Henry L. Stimson

With the recent military operations about Chinchow, the last remaining administrative authority of the Government of the Chinese Republic in South Manchuria, as it existed prior to September 18, 1931, has been destroyed. The American Government continues confident that the work of the neutral commission recently authorized by the Council of the League of Nations will facilitate an ultimate solution of the difficulties now existing between China and Japan. But in view of the present situation and of its own rights and obligations therein, the American Government deems it to be its duty to notify both the Government of the Chinese Republic and the Imperial Japanese Government that it can not admit the legality of any situation *de facto* nor does it intend to rec-ognize any treaty or agreement entered into between those governments, or agents thereof, which may impair the treaty rights of the United States or its citizens in China, including those which relate to the sovereignty, the independence, or the territorial and administrative integrity of the Republic of China, or to the international policy relative to China, commonly known as the open-door policy; and that it does not intend to recognize any situation, treaty, or agreement which may be brought about by means contrary to the covenants and obligations of the Pact of Paris of August 27, 1928, to which treaty both China and Japan, as well as the United States, are parties.

Neutrality and War, *Charles A. Lindbergh*, 1939

Most famous for being the first to successfully fly solo and nonstop across the Atlantic, Charles Lindbergh (1902–74) was also a leader in the movement to prevent the United States from entering World War II. Touring the country on behalf of the America First Committee, a group committed to American neutrality in the war going on in Europe, Lindbergh argued that Roosevelt administration policies intended to assist the British and their allies in fighting Nazi Germany went against traditional American policies rooted in the Monroe Doctrine. Lindbergh and the America First Committee were accused of anti-Semitism and pro-Nazi sympathies. The committee disbanded after the Japanese attack on Pearl Harbor. Rebuffed in his attempts to rejoin the American air force, Lindbergh traveled to the Pacific theater as an observer and ended up flying a number of combat missions.

Neutrality and War

October 13, 1939

Charles A. Lindbergh

Tonight, I speak again to the people of this country who are opposed to the United States entering the war which is now going on in Europe. We are faced with the need of deciding on a policy of American neutrality. The future of our nation and of our civilization rests upon the wisdom and foresight we use. Much as peace is to be desired, we should realize that behind a successful policy of neutrality must stand a policy of war. It is essential to define clearly those principles and circumstances for which a nation will fight. Let us give no one the impression that America's love for peace means that she is afraid of war, or that we are not fully capable and willing to defend all that is vital to us. National life and influence depend upon national strength, both in character and in arms. A neutrality built on pacifism alone will eventually fail.

Before we can intelligently enact regulations for the control of our armaments, our credit, and our ships, we must draw a sharp dividing line between neutrality and war; there must be no gradual encroachment on the defenses of our nation. Up to this line we may adjust our affairs to gain the advantages of peace, but beyond it must lie all the armed might of America, coiled in readiness to spring if once this bond is cut. Let us make clear to all countries where this line lies. It must be both within our intent and our capabilities. There must be no question of trading or bluff in this hemisphere. Let us give no promises we cannot keep—make no meaningless as-

surances to an Ethiopia, a Czechoslovakia, or a Poland. The policy we decide upon should be as clear cut as our shorelines, and as easily defended as our continent.

This western hemisphere is our domain. It is our right to trade freely within it. From Alaska to Labrador, from the Hawaiian Islands to Bermuda, from Canada to South America, we must allow no invading army to set foot. These are the outposts of the United States. They form the essential outline of our geographical defense. We must be ready to wage war with all the resources of our nation if they are ever seriously threatened. Their defense is the mission of our army, our navy, and our air corps—the minimum requirement of our military strength. Around these places should lie our line between neutrality and war. Let there be no compromise about our right to defend or trade within this area. If it is challenged by any nation, the answer must be war. Our policy of neutrality should have this as its foundation.

We must protect our sister American nations from foreign invasion, both for their welfare and our own. But, in turn, they have a duty to us. They should not place us in the position of having to defend them in America while they engage in wars abroad. Can we rightfully permit any country in America to give bases to foreign warships, or to send its army abroad to fight while it remains secure in our protection at home? We desire the utmost friendship with the people of Canada. If their country is ever attacked, our Navy will be defending their seas, our soldiers will fight on their battlefields, our fliers will die in their skies. But have they the right to draw this hemisphere into a European war simply because they prefer the Crown of England to American independence?

Sooner or later we must demand the freedom of this continent and its surrounding islands from the dictates of European power. American history clearly indicates this need. As long as European powers maintain their influence in our hemisphere, we are likely to find ourselves involved in their troubles. And they will lose no opportunity to involve us.

Our Congress is now assembled to decide upon the best policy for this country to maintain during the war which is going on in Europe. The legislation under discussion involves three major issues—the embargo of arms, the restriction of shipping, and the allowance of credit. The action we take in regard to these issues will be an important indication to ourselves, and to the nations of Europe, whether or not we are likely to enter the conflict eventually as we did in the last war. The entire world is watching us. The action we take in America may either stop or precipitate this war.

Let us take up these issues, one at a time, and examine them. First, the embargo of arms: It is argued that the repeal of this embargo would assist democracy in Europe, that it would let us make a profit for ourselves from the sale of munitions abroad, and, at the same time, help to build up our own arms industry.

I do not believe that repealing the arms embargo would assist democracy in Europe because I do not believe this is a war for democracy. This is a war over the balance of power in Europe—a war brought about by the desire for strength on the part of Germany and the fear of strength on the part of England and France. The more munitions the armies obtain, the longer the war goes on, and the more devastated Europe becomes, the less hope there is for democracy. That is a lesson we should have learned from our participation in the last war. If democratic principles had been applied in Europe after that war, if the "democracies" *of* Europe had been willing to make some sacrifice to help democracy *in* Europe while it was fighting for its life, if England and France had offered a hand to the struggling republic of Germany, there would be no war today.

If we repeal the arms embargo with the idea of assisting one of the warring sides to overcome the other, then why mislead ourselves by talk of neutrality? Those who advance this argument should admit openly that repeal is a step toward war. The next step would be the extension of credit, and the next step would be the sending of American troops.

To those who argue that we could make a profit and build up our own industry by selling munitions abroad, I reply that we in America have not yet reached a point where we wish to capitalize on the destruction and death of war. I do not believe that the material welfare of this country needs, or that our spiritual welfare could withstand, such a policy. If our industry depends upon a commerce of arms for its strength, then our industrial system should be changed.

It is impossible for me to understand how America can contribute to civilization and humanity by sending offensive instruments of destruction to European battlefields. This would not only implicate us in the war, but it would make us partly responsible for its devastation. The fallacy of helping to defend a political ideology, even though it be somewhat similar to our own, was clearly demonstrated to us in the last war. Through our help that war was won, but neither the democracy nor the justice for which we fought grew in the peace that followed our victory.

Our bond with Europe is a bond of race and not of political ideology. We had to fight a European army to establish democracy in this country. It is the European race we must preserve; political progress will follow. Racial strength is vital—politics, a luxury. If the white race is ever seriously threatened, it may then be time for us to take our part in its protection, to fight side by side with the English, French, and Germans, but not with one against the other for our mutual destruction.

Let us not dissipate our strength, or help Europe to dissipate hers, in these wars of politics and possession. For the benefit of western civilization, we should continue our embargo on offensive armaments. As far as purely defensive arms are concerned, I, for one, am in favor of supplying European countries with as much as we can spare of the material that falls within this category. There are technicians who will argue that offensive and defensive arms cannot be separated completely. That is true, but it is no more difficult to make a list of defensive weapons than it is to separate munitions of war from semi-manufactured articles, and we are faced with that problem today. No one says that we should sell opium because it is difficult to make a list of narcotics. I would as soon see our country traffic in opium as in bombs. There are certain borderline cases, but there are plenty of clear cut examples: for instance, the bombing plane and the anti-aircraft cannon. I do not want to see American bombers dropping bombs which will kill and mutilate European children, even if they are not flown by American pilots. But I am perfectly willing to see American anti-aircraft guns shooting American shells at invading bombers over any European country. And I believe that most of you who are listening tonight will agree with me.

The second major issue for which we must create a policy concerns the restrictions to be placed on our shipping. Naval blockades have long been accepted as an element of warfare. They began on the surface of the sea, followed the submarine beneath it, and now reach up into the sky with aircraft. The laws and customs which were developed during the surface era were not satisfactory to the submarine. Now, aircraft bring up new and unknown factors for consideration. It is simple enough for a battleship to identify the merchantman she captures. It is a more difficult problem for a submarine if that merchantman may carry cannon; it is safer to fire a torpedo than to come up and ask. For bombing planes flying at high altitudes and through conditions of poor visibility, identification of a surface vessel will be more difficult still.

In modern naval blockades and warfare, torpedoes will be fired and bombs dropped on probabilities rather than on certainties of identification. The only safe course for neutral shipping at this time is to stay away from the warring countries and dangerous waters of Europe.

The third issue to be decided relates to the extension of credit. Here again we may draw from our experience in the last war. After that war was over, we found ourselves in the position of having financed a large portion of the expenditures of European countries. And when the time came to pay us back, these countries simply refused to do so. They not only refused to pay the wartime loans we made, but they refused to pay back what we loaned them after the war was over. As is so frequently the case, we found that loaning money eventually created animosity instead of gratitude. European countries felt insulted when we asked to be repaid. They called us "Uncle Shylock." They were horror struck at the idea of turning over to us any of their islands in America to compensate for their debts, or for our help in winning their war. They seized all the German colonies and carved up Europe to suit their fancy. These were the "fruits of war." They took our money and they took our soldiers. But there was not the offer of one Caribbean island in return for the debts they "could not afford to pay."

The extension of credit to a belligerent country is a long step toward war, and it would leave us close to the edge. If American industry loans money to a belligerent country, many interests will feel that it is more important for that country to win than for our own to avoid the war. It is unfortunate but true that there are interests in America who would rather lose American lives than their own dollars. We should give them no opportunity.

I believe that we should adopt as our program of American neutrality—as our contribution to western civilization—the following policy:

1. An embargo on offensive weapons and munitions.

2. The unrestricted sale of purely defensive armaments.

3. The prohibition of American shipping from the belligerent countries of Europe and their danger zones.

4. The refusal of credit to belligerent nations or their agents.

Whether or not this program is adopted depends upon the support of those of us who believe in it. The United States of America is a democracy. The policy of our country is still controlled by our people. It is time for us to take action. There has never been a greater test for the democratic principle of government.

The Atlantic Charter, 1941

Officially neutral until the Japanese attack on Pearl Harbor, the Roosevelt administration, and with it the United States, became increasingly open in its support of the British and other Allied forces as the war with Germany and Japan went on. The Lend-Lease Act of March 11, 1941, had authorized the president to give war materials to Allied nations in exchange for rights to use various military bases, and FDR had taken full advantage of that authority. After Germany attacked the Soviet Union in June of 1941, the United States and Britain invited the Soviets to join in working out a plan for postwar Europe. The Soviets initially refused, and the plan was formulated by FDR and British prime minister Winston Churchill. Eventually agreed to by the Soviets, along with various national forces allied against Germany, the Atlantic Charter eschewed territorial expansion in favor of popular self-determination, disarmament, free trade, and efforts at social and economic improvement.

The Atlantic Charter

DECLARATION OF PRINCIPLES, KNOWN AS THE ATLANTIC CHARTER, BY THE PRESIDENT OF THE UNITED STATES OF AMERICA AND THE PRIME MINISTER OF THE UNITED KINGDOM, AUGUST 14, 1941

Joint declaration of the President of the United States of America and the Prime Minister, Mr. Churchill, representing His Majesty's Government in the United Kingdom, being met together, deem it right to make known certain common principles in the national policies of their respective countries on which they base their hopes for a better future for the world.

First, their countries seek no aggrandizement, territorial or other;

Second, they desire to see no territorial changes that do not accord with the freely expressed wishes of the peoples concerned;

Third, they respect the right of all peoples to choose the form of government under which they will live; and they wish to see sovereign rights and self-government restored to those who have been forcibly deprived of them;

Fourth, they will endeavor, with due respect for their existing obligations, to further the enjoyment by all States, great or small, victor or vanquished, of access, on equal terms, to the trade and to the raw materials of the world which are needed for their economic prosperity;

Fifth, they desire to bring about the fullest collaboration between all nations in the economic field with the object of securing, for all, improved labor standards, economic advancement and social security;

Sixth, after the final destruction of the Nazi tyranny, they hope to see established a peace which will afford to all nations the means of dwelling in safety within their own boundaries, and which will afford assurance that all the men in all the lands may live out their lives in freedom from fear and want;

Seventh, such a peace should enable all men to traverse the high seas and oceans without hindrance;

Eighth, they believe that all of the nations of the world, for realistic as well as spiritual reasons must come to the abandonment of the use of force. Since no future peace can be maintained if land, sea or air armaments continue to be employed by nations which threaten, or may threaten, aggression outside of their frontiers, they believe, pending the establishment of a wider and permanent system of general security, that the disarmament of such nations is essential. They will likewise aid and encourage all other practicable measures which will lighten for peace-loving peoples the crushing burden of armaments.

DECLARATION BY UNITED NATIONS:

A JOINT DECLARATION BY THE UNITED STATES OF AMERICA, THE UNITED KINGDOM OF GREAT BRITAIN AND NORTHERN IRELAND, THE UNION OF SOVIET SOCIALIST REPUBLICS, CHINA, AUSTRALIA, BELGIUM, CANADA, COSTA RICA, CUBA, CZECHOSLOVAKIA, DOMINICAN REPUBLIC, EL SALVADOR, GREECE, GUATEMALA, HAITI, HONDURAS, INDIA, LUXEMBOURG, NETHERLANDS, NEW ZEALAND, NICARAGUA, NORWAY, PANAMA, POLAND, SOUTH AFRICA, YUGOSLAVIA.

The Governments signatory hereto,

Having subscribed to a common program of purposes and principles embodied in the Joint Declaration of the President of the United States of America and the Prime Minister of the United Kingdom of Great Britain and Northern Ireland dated August 14, 1941, known as the Atlantic Charter

Being convinced that complete victory over their enemies is essential to defend life, liberty, independence and religious freedom, and to preserve human rights and justice in their own lands as well as in other lands, and that they are now engaged in a common struggle against savage and brutal forces seeking to subjugate the world, DECLARE:

(1) Each Government pledges itself to employ its full resources, military or economic, against those members of the Tripartite Pact and its adherents with which such government is at war.

(2) Each Government pledges itself to cooperate with the Governments signatory hereto and not to make a separate armistice or peace with the enemies.

The foregoing declaration may be adhered to by other nations which are, or which may be, rendering material assistance and contributions in the struggle for victory over Hitlerism.

Done at Washington
January First, 1942

The United States of
America
by FRANKLIN D
ROOSEVELT
The United Kingdom of
Great Britain & Northern Ireland
by WINSTON S.
CHURCHILL

On behalf of the Government of the Union of Soviet Socialist Republics
MAXIM LITVINOFF
Ambassador
National Government of the
Republic of China
TSE VUNG SOONG
Minister for Foreign Affairs
The Commonwealth of
Australia
by R. G. CASEY.
The Kingdom of Belgium
by Cᵗᶜ· R. v. STRATEN
Canada
by LEIGHTON
MCCARTHY
The Republic of Costa Rica
by LUIS FERNÁNDEZ
The Republic of Cuba
by AURELIO F.
CONCHESO.
Czechoslovak Republic
by V. S. HURBAN
The Dominican Republic
by J M TRONCOSO
The Republic of El Salvador
by C A ALFARO—

The Kingdom of Greece
by CIMON G.
DIAMANTOPOULOS.
The Republic of Guatemala
by:—ENRIQUE LOPEZ
HERRARTE.
La Republique d'Haïti
par FERNAND DENNIS.
The Republic of Honduras
by JULIÁN R. CÁCERES
India by
GIRJA SHANKAR
BAJPAI.
The Grand Duchy of
Luxembourg
by HUGUES LE
GALLAIS
The Kingdom of the
Netherlands
A. LOUDON
Signed on behalf of the
Govt of the Dominion
of New Zealand
by FRANK LANGSTONE
The Republic of Nicaragua
by LEÓN DE BAYLE
The Kingdom of Norway
by W. MUNTHE
MORGENSTIERNE
The Republic of Panamá
by JAÉN GUARDIA
The Republic of Poland
by JAN CIECHANOWSKI
The Union of South Africa
by RALPH W. CLOSE
The Kingdom of Yugoslavia
by CONSTANTIN A.
FOTITCH

The Four Freedoms, *Franklin Delano Roosevelt,* 1941

Pearl Harbor Speech, *Franklin Delano Roosevelt,* 1941

Delivered as his annual message to Congress, FDR's Four Freedoms speech set forth his argument for America to undertake increased preparations for war and support for British and other forces opposing Nazi Germany. He further argued for defense of four freedoms, which involved liberating people from restrictions on speech and religious worship and freeing them from poverty and fear of war and oppression. All were to be provided not just in the United States but around the world. It was not, however, the Nazi government in Germany but the Japanese navy that finally brought war, through its attack on American forces in Pearl Harbor. Soon after, on December 11, 1941, Germany declared war on the United States. The United States responded with a formal declaration of war against Germany on the same day.

The Four Freedoms

January 6, 1941

Franklin Delano Roosevelt

Address of the President of the United States

Mr. President, Mr. Speaker, Members of the Seventy-seventh Congress, I address you, the Members of the Seventy-seventh Congress, at a moment unprecedented in the history of the Union. I use the word "unprecedented," because at no previous time has American security been as seriously threatened from without as it is today.

Since the permanent formation of our Government under the Constitution, in 1789, most of the periods of crises in our history have related to our domestic affairs. Fortunately, only one of these—the 4-year War between the States—ever threatened our national unity. Today, thank God, 130,000,000 Americans, in 48 States, have forgotten points of the compass in our national unity.

It is true that prior to 1914 the United States often had been disturbed by events in other continents. We had even engaged in two wars with European nations and in a number of undeclared wars in the West Indies, in the Mediterranean, and in the Pacific for the maintenance of American rights and for the principles of peaceful commerce. In no case, however, had a serious threat been raised against our national safety or our independence.

What I seek to convey is the historic truth that the United States, as a nation, has at all times maintained opposition to any attempt to lock us in behind an ancient Chinese wall while the procession of civilization went past. Today, thinking of our children and their children, we oppose enforced isolation for ourselves or for any part of the Americas.

That determination of ours was proved, for example, during the quarter century of wars following the French Revolution.

While the Napoleonic struggles did threaten interests of the United States because of the French foothold in the West Indies and in Louisiana, and while we engaged in the War of 1812 to vindicate our right to peaceful trade, it is, nevertheless, clear that neither France nor Great Britain nor any other nation was aiming at domination of the whole world.

In like fashion, from 1815 to 1914—99 years—no single war in Europe or in Asia constituted a real threat against our future or against the future of any other American nation.

Except in the Maximilian interlude in Mexico, no foreign power sought to establish itself in this hemisphere, and the strength of the British Fleet in the Atlantic has been a friendly strength. It is still a friendly strength.

Even when the World War broke out in 1914 it seemed to contain only small threat of danger to our own American future. But as time went on the American people began to visualize what the downfall of democratic nations might mean to our own democracy.

We need not overemphasize imperfections in the peace of Versailles. We need not harp on failure of the democracies to deal with problems of world reconstruction. We should remember that the peace of 1919 was far less unjust than the kind of "pacification" which began even before Munich and which is being carried on under the new order of tyranny that seeks to spread over every continent today. The American people have unalterably set their faces against that tyranny.

Every realist knows that the democratic way of life is at this moment being directly assailed in every part of the world—assailed either by arms or by secret spreading of poisonous propaganda by those who seek to destroy unity and promote discord in nations still at peace.

During 16 months this assault has blotted out the whole pattern of democratic life in an appalling number of independent nations, great and small. The assailants are still on the march, threatening other nations, great and small.

Therefore, as your President, performing my constitutional duty to "give to the Congress information of the state of the Union," I find it necessary to report that the future and the safety of our country and of our democracy are overwhelmingly involved in events far beyond our borders.

Armed defense of democratic existence is now being gallantly waged in four continents. If that defense fails, all the population and all the resources of Europe, Asia, Africa, and Australasia will be dominated by the conquerors. The total of those populations and their resources greatly exceeds the sum total of the population and resources of the whole of the Western Hemisphere—many times over.

In times like these it is immature—and incidentally untrue—for anybody to brag that an unprepared America, single-handed, and with one hand tied behind its back, can hold off the whole world.

No realistic American can expect from a dictator's peace international generosity, or return of true independence, or world disarmament, or freedom of expression, or freedom of religion—or even good business.

Such a peace would bring no security for us or for our neighbors. "Those who would give up essential liberty to purchase a little temporary safety deserve neither liberty nor safety."

As a Nation we may take pride in the fact that we are softhearted; but we cannot afford to be soft-headed.

We must always be wary of those who, with sounding brass and a tinkling cymbal, preach the "ism" of appeasement.

We must especially beware of that small group of selfish men who would clip the wings of the American eagle in order to feather their own nests.

I have recently pointed out how quickly the tempo of modern warfare could bring into our very midst the physical attack which we must expect if the dictator nations win this war.

There is much loose talk of our immunity from immediate and direct invasion from across the seas. Obviously, as long as the British Navy retains its power, no such danger exists. Even if there were no British Navy, it is not probable that any enemy would be stupid enough to attack us by landing troops in the United States from across thousands of miles of ocean, until it had acquired strategic bases from which to operate.

But we learn much from the lessons of the past years in Europe—particularly the lesson of Norway, whose essential seaports were captured by treachery and surprise built up over a series of years.

The first phase of the invasion of this hemisphere would not be the landing of regular troops. The necessary strategic points would be occupied by secret agents and their dupes, and great numbers of them are already here, and in Latin America.

As long as the aggressor nations maintain the offensive, they, not we, will choose the time and the place and the method of their attack.

That is why the future of all American republics is today in serious danger.

That is why this annual message to the Congress is unique in our history.

That is why every member of the executive branch of the Government and every Member of the Congress face great responsibility—and great accountability.

The need of the moment is that our actions and our policy should be devoted primarily—almost exclusively—to meeting this foreign peril. For all our domestic problems are now a part of the great emergency.

Just as our national policy in internal affairs has been based upon a decent respect for the rights and dignity of all our fellow-men within our gates, so our national policy in foreign affairs has been based on a decent respect for the rights and dignity of all nations, large and small. And the justice of morality must and will win in the end.

Our national policy is this:

First, by an impressive expression of the public will and without regard to partisanship, we are committed to all-inclusive national defense.

Second, by an impressive expression of the public will and without regard to partisanship, we are committed to full support of all those resolute peoples, everywhere, who are resisting aggression and are thereby keeping war away from our hemisphere. By this support, we express our determination that the democratic cause shall prevail, and we strengthen the defense and security of our own Nation.

Third, by an impressive expression of the public will and without regard to partisanship, we are committed to the proposition that principles of morality and considerations for our own security will never permit us to acquiesce in a peace dictated by aggressors and sponsored by appeasers. We know that enduring peace cannot be bought at the cost of other people's freedom.

In the recent national election there was no substantial difference between the two great parties in respect to that national policy. No issue was fought out on this line before the American electorate. Today it is abundantly evident that American citizens everywhere are demanding and supporting speedy and complete action in recognition of obvious danger.

Therefore, the immediate need is a swift and driving increase in our armament production.

Leaders of industry and labor have responded to our summons. Goals of speed have been set. In some cases these goals are being reached ahead of time; in some cases we are on schedule; in other cases there are slight but not serious delays; and in some cases—and I am sorry to say very important cases—we are all concerned by the slowness of the accomplishment of our plans.

The Army and Navy, however, have made substantial progress during the past year. Actual experience is improving and speeding up our methods of production with every passing day. And today's best is not good enough for tomorrow.

I am not satisfied with the progress thus far made. The men in charge of the program represent the best in training, ability, and patriotism. They are not satisfied with the progress thus far made. None of us will be satisfied until the job is done.

No matter whether the original goal was set too high or too low, our objective is quicker and better results.

To give two illustrations:

We are behind schedule in turning out finished airplanes; we are working day and night to solve the innumerable problems and to catch up.

We are ahead of schedule in building warships; but we are working to get even further ahead of schedule.

To change a whole nation from a basis of peacetime production of implements of peace to a basis of wartime production of implements of war is no small task. And the greatest difficulty comes at the beginning of the program, when new tools and plant facilities and new assembly lines and shipways must first be constructed before the actual material begins to flow steadily and speedily from them.

The Congress, of course, must rightly keep itself informed at all times of the progress of the program. However, there is certain information, as the Congress itself will readily recognize, which, in the interests of our own security and those of the nations we are supporting must of needs be kept in confidence.

New circumstances are constantly begetting new needs for our safety. I shall ask this Congress for greatly increased new appropriations and authorizations to carry on what we have begun.

I also ask this Congress for authority and for funds sufficient to manufacture additional munitions and war supplies of many kinds, to be turned over to those nations which are now in actual war with aggressor nations.

Our most useful and immediate role is to act as an arsenal for them as well as for ourselves. They do not need manpower. They do need billions of dollars' worth of the weapons of defense.

The time is near when they will not be able to pay for them in ready cash. We cannot, and will not, tell them they must surrender merely because of present inability to pay for the weapons which we know they must have.

I do not recommend that we make them a loan of dollars with which to pay for these weapons—a loan to be repaid in dollars.

I recommend that we make it possible for those nations to continue to obtain war materials in the United States, fitting their orders into our own program. Nearly all of their material would, if the time ever came, be useful for our own defense.

Taking counsel of expert military and naval authorities, considering what is best for our own security, we are free to decide how much should be kept here and how much should be sent abroad to our friends who, by their determined and heroic resistance, are giving us time in which to make ready our own defense.

For what we send abroad we shall be repaid, within a reasonable time following the close of hostilities, in similar materials or, at our option, in other goods of many kinds which they can produce and which we need.

Let us say to the democracies, "We Americans are vitally concerned in your defense of freedom. We are putting forth our energies, our resources, and our organizing powers to give you the strength to regain and maintain a free world. We shall send you, in ever-increasing numbers, ships, planes, tanks, guns. This is our purpose and our pledge."

In fulfillment of this purpose we will not be intimidated by the threats of dictators that they will regard as a breach of international law and as an act of war our aid to the democracies which dare to resist their aggression. Such aid is not an act of war, even if a dictator should unilaterally proclaim it so to be.

When the dictators are ready to make war upon us, they will not wait for an act of war on our part. They did not wait for Norway or Belgium or the Netherlands to commit an act of war.

Their only interest is in a new one-way international law, which lacks mutuality in its observance and, therefore, becomes an instrument of oppression.

The happiness of future generations of Americans may well depend upon how effective and how immediate we can make our aid felt. No one can tell the exact character of the emergency situations that we may be called upon to meet. The Nation's hands must not be tied when the Nation's life is in danger.

We must all prepare to make the sacrifices that the emergency—as serious as war itself—demands. Whatever stands in the way of speed and efficiency in defense preparations must give way to the national need.

A free nation has the right to expect full cooperation from all groups. A free nation has the right to look to the leaders of business, of labor, and of agriculture to take the lead in stimulating effort, not among other groups but within their own groups.

The best way of dealing with the few slackers or trouble makers in our midst is, first, to shame them by patriotic example; and if that fails, to use the sovereignty of government to save government.

As men do not live by bread alone, they do not fight by armaments alone. Those who man our defenses, and those behind them who build our defenses, must have the stamina and courage which come from an unshakable belief in the manner of life which they are defending. The mighty action which we are calling for cannot be based on a disregard of all things worth fighting for.

The Nation takes great satisfaction and much strength from the things which have been done to make its people conscious of their individual stake in the preservation of democratic life in America. Those things have toughened the fiber of our people, have renewed their faith and strengthened their devotion to the institutions we make ready to protect.

Certainly this is no time to stop thinking about the social and economic problems which are the root cause of the social revolution which is today a supreme factor in the world.

There is nothing mysterious about the foundations of a healthy and strong democracy. The basic things expected by our people of their political and economic systems are simple. They are:

Equality of opportunity for youth and for others.

Jobs for those who can work.

Security for those who need it.

The ending of special privilege for the few.

The preservation of civil liberties for all.

The enjoyment of the fruits of scientific progress in a wider and constantly rising standard of living.

These are the simple and basic things that must never be lost sight of in the turmoil and unbelievable complexity of our modern world. The inner and abiding strength of our economic and political systems is dependent upon the degree to which they fulfill these expectations.

Many subjects connected with our social economy call for immediate improvement.

As examples:

We should bring more citizens under the coverage of old-age pensions and unemployment insurance.

We should widen the opportunities for adequate medical care.

We should plan a better system by which persons deserving or needing gainful employment may obtain it.

I have called for personal sacrifice. I am assured of the willingness of almost all Americans to respond to that call.

A part of the sacrifice means the payment of more money in taxes. In my Budget message I recommend that a greater portion of this great defense program be paid for from taxation than we are paying today. No person should try, or be allowed, to get rich out of this program; and the principle of tax payments in accordance with ability to pay should be constantly before our eyes to guide our legislation.

If the Congress maintains these principles, the voters, putting patriotism ahead of pocketbooks, will give you their applause.

In the future days, which we seek to make secure, we

look forward to a world founded upon four essential human freedoms.

The first is freedom of speech and expression everywhere in the world.

The second is freedom of every person to worship God in his own way everywhere in the world.

The third is freedom from want, which, translated into world terms, means economic understandings which will secure to every nation a healthy peacetime life for its inhabitants everywhere in the world.

The fourth is freedom from fear—which, translated into world terms, means a world-wide reduction of armaments to such a point and in such a thorough fashion that no nation will be in a position to commit an act of physical aggression against any neighbor—anywhere in the world.

That is no vision of a distant millennium. It is a definite basis for a kind of world attainable in our own time and generation. That kind of world is the very antithesis of the so-called new order of tyranny which the dictators seek to create with the crash of a bomb.

To that new order we oppose the greater conception—the moral order. A good society is able to face schemes of world domination and foreign revolutions alike without fear.

Since the beginning of our American history we have been engaged in change—in a perpetual peaceful revolution—a revolution which goes on steadily, quietly adjusting itself to changing conditions—without the concentration camp or the quicklime in the ditch. The world order which we seek is the cooperation of free countries, working together in a friendly, civilized society.

This Nation has placed its destiny in the hands and heads and hearts of its millions of free men and women; and its faith in freedom under the guidance of God. Freedom means the supremacy of human rights everywhere. Our support goes to those who struggle to gain those rights or keep them. Our strength is in our unity of purpose.

To that high concept there can be no end save victory.

Pearl Harbor Speech

December 8, 1941

Franklin Delano Roosevelt

To the Congress of the United States:

Yesterday, December 7, 1941—a date which will live in infamy—the United States of America was suddenly and deliberately attacked by naval and air forces of the Empire of Japan.

The United States was at peace with that nation and, at the solicitation of Japan, was still in conversation with its Government and its Emperor looking toward the maintenance of peace in the Pacific. Indeed, 1 hour after Japanese air squadrons had commenced bombing in Oahu, the Japanese Ambassador to the United States and his colleague delivered to the Secretary of State a formal reply to a recent American message. While this reply stated that it seemed useless to continue the existing diplomatic negotiations, it contained no threat or hint of war or armed attack.

It will be recorded that the distance of Hawaii from Japan makes it obvious that the attack was deliberately planned many days or even weeks ago. During the intervening time the Japanese Government has deliberately sought to deceive the United States by false statements and expressions of hope for continued peace.

The attack yesterday on the Hawaiian Islands has caused severe damage to American naval and military forces. Very many American lives have been lost. In addition American ships have been reported torpedoed on the high seas between San Francisco and Honolulu.

Yesterday the Japanese Government also launched an attack against Malaya.

Last night Japanese forces attacked Hong Kong.

Last night Japanese forces attacked Guam.

Last night Japanese forces attacked the Philippine Islands.

Last night the Japanese attacked Wake Island.

This morning the Japanese attacked Midway Island.

Japan has, therefore, undertaken a surprise offensive extending throughout the Pacific area. The facts of yesterday speak for themselves. The people of the United States have already formed their opinions and well understand the implications to the very life and safety of our Nation.

As Commander in Chief of the Army and Navy I have directed that all measures be taken for our defense.

Always will we remember the character of the onslaught against us.

No matter how long it may take us to overcome this premeditated invasion, the American people, in their righteous might, will win through to absolute victory.

I believe I interpret the will of the Congress and of the people when I assert that we will not only defend ourselves to the uttermost but will make very certain that this form of treachery shall never endanger us again.

Hostilities exist. There is no blinking at the fact that our people, our territory, and our interests are in grave danger.

With confidence in our armed forces—with the unbounded determination of our people—we will gain the inevitable triumph—so help us God.

I ask that the Congress declare that since the unprovoked and dastardly attack by Japan on Sunday, December 7, a state of war has existed between the United States and the Japanese Empire.

FRANKLIN D. ROOSEVELT.
THE WHITE HOUSE, *December 8, 1941.*

SOURCES

In addition to *The Congressional Record* and its antecedents, and federal statutes available in *Statutes at Large*, the following sources were used in preparing selections reproduced in this volume. Selection titles, where not self-evident, are given after their sources.

A. L. A. Schechter Poultry Corp. v. U.S., 295 U.S. 495 (1935).

Act to Increase the Military Force of the Confederate States. HR 367, February 10, 1865. Richmond: Confederate Imprints, 1861–65, reel 8, no. 540.

Addams, Jane. *The Subjective Necessity for Social Settlements: Philanthropy and Social Progress, Seven Essays*. New York: T. Y. Crowell, 1893, 1–26.

———. "Why the Ward Boss Rules." *Outlook* 58 (April 2, 1898): 879–82.

Beveridge, Alfred J. "The Star of Empire." In *The Meaning of the Times and Other Speeches*. Indianapolis: Bobbs-Merrill, 1908.

Bryan, William Jennings. "Cross of Gold Speech." In *Official Proceedings of the Democratic National Convention*. Logansport, Ind.: Wilson, Humphreys, 1896, 226–34.

Buck v. Bell, 274 U.S. 200 (1927).

Carnegie, Andrew. "The Gospel of Wealth." In *"The Gospel of Wealth," and Other Timely Essays*. New York: Century, 1900, 1–47.

Civil Rights Cases, 109 U.S. 3 (1883).

Constitution of Indiana, Article XIII. In *Special and Local Acts of the State of Indiana Passed at the 36th Session of the General Assembly*. Indianapolis: J. P. Chapman, 1852, 24–25.

Constitution of the Confederate States of America. In *Journal of the Congress of the Confederate States of America 1861–1865*. Vol. 1. 58th Cong., 2d sess., Senate Doc. 234: 64–66. Washington, D.C.: GPO, 1904.

A Contract with the People: Platform of the Progressive Party Adopted at Its First National Convention, Chicago, August 7, 1912. New York: Progressive National Committee, 1912.

Covenant of The League of Nations. London: Stevens and Sons, 1920, 189–203.

Davis, Jefferson. Inaugural Address. In *Journal of the Congress of the Confederate States of America 1861–1865*. Vol. 1. 58th Cong., 2d sess., Senate Doc. 234: 909–24. Washington, D.C.: GPO, 1904.

———. Message to the Congress of Confederate States. In *Journal of the Congress of the Confederate States of America*

1861–1865. Vol. 1. 58th Cong., 2d sess., Senate Doc. 234: 8–11. Washington, D.C.: GPO, 1904.

Debs, Eugene. "The Socialist Party and the Working Class." In *Debs: His Life, Writing and Speeches*. Chicago: John F. Higgins, 1908, 357–73.

Declaration and ordinance, passed unanimously, December 20th, 1860. To dissolve the union between the state of South Carolina and other states united with her under the compact entitled, "The Constitution of the United States of America." Charleston: Evans & Cogswell, 1860.

Declaration Known as the Atlantic Charter. Washington, D.C.: GPO, 1942.

DuBois, W. E. B. "The Talented Tenth." In *The Negro Problem: A Series of Articles by Representative American Negroes of To-Day*. New York: J. Pott, 1903, 33–75.

Eastman, Joseph. "The Place of the Independent Commission." 12 Const. Rev. 95, 95–102 (1928).

Harvey, William. *Coin's Financial School*. Chicago: Coin's, 1894.

Hay, John. "Open Door Note." In *Papers Relating to the Foreign Relations of the United States*. Washington, D.C.: GPO, 1901, 129–30.

Hayes, Rutherford B. Inaugural Address. In *Inaugural Addresses of the Presidents of the United States from George Washington to JFK*. Washington, D.C.: GPO, 1961, 135–40.

Hoover, Herbert. "Radio Address on Unemployment Relief." Washington, D.C.: GPO, 1931.

James, William. *What Pragmatism Means; Pragmatism: A New Name for Some Old Ways of Thinking*. New York: Longmans, Green, 1914, 48–81.

Johnson, Andrew. Veto of the First Reconstruction Act. 53rd Cong., 2d sess., Misc. Documents of the House of Representatives, 1893–94. Washington, D.C.: GPO, 1895, 498–511.

———. Veto of the Second Freedmen's Bureau Bill. 39th Cong., 1st sess., 1866, Ex. Doc. 25.

Late Corp. of Church of Jesus Christ v. U.S., 136 U.S. 1 (1890).

Lee, Robert E. "Last Order of Gen. Robert E. Lee." In *War of the Rebellion: A Compilation of the Official Records of the Union and Confederate Armies*, 1st ser., vol. 46, pt. 1: 265–67. Washington, D.C.: GPO, 1894.

Lincoln, Abraham. First Inaugural Address. In *Inaugural Addresses of the Presidents of the United States from George Washington to JFK*. Washington, D.C.: GPO, 1961, 235–39.

———. Address on Colonization to a Deputation of Negroes.

In *Collected Works of Abraham Lincoln.* Vol. 5, 370–75. New Brunswick: Rutgers University Press, 1953.

———. Gettysburg Address. In *Collected Works of Abraham Lincoln.* Vol. 7, 22–23. New Brunswick: Rutgers University Press, 1953.

———. Last Public Address. In *Collected Works of Abraham Lincoln.* Vol. 8, 399–405. New Brunswick: Rutgers University Press, 1953.

———. Proclamation Suspending Writ of Habeas Corpus. In *Collected Works of Abraham Lincoln.* Vol. 6, 451–52. New Brunswick: Rutgers University Press, 1953.

———. Second Inaugural Address. 87th Cong., 1st sess., 1865. House Doc. 218.

Lindbergh, Charles A. "Neutrality and War." In *Radio Addresses of Col. Charles A. Lindbergh, 1939–1940.* New York: Scribner's Commentator, 1940.

Lochner v. New York, 198 U.S. 45 (1905).

Mann, Horace. Annual Report, Together with the Report of the Secretary of the Board. Vol. 12: 42–43, 90–138. Washington, D.C: GPO, 1848. (Twelfth Annual Report of the Massachusetts State School Board.)

Massachusetts Constitution, Article 18. In *Acts and Resolves Passed by the General Court of Massachusetts.* Boston: William White, 1855.

McKinley, William. First Inaugural Address. In *Inaugural Addresses of the Presidents of the United States from George Washington to JFK.* Washington, D.C.: GPO, 1961, 169–77.

Mississippi Constitution of 1868. In *Journal of the Proceedings on the Constitutional Convention of the State of Mississippi.* Jackson: E. Stafford, 1871.

Mississippi Constitution of 1890. In *Journal of the Proceedings on the Constitutional Convention of the State of Mississippi.* Jackson: E. L. Martin, 1890.

Mississippi Ordinance and Declaration of Secession from the Federal Union. Jackson: Mississippian Book and Job Printing Office, 1861.

National Labor Relations Board v. Jones & Laughlin Steel, 331 U.S. 416 (1937).

An Ordinance to Repeal the Ratification of the Constitution of the United States of America, by the State of Virginia. Richmond: C. L. Ludwig, 1861.

Plessy v. Ferguson, 163 U.S. 537 (1896).

Populist Party Platform, from Convention Held July 4, 1892, in Omaha, Nebraska. *The World Almanac*, 1893. New York, 1893.

Preamble, Constitution and By-Laws of Industrial Workers of the World. Chicago: I.W.W., 1905.

Reynolds v. U.S., 98 U.S. 145, 153–169 (1878).

Roosevelt, Franklin Delano. First Inaugural Address. In *Inaugural Addresses of the Presidents of the United States from George Washington to JFK.* Washington, D.C.: GPO, 1961, 235–39.

———. "Fireside Chat on the Reorganization of the Judiciary." In *The Public Papers and Addresses of Franklin D. Roosevelt.* New York: Macmillan, 1941, 122–23.

———. "Commonwealth Club Address." In *The Philosophy of Government: Governor Franklin D. Roosevelt's Speech at the Commonwealth Club, San Francisco, California, September 23, 1932.* New York: Democratic National Committee, 1932.

Schenck v. U.S., 249 U.S. 247 (1919).

Shaw, Anna Howard. "The Fundamental Principle of a Republic." In Wilmer Albert Linkugel, *The Speeches of Anna Howard Shaw: Collected and Edited with Introduction and Notes.* Ph.D. diss., University of Wisconsin, 1960, 259–92. Original source, *The Ogdenburg Advance and St. Lawrence Weekly Democrat*, July 1, 1915.

Sherman, William T. "Special Field Order 15." In *Memoirs of General William T. Sherman.* Vol. 2, 250–52. Bloomington: Indiana University Press, 1957.

Slaughter-house Cases, 83 U.S. 36 (1873).

Stanton, Elizabeth Cady. "Address to the First Annual Meeting of the Woman's State Temperance Society." In *History of Woman Suffrage.* Vol. 1, edited by Elizabeth Cady Stanton, Susan B. Anthony, and Matilda Joslyn Gage, 493–97. New York: Arno & The New York Times, 1969.

Stimson, Henry L. "Note on Chinchow." In *The Far Eastern Crisis.* New York: Harper & Bros., 1936, 96–97.

Sumner, William Graham. "The Fallacy of Territorial Extension." In *On Liberty, Society, and Politics: The Essential Essays of William Graham Sumner.* Indianapolis: Liberty Fund, 1992.

Taylor, Frederick Winslow. *The Principles of Scientific Management.* New York: Harper & Bros., 1919, 5–29.

Twelve Southerners. "Introduction: A Statement of Principles." In *I'll Take My Stand: The South and the Agrarian Tradition.* New York: Harper, 1930.

U.S. Congress. Senate. *Resolution Concerning Election of Senators.* 53rd Cong., special sess., 1893. Misc. Doc. 31.

———. Articles of Impeachment of Andrew Johnson. 40th Cong., 2d sess., 1868. Misc. Doc. 42.

———. *Second Freedmen's Bureau Bill.* 39th Cong., 1st sess., 1866. Ex. Doc. 25.

———. Senate. *Black Code of Mississippi.* 39th Cong., 2d sess., 1865. Ex. Doc. 6, "Freedmen's Affairs," 190–97.

Wade-Davis Manifesto. *New York Daily Tribune*, Aug. 5, 1864.

Washington, Booker T. *Address of Booker T. Washington: Report of the Board of Commissioners Representing the State of New York at the Cotton States and International Exposition Held at Atlanta, Georgia, 1895.* Washington, New York: Wynkoop, Hallenbeck, Crawford, 1896: 190–93. (Atlanta Exposition Speech.)

INDEX

Page numbers for illustrations are in italics.

presidential powers, 423–27
compared with Congress's war powers, 523–24
impeachment of Andrew Johnson (1868), 117–21
increase by Franklin Delano Roosevelt, 438–40
increase in 1871, 137
National Industrial Recovery Act, 457
Populist Party Platform, 324–26
provisions in Constitution of the Confederate States of
America (1861), 20
U.S. Supreme Court rulings on, 466
See also vetoes of acts and bills
presidential term of office, 173, 326. *See also* age limits for
justices
presidents. *See names of specific presidents*
Principles of Scientific Management, The (Frederick Winslow
Taylor, 1911), 306–13, 317
prisoners of war. *See* Proclamation Suspending Writ of Habeas
Corpus (Abraham Lincoln, 1863)
prisoners' rights, 91
Proclamation Calling the Militia and Convening Congress (Abra-
ham Lincoln, 1861), 39–40
Proclamation of Amnesty and Reconstruction (Abraham Lincoln,
1863), 68–70
Proclamation of Blockade against Southern Ports (Abraham
Lincoln, 1861), 39, 41–42
Proclamation Revoking General Hunter's Emancipation Order
(Abraham Lincoln, 1862), 50, 52–53
Proclamation Suspending Writ of Habeas Corpus (Abraham
Lincoln, 1863), 48–49
Professor "Coin," 327
profit motive. *See* capitalist ethic; industrialism
Progressive Party
Declaration of Principles of the Progressive Party (Theodore
Roosevelt, 1912), 360–67
opposition to "machine politics," 349, 356–59
presidential candidate, 513
and territorial expansion, 496
and William James's philosophy of pragmatism, 331–38
prohibition
Prohibition Debate in U.S. House of Representatives (1917),
372, 375–81
repeal, 372, 382
See also temperance movement
Proposed Constitutional Amendment Regarding Religious Establishment (House of Representatives, 1876), 287
protectionism. *See* tariffs to promote industry
public accommodations
Civil Rights Act (1875), 137, 144–45
Civil Rights Act (1875), cases (1883), 175–88
Plessy v. Ferguson (1896), 259–69
public health, 365
Lochner v. New York (1905), 226–34
Slaughter-House Cases, 150–70

public lands
for agricultural and mechanical arts colleges, 207–8
Homestead Act (1862), 198–99
for transcontinental railroad, 200–207
See also land
public schools
as antidote to crime, 238–52
Blaine amendments, 287
in Mississippi, 146, 148–49, 191
"separate but equal," 191, 207
See also Catholic Church schools; colleges
public works projects, 447–51
Franklin Delano Roosevelt's, 441
Herbert Hoover's, 428
Pullman strike of 1894, 339

quota systems for U.S. immigrants, 298, 302–5

race
as criterion for whether or not to go to war, 560
Justice Harlan's discussion of discrimination in *Plessy v. Ferguson,* 259–64
Supreme Court's decision on discrimination in Civil Rights
Cases (1883), 175–84
and territorial expansion by United States, 496–97
See also civil rights
Radical Republicans, 67, 102, 115, 189
Radio Address on Unemployment Relief (Herbert Hoover, 1931),
428–30
railroad corporations
influence on politics, 189
land acquisition, 198, 200–207, 326
Mississippi constitutional provisions, 189–91
political corruption, 404–9
Populist Party's proposal to nationalize, 324, 325
separate facilities for black and white people, 175–76, 259–69
See also interstate commerce; Interstate Commerce Act (1887);
Pullman strike of 1894
Railway Labor Act (1926), 478
Ransom, John Crowe, 316
Reconstruction, 67–193
Act of 1867, 102–14
background, 67
end of, 171
objections to, 67
texts, 68–193
See also African Americans; carpetbaggers; emancipation; freed
slaves; public accommodations; Radical Republicans;
Southern states
Reconstruction Finance Corporation, 441
Redistribution of Wealth (Huey Long, 1935), 452–56
referenda. *See* initiative and referendum system of voting
reformers, 323

This book is set in Adobe Garamond, a modern adaptation by Robert Slimbach of the typeface originally cut around 1540 by the French typographer and printer Claude Garamond. The Garamond face, with its small lowercase height and restrained contrast between thick and thin strokes, is a classic "old-style" face and has long been one of the most influential and widely used typefaces.

This book is printed on paper that is acid-free and meets the requirements of the American National Standard for Permanence of Paper for Printed Library Materials, z39.48–1992. ⊗

Book design by Sandra Hudson, Watkinsville, Georgia, adapted by Barbara Williams, BW&A Books, Inc., Durham, North Carolina

Typography by Newgen North America

Printed and bound by Edwards Brothers, Inc., Ann Arbor, Michigan